A Library
of Literary
Criticism

A Library
of Literary
Criticism

VOLUME 3

McCarthy
to
Sagan

MODERN WOMEN WRITERS

Compiled and edited by

LILLIAN S. ROBINSON

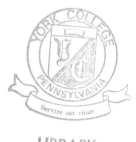

A Frederick Ungar Book

CONTINUUM · NEW YORK

1996
The Continuum Publishing Company
370 Lexington Avenue
New York, NY 10017

Printed in the United States of America

Library of Congress Cataloging-in-Publication Data

Modern women writers / compiled and edited by Lillian S. Robinson.
    p.   cm. — (A library of literary criticism)
  "A Frederick Ungar book."
  Includes bibliographical references and index.
  ISBN 0-8264-0823-0 (set). — ISBN 0-8264-0813-3 (v. 1). — ISBN
0-8264-0814-1 (v. 2). — ISBN 0-8264-0815-X (v. 3).—ISBN 0-8264-0920-2 (vol. 4)
    1. Literature—Women authors—History and criticism.
  2. Literature, Modern—20th century—History and criticism.
  3. Women authors—Biography. I. Robinson, Lillian S. II. Series.
PN471.M62   1996
809'.89287'0904—dc20   94-43197
                                                            CIP

AUTHORS INCLUDED

Volume 3

McCarthy, Mary	U.S.
McCullers, Carson	U.S.
Macaulay, Rose	Great Britain
MacEwan, Gwendolyn	Canada
Maillet, Antonine	Canada
Majerová, Marie	Czech Republic
Maksimović, Desanka	Serbia
al-Malā'ika, Nāzik	Iraq
Mallet-Joris, Françoise	Belgium
Manicom, Jacqueline	Guadeloupe
Manning, Olivia	Great Britain
Mansfield, Katherine	New Zealand–Great Britain
Manzini, Gianna	Italy
Maraini, Dacia	Italy
Markandaya, Kamala	India
Marshall, Paule	U.S. (African American)
Martín Gaite, Carmen	Spain
Martinson, Moa	Sweden
Mason, Bobbie Ann	U.S.
Matute, Ana María	Spain
Mayröcker, Friederike	Austria
Medio, Dolores	Spain
Meireles, Cecília	Brazil
Menchú, Rigoberta	Guatemala
Mew, Charlotte	Great Britain
Meynell, Alice	Great Britain
Meynell, Viola	Great Britain
Miles, Josephine	U.S.
Millay, Edna St. Vincent	U.S.
Millin, Sarah Gertrude	South Africa
Minco, Marga	Netherlands

Mistral, Gabriela	Chile
Mitchison, Naomi	Great Britain
Mitford, Nancy	Great Britain
Miyamoto Yuriko	Japan
Moix, Ana María	Spain
Montero, Rosa	Spain
Moore, Marianne	U.S.
Moore, Olive (Constance Vaughn)	Great Britain
Moraga, Cherríe	U.S. (Mexican American)
Morante, Elsa	Italy
Morejón, Nancy	Cuba
Morgenstern, Beate	Germany
Morgner, Irmtraud	Germany
Morrison, Toni	U.S. (African American)
Mugo, Micere Githae	Kenya
Mukherjee, Bharati	India–Canada–U.S.
Munro, Alice	Canada
Murdoch, Iris	Great Britain
Naidu, Sarojini	India
Nalkowska, Zofia	Poland
Naranjo, Carmen	Costa Rica
Nasrallah, Emily	Lebanon
Naylor, Gloria	U.S. (African American)
Neera (Anna Radius Zuccari)	Italy
Nemes Nagy, Ágnes	Hungary
Nin, Anais	U.S.
Njau, Rebecca	Kenya
Noailles, Anna de	France
Nogami Yaeko	Japan
Norman, Marsha	U.S.
Novak, Helga	Germany
Nwapa, Flora	Nigeria
Oates, Joyce Carol	U.S.
Ōba Minako	Japan
O'Brien, Edna	Ireland
O'Brien, Kate	Ireland

Ocampo, Silvina	Argentina
Ocampo, Victoria	Argentina
O'Connor, Flannery	U.S.
Odio, Eunice	Costa Rica–Mexico
O'Faolain, Julia	Ireland
Ogot, Grace	Kenya
Okamoto Kanoko	Japan
Oldenbourg, Zoe	France
Olsen, Tillie	U.S.
Onwueme, Tess	Nigeria
Oreamuno, Yolanda	Costa Rica–Guatemala
Ortese, Anna Maria	Italy
Owens, Rochelle	U.S.
Ozick, Cynthia	U.S.
Paley, Grace	U.S.
Panóva, Vera	Russia
Pardo Bazán, Emilia	Spain
Parker, Dorothy	U.S.
Parra, Teresa de la	Venezuela
Parra, Violeta	Chile
Parun, Vesna	Croatia
Pawlikowska-Jasnorzewska, Maria	Poland
Peri Rossi, Christina	Uruguay
Petrushevskaya, Ludmila	Russia
Petry, Ann	U.S. (African American)
Piercy, Marge	U.S.
Piñon, Nélida	Brazil
Pitter, Ruth	Great Britain
Pizarnik, Alejandra	Argentina
Plath, Sylvia	U.S.
Plessen, Elisabeth	Germany
Pollock, Sharon	Canada
Poniatowska, Elena	Mexico
Porter, Katherine Anne	U.S.
Portillo del Trambley, Estela	U.S. (Mexican American)
Potter, Beatrix	Great Britain
Poulin, Gabrielle	Canada
Pozzi, Catherine	France

Prichard, Katherine Susannah	Australia
Pritam, Amrita	India
Prou, Suzanne	France
Pujmanová, Marie	Czech Republic
Pym, Barbara	Great Britain
Queiroz, Rachel de	Brazil
Quiroga, Elena	Spain
Raab, Esther	Israel
Raine, Kathleen	Great Britain
Rama Rau, Santha	India
Ratushinskaya, Irina	Russia
Ravikovitch, Dalia	Israel
Rawlings, Marjorie Kinnan	U.S.
Redmon, Anne	Great Britain
Reinig, Christa	Germany
Renault, Mary	Great Britain
Rhys, Jean	Dominica–Great Britain
Ribeiro Tavares, Zulmira	Brazil
Rich, Adrienne	U.S.
Richardson, Dorothy	Great Britain
Richardson, Henry Handel (Ethel F. Robertson)	Australia
Riding (Jackson), Laura	U.S.
Ridler, Anne	Great Britain
Riley, Joan	Jamaica–Great Britain
Rinser, Luise	Germany
Roberts, Michèle	Great Britain
Robinson, Marilynne	U.S.
Rochefort, Christiane	France
Rodoreda, Mercè	Spain (Catalan)
Romano, Lalla	Italy
Rose, Wendy	U.S. (Native American)
Roth, Friederike	Germany
Roy, Gabrielle	Canada
Rukeyser, Muriel	U.S.

MCCARTHY, MARY (UNITED STATES) 1912–

Miss McCarthy has learned the difficult art of setting down everything as it might have happened, without telling a single self-protective lie and without even failing, in the midst of a seduction, to mention the safety pin that holds up the heroine's badly mended underwear. *The Company She Keeps* is not a likeable book, nor is it very well put together, but it has the still unusual quality of having been lived.

Malcolm Cowley. *The New Republic*.
May 25, 1942, p. 737

What is delightful about *The Oasis* is the infectious energy and enthusiasm of Miss McCarthy, who plunges gallantly into the thick of so many complicated ideas and problems with a rebarbative gusto.

There is a violence in this writer which is both exhilarating and amusing. . . . Miss McCarthy's mind has what people are accustomed to calling a masculine width or range. She sees people in terms of moralities—both civic and personal. But it is even more her feeling for words and her talent for epigram which emerges at the end of the book as her particular gift.

Julia Strachey. *New Statesman and Nation*.
February 26, 1949, pp. 211–12

The McCarthy pictures have horror in them, and all her characters live in hell, but there is nothing depressing about reading her stories. Her style has such verve and swiftness, is so compelling, that the reader follows after her, on the scavenger hunt for the revealing incident, the ultimate perception that will give away another person and deliver him, naked and quivering, into his understanding. There is an intellectual satisfaction to be found here, gratification in a style that is so perfect a tool for its purpose.

Lorine Pruette. *New York Herald Tribune*.
September 24, 1950, p. 8

Her highly sophisticated and intellectualized prose leads her into fascinating digressions which make her sound like an essayist *manqué;* it also leads her into frequent epigrams, but instead of the shallow verbal sparkle of drawing room comedy, hers have the psychological penetration of La Rochefoucauld. . . . Like Joyce she has been deeply affected by her early religious training even when fleeing from it. Although she has stepped out of the confessional booth to lie down on the analyst's couch she is still on the same quest for the essential, the quintessential self. Her brief incisive pieces are etched with corrosive acid, it is true; but they still have a savage honesty, a bristling sensibility, and at bottom a pitiless humility.

Robert Halsband. *Saturday Review of Literature*. October 7, 1950, p. 23

It is the anguished urban sensibility that Miss McCarthy's prose writhingly plots. The people in her stories all seem uncontrollably involved in endless showdowns with the people around them, or as often as not just with themselves; and nobody, unfortunately, ever seems to win. But this is the deadly pattern of relationships among "thinking" people.

Miss McCarthy's attitude toward the people in her stories is one of contempt and outrage, but it is not just a shallow, critical attitude. It originates in a deep and almost continually disappointed moralism. She wants people with intelligence to be good and decent and productive, and that they are not arouses the furious broken-hearted chastiser in her.

Chandler Brossard. *The American Mercury*. February, 1951, pp. 232–33

The most important thing in fiction is binding connection, that which makes the characters adhere to one another, as it were of their own affinity, through all the situations the novelist invents. This is love. It cannot be derived from the satirical connection. . . . Yet it is this which Miss McCarthy vainly tries to do in her last two novels (*The Oasis* and *The Groves of Academe*) . . . ; she would have satire do the work of love. Apparently she cannot prevent the substitution, because satire has become for her more than a genre; a virtual ontology which throws up a world of ridiculous objects, even when she herself belongs to that world and berates it only because she is unable to break her dependence on it.

Isaac Rosenfeld. *The New Republic*. March 3, 1952, p. 21

The major distinction Miss McCarthy makes with regard to people, the only distinction that has force and reality to her, is between the intelligent and the stupid. . . . A Mary McCarthy heroine examines her soul with the scrupulous, unashamed persistence of a professional model looking herself over in the vanity-table mirror. . . . In general, it might be said . . . [that her characters] dramatize the disjunction—or rather, the hostility—between Reason and Impulse. This is Miss McCarthy's true subject, a theme which underlies her satirical castigations, which calls forth all her famous brilliance, which gives point to her acerbity and depths to her apparently gratuitous bitterness.

Norman Podhoretz. *Commentary*. March, 1956, p. 272

Unlike other notable hatchet-women (Dorothy Parker, for instance), Miss McCarthy is not a Sophisticate but an Intellectual. . . . And though time and circumstance cast her in with the young radicals for whom Marxian criticism of "the system" furnished that rationalization of their discontents which the previous generation had found in the war against "provinciality," she never committed herself wholeheartedly to that either. In fact, if she ever discovered what she believed, admired, or wanted she never devoted much time to praising or expounding it. But she can justify her contempt for what she does not like—and that is almost everything including other intellectuals—with telling thrusts and shrewd analysis.

Joseph Wood Krutch. Saturday Review of
Literature. May 26, 1956, p. 20

Memories of a Catholic Girlhood, Mary McCarthy's account of her childhood and adolescence, has made clearer to me the traits which make her the particular sort of artist she is. They are, I believe, perfectionism, a fanatical striving for honesty, and a fierce sense of hierarchy—a combination calculated to produce a thoroughly disturbing vision of life. For to the perfectionist, things-as-they-are appear for the most part lamentably worse than they ought to be; the cult of honesty makes it a duty to portray this state of affairs as unsparingly as possible; and in a hierarchical order, it is always easy to disgrace oneself but almost impossible to behave so well as to transcend one's station. . . . The portraiture of her recollections is more tolerant of human frailties than in her fiction and therefore more attractive and richer in vitality.

Charles J. Rolo. Atlantic Monthly.
June, 1957, pp. 90–91

What she has written so far has been of the fashionably acid and shocking kind: it is concerned on the whole, even to the point of ruthlessness, with the discrepancy in an urban and aggressive society between moral jargon and the inanity of pretentious action, with the atrophy of feeling and the protective surrogate of sentimentality and middle-class convention. These defects in our life she has represented with an unmerciful eye for weakness and vulgarity. Memories of a Catholic Girlhood is no less skeptical toward the world of the past half-century in which she grew up, but it is more perceptive, more critical of her own resources of understanding, and therefore, more mature, than any of her previous fiction.

Victor Lange. The New Republic. June 24,
1957, p. 18

What Chaucer did for the fourteenth-century English pilgrim, Mary McCarthy has done for the Vassar girl of 1933. The section of society Miss McCarthy has chosen to cut through obviously limits her field, but one of the virtues of The Group is that it is an unassuming and economically constructed novel which displays a brilliance for the particular, rather than symbolic. . . . And this without a trace of apology or pretense from the author. It is never a fatuous book. Even when it succeeds in reaching beyond its own narrative boundaries of time and place, it remains essentially what Miss McCarthy apparently wanted it to be; a period piece.

Robert Kiely. The Nation. September 21,
1963, p. 163

Miss McCarthy is very good at showing how the life and feelings of women are mixed up in things, particularly those things—clothes, furniture, food, etc.—which make up the domestic routine. Yet, the proliferation of such detail has the effect of robbing her characters of freedom, as though they were all prisoners in a Cartesian universe, enmeshed in those great chains of causation that lead from the First Cause to each tiny effect.

This is the style, then, of a writer on whom nothing is lost and for whom everything figures. Miss McCarthy does not handle words with unusual distinction—in that sense she is not a stylist at all—yet her prose is unmistakable. At its most characteristic her writing has a finely articulated grayness that comes from a series of wonderfully linked, perfectly comprehended minutiae. . . .

In much of Miss McCarthy's later fiction there is an increasing sense of baffled helplessness, an undercurrent of terror at the powerlessness of women to save themselves, or even to help themselves. The sardonic amusement with which she watched Margaret Sargent [*The Company She Keeps*] make a mess out of her life has gradually disappeared to be replaced by the queer, hard, semi-tragic feeling that one finds at the end of *A Charmed Life* and throughout *The Group.*

Thomas Rogers. Commentary. December,
1963, pp. 488–89

Her dependence on autobiographical or semi-autobiographical materials is not in itself a deficiency (although one wonders whether she could write a novel not based on events in her own life), but her technique is. Her enormous vocabulary and erudition show on every page; indeed, scarcely a page appears without some italicized French phrase or esoteric term. But this witty, highly intelligent fondness for words for their own sake sometimes makes of a relatively short narrative a book of several hundred pages. Her treatment of characters, with rare exceptions, serves as a pulpit or platform from which she can lecture on some evil in humanity or some *cause célèbre* with which she is no longer personally involved. Indeed, so cavalier is she with characters, even central ones, that she disposes of them in the best *deus ex machina* fashion; when all else fails, kill them off; it's neater that way, and it saves her the chore of figuring out some logical means of ending the novel. When Miss McCarthy is not attempting a novel, as in her excellent stories in *The Company She Keeps,* or her semiautobiographical narratives in *Cast a Cold Eye* (1950, later incorporated in *Memories of a Catholic Girlhood* [1957], in many ways her best book), she has no noticeable trouble winding things up; there is none of the sometimes forced attempts at polemicizing; there is none of the artificial intrusion of the author in literary or political digressions. In short, whatever strengths are to be found in her novels—vigor, honesty, straightforwardness, intelligence, to name a few—are more than adequately represented in the shorter pieces as well, and not a few additional strengths are added.

Paul Schlueter. In Harry T. Moore, ed.
Contemporary American Novelists
(Carbondale: Southern Illinois Press, 1964),
pp. 62–63

Mary McCarthy's own voice is heard more in all of her work than she is perhaps aware of. . . . Certainly the more it is heard, the more feeling there is. One hates to say it, because one hates even by the remotest implication to seem to abandon fiction to the breast-beating writers, but it is difficult to get away from the point that in some of her novels and tales Miss McCarthy casts *too* cold an eye. One welcomes the feeling in *The Stones of Florence* for the Florentines themselves. The Venetians may have allowed their city to become a fairy tale, but the Florentines care for much more than their monuments, and Miss McCarthy has a fine scorn for the foreign residents in the past and present who have not been able to see this. And in *Memories of a Catholic Girlhood* she rises to a pitch of something like passion that makes it the noblest utterance that she has yet produced.

Louis Auchincloss. *Pioneers and Caretakers*
(Minneapolis: University of Minnesota
Press, 1965), p. 186

Mary McCarthy does "miss" by having too much furniture in her novels and by not leaving enough space for the play of passions and the drama of growth. But if her concern is satiric and her interest lies in creating characters unaffected by time, then these charges are inconsequential. However, if her purpose is to write not satirical novels but novels that are satiric only peripherally, then the lack of resonance and development that is evident in her fiction becomes a flaw. The chief failure of her fiction to the present is that it commits itself neither to satire nor to the "form" of the novel. The result is a somewhat dichotomous grouping of snatches of brilliant satire and of characters whose complexity involves them in a different—and greater—reality.

Barbara McKenzie. *Mary McCarthy* (New
York: Twayne, 1966), p. 179

She shares Emily Dickinson's admission to Colonel Higginson that "candor is the only wile," and she has built a career, as someone has said, on candor and dissent. She has always regarded sex as comic or grotesque, and professes a lack of interest in "happy" sex in fiction. She is unforgiving to her enemies and is no more charitable toward human stupidity than she is to bad writing. She is a David against the social, economic, intellectual and cultural Goliaths of the twentieth century, and she relishes the role.

She has never lost her faith in the Fact and her reliance upon it in her novels. Her fiction is really dramatized theses, orations with figures. Her special purview has been the facts of feminine existence that other writers, especially other women, have shied away from as indelicate. As Maxwell Geismar said of Saul Bellow, she is a novelist in spite of herself, for all her instincts are toward the informal essay raised to the level of fiction. Dwight Macdonald has called her fiction "a series of reviews of people's performances" rather than a direct vision of the performances themselves. In the process of the review we learn her standards and hear her rather stern, sometimes almost puritanical moral judgments. Her criticism, like her fiction, is uncorrupted by compassion, and she writes it with a sense of mission, of vocation. She is an advocate of common sense, the concrete, the real, and the authentic.

Doris Grumbach. *The Company She Kept*
(New York: Coward, 1967), pp. 216–17

The fact is that one returns to Mary McCarthy not for her gossip but for herself, or rather for herselves, those black shadows cast by the fingers of a very gifted writer on the hard wall of experience. These are the I, She, You, the Young Woman, the Wife of her fiction and essays, to whom she gives a name only reluctantly; it is the reader, not the author, who craves the security of the named name. Few writers have fought so hard to preserve the self against intrusion, whether from the otherness of fact or the otherness of other people, and she has done this with the classic devices of her beloved French novelists: the revelations that tell all and nothing, the ruthless self-analyses that defy us to belabor her weaknesses, snobberies and cruelties half so harshly as she has done herself.

Ellen Moers. *The New York Times*.
June 11, 1967, p. 7

[McCarthy's] work is about the painful mixed blessing of freedom for her kind of people—for intellectuals—and in particular, about how hard it has been for intellectuals in our time to behave decently and humanly. For to be free and clever has often meant only to be able to escape from difficult, limiting reality into the realm of flattering abstractions. And yet—for I have said that to speak of what she dislikes is to speak of only half her subject— if she shows what makes her kind go wrong, she shows just as vividly what makes them go right. She shows that sometimes, even in intellectuals free to please themselves, there arises a love for reality that is greater than love of self. This development, because it means that the self must be willing to suffer for something it values more than its own ease, can be one of the moving and beautiful events of a human life—it can be heroic.

At any rate, the conflict between these two tendencies of the mind is at the center of all Miss McCarthy's novels. Because this conflict is her own, her reports on it have the variety, complexity, and intensity of personal experience. But because the freedom to live by ideas, ideas which may lead away from the real as well as toward it, is what distinguishes the whole class of twentieth-century intellectuals, her tales of the troubled Mary McCarthy heroine have developed naturally into social satire.

Irvin Stock. *Mary McCarthy* (Minneapolis:
University of Minnesota Press, 1968), p. 9

To read Mary McCarthy you have to be constantly awake. There is no filler than can be skipped, or relaxed winks to the reader assuring him he needn't work too hard for the next page or two; whatever you miss is to your disadvantage, and most of the essays [in *The Writing on the Wall, and Other Essays*] need to be reread, preferably after a second look at the particular book under consideration.

What keeps one awake is the sound of a voice always talking *to* you, varying itself in pitch and delivery as the subject demands. This is not to praise her for lively shock-value, as in the phrase "I'll bet Mary McCarthy would do a job on *that* one." In fact readers with the image foremost of the Lady Mary as wicked wasp will find it quite irrelevant to this book; whatever cleverness there is, and there is plenty, operates in the service of literature.

William H. Pritchard. *Hudson Review.*
Summer, 1970, p. 372

The big news about Miss McCarthy's new book [*Birds of America*] would seem, anywhere in the course of reading it, to be its warmth. A novelist noted for her use of acid and vitriol has here produced, not precisely a novel but a work, didactic in tone, whose principal characters are a loving son and a lovable mother, in which even divorced husbands are likeable, the ugliness of modernity is hateful, and home, art, old days, old ways, lovely and to be valued. . . .

Not till [the end] does the realization begin seeping into the reader's mind of what Miss McCarthy may really have been about here. Far from extolling established values, she has destroyed them, by putting in their place a new archetype: the woman of the future. . . . The whole of Miss McCarthy's career—rebel against religious orthodoxy, sexual nonconformist, intellectual and political iconoclast, falls into place: *Birds of America* is a parable of her development. Louder than the loudest protests, clearer than the coolest psychological logic, this warm, readable narrative liberates the cold truth about her mind, unique in its own right.

Virginia Quarterly Review. Autumn, 1971,
p. clx

As in her earlier books about the war, *Vietnam* and *Hanoi,* the most impressive quality that Mary McCarthy brings to bear on her subject is a keen moral sensibility. This is her real guide as she picks her way through the legal debris in the Georgia courtroom, sorting its facts, examining its participants, and salvaging the key issues. What emerges [in *Medina*] is not a document that vilifies the rather shallow figures of the trial but a polemic that tries to pull us closer to recognition of the nature of our involvement in this action.

Basil T. Paquet. *New York Review of Books.*
September 21, 1972, p. 37

The first seven chapters [of *The Mask of State*] are on-the-spot accounts of the Ervin Committee hearings. Their factual accuracy proves that Miss McCarthy listened carefully and absorbed the substance of the testimony. When she tells us what happened her perception is fully adequate to providing an understanding of the events.

Admittedly, one whose hunger for facts, accusations and quotations is insatiable would do better to plunge into the brain-addling flood of undigested information which is visited upon the reader of *The New York Times.* Mary McCarthy's aim is to interpret what is being said, and by what manner of men.

What better evidence of Mary McCarthy's journalistic skill can we ask for, than the fact that almost a year later nothing has happened which seriously contradicts her conclusions and perceptions. Despite the energetic ingenuities of all the king's lawyers and all the king's pressmen, we see them shattered now as she described them then. . . .

McCarthy's voice has always been perfectly reliable; the stirring and disturbing tone of the born truth teller is hers, whether she is writing essays or fiction. Her perspective is always feminine: Antigone grown up, her absoluteness not diminished as she takes on sex. She has never been easy on herself or her characters, or tried to make anyone look better. This is true whether she is describing her failure to best an anti-Semite ("Artists in Uniform"), her fears about traveling as a reporter in Vietnam ("How It Went"), or her heroine's response to divorce in "Cruel and Barbarous Treatment.". . .

Where are we, then, to place *Cannibals and Missionaries,* which its publishers present as "a thriller," in the context of Mary McCarthy's work? She is not the sort of writer who would toss off a book as a lark or a diverting experiment, so why has she done it?

It is clear to me that this, the most political, the least autobiographical of her novels, would have been impossible without her experience of traveling to Vietnam as a reporter. Many of the details of that experience, particularly those about physical fear and communal bonding, find their way into this novel in the accounts of the passengers' ordeal. *Cannibals and Missionaries* is the story, among other things, of a committee of liberals who are hijacked while traveling to Iran to examine the atrocities of the Shah's regime. It speaks, with McCarthy's habitually unsentimental voice, to the problem of witness and political responsibility among nonprofessional men of good will. For McCarthy, terrorism is disturbing in the same way that sexual promiscuity would have been for Emily Brontë: it is political activity without manners, without form; therefore it is incapable of yielding much meaning and is inevitably without hope. In some crucial way, it is not serious; it has no stake in the future. . . .

The most important achievement of *Cannibals and Missionaries* is McCarthy's understanding of the psychology of terrorism, the perception, expressed by Henk, that terrorism is the product of despair, "the ultimate sin against the Holy Ghost." Once again, McCarthy is asking the difficult question, confronting the difficult problem. For surely, terrorism threatens us all, not only physically and politically, but morally and intellectually as well. It postulates a system of oblique correspondences, a violent disproportion between ends and means, against which we have no recourse. She comes to terms as well with our peculiar but irrefutable tendency to see human beings as replaceable, works of art unique. For the lover of formal beauty who is also a moralist, it is the most vexed of questions. I'm not sure McCarthy has anything new to say on the subject, but she does not imply that she does.

Often, artists have responded to the prospect of atrocity by creating a well-crafted work of art. One thinks of Milton's "On the Late Massacre of the Piedmontese," a perfect Italian sonnet whose hundredth word is "hundredfold." In response to the truly frightful prospect of anarchic terrorism, Mary McCarthy has written one of the most shapely novels to have come out in recent years: a well-made book. It is delightful to observe her balancing, winnowing, fitting in the pieces of her plot.

The tone of *Cannibals and Missionaries* is a lively pessimism. Its difficult conclusion is that to be a human being at this time is a sad fate: even the revolutionaries have no hope for the future, and virtue is in the hands of the unremarkable, who alone remain unscathed.

Mary Gordon. *The New York Times.*
September 30, 1979, pp. 1, 33–35

Cannibals and Missionaries is susceptible to the recurring criticism that McCarthy is more essayist than novelist. One reader wonders why she wrote this book as a novel; another finds the long periods of inaction tedious. We may again pass over the question of genre. As the term is commonly used, *Cannibals and Missionaries* is a novel. But to say so does not clear it of the charge that it contains so many monologues, both internal and external, that the subjects of conversations and reflections, rather than action and character, sometimes dominate our attention.

There is, to be sure, a lot of talk in *Ulysses, The Sound and the Fury,* and *Portnoy's Complaint.* But McCarthy's fiction hardly resembles Joyce's, or Faulkner's, or Roth's. Although she exposes the minds and actions of her characters, she does not often explore their souls and invite us to *feel* with them. Indeed, we hardly even mourn their deaths—fortunately, since their mortality rate is appalling. We like many of them, but amusement and embarrassment are the emotions we are most likely to feel on their behalf; and we do not willingly identify with most of them. We do, however, judge them. We think about them in terms of what they do and ought to do, not of how they feel or why they feel that way. Our attention is directed to how their minds work, what they know, and how they explain themselves. McCarthy believes (as she says in the interview with Niebuhr) that truth is knowable; her characters are prone to err, but not with impunity and not without presenting their case. They argue and rationalize. They think in essays; sometimes they write letters and journals. And finally, we cannot believe that Sophie's journal entries and Peter Levi's letter are written to portray Sophie and Peter; rather, these characters seem at times to have been created to ponder ideas.

If a weakness of McCarthy's fiction is its essayistic tendencies, its great strength is the accuracy with which she portrays characters, particularly comic characters, giving new life and individuality to universal types. Aileen Simmons belongs to the tradition of the Wife of Bath, going on a pilgrimage and looking for a mate, gregarious, a little overdressed, outspoken, ever-mindful of precedence. Her eye is on the clerkly Senator, an unlikely prospect if ever there was one, but she also contemplates a rich old man, Charles Tenant; like Allison of Bath, she is alert to any opportunity. Frank Barber has literary kinsmen in Parson Adams and Pangloss and, doubtless, some Ur-Parson among the cavemen. Of more recent vintage is the wicked Charles, genuinely liberal, dauntless, and dreadful in his confessions of the human frailties that plague us all. He is a comic character and a homosexual, and the two facts have nothing to do with each other; the gay Charles is offered as character without any statement about his sexual identity, which is a problem only to Aileen. At eighty, he is in any case past his prime, but he is physically fearless and a good foil to the other men with their macho instincts.

Willene Hardy. Mary McCarthy (New York:
Frederick Ungar, 1981), pp. 194–95

McCarthy is at her sharpest when she deals with would-be elites of hangers-on. Even though she has been linked with artistic and intellectual elites, the monetary elites, for instance, have not enjoyed safe passage. The outstanding feature of peripheral members of the monetary elites is the tinge of the *parvenu,* further tarnished by grasping insecurity. Kay Strong Peterson, of *The Group,* serves as a fine contrast to her genuinely elitist roommate the placid, moneyed Pokey. Kay is a member of the *nouveaux riches* who is striving to penetrate the inner circles of the moneyed elites. Shrewdness and money, even though new, have gotten her into Vassar, even into Pokey's exclusive South Tower group—but she is clearly out of her depth. The more legitimately elitist South Tower girls spot her as an outsider, a philistine newcomer, a frenetic acquisitor with lots of money but impoverished tastes. They are aristocratically embarrassed for her when she delights in the check that her bourgeois father sends to her in lieu of attending her wedding. Kay further reveals her reliance on money by spendthriftiness. But unlike Pokey, Kay's purchases skewer her budget. She is not wealthy enough, finally, to buy her way into the inner circles. An airplane, for example is clearly beyond her budgetary reach. Yet she tries to create the illusion of a personal pedigree that she is eternally denied by buying only the most expensive name-brand products. . . .

Her autobiography is replete with a sense of doctrinaire Mary McCarthyism and she feels free to throw boulders even at an afterlife: "I do not mind if I lose my soul for all eternity. If the kind of God exists who would damn me for not working out a deal with Him, then that is unfortunate. I should not care to spend eternity in the company of such a person." But her supersufficiency and claims to integrity seem mere pretense: for McCarthy though a lapsed Catholic, refuses to let the topic die. Uncertain, she is always compelled to launch one more barbed denial. The defense against damnation is a paradigm for the unstable fortress of superiority she has erected to protect herself in the elitist world she chooses to dwell in—a world she both loves and loathes.

Dawn Trouard. Perspectives on
Contemporary Literature. 7, 1981,
pp. 99–100, 102

In *The Oasis,* a group of leftist, libertarian refugees from mainstream America move into an abandoned turn-of-the-century resort in the Pennsylvania foothills, ostensibly to practice what they preach: "certain notions of justice, freedom, and sociability." When the colonists find themselves using force to eject a local party of strawberry pickers who are trespassing on their new property, the experiment runs a cropper. McCarthy assembles the usual bunch: an editor, teacher, critic, Protestant minister, actor, trade unionist, girl student, magazine illustrator, novelist, middle-aged poet, and the colony's maverick, a diabetic Jewish businessman from Belmont, Massachusetts. In one guise or another, they are characters the reader meets in nearly all her fiction. . . .

Cannibals and Missionaries . . . despite its proximity to [McCarthy's] immersion in philosophy, is the least reflective of McCarthy's novels. Ideas bob on its intricately plotted surface like bright decoys, inviting comparison with the natural world but not quite making the cut. A character's journal entry, torn from context at the end of the book, addresses a lifelong question: "Art merely the medium, the element, by which the sacred, i.e., the extraordinary, is conveyed." The politics of terrorism are treated aphoristically: "Today's arch-revolutionaries had no faith in a future life for their ideas; it was gone, like the Christian faith in God's design." In extremis, when the terrorist aims at moral instruction, or *de*-instruction, as McCarthy's pet terrorist, Jeroen, the former Dutch art student who commands the hijackers, does, terrorism becomes "art for art's sake in the political realm."

Carol Brightman. Writing Dangerously:
Mary McCarthy and Her World (New York:
Clarkson Potter, 1992), pp. 110, 592

MCCULLERS, CARSON (UNITED STATES) 1917–67

Maturity does not cover the quality of her work. It is something beyond that, something more akin to the vocation of pain to which a great poet is born. Reading her, one feels this girl is wrapped in knowledge which has roots beyond the span of her life and her experience. How else can she so surely plumb the hearts of characters as strange and, under the force of her creative shaping, as real as she presents. . . . Carson McCullers is a full-fledged novelist whatever her age. She writes with a sweep and certainty that are overwhelming.

Rose Feld. *The New York Times.*
June 16, 1940, p. 6

Miss McCullers's picture of loneliness, death, accident, insanity, fear, mob violence and terror is perhaps the most desolate that has so far come from the South. Her quality of despair is unique and individual; and it seems to me more natural and authentic than that of Faulkner. Her groping characters live in a world more completely lost than any Sherwood Anderson ever dreamed of. And she recounts incidents of death and attitudes of stoicism in sentences whose neutrality makes Hemingway's terse prose warm and partisan by comparison.

Richard Wright. *The New Republic.*
August 5, 1940, p. 195

No one could say . . . that Miss McCullers has not succeeded in making her genuine talent felt, a talent which is less of subtlety than of enfant-terrible insight expressed with quite grown-up precision, as yet unmellowed and unhallowed. It should not be forced in order to take advantage of a passing vogue, for it will surely crack up in the hurly-burly of competition. It is a brave talent; but not, I think, a very sturdy plant. It calls for gentle handling and careful cultivation.

Fred T. Marsh. *The New York Times.*
March 2, 1941, p. 6

She is a suggestive rather than an eloquent writer, and often seems to present us less with a meaning than with a hint. And yet the lines of her work are clear and firm. . . . Though she has an acute observation, she does not use it to make rounded people. . . . Carson McCuller's work has always seemed to me to be a form of self-dramatization. . . . She does not dramatize herself in the sense that she is merely autobiographical; but she does dramatize herself in the sense that she seems to invest the various sides of her personality with attributes skillfully collected from the outside world.

George Dangerfield. *Saturday Review of*
Literature. March 30, 1946, p. 15

Her gifts are limited—as Virginia Woolf's were limited, or Glenway Wescott's.

I do not mention these writers casually, or because I am unfamiliar with them. Like them both, Mrs. McCullers, though operating in a narrow field, ploughs deep furrows. Like them both, if I may pursue the metaphor, she engages in what Southerners used to call intensive cultivation. The trick about intensive cultivation . . . is that the earth runs sterile. Such, surely, was the fate of Mrs. Woolf and Mr. Wescott. Up to the moment Mrs. McCullers has not thus been cursed. She does not, of course, write the kind of gleaming, perfect prose Mrs. Woolf was capable of. But hers is beautifully fitted to her purposes, and that, I suppose, is what good writing means.

Francis Downing. *Commonweal.*
May 24, 1946, p. 148

The art of Carson McCullers has been called "Gothic." Perhaps it is—superficially. Certainly her day-to-day world, her little Southern towns, are haunted by far more masterful horrors than were ever conjured up in the dreary castles of a Horace Walpole. It seems to me, however, that the "Gothic" label misses the essential point. Because Carson McCullers is ultimately the artist functioning at the very loftiest symbolic level, and if one must look for labels, I should prefer to call her work "metaphysical." Behind the strange and horrible in her world there are played out the most sombre tragedies of the human spirit; her mutes, her hunchbacks, speak of complexities and frustrations which are so native to man that they can only be recognized, perhaps, in the shock which comes from seeing them dressed in the robes of grotesques. They pass upon the street everyday but we only notice them when they drag a foot as they go by.

William P. Clancy. *Commonweal.*
June 15, 1951, p. 243

Since all her novels represent some kind of variation on the one theme of human loneliness, a knowledge of her treatment of this theme is necessary to understand the purpose and cast of her writing. We should not take it for granted, however, that her work is in any way systematic or mechanical. Her way is not the course of allegory . . . but the way of myth. She is, after all, a novelist haunted by the elusive nature of human truth, and her underlying theme gives coherence to the variety and surprises she has found in the world about her.

Dayton Kohler. *The English Journal.*
October 1951, pp. 421–22

The same fundamental pattern exists in all Mrs. McCuller's major prose works. The pattern is more elaborate in *The Ballad of the Sad Café* than elsewhere, but the beginnings of it are recognizable in her first novel and its evolution has occupied the whole of her literary career. It is a closed pattern, and one which many readers will view with a reluctance which is a measure of their suspicion that it is, after all, authentic. . . . But it is a pattern with a strange vision of life which Carson McCullers has attained in *The Ballad of the Sad Café;* an eternal flaw exists in the machinery of love which alone has the power to liberate man from his fate of spiritual isolation.

Oliver Evans. New World Writing I.
April, 1952, p. 310

To say that Mrs. McCullers has a Gothic penchant is but to note, and note superficially, her interest in the grotesque, the freakish, and the incongruous. Such qualities, to be sure, exert a large influence on the contemporary imagination. There is another sense, however, in which the Gothic element may be defined more pertinently. The Gothic insists on spiritualization, the spiritualization of matter itself, and it insists on subjectivism. . . .

Protestant as the fundamentalist tradition of the South may be, and Gothic as its experience of guilt and tragedy is likely to appear, it is the peculiar stamp of subjectivism, wistful and bizarre, that emerges like a watermark on every page Mrs. McCullers has written.

Ihab Hassan. Modern Fiction Studies.
Winter, 1959, pp. 312–13

She was an American legend from the beginning, which is to say that her fame was as much a creation of publicity as of talent. The publicity was the work of those fashion magazines where a dish of black-eyed peas can be made to seem the roe of some rare fish, photographed by Avedon; yet McCullers's dreaming androgynous face, looking out at us from glossy pages, in its ikon elegance subtly confounded the chic of the lingerie ads all about her.

Unlike too many other "legends," her talent was as real as her face. Though she was progenitress to much "Southern writing" (one can name a dozen writers who would not exist in the way they do if she had not written in the way she did), she had a manner all her own. Her prose was chaste and severe and realistic in its working out of narrative. I suspect that of all the Southern writers, she is the most likely to endure, though her vision is by no means as large or encompassing as that, say, of Faulkner, whom she has the grace to resemble not at all.

Gore Vidal. The Reporter. September 28,
1961, p. 50

For those who have indicted Mrs. McCullers and the whole school of Southern writers for their absorption in what often, for lack of anything better, is termed the "morbid," there can be, of course, no answer. Recognizing what Tennessee Williams has called "an underlying dreadfulness in modern experience," Mrs. McCullers elects to depict it in its own terms—terms sometimes fraught with an almost overpowering feeling of human suffocation in a world beyond control, yet terms ultimately successful through their very irresistible intensity.

In the labyrinth established for the McCullers characters, a world of "no exit," man is caught up in the dizziness of life, is inextricably drawn toward a crisis in which he either recognizes himself or, failing this, is lost forever in frustration and despair. It is a world of either/or, in which there are few half-way measures, where everything is viewed in nightmarish bold relief. Simultaneously unrealistic and yet supra-realistic, it is the unique and unforgettable world of Carson McCullers.

Catharine Hughes. *Commonweal.* October
13, 1961, p. 75

In every case, whether the lover is grotesque or whether the grotesquerie is in the nature of his love (we remember that Frankie Addams has, in the words of Berenice, fallen "in love with a wedding"), the result is not only suffering but violence. Singer kills himself. The Captain shoots Private Williams. And in the later works the violence persists. In *The Ballad of the Sad Café,* the climax is a horrifying wrestling-boxing match between Miss Amelia and Marvin Macy, after which Macy and the hunchback, Cousin Lymon, systematically destroy and violate everything. The concluding action of *Clock without Hands* starts with the bombing of Sherman Pew's house and his death, events which are followed by the complete collapse of old Judge Clane as he tries to make a speech on the radio; after these bizarre details, the death from leukemia of J. T. Malone provides a quiet and pathetic ending. Indeed the novel is set within a framework of sickness and death which thus become the symbolic symptoms of the society (a punishment for the failure to recognize the existence of time and the necessity of change?).

Grotesque characters and lurid events are not all of Mrs. McCullers's stock-in-trade. She has, as well, a sense of form. In a curiously dead-pan style, she begins each of her longer works with an exact statement of what is going on.

Marvin Felheim. In Harry T. Moore,
Contemporary American Novelists
(Carbondale: Southern Illinois University
Press, 1964), pp. 49–50

The Member of the Wedding (1946) and *The Ballad of the Sad Café* (1951) represent the art of Carson McCullers at its finest. One cannot find in the history of the American novella more beautifully plotted pieces. . . .

Although it is on the authorship of her novellas that Mrs. McCullers's fame will primarily rest, *Clock without Hands* is a memorable book. It makes the mistake of dealing too currently with the segregation problem, so that a sense of newspaper headlines becomes mixed up oddly with the never quite real atmosphere of a McCullers novel, but it is still a vivid picture of the South in the throes of racial crisis.

Louis Auchincloss. *Pioneers and Caretakers*
(Minneapolis: University of Minnesota
Press, 1965), pp. 165, 168

In her best work, Mrs. McCullers has always been concerned with exploring what Hawthorne called the "labyrinth of the human heart," and what she has found therein has not always proved cause for rejoicing. What she conceives to be the truth about human nature is a melancholy truth: each man is sur- rounded by a "zone of loneliness," serving a life sentence of solitary con- finement. The only way in which he can communicate with his fellow prisoners is through love: this affords him a certain measure of relief, but the relief is incomplete and temporary since love is seldom a completely mutual experience and is also subject to time. This view of life and love received its most pessimistic statement, of course, in *The Ballad of the Sad Café,* which added the startling notion that the beloved "fears and hates" the lover. A flaw thus exists in the very nature of love, and frustration is the lot of man.

Oliver Evans. *The Ballad of Carson
McCullers* (New York: Coward, 1966),
pp. 192–93

In a recent survey, *Fiction of the Forties,* Chester Eisinger has traced the main flaw in *The Member of the Wedding* to "its focus on the child's self- centered world in which the macrocosm plays no part." But this, I think, is precisely the source of its strength. Throughout this essay, I have argued that Mrs. McCullers is fundamentally a master of bright and melancholy moods, a lyricist not a philosopher, an observer of maimed characters not of contami- nated cultures. That she writes best of uncomplicated people in fairly straightforward narrative forms is proven positively by *The Member of the Wedding* and "The Ballad of the Sad Café," and negatively by the failure of her last full-length work of fiction. Published in 1961, after ten years of painful composition, *Clock without Hands* tries to link the existential crisis of a man doomed by cancer to the sociological crisis of the South poisoned by racial strife. But because Mrs. McCullers was ill and working against her natural grain, the novel is deficient both in psychological intuition and cultural analysis.

Lawrence Graver. *Carson McCullers*
(Minneapolis: University of Minnesota
Press, 1969), p. 42

In Mrs. McCullers' writings, even when bodies are not freakish, souls are. Souls, she remarks, have colors and shapes like bodies. Indeed, these shapes are so marked that they give the impression of abnormality even in a normal body. Contradictions in the mind show in the body of Jake Blount [in *The*

Heart Is a Lonely Hunter] as though he were a man who had served a term in prison, lived for a long time with foreigners in South America, or gone to Harvard. Something was different from the usual. The great question here is whether fulfilment obtained at the expense of normality should be considered wrong. Should such fulfilment be allowed to bring happiness? The soul of man is small and grotesque. It seeks to love its grotesque counterpart in the flesh. The flesh, however, does not recognize its soul and hates it.

What Mrs. McCullers is offering in this regard is a strange variant of neo-Platonism. In classical neo-Platonism beautiful soul cries out in longing to beautiful soul, finding its happiness in a union beyond the flesh as it reaches out to the bliss of the Transcendent Good. Mrs. McCullers's affirmation is that a Creator has formed an incomplete humanity, one that can only trust that there is sense in creation. Some good, rather than total good, is the meaning available for man.

Radiance, nevertheless, exists in the world and cannot be denied.

Alice Hamilton. *The Dalhousie Review.*
Summer, 1970, p. 216

In McCullers what fills the space usually occupied by man-and-woman love is a sensitiveness that charges other people with magical perceptions. She radiated in all her work a demand for love so total that another was to become the perfect giver, and so become magical. The world is so bleak that it is always just about to be transformed.

Alfred Kazin. *Bright Book of Life* (Boston:
Little, Brown, 1973), p. 52

If the muse of isolation was for Carson McCullers inward-turning and at home only in the South of her childhood memories, it inspired her best writing with a rare sympathy for and insight into hidden suffering which, I think, represent the highest accomplishments of her fiction. For McCullers wrote of man's isolation with an understanding that was as compassionate as it was despairing. She spoke for people, who, in their trapped inwardness, could not speak for themselves, who loved without hope of being loved. Running throughout her works is the unstated conviction that no human being can in his inmost, truest self ever be really known, that he is doomed either to eternal loneliness or to compromise with the crass world outside. . . .

McCullers believed that only through the compassion and empathy of art could such vulnerable inwardness be freed and appreciated for the valuable and rare quality that it was. Her vision of human loneliness is a vision born of love. . . . McCullers possessed what most of her characters tragically lack, a double vision that enabled her to see the inside and the outside of people: a hopeless love for a departed friend beneath John Singer's deferential politeness, a sincere moral outrage beneath Jake Blount's loud talk and belligerent manner, an uncertainty of identity and terror of the future beneath Frankie's foolishness and irritability, and a desperate, lonely passion beneath

Miss Amelia's masculine dress and crafty business practices. In her most successful works McCullers could, as she once claimed, "become" her characters, enter their lonely lives, the places where they lived. And without letting us lose sight of their awkward, sometimes frightening and often amusing outwardness, she let us see into their secret inwardness.

Richard M. Cook. *Carson McCullers* (New York: Frederick Ungar, 1975), pp. 126–28

McCullers's is . . . the definitive use of a specific emotional effect—a pathos that at once lends a strange atmosphere to landscape and character, and helps establish an intimate, unusually searching relationship between tale and reader. This is an impressive achievement—showing the kind of subtlety and even deviousness of intent we are perhaps more inclined to associate with more "difficult" fiction—and its very impressiveness has, I believe, led one or two of McCullers's critics into overestimating her. . . .

The very perfection of McCullers's work depends, after all, upon her own level-headed acceptance of her limitations. She knows that she can describe, quite subtly, one particular dilemma or area of life and she concentrates almost her entire resources on that. There is no place in her fiction . . . for the rich "over-plus" of experience—by which I mean any aspects of behavior that cannot be included under the heading of theme, or any dimensions of feeling that cannot be reconciled with the major effect of pathos. And recognizing this she demonstrates little interest in such matters as the historical and social context, and no commitment either to the idea of a developing consciousness. Her people walk around and around within the circle of their own personalities, their inner world of thought and desire hardly engaging with the outer world at all. They seldom change, except physically, they never reflect more than one aspect of our experience (admittedly, it is a significant one); and to inflate them, their world, or indeed their creator to a major status—to suppose, in fact, that McCullers's novels and short stories are any more important to the tradition than they genuinely are—is, I believe, to be guilty of what used to be called "overkill." It is, in other words, to smother a quiet but effective talent by heaping upon it unearned and patently unacceptable praise.

As for McCullers's actual achievement, though, setting aside all such exaggeration, that surely is certain and secure. She is not a major writer. . . . But she is a very good minor one—so good, indeed, that she seems to reap a definite advantage from her minor status and turn her limitations into virtues.

Richard Gray. *The Literature of Memory* (Baltimore: Johns Hopkins University Press, 1977), pp. 272–73

Mrs. McCullers's fiction, in particular *The Member of the Wedding,* can speak to the adolescent reader in very intense fashion, for what it conveys is the frustration and pain of being more than a child and yet not an adult, with the agony of self-awareness and sense of isolation thereby involved. There is the shock of recognition—something of the same kind of reassurance through identification that books such as *Look Homeward, Angel* or *The Catcher in the Rye* have been known to provide. . . .

The McCullers fiction, I believe, has at its center a fundamental premise: which is, that solitude—loneliness—is a human constant, and cannot possibly be alleviated for very long at a time. But there is no philosophical acceptance of that condition, and none of the joy in it that one finds in, say, Thomas Wolfe or even Hemingway. The solitude is inevitable, and it is always painful. Thus life is a matter of living in pain, and art is the portraying of anguish. Occasionally, a character of hers knows happiness, but never for very long. . . .

Like certain other of her contemporaries, Carson McCullers, it seems to me, constructed her art out of the South, but not out of its history, its common myths, its public values and the failure to cherish them. What is Southern in her books are the rhythms, the sense of brooding loneliness in a place saturated with time. Compare *The Heart Is a Lonely Hunter* or *The Member of the Wedding* with, say, *Winesburg, Ohio,* and the relationship with the region is obvious. Sherwood Anderson's grotesques are more simple; a few clear, masterful sentences and we get their essential quality. Carson McCullers must show her misfits, whether spiritual or physical, in an extended context; there is plenty of time for everything. The Southern quality is unmistakable, in the unhurried fascination with surfaces, the preoccupation with the setting in which the characterization reveals itself. Character is not for McCullers, any more than for Eudora Welty or William Faulkner or Thomas Wolfe, an idea, but a state of awareness. To repeat, there is plenty of time . . . and when the violence comes, as it so often does, it erupts in a place and a context, and it jars, queerly or terribly or both, the established and accustomed patterns. Before and after, there is lots of waiting, lots of time to think about everything.

Louis D. Rubin, Jr. *Virginia Quarterly*
Review. Spring, 1977, pp. 269–70, 281–82

Carson McCullers's most memorable houses are ultimately claustrophobic. Most of *The Member of the Wedding* occurs in the hot, stale kitchen where Berenice guides tomboy Frankie through her transformation into giddy adolescent Frances. The walls are covered with John Henry's grotesque childish drawings which give the room "a crazy look like that of a room in the crazy-house." The same conversations and the same card games are played maddeningly over and over by the three inhabitants of Frankie's domestic world so that the time passes like a sick dream. This world is a living freak show peopled by a transvestite boy, a black cook with a left eye of bright blue glass, and a gangling tomboy. It is a horrifying prison for Frankie, who moves into a completely new house at the end of the novel, leaving her freakish past behind.

Such an escape may be possible because she submits to conventional demands for femininity. The opposite resolution comes in *The Ballad of the Sad Café*. Whereas Miss Amelia's café had formerly been her fortress and treasure-house, and then under Cousin Lymon's influence had opened up to become a warm center for the town's social life, the destruction of Amelia's power transforms the cafe into a prison. Boarded up, painted only on one side, and leaning crazily to the right, it expresses the state of Miss Amelia's life. Sometimes when the heat is at its suffocating worst at the end of the day, a terrible face appears from behind the shutter of the one window left unboarded. Because she would not submit to her biological destiny, Miss Amelia has been left a sexless recluse, enclosed in her old house and only rarely looking out "with two gray crossed eyes which are turned inward so sharply that they seem to be exchanging with each other one long and secret gaze of grief.". . .

Memory plays very little part in the lives of Carson McCullers's heroines, and they live in a world practically devoid of traditional Southern femininity. They are contemporaries of Virgie Rainey and Laurel Hand, yet they inhabit a flat present bereft of myth, history, or even family traditions. Surrounded by the tawdry everyday life of modern Southern towns, they seem to exist in a void, alienated from the few models of femininity available to them. The only warmth provided by women comes from Negro cooks. Mick Kelly's mother rarely appears in *The Heart Is a Lonely Hunter,* and then only to issue impatient or dispirited orders about Mick's baby-sitting chores or the management of the family's boardinghouse. She is a scarcely believable stick figure by comparison with the vivid presence of Portia. The cook's vigorous and compassionate views of the world provide the only adult guidance for Mick and her little brothers, yet Portia is more like a practical older sister or aunt for Mick than a mother. The real maternal figure in the novel is the androgynous cafe keeper Biff Brannon, but Mick shies away from his solicitations. In *The Ballad of the Sad Café* Miss Amelia Evans has been raised motherless and has lost even her father long before the action of the novella begins. Frankie Addams of *The Member of the Wedding* knows her mother only as a timid and sad-looking picture shut up under the handkerchiefs in her father's bureau drawer. Berenice the cook is the wise black mammy figure who has raised the motherless child, but her race prohibits Frankie from following her example as a woman. Without mothers, these feminine protagonists define themselves most comfortably in masculine terms. The crisis for each of them comes as social pressures force them to abandon masculine independence and accept a feminine identity increasingly fraught with anxiety as McCullers progresses in her exploration of the problem from novel to novel.

Louise Westling. *Sacred Groves and Ravaged Gardens: The Fiction of Eudora Welty, Carson McCullers, and Flannery O'Connor* (Athens: University of Georgia Press, 1985), pp. 181–82, 110–11

[Margaret] McDowell calls *The Heart Is a Lonely Hunter* McCullers's representation of her "regret that selfless love is rare and apt to be evanescent." Faith is no option for the characters of McCullers's novel; men and women choose a flesh-and-blood hero to take the place of the prophet from Nazareth. When McCullers lists the theme she believes she had developed in the novel, a "unifying principle or God" plays a major role: "There is a deep need in man to express himself by creating some unifying principle or God," she writes in *The Mortgaged Heart*. "A personal God created by man is a reflection of himself and in substance this God is most often inferior to his creator." Another concept she supports fictionally is that in a "disorganized society these individual Gods or principles are likely to be chimerical and fantastic." Because Copeland, Mick, and Blount create Singer to meet their needs, their god is not divine. He is all too human. Rather than his pointing the way to God through a Gethsemane moment, isolation damns Singer. His song is never heard. McCullers has written an allegory of an individual's search for self, and those internal glimpses remain rare and incomplete. Whatever the stylistic failures of *The Heart Is a Lonely Hunter*, McCullers has successfully explored what she termed the "solitary region of simple stories and the inward mind." Her characters do not carry a pack labelled "Sin" on their backs, but Singer easily may be cast as an allegorical Everyman. The pain of the characters is as internal as it is destructive, and their cries for deliverance go unheard.

Southern Literary Journal. 24:2, Spring, 1992, pp. 34–35

MACAULAY, ROSE (GREAT BRITAIN) 1881–1958

Rose Macaulay is of the very small band of writers in our day whose work counts. She is not for the great multitude who follow after the kingdom of this world and worship success. She lavishes all her art on the failure, the beloved vagabond who loses the world and saves his own soul: the poor in heart for whom is the kingdom of heaven. Unconsciously in writing of her books one finds oneself using scriptural or scriptural-sounding phrases. Nothing else fits her. Whether she will or not the moral of her books—if that is not too heavy and dull a word—is profoundly Christian. Her kingdom is not of this world.

She has written in all some eight books, and in every one there is the triumph of failure, most delicately, gaily and wittily rendered. Each one is a tragedy, but a tragedy presented with the gaiety of the Saints, or of the French widow who wrote of her bereavement "Je pleure mon Albert gaiement." There is that high lift of the human heart in sorrow which is surely a gift of the Holy Spirit. All of Miss Macaulay's heroes and heroines whom I know and love—Benjie in *Views and Vagabonds,* Peter in *The Lee Shore,* Eddy in *The Making of a Bigot,* and Alix in *Non-Combatants*—go out as failures from one point of view or another: prosperity is possibly the thing in human life which Miss Macaulay most abhors.

She has a rich and fruitful theory of life, or perhaps one should say, philosophy of life. She has an abundant and humane humor. She has an exquisite capacity for depicting natural beauty. She is a born lover of the Open Road. Her wit, lambent and tender, plays over the characters she creates. She makes an atmosphere reminding you now of Sterne, now of Stevenson, again of Borrow when he was not controversial. She creates a great number of characters and makes one realize each one. She is wise as well as witty. She has observed life with laughing and moist eyes, and her observations are scattered over the pages of her books. Altogether hers is a rich and manifold gift.

Katharine Tynan. *Bookman.*
November 19, 1916, p. 37

There is one small volume of poems by Miss Macaulay, called *The Two Blind Countries.* It is curiously interesting, since it may be regarded as the testament of mysticism for the year of its appearance, 1914. That is, indeed, the most important fact about it, though no one need begin to fear that he is to be fobbed off with inferior poetry on that account. For the truth is that the artistic value of this work is almost, if not quite, equal to the exceptional power of abstraction that it evinces. Poetry has really been achieved here, extremely individual in manner and in matter, and of a high order of beauty.

One is compelled, however, though one may a little regret the compulsion, to start from the fact of the poet's mystical tendency. Not that she would mind, presumably; the title of her book is an avowal, clear enough at a second glance, of its point of view. But the reader has an instinct, in which the mere interpreter but follows him, to accept a poem first as art rather than thought; and if he examines it at all, to begin with what may be called its concrete beauty. I will not say that the order is reversed in the case of Miss Macaulay's poetry, since that would be to accuse her of an artistic crime of which she is emphatically not guilty. But it is significant that the greater number of pieces in this book impress the mind with the idea they convey, simultaneously with the sounds in which it is expressed. And as the idea is generally adventurous, and sometimes fantastic, it is that which arrests the reader and on which he lingers, at any rate long enough to discover its originality.

Mary C. Sturgeon. *Studies of Contemporary Poets* (London: George Harrap, 1919),
pp. 181–82

She uses the novel for critical purposes; it is significant that *Told by an Idiot,* her last and best book, covers too many generations to allow of detailed characterizations, and will be remembered chiefly for its point-of-view. I do not mean that she cannot create character. She can, and does. But her main gift is for general judgment. Some critics, faced by this puzzle (since it is notorious that no woman can see a joke, keep a secret, or *think*), have hazarded the wide solution that Miss Macaulay does *not* make general judgments for the simple reason that she is a woman and can't. Miss Macaulay, unperturbed, has surpassed herself in a novel where the general judgments are more important than the characters. Of course, her generalizations are false—that goes without saying. All generalizations are false: but some of them are illuminating. Miss Macaulay is always—well, almost always—witty; I confess I did not find her so in *Mystery at Geneva,* but I am told that was a joke I did not see. Men have no sense of humor. In *Told by an Idiot* she fairly blazes with wit. There are, actually, enough good jokes in her first four pages to furnish a whole novel; and if she does not quite keep up that pitch, it is because nobody could. She has chosen a form which gives admirable scope to her *kind* of wit. She takes a whole family, parents, children, grand-children, through roughly half a century, touching off in each decade the absurdities and illusions which at each point have passed for wisdom, and insisting, in a refrain which gains by every repetition, that those absurdities and illusions belong to this year or that because they belong to all years—to the human heart itself. This panoramic method precludes the fond detailing of daily life; it calls for vivid pictures, and it gets them. All the same, Miss Macaulay gropes marvelously deep into some of her characters, especially Rome and Imogen; she has, as it were, packed twenty novels into one.

Gerald Gould. *The English Novel of Today*
(rpt. Freeport, New York: Books for
Libraries Press, 1971 [John Castle, 1924]),
pp. 71–73

Orphan Island is an ingenious comic story of a satirical nature which should have a wide popularity. It should appeal generally, and I venture to think only, to that mass of people to which reading means novel reading. Particularly it should appeal to people brought up in the mid-Victorian era who are trying to throw off their Victorianism, to those for whom a delicate facetiousness stands for wit, and to those who admire skill in workmanship in preference to new ideas; there is, I believe, a large class of persons whose only joy in literature is to be able to say, *"How well that is put—that is what I have always thought (or observed, or deduced) myself."*

I. P. Fassett. *Criterion.* April, 1925, p. 474

Miss Macaulay's genuine and deep-hearted sympathy is often ignored or unrecognized by those who fear her intellectual approach to emotional problems. She is here, to some of us, one of the most satisfactory of modern novelists in her firm conviction that nothing needs firm intellectual handling so much as that queer mess of superstition, allegory, sham science and herd-hysteria which so many people gravely call by such names as "psychological problems." Admirable as is the drawing of the Folyot [*Keeping up Appearances*] household, with its passion for social work and science, its dislike of sloppiness, Miss Macaulay is perhaps even better in her account of the Arthurs in East Sheen. . . . Praise of this brilliant novel would not be complete without a word of admiration for the emotionally subtle portrait of Carey Folyot.

R. E. Roberts. *Bookman.*
May, 1928, p. 129

All these, all the great sites of classical Antiquity, many of the Orient and some in Yorkshire valleys or among Welsh hills go to build up this long, extremely pleasant book [*Pleasures of Ruins*]—a book in form by no means unlike some noble lapidary ruin: each stone an essay, each chapter a craggy, dry-jointed wall of indeterminate height, and one great big chapter, with Rome at its core, towering over the whole. The book ends with a brief "Note on New Ruins." Miss Macaulay does not think much of them. And in the last half-dozen lines she makes a confession which all but the hopelessly decadent and enervate must applaud. She prefers her buildings whole.

John Summerson. *New Statesman and*
Nation. December 12, 1953, p. 765

The Towers of Trebizond could have been written by no one but Rose Macaulay. Her many gifts are here fully expressed and the conflicting elements in her thought and manner are perfectly united.

The narrator of the story, young, intelligent, well-read, and enmeshed in an adulterous love affair, goes off to Turkey on a missionary venture with an aunt, a very High Church Canon and a camel. Miss Macaulay has evolved a style which exactly reflects Laurie's character—an easy, colloquial style, inconsequent but never incoherent, edged and witty, but flowering from time to time into ample passages of description, into dreamy musings, into religious argument. The book is a travel book about Turkey; it is an adventure story alive with high comedy, full of absurd but credible incidents on the shores of the Black Sea or the English countryside. It reads like a gay, learned, eventful, lyrical comedy, with never a dull patch. But it is not a comedy. . . .

Rose Macaulay alone of living writers could have achieved just this effect: this use of high comedy to convey a tragic meaning. She could not perhaps have done it earlier in her career, for in this book the different elements in her thought and feeling are for the first time wholly fused.

C. V. Wedgwood. *Time and Tide.*
September 8, 1956, p. 1073

I have reread Rose Macaulay's *They Were Defeated,* which is to be reissued after long being out of print. It first appeared in 1932. I read it then and believed it to be by far her finest book. That is saying much, for Rose Macaulay is perhaps the most learned woman writer of distinction in our language. I should place her with George Eliot and Rebecca West, for intellectual capacity and for scholarship. Further, she was a literary artist, using words with full consciousness of their potentiality.

I remember telling her of my predilection for this historical romance, and saying that I thought it should be regarded in future as a companion book to Shorthouse's *John Inglesant,* doing for seventeenth-century Cambridge what the Victorian novel did for seventeenth-century Oxford. To my pleasure, she replied that it was her own favorite, and that she was disappointed because the public had not agreed, so far as the sales figures revealed. But there are some books which take many years to impress themselves. Both Somerset Maugham's *Of Human Bondage* and Arnold Bennett's *Old Wives' Tales* lacked immediate success. But now they are recognized as classics among the novels of the twentieth century.

So is *They Were Defeated.* For me, it carries a vast scholarship as easily as does Santayana's *The Last Puritan.* It is a long tale, but I should not say it is told at leisure. It moves quickly, propelled by a passion that sweeps along like a prairie fire. But though the fire is wide it is, by a miracle such as only the human mind (being divine) can work, a cool, serene fire, and it throws a light into every corner of that period of English history; a period which Miss Veronica Wedgwood is exploring in her noble history of the Civil War.

Richard Church. *John O'London's Weekly.*
January 21, 1960, p. 57

Nobody should have known better than Rose Macaulay how dangerous a commodity words can be—especially today, especially the private words of a gifted and known personality. Did she expect these letters [*Letters to a Friend*] to be made public? They were written towards the end of her life to an Anglican priest, Father Hamilton Johnson of the Cowley Fathers' community in Boston, USA. He had known her very slightly through church attendances at the start of the First World War; but in 1916 he left for America and the connection ceased. In 1950 he read for the first time her early novel *They Were Defeated,* and wrote. Rose Macaulay cherished his letters yet thought it courteous to have them destroyed at her death. Her priestly correspondent did not do the same. He enlisted the editorial aid of a Macaulay cousin, Miss Babington Smith, and when he died in March 1961, at the age of eighty-four, the book was already well in hand.

It should be said at once that the publicity which has vapored up about these letters is quite misleading. Readers need not expect to find in them any intimate revelations—though to be sure, something of whatever may have been edited out of the text is set down in the editorial introduction, oddly recalling those censored Latin schoolroom books which Byron describes in *Don Juan.* But there is little to tell—only that Rose Macaulay had had a twenty-year relationship with a married man who died in the early 1940s, and that the artificial compromise of those years seemed to her, in retrospect, vexing and sad.

Nor do the letters offer even the history of a dramatic religious conversion. Rose Macaulay, who came of long lines of clerical ancestors on both sides, had never really been out of the Church's sway. "I am Anglican profoundly," she wrote, "born and bred to it, the heir to it, and now well in it once more. . . . *What* a heritage we have." . . .

It is on the whole a weakened R. M. who shows in these pages; this isn't the image that most of her readers would want to be left with finally. "One should," as she said herself, "consume one's own smoke"; and in the two years of passionate church going, letter writing, confessional visiting, she certainly was not doing that. Happily the story need not end with this volume. For one thing, there is a hint that after 1952 (though a further collection is promised by the present editor Miss Babington Smith) letters to Father Hamilton became "less frequent." And then, in 1956, Rose Macaulay was to publish *The Towers of Trebizond*—surely the most brilliant and valuable novel of all her fifty years' writing. In this fantastic tragical-comedy she was able to look with her familiar sympathetic irony and a fresh tide of wit, and with something deeper too, at all the Macaulay obsessions—travel, the Church, family relationships, women and learning, the pains and the pleasures of love. Certainly there is more in this book on the themes of the letters than in all of the letters themselves. Her genius, after all, worked (as it had all her writing life) through the fictional transmutation, absorbing all problems and doubts, and not through the raw unordered thoughts of the airmail post. Her true smoke consumer had always been here.

Naomi Lewis. *The New Statesman.*
November 3, 1961, p. 659

The Rose Macaulay we know through her witty, satirical books—from the early novel *Potterism* to the last and perhaps most winning of her works, *The Towers of Trebizond*—was as much at home in antiquity and in the seventeenth century, as in her own time; in Italy, Spain, Portugal and Turkey, as in England; in the literature of other lands and ages, as in that of her contemporaries. But from these letters emerges a Rose Macaulay who was certainly not heretofore fully understood. Now we see her in the round, three-dimensional in the range of her intellect, the quality of her opinion and the capacity of her heart. . . .

For an already elderly, established, distinguished woman to transcend not only worldly success and diminishing strength but the political, intellectual and moral chaos of the 1950s and insist, with a wholly unsentimental, a beautifully precise, a consistently humble insistence upon living by the Reason and the Light she had come to see anew, was no minor victory. Those in England who have raised a hue and cry against the publication of Dame Rose Macaulay's letters to Father Johnson [*Letters to a Friend*] must have forgotten how much more heavily valor weighs on the human scales than mere discretion.

Virgilia Peterson. The New York Times.
February 25, 1962, p. 6

"*Trebizond* stands . . . not merely [for] the actual city (though this comes in, and a lovely place it is) but for the . . . romantic and nostalgic vision of the Church which haunts the person who narrates the story." Thus Rose explained to Father Johnson the essence of her new novel, *The Towers of Trebizond,* when she wrote in February 1956 to tell him it was just completed. She was now seventy-four, and five years had passed since she began again as a Christian; when she wrote *The Towers of Trebizond* she had left behind her the difficult initial stages of contrition and readjustment. She now felt, with joy, that she really belonged within what she called in her epigraph "that strange bright city." And she could now perceive with alarming awareness that the Eternal City, for which man has an undying hunger, is barred to all those "who do not desire to enter it more strongly than they desire all other cities," those who by their own choice remain stubbornly within "cities" which are illusory and transient. Rose could not have written *Trebizond* while she still felt herself an exile. But she was now strongly enough rooted in the Church to express a burning longing to help others, by sharing with them— so far as she could—her own experience of a divided life, and of what, in spiritual terms, it had cost her.

In *The Towers of Trebizond* her talent for combining a serious message with light satire flowered to its fullest, as she wove together tragedy and comedy, fantasy and farce. But her sense of humor sparkled so brightly that quite a few people failed to appreciate the book's more heartfelt aspects. Rose was astonished and dismayed when she heard (through one of her cousins, Lady Fletcher) that someone had thought the whole thing was "a leg-pull." "Never was a novel (by me) more passionately in earnest (I mean in its religious and moral parts)" she protested. "I wrote it in a kind of white-hot passion; but perhaps made too many jokes as well, which confused the issue to many readers. [What] I hope . . . most people saw in it [was] . . . the struggle of good and evil in the human soul, and its eternal importance, and the pull and power of the Christian Church on the divided mind, its torment and its attraction."

Constance Babington Smith. Rose Macaulay
(London: Collins, 1972), pp. 203–4

What Not is dedicated to "Civil Servants I Have Known" and Macaulay had indeed known many, for during the First World War she was one herself, in the British War Office. Although "no records of her work have survived" her biographer reveals that her work was connected with conscientious objectors, and also that "the Propaganda Department wound up at the end of 1918, and the final part of her time as a temporary civil servant was probably spent at the Ministry of Information's main office." Propaganda and censorship are at the receiving end of many of her darts in this novel, but her knowledge proved to be a two-edged sword, for while it provided her with the material for satire, it evidently led to underestimate reaction; in a note appended to her introductory Apology, she reveals that publication was delayed to allow for a slight alteration in the text, to safeguard it against one of the laws of the realm. . . .

Although not the best of Macaulay's many novels, *What Not* has an internal tension that renders it disquieting. The author's opposition to attempts to coerce people, even for their own good, conflicts with her fears that these attempts may succeed. The basis for the tension is stated in her introduction, where she says that "wars do not conduce to intelligence. . . . They put a sudden end to many of the best intellects, and many of the minds that are left are battered and stupified." That the fictional means to lift the average level of intelligence could have some success is indicated by her own use of the before/after image; a trainload of commuters introduced at the beginning of the novel is paralleled by a similar group presented later, whose topics of conversation have risen above the purely domestic concerns of those in the first scene. While the author is intellectually sympathetic with the ends promulgated by her Ministry of Brains, she is simultaneously derisive and apprehensive of their means.

But the tension is resolved. The working class, the upper class and intellectuals prove to be ultimately unreformable. Agricultural laborers ignore the preferred re-training, and insist on procreating without thought for the elaborate system of fines established by the Ministry (although imprisonment is under consideration as a punishment, it has not yet been put into effect). "Villagers are so stupid; they will not take the larger view, nor see why things annoying to them personally are necessary for the public welfare." Industrial workers take things a step further; they continue to have as many children as they wish, but strike to force higher wages with which to pay their fines. The members of the upper classes are, like the villagers, undeterred. The rebellion that eventually collapses the Ministry of Brains from within is the marriage of the central character in the novel (her author's alter ego), to the Minister himself—they are both classified "A," but he is forbidden marriage and parenthood because of his two mentally retarded siblings. Their decision is not easily arrived at, and when it is finally reached, the author appends to Kitty's "I don't care. I don't care. What's the good of living if you can't be what you want?" the comment: "Which expressed an instinct common to the race, and one which would in the end bring to nothing the most strenuous efforts of social and ethical reformers." Of Kitty's rueful laughter on the last page of the novel, she adds "It was something; perhaps, in a sad and precarious world, it was much."

The title of *What Not* is taken from the outraged cry of the defendent in a food hoarding case, in January 1918:

> It has come to a fine thing if people cannot live in their homes without being interfered with by the police. . . . You are upset-

ting the country altogether with your Food Orders and What Not.

Macaulay interprets "What Not" as any form of interference often seriously advocated by utopian idealists, but it is her belief that our common instincts must, in the long run, prevail over bureaucratic attempts to eradicate them, in however good a cause. Speaking for her, Kitty says "Amen" to the silliness of the world, for "it would be damn dull one if it wasn't."

Gorman Beauchamp et al., eds. *Utopian Studies* (Lanham, Maryland: University Press of America, 1987), pp. 12–14

In both *The Heat of the Day* by Elizabeth Bowen and *The World My Wilderness* by Rose Macaulay, women artists find themselves forced to reexamine those traditional values which were supposed to sustain them and their world. Behavior and language become discordant as words such as duty, loyalty and national identity become suspect. The war unveils the absurdity of equating the spoken and body language of decorum and civility with emerging feelings about family and cultural unity. The shock of recognition comes with the aftermath of heroics. When men and women are reunited, they discover that the different battles they fought at home or on fields of combat parallel the different moral and psychological territory they have always occupied. Victory cannot conceal the deep fissures war has exposed on the home front. The experience of women in war transforms the domestic novel into personal epics which show the complex difficulties of coming to terms with contemporary England.

Both *The Heat of the Day* and *The World My Wilderness* were written after the war—1949 and 1950 respectively. While Bowen's novel deals with the Blitz itself, Macaulay's shows the aftermath of war and its lingering effects. At the center of each novel is a woman who, as an artist figure, casts doubt on the arts of this righteous war. Helen, in Macaulay's novel, is a painter who also invents twelfth century Provencal poetry, passing it off as scholarly discovery and who prefers gambling to domestic arts. . . .

In Macaulay's novel, the young must first reinvent the present by reenacting its incoherence. Barbary, Helen's daughter by her English husband, followed the Maquis with her French step-brother Raoul and now in 1946, "still waged their war, resisting policemen . . . capitalists, collaborators . . . and trains." Sent to London to be civilized, Barbary and Raoul play a "barbaric war," stealing and hiding from the police, whom they think of as Gestapo in "the waste land" of the bombed-out East End.

For Barbary and Raoul, playing in the ruins makes an art of survival in the emotional, moral, and linguistic confusions that constitute the postwar. Barbary is an artist born of war, transforming its rubble into a personal epic of the "wilderness we carry with us." The form of this woman's epic is ungenteel: postcards of her haunts in the East End ruins peddled to tourists.

Like her stealing, this art assaults those traditions which make her an inheritor of war, but it momentarily empowers her. Otherwise, she suffocates in the "wasteland" of decorous behavior in her father's orderly household. Barbary thus brings to England the anarchy which may have sustained her mother. But as the fall which leaves Barbary in a coma shows, this is no solution, only an escape into inertia. Helen has actually chosen intertia as a strategy to cope with a history in which "the crook in all of us is bursting out and taking possession, like Hyde, while Jekyll slowly dies of attrition. . . .

The language of women's war experience in both novels calls for the presence of children. If women struggle to connect feeling and morality by using the language of their bodies, they are responsible for the birth and lives of their children who will inherit the world of war. Bowen and Macaulay leave their weary heroines in watchful positions, transmitting to their children the empowerment to translate their fathers' traditions into the post-war. As they remain silent and withdrawn, however, these female characters also inscribe the negation of such tradition. Refusing to participate in the creation of fictions based on a language they know to be duplicitous, Helen, Stella, Louie Lewis, and Barbary enact a new kind of fiction: one which acknowledges the necessity of invention, of lying, to create and sustain a self which cannot be known in the language of men.

Phyllis Lassner. *Perspectives on Contemporary Literature.* 14, 1988, pp. 30–31, 34–37

The selections included here exhibit Macaulay's particularly conflicted, complex female modernism, as it figured in her war fiction (*Non-Combatants and Others* [1916] and *Told by an Idiot* [1923]) and her essays (*Personal Pleasures* [1935]). Certain themes dominant in the discourse appear here: the variety of women's responses to war, including women's complicity with and attraction to war making; the politics of canon creation; the relation between gender and literary style. Other themes, less typical of female modernism, express the concerns that kept Macaulay from meshing seamlessly with her male or female modernist colleagues or—because of our postmodern affiliations—with us: Macaulay's turn to religion to express a prophetic critique of patriarchal society within a discourse previously disabling for women; her preoccupation with the literary marketplace; her willingness to subordinate critical analysis to breezy commentary, perhaps as a Trojan horse solution to the problem of publishers' restrictions on female voice and subject matter. . . .

Macaulay defied the constraints of the canon, not only by resisting the glorification of war but also by choosing to write in uncanonized genres: the personal or topical essay and the travel book. In the 1920s, Macaulay published her essays in a tellingly diverse group of papers and journals, including the *Daily Mail,* the *Evening Standard,* and the High Church weekly, the *Guardian.* While a number of the essays quite self-consciously address female readers, others seem to construct a male audience; the implied reader also seems to change with the shifts in tone from a female-oriented breezy casualness to an acerbic satire that seems to invoke a male reader. Collected in 1925 by Methuen, her essays were advertised for "intellectual readers," thus perpetuating in the construction of its audience Macaulay's conflicting identifications with male intellectual authority and female intellectual challenge.

"Following the Fashion" demonstrates Macaulay's play with the gendered conventions of voice and subject matter. In this witty essay, Macaulay transposes the defiant self-assertiveness legitimately woman's prerogative when dealing with "trivial" matters of dress or pastime to the more serious literary arena, conflating social with literary conventions. The result is a biting parody of her modernist contemporaries Ernest Hemingway and T. S. Eliot. . . .

Characteristically modernist in its play with the rupture of the aura brought about by the development of photography, "Album," with its wry summation of Macaulay's life by an imaginary descendant, also expresses in its ironic subtext the vision of female modernism. The insistence on periodizing human character ("she just wrote away, as those Georgians did") establishes her debt to Woolf's construction of modern writing in her influential essay "Mr. Bennett and Mrs. Brown," while it testifies to Macaulay's male-identified allegiance to the Georgian group of writers as Woolf constituted it: "Mr. Forster, Mr. Lawrence, Mr. Strachey, Mr. Joyce, and Mr. Eliot." The essay reflects a sense of the impermanence of social structures and values, recalling not only Lawrence's anatomy of love's progress across the generations in *The Rainbow*, but also Woolf's feminist play with gen(d)erational change in *Orlando*.

Susan M. Squier. In Bonnie Kime Scott, ed.
The Gender of Modernism (Bloomington:
Indiana University Press, 1990),
pp. 253, 256–58

MACEWAN, GWENDOLYN (CANADA) 1941–

Miss MacEwan is twenty-two, and this, her first novel [*Julian the Magician*], is the sort of book Virginia Woolf might have had in mind when she said: "Publish nothing before you are thirty." Like so many young people who want to be writers (or at least published), but who either have no personally experienced subject matter of their own, or have not yet exercised the self-inquiry and patience to discover it, Miss MacEwan takes her material from familiar abstractions and doodles them up with facile, pretentious method.

Using the passion of Christ as her framework, she tells the story of Julian, a magician of unnamed time and place, who seems to perceive, or at least will, similarities between himself and the "great magician." He not only stages his own last supper and arranges for his betrayal and denial, but performs miracles as well, changing wine into water and curing a congenital idiot. (Whether these seeming miracles are inspired by Heaven, fever, or schizophrenia we never know, nor does our not knowing seem to be the point of the story.) Finally, during one performance Julian restores the sight of a blind man. The amazed crowd is ready to proclaim the magician a man of God; but an hour later the man drops dead (probably from pure shock), and the crowd is now ready to hang Julian. He, however, asks to be crucified, and is.

Whatever Miss MacEwan thought she meant by all this parallelogramming, it is obscured by characters who are nothing more than anonymous voices, and, even worse, by imprecise, muddled uses of language, sometimes as bad as, "doves are the pink knives of perfect silence; cleaving the noise, the madness."

Peter Deane. Book Week.
December 15, 1963, p. 14

[MacEwan's] physical urgency [in <i>A Breakfast for Barbarians</i>] is always qualified by a desire to theorize, and she is more interested in "the slow striptease of our concepts" than in "the precious muscle in the thigh." She is also interested in the incantatory, the magical, the ritualistic; her poems frequently begin with a comparatively conversational approach and end in a chant. This progress from calm to storm is often caused by the near-ritualistic repetition of locution patterns, and by the cumulative use of imagery, rather than by a developing logic. . . .

This technique may be sanctified by its age and its ubiquity; it was used by the spell-writers of ancient Europe, and it is still in use among tribal societies in all parts of the world. Its effectiveness depends, however, upon our assenting to language as incantation, and upon our suspending our critical faculties to an intolerable (at least to me) extent. Of course, there are many poems here which do demand intellectual responses; nevertheless, even in these the incantatory tone soon becomes dominant. It is sometimes as if we were being required to listen to an important message to the accompaniment of a rock 'n' roll band; the words, however significant in themselves, begin to lose meaning and become only emotive gestures. Drunkenly we nod; we don't know what the hell it means, but there seems to be passionate sincerity in every syllable. If we were sober we know we'd understand it right away, but someone keeps filling up the glasses.

Robin Skelton. Poetry. October, 1966, p. 55

In reading Gwendolyn MacEwan's poetry it is a temptation to become preoccupied with the original and brilliant verbal surfaces she creates, at the expense of the depths beneath them. But it is occasionally instructive to give at least passing attention to what poets themselves say about their work, and MacEwan has been insisting for some time that it is "the thing beyond the poem," the "raw material" of literature, that above all concerns her. There is, of course, more than one thing beyond the poems, but there is one figure whose existence is hinted at throughout her work and who acts as a key to much of it. This is the Muse, often invoked and described but never named; and in MacEwan's poetry the Muse, the inspirer of language and the formative power in Nature, is male. Ignore him or misinterpret him and her "muse" poems may be mistaken for "religious" ones or reduced to veiled sexuality. Acknowledge him, and he will perform one of the functions MacEwan ascribes to him: the creation of order out of chaos. . . .

The Muse exists both inside and outside time, and like the letters on a page he is static yet in movement. Bodies as alphabets occur earlier in *A Breakfast for Barbarians,* and, again, word-thing metaphors date back to *Selah;* the importance of this body-letter lies in the fact that it is the first letter and the alphabet to which it belongs is unknown. The Muse is always *about* to be interpreted: he can never be completely deciphered.

Margaret Atwood. *Canadian Literature*. 45,
1970, pp. 25–26, 28

King of Egypt, King of Dreams is the story of Akhenaton, ruler of Egypt from 1367 to 1350 B.C., his rise and demise. . . . A knot of reasons propelled him onto the course that is the substance of the novel and the reason for which he is best remembered today. For Akhenaton introduced the concept of monotheism into Egypt and into our lives. . . .

We are left looking at a prismatic man; a mystical demagogue, a cross between Hitler and a flower-child, an individual. Akhenaton is known as the first individualist. Indeed, he is a model for what true individualism can represent and a caution for how it adapts to the social jig-saw.

The novel is rich in character and characters. Nefertiti, his wife, drifts in and out of the story but stays with you a long time after it is over. Ay, Akhenaton's father-in-law, is one of the touchstones of his life. Philosophical and practical, he illumines Akhenaton's character by contrast. . . .

Gwendolyn MacEwan's prose is admirably suited to her subject matter. The story is written in a straightforward manner, the prose is economical and clean, and we are mercifully spared the miasma of irrelevant historical data that so many novelists feel compelled to pour upon us. Here, the story's the thing. A useful glossary of Egyptian names and terms is included.

I found *King of Egypt, King of Dreams* to be a moving book. Akhenaton tries to incorporate the god, the beast, and the man into one. . . . When the intellect fires the imagination, the novel thrives, history becomes redolent with meaning, and for a brief time we are transported out of our temporality.

Randall Ware. *Books in Canada*.
November, 1971, p. 8

"To think" is "to thank" is "to write poetry" was a premise for reasoning out the creative act in human lives advanced by Martin Heidegger. The revelation of its truth has been so far pronounced undefective by all who, like Miss MacEwan, contemplate the *void,* the absolute, including mystics and a handful of literary critics.

Her poetic experience, much like the reflective understanding of theology in faith, issues from a struggle with the nature of Being. This is physically expressed in an ultimate concern for life at its very foundations, and not merely with the objective visible nature of the phenomena of things. The point at which this is startlingly expressed is in her "A Lecture to the Flat Earth Society" [in *The Armies of the Moon*]. This is her main psalm of a disciplic advent of Mind to the very edge of all consciousness which sings that only such a journey can reveal the true nature of what we are and why we are here.

Through fear of death, Man is cast out "into the Primal Dark beyond," and it is only the "consolation of each other's company" that constrains the conquerors of that final possibility from "falling into the sweet and terrible night." As an entity, this high, outerspaceish human consciousness leads a precarious existence. She says it is a "disc which spins its insane dreams through space," forever subject to the gravitational force of moral falling.

Fair enough. But, by saying it is "doomed," she admits the finitude of her existence by alienating mystical experience from all traditional ideas of a trans-human reality known to poetry, theology and other literature.

She parallels the enigma of "Why do we work to feed ourselves to live for fear that we would die" with that of the scientific astronaut, who, in all his passion for knowing, knows intuitively that he is merely playing intellectual golf over the reality which is hidden beyond the physicality of things.

In so doing Miss MacEwan moves us to the transcendental by the reality of nothing and makes us stand before the severity and incongruity of its meaning. In the battle of ideas, to show us how small we really are calls for the positivization of all our passions.

Clyde Hosein. *Books in Canada.*
August, 1972, pp. 5–6

The stories in *Norman* have, as I expected they would, a strong organic unity with one another and with [MacEwan's] novels and poems. The title story in its two parts is clearly there partly as the mythic base for all the stories. Norman, the hero of his author's apocalypse, is a life-spirit. Heraclitean fire, the divine imagination, embodied in gods, demons and men, threatened always by extinction in this present world but always phoenix-like. The freshness of the stories comes largely from the voice, the interworking of innocence and irony. The irony is never bleak or astringent and the view of this present world, though apocalyptic (or because apocalyptic) is comic.

The story which least fits this description is the first one, "House of the Whale." For that very reason perhaps, I find it the most moving and memorable. . . . The other stories, whatever irony they generate, leave us convinced of the triumph of Norman. In fact, the best of them identify that triumph as one of imagination. Events and characters echoing each other clearly signal their archetypal groundings. . . .

The function of the last story and "The Return of Julian the Magician" as poetic scripture on which the other stories are glosses is clear. For me, the stories that embody more lightly their archetypes succeed best. They are generally short—"Fire," "The Oarsman and the Seamstress," "Kingsmere," and "Snow." Verbally, of course, all this work is exciting, but magic needs to be self-concealing to be truly magic.

Robert Gibbs. Journal of Canadian Fiction.
Winter, 1973, p. 93

Two well-known Canadian authors have created magicians; they are, of course, Robertson Davies, in his Magnus Eisengrim trilogy, and Gwendolyn MacEwan, who creates a whole series of magicians which bear a strong generic likeness to one another. It would be hard to find two writers whose approaches to prose fiction are more different; yet their magicians have a few things in common. Both are artist figures, and both are in fact Canadian, although both disguise this plebeian origin under an assumed name. (The implication is that you can't be both Canadian and magic; or you can, but no one will believe in you if you reveal your dull grey origins.)

MacEwan specializes in magician as artist as Christ. (In her first novel, *Julian the Magician,* the magician actually insists on being crucified, just to see if he can be resurrected.) Her characters are not only called magicians, they actually are; that is, they seem able actually to perform superhuman feats. . . .

What we might call "the sacrificial fade-out" seems to be typical of these Canadian demi-gods and magician priests: their death or disappearance is chosen, and seems to have some element of sacrifice in it, but unlike traditional sacrifices, such as Christ's, it doesn't save or even benefit anyone else, and is more in the nature of an abdication or departure. The sacrificial fade-out is a MacEwan specialty. It's present in almost all of her magician stories, including her two novels, *Julian the Magician* and *King of Egypt, King of Dreams;* but it is most explicit, perhaps, in her short story, "The Second Coming of Julian the Magician," a serio-comic treatment of the dilemma of a real magic man in a non-magical age and country.

Margaret Atwood. In David Haines, ed. The
Canadian Imagination: Dimensions of a
Literary Culture (Cambridge,
Massachusetts: Harvard University Press,
1977), pp. 240–41, 244, 245

If it is permissible or even possible to apply a single adjective to the aim of Gwendolyn MacEwan's writing, then the most accurate word would be explorative. All of her publications to date have been concerned with a quest for a particular knowledge or vision and, consequently, with the communication of such knowledge to her audience. Ordinarily, this would not appear to be an onerous task for so gifted an artist; but the repeatedly mystic nature of MacEwan's vision demands from her a much more complex process of communication than that which can be achieved through language alone. In order to grasp the intangible "mystery, joy, and passion of life" that she strives to reveal—in order to appreciate the prophet as much as the poet—statements of emotion, dogma, and personal theory are insufficient. It is not surprising therefore, that MacEwan has provided her readers with many signposts which if heeded, will help to guide them into her "fifth earth," the birthplace of "Orbiting castes and giants and starbeasts" of myth, ambiguity, personal terror, and ecstasy. Through a combination of concrete detail and application of kinetic mythology, that is, "myth alive and reenacted in the spontaneous actions of real people," she is able to blend the human and divine, thereby transmuting ordinary phenomena into arcane revelation. . . . An investigation of . . . [the epigrams and symbols included in her writing] will provide a key to the imagery of MacEwan's prose and poetry and enable the reader to participate more fully in her perceptual and spiritual explorations.

> Jan Bartley. *Invocations: The Poetry and Prose of Gwendolyn MacEwan* (Vancouver: University of British Columbia Press, 1983), pp. vii–viii

MAILLET, ANTONINE (CANADA) 1929–

Antonine Maillet has fast become one of the most popular French-speaking Canadian writers. Her unforgettable monologues in *La Sagouine* have had the longest run of any play in French-speaking Canada and her latest novel, *Pélagie-la-Charrette* (literally translated, "Pélagie-the-Cart"), will no doubt sell more copies in one year than any other French-Canadian work of fiction. *Pélagie* will also soon become both a television program and a full-length feature. . . .

She has written sixteen books—plays, short stories, novels and critical studies. In 1960, she was awarded the Québec government's Prix Champlain for her first novel, *Point-aux-Coques*. Since then, she has received seven other literary awards. With one exception (*Le bourgeois gentleman,* a social satire of a Montrealer who dreams of becoming an English Canadian), all her works involve Acadian themes. The most predominant theme is that of the family storyteller. Various recurrent characters have a unique gift. They are amateur genealogists or "défricheteux de parenté" (family land-clearers). For such "conteux" and "radoteux," childhood acquires a collective meaning.

Personal childhood turns into national childhood as one traces one's history back to the common ancestor from Touraine or Poitou, the birthplaces of the first Acadians.

History is yet another fascinating theme. Antonine Maillet treats history in such a way that traditional heroes are replaced by new ones. . . .

Acadia's most prolific author is what one might call a "literary map-maker." She has mapped out in stunning detail, in realistic and poetic beauty, the landscapes of New Brunswick, centering her creative eyes on the immediate area surrounding the Bays of Bouctouche and Cocagne. Those who have read her works will never forget the dunes, the small natural harbors (the "barachois") and the long white beaches of Acadia, . . . the land of the dikes, of smelt cabins, oyster barrels ("pontchines d'huitres"), crooked rail-fences and piles of corded wood, in the primitive and ancient land. . . .

Antonine Maillet remains faithful to the oral tradition from which she evolved. The storytellers, troubadours and "chroniqueurs" descended from Rabelais and his spirited Gargantua are living in Acadia and very much alive. Antonine Maillet has given them new and unique forms, and in so doing, has risen to the highest reaches of literary achievement. The themes and symbols of her works entertain while at the same time forcing one to reflect on a common ideological concern: the struggle of the underprivileged. In this sense, the Acadians represent all subjugated groups.

The admirer of French writing in Canada cannot help but be struck by the newness of the symbolism used by Antonine Maillet. Her figurative world evolved from different influences than those of Quebec writers. The ocean is the dominant symbol, not the land nor the forest. . . .

Pélagie-la Charrette superbly illustrates the cohesive and representative nature of the writing of Antonine Maillet. The historian in the novelist created a plot founded on historical fact: around 1780, between one-hundred-forty and one-hundred fifty Acadian families scattered throughout the Eastern Seaboard states, made their way back to their homeland only to discover that "la Nouvelle-Ecosse" had quickly become "la Nova-Scotia." Approximately half of the former exiles decided to remain in Nova Scotia and the rest settled in New Brunswick, which was then a land of trading posts inhabited primarily by Indians.

The plot of *Pélagie-la-Charrette* has a double focus: the return to Acadia of Pélagie, Bélonie, and their friends in 1780; the narration of Pélagie and Bélonie the third, who tell the story of their illustrious ancestors. The two perspectives intermingle and provide an appropriate mixture of live action and commentary. And now exactly three hundred years after the repatriation of Pélagie LeBlanc commonly called La Charrette, Acadia is in a state of celebration. The cart has started to move again, but it is now moving in the new "Acadies," the Acadias of hope and survival and not those of exile located in Louisiana and Georgia.

Donald Smith. *Canadian Literature.* 88, 1981, pp. 157–59

Antonine Maillet's dual careers, as novelist and playwright, have been developing in parallel for some twenty years now. She began as a novelist with *Pointe-aux-Coques* in 1958, and also achieved her greatest success with a novel, *Pélagie-la-Charrette,* which won the Goncourt Prize in 1979. However, her most memorable character, La Sagouine, was created for the stage, and around her a mythical universe has developed. The stage has also provided the medium which enabled Maillet to articulate most coherently a complex *Weltanschauung.* For the stage she has created a concert of voices and characters (as Godin has shown to be the case in *Évangéline Deusse*), as well as a succession of monologues in which the narrator/performer explores her memories and her perceptions just as one sight-reads a score—rehearses them, redefines and modulates them. She has also developed a dual intertextual network: the external, explicitly referred to by the author writing as critic; and the internal, reaching from one play to another, with echoes and allusions, or reworking the same "score" in successive versions.

Maillet's dramatic corpus is actually broader and more ambitious than her *oeuvre* as a novelist. Thus in 1978, with *Le Bourgeois Gentleman,* "a comedy inspired by Molière," she introduces settings, characters, and problems entirely different from the Acadian background of her other works. Here she devotes her attention primarily to external intertextuality and transposes ideological concerns from relations between classes to relations between national groups in a colonial context (Albert Memmi's *Portrait du colonisé* may well have served as a source text). But while this latest undertaking is of considerable interest (though not altogether successful), I shall here consider only her Acadian dramatic works (not including three early, unpublished attempts from 1957, 1958 and 1960): that is, the five plays which have been performed and published. Three of these—*Les Crasseux* (1968/1972), *La Sagouine* (1971/1974), *Gapi et Sullivan,* with its expanded version, *Gapi* (1973/1976)—have been considerably reworked. . . . The other two Acadian plays: *Evangéline Deusse* (even though it takes place in Montréal, the chief character is Acadian, a demystified successor to Longfellow's archetypal heroine), and *La Veuve enragée,* published in 1977. . . .

Maillet's dramas are very specific: they offer the defense and illustration of a national theater for a nation that is still as much in limbo as Poland was in Jarry's *Ubu.* They are the representative voice of a social group that is still not heard publicly, of a sex that is still often relegated to the status of "other." But at the same time, this Acadian repertoire, whose major protagonists are old, poor women, is universal in its topoi and its structures: it constitutes in many respects a paradigm for the study of general ideology, of cultural patterns, of the layering of language. It would therefore be rewarding to use it as a basis for further research, dealing for instance with mythopoetic *jonglerie* and other extensions of the dramatic into the *hors-scène.* But such extensions are most often reinvested in the scenic cube, even if this return, this new surging up, carries with it the strange atmosphere of myth or carnival, of a different truth, a different time, a different space. Perhaps this is an example of the theater of the oppressed at work. Perhaps it is the expression of a general rule of any theater which establishes reality against reality by a process of denial.

Pierre Gobin. Modern Drama. 25, 1982,
pp. 46–47, 57–58

Traditionalist, feminist, nationalist—how is one to classify the broad range of Antonine Maillet's important female characters? The answer has to be: partly each, yet not exclusively any of the above. At the risk of offending partisans of all three groups, I suggest that the wonderfully gifted Maillet— surely one of the best storytellers writing in French today—has simultaneously transcended the confining stereotypes of traditionalism, the humorlessness of some feminism, and the narrow vision of fanatic nationalism. At the same time, no author currently writing has created women who are at once more classically feminine, more liberated . . . and more Acadian.

How has Maillet achieved this remarkable synthesis? One thinks, of course, of her humor and her narrative genius, but in addition there is the striking use she makes of female protagonists. When one examines their characters, personalities, objectives, and actions, it is clear that many of these women have much in common with the typically male epic hero. Indeed, "heroine" seems almost too derivative a word to apply to these strong, memorable figures. They come closer to the powerful but unquestionably feminine women that Maya Angelou refers to as "she-roes."

Although Maillet's best known character is doubtless la Sagouine, the kind of epic heroine (let us resign ourselves to the traditional word) alluded to above is better exemplified in her narrative works, of which three will be considered here: *Mariaagélas, Les Cordes-de-Bois,* and—obviously—*Pélagie-la-Charrette.* Two of these sparkling novels proclaim the centrality of their women protagonists right in their titles. The third, *Les Cordes-de-Bois,* in fact does so as well, since the title refers to the entire clan of extraordinary women known as the Mercenaires, whose most impressive (and central) figures are la Piroune and her daughter la Bessoune.

The strictures that threaten the freedom and self-fulfillment of these redoubtable Mercenaire women are reflected spatially in the setting of the novel: a stifling, hypocritical, "well-ordered" village called le Pont after its most prominent physical feature, standing cheek by jowl with the rakishly timber-covered butte called les Cordes-de-Bois, home of and synonym for the Mercenaires. The entire novel will revolve around the opposition, between these two microcosmic universes and the principles they represent. . . .

"La voie des femmes"—the royal road to the rebirth of Acadia! All the heroines in these Maillet novels could in some sense be symbols of Acadia— a small nation, weak in the eyes of a world that knows only physical force, but strong in her desire to live and flourish despite all obstacles. Refusing the right of others either to condemn her to death or to dictate the conditions of her life, this Acadia triumphs over her foes by courage, boldness, humor, shrewdness, and nobility of spirit. There is heroism in her struggle, but also a saving mischievousness that excludes excessive solemnity. She is Maria the bootlegger, refusing the life of the shops, thumbing her nose at the fate others have reserved for her. She is la Piroune, using the buoy bells to broadcast the invitation of a generous heart across the open sea. She is above all Pélagie, hitching up her hem and setting off in a dilapidated wagon towards life and liberty. Her traditionalism does homage to a past born in the Celtic mists of the sea and tempered in the fire at Grand-Pré; her liberation creates a nation that determines its boundaries by the location of its soul; her nationalism is a reflection of the universal human quest for life and freedom. One may smile at her indulgently, but always with admiring affection, for Acadia is still living her epic—glorious, and, in its way, consummately female.

Marjorie A. Fitzpatrick. In Paula Gilbert
Lewis, ed. *Traditionalism, Nationalism, and
Feminism: Women Writers of Quebec*
(Westport, Connecticut: Greenwood Press,
1985), pp. 141–42, 151–52

For Antonine Maillet, the obstacles and the ordeals are several. From an objective point of view we might note the hunger, the needs of all sorts, the hatred of and the contempt for an antagonistic people, the English. The road is long that follows the massive deportation from Georgia back to the homeland; it is a laborious and winding road and often lonesome, rich in fear and dread. In the course of the journey, wagons have been hitched to wagons, wagons of all sizes, small and large, which Pélagie has vowed to lead to safety, seawards to what is now the promised land, once the cradle of her people. At stake is a continuity of life, a permanence, a reaching beyond the limitations of woman as a fragment towards her integration into a whole. . . .

Travel in *Pélagie-la-Charrette* is a horizontal one. It leads Pélagie from South Carolina back home, but this return takes twenty years. The mythological element is underlined first by the death of the heroine, once her task of shepherdess of her people has been accomplished. . . .

The long march of *charrettes* seems to identify the essential mission of the Acadians: to fight, to acquire absolute reality and pride, to link the lost landscapes of Acadia with inner bonds to the spirits of the wanderers, to overcome abandonment and fear. Through a *surdétermination* of the symbol, the wagon also becomes a motherly image of intimacy; an earthly vehicle is transformed into a Messianic device under a charismatic leader. . . .

We find in Antonine Maillet an inversion of *écriture*: her style is at once popular and very elaborate. Myth and history combined provide the dynamic of this novel. One can speak of a female *écriture* only in as much as Antonine Maillet puts mythology in a privileged position over history. Hence her novel illustrates a necessity to imagine and use that imagination to fuse history and myth. This results in an *écriture* which creates an Acadian communal sensibility rather than a strictly female one.

Micheline Herz. In Paula Gilbert Lewis, ed.
Traditionalism, Nationalism, and Feminism:
Women Writers of Quebec (Westport,
Connecticut: Greenwood Press, 1985),
pp. 176–79

[The Goncourt] award was the capstone of a series of widely acclaimed and brilliantly crafted works that had preceded her last book, *Pélagie-la-Charrette.* It may first be appropriate to remark that her first novel was not, as the ethnocentric publisher of *Pélagie* may lead the unsuspecting reader to believe, *Mariaagélas,* actually her ninth volume. As of 1973, the date of *Mariaagélas*'s first edition, Mrs. Maillet had indeed already three other novels in print, as well as a collection of short stories, two plays, a humoristic presentation of the history and civilization of Acadia in the form of a very unconventional tourist guide, not to mention her published doctoral dissertation on Rabelais and the oral traditions of Acadia. Between *Mariaagélas* and *Pélagie-la-Charrette,* the author published another three plays, one of which the now famous *La Sagouine,* and three novels. One of the latter, *Les Cordes-de-Bois* narrowly missed, in 1978 the Prix Goncourt which Mrs. Maillet was awarded the following year. . . .Over such two richly productive decades of literary endeavors, a thematic evolution seems to emerge, from the early novels of individual quest to the epic narrations of the more recent works. Between the opposite poles of this creative trajectory, moreover, another two phases clearly stand out: Mrs. Maillet's masterful adaptation, on the one hand, of the infinite resources of the folk-tale in such novels as *Don l'Orignal* and in the short stories of *Par Derrière chez mon père,* and, on the other hand, a series of plays, among which the internationally acclaimed *La Sagouine* and the lesser-known but equally important *Evangeline Déusse* represent prominent landmarks. . . .

In *Pointe-aux-Coques* (1958) and *On a mangé la dune* (1962), the author set out to explore the sociological, thematic, and, above all, linguistic parameters within which her subsequent works would develop. Very much like the *Pélagie-la-Charrette* of seventeen years later, *Pointe-aux-Coques* deals with the theme of self-discovery and the symbolic journey of returning. . . .

It was inevitable that the narrative vivaciousness of Rabelaisian prose would find an even more spontaneous outlet in the dynamic universe of the stage. *Les Crasseux,* first published in 1968, adapted with considerable dramatic strength the plot of *Don l'Orignal.* In the absence of the novel's pervasive satirical point of view, the play ludically focuses on the dynamics of confrontation between two rival groups whose characterization makes for unforgettable social comedy. But more significantly, the author's artistic endeavors now point to novel preoccupations. Quasi "engagés," her writings have become strategically conscious of their audience. And the stage's dionysian outbursts underscore more and more the socio-philosophical meaning of laughter. While steering clear of the ponderous strictures of political moralizing, Mrs. Maillet's dramas display, indeed, persistent shades of Brechtian determinism. . . .

By the time *Mariaagélas* was published, in 1973, the seeds of Mrs. Maillet's best creations were blossoming into superb prose epics. This richest phase of her creative evolution yielded four novels in which her affinities with Rabelais, her epic and ritualistic apprehension of human destiny and her masterly characterization of female protagonists won her international recognition. . . .

Mariaagélas represented her first full-fledged novelistic portraiture of the heroine as rebel, a grown-up and pugnacious avatar of Radi, the adolescent protagonist of *On a mangé la dune.* The book merits critical attention not only for its magnificent fresco of ancestral traditions, but also for the brilliant mordancy of its social satire, its humanistic ideology and comico-dramatic characterization of a fiercely independent woman during the rum-running days of Prohibition.

Emmanuel à Joseph à Dâvit (1975), tonally autonomous from the novels of this period, harks back to the quiet inspiration of *Par Derrière chez mon père,* but symbolically juxtaposes, in the North-South axis of two neighboring villages, the quietly traditional life of the land and that of the sea, the latter suddenly threatened by the relentless encroachments of modern industrial interests. Peacefully counterpointing this conflict, a nativity story unfolds, ostensibly patterned on the Biblical model, but whose mythical undertones throw a new light on Mrs. Maillet's use of religious themes, and significantly counterbalances her abrasive satire, in other works, of unbending and dotardy religion.

Les Cordes-de-Bois centers on the truculent and sympathetically caricatural portraiture of a matriarchal bevy (the Mercenaire family), and chronicles its hilariously eventful *démêlés* with the religious clan of contentiously prudish Ma-Tante-la-Veuve.

The luxuriance of Antonine Maillet's literary imagination and of her textual strategies is indeed stupendous. . . . [I]ncorporation of oral traditions, ludic didacticism, socio-historical awareness, linguistic revivalism and universal myth-making constitute some of the more salient foundations of her works, and because of a rich career extending now over twenty-three years, it is easier to appreciate the eminence of her contribution to the world of letters, what a critic has recently termed an "imposing presence." Very similar to that of other illustrious regionalists' (Faulkner's, Giono's and Steinbeck's especially come to mind) her vision is able to transcend the immediate sphere of native sources and, through the optimistic medium of self-derisive laughter, the catharsis of insane comedy and the overriding power of humanistic concerns, to explode in the type of pan-human statements of which only true art can partake.

Bernard Arésu. In Makoto Ueda, ed.
*Explorations: Essays in Comparative
Literature* (Lanham, Maryland: University
Press of America, 1986), pp. 211–14, 221

Antonine Maillet's contemporary Evangeline, a woman in her eighties, who is, according to Henri-Paul Jacques, a "philosophe sans le savoir," tells her story of wandering, of exile, and of alienation to passers-by in a Montreal park, site of the modern Acadians' exile, "l'exil des Chômeurs." Her speeches (often monologues) in Acadian French strongly remind us of those of La Sagouine. Among the persons who stop to listen is a Breton who has along a copy of the Longfellow poem in the 1865 Pamphile Lemay translation (published in his *Essais poétiques*), and *not*, of course, in the Marguerite Michaud adaptation for children. While the Breton attempts to tell the story according to Longfellow, Evangeline interrupts to criticize her homonym's behavior and to repair the story-line, or to tell the gospel according to Evangéline, i.e., "l'Evangéline selon Antonine," as Godin puts it. . . .

Maillet's Evangéline is cast in the mold of Pélagie and La Sagouine: strong, brave, wise from suffering; ready for new beginnings; Apollonian, sun-bathed, hopeful, and essentially free. She is an achetypal strong woman, who surpasses the Maria Chapdelaines of this world; and yet she is not unlike them. In short, she is the "true Evangeline" that historians and mythmakers alike will do well to consider, even though the Evangeline *they* know *also* stoically "endurait [les] maux avec patience," listening always to that inner voice that reiterated the command to hope, ever hope. For the "true Evangeline," the "new Evangeline," Maillet's Evangeline has everything that Longfellow's Evangeline had, and more: more stamina, more pluck. Moreover, she speaks neither *English* as in Longfellow, nor smoothed-out French as in a Michaud, but bona fide Acadian French, pure French, the French of her ancestors whose authentic speech goes back to the time of Rabelais. . . .

But *Evangéline Deusse* does not necessarily dwell exclusively on the abusive side of the powerful and oppressive "haves" of this world. It represents a social, linguistic and religious microcosm that embraces various types of Canadian (and especially of Montréalais) minorities as well as their conditions. Acadian, Quebec and standard French are spoken here (though the Breton knows all the old Acadian words; and standard French is also spoken by the Rabbi, though he reads his newspaper in Hebrew. Beyond this, the presence of the rabbi in our play allies the theme of the wandering Jew and the Acadian odyssey, as well as providing a happy replacement of the stock priest (Father Félicien). Moreover, the play also showcases the strength and the endurance of the Acadians, and especially of the Acadian woman; and it shows this *survie* with art, universality and focus. For if Maillet's droll, home-spun Evagéline is another Sagouine, if she is another Pélagie, or another Pélagie-la-Gribouille, "du fond de la baie, descendante de l'héroïne légendaire du Grand Dérangement," Evangéline Deusse, descendant of the founders of the Fond de la Baie, is *also* all Acadian people, all little people striving to make their trees grow in a barren and hostile environment. And, in an even larger sense, an even more profound and permanent way, she is an aged Tiamat, who, from the stuff of a cosmic chaos and her own somewhat ruined body—a body nonetheless sustained by hope, courage and stoic forbear-ance—shapes the course for new beginnings, for a future life. . . .

As such an archetype, Evangéline Deusse joins the salvation types of the Bible. She, like Pélagie, evokes Demeter or the myths of Mother Earth; she is, like Pélagie, like La Sagouine, a central nurturer, because in addition to rearing eleven sons, in addition to the loving care she lavishes on her fragile pine tree (symbol of the Acadian people, if you will), she inspires tenacity, hope, buoyancy, perseverance, wisdom, by her words as by her actions. Hav-ing an *en soi* personality, she is open to the world and ready for its demands as well as for its buffetings. A mainstay, like Pélagie, in the Acadian *geste,* Evangéline Deusse's journey, like Pélagie's, entails a love tryst—but in nei-ther story is the meeting realized. Yet as we have seen, somehow that does not daunt either woman. One may assume that in both cases they love their men, but they have a wider mission.

Janis L. Palliser. *American Review of Canadian Studies.* 18, 1988, pp. 242–45

MAJEROVÁ, MARIE (CZECH REPUBLIC) 1882–1967

Although the proletarian element appeared in her work from the very outset and she tackled the theme in one of her first works of fiction, Marie Majerová still had to run through the whole gamut of the exclusivist writing of her day (exclusivist because it was far removed from the most important questions and problems of life). She had to make her way through the themes of women's subjection and liberation (first, the anarchistically conceived, illu-sory liberation, then true liberation). Moreover, she had to settle accounts with the anarchism of the prewar generation, until, having passed through the great convulsions of the world war, she attained genuine, piercing insight into life.

It is true that all along she had been interested in and in touch with working-class life and the workers' movement. But here again, she had to confront the growing opportunism in the movement: a sterile thing for a poet. For Majerová, the war signified a break. . . . When, with the great revolutionary transformations of the postwar years behind her, she stood in the thick of the most vital working-class movement, she had to sharpen her weapons as a writer, above all in the psychological presentation of her characters.

Even her first major achievement, the novel *Nejkrásnější svět* (The most beautiful world) was not triumphant. The crisis of the postwar revolutionary spirit brought Majerová to a crisis in faith in the social outlook that had cemented her world. . . . But all along . . . there was the striving to find a way forward. And so, as the years went by, the best, most fruitful aspects of her life and work led at last to a second peak in her oeuvre—the great epic *Siréna* (The siren). [1937].

Bedřich Václavek. *Tvorbou k realitě* (Prague:
Svoboda, 1950), p. 87

Whereas [Majerová's] other fiction is predominantly or entirely set in towns or cities, *Nejkrásnější svět* is alone in being more than half purely rural. Without a doubt, Majerová here has paid generous tribute to her native region. With the same remarkable feeling for the typical features of our homeland she had already shown in the poetic prose passages of *Zluhu a hor* [From meadows and hills], she offers in this novel a fluid and colorful picture of the central-Bohemian countryside, with its broad fields and meadows, its gardens and woodlands. . . . But, with all her intimate feelings and rich imagery, Marie Majerová has also succeeded in re-creating country life as it really was in the days before World War I. She has evoked its singular atmosphere, as yet barely touched by the proximity of the neighboring towns, even of Prague itself. She depicts the way of life, with the traditional customs and ceremonies. . . .

She would not, however, be the true socialist writer she is if she had not also paid special attention to the social order of the day, going further than her realist predecessors in exposing and denouncing the evils of deprivation and oppression in rural life. Her countryside is certainly far removed from "one family." . . . Alongside the proud estates . . . [there is] the stark poverty of the bondsmen eking out a bare existence from the fields and the appalling slavery of the landless who, as stable hands or laborers, are cast upon the mercy of the squires and, while currying the favor of their masters, are united in their black hatred of them. . . .

Majerová shows no hesitation to work at rethinking the concept of her book. Hence the present version of the novel, in which she has not only expanded the picture of ferment and growth within our working-class movement . . . but also remolded the characters, especially Roman. Now Roman volunteers for the Russian front intending to desert to the other side. And although he does not succeed, he does at least get a close view of the Great October Revolution. Under its influence he returns home, to Lenka, now an active supporter of her revolutionary view of society, although he arrived at his belief largely thanks to an inquisitive mind, while she did through her experience in life and her ardent sympathy for all oppressed people. To their happy love Majerová has now added their common enthusiasm for the social battle to achieve a new, "most beautiful" world. She has also emended the end of the story, turning the death-bed dream with which she rocks Lenka . . . into a restorative sleep from which the heroine awakens to life. After all we have learned about them, we have no doubt that she and Roman will carry on the fight, undaunted even by the December defeat of the revolutionary workers' movement.

A. M. Piša. *Stopami prózy* (Prague:
Československý spisovatel, 1964),
pp. 44–45, 54–55

Majerová was innately and purposefully a writer who aspired to present a credible and faithful picture of people, their personalities, relationships, and the times they lived in, to achieve a *realism* that arose from a penetrating and informed perception. She found the greatest theme for her endeavors by returning to the past of Kladno. In the broad and *representative* canvas of her chronicle-novel *Siréna* she attempted to show the past and present of the working class, the social conflicts, the sad but significant destinies of her characters. Through the manifold experiences of the Hudec family she sketched the revolutionary march of events.

Throughout the long years she spent in the school of deprivation and strikes, of solidarity and treachery, of love and hate, Majerová learned how to trace the transformation of the countryman into townsman and self-aware *proletarian*. Thus, she does not portray the proletarian as an isolated individual, a victim of misfortune. Instead, he is seen as a member of the working class, which is growing aware of its status and its goals. This is precisely what always attracted her most: to observe how people's motivation and behavior is shaped in unison with the movement of economic and social forces; how people come to terms, instinctively or consciously, with the enormous force of the social process, its currents and explosions.

The most dramatic expression of her endeavor to write socialist fiction was to be her *Havířská balada (Ballad of a Miner)*. This life story of a Czech miner, another member of the Hudec family, follows *Siréna* chronologically, but it is a ballad rather than a chronicle, that is, a story reduced to a few basic situations and relationships, narrated in such a way that the alternating tones of excitement, anguish, and lyricism yield the "heroism, love, and happiness of the common man." The focus is on a man who, in his struggle to eke out a bare living and to defend his human rights and aspirations, comes up against the pressures of an unjust social order. In the end, however, as is the way in ballads, despite all the tragedy in life there remains a sense of beauty and of heroism: the assurance of solidarity, so essential at moments when a man's fate depends on others; the gift of companionship from a comrade's helping hand; the devoted sympathy of wife and family; and finally work, without which life loses all dignity.

Miloš Pohorský. Afterword to Marie
Majerová. *Havířská balada*
(Prague: Mladá fronta, 1968), pp. 151–52

During her long career, [Majerová] never wrote without the socialist idea in mind. Her early novel *Nejkrásnější svět* is indeed conventional; in reading its first chapters and knowing that it is supposed to be the harbinger of Czech socialist realist fiction, one wonders how this could be true. The novel itself would have been long forgotten if it were not for its author's political position. Nevertheless, in spite of the novel's lurid sentimentality, its naïve and dated feminism, the story, particularly in its 1951 edition, deals with the beginnings of the Czech socialist movement. When in the 1930s the Marxist theory of socialist realism rose on the Czechoslovak literary horizon, it fitted Majerová like a glove. In contrast to other writers, she had to make little effort to conform to its tenets. While a [Anna Marie] Tilschová or Pujmanová was obliged to visit factories and mines to learn how to write about them, Majerová could merely remember. Olbracht, a much more competent writer than she, had to use his skill and imagination in creating a servant girl who became a militant Communist; Majerová herself served as a maid in Budapest. . . .

In her last collection of short stories, *Cesta blesku* [The path of lightning, 1954] every one, young and old, glows with unselfish happiness and working zeal. . . . The volume, which contains fifteen short stories, instructs the reader in recent Czechoslovak history and enlarges upon the building-up period and the state's planned economy. All this is performed with great ease and on party-line premises.

Milada Součková. A Literary Satellite
(Chicago: University of Chicago Press,
1970), pp. 71–72

Majerová's career as a writer began with her first poem "Píseň" (A song) in the *Workers' Calendar* for 1901. Negative sentiments dominate as a proletarian mother meditates over the crib: "I hide all the poison and anger in my bosom / and in the corner, in secret, I keep vengeance."

In 1905 Majerová published her first novel, *Panenství* (Virginity). It was based on her own unhappy experience. She denounced the "bourgeois" value placed on a young woman's virginity before marriage, which treats it as a commodity that enhances the capital value of a woman in a society where only money counts. . . .

She examined her Parisian experience in the novel, *Náměstí republiky* (Republic Square, 1914). In this she presents an anti-hero, Libertad, a sensualist and anarchist, who leads a group of similarly inclined hedonists in a commune. They preach the egocentric liberation of the senses from bourgeois moralist prejudices. The hero, Luka Veršinin, is a Russian migrant anarchist, who does not have time to live his life because he wants to sacrifice it to the revolution. In Paris he gradually loses all his illusions about the various ways of achieving this. He becomes a terrorist, and with his last few francs he buys a gun and instead of committing suicide, shoots a couple of French officers during a May Day parade. Looking for action that will change the world he has decided: "Just to shoot them off, piece by piece! Then one will see what can be done."

Marie Majerová was attempting to establish the ideal of the revolutionary hero of radical action. For her the capitalist system was the source of all social evils and of individual unhappiness, therefore it had to be destroyed. Only a future socialist system could guarantee both individual and collective paradise.

In her next novel, *Nejkrásnější svět* (The most beautiful world), she was still looking for ways of achieving the ideal society but her emphasis had changed. In the new Republic the heroine Lenka discovers the proper Leninist way to a successful revolution. She runs away from her tyrannical father who rules a "typical bourgeois family" because she has to break out of the prison of a "bourgeois" family. Personal happiness must be reached through revolutionary activity that will establish a proletarian dictatorship. Only then will everybody be happy and enjoy the beauty of life. . . .

F. X. Šalda, the influential literary critic, who was usually sympathetic to extreme left-wing writers, when reviewing her novel, pointed out what she did not realize, namely that revolutionaries were generally ascetic fanatics and dogmatists. The authoress with her "idyllic epicureanism" did not fit the pattern. . . .

Her novel of 1932, *Přehrada* (The dam), proposed a master plan for a Communist takeover of the country. The plot was set thirty years in the future. At an official opening of a dam, the corrupt politicians and capitalists who had constructed it of inferior concrete become so worried that they panic when an underground revolutionary organization spreads rumors that the dam will collapse and flood the capital city of Prague. The revolutionaries use the occasion to distribute hidden arms to workers and overnight, in a coup, seize power. In the democratic Republic this insurrectional novel brought no repercussions upon the authoress. It was widely read, sold well, and its literary merit was discussed in the "bourgeois" press. Some Marxist critics, however, were embarrassed and criticized it. It was wrong to suggest that the party would use lies for its coup d'état.

Majerová's major novel, *Siréna* (The siren), was published in 1935. It was to become her most translated and celebrated work, later to be filmed and shown around the world. In a loosely connected history of four generations of a family, Majerová attempted to show the problems of workers and the gradual awakening of their political consciousness. It was set in the industrial and mining center of Kladno which she knew well. The novel, accompanied by documents, is well informed about actual working conditions but is hard and often unpleasant to read. The narrative combines naturalism with forced lyricism in some kind of tortured expressionism, or "socialist verism." . . .

Even Marxist reviewers in the 1930s, and again the 1960s, complained about the novel's old-fashioned "bourgeois" narrative technique and its pedantic quality—like that of an illustrated text book. But it was read, especially after the coup d'état of 1948 when it became an obligatory text for educating children, and in party schooling. In 1965, with an additional printing of seventeen thousand copies, it reached its twenty-third edition. It was also translated into the satellite countries' languages and propagated as an exemplary achievement of socialist realism. Soviet readers liked it. Majerová's next story, *Havířská balada* (Miners' ballad), written in 1938, was also criticized for its bombastic style, but later extolled as an exemplary work.

The Communist Party made the work of [this] third-rate writer a national socialist classic.

Peter Hruby. *Daydreams and Nightmares: Czech Communist and Ex-Communist Literature, 1917–1987* (New York: Columbia University Press, 1990), pp. 208–12

MAKSIMOVIĆ, DESANKA (SERBIA) 1898–

If we were asked to find an American counterpart for this Serbian poetess, we would point to Sara Teasdale. Amid the turmoil of our times Desenka Maksimovič goes her quiet way, confessing in pure lyrical verse her boundless love of life and nature. One finds no striving for the New Objectivity in her poetry, no painful bending for originality in thought and form. In her verse we have the tenderest expression of a woman's soul.

Anthony J. Klančary. *Books Abroad.*
11, 1937, p. 512

"The Chronicle of Perun's Descendants" is an unusual and complex poetic work, a sort of epic composed of fifty-eight poems and imbued with lyricism. The poet harmoniously combines elements of South Slavic ancient history and mythology in an attempt to present certain local and universal human problems (discord among brotherly nations, senseless wars, love and hatred, humility and vanity).

The individual poems of this "chronicle" in verse are structured into two cycles centered around a war (thirty-seven poems) and a religious controversy (twenty-two poems), both of which took place in 920. In spite of this clear-cut thematic difference, it is obvious that Maksimovič considers the two cycles as integral parts of one poetic whole. Not only is there no formal division between them, but the poet also utilizes a series of structural devices to emphasize their unity. Thus the Croats and their King (Tomislav) are among the protagonists of both cycles. In addition, the voices of Slavic ancestors, the appearances of old Slavic gods and the church bells sounding crucial events recur throughout the chronicle as musical leitmotifs in a well-composed symphony.

The war theme introduces the Serbs and Croats as allies, united by the will of their gods against Bulgarian aggressors. The theme of the religious controversy (dealing with the period in which [the] Latin service was introduced in Croatian churches) poetically evokes the times when the Croats chose a religious path of their own and broke their ancestral ties. While the chronicle opens loudly and fiercely, with Perun's thunder announcing the supreme god's discontent with the forthcoming bloodshed, the closing poem is gentle and soothing in tone. The moonlight softly falls over the earth, covering the ancient scenes with its fine and transparent curtain, while the poet reminds us that in the face of eternity, as in the dim light of the moon, all human conflicts lose their shape and sharpness, become unreal and pointless.

For a linguist, and for those who admire beautiful poetic language, Desanka Maksimovič's newest work, written in rich metaphoric style seasoned with archaisms, provides a real treat.

Biljana Šljivić-Šimšić. *World Literature Today.* 51, 1977, pp. 305–6

Desanka Maksimović . . . is one of Yugoslavia's leading living poets. The present collection [*Pesme*/Poems] of forty-three poems marks her visit to Canada in 1976. It offers an interesting, representative sampling of her work, dating back to its origins nearly sixty years ago and ranging from highly personal lyrics to moving, powerful reactions to the abundant sufferings of her people. In this last regard "Krvava bajka—A Legend in Blood," inscribed on the monument to the men and boys slaughtered by Nazi occupation forces at Kragujevac (1941), is particularly noteworthy.

The Serbo-Croatian originals are accompanied by facing English translations, done by a variety of translators. Most are literal and linguistically correct and convey some sense of the imagery and content of the originals. A small number are so free as to bear only a remote resemblance to the originals. A preface—both in English and Serbo-Croatian—provides informative biographical and bibliographical information; its rudimentary critical observations would have been better left unsaid.

> E. A. Scatton. *World Literature Today.* 51,
> 1977, p. 306

The venerable Serbian poet Desanka Maksimović has just turned ninety and is as active as she was decades ago. After twenty books of poetry . . . she has just published a collection of seventy-five new poems gathered in five cycles. The most remarkable feature about Desanka (as she is affectionately called) is her steady poetic craft. Little has basically changed from her early days: a concern for basic human values, compassion for all living creatures, an unshakably optimistic attitude, a visceral attachment to nature, and a highly lyric reaction to whatever comes her way. If there is a perceptible change in her most recent volume, it is a melancholy realization of the setting of the sun and a wisdom, even resignation, that emanates from it. After all, the experience accumulated over the decades amid tireless activity that would have felled many a weaker being cannot but convince her of the inevitable. As a result, we have several exquisite poems addressing that point.

Desanka has also been a witness to many changes in the life around her and has left testimonials about them. It is in this light that the title poem "Pamtiču sve" (I'll remember it all) should be understood.

Poets like Desanka appear only once in ninety years.

> Vasa D. Mihailovich. *World Literature
> Today.* 63, 1989, pp. 334–35

In her very first collection, *Pesme*, Desanka Maksimović emerged as a sensitive lyric poet, fascinated with nature, of which she has felt an integral part and in which she has confided and searched for joy, beauty, and comfort ever since. Her prewar poetic work includes mainly love and descriptive poems in which the poet confesses her own youthful anxieties and curiosity in front of the great mysteries of life and love. As she matured Maksimović widened the scope and depth of her preoccupations, and her poetry came to have a more universal character. The suffering of her nation in World War II inspired a series of beautiful, humane patriotic poems, of which *Krvava bajka* (1951; A legend of blood, 1962), occasioned by the German massacre of schoolboys in Kragujevac in 1943, is the best known and most widely translated.

Maksimović reached her peak in the 1960s and 1970s. The collection *Tražim pomilovanje* (1964; I plead for mercy), subtitled "Lyrical Discussions with Tsar Dushan's Medieval Code of Laws," glorifies forgiveness and compassion as the most noble of human virtues. Among those for whom the poet pleads are both the oppressed and the oppressors, the humble and the vain, the naïve and the sly, the poor and the rich, women, monks, soldiers, sinners, and dreamers—all her fellow human beings. In the collection *Nemam više vremena* (1973; My time is running short) the aging poet meditates on death and dying and reminisces about the passing of her loved ones. With calm resignation, Maksimović accepts death as a component of life and prepares herself for the last journey, which for her means returning to nature and merging with eternity.

Like many great literary figures, Maksimović does not belong to any specific twentieth-century literary movement or fad. Anything that might have influenced her is filtered through the prism of her own talent and her strong poetic individuality and is fully and harmoniously integrated in an entirely original poetic whole. With its accent on love, beauty, and universal ethical principles, her poetry, written in a superb style, represents her most valuable contribution to Serbian literature. . . .

One of the few best-selling poets of our nonpoetic era, Maksimović is today the dean of the Serbian literary scene, and her opus has become an integral part of Serbian national culture.

Biljana Šljivič-Šimšić. In Leonard S. Klein, ed. *Encyclopedia of World Literature in the 20th Century* (New York: Frederick Ungar, 1983), pp. 182–83

AL-MALĀ'IKA, NĀZIK (IRAQ) 1923–

Nāzik al-Malā'ika is endowed with a profundity of emotion, a breadth of vision, and a purity of conscience that give her unique qualities as a poet. Her artistic gifts and her ability to use language allow her to soar. She is able to use her talents to give the most honest and successful analyses of her own self, revealing to us the sights and perceptions that haunt her and the painful events she has witnessed. She immerses herself in terrifying visions and then distills them into an atmosphere of melancholy and bitter suffering. It is in this sense of anxiety that the secret of her creativity lies, along with her fertile gift for expression and a breadth of imagination that makes full use of her own fervent emotions and marvelous poetic imagery. In her love she finds herself rapidly stricken by devastating failure; a stream of ideas begins to flow from the profound depths of her soul. Sentiments pour forth, responding to her agitated thoughts and the whims and fancies of her mind. She gives inspiring expression to a very genuine experience that makes you feel the profound fervor of artistic truth and the clash of sentiments. . . .

Nāzik al-Malā'ika also concerns herself with the problems of human existence, showing her usual skill and subtlety. She pours her realism into an attractive artistic mold and then gives artistic expression to her feelings. . . . Unlike some of our writers, she is not prepared to live in an ivory tower . . . but stands in the forefront of contemporary poets who are proclaiming the birth of a new age in which social problems will be aired and portrayed in unprecedented ways. This will be a genuinely humanist literature that will deserve to survive from one era to the next, since it conforms with the dynamic principles of development and is totally free of any artificiality or narrowness of vision.

Khidr 'Abbās al-Sālihī. *Al-Ādāb.*
December, 1958, pp. 22–23

I would like to say a few words about the love poetry of Nāzik al-Malā'ika. When I use the term "Sūfī poetry," what I actually mean is the kind of love poetry she herself writes. Nāzik al-Malā'ika does not tell us in this kind of poetry anything of particular importance about her private life or about the "passions" of the members of her sex. After all, excellent poetry should be neither a psychological or social document. There is no inherent contradiction in the statement that poetry can tell us far more about the person who wrote it than can be gleaned from talking about personality. Good poetry is neither masculine nor feminine. It is true that in her first collection and a few weak poems from her other collections there may be a few obscure references to her experiences in life. However, we only pause at these rather weak examples of her depiction of her life when we want to find out how she has come to mold the more productive experiences of her better poems; once we have that information, that is enough of such weak poems.

She does not tell us a great deal about any love affairs hidden in the recesses of the past; her total concern is to tell us about the present and future. From the point of view of poetry, all that concerns her about these past experiences is that they were idealistic and short-lived. And it is precisely this that makes the whole thing so suitable for transformation in the poet's consciousness into a Sūfī mystical experience, particularly when it is linked to that inward contemplation that sees in the self the "secret of nature." In this way, pain, anger, sorrow, and contempt are changed into a burning desire for the return of the moment in the past, the ideal moment, the overwhelming sense (but without any feeling of revolt) of the deep abyss separating lover from beloved; and that is the essence of the mystical experience.

Nāzik does not achieve this stage in one move. Indeed, it would be futile and even laughable to conceive of her moving upward gradually like a pupil moving from one class to another. We can see that this mystical experience has allowed her to escape from the prison of the self through self-contemplation and to liberate herself from the past by adhering to it. This has given her poetry a new psychological richness, so much so, in fact, that it has almost brought her—as with others—to a stage of sterility and bankruptcy.

Shukrī 'Ayyād. Al-Ādāb. March, 1966,
pp. 41–42

The collection *Lover of the Night* contains both poetry and straight narrative. This fact stems from her own fierce sensibilities: she is eager to say every-thing and hide nothing. And so you will find fine expressions alongside others of much less worth. But, you may say, that is the way it is with all things at the time of birth; that is one of nature's rules. Great classical poets like Abū Tammām and Ibn al-Rūmī pointed this fact out. Nevertheless, I choose to differ with both of them; to me the laws of art require that early faults should be exposed and strangled at birth. . . .

Most poets get their sustenance from the world around them . . . but Nāzik draws her poetic inspiration from within her own heart and soul. When she describes the scene of the horse stumbling in the street . . . she chooses to portray only that part of the total scene which touches her own sensibilities and strikes a chord of sympathy within her. In such a picture what she has seen is a reflected image of her own self. . . .

To turn to her poetic technique, she has succeeded admirably in getting away from the confines of rhyme. Her poems consist of couplets, quatrains, and so on, but you will not find more than two poems in the entire collection with the same rhyme scheme. It is the same with the meters. Most of the poems use the *khafīf* pattern [one of the traditional meters], which is particu-larly appropriate for the expression of grief. But you are not conscious of this correspondence of form and content as you read because this most sensi-tive poet holds your attention principally by describing the sufferings she endures. So you suffer with her.

There are few images in her poetry, but she makes up for this with her own fiery spirit, which produces an emotional revolt without parallel among Arab women poets. This revolt of the mind and the heart takes her attention away from the external world. . . . I believe that her hatred of the world springs from her love of it. If you read through the complete collection from beginning to end—including her translations of works by foreign poets—you will find that it revolves around one single emotion. In fact, it seems that you are faced with an *idée fixe* that has enabled her to go into her theme thoroughly.

Mārūn 'Abbūd. Mujaddidūna wa-mujtarrūna
(Beirut: Dār al-Thaqāfa, 1968), pp. 221–22

It would be a mistake to impose on Nāzik al-Malā'ika's poetry the criteria applied to committed poets. In her four collections, Nāzik is, in her own words, a free poet who "expresses the sentiments of her life and records the strange feelings of her own soul." That is not to say that she disavows commitment. She has written poems within the realm of social sensibility and has dealt with the questions of the hour in a manner that displays a burning national feeling and her own humanitarian attitudes. We need only point to her seething poem "To Wash Away Dishonor" in the collection *The Bottom of the Wave* to demonstrate what we mean. However, she does not impose the idea of commitment on herself, nor does she believe that poetry can endure being tied to a particular school or topic. She has expressed this view very clearly in the introduction to *Splinters and Ashes,* where she says: "In poetry, the golden rule is that it has no rules." In her view the poet is only a poet if he has his own special identity, since that identity is the secret behind his individuality and creativity. He can borrow new styles on condition that he mold them so as to express his own individual personality and his own private world.

In the case of Nāzik al-Malā'ika, the world she writes about is certainly her own private world. There may be images in it that are familiar enough, but the notion of "I" looks down on us from every direction. Her poetry represents a violent revolt against the old poetic tradition. Her immersion in the identity of the self is a reaction against homiletic poetry and occasional verse, with their rhetorical style; it is a withdrawal into the world of the imagination and the unknown, of nature and song.

Rose Ghurayyib. *Shi'r.* Spring, 1968,
pp. 117–18

It was undoubtedly the Iraqi poetess Nāzik al-Malā'ika who, first in the introduction to her collection *Splinters and Ashes* and later in her book *Problems of Contemporary Poetry* (1962), laid the theoretical foundations for the development of this new form [of free verse]. Al-Malā'ika was concerned with freeing Arabic poetry from the regularity characteristic of the traditional forms. With the single line of verse as the basic unit of the *qasīda* pattern, the molds of Arabic poetry imposed their form on the content and quite often deprived the resulting poetical composition of its vital effect. Thus al-Malā'ika advocated the need for a free verse, in which the meter is based upon the unit of the *taf'īlah* (foot) and the freedom of the poet is secured through his right to vary the *taf'īlāt* (feet) or the lengths of his lines as he feels most appropriate for the expression of his message. However, she limited the range of this freedom by requiring that the *taf'īlāt* in the lines be completely similar. This meant that, of the sixteen traditional meters, only seven (*Kāmil, Ramal, Hazaj, Rajaz, Mutaqārib, Khafīf,* and *Wāfir*), which are based on the repetition of a single *taf'īlah,* could be used by the free-verse poets. The other meters were considered inappropriate for this type of poetry. Furthermore, al-

Malā'ika insisted on the use of rhyme in free verse for its rhythmical and organizational value in the making of a poem.

These are, in broad lines, al-Malā'ika's basic principles for the development of free verse. Many poets and critics rejected them on the assumption that they were arbitrary rules no less rigid than those of al-Khalīl's (d. 791) prosodic system. Other poets modified them by using combined meters in their compositions or by inventing their own *taf'īlāt*. In his criticism of al-Malā'ika's theories, Muhammad al-Nuwayhī, a prominent Egyptian critic, advocated the shift of the basis of modern Arabic verse from its traditional quantitative structure to the accentual pattern of English poetry.

> Mounah A. Khouri and Hamid Algar.
> Introduction to *An Anthology of Modern
> Arabic Poetry* (Berkeley: University of
> California Press, 1974), pp. 16–17

In the recent edition of her *Collected Works,* her two-volume *Diwan* of 1970, Malā'ika published for the first time her long poem *Life's Tragedy* which runs to 1,200 lines (in rhyming couplets), written between 1945 and 1946, together with two revised but incomplete versions of the poem composed in the same form of verse in 1950 and in 1965, and entitled respectively *Song for Man I* and *Song for Man II.* The poem, clearly influenced by Abu Madi's "Riddles" and Taha's "God and the Poet," is, as Malā'ika herself was aware in the introduction, an extremely romantic work, the title of which indicates the extent of her pessimism and her agonizing sense of life as an overwhelmingly painful riddle. The theme is the poet's quest for happiness, which is occasioned by the sufferings of the Second World War and which drives her to seek it in vain, first in the palaces of the rich, then in the monasteries of the ascetics, the dens of sinners, in the simple life of the shepherd and the peasant, among poets and lovers, until finally the poet finds her rest in the presence of God who, as in the conclusion to Taha's poem, provides the answer. There is nothing in the least unusual or surprising in the young Malā'ika writing such a poem on a theme of this type in the mid 1940s. What is obviously significant and indicative of her apparently permanent romantic cast of mind is that she should later on feel the need to go back to the poem and to revise it at two different periods of her life. As she says in the introduction, comparison between the styles of writing might give the reader an idea of her poetic development. Indeed the diction of the latest version is much less unabashedly romantic than that of the earliest one, although the earliest version would seem to be much more successful because in it the language is more in keeping with a theme that belongs to the heart of the romantic tradition in modern Arabic poetry.

> Mustafa Badawi. *A Critical Introduction to
> Modern Arabic Poetry* (Cambridge:
> Cambridge University Press, 1975),
> pp. 228–29

In the light of the continuous experiments in this century to break through
the impasse of fixed pattern in the poetic form, it is idle to link the free verse
movement which started formally in 1949 (date of publication of the second
dīwān of N. al-Malā'ika, *Shazāyā wa Ramād*), with the revolutionary political
ideas which erupted at the end of the 1940s. In fact, the first experiments by
the leaders of the later free verse movement were effected before 1948, the
date of the Palestine catastrophe which evoked in many Arab intellectuals a
strong rejection of the sanctimonious relics of the traditional culture, which
included the old poetic form. The formal beginning of the movement of free
verse must therefore be seen as an artistic phenomenon which succeeded
because it was both artistically mature and timely in that it suited the historic
and psychological moment in the Arab world. This does not mean that the
previous successive experiments in form throughout this century had not
been prompted by a revolutionary spirit. The early experimentalists in form,
like the later ones, were all avant-garde who had courage and originality, and
they all rejected the slavery of the modern poet to old, preconceived poetic
forms. The free verse movement at the end of the 1940s was the fulfillment
of these efforts. Because of the spiritual shock caused by the Palestine debacle of 1948, and the general mental, political and social energy it produced,
the new poets were able to imbue their new form with finer poetic qualities
and with more contemporaneous attitudes and visions.

It was N. al-Malā'ika's second *dīwān, Shazāyā wa Ramād,* published in
Baghdad, which headed the free verse movement. Although only eleven
poems out of thirty-two were in free verse, in her preface she propounded
her views on the purpose and artistic supremacy of free verse. . . .

Nāzik al-Malā'ika's poetry vascillates in a fascinating manner between
agony and ecstasy, anger and a rather philosophical matter of fact tone. . . .
[She] employs the paradox of wit with skill: "our sleepless dreams"; "beautiful faults"; "our rough, impossible merits"; "in the fragrant beauty and fruitfulness of our follies." These are all verbal paradoxes, but such poems as
"Al-Sha khṣ al-Thāni" and "Al-Zā'ir al-Ladhi lam Yaji'" conform to the idea
that a poem is paradoxical when it modifies dramatically our preconceived
concepts. In these poems, the longing for the image of a lost lover stands in
contrast with the paradoxical feeling of satisfaction that he never reappeared,
for by not so doing, he remained the same person; his reappearance would
have destroyed the image of continuity which the interruption of the relation
could secure. There is more wit than pathos in these poems, but for al-
Malā'ika, whose natural inclination, one would have thought, was to have
bewailed a lost lover (as she indeed does in other poems), this is an achievement. It is also an achievement for Arabic poetry at the time, for the rather
dry humor, the quiet philosophizing, the matter of fact, intelligent tone, are
miraculously free of the traditional sentimentality which normally accompanied such persistent themes in Arabic.

Salma Khada Jayyusi. *Trends and
Movements in Modern Arabic Poetry,* vol. 2
(Leiden: Brill, 1977), pp. 557–58, 656, 683

After the Second World War, women begin to contribute to [Arabic] literature in a way which, qualitatively speaking, is in no sense inferior to that of their male colleagues. The first woman who plays a central part in modern Arabic literature is the Iraqi poetess, Nāzik al-Malā'ika . . . one of the two founders of so-called free verse, a poetic form based on one of the verse-feet of classical Arabic meter which is repeated, but with the length of the lines and the rhyme scheme being left free. Since its first appearance in 1947 this poetic form has become the most productive one in modern Arabic poetry, above all thanks to Nāzik al-Malā'ika's efforts in her critical writings as well as her poems to refine and develop her theories.

The thorough knowledge of Arabic poetry on which the theories of the "free verse" movement were based was something Nāzik owed to her family background. Both her father and her mother had a certain reputation as poets, and her mother was the first Iraqi poetess to call for an improvement in the position of women. But Nāzik's poetry was also influenced by the conservative attitude of the wealthy circles in Baghdad in which she grew up; the melancholy tone and pessimistic view of life which are especially noticeable in her first collections of poems are partly a product of this. Although she devotes most of her attention to the world of the mind and the spirit, she can, when looking at the outside world, react forcefully and profoundly to political and social injustice. She herself ascribes the melancholic tone of her poems to her fear of death, her lack of inner freedom, the defeats and reverses in the political sphere which her people have suffered and the humiliations which she as a woman has experienced.

> Hilary Kirkpatrick. In Mineke Schipper, ed.
> *Unheard Words: Women and Literature in*
> *Africa, the Arab World, Asia, the*
> *Caribbean, and Latin America* (London:
> Allison and Busby, 1985), pp. 76–77

Free verse was introduced into the [Arabic] poetic canon by a woman. In 1949 the Iraqi poet Nazik al-Malā'ika published a collection of verse called *Shadhāyā wa ramad* (Splinters and ashes). Only eleven of these poems were in free verse, but the iron hold of classical and neoclassical poetry had been broken. True, men had experimented with free verse, but their attempts had encountered stiff opposition. Experimentation had been tolerated in the new, Western genres such as the novel and the short story, but poetry, the literary art of the Arabs par excellence, could not submit to such treatment. Critics condemned all experimentation in poetry as evidence of weakness on the part of the poet, who clearly could not master the arduous techniques of the classical ode, elegy, eulogy, et cetera. However, when Nazik al-Malā'ika risked the critics' scorn and published "Splinters and Ashes," the reaction was astounding. The collection was hailed as a breakthrough, and two of al-Malā'ika's countrymen, Badr Shakir al-Sayyab and Abd al-Wahhab al-Bayyati, started composing poetry in this new liberated form. Only a woman who was barred by gender from entry into the magic circle of the literary canon could risk such a challenge. She was outside criticism, good or bad; she had nothing much to lose but a great deal to gain. In the same year, 1949, the Jordanian poet Thurayya Malhas published a collection of free verse entitled "The Wandering Song," wherein she attacked tradition in literature as in thought. Free verse had come to stay.

Miriam Cooke. World Literature Today. 60,
Spring, 1986, p. 213

MALLET-JORIS, FRANÇOISE (BELGIUM) 1930–

The Rampart of the Béguines tells the story of the corruption of a minor: an adolescent girl is seduced by a lesbian. The scabrous nature of the subject matter is accentuated by the fact that the seductress is also the mistress of the victim's father. One shudders to think of the vulgarity that such a theme might well produce. But there is not a trace of vulgarity in this novel. If it is sometimes impossible to breathe in this atmosphere, the cause lies not in shameful details but in the cold and treacherous suavity of the diction. We learn on page 86 that *Dangerous Relationships* happens to be one of the lesbian Tamara's favorite books. To tell the truth, the reader should have suspected as much for some time. It is also probable that Laclos is one of Mallet-Joris's own stylistic models, and I would add that he is also a model for the psychology and morality of this novel. . . .

As in Laclos, this story of a corrupted young girl, and of the sexual spell cast upon her, appeals not to the reader's baser impulses but to his heart. As with Laclos, beneath the licentious gracefulness and the imperturbable immorality of the narrative, we are invited to watch a rather terrifying surgical operation performed on the human heart. But the writer's hand does not tremble as she holds the scalpel. Even more than sensations of pleasure, she is able to describe the awakening of the will to power and domination; and the central theme of her work is perhaps the antagonism between two people filled with equal energy and possessed by an equal need to affirm themselves and crush others. Is this not also the subject of *Dangerous Relationships*? . . . In my opinion *The Rampart of the Béguines* is the literary revelation of the year.

Jean-Louis Curtis. Les Temps Modernes.
June, 1951, pp. 2287–89

The Illusionist . . . centers on relationship that must generally be considered unnatural. . . . Françoise Mallet writes about it with a directness and simplicity that few, I think, will find offensive and many, moving and enlightening. . . . *The Illusionist* deals with experience that fortunately is, at least at this extreme, off the beaten track, but the sincerity of the young author and the effectiveness of her narrative give her theme general interest and importance.

Mary Ross. *New York Herald Tribune.*
September 7, 1952, p. 12

This author, now twenty-seven, is a writer of scope and force. Her third book [*House of Lies*] is solid, interesting throughout, at times brilliant. And its strong grasp of human motivation, its understanding of the essential isolation of man (to the point where he cannot believe even in another's disinterestedness if it cost him his life) are truly profound. The author's work, stemming from the vital tradition of Belgian woman novelists, is worthy of such splendid predecessors as Marguerite van de Wiele and, more recently, Julia Frezin. Françoise Mallet-Joris is, I believe, the only young woman writing in French today who deserves the title of novelist.

Frances Keene. *The New York Times.*
November 10, 1957, p. 39

François Mallet-Joris has now given us a long, ample novel [*The Empire Celeste*], which is well constructed and rich in observation, thought, and wit. It could almost be said that everything one previously thought about her talent has been surpassed. Such inspiration, such stunning richness, was unexpected. She is indisputably an important novelist, that is to say, a writer who can conceive, bring to life, and direct the movements of very different characters at the same time (but not on the same level or with the same rhythm). She can interest the reader in their destinies and in their variant natures, interweave these destinies plausibly within a general structure, and finally orchestrate all these diverse elements in an ascending line of emotion and interest. This achievement is no small matter, and the novelists who succeed in it are few. . . .

Mallet-Joris seems to have a love for public places, in which varied people with unusual destinies can meet. In her previous novel, *The Lies,* one could feel the writer's tenderness for a big city's streets, a port, a seedy bar. Here she has penetrated, much more profoundly and intimately, a corner of Montparnasse. She communicates its sad and slightly artificial tone, its density, and its shadows on which the phantasmagoric neon flashes. The reader inhabits this restaurant on the Rue d'Odessa, the Empire Céleste, with the author. . . . It is the fixed point through which the major lines of the novel pass.

Gabrielle Gras. *Europe.*
December, 1958, pp. 125–26

With the appearance of these two novels [*The Illusionist* and *The Red Room*] Francois Mallet-Joris, still in her twenties, was hailed as a modern successor to the Marquis de Sade and Laclos. Combining a striking command of novelistic technique with scandalous subject matter, Mme. Mallet-Joris revealed a preoccupation with the politics of conflicting wills which could not fail to recall these masters of the eighteenth century. The publication of two subsequent novels and a collection of short stories, however, has seen the eroticism of constraint take second place to an elaboration of the anatomy of will. Closer to the classical seventeenth century in its analysis of motives and illusions, this inquiry into the will is almost geometrical in form and moralistic in intent.

Rima Drell Reck. *Yale French Studies.*
Summer, 1959, p. 74

One of the things that puzzle me about so many under-aged novelists is how they can manage to sound so much like octogenarians. There have been half a dozen novels recently by French and American youngsters all of which sounded as if they had been written by Somerset Maugham's aunts. . . .

It is only fair to Mlle Mallet-Joris to acknowledge that by current standards in the trade she is practically middle-aged—twenty-seven. Even so, *The Empire Céleste* is her fourth novel and I believe her first was published when she was seventeen or thereabouts, so that she would certainly qualify as precocious. What then accounts for her creative ossification, the grey, ponderous qualities of her imagination, her appearance of having never rejoiced in anything or experienced anything original, rebellious, or idiosyncratic?

There is nothing particularly wrong with Mlle Malle-Joris's theme: that men have illusions about themselves which they defend desperately against the truth. But there is a great deal wrong with what she does with it. For one thing, she employs a sagging old novelistic device—that of passing rhythmically and monotonously from the consciousness of one of her characters to that of another, so that there are at least seven or eight times too many fictional points of view. For another she is much given to the author's aside, the little Godlike observations on what fools mortals be, or the elephantine invocations to the muse of sociology.

Richard Gilman. *Commonweal.*
December 25, 1959, pp. 377–78

The award of the Prix Femina to this novel [*Café Céleste*] was a recognition of the broad sweep of her talent, since here all the dimensions of life are present. Her technique which owes a great deal to the realists and naturalists of the nineteenth-century, perhaps the most to Zola, successfully creates a believable world. Beyond the technique, however, is that feeling of involvement with all mankind which is her legacy from Tolstoy and Dostoevsky. . . . This excellent novel . . . is one of the best that France has sent us recently.

Vernon Hall, Jr. *New York Herald Tribune.*
January 10, 1960, p. 6

Since they feel no pity for others, either because of a natural hardness of heart or because of a repulsion for any kind of weakness, the characters of François Mallet-Joris expect none in return. They feel compelled to defend themselves against the possible annexation of their inner self by others. Total indifference is a form of defense granted to only a privileged few. Against the merciless look which seeks to judge, and which will succeed in judging, often unjustly and without appeal, if one allows it to, a secure shelter is to be found in lies. Each one, then, chooses a mask for himself, a flattering attitude, and strives to play his part in an effort to see at last in the eyes of those who watch him the reflection of an image he has chosen. Thus we witness throughout the novels a tragic masquerade, for, instead of the awaited liberation, each person brings about his total enslavement by others. He needs them constantly, he needs their eyes in which to seek reassurance that his mask fits, that his comedy is accepted. . . .

Can the lie, then, become a kind of second truth? No. Because deep within every person there remains a realm lighted by the consciousness of a struggle between what he is and what he appears to be. It is surprising to find so little self-analysis in novels where the narration in the first person, or interior monologue, plays such an important part. Introspection is foreign to these characters because they are afraid of it. The look they give themselves strives to remain directed outward toward their reflection. François Mallet-Joris observes the rules of the game with consistency: for instance, she does not describe the physical appearance of Hélène, the young heroine-narrator of *The Rampart of the Béguines* and *The Red Room* unless the girl can glance at herself in a mirror. As long as the images reflected by mirrors or by the eyes of others coincide with one's chosen role, all is well, and the falsehood behind which each one hides could be no more than a pleasant comedy. But let one pair of eyes refuse this image, and the inner struggle, ignored for a while, is felt with renewed sharpness. This beautiful and perfect Tamara might become so if Hélène's eyes did not return a different image, the real one, the secret one.

Geneviève Delattre. Yale French Studies.
Spring-Summer, 1961, pp. 123–24

The Characters, despite my minor reservations about it, is a miraculously well-written novel; yes, miraculously, and not by chance, because it is inspired by the very pulse of the seventeenth century. . . . Our Françoise pushes her daring to the point of writing in black and white, "The marquise went out at six," the kind of information Valéry cited as typically novelistic, prosaic, and unworthy of his pen. And her lovely ways of standing up to the veto of an illustrious shadow, with a wink of the eye and a stroke of the pen, leads one to suppose that the awkwardnesses of Mallet-Joris are not entirely involuntary. . . .

Louise de La Fayette believes that it is enough to love the king and to be loved by him. . . . When the king abandons her, she can no longer share this grandeur with anyone but God, toward whom she continues to rise, while the king confines himself to the necessities of his earthly functions, which become heavier and heavier. Both resign themselves to ineluctable sacrifice, but Louise keeps her soul intact, ennobled and fortified by her trials, while the king has the weakness of someone who "can be cruel when he is disappointed."

This double movement, begun well before the beginning of the story and prolonged well beyond its conclusion, is handled with an admirable density in the presentation of the few decisive weeks that contain the strictly narrative content of the novel. This rapid, suspenseful movement encapsulates without diminishing the destiny of two lovers who are condemned to seek each other and almost immediately to lose each other through parallel but inverse fates, just as a single day in classical tragedy contains the supreme temptation and sudden catastrophe in which the heroes unmask themselves for eternity. For this novel has the rigor of a classical tragedy.

Alexis Curvers. *Revue Générale Belge.*
November, 1961, pp. 85, 87, 89

A Letter to Myself is as persuasive as the best of novels, and it is more than a novel. Free from any theorizing or dogma, fuss or posturing, it describes an experience in which living and writing are bound closely together, one substantiating the other. The book may well be a turning point in the present orientation of the French novel.

To compare one woman writer to another, just because they are women, is a pointless game. But if the mantle of Colette is to fall on another woman writer in France, Françoise Mallet-Joris, different though she be, is certainly at the moment, the most likely heir. Her earlier novels had testified to her unusual acuity of vision, her rich sense of the concrete, and her undeniable ability to create character. *A Letter to Myself* reveals the scope of her imagination and sensibility.

Germaine Brée. *Saturday Review of*
Literature. May 23, 1964, p. 42

Always in motion, in continual evolution, the work of Françoise Mallet-Joris can nevertheless be summarized by two words—lies and revolt. These are the permanent themes, the obsessions, the indispensable pillar sustaining the edifice. The greatness of Mallet-Joris's art is precisely that she has remained faithful to her themes without ever rewriting the preceding book in different words. . . .

Hélène [in *The Red Room*] reminds one somewhat of Dominique in *A Certain Smile,* but Françoise Sagan's heroine is only experimenting, while Hélène remains a prisoner of her passions. *A Certain Smile* is a much more desperate book than *The Red Room,* because in *A Certain Smile* cheating does not give rise to revolt. Convinced of the stupidity of every reaction, Sagan offers her heroines lies, while Mallet-Joris condemns hers to perma-

nent revolt. Delivered to whatever fate wishes of them, the characters of
Sagan are contented to exist, resigned to submit to their destiny; those of
Mallet-Joris live, that is to say, choose. . . .

One might think that revolt is often simply a game one plays for oneself
and therefore a lie. The characters of Sagan think so. Mallet-Joris does not
deny this point of view, but she believes that the refusal to be weak and the
fight against cowardice lead one toward an individual and personal truth. . . .
In an age that is trying to the point of exhaustion to give men—even to force
on them—a collective happiness this young woman is rehabilitating the very
concept of individualism in her books.

Michel Géoris. Le thyrse. November, 1964,
pp. 489, 491, 498

Françoise Mallet-Joris, the Franco-Belgian author who has already situated
two of her novels in the period of Richelieu, here [in Three Ages of Night]
returns to those times to tell the story of three unhappy witches. Two of them
were burned at the stake, while the third sent her lover there and ended her
own life in a convent. From trial documents, medical reports, and studies of
demonology, Mme. Mallet-Joris has reconstructed these three lives. The
basic facts are historical; that they can conjure up real people and real times
is the part of fiction—a writer's brand of magic. . . .

The author peruses the records of these lives and . . . as a writer trained
in the method of analysis that has long been the glory of French fiction, shows
how these three became witches. She treats them as a moralist, too (and this
is also in the French tradition), since these women, if not sorceresses, were
still servants of the devil, all guilty of monstrous pride. . . . All the human
specimens that surround the heroines are shown to be base, cruel, or stupid.
Yet we feel sorry for them, as doubtless does the author, for they are made
evil by life and the times.

Their times were not the Middle Ages, the author reminds us, but the
sixteenth and seventeenth centuries: the period of the Renaissance, the age
that produced Montaigne and Descartes. Exploring this phenomenon with
Françoise Mallet-Joris is like descending into hell. We pass through circles
of the damned, witness fits, tortures, and executions, with the smell of burning flesh reaching our nostrils. Deploying the resources of a Flemish imagination, the author evokes a background of fantastic horror for her witches. . . .

Laurent Le Sage. Saturday Review of
Literature. August 23, 1969, pp. 40–41

Allegra—a long and detailed novel, the kind that the author of The Lies likes
to write—is a book with a soul. It has a "family of women"—the mother, the
grandmother, the three daughters—and numerous other characters, all of
them picturesque; it has adventures, truth, everyday reality, humor, and
drama, too, and romance—in short, it has life! Something lights up this book
from within, which is neither love precisely nor faith: one might call it a state

of grace. This grace can be sensed every time a mute little boy named Rachid makes his appearance. . . .

Certainly, the romance between Rachid and Allegra is only the main thread of a book constructed like a patchwork of various sequences, very carefully linked (although sometimes perhaps there are too many of them). Yet this song, this murmur of sweetness, is what always makes itself heard. Mallet-Joris herself admits that style is not the essential thing for her. She weighs, she measures, she constructs well, she has the gift of making characters "come alive"; but her concern for underlining every nuance makes her writing somewhat heavy. But as soon as the child reappears, her book suddenly soars. Her writing becomes airy and poignant: the state of grace. Few other writers can describe childhood with her profound, tenuous, almost miraculous ease.

Matthieu Galey. *L'Express.*
February 2–8, 1976, p. 64

The novels of Françoise Mallet-Joris are in the tradition of the great French novels. Unlike the depersonalized, anonymous creatures who people the novels of Kafka or of the French new novelists, Mallet-Joris's characters elicit the sympathy and comprehension of the reader. They are distinct individuals; they come from specific backgrounds and are products of their class, education, and psychological makeup. As in the case of the novelists of the nineteenth century, the author has succeeded in creating characters worthy of the reader's interest, an unusual accomplishment in the twentieth-century novel.

Yet, it is not only because of the idea of normative human behavior, but also because of the notion of causality and coherent chronology that Mallet-Joris's novels remain within the framework of the traditional novel. Her plots are well constructed, she tells her stories as a sequence of events, proceeding from well-explained causes to well-determined results, satisfying in this manner a need for understanding and a desire for a rational organization of the world. Unlike the new novelists who contend that such organization betrays the immense complexity, lack of logic, and indiscriminate piling up of events that, for them, constitute reality, her organization reflects her belief in God and in a well-ordered universe.

Like the great novelists of the past, Mallet-Joris does not content herself with merely telling a story, but seeks to take the reader beyond the world of external appearance to plunge into the more profound reality of dreams and of the subconscious. In her novels she has retained the qualities of interest, wonder, and surprise, which formerly characterized the novel but which, in our day, have been relegated to genre novels like the romance and the detective story.

Despite their debt to the past, however, Mallet-Joris's works bear the distinctive mark of the twentieth century. Like Proust, the author has ascribed to the novel functions that go beyond those of the traditional novel. Her novel, like the Proustian work, is an attempt to give a permanent, concrete form to fleeting sensory impressions. It seeks to provide a mystical experience, deciphering the signs we find around us in the visible world to reveal the ideal that is hidden behind them. . . .

It is not only because of their metaphysical and philosophical preoccupations that Mallet-Joris's novels bear the stamp of the second half of the twentieth century but also because, in them, there still remain questions that are unanswered, as well as inexplicable elements that are characteristic of modern uncertainty. Mallet-Joris also presents characters whose motivations and behavior are never completely explained, but who are shown merely on their journey through life, possessed of a secret that is incommunicable to others and which, in her opinion, belongs, finally, only to God. To express these modern ideas, Mallet-Joris joins to the traditional chronological unfolding of a story certain contemporary techniques such as simultaneity—presentation of various events occurring at the same time—and the passage from interior monologue to description, from subjective opinions to objective descriptions, without introduction or transition. She also uses the cinematographic technique of the cutting and fading of scenes without any transitional description.

While the contemporary novel has become more and more removed from human concerns, Mallet-Joris's novels remain concerned with typical human needs and desires. Whatever the format of the novel may be—from the tight, classical concision of *Les Personnages* to the many characters and subplots of *Dickie-Roi*—in each Mallet-Joris has demonstrated that plot, characterization, description, evocation, analysis, quest for an absolute and metaphysical disquietude can coexist successfully with certain techniques of the new novel. Françoise Mallet-Joris's novels, testimonials to the past and bearing the mark of the twentieth century, are stamped with the author's sensibility and are unique in modern literature.

Lucille Frackman Becker. *Françoise Mallet-Joris* (Boston: Twayne, 1985), pp. 126–28

MANICOM, JACQUELINE (GUADELOUPE) 1938–76

Mon Examen de blanc (My exam in whiteness) . . . is presented as a "straight" novel, with occasional flashbacks; the heroine who studied medicine in France having returned to the island to devote herself to her poorer compatriots. The second is the "diary" of an obstetrics nurse in a . . . lower class ward of a Parisian hospital. Both are straightforward treatment of modern medicine's callous treatment of female bodies, particularly lower class or colored. For "modern medicine," read the white male doctors" who are, in her books, the champions of an oppressive patriarchal colonial system. The Parisian hospital or the Guadeloupean one become the microcosmic version of French society, racism the instrument of sexual and political repression. That the indictment struck close to home was obvious when the powers that be had her demoted from the operating room and put to emptying bedpans at lower pay.

There is no question that the "scandal" created by the publication of [a] semi-autobiographical diary greatly contributed to her visibility and to the success of the novel. For this committed trade unionist, literature was, foremost, a social weapon. There is, in her mental universe as it is inscribed in her fiction, a radical cleavage between the masculine and the feminine principles. One aggresses and destroys life. The other nurtures and transmits it. Yet, women cannot be effective nurturers if they, in turn, are threatened by the aggressors. Hence, in order to achieve social and political liberation, a woman must start with physical liberation. She must learn to rule her own libidinal economy autonomously.

[T]he East Indian heroine of *Mon Examen* is exemplary. The "exam" of the title, a local phrase, has to do with passing in the White universe, not so much physically as mentally. One interiorizes all the rules and ideological mythologies (in the Barthésian sense) that will make one a good French citizen: *assimilé,* in short sold to the principles of *mission civilisatrice.* Accordingly, Madévie falls in love with a White, upper class, racist and sexist medical student in Paris and becomes his pliable object, an exotic sexual toy. However, in stark contrast with the *lactification* principle so denigrated by Fanon, she decides to abort and come home. She will eventually become involved with a local Black trade unionist.

The lover is gunned down by the riot control police as he leads the peaceful protest march of striking workers. This incident, by the way, is taken directly from the 1967 riots when several marchers were shot. Thus personal history meets national history. It is crucial for us not to interpret the ending as a symbolic switch of ideology, an either/or choice between racist assimilation *(lactification)* and Negritude. The sessions having to do with the trade union meetings specifically warn against simply exchanging one ready made ideology for another. The racial awakening is mediated, above all, by the class conflict. In Manicom's universe, to achieve justice and equality on the islands, one must transcend race as well as sex: women *and* men as free equals.

Clarisse Zimra. *Journal of Ethnic Studies.*
12:1, 1984, pp. 65–67

Manicom's book, *Mon examen de blanc,* is perhaps the most militant "feminist" West Indian work to date. She exploits to the full the possibilities inherent in the central situation of the novel: an operating/labor room, a hospital in Guadeloupe where a white male gynecologist/surgeon is assisted by an *Antillaise, femme de couleur* (she is of East Indian origin), an anaesthetist. The relationship between the two colleagues—equally educated, equally skilled, but unequal for other traditional, hierarchical reasons—is cleverly constructed and subtly manipulated by the narrator in order to comment on both the feminine condition and the position of the West Indian *assimilé(e)* and Antillean society in general. Manicom uses the closed space symbolically to represent the heroine's dilemma. . . .

Manicom was an avowed feminist and also actively involved in politics and her multi-faceted metaphor functions effectively on several levels in terms of racial, sexual and nationalist politics. The relationship between Madévie, the French West Indian woman of color, and Cyril, the white Frenchman, thus extends beyond a simple preoccupation with any one of these aspects and makes many points at once. In terms of consciousness the protagonist/narrator of *Mon Examen de blanc* has come a long way. But there is still a long way to go. The neuroses and problems have been diagnosed but not removed. Manicom's work recognizes that the situation is indeed complex, but suggests that the solution is to be found in political action and commitment. Manicom sketches the possible lines of a revolt.

> Elizabeth Wilson. In Carole Boyce Davies
> and Elaine Savory Fido, eds. *Out of the
> Kumbla: Caribbean Women and Literature*
> (Trenton, New Jersey: Africa World Press,
> 1990), pp. 50–51, 53

Madévie's exorcism of the ghosts of Xavier and her unborn child through political commitment to the people of Guadeloupe is the most unambiguous example of a transcendence of the traps of *lactification* to be found in these texts. Her growing understanding of the Guadeloupan people—of whom she had known precious little before her affair with the politically-committed and martyred Gilbert—parallels her awakening to a realization of the gender and race issues that had loomed so large in her relationship with Xavier. Madévie's ability to see her present self in opposition to her "double," the Madévie of Paris and Xavier, allows for an ironic presentation of her process of awakening to new realities and of her hard-won ability to stand on her own. Gilbert's death in many ways reinforces these new realities, removing him from the scene as a male "crutch" in her political and personal development.

> Lizabeth Paravisini-Gebert. *Callaloo.* 15,
> 1992, p. 71

MANNING, OLIVIA (GREAT BRITAIN) 1915–80

Miss Manning's husband Cartwright [*My Husband Cartwright*] has already endeared himself to readers of *Punch,* so I trust this collection of his misadventures will bring him many new friends—not acquaintances, for Cartwright is not a man who believes in acquaintances; he is a man who loves his fellow-men, even to the length of lending them money, which often they forget to return. . . . Miss Manning's picture of his likes and dislikes (for he dislikes ancient ruins, preferring to sit in a dark bar talking politics with a friend) is intensely human. It is warm, charming and alive—like Cartwright himself.

Fred Urquhart. *Time and Tide.*
December 22, 1956, p. 1591

The *Great Fortune* of Miss Manning's title is Life itself. Above all a humanitarian, her interest in people is not selective—idealists, eccentrics, self-assured prigs and the lonely and deprived are all subjected to her cool unsentimental appraisal. This is an excellent recipe for a novelist.

Her new novel will consolidate Miss Manning's reputation as a very accomplished writer indeed. Its delicate balance, superb interplay between scene and character, and the general sense of control and economy mark it as the work of a true craftsman.

The book is particularly memorable for its brilliant evocation of Bucharest in the period between the outbreak of war in 1939 and the fall of Paris.

John Barrows. *John O'London's Weekly.*
February 18, 1960, p. 186

The Great Fortune is a witty, charming, and civilized novel. The first volume of a trilogy, it is about the English colony in Bucharest during the winter and spring of 1939–40, and in particular about Guy Pringle, an English lecturer at the University, and his relationships with his wife Harriet and his friends. . . .

I think . . . Miss Manning shows an insight into English character which is deeper than may at first appear. The book is deceptively restrained and light: the local color nicely done, the subsidiary characters funny. The writing is an object lesson in good manners. Miss Manning controls her narrative with the gentlest possible touch; one is never pushed or hurried, but has that rare and blessed sense of there being spaces between words: this is a matter of texture, and few writers have mastered it; but when you meet one who has, you notice it at once.

K. W. Gransden. *Encounter.*
May, 1960, p. 78

Perhaps the most eloquent fictional voices of our day will turn out to be the writers of the grave sort of comedy in which the laughter is as painful as it is rare, and tends to bleed inwardly. It is the way Evelyn Waugh has moved, and there are twinges of the same quality in *The Spoilt City,* Olivia Manning's latest novel—the second on the theme—about Bucharest in the shadow of war.

This book and its companion, *The Great Fortune,* deserve to win a place among the remembered novels of our time even though they have no technical interest beyond that of conventional craftsmanship. They are a swan-song for so many things; for the 1930s, for the English amateur cosmopolitans like Guy Pringle, for the whole way of life such expatriates represented. Armed with his high, naïve intelligence, injected with good intentions, Pringle thinks he can protect the darkening world, but in the end can only protect himself, which is not what he wants at all. He is insulated from disaster and can never really believe, as a Rumanian puts it, "the things that happen to others."

Norman Shrapnel. *The Manchester Guardian Weekly.* May 17, 1962, p. 6

Olivia Manning has an exceptional capacity for wriggling into the skin of a character unlike herself and staying there with a minimum of obvious effort. This capacity is all the more impressive for being—I have to admit it—rarer in women novelists than in men. One does not have the feeling with her, as one does with most of our other distinguished women novelists, that each novel is one more disguised installment of the author's personal life. If Miss Manning identifies herself with any of the characters in *The Play Room,* she has dissembled so adequately that it becomes irrelevant. The artifice is perfect, the consistency flawless.

Not that this is entirely to the book's advantage. While admiring its pristine, economic style, vivid yet cool, I find myself wondering a little what, of value or originality, Miss Manning is trying to say? Briefly (and the novel is brief, though not simple) it views events through the eyes of a teenage girl, Laura, bored and ill-at-ease in a drearily genteel home, seeking excitement and also a meaning to life with Vicky, an adored school-mate. Laura watches uneasily as Vicky takes up with a psychopathic baddy, half foreseeing—yet, with the ignorance of adolescence never really fearing—the terrible real-life fate that overtakes Vicky on the lonely wastelands beyond the factory estate.

This climax, powerfully and even movingly described, convinces: these things *do* happen. But other things about Vicky tend to make her seem a synthetic character, a symbol, perhaps, or a slightly obvious "example" of her generation and class. She is beautiful, which is unfortunately not an effective attribute for a character in a novel; she rides the motor-bike on which her only brother was killed; charmingly amoral, she has a passionate lesbian relationship with another schoolgirl: there are moments at which one wants to say "Come off it!" Laura may well see her as a kind of devil-angel, but must we? The suggestion of symbolism is reinforced by an odd incident in Laura's life which prefigures Vicky's end; on holiday with her young brother, Laura comes across a bizarre man-woman figure who makes suggestive remarks and shows them a room full of pornographic dolls. Again, this incident is brilliantly written in its way, but there is, too, something contrived about it. One is not convinced that the dolls really cropped up naturally in Laura's formless experience. I felt they were put there, just a shade too neatly, by Miss Manning.

Gillian Tindall. *The New Statesman.* April 11, 1969, p. 522

A solid, monolithic theme projects from Olivia Manning's *Balkan Trilogy* and that is "uncertainty." The series concerns itself neither with abstract or metaphysical theories of time, refashioned or shifting ideologies, nor various plays for power or status; but with the often bare, ironically conditioned facts of living in uncertainty—uncertainty not as an accident, but as a constant of life—in a world over which hangs the certainty of ruin.

[Of contemporary British novel sequences], Miss Manning's is the least self-conscious, the least arty, in a sense the easiest, but one of the most knowledgeable about common experience. It strives not for effects but for a single effect: to show a society teetering on, about to plunge into, an abyss, and to show people caught up in the making of history at a time when the mere debacle of the First World War was about to yield to the holocaust of the Second. Yet to show all this with something rivaling an antiepic, antiromantic sweep, to show how in this extraordinary decade the everyday world, through uncertainty, runs down.

For most of the trilogy Miss Manning's extraordinary world is Bucharest during the early years of the war, a city crammed with its complement of adventurers, expatriates, emigrés, opportunists, money barons, civil servants, and princes who suddenly find themselves on the threshold of history. Part comic-opera Ruritania in its feudality, its gilt and gaudiness; part political nightmare in its ferment of royalist, liberal, and fascist factions, Bucharest reflects the pretensions and tensions of a Rumania as heterogeneous as Durrell's Alexandria or Burgess's Malaya. It is a presence, a force of some magnificence before it squanders "the great fortune" (the title of the first volume in the sequence) to become "the spoilt city" (the title of the second). Pressured from within and without, part of a country neutered by its fence-sitting neutrality, ransacked of its dignity, culture, wealth, and civilization, Bucharest becomes the battleground for a kind of primal survival, and, as Miss Manning makes symbolically apparent, a Troy fallen anew.

Robert K. Morris. *Continuance and Change: The Contemporary British Novel Sequence* (Carbondale: Southern Illinois University Press, 1972), pp. 29–30

The second volume of Olivia Manning's Levant Trilogy [*The Battle Lost and Won*] displays all her impressive talent. The writing is spare, witty and dry; the characterization so precise and so discreet you are hardly aware of the skill. This is naturalism deployed with a high degree of art. Miss Manning catches the essential feeling of place and action, and has succeeded brilliantly in the unusual feat for a woman of describing war. The battle scenes, for various reasons, are among the best in the book. Miss Manning's readers are prepared for her skill in conducting her cast through a series of comic maneuvers in exotic but seedy surroundings, and the Cairo sequences in this novel are convincing and entertaining, though they lack the clarity of mood and vividness of feeling of the desert war scenes. This must be intentional, for Olivia Manning looks at Alamein through the eyes of a young man to whom fighting is exhilaration, and the companionship of his men a more genuine form of love than marriage to the forgotten wife at home, or mild desire for a glamour girl glimpsed on leave. . . .

The prevailing negative mood of *The Battle Lost and Won* makes its deliberately small-scale figures seem less alive than they have done in her previous novels. It is as if a cast of minor characters were assembled waiting for the leads to appear. Perhaps we are meant to have precisely this sense of anti-climax. But the greater vitality of Simon and the soldiers, Ridley who "had to love something" and the inarticulate driver Crosbie whom Simon loves for the same reason, gives the lie to some of the novel's intimations of cynicism. What Miss Manning is saying isn't, to me, at this moment, entirely clear: what is clear is the imaginative skill with which she has created the prevalent mood, in landscape, in action, in dialogue. The book's intentional lassitude reflects no lack of vitality in the author. Those readers who find *The Battle Lost and Won* less sustainedly comic, more moving but in some ways more frustrating than her earlier work, will wait eagerly for its sequel.

Rachel Trickett. (London) *Times Literary Supplement.* November 24, 1978, p. 1358

This third installment [*The Sum of Things*] of *The Levant Trilogy* completes the cycle (preceded by *The Balkan Trilogy*) of the late Olivia Manning's six-volume chronicle of the Second World War. To this reviewer the last is also the best novel of the trio: the reason is that its material, the social comedy of Cairo, and the inner life of the principal characters, including the culminating self-discoveries of the Pringles, is of the kind best suited to the author's gifts. The battle sequences, such as those of the two preceding volumes, although well researched, have been better handled by other pens, though the title, drawn from Housman's First World War "Epitaph on an Army of Mercenaries," "What God abandoned, these defended/And saved the sum of things for pay" pays due tribute to the importance of the theme of the desert war in the cycle. In this volume the accounts of military hospitals, of the wanderings in Palestine and Syria of the heroine (whom her husband supposes to have been drowned in a torpedoed ship), and of a religious ceremony in the Church of the Holy Sepulcher in Jerusalem, offer descriptive writing of a quality which the author has never surpassed. These novels will inevitably be contrasted with Lawrence Durrell's *Alexandria Quartet,* and by comparison *The Levant Trilogy* lacks mystery and imaginative invention. It presents a scene the details of which will be instantly recognizable to the visitors to Egypt of that period. At the same time it displays an integrity in its characterization and a delicacy in its descriptions which by comparison expose the not infrequent passages of inflated writing in the *Quartet.*

Ian Scott-Kilvert. *British Book News.* January, 1981, p. 56

The Great Fortune commences by dramatizing, in the assassination and funeral of Calinescu, some of the profound fissures in the internal structure of

Rumania, fissures ominous with meaning for the near future: like the characters in the novel, we know from the outset that we will apprehend a great deal in this strange country sick with its own peculiar political disease. The novel closes with a charade, a production, under Guy Pringle's direction, of Shakespeare's *Troilus and Cressida,* which, although it is filled with comic irony, is surely not intended simply to comfort us. Meanwhile Olivia Manning analyzes with great intelligence, partly by letting her characters become themselves and partly by maintaining our sense of a disengaged narrator who has the necessary overview to recreate for us the urgent history of the time, the multiple forces that are now converging on one vulnerable center. . . .

At the end [of the trilogy] amidst the moral squalor of self-concern which constitutes a large part of the desperate British departure from Athens, Harriet, aboard ship for Cairo, finds in Guy a tentative hope, a small sense of the future which, by its very limitation, seems appropriate to their circumstances and to themselves: "If Guy had for her the virtue of permanence, she might have the same virtue for him. To have one thing permanent in life as they knew it was as much as they could expect."

Such a passage, restrained, coolly and acutely realistic, properly contingent, marks a fitting conclusion to the world of *The Balkan Trilogy* and to the marriage which stands at its center. And that marriage, we now realize, has become more and more important to us in the moral decay, the timid compromises, the fearful threats and the small margins for hope that comprise the terrain of a certain corner of Europe between the fall of 1939 and the beginning of 1941.

Harold J. Mooney. In Thomas F. Staley, ed.
Twentieth-Century Women Novelists
(Totowa, New Jersey: Barnes and Noble,
1983), pp. 41–42, 57–58

The short, valedictory "coda" to Olivia Manning's six-volume novel sequence, *Fortunes of War,* writes finis to one of the most remarkable books published in the past twenty-five years, while leaving inconclusive the fates of its equally remarkable hero and heroine, Guy and Harriet Pringle, whose four-year odyssey in the Balkans and the Levant the series has charted.

This is, of course, as it should be. From the first pages of the first volume—when, "in the confusion of a newly created war," a young, wondering Guy and Harriet roll toward Bucharest, their night train skirting a dark pine forest, "the light from the carriages [rippling] over the bordering trees"—to the last pages of the last—when, in 1943, "his youth behind," twenty-one-year-old Lt. Simon Boulderstone stands at the rail of a destroyer, watching "the glimmer of the blacked-out shore, the last of Egypt"—*Fortunes of War* has been unwavering in its depiction of the human condition as openended. In Miss Manning's fiction, life is a continuing quest and question: a kaleidoscope of paradoxes and ironies that shape and shift character and in turn are shaped and shifted by them. Under normal circumstances such patterns take on unexpected permutations. How much more unexpected personal change is when carried out against the ever-changing and most impersonal of backdrops—war.

For the world at war is Miss Manning's world. And, as true to life as to her novelistic vision, the "stray figures" who happen into it—to grapple, ordinary as they are, with the extraordinary; to love, marry, mature, succeed or fail, live or die—are merely left to anonymous time and history after the great tragic backdrop has been removed. Yet, like the controlling image of the Levant trilogy—the pyramids—all of *Fortunes of War* is a monument to days that once shook the world and now slip, year by year, further from our memory. What makes Miss Manning's record so viable—nay, phenomenal— is the labor and art which have gone into perfecting the smallest details of its construction. Though each of the novels is self-contained, taken together their effect is solid, overwhelming, enduring. This, in part, is due to the heft of Miss Manning's well-wrought words—over half a million of them. But there is more. Scene by scene, character by character, theme upon theme, the six parts of *Fortunes of War* are pieced together to become a pyramid of its own—the foundation laid in *The Great Fortune* and rising to the apex in *The Sum of Things*.

Twenty years of actual time and four of fictional time separate these first and last volumes, and throughout it all Miss Manning sticks by the original paradox that furnishes the groundwork for the series: the idea that Guy and Harriet can build their lives (together and independently) in a world that is progressively breaking down. . . .

True to her thesis throughout *Fortunes of War,* Miss Manning has taken [her characters] through many experiences and changes to find some sense of permanence in a marriage acceptable to both. What the Balkans and Egypt and the war have taught them about that, and about a dozen other things, is considerable: yet it can only be measured by the distance they have come and the height they have climbed. How much further they had to go—if they were to go further—we shall, alas, never know. Olivia Manning died of illness not long after completing the final volume in the series: refusing to surrender in her own lost battle before seeing to it that her greatest hero and heroine were on the way to winning theirs.

Robert K. Morris. In Jack I. Biles, ed.
British Novelists since 1900 (New York:
AMS Press, 1987), pp. 233–34, 251–52

MANSFIELD, KATHERINE (NEW ZEALAND–GREAT BRITAIN)
1888–1923

Some time ago I read Miss Katherine Mansfield's *Bliss*. I was good enough critic to see that she was an artist, in absolute command of her means, making her effects surely and (for the reader's eye) with ease, using words rightly, composing beautifully. But I was dissatisfied and in a way irritated. Always I wanted more. Always I asked for a definite outcome, for something final. The first piece in the book was called "Prelude," and as I finished it, admiring, I asked: Prelude to what? And almost everything was a prelude. What was the end of Mouse? Of the little Governess? What did Bertha do or not do that night when she knew that Harry was faithless? Miss Mansfield, I thought, was not doing her share, was leaving altogether too much to me (That subtle critic, the present reader, perceives that I was extremely stupid, but let him have patience). Then some time later, I read "the Daughters of the Late Colonel" in *The London Mercury*. I finished it in open-mouthed admiration for the genius which had told me so much, and this time I had no wish for more. That was not because I was uninterested in those pitiful women so delicately yet so completely presented to me, but because the presentment *was* complete, the phase of life fully rendered, the atmosphere given once for all. It was a final achievement. Further speculation would be vulgar, stupid. Being quite clear about "The Daughters of the Late Colonel," I had the sense to return to *Bliss*, recognizing that the expression of a phase of life, the conveying of an atmosphere, was the final purpose of this writer. There was no intention of telling a story or of asking the reader to tell one to himself. I read *Bliss* again completely satisfied. The artistic intention was achieved in every instance; there was no room for anything more.

G. S. Street. *The London Mercury.*
November, 1921, p. 54

Miss Mansfield's collection, *Bliss,* boldly labeled "stories," is remarkable for not being tedious. It is far from tedious. She has so penetrating a mind and such a talent for expression that she would be interesting whatever form she were using and whatever subject she were writing about. It is not that she has a markedly personal view of things, a passionate or a philosophical attitude; she is restrained, and leaves her affections and her admirations too much to be guessed and deduced. It is not that she has a rich prose style; she checks the natural music in herself, and contents herself with a perpetual stream of exact statements as terse as she can make them. Every word counts to the intelligence and the eye, but none to the ear. But the fabric of her writing has no weak or dull places. She beats all the writers of dyspeptic "economical" "realistic" "studies" on their own ground. Every story is a tissue of accurate observations accurately expressed. Miss Mansfield has an extraordinary visual, and, if one may say so, olfactory, memory; her stories may vary in reality, but her material settings—in which one includes everything from vegetation to the human garment of flesh—never. Almost every page contains minor felicities which a man with the penciling habit would be inclined to mark.

J. C. Squire. *Books Reviewed* (London:
Hodder and Stoughton, 1922), p. 10

By any standard, Miss Mansfield is a very great short story writer. In one particular she is the greatest of all. Her stories affect the reader not as transcriptions of life but as life itself. Other writers—Mr. Wells, Mr. Kipling, DeMaupassant—come back from hunting with a fine prey, but the prey is dead, even dressed and cooked. Miss Mansfield's spoil is still living. . . . In *The Garden Party* as in *Bliss,* Miss Mansfield gives the reader beyond his usual pleasures a pleasure which properly belongs to the artist, for, after selecting and arranging, she relinquishes the final stage, which might be called interpretation, to us. . . .

A . . . consequence of Miss Mansfield's abnegation is that she cannot afford to write lengthily. *The Garden Party* includes another installment of the sensations of that family which we first met in "Prelude," and already, I think, the reader must be confused and tired of them. Superb as Miss Mansfield's art is, it is too impressionistic for a novel, and as "Prelude" swells beyond the normal size, as details grow richer, the field of observation, the eye of the reader is strained. Nothing is happening. The details are all significant—but of what? We begin to fail to adjust to them and relate to them, and Miss Mansfield, keeping silence, threatens to overwhelm us with facts that cannot be explained. It is a Frith picture, which can only be looked at in bits. . . .

To consider limitations upon the efficacy of Miss Mansfield's impressionism is not to censure Miss Mansfield. Her style, as her imitators will some day prove to us, is infertile, and its developments soon exhausted. But Miss Mansfield's own writings are immortal. *The Garden Party* ranks with *Bliss* as one of those rare volumes which are not only exceedingly good but are indisputably good. The gods of one generation are idols to the next. You can never tell—or hardly ever—what will last. Miss Mansfield's stories are the obvious exception.

H. C. Harwood. *The Outlook.* February 25, 1922, p. 154

One asks involuntarily, is Miss Mansfield's new book [*The Garden Party*] as good as her last? It would need, of course, to be very much better to give one the same shock of delighted surprise; and there has hardly been an interval long enough for any great development in her genius. Therefore it is not unnatural that one's first judgment of it should be a trifle unenthusiastic. The more obvious qualities in that earlier book remain the same in this, and Miss Mansfield's more obvious qualities tend to be a trifle unsatisfying. Her themes lacked substance: not that there was an inherent lack of substance in her chosen characters and situations but rather in what she got out of them— though there can be no doubt that she got out of them precisely what she intended to. She is too fine and altogether too wise and severe an artist to do otherwise; it might be said, almost without exaggeration, that she never fails. But those earlier stories, unsatisfying as they were, had a conquering glitter and variety. Now, either these qualities have faded or I have grown used to them. Perhaps the second alternative is the true one. They are like drugs; if they are to have the same effect the dose must be increased.

Edward Shanks. *London Mercury.*
April, 1922, pp. 658–59

There is no doubt that the stories of Katherine Mansfield are literature. That is, their qualities are literary qualities. No one would think of dramatizing these stories, of condensing them into pithy paragraphs, or of making them into a scenario for Douglas Fairbanks. They do not dissolve into music, like Mallarmé, or materialize into sculpture like Hérédia. The figures are not plastic; the landscapes are not painted, but described, and they are described, usually, through the eyes of a character, so that they serve both as a background and as a character study. In the same way Katherine Mansfield does not treat events, but rather the reflection of events in someone's mind. Her stories are literature because they produce effects which can be easily attained by no other art. . . .

These stories, at least the fifteen contained in [*The Garden Party*], have a thesis: namely, that life is a very wonderful spectacle, but disagreeable for the actors. Not that she ever states it bluntly in so many words; blunt statement is the opposite of her method. She suggests it rather; it is a sentence trembling on the lips of all her characters, but never quite expressed. . . .

The method is excellent, and the thesis which it enforces is vague enough and sufficiently probable to be justified aesthetically. Only, there is sometimes a suspicion—I hate to mention it in the case of an author so delicate and so apparently just, but there is sometimes a suspicion that she stacks the cards. She seems to choose characters that will support her thesis. The unsympathetic ones are too aggressively drawn, and the good and simple folk confronted with misfortunes too undeviating; she doesn't treat them fairly. . . .

This second volume, compared with the first [*Bliss*], adheres more faithfully to the technique of Chekhov, and the adherence begins to be dangerous. He avoided monotonousness only, and not always, by the immense range of his knowledge and sympathy. Katherine Mansfield's stories have no such range; they are literature, but they are limited. She has three backgrounds only: continental hotels, New Zealand upper-class society, and a certain artistic set in London. Her characters reduce to half a dozen types; when she deserts these she flounders awkwardly, and especially when she describes the Poorer Classes. Lacking a broad scope, she could find salvation in technical variety, but in her second volume she seems to strive for that no longer.

Malcolm Cowley. *The Dial.* August, 1922,
pp. 230–32

Had Miss Mansfield lived she would surely have produced work far superior to most of the pieces in this volume [*Something Childish*]. Of course, this is only comparing Miss Mansfield at her best with Miss Mansfield not quite at her best; compared with the productions of other, less gifted, writers, her most tenuous sketch is of importance.

This is one very good reason for reading everything Miss Mansfield wrote. I do not mean that the tragic shortness of this life makes us eager to search for the germs of future achievements even in her notes and sketches; though this is true. But if we ask what it is that we value in the writings of Katherine Mansfield, the answer is: a unique temperament, an original vision of the world. She offers us no interpretation of life, no profound brooding over the human comedy, but a vivid record of appearances, a thousand swift impressions of the world of men and things which no other person could give us. "What is there to believe in except appearances?" she asks in one of these stories; and adds: "The great thing to learn in this life is to be content with appearances, and shun the vulgarities of the grocer and philosopher." Obviously, appearances can be made the symbols of any profundity you like, and I am far from asserting that Katherine Mansfield gave no significance to her impressions. But with a writer of this kind we are more interested in the unique personality behind the work than in the work itself; and in the case of Katherine Mansfield the same personality can be detected in the earliest and slightest of her writings as in the latest and most solid.

Richard Aldington. The Nation and Athenaeum. September 6, 1924, p. 694

Ten years ago the name of Katherine Mansfield was hardly known in our literature. Since then, because of her short stories, it has been associated with Anton Tchekhov; and now that an abrupt end has come to her great brilliance and the promise of yet greater brilliance, she is, according to some, entitled to a place alongside Amiel and Bashkirtseff because of her private diaries. Doubtless the two volumes of letters [*Letters*] to her intimate friends which her husband, Mr. Middleton Murry, has selected with a devotion that remains unwearied, will cause her name to be linked in a third direction, with that of John Keats.

For Katherine Mansfield, like the author of "Endymion," wrote her last letters after her fatal illness had manifested itself and when her doom appeared inescapable. Keats was no more rebellious and alternately resigned than she, and exiled from active life and home and friends, they began to pour out their hearts on paper, honestly and earnestly, passionately and affectionately, and with a regularity that made each of them as a correspondent uncommonly prolific. But when every possible comparison has been offered, Katherine Mansfield still remains essentially a unique and solitary figure. A tragic figure, it need hardly be said. She had a precarious foothold on the border between two worlds, and while others in that state are often wholly high-spirited and gay, or utterly dismayed and dispirited, she was so seldom at one or the other extreme as to present a greater paradox than any individual to be found in a sphere—that of art—which is overcrowded with paradoxical people. . . .

Katherine Mansfield, with all her senses preternaturally acute because of her precarious position, saw life much more vividly than most of us see it, but her ultimate desires were the ordinary man's or woman's. . . . And after all was she not already in her imagination a "child of the sun"? She loved light and the things of light—animals, birds and summer, Dickens, Tchekov, and birthdays. Her stories are themselves like sun-rays lighting up the little obvious and yet hitherto invisible things in the garden—the dusty particles that crowd the green air, the bits of sparkling grass or shell on the path. She distorted nothing. Thus, her letters, written in the nervous, staccato and yet liquid English that was in all her stories, and crowded with brilliant detail and vivid phrases, are an expression of the rare art that began with *Bliss and Other Stories, The Garden Party, The Doves' Nest* and *Something Childish,* and that the *Journal* illuminated technically; a finite perfect art, which reminds us in some ways of Jane Austen, and to which, alas, there are to be no further contributions.

Thomas Moult. *The Bookman.*
December, 1928, pp. 183–84

"To be crystal clear," "to be 'simple' as one would be simple before God"— that was Katherine Mansfield's prayer; and before she prayed it was granted, for only single-mindedness could so pray. That quality by which we learned to know her in her stories is in these poems [*Poems*] so that, in spite of their uncommon kind, they seem familiar. They are more valuable for her personality in them than for themselves.

They are little poems, fancies rather than imaginings, with no fire that kindles us, but a cool clear glow that hushes us.

It is understandable that some of the poems could be written, evening after evening, on set themes, for they are not hot geysers issuing at some inscrutable timing of darkness; they come from cool wells, deeply kept; the sinking and lifting of a dipper finds them. Katherine Mansfield held all the beauty of the world that had crossed the threshold of eye and ear, and its meaning for her; she had a throng of words and images clamoring for use; she had inalienably her candid spirit; and so she had these poems. Utterance was necessary, but only a few of these poems were. Many of them are too cool and faultless, as if they knew too well what they aimed at and what they avoided. Faultier, they might have been greater.

Orgill Mackenzie. *The Adelphi.*
October, 1930, pp. 76–77

It is first of all essential to isolate the two Katherine Mansfields if one is to come to any honest estimation of her work; it is necessary to set ruthlessly aside that lovely, proud, appealing woman who, with the aid of her best stories, has for a long time been a literary tradition to us. To respond to that figure's austerity, its pride and melancholy, and its heart-breaking loneliness brings one no closer to her talent but rather serves to exclude one utterly from any scrupulous appraisement of the work. This, to an extent, is true of many minor artists, but because of the circumstances of Katherine Mansfield's life and death it seems to me peculiarly true of her. . . .

The other Katherine Mansfield is here in these six-hundred-odd pages [*The Short Stories of Katherine Mansfield*]—work, by the effort of the will, detached from the women one was drawn to because one found facsimile of one's own weaknesses in her journal and from the woman one pitied because one knew her to be ill and lonely and afraid. These pages, delicately, tenderly and carefully composed, are animated by situations so futile that it is difficult to believe they were ever, not of importance but of interest even; stories terminating compactly on infinitesimal disappointments or with ladylike surprises, sketches of county types or foreign types or landscapes not so very different in technique from the sympathetic aquarelles that English ladies on the Continent sit down and do. . . .

It is perhaps unfair to judge a writer's work by what he failed to write rather than by what is there. But had Katherine Mansfield succeeded in doing what she obviously *knew* could and had been done she might have been as enduring as Jane Austen and as invaluable to the history of her time. For there is in these unhappy little stories a thing that makes them different, that saves them oddly from being exactly what they are. It is there on every page, cried out in trembling and desperation, the awful, the speechless confession of her own inadequacy. Not the inadequacy of herself as a human being (although if one did not sternly separate the two it might revert to that in the end), nor her inadequacy as a critic, but the hopeless, the miserable inadequacy to see in any other and wider terms the things she sensed so acutely; the inadequacy to translate into any convincing language the griefs or joys she witnessed or experienced.

Kay Boyle. *The New Republic.*
October 20, 1937, p. 309

[Katherine Mansfield's] apprehension of a world in which all people are hermits in their individual egos implied a reliance in her work upon private standards and judgments. Her intuition of the nature of human society— though here "society" has the reverse of its usual sense, its characteristics being scarcely social—with which she was concerned as a writer, conditioned her treatment of it. With all her life emphasizing the subjective, the sensibility of the individual, she could not have imposed on her work an objective pattern, based on public values in which she did not believe, and against which, in New Zealand, she had revolted. She was working outwards, and her fragmentary composition was inevitable. Her patterns were private. Her work was organized by her own understanding of men and women, of their isolation, and by her tenderness, the existence of which in herself denied the truth of her view of others. She believed that true understanding was only to be attained through the receptivity of the pure heart of the artist, who, in her private myth, stood at the center of life, the interpreter of man to men.

Keith Sinclair. *Landfall*. June, 1950,
pp. 137–38

The material of Katherine Mansfield's stories, based so directly on her own experiences, is in the central tradition of the English novel, the affairs of everyday heightened by sensitivity and good writing. Her range is even more restricted than Jane Austen's few families in a country village. For her, one family and a few relationships she had known were enough to express a universality of experience. Essentially the stress is on character and the subtle interrelationships of people in small groups, bound together by bonds of emotion. To express these she concentrates her writing, discarding the heavy lumber of narration and descriptive backcloths. In the end she has not more than half a dozen themes. . . .

Several critics have pointed out the poetic qualities of Katherine Mansfield's writing. The American critic Conrad Aiken, himself a poet, as early as 1921 in a review of *Bliss and Other Stories* made the essential point. Katherine Mansfield writes the short story with the resources and the intention of lyrical poetry. Her stories should not be (and were not written to be) read as narratives in the ordinary sense, although considerable narrative movement is implied in the majority of them. She conveys, as a lyric poet conveys, the feeling of human situations, and her stories have all the unity and shapeliness and the concentrated diction of implied emotion that characterizes the well-wrought lyric. As with the lyric, her stories yield their full meaning only on re-reading, when the reader can link up the implications of phrase upon phrase that are not always apparent on the first run-through. And like the lyrics of a poet the stories illuminate each other. . . .

There is nothing vague or nebulous—or naïve—about her writings. She is assured in her craft, and knowledgeable even to the placing of a comma. She writes with precision, knowing the effect she intends, and achieving it in all her best work with an accuracy and an inexplicable rightness in prose expression that is perhaps in the end the only real secret that died with her.

Ian A. Gordon. *Katherine Mansfield*
(London: British Council/Longmans,
Green, 1954), pp. 18–19, 25, 29

Katherine Mansfield is for me something unusual in the history of the short story. She is a woman of brilliance, perhaps of genius; she chose the short story as her own particular form and handled it with considerable skill, and yet for most of the time she wrote stories that I read and forget, read and forget. My experience of stories by real storytellers, even when the stories are not first-rate, is that they leave a deep impression on me. It may not be a total impression; it may not even be an accurate one, but it is usually deep and permanent. I remember it in the way in which I remember poetry. I do not remember Katherine Mansfield's stories in that way. She wrote a little group of stories about her native country, New Zealand, which are recognized as masterpieces and probably are masterpieces, but I find myself forgetting even these and rediscovering them as though they were the work of a new writer. . . .

Most of her work seems to me that of a clever, spoiled, malicious woman. Though I know nothing to suggest she had any homosexual experiences, the assertiveness, malice, and even destructiveness in her life and work makes me wonder whether she hadn't. It would be too much to exaggerate the significance of her occasionally sordid love affairs, of which we probably still have something to learn, but the idea of "experience" by which she justified them is a typical expedient of the woman with a homosexual streak who envies men and attributes their imaginary superiority to the greater freedom with which they are supposed to be able to satisfy their sexual appetite. . . .

There is one quality that is missing in almost everything that Katherine Mansfield wrote—even her New Zealand stories—and that is heart. Where heart should be we usually find sentimentality, the quality that seems to go with a brassy exterior, and nowhere more than with that of an "emancipated" woman. In literature sentimentality always means falsity, for whether or not one can perceive the lie, one is always aware of being in the presence of a lie.

Frank O'Connor. *The Lonely Voice* (New York: World, 1963), pp. 128, 130–31

[Katherine Mansfield's] characters may be stooges, but her women are not toy characters who bend with the weight of life and its struggles but are sturdy and strong. When women are busy with the house, clothes, children and peculiarly feminine worries, anxieties and cares, man's world and its economic activities and business trifles is let alone. Women live in a real, throbbingly real world. They are not puppets dancing to the tune of their creator.

Her readers come to know about men from the thoughts and utterances of her women. Katherine Mansfield handles her male characters as competently as her female ones. However, their position in the stories is subordinate to that of children and women, and their presence in the household is not looked upon with favor. The impression she gives is that men's characters leave much to be desired. The desire of women to be left alone is noticeable in most of the earlier sketches and stories, and in the perfect visions of the later period. In some of her earlier stories the predatory attitude of men who seek to pounce upon women at the earliest opportunity is strongly emphasized. . . .

It was Miss Mansfield's singular destiny that she should be uprooted from her native soil and planted on the somewhat uncongenial European soil. These were the ironical antitheses of her destiny; to marry Mr. Bowden and to live apart from him, to be born in comfortable circumstances and to spend many years in straitened ones not unassociated with turmoil, anxiety, separation, dependence, and insecurity. These very ironies of her life lend enchantment to her piquant and romantic life. At any rate, she was not born to be happy. She died young in the fullness of her youth. Like Keats and Chekhov, she suffered from the torment of a slow death.

In the annals of literature, she will be remembered if not as a great short story writer, at least as an experimenter, innovator and inspirer of the great art. She will be remembered with fondness, with affection, and with admiration not only by Englishmen and New Zealanders, but all who love literature. . . . It is an irony of fate that she died a premature death; inevitably all her ambitions of reorienting art collapsed; all her hopes returned with the return of the spring, but the spring of 1923 never returned for her.

Nariman Hormasji. Katherine Mansfield: An Appraisal (London: Collins, 1967), pp. 96–97, 152–53

As a critic, Katherine Mansfield possesses in great measure what many of her contemporaries and successors lack: a warm, human approach to books and authors, a vivid critical personality, and a practical directness of motive and language. One may search in vain through the hundreds of pages of her collected reviews in *Novels & Novelists,* or through the random remarks on writing and writers in her letters, *Journal,* and *Scrapbook* without encountering mention of symbolism, naturalism, decadence, aesthetics, point of view, and similar terms of early twentieth-century criticism that often tend to obscure the treatment of the work of art itself. . . .

As in her letters, Mansfield reveals a strong and sharp personality in every line of her criticism. There is no temporizing with inferior work, no praising of friends because they are friends, no puffing of a private coterie or attacks on the favorites of hostile critics. Though most of Mansfield's criticism comes from the pages of her husband's *Athenaeum,* the reviews speak with her voice and offer her judgments, not the collective judgments of the periodical. . . .

Katherine Mansfield is not a great writer, though in a very few stories she approaches artistry of the first rank. Her significance to the contemporary critic is as an authentic and original talent in fiction. Like Virginia Woolf in the novel, Mansfield felt the need to break windows. Her emulation of her Russian predecessors in her inimitable English prose helped alter the reading tastes of an English public surrounded by insipidity and pretension in the short fiction available at the time of the First World War. Like Joseph Conrad and James Joyce, she wrote at a time when a breakthrough in the representation of reality was not only desirable but also possible in the English short story: when the tools of psychology might be employed to construct meaningful symbolic structures in fiction; and when literary characters might be examined from the inside as well as from the outside, whole or fragmented into aspects of themselves. She wrote at a time when the furniture of fiction was largely being scrapped in favor of concentration on essences: the spirit that moved human beings rather than the scene in which they moved. Her recognition of these new directions came early. Her determination to follow them, not as a member of a coterie but because she understood that they were the only paths open to her kind of talent, has assured her a small but secure place in literary history. Much more than the influence of her literary criticism, her short stories have played a large part in shaping the contemporary short story in our language.

Marvin Magalaner. *The Fiction of Katherine Mansfield* (Carbondale: Southern Illinois University Press, 1971), pp. 7–8, 131–32

Katherine Mansfield became famous only after her death, and it was as much for the extraordinary talent and personality revealed in her letters and journals as for the qualities of her stories. I think the fame was deserved; but it rested on style rather than substance, and for that reason it has survived better in France than in England. In England art is seldom valued for its own sake; it is a vehicle, like a coal truck; and from Dr. Johnson to Dr. Leavis the English critics have almost without exception seen their primary task as being to check the quantity and quality of the coal.

In Katherine Mansfield's letters and journals are displayed qualities of mind, imagination, sensibility, intelligence, wit—all finding verbal expression, coming to life on the page, running irresistibly day by day off the tip of the pen. This is not the same as saying that she is always revealed as a good person, a nice person, that she is always controlled, or fair minded, or strong, or sensible. She is afraid, defeated, hysterical, waspish as often as she is affirmative, joyful, witty or wise. But whatever the state of her mind or soul, there is always distinction in the writing, distinction of intellect and of personality transmitted through all the rare and lovely skills of the natural writer. She has more than talent. She has genius—and only a part of that genius gets into the stories. Fiction writers usually do their best work after the age of forty. Katherine Mansfield died at 34, leaving about ninety stories, some of them unfinished—a total of perhaps 250–300 thousand words. It is clear that she needed a longer life to produce the best work she was capable of. Nevertheless she has a distinct place as one who made certain discoveries about the form of fiction. It is the nature of these discoveries that still call for critical definition; and at the same time, if they are to be usefully discussed, it becomes necessary to disengage the Mansfield image from some of the mythology that has surrounded it since her death in 1923.

To speak of Katherine Mansfield's discoveries in fiction is not to speak of something achieved in full consciousness, or critically articulated. In her conscious intentions she was often very conventional. She was always setting out to write a novel. What became "Prelude" began as a novel with the title *The Aloe.* As she wrote "Je ne parle pas français" she called its sections chapters, apparently expecting it to grow into a book. She planned a novel called *Maata,* and another called *Karori.* All these came either to nothing or to smaller items which, not being novels, we call stories, but which would be better described as fictions. It was not lack of stamina which brought this about. She had ample energy and fluency and determination as a writer. It was her instinct as an artist that gave her fictions their modern shape. She taught us the fiction as distinct from the narrative, and it is in this sense that she is an innovator.

C. K. Stead. *The New Review.*
September, 1977, p. 27

Virginia Woolf disliked "Bliss," commenting in her diary that Mansfield's "mind is a very thin soil, laid an inch or two deep upon barren rock . . . she is content with superficial smartness, and the whole conception is poor, cheap, not the vision, however imperfect, of an interesting mind . . . the effect was as I say, to give me an impression of her callousness and hardness as a human being." Woolf's criticism is to some extent acute. Mansfield's smartness can be superficial, and [her] London and Paris stories do seem to come from a callous human being; they contain no warmth, only a hard critical examination. Witty, well-observed, honest, but narrow and limited. Yet callousness and inhumanity are exactly what she wants to portray. She captures the small daily cruelties, unawarenesses, vanities, that together make a cruel and hateful world. Here there is no connection between rich and poor, man and woman, fortunate and unfortunate. In this urban world, nature has no place; Rosemary Fell buys hothouse flowers from an expensive florist. William's Isabel treats a pineapple as a new toy. This is indeed the world of ugliness, stupidity, and corruption that Mansfield bewailed to Ottoline Morrell, and her view of it is sharply etched and convincing.

Yet this is the world to which she was born an outsider. Her view is harsher than Woolf's because she remains always more distant from this life, because she sees it with horrified clarity. It is this world that caused the War, this world she sees persisting after her brother and so many others were pointlessly destroyed by the War. Retreating in anguish, she turns back to [New Zealand,] the once-despised world of her childhood, now immeasurably more appealing.

Constance A. Brown. *The Centennial Review.* Summer, 1979, pp. 338–39

The method of "Prelude" was innovatory for 1918—four years before *Ulysses* and *Jacob's Room* were published. It is a symbolist method which was adopted quite consciously, as can be seen from the nature of the changes that were made as the 1915 version evolved into that of 1917. In returning to the symbolist ideals formulated in her early years, and in adapting them to short prose fiction, Katherine Mansfield effected a revolution in the short story comparable to that achieved by Joyce in the novel. Like novelists writing of Joyce, numerous short story writers have testified to her influence on the formal directions of the story.

"Prelude" can be described as symbolist firstly because in it, in accordance with Symbolist theory, the author conveys abstract states of mind or feeling only through concrete images, which act as "objective correlatives" for them. She rejects "descriptive analysis" in favor of "revelation through the slightest gesture," according to a prescription noted in one of her 1908 notebooks. In her work, this idea of the "concrete image" through which emotion is to be expressed can be extended to include the composition of an entire story. Thus in her best writing each detail of character, setting and scene contributes to the evocation of a specific mood or feeling, and detail is not primarily mimetic.

She worked deliberately towards this art of exclusion and suggestion, as we can see by comparing the extant draft of "The Aloe" with "Prelude." The revisions that she made are almost always designed to eliminate analysis or explanation, so that themes are conveyed through the concrete texture of the story—through dramatic action, stylized interior monologue, scene and imagery. She repeatedly cut from "The Aloe" analysis of motive, so that her characters could be revealed, not explained. . . .

"Prelude" is also symbolist in its structure. Critics have normally described the organization of the story as "random," seeing this as her innovatory contribution to the art of the short story. In reality, the story is anything but random. Each episode is played off against the next to form a complex pattern of thematic parallels and contrasts. In Sections V to VII, for example, the role of woman is explored through a series of discriminations about the affinities and differences between Linda Burnell (the central figure), her mother Mrs. Fairfield, and her sister Beryl. Linda's status as a woman midway between her insecure, unmarried sister and her stable and creative mother is affirmed through a complex web of relationships. . . .

This use of parallelism and contrast is inseparable from the patterns of imagery which prevade the story, extending to almost every detail, down to the up-ended tables and chairs of the opening paragraphs. The main image of the story, as the title of the first draft suggests, is the aloe. That its exact "meaning" has never been agreed on is evidence of its continuing power to stir and disturb the imagination of the reader. . . . In the full context of the story the aloe emerges most convincingly as an image of the fundamental life-force itself, including sexual force in human life. It represents the essential will or energy behind appearance, which is why not all the characters of the story approach it, for not all are capable of penetrating to the deeper issues of life. . . . Through the controlling symbol of the aloe Katherine Mansfield thus expresses in "Prelude" a view of life which underlies all her major stories. The aloe is, like life itself, often unlovely and cruel, offering for long periods nothing but "years of darkness," yet it also holds within itself the possibility of that rare flowering which justifies existence, "which, after all, we live for."

Clare Hanson and Andrew Gurr. *Katherine Mansfield* (New York: St. Martin's, 1981), pp. 50–52

Although feminist criticism has produced a vast number of studies about the life and work of Virginia Woolf, it has devoted far less attention to Katherine Mansfield. Mansfield's contributions to the development of modern fiction have been largely taken for granted. Her innovations in the short-fiction genre (especially the "plotless" story, the incorporation of the "stream of consciousness" into the content of fiction, and the emphasis on the psychological "moment") preceded Virginia Woolf's use of them, and they have been absorbed and assimilated—often unconsciously—by writers and readers of the short story. Mansfield never became one of the "lost" or "neglected" women writers needing rehabilitation by feminist critics. Unlike some of the female modernists who are currently being reclaimed by feminist scholars—writers whose highly experimental work was published by small presses and avant-garde journals and never reached a large public readership—Mansfield developed a huge following, which began to take on the features of a cult by the 1930s. Although this mass popularity subsided, even during the 1940s and 1950s she retained a "respectable" critical reputation. Her stories were included in most college anthologies of fiction; if anything, Mansfield was the anthologist's "token" woman. Her frequent use of irony and her insistence on organic unity in fiction made her writing especially amenable to the methods of the New Critics. That scrutiny ensured the continuity of her reputation, but also guaranteed that her work would be treated in isolation from its social, political, and historical contexts.

The initial problem for feminist criticism was to rescue Mansfield from everyone's assumed familiarity with her. . . .

Although a good part of Katherine Mansfield's impetus toward a new genre of short fiction reflects a need to express a specifically female vision that could not be incorporated into the traditional structure she had inherited, it would be a mistake to consider it an entirely conscious program on her part. If anything, she strove to separate herself from any definition as a feminist theorist.

Sydney Janet Kaplan. *Katherine Mansfield*
(Ithaca: Cornell University Press, 1991),
pp. 2–3, 10

The Garden Party and Other Stories was published by Constable on February 23, 1922, and in New York later that year. After having already published two largely successful volumes, what could Mansfield possibly have wanted to do? [She] wanted to demonstrate her maturity as an artist. She still felt a need to be accepted by the public, and she wanted to exhibit what she viewed as perfection in her own work. Whereas in *Bliss* she had concentrated on the imagination, she now wanted to write about feeling. She also wanted to show a more positive outlook on life, and for her to do this, she had to focus on childhood. The stories in *The Garden Party and Other Stories* are much brighter than the others [Mansfield] had written. It seems strange but true that as her health declined, her stories brightened. She began to withdraw into herself, and, [as Marvin Magalaner put it] "like Wordsworth, invalided and isolated, she nurtured her youthful experience and made it the center of her work in her later fiction. The depiction of children—herself and those she had known—became her trademark." . . .

Although her later fiction has a large emphasis on children, her primary emphasis is on the interpersonal relationship between characters. She writes, in this volume, a good deal about feeling in these interpersonal relationships Magalaner remarks that "a heightened sensitivity to personal relationships in fiction is perhaps Mansfield's foremost asset as a writer of short stories."

Patrick D. Morrow. Katherine Mansfield's
Fiction (Bowling Green, Ohio: Popular
Press, 1993), p. 72

MANZINI, GIANNA (ITALY) 1896–1974

That the art of Gianna Manzini, in the apparently static nature of its subject matter, becomes increasingly anxious to strike new chords and vibrations on the precious keyboard of its own sensibility, which runs from the *accent grave* of the primal instincts, the impulses of the blood, to the *accent aigu* of the soul, is something that I have said of her books several times. This anxiety and effort have been able to translate themselves gradually into authentic gains, albeit in that entirely intimate and discreet way that her essentially autobiographical and lyrical art involves. . . .

Manzini's progress is in the direction of the profound, of excavation, not only psychological, introspective, but formal, expressive, her prose increasingly freeing itself from those narrative schemas of the early books (*Tempo innamorato* (Time in love), 1928; *Incontro col falco* (Encounter with the falcon), 1929, perhaps more through the uneasiness that derived from its fundamental lyricism than through certain links to their common Tuscan tradition.

Once this uneasiness of the closed narrative disappeared, Manzini's compositions became more or less to be configured as "narratives in the making"—not so much because the imagination, so ready in her to be unleashed in the most ardent analogies, takes a decisive leap forward, but because of that theme which is the basis of all her themes: the loneliness of human creatures (and of woman in particular) and the consequent effort to escape into memories, images, dreams, and the return . . . to reality. This theme is treated by her with the freedom of a musical theme, as an "improvisation" that invents its own design . . . (a type of narrative that has little or nothing in common with the "open" form that we hear so much about among the "ultramoderns."

And if at times in these compositions the third person narrative recurs and that design follows a certain objectivity, this is due to that highly lucid critical consciousness that accompanies Manzini in her remembering and evoking, that desire not so much to look at oneself in the mirror of one's own sensations as to separate oneself (at least at times) from oneself to get deeper into that counterpoint of reality and fiction. In short, from *Boscovivo* (Livingwood) (1932) to *Un filo di brezza* (A thread of breeze) (1936) to *Rive remote* (Distant banks) (1940), from *Lettera all'Editore* (Letter to the publisher) (1945) to *Forte come une leone* (Strong as a lion) (1947) to *Ho viso il tuo cuore* (I have seen your heart) (1950), from *Il valtzer del diavolo* (The devil's waltz) (1953) to the many portraits of animals (*Arca di Noe* (Noah's ark), (1960), to the "novels" cited, her path as a writer has consisted in making increasingly intrinsic this relationship between inspiration and invention, in blowing her own images into an ever more succinct crystal of words.

Arnaldo Bocelli. *Il Mondo* (Rome).
November 26, 1963, p. 10

There does not always seem to be as broad a series of themes, variously implicated in a rigorous phenomenology of reality within which to develop narrative discourse, as would correspond to the breadth of Manzini's production. Rather, observing Manzini's poetic world in its complex entirety, it is much more feasible to speak, rather than of themes, of subtle existential suggestions in a psychological key, able to arouse the exciting lyrical-descriptive process in a writer like Manzini, who is interested in the most difficult mechanisms of consciousness and, consequently, in the most varied and unexpressed manifestations of the spirit.

It thus becomes clear why, by cultural background and personal concern for the most arduous psychological research, Manzini, incisive reader of the human soul, was not very interested in the practical world of daily life and, when it has to enter into the writer's narrative, it is there only to arouse a whole series of occasions able to stimulate precisely that mechanism of consciousness in whose intense dynamic, explored in its most minute traces, the writer found the elements to express and enrich her lyric world. . . .

In the way she divides up the tales collected in *Cara prigione* (Dear prison), in 1958, Manzini proposes certain ideal thematic lines along which her narrative practice had developed, particularly in her short fiction. . . . The motifs of this collection are *Sorriso e morte* (Smile and death), *Veleni* (Poisons), *Figure* (Figures), and *Improvvisi* (Surprises). It is a matter, obviously, of interior motifs, which make up Mazzini's poetic world. . . .

The autobiographical motif also emerges in Manzini's entire production as an essential moment in the context of an allusivity always held in check by the superior claims of style. . . .

The isolation of Manzini's characters is not always of the dialectical or problematic sort, but is above all of the existential sort. It is not born in these creatures, who respond to the slightest nuance of feeling, out of a precarious relationship to society, but from an impossible relationship with themselves, an existential condition of anguish that arises from a sense of uncertainty or dissatisfaction in whose traces the individual as a historic entity and hence and ethical one, is dissolved to leave room for a vibrant and painful cluster of feelings or hopes destined to remain unfulfilled.

Enzo Panareo. *Invito alla lettura di Gianna Manzini* (Milan: Mursia, 1977), pp. 105–7

Studying Gianna Manzini in the setting of contemporary Italian literature elicits two essential considerations: one is of the poetic and literary quality of her prose; the other is of its experimental and innovative character. Whereas the first aspect places Manzini in the well-established literary tradition of "prosa d'arte (artistic prose), the author's tendency to experiment shows her unrelenting exploration of the different, expanded functions of the novel itself.

Manzini's works have not been translated into English, perhaps because of the peculiar problems that her prose would present in another language. Critics have often labeled her art as "difficult" and considered her an "elite" sort of writer. The term *prosa d'arte* refers broadly to certain characteristics of refinement and linguistic preciousness present in most Italian prose produced between the two wars. . . .

Manzini skillfully exploits the possibilities of her narrative. She searches for internal rhythms and linguistic shades that resemble the "visual fragmentism" and "descriptive impressionism" found in contemporary Tuscan writers and poets. But, at the same time, she deepens her interest in the structural aspects of fiction, searching for methods that would allow a freer intellectual and emotional interchange between characters and author. For the most part, she accomplishes this open flowing by introducing a circular and diffusive voice that allows the interplay of various narrative levels (dialogue, direct narration, flashback, string of associations), thus creating a crisis of objectivity inside the novel itself. Manzini's novel *Lettera all'editore* (Letter to the publisher) (1945) is a manifesto of her poetics. Structured as a work-in-progress—as Gide's *Faux-monnayeurs,* Pirandello's *Sei personaggi in cerca d'autore,* and Bontempelli's *Vita intensa*—the novel is self-reflective and constructs its own plot, thus enabling reality to enter fiction and precluding a closed structure. The critic Emilio Cecchi immediately recognized *Lettera all'editore* as an example of Italy's most innovative narrative style and saw it as an attempt to achieve new forms of expression and to create a new type of novel. . . .

Most of Manzini's attentive readers and critics agree that her works reflect a combination of "emotion and intelligence, culture and nature, refinement and instinct." Gianfranco Contini states that her highly refined prose goes beyond that of D'Annunzio or *La Ronda*; according to Contini, Manzini successfully integrates "analogical discourse with the melodic lyricism of her monologue" and creates an intellectual theme for this blend. The result is a unique and eminently feminine style. Giansiro Ferrata sees the intense richness of a feminine point of view as the writer's mark of distinction and originality. On the other hand, Anna Nozzoli claims that Manzini's narrative style and choice of characters are so highly conditioned by her interest in a metaphorical representation of reality that female characters fail to acquire "narrative autonomy" or to establish their personalities with realistic and psychological conviction. Although Nozzoli's analysis brings the salient aspects and motives of Manzini's female characterization to light, the critic fails to consider sufficiently the function of the author's "analogical discourse" as an explorative operation. . . .

Manzini devotes her last two works to the memory of each of her parents. By summarizing their lives, she also portrays her own existence as a daughter and writer; in addition, she recapitulates her aesthetic ideas, while stylistically and linguistically highlighting her commitment to literature and future life. The tradition of artistic prose permeates all her narrative works and consistently maintains an original blend of lyricism and language that sustains her ardent vision of reality. Her unrelenting search for words that emotionally and intellectually re-create existence, energy, and a potential for discovery finds its most fulfilling experience in linguistic signs of "light." Manzini's faith and devotion to writing enable her to conceptualize ineffable and hidden aspects of reality through her poetics.

Giovanna Miceli-Jeffries. In Santo L. Aricò,
ed. *Contemporary Women Writers in Italy:
A Modern Renaissance* (Amherst:
University of Massachusetts Press, 1990),
pp. 91–93, 104–5

MARAINI, DACIA (ITALY) 1936–

[*La vacanza* (The vacation)] is a sensitive, gripping story told with a control and clarity of style which more than attests to the seriousness and maturity of its young author. Its greatest merit lies perhaps—as Moravia states . . . —in the delineation of the character of the protagonist. The fourteen–year-old, convent-bred Anna can be placed, without apology or fear of the comparison, beside Moravia's own Agostino and Luca and Elsa Morante's Arturo, among the more successful characterizations of the adolescent in Italian literature. . . . The events of [a] brief period spent in a decaying, corrupt world in which the only morality is self-survival . . . are narrated by Anna simply, matter-of-factly, without comment or reflection. . . . Her passivity and indifference temper the pathos of a childhood of anonymous neglect, the depravity of sexual perversion, the fearful horror of war, and save the novel from sentimentality and sensationalism.

Zina Tilone. *Books Abroad.* Summer, 1962,
p. 311

The Age of Malaise provides you with comfort and chic, for it isn't new, it is merely *à la page*. And what is more *à la page* these days than malaise? The world and the emotions of this novel have become familiar to us, in various ways, through . . . Camus and Françoise Sagan . . . and Fellini. Miss Maraini's influences are evident, but since she is clearly in possession of them rather than they of her, *The Age of Malaise* does not seem unoriginal. It seems original, though in a very definite vogue out of which it never manages to climb. It never becomes itself deeply. . . . It seems to me that Miss Maraini's intention is to debunk the Age of Malaise, to reveal it as the veneer coating all the traditional vices and vanities. . . . It is the work of a very gifted young writer.

Alfred Chester. New York Herald Tribune.
May 5, 1963, pp. 5, 11

Its naturalism, less intellectually contrived than Moravia's, belongs rather to the Italian cinema. . . . Light, warmish Roman rain seems to drizzle throughout the book. . . . The publishers mention *La Dolce Vita,* but there is not a touch of Fellini's histrionic spuriousness. Signorina Maraini's vision is sincere, direct, pure as rain.

There is missing [from *The Age of Malaise*] only the last thrust, the last initiative, of imagination. Christianity has long ago been washed away from this Italy, leaving only compassion; and in a sense Signorina Maraini's characters are more compassionate than imagined. Failing to apply the last ruthlessness of artistic intelligence, she stops the book short of tragedy and never penetrates to the actual structure of the loneliness which surrounds her people even in the dreadful sociability of Italian manners.

Brigid Brophy. New Statesman and Nation.
May 10, 1963, p. 717

As presented by the author, Enrica is certainly representative of a generation that is unable to find meaning in life or new values in a world robbed of its dignity and humanity by too many blunders, too many wars, too many betrayals. The evidence presented in [*The Age of Malaise*] speaks eloquently to this point: we have become incapable of enjoying even the rawest physical pleasure; we are unable to find a sense of purpose in the futile struggle of everyday living; finally, we have allowed ourselves to be turned into neurotic automatons. In that sense, the novel's characters reveal the sickness of our condition. . . . It is easy to see why the novel should have attracted the sympathy of Alberto Moravia. It is his own early novel, *The Time of Indifference,* that has considerably influenced Miss Maraini's sensibility, and it is Moravia's cold, semiclinical, grayish style that the young author has made her own, ably using it to depict the monotony of her sordid, hopeless world.

Sergio Pacifici. Saturday Review of
Literature. May 11, 1963, p. 74

The title of Dacia Maraini's novel [*The Age of Malaise*] is, perhaps intentionally, ambiguous. Does it refer to Our Times, or to the period of adolescence? This may seem a minor point, but the titles of novels nowadays can imply a sociological generalization which may not necessarily be warranted by the text.

Miss Maraini's seventeen-year-old heroine . . . tells her own story in a laconic style with no emotional comment—her malaise, it seems to me, is quite insufficient. Miss Maraini is trying to suggest the unformed and bewildered heart which has as yet no imaginative content, and she relies on objective correlatives—what is going on in the physical environment—to suggest, or replace, feeling. . . . Miss Maraini has talent and skill, but she may have set herself an impossible task. It is difficult to be interesting about total emptiness, very difficult indeed in the first person, lacking the maturity of self-satire. This is a clever picture of total negation. I find the attempt impressive. But I am asking myself if the negation does not extend far beyond the book.

Kathleen Nott. *The New York Times*.
May 26, 1963, p. 5

While economists tell us Italy is in the midst of a boom unparalleled in its history, Italian films and novels go on declaring that emptiness and desolation lurk beneath all the glittering prosperity. *The Age of Malaise* by Dacia Maraini could be a scenario for one of the earlier and more modest films in the "realistic" style of De Sica, with the same flat, bleak story of humble people carrying on with a forlorn stoicism under oppressive circumstances. Neither its material nor its mood is appealing, but the spare and unrelieved veracity of its telling establishes Miss Maraini as one of the younger Italian writers worth watching. . . . For [the novel's heroine], her sexual encounters are as meaningless as all the other prospects life holds before her. All values, except that of survival, have disappeared from her world.

William Barrett. *Atlantic Monthly*.
July, 1963, p. 132

Rosamond Lehmann wrote a more stylish English version of this story before Dacia Maraini was born; Françoise Sagan more recently a French version with ritzier props, but no greater passion. [*The Age of Malaise*] deals with an authentic tedium in an authentic fashion. This is the Italian style, a class up from Pasolini's sub-proletariat. The writing is laconic, but never flabby. The detail, from furnishings to cars, from clothes to food, has the Fleming touch, without the advertising. . . . This may be a book about trivialities, but it is not a trivial book. It is calculated and detached, with a nervous tautness of narrative. Only a real writer could have brought it off.

Alan Ross. *London Magazine*. August, 1963,
p. 88

The work of Dacia Maraini . . . identifies itself with the present stage of Italian feminism through a creative effort in which the contemporary experience of women is probed with systematic and steadfast purpose. Moving from existential alienation to social commitment, Maraini's experience as a writer undergoes a process of evolution in ideology and formal elaboration commensurate with her perception of woman's changing position in society. From this process, two forms of writing emerge: a narrative effort distinguished by psychological treatment of individual rapport with reality; and a utilitarian, didactic approach to poetry and drama motivated by the precise aim of furthering the cause of women's rights. . . .

The initial or prefeminist stage of Maraini's work is represented by a volume of short stories and three novels, of which two are immature and largely derivative efforts. In *La vacanza* (The vacation; 1962), written when the author was twenty years old, and *L'età del malessere* (1963) the characters' disposition oscillates between total estrangement and a futile search for self-assertion through sexual activity. Both narratives focus on adolescent women who move aimlessly from one experience to the next, subjecting themselves, often with masochistic condescension, to emotional and sexual exploitation by older men or youngsters of their age. Their sense of alienation, accentuated by the erosion of personal relationships within the family, takes on meaning as an expression of social and psychological disorientation rooted in a passive consciousness that refuses to come to terms with reality. . . .

The novel *A memoria* (From memory) attests to a transitional stage in Maraini's writing, a stage in which the search for innovative expression is accompanied by a fresh but still problematic existential outlook. One of the more interesting experimental efforts of the post-war avant-garde, the work offers a successful approach to narrative structures consistent with the technical innovations of the French "new novel." Of particular interest is Maraini's receptivity to the *regard* narrative of Robbe-Grillet and its felicitous results in projecting a impersonal rapport with the external world. A *memoria* is structured with three levels of narration, each identifying the existential consciousness of the fictional *personae* through a resourceful treatment of the following elements: diary entries in which Maria (the narrator) records her experiences with cold objectivity; extended dialogues through which Maria's difficulty in relating to her husband is given graphic evidence by the repetition of the same point, each time with a different twist; a series of letters from a friend to the narrator written in a fragmented, highly elliptical style requiring the reader's intuitive participation to yield meaning. . . .

From a feminist viewpoint, A *memoria* is a disturbing, ambivalent work permeated with contradictory notions. On the surface, the portrait of an assertive and independent woman who has shed the lethargy of her counterparts in *La vacanza* and *L'età del malessere* seems to point to feminist awareness. Moreover, Maria's sense of initiative and her appropriation of masculine traits unfold in the context of persistent, competitive analogies with Pietro's disposition. Yet Maria is hardly a positive character. The veneer of independence and sexual freedom hides . . . a disturbed person who is incapable of giving her life a structured and purposeful direction.

The contradictions reflected in *A memoria* are resolved in Maraini's feminist novel, *Donna in guerra* (Woman at war; 1975). The title itself is noteworthy: it brings up to date [Sibilla] Aleramo's *Una donna* with a militant qualifier that immediately directs the reader's attention to the Italian feminist movement, which coalesced in 1968 amidst widespread and often violent protests by students, factory workers and groups of women. No doubt, the work is the outgrowth of Maraini's association with the movement, but examined closely, it contains few traces of the militancy suggested by the title. *Donna in guerra* is, rather, a thought-provoking narrative in which a woman's individual consciousness and her yearning for self-fulfillment are probed with calm and rational objectivity.

Written in the form of a diary, the medium to which feminist authors have turned with increasing frequency in recent years, the story documents the gradual disaffection in the relationship of a young couple. Essentially the difficulty arises from a clash of attitudes involving Giacomo, a kind but inflexible man whose traditional perception of marriage attaches little value to a woman's needs, and his wife Vannina, who grows weary of feigning happiness while accepting her gray existence with resigned indifference. . . .

Much more significant than the inversion of roles found in *A memoria* is the emergence, in this work, of a woman who relies on reasoning and reflection rather than instinct, not only to solve her predicament but to take cognizance of social injustices, especially the injustices perpetrated against women.

Augustus Pallotta. *World Literature Today.* 58, 1984, pp. 360–61

In *Memorie di una ladra* (Memories of a thief) Maraini depicts the life of a willful outsider. The seemingly indestructible narrator, Teresa, survives innumerable beatings, bombings, inhumane prisons and insane asylums, and family persecution, to mention only a few of the adventures in this action-packed, linear plot. The picaresque genre derives from criminal confessions, causing Claudio Guillén to identify it as the "confessions of a liar." However, if the confessional pieces of Guiducci display the aporia of the belief in the view that the personal self can be kept separate from the social, the picaresque tradition has always reaffirmed that there is no material survival outside of society. Like the traditional picaro, Teresa prefers estrangement and roguery to any traditionally prescribed female role, but she will always somehow adjust to social demands, however defined, which are imposed upon her. Once again revolt will reveal itself as cooperation.

Memorie di una ladra is a result of extensive research done by Maraini in the late 1960s on the deplorable conditions in women's prisons. In an interview that introduces Bompiani's reedition of the work, she speaks of how reeducation in women's prisons aims at producing model housewives.

But in the episodic, action-packed narrative itself, such ideological points are given short shrift by the practical, down-to-earth Teresa who moves from one adventure to another, never improving except to learn from experience how to become a better thief. Like the traditional picaresque orphan, Teresa is thrown unprepared into a harsh society whose values she has to learn anew. Society, its hardships, inequalities, and oppressions, becomes the natural foe of the picaro who, in his judgments, displays a strong sense of moral rectitude. Typically, Teresa rails incessantly against the cowards, many of them male, who betray her both in sex and in burglaries, and thus have "forced" her to go to jail. Her sense of honor is based on the rigid standards of "omertà," the underworld's code of solidarity, which is based on remaining loyal and silent while taking the rap alone. . . .

In *Donna in Guerra*, Maraini confronts the theme of accepting responsibility for one's life, as difficult as that may be, in her depiction of the transformation of a withdrawn, dependent female who hides behind her traditional subservient role into one ready to accept the risks involved in assuming responsibility for one's life. . . .

Donna in Guerra reverses the archetypal romance quest. The adventures and separations do not lead to the marriage of the essentially passive protagonists. Instead, a married woman, after a series of adventures and a brief separation from her husband, decides to divorce and, in her own words, start all over again. . . .

Donna in Guerra, however, ends with a call for solidarity and courage to continue to overcome one's limits.

Carol Lazzaro-Weis. *Italica.* 65, 1988,
pp. 298–300, 302, 304

Donna in guerra (Woman at war) covers a brief period of a couple's relationship. Vannina, an elementary school teacher in Rome's periphery, grows increasingly weary of her unsatisfactory marriage. Giacinto, her mechanic husband, is a seemingly kind and pensive individual whose traditional perspective fails to recognize a woman's needs. Their life together initially appears to be without problems, until a summer vacation unexpectedly exposes Vannina to a world entirely different from the one she knows.

Written in the form of a diary, the novel reflects not only Vannina's personal experiences but also the overall condition of women in Italy. Examples that illustrate themes of social injustice surface, and gender stereotyping invariably comes into play. Vannina's brief association with an underground Leftist group accentuates a sociopolitical scenario. Although proclaiming themselves revolutionary thinkers concerned with people's rights, the men in this ideological organization show themselves to be increasingly insensitive to the plight of women. Vannina herself witnesses labor exploitation of the worst kind in the slums of Naples, where she conducts interviews with housewives engaged in poorly paid piecework. While it is almost impossible to isolate the common denominator in literature written by women, the most

recurring remains the motif of conflict. When these authors or their protagonists identify with others, they demonstrate sympathy for those involved in
some form of class struggle.

Informing her text with a strong feminist charge, Maraini adopts a narrative technique that noticeably deviates from the canon. In order to demonstrate the need for an end to patriarchal stereotyping of women, she adopts
a narrative technique of reversal. She eschews narration as the dominant
mode of communication, and her vocabulary often reflects an everyday inventory of slang and vulgarities. . . .

[The] stylistic method [of relying on dialogue] combines with the first-
person presentation of the narrator and underlines the urgency of the author's
communique. The diaristic form alone normally provides a confession, a description of an individual's life, and a narrator's perspective. In the case of
Donna in guerra, readers also have the advantage of another point of view.
They actively become "producer[s] of the text" and draw inferences from
the dialogue in order to make better sense of the words. This author/reader
coproduction of the "unformulated text" charges the novel with a more forceful message. . . .

The message . . . may be considered twofold. First of all, *Donna in
guerra* illustrates the difficulties women experience in a totally male-oriented
society. If a woman does succeed in liberating herself from an oppressive
situation, the overall problem of gender stereotyping remains unsolved . . .
Secondly . . . solutions to the plight of women require the cooperation of
both the male and the female; otherwise, women will always find themselves
in perilous predicaments. This is the subtext of many of Vannina's experiences; for the most part, she acquires a sense of peace and calm either in
the company of other females or with those males, e.g., Orio, who have not
been totally coopted by patriarchy. Thus, the title *Donna in guerra* refers
precisely to the continuing struggle women must wage against patriarchy,
just as Vannina, by freeing herself from Giacinto, has won a battle but not
the war.

Anthony J. Tamburi. In Santo L. Aricò, ed.
*Contemporary Women Writers in Italy: A
Modern Renaissance* (Amherst: University
of Massachusetts Press, 1990), pp. 139–40,
148–49

What distinguishes the diction in Dacia Maraini's entire artistic production
is the need to act, in the name of all women, on the totalizing reality of the
masculine world. Maraini's linguistic enterprise . . . arises from her recognition of her own inauthenticity as a speaking subject and her marginalized
position in society in that woman, silenced for centuries, has been deprived
of a space in which to approach her own process of signification. Object of
a reality that is not her own, woman, according to Maraini, has been "spoken"
by man, has been represented in his image and, impelled by the forces that

have conditioned her, she has found herself face to face with a mere simulacrum of female identity, a deformed reflection of her own I. In her works, Maraini is committed to reclaiming her own body, the site of unrestrainable impulses and the vehicle of a knowledge capable of overthrowing the preestablished order By thus demanding a corporeality that has always been denied to woman, her writings inscribe the signs of the female imaginary upon the language. Through the figurative word, in an excess of erotic charge revelatory of an intimate and secret world, the myths of the sacredness of the family, of institutionalized love and the relations between man and woman based on ownership all fall away.

In her first collection of poetry, *Crudeltà all'aria aperta* (Cruelty out in the open), the poetic discourse takes an interesting turn as it clashes against the imperative of memory of the father, to whom the I is chained by a relation at once amorous, visceral, and profoundly narcissistic. Love for the father, the original source of pleasure and desire, nonetheless creates strong tensions at the level of discourse with the nascent awareness of his betrayal. The image is fragmented under recalcitrant memory silenced by suffering. Poetic experience strips the false consciousness of the woman where inauthenticity and discrimination have for centuries fostered the sense of alienation. In the words of Biancamaria Frabotta, women's poetry is born from the recognition that there are no other ways that can make the raising of consciousness other than looking this lack in the face in an attempt "to penetrate again into the horrors of non-being." . . .

By engaging political experience with the "private," Maraini's discourse becomes narrative and confessional, hence a spontaneous communicative act in which the raising of the individual consciousness entails the collective interests. . . .

It is not until her second collection of poems, *Donne mie* (My women), published in 1974, that Maraini will approach a true dialogue with women on the subject of love. With this collection and following the advent of post-68 neofeminism . . . it becomes necessary to remake everything according to a plan of virulent social criticism. In open polemic with the system, poetic expression, more than form, aims at a provocative language, populist. . . . While the poetic voice in *Crudeltà all'aria aperta* is still circumscribed within the orbit of private experiences, in *Donne mei,* rage, as the legitimate reaction of knowledge and loss of the beloved object, it transcends the limits of the individual to find, in the reflection of one's own image delineated in all women, a new charge of love.

Grazia Sumeli Weinberg. Italica. 67, 1990,
pp. 453–54, 464

Dacia Maraini, the author of numerous novels since 1963, portrays in *La lunga vita di Marianna Ucrìa* the life of a Sicilian family during the first half of the eighteenth century. Marianna is a deaf-mute who, in her dreams and sensitivities, must deal through written communication with married existence and with the problems of sisters and cousins. The novel recounts varied incidents within the egotistic, closed family circle in prose of great intensity, written in descriptive form and with realistic detail. Marianna longs to be able to hear the sounds of nature, the songs of birds, and prays that she will not lose her eyesight and that her heart will remain strong. She feels, however, that members of the family make fun of her and that even Christ laughs at her. She is extremely self-conscious, and through her imaginings she has developed a heightened sense of intuition. To escape her unhappy marriage, she becomes an avid reader, regularly choosing novels about love. At the end of her long life after the death of her husband, she has a lover, a judge, who seeks to marry her. She escapes to Naples, much to the horror of her family, who feel abandoned. The story ends with the question "What to do?" regarding the proposed marriage. Marianna remains despairing, *muta*.

In Maraini's forceful psychological study we also find a wealth of brief descriptions of members of Marianna's family from a physical and mental point of view. There are, in addition, passages describing the beauties of external nature, which she deeply appreciates. Attention to color and above all to fragrances and odors in the depiction of surroundings is notable as well. The use of comparisons further enhances the narrative's realistic passages: "i singhozzi senza voce sono come lampi senza tuoni." The vocabulary is rich and at times dialectal. The novel furnishes a kaleidoscope of upper-class Sicilian life and society, breaking the account up into forty-three short chapters. Although there are happy times with balls, parties, and grape harvests, the pervading atmosphere is one of tragedy and unhappiness for this proud family with its long royal heritage: "il sapore amaro e crudo della vita." There are also political references to dramatic events of the day in Palermo.

Maraini awakens the reader's sympathy for such a tragic figure as the deaf-mute and gives vivid local color to a narrative consisting chiefly of everyday existence. *La lunga vita di Marianna Ucrìa* differs from many other novels both in its subject matter and in its touching portrayal of Sicilian life.

Patricia M. Gathercole. World Literature
Today. 65, 1991, p. 286

The work of Italian novelist, poet, essayist, screenwriter, and playwright Dacia Maraini is not well known in the English-speaking world despite the fact that six of her eight novels have appeared in English and at least ten of her more than thirty plays have been performed outside Italy. Since Denise Stoklos's production of *Mary Stuart* (Maria Stuarda, 1980) at La Mama in 1987 and Michael Smith's production of *Clytemnestra's Dream* (*I Sogni di Clitennestra,* 1978) at the Judith Anderson Theatre in New York in 1989, her work has begun to gain some recognition in the United States. Internationally she is the most widely performed living Italian playwright after Dario Fo and Franca Rame. . . .

Like her compatriot Franca Rame, Maraini combats . . . male-centered avant-garde practice with a strong materialist, socialist feminist perspective.

In much of her poetry, fiction, and polemic for a "theatre of words," however, she is closer to the Utopian, radical feminist aesthetic of *écriture féminine*. . . .

Most of the female protagonists of Maraini's novels and plays discover their strength and capacity for self-determination through both interior, individual and public, political action. The shift between a historical, economic, and class-based analysis of women in society in some of her plays to a more psychological and aesthetic concern with themes such as seduction and sexuality in others suggests similar dual tactics are at work in what might be defined as "scrittura femminile," a particularly Italian version of *écriture féminine*. . . .

Mary Stuart (1980), a reworking of Schiller's classic play, is Maraini's most widely performed text, having been staged in fifteen countries, including England and Australia, and in a one-woman version by Brazilian actress Denise Stoklos at La Mama in New York in 1987. It explores the theme of women's traditional isolation and confinement, examining the way in which Mary Queen of Scots and Queen Elizabeth were both trapped in their public and traditionally male political roles and denied realization of themselves as women.

Tony Mitchell. Theatre Journal. 42, 1990,
pp. 332–33, 343

MARKANDAYA, KAMALA (INDIA) 1924–

Of the writers who have but lately come into the limelight, Kamala Markhandaya is perhaps the most outstanding. Her first novel, *Nectar in a Sieve,* has been compared with Pearl Buck's *The Good Earth,* though a nearer and apter analogy would be K. S. Venkataramani's *Murugan the Tiller.* Miss Markhandaya takes us to the heart of a South Indian village where life has not changed for about a thousand years. Now industry and modern technology invade the village in the shape of a tannery, and from this impact sinister consequences issue. Poverty and misery, the advancing disease of overpopulation, the wailing of the helpless—what "nectar" out of this muddied ocean? . . .

But the heart that is tempered in the flames of love and faith, of suffering and sacrifice, will not easily accept defeat. Rukmini the narrator-heroine is also a Mother of Sorrows. She receives shock after shock: for example, her husband's infidelity, and her daughter's sacrificial going on the streets to save the family from starvation. . . . Calm after storm, spring after winter—such is the unending cycle. One must persevere, one must hope, even if it were only in trying to discover "nectar in a sieve"!

If *Nectar in a Sieve* recalls Venkataramani's *Murugan the Tiller,* Miss Markhandaya's *Some Inner Fury* recalls his *Kandan the Patriot.* Where Venkataramani is poetical and masculine, Markhandaya is suggestive and feminine. If her writing is less rich in imagery, it has more ease and more of the light of love.

> K. R. Srinivasa Iyengar. *Indian Writing in English* (New York: Asia Publishing House, 1962), p. 331

We follow the peasant-youth, Ravi [in *A Handful of Rice*], through his rootless life in the city until he settles in the house of the tailor, Apu, and marries Apu's daughter. Most of the book is set in this family, mere inches from the poverty-line. Apu's industriousness holds it together, but, with his death it slides slowly downhill. What Ravi has learned of life keeps him from returning to his former criminal companionship, yet at the end he joins, in spite of himself, in the mob in a food riot.

We feel here that we have been given an insight into a way of life that we have hitherto known only through the newspaper or the television report. Ravi is a human being, not so very unlike us, instead of some strange cipher in a distant land. His problems, his family, his thoughts and hopes are not very different from ours. This mediation of common humanity to all mankind is one of the important functions of literature that is set outside the charmed circle of Western society. Achebe has done it for West Africa. Using a similar style—short, no-nonsense sentences, thoroughly professional—Kamala Markandaya has done the same for India in a memorable book.

> T. A. Dunn. *Journal of Commonwealth Literature.* July, 1968, p. 127

Of all the contemporary Indian novelists writing in English, Kamala Markandaya is the most accomplished, both in respect of her sensitive handling of a foreign medium and her authentic portrayal of the Indian scene. What distinguishes her most incisively from other Indian novelists is her acute awareness of a gradual shift in values that has been taking place in this subcontinent during the past two decades or so. . . .

Kamala Markandaya's novels attempt to present in symbolical characters and situations this thrust toward modernity, which often assumes in her work the guise of a malignant tumor infecting the vitals of a culture traditionally quietistic. It is this evil force that drives her rustic characters from idyllic tranquillity to the disquieting pressures of city life. The exodus from the villages here symbolizes the disinheritance of the human soul, its recantation of the age-old commitment to faith, peace, compassion, and truth.

Change is, therefore, the focal theme in her novels; it is the pivot round which her fictional world revolves. There is hardly a novel which does not derive its aesthetic validity from the interlocked polarities of religion and science, possession and renunciation, empiricism and transcendentalism.

Nectar in a Sieve, her first novel and her magnum opus, captures this dichotomy of values in a most compelling manner. Rukmani, devoted wife of a tenant farmer, living in the soulful quietude of her little village, suddenly finds within this Garden of Eden a serpent in the form of a tannery that begins to rear its ugly head, devouring green open spaces, polluting the clean, wholesome atmosphere, and tempting simple, gullible peasants into greed, ambition, and immorality.

Shiv K. Kumar. *Books Abroad.* Autumn,
1969, pp. 508–9

Kamala Markandaya, with six novels to her credit, is one of the more prolific Indian-English novelists—only Mulk Raj Anand or R. K. Narayan have published more novels. She has dealt with various strata of society: *Nectar in a Sieve* deals with the village and its poverty; *Some Inner Fury* is narrated by Mirabai, a young girl from an affluent, Westernized family who is parted from her English lover by the fury of the Quit India movement; *A Silence of Desire* has urban middle class characters, while *A Handful of Rice* deals with urban poverty. In *Possession* the scene alternates between Lady Caroline Bell's elegant home in London and Valmiki's impoverished home in a south Indian village. Her latest novel, *The Coffer Dams,* deals with the English in India—not the colonialists, but a British construction firm invited to build a huge dam in the country.

In her first five novels, one notices a tendency to "explain" India to the foreign audience—the familiar characters of the popular image of India are all there—the poor but uncomplaining villager, the Maharaja who has lost his heritage with the integration of his state with India ("Jumbo" in *Possession*) or the "holy man" (in *A Silence of Desire and Possession*). She does make an attempt to present the traditional way of life—the strength that comes of acceptance is stressed both in *Nectar in a Sieve* and in Sarojini's attitude in *A Silence of Desire.* But how deep is her understanding of tradition? She has been praised for her mastery of English, but the question is whether the language expresses the sensibility of her characters. *Some Inner Fury* is the best of her novels precisely because the heroine belongs to that class of society from which Miss Markandaya herself comes—English expresses her sensibility adequately. But the same cannot be said about her other novels, where not only the language but the presentation of life is inadequate—Miss Markandaya does not seem to know her village as well as the balls and offices of *Some Inner Fury.*

Shyamala Venkateswaran. *The Literary
Criterion.* Winter, 1970, p. 57

It is difficult to say what I want to say about *The Nowhere Man* without seeming patronizing. The major though not all the minor characters are round. The book's heart is in the right place. The subject is important and interesting—a Hindu immigrant in South London, here since before the war and feeling himself almost an Englishman until he encounters post-war racial antagonism. What is lacking is sparkle. The book could do with some of Ruth Jhabvala's sharpness. And I found myself wishing William Trevor could take over the relationship between the Hindu widower in his fifties and the ten-year-older distressed but defiant English gentlewoman. Kamala Markandaya would profit from some of Margaret Atwood's speed-writing. Instead she slows things up by using non-sentence sentences. Like this. Too often. To no good purpose. I've liked and admired some of her earlier books, but I was disappointed by this.

John Mellors. London Magazine.
August–September, 1973, pp. 150–51

In several of Kamala Markandaya's novels, sexuality plays a most important role. One does not have to be a prude to feel that the sexual emphasis is overdone in *Some Inner Fury* (1955) and *A Silence of Desire* (1960), two of the earlier novels; and in *Nectar in a Sieve* (1954), the first novel to be published, sex, though manifestly present, is not integral to the action. However, by the time Markandaya gets to *Possession* (1963) she is in firm control of her material and sex emerges as a powerful agency which functions as symbol and metaphor as well as in its own right as part of the action. Fury and desire are transmuted into a force no less dynamic but more precisely observed—an essential element in the novelist's equipment. In the poignant and harrowing *A Handful of Rice* (1966), sex is certainly not unimportant, but it does not have the central position that it has in *Possession,* and one has to wait for *The Coffer Dams* (1969) to find a similar powerful, symbolic sexuality. In the novel of old age, *The Nowhere Man* (1972), moving though it is, sex is important in a recollection rather than as immediate action, although it is handled with a subtlety that foreshadows *The Golden Honeycomb;* and in *Two Virgins* (1973)—the nearest Kamala Markandaya has come to a pot-boiler with an eye on the mass market—sex is abundant but rather pointless. In the latest and longest novel, *The Golden Honeycomb* (1977), Markandaya returns to symbolic sexuality but, since she has given herself more space to maneuver, treats it in a more complex and subtle way. In this work of triumphant maturity, sex becomes the transforming force that through the green fuse drives the flower, omnipresent but not insistent, far removed from the violent cries and groans of the earlier novels.

James Dale. World Literature Written in
English. 21, 1982, pp. 347–48

Kamala Markandaya's novels deal with the modernization of India, especially through its interaction with the West. We can discern a pattern—not a smooth progress, but a troubled swinging between tradition and modernity, between cultural exclusivism and a pluralistic cultural identity in her novels. Structurally, her novels reflect this state of cultural ambivalence through a conflict pattern, which forms the basis of her plots—conflict between village and city in *Nectar in a Sieve, A Handful of Rice* and *Two Virgins*, or a clash between tradition and modernity in *The Coffer Dams* and *A Silence of Desire,* or the reactions of an individual to the colonial presence in novels like *Some Inner Fury* and *The Golden Honeycomb*. This pattern of unresolved oppositions forms the basis of Markandaya's plots and is in effect her own problem and the problem of novelists like Ruth Prawer Jhabvala—"the dilemma of people caught between cultures, uncertain about what direction to take and how far to take it." Later when Kamala Markandaya settles down in London, she reconciles herself to her new cultural atmosphere, but yet maintains her ambivalent attitude. . . .

A study of the cultural archetypes and images in the novels of Kamala Markandaya highlight the cultural miscegenation in her art and attitude. Even though Kamala Markandaya limits herself to the depiction of Indian landscape, she relies on the Indian heritage, as well as the Western culture for the choice of images and symbols. . . .

In Markandaya's novels, the journey of her fictional hero from the village to the city, or from tradition to modernity, or in essence from innocence to knowledge falls into some common archetypal pattern. The whole culture with all its complexities and contradictions is thus metaphorically presented. . . .

Through . . . archetypes and images, Kamala Markandaya expresses her fear about the taint of a cultural miscegenation on Indian heritage. She brings out the dangers of dehumanization involved in a commitment to civilization. Change, even for the better, always has to be paid for, and the price paid for the social benefits of twentieth-century technology has been exacting, and the predicament would seem to be an enduring part of the consciousness of modern India, "the ache of modernism," to use Hardy's phrase. But at the same time she does welcome an India that has absorbed the best in Western culture. She accepts the West without complaint, though not without criticism. Kamala Markandaya's fictional world, revealed through these archetypes is an Eden, balanced on a knife-edge between the twin chaotic threats of nature and civilization.

P. Geetha. *Journal of Commonwealth Literature*. 26, 1991, pp. 169–70, 177

Kamala Markandaya structures her novel *Nectar in a Sieve* around the conflict of cultures. A commonplace criticism of this novelist identifies these conflicting cultures in the largest terms, such as between Indian fatalism and British rationalism, or between the encroachments of industrialization, as represented by a hated tannery, and the peaceful rural life of tenant-farmers. Yet Markandaya is careful to modulate these larger conflicts with a series of narrower oppositions—town values versus country values, illiteracy versus literacy (land versus learning)—reverberating even in the minor key of the open fields of the Indian peasant as opposed to the closed doors and shutters of the local Muslim colony. Each of these conflicts, major and minor, produces an incremental step in the learning process for the narrator. . . .

From the cauldron of conflicting cultures, the protagonist of *Nectar in a Sieve* has divined a way of assimilating the mighty opposites of hope and will. The flashback technique joins the final movement of the novel to the opening movement. These movements force an integration of a return to the land, which revives Rukmini's spirit, with a willingness to make a promise for the future. "Things fall apart" in this novel where cultures conflict, but the author puts them back together through her central character's ability to reconcile the potentialities of these cultures and to overcome their restrictions. *Nectar in a Sieve* reinforces the ideas represented by the circle—a belief in immanence—and the arrow—an acceptance of progress. As repeated in the emblem of the land and the hospital, and the concepts of extended family and science, Kamala Markandaya has shown the way for clashing cultures to undertake the difficult process leading to reconciliation and rehabilitation. . . .

The imaginative journey that is *Nectar in a Sieve* absorbs binary cultural impulses about time and belief into a unitary image, the arrow in the circle, a powerfully suggestive expression for the integration of Eastern and Western perceptions of human experience.

Louis R. Barbato. Ariel. 22:4, 1991,
pp. 7, 14

Basically . . . her novels embody a feminine protest, one that marks a rare symbiosis of the Indian woman's plight and the Western woman's struggle. Perhaps because of this unlikely alliance, her women are shown always to handle their situations, no matter how difficult, with grace. They may appear as passive sufferers, as in the case of Rukmini in *Nectar in a Sieve,* or as targets of male domination and ego in *A Silence of Desire,* or as victims diminished by physical violence that the superficially modernized urban males perpetrate on village innocence in *Two Virgins.* But always they are survivors, and ultimately the women themselves take hold of their own circumstances. The female characters invariably emerge as rebels who question the conservative ethos around them. The more obvious examples are a village woman like Rukmini, a small town woman like Sarojini in *A Silence of Desire,* the more sophisticated Mira of *Some Inner Fury,* and the English women like Helen of *The Coffer Dams* and Caroline of *Possession.* . . .

Markandaya's key novels establish her ability to penetrate the female psyche, especially that of Indian women. Her characters range widely, from illiterate peasant women to westernized city women, from British women to Indian royalty. The novels explore all segments of the woman's world, from the peasant village to the Indian city to the lands beyond the Black Sea. Markandaya's peculiar strength, as William Walsh has noted, lies in "the delicate analysis of the relationship of persons, especially when they have a more developed consciousness of their problems and are attempting to grope toward some more independent existence."

Of course, this discussion was not intended to suggest that Markandaya has self-consciously created a world governed by clichéd patterns of feminist fiction. Her world is an all-inclusive one—albeit a woman's world—in which she explores the tangled web of human relationships. When Markandaya "broke away into exile"—to use a feminist expression—she broke all barriers to weaving stories in the set models of Indian fiction in English such as we find in the work of Narayan, Anand, Rao, and Bhattacharya. She wrote as herself—a woman—and brought to bear her individual "female imagination" on the Indian fictional world she created.

Ramā Jha. In Robert L. Ross, ed.
International Literature in English: Essays on the Major Writers (New York: Garland, 1991), pp. 252, 257

Kamala Markandaya's *Possession* ultimately presents us with a much richer picture than has been available to us in critical perspectives dominated by binary oppositions. Analysis through a Lacanian lens offers a challenging way to read her novels. The Lacanian topology of the subject, structured by the symbolic, the imaginary, and the real, orders that link like a Borromean knot, provides an alternative to the "binarity" of deconstructive readings. Since our subjectivity is not simply constructed, but reflects the complexity of the conflicting ideological components that make up our identities, Markandaya insists on a much more subtle engagement with the issues that dominate the East-West dialogue. *Possession*, in my reading, therefore, is not a "failed" novel as some critics would have us believe. Rather, her sophisticated writing across cultures provokes us to find new ways to pose the question of our unconscious desire and sexual and racial "Othering."

Ramchandran Sethuraman. *Ariel.* 23:3, 1992, p. 119

MARSHALL, PAULE (UNITED STATES) 1929–

In the approach from Fort-de-France to Trois Ilet, the Martiniquan land lifts off the Caribbean in soft folds of tiered country. One imagines that the fictitious Bournehills of Paule Marshall's *Chosen Place, Timeless People* presents to the mind's eye a similar prospect from the vantage of the sea. But the perception of a specific geographical place in the Caribbean might matter less to Marshall's overall intentions for this novel than the sheer magnitude of mimetic life that it captures. A study of politics and society in an English-speaking Caribbean community and the turbulence that is stirred when representatives of corporate America are introduced to it, *Chosen Place* was published in 1969. The novel is now available again in Vintage paperback after having been out of print for several years. The plausible reasons why the novel was, for all intents and purposes, "lost" until the fall of 1984 will not occupy my attention beyond this note, but I observe the absence as more than odd, given the nimble orchestrations of this work. In fact, when I recall my own limited acquaintance with the fabled Caribbean "Horseshoe," most northerly point projecting ninety miles off the southeastern tip of the United States, I imagine *Chosen Place* as its most definitive mimesis. . . .

In 1981, Feminist Press reissued Marshall's *Brown Girl, Brownstones. Chosen Place,* in perspective with *Brown Girl, Praisesong for the Widow* (1983), and the writer's short stories, not only corrects the limited view of her career that we have at the moment, but also comprehends Marshall's project as a writer within an enlarged scope of fictional operations. With *Chosen Place,* it is as if Marshall brings to a head her own writing past and future in rich continuity with the present. To that extent, I would consider this novel not only the "impression point" against which we might gauge and contemplate Marshall's efforts up to the moment, but also one of the most engaging works of fiction created by an African-American writer within the last half century of American creative effort. With that in mind, we can well regard Paule Marshall's career as a significant point of intersection between feminist and creative discourse. . . .

Set against a background of vegetal lushness, *Chosen Place* might well have been inspired by the author's ancestral home Barbados that also provides the scenery for some of her short stories as well as the source of memory and myth in *Brown Girl, Brownstones.* Whatever Caribbean scene the novel brings to mind, we perceive Bournehills, the fictitious country of the novel, as a continuum of geopolitical and cultural moments surrounded by Marshall's order of the timeless. The Caribbean itself converges with the Atlantic, and their interaction describes a point of dramatic emphasis. This shifting tempo of breaking waters and altering colors in a confluence closes the links of the notorious "Middle Passage." The currency of exchange between waterways engenders a wealth of metaphorical referents. In that way, Old World, sub-Saharan Africa connects geographically and figuratively with Bournehills of the New World. The geographical nexus of motives is completed by Stanford and mainline Philadelphia, points of origin for two of the main characters; both the United States and the Caribbean are read, consequently, by way of the economics of captivity and their implications for the contemporary world. With Bournehills at the center of Marshall's scenic apparatus and Bourne Island and Spiretown related to it in triangular proximity, we move freely between seaport, hillside, and suburban aspects of a continuous cultural and geographical progression.

The sociology that Bournehills generates is as complicated as its terrain. There are the common people, who have names and faces in the novel, and there are more of them than most contemporary fiction attempts. The various ritualistic activities of Marshall's fictional world so refine our sense of the people that a reader's intimations of anonymity complement the affecting presences of the work rather than hinder their impact. Above the folk in the social hierarchy is the local ruling class, which dominates in the name of the absentee landlords. Treacherous both to their own people and the overlords, the local rulers are occasionally attractive, well-educated abroad, own expensive things, some of them droll and amusing. Beyond the surrogate rulers, or lateral to them, are the social critics of local society, Merle Kinbona among them, and they are the "conscience" of their people, even as their own is troubled. These free-floating agents, suspended between cultures, provide the basic stress points on which the action turns.

> Hortense J. Spillers. In Marjorie Pryse and
> Hortense J. Spillers, eds. *Conjuring: Black
> Women, Fiction, and Literary Tradition*
> (Bloomington: Indiana University Press,
> 1985), pp. 151–52, 154–55

Like *Maud Martha,* the emphasis in *Browngirl, Brownstones* is on the black woman as mother and daughter. In an interview with Alexis DeVeau in 1980, Marshall recalls that she wrote her first novel in the late 1950s as a relief from a tedious job. She wrote the novel not primarily for publication but as a process of understanding, critiquing, and celebrating her own personal history. In understanding "the talking women," who were the most vivid memories of her youth, Marshall also demonstrates through her portrayal of Silla Boyce how the role of *mother* for this black woman is in conflict with her role as *wife,* because of the racism that embattles her and her community. Marshall's novel, as well as Brooks's, was certainly affected by society's attitude that black women were matriarchs, domineering mothers who distorted their children who in turn disrupted society—a vortex of attitudes that culminated in the Moynihan Report. In attempting to understand her maternal ancestors, then, Marshall had to penetrate the social stereotypes that distorted their lives.

Few early Afro-American women's novels focused on the black woman's role as mother, because of the negative stereotype of the black woman as mammy that pervaded American society. But instead of de-emphasizing the black woman's role as mother, Marshall probes its complexity. She portrays Silla Boyce as an embittered woman caught between her own personality and desires, and the life imposed on her as a mother who must destroy her unorthodox husband in order to have a stable family (as symbolized by the brownstone). This analysis of the black mother prefigures other analyses of this theme in the 1970s, especially Toni Morrison's *Sula* and Alice Walker's *Meridian.* And Marshall shows that racist and sexist ideology is intertwined, for Silla's and Deighton Boyce's internalization of the American definition of woman and man runs counter to their own beings and to their situation as black people in American society, and precipitates the tragedy that their relationship becomes.

Silla, however, is not an internal being like Maud Martha. She fights, supported by her women friends who use their own language to penetrate illusion and verbally construct their own definitions in order to wage their battle. As a result, Selina, Silla's daughter, will, by the end of the novel, have some basis for the journey to self-knowledge upon which she embarks, fully appreciating the dilemma which her mother and father could not solve.

Like Brooks's novel, *Browngirl, Brownstones* emphasizes how the black community, its customs and mores, affects the process of the black woman's exploration of self. But Marshall's novel also stresses the importance of culture and language as contexts for understanding *society's* definitions of man and woman. She veers sharply away from much of the preceding literature, which emphasized advancement for black women in terms of white American values. She portrays the Barbadian-American community both as a rock her characters can stand on, and as the obstacle against which they must struggle in order to understand and develop their own individuality. Finally, though, Selina's decision to return to the Caribbean is her attempt to claim her own history as a means of acquiring self-consciousness. In *Browngirl, Brownstones*, an appreciation of ethnic and racial community becomes necessary for black women in their commitment to self-development.

> Barbara Christian. In Marjorie Pryse and
> Hortense J. Spillers, eds. *Conjuring: Black
> Women, Fiction, and Literary Tradition*
> (Bloomington: Indiana University Press,
> 1985), pp. 238–40

Through Selina's physical journey, Marshall asserts the need for Blacks to make the spiritual and psychological journey back into their past. John McCluskey, Jr., states: "The refrain of the woman who with love and compassion must be willing to define herself and the responsibility such an act demands rings throughout her (Marshall's) work. The refrain is not flattened by resignation, but sharpened by affirmation, by an insistent 'I am!' All the while, however . . . the awareness of sociocultural history adds a new dimension to personal identity, defines quest and mission." Selina positively affirms her desire for individuality and independence that parallels her mother's. She asks Silla: "Remember how you used to talk about how you left home and came here alone as a girl of eighteen and was your own woman? I used to love hearing that. And that's what I want. I want it!" Selina has come to a deep realization of her personal and collective self, which she will incorporate in shaping her quest for meaning and fulfillment and in these ways the protagonist of *Brown Girl, Brownstones* has progressed from a fragmented individual self, through a turbulent awakening to a realigned whole.

> Geta J. Leseur. *Obsidian II*. 1, 1986, p. 129

[The novels of Paule Marshal]—*Brown Girl, Brownstones* (1959), *The Chosen Place, The Timeless People* (1969), and *Praisesong for the Widow* (1983)—deal with female protagonists' quests for identity in different epochs of their lives. . . . Marshall highlights age, continual process, and female mentoring and its relationship to empowerment and subsequent articulation as significant elements of her women's quests. . . .

Whereas *Brown Girl, Brownstones* generally limits the interplay of divinity and everyday reality to Selina's consciousness, *Praisesong* extends the perceptions from the point-of-view character to the controlling, creative consciousness of the narrator and the very structure of the work. The whole ritual which leads to Avey Johnson's rebirth is for "'the Old Parents . . . The Long-Time People,'" as Lebert Joseph calls the vodun spirits. Eugenia Collier points out that Lebert Joseph himself embodies an African deity, Legba. The renewed belief in and experience of myth is essential to Avey's recovery of integrity.

To recover her wholeness, Avey must recognize her participation in a racially or culturally specific myth rather than a universalist structure. Initially, she resists this identification, considering it part of the streets which threaten her family: For over twenty years, after a dream about the death of her daughters in an incident like the Birmingham church bombing, she simply forces herself to stop dreaming. In a sense Avey desires that alienation which is forced upon so many modernist protagonists. But even this lifelong, chosen repression does not alienate the Marshall individual to the point at which Ellison's invisible man or Morrison's Sula begins to function; when the individual absolutely requires sustenance, the subconscious knowledge of kinship reemerges. During the crossing to Carriacou, the island where her true self is reborn, Avey recovers her connections to a defining element of her ancestral history, the Middle Passage: "She was alone in the deckhouse. That much she was certain of. Yet she had the impression as her mind flickered on briefly of other bodies lying crowded in with her in the hot, airless dark. . . . Their suffering—the depth of it, the weight of it in the cramped space—made hers of no consequence." Avey finds her own suffering diminished, its meaning modified by the knowledge of her heritage. The Middle Passage occurs again and again as a touchstone in Afro-American writing. Equiano's and Douglass's narratives, Baldwin's *If Beale Street Could Talk,* Hayden's "Middle Passage," and Baraka's *Dutchman,* to name but a few works, explore the Passage's literal history and figurative meanings for black identity.

The Chosen Place, The Timeless People shares this mythic resonance, but its presentation of each person as a cultural microcosm allows it to avoid *Praisesong*'s thinness of characterization. Combining the mythos of *Praisesong* and the convincing individuality of *Brown Girl, Brownstones* with an added political and social consciousness, *The Chosen Place, The Timeless People* is the most richly textured of Marshall's novels. The novel dispenses with the direct family resemblances so crucial to *Brown Girl* in favor of more inclusive connections. . . .

Paule Marshall's female questers . . . achieve energized, articulate identities, with each quester resolving the problems of her particular stage of life.
An adolescent, Selina separates from her parents without rejecting them,
acknowledges her community while denying its right to determine her personality. The middle-aged Merle recovers from her disappointments in her own
character and her husband's personal rejection. Revitalized, she journeys to
Africa to establish a relationship with their child; her renewed self-respect
and consequent interest in her personal life does not signal a retreat from
her political commitment, however. For Merle, Bournehills is home, and she
intends to return to her political commitments there. As an older woman,
Avatara must throw off the psychological bondage of many years' loyalty to
a false ideal which had seemed the only means of survival. Instead of being
handicaps, her age and family position grant her the authority to educate the
youngest part of her immediate community, her grandsons. Marshall has thus
expanded the nature and duration of the classical quest pattern. The quest
is no longer an isolated if perhaps lengthy incident in the quester's life but a
lifelong commitment and, in her first two novels, a continuous modification
of identity. While speaking in her own voice of her own experience, each
quester addresses a wider community, until, in the final scene of *Praisesong,*
the empowered woman quester becomes a griot speaking in tribal language
of universal concerns.

Missy Dehn Kubitschek. *Black American*
Literature Forum. 21, 1987,
pp. 44, 47–48, 59

The heritage/ancestry relationship is clearly worked out by Paule Marshall
only in her most recent work *Praisesong for the Widow* (1983). In her first
work, *Brown Girl, Brownstones,* the conflict for the girl Selina, arises from
continual tension between her mother's rigidity and her father's contrasting
emotionalism, between the conflicting worlds of Afro-Caribbean society in
New York and her separate American experience. The girl's understanding
of culture is shaped by the many conversations of the Caribbean working
women in the kitchen, the Caribbean diet that is the mainstay of the household, the dialect from which she learns rhythm and poetry and relationships
with other Caribbean people, like Suggie, who expose Caribbean sensuality.

Marshall herself spent vacations as a child and as an adult with family
in the Caribbean. Her dedications tell the story of this connection with family
still Caribbean-based, still strong. *Reena and other Stories* is "In memory of
my aunt Branford Catherine Watson (Bam-Bam), a West Indian market
woman who thought nothing of walking fourteen miles to town and back in
a day." *Praisesong* is "For my Grandmother," the character she immortalizes
in her short story "To Da-Duh in Memoriam." It is perhaps necessary to
begin this discussion, as Eugenia Collier does, by charting the passage of
Marshall's questing character. The child in the story has been taken ostensibly to one of those "vacations" home which we know have more to do with

family identification and history than they have to do with holidaying. The story dramatizes the tensions between ancestry and youth, tradition and modernity, African civilization with its tradition of respect for humanity and Western civilization with its often callous disregard for life. The child's identity is a source of the debate which Marshall unfolds. Da-Duh is in a losing battle, pitted against the skyscrapers of New York and the war planes which swoop over Barbados towards the end of her life. For her part, Da-Duh wants to do no more than expose her granddaughter to all the features of her Caribbean, but the child has numerous examples of bigger and better things to counter Da-Duh's canefields. Yet, while the canefields are presented as idyllic, the reality is much more complicated than Collier reads it. For the irony is that canefields are so wedded to Caribbean slavery and oppression of Africans that the child's rejection of them is an important departure from that particular experience and history. Yet her acceptance of America's technological might is another form of slavery. Importantly, Marshall captures that falling away that often occurs between generations. For whereas the grandmother's experience is of slavery and British colonialism, the insidious and also "colonial" relationship to America is also implicit in the child's acceptance of American dominance. Da-Duh's resignation evinces her understanding of this new master/slave dialectic. . . .

This struggle to maintain heritage in the path of encroaching Western values is pursued relentlessly in all of Marshall's works and is crystallized in *Praisesong,* where the struggle between generations begun in "Da-Duh" takes on greater significance. Here, the protagonist is engaged, with her Great Aunt Cuney, in a dream battle, the outcome of which is that Avey must have a complete immersion into her African heritage in the Caribbean in order to maintain equilibrium. Avey's journey is beset by psychological trauma and physical agony but ends in a soothing resolution during the phase of acceptance and belonging. There is a definite Pan-Africanist focus in the relationship to heritage in *Praisesong* and in several other Marshall works. . . . Just as *Brown Girl, Brownstones* ends in conflict and departure to the Caribbean, *Praisesong* ends at the point of return to the U.S.A., the journey having been completed. The difference is that a much more controlled protagonist makes the journey in the latter. Avey is now beyond the impetuousness of youth and more fully engaged in the rituals of identification.

Carole Boyce Davies. In Carole Boyce
Davies and Elaine Savory Fido, eds. *Out of*
the Kumbla: Caribbean Women and
Literature (Trenton, New Jersey: Africa
World Press, 1990), pp. 61–62

MARTÍN GAITE, CARMEN (SPAIN) 1925–

When we finish reading a first book . . . we are always left looking toward the future, trying to make conjectures. And when the book [*The Spa*] is so well written, so beautifully written with such truth and urgency as is Carmen Martín Gaite's, we are compensated and have something to be joyful about. Carmen Martín Gaite is a perfectly formed writer, in spite of "The Spa" [the title story]. . . . For me, "The Spa" is not the best of the four stories that make up this first book, precisely because, without leaving its narrative qualities aside, she has attempted a more abstracted and intellectualized undertaking that is more in the line of Kafka than in the line of her own nature. . . . "The Spa" seems to me to be somewhat confused, whereas the style of the others stories ["The Information," "A Day of Freedom," "The Girl Below"] is crystal clear, very intimate, with a delightful and highly cultivated feminine insight, with very specific features. The complexity of the subconscious does not seem to be the dominant feature in Carmen Martín Gaite, who is outstandingly endowed with the qualities of sobriety and economy of language, tenderness and transparency. . . .

The young writer [of these stories] possesses an uncommon descriptive elegance of a writer who is well adjusted and alert, without affectation and irregularities of composition. It is, therefore, logical that her stories—principally, the last three—turn out to be stimulating. Her concise, sober prose attains a lean and well-modulated emotional level.

R. de G[arciasol]. *Ínsula.* September 15, 1955, p. 9

We have [in *Threads of Discourse*] a form of interior duplication: a written narration which consists of an oral narration in which speaking, writing, and reading are frequent topics of conversation. The relationship between the two interlocutors is analogous to that of the writer and the reader. Carmen Martín Gaite hopes to find in the reader her own ideal listener and to enlist his or her collaboration as a silent participant in a dialogue, just as Eulalia and Germán are, alternately, listeners rather than speakers. At one point Eulalia reflects upon the joy of reading which she describes as a dialogue with an absent person, adding that when a reader responds to a book it is as if he had actually seen the author's face and heard his voice. Ideally, the sharing of experiences which occurs on one level between Eulalia and Germán will be paralleled by the communication on a second level between author and reader. . . .

The key image in the novel is that of the thread, the *hilo* of a conversation, of interpersonal relationships, of one's own identity, and of life. It gives or can give continuity to an otherwise fragmented existence by connecting one's actions so that they cease to be isolated happenings. . . . "We have a thread that is lost" is the refrain of one of Germán's friends who sees this loss as the basic cause of contemporary alienation. The solution lies in communication. Participants in a conversation are depicted as grasping the two ends of a thread which they pass back and forth, weaving a fabric, embroidering a design.

Kathleen M. Glenn. *Romance Notes.*
Spring, 1979, pp. 281–82

Between Curtains's most notable structuring feature is its proliferation of points of view and even of narrators. It shares with the modern novel its loss of confidence in a single, authoritative narrative voice, and for a peremptory, reportorial embrace of reality it substitutes an assemblage of private perceptions (*Inner Fragments* is the apt title of Martín Gaite's 1976 novel), much like the beveled mirror in which Pablo sees multiple, cubistic images in motion. The traditional third-person narrator is not absent, and Martín Gaite's experiment is not nearly so radical as others of her day, but her self-conscious text is enslaved by no laws of mimetic composition and accomplishes its design as much through the playful invention of expressive modes as with the dutiful representation of reality.

Lest the reader-critic take umbrage at the notion of a serious social-realist novel vested with playfulness in its execution, it is only fair to point out that Martín Gaite openly associates herself with that bevy of modern artists who suffer no sense of shame or erosion of purpose when they view art as a game.

John W. Kronik. In Mirella Servodidio and
Marcia L. Welles, eds. *From Fiction to
Metafiction: Essays in Honor of Carmen
Martín Gaite* (Lincoln, Nebraska: Society of
Spanish and Spanish-American Studies,
1983), p. 52

By letting [an] image of the past come alive and leap out of the fixed limits of the mirror onto the flowing space of her consciousness, Martín Gaite embarks on that inward odyssey that Adrienne Rich [American feminist poet] has so eloquently called the journey of the woman artist through "the cratered night of female memory to revitalize the darkness, to retrieve what has been lost, to regenerate, reconceive and give birth" ["Re-Forming the Crystal," in Rich, *Poems: Selected and New, 1950–1974*]. Thus, in countless pages of the novel, we see her peeling away layer after layer of the past, savoring its taste and touching its contours. And it is precisely through this process of retrieving not the photographic image of the past, but its flavor, nuance and subjective reality, that Martín Gaite has further multiplied the many readings one can find in her text [of *The Back Room*]. . . . Martín Gaite's singular ability to capture the pulsations of the period and her great facility for converting the mundane into the interesting, transform *The Back Room* into not just a hybrid of the fantastic, sentimental, historical and autobiographical, but rather, a unique Bildungsroman for a whole generation of Spanish women who will undoubtedly see themselves reflected in the minute descriptions that the author provides of her own upbringing.

Linda Gould Levine. In Mirella Servodidio
and Marcia L. Welles, eds. *From Fiction to
Metafiction: Essays in Honor of Carmen
Martín Gaite* (Lincoln, Nebraska: Society of
Spanish and Spanish-American Studies,
1983), pp. 167–68

One reading suggested by [*The Back Room*] is that the reality of the Franco years cannot be apprehended by a static presentation of dates, statistics, and events; it cannot be reduced to univocal statements. The dynamic interplay of texts in *The Back Room,* on the other hand, does allow us to apprehend that the literary text is integrally woven into the sociohistorical text of the country. Above all, it points toward the plurality of meanings inherent in the very concept "text." . . .

The title of Carmen Martín Gaite's short story collection, *Las ataduras* (The bonds) . . . employs a symbolic correlation between the clinging vine and feminine bondage, but the metaphor is minimally developed, barely insinuated in a manner that might prove hermetic if not for Aldecoa's extended development of identical images. Martín Gaite's correlation probably was left implicit because of the prevailing censorship in 1960. Written in an era that Martín Santos's widely discussed novel aptly termed a "time of silence," Martín Gaite's novelette makes use of silences, omissions, and ellipses to communicate her nonconformity. In this story, the symbolism of the clambering vine is conveyed through ironic juxtapositions and the incongruity of the heroine's reaction. It is unclear to what extent the novelist relied upon an implied intertext (i.e., fixed phrases of popular discourse) as an aid for the reader's interpretation.

Because Martín Gaite wrote under strict censorial control by a regime distinguished for its hostility to feminism and the liberation of women, the symbolic import of this story is less visible than that of Aldecoa's novel. The full significance of the vine must be extrapolated from the relationship of the metaphor to the title of the novelette ("Las ataduras"), which is also the title of the short story collection as a whole. Seemingly unrelated titles were sometimes utilized as clues to a work's allegorical meanings (concealed from the censors), and this tale provides a good example of the technique.

Janet Pérez. In Noël Valis and Carol Maier,
eds. *In the Feminine Mode* (Lewisburg,
Pennsylvania: Bucknell University Press,
1990), pp. 88, 90

[Martín Gaite is] the most studied contemporary woman writer of Spain. It is clear that her stature rests on a body of work that is complex and varied but which reveals certain overriding consistencies. These include her effective, "conversational" prose, mastery of multiple techniques, skill as a social observer, and astute depictions of the lives of women.

The most pervasive quality in Martín Gaite's fiction is that it seems to be addressed, even spoken, to a respected colleague. For this author, the reader is a conversational partner who enables her to fulfill an urgent desire to communicate. In unpretentious yet expert prose, she captivates with storytelling skill at the same time that she engages the reader in assembling meaning from cues that range from the documentary—as in *Entre visillos,* to the playfully ambiguous—as in *El cuarto de atrás.* A related question of the characteristics, boundaries, and power of oral and written narrative is both explored and actualized in two of her novels, *Retahílas* and *El cuarto de atrás,* which consist of cathartic conversational interchanges. The precursor of these novels, *Ritmo lento,* focuses on the failure of a "talking cure" with a deficient conversational partner, a psychiatrist whom the patient holds in low regard.

Throughout her work Martín Gaite has experimented with new techniques and repeatedly has been ahead of her time in her choice of literary directions. Her first novella, *El balneario,* introduced techniques in 1954 that would not become widespread for at least twenty years, including a fantastic episode and an oneiric exploration of the main character's subconscious mind. Along with other members of the Generation of Mid-Century, she participated in the documentary realism of the 1950s; her cinematic descriptions and seemingly tape-recorded dialogues are among the most accomplished of her group. Her 1958 *Entre visillos* is the best example of this method, which is also represented by her 1960 *Las ataduras.* She went on to help introduce a new type of social novel in 1962 with *Ritmo lento,* in which objective realism was replaced by a synchronic narrative collage that probed the psychology of a maladapted yet superior individual. Martín Gaite created a new genre with her 1974 *Retahílas,* a series of spontaneous, interlocking verbal missives created by chance over the course of one night, and couched between the text's two objective "bookends." Her action-adventure story *Fragmentos de interior,* published in 1976, was a very early entry into the escapist action genre, a literary category that only recently has been taken seriously by the critical elite. In her 1979 *El cuarto de atrás,* the conversational format of *Retahílas* recurs, both with several twists: one of the conversational partners represents Carmen Martín Gaite herself, and the other may be an apparition. Neither the narrator nor the reader can resolve the ambiguity of this metafictional text, which mysteriously "writes itself."

Her techniques have always abetted Martín Gaite's observation of Spanish society. Over four decades she has been an anthropologist to her own culture, a social critic who analyzes Spanish society of the twentieth century with the trained eye that she uses in her nonfiction explorations of eighteenth-century Spain. Her social analysis began in the mainstream of Spanish neo-realism of the 1950s, which focused on everyday, "non-literary" people. In the 1960s she depicted the psychology of an individual who was sanctioned for being superior to the mediocre values of society. In the 1970s, Martín Gaite overtly criticized the decay of contemporary society, and especially the deterioration of language; the superficiality of the European youth culture also came under her scrutiny. When censorship ended, Martín Gaite retrieved recollections of the bizarre nature of life for her generation, who came of age in the civil war and lived in its repressive aftermath for close to forty years. Beyond her fascination with society as a whole, Martín Gaite is more specifically concerned with the lives of women. It can be argued that her acuity as a social observer is directly related to her gender and to the alienation felt by intellectual women of her generation in Spain, who could not help but resent the traditional social directives that would have had them limit their sights to being the mirror of a man. There are woman heroes in Martín Gaite's fiction, and they pursue what have been termed "quest plots" in their lives, seeking to fulfill personal ambitions and to accomplish individual goals.

Not only have Martín Gaite's depictions of women been sensitive and compelling, they have been audacious. In the 1950s she ventured that proper spinsters can have repressed but furious longings for adventure *(El balneario),* and she devoted a serious novel to a year in the life of a provincial adolescent girl. The protagonist of her 1962 novel *Ritmo lento* criticized the prevailing notion of women as possessions, and with even greater insight, she attacked women who perpetuated this injustice. When social mores relaxed in the 1970s, Martín Gaite did not romanticize women's new freedom: she reported honestly on the ageist double standard that discriminated against women in *Retahílas* and in *Fragmentos de interior,* and ridiculed the "liberated woman" who traded sexual favors for job advancement in the latter novel. Martín Gaite's most recent representation of a woman was based on a presentation of her own autobiography and depicts a famous woman writer granting an interview to a male admirer. . . .

Perhaps no less than her accomplished prose style, they underly the success of the person who helped to invent a new category in contemporary Spanish literature: the master writer who is a woman.

Joan L. Brown. In *Women Writers of
Contemporary Spain* (Newark, Delaware:
University of Delaware Press, 1991),
pp. 86–89

The conversations of Martín Gaite's narrative texts are not heard but read. Though texts like *Retahílas* and *El cuarto de atrás* may appear to be spoken, they are not unmediated speech. (This playful deception is undermined in *El cuarto* when pages of a manuscript multiply simultaneously with the interlocutor's spoken discourse.) The unique power of these later narratives by Martín Gaite is their dynamic blend of orality and textuality, their refusal to opt for the either-or of "langue" or "parole." They exemplify most distinctively, among narratives by women at this time, the creation of text as play and production (theorized most clearly by Barthes) and writing as a process of opening meaning, a maneuver described by Derrida as inherent in writing. The ludic nature of Martín Gaite's later narratives, especially *El cuarto,* consists thus in a playing with the strategies of both speech and writing while opting for neither as mutually exclusive. In this way, *Retahílas* and *El cuarto,* by performing the Derridean move of putting into doubt a system of oppositions, break the boundaries of those oppositional structures that have underwritten logocentric texts and culture, thus opening the way to meanings outside them.

This impulse to write beyond the boundaries of a mutually exclusive orality and textuality is paralleled in Martín Gaite's work by an analogous desire to break through oppositions governing cultural definitions of gender. Yet, though critical attention to Martín Gaite's contribution as a social critic has also been extensive, her importance as a vanguard figure in the transformation of narrative strategies specific to the interplay of gender and textuality has not been as widely documented. It is this aspect of Martín Gaite's work, the one that is most crucial for the establishment of theoretical links with preceding and succeeding narrative strategies by other women writers. . . .

By reshaping their intertexts through reclamation and revision, these two later narratives by Carmen Martín Gaite employ a synthesis of voice and pen determined to "make things happen" and "invent something new."

Elizabeth J. Ordoñez. *Voices of Their Own:*
Contemporary Spanish Novels by Woman
(Lewisburg, Pennsylvania: Bucknell
University Press, 1991), pp. 78, 100

El cuarto de atrás is predicated on the escapism characteristic of children's fantasy literature, as Martín Gaite would be the first to point out. As she notes in an interview: "When one experiences the dazzling impact of reading at an early age, the effect is akin to that of an arrow wound. Reading provides insight into a secret world that liberates one from the hostile pressures of the environment, from the routines and deception that the confrontation with reality produces." In line with the thrust of Martín Gaite's observation, *El cuarto de atrás* consistently draws attention to the haven provided by the world of fantasy, romantic fiction and the fairy tale in the narrator's mind. Intriguingly, however, the worlds of fantasy and reality are never presented in the novel as separate worlds; there is, indeed, often an uncanny interrelation, and even identity, between them.

Martín Gaite's use of motifs derived from the "novela rosa," therefore, has the specific purpose of overturning the patrocentric fallacy. *El cuarto de atrás,* like the discourse of feminism, refuses simply to reflect passively the patriarchal myth and thereby produces a text which is at once metafictional and feminist. *El cuarto de atrás,* thus, narrates the history of a "psychic growth." When the novel concludes, as Ruth El Saffar notes, the reader is reassured that the association between dreaming and "madness and danger" has been dispelled; the narrator "has transformed her tossing and turning, through the recording of a mysterious dialogue born out of insomnia, into a virtue." Metatextuality, the "novela rosa" and the fairy tale have, thus, been triumphantly woven into a new syntax designed to liberate womanhood from the law of the patriarchal *master* text and produce a new *mater* text.

Stephen M. Hart. *White Ink: Essays on Twentieth-Century Feminine Fiction in Spain and Latin America* (London: Tamesis, 1993), pp. 72, 78

MARTINSON, MOA (SWEDEN) 1890–1964

Moa Martinson's first novel, *Women and Appletrees (Kvinnor och äppelträd)*, was published in Sweden in 1933. Sweden's working-class readers were already familiar with the essays and serialized stories she had published in proletarian journals. *Women and Appletrees* secured their devotion and enlarged Martinson's audience in Sweden's then hierarchical society. Critics could not ignore Martinson's remarkable first novel, but this largely male bourgeois literary establishment was clear in its consensus: *Women and Appletrees,* while realistic and poignant, was undisciplined, muddled, hastily written. In her varied succession of novels, short stories, and poems, Moa Martinson paid no attention to critics; neither did her readers. Even after her death in 1964, her immense popularity in Sweden hardly diminished. In 1973, her publishers began reissuing her novels, *Women and Appletrees* appearing in both hardcover and paperback in 1975. A new generation of readers and critics warmly appreciated her vigorous, inimitable style, which combines her witty, deeply felt response not only to life's almost intolerable burdens but also to its limitless joys. . . .

Although Martinson begins her novel with Mother Sofi's generation in rural Sweden in the 1840s, it is chiefly her own, from the 1890s to shortly after World War I, that she depicts through her autobiographical characters, Sally and Ellen. *Women and Appletrees* is a novel about women's struggles to endure and overcome the poverty, brutality, and loneliness they suffered in the slums of industrial Norrköping and Stockholm, and in the farming villages between them.

The experiences Martinson relates, her own and those she heard from others, particularly her mother and grandmother, are exuberantly vigorous, for she writes as if she were telling them to an immediate audience. The novel, thus, is written in a flexible, conversational style, one story following the other. Martinson only interrupts the flow of the stories to intersperse dialogue, growing out of and enhancing them, or to universalize a specific happening, offering choric commentary about life, nature, war, and society.

Her use of this convention is perhaps didactic and may be somewhat jarring to modern readers as they move from her fictional creation to her commentary or interpretation. It is here that Martinson's time clock—her shifts from the present to the past, or to the historical or eternal present, when the text compels them—must engage closer attention, or the novel might seem to lose artistic precision. That it does not (anymore than a dexterous use of stream of consciousness) shows her skill.

To sustain the sense of immediacy that she depends on, Martinson uses repetition, gives hints of future action that spur the reader's attention, inserts details that might seem irrelevant, but which evoke time and place, compelling her listener-reader to identify with her intensely personalized characters. The rhythm of her sentences is that of spoken Swedish, the sing-song music of this tonal language. . . .

In the oral tradition that Martinson uses, symbols have even greater importance in the novel's construction. The title she chooses—*Women and Appletrees*—immediately elicits a sensual response; the image, elemental, evocative, has a wondrous simplicity. Martinson uses the apple tree in each of its seasonal changes—mossy greenness, flowering beauty, burnished glow, bare sturdiness—to emphasize her main characters' strength and imagination to endure their hard lives and triumph over them. . . .

Sweden's literary critics largely dismissed [Martinson's] novels as limited and undisciplined. In her updated preface to *My Mother Gets Married,* Moa quotes a critic who ridiculed her novel as "food for the dump." Another critic more generously echoed the opinion of his fellows in his assessment of her novels: "a gaudy splash of color" in the "thirties' naturalistic *statare* school of romanticists." This attitude has deservedly and fortunately changed. Her novels have been praised by critics in books as diverse as literary histories and anthologies of radical working-class writers. This criticism is especially true of her autobiographical trilogy, including the already mentioned *My Mother Gets Married, Church Wedding (Krykbröllop,* 1938), and *The King's Roses (Kungens Rosor,* 1939). Moa Martinson's most perceptive critics have always been women. . . .

Margaret S. Lacy. Afterword to Moa
Martinson. *Women and Appletrees* (New
York: Feminist Press, 1985),
pp. 199–202, 209–10

In her 1956 foreword to a new edition of her fourth novel, *My Mother Gets Married,* published in 1936, Moa Martinson, out of love and deference for her mother, writes that the main character in the book is her mother. Strong as Martinson makes the characterization of Hedvig, her mother, it is clearly Martinson's own self-portrait, Mia, who is the central character in this first volume of her autobiographical trilogy. All of the experiences in the novel are described through Mia's eyes, and only she reflects upon these experiences that occur in two years of her life. She is nearly seven when the novel begins and nine when it ends. The action takes place in Norrköping, an industrial city in Sweden, and in factory suburbs and on farms surrounding it, just before the turn of the century. *Church Wedding,* the second novel of the trilogy, chronicles Mia's next five years in the same setting. The novel ends with Mia's letter to a former schoolmate who has emigrated to America; Mia turns down Lasse's offer of marriage. The last novel, *The King's Roses,* like the first, covers two years in Mia's life. From fifteen to seventeen, Mia has been a children's maid in a neighboring parish, a waitress in a large restaurant in Norrköping, and for a brief time, a student waitress in Stockholm. At the end of the trilogy, Martinson provides a tantalizing glimpse of Mia ten years later. Twenty-seven years old, Mia is married to a shiftless drunkard; she is striving to take care of her children; and in her home south of Stockholm, she is holding meetings for farm workers to better their living and working conditions.

My Mother Gets Married, like *Church Wedding* and *The King's Roses,* encompasses a narrow world, but it is one that gives the illusion of roominess because it is shaped by an oral tradition that blends fairy tale and folklore with realistic events and detail. The stories that Martinson relates through her persona (Mia) grow out of the child's quest for adventure, and for knowledge that will enable her to understand a harsh reality, one filled with all the dreadful adjuncts of poverty: hunger, cruelty, disease, dirt, ignorance, superstition, violence, often early death. These are like the mythical monsters of the fairy tale that the child must deal with in order to bring some kind of order out of confusion, to rejoice over small victories, and to keep dignity with a plucky response.

My Mother Gets Married is artistically Moa Martinson's best book. Because it is told solely from Mia's point of view, the novel not only has a consistent psychological position, but also a tightly knit structure that admits little of the didactic interpolation that jars the modern reader in Martinson's first novel, *Women and Appletrees.* Except for the leading characters, the rest are emblematic. Martinson skillfully uses this device of folklore to widen her perspective. Thus, characterizations of people, such as "the red-haired woman," "the neighbor with her peaked cap," "the landlady" of the "sugar-syrup house," "the farmer," and "Aunt" universalize them and their experiences. . . .

Moa Martinson's role as a novelist of woman's enduring strength is secure. Despite its harsh theme, *My Mother Gets Married* can be drolly humorous. Mia's resourcefulness engages readers at once and continues to charm them. She is feisty, quick, and imaginative. Like her mother and her grandma, Mia never gives up any battle even when she knows she cannot win. Sometimes dishonest with others, Mia is always honest with herself. She is often baffled by the contradictory behavior of "the grown-ups," but she never loses her sense of wonder and hope. Moa does not sentimentalize Mia; she is a consistently believable child. In creating the character of Mia, Martinson draws upon memories, always colorful, often harrowing, of her own childhood, and filters them through her adult sensibility. It is the autobiographical character of Mia that will make Moa Martinson's novel, *My Mother Gets Married*, endure.

> Margaret S. Lacy. Afterword to Moa Martinson. *My Mother Gets Married* (New York: Feminist Press, 1988), pp. 277–78, 284–85

Although it suffers from some awkward and didactic prose, Martinson's first volume in her autobiographical trilogy is a potent, wrenching portrait of the impoverished Swedish working class. Mia's mother gets married for the first time when Mia is six years old, and through the child's piercing eyes are revealed "neverending hardships like mean teachers, bad men who beat their women, and 'aunts' who got big and moaned and groaned about it." As Lacy, who also translated Martinson's *Women and Appletrees,* notes, the narrative style is shaped by an oral tradition that blends fairy tale and folklore with realistic events and detail. Except for the principals, the characters are emblematic and therefore universal: "the red-haired woman"; "the farmer." Martinson's reputation as a champion of the proletariat is here affirmed as she reimagines through her persona Mia her own grievous roots in a male-dominated, largely aristocratic society: the stigma of illegitimacy, poverty's attendant ostracism, filth, illness, hunger and superstition, and her frequent brutalization by alcoholic and philandering men.

> Penny Kaganoff. *Publishers Weekly.* December 9, 1988, pp. 57–58

As Margaret S. Lacy points out in her afterword, *Mor gifter sig* (the title of the Swedish original, published in 1936) is generally considered the most artistically successful of Moa Martinson's fiction. This classic of Swedish working-class literature is the first volume in a trilogy which also encompasses *Kyrkbröllop* (1938, Church wedding) and *Kungens rosor* (1939, The king's roses). All three volumes are autobiographical: in *My Mother Gets Married,* the first person narrator, Mia, is obviously Moa herself. However, the heroine (in more senses than one) of the book is the mother, Hedvig.

The setting of the novel is the Swedish provincial city of Norrköping and environs, around the turn of the century. Mia, with her mother and stepfather, moves from one-room apartment to one-room apartment, one shabbier than the other. Toward the end, temporarily forsaken by the shiftless stepfather, they take refuge with various relatives. All during this time, the mother suffers through repeated pregnancies, none of them resulting in a child who survives its first year.

The novel is a wonderful description of poor people's Sweden around the turn of the century, and of a world seen through the eyes of a child. One enjoys the story and gets to like the plucky, inquisitive Mia and her strong, gallant mother. Their personalities light up the outward grimness, which is also alleviated by episodes of shining happiness, such as Mia's love for her little schoolmate Hanna, the help the mother is able to give a neighbor who is too young and ignorant to cope with her infant, and the story of Mia's trip to the family of a cobbler in Kolmården.

Yvonne L. Sandstroem. *Scandinavian
Studies.* 63, 1991, pp. 252–53

MASON, BOBBIE ANN (UNITED STATES) 1940–

The stories of Bobbie Ann Mason have appeared in publications such as *Redbook, The New Yorker, The Atlantic Monthly,* and the *Washington Post* magazine. They are the kind of stories in which little seems to happen, the prototypical *New Yorker* format set in the modern Southern landscape. She tends not to describe big events, dramatic moments of confrontation or self-awareness. Instead, she writes with a precise and evocative sense of detail: she defines by accumulation. Her characters live in the world of K-Marts and cable TV, but they come from another world altogether. They are beset by a change that is too rapid and all-encompassing, caught between the culture of their heritage, which no longer holds except in memory or guilt, and that of the present, which has effectively displaced, transformed and cheapened the traditional. Understatement is at the heart of her style, and it results in a restrained tension throughout. She depicts her characters in [their] entropy, losing their strengths, their beliefs, and finding nothing substantial to replace them. While her details and sense of place give her stories their distinctly Southern identity, her characters suffer from a kind of universal modern malaise. These concerns are often stated in rather ordinary terms, which perhaps belie their importance. A bowl of strawberries, a dying dog, the habits of cats, chicken lice, New Wave music, all achieve a level of significance not at all forced in the telling. . . .

The fiction of Bobbie Ann Mason shows a world in transition. Her land is rich in tradition, but her people don't know quite what to do with it. As one says, "You think things are one way and then they get turned around and you lose track of how they used to be." Her characters are neither *in* nor *out* of place: those who stay feel provincial and yearn for something better; those who leave feel rootless and fragmented and turn back for some order. She does not advocate a sentimental return to the past, but she does propose a kind of emotional commitment which she too often finds lacking in the present, a willingness to share and support which she associates with family and place, with tradition and history. Her stories are open-ended, inconclusive, but their structure mirrors the world they describe.

Edwin T. Arnold. *Appalachian Journal.* 12,
1985, pp. 135–36, 139

It's generally claimed that Bobbie Ann Mason is writing about the guts of the guts of the country, but to assume that *In Country* is therefore a nouveau pastoral dream of, when all's said and done, good hearts in simple people is like thinking Springsteen's "Born in the U.S.A." is a simple, warm-hearted, up-beat song and suitable for use at Super Bowl half-time festivities and as the basis for jingles urging us to vote America by buying Detroit-made cars. I mean, let's look at what the words are really saying. I have no heart left for life in America at all, and no hope for any of her characters, or real-life people like them, when Mason is finished with them. They are grotesques, and their country is Franchise City. Maybe they are; maybe it is; Mason's prose does not work to go deeply into these lives but to distort their surface images as though they were being reflected off loose hubcaps. Diane Arbus, not Sherwood Anderson.

Which is legitimate of course; it's anyone's right, and maybe modern U.S.A. as it is lived by lots of people is thus most truthfully portrayed. What puzzles me, however, is why readers and reviewers continue to use words like "charming" and "deeply respectful" to describe a vision that is so terrifying, stripping, disheartening. It's not the story line of this novel, which is a conventional trajectory of hope. A just-on-the-verge-of-life, eighteen-year-old, small-Kentucky-town girl, Sam, is seeking the future by trying to know the past. For what substance and enlightenment she finds she may as well be seeking lost Atlantis, but all she wants is to understand an event less than twenty years old, and lived by many: the Vietnam War. "In country" is where her farm-boy father was killed before she was born; where most of the men, vets, she knows in her small town were mentally, physically, or emotionally damaged, including her Uncle Emmett, who may have been exposed to Agent Orange, and with whom she still lives—he's her family, she's his. At least poor Emmett has many of the symptoms—acne, headaches, gas—which he, through fear and disillusionment with "them"—"they" won't care, "they" won't listen—tries to laugh off. Sam has fastened not only on trying to get Emmett to go to the V.A. hospital for tests, but on anything about the war; she wants Vietnam, even its trees, or birds, to come real for her, to be explained or described. . . .

The source of deepest terror in this novel is not the plot or the characterization, but the style; and the recurrent, pervasive image of terror is brand-name junk. The nature of that junk, a piece of which appears in almost any sentence, is oxymoronic: this reiterated trash—Pontiac Thunderbird, Dairy Queen, Dodge Dart, Burger Boy, Exxon, K-Mart, Ford Cobra, Holiday Inn, Howard Johnson's, MTV, Billy Joel, the Kinks, re-runs of *M*A*S*H*, *Reader's Digest*, plastic quarts of Coke and Pepsi and Mountain Dew, Doritos, chips 'n dip, Egg McMuffins, Ready-to-Heat Tacos, Gerber's "Blueberry Buckle," styrofoam cartons, Saran Wrap, Velcro, Acrylic, Tupperware, Formica—is terrifying because it's stuff that is cheap, flimsy, ugly, and utterly temporary, carrying no message, no texture, no touch, no history, no beauty, no way back or forward, no help for human life and, at the same time utterly

permanent. Non-biodegradable nothingness laid as solidly across life and mind as the Interstates and Malls are laid across what used to be farm land.
Alice Bloom. *New England Quarterly.* 8,
1986, pp. 519–21

Shiloh and Other Stories, her major work of fiction . . . was nominated for the National Book Award in 1983. Throughout this collection Mason dramatizes the bewildering effects of rapid social change on the residents of a typical "ruburb"—an area in Western Kentucky that is "no longer rural but not yet suburban." Again and again in these stories old verities are questioned as farm families watch talk-show discussions of drug use, abortion, and pre-marital sex. Old relationships are strained as wives begin to lift weights or play video games with strange men. In such contexts the sense of self is besieged from all sides and becomes highly vulnerable. As O. B. Hardison has observed, "Identity seems to be unshakable, but its apparent stability is an illusion. As the world changes, identity changes. . . . Because the mind and the world develop at different rates and in different ways, during times of rapid change they cease to be complementary. . . . The result is a widening gap between the world as it exists in the mind and the world as it is experienced—between identity formed by tradition and identity demanded by the present."

Mason's stories document many efforts to bridge such a gap. Although the behavior of her characters is diverse, two basic patterns are apparent. When faced with confusion about their proper roles, they tend to become either doers or seekers. They stay put and attempt to construct a new identity or they light out for the territories in the hope of discovering one.
Albert E. Wilhelm. *Southern Literary
Journal.* 18, 1986, pp. 76–77

Compared with Southerners who generations earlier lived in traditional small-town communities unvexed by the problems of modernity, Mason's characters possess much more individual freedom. Their places in society, unlike those of their forebears, are no longer so rigidly defined. But this freedom comes with a cost. Her characters frequently suffer from severe insecurity; many wallow in feelings of aimlessness and confusion. To compensate for the absence of a moral vision that could give their lives direction and commitment, they look to self-fulfillment as the ultimate ideal. One judges others (and treats them accordingly) not by the integrity of their actions but by the role they play in helping—or hindering—one's quest for self. In such a world, cherished bonds and commitments dissolve seemingly on characters' momentary whims. Priorities seem askew. . . .

For Leroy and most of Mason's other characters, history, except during moments of extraordinary crisis, is not a shaping force, alive and vital. Certainly the Civil War experience no longer defines Mason's Southerners. While several other characters—Kay in "Offerings" and Nancy in "Nancy Culpepper" for instance—gain a larger perspective of their lives by investigating the relevance of their Southern roots, none appears rewarded with a fullness of vision that will carry them forward to further growth. While Mason often establishes in her stories a tension between a traditional past and a modernist present, very similar to the paradigm found in much of the literature of the Southern renascence, she does so only to show how this tension no longer carries any significant weight and authority. The present order is so overwhelming and so pervasive in the modern consciousness that the ways of the distant past pose little challenge to it; only in moments of crisis or in unusual situations does the tension surface, and then it usually leads merely to momentary, not ongoing insight. . . .

Thinking back on the 1960s, or indeed on any period that seriously challenges one's present life, it is not for Mason a foolproof means of growth. Certainly there are a number of characters in her stories who are acutely aware of the significant changes that their lives have undergone but who nonetheless are anguished and unhappy. These people, who often focus their attention for fulfillment entirely on the present moment, have cultivated a detachment from the past so that whatever meaning it potentially carries is reduced merely either to nostalgia or intellectual curiosity. In both cases, history becomes a set of experiences that bears little relevance to one's present life. Such detachment is what plagues Jack Cleveland in "Lying Doggo" until the very end of the story when he opens himself up to the wisdom of the past (from his days of counterculture experiment with his wife) and celebrates a quickening of knowledge and spirit. Jack's growth is similar to Edwin Creech's: both have been renewed by their acceptance into their lives of a vital sense of history. Both, furthermore, draw upon the events of the 1960s and 1970s, a period drastically different from the time in which they now live; and both discover that his searing dichotomy between past and present offers perspective and dialectical challenge.

Robert H. Brinkmayer, Jr. Southern Literary Journal. 19, 1987, pp. 22–23, 26–28

Much has been written about the loss of identity experienced by the characters of Bobbie Ann Mason's short stories; the people of Shiloh and Other Stories in particular seem to be confused by the onslaught of pop culture, the media, and other forces of social change. The males, perhaps, seem the more affected, and more ineffectual in their attempts to seize or to create some new center for their lives. The women, at least most of them, react to their frustration and discontent more forcefully; they are or become downhome feminists, and the degree of their feminist responses within their culture is largely determined by education, by economic empowerment, and by age, or by some combination of the three. . . .

It is important to see that the downhome feminists of these stories do not want what their city cousins want: equal legal and political rights, equal access to careers, equal pay, government support of child care, and so on.

Mason's women simply want breathing space in their relationships with their men. Sometimes only divorce, always initiated by the women, will provide the degree of change these women seek but sometimes their assertiveness merely aims for a change of pace—casual adultery, for example. . . .

Bobbie Anne Mason has an uncanny ability to capture the state of mind of the women of rural Western Kentucky in the 1970s. As that culture becomes more homogenized, more integrated with the general American culture, these women will lose their special identity and their special problems. They will become more like Nancy Culpepper and the narrator of "Residents and Transients" as they become better educated and more economically independent. They will have more complex relationships with their men and families; their lives will be more refined, more introspective—and the trade-off in vigor and earthiness may leave them far less interesting.

G. O. Morpheus. Southern Literary Journal.
22, 1989, pp. 41–42, 49

Mason's grainy portraits of small-town America, written in a deadpan prose, are an appropriate *mise-en-scene* for examining the interplay between people and popular culture, and this is where Mason works, though she appears to eschew any profound meaning in popular art. . . .

For Mason, part of what makes up "the quality of experience in everyday life"—at least in her fiction—is not only the generic furniture of mass culture but the "significance" of popular art ("what it means ultimately") as well. In other words, no matter how banal, demeaning or forgettable, popular culture is formative, and in Mason's fiction it appears as the foreground on which her characters move. Mason's treatment of popular culture—and popular music in particular—in *Shiloh and Other Stories* and *In Country* provokes aggressive questions about that culture, its effect on us and about the nature of art in a high technology society: how does pop culture enter into the lives of people and what is its function there? If people even bother to take it in, or if they unknowingly absorb it, what then do they do with it? How good or schlocky does a piece of pop culture have to be in order to make it into fiction? Is pop culture less significant when it is just part of the day-to-day than when it bears hard on the day-to-day?. . .

Mason has recently referred to her "'writing as my version of rock'n'-roll. . . .' Both are 'a kind of positive energy' that embody . . . 'hope for a better world.'" Because Mason writes fiction and not rock songs, in hoping for a better world she looks first to find out what can make life limiting and unfulfilling. Across the neon and billboard rural landscape move men and women—numbed by their own limited intentions—whose acquiescence illustrates a persistent American irony: the promise of utopia and success set against the fact of separation and failure. Mason depicts this irony variously, but perhaps most sharply by examining how popular culture affects lived experience. The best popular culture has always justified itself by disturbing the peace on the one hand and on the other by commenting on the reality most said it blurred if not denied altogether. The worst popular art creations, and perhaps the most destructive, are "designed not to trouble, but to reassure; they do not reflect reality, they merely rearrange its elements into something we can bear." Mass culture of this sort is flimsy, escapist, superficial, but often as dangerous, as manipulative and as interesting as the most provocative "high art." Baldwin comments that popular culture "can only reflect our chaos: and perhaps we better remember that this chaos contains life—and a great transforming energy." In *Shiloh,* popular culture most often functions divisively, isolating the characters or tranquilizing them; but in her novel, Mason shows how popular art, especially popular music, can be a means of continuity and communication. Mason wouldn't disagree that popular culture reflects our chaos, but she seems more drawn to those elements and kinds of popular art which create it (producing a vital spark in the culture) and those which destroy it (creating a cultural exhaustion that just might lead to growth through decay) but mostly to what happens to people as these impulses vie for ascendence.

Leslie White. *Southern Quarterly.* 26, 1988,
pp. 71, 78–79

Mason has never outgrown her intense feelings for rock 'n' roll ("If you grow up on Chuck Berry and Little Richard, it never leaves you," she said in one of her interviews), and indeed rock music continues to be a shaping experience in her life and literature. "Is music important to you personally?" asked one of her interviewers. "Oh yes!" Mason replied. "Writing is my version of rock 'n' roll." Rock music is everywhere in her fiction—being listened to, discussed, and dreamed about—and in her interviews Mason always appears eager to assert her allegiances to her rock heroes. . . .

Mason's fascination with rock music clearly transcends merely musical enjoyment—though of course there's clearly much of that too—and might be best understood as a crucial element in her larger interest in and sympathy for popular culture. Despite having a Ph.D. in English literature and a book on Nabokov, Mason recoils from what she sees as the hypocrisy and elitism of "high culture." Her feelings are clearly embodied in her fiction—a fiction of what might best be called "ordinary folks," working-class people and their concerns. "They're the people I'm drawn to," she told Wendy Smith, and she went on to say that early in her career she consciously chose to write about these people in large part because she "was so sick of reading about the alienated hero of refined sensibility." "It's important to me," she told Smith, speaking of her ties with her characters, "and I can relate to their problems more easily than I can to more middle-class concerns. I think the lives of people like this have just as much depth and sensitivity as anyone else's."

Robert H. Brinkmeyer, Jr. *Mississippi
Quarterly.* 42, 1988–89, pp. 5–7

Bobbie Ann Mason explains that she did not consciously choose to write about Vietnam, that she had characters and action in mind before she realized that they had something to do with the war. She says, "I think it came out of my unconscious, the same way it's coming out of America's unconscious. It's just time for it to surface." *In Country* shows how the conscious and subconscious minds of three generations of men and women have been affected by the Vietnam War. . . .

Although the novel focuses on seventeen-year-old Sam Hughes' search for the meaning of the Vietnam War, particularly the death of her father, it explores the personal loss of other members of the Hughes family and the changes brought by the war to the community and the nation. *In Country* is structured around two quests. Sam, her grandmother MawMaw, and her uncle Emmett make a three-day journey by car to Washington, D.C. to see the Vietnam War Memorial. This quest is the result of another—Sam's going both literally and figuratively into the wilderness, or "in country," to test her ability to survive. "In country" is the phrase veterans use to refer to their time in Vietnam, and Cawood's pond, a dangerous swamp, is Sam's symbolic Vietnam. . . .

The archetype of Sam's journey may be Psyche's search. Sam is, like Psyche, the feminine principle: "Psyche divinized is consciousness raised. Her journey is the feminine journey from blind, instinctual attraction to a knowing, individualized love." Sam moves from caring for Emmett because he is family and a real life version of the damaged veterans on television to real love for her uncle and understanding of his deep sorrow.

Sam's quest, like Psyche's, is motivated by distrust, jealousy, hatred, and fear. Her distrust of the social system, her jealousy of Irene, her hatred of the war, and her fear for Emmett's health and sanity have separated her from her family and friends and have created division within herself. Sam's going in country enables her to deal with these feelings as Psyche's solitary ordeals purge her. Like Psyche, "by attending to the self in isolation, rather than repressing its demands or seeking distractions, [Sam's] process of discovery is furthered.

Sandra Bonilla Durham. *Southern Literary
Journal.* 22, 1990, pp. 45–47

MATUTE, ANA MARÍA (SPAIN) 1926–

The name of Ana María Matute was completely unknown to us before it was heard in the voting proceedings of the Nadal Prize of 1947. . . . Her novel, which played a big part in those proceedings, has just been published, and followers of this prize—so unjustly and stupidly attacked these days by a legion of resentful people—can judge for themselves the merits of *The Abel*

Family, whose young author is no more than twenty-two years old. I mention this fact about her age not because I believe that it is enough information for us to agree about a novel that is of decent quality—and *The Abel Family* is much more than that—but because one cannot demand from a novelist in her twenties what can be expected in one who is sixty. Let us say right away that the first half of *The Abel Family,* the whole section that takes place in a mining town, strongly attracted our attention from the first pages, and revealed a novelist to us. The sober description of the environment, the slightly acidic portrayal of the characters, the modern sense of narrative and dialogue, and above all, the bold and contradictory strength of certain characters—like Valba and her brothers and sisters—succeed in capturing our interest. The author achieves naturalness in the narration and knows how to avoid overly elaborate literary effects. The harsh and bare world of the Abels—the father and the six children—is captured in its exact and mysterious waves of light and shadow, of goodness and evil. . . . The author soon decides that they should abandon the village and escape to the city. One after another they flee their land and themselves. The reader laments this disbanding and thinks that it is a pity that the author has not maintained up until the end of the novel the dry and harsh, although harmonious, atmosphere of the piece of unyielding land that the Abels inhabited in the village. If the author had not given in to the easy recourse of moving her characters to the city to search for new contrasts and accidental happenings, and if she had granted more space to passion in her work, we would probably have been able to say of Ana María Matute that she was the Spanish Emily Brontë. But the Abels's reaction in the city disconcerts us, and the arid harmony of the violent world of the village loses its freshness and ends up disappearing. Everything falls apart, not only the house in the village, but the intense world, the beautiful flame of the Abels. In the city they soon seem like rag dolls, wretched puppets who do not persuade us. We stop loving them and close the book thinking that a great novel has been stymied. But the name of Ana María Matute will not be forgotten by us. In her is the mark of a true novelist.

J. L. Cano. *Ínsula.* February 15, 1949, p. 5

We have before us a short, exemplary little book [*The Stupid Children*], a minuscule wisp of a book, a violent and very tender book, a deep and venomous book that by itself would be enough to give a stamp of uniqueness to its author. Ana María Matute, in a most potent and honest voice, forces her bitter and naked soul to cry out amid a panorama, that is, a literary panorama, in which women writers, for the sake of appearing pious and proper, sweeten—or weaken—the voice that God gave them and dress up in—or hide behind—the vain clothing of empty whited sepulchers.

Joyously, openly . . . we proclaim our admiration for these stupid children who have sprung from the head of Ana María Matute, a woman who has learned how to prolong, to unforeseen limits, the cruelty, the ingenuity, and the astonishing amazement of children. Up until the age of ten we are all geniuses, according to Huxley. Ana María Matute, with the knowledge of her thirty years on her shoulders, has had the good sense—and the good fortune (everything is not preplanned)—to leave her heart in girlish braids. And from this attitude has been born the most important book, in any genre, that a woman has published in Spain since Doña Emilia Pardo Bazán.

. . . *The Stupid Children* will leave an indelible mark on Spanish letters. . . . And as we do with Federico García Lorca with his *Gypsy Ballads,* we will be able to do with Ana María Matute—to blame her for the mindless sterility of her followers, who will not be few in number. Kant said that genius is the means through which nature gives rules to art. And the art of Ana María Matute, in this brief, exemplary little book, comes ruled by her memory of childhood, which constitutes for our author all its authentic and fresh nature.

Camilo José Cela. *Papeles de son armadans.*
July, 1957, pp. 107–8

[Matute] is a writer who gives a feeling of grandeur rather than one of novelty. *Fiesta in the Northwest* and above all *First Memory* vividly recall to us the work of Truman Capote, in particular his *Other Voices, Other Rooms.* Both the Spaniard and the American recount difficult adolescences, childhoods that stick to adults like mud to the souls of boots, paradises that are green and black at the same time, incorruptible destiny. Even more, the loneliness of people, those tragic lands: Castile and Louisiana. In Matute and also in Capote, children create the myth of the all-powerful father, a myth that one day collapses and pushes Joel Knox to pederasty *(Other Voices, Other Rooms),* Juan Medinao to the weak and systematic forgiving of offenses *(Fiesta in the Northwest).* . . .

First Memory tells about how one becomes an adult; *Fiesta in the Northwest,* why and how one does not become one. Juan Medinao will never leave his childhood, which has branded him, and in some manner, stopped him. But what childhood? In fact, from the age of five, with his twisted legs and big head, he is an old man. . . . In *Fiesta in the Northwest,* escapist dreams play the same role that the myths of Borja and the imagined cities of Matia do in *First Memory:* one must conceal the world of men and things in order to tolerate them.

And it is true that the world here below is cruel to Juan, whose father is a usurer. Over the wretched and resigned laborers, who are passively hostile, in that corner of Castile, Juan senior exercises unlimited power and behaves forcefully, brutally, with frenzy, like those landowners in Bolivia or Ecuador for whom the peasants are not quite men. Juan junior is traumatized because of this. . . .

Harsher, tougher, and more violent than *First Memory, Fiesta in the Northwest* is a book of brutality, of cruelty, of man's misery. Of their hunger and of their death. It is also a more ambitious and complex novel than the first. Here Castile is present, and out of that province Ana María Matute wanted to create a backdrop for her characters. Like Juan, Castile never changes, and like him, it is miserable and tragic. For Juan, for Dingo, nothing is ever new; everything is always beginning again and everything is repeated; after thirty years, after time immemorial, there are these broken-down roads, the mud after the rain, children who die of hunger. Nothing alters the landscape or changes the destiny of the people. Ana María Matute has written a novel about time that does not pass.

Yves Berger. *Nouvelle Revue Française.*
May, 1961, pp. 896, 899–901

Tres y un sueño (Three and one dream) . . . is a book which combines fantasy worthy of Lewis Carroll with satire comparable to that of Rubén Darío's "*El rey burgués*" and picaresque cruelty unsurpassed even in some of Camilo José Cela's darkest pages. It is marked by an intensity of feeling and a style which is occasionally lyrical, usually somber and terse. . . . The case for the existence of a transcendental reality in the world of fantasy is persuasively presented.

Daniel S. Keller. *Books Abroad.* Winter,
1962, pp. 61–62

The literary talent of Ana María Matute seems to be the most powerful among recent novelists. [In *Historias de la Artámila*] the author reaches the full maturity of her inspiration. In previous, very valuable works, Ana María Matute often ran the risk of being too *précieuse* not only in language but also in the mental subtleties expressed; now her language becomes direct and wonderfully simple without ceasing to be tremendously creative and poetic, and the types of feeling that are depicted are uncomplicated and fundamental. . . . There is a Chekhovian quality in this beautiful book, an emphasis on the intense lyrical and emotional impact of little things and apparently insignificant happenings. . . . Ana María Matute combines this appreciation of little things with a sensitive and realistic presentation, through the memory of personal experience, of the present tragedy of the Spanish people. This is a book of protest, subtle and lyrical but nonetheless strong and brave.

Rafael Bosch. *Books Abroad.* Summer, 1962,
p. 303

The theme of children caught in an adult world which they do not understand, and reacting to it with innocent craft and cruelty, made an English novel so famous in the 1920s that it continues as a paperback classic. Ana María Matute has spun the development of very different lives in her Spanish story [*School of the Sun*], but the plot, while developed with less complexity, recalls *High Wind in Jamaica,* and is good enough to stand comparison with Richard Hughes's earlier book. . . . This is a slighter book than *High Wind in Jamaica,* but its brooding sense of the tragedy of innocence in evil is as true, and its telling is skillful. . . . Ana Mariá Matute has produced one of the more competent of the novels which have come from the younger generation of Spanish writers.

Mildred Adams. The New York Times.
April 21, 1963, pp. 4, 30

The impression [*The Lost Children*] makes is not one of bitterness and horror, but of the strength of life and the unfailing resurgence of the human spirit. The explicit pessimism of Miss Matute's novel is somehow illuminated from within by a celebration of the power and vitality of mankind. . . . Miss Matute [has an] exact observation which sees so deep into an ordinary situation that it becomes fresh [and she] clothes this story in clear light as uncompromising as it is unsentimental. Like *Ship of Fools,* . . . *The Lost Children* reveals the understructure of the world, the beams and girders that sustain society as it is; or, if you prefer a more dynamic metaphor, it shows us the lines of force binding people together and holding them apart. . . . This book . . . has a classic power expressed in brilliant prose.

Elizabeth Janeway. Christian Science
Monitor. May 20, 1965, p. 7

Her mode—her choice—is what in the axiological language of form we call the trivial. . . . Her method [in *The Lost Children,* i.e., *The Dead Children*] is to combine the stammering, mind-refusing world of childhood with the almost idiot, brute world of the senses. Hence we get a queer "poetic" prose which even in the most conventional narrative is stiffened by a complex degree of imagery and refrain, all to account for a very simple state of mind. . . .

In *School of the Sun* [i.e., *First Memory*], Miss Matute's heroine reads in [J. M.] Barrie's [*Peter Pan*] that Peter "'did spring cleaning at the time of the gathering of the leaves in the forest of Lost Children.' And the same Lost Children were all too grown up, suddenly, for playing, and too childlike, suddenly, to start life in a world we didn't want to know." The shift in personal pronoun here is indicative of the author's commitment, and in her new book we have the same stubborn, stuttering, mindless refusal to know the world beyond the senses, beyond the preoccupation with immediate, unreflected experience that makes this 500-page book no more—and no less, for it is remarkably written—than a lyric cry, a long cortical spasm.

Miss Matute's retreat from history—from the notion that not only do things happen, but that their happening has a meaning, that a set of values can be assigned to them—her preference for unmediated Experience, reminds us of a famous moment when Dorian Gray, appalled by the "truth" of Lord Henry Wotton's shocking words, stares at a spray of lilac he has just dropped on the gravel path. . . .

The young Spanish novelists, and Miss Matute chief among them in her long, terrified lament, have fallen into Dorian's trance. The lobotomy-by-childhood, the anesthesia-by-intensity which *The Lost Children* so insistently evokes gives us, as no ideological intervention could do, the measure of the "high import," the terror and the surrender to which the Spanish writers have been, and are still, subject.

Richard Howard. New Leader. July 5, 1965,
pp. 19–20

[Matute] has a very personal style, rich in imagery, often poetic, that does not lend itself as readily to translation as do less imaginative works. In Matute there is always the hint that behind the surface realities of the everyday world hovers another existence, strange and secret. Her fiction rests on a solid substratum of realistic and concrete detail, but Matute's special talent lies in extracting the invisible interior reality from the visible reality of the external world. These qualities, at times iridescent and at times somber, appear in all of her writings, but they reach their maximum expression in her imaginative creations like *The Stupid Children* and *Three and a Dream*. In both of these the author is dealing with children, or grownups with childlike minds, having sensitive feelings but forced by the harsh realities of life in live in a world of fantasy. These studies, at times touched with surrealism, reflect one of the author's preoccupations: the shock which adult hypocrisy gives to youthful minds. . . .

[Matute] is more concerned with the recurring season, the anguished eroticism and frustrations of adolescence, the disappointments of age, relations between the rich and the poor, the tensions between the past and the present, than she is [with] current events and fashions. . . .

The Matutean concept of life is not a rosy one. Despite the long golden hours dreamed away in the lost paradise of youth, we are caught in a trap and destined to a tragic end. Her attitude is in many respects similar to that of the late Pio Baroja, who saw no solution for man's major problems.

George Wythe. Books Abroad. Winter, 1966,
pp. 19–20

Matute's work is multifaceted, but its two extremes and most frequently represented variants are the stories of fantasies and the works whose theme or background involves either the Civil War or the Castilian peasant. Her interest in this is constant, lifelong, as shown by the study of her work from the earliest preserved juvenilia and her writings of pre-adolescence, up to the latest publications. Despite certain changes or modifications in her evolution as a writer, Matute's style has always been extremely personal and subjective, dominated by a primarily lyric vision of reality, or a deceptively childlike conception. Beginning with a fairly traditional structure, Matute has gradually tended to ever greater experimentation with the novelistic architecture, point of view, and treatment of time. The importance of formal plot, never a major element in her novels, has decreased, while the novelist's interest in psychology (a constant in her work) has grown ever stronger, with special emphasis on the problems of motivation, and an almost obsessive interest in the key formative factors and experiences which make people "what they are" such as the half-buried childhood trauma which may suddenly erupt in an apparently inexplicable act of adult violence. . . .

Matute continues to be intrigued with time, both as a theme and as a narrative possibility, being apparently particularly fascinated with the "threshold" moment or experience (of passage from childhood to adolescence, or adolescence to adulthood). At the same time, there is some experimentation with the contrary possibility, the unreality of time, and the possibilities of annihilation. Likewise, (and more frequently of late), the reader encounters factors which render meaningless the passage of hours, days, and years. A key motif, Cain and Abel, is obviously related to two of the previously mentioned obsessive concerns, social conflict and the Civil War (often symbolized by the violence between brothers). It may well be significant that in the early works, this conflict is almost inseparable from the soil; later it becomes (by implication) more closely related to other means of production. Matute is far from being either an ideologist or thesis novelist; in fact, it would be difficult to find anything resembling doctrine or dogma in any of her works, aside from such thoroughly Christian formulas as "Love one another." Her idea of charity . . . is much broader than simple almsgiving, and extends to many areas of human relationships, but especially to the concept of equal rights of all to the necessities of life, and to be treated with dignity and justice. Matute is sufficiently fair in her treatment of the Civil War that, even though by family, background, upbringing, and class contacts she should belong to the Nationalist (or Franco) faction, her implicit sympathies are with the vanquished, with the poor and suffering of all creeds, and with all whose rights and liberties are curtailed. Her concept of true Christianity, as expressed in "Love thy brother," implies acceptance, understanding, and sharing.

Janet Díaz. Ana María Matute (New York:
Twayne, 1971), pp. 145–47

The world of *The Trap* (1969)—the last novel in the trilogy *The Merchants* [the first two being *First Memory* and *The Soldiers Cry at Night,* respectively] by Ana María Matute—is characterized by an isolation between the self and others; between the self and itself; pervasive solitude; separation caused by death, divorce and faulty communication. The universal separation symptomatic of alienation is communicated and reinforced in this work of fiction by a form and structure which corresponds to and discovers the thematic content. . . .

The theme of alienation emerges in the novel through each character's delving into the storehouse of memory, as well as acting in the present. However, external action for its own sake is underplayed, the novel concentrating instead upon static internal action as a means of portraying fragmented, alienated characters. . . .

The principal challenge of the writer who sets out to portray this modern predicament is how to create a form which not only corresponds to the existential situation but also enhances it. The technique of presentation employed in *The Trap* could be termed an aesthetics of alienation. It would be difficult to conceive of a form more suited to the portrayal of the problems of alienated consciousness. This is consonant with one of the strengths of Matute's art, according to Enrique Sordo: "Ana María Matute's art has among other essential qualities, that of sticking closely to the theme that is being narrated. . . ." The novel is divided into chapters corresponding to the four principal characters' perspectives. . . . Most importantly, each character seems to be isolated within his own private world. Any of the rather sparse dialogue which does occur is encased within the recollections of each character. . . .

Matute has been criticized by Joaquín Marco for her use of nonfunctional language in *The Trap*. At times, though, linguistic nonfunctionality seems to be both medium and metaphor for the breakdown in communication plaguing modern society. Matia's diary is indecipherable to her, seemingly written in an unknown language. We are witnesses to a modern despair and distrust of the powers and faculties of languages and its ability to effect communication. Isa's aunts employ a private "semi-language" of unintelligible monosyllables and guttural sounds. Repeatedly language, like the culture in which its exists, is dehumanized. It is transformed into hollow sounds which have ceased to signal meaning and serve only as constant reminders of the impossibility of authentic communication. So the very use of a specific kind of language or non-language underscores the fatal isolation and separation of the characters from one another.

Although the principal plot of *The Trap* is rather simple, it is contained within a complex labyrinthine structure of flashbacks and musings which at once parallels and reconfirms the characters' alienation from their world and from each other. The use of a baroque-like, involuted style and structure, probably inspired by the works of Faulkner, is able to portray and to be strongly analogous to a disturbingly alienated outside world. This world view is expressed through imagery and action, as well as conceptualized through structure in *The Trap*. Dialectical analysis reveals the indissoluble interrelationship between an alienated literary and nonliterary culture, between this world of fiction and the real or external world outside it.

Elizabeth Ordoñez. *Journal of Spanish*
Studies: Twentieth Century. Winter, 1976,
pp. 180–81, 187–89

First Memory (1960) represents a new direction for the Spanish novel and the New Wave because, unlike its predecessors, it is the first to encourage a new variant of style I shall call "subjective Realism." A work of astonishing beauty, *First Memory* is deceptively simple. . . .

Critics may warn readers of a writer's stylistic excesses, but for me Matute is the only writer up until 1960 who has developed an original style and unique facility to transform her experiences and feelings into an *artistic* and subjectively Realistic fictional world. When asked about any writers that influenced her career, at first she said she did not know of anyone and then volunteered these names—Sartre, Camus, Malraux, Hesse and Knut Hamsun. She also felt certain Spanish publishers such as Lumen, Seix Barral and Destino have furthered her career since these publishers are particularly against government censorship. Also, thanks to many literary prizes she has won, she finds there is greater interest in her life and work, and consequently, she has become prolific as a writer. Matute's consummate skill at avoiding direct questions about her work in no way parallels her unique artistry as a writer. Careful not to discuss the war, she feels *First Memory* is ultimately not a "war novel" but one about a young girl's adolescence. . . .

Whatever the verdict may be about her attaining literary greatness in the future, and Matute is probably only just now entering her most significant period, she surely now represents the epitome of the true artist, the seeker of truth, the master story teller, humanity's lover, the nobility of the soul.

Ronald Schwartz. *Spain's New Wave Novelists* (Metuchen, New Jersey: Scarecrow, 1976), pp. 115–16, 127, 130

Matute suggests that the causes for most of the current loneliness and frustration of her characters may be found in the past. She indicates that many of them are extremely concerned with the strong influence of the past in their lives when she permits their stories to be told, in first and third persons, by means of retrospective narration. Some of her characters . . . are attracted to the past because their earlier lives, in spite of holding the origins of their current low status, are much less problematic than is the present. The past, though frequently unpleasant, represents a security which these people no longer can know.

Her novels also show a close relationship between the extent of her characters' involvement in historical events and their limitation by the past. Pablo Barral [in *In This Land*] and Daniel Corvo [in *the Dead Children*], . . . fought to reduce the inequalities that they suffered and observed. At the war's end they believe that further efforts are useless, and they refuse to participate in the life of postwar Spain. Other characters who have made lesser commitments apparently feel less limited by their earlier failures. From the foregoing it is possible to conclude that in the fictional world of Ana María Matute those who have participated actively in the past are often doomed to be destroyed by it.

J. Townsend Shelby. *Revista de Estudios Hispanicos.* May, 1980, pp. 91–92

Ana María Matute's *La trampa* (The trap), published five years before [Carmen Martín Gaite's] *Retahílas,* in 1969, is, to date, the author's most interesting presentation of a woman's psychology. Curiously, there are a number of interesting parallels in the external structure of the two novels. In both, we find that the protagonists' self-examination is initially triggered by certain events in their grandmothers' lives. In *Retahílas*, Eulalia's dying grandmother wants to be transported back to her country estate; Eulalia accompanies her and finds in her escape from the city the emotional distance needed to begin her self-exploration. In *La trampa*, Matia's grandmother, a central character in *Primera memoria* (First memory) (1960), willfully celebrates her one-hundredth birthday at age ninety-nine and requests that her family return to the island to spend it with her. Matia, like Eulalia, is suddenly submerged into a reality filled with childhood evocations and recreates during the course of three days the main events in her life from the termination of *Primera memoria* to the present time. In this novel, Matute has set out a difficult assignment for herself by picking up the loose threads of Matia's life, totally set aside in the second novel of her trilogy, *Los soldados lloran de noche* (The soldiers cry at night) (1964). The jump from portraying a fourteen-year-old girl in *Primera memoria* to a woman in her forties in *La trampa* is not easy to master, and Matute has achieved it with a certain amount of success although there are still many questions which remain to be answered.

Matute does not view herself as a proselytizing feminist in this novel, nor does such a role correspond to her definition of the novelist's task. If, according to her theory, "el escritor enciende luces rojas. Porque el escritor no es un moralista, ni un sociólogo ni un doctrinario. El escritor es un hombre que duda, se pregunta a sí mismo y provoca en el lector un angustia, recelos y repulsa que pueden ser beneficiosos" (the writer sends out red signals, the writer isn't a moralist or a sociologist or a doctrinarian. The writer is a person who doubts, questions himself, and provokes in the reader an anguish, distrust and sense of repulsion that can be beneficial), this is what she achieves in *La trampa*.

Linda Gould Levine. In Beth Miller, ed.
*Women in Hispanic Literature: Icons and
Fallen Idols* (Berkeley: University of
California Press, 1983), pp. 301–2

As is the case with many postwar writers, Matute frequently makes orphans her protagonists, thereby symbolizing their solitude, alienation, and vulnerability. Most of her major characters are children or adolescents; the rare adult protagonists are usually engaged in retrospective recall of childhood and adolescent episodes. The myth of Cain and Abel, symbolizing the endemic causes of the Civil War (conflict between brothers), is an obsessive motif in her fiction. Seldom does Matute portray women in the role of wives or mothers, and when she does, they are minor characters. Rarely, if ever, are they happily married, and often they are widows. Motherhood is portrayed not as fulfillment but the cause of endless sacrifice. The unbroken family is a rarity in Matute's fiction, and happiness beyond the charmed fantasy world of childhood is fleeting if it exists at all. Her typical protagonist is an androgynous, half-tamed, and rebellious adolescent, usually with a Peter Pan complex. Most often her narratives trace the passage to adulthood, the loss of inno- cence, illusions, or idealism constituting the essential core of a pre-adult mentality. The character who has surrendered to materialism, convention- alism, or practicality ceases to interest Matute.

> Janet Pérez. *Contemporary Women Writers of Spain* (Boston: Twayne, 1988), p. 132

MAYRÖCKER, FRIEDERIKE (AUSTRIA) 1924–

Friederike Mayröcker presents twenty years of her own poetry here [in her collection *Tod durch Musen* (Death by muses)]. She classifies the contents of this volume as "poetic texts." With this term, the author makes the claim that her texts belong to a genre of poetry that stands in contrast to classical poetry, and, as nonclassical or experimental poetry, that distinguishes itself from it. We would nonetheless gladly call her a poet. Friederike Mayröcker has every right to make this claim: it is truly amazing how even her earliest texts, which when compared with her later "provocative-texts" can still be viewed as "experience-texts," already reveal the productive tendency that is characteristic of experimental texts. A tendency that continues and keeps growing right up through the latest creations, all the while becoming more differentiated and so very refined that already for this reason alone the collec- tion deserves an "Afterword.". . .

The twenty-year journey through these "poetic texts" has led from early language creations bearing the imprint of experience to her most recent works, in which stimulus and response have given rise to a distinctive quality. Accordingly, one can conclude that the Experiencing Self of the poet, that initially can be evaluated as narrowly related to the self—even in the posses- sive forms of mine and yours—fades away more and more, or appears only occasionally in the form of a quotation. And accordingly, one can conclude that the simple message of the earlier texts, a message that emerges almost devoid of punctuation, has developed in the more recent texts into a fibrous, sinuous ordering of words that are splintered, subdivided, compacted, and yet at the same time elegantly interpreted. Not since e. e. cummings has so much attention been drawn to the use and functions of punctuation as today in the works of this Viennese author. Thus, one becomes aware of the fact that the lack of such simple punctuation marks as commas and periods corre- sponds fully to the will to avoid "simple sentences." In the place of simple punctuation marks, there emerges an accumulation of semicolons, parenthe- ses, exclamation points, dashes, markers of separation and connection, co- lons, demarcations of omission, and finally, slashes, which appear more and more frequently. When one focuses on the role of the semicolon—actually a rather hybridized, and thus not very attractive sign, typographically speaking—as a potent organizing agent linking variously compounded sentences, the "images" of the most recent texts begin already in and of themselves to show great promise. The structure of the texts becomes visually salient as well. . . .

It is very informative to observe the development of a manner of writing that has been called, and justifiably so, an aesthetic—and thus, an intellectual—manner of writing. In the two decades that she has been writing, Friederike Mayröcker has proven on numerous occasions that experimental poetry is anything but dry and boring—as critics often accuse her of being—but rather, on the contrary, that her texts too can possess the richness of stained glass window panes: window panes, however, upon the structure of which a significant portion of the aesthetic information has been transferred. We marvel at the weightless beauty of soap bubbles that reflect their surroundings and that have the capacity, due to their fragility, to increase our sensuality and our sensitivity. But above all, we marvel at the ripe texts in which the inventions of colorful metaphoric processes enable us to peek through into the sphere of values in which the power of creation and the power of evaporation, captured in the element of change, are kept in perfect balance.

Eugen Gomringer. Afterword to Friederike
Mayröcker. *Tod durch Musen* (Darmstadt:
Luchterhand, 1973), pp. 193–95

In the twenty-nine texts contained in her book *Mini-Monster Dream Lexicon: Texts in Prose* (1968) Friederike Mayröcker juggles two models at a time, a stable model for structure and a variable model for form. Stable is the structural model of prose, a concept that envisions prose as language that is uniquely linear in its progression in sentences and paragraphs; variable is the model for form as a sort of outline based on a notion of forms in which prose is employed. The author refers to such forms explicitly as: "Conversations" *(Angel's Talk; Simultaneous Conversations);* "Film-like Renderings" *(Fiction Film; Ten-Second-Plays; Telephone Theater; Comedy Rehearsal; Recording Service; Tele-Vision);* "Protocols" *(Activity Report; Daily Reports);* "Things Instructional. Things Lexical. Didactic Texts" *(Dream Lexicon; Demonstration).* Or she sets up hints about the contents, which awaken an image of certain modes of depiction: *Science-Fiction Text; Things Personal; Half-Length Portrait of H.C. Artmann; Landscape; Things from the Country; Retrospectives; A Topological Text; English Prose; Prose on Airplane Types.*

In what manner, then, are these two models, one stable and one variable, put to use? This question only serves a purpose if the texts themselves, in terms of both form and language, and in spite of the models, produce something other than the following: a conversation (in prose); a radio play (in prose); a report (in prose); a description (in prose), etc. Just such a deviation from the images conjured up through the models and thus from the expected result, is, without exception, the case here.

The texts stand at a distance from the models, the model remains in view, and yet the text remains free; it does not subjugate itself to the model. This applies equally to the prose structure of the model and to the respective formal model.

Ernst Jandl. In Karl S. Weimar, ed. *Views and Reviews of Modern German Literature* (Munich: Delp Verlag, 1974), p. 51

Clearly the dialogue or dialogic speaking presents an adequate possibility. . . . Friederike Mayröcker also kept to this path when she switched over from a lyrical to a prose form in the early 1970s. Her volume entitled *ever a summit clouded over* (begun in 1971, published in 1973, and classified as a "story") is composed of 23 chapters: just this kind of evaporated texts, comprising only a very few pages each, and once one has begun to pick up on their scent, exhibiting an exciting internal structure of language. They are made up of what at first appears to be fully enigmatic sentences, into which things are inserted, onto which things are attached, again and again, like a basso continuo: "he said." Chapter 9 begins, for example, following the heading with the words: "broad-chested through the gaping chaos, he said, we cleared the way." The tireless repetition of the phrase "he said" keeps the male addressee from tiring, and keeps the female addressee—who responds in gesture, plot, and speech—ever-present. This dialog form is one of the many that are possible, and that the poet has already played out in her poems, and that she has continued to further develop. Her second prose volume, *The Light in the Landscape,* begins and ends in the form of an epistolary novel (with its opening lines: "Dear M.W. Having met you, I am very impressed, you'll be grateful to know. I just wanted to write and tell you that . . ."). And as in her first prose volume, she injects it with an almost stereotypic dialogue figure ("said the World Biographer" is the recurring phrase here). And beneath the title of this book, the following motto is printed:

This is the record of a transformation
To which all apparent forms of human life
are made subject, in the consciousness
of brotherly unity
with that which emerges out of the present, past, and future.

Gisela Leidemann. *Die Zeit.* October 14, 1977, n.p.

In the case of the Austrian writer and poet Friederike Mayröcker, the "effective view to the outside" seldom follows the look "into the interior." The view to the outside appears predetermined by the external world within it. "Internal and external" have merged with it to such a degree that the dialectic process of sense perception is nearly one of indifference. It is decisive not only for the narrative content—which is much more static than it is dynamic—, but above all for its mode of expression: its style, its syntax, its grammar, its metaphors, to select just a few aspects.

It is not easy to offer the reader a synopsis of the book *Almost Markus M.'s Springtime.* There is even a warning in the jacket notes: "Anyone who has the desire to find out the storyline of this book, because he is used to stories and would like to start there in approaching this book, will—as is the case with the other stories by Friederike Mayröcker—experience some difficulty."

For there is no story; it is established elsewhere. Leaving aside the illogical nature of this last sentence—if there is no story, then it can not be established elsewhere!—we find ourselves confronted with a text that has no clearly definable plot and describes no clear-cut events, that has no definite beginning, and is open-ended, but that is bursting with developmental processes that permit, no, that demand a multivalent interpretation. Reader and author share in the repertoire of potentialities and issues of conjecture that are embedded in this text.

Lisa Kahn. Literatur und Kritik. 165–66,
1982, n.p.

When the two Austrian authors Ernst Jandl (born in 1925 in Vienna) and Friederike Mayröcker (born in 1924 in Vienna) received the Radio Play Prize for the War Blind for 1968 in honor of their collectively produced stereo radio play *Five-Man People,* the press devoted a great deal of interest to this progressive award decision. *Die Welt* wrote: "Confirmation of a new direction in radio that distinguishes itself in principle from the naturalized radio play. A new era begins with *Five-Man People.*" The jury for the radio play prize did not have the script, but evaluated the audio composition. They awarded the prize to the authors with a vote of seventeen in favor and one against, and mentioned with praise the young director Peter Michel Ladiges who had transposed the unusual harshness of the stereophonic score into an adequate realization in the debut broadcast on Southwest Radio in November of 1968.

The jury justified their decision as follows:

> Ernst Jandl and Friederike Mayröcker, who are known as representatives of experimental poetry, together with Peter Michel Ladiges, have applied in an exemplary manner and for the first time within the genre of the radio play the potentialities of concrete poetry. They reveal exemplary processes in language and in plot, in which the course of human life, as it is programmed in accordance with the norm, is not portrayed, but rather, is evoked. In so doing, they utilize and master the potentials of stereophonics. Language provides the authors the material with which they play and, at the same time, makes for an unmistakable brand of communication that has an impact on the times as much as it reflects them.

On the occasion of accepting the Radio Play Prize for the War Blind, Ernst Jandl mentioned two important factors that constituted the foundations for the radio play: stereophonics and teamwork. Jandl explains:

> Teamwork, that means: a text that was intended to be spoken by a number of speakers as a radio play, had to evolve out of dialogue; the two authors' familiarity with one another guaranteed the necessary openness—no one shied away from saying anything—and at the same time, the necessary control—no one shied away from voicing criticism or blame. Stereophonics proved itself to be an exceedingly useful engine; from left to right, we fixated on five points; these evolved into the speakers, the direction, the stations, the goal.

This was the starting-point from which Ernst Jandl and Friederike Mayröcker created the stereo-radio-play *Five-Man People,* a work that marked a breakthrough for the new radio play.

Birgit Johanna Lermen. Wirkendes Wort. 32,
1982, pp. 179–80

Mayröcker's work has been characterized as "poetic phenomenology," and indeed she does offer a fresh and highly imaginative mode of perception. Fragments from experience and memory, dream and fantasy, perceptions, reflections, and heterogeneous elements of thought and feeling are brought together in an atemporal amalgam in which time levels of recent and remote pasts are superimposed on present, future, and future-perfect possibilities of consciousness. Reality is portrayed as discontinuous, nonchronological, fragmentary, and ambivalent; precisely this open-endedness is more central and significant than anything that can be objectively established. The theme of her works is most basically the sensibility of the writer, and the most persistent motif to emerge is the portrait of an artist, that is, a view of the creative process itself. Autobiographical elements are included but are so transformed that rather than any "confessional," the recovery of the self's own history becomes a fictional documentation of the creative process as a series of imaginative possibilities. The "sea-change" is so thorough that at times the text seems to produce the author rather than the other way around; but the author of course produces both—the text and thereby also the artist-self. Art functions not as a fanciful supplement to the world of practical activity or as an accessory to the "truth" of science or religion but rather as a fundamental mode of apprehending that world, as the container rather than the contained. The organizing sensibility, which is literary and aesthetic, at once involved and dispassionate, is concerned not with the self as such but with the quality of modern life in general and particularly with modes of perceiving it.

It was with *Tod durch Musen* in 1966 that Mayröcker won wide public recognition. As her first major publication it presents the author's selection of poems from the years 1945 to 1965, which has since been expanded and published in a hardback edition of *Ausgewählte Gedichte* (1979, Selected poetry). The widely acclaimed *Tod durch Musen* receives its title from the opening cycle, which consists of nine "models" addressed to the nine muses and stands as metapoetic commentary on the creative process, which is conceived as one of devastation. The muses, as the source of art, are also the source of death, for creating a text entails creating also an artist and thus "killing" the person. . . .

The term [perpetual motion] could serve to describe Mayröcker's entire literary production, which, over the past three decades, demonstrates change and development while maintaining an essential continuity and unity. The author's variable course through diverse genres represents an exploration of linguistic media and a testing of the limits of form, for a writer is first and foremost an artisan of language who aspires to consummate mastery of the means. From the intense encounter with art in *Tod durch Musen* to the richness of poetic perception in *Das Licht in der Landschaft* (Light in the landscape), from the materialistic reduction of culture in *Metaphysisches Theater* (Metaphysical theater) to the visionary expansion of language in *Die Abschiede* (Farewells) the texts are implicated one in another, evolving from and revolving around one central theme: perception-transformation-creation. It is a phoenix-like death and resurrection of the work of art (and the artist) out of the ashes of life, and it could be viewed as a dialectic, were not the term preempted by causal and teleological systems of thought. What appears as dialectic might be better described as reciprocal interaction of forces, an activity which rejects the limitations entailed in categorization and abstraction. Transformation is, of course, the crux of the matter, and the creative process will probably always remain the mystery it is portrayed to be in the prototypical instance of music and silence in *Heiligenanstalt*.

Art is not a theory but rather continual exploration, and one would "explain" it only in order not to have to experience it, whereby a critical notion is inserted, or rather, built in, by scrupulous self-regulatory powers. Art is experience—certainly for the creator, but also for the receiver, who is an accomplice in the discovery and invention of meanings. If a reader occasionally loses his/her bearings in a text, that is not so different from his/her encounters in the world, and an artist exploits the uncertainty of the situation as a source of creative strength. Reality inheres not in a counterfeit integration of life but in a scattering of random souvenirs, whose charm derives from the inviting spaces between them. Valorization is by experience, not by institutional analysis, and the critic can only hope that the "imperfections" of the present stage will direct the reader to the greater freedom and vitality of art.

Beth Bjorkland. In Donald G. Daviau, ed.
Major Figures in Contemporary Austrian Literature (New York: Peter Lang, 1987),
pp. 314, 332–33

Friederike Mayröcker's most recent prose work [*Men Herz, mein Zimmer, mein Name* (My heart, my room, my name)] consists of just one mammoth sentence stretching the length of the entire book. Although the author again uses her well-established techniques such as arranging her thoughts by means of associations or quoting from letters, conversations, books, and found material, the piece is nevertheless highly structured, as evidenced by the many repetitions of key phrases placed at critical junctures. First-time readers of Mayröcker might still tend to be confused and frustrated by what appears to be a wild jumble of words and ideas, and admittedly many passages remain obscure and nebulous: but old hands will continue to be amazed at her dogged attempts to examine her psyche publicly.

In conversations with a certain (fictive?) invalid, Rosa, and with her "ear confessor" *(Ohrenbeichtvater)*, the first-person narrator, easily identifiable with the author, describes all her simultaneous inner thoughts and feelings. In so doing she blurs our usual distinctions between dream and reality, between memory and the present, between imagination and the concrete. The reader can thus begin to grasp a new sense of time and dimension, similar to the images of several films being projected at the same time onto one screen, a concept that is only hampered by the mechanics of the printed line. As she states several times, the whole writing process is a type of narcotic for Mayröcker, and the specific procedure she uses in *mein Herz mein Zimmer mein Name* conveys a sense of a relentless and breathless writing activity which obviously is absolutely essential for her to maintain her profession and to search for her own identity. This helps explain the title: by using the thoughts and emotions within her heart combined with the written materials in her room, she hopes to find the persona that carries her name.

Robert Acker. World Literature Today. 64,
1990, p. 109

MEDIO, DOLORES (SPAIN) 1917–

The contemporary Spanish novel is notable not only for the so-called Renaissance of the past twenty years, but also for the presence of an unusual number of women novelists, some of considerable talent and prominence. . . .

Probably the most popular woman writer in Spain today is Dolores Medio. She is popular in both the American and Spanish connotations of the word, in terms of appeal to the public and of primary concern for the *pueblo*. Her works are popular also in that they are neither complex nor abstruse but accessible to the average intellect. She writes very deliberately "al alcance de todos los lectores," [accessibly to all readers] and it is part of her personal theory of the novel that it should be so written. . . .

A major trend in the post-Civil War Spanish novel is the *novela social,* with its impulse toward social reform. Armando López Salinas, Jesús López Pacheco, Angel de Lera, Jesús Fernández Santos, Antonio Ferres, Fernando Avalos, Juan Marsé, Mauro Múñiz and other young novelists of the *nueva ola* have written of the problems of specific occupational groups, often emphasizing social determinants. *Funcionario público* (Civil servant) is part of this trend, and (if "housewife" be considered an occupation), *Bibiana* could be added to the list. Critical allegations to the contrary notwithstanding, it does not seem to me that *Diario* can be considered a study of the teaching profession; even when the love interest is removed, it is too personal and too intimate a document. . . .

In technique, many current Spanish novelists follow a recent French model. They give verbal allegiance to the objectivist theories of the *roman nouveau* (as exemplified by Robbe-Grillet and Sarraute), eliminating traces of the author's personality, value judgments, analysis, and other subjective material. Description is external and scientific, often mathematically exact. Subjective states are seen only via their physical manifestations. Part of the *objetivista* creed holds that the psychological novel is a vein which has been exhausted and was never particularly rewarding; a premise which Dolores Medio rejects. She is less extreme than most in her use of *objetivista* techniques, adapting them in combination with traditional narrative and interior monologue, perhaps reflecting her fondness for Joyce and Proust. Her use of these combined techniques is most clearly seen in *Funcionario público, El pez sigue flotando* (The fish stays afloat), and *Bibiana.* Chronologically her novels reveal a growing awareness of technique and a progression from the more traditional forms to her present eclecticism.

Janet Winecoff. *Kentucky Foreign Language Quarterly.* 13, 1966–67, pp. 170–71, 174–75

Two major groupings divide the body of her work, each distinguished by similar attributes in the leading character. One group presents a female figure reminiscent of the author herself. This person is young, observant, solitary, and given to comments about life. Her psychological (and at times physical) distance from the action is enough to permit her to comment on it, and even scrutinize her own feelings with some degree of objectivity. These novels are patently autobiographical in character, and the women's analytical tendencies permit a freer expression of the author's own views on the subject under consideration. Such works include *We Riveros,* portions of *The Fish Stays Afloat,* and *Diary of a Schoolteacher.*

The second group, by far the more numerous, develops a character who is simultaneously important as an individual and as a representative of a large group, generally the middle or lower class. No distinguishing features or outstanding traits differentiate these people from the thousands like them; their very averageness is the quality that Miss Medio seeks. This group includes *Pubic Servant,* portions of *The Fish Stays Afloat, Bibiana,* and the short stories. . . .

Patterns of contemporary life are measured through personal reaction and the effect that wide-sweeping political or social changes would have on the individual. Emigration, rapid mechanization, big business and its inevitable dehumanization, the sudden acquisition of wealth are all subthemes of the individual's relationship with society. Rapid changes cause a sense of unease and insecurity: "Giddy-up, Nicolasa" or "A Handful of Dry Grass" bears witness to the nostalgia and pain with which the characters leave the old ways behind.

The style with which Miss Medio presents these ideas is basically simple and realistic. Her prose is deliberately clear and concise, so that the reader can easily follow the train of thought. There is also some experimentation in form whenever it can be used to best advantage: interior monologue allows for the withdrawal of author intervention; popular speech, thought patterns, and extensive use of dialogue give the main emphasis to the character and allow the reader to form his own conclusions. Miss Medio often creates a situation which forces the reader to abandon his omniscient perspective, placing him on the level of the character.

The novelist is very aware of the responsibility of the artist vis-à-vis his public, since the work of art is a perfect teaching situation. Although she does not believe in the novel as a deliberate means of propaganda, her obvious sympathy for the characters and the elucidation of problems inherent in the classes which she describes create an awareness of inequities which need to be remedied. At the very least it is a call for solidarity through mutual suffering, understanding, and love.

Although it is entirely possible that Miss Medio will change her style and even modify essential themes, we may predict that her abiding interest in the ordinary person and his relationship with the contemporary social structure will continue to be a major concern in her literature and her personal philosophy.

> Margaret E. W. Jones. *Dolores Medio* (New
> York: Twayne, 1974), pp. 147, 149–50

Dolores Medio, a native of Oviedo, born in the early 1920s is a very popular but lesser known writer of distinct talent. Her most influential work is a social novel, *Nosotros los Rivero* (1953; We Riveros); dealing with the lower-middle class of Madrid and their problems. Although that work suffers several defects, notably an insufferable air of idealism and excessive romanticism, Medio's novels generally maintain her popularity, as her latest fictional effort, *Bibiana* (1967) certainly proves. Medio is well-acquainted with Madrid and especially its lower-middle class and presents an evocative tableau in terms of dialogue and colloquialisms of contemporary Madrileños participating actively in their society.

> Ronald Schwartz. *Spain's New Wave
> Novelists, 1950–1974: Studies in Spanish
> Realism* (Metuchen, New Jersey: Scarecrow
> Press, 1976), p. 310

Dolores Medio . . . won the Nadal Prize for her novel *Nosotros, los Riveros.* This novel, like others of hers, shows the rebellion of women against social stereotypes. The desire to be like men is natural when women begin to see the differences in treatment between men and women:

> When Maria asked "Why doesn't Ger help us with our work?" Her sister answered "Ah, no, Ger is a man; he must study; he is the only son in the family and mother has all her dreams riding on him." If you were to ask Aunt Mag, "Why are you taking out the garbage? Ask Ger . . ." she would answer, "Ger, Nita? Are you crazy, he might get his clothes dirty. Besides, he is a man. Leave him alone with his books. He has enough to do with his studies. . . ." "Your brother is always right," Mrs. Rivero would always say, "Besides, since he is a man." . . .

Years later, this same girl, now a popular writer, returns to the home she had abandoned. She has been able to rise above her environment and has triumphed. This same type of personal success, perhaps in a more modest way, can be observed in *Diario de una maestra* [Diary of a Schoolteacher] published in 1961. This novel develops, point by point, the search for identity and purpose in life by a girl of humble means who is, at the beginning, bound by romantic ideas about love. Like Lena Rivero, the protagonist of *Nosotros, los Rivero,* Irene is a girl who becomes independent when she goes to study at the University of Oviedo. There she meets her "great love," one of her teachers. He becomes her lover for a while until work and the Spanish Civil War separate them. Her greatest criticism is directed toward men who speak of great ideals but who at the moment of self-sacrifice turn coward. On the other hand, women are capable of giving themselves completely to a great love affair or to some other cause in spite of great difficulties. Our protagonist is such a woman, loyal to her lover and to her ideals. Her lover, on the other hand, would give up his ideals for a more comfortable existence.

She waits for twenty years for him to return home, then, when they meet, she realizes that he has changed and that she will have to face the future without her old illusions. Dolores Medio, in her post-war novels, shows the revival of interest in [individual] human beings.

Lucia Fox-Lockert. *Women Novelists in Spain and Spanish America* (Metuchen, New Jersey: Scarecrow Press, 1979), pp. 9–10

Funcionario público (1956; City employee), one of the better achievements of the "social" novel, relates the plight of Pablo Marín, a poorly paid telegraph operator in Madrid, who lives with his wife Teresa in a sub-let room, suffering economic hardships and postwar shortages of housing and opportunity, until he is rendered impotent by the fear of having a child (the landlady will not allow children and they have nowhere else to go). He escapes from the grim realities of daily routine by fantasizing about a young woman whose diary he chances to find, overlooking the growing frustration of Teresa until finally she leaves him. Unlike most documentary social literature, this novel had a tangible impact, resulting in a pay raise for communications workers. *El pez sigue flotando* (1959; The fish keeps floating), Medio's third novel, presents a microcosm of Madrid via a vision of the tangential lives of characters in ten flats of a Madrid apartment building. The stories are fragmented, the reader's vision often not extending beyond what might be visible from one of the apartment windows. Essentially realistic, in spite of the experimental technique, this novel emphasizes once again the economic strictures of a majority of the characters, financial worries and deprivation, as well as isolation, loneliness, disillusionment, and emotional frustration. *Diario de una maestra* (1961: A schoolteacher's diary), considered one of Medio's most significant works, is frequently autobiographical, reflecting the novelist's own experiences, attitudes, personality, and philosophy, with a thin literary disguise. *Atrapados en la ratonera. Memorias de una novelista* (1980; Caught in the Mousetrap. A Novelist's Memoir) which covers many of the same years in Medio's life, allows the critic to compare autobiography with fictional disguise. *Diario* spans a period from the protagonists's university studies and the beginning of her romantic liaison with her professor, Máximo Sáenz, until some eleven or twelve years later, when Max is released from political prison some eight years after the end of the Civil War. In the interim occurs the teacher's experience in the village, her conflict with the reactionary attitudes and suspension from her post, her attempts during the war to rejoin Max, and later her work in a war hospital in Oviedo. Surviving via a variety of jobs until restored to her teaching position, she continues to sacrifice in order to send tobacco and food to Max in prison, living for the day of his release. When at last the longed-for reunion arrives, Max is beaten, aged, disillusioned, and no longer interested in a life together. He stays barely long enough to inform her that he is going to America, leaving her stunned. On the verge of suicide, she is recalled to her pedagogical obligations by a handicapped child she had been helping.

Bibiana (1963), first volume of the trilogy *Los que vamos a pie* (Pedestrians), takes its title from the name of its protagonist, a rather simple, middle-class Barcelona housewife whose life revolves around her husband and children. Emphasis is placed upon daily routine, including many household chores—cleaning, cooking, marketing, doing the laundry—and Bibiana's relationships with her husband and adolescent offspring, who all somewhat look down on her, seldom realizing how they depend on her. There are few breaks in Bibiana's routine, except when she is inadvertently involved in a political meeting (a reflection of Medio's own experience, which landed her in jail), and another time when she is interviewed for a radio program. *La otra circunstancia* (1973; The other circumstance), a continuation of the trilogy, shifts its focus from Bibiana to her husband, Marcelo, and presents a later period of relative ease when economic hardships have given way to a certain prosperity and consumerism. Other problems appear, however, especially for Bibiana, with her daughter's corruption and husband's disaffection. To date, the trilogy has not been completed.

Also in 1973, Medio published *Farsa de verano* (Summer farce), a novel resembling *El pez sigue flotando* in its bringing together of a diverse group of unrelated people in the same space and time. Vacationers on a package tour are portrayed with their individual stories, preoccupations, and characters. Their realistic, everyday lives are interrupted unexpectedly by a tragic accident. *El fabuloso imperio de Juan sin tierra* (1981; The fabulous empire of Juan the Landless) is Medio's latest novel to date. Set in an Asturian village, it portrays the return of a long-absent former villager about whom many stories circulate. The emigrant's reappearance provides a pretext for re-creating memorable events of earlier years via conversations and recollections with residents Juan had known when an adolescent. Somewhat in the vein of Delibes' novel, *El camino,* with its evocative reconstruction of village personalities and relationships, anecdotes, and speech, this work of Medio's excels in its capture of colloquial, regional conversation and humble slice-of-life human interest stories. Medio has also published several collections of short stories, including *Compás de espera* (1954; Waiting time), marked by its preoccupation with social inequities, class divisions and prejudices, economic injustices, and victimization of the weak by those more fortunate. *El bachancho* (1974), another story collection, includes many previously published in defunct magazines, mostly on social themes and depicting the problems of the poor from a realistic standpoint. Three novelettes or long stories—two published some years earlier—appear in *El urogallo* (1982; The partridge). The title novelette relates the capture of a Republican guerrilla in the Civil War by baiting a trap with his fiancée (an allusion to a hunting technique in which the female is similarly used). *Mañana* (Tomorrow), first published in 1954, presents a young woman trapped in a monotonous existence who has her unexpected opportunity for a better life with a man ruined by ironic chance. *El señor García,* the third novelette of the collection, originally appeared in 1966, and like *Funcionario público,* depicts the plight of an underpaid office worker. García is led to believe that he will be promoted to office manager, resulting in the raise in the value of his personal stock and some limited adulation from co-workers. Ironically, the position goes to a relative of the boss and García returns to his dull existence with his deflated hopes.

Medio is not feminist by ideology, but with her emphasis on class and social issues, together with the female role model presented by her resolutely independent single protagonists in *Nosotros, los Rivero, El pez sigue flotando,* and *Diario de una maestra,* she makes more of a feminist statement than most of the women who precede her. Significantly, also, she is the only woman writer of her generation to transcend stereotyping of the "old maid" and to present the single state in a positive light. Intellectual integrity and altruistic dedication to the collective good within the realistic critical tradition are hallmarks of Medio's career, followed by a keen appreciation of the ironies of everyday life, the contradictions of emotions and decision.

Janet Pérez. *Contemporary Women Writers of Spain* (Boston: Twayne, 1988), pp. 123–25

Medio has been associated primarily with the"social novel" in Spain, a postwar literary movement that sought to provide a critical view of contemporary Spanish social, economic, and political reality in order to provoke reaction and reform. There are undeniable points of contact with the goals of the social novel, but exclusive association with this movement would not be completely accurate, since both style and intent may ally her more closely with the nineteenth-century Spanish realists and naturalists. Her descriptions of her own technique certainly suggest the procedures of the nineteenth-century novelists she so admired—observation, documentation, literature as a chronicle of contemporary life—and she has stated that one can study the contemporary history of Spain better through the daily lives of her characters than in a textbook. Her interest in the theories of heredity and environment, clearly evident in *Nosotros los Rivero,* recall similar procedures of the nineteenth-century naturalists, particularly Leopoldo Alas (Clarín), a fellow writer from Oviedo whose influence is apparent in her work.

Medio's fiction is set in contemporary Spain; her favorite subjects, the common people (with whom she identifies), are individually and collectively the protagonists of her literature. The preference for the common person translates into a preponderance of lower- or middle-class characters, caught in the web of problems generally associated with modern times.

Dolores Medio is one of the generation of postwar novelists whose major works appeared in the 1950s and 1960s. Like the other writers of this period, she shows a great interest in displaying contemporary Spanish life through the experiences of the average person, who is generally a victim of forces beyond his or her control. The plots invariably show the effects of the postwar conditions on humanity, and use the themes of solitude, disillusionment, shattered hopes, lack of communication, and financial difficulties to reinforce the characters' more personal stories. The interweaving of historical moment with individual concerns, the influence of environment on character development, and the juxtaposition of social pressures and personal goals suggest that Medio considers the clash between exterior demands and individual aspirations to be important in her fictional works. Her critical intentions appear most clearly in her use of characters who transcend their individuality to represent their class or group. The individual can thus provide commentary on society as a whole, while retaining enough singularity to allow human interest and psychological depth to the story.

Medio is also recognized as a member of this generation because of her connections with social realism: her critical stance, certain normal techniques (realism, objectivism), and contemporary lower- and middle-class themes. However, she has not yet been fully appreciated in her role as feminist writer.

Her works clearly document and comment on the position of the Spanish woman in the early postwar years, a portrayal made even more poignant by the realization that much of what her female characters undergo is a faithful reflection of her own experiences. Thus a major contribution to Spanish fiction and to women's studies centers around the female characters in Medio's works, which may be divided into two rough groupings. The young, successful professionals (Lena, Irene, Marcela) evoke aspects of the writer's own life; they often go through an initiation process, generally precipitated by some personally or nationally traumatic experience. Others, either a principal character (Bibiana) or one of the myriad secondary females who populate these works, appear in a static role that seems to reflect on the inequitable situation of women in contemporary Spain. Their lack of power to influence others, much less to direct their own lives, is made apparent in every aspect of their existence. Even the more liberated women—those who seem to have more control over their lives or who have more contemporary, if cynical, outlooks (such as Bibiana's daughter)—have lives that are filled with personal and professional problems and questions, suggesting that mere liberation is not a total solution to human problems.

Medio's fiction can be appreciated as a reflection of the literary preoccupations of her time—social realism, objectivism, critical intentions, as a faithful representation of contemporary social and historical reality that she herself experienced, and as a commentary on more universal, human concerns.

Margaret E. W. Jones. In Joan L. Brown,
ed. *Women Writers of Contemporary Spain*
(Newark, Delaware: University of Delaware
Press, 1991), pp. 61, 69–70

Solitude and silence circumscribe the mature lives of all our protagonists. Matia, of *La trampa,* lost her voice at an earlier age, but at maturity she becomes even more painfully aware of the "ultimate solitude," which, like an archipelago, makes of each individual an island entirely separate from others. The diary she is writing is analogously ruptured and jumbled, as is the overall narrative that encloses her. Matia is disturbed by this chaos, unprepared for the discursive subversiveness that it might portend: "Lo leo, lo tomo, escribo otra vez: y lo que leo, lo que escribo, me parece indescifrable. Lo releo, y no entiendo una sola de estas líneas. Como si estuviera escrito en un desconocido idioma" (I read it, I take it, and I write once more: and what I read, what I write, seems indecipherable to me. I reread it, and I don't understand even one of these lines. It's as if I were writing a foreign language). Clearly, this despair signifies more than individual anguish before the blank page; it says something about our contemporary distrust of language and our hopelessness before the elusiveness of meaningful communication. For a woman, it is even more compelling, suggesting also and again the double bind that requires woman's submission to an alien contract if she is to speak at all. . . . This imposition, founded upon cultural definitions of the speaker's (or writer's) lack, forces her to speak in a tongue figuratively foreign to her and outside the context of her own desire. . . .

In many ways the particular situation of Matia—and the general condition of other dispossessed and displaced women like herself—is symbolized by the maternal condition itself, which Diana Hume George has named "exile." Matia, as both literal and figurative exile—as well as mother—is a "double site of loss." And as writer in search of her lost language, the poignancy of her condition sums up the particular wasteland that the mature Spanish woman writer often came to occupy at mid-century. So although a mother, Matia finally comes to maturity with the same sense of loss, solitude, and silence as her childless predecessors, the protagonists of *La playa* (The beach) and *La enferma* (The sick woman). Having internalized alien discourses on aging, femininity, motherhood—in a word, on women—the lives of all three are inscribed into a similarly constricted plot of shrinking possibilities and loss of voice.

Elizabeth J. Ordoñez. *Voices of Their Own: Contemporary Spanish Novels by Women* (Lewisburg, Pennsylvania: Bucknell University Press, 1991), pp. 69, 72

MEIRELES, CECÍLIA (BRAZIL) 1901–64

From Cecília Meireles's *Absolute Sea* flows the sensation of a poetic reality that is to be esteemed above all for its lack of subordination to any current of modern poetry whatsoever. From the modernist battle . . . there resulted the prolongation, throughout almost all of contemporary poetry, of a sort of rupture between form and poetic substance. Because the "ancients" had buried themselves beneath a petrified form, the renovators only rose up in favor of poetic essence, disdaining or overlooking what was equally poetic in the beauty of formal construction. To be sure, today we can see a tendency toward the entirely opposite direction. Poets who have come from modernism, like Carlos Drummond de Andrade, have undertaken vast stylistic experiments. . . .

Out of the delirium and the deprivations of so many formless verses, [Meireles's] work takes on the appearance of something varied and complex, with a certain restful manner, with its rhythm, its musicality, its assonances, and its cadences. Hers are not verses to the twilight, impelled simply by the forces of surrealist inspiration. She orders them through technical standards for artistic beauty. No device of poetic art is foreign to her. From the venerable Portuguese classics, through the romantics, Parnassians, symbolists—she knows them all, and she borrows from all of them to create the structure of her own poems. Thus she demonstrates a great variety of form: in meter, rhyme, vocabulary, and syntax; or in the simple poetic constructions of free verse.

Álvaro Lins. *Os mortos de sobrecasaca* (Rio de Janeiro: Editôra Civilização Brasileira, 1963), pp. 55–56

Cecília Meireles's art is essentially classical. Not because of influences or conscious imitation; it seems just to have been born this way. In a poem of hers one senses the perfect wedding of expression to the idea and of the form to expression. The fact that her themes in general are not conditioned by the present moment and that her verses are free from what is called local color also contributes to this [classicism].

Lyrical to the bone, she undertakes in a large number of poems a self-explication. She addresses herself to other humans, to be sure, as do all poets. But she speaks above all to herself, with the goal of finding in this microcosm the reply to questions that the universe hurls at her. Out of the necessity of the continual confrontation with herself must come the multitude of mirrors that populates her books.

Another of Cecília Meireles's special qualities . . . consists of capturing in short poems, of just a few lines, a fleeting instant, illuminating it with a magical light and, by placing it in a perspective of eternity, giving it a majestic amplitude.

Incessantly distracted by phenomena, torn by emotions, metamorphized by the succession of time, the artist makes a continual effort in defending herself against an inevitable fragmentation and entrusting the segments of her intimate mosaic to something imperishable. This is why the concept of memory and its variations is a constant in her poetry. She perceives events and senses them transformed into future recollections. Hence, we find in them a bitter and strange taste, the painful reaction to what for others is barely an experience. [1956]

Paulo Rónai. *Encontros com o Brasil* (Rio de Janeiro: Ministério da Educação e Cultura, 1958), pp. 59–60

During the full effervescence of the modernist movement, it was [Meireles] who was singled out by many as one of the renovators of poetry, especially since her poetry did not partake of that rupture with the past, of that polemical spirit which characterized the new writers during the phase of frenetic artistic liberation. What we find from the beginning in Cecília's fluid style is the echo of the "classic clarities," as Manuel Bandeira has said, "the best of the subtleties of Gongorism, the clarity of metrics characteristic of the [Brazilian] Parnassian school, the outlines of the syntax and the intonations of the symbolists, the unexpected juxtapositions of the surrealists. All of this well assimilated and fused together through a personal technique, sure of itself and of what it wants to say."

The variety of poetic forms she uses is splendid: sonnets, *quadrinhas*, ballads, rondelettes, and so forth, as well as a rich variety of meters and of rhymes she invented. One can see the growingly rigorous refinement of her poetic form in *Solombra* (Sunshadow) a collection of twenty-eight poems written in the sinuous meter of the alexandrine and the rigorous structure of thirteen verses each, divided into four tercets and a single final line. Despite this apparently rigid and restricting form, lightness and fluidity emanate from this poetry. Admirably mixing the old and the new, Meireles unveils a broad lyric field, one perfectly attuned to modern literary movements.

Nelly Novaes Coelho. *Tempo, solidão e morte* (São Paulo: Conselho Estadual de Cultura, Comissão de Literatura, 1964), pp. 9–10

Seeing [her posthumously published poems] free themselves from their human matrix, it is as if I were seeing her poetry for the first time in the open light, without the perplexity that was awakened in me somewhat by the enchanted or enchanting being called Cecília Meireles. . . . She never seemed to be a quite real creature: no matter how much I try to grasp the physical traces of her presence among us, characterized by gestures of courtesy and sociability, I am left with the impression that she was not where we saw her, that she was without substance, creating a fascinating illusion that would serve us as compensation for knowing that her nature was intangible. Distance, exile, and travel shone through the benevolent smile with which she participated in the game of good social manners, and it was a smile of such beauty, amplified by such extraordinary greenness in the eyes and a voice of such pure melodiousness, that it confirmed even more, through the ingenuity of the trick, the unreality of the individual.

Where was the real Cecília, the one who, answering someone's question, admitted that her principal defect was a "certain absence from the world"? Absent, to be sure, from the world as a theater in which each spectator feels himself compelled to take a frenetic part in the spectacle. But not absent from the world of essences, in which life is more intense because it unfolds in a pure state, without compromises, free from the contradictions of existence—a state in which knowledge and beauty become integrated and dissolve into a perfection of peace. To attain this world, Cecília traveled among select forms that she interpreted more than she described. Her notions of nature are sketches of metaphysical pictures, with objects serving as songs of a transcendental content where the unity of being reaches consummation with the universe. . . .

Carlos Drummond de Andrade. In Cecília Meireles. *Crônica trovada da cidade de Sam Sebastiam* (Rio de Janeiro: Livraria José Olympio Editóra, 1965), pp. 14–15

As assessed by Brazilian criticism, the poetry of Cecília Meireles is especially noteworthy for its aesthetic independence, its spiritualistic and idealistic trends. Mário de Andrade saw in her work an outstanding eclecticism, "a mysterious ability to succeed . . . which selects among all existing trends only what enriches or makes expression easier." Osmar Pimental believes that because she [rejects] the accidental and anecdotal, she can concentrate her attention "on the fundamental themes of lyricism." Classically balanced in its metrical architecture, modern in its appeal to the sensibility of the twentieth century, Cecília's poetry seeks original solutions for lucid suffering and constitutes a lyrical geography that "belongs both to everyday life and to dreamland." In her language she "instinctively seeks what can give transparency, pureness, fluidity and transformation, and she goes, with her naked soul, through the world with her freedom and lucid dream."

The two favorite paths of Cecília's art, as seen by José Paulo Moreira da Fonseca, are confession and song. Finding her musical treatment more Portuguese than Brazilian, Fonseca believes that Cecília "likes to dilute the poem-thought, in an atmosphere with a continuous intermingling of images, ideas and feelings, in an almost seamless flow." She does not isolate her imagery into neatly designed outlines; this lack of isolation allows the intermingling of both the external and the internal world, an intermingling which permits her metaphysics to reduce everything to the universal essence, "where nothing fights, where nothing suffers, where nothing stirs." This reduction is part of what Nuno de Sampaio calls her mysticism, which prefers prophecy to defined truth, instruction to thought, and adoration to explanation. . . .

The basic difference between Carlos Drummond de Andrade and Cecília Meireles is seen in their individual interpretations of the rose: for Andrade the rose is a symbol of communion with men; for Cecília it was an image of disinterested beauty. The world of Andrade is one primarily of social conscience and moral involvement; the world of Cecília, on the other hand, was one of unceasing natural motion, "continuous replacement of forms and appearances" transcending "the limits of individual life before and after." Yet despite their differences, temperamental and aesthetic, Andrade and Cecília were alike in the fact of their supremacy: each dominated [a] phase of the Modernist Movement.

> John Nist. *The Modernist Movement in*
> *Brazil* (Austin: University of Texas Press,
> 1967), pp. 202–4

Cecília Meireles cannot really be grouped with the modernist poets who revolutionized Brazilian poetry in 1922; she is more a continuer of the line of the symbolist poets active at the turn of the century. Her poetry is extremely personal, much of it a search for herself within the environment she saw around her. Three predominant themes are space, sea, and solitude, handled stylistically by variations of form, sound, and color. In her work there is a pervasive lyricism, characteristic of much of Luso-Brazilian poetry; and she sometimes felt drawn to Portuguese medieval poets, with the result that some of her verse has the tone of troubadoresque poetry.

Critics have praised her style as a high expression of lyricism but have shown dissatisfaction with her tendency to make the poetic moment too explicit. In this she strayed from the path of her symbolist antecedents and was at a distance from her modernist contemporaries. . . . Cecília Meireles was always preoccupied with being understood, which might have come from the fact that she was also the author of several children's books.

Gregory Rabassa. In W. B. Fleischmann, ed.
Encyclopedia of World Literature in the 20th Century (New York: Frederick Ungar, 1969),
p. 404

[Meireles's] literary origins placed her in the midst of the movement of renovation centered around the review *Festa*. . . . Deriving its impetus from symbolism, the *Festa* group still defended the concept of universality on a spiritual basis, interpreting its literary manifestation as a perennial segment of energy between peoples. And the initial phase of Cecília Meireles's poetic career clearly reveals the influence of the great symbolist poets of the world, including our own. It is an airy and vague poetry, languid and fluid, set in an intimate atmosphere of shadows and dreams, while at the same time it is mystic and sensual. Such are the characteristics of the poetry in the volumes *Specters, Never More and Poem of Poems,* and *Ballads for The King,* especially the last two, in which the symbolist inheritance is seen in the clear influence of Maeterlinck, Verlaine, Antônio Nobre, Cruz e Sousa. Years later, when Editôra José Aguilar published her *Poetic Works* in 1958, the poet chose not to include these books of her early career. Critics, however, cannot help but consider them, for they reveal many of the roots of her later themes.

Her poetic stature was affirmed with the publication of *Voyage,* a work that was awarded a prize by the Brazilian Academy of Letters in 1958. Her central theme is the consciousness of the flight of time and the longing for eternity, two elements which are the points of departure for baroque literature, as Fritz Stich has indicated. Baroque writers, in the face of the precariousness of the things of the world, either celebrate life passionately, in the tradition of Góngora, or recoil into a kind of spiritual self-contemplation, along the lines of Quevedo. I quite agree with Dracy Damasceno's observation that Cecília Meireles's poetry is in the tradition of Quevedo. In her poetry this spiritual self-contemplation leads to the themes of melancholy, disenchantment, renunciation, farewell, indifference, the lack of human comprehension, silence, solitude, and her own death. . . .

Leodegário A. de Azevedo Filho. *Poesia e estilo de Cecília Meireles* (Rio de Janeiro: Livraria José Olympio Editôra, 1970),
pp. 179–80

The Symbolist creed which serves as a background to the poetry of Cecília Meireles can be summarized in terms of the emphasis that it placed on the individual sensibility of the poet and on the means used by the poet to communicate an experience of the supernatural through the language of man. The subjective element in poetry was finally given its just due by the Symbolists after having been banished by the Parnassians. All that was political or public was necessarily contrary to this aesthetic of the self, so concerned with the pure value of sound in poetry.

In Brazil no modern poet felt the legacy of Symbolism more than Cecília Meireles. It was natural that she should be drawn to this poetic creed with its emphasis on the self, the mysterious and the nebulous, given her heightened sensibility, her natural bent toward mysticism, and the fact that since early childhood she had been, as she herself has said, a constant companion of death. In addition, early within her poetic career, Cecília Meireles found further reenforcement for her Symbolist ideas from the group of writers in Brazil known as the Spiritualists. These writers, also known as the *Festa* group, were seeking spiritual renovation of Brazilian arts and letters and greatly admired the Brazilian symbolists Cruz e Sousa and Alphonsus de Guimaraens. . . .

Cecília Meireles's early works are indicative of her special debt to Symbolism. Moreover, they serve as an indication of what was to be her future poetic path. These early works reveal a refined sensibility and an ear exceptionally concerned with the aural architecture of the poem.

Rubén García. Romance Notes. 21, 1980,
pp. 16–17, 22

While [I do] not refute the importance of the symbolist tradition in her work, [I do] propose that there is a social statement in her poetry. One way to approach the social concerns in Miereles's work is through an examination of her woman-mirror imagery. One of her best poems containing this imagery is "Mulher ao espelho.". . .

This idea of the self dictated by societal norms is an important theme in Meireles's "Mulher ao espelho." In the poem while the poet expresses indifference towards who she has become she nevertheless recognizes that her image has been shaped by tradition and that it has assured her acceptance in society. . . .

Although society imposes restraints upon the poet, it is her objective to discover who she is. The image of the mirror serves to define creatively the poet's pursuit of self-knowledge as vital to her existence in society. The shift from the feminine plural forms used throughout the poem to the masculine plural forms *uns* and *outros* implies that it is not only the lot of women but of all mankind to search for their real identity. Thus, the mirror is neither an instrument of self-admiration nor of self-examination for the sake of society, as suggested by Berger, since the poet understands that she is a product of society; she is, in effect, its reflection. Rather, the meaningfulness of the mirror image in "Mulher ao espelho" resides in its capacity to assist the poet's search for her other self.

Darlene J. Sadleir. *Romance Notes.*
23, 1982, pp. 119, 121–22

MENCHÚ, RIGOBERTA (GUATEMALA) 1959–

I, Rigoberta Menchú is the memoir of [a] young Indian, who was drawn into the rebel ranks by the almost fanatical military onslaught against her people in the 1970s.

Her book is a fascinating portrait of the culture of her Quiché tribe, one of the largest in Guatemala. For centuries observers have known that following the Spanish conquest, the Mayans of Guatemala remained deliberately apart from Latin society. Rigoberta Menchú explains: "We must hide so much in order to preserve our Indian culture and prevent it from being taken away from us."

The survival imperative is indeed the single greatest force in her life. Indians seem passive toward exploitation, persecution and mistreatment, she suggests, in order to retain their identity. Their unwillingness to learn the customs or language of their oppressors, their resistance to formal education or even to using Western machinery, are part of this attempt to preserve their uniqueness. So the endurance of their community, the preservation of their ancestral customs, the continuation of their deepest traditions become far more important even than temporary enslavement.

But Menchú's book shows how that attitude has begun to change in the face of the army's bestial rampages. She had already lost two brothers to the common hazards of Indian life in Guatemala—one to malnutrition, the other to pesticide poisoning in a coffee field. But not until the military tried to seize their ancestral lands by force were she and her family finally moved to action. For protesting this unlawful activity, the army under Gen. Romeo Lucas García tortured her younger brother for sixteen days until he died; it then killed her father by setting the Spanish Embassy on fire while he was occupying it to denounce army massacres. And when Rigoberta's mother dared to organize her compatriots, the soldiers beat her, raped her and chopped her to pieces.

Rigoberta Menchú's narrative is a searing one. It is, however, marred in places by unnecessary repetitions, lapses in chronology and a distracting lack of clarity, which could have been avoided by more systematic editing. Even so, her work is an extraordinary feat, taking us inside the mind of a modern Mayan and explaining the most intimate details of Quiché life.

Stephen Schlesinger. *The Nation.*
May 4, 1985, p. 538

Rigoberta Menchú, a Quiché woman from northeastern Guatemala, was not yet twenty-three years old when she was forced into exile because of her efforts to help organize the indigenous working people of the country to defend themselves against exploitation and to fight for progressive change. Knowing that for indigenous people Spanish was the language of cultural, economic, and political domination, she determined to learn it as a tool of liberation. In less than three years, she did so. This book is the result of some twenty-four hours of interviews, conducted with her in Spanish by ethnographer Burgos when Menchú arrived in Paris in January 1982. The book is, as Menchú says, more than her own personal story; it is "the story of a people." For folklorists and students of culture, it offers extraordinary insights into the nature of traditional culture and its dialectically linked conservative and progressive functions in relation to the mechanisms of cultural domination and the process of political-cultural liberation.

At the first level, Menchú offers a richly detailed account of the culture of the Quiché: of their close relationship to nature; of the rites associated with birth, marriage, death, planting, and harvesting; of the training of male and female children and the social and cultural roles of men and women; daily amusements and fiestas; organization and governance of community life; clothing; the systematic transmission of traditional beliefs, values, and observances; and the relationship between the oldest levels of culture and new hegemonic systems and structures such as the Catholic Church, upper-class cultural and economic life and institutions, and a succession of reactionary national governments.

Set against her movingly detailed description of her culture, Menchú's account of the systematic exploitation of her community (and indeed of most of Guatemala's indigenous people) is at times almost unbearably graphic. . . .

From a cultural perspective, the inherent danger of such a narrative as Menchú's is the temptation to set up a strawman contest between an idealized traditional culture and an alien and inhumane hegemonic system. The story Menchú tells is far more than descriptive, celebratory, and plaintive, however, for she provides a remarkably tough-minded dialectical analysis of the culture's sometimes dysfunctional internal dynamics. However admirable the continuities, however rich the traditions, however beautiful the clothing, music, and rituals, it is a culture whose proud traditionality and understandably self-protective insularity in some ways heighten the vulnerability of the community. Rigoberta's father, denying her desperate wish to educate herself and learn Spanish, tells her it is "better that we suffer together" than to accept the inescapable *"ladinización"* imposed by the schools. She reveals the limits of her own world view as she comes to understand that the hated *ladino* sector of the social structure is by no means monolithic—that indeed her community's interests are linked more closely with those of the *ladinos pobres* than with those of the acculturated *indios ladinizados,* as purely cultural considerations might imply. She also unflinchingly lays bare the *machismo* that is part of every level of Guatemalan culture—indigenous, *ladino* and *blanco*—and in the process builds a strong feminist theme into her narrative.

Equally useful for folklore students to understand, however, are the links Menchú explores between the social, economic, and cultural exploitation of indigenous people and the positive role played by traditional culture in the birth of political consciousness and the struggle for liberation and equality. For if the dominant culture can manipulate traditional culture in order to divide and oppress indigenous people, the culture itself (this is the other half of the dialectic) also offers resources of identity, continuity, security, community integrity, solidarity, and flexibility. Thus the culture that at times increases vulnerability also consistently orients, empowers, and sustains. "When we began to organize," says Rigoberta, "we began to use those things we had hidden and preserved." In remote times they achieved a level of self-conscious defiance and self-transcendence through the mocking "Dance of the Conquistadores." In these latter days they construct a "ceremony of self-defense" when they organize to fight the invading troops of the right-wing national government, and a "ceremony of farewell" when the entire community later decides (paradoxically) that they must disperse *as* a community to guard and be faithful to "those things we have received from our ancestors."

For a generation of students raised on the "we-had-to-destroy-it-to-save-it" historical ignorance, cultural intolerance and political arrogance of the Vietnam era—renascent in current U.S. policy in Central America—Menchú's book could be a godsend. It reveals and dramatizes in an especially powerful way the inescapable interpenetration of the personal, cultural, and political dimensions of human experience.

David E. Whisnant. Journal of American Folklore. 100, 1987, pp. 29–30

Rigoberta Menchú has a "mission"; a purpose (a form of theorizing?) under/ or over/writes her actions. She comes to Paris as a representative of the Popular Front to speak to solidarity groups. Unlike the anthropologist/interviewer/"theorist" Burgos-Debray who speaks her own language, Menchú conducts this speaking in Spanish, the language of the servant's colonial master, of her exile in Mexico, and not her "own." She speaks in "other words," from "inside" the discourse of the colonizer. She takes on this language in order to speak from their position, an/other subject position, but to occupy it as an Indian, in the interests of her people. The interviewer explains: "Rigoberta learned the language of her oppressors in order to use it against them. For her, appropriating the Spanish language is an act which can change the course of history because it is the result of a decision: Spanish was a language which was forced upon her, but it has become a weapon in her struggle. She decided to speak in order to tell of the oppression her people have been suffering for almost five hundred years, so that the sacrifices made by her community and her family will not have been made in vain." So, this text that is Spanish, created by Rigoberta Menchú and Elisabeth Burgos-

Debray, the language of which is not entirely "natural" (spoken by an Indian and written by a Latin American anthropologist), has been translated (though not entirely) into English by Ann Wright, who describes it as follows: "Rigoberta's narration reflects the different influences on her life. It is a mixture of Spanish learned from nuns and full of biblical associations; of Spanish learned in the political struggle replete with revolutionary terms; and, most of all, Spanish which is heavily colored by the linguistic constructions of her native Quiché and full of the imagery of nature and community traditions." Many texts from other cultures come to us in this way—in another language, translated in two or three (re)moves from the "original" language, and presented through the optics of alien discourses, languages against which the speaker speaks. These are only a few of the reading problems the text presents, but not uncommon ones because they simulate woman's position in general, always speaking in an/other language, in an/other relationship to the language of power (the "original," author-ized speaking), and they ask us to confront the troublesome status of texts in general, those "mixed bloods," the origin and meaning of which remain unsettled and open to discussion.

Not unrelated to this is Rigoberta Menchú's discussion of the theory/practice opposition, part of a longer conversation between "theorists" (feminist intellectuals of the elite class) and "political activists" (poor and working-class women engaged in fundamental struggles). . . .

In *I, Rigoberta Menchú* feminist critics can read the story of a theory/practice relationship in which the exigencies of daily life (practice) require a rewriting of Law (theory), and the authorizing function of Law redefines or corrects the already-constituted actors and their relationships. The effectiveness of feminist literary criticism rests in contra/diction, its ability to remain incomplete, to be a moving energy of practice, the enactment of tactics not intended to survive their occasion struggling against the singular identity of Feminism that makes nominal representation possible, that permits me to think even for a moment that the Quiché Indian woman, despite what she might choose to tell me, has no theory, and that makes it impossible for me to say what the "place" of feminist criticism is or might be. Likewise, according to this (il)logic, it [is] impossible for me to formulate, to fix as literary history, or to predict the implication of a feminist critique that erupts, attacks, disappears—appears, now here, now here again, occurring and recurring ir/regularly, unpredictably, and contra/dictorily.

Elizabeth Meese. *(Ex)tensions: Refiguring Feminist Criticism* (Urbana: University of Illinois Press, 1990), pp. 102–3, 128

Clearly, the question of Rigoberta's representativity becomes a major key to grasping the implications of her text. There is the question of whether she represents more than herself, more than her family, a sector of her group, the Guatemala Mayans, and so on. Then there is the question of her story's referentiality, its "truth content"—how the impression of veracity is achieved, and whether that impression can be confirmed. Rigoberta convinces, and she does this, however, despite her own efforts to raise the possibility of ambiguity, half-truth, and outright error. But if the text goes "beyond ideology," then what are the determinants of Rigoberta's perspective and what kind of truth might we find in her telling?

First, we have the problem that on the one hand she wants to tell her story to win sympathy to her people's cause, but on the other hand she is afraid to tell the whole truth, because her people know from experience the way others have used what they could find out about them. Second, we have the problem of the fact that she tells her story to a Paris-trained anthropologist and that this anthropologist clearly affects the text, ordering the material according to her own sense of priorities, framing the chapters and determining the questions she asks. We have the problem of Rigoberta's own motivations, as a politically minded cadre who has been trained to see reality in a certain way and to seek certain outcomes for her people. Then too we may question the ways she sees her culture, about the relation between what she claims are Mayan beliefs and what they may authentically be, even in their transformation through time. And we have also the linguistic question— the use of Spanish by one whose real language is Quiché. These and other matters of representation have clearly absorbed the critics with every aspect of her text, starting with the title of her book and its by now almost classic opening lines.

Marc Zimmerman. *Latin American Perspectives.* 18:4, 1991, p. 31

Representation for Menchú . . . is something quite different from classical political representation or the aesthetic reflective mimesis of nineteenth-century European realist fiction. The nahual, more than a representation, is a means for establishing solidarity. It projects the absence of domination through instrumental rationality, put negatively, and the general practice of love, put positively. It is something akin to the solidarity provided by Jesus in early Christian lore, whose significance also lies in the body, that is, Christ's embodiment of love. This is precisely the sense in which Menchú's community fuses Christianity with its own rituals in a syncretic body of practices for survival. . . .

Menchú's testimonio does not fetishize otherness as do the hegemonic postmodern texts referred to above. Instead, she gives a personal specificity to those marginalized and oppressed elements of which she herself is one. She is not an elite speaking for or representing the "people." Her discourse is not at all about representation or about deconstructing representation by the violence to the marginal. Instead, it is a practice, a part of the struggle for hegemony. In embracing Christ as the symbol of revolutionary consciousness and conscience, Menchú's community also embraces him as the most important of a panoply of "popular weapons," which include both Christianity and Marxism, two master discourses which in the struggle for survival are made to yield their overriding authority. It is the practical aesthetics of community-building, of solidarity, that determines how and to what extent such master discourses are brought in the service of recognition and valuation of the marginalized.

George Yúdice. *Latin American Perspectives*. 18:3, 1991, pp. 27–29

How . . . are we to take Rigoberta's protestations of silence as she continues to talk? Are there really many secrets that she is not divulging, in which case her restraint would be true and real? Or is she performing a kind of rhetorical, fictional seduction in which she lets the fringe of a hidden text show in order to tease us into thinking that the fabric must be extraordinarily complicated and beautiful, even though there may not be much more than fringe to show? If we happen not to be anthropologists, how passionately interested does she imagine the reader to be in her ancestral secrets? Yet her narrative makes the assumption that we are (or, in the case of secrets, would be) interested, and therefore piques a curiosity that may not have preexisted her resistance. That is why it may be useful to notice that the refusal is performative; it constructs metaleptically the apparent cause of the refusal: our craving to know. Before she denies us the satisfaction of learning her secrets, we may not be aware of any desire to grasp them. Another way of posing the alternatives is to ask whether she is withholding her secrets because we are so different and would understand them only imperfectly; or whether we should not know them for ethical reasons, because our knowledge would lead to power over her community. As in the case of Nietzsche's meditation on the nature of rhetoric in general, the choice between ethics and epistemology is undecidable. Because even if her own explicit rationale is the nonempirical, ethical rationale (claiming that we should not know the secrets because of the particular power attached to the stories we tell about ourselves) she suggests another reason. It is the degree of our foreignness, our cultural difference that would make her secrets incomprehensible to the outsider. We could never know them as she does, because we would inevitably force her secrets into our framework. "Theologians have come and observed us," for example, "and have drawn a false impression of the Indian world."

Doris Sommer. *Latin American Perspectives*. 18:3, 1991, p. 34

Testimonio is concerned not so much with the life of a "problematic hero"— the term Georg Lukács uses to describe the nature of the hero of the bourgeois novel—as with a problematic collective social situation in which the narrator lives. The situation of the narrator in *testimonio* is one that must be representative of a social class or group. In the picaresque novel, by contrast, a collective social predicament, such as unemployment and marginalization, is experienced and narrated as a personal destiny. The "I" that speaks to us in the picaresque or first-person novel is in general the mark of a difference, an antagonist to the community, in the picaresque the *Ichform* (Hans Robert Jauss's term) of the self-made man: hence the picaresque's cynicism about human nature, its rendering of lower-class types as comic, as opposed to the egalitarian reader-character relation implied by both the novel and *testimonio*. The narrator in *testimonio,* on the other hand, speaks for, or in the name of, a community or group, approximating in this way the symbolic function of her epic hero, without at the same time assuming the epic hero's hierarchical and patriarchal status. René Jara speaks of an "epicidad cotidiana," an everyday epicality, in *testimonio.* Another way of putting this would be to define *testimonio* as a nonfictional, popular-democratic form of epic narrative.

By way of example, here is the opening of *I, Rigoberta Menchú,* a well-known *testimonio* by a Guatemalan Indian woman:

> My name is Rigoberta Menchú. I'm 23 years old. This is my testimony. I didn't learn it from a book and I didn't learn it alone. I'd like to stress that it's not only my life, it's also the testimony of my people. It's hard for me to remember everything that's happened to me in my life since there have been many bad times but, yes, moments of joy as well. The important thing is that what has happened to me has happened to many other people also: My story is the story of all poor Guatemalans. My personal experience is the reality of a whole people.

Rigoberta Menchú was and is an activist on behalf of her community, the Quiché-speaking Indians of the western highlands of Guatemala, and so this statement of principles is perhaps a little more explicit than is usual in a *testimonio.* But the metonymic function of the narrative voice it declares is latent in the form, is part of its narrative convention, even in those cases when the narrator is, for example, a drug addict or criminal. *Testimonio* is a fundamentally democratic and egalitarian form of narrative in the sense that it implies that any life so narrated can have a kind of representational value. Each individual *testimonio* evokes an absent polyphony of other voices, other possible lives and experiences. Thus, one common formal variation on the classic first-person singular *testimonio* is the polyphonic *testimonio,* made up of accounts by different participants in the same event.

What *testimonio* does have in common with the picaresque and with autobiography, however, is the powerful textual affirmation of the speaking subject. This should be evident in the passage from *I, Rigoberta Menchú* quoted above. The dominant formal aspect of the *testimonio* is the voice that speaks to the reader in the form of an "I" that demands to be recognized, that wants or needs to stake a claim on our attention. This presence of the voice, which we are meant to experience as the voice of a real rather than a fictional person, is the mark of a desire not to be silenced or defeated, a desire to impose oneself on an institution of power, such as literature, from the position of the excluded or the marginal. Jameson has spoken of the way in which *testimonio* produces a "new anonymity," a form of selfhood distinct from the "overripe subjectivity" of the modernist Bildungsroman. But this way of thinking about *testimonio* runs the risk of conceding to the subjects of *testimonio* only the "facelessness" that is already theirs in the dominant culture. One should note rather the insistence on and affirmation of the individual subject evident in such titles as *I, Rigoberta Menchú* (even more strongly in the Spanish—*Me llamo Rigoberta Menchú y así, me nació la conciencia.*

John Beverly. In Sidonie Smith, ed.
*De/Colonizing the Subject: The Politics of
Gender in Women's Autobiography*
(Minneapolis: University of Minnesota
Press, 1992), p. 95

MEW, CHARLOTTE (GREAT BRITAIN) 1870–1928

The Farmer's Bride is a book of forty pages containing seventeen poems. This at present is Charlotte Mew's only published work. The whole of Mrs. Browning's remains can hardly be compressed into five hundred pages of double column. Such poets would not, or could not, learn condensation or practice forbearance. They shirked weeding their own gardens which thus fell to seed, and the flowers are now lost in a tangle of forsaken undergrowth.

Charlotte Mew will not burden futurity with an "Essay on Mind" in two long books of rhymed couplets and with notes, nor with a "Battle of Marathon" in four cantos, nor an "Aurora Leigh" in nine books. Her poetry reveals plainly that she is too modest a person and too authentic an artist. Her imagination could not wander through hundreds of lines of blank verse, or, if it tried, discretion would certainly laugh it back homewards. . . .

She does not tire you with personality; but continually interests you in its strange reflections. There is a rumor through the whole book of Death (that favorite subject of all poetry), as of a fact in the background, not to be forgotten, yet not a reality. . . .

Charlotte Mew's poem "The Changeling" is one of the most original of its kind in modern poetry. It has nothing in common with Christina Rossetti, Stevenson, Walter de la Mare, or any other writer of fairy poetry. It is neither written down nor up: it is factful, not fanciful. It is not quaint or sweet, but hard and rather dreary. You do not smile; you shiver. This child has been born a changeling just as another may have had the misfortune to have been born an idiot, and it tries rather blunderingly, apologetically, and with a touch of bitterness to explain its inevitable fate. . . .

No words are wasted on describing its emotional effect. The method of this poem is to stir the reader to great apprehension and then abruptly leave his imagination to follow its natural course. . . .

No argument, or quotation, can prove that the poetry of Charlotte Mew is above the average of our day. She writes with the naturalness of one whom real passion has excited; her diction is free from artificial conceits, is inspired by the force of its subject, and creates its own direct intellectual contact with the reader. Her phraseology is hard and concentrated. To praise her poetry is to offer homage where it is due; and to recommend it is to desire for others the enjoyment one has oneself experienced.

Harold Monro. *Some Contemporary Poets*
(n.p.: Leonard Parsons, 1920), pp. 75–82

Women have not often been great poets, but they often have had one or two special qualifications. If their poetry has been narrow, on the other hand, it has been seldom flat; and in that narrow space—feeling, moreover, no call to be vigorous—they can the more easily achieve a high degree of finish. Charlotte Mew's verse [*The Rambling Sailor*] is a distinguished example of this class: ladylike, intense, rather confined; with only here and there a spirited and lucky venture into the objective. Her style is sophisticated, but single; an instrument evidently valued for itself, contrived merely to render in each poem one vibration of sincere feeling, not very loud.

Life and Letters. October, 1929, p. 398

Looking back on Charlotte Mew's published work it is difficult to understand how it was that so gifted a woman should have produced so little in the sixty years given to her. Many writers give up in despair at failing to place their work, but such was not her case. From the very first she found a ready market for her stories—the poems were a later development of her talent. She wrote a one-act play in Cornish dialect, *The China Bowl,* which shows her sense of drama at its best; Violet Vanbrugh intended producing it, but almost at the time she made the decision circumstances prevented her from carrying it out and to Charlotte's intense disappointment no more was heard of it. I think from what she said this was one of the great disappointments of her life, and, characteristically, being disappointed she threw the manuscript into a drawer and left it there. She herself attributed her small output to the difficulties of domestic life, doing the housekeeping and looking after "Ma," and the constant interruptions when she sat at her desk—Jane, the factotum, who was with her for years, knocking on the door to ask if she should "finish up" the rice pudding for her dinner? and should she run out for some kippers? or would Miss Lottie mind going herself?

I think myself that as she grew older she no longer had the power of concentration required to sit at a desk for hours at a time, that she lost interest in story writing which had been her main work till about 1916, after which she wrote no more prose at all and very little verse. The sustained prose work dwindled from the long stories printed in *Temple Bar* in the 1890s, to short studies and occasional essays in the early 1900s and then to odd poems, and slowly work came to a standstill. Also, I think she was afflicted with a certain dilettante outlook, perhaps the result of her education, which was the limited one of the 1870s and 80s, and also was partly influenced by her mother's attitude to a daughter with a career. No one in the family except Anne took her work seriously.

She was almost fifty when her first book *The Farmer's Bride* (1916) appeared, and although she was greatly encouraged by its reception she wasn't capable by then of writing much more. Few of the poems which were published posthumously in *The Rambling Sailor* (1929) were written after 1916. She always spoke of stacks of manuscripts salted away in trunks, but after her death very little was found. Perhaps there was some truth in the remark she once made casually to me one afternoon at tea in Gordon Street. She was sitting making spills, which she used to light her endless cigarettes, and which were also made for the parrot to chew and amuse himself with. Seeing some writing on some of these, I asked if she used up old letters that way, and she replied—"I'm burning up my work. I don't know what else to do with it." Anne and I often wondered together whether she might be really destroying some original work, or whether it was just intended to whip us up. Who knows?

Only 500 copies of *The Farmer's Bride* were printed and they took five years to sell out, and yet out of that tiny edition came a great reputation. We published what was to us this big edition—many of the books that came from the Poetry Workshop had only 250 copies for their first edition—because we felt that in Charlotte Mew there was a poet whose work would justify our faith. Time has shown that we were right.

Alida Monro. *The Adelphi.*
August, 1953, pp. 286–88

Born in 1869, the poetess—tiny, bird-headed, iron-haired, bright-eyed, tweed-suited, velvet-collared, Oxford bow-ed and porkpie-hatted, just failing all her life long to keep up appearances—inhabited in extremely "reduced circumstances" the family house in Bloomsbury, together with a shriveled and even tinier "Ma," a sister Anne who painted firescreens, and a ninety-year-old parrot with a festering claw. A third sister and only brother of this somewhat Brontë-ish household languished in insane asylums, and Charlotte and Anne had vowed themselves to chastity in order not to pass on the hereditary taint. . . . After the death of Anne in 1928, Charlotte's own reason became partly affected and she died by her own hand.

From this unhappy, enclosed, and haunted life, what poetry might be expected to come? Gentlewomanly landscapes, or ballads about cavaliers or fairies, or at best over-excited emotions brashly expressed? In timid, second-hand conventional techniques and forms, or perhaps in "free verse" with no form at all? Perhaps, if the gods were temporarily indulgent, a lucky-strike lyric and a little period charm? Nothing could be further from the actuality. Charlotte Mew is one of the most original and inventive of poets, her forms strong and entirely individual; her forte is the long semi-dramatic poem, in which she shows a control and sense of balance and effect that are quite astonishing; and her most successful subjects are such matters as "Madeleine in Church" (a prostitute's colloquy with the Virgin), or "The Fête" (a boy's first sexual experience). A single poem by "queer lonely unhappy" Miss Mew tells us more about human beings and their relationships, one to another, more about this world we live in, more about "reality," than the whole corpus of Mr. [Wallace] Stevens's writings.

Hilary Corke. Encounter. June, 1954,
pp. 78, 80

There is no worked-out, rigorous structure of thought behind Charlotte Mew's work. It is impossible to abstract from it, for example, a defined sense of her political attitudes. In this respect, little more than a sense of a quirky and individualistic personality emerges from her work. . . . Perhaps it is the very simplicity of her approach to timeless themes which explains in part the curious neglect the work has suffered. Her individuality, her passionate sincerity and the particular circumstances of her life do not permit her to be categorized with the writers and poets who were her contemporaries. Too experimental for Edward Marsh's taste, it was indeed a loss that her work was not included in *Georgian Poetry* whose phenomenal success would have kept it more in the public eye. The Poetry Bookshop published *The Rambling Sailor* posthumously in 1929. Though "The Farmer's Bride" and to a lesser extent "The Changeling" were frequently printed in anthologies including *Poems of Today,* widely used in schools, a revival of interest in her work was long overdue by 1953 when her *Collected Poems* was published by Duckworth, and Patric Dickinson broadcast a radio program about her work. In Rose Macaulay's novel *The Towers of Trebizond;* first published in 1956, the Turkish students declare, "We study English Poetry . . . Dylan Thomas, Spender, MacNeice, Lewis, Eliot, Sitwell, Frost, Charlotte Mew." The listing after Frost, whose innovatory "talk" poems developed out of dramatic monologue, is significant. Charlotte Mew's keynote is immediacy, derived from her distinctive use of the dramatic monologue. Frank Swinnerton, asked by Siegfried Sassoon to review her *Collected Poems* in *John o' London's Weekly* because he himself was too unwell to do so, extolled her poems in a way that needs only the number of years changing today: "Since the poet's range is comparatively narrow I should have expected them, after thirty years, to seem a little old-fashioned. Instead, they come burning from the printed page as they always did." As do her stories and essays. These she composed throughout her writing life, contributing to *Temple Bar, The Englishwoman* and other publications of the day. These writings are collected here for the first time, and to those already familiar with her poetry they will reveal new dimensions to her talent and provide new pleasures.

Val Warner. Introduction to *Charlotte Mew.*
Collected Poems and Prose (Manchester:
Carcanet/London: Virago, 1981), pp. xvi,
xx–xxi

The Farmer's Bride and all the poems which were to follow it, where Charlotte Mew speaks in different voices, raise the question—why do poets impersonate at all? They may do it because they have a great deal to hide, or because (like Browning) they haven't quite enough. They may (like Byron) be too energetic or too self-indulgent to contain themselves, they may (like Eliot) want to escape from emotion, or (like Yeats) from the unsatisfactory limitation of self. To Charlotte Mew impersonation was necessary, rather than helpful. "The quality of emotion," she thought, was "the first requirement of poetry . . . for good work one must accept the discipline that can be got, while the emotion is given to one." And what she needed to give a voice to, as she also explained, was the *cri de coeur*—that is, the moment when the emotion unmistakably concentrates itself into a few words. Examples which she gave are Marguérite Gautier's *"Je veux vivre"* and Mrs. Gamp's "Drink fair, Betsy, wotever you do." "One has not only the cry but the gesture and the accent—and so one goes on—calling up witnesses to the real thing." A cry has to be extorted, that is its test of truth. It might make a poem, or it might not. Charlotte once saw a woman walking across Cumberland Market, in Camden Town, "with a tiny child holding on to her skirt, trying to keep up with her and chattering in a rather tired treble, like a chirpy little sparrow, as they went along. Suddenly the woman stopped and struck the child, with a thickly spoken 'Now go and make yer bloody 'appy life miserable and stop yer bloody jaw.'" This too was a *cri de coeur*. As to the farmer, she believed that "as far as I had the use of words, they did express my idea of a rough countryman feeling and saying things differently from the more sophisticated townsman—at once more clearly and more confusedly."

The Nation's readers, even if they thought the farmer's restraint unlikely, responded to the raw sensation of wanting and not getting, against the background of the season's return.

Penelope Fitzgerald. *Charlotte Mew and Her
Friends* (London: Collins, 1984), pp. 104–5

The recent publication of Charlotte Mew's *Collected Poems and Prose* attests to a reawakened interest in an elusive—even mysterious—figure at the intersection of two eras. Considered a genius by Thomas Hardy, Mew did not publish her first book of poetry until 1916, when she was nearly fifty years old and about to end her writing career. That career had begun in the last decade of the nineteenth century, when she published short stories in *The Yellow Book* and other journals, meanwhile establishing a reputation as a quirky, fiercely independent New Woman in voguish London circles. Yet a biographical sketch by her friend Alida Monro describes her as self-deprecating and morally prudish; a more recent sketch by Penelope Fitzgerald tells of "the threat of insanity and . . . the dark thrill of self-inflicted frustration" caused by tensions between her religious, ladylike background and her lesbian inclinations. Her family and upbringing discouraged her from thinking of herself as a writer or of promoting her own work. Twelve years after Harold Monro's Poetry Bookshop published her first book, she had retreated to obscurity, despair, and finally suicide, her work nearly forgotten and certainly eclipsed by the school of Pound and Eliot. Leaving a tightly guarded literary estate and a life that, as Fitzgerald says, "refuses quite to be explained," Charlotte Mew seems to have invited scholarship that tends toward mystery-solving pieces: searches for motives, connections, relationships. Very few critical studies of her life and work have appeared, though Fitzgerald's forthcoming biography may end the speculations about Mew's personal life and encourage further study of this haunted, gifted writer.

In historical context, the span of Mew's lifetime is itself important, in that it includes most of the Victorian Age, World War I, and the 1920s (1869–1928). Though her books appeared much later, most of her writing was done in the twenty years before the war, at a time of delicate social and aesthetic transitions. One can see in Mew's poetry the transformation of the Victorian imagination: the defiance and realism of the New Woman who yet retains shades of Pre-Raphaelite theatricality and tragedy. One group of her poems centers on a specific social-sexual conflict perhaps hinted at in the paradoxes of her personal life: the Victorian treatment of the Fallen Woman theme. In these poems the treatment of eroticism veers away from the despair of Swinburne and the courtly love variations of Rossetti, while showing the influence of both these poets. Mew brings to the Fallen Woman—that is, the explicitly sexual woman—a unique understanding as well as remarkable craft.

Linda Mizejewski. *Texas Studies in Literature and Language.* 26, 1984, pp. 282–83

MEYNELL, ALICE (GREAT BRITAIN) 1847–1922

Alice Meynell published her first volume in 1875. She is an early example of the reticence that is now conspicuous in most branches of English poetry. . . .

Mrs. Meynell . . . and other poets . . . seem to have devoted themselves so exclusively to their art that they have not realized it as an outcome of the habit of Life that all poetry is intended to express.

Harold Monro. *Some Contemporary Poets* (n.p.: Leonard Parsons, 1920), pp. 41–42

Mrs. Meynell is a writer with an extraordinary power of raising the simple and the lowly to those lofty regions of the moral nature in which honor, dignity, and serenity—far from unimpassioned abstractions—sustain a triple sovereignty. If she touches grammatical questions you cannot for a moment think them mere grammatical questions. . . . Mrs. Meynell is one of our best critics, one of the subtlest, the austerest, the most constant in a regard for the obligations of the art of letters. Nothing slack or uneasy, nothing trivial or frivolous, may endure her glance; and she does not mitigate it even when she confronts so especially admired a writer as Jane Austen. . . . Her essays on Coventry Patmore and George Meredith [*Second Person Singular*] are as independent in their praise as these others in blame; and all alike serve to remind us that a fine critic does not teach us what to believe or what to think or what to welcome, but how to judge for ourselves.

John Freeman. London Mercury. February,
1922, p. 434

Mrs. Meynell must place herself slightly at an oblique angle, and view the moments which possess her mind a little from one side. She shoots beside the mark rather than at it; and her arrows, like the bright glances of the robin, fly the straighter because they seem to spy their object from one side. This gave a bird-like quality to her writing, which is at once intense but detached.

We gain from her work, then, this: not, at first, an extension of our humanity but an added sharpness to our consciousness. But insofar as this consciousness is concerned with experiences not peculiar in themselves, but common to all men, it is enriching. The experience of Strephon in "St. Catharine of Siena" is an experience of mankind; Catharine herself is feminine humanity. Hackneyed or official themes are transformed by this insight. Shakespeare's Tercentenaries became two dates in Mrs. Meynell's own life, and the death of Edith Cavell is seen as perhaps Edith herself saw it: a nurse who watched at her own death-bed, a woman who quietly waited for the dawn. We penetrate beyond the heroine of the copy-book to the natural woman, and go with her to her execution. This is the quality which raises Mrs. Meynell's verse to the highest point possible to its own order. Each poem, too, is carefully reasoned, and the reader who does not follow the argument will miss the whole; for intellectually no less than emotionally the verse has point. This intellectual concentration is a dangerous quality. "Via et Veritas et Vita" is an epigram, but a good one. "Veni Creator" and "Why wilt Thou Chide?" seem, or seem near to, intellectual conceits. The latter poem apparently offers an impossibly subtle consolation. Renunciation, consolation—how the theme recurs!

Osbert Burdett. Critical Essays (London:
Faber and Gwyer, 1925), pp. 132–33

Mrs. Meynell was never a professional writer, making daily recourse to a desk and producing books at regular intervals. She led an active and varied life. She bore and brought up a large family; she read and traveled; she entertained a large circle of friends; and Francis Thompson, whose noble poem "Her Portrait" was inspired by her, was only the most conspicuous of many writers, particularly young ones, who went to her for counsel and encouragement. She lived as well as wrote, and she would not have chosen to do otherwise. Yet there was no question with her of writing in spare moments. She wrote when she felt inclined; she spent great pains on preparation and revision; she had no desire to produce a great body of work. It is not easy to conceive any alteration of circumstances—even that economic pressure which she was happily spared—which would have led her to write more profusely or less carefully; and it may be assumed that what we have from her is all that she was born, or felt inclined, to give. By temperament and theory she was destined to do a few things as nearly perfectly as she could. Her philosophy was a kind of Christian stoicism, and she aimed at equanimity and self-control in her art as in her life.

There have been those whose careful and cunning artistry, tact and taste of expression, have arisen from a defect of passion. There was no defect of that in Alice Meynell; she had much to control, and control never froze the springs of emotion in her. In old age she retained the quick sensitiveness of youth, sweet and generous impulses, instant responsiveness to cruelty and injustice.

J. C. Squire. *Essays on Poetry* (London: Hodder and Stoughton, 1925), pp. 98–99

Her poems were mostly the product of more leisured days, in youth and old age. The freakish taste of anthologists has made her best-known poem one with an almost disagreeable sentiment: ("She is so circumspect and right; she has her soul to keep.") The editors of the Centenary Volume have chosen the verse less surely than the prose. "Renouncement" (written at the enforced breaking of her youthful friendship with a priest) is popular, I think, because it treats of the widely felt grief of separation, also perhaps, because it encloses a hidden resentment; but "Parted" is a much finer poem about the same experience. . . .

Hers is a craftsman's poetry, written with a fine tension on pensive and private subjects; such work will always give pleasure. But in prose she found greater scope.

Her writing shows curiously little fantasy. It contains portraits, but not a hint of fiction. It is not the literature of dreams but of ideas and observations, coming from an unusually sensitive and vigorous mind. Now that we are sufficiently far removed from Meredith's praise and Mr. Beerbohm's protest, we can discover for ourselves something of the stimulation that the contemporary reader found in her work.

Naomi Lewis. *A Visit to Mrs. Wilcox* (Sarasota, Florida: The Cresset Press, 1957), pp. 209–11

MEYNELL, VIOLA (GREAT BRITAIN) 1886–1956

Of the making of many books there is no end. But in all their thousands how few of them there are that in any striking fashion differentiate themselves from the rest. But the rarest of all pleasures that comes a critic's way—that of being able to assert with surety and conviction that he has found something with the stuff within it that makes for greatness—is the happy result of a perusal of *Modern Lovers*. With how much of it we cordially agree! . . . The two books with which it makes an odd comparison are *Wuthering Heights* and, of all the stories in the world in this connection, Schnitzler's *The Road to the Open*. No two stories of course could be more dissimilar. But it is the curious intermixture of weirdness and strangeness and harshness that seemed built into the very stones of the grim house upon the heights in conjunction with Schnitzler's cynical modernity that makes this particular novel unlike any other novel we have ever lit upon.

The Outlook. January 17, 1914, p. 84

She, like so many modern writers, rejects the realistic novel, the novel of ordinary manners; and, like them, in doing so she feels the need of some removed and, in the good sense, unreal setting for her stories. The classic examples of such settings are Mr. Conrad's ships at sea and his isolated and mysterious Asiatic lagoons. Here the novelist's characters are to be set free from the stream of everyday life and allowed to develop and act in an ideal manner. . . . Miss Meynell's attempt and partial failure here to remove and isolate her characters gives her book [*Antonia*] a bewildering and nightmare quality. The society in which the action takes place is cosmopolitan and bizarre in the extreme, but it remains attached to the world we know: not in any society, from whatever corners of the earth its members may have been brought, do people consistently behave as Miss Meynell makes them behave here, while simultaneously they are taking trains, shopping in Paris, and sending for doctors because the wife of the concierge has a touch of pleurisy. I shall not outline the story, the love passages of Antonia Borch with Oswald Brook, and her subsequent marriage to Prince Mitrany, because I do not pretend to understand it; least of all do I understand why the marriage should be so tragic a matter, though this is clearly the point of the book. But Miss Meynell's nightmare is vivid and, in its strange way, engrossing. In the intervals of doing the most common things her characters perform extraordinary gyrations of the spirit, which, incomprehensible as they are in themselves and in their further significance, have an undeniable interest. And Miss Meynell writes both eloquently and powerfully.

Edward Shanks. *London Mercury.*
November, 1921, p. 96

Miss Viola Meynell is distinguished by a gift for the broadly comic. Her girls who say: "Well, I don't know; I think people always like to do the things they're fond of doing," and "I put it down to the want of ignorance, don't you think so?" are adorable; and her elocution mistress might almost have come out of *Martin Chuzzlewit.* . . .

Women novelists have, on the whole, I think, succeeded better in the satiric delineation of men's foibles than in the direct delineation of their virtues (witness Jane Austen). I do not want to suggest any generalization to the effect that this always must be so. But certainly, among the women writers of the day, and not least in Miss Meynell's work, I am troubled by a feeling that the male characters are too frequently relegated to a low moral level, a level of egoism and mere self-absorption. In *Columbine* the hero is amazingly self-centered: he sees everything as it affects his own personality, nothing objectively. In *Modern Lovers* the hero has faults to which one cannot help suspecting his creator was either blind or over-indulgent. It is not in the least that one wants didacticism, vice denounced, or virtue embarrassed with laudation: all one wants is the recognition, *felt* in the texture of the representation, revealed through it, that there is something abnormal, unrepresentative, unpleasant, in these egoistic excesses. *Narcissus* deals with two brothers, Victor and Jimmy. The relationship between them is one of the best things about them. Miss Meynell exercises upon it her rare gift of stressing sentimental values without ever becoming in the bad sense sentimental. She has a wonderful touch for the deep and recondite pleasure of simple things: the spiritual atmosphere of a living-room, the reading of a book.

Gerald Gould. *The English Novel of Today*
(London: John Castle, 1924), pp. 126–27

MILES, JOSEPHINE (UNITED STATES) 1911–85

Miss Miles's poetry seems to me to evolve upward (though doubtless not in the order in which the poems are written) from something that is little more than the enjoyment of vernacular speech—which obviously delights her ear—through a kind of sharp, humorous, and often resonant character-picture, by way of enigma, to the lyric proper. At each level she shows some if not all of the traits which are most personal and peculiar to her as a writer and which give the over-all tone of her work. The traits I think of are: the delight in the vernacular, which she makes serve a sophisticated craft; the quality of her humor, which Louise Bogan compared to the "dissenting 'dryness' of the country store or town meeting"; and her belief in the importance of particular event, circumstance, place—the net in which she snares her subjects, and the idea informing her love of vernacular speech, of the particular flavor of the language she hears.

Barbara Gibbs. *Poetry.* October, 1946, p. 49

Thoroughness, courage, and at least a perceptible originality have for some time made Josephine Miles one of our most interesting commentators on the poetic mind. . . .

The present study [*The Primary Language of Poetry in the 1940s*] shows the linguistic method for which she is best known as neither feeble nor triumphant; one is inclined to view her particular approach cordially but nevertheless coolly. Her book falls into three chapters: the first and longest contains by far her most valuable work, which, it is noteworthy, arises not from her statistical method of commentary on the art of poetry by aid of linguistics but from her own poetic spirit, that not infrequently inspires imaginative language of no mean order. In other words, although Miss Miles appears to give first place to a scientific method, and second place to a philosophic one, the aesthetic method of criticism actually serves her best; when her own hand is happiest, criticism turns out to be neither science nor philosophy but art.

Henry W. Wells. *American Literature.*
May, 1952, p. 265

Her work is terse, quirky, and often quite abstract; rarely does it have the sonority and rhythmic charm which, in some poets, can make us patient of difficulty. Yet if one sticks with these poems, it soon transpires that they are the real thing. Beyond the dry obliquities of the language, the shying-away of the half-rhymes, the condensed secretarial grammar, lies an intense, intelligent and original sensibility with certain persistent concerns. Once this is perceived, the mannerisms are largely redeemed.

I find two main subjects here [*Prefabrications*]. The first is human communication, and it is studied in short, penetrating poems about loneliness, animosity, understanding, and love. The second is human dignity, as conceived by a skeptical, democratic intelligence. These subjects are pursued in a milieu of super-markets, shoe-stores, highways, and beach-cabins; Miss Miles accepts the fearful jerry-built landscape of California as the real world of her poems, and finds her symbols in it.

Richard Wilbur. *Saturday Review of Literature.* February 18, 1956, p. 50

A conceivable interpretation of her title [*Prefabrications*] is that she is countering the jerry-built constructions of the modern world, those that shut out sun and sea, with the pre-logical fabrications of the poetic imagination. Man, at war with nature, including human nature, has become a prisoner in time. Only by an act of the imagination or, equivalently, by an act of love can he reestablish contact with his primal source and regain the power to set himself free. Miss Miles's approach is oblique, metaphorical—she is not one for direct assault—but over and over again we hear the light-voiced cue. . . .

The people of her fancy are sensitive, disturbed, but not doom-ridden; their hearts are nimble; the sea and the rain and the wind have news for them.

Stanley Kunitz. Poetry. June, 1956, p. 190

Josephine Miles presents the anomaly of a poet and a good one who as a literary scholar and historian has been chronically given to a statistical method of analysis. Because she is a poet and this character seems to carry over into her scholarly labors, even in their most forbidding phases, her articles and monographs, now a long series, have always had their peculiar interest and have offered their peculiar kind of profit—though, for me at least, there were moments, especially in the beginning, when it seemed as if verbal statistics were being recited with a strange feverish insistency, an out-of-place lyric throb. . . .

What then are the conspicuous merits of the descriptive tour of English poetry [*Eras and Modes in English Poetry*] which Miss Miles conducts according to these lights? I believe they are considerable, and peculiar. They are related first of all to the fact that she does eschew the recent American enterprise of organistic analysis and evaluation of individual poems. We must not go to Miss Miles for that. Rather, the peculiar aim of her technique is the description of large areas of poetry—"eras and modes." She is out precisely to make generalizations, to formulate viable historical concepts. . . . [H]er method of verbal statistics, richly informed or supplemented by her own special insights, is a union of the formal and contentual which at its best comes close to being a masterly union for generalizations about poetic history.

W. K. Wimsatt. Journal of English and
Germanic Philology. April, 1958,
pp. 321–22, 325–26

Miss Miles early found her own style and attitudes, and she has worked with integrity and pleasure to make the world her verse defines as large as possible. Her poems, though, are characteristically as small as possible; few have made a couple of quatrains say so much, or with such grace. Miss Miles's tone—gravely insouciant, sweetly tough—is all her own. Her rectitude of feeling and exactness of language evoke continual felicities. The reader's pleasure grows with her maturing mastery, for good as are the early works, her more recent poems are her best.

Miss Miles confronts experience both openly and inwardly, and finds poems everywhere. With her ear for the colloquial and eye for the surprising delight in the ordinary, she makes poems both witty and compassionate about motels, advertisements, election campaigns, California's exploding population, drivers in traffic, buying a pair of shoes. She can sketch persons memorably in brief, characteristic actions, and she understands her people with a sympathy that is unsentimental. A complementary voice—passionate, contemplative, self-knowing—alternates with and reinforces the language that renders her exterior world.

Daniel G. Hoffman. *Saturday Review of Literature.* October 29, 1960, p. 31

In the case of Miss Josephine Miles, I find myself confronted with thirty years of poems of a kind that I have never much liked. [*Poems 1930–1960*]. Yet after reading Miss Miles, I find also that all my standards, never very strictly defined, have been upset, so that I am not exactly sure what I like and what I don't. Though, like most people who read poetry at all, I was aware of Miss Miles's name and of her rather muffled but nonetheless quite apparent reputation, I have never until now taken a good look at the totality of her output. The first quality of her work that struck me was a uniform sort of unrelieved and often drab intellectuality. There are plenty of intelligent comments, plenty of shrewd, narrow-eyed observations, but I kept wishing for a little more feeling and a little less knowledge. The poems are so self-contained that they come to seem automatic, including as they do all the things that poems need in our time in order to exist respectably: they have beginnings, middles, and ends, and one is never in any doubt about which is which. There is none of the opening out into a Beyond greater than anything the poems have to tell: nothing to assure the reader that what *he* brings to the poems of his own life is at all important—Miss Miles has neatly packed everything for him. And yet I did not continue to feel this way for long. I came to believe what Miss Miles says, and believe it in a way that also includes a large measure of admiration for the gentle assurance with which she deals with her material. If there is such a thing as making a cardinal virtue out of deliberately letting alone larger subjects in favor of smaller ones, Miss Miles has made a modest and authentic triumph of it, and any reader who is at all alive will be enriched by her quick, penetrating looks from the odd angles of hidden corners.

James Dickey. *Sewanee Review.* Spring, 1961, pp. 330–31

American satirists, at the moment, are few and far between, and when they do turn up, their line of attack is likely to be oblique rather than direct. Josephine Miles, for a good many years and in three books, has shown a satiric gift of the most subtle kind. That this gift has been nourished by a California background makes it all the more rare; Miss Miles teaches at Berkeley. Her new book, *Prefabrications,* is principally focused upon details of day-to-day life—those details that it is almost impossible for a poet of any time or place to get at without showing signs of pressure and strain. Miss Miles writes with ease and with insight about the parking lot, the motel, the Los Angeles high school, the building project, the supermarket, and the service station. Through some delicate imaginative adjustment, the intermittences of the heart and the clear light of the intellect become involved with these locales. Miss Miles is able to produce *Zeitbild* of a true kind, because to her the spirit comes first.

Louise Bogan. A Poet's Alphabet (New
York: McGraw-Hill), 1970, p. 226

Miles does not (only) contain multitudes, but is part of a multiply supported, threatened, and ramified world. . . . [E]ven the world of educated people cannot be cognitively mastered by one technique or language or consciousness; and the rest of the world, in which educated people also live, seems, to put it mildly, no better suited to becoming a pastoral object of judgment for "serious and high-minded people." Miles's university is a complicated and sometimes protective institution; it is linked to, even when it momentarily lets her forget,

> other institutions
> More terrible, where I would do less well.
> Hospital, asylum, prison, prison camp.
> And I fall into a reverie of dismay:
> Failure to aid survival, failure to foster. . . .

("Institutions")

Miles never undervalues the prosperous milieu of her work ("O small and flowering garden of free friends!") and never pretends not to be or not to enjoy being a woman of culture. At the same time, partly from her experience of physical disability, she is knowledgeable about the intermittent alliances of intellect and force that guard the gates of the university. . . .

Perhaps because of this masking effect, one of the few strands of liberal politics that does not appear very explicitly in Miles's poetry is feminism. The presence of males, like the presence of activists and busy people and entrepreneurs and money and violence, is vigorously conspicuous. It is not that Miles necessarily approves of all these things but that, in the world of many of these poems, they *are* the discourse: they are the "on" switch, and their opposites can seem like mere negations. Again, this cognitive strategy must be the appropriate one for the resolute mind pressing toward "well" or "mobile" from "not well" or "immobilized." But when the less clamorous problem of gender, perhaps hardly felt as a separate problem, tends to be subsumed under the same strategy, the result can be something more surprising: a world divided, not between the male and the female, but between the male and the not male.

The most marked example of the not-male is the speaker in "I am trying to think what it means to be right." A housewife, she is terrified, in a ghostly yet domestic way. . . .

What is really frightening her is the real world—politics and violence, "soft southern voice, soft asian robe." "The yard outside, world outside cry." But in spite of the demonic insidiousness with which the violent outside world is rising up against her in her own mind, her only response is to try to shut it out more absolutely and blankly. . . .

In this poem, the female space is merely a desperate, cruel denial of the active male world—and the female space is, finally, entirely shaped by and impregnated with the male world, as any mere negative is by the thing it denies.

Eve Kosofsky Sedgwick. *Epoch.* 31, 1982,

pp. 69, 72–73

Just as the Latin love lyric seems the source of Robert Creeley's prosody, so, then the source of Josephine Miles's verse seems to be the classical epigram. Creeley's work is sardonic regarding self but asking compassion for others, while understanding that the world has very little mercy for anything. Miles, on the other hand, is consistently ironic in tone, satirical in intent, and never compassionate, though (perhaps this is greater) always accepting. . . .

I said she is never compassionate, and I mean that in its purist sense. She accepts, sees beyond the merely human into something bigger. Hauntingly, the lines, "A radioactive fish is one charged/ With more universe than he can bear," rings loud jangling bells of resonance for me with Robinson Jeffers, another great California poet, whose philosophy of "inhumanism" (conceived far, far ahead of his time) held that man is only a small part of the universe and that to conceive of "universal" problems in terms of man is not only egotistical but deadly for its inconsequentiality of vision.

Jeffers too tried to combine the dramatic and the human with a vision of statesmanship and the lyric intensity of musical verse. Jeffers's vision of government and power was one which extended beyond national boundaries. He abhorred war and saw, equally, Roosevelt, Mussolini, and Hitler as warmongers and villains. These views caused half a dozen of the poems in his collection, *The Double-Axe,* to be cut out of the book by his long-time editor and publisher, and a disclaimer against the views in the rest of his poems to be published in a foreword to the book. But his poems were not political diatribes. They were lyrics of deep intensity. Perhaps Jeffers was the only poet of his generation who completely succeeded in the combination. But if we look at his critical fate, we see that the combination of those three poet-roles, dramatist, statesman, and singer, is not terribly attractive to the world or to the critics of poetry. Alas, for both Robert Creeley and Josephine Miles, the lyric does not overwhelm and charm the beasts to sleep. The wit and wisdom are sharp and go past easy compassion or mercy, while the view of mankind accepts everything including such immense failure of history that most do not want to hear it. That clear vision of our politics and history is rejected by most readers of poetry. . . .

Both Creeley and Miles create a language purity in their poetry which does not obliterate meaning. It is moralistic but not didactic. The fashion in poetry and criticism today (structuralism) moves toward a false concept of technological accomplishment, I think. For the function of language has al-

ways been and always will be the communication of ideas, feelings, knowledge. To work towards a language which abandons these values is to work
against language rather than to progress. Yet John Ashbery, one of the most
highly touted poets in this country today, does this. What I find so remarkable
in the work of both Miles and Creeley *is* that movement towards purity,
established by Dickinson, but without losing substance, meaning or history
with the fragmentation. Their poems do what I conceive that (to me) mysterious entity, the "chip" to be able to do: In a tiny space, carry enormous
amounts of information and energy.

And maybe that is the new function of the poet, his new role, or the very
one Plato was worried about: to be the "chip" which holds all information in
an infinitisimal space, which gives the power of a whole galaxy in a feather
or a shoe. If so, then surely Josephine Miles is one of the New poets, for her
language and vision do present that concentration.

Diane Wakowski. Epoch. 31, 1982,
pp. 78–80

Although her poetry has seldom dealt autobiographically with the themes of
personal initiative and courage, it has explored them through a variety of
other materials. Many of the characters in her poems do things which they
could never do without an image of heroic selfhood, a belief that it is necessary and right to fight the odds and defy circumstance. But she shows us that
this vision, however necessary and laudable it is, can also be limiting in the
way it can centralize the self and oppose it, even blindly, to everything else.
She has never tried to say in so many words what a proper spirit for heroic
effort would be; instead she has worked to create that spirit through the
ironies and tensions of her poems. It is a state of constant argument between
heroic willfullness and a cooler, more expansive vision—one that looks
around with a certain detachment and is willing to let the universe lay
down its blessings and afflictions where it will. This argument, in statements remarkably strong and fresh, is what she gives us in, for instance,
"Sisyphus.". . .

There is a violence when the novelty rushes in: violence of matter against
thought, of the impersonal against the person. And it is only basic honesty
to admit that aesthetic exhilaration is bound up with it. What's remarkable
to me, and characteristic of Josephine Miles's work, is that the considerable
violence of this poem is all in its fictional situation; there is no violence at
all in the language itself. I used to think that this fact of Miles's poetry
constituted a moral advantage. I thought that by limiting the violence to
her fictions, and then writing calmly in its presence, she could draw clearer
boundaries between the unknown and the known, the alien and the human,
than could those of us who engage violence with and in our words. I realize
now, though, that the advantage is not in her method. Where we might let
the violence take control of our imagery, she occasionally creates a fiction

whose subtle violence overrides what her language can do; "Oedipus" is an example of this.

Josephine Miles's real advantage is the same as Neruda's or Adrienne Rich's: she controls the violence more often than not. . . . This poise is classical and classic; it does not try to suppress the violence of nature and creation, but it does answer that violence, by showing how opposite and antagonistic elements can be brought into balance within the play of their force. Such answering is one of the fundamental acts of her poetry, and it is moral action on the most fundamental level. All of the specific ethical and political stances of her poetry can be seen as extensions and elaborations of it.

Rory Holscher. *Epoch.* 31, 1982,
pp. 82, 84–85

For the past several years I have been thinking about how lyric poetry might include other lives and ordinary events without becoming narrative and without usurping the world by transforming it into something too tidy or too emblematic of the self. These issues are ethical and political, as well as poetic, involving the question of how poetry engages the languages and the cultures of its world, shaping but not colonizing what it shapes. Related concerns are explored by contemporary writers as varied as Heather McHugh, Robert Hass, and C. K. Williams. But the poet to whom I am drawn most strongly and most consistently as I consider how poetry might be both inclusive and lyric is one whose name is rarely mentioned outside of Berkeley, California— Josephine Miles.

It is not simply the shape of Miles's life as a poet that I admire, although it is worth mentioning that she first published in the 1930s, when her poems from the 1935 *Trial Balances* won the Shelley Award, and that her work appeared steadily, growing in power and scope, through her final volume, the 1983 *Collected Poems,* published just before she died. Miles learned her craft along with, as well as from, American poets like Moore, Williams, and Stevens (although her one statement on the poet that meant most to her in her early years invokes Yeats). Most strikingly her mature poems carry forward the insights of the older poets she admired, especially in her reclamation of the gestures of American speech. . . .

Miles is maintaining a delicate balance: the language she preserves belongs to those who use it; it is a source of vitality *from people.* At the same time, Miles reveals an acute awareness of the impositions of poetry. In shaping, in appropriating from people, she is contributing to, but also changing, what she has heard. . . .

There is an ethical issue at stake here. Miles proposes that to add a "sense of meaning" is both to preserve and to change what is inarticulate, at the same time that she sees the shaping intelligence as "natural," as "contribution" rather than imposition. From her earliest volumes Miles's poems have exhibited a similar self-consciousness about what she has called "the necessity of pattern-making" coupled with a sense of the importance of set-ting "unlikeness over against likeness."

Later poems—especially from the 1960s and 1970s—take up the question of poetry's ability to renew without denying the reality of which it is part in a way that is more overtly political. And yet even Miles's most apparently didactic pieces are subtly aware of the complexity of ethical issues, especially those involving what I have been trying to call the ethics of language. To illustrate, I might cite any number of poems from Miles's 1979 volume, *Coming to Terms*. Again, the very title of the volume suggests not only the poet's negotiations with and within the world, but also an awareness of the conditions or terms within which poets operate, that is, of the limits of language. Further, though, the title bespeaks an awareness of the precision of language, and what is at stake in our knowledge of language. . . . Miles's poems, like her career as a whole, might equally be called "hard won and complex." And yet these poems are also moving, both in the sense of touching us and in the sense of going somewhere. Surely hers should be one of the voices to which more people listen: a singular voice to take away the sting of the singular.

Lisa M. Steinmann. *Chicago Review.* 37,
1990, pp. 130–33, 138

MILLAY, EDNA ST. VINCENT (UNITED STATES) 1892–1950

One would have to go back a long way in literary history to find a young lyric poet singing so freely and so musically in such a big world. Almost we hear a thrush at dawn, discovering the ever-renewing splendor of the morning. . . . The surprise of youth over the universe, the emotion of youth at encountering inexplicable infinities—that is expressed . . . and it is a big thing to express.

Harriet Monroe. *Poetry.* December, 1918,
p. 167

A sensitive spirit on a romantic pilgrimage through an over-sophisticated civilization from which most of its romance has been robbed—this is the keynote of her work, as it is the keynote of many other modern poets not so finely tempered or so feverishly alert. . . . Sensitively, and with swift strokes, she has set down, if not the Odyssey of a heart, at least a record of all its poignant moments, its strange terrors, its little absurdities, and much, too, of its mocking emptiness.

John Hyde Preston. *Virginia Quarterly
Review.* July, 1927, p. 343

Taking the vocabulary of nineteenth-century poetry as pure as you will find it in Christina Rossetti, and drawing upon the stock of conventional symbolism accumulated from Drayton to Patmore, she has created, out of shopworn materials, a distinguished personal idiom: she has been able to use the language of the preceding generation to convey an emotion peculiar to her own. . . . There are those who will have no minor poets; these Miss Millay does not move. The others, her not too enthusiastic but perhaps misguided partisans, have seen too much of their own personalities in her verse to care whether it is great poetry or not; so they call it great. . . . Miss Millay is one of our most distinguished poets, and one that we should do well to misunderstand as little as possible.

Allen Tate. *The New Republic.* May 6, 1931,
pp. 335–36

Her work is not rich enough in overtones and in contrapuntal cross-references to be great musical verse; not sufficiently marmoreal for great plastic verse; nor of such comprehensive ordering power as to be great poetry of ideas. At its best, it falls just short of that intensity which is found in the highest moments even of some contemporary poetry. There is a word slightly in the way or else the image lacks the needle point. It never quite, to use E. E. Cumming's phrase, "lifts the top of your head off."

Philip Blair Rice. *The Nation.* November 14,
1934, p. 570

Millay may be happy or unhappy or angry or loving or perplexed; she may be in any one of a hundred different moods; but when she is writing a poem she is never debilitated or unconscious. Whatever her mood, she is intensely alive in every one of her five senses, and all her senses are fused in a single controlling mood and purpose. Her poems represent only those moments in her life when she has succeeded in becoming utterly at one with herself and intensely aware of the world.

Elizabeth Atkins. *Edna St. Vincent Millay
and Her Times* (Chicago: University of
Chicago Press, 1936), p. 148

In Edna Millay's high lyrical talent, the Yankee note, which one felt from the first, increased in depth and clarity as time went on, as the flippancy of her earlier verse,—its conscious naïveté mingled with wonder,—yielded to profundity of feeling. She had begun with fairy-tale fancies and travesties of nursery-rhymes, in which she turned the moral inside out; but this mood of an infantile mischief-maker had always been half-rapturous and the rapture grew, together with her force of passion. An accomplished and disciplined craftsman, Miss Millay was a learned poet, with the Yankee love of Virgil, Catullus, Chaucer, and especially the Elizabethans whose vein she recaptured in her tragic sense of youth and the brevity of life.

Van Wyck Brooks. *New England: Indian
Summer* (New York: Dutton, 1940), p. 540

A writer must be judged by his best. Edna Millay's best came at a time when many needed her excitement. Whether her capture of that audience was a good or a bad thing for the course of poetry one cannot say with any conviction. Certainly her intimate treatment of the frankly sensuous was some part of an age's contribution toward broadening the range of subjects permissible to poetry. That much is surely good. . . . But neither merit nor lack of merit defined her position in the poetry of the 1920s. It was not as a craftsman nor as an influence, but as the creator of her own legend that she was most alive to us. Her success was as a figure of passionate living.

John Ciardi. *Saturday Review of Literature.*
November 11, 1950, p. 77

She wrote some bad verse when she was young and some worse verse when she was older, as who has not. . . . She could be silly, cute, arch, hysterical; she could commit ghastly errors of taste. She also could and did, write so memorably that her language was on every tongue. . . . She was a fine lyric poet, also in the classical sense, a fine elegiac poet. . . . She expressed a great deal more than the spirit of a tinsel age: there was the silver of an individual voice, the legal tender of no base emotion.

Rolfe Humphries. *The Nation.*
December 30, 1950, p. 704

Let me register this unfashionable opinion here, and explain that Edna Millay seems to me one of the few poets writing in English in our time who have attained to anything like the stature of great literary figures in an age in which prose has predominated. It is hard to know how to compare her to Eliot or Auden or Yeats—it would be even harder to compare her to Ezra Pound. There is always a certain incommensurability between men and women writers. But she does have it in common with the first three of these that, in giving supreme expression to profoundly felt personal experience, she was able to identify herself with more general human experience and stand forth as a spokesman for the human spirit, announcing its predicaments, its vicissitudes, but, as a master of human expression, by the splendor of expression itself, putting herself beyond common embarrassments, common oppressions, and panics.

Edmund Wilson. *The Nation.*
April 19, 1952, p. 372

It was her anxiety (I feel) that an intellectual passion keep pace with an emotional passion which so increasingly troubled and labored her mature work. She was essentially a lyric and emotional poet, and her art, which belonged to that side of her nature, suffered in the attempt to express her maturer convictions, and under the weight of an active social consciousness.

And it is her own poetic vitality, her immense capacity for delight in the world of nature which she observed so lovingly and accurately and so unforgettably made plain, the intensity of her relationships, her responsiveness, her vulnerability, and above all else her unshaken dedication to her art, which made her, in the face of what she feared but never capitulated to, and under the bludgeoning of ill-health and an encroaching neuroticism, the truly great lyric poet which she was.

Sara Henderson Hay. *Saturday Review of Literature.* June 5, 1954, p. 20

. . . along with her New England stoicism we have certain concomitants of reverence for life, indignation at its gross abuse. The murder of Lidice, the murder of Sacco and Vanzetti, the murder of Hiroshima, "logic alone, all love laid by," connect themselves with a score of poems that capture her heart. "And on the gravel crawls the chilly bee." . . .

This is the great, not the genteel, tradition. Varied, felicitious, sustained, Edna St. Vincent Millay explores the tragic sense of our time and "the joys of an unhappiness that confesses itself." Hers is the serious poetry, the profound affirmation, that the genteel tradition forbade. New England is in it, "clean cliff going down as deep as clear water can reach." "There, thought unbraids itself, and the mind becomes single." This book [*Collected Poems*] is a monument to straightness and singleness of soul.

Francis Hackett. *The New Republic.* December 14, 1956, p. 22

Dylan Thomas said that "Out of an inevitable conflict of images . . . I try to make the momentary piece which is a poem." Unwittingly he defined the conspicuous technical deficiency of Edna St. Vincent Millay: there is no conflict of images, since such a conflict is "inevitable" only in major poets, and consequently there is no richness, no secret tension to relate the mystery of the poem to the mystery of human experience. There is no mystery in Millay's experience, nor was there in ours at the time we applauded her as our spokesman. It was not peace, momentary or eternal, that she recorded, but merely the outcry. At eighteen, when most of us looked upon peace as complacency and hysteria as honesty, she was our very selves.

Not so today. The recent edition of her *Collected Poems* . . . has left me feeling wistful about the girl I was. With the splendid exception of a handful of sonnets (artistically inexplicable) she was to our youthful solitude what Jerome Kern was to our youthful romance. It saddens me to write it, "for today I'm dreaming of yesterday." Millay will be, if she is not already, a period piece, a cultural curio like roses made of hair and protected under glass. Nothing quite like her will ever happen again.

Bette Richart. *Commonweal.* May 10, 1957, p. 159

Her sense of impermanence and impending loss was by no means confined to love. The theme of death runs all through her poetry. But it was not in any sense a fear of or what some of her critics considered an obsession with death. She herself called death a "Supreme Nuisance, an obstacle in the road of life, insurmountable and unskirtable. . . ." If she is obsessed with anything, it is with life.

Her chief emotion about death is resentment of a blind and irrational force that will so rudely cut off life. "Down, you mongrel, Death!" she says in one of her poems. She resents death so much that is is not enough for her to know that there is a constant cycle of rebirth in the world.

Miriam Gurko. *Restless Spirit: The Life of Edna St. Vincent Millay* (New York: T. Y. Crowell, 1962), p. 130

[The] sense of vulnerability provides one of the richest linguistic patterns in her poetry, for in spite of her efforts to repress and protect a part of her emotional life, Millay is exposed and betrayed through a language pattern which calls attention to the emotional conflicts and tensions, the psychic realities of her existence. This pattern of self-revelation appears consistently throughout her work, though sometimes disguised by attitudes associated with the public image. . . .

It is understandable why Millay's two extended narratives of woman's psychological disintegration are presented in sonnet sequences. Millay persistently resorts to the constraints of traditional verse forms. Given her time and place in the history of American poetry and given the external evidence of her unconventional childhood and youthful radicalism, one would expect to find her in the company of the avant-garde of American poetry. But Millay is no true Imagist. She eschews the freedoms of form which Ezra Pound had defined as essential to the new poetry. The sonnet, her best form, is a fit vehicle to convey her deepest feelings of woman's victimization. Through it, Millay imaginatively reenacts her constant struggle against boundaries. The wish for freedom is always qualified by the sense of restriction; couplets and quatrains suit her sensibility.

In Millay's poetry, women, in their quiet lives of fatal desires and futile gestures, are tragic and heroic. She identifies herself with suffering women, women whose dreams are denied, whose bodies are assaulted, whose minds and spirits are extinguished. She states her consciousness of the universality of women's vulnerability and anguish in "An Ancient Gesture," contrasting Penelope's tears with those of Ulysses. . . .

From the earliest volume, *Renascence,* where even her youthful awakening is accompanied by its grief-laden songs of shattering, through her posthumous harvest of mature experience, Millay records, unrelentingly, her life of pain and frustration. If she too loudly insisted on the public self's claims for freedom to love and think and feel and work as she pleased, she nevertheless quietly throughout her work continued to send out her linguistic distress signals. It is her profound insight into her self's inevitable capitulation that makes Millay ultimately so vulnerable and her poetry so meaningful.

Jane Stambrough. In Sandra M. Gilbert and
Susan Gubar, eds. *Shakespeare's Sisters:
Feminist Essays on Women Poets*
(Bloomington: Indiana University Press,
1979), pp. 184, 198–99

I call Millay the "Saint" of the modern sonnet because she strove for perfection in a form that was considered old-fashioned, if not obsolete in the early part of the twentieth century. More specifically, in the same sense that she was supportive of a form that was being demeaned if not actually under attack, she was the *patron*-saint of the modern sonnet. She wrote a good many individual love sonnets that have immortalized her images as a celebrant of sexual love for its own sake, plus a number of "intellectual sonnets," like the one on Beethoven's Fifth Symphony, or the one on Euclid's vision of naked Beauty, or the tribute to all women activists, dedicated to Inez Milholland, a dashing young Suffragist who died while campaigning for the Cause. This was read by the poet herself in Washington, D.C. at the unveiling of a statue of the three leaders in the cause of equal rights for women.

But beyond these individual fourteen-line poems, Millay is the author of three sonnet sequences, the first of which is notable for its homely language, its narrative quality. This sequence is the only one that Millay ever wrote employing the third person singular, and while an unusual genre piece composed with insight into the stoical character of a woman, it did not have the appeal or the pure artistry of her intimate yet objective personal sonnets, or those written out of deep philosophical conviction, as the other two sequences were. I am referring to "Fatal Interview," and "Epitaph for the Race of Man," which reach near-perfection in the sustained intensity of an emotional experience found in the former, and the powerful philosophic thought in the latter. . . .

Her most valuable contribution to twentieth-century poetry . . . is the modern sonnet. By "modern" I mean a fresh handling of the form while keeping the form itself intact—modern in language and feeling while still classical in form. . . .

Though it is true that she has always been overplayed or underplayed, lauded beyond all bounds or dismissed as a youthful exponent of free love expressed in conventional forms, the sequence comprising "Epitaph" has been generally neglected in either case. But the timelessness of the theme, ironically more applicable today than it was in 1934; the flawlessness of the technique; and the depth of feeling combine to make this eighteen-sonnet poem profound and enduring.

At the end of her life, in her last volume, written when her world had fallen apart, Millay wrote a sonnet beginning, "I will put chaos into fourteen lines." It is significant as proof of the form to which she was deeply devoted.

And it is proof, in the excellence of her posthumously published volumes, *Mine the Harvest,* that her greatest contribution to twentieth-century poetry is the modern sonnet.

> Jean Gould. In Alice Kessler Harris and
> William McBrien, eds. *Faith of a (Woman)*
> *Writer* (1984; Westport, Connecticut:
> Greenwood Press, 1988), pp. 129–30, 141

MILLIN, SARAH GERTRUDE (SOUTH AFRICA) 1889–1968

In *God's Stepchildren,* Mrs. Millin has created high tragedy out of the trite materials of melodrama, and has showed significantly how a problem novel can be made the work of authentic art. Her theme is the tragic clash of caste and racial prejudice in the social dilemmas of miscegenation in South Africa, as reflected in the life-tragedies of four generations of the high-caste descendants of an English missionary who married in blind but righteous deliberation a Bushman girl, daughter of the former missionary housekeeper. From this one irrevocable challenge of Nordic folkways, there flows a sequence of tragedies such as has been rarely drawn in the whole range of modern realism. Modern enough in substance, and local enough to be a sort of dramatic epitome of the colonial life of South Africa, these tragedies are so firmly conceived that they are Greek in their simple inevitability and high Elizabethan in their rush and poignancy. . . . *God's Stepchildren* is the classic of its theme in our English literature.

In some of her deepest insights she seems merely to make blood the symbol of fate, and to use nature as a sort of sacrificial scapegoat for the sins of society. I know of no other English novel on this difficult theme with human values so fairly and sympathetically drawn. It effects truly a catharsis of pity and terror, and passes our social obsessions through a sort of purgatorial discipline.

> Alain Locke. *The Survey.* May 1, 1925,
> pp. 180–81

If opposites attract, then Sarah Gertrude Millin loves Olive Schreiner with a great passion. It is a safe bet, though, that she doesn't. I have yet to hear of a cold-blooded classicist who did not loathe the hot romantic. The contrast is not as clear as these labels indicate. Olive as a romantic has a low boiling-point in comparison with Sappho, say; Sarah as a classic is not quite cold. Her coldness is not the coldness of marble; it is the absence of heat in a fish.

Yet the two are sufficiently opposed in style and temperament to make all homage paid to the one a token that equal homage is due to the other.

Olive Schreiner was a great genius but a weak artist; Sarah's genius is less, but her artistry greater.

Even in her youth, when Sarah Gertrude was writing novels of the least ambitious kind—novels about "lurv"—her matter-of-factness kept breaking in. You can dip into her earliest books without being nauseated. *Middle Class,* for instance, in spite of its war-scarred, silent hero and his faithful Zulu, has credible and laudable moments. Its heroine and her female acquaintances are interesting—interesting, that is, to anyone who wants to know, not what a 1920 flapper of Gouldburg was like, but what she thought she was like. The creature hasn't changed much. The teenage tiger of to-day is remarkably like her mother, the "white monkey," of yesteryear. . . .

Mrs. Millin's early writings—*Middle Class, Adam's Rest, The Jordans* and *The Dark River* (novels whose very names she religiously suppresses today)—may not be much; but they are not much to be ashamed of.

Then came *God's Stepchildren,* by which time Mrs. Millin had grown up. The strong silent men have disappeared; the flappers have ceased from flapping; she writes of men and women ugly enough and unhappy enough to convince us that she has sensed the skull under the hair, the bone under the silk stocking. But she seems virginally unaware, still, of the flesh between. "Lurv" has been displaced by the Devil, who reduces half-witted idealists to miscegenating baboons. God was never half so nasty to His stepchildren as Mrs. Millin is to her social misfits and anthropological specimens. . . .

Well, she is young yet—compared with Goethe and Bernard Shaw. She may still produce a work worthy of comparison with [Schreiner's] *The Story of an African Farm.* At present, all she has produced is prose—prose of a very high order, excellent prose; prose which, to echo her favorite trope, is really and actually prose. And it is nothing more.

E. Davis. *South African Opinion.*
February, 1947, pp. 26–27

[*The People of South Africa*] is a terrible and compelling book, terrible because it concerns a question which the author feels is "beyond solution"; compelling because its problems are so bound up with the whole history and destiny of our civilization.

Mrs. Millin is a biographer and novelist as well as a historian, a South African brought up in Kimberley and making her home in Johannesburg; she has absorbed the issues of what she writes as long as she can remember, and she knows moreover that history is a matter of individuals, of a Rhodes, a Smuts, a Ghandi, and the ignorant black man begging for a job at the back doors of the white man's cities. . . .

The reader can hardly avoid finishing Mrs. Millin's book with two convictions: one, that something must be done to relieve the sufferers, black, white, and yellow, in South Africa's society; the other, that it is already too late, that we must prepare ourselves for a ruinous denouement. Here, she says, are the two sides—in South Africa there are sometimes more than two sides to a question—of the problem; if the world can be a better judge of wrong and right than the South Africans themselves have been, let the world step forward and see justice done.

Sylvia Stallings. New York Herald Tribune.
February 14, 1954, p. 1

Mrs. Millin evinced a major talent which soon stood out from the ruck of South African writing at the time. But her impact on South African literature was more than that of a richer talent elevating the standard of contemporary South African letters. Mrs. Millin cut a path away from the prevailing romanticism and blazed the trail to South African realism: in a series of distinguished novels, she charted the sterner course which has since been followed by writers like Pauline Smith, William Plomer, Daphne Muir, Stuart Cloete, Alan Paton, Laurens van der Post, Peter Abrahams and many more. As the Witwatersrand University noted when it conferred the honorary degree of Doctor of Literature upon her in 1952, "Mrs. Millin has become par excellence the interpreter of South Africa to the English-speaking world. This is not only because of such an essay in objectivity as *The South Africans*—it is also, and chiefly, because of her novels of South African life."

Mrs. Millin's best novels are set in the small towns of South Africa, not the cities. She searches for elemental lines in her portrayal of South African life, and she seems to find them more clearly in the restricted orbit of the platteland, thrown into startling relief by the vast South African background.

It is this background that is the most significant element in Mrs. Millin's work. Nowhere else in literature—not even in the best Afrikaans novels nor in Olive Schreiner's *Story of an African Farm*—is there such a portrayal of the South African scene as Mrs. Millin's books in their totality provide. From their pages the land emerges stark and true—earth that takes well to diamonds and gold, but does not easily bear pastoral tranquility; sparsely populated, low in fertility, tragic in history; a country that does not, as General Smuts once remarked, go forward in a straight line like other lands. It is not the convenient South Africa of guide-books and advertising posters that is here revealed, but a country restless with racial tensions and the fateful need to choose between the kraal spirit and the open horizon.

Edgar Bernstein. In South African P.E.N.
Yearbook, 1955 (Johannesburg: South
African P.E.N. Centre, 1956), pp. 101–2

Mary Glenn seemed at first to be a longer and more complicated novel than it in fact became. Sarah Gertrude destroyed her manuscript when half the book had been written. She had analyzed too many characters too closely, she thought, and the novel had thus become unclear; clarity was her chief aim and she could not bear the thought of a confused book. The finished product, therefore, was an extremely short novel—less than forty thousand words in length—which was completed in only six weeks. Its style is as terse and relentless as the book is brief and a good deal of its power lies in the spareness of the narrative. Each part of the novel pertains to its central theme. . . .

The color question hardly affects *Mary Glenn*. With the exception of a few references to Africans, the book need not be located in Africa; and with the exception of a few hauntingly evocative descriptions of the stark countryside where the Glenns and Van Aardts search for Jackie, Sarah Gertrude makes no attempt to draw upon local color for effect. Her stern indictment of the social *mores* of Lebanon is not directed at small-town life in South Africa alone but could be applied to other societies. Despite its strange combination of psychological perspicacity and uncertainty about narrative attitude, *Mary Glenn* is evidence of Sarah Gertrude's growing competence. . . .

Written entirely from Sarah Gertrude's own point of view, *The South Africans* is a collection of prejudices and personal conceptions of South African life. Often her views are misconceptions, but the uninformed reader is offered no alternative opinions nor indeed the opportunity to investigate the original contention. In a sense the book tells more about the author than it does about the subject. With the exception of her autobiographical volumes, *The Night is Long* and *The Measure of My Days, The South Africans* is the most self-revelatory of all Sarah Gertrude's works, betraying many of her own attitudes toward issues that confronted South Africa. The book contains some remarkably sensitive and perceptive insights into certain aspects of South African life, but it lacks the dispassionate qualities and objectivity necessary to make the study truly illuminating. Sarah Gertrude is too close to her subject and too obviously shares the attitudes being examined for the book to achieve the measure of detachment that is so vital in sociological analysis. . . .

It has been observed before that, in her novels, Sarah Gertrude tends to see people more in terms of types than as individuals, but in no novel is such blatant disregard for the individual exhibited. When *The South Africans* deals with other races, it is often more complimentary but always no less undocumentedly authoritative. The sections of the book which deal with the various racial groups in South Africa are a study in stereotypes, as unsupported as they are general. When *The South Africans* deals with the countryside or with certain eras or with the spirit of the cities, it is superb in the power of its intuitive impressionism. In its studies of the peoples of South Africa, gross over-generalization destroys its credibility and finally, its integrity. . . .

One of the most encapsulated and striking statements of Sarah Gertrude's horror of Africans is a book she published in 1962, *The Wizard Bird*. It was her first novel in ten years; she had long since stopped attending to her literary career, but she still had a contract with the London publishing house of Heinemann, which had begun to press her for the book she owed them. Thus, she set about writing her sixteenth novel not out of any artistic reawakening, but rather for the simple fulfillment of a contract. Given her preoccupation with what she saw as the threat posed by black Africa, it is hardly surprising that she should have chosen that subject as her theme. Sarah Gertrude had in former days been able to construct competent novels around even the most political themes, but unlike her previous fiction, *The Wizard Bird* is so preoccupied with its message of hate that even the barest necessities of art are largely ignored. The dialogue—previously one of her great strengths as a novelist—is painfully stilted, while the story is handled with an almost total lack of subtlety. Sarah Gertrude apparently experienced great difficulty in writing a novel after so many years, and this is evident in the book's awkwardness. Any merit that *The Wizard Bird* has lies in its ability to expound Sarah Gertrude's viewpoint, for it is too rough to achieve even the stark effect it might otherwise have had.

The *Wizard Bird* is filled with disgustingly grotesque scenes. Throughout her fictional works, Sarah Gertrude had shown a certain taste for the grotesque, but this novel carries it to the point of obscenity. The African protagonist, Chibisa, is little more than a caricature of horror: a man with the merest veneer of English civilization over a savage, cruel, and disturbed nature. In choosing an insane man as the paradigm for the leaders of the newly independent African nations, Sarah Gertrude blatantly reveals just how unbalanced she has become on the subject of Africans. The open disgust with which she describes the interracial marriage of Chibisa and Allison and the anguish with which she writes of the girl's horror at the prospect of miscegenation are a reminder of a similar view expressed in *God's Stepchildren,* but there is a hysteria in *The Wizard Bird* absent in the earlier novels. This book is the first of Sarah Gertrude's published works to reveal her new, uncontrolled attitude towards Africans which is so much more desperate than even her wildest pre-war statements. It is fitting that Sarah Gertrude should have alluded in *The Wizard Bird* to a play by Shakespeare that was obsessing her more and more these days, *Titus Andronicus,* for it also is crude and obscene in its violent and repulsive grotesques. It is no more just to judge Sarah Gertrude by *The Wizard Bird* than Shakespeare by *Titus Andronicus,* but the novel is nevertheless an indication of how much her literary—to say nothing of her political—judgment and talents had declined in the past decade.

Martin Rubin. Sarah Gertrude Millin: A
South African Life (Johannesburg: Donker,
1977), pp. 94–95, 100–101, 269–70

In South Africa, where a party riddled with Nazi sympathizers came to power in 1948 and set about a program of racial legislation whose precursor if not model was that of Nazi Germany, political prudence dictated that the rationale for race-classification, race-separation and race-dominance not be couched in terms of eugenics and biological destiny. In fact the public language of the National Party in South Africa as it has developed since 1945 has undergone Byzantine elaborations in a retreat from voicing the key opposition—*über* versus *unter*—that was uttered with such confidence by Nazism in its heyday.

If we return to the discourse of racism before 1945, what strikes us first about it is its nakedness, its shamelessness. "The old predatory instinct [has] subserved civilization by clearing the earth of inferior races of men," wrote Herbert Spencer in 1851. "A wooly-haired nation has ever had an important 'history,'" wrote Ernst Haeckel in 1873. Missionaries "turn healthy, though primitive and inferior, human beings into a rotten brood of bastards," wrote Adolf Hitler in 1924. "The Griqua type of half-caste . . . is lower than the Kaffir," wrote Sarah Gertrude Millin in 1926. We no longer come across ideas like these expressed in public, even in South Africa (who is in a position to judge to what extent they live on in the private realm?). . . .

What we may tend to ignore about ideas like these, however, is that they were . . . the intellectual currency for a long time, and were based on a great deal of what passed for scientific research. They formed part of one of the dominant myths of history from the mid-nineteenth to the mid-twentieth century, the myth that Western Europeans were biologically destined to rule the world. . . . I will attempt to trace the lineage of one element of this myth, the complex of ideas that informs the notions of *blood, flaw, taint,* and *degeneration,* particularly as these notions occur in the work of Sarah Gertrude Millin, a writer of considerable achievements, certainly the most considerable novelist writing in English in South Africa between Olive Schreiner and Nadine Gordimer, neglected nowadays because her treatment of race has come to seem dated and even morally offensive. Millin's ideas on race . . . are not a hotchpotch of colonial prejudices but the reflection of respectable scientific and historical thought, only barely out of date in her time; further, her emphasis on race is at least in part a response to formal problems that face any colonial writer working in the medium of the novel. . . .

The fundamental problems that Millin faced as a novelist are those that any colonial novelist of her generation faced: the problem of deciding what elements of the European novel are relevant to the colonial situation; and the problem of finding a social field rich enough to bear the transplanted European novel. These two problems are closely intertwined. Because colonial society is typically "thin" and does not permit the play of social nuance that the novel of manners is built upon, the colonial novelist has to look beyond the field of social interaction. The Romantic novel, with its emphasis on solitary destinies and on landscape, thus provides a more congenial model: Emily Brontë rather than Jane Austen. As American novelists of the first and second generations discovered, however, it is not easy to make novels out of the careers of people outside society. The problem is succinctly stated by R. W. B. Lewis: "What kind of change is possible for the solitary figure surrounded by space?" The history of nineteenth-century American fiction can be written as the history of responses to this question. . . .

A typology of characters on an ethnic rather than a class basis is an inviting solution for the novelist seeking a system of characterological oppositions out of which to generate writing. But such a solution entails a radical rethinking of the novel as a form. The solution which tends to emerge in colonial practice is a mixed one: an ethnic typology for those parts of the novel set in the wilderness, a class typology for those . . . set in society. This is the solution Fenimore Cooper arrives at in his Leatherstocking novels (where society is represented in microcosm by the band of white adventurers), and this too is Millin's solution in novels and superficially diverse as *God's Stepchildren* and *The Fiddler*. The utter failure of a novel like *King of the Bastards* can be explained as the result of too much of the "solitary figure surrounded by space," too much reliance on an ethnic typology of tribe after tribe after tribe which Millin has to elaborate out of her entrails as she writes.

[The] view of Millin as a woman imbued with the racial prejudices of white South African society and using her novels as a means of propagating and justifying these prejudices must therefore be tempered by a view of her as a practicing novelist adapting whatever models and theories lie to hand to make writing possible.

J. M. Coetzee. *English Studies in Africa*. 23,
1980, pp. 41–42, 57–58

Even though race plays no part in *Mary Glenn,* it does emerge in much of Millin's writing, particularly in *God's Stepchildren* (1924), which may well be artistically her best novel. Through the record of four generations, the narrative reveals that miscegenation produces a bitter crop. Her treatment of the half-caste in this book has brought on accusations that she was propagating the doctrine of racial purity, especially in light of her support of the National-ist party and its implementation of apartheid during the last decade of her life. There appeared in 1977 an excellent biography, *Sarah Gertrude Millin, a South African Life,* by Martin Rubin, an American scholar who does much to explain Millin's obsession with race during her old age and to restore her reputation in spite of her personal eccentricities. Possibly this new edition of *Mary Glenn* will also aid in this restoration; for, whatever her racial aberrations, she remains an important figure in both South African and Common-wealth literature. . . .

It would be difficult to find writers more divergent as artists than Millin and [Olive] Schreiner. On one hand, Millin is a craftsman, a writer for whom every word and action count; in fact, reading her work brings to mind the "unfurnished novels" of Willa Cather. On the other hand, Schreiner gives the impression of formlessness, at times seeming to lose track of her narrative; but careful reading proves otherwise. Although in Millin's fiction the narra-tion and the idea never separate, Schreiner's stories scatter, as she wills them to do, to give room for her characters' struggles with philosophical ideas, sociological problems, theological questions, and so on. Schreiner also sets her women in conflict with a society which has assigned them to second-class roles, and then they either rebel or fail, or both. Millin, though writing about the same society, seems less concerned with women as women or men as men but more involved with universal responses to a world into which humans find themselves relegated. Both writers are ironists, observing and recording along with Heinrich Heine how heavily the irony of God weighs upon man. But even in this respect they differ, for Millin's irony tends to be less weighty, less practiced than does Schreiner's; yet the broad strokes work for Schreiner.

Rubert L. Ross. *World Literature Written in English.* 24, 1984, pp. 240–41

MINCO, MARGA (NETHERLANDS) 1920–

For anyone who has read some of the autobiographical horror-stories written after the last war, this book [*Bitter Herbs*] may seem uneventful and gentle. After all, in a horrible era of mass murder it describes the destruction of one single Jewish family in Holland—and not even that. We are introduced to various members of the family, the author's parents, brother and two sisters and the last sentence of the book informs us: "They would never come back— not my father, not my mother, nor Betty, nor Dave or Lottie." That is all— we are not even informed how they perished. The author's own adventures are not too hair-raising either. She saw her parents move into the ghetto, eventually she went into hiding and succeeded in remaining alive. There were no hot pursuits by the Gestapo and bloodhounds; nor were there any last minute, hair-breadth escapes.

Nevertheless, this little book is moving and memorable. Mrs. Minco was a young girl when the Germans occupied Holland and she manages to recall her own childish astonishment at the terrible events that followed. In other accounts, written by people more politically minded or more outraged, re- volted and angry, the destruction of the Jews is turned into a duel and a fight (however unequal and pathetic) in which the author wins in the sense that he manages to escape with his life but, usually, loses everything worth living for, including his faith in human decency and sanity. There is no duel, no fight, no conflict in this book; not a word of complaint or self-pity; not even an angry outcry against the Nazis. There is childish astonishment only and a matter of fact description of simple day-to-day events and this deceptively naive quality of the writing gives a truly nightmarish glare to the narrative.

When the family learn they will have to wear yellow stars in the future, they do not criticize the German orders; they are only worried if Father has bought enough stars to do all their summer-frocks, too; they are put out by the idea that a yellow star looks awful on a red blouse. When the men are called up to work in a labor camp, the young brother looks forward to the coming "adventure" and is pleased that he is going to "see the world." They all knew very well what was happening in Poland but—of course—"things won't come to that with us." When all is over a mad uncle keeps going out to the tram—several times every day—hopefully and cheerfully to wait for those who will never return.

Their incorrigible optimism enhances the nightmarish effect of this impressive little book, because it reminds the reader that the wartime crimes of the Germans were not only wicked and inhuman but were also so utterly pointless and stupid that anyone's normal reactions to the goings-on seemed unreal and abnormal.

(London) Times Literary Supplement.
November 11, 1960, p. 1164

Marga Minco's novel The Glass Bridge appears on the surface to be the story of a victim: a young woman in hiding in German-occupied Holland. It reads, for the most part, like one of the many documentary accounts of those who have been through such an experience, in the style of a simple story of events, stripped of artifice. The narrator's parents and, later, the rest of her family are rounded up and disappear, and on both occasions she escapes through the accident of being absent at the moment of danger.

The descriptions of her loss are given without sensational weight:

> A man who lived opposite us came to tell my aunt and uncle: at four-thirty they had cleared out several houses, my parents' house among them. At that very moment, I had probably been sitting in the school building working on a multiplication exercise, and looking to see whether the answer was divisible by thirteen. It hadn't been.

Her attempted rape by the resistance worker who provides her with false papers and a place to stay is offered with a similar numbness. The story is one of survival and loss and the tone is of a bemused acceptance of the world as it is. A brief affair with a second resistance fighter . . . [is] described in equally muted prose.

It is only through her growing fantasy about the dead girl whose identity she has been given that we get a sense of the deep damage that has been done to the narrator. She expresses concern about . . . Maria Roselier's life and death in a way that is absent in her memories of those who were dear to her.

Her curiosity about the girl who died young but not at the hands of the Nazis, continues long after the war is over; it is as if Maria's tragedy is greater than her own, and the guilt of surviving engenders an intense relationship with [her].

Jenny Diski. The New Statesman.
May 27, 1988, p. 35

To its credit, The Glass Bridge belongs to a category of Holocaust fiction that favors the subtle unraveling of plot over lurid scenes of torture. Rendered in a lucid translation by Stacey Knecht, the Dutch journalist and novelist Marga Minco's slender novel tells the story of a young Jewish woman named Stella, who survives the Nazi occupation by assuming a false identity; through the agency of Carlo, a Dutch Resistance agent, nineteen-year-old Stella receives papers in the name of Maria Roselier, a young woman who, before her recent death, lived . . . near the Belgian border. As the new Maria Roselier, Stella falls in love with Carlo. She suspects the name is familiar to him, but he is honor-bound to keep silent. Unfortunately, the authorities catch Carlo carrying blank identity cards and he is executed soon thereafter. Twenty years later, long after she has lost not only her lover but her beloved father and brother, Stella finally visits [the village where Maria was from] and discovers how Maria's personal, unpolitical fate assured her own seren-dipitous survival. Ms. Minco's story is filled with finely-wrought descriptive passages, particularly her account of the young Stella sliding down the ice-covered arched bridge of the title with her father standing at its highest point, neither retreating nor advancing. The image of Stella borne forward and away from her father reinforces an observation expressed later in the story: "The idea that, time and again, our decisions are made for us, is often unbearable to me."

Barbara Finkelstein. The New York Times.
August 20, 1989, p. 20

Marga Minco's subject is the aftermath of the German occupation of the Netherlands in the Second World War and "survivor's guilt." In *An Empty House* (1966), the young Sepha emerges from a succession of hiding places to discover that she is quite alone in the world. She copes with the loss of her entire family in the concentration camps by keeping the Red Cross announcement of their deaths "in a drawer which she never opens." While hitchhiking from Friesland to Amsterdam in 1946 to marry Mark, her Catholic lover from one of the "safe houses," she falls in with Yona, another Jewish survivor, who is obsessed by the fact that she is alive while others are not. Sepha makes the mistake of putting her address into the girl's pocket. When Yona "falls" into a canal following her discovery that what was once her family home in Amsterdam is now only a façade, Sepha is assumed to be a relative and summoned to her hospital bedside. Afterwards Sepha is unable to free herself from the tortured girl in whom she recognizes her *alter ego.*

Sepha marries Mark and attempts to rebuild the empty house of her life "with stones that have no past." It is not, however, until Yona's fatal fall from a moving train in 1950 that she is able to abandon her "luggage" of guilt for which "there is absolutely no cupboard."

Like Aharon Appelfeld in *Badenheim 1939*, Minco hints at, rather than spells out, sadness and suffering. Sepha's post-war search for herself is de-picted against a past she is unable to forget. The clatter of dustbins reminds her of the rattle which was used to scare the rats from the frozen corpses of those who perished in the "hunger winter"; a group photograph of a non-

Jewish farmer's "fit as a fiddle" relatives recalls her own once complete family; a Canadian soldier conjures up her Uncle Max from Assen whose twelve-year-old twin sons are gassed at Sobibor.

The Fall (1983) covers a much later post-war period. Frieda Borgstein is eighty-five and iron-willed, but it is chance rather than determination which has made her a survivor. In 1942 she waits in the hallway of her home, with her husband and children and their packed suitcases, for Hein Kessels, a close friend and member of the Dutch Resistance, who has promised them safe conduct to Switzerland. Frieda goes upstairs at the last minute to fetch a sweater for her daughter—"Why had she stood so long in Olga's room?"—and hears the front door slam. Panicking, she falls down the stairs to find that the others have gone without her. Her twisted ankle, preventing her from following them, saves her from deportation and death: the Borgsteins have been betrayed.

On the day before her eighty-fifth birthday party, Frieda—like Yona—has a second, fatal fall. The model Home for the Aged in Amsterdam in which she now lives is awaiting inspection by "a busybody from the provincial department," when Frieda decides to brave the sub-zero temperatures to buy pastries. The outcome of her mission, on which she carries the silver-framed photograph of her late husband in her handbag, is determined by a series of apparently unrelated and dramatically unfolded events. The Dutch word *val* means "trap," "fall" and "coincidence" as well as "downfall." Frieda dies before she discovers that the "busybody from the provincial department" is none other than Hein Kessels, whose double-crossing of her family she never understood. It is only after her funeral that we learn that he was followed to the Borgstein home in 1942 by the Nazis, and that he was himself betrayed.

The two turning-points in Frieda Borgstein's life are described in spare prose (sometimes spoiled, here, by clumsy translation) and in little over one hundred pages. As in *An Empty House,* the characters jump off the page and emotions are summoned by restraint.

Rosemary Friedman. (London) *Times Literary Supplement.* June 15, 1990, p. 654

MISTRAL, GABRIELA (CHILE) 1889–1957

In the emotional power and grace of form of her lyric work, Gabriela Mistral is considered by many competent critics the foremost among living women poets in Spanish America. . . . An important part of Gabriela Mistral's work are her prose poems, of an apostolic simplicity, beauty, and strength which remind one of Tagore at his best, but with a simplicity of style and a directness of appeal which are all their own.

Gabriela Mistral is primarily a mystic, and temperamentally akin to the two great feminine prototypes of Mysticism: the Spanish Santa Teresa, and the Mexican Juana Inés of the Cross. But hers is not the mysticism of quietism and seclusion, but rather that practical mysticism which expresses itself in a protest against formalism and literalism and in which the gloom and austerity of the prototypes are entirely lacking. Nor does her creed, "I am a part of everything and everything is a part of me," brook limitations. And from this creed, quickened by the passion of a soul luminously Latin, has sprung a state of mind permeated with simple human piety and sympathy, which distinguishes the fundamental thing of life—above all the child, the mother, the workman, the chief forces of conservation and progress.

Pan-American Union Bulletin. July, 1924,
pp. 657–58

When she was a teacher at Andes, a village near the mountains, she became known throughout her native land through a literary gathering that took place at Santiago, the capital, and was sponsored by the writers' society of that city. Carried away by her admiration for two European poets, Gabriele D'Annunzio and Frédéric Mistral, she had submitted to the conference some remarkably beautiful poems entitled *Sonnets on Death.* She presented them under the pseudonym of Gabriela Mistral that was to be famous all over the world and bury her real name forever. They were published in Chile in 1922. Immediately there was the greatest enthusiasm for her poetic talents, seldom found in South America in so striking, so appealing, so profound a form. Her lyrical talent was recognized as among the very highest in all Spanish literature. . . .

Although her poetry is little known in the English language, it enjoys universal favor among our peoples. . . . In all of [her poems] there is a unique delicacy, gentle resignation and an inclination that is spontaneously ethical. Her principal influences are the Bible, Tagore, the Mexican poet Amado Nervo, and the outstanding Spanish-American poet, Rubén Darío.

Living Age. November 29, 1924, pp. 495–96

From the earliest studies of Garbriela Mistral's poetry, critics have often observed that her work reflects her strong drive toward mysticism, which at times she fully attained. The well-known Mexican writer Eduardo Colín, in an article published . . . in 1933 . . . speaks of the "terrestrial mysticity" of our poet. But the understanding of Gabriela Mistral's mysticism was most definitively expressed by the Chilean writer Francisco Donoso: "Almost all of Gabriela Mistral's poems have the accent of a prayer, a loving or confident prayer at times, a desperate petition on other occasions when her feelings are overwhelmed by some tragic vision. . . . Not only in purely subjective matters do we notice this mysticism of Mistral's; in all the objective subjects she sings about one can discover the drift of mystery and religiousness that moves her. . . ." It would not be out of place to note that Mr. Donoso is a priest, which gives his observations a value they would not have coming from someone else. . . .

["Nocturne"] is a composition that is too human to have any real root in mysticism. She wrote it when she was still obsessed by the tragedy that overshadowed the best years of her life. And if in it she engages in a dialogue with God, she does so more for its rhetorical value as an expedient to move the reader, than for the purpose of revealing a state of union with the Creator. The same thing could be said about "The Plea." In this poem she also engages in a dialogue with God, but only to beg him to grant the soul of her lover-suicide an impossible pardon. No composition could ever be mystical that thus forgets the dogmatic theology that must necessarily support mystic poetry, especially if the writer is a Catholic. In general, the same thing could be said about all these poems that mention God. Instead of singing of the joys of union with Him, or expressing the desire that such a union take place, she only wants to calm the human disquietude that was left by the tragedy that made her a widow before she even married. God is petitioned by the writer in order that He concede to her as an individual or to the soul of her lover the grace of pardon or the acceptance of her uncommon love. . . .

Raúl Silva Castro. *Estudios sobre Gabriela Mistral* (Santiago: Editorial Zig-Zag, 1935), pp. 61, 69–70

[*Desolation*, 1923] is full of passion and tragedy—the suicide of a lover, the anguish of the woman who quarrelled with him and lost him, the deep longing for his child which she would never bear. With these themes go her love for and keen observation of country places and country children and her sense of the teacher as a consecrated being. The tone is simple, direct, almost primitive. She talks to Christ as freely as to a child. Her expression is devoid of modern mannerisms and romanticist pretensions; her lyric tone is pure. Friendly critics say that her masters were the Bible, Dante, Tagore, and Tolstoy.

Her later volumes carry the same clarity of expression, the same threads of mingled mysticism and paganism, the same moving force of love and tragedy. She has not had an easy life, and the anguish of it is laid open and served up bleeding. Her sympathies are with the downtrodden and forgotten—the shy, wild children in lost Chilean valleys, the Basque orphans scattered "among strange peoples in countries of impossible tongues and bitter climates." The Spanish war she took—as did so many other poets—as a personal catastrophe, and she castigated her continent for not welcoming its exiles. This point of view did not increase her popularity with people who had already objected to her frankness and her anti-clerical sentiments. . . .

The uncomfortable suspicion persists that the Nobel Prize may have been awarded to Miss Mistral this year because her poetry, being fine, was also safe and in the main non-controversial. Her poems are deeply human, and in style and content they raise a minimum of uncomfortable questions.

Moreover, Miss Mistral is a woman, and not many Nobel prizes have gone to women poets; she is a South American, and no Nobel prize has previously gone to a South American. This year above all others, with poets in other places submerged by the war, a South American woman poet could be safely chosen, particularly as her fellow-poets held her in such warm regard.

Mildred Adams. The Nation. December 29,
1945, pp. 739–40

In Spanish speaking countries Gabriela's name (and almost everyone in referring to the poet said simply *Gabriela*) had long been a household word. She had become one of the most popular poets of her tongue. Although her first publication was achieved in our country, in Continental Europe her poems were more widely translated than in England or the United States. Even after she was awarded the Nobel Prize for Literature, why so little of Gabriela was translated into English, I do not know. Much of her poetry is simple and direct in language, never high-flown or flowery, and much easier, I think, to translate than most poets writing in Spanish.

Langston Hughes. Introduction to Selected
Poems of Gabriela Mistral (Bloomington:
Indiana University Press, 1957), p. 10

There has been no lack of critics to point out a certain carelessness, a certain formal irregularity in the work of [Gabriela Mistral]. In so doing, they have not realized that what they were seeing was a deliberate stylization, a kind of voluntary lack of grace (let us so call it), which corresponds to a conscious reaction against modernist decorativeness. Those who believe that the poetry—as well as the prose—of Mistral is somewhat improvised are mistaken. Also mistaken are those who assume that her provincial life and her duties as a teacher were reasons for a lack of poetic refinement during her early years. Like Juan Ramón Jiménez, Gabriela can be counted among those poets of our language who . . . [have tried] to find the word for which no other word can be substituted, the necessary music, the true color.

Gaston Figueira. De la vida y la obra de
Gabriela Mistral (Montevideo: n.p., 1959),
p. 43

The sequence *Pain* from the book *Desolation* can be seen as the very center of [Mistral's] work. It is her living history, dedicated to "his shadow." . . . This loved one is a shadow, is the foggy breath of the grave. And with ghosts, with the residues of death, it is possible to be more intimate, more sincere, than with the living. For the living maintain a distance that is impossible to cross, not even in the warmest and most absolute contacts. There is always something finally unbreachable . . . that keeps them withdrawn and secret. Love brings us together more than anything in this world, but the final possession seems to come only in death.

Anyone who has loved beyond any limit, beyond any hope, is on his own ground when the loved one is already a shadow. Life then ceases to be a succession of savage islands. . . . It becomes whatever is most genuinely shared, even in its ultimate consequences. This is what happens in Gabriela Mistral's love poetry, from *Desolation* to *Wine Press*. . . . And this sharing, which is consummated and perfected beyond death, could have had its origins only in a life of love, in the insecurity of jealousy and the sadness of a soul in love, in the experience of the encounter with the beloved one that was also the beginning of a knowledge of the destiny that lay before her.

Luis V. Anastasia Sosa. *Revista
Iberoamericana de literatura*. Nos. 2–3,
1960–61, pp. 18–19

The strength of [Mistral's] mystic transformation [in *Wine Press*, her last book] is greater than the roots of mourning. Gabriela Mistral bears the burden of unconfessed guilt, which causes her anguish and places obstacles in her way. The symbol of this guilt . . . is the *door*, just as the symbol of earthly anguish that guilt produces is *mourning*. Doors represent the hostile dividers that keep man a prisoner, exiled from God and from his fellow men. Like other "walls" mentioned in *Wine Press*, these doors take on demonic powers; they are endowed with human intentions in the face of which the poet becomes agitated and troubled, like someone who is experiencing bad dreams. In the grip of a Christian death man will shatter this barrier and, with his recently won freedom, will set out to pursue his struggle against *doors* and *mournings*. Thus, there always exists the hope for divine intervention. Here we have the secret dynamism of Gabriela Mistral's mystic poetry; it contains a salvation. . . .

There are few poems in which this message appears with greater clarity and simplicity than in "Christmas Star." Let me mention in passing, without attaching too much importance to it, that the subject of this poem was also used by Pablo Neruda in his "Ode to a Star." Naturally, Neruda was interested in the lyric projection of the idea; and in the image of a man casting the star upon the ocean he pays homage to a terrestrial power. Mistral, on the other hand, by beginning with the image of the little girl who falls with the star in her hand, describes the transmutation of a being into a divinity. Incarnated in the star, the little girl goes off into the distance, toward a supernatural world.

Wine Press thus reveals the necessary opposition of principles that provides the basis for an essentially Catholic conception of the world. This opposition takes the form of a duality of powers that, by struggling with each other, resolve themselves in the end through the knowledge of God. . . . Exile and return, mourning and rebirth—these are common forms used by the poet to describe her life and to suggest, at the same time, the faith that will save her.

Fernando Alegría. *Las fronteras del
realismo: Literatura chilena del siglo XX*
(Santiago: Editorial Zig-Zag, 1962),
pp. 166–67

The influence of [Gabriela Mistral's] native village removed the horizon from her great flight; her background kept her from drawing near the great sources of intellectual beauty. Yet it gave her poetry the most original qualities: a strong personality, passion, a tragic sense of life, solitude. Thus, her poetry will remain as a great human document. I was close to her and was at times influenced by her poetry, but I will never be able to define her work with exactitude. . . .

Gabriela was a distinguished teacher and a writer who crystallized an era. The strength of her renovation of literature is a model for young writers. Her devotion to teaching and her worthy life are exemplary. . . . She lived alone, between sorrow and happiness, between the thorn and the corolla, between the worm and the star. Let us not forget that she was born in a country of liberty and that it was her lot to live through one of the most violent periods in history. She offered words of consolation for the oppressed of the world, the Jews of Poland, the exiled Basque children, the orphans of the revolutions, those who suffered in concentration camps. But she could also be silent, when it came to the dictators of her continent whose vanity she wounded by never having any dealings with them. With natural modesty, she realized, like no one else, the role of the writer in society.

Arturo Torres-Ríoseco. *Gabriela Mistral*
(Valencia: Editorial Castalia, 1962),
pp. 25–26

When I speak of the "biblical roots" of Gabriela Mistral's poetry, I am thinking about various aspects of her work: her use of themes from and allusions to the Bible, her biblical style, and her religious inspiration. The Bible of Gabriela is the whole Christian Bible: the Old Testament with its cries of pain, and the New Testament, the Gospels with their songs of tenderness. She responds to the terrible prophetic tones of the Old Testament and also to its passages of softer emotion, such as the Book of Ruth. And the Gospels inspire in her songs to children, the children of her soul, and lead her closer to the peace that Christ offers.

The Bible has been the source of literary motifs for many post-modernist writers. I recall at this moment Gabriel Miró's *Images of the Passion,* and Juana de Ibarbourou's *Images from the Bible,* two works from either shore of Hispanic literature [that is, he was Spanish, she Uruguayan]. But these poetic prose pieces are merely dressed up with biblical material, as in Rubén Darío's "The Wolf's Motives," in which he used the poetic elements of the legend of Saint Francis. But for Gabriela, as for Amado Nervo, the Bible is not only the strongest and the most beautiful of books; it is God's book of life.

Gabriela is the only woman mystic in Latin American poetry since the remote days of the baroque, of Mother Castillo of Bogotá. Thus, as Amado Nervo is the only mystic of modernism, Gabriela is the only mystic of post-modernist poetry. And only recently in the poetry in Spain, with Dámaso Alonso, has the Bible again become the source of mystic and not merely aesthetic inspiration.

Gabriela's poetry begins with the primitive cry of her suffering. And the Biblical roots of *Desolation* are principally those of the Old Testament. But this anguish and the frustration of maternity yields to a sweet spiritual maternity, directed toward all children, the poor, the Indian, and the abandoned; at this point the New Testament is her principal source. Later in her life, at the time of the death of her mother, she undergoes a religious crisis, and as she turns toward the Catholic religion of her childhood, in a sincere return, the Gospels become the light of her resigned submission.

Carlos D. Hamilton. *Cuadernos americanos.*
No. 118, September–October, 1962,
pp. 202–3

Gabriela Mistral's poetry stands as a reaction to the Modernism of the Nicaraguan poet Rubén Darío *(rubendarismo)*: a poetry without ornate form, without linguistic virtuosity, without evocations of gallant or aristocratic eras; it is the poetry of a rustic soul, as primitive and strong as the earth, of pure accents without the elegantly correct echoes of France. By comparison with Hispanic-American literature generally, which on so many occasions has been an imitator of European models, Gabriela's poetry possesses the merit of consummate originality, of a voice of its own, authentic and consciously realized. The affirmation within this poetry of the intimate "I," removed from everything foreign to it, makes it profoundly human, and it is this human quality that gives it its universal value.

Passion is its great central poetic theme; sorrowful passion similar in certain aspects—in its obsession with death, in its longing for eternity—to Unamuno's agony; the result of a tragic love experience. *Pathos* has saturated the ardent soul of the poet to such an extent that even her concepts, her seasons are transformed into vehement passion. The poet herself defines her lyric poetry as "a wound of love inflicted on us by things." It is an instinctive lyricism of flesh and blood, in which the subjective, bleeding experience is more important than form, rhythm, or ideas. It is a truly pure poetry because it goes directly to the innermost regions of the spirit and springs from a fiery and violent heart.

The second important poetic motif is *nature,* or rather, *creation,* because Gabriela sings to every creation: to man, animals, vegetables, and minerals; to active and inert materials; and to objects made by human hands. All beings have for her a concrete, a palpable reality and, at the same time, a magic existence that surrounds them with a luminous aura. In a single moment she reveals the unity of the cosmos, her personal relationship with creatures, and that state of mystic, Franciscan rapture with which she gathers them all to her.

There is also an abundance of poems fashioned after children's folklore. The stories, rounds, and lullabies, the poems intended for the spiritual and moral formation of the students, achieve the intense simplicity of true songs of the people; there throbs within them the sharp longing for motherhood, the inverted tenderness of a very feminine soul whose innermost "reason for being" is unfulfilled.

Margot Arce de Vázquez. *Gabriela Mistral: The Poet and Her Work* (New York: New York University Press, 1964), pp. 21–22

Among the poetic themes Gabriela Mistral elaborated consistently—love and anguish, life and death, nature and man—none occupies a more pivotal position than her treatment of the meaning of God. The Old Testament God and Jesus Christ, in their respective sternness and charity, appear to share qualities of omniscience and omnipresence. Yet, for Yahweh the poet reserves characteristics rooted in tradition, Scripture, and the collective unconscious. Yahweh's strength negates all possible appeals for mercy and benevolence. Yahweh has absolute power over the life-taking and life-giving aspects of human existence. If man were condemned to face forever the anger of a post-Edenic deity, compassion and love would matter little. What Yahweh tendered grudgingly, Jesus Christ offered in abundance. The Sinaitic God, therefore, made man aware of his own anguish and insignificance; Christ's sacrifice imparted to man the unique experience of knowing a divine being who shared human pain. This explains Gabriela's appeals to a tortured Jesus Christ, who knew human suffering and promised redemption. If the end is worthwhile, she felt, then the means must be justifiable. Still, when she ultimately chose the Christian path, she did not cease to recognize that Christian and Jew had a common heritage of suffering. Nor did she disregard the bond of suffering that linked her to both traditions. . . .

In the quest to reinforce her belief that the divinity of man is a virtue dependent on man's capacity for good or evil and not a grudging concession from Church and clergy, she broke away from institutionalized religion. In Theosophy, which embraces Christian and Buddhist tenets, and holds truth to be the highest form of religion, she was able to maintain her love for Jesus Christ and her oneness with all creatures. To all intents and purposes, then, the study of Theosophy took her closer to God by taking her closer to the spirit of God that resides in all men. What is more crucial, Theosophy frees the individual from the necessity of blindly accepting the judgments of a priestly caste. Gabriela rejected the condescending and selfish edicts of the Church in Chile, because the Church did not seek to elevate its worshipers but, instead, offered sentimentality rather than piety, asked for faith and offered no means by which the faith could be sustained. Inimical to theology, Theosophy depends upon an open, inquiring mind which affirms the rational nature of religion. . . .

Confronted with a religious crisis after 1924, Gabriela Mistral was forced to reconcile her early aversion to the Church with the possible benefits of the Church to society. She had to reconcile also her conscious choice of Theosophy and Buddhism with the discrepancies she could not help but see in them. Impinging on these issues were the three irreconcilable deities of

Judaism, Christianity, and Buddhism, each with his own brand of righteousness, pain, and charity. Apart from offering personal fulfillment in a religious life, religion must also point the way to the betterment of society as a whole. In this latter consideration Gabriela Mistral found the key to the true religion. Influenced in part by Bergson, in part by the Christian Socialists, she began to believe in a dynamic Christianity that would put service and charity above the personal needs of a priesthood.

Martin C. Taylor. *Gabriela Mistral's
Religious Sensibility* (Berkeley: University
of California Press, 1968), pp. 114–17

[Gabriela Mistral] had an immense influence on every intellectual and literary group throughout [Latin] America. For thirty years there was no important event, even in other countries, that was not given a defining set of guidelines by Gabriela, or for which she did not proffer words of encouragement, or against which, if necessary, she did not raise her voice in protest. Through her very presence or through her newspaper articles and her "teaching messages," she made her voice heard. As Mariano Picón-Salas said, "It was nothing less than defining in the face of the political divisiveness of the Latin American world a common spiritual and moral legacy, an inheritance of culture and an aspiration for justice that was valid for the entire continent. The contagious fire of the creative passion of this woman seemed to convince the most wicked of men."

Thus, it is significant that Gabriela Mistral's . . . efforts did not become reduced to mere feminist activities. The strong current of love for humanity, which forms the center of her literary work, was not simply the elegant gesture of the woman writer; rather, it paralleled her fervent dedication to all causes that could better the lot of the helpless and the humble, to all strivings for greater social justice in the world. This messianic attitude, present in many of her poems and militantly active in every act of her existence, was already evident in this youthful proclamation: "I am a Christian, and in favor of total democracy. I believe that Christianity, with a profound social sense, can save peoples."

Salvador Bueno. *Cuadernos
hispanoamericanos.* No. 242, February,
1970, p. 389

The distinctive note of *Desolation* is its unique intensity. The muse certainly seems to be the mistral, the fierce, tearing wind of southern France, which like the equally fierce *puelche* [easterly wind from the Andes] of her native Chile, carried everything along with it. The critics who determine value by adherence to rules looked askance at these explosions. But Gabriela, in true Hispanic fashion, turned her back on easy elegance, deliberately eschewed the smooth flowing, and reveled in the rough-hewn and rugged. A disheveled and burning passion must find its own form. Its muse is not the orderly collected muse of Virgil. Even some of her tender notes are almost ferocious. The dynamic Hispanic genius pays little homage to formal tidiness. The cool-headed poets, content with the resonances of the ivory tower, cannot gain entrance to this hall of the winds, the mistral and the *puelche,* with its primitive earthiness and craggy rural tones. Gabriela's frankness and openness scandalized the routinists.

The vocabulary of Gabriela Mistral is extraordinarily rich and original. Guillermo de Torre, in accordance with the distinction that Leo Spitzer made between the meaning of *habla* ("speech") and *lengua* ("language"), affirmed that it was *habla* and not *lengua* that Gabriela spoke, for speech to her was an individual act of will and intelligence. Marcel Bataillon . . . considered Gabriela "one of the greatest Spanish poets of our time," and said that he had found even more reasons to love the Spanish language after reading Gabriela, "whose skill as a poet, a maker of words in the true sense, had once again proved the infinite possibilities of expression Spanish had in the hands of great artists."

Oxford's William J. Entwistle also praised the simplicity and rustic quality of the language of *Felling of Trees.* He said that, like Saint Teresa of Ávila, Gabriela had created a "rustic revolution" in Spanish by avoiding the bookish speech sanctioned by the Academy. She had the courage to use words that were not in its dictionary. There are other points of similarity in the *habla* of Gabriela and that of Saint Teresa. With the most concrete and homely imagery, both were able to attain great spiritual effects. With their feet planted firmly on the ground, they were able to soar, to create a happy union between the earth and the spirit. . . .

Gabriela writes with a dead earnestness and a profound modesty. Hardly ever do we hear a light gay note, a dancing rhythm to balance the gray and black hues of her ardent passion. She differs from other women poets of her time, often painfully self-centered and extremely conscious of their "femininity," in that she seldom mentions herself unless it is to tell us of her plainness. In her poems as in her life she is the arch enemy of *vanitas.*

Margaret Bates. Introduction to *Selected
Poems of Gabriela Mistral* (Baltimore:
Johns Hopkins University Press, 1971),
pp. xx–xxi

It is possible that with the passing of time the oral poetry of Gabriela Mistral will be considered the most profound and valuable expression of her creative genius. By "oral poetry" I mean the improvised talks she gave at university halls or at private gatherings, the conversations she carried on all night, sipping her scotch whiskey and smoking cigarettes, as well as her famous *Recados,* articles written on the spur of the moment covering a wide variety of subjects, in which, more than a style of writing, a tone of voice is recognized.

Her written poetry is, of course, something else. *Desolation,* heavy as it is with ritual images and archaic ornamentation, is basically a testimony of love and religious crisis. The book's popularity was due mainly to its dramatic eloquence and anecdotal content. *Tala* (1946), on the other hand, is an intricately woven structure of symbols conveying a state of alienation in a Hispanic-American world of ancient mountains, forests, and oceans; it is also an austere verbal discourse composed of both modern and neoclassical rhetoric. . . .

How does one go about trying to define Mistral's ideology [since] we cannot count on a sufficient number of texts to provide a solid foundation? Something can be accomplished if, instead of dealing with the bulk of her prose output, we follow only certain currents of her thought in one particular field—political in this case—ideas that are easily recognizable and, perhaps, universally acceptable. As a contribution to this study, I would like to propose five categories which may be judged essential to the definition of her social ideas:

1. Human rights: specifically, the problems of political and racial minorities.
2. Social Christianity: the social responsibility of the church in reference to economic and political injustice and its duty to defend and protect civil rights within the structure of a liberal democracy.
3. Antitotalitarianism: opposition to all forms of political extremism and to militaristic aggression.
4. Pacifism: support of the nonviolent movement as represented by Mahatma Gandhi; condemnation of imperialist wars and of the proliferation of nuclear weapons.
5. Americanism: conceived as an exaltation of indigenous communal organization and promotion of agrarian reforms.

These five currents of critical thought, abundantly supported by examples taken from books and articles and from speeches, suggest an ideology with a Christian basis rooted in the theories of Henri Bergson, Teilhard de Chardin, and Jacques Maritain.

> Fernando Alegría. In Beth Miller, ed.
> *Women in Hispanic Literature: Icons and*
> *Fallen Idols* (Berkeley: University of
> California Press, 1983), pp. 215, 219

Gabriela Mistral has all too often been taken to task for allegedly offering in her work too literal or mimetic a representation of woman. If this were true, one could understandably quarrel with the type of statement she would then be making about womanhood. Her insistent theme of maternity as female fulfillment would therefore take on unpleasant overtones befitting the Freudian dictum "biology as destiny." However . . . I argue that Mistral's treatment of the maternal function should be separated from any possible implication about how real-world women are to realize their potential. After all, we shall be looking here at autonomous poetic texts and, moreover, at texts of a highly metaphorical nature—not at all at a set of directives concerning how women ought to feel or behave.

I propose starting instead at the larger poetic system wherein woman and maternity are simply elements, albeit prominent ones. This system in its scope goes far beyond the question of women's social role. In effect, it is so globally inclusive that, as we shall see, it seeks to take in the entire cosmos. At issue, then, is an immense spiritual quest whose goal is the generation of meaning and whose proof lies in the symbolic code or system developed by the poet. Within such a code, woman and procreation are present as meaning-bearing signs in a larger, all-encompassing poetic language.

C. Virgillo. In C. Virgillo and Naomi
Lindstrom, eds. Woman as Myth and
Metaphor in Latin American Literature
(Columbia: University of Missouri Press,
1983), pp. 138–39

Until the recent publication of two bilingual anthologies of poetry by Latin American women, Mistral's poems had received recognition only because they appeared to conform to female stereotypes. Male critics pointed to the merit of her "feminine" themes—"love of God, nature, the mother, the world's just causes, the humble, persecuted, suffering, and forgotten" (amor a Dios, a la naturaleza, a la madre, a las buenas causas del mundo, a los humildes, perseguidos, dolientes y olvidados). Aesthetic appreciation focused on her "great sensibility" (gran sensibilidad). Scant attention was paid to meaning and to how that meaning technically was achieved.

Other qualities of Mistral's poetry are noted in a curious way. For example, in their widely used anthology, Enrique Anderson-Imbert and E. Florit single out as a chief virtue Mistral's poetic "vigor," suggesting that vigor—a sinewy sort of cerebral strength celebrated by Huidobro in his famous dictum—was distinctly a property of the male mind. Mistral's vigor was, according to Florit and Anderson-Imbert, "more the vigor of a poet than a poetess" (vigor de poeta más que de poetisa). Thus it seems that the adoption of a masculine pseudonym did nothing to deflect injurious criticism. Not surprisingly, Mistral's "crazy women" poems (Locas mujeres) and other works of hers went unrepresented in most anthologies. Nor did critics take note of Mistral's anger in the exclamations of the short lyric poem "I Have No Solitude" (Yo no tengo soledad), published in *Ternura* (Tenderness) (1924). In that poem, anger mixes subversively with maternal impulses. In "Lluvia lenta" (Slow rain), Mistral evokes a distilled anger, a bitterness dripping-slow like rain that drills into the soul. It is nothing less than a cosmic affliction that women alone must bear and about which men—secure and sheltered in the home, childlike in their comfort, ignorance, and privilege—know nothing.

"Within the home, men / do not feel this bitterness, / this cargo of sad water / sent from on high." (Dentro del hogar, los hombres / no sienten esta amargura, / este envío de agua triste / de la altura.) "Man as mothered child— Mistral's maternal instinct harbors suppressed outrage."

Harriet S. Turner. In Noël Valis and Carol Maier, eds. *In the Feminine Mode: Essays on Hispanic Women Writers* (Lewisburg, Pennsylvania: Bucknell University Press, 1990), p. 232

MITCHISON, NAOMI (GREAT BRITAIN) 1897–

In writing a historical novel of Gaul in the time of Julius Caesar [*The Conquered*], Mrs. Mitchison has made a bold experiment that must be said, on the whole, to have succeeded. . . . There is in this story a fine objectivity, a close grip upon facts, not large historical facts, but the little facts that count for so much in romance, that carries conviction; and that and the writer's sound prose largely help to make it the surprising performance it is. Even its very faults as a story, a piece of drama . . . only help the author in her main purpose, for they leave us with the impression of long, dragging years of ineffectual heroism, divided loyalties and broken vows, the sudden sharp cruelties of fiery nationalists and jealous clans and the long heartbreaking cruelty of empires. This, I take it, is what Mrs. Mitchison intended when she put together so deftly this finely consistent prose narrative, and she may be said to have succeeded in doing something new that was really worth doing, for with this story she has occupied the space there is between the narrative poem (which may be in prose, if it is conceived as a poet conceives his work) and the historical novel. I hope she will contrive to stay there, for she has conquered the method, and the material, I imagine, is almost inexhaustible.

J. B. Priestley. *London Mercury.*
September, 1923, pp. 545–46

Black Sparta. . . . Twelve stories, with verses interspersed, of Greece in the fourth and fifth centuries. Mrs. Mitchison has put so much thought, work and feeling into them that I am sorry not to find the result more satisfactory. Transposition is, no doubt, the best device for making the ancient world alive, but Mrs. Mitchison transposes not into the key of modern life but into the key of a particular fiction—the kind in which the characters unroll their subconsciousness in a gurgling [Greek], which reminds me more of Mrs. Pace in the *Weekly Dispatch* than of any Greek I have ever read. Now and then it comes off: the genesis of a Pindaric ode in "Lucky Thessaly" is well conceived and executed. But as a rule I have the feeling that Mrs. Mitchison has not apprehended her Greeks but compiled them out of elements which, apart from the conscientious homosexuality, are quite un-Hellenic. This would matter less if the stories were more interesting.

Life and Letters. August, 1928, pp. 230–31

Mrs. Mitchison does herself injustice when, in her foreword, she explains the neat little summaries which follow each section of her book by saying that "it is difficult to remember just what happened." The defect of *The Corn King and the Spring Queen* does not lie in any want of vividness. Her descriptive power never fails her. To a reader with even a moderate gift of visual memory there will remain at the end of his reading a complete and brightly colored tapestry of great intricacy upon which, against backgrounds often of entrancing beauty, a number of queer figures, lively rather than life-like, appear in a vast variety of attitudes graceful or grotesque. One observes them with an admiring curiosity, but their cruelties excite one's horror as little as their loves engage one's emotions; their plots bring no catch to the breath; their fighting leaves the blood unstirred; even their obscenities do not shock. . . .

Yet, although the author's interest seems to have been devoted to archaeology rather than to the human aspect of her characters, and though a didactic tendency has led her to clog the narrative with redundancies, it is impossible not to admire the book. It is never for a moment dull.

The Adelphi. September, 1931, pp. 549–50

Though not the best of . . . novels, *We Have Been Warned* is most interesting. Its theme is left-wing politics in England, the activities and personal relationships of middle-class people feeling the draft of conscience and Communism, Oxford Socialist dons, the local Communist Party, strikes, Intourist trips to Russia, hunger marches to Hyde Park. Mrs. Mitchison knows her people. Some of the reporting is good, particularly the chapters about Russia. The different shades of red opinion in this country and the changes of scene between Oxford, London, Scotland and Russia make the book varied and readable, and help also to disguise the muddled sentimentalism of the writing. But at times the Sunday-school atmosphere becomes overpowering.

G. W. Stonier. *Fortnightly Review.*
June, 1935, p. 763

It is, at first, almost a relief to see that a new novel [*When We Become Men*] about African problems is by a name long familiar in our own literary circles, someone on whom one has at least some background information by which to measure not so much the treatment as the voice adopted. In fact, however, Mrs. Mitchison has deliberately invited attack from both political and literary sides of the African fence: she has become a member of the Batswana tribe in Bechuanaland, thus entitling herself to write not as an observer but through the eyes and hearts of the African; and she has chosen tribalism, in the "new and free" form which she believes may perhaps provide the ultimate answer to that unhappy continent's search for a just society, as the center of a novel about pressures of old and new, democratic and feudal, which will very probably provoke all factions to denounce her picture of African life as unconvincing. . . .

Much of Mrs. Mitchison's argument is bound to sound not only facile but also unconvincing, stated self-consciously through the lips of young Africans. Indeed, until she is halfway into her novel one cannot help noticing both the extraordinary naivety of her style and the imaginative gaps the reader has to bridge for himself in accepting the tribal background. But the story moves fast and professionally, the characters do begin to live outside their utterances, and Mrs. Mitchison's experience as a writer for children is perhaps an asset in showing us, who may not know more than the newspapers tell us, a good deal of authentic detail about the way of life with which she has fallen in love.

(London) Times Literary Supplement.
January 7, 1965, p. 5

The Corn King and the Spring Queen (1931) is a giant book that can in a sense be summarized. Mitchison acknowledges this by the clear and simple summaries she provides at the end of each of its nine parts, "because it is a long and crowded book and it is rather difficult to remember just what happened from time to time." Summary is legitimate, then, but it does not begin to substitute for the long and absorbing experience of reading it. And a summary as short as the following can say very little.

In the novel, Mitchison balances two stages of civilization, treating them alternately. There is the ancient Scythian kingdom of Marob, ruled by Tarrik, the Corn King, and Erif Der, a witch, who becomes his Spring Queen at her father's urging, to destroy and supplant Tarrik but who in the end loves and saves him. Tarrik and Erif are barbarians, susceptible to magic, in tune with the seasons and their rituals, and necessary to the prosperity and fertility of Marob. Consciously rational Greeks on the whole despise the barbarians of Marob, and Erif's magic does not work on the clear, rational mind of Sphaeros, the Stoic philosopher, for example. The narrative moves repeatedly from Marob to Sparta, and many of the characters journey there also. Here a long period of decadence has destroyed ancient ways, creating an oligarchy, a dictatorship of the wealthy, the enslavement of the poor. Agis and Kleomenes, successive Spartan kings, seek to lead a revolution which will restore the ancient ideals of equality and fellowship, but although like Tarrik (and later Jesus) they are kings willing to die for their people, the sacrifice of their deaths does not bring about the desired result. The ideal of Sparta is lost. . . . Tarrik and Erif Der are cleansed of their troubles and restored to Marob, Corn King and Spring Queen again, but with a flow of Hellenic enlightenment that transforms them as individuals, but is not fully passed on to their successors, who are less troubled, and more fortunate.

Although Marob is an imaginary kingdom, necessarily, as written records would never be made of that kind of civilization, Sparta is carefully documented here. Mitchison's fictions of the Hellenic world return repeatedly to the antithetical claims to allegiance of Athens and Sparta, a kind of democracy in however exhausted a phase, and a place of iron discipline and austerity, and a certain totalitarian quality. In the 1920s and 1930s Mitchison recognized this totalitarian quality in Germany and Italy, with the rise of the Fascist dictatorships, and to some extent in Russia too; on her 1932 visit to the USSR she notes at one point in her diary, with sad disapproval: "A lot of Sparta about this."

Any attempt to "cover" Mitchison, even on this scale, would be ludicrous, for she has published more than seventy books. . . .

The stories range from primitive man and the cave-painters of Lascaux, through an ancient Greek tale of citizens enslaved, to Scottish and African tales of a more recent vintage. There are repeated treatments of physical and psychological slavery, and the exercise of unjust or irrational power in human relationships is often illustrated by cases of rape: particularly interesting are the pragmatic solutions variously arrived at, often by the women involved, to cope with the reality and the aftermath of such incidents. The African stories underline different cultural attitudes to sexuality, and to polygamy, and something of the nature of western imperialism.

The selection ends with "Remember Me," an account by a survivor of a "minor" nuclear holocaust in Scotland; it is remarkable for the authenticity and quiet desperation of the narrative voice, and the finely judged use of significant detail. This subject is typical of much of her more recent work, which tackles huge issues of conservation, ecology and famine, sometimes in a kind of science fiction. The selection juxtaposes Mitchison's abiding preoccupations, as in her most recent longer fiction. *Not by Bread Alone* (1983) investigates possibilities of great advances in world food production, with terrible consequences when new foodcrops become susceptible to new diseases; and her most recent work, *Early in Orcadia,* attempts to recreate the lives and outlooks of early settlers in Stone Age Orkney primitive man, but always centrally, discernibly human.

Isobel Murray. In Cairns Craig, ed. The
History of Scottish Literature, Vol. 4
(Aberdeen, Scotland: Aberdeen University
Press, 1987), pp. 112–14

Valued she may be as a novelist, but Naomi Mitchison is largely ignored as a poet. Much of her poetry remains unpublished, but one volume, *The Cleansing of the Knife* is currently available. In conversation recently, Mitchison said that she felt her poetry comes from a deeper source inside herself than her other writing, even the best of the novels. Her poetry is engaged with the real world, the actions and objects of everyday life, but not limited in range to practical existence. In such poems as "The Alban Goes Out: 1939," the title poem, "The Cleansing of the Knife," and "The Talking Oats" and the introductory poem to *The Bull Calves* Mitchison attempts to articulate a vision of Scotland, past, present and future. While mindful of the disintegration endemic in Scottish history, she aims towards an integrated, wholesome, fulfilling future. The poems are largely "spoken" by involved observers; often her own voice is heard, sometimes in the background, sometimes speaking directly. Nancy Gish, reviewing "The Cleansing of the Knife" accuses Mitchison of speaking in her own voice *about* Scotland, and lapsing therefore into sentiment and moralizing. But the voices used are of someone directly caught up in the events described, and Mitchison is too concerned with the need to understand and *act* to allow sentiment to blunt the vision. Her central message is of loyalty, responsibility, of the debt owed by each to the community, local, national, world-wide. . . .

Her own community of Carradale provides the setting for these poems, acting as a microcosm for Scotland as a whole. In her short poems, too, are fine achievements. "Adoption of a Parliamentary Candidate, Lochgilphead: 1939," "Comfort," to name but two. The time is ripe for the re-evaluation of her work, including her poetry.

Joy Hendry. In Cairns Craig, ed. *The
History of Scottish Literature,* vol. 4
(Aberdeen, Scotland: Aberdeen University
Press, 1987), pp. 299–300

Originally published in 1931, this dense, epic-length fantasy [*The Corn King and the Spring Queen*] is a quest story cunningly woven of history and myth. Erif Der, a witch in a Black Sea land, falls in love with the king whom she was supposed to topple. As Spring Queen, she takes revenge on her scheming father, introduces death into the cycle of the seasons and must seek purification of her soul. Another seeker is Kleomenes, rebel king of Sparta, who is willing to put up his own children and his mother as hostages for the sake of the revolution in which he fervently believes. Berris Der, brother of Erif and an adventurous painter-sculptor hopelessly in love with a Spartan woman, represents a third type of quester. There are many others in a crowded canvas stretching from Asia Minor to Egypt. In scenes of beauty and power, Mitchison breathes life into such perennial themes as courage, forgiveness, the search for meaning, and self-sacrifice.

Sybil Steinberg. *Publishers Weekly.*
March 30, 1990, pp. 53–54

MITFORD, NANCY (GREAT BRITAIN) 1904–73

Nancy Mitford's new novel *The Pursuit of Love* has a theme which might have made as portentous and boring a story as any novelist could well wish— nothing less than a girl's progress to true happiness via two unsuitable marriages. But Nancy Mitford has been original enough to tell her story as a perfectly straight narration (a method employed by some of the better writers in the past) and since her sense of humor is much deeper than her sense of the significant, she has written a book which is filled with laughter. Linda's pursuit of love is recounted by her cousin Fanny, who shared in all her early pleasures and anxieties, and who can therefore give a clear description of Linda's family, headed by Uncle Matt, an eccentric peer who used to hunt his children (with their friendly co-operation) with bloodhounds. The friendship of Linda and Fanny brings a gossipy character to the narration. Like gossip it is full of high spirits and pleasant malice. Like gossip, on the other hand, it is too diffuse. But because it is all written with such perfect freedom from nonsense, the book sometimes takes on the character not of a novel but of a light-hearted and accurate biographical study. *The Pursuit of Love* is an unexpected book. It is not great literature. It is not great wit. But it has more truth, more sincerity, and more laughter than a year's output of novels in the bogus significant style. And behind its screen of humor there is a just picture of the English upper classes of the twentieth century.

The Spectator. January 4, 1946, p. 20

Patience is needed . . . even with Miss Nancy Mitford's *The Pursuit of Love,* which is rewardingly funny in many places. This is the least, and indeed the most, one can say of it. It begins extremely well with a picture of the children of an aristocratic family called Radlett. Its early pages introduce, in Uncle Matthew and Captain Warbeck, two of the best comic figures in any modern novel. I cannot recall a funnier picture of the violent foreigner-hating patriarch than Uncle Matthew; his early morning foibles are beautifully recorded. . . . But, alas, though Uncle Matthew dodges in and out of the whole book, the later pages are given over to the affairs of one of his daughters, Linda. . . . The less successful episodes in her pursuit . . . are convincing enough; but at a moment of despair she is picked up by a French duke and installed as his mistress, and thenceforward the novel has the sentimental staginess of the late W. J. Locke.

Henry Reed. *New Statesman and Nation.*
February 2, 1946, p. 90

This is the time of year when, according to one of the oldest and most sacred superstitions of publishing, the reading public is to be found slouched on its back in a string hammock, victim of a sudden and unappeasable appetite for light novels. These works are to the robust fare of midwinter what a raspberry ice is to roast beef and Yorkshire pudding; they are expected to cool the prostrate reader, not nourish him. . . .

At first glance, *Love in a Cold Climate*, by Nancy Mitford, is an excellent specimen of this genre. . . . The title itself could scarcely be more adroit; now, in the dog days, it will help to sell thousands of copies, whereas in January it would have sold few or none. The novel has, moreover, the advantage of being about exceedingly well-bred people who behave exceedingly badly, and what could be more refreshing than to hear, for the fiftieth time, the good news that our supposed betters are at least as wicked as we are, and maybe wickeder? . . .

If, at second glance, *Love in a Cold Climate* is something less than perfect, if it fails to make us feel twenty degrees cooler inside, the blame must fall, in part, on this same rich, Stanley-of-Alderley blood, for it is the duty of the comic novelist to be detached and Miss Mitford's difficulty is that, as a member of the family, she cannot be detached. She begins by being witty— and she can be very witty indeed—at the expense of Lord and Lady Mont- dore and their hollow and outrageous circle, but almost immediately one senses her mounting personal disgust at horrors that a lower-middle-class writer, stemming from the Blimeys of Billingsgate, would either work up into farce or, more likely, lock in his breast as loyally as any upstairs maid. Poor Miss Mitford is unable to choose any such easy ways out. . . .

In the end, Miss Mitford takes her revenge on the Montdores by meting out a variety of harsh and astonishing punishments. Lord Montdore sinks into smiling and unregretted senility. Polly, the cold, lovely daughter of the house, on whose unwillingness to marry the plot of the novel centers, at last insists on marrying her mother's lover, an aging, sickly, snobbish widower, who once, when Polly was a little girl, attempted to corrupt her and suc- ceeded only in making her fall in love with him. Lady Montdore is captured by her husband's homosexual cousin and heir, and transformed by him from a stout, red-cheeked woman of sixty into the sort of thin, shrill old lady of whom people whisper, "Isn't she marvelous? They say she's past seventy." As for Uncle Matthew, who wishes that nearly everyone he knows were dead—But perhaps it is plain by now that Miss Mitford has violated most of the conventions of the light novel in writing what is still unquestionably a light novel, and that while *Love in a Cold Climate* can be recommended as a means of passing a long summer afternoon, it has an ending about as happy as that of *Hamlet* and can guarantee no one the prospect of pleasant dreams.

Brendan Gill. *The New Yorker.* July 23,
1949, pp. 70–71

One of my French friends used to talk about *"le high-life,"* making it rhyme mysteriously with fig-leaf. I was reminded of that in reading *The Blessing* for it is high-life with a decided French accent, and a very diverting picture it is, too. The important question here is, as always with a light novel, is it amus- ing? The answer is an unqualified Yes. It is extremely amusing. It is also sophisticated, sometimes brilliant, sometimes ribald, and very European in its view. I suppose it could be read on other levels that pure amusement; as a study, contrasting French and British ideas of marriage, for instance, or as a picture of a thoroughly spoiled child and the psychological evils of divorce, or as a devastating indictment of that worst of all English institutions, the indomitable Nanny, but I doubt if it will be. It is amusement that comes first and what one remembers afterwards is an undercurrent of wicked, rippling laughter. Miss Mitford's wit is what the French call *malin*—sly, clever, mischievous rather than malicious. There is a fine touch of irony in her title, *The Blessing,* applied to one of the prize brats of fiction, dear little Sigismond who does his best to disrupt his parents' lives, having learned that he gets more out of them when they are separated than when they are together. . . .

Like a great many other people, I love to read about the gentry. I always like the Cinderella story better when she gets away from the cinders and those dull sisters and we get on to the ball. There is quite a bit here about dining out and fetes and parties, a background that is perfectly familiar to Miss Mitford who knows her Anglo-French upper crust to its last crumb. She was born to that world and is good at her tongue-in-the-cheek reporting.

Her analysis of the characteristic French and English virtues and faults is, on the whole, shrewd and just, but she is, I strongly suspect, one of those she describes: "They belonged to the category of English person, not rare among the cultivated classes, and not the least respectable of their race, who can find almost literally nothing to criticize where the French are concerned." Though not of that exalted company, I agree. In spite of its airy account of infidelities, the mood is moral. "A woman who puts her husband first seldom loses him," Grace is told and, despite Sigi's machinations, we get a happy ending. Under its sophisticated, sometimes brittle, surface, there is a good deal of wit and wisdom concealed here. This a fine mixture of English charm with Gallic humor. And quite a dish it is!

Rosemary Carr Benet. *Saturday Review of Literature.* October 6, 1951, p. 33

Nancy Mitford, having exhausted the comic possibilities of love in a cold climate, has moved on to less frigid shores. I am not sure the sea change is beneficial. *The Blessing* is a curious little novel, French with an odd accent. It is as if Miss Mitford's characters, having crossed the channel, were determined to be as briskly gay about sex as they had always heard the French were; and a determined gaiety can grow wearing, particularly when it involves popping in and out of baroque bedrooms. *Love in a Cold Climate* had mockery and cruelty and wit, and it glittered like ice. *The Blessing* is only hard, and frivolous like rock candy.

However, even a confection can have its virtues, and this book has several, all satiric. . . . And there is all that grandeur which is the Mitford trademark.

Phyllis McGinley. *New York Herald Tribune.* October 14, 1951, p. 10

Now, into a fray involving a presumably beleaguered English aristocracy, has leaped the Honorable Mrs. Peter Rodd (Nancy Mitford) with results disquieting for the domestic tranquility of England (never say "Britain" without revealing that you are hopelessly middle class!). Miss Mitford, who regularly shocks and delights England and America with her perky novels, now sallies forth as editor of and major contributor to a lively volume of essays [*Noblesse Oblige*] about the mores and speech habits of what many others had passed off as a moribund English aristocracy.

The flurry began with the publication in an English philological journal of a study called "Linguistic Class-Indicators in Present-Day English," by Professor Alan Ross of Birmingham University. Miss Mitford gleefully took the main drift of the professor's study and applied it to her own observations of aristocracy . . . with delightful comic effect. Her own essay, entitled "The English Aristocracy," was first published in *Encounter,* a magazine with distinctly upper middle-class appeal. Miss Mitford's major assertions are that in England there still exists a marked class structure; that the English aristocrat is "a wily old bird" who has lulled an unsuspecting world into believing that he is on his last legs politically and financially; that this clever aristocracy presumably is just biding its time until some happier day arrives; and that its sturdy survival is clearly manifest in certain linguistic habits. This upper middle-class speech and manner she designates as "U" and those of everyone else as "non-U." According to her neat distinctions, it is, for example, U to say "table-napkin" but unmistakably non-U to say "serviette." Only a non-U person would speak of a "teacher"; the U terms are "master," "mistress," or more specifically "maths-mistress." Professor Ross, whose study appears in a condensed version in this volume, informs us that one who spoofs at such U niceties by calling them "la-di-da" is most certainly non-U.

John R. Willingham. *The Nation.*
September 15, 1956, p. 224

The book [*Voltaire in Love*], warns the author in a disarming note, is neither a biography nor a study of Voltaire's literary and philosophic achievements. . . . It concentrates instead upon Voltaire's love affair with the Marquise Emilie de Châtelet. . . .

Miss Mitford contributes much of her own. Her style is, as always, vivacious, the narrative headlong, the incidental humor often suitably wry, as in her quotations of Voltaire's letters. . . .

Miss Mitford is not concerned in her biographies with the inner motivations of her subjects. They enact their story upon her pages, they speak their lines, and they keep the reader absorbed and awake. In their way, because they are stamped in their creator's individuality, Miss Mitford's books are works of art.

Frances Winwar. *The New York Times.*
February 23, 1958, pp. 3, 38

Everyone should be told that this [*Don't Tell Alfred*] is one of Miss Mitford's very best. Not, perhaps, wholly as perfect as *The Blessing,* but definitely a runner-up. And many of the same enchanting characters appear as in *The Pursuit of Love* and *Love in a Cold Climate,* and their children are giggles from the same guffaw. Fanny, the heroine of *Don't Tell Alfred,* is the happily married mother of four sons. Middle-aged, a trifle moth-eaten, she is in town for a day's shopping when Alfred, her husband, pastoral theologian at Oxford, is, quite unexpectedly made British Ambassador to Paris. . . .

All in all, this novel is crammed with vitamins, with wit, nostalgia, and trenchant comment. Miss Mitford understands the intricacies of French politics better than anyone else alive and explains them painlessly. Indeed, she provides sheer rollicking fun as well as a deep down tenderness for human foibles that she deftly conceals. She is perhaps the nearest our blurred, woolly and sadisto-sentimental age has gotten to the sane simplicity of Jane Austen. There is, in Miss Mitford, the same Chanel-like clarity of thought and line, the same deceptively unadorned style that is present almost by its absence. For she is, under it all, a serious writer, an artist who senses and sees the quirks and quiddities of the human condition.

Anne Fremantle. *Commonweal.* June 30,
1961, pp. 357–58

MIYAMOTO YURIKO (JAPAN) 1899–1951

Miyamoto Yuriko, a leading proletarian writer of the first half of the Showa period, stands out . . . as an exceptional figure, as a writer who placed women's concerns at the center of her literature and integrated them with the socialist movement of her time. She began her writing career as an idealistic humanist who was disturbed by the alienation of elite intellectuals from the masses; yet in her attempt to grow into a real intellectual, liberated from the conditioning forces of her bourgeois background, she came to realize that being a woman imposed an obstacle as great as any other she confronted. She came to believe that overcoming the class nature of her philosophic and aesthetic ideas and becoming a truly liberated woman were both crucial to living a rich and meaningful life. She saw the family and marriage systems as feudal institutions preserved in the interests of modern capitalism and considered them to be the primary forces oppressing women. At the same time, she noted the failure of women intellectuals to grasp the class nature of their ideas and their cynical and reactionary retreat into false femininity. For Yuriko, being a humanist meant being a feminist and communist revolutionary, and the humanist, feminist and revolutionary struggles were necessary truly to liberate human beings. . . .

What principally characterizes [Yuriko's first] novel [*Mazushiki Litobito no Muac* (A flock of poor folk) is the author's tendency toward introspective self-searching, together with her idealism and strong faith in human goodwill, characteristic traits which were to stay with her the rest of her life. Reflecting the strong influence of Tolstoy and such writers of the Shirakaba group as Arishima Takeo, she expresses in this work a youthful and hopeful belief in the union of consciousness and practice, and her determination to contribute to human welfare. In this respect she differs from the naturalist writers and urban intellectuals of the late Meiji period (1868–1912), whose discovery of the deep chasm between themselves and the peasants, and of the evil of a system which separates people so absolutely merely led them to an overall pessimism and desperation about human nature. . . .

In *Nobuko,* the protagonist's decision to give up her husband and go against the desires of her family was for the sake of her personal growth and happiness. Although well aware that her action would invite criticism as an egotistical act, Nobuko felt at that time that marriage was detrimental both to women's happiness as individual human beings and to their creativity. It was necessary to be independent from men, emotionally as well as economically, in order to secure a room of one's own. Yet Nobuko's solitary life makes her experience the frightening loneliness and emptiness that exist in life without love. She comes to reconsider whether marriage itself is the problem or whether it exists in deviation from an ideal form of marriage.

In *Futatsu no niwa* (*The Two Gardens,* 1947), an autobiographical sequel to *Nobuko,* Yuriko traces her life after her divorce to her decision to visit the new Russia. Although she was now writing novels steadily and enjoying a newly independent life as a professional writer, she (Yuriko-Nobuko) suffered from loneliness and a sense of sterility which came from the absence of total involvement in human relations. . . .

When Yuriko started writing as a feminist . . . with her own life as the central theme of her novels—and that started with her postwar novels—the gap between politics and literature and that between history and individual life were eliminated. She had discovered new modern heroes, the oppressed class of women struggling for liberation, a class emerging to play an important role in the history of human liberation. By writing autobiographical novels from a revolutionary feminist perspective, she achieved a unique combination of literature and politics, of history and individual life. The result was the overflow of her creativity. *The Banshū Plain, Fūchiso, The Two Gardens,* and *Road Sign* were written within the short years of bubbling creativity between the end of the war and her death in 1951. They were all autobiographical works and extensions of *Nobuko,* tracing her personal growth as a woman writer and woman communist, but these later works were distinguished from *Nobuko* by their communist-feminist perspective. She had plans for writing two more such novels, plans left unmaterialized by her sudden death.

The form of Yuriko's novels is closest possibly to the *Bildungsroman,* a form of novel which traces the moral as well as social development of an individual. Her works, most simply are a communist and feminist variant of the *Bildungsroman*. The recent autobiography of Simone de Beauvoir also resembles her works in its basic attempt to trace the inner as well as the social growth of the author-protagonist, and to place her in history. By placing inner growth within a concrete historical and social framework, history and individual life are uniquely interfused, creating both a personal drama and social intellectual history; Yuriko's hero is an honest reflection of herself, yet she emerges as a universal modern hero. Although Yuriko's hero is by no means portrayed as an ideal, superhuman woman, she is a positive hero whose faith in female and human liberation through communist revolution is unshakable.

Yuriko's works present the drama of a woman developing from a member of the bourgeois elite, dependent on men, into an independent, mature woman writer and communist, even as they mirror realistically an important page in the social, moral and intellectual history of modern Japan. Thus Yuriko created a new form of autobiography, one in which the protagonist emerges as a historic figure of the age, experiencing fully its limitations and possibilities. Her writings interlace uniquely the tradition of the I-novel with the historical social commitment derived from her political activities.

> Noriko Mizuta Lippit. *Reality & Fiction in Modern Japanese Literature* (Armonk, New York: M. E. Sharpe, 1980), pp. 146–48, 151, 160–61

The first of Miyamoto Yuriko's four post-war autobiographical novels, *The Banshū Plain* (Banshū Heiya, 1946), is a travel narrative which presents a panoramic view of Japan in the first weeks after the surrender, and explores its protagonist's relationships with female characters in the context of the extended family. Two others, *Two Gardens* (Futatsu no niwa, 1947) and *Guidepost* (Dōhyō, 1947–1950), are set in the prewar period, with the latter retracing in three volumes Miyamoto's experiences in Moscow and the evolution of her commitment to socialism and feminism. In striking contrast to the breadth of scope and retrospective cast of these novels is the immediacy of theme and circumscribed focus of *The Weathervane Plant*. The novella's subject is the relationship between husband and wife, reunited at the war's end after a twelve year separation resulting from the husband's imprisonment. . . .

The Weathervane Plant is set in the autumn immediately following the end of the Pacific War, with a plot that unfolds over a time span extending from late October to early December, 1945. Its protagonist, a woman novelist named Hiroko, is modeled after Yuriko herself, while the male character, Jūkichi, is modeled after her husband, Kenji. The first four chapters explore, from the wife's perspective, the process whereby Hiroko adjusts to life with Jūkichi after his long absence, often doubling back to touch on some aspect of the two characters' experiences during the war. In three later chapters the focus expands, as if in concentric circles, to include Hiroko's relationship with other women (Chapter 5) and her relationship to society at large, in the contrasting forms of the wartime government-organized Japanese Literature Patriotic Society, (Chapter 6) and the postwar Communist Party (Chapter 7). . . .

While the notion of women's writing as "double-voiced discourse" helps to illuminate mechanisms which perpetuate dynamic tension in *The Weathervane Plant,* it also brings into relief new dimensions of Miyamoto's significance in the broader context of modern Japanese literary development. As an I-novelist and realist Miyamoto has been criticized for conventionality of style in the same breath that she has been lauded for the boldness of the life which her work, in its totality, unfolds. In this vein, Katō Shūichi's evaluation is representative: "Miyamoto's novels are drawn directly from her own life; the uniqueness of that life meant that they expanded the world of Japanese literature."

Yet the very limitation of imaginative scope which may be perceived as a lack in Miyamoto's fiction takes on fresh significance when we consider her "other" voice, her contribution to a Japanese feminist literature which she herself pioneered. Here, Miyamoto's absorption with the details of everyday experience may be linked to her sense of woman's struggle for self-realization in the face of ineluctable social constraints. . . .

As the saga of the evolution of a Japanese feminist, the life story narrated in Miyamoto's oeuvre is of compelling historical interest. It is for the clarity with which the elements of that struggle are revealed, and in those moments when we cannot fail to be moved by the intensity of her protagonist's quest, that Miyamoto's work achieves its enduring literary power.

Brett de Bary. *Journal of the Association of Teachers of Japanese.* 19, 1984–85, pp. 10–12, 24–25

While many Japanese writers fell silent or wrote harmless material, if not military propaganda, during the late 1930s, Miyamoto Yuriko remained determined to express her belief in communism and the liberation of women in her writing. She was one of the few writers of this period who held firm to her radical views, despite great pressure and physical torture by authorities. With the close of World War II, Yuriko emerged as a leader of the intellectuals, and her literary career had followed a long and dramatic course that was rare among Japanese women writers.

Although most of Yuriko's major works of fiction are autobiographical, they do not tend to focus on the awakening of a female protagonist within the confinement of the family institution, a subject explored by many women writers of the previous generation. Her themes reflect the turbulent times in which she wrote, and her heroines' social and political concerns as well as their inner struggles are carefully examined. In this sense, and in the breadth of her intellectual and emotional experiences, Yuriko might be compared with Simone de Beauvoir: As a feminist and as a writer, Yuriko, like de

Beauvoir, challenged the institutions and mores of the middle-class milieu into which she was born and about which she wrote in her fiction. . . .

Nobuko is a record of the familial and internal battles that Yuriko fought as a young woman, and it is her best and most widely read novel. At one point the heroine of the story declares that she must escape from a marriage she had entered to escape her overbearing family, closely paralleling Yuriko's own struggle and her decisive move to end a relationship she later likened to "being bogged down in mud." Yuriko's divorce was a move to freedom, and her relationship with Yoshiko helped her fulfill a desire to grow and expand her horizons. . . .

During the war years, Yuriko had been working on manuscripts, gathering information and writing about the cruel treatment she and her comrades had received at the hands of the police. The experiences of these individuals, their sufferings and their joyous celebrations when the country was finally liberated from military oppression, are masterfully rendered in the two novels, *The Banshu Plain* and *Weather Vane Grasses*.

During the following year, Yuriko put the finishing touches on a novel that takes up where she had left off in *Nobuko*. This work, entitled *Two Gardens,* along with her next major novel, *Signpost,* completed her autobiographical trilogy. The works bear witness to a woman's struggle for personal freedom and growth and her developing political consciousness. Considered her most significant fiction, the novels of this trilogy are also particularly important for illuminating Yuriko's concerns as a woman and an artist.

Yuriko never fully regained her physical health following her years of imprisonment, and she died suddenly at age fifty-two, at the height of her creative power. At the time of her death she was widely regarded as the conscience of the intellectuals and a writer deeply concerned with the condition of Japanese women. A writer devoted to her personal relationships and political commitments as well as to her art, she is remembered today both for her written works and her lifetime of political activism.

Yukiko Tanaka, ed. *To Live and to Write:
Selections by Japanese Women Writers
1913–1938* (Seattle: Seal Press, 1987),
pp. 41, 43, 45

MOIX, ANA MARÍA (SPAIN) 1947–

Ana María Moix presents to the reader a clearly discernible fictional structure in which she conscientiously rearranges a basic set of prototype patterns to reveal certain unchanging problems which beset the individual. Time as a concrete force is a major preoccupation. The characters are drawn obsessively to the past, in a frustrating attempt to merge two blurred, imperfect images (the child and the adult) which have undergone an unnatural separation. The childhood years may symbolize one's lost purity, vanished innocence, or an ideal that has disappeared long since: memory provides an invisible dimension through which to approach the riddle of one's fragmented existence. . . .

Both Julia and Ismael offer excellent examples of the attempt to reassemble the disparate pieces of their lives, but significantly neither is successful. . . .

The characters who populate Ana María Moix's special world are *marginados,* alienated not through contact with social pressures, but because of their inability to resolve an inner tension stemming from the conflict between appearance and essence. Specific patterns reveal this state to the reader: unchanging character types (the doubles; the strong/weak pair); symbols (the Chinese puzzle box, the crayon box) or situations (bisexuality; ambivalent behavior, the return to the past). Her reuse of the same characters, themes and even plot incidents from book to book is not a sign of limitation, but of an obsessive fascination with certain combinations possible in existence. That she has managed to fashion a complete, coherent fictional world with a relatively small number of books is proof of her ability to translate a synchronic view of reality to the reader. It may be assumed that subsequent contributions may change in plot or form, but will continue to enrich this ideological vision by adding a new layer to the already complex fictional reality.

Margaret E. W. Jones. *Journal of Spanish Studies.* 4, 1976, pp. 111, 115

[A] pessimistic perception of woman's entrapment and alienation is dramatically explored by Ana María Moix in *Julia,* where the adolescent turns from heterosexuality and activity to an essentially lesbian and passive relationship in a desperate attempt at human contact. *Julia* is the portrait of a young girl's love for her mother, of her feelings of rejection by that mother and of her latent homosexual love towards Eva, her teacher. The extraordinary innovation of the novel is that it dares to touch on the theme of the homosexual female, a theme that has generally been avoided in literature until very recently, particularly in Spain where such topics have until now scarcely been broached. . . .

The emotional development that Ana María Moix describes in her novel is precisely that of a child rejected by the mother who prefers her male children to the clingy and unhappy little girl who follows her, whimpering and crying for attention. It is the story of Julia's search for a substitute mother and of a traumatic sexual violation at the hands of her brother's friend.

The novel begins with Julia, now a twenty-seven-year-old girl, unable to sleep and having the same nightmares that she had as a child of five. She awakens, terrified by gigantic monsters who have destroyed everything in their path and have now invaded her room. Julia is unable to push these figures away. In desperation she screams for Eva, her teacher, in the same manner as she had screamed for her mother during her childhood. Julia knows, however, that Eva is too far away to hear and that she cannot come to comfort her. Nevertheless, she fantasizes that Eva will come and that she is able to hug her and hide her head in the security of her embrace. At the same time Julia knows that she is too old to be tormented by such fears, too old to need Eva and that, indeed, it is high time for her to habituate herself "a vivir sin pensar en nadie, sin esperar a nadie, sin necesitar a nadie." The transition from childhood to adulthood which Julia must of necessity undergo seems, therefore, from the very start to be a transition from one state of loneliness into a more intense state of loneliness in which all hope for communion with another human being must be given up. Adulthood is an intensification of the torments of the child's threatened and confusing world. . . .

The Julita that is triumphant at the end is the Double or *Doppelgänger,* who represents the self that has been left behind, overlooked and unrealized. It is the self that must come to terms with and that can never be taken for granted. It is the self that appears when the first self is in a state of great vulnerability. Often the two selves can only exist for each other. In the vast majority of cases the second self helps to strip away all the masks of self-deception and compels the Ego towards self-awareness and self-fulfillment. It is this second self that the child Julita embodies. In Ana María Moix's novel the resolution of the long quest for acceptance of the second self ends in failure. Having become acquainted with the strange projection of her emotional structure, Julia does not achieve an expanded vision of who or what she is. In knowing the other, Julia has become a victim rather than a beneficiary of the hidden insight that her unknown self could offer. If the other is also the I, as in this particular story, then the I in *Julia* is overwhelmed and engulfed by the other.

Sara E. Schyfter. In Randolph D. Pope, ed.
The Analysis of Literary Texts: Current
Trends in Methodology (Ypsilanti, Michigan:
Bilingual Press, 1980), pp. 43–44, 49

The relationship between women is . . . a central aspect of Ana María Moix's novel *Julia,* in which the protagonist Julia has a deep involvement with her university literature professor, Eva. Eva's importance in the novel is not merely limited to her role as an intellectual model for Julia; she also represents the mother, friend, and lover that Julia actively seeks. To this degree, Moix radically deviates from the presentation of the female protagonist seen in Martín Gaite and Matute by introducing the tabu theme of lesbianism into the core of her work. By means of an interior monologue narrated exclusively in third person throughout the novel, Moix captures the anxieties of her twenty-year-old protagonist, whose continual nightmares center on her rape at the age of six by Victor, a friend of the family. As a result of this traumatic experience, together with the sense of emotional deprivation she experienced as a child, she develops an intense physical aversion to men and an obsessive need to find a strong female figure with whom to identify and in whom to find solace. Her monologue is filled with multiple images reflecting her sense of guilt at wishing the death of her parents; her fixation with the past and her other self, the Julita of six, whose very existence in her mind is a continual evocation of her rape; Freudian metaphors of phallic symbols, which threaten to consume her; and ultimately a need for self-destruction as a means of freeing her from her divided self.

In the first reading of the novel, neither the rape itself nor the lesbian theme is apparent; Moix herself has spoken of "the sensitivity of the critics" in not mentioning the homosexual overtones of the novel. Considered from within the context of Spanish culture and its cult of machismo, lesbianism is a difficult issue to deal with. . . .

In Moix's novel, lesbianism finally emerges as a theme treated with sensitivity and care, although definitely with a somewhat guarded allusiveness. . . .

If one can speak then of a definite sense of continuity in Moix's recent prose works, it is also apparent that her demythification of conventionality and her audacity in dealing with sexual topics become much more pronounced in her second novel. If *Julia* provides a guarded treatment of the theme of lesbianism, together with clear references to "the anti-baby pill," male homosexuality, and rape, *Walter, ¿por qué te fuiste?* represents a more daring and inclusive view of several other sexual themes, previously taboo in Spanish literature: male and female masturbation, bisexuality, sodomy, and menstruation. Within this context, it is not surprising that forty-five cuts were made in the novel by the censors prior to its publication, although many were also of a political nature. As previously stated, *Walter* is technically a much more difficult novel to approach than *Julia*. The connection with outside reality maintained in *Julia* through the external unities of time, place, and action is much less apparent in *Walter,* and what is left is a narrative discourse presented from various perspectives. . . .

When one considers that Moix completed this novel in one and a half months, after having thought about it for four years, the intensity and facility of her narrative skills is awesome. Alternately using a lyrical and satirical style, she both captures the inner fragmentation of Ismael, the male alter ego of Julia herself, and unmasks anew the bourgeois society of Barcelona of the 1960s.

Linda Gould Levine. In Beth Miller, ed.
*Women in Hispanic Literature: Icons and
Fallen Idols* (Berkeley: University of
California Press, 1983), pp. 304–5, 309–10

The uniqueness of Moix's rendering of the conflict between the child and the adult lies not so much in her use of the double as in the absoluteness of the incarceration of her characters. About the same time she wrote her two novels, Juan Goytisolo produced his works of inner duplication. But while the division between Alvaro and Alvarito becomes an aggressive attempt on the part of Alvaro to exorcize and destroy his inner self, the fragmentation of Moix's Julia results in the submission of the first self to the invasive attacks of a double. Consequently Moix's character suffers dual victimization: one applied on a collective level by restrictive social norms, and one exercised on a psychic level by the power of unfulfilled desires. Moix expands and complements the disintegration of Julia by reproducing it with significant variations in Ismael. The creation of Walter extends the doubling process beyond these twin female-male characters to include in some way her entire cast of young people. Through her intricate and effective use of division, duplication, and doubling, Moix paints a powerful portrait of comprehensive alienation.

> Catherine G. Bellver. In Ricardo Landeira
> and Luis T. Gonzalez-del-Valle, eds. *Nuevos*
> *y Novísimos: Algunas perspectivas críticas*
> *sobre la narrativa española desde la década*
> *de los 60s* (Boulder, Colorado: Society of
> Spanish and Spanish American Studies,
> 1987), p. 40

Ana María Moix's recent collection of short stories, *Las virtudes peligrosas* (Dangerous virtues), poses innumerable questions and problems of interpretation for the reader who has followed her literary trajectory of the last seventeen years. It is a trajectory marked by periods of great productivity and years of silence, by alternating currents of escapism and social confrontation, intense sadness and biting parody, poetry and fiction—an intricate web of hermetic images which pulls the reader into its very center and then leaves her stranded. To open the door to Ana María Moix's world in 1969, as well as in 1986, is ultimately to follow the Dantesque motto and leave "all hope" behind, for there is no redemption possible for the explorer of her verbal Inferno, only repetition and entrapment, at the hands of her "palabra enemiga."

Nowhere is this sense of the destructive force of words more apparent than in *Las virtudes peligrosas*. It is a haunting book which Moix seems to have written almost against herself, as if the cry for silence so poignantly desired throughout the pages of *Walter ¿por qué te fuiste?* were finally defeated and its author compelled, again, to transform her obsessions into fiction. Five short stories, five abstract and depersonalized worlds, marked by characters without names, settings without time and space, conflicts without origin, words without passion—a complex artifice of absence which, nonetheless, tantalizes the reader with its aura of mystery suggested by the titles themselves: "Las virtudes peligrosas," "Érase una vez," "El inocente," "El problema," "Los muertos." The intent of this discussion is to penetrate, or perhaps, infiltrate, the "enemy lines" and suggest strategies for interpreting the complexities of Moix's recent book, as well as for situating it within the context of her previous body of fiction. . . .

[E]xplicit vindication of an autonomous female identity, momentarily and paradoxically liberated in Moix's text about the entrapment of texts, brings the author back three-hundred-sixty degrees to the center of her own feminist writings in *Vindicación feminista* in the 1970s. During that period her monthly column "Diario de una hija de familia" provided an irreverent view of tradiional Spanish machismo and cultural values. This satirical destruction of codified norms has enabled the reader to delight in Moix's creations at the same time that we sense her struggle with the futility of words and the voids they create.

It may indeed be true, as Blackmur has hypothesized, that "the next age will not express itself in words . . . at all." Although Ana María Moix seems to subscribe to this view, she nonetheless offers us some redemption from our verbal insufficiencies. Her unusual configurations of irony and satire compose a compelling textual mirror into which we are inexorably and comically drawn. Let us hope we emerge intact, instead of "two thirds" trapped within.

Linda Gould Levine. In Ricardo Landeira
and Luis T. Gonzalez-del-Valle, eds. *Nuevos
y Novísimos: Algunas perspectivas críticas
sobre la narrativa española desde la década
de los 60s* (Boulder, Colorado: Society of
Spanish and Spanish American Studies,
1987), pp. 97, 108

The Franquist state and its "generational" legacy deny Julia the "outside" space necessary to bring her fully into the present. Her dependency upon female *presencias* for a feeling of well-being is simply confirmation of her effective absence in the present. Julia the desperate imaginer is incapable of transferring the received images of her experiences or her thoughts to an outer realm and thus must experience the emptiness and absence of life. Her sickness, therefore, is also the sickness of a regime, the ultimate and exclusive "outside" that denies its citizens the physical space to express their political ideas and the psychic space to establish themselves as strong and independent personalities. In spite of Julia's insignificance in the social context that threatens to destroy her spirit, the novel evinces, nevertheless, an after-the-fact transcendence originating in the "aberrant" epistemology that constitutes Julia's neurosis. Julia's suicide attempt has the dual effect of resurrecting in her imagination the vision of her younger self, Julita, that she had hoped was long dead ("había intentado matar a Julita, y sólo permanecía," but also of momentarily erasing the past "sin pensamientos, sin recuerdos, . . . desterrado a un lugar sin nombre, desconocido, fuera del tiempo y del espacio de los demás." Given the epistemological context in which the narrative proceeds, the presence of these unwelcome absences may herald a more hopeful ending to this novel than is at first apparent. The conclusion also serves to underscore Moix's aversion to an association with a literary generation alleged to have emerged at the very moment of the writing of her novel.

C. Christopher Soufras, Jr. In Ricardo
Landeira and Luis T. Gonzalez–del–Valle,
eds. *Nuevos y Novísimos: Algunas
perspectivas críticas sobre la narrativa
española desde la década de los 60s*
(Boulder, Colorado: Society of Spanish and
Spanish American Studies, 1987), pp. 222–23

The younger sister of the well-known novelist Terençi Moix, Ana María began as a writer of experimental poetry, in the vein of pop and op art, inspired by images, characters, techniques, and vocabulary of the mass media, exemplified in *Baladas del dulce Jim* (1969; Sweet Jim's ballads) and *Call Me Stone* (1969). *No Time for Flowers* (1971), a series of prose poems with a distinguishable narrative content, is her last book of poetry. A hybrid, it employs the interior monologue (used more extensively in her next novel) with many intertextual materials drawn from popular songs, Lorca, and other easily identifiable references. Her three books of poetry were republished as *A imagen y semejanza* (1983; In the image and likeness). Moix's first novel, *Julia* (1970), portrays the world of the Catalan bourgeoisie in the immediate postwar period—the world in which the author was born and raised. Some characters and events are autobiographical but have been subjected to considerable literary elaboration. A psychological mystery-intrigue, the novel is presented as the interior monologue of the emotionally disturbed and sometimes suicidal young protagonist. During a sleepless night Julia relives the main events of her last fifteen years, and most particularly her quest for personal freedom. The roots of her self-destructiveness are traced to the decadent, oppressive, and ambivalent atmosphere in which she was raised. Julia's tortured remembrance of the past includes her relationship with her two brothers (Rafael who died in adolescence, and the homosexual Ernesto), her adored, egotistical mother, despised grandmother, and anarchist grandfather. An overdose of drugs, an almost-successful suicide attempt, intensifies the process of Julia's alienation. Her phobias, superstitions, and the presence of a double, Julita (her five-year-old self), are further symptoms of Julia's problem. Moix presents a distinctly feminine viewpoint, indicting traditional values and institutions as she examines the impact upon her persona of a society in transition, adolescent and student rebellion and the question of lesbianism broached when a schoolmate makes sexual advances. . . .

Moix continues her satire of the Catalan bourgeoisie in *¿Walter, por qué te fuiste?* (1973; Walter, why did you leave?). While this novel is not strictly a sequel to *Julia,* some members of the same family appear again, together with episodes from some of the writer's earlier stories. . . .

A recurring motif in Moix's fiction is escape, whether by drugs, madness, suicide, alcohol, sex, metamorphosis, or—in Ismael's case—life in the circus.

Paired with the difficulty of adaptation, it serves to underscore the loss of innocence, purity, ideals, and eventually youth. Childhood is both paradise and prison, and its tragic aspects are lucidly reflected in Moix's second novel.

Janet Pérez. *Contemporary Women Writers of Spain.* (Boston: Twayne, 1988), pp. 157–59

Ana María Moix first came to the attention of a broad public in Spain through her appearance in the influential 1970 anthology of José María Castellet, *Nueve novísimos poetas españoles* (Nine extremely new Spanish poets), which gave a name and a definition to a significant departure in contemporary Spanish letters. At the age of twenty-one she was among the youngest, and the only woman, to be published in *Nueve novísimos,* and by twenty-six she was already the author of three books of verse, a book of stories, two novels, and a collection of interviews with writers and artists. From 1973 until 1985 Moix did not publish any new book-length work, with the exception of a story for children, a silence little anticipated by those critics who had written of her early promise, and the cause, it would seem, for the scant attention devoted to her work during that long period. Yet it is during this time that Moix served as the cultural coordinator for *Vindicación feminista* (Feminist rights), contributing essays, reviews, and short fiction, and marking her own position in relation to the feminist movement in Spain promoted by that landmark journal. In 1985, however, Moix published *Las virtudes peligrosas* (Dangerous virtues), a new collection of stories that gives evidence of an important shift from her early work; and at the same time, her writing has begun to reenter the focus of critical attention. . . .

Such criticism as there has been has concentrated on Moix's prose, rather than her poetry, making an implicit judgment with which I concur: Moix's great achievement to date has been *Walter, ¿por qué te fuiste?,* and, I believe, her short stories. Nevertheless, if *Walter* may be seen to arise out of the striking, but on the whole less successful *Julia,* tempered by the experience of the first book of stories, *Ese chico pelirrojo a quien veo cada día* (That red-headed boy that I see every day) (1971), Moix's early poetry must also be considered as part of the turbulent material out of which the later novel was formed. . . .

The close interconnection of distinct texts is especially visible in the novels, which both treat the growth and death of isolated members of a single extended family centered in Barcelona in the later Franco years. . . .

The narrative pathway of *Julia* . . . follows a tortuous route. It begins with the injunction against divulging the secret of the rape. This obstruction to Julia's access to language is then converted into the symptom, or trope, of stifled breathing. Finally, language returns in the narrative of Julia's recollections, but only by becoming itself an obsession that exceeds Julia's control. The troubled current of Julia's reminiscences is, on the one hand, her defense against the perceived menace of the late night hours and her lonely room, and on the other, her language represents the deferred speech of Julita. In short, if Julia cannot control her recollections and their narration, Julita can and does, drawing any and all reminiscences to herself, the six-year-old victim of a rape who has become the Fate of the narrative.

> Andrew Bush. In Joan L. Brown, ed.
> *Women Writers of Contemporary Spain:*
> *Exiles in the Homeland* (Newark, Delaware:
> University of Delaware Press, 1991), pp. 136,
> 138, 141–43

MONTERO, ROSA (SPAIN) 1951–

In *Te trataré como a una reina* (I'll treat you like a queen), published in 1983, public authority to read and interpret the world is best represented by the four "documents" which are inserted into the novel. All project a male perspective and system of values; all are distorting mirrors which reflect false images of women. A corrective is provided, however, by the main body of the text. Ironic juxtapositions and different perspectives on the same events are used to subvert masculine pretensions and invalidate male-generated images. Montero furthermore shows how women, long the victims of cultural conditioning and myths that have been perpetuated by patriarchal society, also misread the men who are close to them and pay dearly for their misreading. . . .

By undermining the writing of her male characters, presenting different perspectives on the same events, using ironic juxtapositions, and resorting to often scathing satire, Montero exposes the ways in which men abuse their power to read the world and those who are close to them. All the female characters of *Te trataré como a una reina* suffer from male stereotyping and male-generated myths which consign them to specific scripts and roles. The repressive nature of those scripts and the limitations of the roles they offer reduce women to the status of supporting players. They are victimized by their own and by others' misreading in Montero's tragicomedy of errors.

> Kathleen M. Glenn. *ALEC (Anales de la*
> *literatura española contemporánea)*. 12,
> 1987, pp. 191, 201

Crónica del desamor (1979; Chronicle of falling out of love), her first novel, follows an autobiographical format and concentrates upon feminist issues, many of them taboo during the Franco regime: contraception, abortion, homosexuality, and the unwed mother, among others. Problems of the working woman, and especially the issue of fair and equitable salaries, are also raised. Many types of relationships are explored, from male-female to friends of the same sex and parent-child, particularly one involving a feminist daughter.

A series of women appear, whose common denominator is their unhappy relationships with males. They are women who are alone, or lonely, who separate from one man, idealizing another, or who attempt to find self-realization in work or eroticism, who grope toward liberation. The strictly up-to-the-moment chronology is reflected in references to the "supposed democracy" and a rather cynical attitude toward political parties as no longer functional. Many of the characters seem to function as much as embodiments of current attitudes as authentic individuals, and there are occasional touches of contemporary *costumbrismo*.

La función Delta (1981; The Delta function) is mildly experimental in technique, employing the structure of two interrelated diaries, or chapters headed by chronological references (in one case, names of days of the week, in the other, dates). The dated entries are shorter and more numerous than those headed by names of days, which total seven and give very little sensation of being written as portions of a diary. Lucía, a woman in her sixties, terminally ill with cancer but undergoing radiation therapy, is the author of both diaries, one of them dealing exclusively with her reaction to her existential situation, her feelings about old age, death, and the one friend who still visits her. The second diary, more fictitious in its retrospective concentration on a crucial week in her life some three decades earlier as well as more self-consciously literary in its elaboration, concentrates upon the premiere of the movie in which she made her debut as a director at the age of thirty, and also explores her relationships with two lovers. Both feminist and existential in its orientation, the novel treats women's problems from a standpoint of obvious acquaintance with sociological and psychological theory. An absorbing testimony of the complex situation of women in Spain at the time of writing, it is of special interest for its tackling of another subject seldom treated, the problems of dying.

Te trataré como a una reina (1983; I'll treat you like a queen) portrays the decadent, run-down, and degrading atmosphere of a Madrid nightspot in the red-light district, surrounded by cheap apartments, seamy clubs, and a general commerce in drugs and prostitution. The "Tropicana" bar sign, an illuminated postcard totally out of place, symbolizes the desire to escape to an exotic tropical paradise as suggested by the neon palm trees and boats (to Havana, in the case of Bella, a fiftyish barmaid). As a metaphor, it indicates the artificiality or impossibility of the escape offered, while drawing attention to the desperate limitations of the existences around it, characterized by solitude and poverty both spiritual and economic. The only escape is madness, death, or prison, or at best, a return to the miserable, backward village from which the characters first fled.

Janet Pérez. Contemporary Women Writers
of Spain (Boston: Twayne, 1988), pp. 163–65

In *La función delta,* Rosa Montero's novel of 1981, the voice of the female body as it lies dying is permitted the luxury of reliving the apprenticeship, mastery, and ripeness of female-defined sexuality. Lucía's lovers, past and present (Hipólito, Miguel, and Ricardo), roughly correspond to these three states; and as accomplice, fellow adventurer, and loving companion respectively, each man grapples with the text of woman's body. Hipólito largely misreads Lucía and her intentions; Miguel reads Lucía's body and her desires with an open tenderness; Ricardo reads Lucía's text (and her body) with irreverential yet affectionate honesty. Ricardo, as Lucía's last interlocutor, offers insights into the problems of male lovers/readers confronting female bodies/texts. He tends to view mood shifts and contradictions as unreliability or lack of verisimilitude. Thus the claims of Lucía's body and her text may be judged by categorical imperatives alien to legibility and comprehension. More disastrously, still, in Montero's later novel, *Te trataré como a una reina*, the bodies of women and men merge without communication; metaphorically speaking different languages, there is no alternative but eventual rupture of all intimacy between them.

> Elizabeth J. Ordóñez. *Voices of their Own:*
> *Contemporary Spanish Narratives by*
> *Women* (Lewisburg, Pennsylvania: Bucknell
> University Press, 1991), p. 204

While the popular suppositions about Rosa Montero—that her novels depict her own life and that they are based on factual reporting—are largely true, it would be naive to accept them as wholly correct. Refutation of the assumption that her works are slavishly autobiographical can only come from the author, and it does. Montero distinguishes between the "autobiographical" and the "biographical," and explains with reference to her first novel that her "biographical" fiction is an imaginary and intermingled account of events that have happened within her social group. The author also counters the notion that she writes journalism in the guise of novels. She is acutely aware of the requirements of the two genres and considers them to be diametrically opposed to one another. Although she credits journalism with teaching her a certain dexterity with words, she feels that the clarity and precision of journalism are detrimental to good novel-writing, and that they must be overcome in the more abstract and ambiguous realm of fiction.

In fact, in her novels Rosa Montero grows progressively stronger in her rejection and subversion of the conventions of journalism. Her development from journalist to novelist is incremental, as I will attempt to show in the following chronological discussion of her four major novelistic works. From her first heavily journalistic narrative to her most recent antijournalistic novel, Montero's fiction demonstrates a gradual renunciation of journalistic clarity. Ironically, in addition to the nonjournalistic narrative techniques that assume increasing importance in her novels, Montero also overtly parodies newspaper reporting and newspaper management with mordant humor and the outrage of an idealist. . . .

The ground-breaking story of the *Crónica del desamor* is the situation of women in modern Spain, a "chronicle of disaffection" that in 1979 constituted a revolutionary exposé. Women's plots are the subject of Ana's projected book; someday she plans to write about "manos babosas, platos para lavar, reducciones de plantilla, orgasmos fingidos, llamadas de teléfono que nunca llegan, paternalismos laborales, diafragmas, caricaturas y ansiedades. Sería el libro de las Anas, de todas y ella misma, tan distinta y tan una" (greasy hands, dishes to be washed, staff cutbacks, feigned orgasms, telephone calls that never come, diaphragms, caricatures, and anxieties. It would be the book of Anas, of all of them and of herself, so different and so singular).

Details of female existence that were always kept out of literature, such as menstruation, sexual harassment, and visits to a (male) gynecologist are described in detail, in frank language, and often with black humor. . . .

La función Delta . . . is much more complex than its predecessor. Whereas her first novel poses as a chronicle of the real world, her second explores the elusive nature of reality. *La función Delta* is narrated in two strands. One is a first-person account of the daily life of a sixty-three-year-old woman named Lucía Ramos in the year 2010, as she approaches death in a hospital. The second narrative consists of Lucía's recently begun memoirs, in which she is describing a crucial week in her life in the 1970s, when she was thirty years old. An account of the protagonist's life gradually emerges from her parallel narrations, which do not converge until the work's close. However, Lucía's story is not straightforward. Her perceptions of both her past and her present are subject to changing interpretations as she gradually falls in love with a lifelong friend, Ricardo, who also becomes her literary critic. The question of "reality" with regard to both the past and the present is further complicated in the novel by the fact that Ricardo, who frequently challenges Lucía's recollections and interpretations, is himself a superb storyteller who delights in "recalling" imaginary events. The metafictional aspects of the novel focus overtly on the nature of narrative and on the continuum of truth on which "reality" and "invention" are opposite poles.

Within this metaliterary orientation, Montero allows the reader to retrieve the milestones of the protagonist's life easily; the central events in Lucía's life are not disputed, although their significance is subject to different interpretations. . . .

Throughout Rosa Montero's evolution from journalist to novelist, she has maintained her preoccupation with social issues. Foremost among these are the roles of women, relations between the sexes, and the abuses committed by those with power. Beyond these observable phenomena, Montero is concerned with the conflict between ideals and reality and with the social construction of "truth." . . .

The fiction of Rosa Montero has grown in complexity and sophistication since her first novel was published in 1979. She has emerged from a background of political journalism to become one of the most interesting and provocative novelists of the post-Franco era.

Joan L. Brown, ed. *Women Writers of*
Contemporary Spain: Exiles in the
Homeland (Newark, Delaware: University of
Delaware Press, 1991),
pp. 242–43, 245–46, 255

In *La función Delta,* Montero applies creativity and imagination as she interweaves universal doubts and questions. The use of the double diary—a journal recording the sixty-year-old Lucía's stay in the hospital and a memoir evoking the memory of a crucial week in her life thirty years earlier—brings a futuristic setting to the novel: the memoirs describe events that took place in 1980, so the sixty-year-old woman is keeping her journal in the year 2010. The story of the protagonist as a young woman unfolds during the Easter holiday, a much-celebrated week in Spain, while the narrator-protagonist's story is told over a period of months in the hospital. Ricardo, her faithful visitor, offers a running commentary of the writing in progress and adds yet another perspective to the "objective" personal commentary of the double diary. Consequently, an important dimension of the story becomes the question of the narrator-protagonist's own reality and how she chooses to remember and record it. Montero herself calls her second novel "an effort to take a step forward in the apprenticeship of narrative." This "apprenticeship" consisted of working with a more complex structure and creating characters who would be "less linear" than those in her first novel, *Crónica del desamor.* Montero's familiarity with the experimental narrative techniques of her time and, more importantly, her willingness to use them are evident in *La función delta.*

Montero wrote her first novels in the late 1970s, when Spain was emerging from Francisco Franco's thirty-year dictatorship. In 1977 Spain held its first general elections in forty-one years, and all aspects of Spanish life that had been so strictly controlled by the conservative national regime were infused with a feeling of openness and modernity. . . .

The reader who enters this author's richly textured world cannot help but be influenced by her fresh presentation of these themes. Montero is not only a talented "chronicler" of her own rapidly changing world, but also a thought-provoking writer who repeatedly challenges her readers with their own reality.

Kari Easton and Yolanda Molina Gavilán.
Afterword to Rosa Montero. *The Delta*
Function (Lincoln: University of Nebraska
Press, 1991), pp. 264–66

Agua Fría, the heroine of Rosa Montero's *Temblor* (Earthquake), leaves the innocence of childhood and its symbolic white tunic. She is forced to enter the priesthood of the Talapot and passes her apprenticeship in the temple's various circles. Escape initiates a journey through a deteriorating, chaotic world teetering on the edge of oblivion. Only with a primitive tribe does she find security. Married and pregnant, Agua Fría discovers that this world too is beginning to fade. She returns to the Talapot, which is soon destroyed together with the Law and its religious superstitions. Her husband is killed, and she chooses to journey toward freedom rather than return to the tribe.

The basic plot describes the rite of passage from childhood to adulthood, but the reader finds other underlying themes. It is no surprise to learn that the novelist has a background in psychology; she also has a reporter's eye for detail. Symbol, myth, and allegory are important in the narrative's development. The role of religion and its rites is interwoven into the mythological tale. Particularly symbolic are the stages of priestly preparation. The temple, which originally had one hundred stories, has only three, then two, then one. Candidates must pass through three circles; in the exterior, discipline, obedience, and silence predominate. Circle two, that of shadows, is also that of knowledge. Here apprentices learn the art of meditation. In the third circle, that of wisdom, only women, the superior sex, study hypnosis. In the interior circle light exists only in the library, where the books of knowledge teach about what are today's modern inventions.

Agua Fría's journey after her escape reminds the reader of the *Odyssey* and the Bible. A trip by caravan is typical of those of ancient or perhaps even modern times. Agua Fría, as she is instructed, travels always toward the North. Occasionally she is tempted to stop; the search for life's meaning urges her on. Toward the novel's conclusion she is tempted to remain with the primitive tribe, because for a time the world remains physically stable. Men, unfamiliar with the contemporary domination of women, rule there. In Agua Fría's world women are the superior race; a major reason is their ability to bear children in a world whose population is disappearing.

Montero criticizes religion's role in people's lives. Its laws form a negative element in the ultimate struggle between being and nothingness. Who can determine whether design or chance governs the world? The search for the meaning of death is part of Agua Fría's journey. Names of people and places tend to be exotic; they supply a Middle Eastern–Oriental flavor. Although approximately ten years pass, time is nevertheless vague; this world is hazy and undefined. The reader who enjoys novels written at several levels of meaning should appreciate *Temblor*. It raises literary and philosophical issues and questions worthy of discussion.

Joan T. Cain. *World Literature Today.* 65, 1991, p. 275

Temblor is set in a world which is recognizable from the brave, new worlds of science fiction, yet it is peopled by monsters and by men and women who are reminiscent of Neanderthal man. . . .

There are, however, some basic differences between *Temblor* and the archetypal science fiction tale. The most obvious difference is that the protagonist is a woman, although here, Montero's novel approaches the remiss of an offshoot of the science fiction novel, feminist science fiction. Agua Fría is the center of the action; she leads the tribe who adopted her to a secret realm where the mystery of the origin of the disintegration process will be revealed. Since her mission is successful and she finally destroys, against all the odds, the evil regime of the "sacerdotisas," it is fair to argue that she exhibits all the traits normally associated with the hero-quester in patriarchal tales. Yet, Agua Fría, even in this her most masculinist side (the salvation of the world), shows feminine characteristics. She begins her quest as a twelve-year-old adolescent with barely emerging breasts, at the time of the death of both, of her mother-figures (her natural mother), and her spiritual mother and, to round off the allegory, at the time of her first menstruation. Despite these defiantly female paradigms, her quest is related to the salvation of the universe. . . .

Temblor takes this feminocentric gesture one step further. It is clear, right from the beginning of the story, that sexual gender is one of the most important, if not *the* most important, issue. Montero's novel focuses specifically on sexual difference and projects the epistemological divide separating man from woman as the single most significant juncture wherein identity, human values and human courage to change life is located.

Stephen M. Hart. *White Ink: Essays on Twentieth-Century Feminine Fiction in Spain* (London: Tamesis, 1993), pp. 132–35

MOORE, MARIANNE (UNITED STATES) 1887–1972

The grim and haughty humor of this lady strikes deep, so deep as to absorb her dreams and possess her soul. She feels immense incongruities, and the incongruity of her little ego among them moves her art not to grandeur but to scorn. As a satirist she is at times almost sublime—what contrary devil balks even at those moments, tempting her art to its most inscrutable perversities?

Harriet Monroe. *Poetry.* January, 1922, p. 215

This volume is the study of a Marco Polo detained at home. It is the fretting of a wish against a wish until the self is drawn, not into a world of air and adventure, but into a narrower self, patient, dutiful, and precise. . . . Miss

Moore has preferred, to date, to express simply the pictorial aspect of the universe, and she has fulfilled perfectly each self-imposed task.

Winifred Bryher. *Poetry.* January, 1922, pp. 209–10

This exacting moralist, who enforces with such intricate resonance the profound convictions of her ethical and emotional fastidiousness, has dumbfounded most of those readers whom she has not completely subjugated. . . . (She is) a poet whose style, at once intensely cultivated and painstakingly honest, never fails to charm me and whose mastery of phrase and cadence overwhelms me.

Yvor Winters. *Poetry.* April, 1925, pp. 39, 44

She is difficult because she will not buy triumph at "horrifying sacrifice of stringency"; she refuses to descend to the level of those to whom "the illustration is nothing without the application"; and she demands of her readers that their minds shall follow hers in leaping by fifths and sevenths from point to point like the jerboa in her poem. She has affinities of spirit with Henry James—the same thoroughness and elegant restraint, the same astute detection of minute differences, the same gradual foliate disclosure and sharp clarity of definition. But all these qualities are condensed into the "contractibility" of verse. Her subtlety of ear and delicacy of rhythmic perception, the variations in her use of full, light, vowel, end, and internal rhymes, and her ingenious designs of syllabic divisions, are all functional parts of the setting in which she arranges her brilliant "jewelry of sense."

Elizabeth Drew. *Directions in Modern Poetry* (New York: Norton, 1940), p. 68

Only Marianne Moore could write a poem about the mind and fill it with thoughts that glow like buried treasure just brought to light. . . . Literally and figuratively, light is the source of her enchantment. What she sees provides symbols for the unseen, the inner vision. . . . Her poetry dreams with its eyes wide open and weaves its spell out of the visible, the tangible, the intelligible; a wide-awake magic; proof that a passionate intelligence can be haunting. . . . In her poetry the appearance of things—the way they greet the eyes and ears; what they feel like to the touch; their characteristic impact—come to us in a blaze of reincarnation. . . . Through art such as this, with its demand upon the attention of the whole person, we are restored not to a state of nature, but to that totality of experience which is a sign of organic development.

Lloyd Frankenberg. *Pleasure Dome* (Boston: Houghton, 1949), pp. 121–23, 133

Miss Moore has great limitations—her work is one long triumph of them; but it was sad, for so many years, to see them and nothing else insisted upon, and Miss Moore neglected for poets who ought not be allowed to throw elegies in her grave. I have read that several people think So-and-So the greatest living woman poet; anybody would dislike applying so clumsy a phrase to Miss Moore—but surely she is. Her poems, at their unlikely best, seem already immortal, objects that have endured their probative millennia in barrows; she has herself taken from them what time could take away, and left a skeleton the years can only harden.

Randall Jarrell. Poetry and the Age (New York: Knopf, 1953), pp. 183–84

Philosophically, she might have been a bore, had she not been rescued by erudition. One unique quality of her work is that she has made learning more lively than any poet save Dame Edith Sitwell. Pound and Eliot have convinced us that immense knowledge is valid equipment for poets, but they have not the winsome finesse with which Miss Moore and Dame Edith display the emeralds and rubies that the mind alone collects.

Bette Richart. Commonweal. December 28, 1956, p. 338

The dexterity and intelligence of . . . poems in *Like a Bulwark* are nimble variants of that keyboard, that system of transitions between fact and moral fantasy which characterizes Miss Moore, with its counterpoint which can encompass and utilize every combination between those chosen limits.

The system of transitions was established in the themes of Miss Moore's earliest poetry. Her symbolical use of animals is the perfect expression of a spontaneous but orderly mind. The orderliness manifests itself in the precise style of writing, the spontaneity in this fantasy where questions of conduct and manners are referred to the animal world. Miss Moore's fantasy is a controlled fantasy, a high seriousness that refuses to be merely solemn.

Charles Tomlinson. Southwest Review. Autumn, 1957, p. 677

There is an effect in her prose of propriety and exactitude which we might be tempted to compare with the powerful economy of intelligence in Jane Austen. We notice that Miss Moore's approval or admiration may appear in her saying that an author's work "detains attention" or "commends itself." A sentence may begin, "Appreciation which is truly votive and not gapingly inquisitive"; or we learn that imagination "precludes" banality. Were one to read no further (no further in the same sentence), the temptation would be to believe oneself reading an author of the late eighteenth or early nineteenth century. But no, it is not Jane Austen's or Fanny Burney's example that provides a prefiguration of these delicate, exact apostrophes or salutations. Personal conviction moves through more rapidly; there are no safe, however valid or intelligible, assumptions. It is rather, perhaps, the more romantically independent if equally responsible affirmations of Charlotte Brontë that we may be momentarily—and only momentarily, and very pleasantly—reminded of. But decidedly Miss Moore's thinking, tempo, expertness is of our own time, though not limited by it, as more ambitiously "modern" writers end in being.

Laurence Stapleton. *South Atlantic Quarterly.* Summer, 1958, p. 370

Hers is a poetry in which as much as possible is left unsaid. So often are her transitions left to the reader to fill in, one may puzzle over certain poems for days and get nowhere with them, or at best, not far. There ought to be enough matter remaining in the *Collected Poems* to nourish a dozen imponderably dull doctoral theses. But those who read for wisdom may be content to notice the sculptural outlines, though ignoring some mysterious grains. In a few Marianne Moore poems whose logic remains obscure to me, I have felt borne along by the power of her metric. Lines may be jagged in appearance, difficult in allusion, and hard to connect one with another; and yet the poem will still stride forward with authority. It is as if Miss Moore has found out that a poet can raise almost any difficulty for the reader and still keep the reader under control, as long as there are many more stressed syllables than unstressed ones. (Where at times the new free-verse falls apart and becomes simply boring, as sometimes, for instance, even Robert Duncan will do, there are usually few heavy syllables, many lines with many weak ones. And there isn't any powerful metric drive—as Miss Moore has, almost always. She can maintain a steady wham, wham, wham of short stubby monosyllables; she throws stresses on an *a* or a *the* or an *of* by putting them in tight patterns and making rimes of them.)

X. J. Kennedy. *The Minnesota Review.* Spring, 1962, p. 376

Since Miss Moore frequently recommends that the individual maintain a certain distance from his fellows, a poised and dignified independence, we may assume that she thinks the price not too heavy. When shut off to some degree from others, we cannot fully comprehend nor be comprehended by them; yet only such separateness can enable us to adopt that cliff-life stance of independence she advises. We may deduce that the dichotomy of soul and body, of spiritual and material, gives rise to those paradoxes which Miss Moore sees neither as quaint or clever absurdities, nor as tragic flaws, but as inevitabilities of human experience. Miss Moore herself chooses to view a paradox not as a problem to be solved but as a situation to be explored for significances. In this exploration arises her poem, whether as a record of discovery or as a report of a search in progress.

Bernard F. Engel. *Marianne Moore* (New York: Twayne, 1964), p. 23

We've all been given courage by her beautiful daring, her abundance, her naturalness that is as cunning, various and splendid as Nature's own. And her moral responsibility. She is a rascal and a revolutionary of form, of aesthetics. She is an uncompromising idealist as to content, to truth. Especially we *women poets,* as we are called, are grateful and lucky in possessing the grand and indelible example of her work and of her life. She is inimitable because she devises her own contests, makes her own rules and, at the point least expected, disconcertingly reverses them, so as to demonstrate that "it is not the acquisition of any one thing that is able to adorn."

May Swenson. In Tambimuttu, ed.
Festschrift for Marianne Moore's Seventy-Seventh Birthday (n.p.: Tambimuttu and
Mass, 1964), p. 48

In reading certain poems of Marianne Moore, it is necessary to distinguish between two kinds of vision operating in them. There is the bird's-eye-view which presents a general panorama and fails to recognize discrete particulars; and there is the close-up, accurate study which recognizes the latter and does not subordinate them to a general picture. Often the two kinds of perception may be observed to be at work in the same poem, each contributing its own images. And, briefly, the images purveyed by the general view most often give rise to false conclusions and express sentimental feelings, while those that are the product of the accurate detailed study give rise to careful moral judgments and express, with some reticence, discriminated feelings. . . . When there are two views or attitudes present in a poem the cruder one is generally dismissed, usually implicitly, in favor of the accurate one; or the former is corrected by the latter. A study of the poet's use of this twofold approach not only throws light on the poems where both approaches are clearly present but helps to reveal an important feature, the essential code, one may say, of the poet and her work: that truth and feeling must rest upon minutely perceived, finite detail.

A. K. Weatherhead. *English Literary
History.* December, 1964, p. 482

Juxtaposition of incongruities is of the essence. But not in the ways of other modernists. She is not working with a sensuous language for violently mysterious effects, or juxtaposing words for the sake of shocks of collision. Rather, her language is strictly tempered and clear, almost classical in its moderation and lack of rhetorical splurge. Verb is firmly connected to noun, there is no straining of language within the sentence unit for a tremor of associations setting up strange trains of disrelations. But she did put these clear lines together in such a way that the firm orderly thought or epigramlike description is set next to another in a manner not to have been foreseen. The surprise, the shock, exists in between the spaces that have been leaped over by a swift imagination. Transitions thus seem more like transpositions, a strange flowering of truth upon fact.

Jean Garrigue. *Marianne Moore*
(Minneapolis: University of Minnesota
Press, 1965), p. 13

This policy of accurate comparison, bringing, if need be, the prune, the alligator, the shad, the porcupine, the frog to the service of a discussion of a cat, does not worry about congruousness just as Braque does not worry about perspective, being intent on a different way of filling its elected spaces. Congruity, like perspective, deals in proportions within an overall view. Miss Moore's poems deal in many separate acts of attention: optical puns, seen by snapshot, in a poetic normally governed by the eye, sometimes by the ears and fingers, ultimately by the moral sense. It is the poetic of the solitary observer, for whose situation the usual meanings of a word like "moral" have to be redefined: a poetic whose effort to define itself has for two centuries constituted a tradition of some centrality. To understand that tradition is to perceive Miss Moore's place in the story of the mind of Europe, neither as eccentric nor as peripheral as she is sometimes made to seem.

Not more than two centuries' weight, though two centuries of continuous revolution, lies behind the ideal of describing accurately the thing seen.

Hugh Kenner. *Southern Review.* Autumn,
1965, p. 755

Well, what kind of Heaven would Miss Moore's be? Much, most probably, like the earth as it is, but refined by responsiveness and intellect into a state very far from the present one; a state of utter consequentiality. For what is Heaven, anyway, but the power of dwelling eternally among objects and actions of consequence? Miss Moore's Heaven would have a means of recording such objects and actions; it would have a history, and a way of preserving its discoveries and happenings: it would have books. But it would be, first of all, a realm of Facts: it would include an enormous amount of matter for there to be opinions about, and so it would make possible vivid and creative and personal parallels between things, and conclusions unforeseeable until they were made. It would take forever from Fact the deadness of being *only* fact, for it would endow what Is with the joyous conjunctions that only a personality itself profoundly creative, profoundly accessible to experience—a personality called a soul—can find among them. Truly, would we have it otherwise in the Eternal City?

James Dickey. *The New York Times.*
December 25, 1966, p. 1

Unless you are already a devotee of Marianne Moore's poetry, this [Tell Me, Tell Me"] is not the book to start with: manner has turned into mannerism, and her optimism has become extensive. There are a few beautiful lines to remind you of one reason why her poetry is held in high regard. . . . Her accomplishment is to describe well and without malice things that catch her fancy and to do this in a way that suits her fancy whether it suits anyone else or not. The best of excerpters, she takes ideas and phrases from her wide and happy reading and sets them in a firm, moral mastic, thereby composing very fanciful, and here and there delightful, mosaic poems. "Jewel" and "gem" are words she likes, and the last poem in this book is "Sun." The first line of the first poem, which is addressed to the Brooklyn Bridge, goes: "Enfranchising cable, silvered by the sea." But in fact the bridge, cables and all, is repainted every ten years or so, and of course the paint is constantly being sullied by New York's aerial sewage. Is this substantial truth less interesting, really, both in itself and as a subject for a poem, than a whimsical sea-silvering of the unpleasantness?

George P. Elliott. *Hudson Review.* Spring,
1967, pp. 139–41

"It was my seventy-ninth year to heaven." Try to imagine such a line in Dylan Thomas, or in almost any recent poet, and at once the special achievement of Marianne Moore is clear, not the good genes and teetotaling that permit the longevity of the person, but the sensibility that permits the longevity of the poet and the poems. From her nearly eightieth year comes *Tell Me, Tell Me.* Miss Moore's curiosity is still urgent, as in the title; her grasp on the elemental still strong as in the sub-title, *Granite, Steel*—and, as in the rest of the sub-title, *and Other Topics*—she shows again her old-fashioned willingness to hazard that poetry treats "Topics": what the mind makes of things. This is a career growing as long and as exemplary as Titian's, with the same strength, that comes from not cutting off any good human capacity. One wants to make the comparison with Titian despite the absence of the gorgeous heroic in her verse, because so much has been said of the quietness and individuality of her art that we are in danger of forgetting its classic completeness, its refusal to make those exclusions of perception, thought, or feeling that give much contemporary verse its eccentric and sometimes specious drama.

S. P. Zitner. *Poetry.* September, 1967, p. 423

The function of a poem, when Miss Moore writes it, is to provide for distinctive energy of mind a sufficient occasion; a direction. The mind moves from its presumed rest; ranges abroad through materials congenial to its nature; comes to rest again. This is the figure the poems make; a sequence, a curve, the trajectory of a mind well aimed. If we ask why one curve is chosen in preference to another, there is no ready answer: it is so. The assumption is that energy of mind is good, and its release in action is good. The note is experimental, exploratory.

Denis Donoghue. *The Ordinary Universe*
(New York: Macmillan, 1968), p. 47

Epigrammatic brilliance, intellectual fastidiousness, and an unwillingness to falsify one's sense of one's own limitations may have an exemplary value of their own, in art as well as in life. Marianne Moore does not tell us the meaning of history, the nature of sin, or the right way to conduct our lives. She keeps things in order; she observes and annotates; she exercises the courage of her peculiarities. She gives us imaginary gardens with real toads in them; she also gives us the sick horror of decency trying to confront honestly the fact of modern war, and the undramatic, faintly humiliating, matter-of-fact discovery that decency recovers from that confrontation.

George W. Nitchie. Marianne Moore (New
York: Columbia University Press, 1969),
p. 178

Marianne Moore and Emily Dickinson do not stand to each other in a relationship as undeniable as that between Miss Moore and Henry James. I doubt if one who had mastered the urbane obliquity of James would care altogether for the abrupt and unceremonious withdrawals into enigma of Emily Dickinson. It has often been remarked that Marianne Moore's style develops out of highly civilized prose. Her sentences are beautifully articulated, more condensed than prose normally is, and with an odd sidelong movement that in prose would probably disconcert; but no one could mistake the element from which they have arisen. Their affinities are with conversation. . . . Emily Dickinson was afraid to converse: she utters a few astonishing words from behind the door and then closes it in palpitation. She too wants her "heightened consciousness" to find its response—but from whom? . . .

And yet, given this all-important distinction between the two poets, their choice of language seems to unite them unexpectedly. Both are incontrovertibly American—or perhaps one should say American of a certain tone and temper which, like much else in the modern world, may be dissolving. They are individual, ironic, and above all fastidious. They place a high value on privacy and know the power of reticence. Their poetry is exact and curious like the domestic skills of the American woman in ante-bellum days. It has the elevation of old-fashioned erudite American talk—more careful in its vocabulary, more strenuously aiming at correctness and dignity than English talk of the same vintage.

Henry Gifford. In Charles Tomlinson, ed.
Marianne Moore (Englewood Cliffs, New
Jersey: Prentice-Hall, 1969), pp. 172–73

I think it has been insufficiently emphasized that a good deal of Miss Moore's verse, particularly the earlier, is not stanzaic at all, or rhymed—or, indeed, regularly, or approximately regularly, syllabic. Nevertheless, perhaps it is here that her contribution to modern experimental poetry may be seen at its purest and most remarkable, for what she is writing is not prose or the prose-poem but poetry with prose's rhetoric, complexity and ease, poetry without adventitious musical aid, whose units are arguments and paragraphs. . . . The baroque cleverness and ornament is to delay and enrich a closely-argued journey towards the clinching spire or altar of meaning and emotion.

Roy Fuller. *Owls and Artificers* (London: André Deutsch, 1971), pp. 49–51

The word "precious" is usually a term of condemnation. For Marianne Moore it is the highest possible praise. Life itself is seen as "An Egyptian Pulled Glass Bottle in the Shape of a Fish" and she does not permit it to be seen in any other way. She, like Stevens, has often been compared to Edith Sitwell, but Edith Sitwell's bric-a-brac universe is a form of rather savage metaphysical sarcasm. Marianne Moore approves of hers. She not only likes it that way but she is incapable of seeing it otherwise. This in itself is an ironic and witty commentary on the world as it really is. It even has a scarcely audible note of tragedy, but it's doubtful if that is intentional. I've often wondered if Tennessee Williams got the idea and the title for his play, *The Glass Menagerie,* from the contemplation of Marianne Moore and her poetry. Certainly the play could stand as a perfect criticism of both person and poems. . . .

Other women of her generation, notably Elinor Wylie, tried to claim the heritage of Emily Dickinson, but today their verses seem thin stuff indeed, while Marianne Moore's survives. More apparently inhuman poetry has probably never been written. . . . There is a progression in the development of a carapace for the sensibility. Emily Brontë, Christina Rossetti, Emily Dickinson, Marianne Moore. They all write about the same thing, the vertigo of the sensibility in a world of terror.

Kenneth Rexroth. *American Poetry in the Twentieth Century* (New York: Herder and Herder, 1971), pp. 68–69

Marianne Moore is not an original thinker. Her "message" of freedom through sacrifice could not be more commonplace, as she herself would agree. Yet she may make it strike us with an original force because it is arrived at in the poems themselves only through difficulty. It is hard for her to sacrifice silence. Then again, it is hard for her to sacrifice speech. Sacrifice alternates with sacrifice, and the freedom with which we are able to put them together, reclaiming both speech and silence "in/the name of freedom" and as a taboo against psychical oppression, is the freedom of Moore's verse. We may take freedoms with her verses because she has given them to us. She covets nothing that she has let go.

What is commonplace as idea is not necessarily commonplace as a personally held and acted-upon conviction; in fact, commonplace, as Marianne Moore embraces it, is rare. It is for the intensely personal valuation that Moore has performed upon the common places as well as the exotic places of the world that we feel gratitude and enlightenment, if we are able to feel them. "In Distrust of Merits" shows us commonplace abhorrence of war and the Self who participates by not participating, yet it has a felt intensity, a "mountainous wave" of unconscious fastidiousness "that makes us who look, know depth." "He/sees deep and is glad, who/accedes to mortality" ("What Are Years?"). It is an easy thing to *say*, but difficult to *see*. . . .

Marianne Moore's work is a lifelong exposition of paradox, and no matter how much careful observation she lavishes on the objects that illustrate her various paradoxes, no matter how much precise illusion is given shape through her disarming rhetoric, the paradoxes still remain and are always interesting. Perhaps paradox itself is the rock crystal thing that the hero is seen to see. It is accuracy and mystery well married; it is naked in its objective transparence, but armored in the untouchable axial law that made it. . . .

There is only one poem called by Marianne Moore "The Hero," but in effect all the poems she wrote might claim this as some sort of subtitle. It is telling that the hero of the poem "The Hero" is an anonymous character, for the hero can be anybody at any time who shares the hero's devotion to vision and to the "rock crystal thing." Heroes have pasts and futures. This is clear from the poem; all her past sensations gather in her, preparing her with responses to her fathering fate, her apprehensions, her convictions. We must acknowledge the value of childhood and of limitations in general, turn the wishes born of both into actions. These actions are heroic when they express both the personal desire of the hero, fulfilling some need in her, and connect also with the desires of a community of potential heroes. Thus the wish and the limitation become a dance, a poem, a Brooklyn Bridge or icosasphere, Bach's Solfegietto, or a knight in quest of modest armor. . . .

We shall always come back to "science" in the work of Marianne Moore, because science was to her a method of knowledge indispensable to her comprehensively evaluative mode of poetry. Moral sense may be uppermost, but it must be informed with the greatest possible exactitude about the state of things in the physical world. In order to make spiritual acknowledgment of creation, it must make technical acknowledgments—how it was done, how it is to be done. This technique links the past and the future as well as the matter and the spirit of all worldly phenomena. If "science" is accurate observation of the world's developing, temporary balance, and eventual dissolution, and "prophecy" the accurate observation of those processes on a spiritual level, then poetry, if it is to contain the truest of all observations, must put them together. The confusion is accurate and necessary. Confusion, submitted to poetry by unconfusion, confusion affectionately admitted, leads to the development and expression of the whole soul.

Pamela White Hadas. *Marianne Moore:*
Poet of Affection (Syracuse: Syracuse
University Press, 1977), pp. 213, 216, 219,
223–24

It holds true . . . of Marianne Moore's poetry at all times that the form, the instrument designed, varies with the intended point of view and the scope of experience looked into or out upon. Naturally she did not always succeed in these experiments; in some of her early poems (like "Snakes, Mongooses") discursiveness may defeat the shape of the whole. But she always obeyed a counsel that she offered younger writers: "Be just to initial incentive." If the subject had attraction, she would not desert it; and sometimes the effort of execution sets up a tension with the intended theme. The tension keeps even the lesser poems alive because the subject of the poem is never sought for but comes as an involuntary summons. The reader too becomes aware of the interaction between the beckoning subject—inhering not in any one theme or image, but in all the words together—and the objectifying figure of spoken sound.

Marianne Moore's poetry shares some technical qualities with the three modern poets most closely associated with her—T. S. Eliot, Ezra Pound, and William Carlos Williams. All these poets developed new rhythmic patterns, freeing verse from the over-use of iambic pentameter and the cul de sac of elaborate post-Swinburne stanzaic forms. All of them introduced a conversational tone, a greater proximity of poetry to spoken language. They could all convert seemingly "nonpoetic" material into the substance of art.

At the same time, the differences among them are as marked; otherwise none would have been a true writer. . . . She does not juxtapose motifs from the past (of art, literature, history) with fragmentary present scenes in the way that Pound and Eliot had. Instead, if she uses past events or quotations from earlier writers, it is to bring them directly within the range of her observation. . . . Likewise, although she sometimes invokes myth for its suggestive power, she does not rely upon it for unifying heterogeneous subjects. Dialogue in her poems, when it occurs, sounds like people talking in the present, not being overheard or remembered. As she remarked, she never considered herself an "imagist," but every page of her work presents images for which alone the poem deserves to be remembered.

Lawrence Stapleton. *Marianne Moore: The Poet's Advance* (Princeton: Princeton University Press, 1978), pp. 221–22

In Moore, sincerity is a blend of eagerness and restraint, of ambition and humility. She leaps, precipitously, into speech, and then checks herself, paradoxically producing more speech by recording her revisions. . . .

For Moore, integrity is the opposite of tedium, and sincerity and gusto are two sides of the same coin. As sincerity is connected with the urge for truth and accuracy, gusto is, as Hazlitt says, "power or passion defining any object." Moore's "gusto" is also like the classical *energeia,* which modernists appropriated. It is the emotional byproduct of the flux and tension of form. This flux and tension are set in motion by sincerity, which accepts no single-minded description of reality. But Moore's gusto is not, as is the energy in Pound's vortex, the eye of the storm, a perfect center created from the collision of perspectives. It is the feeling of pleasure accompanying bafflement,

the energy released in the poem by the resistance of an object to each onslaught of form. Her acts of description and definition repeatedly give way
to exclamation of delighted defeat. The desire for possession is displaced by
passion and admiration. Gusto is an emotion connected with failure, not
with mastery, with relinquishing, not attaining, "what one would keep." Few
writers deal with failure so enthusiastically. Moore celebrates the world's
elusiveness, its superiority to our acts of appropriation, seeing the world's
freedom as intrinsic to our own. And "gusto thrives on freedom," on the
repeated discovery of difference. Thus her poems do not seek a still center
in the turning world; they are distinctly temporal, and turn with it in constant
astonishment. . . .

Moore's greatest poetry does not deal directly with the major myths of
our culture, with tragic or comic themes. Her truths, excerpted from her
poems, may seem proverbial. But if we consider her subjects and themes as
occasions for significant imaginative acts we can have no doubt about the
value of her art. Like "impassioned Handel" in "The Frigate Pelican" who
was "meant for a lawyer and a masculine German domestic/career—" but
who "clandestinely studied the harpsichord/and never was known to have
fallen in love," Moore is "unconfiding" and "hides/in the height and in the
majestic/display of her art." Like the frigate pelican and his fellows, without
cosmic purpose ignoring the more obvious lures of the romantic sensibility,
she "wastes the moon." . . .

Moore's poetry is opposed, above all, to complacency, inertia, dejection.
Her objective in the aesthetic of sincerity and gusto is to keep the mind alert
and free, the world large and abundant.

Bonnie Costello. *Marianne Moore:*
Imaginary Possessions (Cambridge: Harvard
University Press, 1981), pp. 3, 13–14

Marianne Moore was an unaccommodating woman who wanted to be accommodating. With an alertness to the spirit of her own times, she went confidently about the pleasures and the work of writing poetry that is
unmistakably individual. The style is so idiosyncratic that it has had no poor
imitators, and, unlike many singular writers, she is difficult to parody. Taking
part in the modernist movement, she created radically new forms that share
in the reality that is the substance of the verse but also are integral to its
significance. She was, like her contemporaries, Eliot and Pound, an avid
student of both well-known and obscure or nearly-forgotten works of the
past; selective and pronounced in her tastes, she wrote poems that are transformations of the old forms or texts with the freedom of one who has discovered them for herself, made them her own, and given them new life. There
is about much that she wrote the air of private, personal enthusiasms as
well as devotion to nuances and snippets of learning inseparable from her
enthusiasms. These qualities combine to give her poems a density or opacity
often requiring a care comparable to her own if one is to enjoy them. Many

readers are, nonetheless, irritated or discouraged, while those who are over-serious and dedicated in the pursuit of the poem may learn that they have misplaced their care and lost the poem. Yet by attending to her forms, her discriminations, and her sensibility, we find that she is often also a powerfully lucid, even translucent poet, and the poem "a rock crystal thing to see." (One hears Moore saying wittily about her characteristic use of details she collected and assembled in the verse: "they are like flies in amber.") She objected to the work's being dulled by generalization or bisected without regard to continuities and to "the principle that is hid." In her writing, the literal and factual give point to the figurative. Style is an act of compression, but the truth of the whole poem cannot deny the truth of the particulars. Words are an act of faith, and their value for the reader depends on the genuine value they had for her.

Elizabeth Phillips. *Marianne Moore* (New York: Frederick Ungar, 1982), pp. 228–29

When Marianne Moore died in 1972, having outlived William Carlos Williams, Wallace Stevens, and T. S. Eliot, she had changed the course of American poetry. She had also left her mark on the reading public in an amusing but entirely appropriate way. Almost anyone who has paged through an anthology of poetry or of American literature responds to her name by quoting one of the lines in "Poetry"—"'Imaginary gardens with real toads in them.'" It is amusing and appropriate that people quote Marianne Moore when she is quoting someone else, since their confusion says a good deal about the history of Moore's difficult poetry. Anthology editors find Marianne Moore's poetry useful. Some of her poems illustrate syllabic verse; most are neither too short nor too long for anthologies; and "Poetry" adds an elegantly irreverent touch to collections of poems about poetry. In spite of these frequent appearances, though, Moore's craft distracts her readers. They admire her technique and then miss the excitement, the challenge, and the playful wit of the poems. She becomes a sort of national mascot.

It is easy to see why Moore's poetry appears so frequently in anthologies but difficult to understand why she continues to be known more for her personality or for quotable phrases than for the body of her work or for her importance to other poets. It is also difficult to account for the fact that today Moore receives less critical attention than do her contemporaries, who, in the early decades of the twentieth century, had admired her work for its genius and daring. In spite of recent studies that treat Moore intelligently, the entire history of Moore criticism reveals a pattern of misperception installed as fact. Moore's contemporaries, unlike later readers, recognized both the surface brilliance of her poetry and the subversive nature of her endeavor. Not many years later, academic critics met with frustration when they tried to fit Marianne Moore into the paradigm of high modernism that they were busily developing. Unwilling and unable to ignore Moore's work entirely, that second generation of readers developed a mythic Marianne Moore whose role

in the canon of modernism reflected their perceptions of her personality. . . .
[Moore's] use of quotation and her subtly imitative form developed out of
a life-long habit of collecting, recording, and indexing quotations. Moore
deliberately blurred the chronology and sometimes the identity of those quotations in order to enact rather than shy away from the complexity of her
subject. The stance is assertive rather than defensive. The essays also account for Moore's ability to embrace the fragmentation that so many modernist writers tried to diminish and control.

> Taffy Martin. *Marianne Moore: Subversive*
> *Modernist* (Austin: University of Texas
> Press, 1986), p. 1

Now that *The Complete Prose* is available we can begin to evaluate Moore's
role as a perceptive, often brilliant reader of her contemporaries; including
nearly four hundred prose pieces written over the course of sixty years, the
collection is an invaluable archive for scholars interested in Moore's *oeuvre*.
Not all of it is of the same quality or interest. Throughout, however, we
encounter a modernist sensibility of acute intelligence, unfailingly attentive
to the culture of her time. Like the critical efforts of her contemporaries—
Pound, Eliot, Williams, and Stevens—Moore's critical essays carve out an
important version of the foundations of modernism.

> Celeste Goodridge. *Hints and Disguises:*
> *Marianne Moore and Her Contemporaries*
> (Iowa City: University of Iowa Press,
> 1989), p. 5

Marianne Moore's poems have a social presence, you might even say a so-
ciable presence. That presence is distinct from Moore's tiresome public caricature as a genteel, fey, impishly brilliant old lady in a peculiar hat—and yet
gentility and idiosyncrasy are unquestionably part of the true social presence
in the poems. Like many stereotypes, this is one we can neither quite feel
comfortable with, nor altogether reject. In Moore's best work, the outer force
of manners penetrates beyond a charming or complacent gentility, to become
a profound moral force, as in the great novelists; and the inner force of
idiosyncrasy becomes the sign of a passionate, obdurate selfhood. I think
that to understand the peculiar strengths or limitations of this poet, we have
to look at her work in the light of such matters as the relation of language
and poetry to social life and even to social class. These matters seem all the
more important because Moore was a Modernist, one of the generation of
poets that raised new questions about the kind of poetry that might be suitable
for an American and democratic culture.

Partly because of our own social habits and predispositions, we readers
often respond to Moore's work in social terms; people dote on her poems,
or find them annoying, a little as if responding directly to a person and her
remarks. . . .

The sudden, even unexpected penetrations of emotion in Moore's work flare up from the tireless pressure of the poet negotiating and considering between her own way of talking and our way of talking, between discourse and discourse's imaginary re-making, the suspended life of a town and that life's forever hoped-for resumption. These oppositions embody the shared, socially visible quality of peculiarity underlying the peculiarity of each distinct human soul.

Robert Pinsky. In Joseph Parisi, ed.
Marianne Moore: The Art of a Modernist
(Ann Arbor: University Microfilm, 1990),
pp. 13, 24

Besides recognizing more fully Marianne Moore's adversarial inclinations, I believe we need to apprehend her as something of a feminine visionary. Secular as her writing may be when we compare it with, for example, that of H.D., Moore is nonetheless a poet who imagines alternatives to the way we live, think, feel, and does so in modes which we may identify as gynocentric and discover as well in the work of other women poets. Let me list, very briefly, a few of the more significant qualities which Moore shares with other women writers, not in order to imply that gender is a rigidly determining category for the artist but to suggest the shade of difference it may make and to offer a context which will clarify what Moore attempts to do with the figure of the maternal hero. First, Moore's assertion that "The Past Is the Present" and her inclination to skip and jump among the centuries within a given poem indicate that she deviates from the high-Modernist assumption that the modern world has been sundered from the past. . . .

Her imagery of disguises, veils, and armor is shared by innumerable women artists. Her style, with its charm, brio, and dash, its elusiveness and its profoundly comic valence, might be threaded back to Anne Bradstreet and Dickinson, in neither of whom does Puritanism preclude humor. "God be with the clown," said Dickinson, and there is a whole story to be written of the ways women writers use humor as a means of resistance and pleasure in a literary culture which privileges tragedy. Then there is the curious way Moore plays with gender distinctions as if, at times, she did not take them quite seriously. . . .

If each of these devices is a way of imagining the world as other than it is (less rigid, less oppressive, less sad, and above all less governed by authorities exterior to personal judgment), it remains the case that Moore is in no sense a poet of explicit protest. On the contrary, her consistent stance toward the world is one of a rather determined affection. Her social or political jibes are not diatribes. Philosophically she prefers admiration to confrontation. But with this we return to the maternal hero, a recurrent figure in Moore's poetry, as affection is a recurrent tone in her temperament, balancing—perhaps explaining—the acerbity which is its countertone. The maternal hero is affectionate, nurturing, protective; she needs to be, for there are enemies at hand. The maternal hero is courageous but also patient; is often an artist of some sort; and is plainly a figure for the poet, Marianne Moore, in her satiric-visionary phase.

Alicia Ostriker. In Joseph Parisi, ed.
Marianne Moore: The Art of a Modernist
(Ann Arbor: University Microfilm, 1990),
pp. 55–56

The most overreaching commitment of Moore's earlier poetry is her refusal of the forms of hierarchy inherent in a specular writing—of a "heroics" that "confuses transcendence with domination" or an aesthetic in which something is "great because something else is small." And whereas this commitment to non-hierarchical forms of meaning is sometimes expressed in the thematics of Moore's writing, it is carried out most fully in the very forms her writing takes—in quotation of statements from insignificant and anti-poetic sources, in subversion of meanings based on hierarchical dualities, in refusal of singular or climactic resolutions, and in representation of the otherness of others. Indeed, Moore's early use of syllabic verse may well be an effort to give each word and syllable significance apart from structures which unify them—the "rising throbbing curve of emotion" of a more traditional lyric versification.

Moore, who hesitates to criticize publicly her male Modernist peers, nevertheless openly reproves them for their poetic speakers' relations of dominance to the others they depict: the "king, steward, and harper, seated amidships while the jade and the rock crystal course about in solution." But whereas Moore criticizes her male peers for these postures, she also faults female poets for engaging in these same structures of domination, albeit differently. In an essay on Elizabeth Bishop, she observes that "some feminine poets of the present day seem to have grown horns and like to be frightful and dainty by turns, but distorted propriety suggests effeteness." Conversely, Moore commends Bishop for not cutting "into the life of a thing" and for not "degrading" a "garment of rich aesthetic construction . . . to the utilitarian offices of the barnyard." . . .

Moore's well-known election to uphold affirmative rather than negative assertions is most likely attributable to familial, religious, class, and educational influences as well as to her gender. Indeed, Moore's culminating aesthetic of "agreeing difference" enables her simultaneously to assume an expansive and agreeable attitude and to disclose critical differences and discrepancies. Moore can at once approve and disapprove of her culture. Furthermore, by not taking a position with respect to any one attitude or idea, Moore avoids establishing a singular stance and thereby reinscribing unacceptable terms of her culture and of her gender. . . .

Moore's poetry of understatement is structured by her paradoxical attempt to give expression to a universality and also to herself as a woman. While in this earlier poetry Moore works against the symbolic or specular propensities of lyric poetry, she remains compelled by the possibility of self-representation through recognizable forms of cultural representation. As such, Moore produces a poetry that marks with precision and imagination her position "elsewhere" from the estranged others and quoted expressions of her writing. But although Moore produces a set of highly significant poems, she finds them inadequate to her needs for a more definitive form of communication, turning in her later poetry to overstatement.

Both H.D.'s and Stein's writings have been more enthusiastically embraced by feminist criticism than has Moore's. Indeed, the reification of feminine presences in H.D.'s poetry and of language structures in Stein's writing make their work significant disruptions of existing forms of signification. The subversiveness of Moore's poetry is far more elusive. Rather than attempting to effect a totalizing vision or to remake language, Moore's writing offers a rich ambiguity—an ambiguity which constitutes through its elected and non-elected silences the play of her "radical otherness." In her refusal to perform surgery on a singular aspect of the literary tradition and system of representation, Moore produces a poetry which finally does not avoid, nor repeat, gender, but re-presents it.

> Jeanne Heuving. *Omissions Are Not Accidents: Gender in the Art of Marianne Moore* (Detroit: Wayne State University Press, 1992), pp. 12–13, 16

It is time for another look at the poetry of Marianne Moore because it is a new discourse, a woman's voice, and one that offers a poetry of triumph, not of despair. It is also important to reexamine Moore's discourse for all of the good reasons T. S. Eliot offered in his introduction in 1935. She is a genuine poet who has "saturated her mind with the perfections of prose." She is an original in every sense of the word. She has a particular gift for detailed observation, for finding the exact words for the experience of the eye. She is an intellectual who achieves an intense, if restrained, emotional value. She is an elegant versifier, whose forms are anything but free. But perhaps most of all, she is a fantasist of great precision; the minute details of her work are never an end in themselves but always have a service to perform in the transmission of her complex but confident and uplifting themes. . . .

Moore never saw herself as the hopelessly beleaguered and lonely being at the mercy of the chaotic particulars of reality. She knew her place in the universe, in the Great Chain of being. She held a prevailing faith, one that was undogmatic and even largely unscriptural. It is never obvious in her work because it permeates it; it was part of the fiber of her every theme. One might call it a kind of clairvoyant Christian awareness of transhuman reality dependent on grace and intuition rather than on doctrine or creed.

> Darlene Williams Erickson. *Illusion Is More Precise Than Precision: The Poetry of Marianne Moore* (Tuscaloosa: University of Alabama Press, 1992), pp. 217, 221, 223

MOORE, OLIVE (pseud. CONSTANCE VAUGHN)
(GREAT BRITAIN) 1905(?)–70(?)

This is a first novel, [*Repent at Leisure,* later reissued as *Spleen*] if indeed it can properly be called a novel, but there is nothing amateurish about it, nor, as the publisher truly points out, any uncertainty in the technique. The author, on the contrary, seems to be absolutely confident of what she wants to do and does it without a faltering step. Whether the reader will appreciate, or even understand it, is another matter. It is a weird conception, and granting that it was worth doing at all, it is well done.

Briefly, the story is of the workings of the mind of a woman with a strong father fixation who, finding herself with child, gradually develops an early resentment of pregnancy into a fixed desire to give birth to a child that shall somehow be different from the rest of the human race—something altogether new in children. Her son is born different in that, though well-formed, he is crippled and imbecile, and the rest of the book is the mental history of the woman's twenty-year expiation of the hysteria of her pregnancy on an island near Capri, where she lives with the child, growing in mysterious horror of him with his growth. Her expiation ends, for no very apparent reason, with the news that her husband has died and she has inherited his wealth. She returns to England, leaving the child, now a man, on the island, obtains some mysterious consolation from seeing in a gallery the portrait of herself and the child done years ago by a German artist with whom there had once been the flickering of a brief romance, and indicates that her late husband's estate is to become a home for slum children.

Presumably by way of emphasizing the unusual quality of this strange tale, the publishers have put it in a jacket of shiny silver paper, which catches the light and annoys the reader, and have spelt the title and author and some of the proper names in the text without capitals.

Saturday Review of Literature. December
20, 1930, p. 475

Each of Moore's novels [in her *Collected Writings,* reissued 1992] takes place in a different world and each has its own idiom and texture. The world of *Fugue* has some echoes of the one established by Jean Rhys, but it would be a mistake to try to push the resemblance too far. *Fugue* has a plot in the sense that things do happen, but what happens is not the point. The reader is even left uncertain as to whether the fugue of the title refers to the musical form, the abnormal psychological state, the characters' flight or all three. It is a tour de force, but, as with *Spleen,* it is a hard novel to like.

The Apple Is Bitten Again gives us Moore's wit without the distractions of plot and character. A compendium of sixteen notebooks, the eighty-some-page volume might make been designed to give the lie to Gertrude Stein's dictum that "remarks are not literature." The best things in *The Apple* are remarks. Some are self-consciously clever cocktail-party conversation, some are wholly new thoughts on the universe of physical, social and mental things. Some, of course, are both. All are fun to read. As ever, there is Moore's deprecation of women, produced in the tone of one who is herself at once free of gender and ironically aware that someone else may not notice this. The position (to the extent that it is one) is summarized at the end of Notebook Number Fifteen, a meditation (or parody of one) on intelligence, mind, soul and what Moore calls Local Brain. She concludes:

> It seems not for nothing that the apple comes always to the rescue of humanity.
> One woman, meaning well, bit an apple. Circumstances were against her (she was ahead of her time) and it turned to superstition.
> Another woman bites an apple. Circumstances are against her and she still may be ahead of her time, and gives back Reason through the medium of Common Sense.

Whoever this woman may be, she is not Olive Moore, who gives much, in her four slim volumes, but rarely reason and common sense. Say rather vision, madness and wit in a package suggesting that, like other olives, her work is a piquant but acquired taste.

Lillian S. Robinson. Women's Review of Books. 9, July, 1992, p. 35

Olive Moore was the pseudonym of Constance Vaughan, about whom very little is known, except that she was part of the Bloomsbury group in the 1930s. Set in London and Strasbourg, *Fugue* is the last of her four novels. It is the story of an independent, sexually liberated woman, Lavinia Reade, and her attempts to escape the restraints both of conventional society and of her intellectual contemporaries and lovers. Her curse is "being so very much alive among the dead."

The novel begins outside Strasbourg, with Harrion, Lavinia's last lover and the father of her second, as yet unborn, illegitimate child. (The first is in the charge of a "highly recommended . . . great sturdy female"; Lavinia has no time for motherhood.) The narrative flits back and forth across time and the English Channel, in a series of reflections, sometimes from Harrion's point of view, mostly from Lavinia's.

For all her liberation, her belief that "Wide and hospitable legs . . . are a proof of strength and independence," Lavinia's deepest sentiments seem pre-feminist and Romantic. She compares her own set of friends to "those enchanting prismatic toys . . . [whom] you must clap and praise," whereas a real man "works with arms and muscles" on the land and "does not treat [a woman] like a goddess for bearing a child or two."

Harrion is even more confused, content only when he can be indifferent to all around him. His callousness, insecurity and desire for an inexplicable fulfillment make him a less predictable figure than Lavinia, whose witty aphorisms often fall flat in comparison to the despairing, obsessive musings of her lover.

This discursive, breathless novel sometimes loses itself in its attempts to light on as many issues as possible. We are made dizzy by discussions of art and life, man and woman, the thinker and the doer, high and low society. The best moment lurks in the simplest contrast: Lavinia, rejoicing "in an eternity," "gazing down at the Bacchic frieze of day, the tumbling children and the burdened fields," while Harrion, preferring the company in a Paris crematorium, sniffs the "stench of grease and putrescence . . . with nostrils distended like an animal."

D.H. (London) *Times Literary Supplement.*
April 16, 1993, p. 22

MORAGA, CHERRÍE (UNITED STATES) 1957–

In *Giving up the Ghost,* Cherríe Moraga broke a twenty-year silence in the Chicano theater movement by placing Chicana lesbian sexuality center stage. The text explores the ways in which both lesbian and heterosexual Chicanas' sense of self as sexual beings has been affected by their culture's definitions of masculinity and femininity. The theme of writing emerges at the end of the play. Marisa's writing is both provoked and interrupted by her memories of Amalia and sexual desire, just as the text itself. Marisa's secular "confession" to the audience is the product of her need to exhume and examine her love for this woman and all women. The text presents both the failures and the promises of building community. Just before Marisa speaks of her "daydream[s] with pencil in . . . mouth," she articulates the need for "familia," redefined as women's community: "It's like making familia from scratch / each time all over again . . . with strangers / if I must. / If I must, I will."

The love of Chicanas for themselves and each other is at the heart of Chicana writing, for without this love they could never make the courageous move to place Chicana subjectivity in the center of literary representation, or depict pivotal relationships among women past and present, or even obey the first audacious impulse to put pen to paper. Even as that act of necessity distances the Chicana writer from her oral tradition and not so literate sisters, the continuing commitment to the political situation of all Chicanas creates a community in which readers, critics and writers alike participate.

Yvonne Yarbro-Bejarano. In María Herrera-
Sobek and Helena María Viramontes, eds.
*Chicana Creativity and Criticism: Charting
New Frontiers in American Literature*
(Houston: Arte Publico, 1988), p. 144

In my view, in *Giving up the Ghost,* Moraga puts into play the concepts "man" and "woman" (and the parodic "butch/femme"), with the intuitive knowledge that they operate in our subjectivities, so that it is difficult to analyze them, except in the way she has done. Women speaking with each other in a spiralling way, not quite face-to-face, but with the recollection that at least once they were so close to each other that they could effect a transfusion so as to avoid the extremes—that is a muted "woman's" speaking position, and a male-identified subjectivity. It is to Moraga's credit that she puts the dyad man-woman into play in such a way that she brings into view three relational trajectories—the lesbian butch who is killing herself by the implied rejection of her literal body, the mother-daughter relation where the daughter may be forced to take the son (or father's) position so as to get close to her mother, and the hope that the heterosexual woman will not be put off by the lesbian due to homophobia.

For young Chicana writers (and critics) the crisis of meaning as women has increasingly led to a measuring "after-the-fact" of the speaking subject's meanings. The most exciting explorations are those that "measure" the intricacies of relationship between and among women. Yet if actual social experiences have the potential of effecting a complex and heterogeneous subjectivity, the symbolic contract within which "woman" is the repository of meaning and not the agent, constantly presses her to align herself with the symbolic; in this way she is forced to live the life of a "woman/mother." To refuse to live the life of a "woman," which is both literal (body) and symbolic (iconic/linguistic configurations), throws her into a crisis of meaning. As young Corky makes clear, if you don't want to be a girl, society as well as she then take it that you want to be a boy. Corky's "error" is that she does not refuse both. How could she? Perhaps, as the older and wiser Marisa suggests, we must make "*familia* from scratch." Marisa, who wanted to save her own mother and later Amalia, by having them remember their own "forgotten places" beyond womanly duty, would, unlike Marge, be capable of saying to Olga Ruiz: "Where are you? Where am I? Where to find the traces of your passage? From the one to the other? From the one into the other?"

Norma Alarcón. In María Herrera-Sobek
and Helena María Viramontes, eds. *Chicana
Creativity and Criticism: Charting New
Frontiers in American Literature* (Houston:
Arte Publico, 1988), pp. 156–57

Cherríe Moraga . . . structures the metaphoric construct of rape in her two-act play *Giving up the Ghost* to articulate its function as a political signifier of women's inferior status with regard to men. . . .

Moraga encodes in her play, through the construct inherent in the act of raping, the consequence and process of making, en-gendering, a group of humans—women. In this process of en-gendering, fabricating, that is, making a gender, the end result is a hole and absence: women as invisible, voiceless, worthless, devalued objects. They are silent entities dominated by ingrained patriarchal vectors where the Name of The Father is Law, and years of socialization to obey the Father's Law transforms the female subject into a quavering accomplice in her own rape. That is to say, women are socialized into being participants in their own oppression. . . .

The protagonist experiences a process of dismemberment: she first loses sensation around her kneecaps; furthermore, her genitals assume a life of their own—they flap "in the wind like a bird / a wounded bird." As she slowly loses her identity as a human being, her face merges into a mass of flesh without any of the distinctive features that normally serve to highlight and express her individuality. She is transformed into what street jargon expresses as "a piece of meat": "a face with no features / no eyes no nose no mouth."

The violent act visited upon the young woman on the verge of adolescence produces a *hole,* a nothingness, an empty space. The female child is obliterated at the precise temporal juncture of becoming a woman. The artistic recreation of the rape scene encodes a political metaphor for society's marginalization of women. It traces, in a few powerful lines, the socialization process visited upon the female sex which indoctrinates them into accepting a subordinate position in the socio-political landscape of a system. The violation itself symbolizes the final act which obliterates women from the system. The process of raping, "making an absence," transforms women into silent, invisible, nonexistent entities—as holes to be filled by males.

María Herrera-Sobek. In María Herrera-Sobek and Helena María Viramontes, eds. *Chicana Creativity and Criticism: Charting New Frontiers in American Literature* (Houston: Arte Publico, 1988), pp. 172–73, 175

Cherríe Moraga's *Loving in the War Years: Lo que nunca pasó por sus labios* is a timely and important work. It is a compendium of nearly a decade of Moraga's works that includes short fiction, poetry, and testimonial essay. Two of those essays, whose length comprise the majority of that book, contain the essence of Moraga's thinking, incorporating dreams, journal entries, and poetry as part of her testimonial discourse. One of the essays in particular, a work she has entitled "A Long Line of Vendidas," addresses some of the issues I have just mentioned [gender in relation to class, ethnicity, culture, and family]. . . .

The naming of this essay (a title appropriated, whose meaning is then reassigned, an ironic and contemporary use of the term "vendida") not only connects Moraga to a mestiza Chicana past but also questions, reevaluates, and finally takes issue with it. As we shall see, the customary uses of the *vendida* myth are restructured in Moraga's analysis in order to forge a reevaluation of the Malinche legend from which it derives. . . .

By choosing to represent the book bilingually, she again likens herself to Malinche, her bilingual and trilingual forebear. "Lo que nunca pasó por sus labios" suggests that a silence is about to be broken, though the multiple possibilities of "sus" (her, his, their, your) do not reveal exactly who will break it: Moraga? Malinche? Chicana lesbians? All of them? In this way, her essay approximates the titles of Latin American women's testimonial discourse: "Let me speak!" "They Won't Take Me Alive," "Tales of Disappearance and Survival." All of these indicate a strength, a fortitude, and a resolve to break silences and assert one's voice. . . .

When Moraga discovers a bicultural group whose most comfortable language is what I prefer to call "bilingual" (bilingual as a noun as well as an adjective), she finally is in a position of not feeling shame for "shabby" English or "incorrect" Spanish. Having come from a home where English was spoken, Moraga acknowledges that this claim on, and longing for, her Spanish "mothertongue" had no rational explanation. After all, she did not have her language stripped from her, as had so many children of the Southwest. Here, it is more appropriate to consider it the ancient language of her heart. In this sense, language is not simply a means of communicating ideas, passions, feelings, and theories, but is also symbolic, representing, among other emotions, love for one's culture. As it becomes a touchstone for that culture, especially in circumstances of exile, one must also relearn its nuances as one learns to accept the entirety of one's culture, both its positive and its negative. "I know this language in my bones . . . and then it escapes me." Humiliated and mortified, Moraga must call the Berlitz language school in New York City in order to return to her Spanish, to her love of her mothertongue, to a love for her mother, to her love for her culture, to her love for her raza, to her "deep racial memory of love." "I am a different woman in Spanish. A different kind of passion. I think, *soy mujer en español*. No macha. Pero mujer. Soy Chicana—open to all kinds of attack." One of these attacks, no doubt, is the accusation that she does not belong and does not speak the language of her mother, even if she feels it in her bones. She articulates the contradiction she faces with one of her journal entries after the Berlitz episode: *"Paying for culture. When I was born between the legs of the best teacher I could have had."* The painful journey she embarks upon in order to discover this truth allows her a return to her mother, to her people, to "la mujer mestiza," to a new awareness of what it means to be Malinche's daughter.

Nancy Saporta Sternbach. In Asunción
Horno-Delgado et al., eds. Breaking
Boundaries: Latina Writings and Critical
Readings (Amherst: University of
Massachusetts Press, 1989), pp. 51, 58–59

As one of several Bay Area feminists who made their reputations in other genres but are now (or again) writing for the theater, Cherríe Moraga has expressed a desire to create plays that inspire new vision while they challenge political correctness.

And in many respects her new work, *Heroes and Saints* . . . does just that. An unusual blend of realism, surrealism and political theater, it is written partly in English, partly in Spanish. Moraga sets the play in a San Joaquin Valley town where growers threaten to shoot farmworkers who are protesting pesticide-related deaths by hanging their dead children from the grapevines crucifixion-style. But rather than proceed by making a frontal attack on toxic sprays, Moraga chooses to emphasize the human drama of a Latina family suffering the effects of the poisons. One daughter, Yolanda, loses a baby to them. . . . Another, Cerezita, herself suffering from a birth defect, is—in what could have been fierce poetry had it been realized less awkwardly— simply a head poised on a wheeled cart. The mother, protecting this daughter, tries to keep her from the world. But following one of a number of extraordinarily powerful moments. . .this one a highly erotic love scene between the head and a sympathetic priest in which the young woman tries and fails to recover a sense of her body, Cerezita carries the corpse of her sister's baby to the fields and is shot.

Ultimately, it's clear that this is not only not agitprop but that the fight against pesticides is not even the central conflict. The real action of the play is the daughter's rebellion against the mother and what she stands for, which is framed as a social and political fight, not a psychological one. The mother is reactionary, a sexually and otherwise repressive, fatalistic figure who must be overthrown. And it's here that *Heroes and Saints* fails in its aspirations. When Moraga contrasts the mother with an older woman activist based on Dolores Huerta, we know we are seeing the acceptable role model. Moraga isn't able or doesn't wish to get inside the way the mother has internalized her oppression as she gets inside Cerezita's yearning or Yolanda's agony, although elsewhere she has written with compassion and intelligence about the difficulties of change.

Hal Gelb. *The Nation.* November 2, 1992,
pp. 518–19

Throughout *Loving in the War Years,* Moraga uses *familia* to refer to both her family and the Chicano community. . . . Although Moraga provides a compelling rationale for the association of family and community, neither the narrative nor the expository sections of *Loving in the War Years* simply endorses the nationalist rhetoric of *familia.* Moraga feels compelled to expose the implications of this rhetoric for sexual and gender politics. She writes that "we fight back, we think, with our families—with our women pregnant, and our men, the indisputable heads. We believe the more severely we protect the sex roles within the family, the stronger we will be as a unit in opposition to the anglo threat." But Moraga doubts that "the Chicano male [holds] fast to the family unit merely to safeguard it from the death-dealings of the anglo." . . . She argues, in fact, that the metaphor of *familia* keeps Chicanos from seeing the oppression that exists "in our culture and in ourselves."

Moraga's dedication—as a lesbian and a feminist—to exposing the soft underbelly of ethnic nationalism led her away from both her family and the Chicano movement. And yet, for her, "being Chicana and having a family [remain] synonymous." The images of homecoming in the opening of *Loving in the War Years* presage Moraga's ultimate "[return] to the love of [her] race," which she describes in the epilogue of her autobiography. By the end of *Loving in the War Years,* it is clear that Moraga will never again stand on the sidelines when her *brothers and sisters* take the streets. . . .

Undoubtedly, separatists' use of the metaphor of family constrains expression of dissent within any social movement, but Moraga's frame of reference is epistemological, not simply interpersonal. For Moraga, to analyze one's *familia* poses a cognitive dilemma, for . . . how can one get enough distance to think about something so intimate? Just as Moraga believes she needed to leave her literal family in order to learn the truth about her father, so she believes that she needed to step out of *la familia chicana* in order to understand (or even "see") it. Moraga implies that no one inside the movement could be conscious of the ideological forces at work within it—hence the need for the intellectual to retreat to the sidelines (if only temporarily).

Lora Romero. *Yale Journal of Criticism.* 6,
1993, pp. 121–22, 126–27

The Last Generation, a comprehensive new collection of prose and poetry by Cherríe Moraga, embraces a myriad forms and audiences. It includes personal narratives, insightful dreams, poetic forays into the author's past, political visions of her community's future, and prose transliterations of talks and presentations given at various conferences and symposia.

Just as the themes interweave like common threads in the five different sections of the book—"New Mexican Confession," "War Cry," "La Fuerza Feminina," "The Breakdown of the Bicultural Mind" and "The Last Generation"—each section contains a mix of the writing styles that intimate the personal (poetry, letters and personal narrative) and demand the political (essays which call us to change ourselves and our world). Those familiar with Moraga's earlier books will recognize the dissolution of the boundaries between creative and academic writing. *The Last Generation* further dissolves these boundaries by "talking breed talk" to a culture whose "Third and Fourth and First Worlds are collapsing into one another."

This book, Moraga explains in the introduction, emerges from the ashes of "disregard, censure, and erasure." She writes "out of a sense of urgency that Chicanos are a disappearing tribe, out of a sense of this disappearance in my own familia." A "mixed-blood," a mestiza of Anglo and Mexican American heritage, she has written previously about the contradictions of being a light-skinned Chicana activist in the dominant culture of "Amerika." She now mourns the fact that the younger generation of her family and community have been taught not to be Mexicans, but Americans. Moraga's refusal to accept this prompts her to write "as I always have, but," she adds, "now I write for a much larger familia." . . .

Throughout *The Last Generation* Moraga examines the colonization, patriarchal authority and homophobia that stifle the world we inhabit, and makes direct comparisons between these forms of oppression and the ecological destruction of the planet. She offers her world view as an admonition— and incitement to collective activism—entreating "a resurrection of the ancient in order to construct the modern." . . .

As a Chicana writer and educator whose schooling was completely devoid of Chicano poetry, fiction, or drama, I want to believe that I am of "the last generation" to have experienced that void. Cherríe Moraga was one of the first to fill that emptiness by helping to establish a canon of Chicana literature, and the prose and poetry of her newest book show she intends to keep those political and intellectual fires burning bright for us all.

> Marie-Elise Wheatwind. *Women's Review of Books.* 11, January, 1994, p. 22

MORANTE, ELSA (ITALY) 1918–85

Elsa Morante is the wife of novelist Alberto Moravia. Her work, however, does not betray the slightest trace of conjugal affinity or influence. She is not interested in psychological realism, nor in the conflicts of urban life. She is a visionary teller, who writes, an Italian critic has observed, "as if contemporary literature did not exist"; and Robert Penn Warren has called what she is after "the real fictional magic."

> Paolo Milano. *The New York Times.* October 7, 1951, p. 5

Elsa Morante . . . reveals in this first novel [*House of Liars*], a concern for that theme which has attracted and preoccupied almost every major novelist of our times, the problem of personal disintegration and paralysis of action. . . . At first glance the novel would appear to be a belated realistic novel of the late nineteenth century. But it does not require much reading to become aware that the psychology which motivates the characters is completely, darkly modern, and that in using a somewhat dated setting and technique, the author has achieved a horror effect, like that sometimes provoked by a surrealist painting in which a familiar everyday object is placed in an utterly incongruous position.

> Serge Hughes. *Saturday Review of Literature.* October 20, 1951, p. 19

Miss Morante is writing out of her epoch [in *House of Liars*]. She is giving us, in too extended form, a cross between a Gothic tale and a picaresque novel. . . . The writer is an observant, stick-to-itive young woman: nothing escapes her. And she recreates the Palermo of two hundred years ago . . . with painful exactitude. Her splendid vignettes of the particular insular culture she seeks to explore are full of smoky fire. . . . Miss Morante writes about what she knows, and she seeks fictional pegs simplified to suit her literary purpose. By projecting the Sicilian world against a screen she will at times silhouette and exaggerate certain details; at other times by putting a light behind a slide she will seem to diminish other views, making them appear as perfect and as unreal as detailed miniatures.

Frances Keene. *The Nation.* October 27,
1951, p. 357

[Elsa Morante is] a woman . . . whose work has masculine imaginative power. . . . [She] has continued slowly to deepen and explore her own particular vein . . .; her rich style is one that many of her contemporaries might envy, and sensitivity tends to save her from mere intellectual exercise. She offers escape and fascination; she is not just a painter of the scene and time into which she was born.

Frances Frenaye. *Books Abroad.*
Winter, 1958, pp. 27–28

Elsa Morante's *Arturo's Island* does well what many novels do badly, or rather what they often cannot—however much they may pretend—do at all. It is hard for any writer of our time to persuade us convincingly that men grow out of soil instead of cement, and of all falsities a spurious earthiness can be among the worst. . . . This novel is different. It really does strike roots in the thin and painful soul of reality. . . . The shifts of the plot, and with them the moods of the book, change like a darkening or clearing sky.

Norman Shrapnel. *Manchester Guardian.*
May 15, 1959, p. 6

[*Arturo's Island*] is a poetic story, with all the charm the improbable has when it is told in the tone of probability. It is beautifully managed; the child's eye view is never lost for a minute, the impersonation never falters. Elsa Morante has that kind of stern, firm, factual imagination which such a book as this needs, if the reader is not to suspect that he is being slid into a fantasy or a dream. The theme of the book is remoteness; the remoteness of the island from the world of politics and war, the remoteness of the child from the parent, the remoteness of homosexual desire from marriage, from birth, from all the domestic symbols. It is extraordinarily clever of the writer to have set her lost world within touching distance of the real one; Naples is no more than a short boat trip away, but it might be a million light years.

Arturo's Island . . . has the mesmeric, lingering quality which inhibits immediate assessment.

Pamela Hansford Johnson. New Statesman
and Nation. May 23, 1959, p. 734

Although it would be a mistake to push the comparison too hard, the hero
of . . . *Arturo's Island* bears a certain resemblance to Huck Finn . . . and in
the early part of the novel there are passages as idyllic as anything in *Huckleberry Finn.* . . . *Arturo's Island* [however] . . . is a study of disillusionment
in a sense that *Huckleberry Finn* . . . is not. Both boys are exposed to evil
in varied and terrible forms, but Arturo is profoundly changed, whereas
Huck isn't.

The novels also differ in the way evil is experienced. . . . The innocent
Arturo . . . encounters evil . . . not in strangers but in himself and those
close to him. . . . *Arturo's Island* is a psychological novel as *Huckleberry
Finn* is not, and Miss Morante's great strength lies in her ability to render
Arturo's emotional states. . . . It is on the poetry, on the ingeniously-wrought
figures of speech that Miss Morante relies for her crucial effects. . . . *Huckleberry Finn,* as everyone remembers, peters out; at the end, as Ernest Hemingway said, Mark Twain cheated. *Arturo's Island* rises to an overwhelming
climax. That is not to say that it is a better book than *Huckleberry Finn* but
merely to call attention to the fact that it is in a tradition of more conscious
craftsmanship.

Granville Hicks. Saturday Review of
Literature. August 15, 1959, p. 16

Both [*House of Liars* and *Arturo's Island*] . . . have an impressionistic rather
than a dramatic style, as well as a theme dealing with the fraying away of
human ties. But *Arturo's Island* is a much more successful creation. Perhaps
Miss Morante's style was too efflorescent, too cluttered with tiny virtuosities,
for the narrative pace of her earlier, more realistically framed tale. Now she
has chosen a milieu that luxuriates in the oblique, the opalescent, the delicately enchanted—just the sort of thing she can do best. . . . Miss Morante
possesses the Italian gift of distilling universality out of the primitive. But
she has also a fine feminine instinct for the singing detail.

Frederic Morton. The New York Times.
August 16, 1959, pp. 4–5

Under the title of *Lo scialle andaluso* (The Andalusian shawl), Elsa Morante
has collected thirteen of her stories, written in the course of about twenty
years: from "Il ladro dei lumi," (The thief of the lamps), which dates back to
1935, when she was very young and is the only unpublished one, to a selection
of those already included in a previous collection, *Il gioco segreto* (The secret
game), from 1941, dated between 1936 and that year, to others that appears
in newspapers and magazines between 1945 and 1951, which is the date of

the title story. They are therefore stories that preceded and partly accompanied her major efforts, the novels *Menzogna e sortilegio* (Lying and enchantment) (1948) and *L'isola di Arturo* (Arturo's island) (1957) and, as such, they include . . . all the characteristics of her personality. . . .

Although the short story is not the most congenial register for Morante, this collection documents her evolution rather well. This development is not so much toward a deepening as an ever more secure individuation and modulation of that original motif, which becomes the very reason for her narrative[:] The motif of life as the search for a reality beyond any illusions, but which then becomes impossible to survive except through fictions. . . .

In the early stories ("Il ladro dei lumi" [The thief of lights] "L'uomo dagli occhiali" [The man with the eyeglasses], "La Nonna" [The grandmother], "Via dell' Angelo" [Angel's Street]), that motif—which subsequently, as it clarified itself, was to find appropriate expression in simultaneous use of realistic and allusive modes, still appears to be turned inward, or rather enveloped in a gothicizing fable-manner that seems to hark back to figurative and pictorial rather than literary examples. . . .

Of these early stories, the one in which the various elements begin to come into balance and Morante's essential motif to flourish is "Il gioco segreto" (which lent its title to her first collection). . . . It is a story that is, in fact, carried out with the levity of a game, but deeply committed, so that its allegory has nothing about it of the forced quality of its predecessors. . . . That is why this "Gioco segreto" although chronologically one of these short stories (it dates from 1937), signals Morante's passage from her prehistory to her history as a narrative artist.

Arnaldo Bocelli. *Il Mondo* (Rome).
December 31, 1963, p. 10

The extraordinary popular success [in Italy] of Morante's latest novel [*La Storia*] cannot be explained simply by the fact that it was published directly in paperback and at a relatively low price (because the author agreed to receive five percent royalty instead of the customary ten percent). Clearly, *La storia* is written with the conscious intent of reaching all the people of Italy, whose story it tells.

Set in Rome between 1941 and 1947, in the midst of the most historic events of the modern world, it is the story of those who do not make history, the subproletarian masses, dispossessed and irrelevant. A feeble-minded half-Jewish schoolteacher and her epileptic child conceived when her mother was raped by a German soldier are at the center of an immense tableau of human and other living beings, all victims, often conscious and sometimes mutually responsible, of a hierarchy of oppression and caught up in an endless chain of power and chance. "A Scandal Lasting for 10,000 Years" is the subtitle on the volume's cover and is one major theme of the novel.

There are no heroes in Morante's anti-heroic epic of oppression and endurance, which in both style and ideology stems from the great neorealist tradition. Children, animals and adults are given equal narrative importance and individual characterization. They express themselves variously in Italian, in dialects, in non-semantic codes and in appropriate combinations of the above. In contrast to the terse historical chronicles of worldwide events that preface each chapter, the characters apprehend reality not in the pseudo-chronological time of history but existentially, in a purely perceptual manner, through intimations, memories, hearsay, visions and rumors of events to come. Thus the ambiguous title word, meaning at once "history" and "story," reflects the formal conception of the novel and its other major theme— namely, the influence of power-motivated historical events upon the random path of individual destiny.

Teresa de Lauretis. *Books Abroad.* 49, 1975,
p. 527

The problem with all this is what exactly it may have to do with history. Each year of the novel's action is prefaced by a three- or four-page summary of the year's principal events in world politics. These summaries reflect a kind of simplified popular Marxism that has become all too familiar in the 1960s and 1970s: Schematically and tendentiously, world disasters are attributed to the sinister machinations of big industry everywhere; and, by the concluding summary, even the clichés of the ecological apocalypticists (the poisoning of the environment with plastics, and so forth) are trundled out. The question is not whether there are grains of truth in such formulas but whether they help the novelist in his work—and in this crucial respect I am afraid their effect is calamitous.

There is nothing beloved in the novel, be it cat, dog, child, man or woman, that does not end up being hideously destroyed, and the novelist will go twenty pages out of her way to catch a good last agony, even pursuing one quite peripheral character all the way to the Russian front in order to evoke his hallucinations as he expires from frostbite. Again and again, Morante is unable to resist a pathetic overload of detail and commentary. . . .

When you assume that all history is a variation on the single theme of fascism, and that all evil—even, it would seem, a child's epilepsy inherited from the mother—is perpetrated by monolithic Powers not even allowed access to the scene of the novel, all that remains of historical experience is the pangs of victimhood; and those, after abundant repetition and heavy insistence, are likely to leave readers numbed—and with a sense that the sharpness of authorial indictment has finally been eroded by sentimentality.

Robert Alter. *New York Times Book Review.*
April 26, 1977, p. 34

The publication in 1948 of *Menzogna e sortilegio,* a lengthy novel which immediately elicited favorable reviews, granted Elsa Morante a position of privilege in the postwar Italian literary world. Subsequent works made her name a household word, especially *La storia,* which consistently appeared on the country's bestseller lists in the early 1970s and became a subject of heated discussion in both literary and political circles. However, even in the midst of lavish praise for *La storia,* many regarded *Menzogna e sortilegio* [as] Morante's best creation. The novel has at times been read as a haunting portrayal of the pleasures and displeasures imbedded in triangular relationships, or as a nostalgic transfiguration of bourgeois tales into myth. In this article I will concentrate on the problems of reading and writing which underlie the narrative: reading as pleasurable mystification or disruptive questioning; and writing as cognitive undertaking, deceptive ruse, or authoritarian, inquisitorial exchange.

All the characters in *Menzogna e sortilegio* are engaged in one way or another in reading personal events novelistically or in understanding fiction referentially. The most voracious consumer of the written word is undoubtedly the narrator herself, Elisa De Salvi. In the course of her adolescence Elisa moved from outer gregariousness to inner brooding, her imagination providing the essential refuge for a perhaps indulgent existential uneasiness. Sequestered in her padded room, Elisa tells us, she willingly fell victim to the allure of books, and her career as a reader began. Her choices ranged from chivalric romances to saints' lives, from extravagant legends to romantic outpourings, each text promising relief from a sense of disorder in life and release from feelings of discontent. And yet there was a subversive penchant in her innocuous, voyeuristic pastime. Because she was angry with her life, Elisa hungered for adventures and sublimated worldly desires in worldy temptations. Fictional kings and queens acquired familial physiognomies; court knights, dukes, and prophets evoked domesticized identifications; and her days came alive with a disquieting, protean charm. . . .

It is this reading that Elisa decides one day to reject. She needs only to survey her past few years to realize that the rhetorical indulgences that were nourishing her fantasies were actually stunting her growth . . . and that her readerly desires—which had slowly imprisoned her both in her own and in her parents' world—were paradoxically fostering her psychological self-erasure. She has reduced herself, she admits, to the condition of a zombie buried alive in her own house. In order to move away from this dysphoria and put an end to this self-imposed exile, she recognizes that she has to leave the world of daydreams and enter the world of reality, and, in the process, to change her diet of lies into one of truth.

However, release may come only when Elisa is able to identify the roots of her compulsion to fantasize and the source of her enthrallment with the past. . . .

Only after diagnosing the disease can Elisa prescribe the therapy: re-memoration [of things she knows] and anamnesis [of things she can recollect through oneiric absorption] will be her daily medicine, and writing this reflection will be her cure.

Valeria Finucci. *Italica.* 65 (1988), pp. 308–9

"Alibi" is the title of a poem and is also the name of a collection of Morante's poetry. She deliberately used this word in her well-known essay—reply to "nine questions on the novel." Critics often refer to this essay when they define her position on art and the role of writers in presenting "incorruptible poetic truths." Not one, however, has focused on the definition of *alibi* in relation to her own poems and narrative. Morante stated:

> Instead of invoking the muses, the modern novelist is led to arouse a *reciting-I* (protagonist and interpreter) that can serve as an *alibi*. Almost as if to say, in his or her own defense: "Of course that which I represent is not *the* reality but a reality relative to the I of myself, or to another I, different in appearance from myself, which in substance, however, belongs to me, and in which I now impersonate myself entirely.

This statement is most revealing, especially for its use of such terms as *alibi* and *reciting-I,* which, while referring in general to narrative voices in novels, can and should also apply to Morante's own writings. The term *alibi* includes such major Morante figures as Andrea and her narrator-protagonists Elisa, Arturo, and Manuele; whether male or female, they all function in various degrees as the author's dramatic personae. In brief, they are all modifications and complements of the same autobiographical, narrating subject. Andrea from *La scialle andalusa* (The Andalusian shawl), Arturo from *L'isola di Arturo* (Arturo's island), and Manuele from *Aracoeli* represent Morante's most important male alibis. They both hide and reveal the author's intimate desires, fears, delusions, and personal experiences related to love and rejection; through them, the writer accentuates the drama of addiction to expressive love and the anxieties of emotional exclusion. . . .

Analyses of Morante's alibis in her poetry and prose give no sure familiarity with the real author. Nevertheless, they facilitate a highly valuable exposure of a writer who has consistently focused on the traumatic experiences of love, rejection, and solitude. In these alibis, the implied author—or better, the autobiographical narrating subject—grows increasingly neurotic and obsessed with feeling unattractive, abandoned, and unloved. Cesare Garboli states that in reading Morante's narrative he easily juxtaposes and confuses the author who emerges from the work with the real-life person whom he knows. According to Garboli, the actual Elsa Morante remains like a beautiful mystery that is hard to define. Morante's alibis are certainly approachable and relatively easy to analyze, but their real author remains a mysterious and fascinating Sheherazade who preferred to reveal herself through her stories, myths, and fables. Elsa Morante has in fact chosen to remain wrapped in a veil of fiction and narrative lies that intend simultaneously to reveal and hide universal and poetic truths.

Rocco Capozzi. In Santo L. Aricò, ed.
*Contemporary Women Writers in Italy: A
Modern Renaissance* (Amherst: University
of Massachusetts Press, 1990), pp. 11–12, 22

MOREJÓN, NANCY (CUBA) 1944–

It is interesting to note that although in many cases the objective principle of the oral testimonial form is of a historical nature, the researchers have situated themselves as participating in an artistic experience, which broadens the dimensions of their inquiries. In *Lengua de pajaro* (Bird's tongue), Nancy Morejón and Carmen Gonce relate their experiences during a historical study of the industrial community of Nicaro in Cuba, which confirms the feelings of Barnet and others for whom the *testimonio* has been a profoundly moving experience on many levels.

> How are we going to encapsulate in our historiographical criteria, our cold inquiries, our ready-made questions, the oral testimony of those individuals who for the first time were reflecting on their own lives, recognizing themselves as a "society," narrating with a certain dose of exaggerations a sort of epic wonder each historic event?

The idea of the "epic wonder" and the study of a "character" by means of the narratives that unfold in interviews can lead, depending on the author's project and creativity, to a work of great literary value.

Margarite Fernández Olmos. *Revista/Review Interamericana*. 11, 1981, p. 71

Nancy Morejón . . . is serious in her commitment to literature and to her people, yet she shares with Louise Bennett, María Arrillaga, and Elsa Tió a typical Antillean humor, with its particularly Cuban form of joking and teasing. During my interview with her in San Juan, she was eager to read from her work and to share herself. She has written literary and theater criticism for Cuban newspapers, and has done translations and editorial work for a government publishing house.

Morejón belongs to a generation of Cuban poets who learned their lessons in traditional meter and verse before experimenting with their own creativity. This accounts for the variety of technical skill in her poetry, and also for the debts she repays to her literary predecessors in selected epigraphs, such as the one by Walt Whitman in "Aguas de Corinta" (Waters of Corinth), and her choice of content, for example in "Disillusion for Rubén Darío," referring to the Nicaraguan precursor of Modernism. Her versatility is not limited to her tone and literary style, but also includes a wide range of subject matter. She can be romantic as in "Impressions" where she recreates the presence of two lovers in a boat, lying in the sun, or, she can be political as in a series of very different poems wherein she pays tribute to the Cuban Revolution, and its protagonists.

In her most widely recognized poem to date, "Black Woman," Morejón pays homage to her womanhood and to her blackness in an epic-style, free verse poem which finds its strength in the personal affirmations that punctuate her tale of forced enslavement, beatings, humiliation, child bearing, rebellion, and finally, independence. The first person narrative voice is a powerful device that engages the reader with its immediacy. Morejón recreates the original impressions of an African woman deposited on Cuba's shores after a seemingly endless ocean odyssey. The slave draws strength from her past in order to survive and recalls "cuánta epopeya mandinga" (the body of African stories and folktales) she left behind. . . .

Morejón uses both Cuba and America's stark history lessons in slavery, debasement, and lynching to create carefully controlled poems that inspire outrage through the very coolness of their metaphors and measured tone.

Morejón also dedicated a poem to the Jamaican people, although different from Bennett's witty and amused portraits of her people. She gave the poem the English title "Farewell," lending an ironic twist to the imagery from the popular song, "Jamaica Farewell," which alludes to the much traveled and emigrating Jamaican, always leaving the island for work abroad. Apparently inspired by the victory of Socialist Michael Manley, Morejón rejoices in the prospect of the new Jamaica, whose native sons and daughters can finally return from abroad to help build the island's future. The poet encourages them to "Say goodbye, a Jamaican goodbye."

And for Chile, defeated only temporarily, she wrote "Eres tú."

Gloria Feiman Waldman. In Doris Meyer and Margarita Fernández Olmos, eds. *Contemporary Women Writers of Latin America* (Brooklyn: Brooklyn College Press, 1983), pp. 52–53

The contemplation of everyday experiences rarely occurs through a reader's own volition, primarily because one takes those experiences for granted. Many writers, particularly poets, often present a fresh vision of ordinary life, forcing the reader to contemplate anew what has become so familiar. A constant in the poetry of Nancy Morejón is precisely defamiliarization of the everyday. In fact, the young Cuban poet elevates the quotidian to the highly poetic, and understatement is the primary figure of speech through which her view is communicated. While much of her work exemplifies this treatment of the quotidian, three poems in particular will be the focus of this study: "The Supper," "Richard Brought His Flute," and "Black Woman."

These three works reveal in part why this writer of the post-revolution era is the poetic voice most approximating the depth and sincerity of Nicolas Guillén's verse on revolutionary struggle or black people. At the same time, however, Morejón's gift for poetry establishes her as a singular talent with a definitive poetic style of her own.

Generally speaking, Morejón's poetry is highly lyrical, expressing intimately her own poetic world. On the whole, those verses that poeticize common, everyday realities know no thematic boundaries, ranging from traditional reflections on love—both fulfilled and unrequited, both erotic and spiritual—to a less conventional thematic stance related to the Cuban revolution. Moreover, it is not uncommon for one poem to contain several of the thematic projections comprising the whole of her trajectory.

Despite the division of her work into various subtheses, two overarching emphases stand out in the poetry—blackness and revolution. . . .

Morejón's very emphasis on what is not considered "highbrow" culture places her in the tradition of such Spanish-American poets as Pablo Neruda and Nicolás Guillén among others. Hers is an insistence on the impurity of the literary act—both of writing and of reading. As such, her poetry can incorporate unconventional literary expression. As is indicated here, these non-traditional expressions characterize much of her work, especially with regard to mundane endeavors. However, what continues to insure the poeticalness and, therefore, the longevity of her work has not been solely the thetic emphases, but rather the manner in which she shows her appreciation for the quotidian.

Yvonne Captain-Hidalgo. Callaloo. 10, 1987,
pp. 596, 604

MORGENSTERN, BEATE (GERMANY) n.d.

Morgenstern's central themes are . . . isolation and alienation in a highly structured society. Many of her stories focus on individuals who don't or can't conform to social expectations. They are outsiders who feel rejected and stigmatized by their peers. Some struggle, sometimes to the point of self-destruction, for some form of social recognition to counterbalance their sense of inadequacy or failure. Others struggle just to make contact.

In "Ein gutes Mädchen" (A good girl), Ilsemarie, an unpopular, unattractive, ungifted student, sees her role as a FDJ leader as her only chance to excel. When her efforts are met with indifference, she becomes increasingly determined and finally obsessed with forcing her classmates, if not to admire her, at least to accept her authority. Her stubborn pursuit of this goal leaves her physically ill and completely alienated from her peers.

The sense of alienation is explored in several stories which center on attempts to communicate. Many of Morgenstern's characters try desperately to break through their isolation and finally talk to, rather than past, one another. While some fail, in "Jenseits der Allee," two women do manage to establish contact with one another. Carefully exploring one another's tastes and opinions, and backing away from any points of disagreement, they tentatively establish some common ground on which to begin a friendship. In other stories, characters simply move past one another, enclosed in their inability to grasp or communicate their emotions. Unable to break out of their isolation, they smother their sense of frustration in anger, alcohol, or denial.

Morgenstern's narrative style is very low-key and controlled. She uses small pieces of conversation and details of daily life to construct her stories mosaic-fashion. Very little happens in these stories; what little action does take place serves to reveal character. Several stories simply present people thinking or talking. The narrative perspective alternates between dialogue, private thoughts, and purely external description, producing a sense of emotional distance from the characters.

Morgenstern does not pass moral judgment on her characters. While "Ein gutes Mädchen" and "Bruno," another story in the volume, both involve individuals who deform themselves in an attempt to fit into a social mold and who try to use that mold to control others, the characters appear as much victims as those they try to manipulate; they are trapped within a rigid set of conventions. Morgenstern's stories do not interpret events or offer simple explanations; the author chooses and arranges her details with great sensitivity to many very different characters in a wide range of conflicts, and leaves the reader with no easy answers.

Dorothy Rosenberg. In Margy Gerber et al.,
eds. *Studies in GDR Culture and Society,*
Vol. 4. (Lanham, Maryland: University
Press of America, 1984), pp. 190–92

The memory of her childhood and of the people surrounding it proves [In *Nest im Kopf* (Nest in the head)] to be both compelling and deceptive to the nearly forty-year-old Anna as she decides to return to the rural East Germany of her youth for a week's visit. She finds herself in search of the security of the parental nest, the time in her life when the world still seemed whole and in harmony with God and the universe. In returning, however, she also finds that this time of innocence exists only in her memory and is more the product of her imagination than of reality. Even the pietistic morality of the Saxon *Gotteshuter* community which had resolutely carried on the faith of the fire-tested Jan Hus for centuries had offered no certain protection from the imperfections of the world.

The discovery of this realization is part of a series of encounters Anna has with the people and the objects of her youth. The limits of this world are the family, relatives, past and present, neighbors, and, in its farthest extent, the village. The world that lies beyond intrudes only in its pale reflection and remains the world of Caesar, unquestioned and unexamined. It is only *Kinder, Küche,* and especially *Kirche,* since Anna grows up in a rectory, which dominates in this world. Even evil has no place here, and the seduction of the pubescent Anna by one of the pious brothers of the community becomes a matter of routine rather than drama. The shadowy figures of this narrow world slide in and out of the pages of the novel in a series of repetitive scenes. The telescoping of time and events eventually becomes more confusing than illuminating.

What remains is an immersion into a community so tightly capsuled in its own vortex, so *weltfremd* that even the dramatic and compelling changes in the outside world are unable to affect it. This is an inner world which accepts the changes that it can, avoids those it cannot, and adjusts to those which it can neither accept nor avoid. It is from this intimate and uncritical perspective that we encounter the events involving the members of Anna's family. It is these finely drawn, almost lovingly exquisite descriptions of people and the events in their lives which give the book its special character. Although Anna claims at the beginning of the novel "that people interest me," it is a sentiment which the reader can share only intermittently.

One cannot but wonder if Morgenstern's foray into a realm of East German life seldom before explored to such an extent in fiction is an indication that the elusive and tortured concept of "Erbe," designated to manifest the seamless passage of tradition into the new society of the present, has now been extended to include the realm of pietism and sectarian religion. The self-assured and confident Anna, who finds that her being "well and expensively dressed" is a vital part of her present accomplishments, remains in essential harmony with her pietistic upbringing; the distance from the *Gotteshut* of her childhood is a matter of growth and not of conflict.

Hans J. Fabian. World Literature Today. 63,
1989, p. 672

MORGNER, IRMTRAUD (GERMANY) 1933–90

Irmtraud Morgner's very long and complex montage-novel, *Life and Adventures of Troubadora Beatriz as Chronicled by her Minstrel Laura* (1974) can be read as a textual field of struggle between oppositional knowledge and the theoretical and unitary discourse of traditional Marxism. Western critics have read the text as a compromising affirmation of the status quo and the GDR's "evolution" toward sexual equality on the one hand, and as a radical critique of that society, its patriarchal structures, and legitimating discourse on the other. The text actually takes up the question of women's emancipation within a socialist society more directly and more polemically than any other literary text to come out of the GDR. However, in spite of the polemics against patriarchy, and indeed, perhaps because of them, the text actually constrains the emancipatory possibilities which it opens up. The ruptures introduced into the text and the GDR by other insistent "feminine" desires are foreclosed by the discursive limitations of orthodox Marxist rhetoric and by the supposed historical necessities that govern the development of GDR society.

Life and Adventures is thematically and structurally marked by the tension between the necessities of the GDR's "really existing socialism" and the unnamed and unassimilable desires, which intervene and which would defy the conceptual and political grasp of conventional wisdom and social structures.

The tensions develop around the fantastic legend of Beatriz de Dia, the medieval troubadora who enters the GDR in the late 1960s after having awakened in France from an 810-year sleep. Beatriz's bonds with mythical and "real" female characters represent the structural and thematic intervention of unconscious and "irrational" desires into the repressive stability of GDR socialism and traditional textual authority. The complex and sustaining relationships among the women expose the micro-structural bases of patriarchal oppression by raising questions of family structure, sexuality and patterns of emotional and political dependency, questions which situate the constitution of power at the level of psychosexual relations. Their questions and unorthodox relationships begin to threaten conventional Marxist conceptions of the meaning of emancipation. Indeed, the threat which Beatriz and female bonding pose to social stability and ideological certainties is emphasized throughout the text by the fears and rationalized denials with which various GDR characters respond to that challenge; for many of the male characters, Beatriz and her fantastic presence clearly represent a world without absolutes, without Fathers, without surrogate gods of any kind, a world which is not only threatening, but unimaginable. Beatriz brings the fantastic, the extravagant, the impossible and the erotic to bear on the apparently "natural" order, its discursive underpinnings and its literary representation; her exploits and textual interventions have the potential for exposing the political nature of conventional distinctions between the reasonable and unreasonable, between natural and unnatural, between truth and fiction.

Biddy Martin. *Studies in Twentieth-Century Literature*. 5, 1980, pp. 60–61

The novel *Amanda* explores and bears witness to a new potential within the genre; a seemingly tiny world, namely that of everyday life in the DDR in the 1970s, is connected to big world problems. This is clearly a trend that generally distinguishes our most significant works of literature in recent times. In the hands of Irmgard Morgner—and by this we mean not merely her style of writing—this means: The reader must follow the author into the realm of the fantastic, but also to the place where the daily efforts of a single mother raising a child are very precisely depicted. It is a witch's novel, for the main character—Laura Amanda Salman—appears from the beginning to be separated into an earthly half, the streetcar driver Laura, and a witch half, Amanda.

In her 670-page book, Irmtraud Morgner can be analyzed in accordance with a statement that is attributed to "a certain Anna." While attending the "46th Round Table meeting of the faction of witches and fools" (which has gathered initially at the French Cathedral on the Academy Square in Berlin), the aforementioned Anna opens the discussion with two statements which could serve as the novel's motto: "Until now, the philosophers have interpreted the world from a masculine perspective. But what counts now is that we interpret it from a feminine perspective as well, so that we can work toward humane change." To read this as merely an ironic or perhaps even humorous variation on Marx and Engels's well-known second thesis on Feuerbach would be to miss the seriousness with which the author defends the central concerns of her book. Still, her conscious reliance on the statement "The philosophers have only *interpreted* the world differently, but what counts is that they *change* it" cannot escape notice. In the search for much-needed solutions to the actual human problems faced in the early 1980s, nothing short of the real emancipation of women within actual East German society can be acknowledged as having made a decisive contribution. And these problems, too, are mentioned in connection with a famous formulation: "The rulers of the earth commanded three world wars. The planet was still rich after the first, still intact after the second, and uninhabitable after the third." Within this context, the words of a United States Secretary of State who believes that there are more important things than peace are met with the following challenge: "War, as a classical means for realizing political goals, must be made taboo."

The frame narrative can be viewed as an important attempt to find a possible way of dealing with completely relevant problems—which are often answered within the sphere of political journalism, manifestos, or in any case through public, political activities—within the work of art itself. Irmtraud Morgner, in her use of frame narrative, makes the noble attempt to close or at least to narrow the gap that exists between the time period taken up in the epic work and real world happenings. Facts from real world events—including the confrontation course and missile strategies adopted by the Reagan administration, as well as global environmental problems—can generally be attributed to the early 1980s, that is, to the period of time in which the novel was completed. In this way, the novel reveals its direct connection to everyday life in East Germany, complete with its utopian-fantastical excesses. As a result, of course, the novel contains a didactic-activist element. The author expresses with clarity and directness her subjective and partial opinion concerning both existential questions of humanity and problems in everyday life, the latter of which seem slight in comparison. And in this way, she and her work assume their own position within the multifaceted realistic literature that exists in 1983 in the German Democratic Republic.

Klaus Kandler. In Siegfried Romisch, ed.
DDR-Literatur '83 im Gesprach (Berlin:
Aufbau, 1984), pp. 155–56, 162

Irmtraud Morgner's optimistic world view in *Leben und Abenteuer der Trobadora Beatriz nach Zeugnissen ihrer Spielfrau Laura* (1974) has changed to a deep-seated concern about the world's chances for survival. Her new novel, *Amanda. Ein Hexenroman* (1983), is an expression of this concern for humanity's future, with emphasis on women's part in shaping that future. . . .

Amanda was not written to expose the wrongs historically done to women—although it does that too—but rather to give an illustration of women gaining the confidence and influence they need to help lead humanity away from the path to self-destruction. . . .

Morgner's humor sets her writings apart not only from Wolf's *Kassandra*, but from the larger body of German literature by women written in the last decade as well. It is a quality of her style and a vehicle for her thoughts, not a gratuitously inserted element. "Sie lachte nur bei ernsten Gelegenheiten," Beatriz, the chronicler of *Amanda*, writes of her former *Spielfrau* Laura: a fitting characterization for much of Morgner's writing in her new novel. . . .

As with Morgner's humor, her fantasy, too, has a socio-critical function. . . . In the free space for creation that Morgner's fantasy opens up, she has given her own interpretation to images from the prehistoric past. Outstanding among these are the figures of Beatriz, Arke (a Morgner invention), and Pandora. These three females, who, in fantastically imaginative ways, incorporate and reveal new possibilities for rescuing humanity today, deserve closer scrutiny. . . .

Morgner relates her theories in *Amanda* to the contemporary world situation and stresses that those women and men who have begun asserting the new value system she has outlined metaphorically have already made some progress in establishing this system. . . .

Will the European peace movement on which she built her hopes in *Amanda* last long enough to fulfill the promise it holds to lead in "the whole victory" for Morgner, for women, for humanity? The name of that victory is *Frieden* (Peace)

Sheila K. Johnson. In Margy Gerber et al.,
eds. *Studies in GDR Culture and Society,*
vol. 4 (Lanham, Maryland: University Press
of America, 1986), pp. 45–47, 61–62

I have found that [the animosity toward women] does not lie in the satirization of the women's movement, but rather, as Janssen-Jurreit once observed, in the analysis that is left out. I arrived at this conclusion, among other things, while conducting my comparative analysis of Irmtraud Morgner's *Life and Adventures of Beatrice the Troubador,* 1974, a novel that closely resembles Günter Grass's *Butt* in terms of its cultural-political pretentions and its form. Above all, I am referring to each work's use of fantastic elements and employment of montage-technique.

I have also found that these two figures are well suited for examplifying and concretizing the results of my comparison. And that the question persists whether there is a difference between masculine and feminine modes of writing.

I begin with Morgner, an East German author who was born in 1933. Uwe Parnitzke is the male figure who lures the female Provençal troubadour out of her 800-year slumber, awakening her to life in the summer of 1970. Already impressed by what Uwe has to say in his lecture about socialist society, she is even more impressed by what the female narrator calls "Uwe's divorce confessions." "What a marvelous land this must be," thinks Beatrice, "where men like him are twice made subject to such abuse." Here I come, she cries, heaving a sigh of relief after her terrifying experiences in the modern French "society for keeping women."

Uwe Parnitzke is what Morgner calls a "victim of a time of upheaval." In contrast to most men, he is subjected to far-reaching contradiction and divisiveness. His relationships to women fall victim to the conflict between the male role he has inherited and acquired on the one hand, and, on the other, his insight into the need to free himself from the gender role with which he is already struggling, due to his natural inclinations. Against his will, he is anchored in the past and its customs, to which belongs the exploitation of women. This dilemma makes him into a "victim of progress," and not only in the political sense. His own conscience holds him back, for it is more progressive and "more humane" than the customs to which he has adapted himself.

All the characteristics that women love in him are those "that he unofficially perceived to be signs of weakness. And probably resisted." Uwe, the journalist, perceives his first wife, Laura, to be superior. "And himself to be inferior, as a result: and that depressed him," the text tells us. It is not the actual feeling that depresses Uwe, but rather his reflections about it and his bad conscience for it. Laura is at the moment a professionally employed Germanist. Valeska, his second wife, wants to do justice to "Uwe and his type" and does not personally blame him for his ethical habits because "history, that which has evolved, can not be condemned." She realizes that Uwe has quite a load to carry with the problems of this time of upheaval, this time when "history is being outgrown." Writing helps her to come to terms with it all. Despite Uwe's convictions, he finds it oppressive when his wife earns more money than he. His revival only comes when his wife lies ill and is dependent on his aid. For Laura and Valeska, there remains no other choice: they seek a divorce from their crumbling husband.

Sexuality is another factor in this divorce decision. Uwe cannot seriously believe that a grown woman like Laura or Valeska could be disgusted by "giant muscle-men." That stands in the way of his sexuality. "He can only sleep face down, only love face up." He probably never even comes: these are the words of Uwe. Valeska's comment: "He was the most beautiful man I ever knew. If only we had met a hundred years later, then we could have enjoyed each other for a long, long time."

Synnove Clason. In Alfred Schöne, ed.
Kontroversen, alte und neue (Tübingen: Max
Niemeyer, 1986), pp. 104–5

Morgner's importance to East German literature, to the critique of socialism and patriarchy, and to feminist aesthetics has been recognized internationally, though it would be wrong to equate her feminism with its various counterparts in the West. Her debt to the utopian thinking of Ernst Bloch is apparent. The highly complex style of this selection, which is taken from Morgner's epic novel *Leben und Abenteuer der Trobadora Beatriz,* reflects the author's desire to teach her readers to defy traditional definitions of empirical reality by playing with imaginative possibilities. An earlier English version, titled "The Rope," omitted the passages involving electron scattering. The story works well without them, but it is precisely in the playful use of the language of nuclear physics that Morgner creates a metaphor for Vera Hill's situation as a woman in the male-dominated scientific-industrial establishment.

The title of this excerpt ["The Third Fruit of Bitterfeld"] alludes to the East German industrial city associated with the famous 1959 conference that launched "the Bitterfeld Movement" to integrate the world of production into the creative arts. It is the third piece in the novel to describe the life of a working woman.

Nancy Lukens and Dorothy Rosenberg, eds.
*Daughters of Eve: Women's Writing from
the German Democratic Republic* (Lincoln:
University of Nebraska Press, 1993), p. 136

MORRISON, TONI (UNITED STATES) 1931–

The tone of much black writing is forensic, a public tone that speaks across ethnic and political gaps, that at one time or another has been used to persuade or frighten whites into action and to cajole or exhort other blacks into solidarity and revolution. Toni Morrison's tone, in this lyrical story [*The Bluest Eye*] about growing up black and poor in a northern Ohio town, is a more private tone, the tone, as it were, of black conversation. All of which is not meant to imply that Mrs. Morrison has no political consciousness, far from it, but only that she has found a way to express that consciousness in a novel instead of a harangue. She has the skill to convince you that she is telling it like it is without constantly telling you that's what she's doing—and that you'd better pay attention to her.

This story commands attention, for it contains one black girl's universe: alienation from the white world in a candy store, a sad neighbor girl made pregnant by her father and eventually driven mad, class conflict among black playmates, deracinated adults fighting each other and splitting up, a father who denies his son, and most of all that sad little girl, who wishes her eyes were blue, the bluest eyes in the world.

The girl never got those eyes; she was spiritually destroyed instead, and no marigolds bloomed either that year. To the narrator, those twin losses seem connected: "I even think now that the land of the entire country was hostile to marigolds that year. The soil is bad for certain kinds of flowers. Certain seeds it will not nurture, certain fruit it will not bear, and when the land kills of its own volition, we acquiesce and say the victim had no right to live. We are wrong, of course, but it doesn't matter. It's too late. At least on the edge of my town, among the garbage and the sunflowers of my town, it's much, much, much too late."

Raymond A. Sokolov. *Newsweek.*
November 30, 1970, pp. 95–96

I've just finished reading Toni Morrison's book, *The Bluest Eye,* and my heart hurts. It's all I can do not to lie down and cry myself into some kind of relief from the life-pain of Pecola, the central character. She is a girl born black, poor and, by majority standard, ugly. It is also an account of the people that surround her, especially Pauline, her mother, and Cholly, her father. They are the kind of people that all black people know of—or are—to varying degrees. . . .

Toni Morrison has not written a story really, but a series of painfully accurate impressions. How all of the people she talks about arrive where we meet them is what she is about with such great precision. She gives us a sense of some of the social elements of some of the people, black and white, that contribute to the erosion of innocence and beauty. To read the book, however, is to ache for remedy.

In *The Bluest Eye* she has split open the person and made us watch the heart beat. We feel faint, helpless and afraid—not knowing what to do to cover it up and keep it beating. We think of remedies past and remedies in progress to apply somehow while the thrashing heart still beats. We must think faster and work harder and hope that maybe a new breed of people, tight with God, in some dark privacy, has a plan ready to set it all—all right.

Ruby Dee. *Freedomways.* 3, 1971,
pp. 319–20

The Bluest Eye was set among unforgiving provincial black people in a small Ohio town and charted the experience of two little sisters as they watched a friend first become a pariah and then sink into madness. The book's general outline—how witnessing and understanding tragedy forces the surrender of innocence and topples wide-eyed, precocious kids into unwilling maturity—is a familiar one in American, especially Southern, fiction; but its language was unique, powerful, precise and absolutely convincing, both spare and rich at once.

Now comes *Sula,* which features another pariah, spans the years 1921 to 1965, and seems to take place in the same setting. . . . While the setting and the characters continually convince and intrigue, the novel seems somehow frozen, stylized. A more precise yet somehow icy version of *The Bluest Eye,* it refuses to invade our present in the way we want it to and stays, instead, confined to its time and place. . . .

Reading it, in spite of its richness and its thorough originality, one continually feels its narrowness, its refusal to brim over into the world outside its provincial setting.

Sara Blackburn. The New York Times.
December 30, 1973, p. 3

[In *Sula*] Morrison at first seems to combine the aims of the Black Freedom Movement and women's liberation. Sula and Nel discover when they are 11 years old "that they were neither white nor male, and that all freedom and triumph was forbidden to them." When they grow up, Nel slips on the collar of convention. She marries, has two children, becomes tied to her "nest," a slave to racism and sexism. Sula goes to the big city, gets herself an education, and returns a "liberated" woman with a strange mixture of cynicism and innocence. . . .

But the perspective Morrison gives us upon these two black women is not pure black freedom or pure women's liberation. We may wish that Nel had absorbed some of Sula's independence of mind and willingness to take risks, and had not plunged so completely into the humdrum atmosphere of conventional family life, with all its sexist and racial overtones. Yet we cannot approve the freedom that licenses Sula casually to steal Nel's husband and condemn her childhood friend to a ruined life, while she just as casually abandons him. That is not freedom but selfishness, and it is immoral, however contemptuous we may be of the pitifully conventional virtues of married life, or however much we may feel that marriage oppresses women. Besides, the freedom that Sula achieves is as much a prison as it is liberation. Totally free, she becomes obsessed with herself, unable to love, uncontained by the normal rules and boundaries we have come to associate with human beings.

Morrison does not accept—nor does she expect us to accept—the unqualified tenets of either of the two current freedom movements. There is more to both society and the individual, and she subjects each of these to a merciless analysis.

Jerry H. Bryant. The Nation. July 6, 1974,
p. 24

The ordinary spars with the extraordinary in Morrison's books. What would be a classically tragic sensibility, with its implacable move toward crisis and the extremes of pity and horror, is altered and illuminated by a thousand smaller, natural occurrences and circumstances. There is death, and violence and hubris; but young girls bicker about menstruation and complain when their mothers insist that they apply clothespins to their noses as a beauty tactic. Spring brings ants and peach pits and scratched knees; fall, cod-liver oil and brown stockings. The very ordinary restlessness of two girls on a

summer day suddenly gives way to tragedy; death joins the stock of adolescent secrets they share. But teenage boys continue to strut on street corners;
and errands must be run for parents. Morrison has a musician's sense of
tone, texture, and emotional balance. Her themes are the stark and painful
plots; her improvisations are the sounds, smells, tastes, habits, idiosyncrasies
that surround them. . . .

Toni Morrison's books are filled with loss—lost friendship, lost love, lost
customs, lost possibilities. And yet there is so much life in the smallest acts
and gestures—Sula and Nel giggle over an old joke, the whores gossip in
front of Pecola—that they are as much celebrations as elegies.

Margo Jefferson. *Ms*. December, 1974,
pp. 34–35, 39

With the publication of *The Bluest Eye* in 1970 and *Sula* in 1974, Toni Morrison has laid claim to modern portrayal of the preternaturally sensitive but
rudely thwarted black girl in today's society. *Sula* is more fully dominated
by the title character, and Sula's characterization is the more complex; in
both novels, however, the protagonist is forced into premature adulthood by
the *donnée* of her life. Pecola's comprehension of her world is never articulated for either the other characters or the reader; Sula, too, remains a partial
enigma both in and out of her narrative. But the pain that each experiences
is made vivid and plain. Taken together, the two novels can—and I think
must—be read as offering different answers to a single question: What is to
become of a finely attuned child who is offered no healthy outlet for her
aspirations and yearnings? Pecola escapes in madness; Sula rejects society
for amoral self-reliance. For both, sensitivity is a curse rather than a blessing.
Morrison's second novel, though richer in many ways, is essentially a reworking of the material of the first with an alternative ending. Though her
characters' problems are conditioned by the black milieu of which she writes,
her concerns are broader, universal ones. Her fiction is a study of thwarted
sensitivity. . . .

Both Morrison's novels find beauty in sensitive response and show its
inevitable doom in a world in which only the hard, the cagey, and the self-
interested can triumph. Although both Pecola and Sula fill essential roles in
their communities, it is not the admirable in their characters that has an
influence. Pecola serves as the bottom-most societal rung whose lowliness
raises the self-esteem of everyone else, while Sula's acknowledged "evil"
encourages other's righteous sense of comparative superiority. Sensitivity is
lovely, but impractical, says Morrison. It is a pragmatic outlook, if not a
particularly happy one.

Joan Bischoff. *Studies in Black Literature*.
Fall, 1975, pp. 21, 23

Song of Solomon by Toni Morrison is a fine novel exuberantly constructed
and stylistically full of the author's own delight in words. Morrison has a

strong narrative voice and much of her novel's charm comes from an oral tradition, her love of simply telling, for example, how places and people got their names and how these names—Not Doctor Street, Ryna's Gulch, a boy called Milkman, Mr. Solomon, women known as Pilate, Sing and Sweet—contain history. There is an enchantment in Morrison's naming, a heightening of reality and language. Though each name is almost mythical it can be explained factually, thus the grandmother named Sing was really part Indian, Singing Bird, but not quite, the illegitimate daughter of a white gentleman, she was Byrd. In *Song of Solomon* lives are as strange as folk tales and no less magical when they are at last construed.

Toni Morrison has written a chronicle of a black family living in a small industrial city on the shores of Lake Michigan, but the method of the book is to enlarge upon the very idea of family history, to scrape away at lore until truth is revealed. And so we see that all the fears and misunderstandings that have shaped, say, the hostile marriage of Macon Dead and his wife Ruth, are as open to interpretation as the influence of dialect and The Good Book upon an old ballad. Milkman Dead, their son, finds that he is burdened by the truth about his parents and elated by a trip to Virginia to discover the remote romantic tales of his family's past. Morrison's novel demythologizes the Dead family, but even as Milkman learns the truth—there was no gold hidden in a southern cave, no lurid scene in which his mother threw herself naked upon her father's corpse—the new myths are created. There was, in fact, Milkman's great-grandfather, Solomon, a prodigious Biblical lover who enters into legend. "O Solomon don't leave me," the black children sing in their play, a corrupt version of Solomon's story, but of course their game, their song has the vitality of life over legend and so does Morrison's novel.

Song of Solomon is so rich in its use of common speech, so sophisticated in its use of literary traditions and language from the Bible to Faulkner, that I must add it is also extremely funny. Toni Morrison has a wonderful eye for the pretensions of genteel blacks and the sort of crude overstatements made by small time revolutionaries. Like many fine artists she dares to be corny—there is a funeral scene worthy of Dickens in which a crazed old woman sings "Who's been botherin' my baby girl" over her daughter, a poor deluded creature who has died of a broken heart. And like many great novels at the core it is a rather simple story of a boy growing to maturity. On the day Milkman Dead is born a mad insurance agent, Icarus-like, is trying to fly off Mercy Hospital. Milkman is finally weaned from the romance of the past and his own self-concern, a grown man ready for life, ready to fly. As for myth, Toni Morrison knows it's dead material unless you give it life—that's art.

Maureen Howard. *Hudson Review.* Spring,
1978, pp. 185–86

Toni Morrison's works are fantastic earthy realism. Deeply rooted in history and mythology, her work resonates with mixtures of pleasure and pain, wonder and horror. Primal in their essence, her characters come at you with the force and beauty of gushing water, seemingly fantastic but as basic as the earth they stand on. They erupt, out of the world, sometimes gently, often with force and terror. Her work is sensuality combined with an intrigue that only a piercing intellect could create.

Two of her three novels, *The Bluest Eye* (1970) and *Sula* (1974), reveal a consistency of vision, for they illustrate the growth of a theme as it goes through many transformations in much the same way as a good jazz musician finds the hidden melodies within a musical phrase. Both novels chronicle the search for beauty amidst the restrictions of life, both from within and without. In both novels, the black woman, as girl and grown woman, is the turning character, and the friendship between two women or girls serves as the yardstick by which the overwhelming contradictions of life are measured. Double-faced, her focal characters look outward and search inward, trying to find some continuity between the seasons, the earth, other people, the cycles of life, and their own particular lives. Often they find that there is conflict between their own nature and the society that man has made, to the extent that one seems to be an inversion of the other. Her novels are rich, then, not only in human characterizations but also in the signs, symbols, omens, sent by nature.

Wind and fire, robins as a plague in the spring, marigolds that won't sprout, are as much characterizations in her novels as the human beings who people them.

Barbara Christian. *Black Women Novelists*
(Westport, Connecticut: Greenwood Press,
1980), p. 137

Toni Morrison . . . has achieved major stature through the publication of only three novels. *The Bluest Eye* (1970) and *Sula* (1973) are brief, poetic works which explore the initiation experiences of their black, female, adolescent protagonists. *Song of Solomon* (1977) is a much longer but still lyrical story relating Macon (Milkman) Dead's search for familial roots and personal identity. Milkman's development is framed and illuminated by the maturation stories of three women important in his life, and the presence of these subplots in the tale of a male protagonist is a good indication of the importance of female initiation in Morrison's thought.

For Toni Morrison, the central theme of all her work is [beauty and love]. . . . Certainly, this theme is evident in *The Bluest Eye, Sula,* and *Song of Solomon,* their female characters searching for love, for valid sexual encounters, and, above all, for a sense that they are worthy. . . .

Morrison's early works explore the results for black women when the values are real and powerful but are designed primarily for middle-class whites. This concept certainly appears importantly in *Song of Solomon,* but that book also explores what happens to women whose values (and value) are determined by the men who control their lives. From the outset, these values are known by some of Morrison's female characters to be useless, even damaging, to them. . . .

In Toni Morrison's novels, she joins her basic theme with the initiation motif, and the initiation experiences, trying and painful as they are, fail. . . .

In her fiction, then, Morrison has united her theme, the explorations of love, and a traditional device, the initiation motif, along with a series of brilliantly dramatized foreshadowing events, skillfully made frames, and splendid characterizations. The resulting novels are compelling statements of the failure of human values. The inversion of a traditional motif—that is, the treatment of failed initiations—is successful, its effect devastating. The achievement is remarkable, making it clear that Toni Morrison is, indeed, a major American novelist.

Jane S. Bakerman. *American Literature.*
January, 1981, pp. 541–42, 563

Because Toni Morrison is black, female, and the author of *Song of Solomon* . . . one expects from her a fiction of ideas as well as characters.

Tar Baby has both. And it's so sophisticated a novel that *Tar Baby* might well be tarred and feathered as bigoted, racist, and a product of male chauvinism were it the work of a white male—say, John Updike, whom Morrison brings to mind.

One of fiction's pleasures is to have your mind scratched and your intellectual habits challenged. While *Tar Baby* has shortcomings, lack of provocation isn't one of them. Morrison owns a powerful intelligence. It's run by courage. She calls to account conventional wisdom and accepted attitude at nearly every turn of her story. She wonders about the sacrifice of love, the effects of racial integration, the intention of charity. Continually she questions both the logic and morality of seeking happiness or what Freud said passes for it, freedom from pain, by living in social accommodation. Although Morrison tells a love story—indeed, she tells two or three stories about love— her narrative lines run to complexities far beyond those of physical or emotional bonding. . . .

To believe Toni Morrison's characters isn't to believe their dramatic behavior. They are real people—in a story. The reason we can't credit their behavior is that, except for the most minor of figures, their actions are determined by Morrison's convictions, not their histories. Such is the curse of novels of ideas.

Webster Schott. *Book World.* March 22,
1981, pp. 1–2

All of Morrison's characters exist in a world defined by its blackness and by the surrounding white society that both violates and denies it. The destructive effect of the white society can take the form of outright physical violence, but oppression in Morrison's world is more often psychic violence. She rarely depicts white characters, for the brutality here is less a single act than the systematic denial of the reality of black lives. The theme of "invisibility" is, of course, a common one in black American literature, but Morrison avoids the picture of the black person "invisible" in white life (Ellison's Invisible Man trying to confront passersby). Instead, she immerses the reader in the black community; the white society's ignorance of that concrete, vivid, and diverse world is thus even more striking.

The constant censorship of and intrusion on black life from the surrounding society is emphasized not by specific events so much as by a consistent pattern of misnaming. Power for Morrison is largely the power to name, to define reality and perception. The world of all three novels is distinguished by the discrepancy between name and reality. . . .

Morrison's use of mythic structure, more and more overtly as her work develops, is central to her existentialist analysis. The heroic quest for identity achieved by conquest in and of the outer world embodies the human need for transcendence and self-definition; at the same time, the mythic sense of fate and necessity corresponds to the experience of facticity, both as irrevocable consequence and as concrete conditions for choice. Between those two poles—free heroism and determined role—move Morrison's characters. Further, mythic patterns are especially appropriate to her social concerns, since the mythic hero by his nature both embodies and transcends the values of his culture. These connections would be significant in most presentations of existential themes, but the special situations with which Morrison is concerned further complicate her use of myth. On the one hand, traditional myths claim to represent "universal" values and experiences; on the other, they clearly exclude or distort minority experiences by offering inappropriate or impossible models (e.g., Shirley Temple). . . .

Morrison, then, must capture "universal" aspirations without denying concrete reality, construct a myth that affirms community identity without accepting oppressive definitions. In the process, she must take the outline of the mythic structure, already so well suited to the existentialist quest for freedom and identity, and adapt it to the historical circumstances that surround this version of the quest. She values the myth as a way to design, not confine, reality; it remains to be seen how much further she can carry that notion.

Cynthia A. Davis. Contemporary Literature.
Summer, 1982, pp. 323–24, 341–42

Reading *The Bluest Eye,* I feel as if I have been in the abandoned store on the southeast corner of Broadway and Thirty-fifth Street in Lorain where Pecola Breedlove lives, as if I have been over the territory traversed by the eleven-year-old black girl as she skips among tin cans, tires, and weeds.

Morrison's skill in creating this very specific place accounts, in part, for my sense of the strangely familiar, the uncanny, when I read her novel—but only in part. While reading, I am familiar not only with Pecola's neighborhood but also, in a more generalized way, with Pecola's story. The sequence of events in this story—a sequence of rape, madness, and silence—repeats a sequence I have read before. Originally manifest in mythic accounts of Philomela and Persephone, this sequence provides Morrison with an ancient archetype from which to structure her very contemporary account of a young black woman. . . .

Although the stories of Philomela, Persephone, and Pecola do not form a composite whole, each of them, with its varied and individual emphases, contributes to a much larger woman's myth, which tells of denial and disintegration, which unveils the oft-concealed connections between male reason, speech, presence and female madness, silence, absence. As a young black woman, Pecola assumes an especially poignant position in this growing complex of mythic representations; she is absent (and absenced) in relation to the norms of male culture and in relation to the norms of white culture. Ultimately, I read Pecola's story as a tragic version of the myth; this twentieth-century black woman remains behind blue eyes, an inarticulate, arm-fluttering bird. But I cannot read *The Bluest Eye* as tragedy; Claudia, our sometimes-narrator, *speaks,* as does Morrison, our full-time novelist. Thus, although the novel documents the sacrifice of one black woman, it attests to the survival of two others—a survival akin to that of Philomela or Persephone—filled with hardship, but also with hope.

Madonne M. Miner. In Marjorie Pryse and
Hortense J. Spillers, eds. *Conjuring: Black
Women, Fiction, and Literary Tradition*
(Bloomington: Indiana University Press,
1985), pp. 176, 189

If Morrison's protagonists are always the "single, separate persons" of American individualism, then the community from which they have become isolated and alienated is always the community of shared beliefs, practices, stories, and histories that is the folk heritage of Afro-Americans. Toni Morrison is an inheritor as well as an innovator. Her predecessors—especially Zora Neale Hurston and Ralph Ellison—actively sought to bring the rich resources of the folk heritage under the transforming hands of the novelist. The lessons of these masters have not been lost on Morrison.

This is not to suggest that she merely "picks up where they left off." Rather, I think, inspired by their example, Morrison has looked very carefully at the way folk processes inform Afro-American life, and she produces highly concentrated images of that relationship that advance her complex vision of its meaning. Like Hurston and Ellison, she lives in this culture comfortably and finds in it all the resources needed for a full and satisfying moral universe. Nonetheless, what she sees when she looks at the behavior of black folk is different from what Hurston and Ellison see, and so her images—her inclusions and exclusions, her emphases and contrasts—are significantly different.

Like Hurston's and Ellison's, Morrison's fiction relies heavily on images of folk processes of communication. In *Song of Solomon* in particular, fictional replications of these folk processes dominate the narrative. Milkman's search for the meaning of his life is carried out through a set of interactions that increase in intensity—a verbal battle, a physical challenge, a hunt, a love affair—among others. But what hurls Milkman into this series of experiences is a story, his father's story of lost treasure. Seeking material value, Milkman discovers history—his place in the story of his ancestors—and that discovery gives him self-understanding.

Storytelling is the primary folk process in Toni Morrison's fictional world, and *Song of Solomon* contains many stories. Surrounding the central narrative of Milkman's growth to effective manhood are the stories that fill out the context that defines that manhood: the story of the black community and its place in the city; the story of his parents' marriage; the story of his friend Guitar's family; the story of the Seven Days; and, of course, the story of his ancestor Solomon.

Joseph T. Skerrett, Jr. In Marjorie Pryse and
Hortense J. Spillers, eds. *Conjuring: Black
Women, Fiction, and Literary Tradition*
(Bloomington: Indiana University Press,
1985), p. 193

Morrison's novels, of those of the major writers, have moved furthest away from the rebellious-woman stance of the mid-1970s, for she has focused, in her last two books, on men as much as women. Still she makes an attempt in both novels to figure out the possibilities of healing and community for her women characters. In *Song of Solomon* Pilate is such a character, although she derives her accumulated wisdom from her father and primarily benefits Milkman, her nephew, rather than any other woman in the novel. Jadine in *Tar Baby* is portrayed as the woman who has taken a position so far removed from her community that she becomes a part of the West. In her search for self, she becomes selfish; in her desire for power, she loses essential parts of herself. Thus Morrison has moved full circle from Pecola, who is destroyed by her community, to Jadine, who destroys any relationship to community in herself.

Barbara Christian. In Marjorie Pryse and
Hortense J. Spillers, eds. *Conjuring: Black
Women, Fiction, and Literary Tradition*
(Bloomington: Indiana University Press,
1985), pp. 242–43

From a newspaper clipping about a fugitive slave in Ohio who killed her own infant rather than see her returned to bondage in the South—"Now she would never know what a woman suffers as a slave . . . I will go singing to the gallows"—Toni Morrison made *Beloved.* From a photograph in James Van der Zee's *Harlem Book of the Dead* of the body of a young girl, shot at a party by a jealous boyfriend, who died refusing to identify her assailant ("I'll

tell you tomorrow"), Toni Morrison has made *Jazz*. All you need is radiance
and genius. . . .

Jazz is a book of dispossession and of haunting. Novel by novel, Toni
Morrison reimagines the lost history of her people, their love and work and
nightmare passage and redemptive music. It's a brilliant project, a ghostly
chorale, a constellation of humming spheres with its own gravity and now
this brand-new star, which is even trickier than usual. If jazz is a music the
performer composes himself, then this novel she calls *Jazz* is a book that
composes itself: "I have watched your face for a long time now, and missed
your eyes when you went away from me." It also *surprises* itself. . . .

I find that I want to roll around in Morrison's books, not a reviewer but
an epicure, even a voluptuary. Give me, instead of overviews, her banquet
of buttercakes and babies' ghosts, conjuring and "graveyard loves," Chicken
Little and cooked flesh, a spittle-web of spiders and the breath of snakes,
laws of hospitality and "men with the long-distance eyes"—after which, I
want to fall into that Shadrack sleep "deeper than the hospital drugs; deeper
than the pits of plums, steadier than the condor's wing; more tranquil than
the curve of eggs." This, of course, isn't criticism; it's gourmandizing. But
don't you already know as much as you want to about African oral traditions,
Uncle Remus, sermons, slave songs and the blues?

Morrison has said that their music no longer belongs exclusively
to her people, so novels are going to have to sing those origin myths and
archetypes. . . .

What could be more political than the fact that Morrison—with her wit,
poetry and passion, breadth of sympathy, depth of feeling, range of interest,
grasp of detail, powers of imaginative transformation, command of time, character, scruple, generosity and radiance, and magical mastery of the Mother
Tongue—turns out to be the best writer working in America? . . .

Beloved (1988) imagines what's left out of the slave narratives. Morrison
even went to Brazil to look at choke-collars and leg-irons you won't find in
any of *our* museums, and then she wrote a ghost story about history. At its
center is an act as awful as anything reported by the Hebrews, the Greeks or
the Elizabethans. Inside *Beloved*'s circle of space/time—spellbound, dream-
dazed—the living and the dead talk to and lay hands upon each other. Madness and memory cohabit. From this history, like a collective unconscious,
the dead, like the repressed, return. . . .

Ghost story, history lesson, mother-epic, incantation, folk and fairy
tale—of lost children and men on horseback; a handsaw, an icepick and a
wishing well; Denver's "emerald light" and Amy's velvet; spiders and roost-
ers and the madness of hummingbirds with needle beaks as dead babies are
offered up to a shameful God; a devouring past of everything that is unfor-
given and denied; a hunger to eat all the love in the world—*Beloved* belongs
on the highest shelf of our literature even if half a dozen canonized Wonder
Bread Boys have to be elbowed off. I can't now picture our literature without
it, between Whitman and Twain, the Other in Faulkner, an African Flannery

O'Connor, and who knows what other cultures she's looked into, which masks she's put on like a shaman, her secret antihistamines. Where *was* this book that we've always needed? Without *Beloved,* our imagination of America had a heart-sized hole in it big enough to die from.

John Leonard. *The Nation.* May 25, 1992,
706–7, 712, 714–15

MUGO, MICERE GITHAE (KENYA) 1942–

The Trial of Dedan Kimathi, a play Ngugi [wa Thiong'o] wrote with Micere Mugo, is particularly insightful in its portrayal of the functional relationships of languages in Kenyan contexts. An example of songs from the play, as well as examples of dramatic dialogue, will serve to illustrate how the authors have achieved this.

The play reconstructs the period of the Mau Mau struggle for independence in the 1950s. Dedan Kimathi was one of the guerrilla leaders who was captured, put on trial, and then executed by the colonialists. The ethnic group inhabiting the area in which the major struggle took place is the Gikuyu; most Mau Mau leaders were also members of this group. While the authors emphasize a nationalistic rather than an ethnic theme, the plot is set in an area where a non-national language, Kikuyu, is the mother tongue, and Kiswahili and English are the second languages.

Although the play's medium is English, it is framed by songs in Kiswahili. The lyrics are strongly political. . . . This same political theme is conveyed in the play's final song. The authors' choice of Kiswahili here reflects its use in expressing concepts of unity and nationhood. To use English would be to use the language of the oppressor to protest oppression; singing in any other Kenyan African language would ethnically mark it.

Jane E. Zuengler. In Braj B. Kachru, ed.
The Other Tongue: English across Cultures
(Urbana: University of Illinois Press, 1982),
pp. 118–19

The purpose of *Dedan Kimathi* is obviously very far from being the ideological consolation of the Kenyan élite, which is portrayed as the enemy of Kimathi and the willing collaborator with colonialism. Indeed, the play is a fervent protest against neo-colonialism, a call to renew the struggle for a genuine national liberation. It seems to have been inspired by, and certainly calls forth, an extreme loathing of the white settlers and their black and Asian bourgeois allies. (The portrayal of the Indian banker, with his caricatured accent, seems to reinforce a racism which the authors are purportedly denouncing.) *Dedan Kimathi* thus has an overt polemical intention . . . but its very fervor, which at times becomes hysteria, and the dramatists' decision to focus dramatically on the martyrdom of a Christ-figure, in the context of sustained religious imagery, also suggests an unconscious (or only partly conscious) ideological function related to the specific socio-historical circumstances of the play's writing and production.

I suggest that the rhetorical excess of *Dedan Kimathi* is in proportion to the absence of any mass-based political movement in Kenya capable of realizing successfully the political objectives advocated by the play. Unable to make an appeal to any really existing oppositional force in Kenyan politics, unable to delineate or assume the existence of any mass movement dedicated to the overthrow of neo-colonialism, the dramatists resort to an overcompensatory rhetorical mode, in which the affective force generated by the drama breaks through, so to speak, an unpropitious reality to celebrate an emotive but imaginary liberation. As the atheist may say of religious fervor, that it is never so great as when the God invoked is at his most absent, so *Dedan Kimathi* exploits the rhetorical excess characteristic of melodrama to depict and celebrate a kind of liberation which is not within immediate prospect in Kenya. Lacking a real revolutionary party or movement to give substance to their dream, the Kenyan dramatists must resort . . . to the cult of personality, epitomizing revolutionary struggle and redemption in the person of Kimathi. As Christ-like redeemer, he is possessed of a virtually magical, miracle-working power which in effect transcends historical limitation, even though the authors can truthfully assert that they are making no greater literal claim than that Kimathi's example is an inspiration to the struggling masses.

Brian Crow. *Ariel.* 14:3, 1983, pp. 30–31

In Ngugi wa Thiong'o's and Micere Mugo's *The Trial of Dedan Kimathi*, time and space coalesce in a symbolic drama of growth and development. Past and present events surrounding the "Mau Mau" revolt are recreated on stage to provide a historical perspective to and continuity of the anti-colonial movement in Kenya. Spatial shifts from distant guerrilla encampments in the Nyandarua forest to local prisons and courtroom installations in Nairobi emphasize the breadth and depth of the "Mau Mau" rebellion. The rapid montage design of the play overrides the accustomed cause-effect rational processes of the audience and consequently prohibits simplistic and limiting interpretations of staged events. In this structure, the characters are similarly transformed from their spatial and temporal individuality to symbolic, collective proportions.

The Trial of Dedan Kimathi is composed of two narrative plot movements: the first focuses on the capture, imprisonment and subsequent trial of Kimathi wa Wachiuri; the second features the transformation of two young Kenyans from childhood to adulthood in a symbolic "rite of passage." Both of these plot movements utilize the character of Kimathi wa Wachiuri as a symbol of the "Mau Mau" movement. . . .

[The] cultural and historical background provides the emotive force and the essential credibility to the symbolic character. Throughout the play he remains a stable and repeatable character in recognizable form who stands for the larger set of meanings understood by the common peasants as the "Mau Mau" movement. . . .

Utilizing the historical impressions of the Kenyan people as a foundation, Ngugi wa Thiong'o and Micere Mugo identify Kimathi as the armed resistance movement. As such, he embodies the peasants' armed resistance to British colonial oppression; he incorporates their hope for military and political expertise; he represents their profound love and respect for nature and the land; he personifies the people's need for a fearless, indomitable leader; he possesses great physical strength and ability to endure pain and suffering; he knows the natural environment and can survive on its bounty; and he has the moral courage to actively pursue their dreams of freedom from colonial oppression. For Ngugi wa Thiong'o and Micere Mugo Kimathi represents a stable model of Mau Mau against which the thoughts and actions of the other characters in the play are measured. For the initial courtroom scene in the Opening, where he is accused as a traitor and "provocateur," to the closing courtroom scene in the Third Movement where he is sentenced to death by hanging, Kimathi wa Wachiuri remains a steadfast symbol.

Change and transformation are however essential to the major thematic thrust of this drama. With Kimathi's trial and imprisonment as backdrop, Ngugi and Mugo chart the movement of a young boy and girl from their life of petty oppression of others to a life of self-sacrifice and social responsibility. They are turned away from victimizing each other in a microscopic parody of the wholesale victimization of the Kenyan peasants by European and African bankers, businessmen, politicians and clergy. While the scale of their oppressive behavior is hardly equivalent, it is symptomatic of a much larger dimension of oppression of the Kenyan people which Ngugi wa Thiong'o implies is current.

E. A. Mazel. *Canadian Journal of African Studies.* 17, 1983, pp. 239, 241–42

MUKHERJEE, BHARATI (INDIA–CANADA–UNITED STATES) 1942–

Mukherjee's two novels, *The Tiger's Daughter* (1973) and *Wife* (1976) reflect a world which refuses to hold together both at the individual and the cultural level. They are novels of and about isolation. Though peopled with innumerable characters, the protagonists do not relate to the others and are preoccupied in exploring the nature of their own identities. The two novels may appear to be similar at first reading, or as M. Sivaramakrishna views them, the second a continuation of the first, but it is unfair to treat them as such for the texture of both the novels is very different. Again when one begins to think in terms of disintegration and decay, it is possible to find parallels in the work of Conrad and other literary figures of the contemporary world, but that too would be bypassing the main concerns of the novels.

The question then arises: how does one approach these novels? How do the characters develop and what is the significance of the structure of the narrative? What kind of a sensibility do they express? Are they as Sivaramakrishna views them "explorations of the kind of sensibility which is inarticulate not because language fails but because the emotions are basically intractable to communication"? Perhaps, but they are more than that for these voiceless emotions arise out of a questioning of cultural issues, and the journeys which Tara *(The Tiger's Daughter)* and Dimple *(Wife)* undertake are journeys at a cultural level. Mukherjee's novels (like those of Ruth Jhabvala), are representative of the expatriate sensibility. This alone offers an understanding of the ambivalence present not only in the psychology of the protagonists but also that of the author; this helps us understand the satiric interludes, the ironic juxtapositions, the shifting point of view and also the final disintegration.

It is not easy to define the expatriate sensibility for it can be variously defined. Does it imply a total rejection or a ruthless questioning of tradition or a love/hate relationship with the native heritage? It would be differently expressed and fused in the texture of thought in each individual work. . . . The sense of time, as it exists in Mukherjee's novels, is important for the understanding of Dimple's life. The present and the past do not interact in *Wife.* In *The Tiger's Daughter* they do interact but the interaction is nonproductive. Again there is the significance of the authorial point of view: the heroines are the focus and both the episodes and the characters are seen through their responses and relationships. There is a questioning of the Indian situation, of how do the post-independence generations relate to their own country, how do they get past the colonial experience, and free themselves from the Western attraction. For both Tara and Dimple, however, there seems to be no way out: the distance they have covered cannot be retraced. They are immigrants both in place and mind, theirs is the foreignness of the spirit.

Jasbir Jain. *Journal of Indian Writing in English.* 13:2, 1985, pp. 12–13, 17–18

Bharati Mukherjee's third volume of fiction is finally out, a decade after the second novel: *The Tiger's Daughter* was published . . . in 1972 and *Wife* . . . in 1975, both about to be reissued by Penguin. And yes, it is different from the first two. It is not just that it is a volume of short stories: with *Darkness,* Bharati Mukherjee comes to terms with North America. . . .

The title of the volume echoes Conrad's *Heart of Darkness,* drawing our attention to violence at the heart of human affairs. "The Father" is a successful Indian businessman in Detroit who discovers that his very Americanized daughter, in her late twenties, is pregnant. He is pleased to think he is modern enough to come to terms with it and tries to persuade his wife to accept it. But when he discovers there is no father, that his daughter wanted to be an unmarried mother because no man was fit enough, his mind snaps: he beats her up and has to be restrained by his wife. This act of violence may be too sudden for the reader to take—I feel there has not been enough of a building-up and a letting-down. But then the violence is the key to a tapestry-like painting needing to be deciphered. Mukherjee herself provides us with clues. In "Saints," "Wayne holds Mom's head against dusty glass, *behind which an emperor in Moghul battledress is leading his army out of the capital"* (my emphasis). The last story in the volume is a description of the painting. The five-page work describes the Begum's wife: "In her capacious chamber the Begum waits, perhaps for death from the serving-girl, for ravishing, or merely the curtain of fire from the setting sun." We see the European adventurer, the Portuguese priests who have religious paintings for him: "They want to trick the emperor into kissing Christ who on each huge somber canvas is a white, healthy baby. The giant figures Hindu icons hidden in the hills." The painting is about the violence of history, feudal oppression, patriarchal oppression, colonialist adventurers, European efforts to get a foothold on the wealthy East. We should not, then, be surprised at the violence at Bangladesh nearly 400 years later. . . .

At the end of "Courtly Vision," we realize that the painting is hanging on a wall in an art gallery somewhere in the U.S., perhaps in New York City, waiting to be bought for a mere 750 dollars. Within "Courtly Vision," there is a further clue to Bharati Mukherjee's writing:

> Give me total vision, commands the emperor. His voice hisses above the hoarse calls of the camels. You, Basawan, who can paint my Begum on a grain of rice, see what you can do with the infinite vistas the size of my opened hand. Hide nothing from me, my co-wanderer. Tell me how my new capital will fail, will turn to dust and these marbled terraces be home to jackals and infidels. Tell me who to fear and who to kill but tell it to me in a way that makes me smile. Transport me through dense fort walls and stone grilles and into the hearts of men.

This is what the literary artist has done: she has penetrated below the surface, found the reality, and told the truth on several grains of rice. The leader wanted to be told the truth, even the bad news. But Bharati Mukherjee does not only focus on the bad news. She also celebrates life, the creative possibilities contained within people, the ability to give up fixed worlds, to break out of cages and relate to a complex, multicultural world. The painting is a two-dimensional cage. The writer-artist frees the people from two-dimensionalism, the writer-artist sees the meaning and the potential.

Peter Nazareth. *Canadian Literature*. 110,
1986, pp. 184, 189–90

Bharati Mukherjee can take her place among the best South Asian and American writers of today. Her work ranges from very good to dazzling. Her handling of her subject, of what she calls "the pain and absurdity of art and exile . . . exile among the former colonizers: the tolerant incomprehensions of hosts, the absolute impossibility of ever having a home, *desh*. . . ." (epilogue to *Days and Nights in Calcutta*) is uncomprisingly honest and often deeply painful. . . .

Days and Nights in Calcutta (1977), coauthored by Bharati Mukherjee and her husband Clark Blaise, consists of two distinct parts. There are two narrative, in some ways two philosophical essays, based on selected experiences and episodes that took place during an extended visit to India (most of it in Calcutta) in the early 1970s. It is in this book that Mukherjee describes the difficulties of being a South Asian writer in Canada and describes the constant search by many immigrants and expatriates for a secure and familiar place. She continues and develops this discussion in the introduction to her brilliantly written, chilling collection of short stories, *Darkness* (1985).

Her first novel, *The Tiger's Daughter* (1971), portrays Tara Banerjee Cartwright, a Western-educated, well-to-do Bengali woman married to an American. Tara's petulance and constant nervousness regarding her role as the Bengali wife of an American visiting her family in Calcutta, overshadows her well-intentioned efforts to understand her world of diverse cultures. . . .

Tara . . . is caught in the physical violence of Calcutta as she tries to untangle the confusion of different cultures. Dimples [in *Wife*] loses her sanity when faced with a culture she doesn't comprehend and that refuses to make room for her. Both are lonely, isolated women and their sense of loss is translated and re-created in the lives of the more gutsy, but almost bizarre characters who appear in *Darkness*. Some of us may feel quite uncomfortable around Mukherjee's characters. We look around us and we see fellow South Asian immigrants at social gatherings, special grocery and sari stores, and even professional conferences. And we say, "No, come on . . . who here would kill her husband as he eats his cereal? And who would be so silly as to be caught in the midst of a political confrontation? Who would brutally attack his unmarried daughter, not because she is pregnant, but because she is pregnant through artificial insemination? This is only well-written South Asian American gothic. After all, aren't all South Asian Americans successful citizens of America with periodic attacks of anxiety regarding their children's cultural identity?" Yet we know that in her own imitable fashion, Mukherjee has taken her own fears and struggles, as well as the fears and struggles of many among us who have remained without a voice to speak of the immigrant experience, and presented some of the more violent and grotesque aspects of cultural collisions.

Roshni Rustomji-Kerns. *Massachusetts Review*. 29, 1988, pp. 656–59

Mukherjee's writing career began in 1971, with *The Tiger's Daughter*, and her seventh book *Jasmine* was published in 1990. Her popularity shot up when her second book *The Middleman and Other Stories* bagged the 1988 National Book Critics Award in America. This collection seeks to dramatize the "immigration experience" in America. In a recent interview, Mukherjee has clearly stated her aim in her writings:

> We immigrants have fascinating tales to relate. Many of us have lived in newly independent or emerging countries . . . when we uproot overselves from those countries and come here, either by choice or out of necessity, we suddenly must absorb 200 years of American history and learn to adapt to American society. . . . I attempt to illustrate this in my novels and short stories. My aim is to expose Americans to the energetic voices of new settlers in this country.

In fact, Mukherjee had to come to terms with her own identity in an alien land, caught as she was between two conflicting cultures. Also, she had to contend with racial discrimination during the years she spent in Canada, precisely between 1972 and 1980. She managed to overcome both the crises and this brought in her a sense of elation and confidence.

R. K. Dhawar. Indian Women Novelists
(New Delhi: Prestige, 1991), p. 23

In an era where air travel has made the distant close, the remote accessible, and rich and poor mobile, the migration of an underclass to more privileged countries is a commonplace. Individual movements across national and ethnic boundaries, and the consequences borne by their participants, comprise the core of Bharati Mukherjee's stories. With few exceptions, the motley, restive group of refugees, emigrants, fugitives, mercenaries, professionals, and others populate the territories explored by three novels and two collections of short stories. Without exception, the international and contemporaneous perspectives of her work are readily perceived.

Her characters are moving, about to move, recently moved or already moved. Mostly immigrants who seek a better life in the United Sates and Canada or would be emigrants dreaming of futures in the West from homes in less developed Asian countries, their odysseys, together with their physical and emotional passion for survival in alien quarters, are the stuff of Mukherjee's narratives. She scours the complex multicultural worlds of her foreigners, the new North Americans, to portray their displacement and adaptation, those of whom she speaks in her article on immigrant writing: "They have all shed past lives and languages, and have traveled half the world in every direction to come here and begin again." Mukherjee's immigrants may be divided into those whose experience of the discontinuities of displacement are such that they either cannot re-place their reality or develop a tragically misplaced one and those, who in their determination to see America as their home, exuberantly will themselves to become Americans over and above their original nationalities. . . .

"Voice" . . . has a special place in Mukherjee's aesthetics. "To me there are no Indian themes, American themes or English themes. What I'm trying to produce is a voice perhaps." Passionate and intense, riveting, urgent, and incisive at its best—at its worst, Mukherjee's voice is too taut and brittle to sustain credibility. Notwithstanding the importance she places on voice and the consequent belittlement of thematic identity, Mukherjee does see herself today as an American writer influenced and inspired by the melting pot of her adoptive country. . . .

In Mukherjee's fiction, a woman's sexual involvement often functions as a measure of detachment from native mores and, correspondingly, of her assimilation and Americanization. Sexual openness is seen as part of the freedom from tradition America offers. Although Leelah, narrator of "Hindus," points to the inescapable obstacle posed by the past in the process of assimilation in her remark, "No matter how passionately we link our bodies with our new countries, we never escape the early days," the seduction exercised by a more open and anarchic environment and the liberation of sensibility, if only partial at times, are particularly evident in Mukherjee's women. But with their more conservative backgrounds, South Asian men and women react in different ways: women, by expressing their sexual needs more candidly; men, by believing their countrywomen are freer in America than in their native land or are more uninhibited and self-sufficient than they have been brought up to be. . . .

For Mukherjee, "there are people born to be Americans. By American I mean an intensity of spirit and a quality of desire. I feel American in a very fundamental way, whether Americans see me that way or not." In the challenges posed by America to her expatriates and immigrants, Mukherjee shows that, inevitably, it is America that is affecting them in varied ways; so far only in a few stories is immigration handled from the mainstream culture's point of view. Her abundant imagination brings the tensions and forces within the multicultural and multiethnic spheres of her new Americans to vivid life. Mukherjee recreates their world—more often than not relegated to marginal status by mainstream North America—throbbing, exuberant, and dynamic with the energy and passions of "aliens" determined to survive, succeed, and ultimately, belong.

Liew Geok-Leong. In Robert L. Ross, ed.
International Literature in English: Essays on the Major Writers (New York: Garland, 1991), pp. 488, 494–95, 498

Her later works, comprising the novel *Jasmine* (1989) and the stories in *Darkness* (1985) and *The Middleman* (winner of the 1988 National Book Award), are her most rewarding. Almost all of them directly or indirectly deal with the disconcerting experience of migrating to North America. Although her first novel, *The Tiger's Daughter* (1972), is set in India, its protagonist is a passive young Bengali wife of an American, and it portrays her Chekhovian disillusion with India during a family visit. Mukherjee's second novel, *Wife* (1975), describes a weak-minded Bengali woman who migrates to New York with her engineer husband in search of a better life; but her sensibilities become so confounded by her changing cultural roles, the insidious television factitiousness, and the tensions of feminism that, ironically, she goes mad and kills her husband.

Many of Mukherjee's later works expatiate upon this South Asian immigrant experience in North America, much of which is painful. Especially painful is the topic of racism; indeed, one possible reading of the title of her anthology *Darkness* is as a reference to racial prejudice, which is, after all, a darkness of the mind toward the darkness of another person's skin. Those works set in Canada, however, are more bitter than those set in the United States, especially on the topic of racism. . . .

Mukherjee's U.S. stories may be intended to be kinder and gentler than her Canadian ones, but she is aware that America is "violent, mindlessly macho, conformist, lawless. . . . No dark-skinned person has the right to feel comfortable inside American history. Yet I do." And she prefers America's "melting pot," girded by its "human rights laws," to Canada's discrete "mosaic." . . .

In Mukherjee's fictions of the South Asian experience in North America, especially in the United States, a few may actually be optimistic, though not painless. The *Middleman* tale "A Wife's Story," for instance, tells the positive variant of the novel *Wife:* the short story's protagonist is an Indian woman who absents herself from her husband to do graduate study in New York, and although she encounters racial prejudice and sees her women friends being sexually exploited, she is able through her liberating camaraderie with both men and women to discover in herself a power, confidence, and sexuality which she did not realize she was capable of. But it is Mukherjee's novel *Jasmine* (1989) that contains her most optimistic depiction of the South Asian experience in North America. . . .

As Mukherjee has explored her immigrant world, her scope and language have evolved appreciably. Her early works are limited to the minds of young women, sensitive, educated, middle class. In her recent works, she empowers herself to appropriate the mentalities of men as well, of whites, of soldiers of fortune. Her narrative voices also have increased many fold. . . .

Both Naipaul and Mukherjee, one providing an example that the other has made into many, have written ironical and cautionary fictions about the uneasy passage of Asian Indians to participate in the American dream. Mukherjee evinces a somewhat more positive view than Naipaul of immigrant life in the United States, glimpsing occasionally the redeeming possibilities of love and the self-affirming opportunities for the pursuit of happiness—though neither love nor happiness is ever obtained without pain or without a price. More often, however, the American Dream is found to be meretricious, easily becoming a nightmare of violence, prejudice, and exploitation; sometimes the dreamer discovers that in dreams begin responsibilities of self-defining of which he or she is incapable. Frequently, therefore, the immigrant only ends up being exploited and victimized, deracinated and *dépaysé*, neither here nor there.

C. L. Chua. *Reworlding: The Literature of the Indian Diaspora* (Westport, Connecticut: Greenwood Press, 1992), pp. 54–57, 60

Focusing on immigrant characters from India, Pakistan, and Bangladesh, Mukherjee does not shy away from the enormous cultural and religious diversity represented by those groups; yet she underscores challenges common to all these immigrants. Her story "Hindus," for example, uses language as a metaphor for an imposed sense of "otherness." In the bright urbane worlds of Toronto and New York some people carelessly confuse Hindi with Hindu. Leela, a Bengali Brahmin, is alert to such insults, intended or unintended. She begins to see language as a new caste system when, in an art dealer's office, she is complimented for knowing "Hindu," which is "such a hard language." Indeed. This dismissive attitude allows some people in the dominant culture to adopt a casual manner disrespectful of both a language and a religion. Leela knows what these slights mean; she says, "No matter what language I speak it will come out slightly foreign, no matter how perfectly I mouth it. There's a whole world of us now, speaking Hindu."

This forbidding sense that words can imprison as well as release is a keystone for writers. Mukherjee examines these "new pioneers," . . . as she calls them, in their urban settings. As always in immigrant literature, these settings are more than decorative features; rather, these cityscapes underscore the isolation which surrounds the characters. Within the canyons of Toronto and New York, their yearning to acculturate pushes up against the desire to embrace cultural ghosts of the lost homeland. In the story "Nostalgia," for example, Dr. Manny Patel is bothered by this longing for the old land and the old ways. He visits an ethnic neighborhood inside the city; he parks his Porsche, a gleaming symbol of his successful transition to the New World, and wanders into the "little India" of the Sari Palace and the New Taj Mahal, where thoroughly acclimated citizens can purchase bhindi and cardamom, dal and marsala tea. He finds there as well an experienced team of hustlers who sexually entice him, then blackmail him. . . .

Canada—indeed all of North America—is being redefined and enriched by this [multicultural] movement. As always in history, immigration alters national identity, and this is nowhere truer than here. [Joy] Kogawa and Mukherjee insist that we hold in mind one small geographic fact: this is still the fabled "New World," and many new explorers are still coming to discover it. Finally, these new voices issue lyric, powerful warnings that plurality without unity may well be as bad as unity without diversity.

Thus *Darkness* and *Obasan* are more than testaments to the ongoing literary renaissance in Canada; they are beautiful textbooks that remind us to appreciate differences as well as similarities. How old citizens and culture groups welcome the "new pioneers" will say essential—and we hope eloquent—things about the New World's ethical development.

B. A. St. Andrews. *World Literature Today.*
66, 1992, 56–58

MUNRO, ALICE (CANADA) 1931–

It is apparent . . . that *Something I've Been Meaning to Tell You* reveals the same divided universe as do *Dance of the Happy Shades* and *Lives of Girls and Women.* And it asks Munro's characteristic questions. "Walking on Water" and "Forgiveness in Families" both play with the old question "Who or what is mad?" In "Memorial," the central character, who has been confronted anew with the rigidly defined world of her sister, thinks "the only thing we can hope for is that we lapse now and then into reality." The sister, with her absolute control of house and family and friends, never lapses, and the toll this takes on her spirit is represented by the ironic death of her son in a freak accident; even to this tragedy his mother cannot respond spontaneously.

Alice Munro's work bears the marks of a distinctive, vital, and unifying vision. Though this vision shows itself more complex and subtle with each of her books, the basic terms remain unchanged. Man finds himself divided into two camps, and the price of this division for both sides is loneliness and pain. The external deformities and violences of "the other country," the place of outcasts, are simply transferences of the unseen, hidden disfiguration of "the world," place of "survivors." Which group suffers most is a question without significance in a universe where men, the pathetic victims of chance, offer each other not kindness or encouragement, but suspicion and hate.

Rae McCarthy Maclendon. *Modern Fiction
Studies.* 22, 1977, pp. 373–74

[Virginia] Woolf argues that the "great mind is androgynous" and thus women must achieve this "token of the fully developed mind" if they are to become first-rate writers. In *Lives of Girls and Women,* Munro demonstrates that the masculine image as understood by Jung is as much a part of the growth of Del's creative identity as it is of her physical and sexual nature.

One of the ironies of *Lives* is that throughout the stories the male portrait is at variance with the assumption of male superiority and freedom held by Del and her Jubilee society. Only at the level of the personal (the mask which according to Jung the ego assumes to meet the world) do positive male characteristics appear. . . .

When the novel begins, Del as a child observes the "troubling distorted reflection" of Uncle Benny's world but she can still regard it as "the same but never the same at all." It was not in *her* world that "people could go down in quicksand, be vanquished by ghosts or terrible ordinary cities." At the end of the novel in Bobby Sherriff she faces the distortion of Uncle Benny's world as now that of her own, the real world, in which the self must seek to right the inward balance in order to be able to view the world and act creatively in it. At this point the irony provided by the discrepancy between Del's vision as a child and as a narrator subsides. In the new narrative voice there appears a signal of a change coming in the life of Del Jordan which will free her from her unquestioning admiration and adulation of the masculine persona and her initial physical and sexual animus image. The painful and continuing struggle toward consciousness and individuation on which she is now embarked contrasts sharply to her dream of boarding the bus "like girls in the movies." But it is the inner journey that will enable Del to record the surface truths of Jubilee in such a way as to communicate their inner reality and thereby to realize her desire for "every last thing, every layer of speech and thought, stroke of light on bark or walls, every smell, pothole, pain, crack, delusion, held still and held together—radiant and everlasting." This, in effect, is what she has done for us in the preceding chapters.

While, according to Munro, "not very many writers [except] the great ones can create characters of both sexes," the masculine portraits in *Lives of Girls and Women* are sound demonstrations of the way the female consciousness interacts with the male at different levels of being. If properly understood by the reader, the masculine image enlarges one's perception of Del Jordan and one's admiration for the art of her creator.

Nancy I. Bailey. *Canadian Literature.* 80,
1979, pp. 113, 120

When an Alice Munro story knocks you back in your chair—and several in her new collection, *The Progress of Love,* have the power to push on you good and hard—it's often because she's upended this "auditorium" perspective Munro writes across generational lines, making the past so vivid it undermines our belief that the present is the true locus of experience. She writes histories of lives that ought to seem foreign. Many of her characters come of age in a world of wing collars, outdoor plumbing and icehouses. Yet Munro's people are contemporary with their own choices, uncertainty and pain, and that makes them our contemporaries. If their decisions have come to look inevitable from their grandchildren's point of view, from within the lives of the actors themselves, they are nevertheless urgent, risky and up for grabs. . . .

Alice Munro is very much a sculptor, and these new stories might best be regarded as bas-reliefs, where the artist has won from resistant material lively scenes of human activity. As an art form, bas-relief is always technically astonishing: the figures are caught in mid-motion, the sensations of depth and distance are evoked although little of either is permitted by the medium. You wind up wondering how so much can go into such a small space. If Munro's short fiction shares the virtues of bas-relief, though, it also shares the limitations of this form. After all, viewed from certain angles, those just barely three-dimensional figures suddenly look incomplete, not fully disengaged from the raw substance. And that's the problem within *The Progress of Love,* where the meanings of many characters' lives remain unclear, waiting, in effect, for Munro to extract them from the stone.

Brina Caplan. The Nation. November 8,
1986, pp. 497, 499

Contradiction and exhilaration, release accomplished through a joke and a partial truth—that leads us to the heartland of Alice Munro's fiction. Often Munro's heroine tries to guard herself, to stay within the safe, approved parameters of a social group. But she knows very well that an enemy lurks within and has a sneaking fondness for that shadow self, that outlaw or jubilant *saboteur.* She knows her integrity is compromised as she denies a messy, "vulgar" past for reasons of protective coloration and she feels bad about her craven ladyhood. She wants to smash the garrison, to say or do the outrageous thing that will acknowledge whatever has been left out. But she is also afraid of appearing ridiculous. Often, it seems to me that Munro (like [Mavis] Gallant and [Margaret] Laurence) regards that self-protectiveness, the fear of appearing ridiculous or incoherent, as an especially Canadian trait. . . .

Munro's view of the artist as one who moves through society, and is outside of it as well, is developed in the comic figure of Milton Homer from the story "Who Do You Think You Are?" That he is a marginal figure is illustrated by the wooden platform at the side of Rose's house and various other yards and porches, where Milton is allowed to perform his antics. That society accords the artist an occasional, quasi-religious centrality is shown by Milton's admission to the parlors of Hanratty when the birth of a child necessitates his rites of naming and invocation. . . .

Alice Munro is . . . a "warm" writer in the sense that a strong feeling of intimacy is generated between reader, character and author. An identification of writer and protagonist allows Munro to be hard on her characters without distancing the reader. Thematically, Munro's fictions are more equivocal than Laurence's. One of Munro's great subjects is embarrassment, or shame; often she will occupy herself with the tension between a character's ambition (her exalted view of self) and her self-criticism, which often relates to over-weening pride. Her eye is on the margin, the point at which something repressed or not seen suddenly materializes in consciousness. Again, she is what I would call a writer of peripheral vision; and when insights do arise from that zone, they remain somehow in suspension or in motion. Although they suggest patterns, they do not immediately make everything else clear and coherent. Munro is always checking and testing: the Munro "signature" is that moment in the story where she points out that she has missed something, that the full truth of the matter has eluded her. She is open in *that* sense, open to open-endedness, to fresh interpretations.

Constance Rooke. In Shirley Neuman and
Smaro Kamboureli, eds. *A Mazing Space:*
Writing Canadian Women Writing
(Edmonton: Longspoon, 1986), pp. 262–63,
266–67

Alice Munro constantly surprises us with new characters, modes and insights, but there are summary generalizations about her art that can be offered. She achieves thematic richness by establishing oppositions, incongruities and paradoxes, often breaking down chronological sequences or allowing the sophisticated adult to recall the freshness and vivacity of the child's experience in order to juxtapose such contraries as the strange and the familiar and the touchable and the mysterious, or alien. She develops a dialectical interplay that defines the relation between the contending opposites in a spiral movement that involves progress and retreat, affirmation and irony; to achieve this she typically places her protagonist between two forces or loyalties, and the resulting creative friction produces the dramatic developments and solutions that we see in Del, Rose, and others, who, being intelligent and imaginative, go through sea-changes. . . .

Besides having the pleasure of recognizing the circumstances and incidentals of their lives in Alice Munro's art, Canadians may feel an allowable pride that a writer of such stature is at work among them, and also gratitude for being helped to answer such questions as "Who do you think you are?" and "Where is here?" It is ironical, but significant, that this very Canadian writer has achieved what she has without striving self-consciously to be "Canadian." Being open to all influences has allowed her to respond to those that are most useful to her own genius and to write fiction as distinctively Canadian as any of the canon. But to leave the matter there would be to mislead and do Alice Munro less than justice. She is more than a Canadian writer, or a writer for Canadians. By seizing on the significant touches of nature in our small world she makes the whole world kin. As the history of her publications shows, her work is not only accessible to, but valued by and therefore in a sense the property of all who read literature in English. She is making substantial additions to, and thus consolidating and renewing, a long and illustrious tradition.

W. R. Martin. *Alice Munro: Paradox and*
Parallel (Edmonton: University of Alberta
Press, 1987), pp. 205–6

The real of the story is continually jostled by other problems besides the real that beset Munro's imagination. The real is always transformed by fiction—

the act by which it acquires soul—and it is somehow bound ineluctably to the discourse of legend, as much as it is obsessed by the need for truth. Each in a certain measure corrects the other, for Munro is perfectly aware of how fiction can obscure truth, just as legend can alter the real. What is even more important, finally, is that these are not always referential terms, as one might speak of "the truth" or "the real." They are designations of kinds of discourse, each one affecting our perception of event and character. What holds them together is a certain feeling, the soul of the story. . . .

Munro once remarked that one must not expect a writer to progress in the elaboration of her work. Although a writer's maturity may deepen, as well as the skill with which the craft is developed, there is a certain sense in which Munro is unassailably correct. For the story in its essence is neither its polish nor the writer's wisdom. It is more elusive, "happening somewhere, not just in [the writer's] head, and in its own way, not [the writer's]. And the story that is finally written "is still only an attempt, an approach, to the story." It keeps, then, some part of itself, its soul, that must escape the grasp of the writer, and toward which, in the end, the critic can but gesture. What is called "soul" may only be perceived in the story's discourse, that continually summons into the text a surface that reflects a hidden depth. In conversation with John Metcalf she denies that this surface is able to evoke "a religious feeling," but its intensity seems to be akin. It is toward that center, that radiant core of energy, that Munro's stories have continually endeavored to reach.

E. D. Blodgett. *Alice Munro* (Boston: Twayne, 1988), pp. 157–58

Munro's definition of the artist . . . stresses a . . . recurring paradox: that the artist *herself* must be a double person, both a voyeur and an actress, both a member of the audience and an imperiled performer of dramatic tricks—in short, a person who exposes not only others but also herself. This paradoxical definition is another parallel that connects many of her stories. Munro explicitly defines "a fiction writer" as a member of a theatrical audience, fascinated by "the way people live in the eyes of others. Every life is a drama, everybody is on stage." One of these "others" is the sharp-eyed voyeur who not only watches the stage, sporadically illumined, but also penetrates the "hidden rooms" and secrets concealed by the protective surfaces of walls or clothes. Watching in the darkness or peering through doors and windows and knotholes, she sees other people's sexuality and nakedness. But by taking the stage, she also repeatedly exposes *herself* to the possible shame of public ridicule. She attempts miracles. She splits herself in half and tries, like Miss Farris and Eugene, to walk on water. In "Simon's Luck," the feminist critic's long list of female artists who committed suicide includes Virginia Woolf, who drowned herself. Thus, if the artist-actress fails in the performance of her double role, she might break through another concealing surface and drown, like Edna Pontellier, the failed artist in *The Awakening*.

This possibility suggests the dangers inherent in what is concealed. These hidden dangers are another parallel between many Munro stories. Under clothes, there is the hungry, sexual body; under the bedclothes, there is the pregnant mother; underwater, there is death.

Ildikó de Papp Carrington. Controlling the Uncontrollable: The Fiction of Alice Munro (De Kalb: Northern Illinois University Press, 1989), pp. 210–11

Loneliness in the work of Alice Munro occurs in a broader context and is . . . the consequence of a darkly deterministic worldview. The flat, featureless landscapes of her Southern Ontario towns are mirrored in the lives of her depleted but idiosyncratic characters. The spectral and alien lives of the men who inhabit this world appear to her female protagonists as riddles incapable of solution. Married or not, her men are outsiders. With varying degrees of distance, husbands haunt the outskirts of domestic arrangements as if their humanity was beyond the pale.

Munro's women appear to take the measure of their own unhappiness from the depth and distance of male isolation. In her earliest stories, Munro's pattern for men is already in place. The recluse, who dominates the consciousness of Munro's younger female characters, demarcates the extreme of social distance. Reclusive isolation attracts Munro's women as an image of freedom from the world of domesticity and repels them as evidence of the seemingly unbreachable psychic and affective distance between men and women.

Reamy Jansen. Cross Currents. 39, 1989–90, p. 399

The dust jacket for Friend of My Youth quotes Cynthia Ozick calling Alice Munro "our Chekhov." In the New York Review of Books Robert Towers compares Munro's technique to foreshortening in the fiction of Henry James. Chekhov and James are not at all bad company for a fiction writer. Alice Munro is, nevertheless, a Canadian woman writer.

Whether or not Munro's reader thinks of the stories here or any of her short fiction as feminist depends upon the friends of that reader's youth: not only the particular images, ideas, and acquaintances—that is, the facts—of one's young life, but also the tendencies of one's generation. The narrator of "Friend of My Youth" explains the difference between her mother's interpretation of a story and her own this way:

> The odd thing is that my mother's ideas were in line with some progressive notions of her times, and mine echoed the notions that were favored in my time. . . . It's as if tendencies that seem most deeply rooted in our minds, most private and singular,

have come in as spores on the prevailing wind, looking for any
likely place to land, any welcome.

Some of Munro's woman characters are highly educated; others are not.
They are all subject, however, to deeply rooted tendencies that both give
power and take it away.

   The narrators of the stories in the present collection reflect on sex and
men, death and mothers from a perspective of middle-aged womanhood.
Dedicated to the author's mother, who died when Munro was a young woman,
the book—Munro's seventh—continues to present sex with honest uncertainty and brings this same clarity to the subject of death: death of husbands,
wives, friends, but especially of mothers. Unlike Munro, I do consider myself
a feminist and as such have more faith in the gender politics of Munro's
fiction than that of, say, Margaret Atwood.

Barbara J. Eckstein. World Literature Today.
64, 1990, p. 639

Alice Munro has said, "I think that the kind of writing I do is almost anachronistic, because it's so rooted in one place." Although there are exceptions,
that place is essentially southwestern Ontario, in towns with fictional names
such as Jubilee, Hanratty, Dalgleish, and Logan. Munro writes of small communities and their people, of social territory she calls "absolutely Gothic"
and about which she emphasizes, "You can't get it all down." From the beginning of her career she has not been concerned with merely describing places,
people, and incidents but with the creation of probing, self-conscious, female
narrative voices that treat the telling of any story as significant as the tangible
details of the story itself. Such voices speak from the point of view of third-
person omniscience as well as through limited, first-person utterance; thus
Munro consistently emphasizes that the relationship between her own stories
and those of her protagonists is one of process as the perceiving consciousness shapes and defines the world. She is especially concerned with the
articulation of paradox—those oppositions within character and event that
complicate and enrich existence because they must be lived with rather than
resolved. The ordinary world in Munro's stories is replete with contradictions, with people and circumstances that refuse to be contained within safe
and predictable patterns of voice and experience. Munro's narrators learn to
include in their visions both the ridiculous and the sublime, sudden shifts in
familiar ways of doing and seeing, life that is, according to one protagonist,
"dull, simple, amazing and unfathomable—deep caves paved with kitchen
linoleum." . . .

   It is in "Meneseteung" (the name of a river that flows into Lake Huron)
that Munro provides one of her most telling portraits to date of a woman
who attempts to move beyond gender divisions of happiness. Munro's ironic
narrative in this story is the saving grace of nineteenth-century poetess
Almeda Roth for whom price paid and vision gained are terribly intertwined.

The language and poetic form Almeda has been given contain her even as she creatively proclaims herself out of a position of servitude as her father's housekeeper. When he dies, the people of her town, led by newspaper gossip columns, expect her, suitably, to turn to another male authority figure. She seems primed to do so until one night when she witnesses the beating of a woman by her man. With some echoes of Rose in "Royal Beatings" in *our* ears, Almeda hears the woman partake in her own degradation: "She keeps crying 'Kill me! Kill me!' and sometimes her mouth seems choked with blood. Yet there is something taunting and triumphant about her cry. There is something theatrical about it." The woman does not die this time, but Almeda chooses to live by turning away from the proffered hand/fist of her suitor. In doing so, she breaks those chains that bind and distinguish primarily in terms of a power struggle that men will always win if women continue only to "pay attention." Conventional opinion has it that this "lady of talent and refinement" goes mad, but "she knows that she is sane." Almeda Roth is an ancestor for women of Munro's century, for Del Jordan and all the others who would live and create in a world that is both real and true.

J. A. Wainwright. In Robert L. Ross, ed.
*International Literature in English: Essays
on the Major Writers* (New York: Garland,
1991), pp. 304, 312

As I read and reread the stories, I began to discern the outlines of a composite figure—a mothering clown that I decided to call a mock mother. The mock mother is constructed as a result of the impossibility of picturing the "real" mother. Often she performs as a kind of trickster who challenges our old ways of looking at the relation between the work of art and the human body. Unlike the spread-eagled male body made famous by Leonardo da Vinci, this body is not static. The belly expands and contracts, sometimes an arm or a leg or a breast is amputated, the iris moves in and out, the blind spot floats over various parts of the body, and the body may be stood on its head or perform acrobatic stunts. What happens if you substitute this figure for the spread-eagled male with the centrally placed penis who is so often seen as an analogy for the work of art? The first thing that surfaces is an awareness of the danger of objectification. If we don't feel this danger when we look at the body of a male it is surely because male consciousness is seen as the peak of our civilization. The first step to take to avoid the trap of turning the maternal body into an object, is to see that the mother is in the act of looking at *herself*, even when she is also looking after her children. . . .

Munro's stories are best served by approaches to motherhood that separate (as does Adrienne Rich) the experience and the institution. The yearning for an archaic maternal past is acknowledged by Munro, but it is seen from an ironic, anti-nostalgic distance. Voice mixed with milk will not show up on paper unless there is at least a little gall. Unless the voice uses a little black ink, moreover, the woman will not achieve either identity or fame. In "The

Progress of Love" Fame's mother describes how "One drop of hatred in your soul will spread and discolor everything like a drop of black ink in white milk." Milk is an inherently absurd image to many of the people in Munro's stories. While Fame milks the cows, her visiting aunt wonders aloud if it hurts the cow and adds: "Think if it was you." Fame is "shaken by this indecency," but Munro's own fame is built on just such daring connections.

Margaret Redekop. *Mothers and Other Clowns: The Stories of Alice Munro* (New York: Routledge, 1992), pp. 4, 6

Where, in her moral/social realism, Gallant uses the personal to parallel the political, juxtaposing memory and morality in an ethics of grieving, Munro charts not world history but ancestral worlds and private histories. Her realism, then, involves the anti-entropic documentation of life as a stay against the natural process of decay—as a kind of shoring against its ruins. She says that "with me it has something to do with the fight against death, the feeling that we lose everything every day, and writing is a way of convincing yourself perhaps that you're doing something about this." Although Munro's fiction is engaged in this fight against death, the goal of that fight is not a sentimental and escapist notion of conquering death with literature; she is not inscribing a Freudian theory wherein, writes Jacques Derrida, a view of "death as an internal necessity of life" produces a "domesticity of death" that is "nothing but a consoling fiction." Rather, Munro stages the fight so that what she has called "the fact of death" might be accommodated within life, but figured in such a way as to represent life as a resistance to order and "all attempts to render it comprehensible." This accommodation is not, then, what Derrida refers to as "the poetics of the proper as reconciliation, consolation, serenity"; Munro's poetics of elegy is a poetics of the *im*proper, the *un*familiar, the *un*resolvable. . . .

Though her fiction involves "the fight against death," Munro's approach is not to sentimentalize the subject(s) of loss and mourning; rather, she figures grief in the form of fiction-elegy and suggests that "the fact of death" might be accommodated within life and within our fictions without false consolation. The reader is invited to participate in this fight and to evaluate various reconstructions of the past for their capacity both to achieve a fictional truth and to provide a model of mourning that might find a place in "real life." Munro charts the movements of a mind in mourning, a mind in motion, reconsidering the past and its relation to the present so that memory is not a trap but something that can be learned from. Her narrators and characters perform their "figuring out" in the act of story-telling.

Karen E. Smythe. *Figuring Grief: Gallant, Munro and the Poetics of Elegy* (Montreal: McGill-Queens University Press, 1992), pp. 107–8, 152

MURDOCH, IRIS (GREAT BRITAIN) 1919–

Iris Murdoch had a late start, publishing her first novel in her middle-thirties, when she had already a reputation as a philosopher and literary critic. Her work is not in the least uneven, but has blossomed out most smoothly and steadily, with each new novel better than the one before. Her first, *Under the Net,* in which one can discern some affinity with the work of Raymond Queneau and of Joyce Cary, was received with more acclaim than understanding. It was even thought to have something to do with the cult of the Angry Young Men. It is certainly an enigmatic book. Miss Murdoch has never (so far as I know) made any statement about her intention as a novelist, and it may be that it pleases her to fox her critics somewhat. One needs, I think, to look at each of her books in the light of the others. She has simplified her technique as she has gone forward, and improved it. Her last book *The Bell* is a triumph, and that very rare thing in literature, a work of compassionate satire.

Maurice Cranston. *The London Magazine.*
November, 1958, p. 26

Miss Murdoch's new novel [*A Severed Head*] is very strange indeed; both in itself and as coming from her. Like Mr. Angus Wilson in *The Middle Age of Mrs. Eliot,* she seems almost to have made a deliberate effort to pare away the characteristics by which she was becoming best known. . . .

Under the Net was in a sense a refusal to write a novel at all (as all picaresque novels are); the life shown in it is too fragmentary to be forced into the conventional novelist's pattern of turning-points and crises, problems and solutions, significant incidents and revelatory experiences; there is only a series of contingent adventures. . . .

In *The Flight from the Enchanter,* Miss Murdoch seemed to have come to terms with the novel far enough to permit herself a more elaborate plot, and to choose an impersonal narrative form which allowed her to generalize about her characters (Rainborough, for instance) in a series of epigrammatic asides which Hugo could hardly have sanctioned. . . . When *The Sandcastle* appeared, many people welcomed it as a sign that Miss Murdoch's writing had become more "realistic." It would be truer to say that it had become more conventional. The world of *The Sandcastle* is not necessarily more everyday than that of the earlier novels—the gipsy-like man who appears announcing disaster is quite as fantastic as anything in them—but it is more neatly and recognizably an artifact. It is the coherence as well as the plausibility of the plot that reassured critics that Miss Murdoch had, as it were, settled down to her trade. . . . The basic moral issue of *The Bell* is that of fundamentalist or interpretative ethics, as reflected in James's and Michael's sermons. It raises the infinitely difficult question of how far one can be guided by rules as opposed to experience, how far it can be good to renounce the world without knowing it, how far one must know one's own limits before setting oneself any moral objectives at all. . . . It is in every way an astonishing book, and one of its most impressive features is the extreme ease with which so tightly disciplined a conception is carried out. Even the style is supremely confident. . . .

In the light (if it is a light) of this, what can one make of *A Severed Head?* Obviously, Miss Murdoch has become more formal still—perhaps following as large a change of course as was marked by the publication of *The Sandcastle.* In her two previous novels the figures move to some extent in a pattern; in *A Severed Head* they go through an elaborate minuet worthy of Mr. Henry Green, in which six partners try out every possible heterosexual combination except one (Honor Klein and Alexander). Indeed the novel contains, in a sense, nothing but form. . . . The characters' backgrounds and occupations seem merely designed, as in the most crudely romantic novel, to give them the money and the leisure to pursue an intricate scheme of personal relations; and their personalities vanish in the midst of their own involvements. . . . The imperfections of *The Sandcastle* were a small and (if the suggestions of this article are true) a necessary price to pay for the smooth perfection of *The Bell;* the sequel to *A Severed Head* may be equally remarkable.

Francis Hope. The London Magazine.
August, 1961, pp. 84–87

To begin with, the surface of the novel [*An Unofficial Rose*] is of a grating "gracious living" vulgarity that is hard to bear. It is not so openly vulgar as the sort of expenses sheet pseudo-elegance of her last novel, *A Severed Head;* but it was still possible there to suppose that all the talk of vintage wines and Meissen birds was ironic in tone. In *An Unofficial Rose,* although the statement of the novel is ambiguous, the tone is not ironic. . . . In civilized sensitiveness we are in the world of Virginia Woolf, although Miss Murdoch perhaps regards her characters with a slightly more aloof irony. What rings false, however, when her world is set down beside Mrs. Woolf's, is that none of her characters regards his or her way of living in its social, economic sense with any questioning whatever. Surely the unease of Mrs. Ramsay or even Mrs. Dalloway gives us a truth about this whole class that Miss Murdoch's world lacks. Indeed Miss Murdoch's characters approach such things as the Boulestin Restaurant or a château-bottled wine with an awe and an underlining which suggests that their creator is not entirely at ease in her chosen environment. The degree to which Miss Murdoch seems to have sold herself to this women's glossy paradise is betrayed by the distinction so harped upon between shrub roses and hybrid teas, a distinction embodied in the title of the book. There have been few more arrant snobberies since the war than the worship of the beauty of the shrub roses. . . .

To such a detective story I am inclined with my namesake Edmund Wilson to answer—who cares who murdered Roger Ackroyd? All I trust is that this review is sufficiently harsh, for in Miss Murdoch, the author of *The*

Bell, we had the only English post-war novelist to set beside our other hope, Mr. William Golding, the author of *Lord of the Flies.*

Angus Wilson. *The Manchester Guardian Weekly.* June 14, 1962, p. 11

It seems to me that on the symbolic level Miss Murdoch fails dismally, because she has forgotten what a symbol is *for*—which is to make something clear that would otherwise not be. There is more symbolism in . . . Thurber's Unicorn at the bottom of the garden, than in the whole of *The Unicorn.* If you put a character into a symbolic robe instead of a simple little button-through, it must reveal something about the character; it cannot be a garment chosen equally at random from a celestial wardrobe. And these symbols fail in their own terms because they reveal no higher reality, make no final point: they are less than human, not more. She thinks she is creating archetypes when she is only producing arch types. . . .

What, then, is to be done with this maddening woman, in whose talent I still stubbornly insist on believing? I think what she badly needs is a change of medium—and quick, before she succumbs to the prevailing malaise and bores us all into the ground with a Trilogy. If she is going to be a fantasist with no feet on the ground and no sense of humor, it seems to me that she must tackle the one field where fantasy has a discipline: I think (quite seriously) that she should try science fiction.

She simply cannot go on doing this celestial knitting—not in a world where the crisp brilliance of Muriel Spark and the wit and insight of Mary McCarthy are there to put her to shame.

Katharine Whitehorn. *Encounter.* December, 1963, p. 82

Each of Iris Murdoch's first four novels has, as its title, an image of the kind of illusion its characters face. The first novel, *Under the Net* (1954), tells the story of Jake Donaghue's wanderings about Bohemian London and Paris as he attempts to find or construct a satisfactory way of life. But planned ways of life are nets, traps, no matter how carefully or rationally the net is woven, and Jake discovers that none of these narrow paths really works. The nets in the novel range from logical-positivist philosophy and left-wing politics through miming theatricals to film scripts and sophisticated blackmail. In the second novel, *The Flight from the Enchanter* (1956), Miss Murdoch deals with a different sort of illusion. All the characters are under spells, enchantments, held in a kind of emotional captivity by another person or force. The principal agent of enchantment, an ephemeral cosmopolite named Mischa Fox, exercises a spell over a number of the other characters in the novel; yet he feels no responsibility for the effects of the spells he exercises and the spells provide no real meaning or satisfaction for the characters caught in them. Emotional enchantment works no better than the weaving of conscious and rational nets, and the characters are eventually forced, by their own natures, to flee enchantment as they must unravel nets. The third novel is called *The Sandcastle* (1957). The title is emblematic of the love affair a married, fortyish schoolteacher tries to build with a young artist named Rain. But the affair cannot last; it is a castle of sand. As Rain explains, when talking about her Mediterranean background, she has known only dry, dirty sand, unsuitable for building castles of any shape or form. From the schoolteacher's point of view, Rain provides too much energy, too much vitality, for him to cope with in his circumscribed world, as a deluge of rain can wash away a sandcastle. And, significantly, there is a torrential rain on the day when the school teacher displays his inability to deal with all the complications of the affair. The elements of the affair—the grains of sand and moisture—exist, but the sand is either too dry or too wet. Human beings are unable to control the moisture, to build a lasting shape out of the illusory dream, and the castle either crumbles or is washed away.

In Miss Murdoch's fourth novel, *The Bell* (1958), a group of people in a lay religious community attempt to place a bell on the tower of a nearby abbey. The bell is a postulant, a means of entering the religious life for each of the people involved. But the bridge leading to the abbey has been tampered with and, in its journey, the bell topples into the lake. The bell itself, the effort of human beings to construct and particularize their own means of salvation, is undermined by human action, emotion, and behavior. At the same time the traditional bell, the bell that once actually pealed from the abbey tower, is recovered from the lake by two of the latest devout characters and sent to the British Museum as a historical curiosity. The tradition of the past is meaningful only for antiquarians, is removed from the central issues of experience, while the contemporary bell is another illusion, the image of another unsuccessful human attempt.

James Gindin. *Postwar British Fiction: New
Attitudes and Accents* (Berkeley: University
of California Press, 1963), pp. 178–79

All Miss Murdoch's novels can in an important sense be seen as studies of the "degrees of freedom" available to individuals. . . . The kinds of freedom studied vary, and the style and matter of the novels also vary greatly, but there is, I would maintain, a surprisingly constant unity of theme underlying the ideas of all the seven novels we have so far. Between the first two novels, *Under the Net* and *The Flight from the Enchanter,* and the third, *The Sand-castle,* there is a break—not only a stylistic attempt to move from fantasy-myth to depiction of character, but a break in subject-matter. The first two books have a social dimension, an emphasis on the possibilities of man's freedom in society at large and mechanized, an interest in work, in the sense of jobs, which is not importantly present in the later novels, which are more concerned with freedom within personal relationships, with Jamesian studies of one person's power over, or modification of another person—although both ideas are of course present in most of the novels.

The Flight from the Enchanter is certainly concerned with one individual's power over another within relationships as well as socially, and the problem of freedom in work, or how work limits freedom, recurs both in the organization of the community in *The Bell,* and in Mor's struggles with his job and the Labour party, or even Rain Carter's painting, in *The Sandcastle.* And the problem which Jake Donaghue encounters from time to time in *Under the Net,* the problem of economic freedom, of whether he can accept large sums of dishonorably earned money in order to live free of economic necessity, also, in a different form, besets Randall in *An Unofficial Rose,* who buys a kind of freedom with the money obtained from the sale of his father's Tintoretto.

But the general idea with which I want to begin the study of the freedom of the characters in the novels is that this freedom is worked out, very broadly speaking, in terms of a constant—and, in the nature of things, incomplete and unresolved—interaction of their own attempts to act, or to order their experience (a process which constantly degenerates into "deforming" reality by fantasy) with the transcendent "reality."

A. S. Byatt. *Degrees of Freedom: The Novels of Iris Murdoch* (Totowa, New Jersey: Barnes & Noble, 1965), pp. 11–12

I feel obliged to clarify further my use of the term *philosophical novelist* as it applies to Iris Murdoch. Unlike L. H. Myers or Thomas Mann in *The Magic Mountain,* she does not openly discuss philosophical ideas in her fiction. When her characters consider problems in ethics and morals, the problems are never presented as abstract doctrine. Her philosophical interest is always social morality rather than a moral code or set of principles that the reader is invited to apply to action and plot. Blending moral action and narrative structure, her novels convey a great urgency. The theme of prose fiction since the eighteenth century has been man's life in society, and the prevailing narrative method has been empirical. By refusing to sacrifice the individual to a principle or a universal, Iris Murdoch has contributed to and possibly enlarged the great tradition. Her philosophical essays make clear that without theory there can be no morality; with Socrates, Buber, and Marcel, she believes that the clarification of thought must precede man's redemption. This theoretical bias gains expression in the novels in the form of closely observed character interaction. The portrayals of Michael Meade in *The Bell,* Emma Sands in *An Unofficial Rose,* and Otto Narraway in *The Italian Girl* reveal that ethical systems matter far less than personal conduct. The final test of any professed morality is direct social experience. Life is not a thought system, and any attempt to reduce it to one involves a falsification. But by dramatizing concrete situations, the novelist shows personal conduct fortifying and even creating moral value.

The priority of distinct, incarnate beings and the attendant belief that man is his own measure also rule out a political reading of the novels: Iris

Murdoch's primary emphasis as a moralist is the free discovery of self and of other selves within the living tissue of human imperfection. Although she has stated an academic preference for Guild Socialism in one of her essays, I do not find the criticism of political institutions a major accent in her novels, with the possible exception of *The Flight from the Enchanter*. Like Amis, Wain, and Sillitoe in this aspect, she never uses such terms as *the proletariate* and *dialectical materialism*. But, unlike these writers, she studies the individual as a conscious entity responsible for making decisions that acknowledge the same degree of consciousness and reality in others. In this respect her awareness of social life may be called philosophical, for she sees the concrete presence of other people as something to be thought as well as perceived through the sense. The emphasis in her work on immediate experience suggests the term *novels of social education* rather than *novels of ideas,* per se. And her philosophical attitude is permeated by her artistic method, which combines objectivity and closely observed social relations: in our contingent world, dynamic interpersonal relations furnish the only escape from materialism and abstraction and the only likely approach to transcendent values.

> Peter Wolfe. *The Disciplined Heart: Iris
> Murdoch and Her Novels* (Columbia:
> University of Missouri Press, 1966),
> pp. 23–24

A lot of dirty water has fallen since Miss Murdoch first caught Jake under the net of merciful exposure [in *Under the Net*]. Eight novels have followed that first one published in 1954, and within the last five, the course of the stream Miss Murdoch is pursuing is clear and very treacherous. Miss Murdoch has turned from investigating the sane to propagating the grotesque as a high religion of behavior. She has gone from situations in which people are troubled by empty-of-center idiosyncrasies to situations in which characters justify their aberrations as superior ways of attacking life. . . .

The good news about Miss Murdoch's newest novel [*The Red and the Green*] is that she has dropped some of her tricks. The detailed fantasies and the spiral comic twists of her plot furniture she now reveals in a manner that no longer overwhelms the reader. In this sense, Miss Murdoch has "prepared" the reader for her characters' devious behavior and consistent inconstancies. . . .

Miss Murdoch has moved forward in this work, for which all of her readers will be grateful. Perhaps it is more accurate to say she has moved backward—back to the deeper feeling displayed in *The Bell,* without recourse to intellectual comedy or wit to hide the pain of her feelings; and backward to the simplicity of style of *The Sandcastle*. Certainly she is still dealing with deviant behavior, but she has dropped much of her devious and gimmick-ridden manner. Her interest in character has grown closer to acceptance of it for its own value.

> Martin Tucker. *The New Republic*. February
> 5, 1966, p. 26

With a living writer one must remind oneself to resist the progressivist or growth-rate fallacy. *The Time of the Angels* is an absorbingly interesting novel by the most seriously and, I think, consequentially entertaining of contemporary English novelists. Is it Iris Murdoch's best novel? I think not. Returning to the Gothic mannerisms of *The Unicorn* and *The Italian Girl,* it is also flawed in rather the same way; plot-rigging is flagrant, and main narrative resolutions are blatantly forced (though by now a certain kind of boisterous melodrama might as well be recognized as one of this author's stable and generally effective defenses "against dryness"). Being her latest book *should* this be her best, glibbest, most perfect? Certainly not. It is enough to say that *Angels* is as serious and vivacious, as secure in its diversely compassionate characterizations, as touching and forgiving in its pictures of the spiritual ordeal of human life, as the most admired of its predecessors. What more at present can one say than that a season without its new Murdoch would seem a dry season indeed?

Of course the possibility remains—this book renews it—of thinking that Iris Murdoch is mistaken in her calling and is no novelist. . . . But . . . if Iris Murdoch does not touch our consciousness of real life and move us with her projections of familiar experience, who in our literature does? Who *has* avoided her lapses into abstraction, contrivance, sensationalist over-management? Who *can* write—or see—like Tolstoy, or who work the Jamesian apparatus? Or is it equally possible that new uses and mutations of the still open form of the novel remain to be created and secured, and that the clear facts in the case of Iris Murdoch—her executive energy, the self-amplification and assurance of her fictional world, the promptness and persistence of her reception—are as good evidence as can be had for thinking that some part of major literary history (at once a history of forms and a history of consciousness and sensibility) is moving through the channel of her performance? On whom, in this case, is the critical *onus probandi?*

Warner Berthoff. Massachusetts Review.
Summer, 1967, p. 581

More than any other novelist around [Iris Murdoch] brings to the surface the question . . . Can people who think as we have come to think write good novels? For she maintains a potentially reductive double reality—representative figures, revolving perspectives that bring the writer near to being a central character. She invites, and investigates, the question, Is it perceived order or performance? She responds naturally to the mind as force, but has to look for what it can apply itself to and wonder how it can maintain its humanity against its destructive tendency. So action and scene inevitably overshadow identification with character.

Unquestionably, defense by reduction hurts an expansive form like the novel. The unevenness of Miss Murdoch's work suggests how unsure anyone is what will help it. For Miss Murdoch is, in Waugh's phrase, a "good trier."

(She would please some readers more if she were not always writing the novel she does not yet know how to write.) . . .

Miss Murdoch has by now progressed enough with her fictional world for it to have its own fable, told with increasing awareness and willingness to face new difficulties created by old solutions. The fable in its developed form goes like this. People of above-average competence, with no resources outside themselves, begin as egoists doing what comes naturally, and in the process injure and get injured. This first impulse exhausts itself in unsatisfying activism, which finally seems pointless. In this injury-inflicting world, eros is overmatched against aggressiveness. At some stage the individual naturally—not on existentialist principle—begins to think of regrouping, gathering his scattered forces and centering on his best possibilities. The effort, because it is a counterattack, becomes a private attempt at rebirth, vulnerable because unsupported in the confusing social fabric.

At this point Miss Murdoch's most original insight appears. G. S. Fraser has noted her skill at giving solidity to the normal. But normalcy is more than solid: it is the ultimate test of the unsupported will. Yet this norm, for which the personality is willing to fight so hard, seems in itself unattractive—amounts at bottom to an active, resentful, self-distrusting directionlessness. The characters who invoke this impulse against unconventional efforts to deal with defeat see in the attempted rebirths at best absurdity and worst danger to sanity. The skill Miss Murdoch has developed in giving life to the struggle between these two claims is her own greatest claim to significance.

James Hall. *The Lunatic Giant in the Drawing Room: The British and American Novel since 1930* (Bloomington: Indiana University Press, 1968), pp. 181–83

In Iris Murdoch's new novel, *The Black Prince,* the . . . broad theme [of the conspiracy theory of reality] wears, at first glance, a familiar shop-soiled air. Here are editorial prefaces and appendices, a middle-aged man in pursuit of a girl-child who hardly exists outside of his writing about her, a sprinkling of chess-symbolism, numerous diversions and dissertations upon aesthetics and the morality of literary creation, some dusty scholarship, and a catch-as-catch-can title (Edward II, Hamlet, the Prince of Darkness, perhaps an extra piece for the chess-board . . . Bradley Pearson takes a shine from all of these). A great deal of the book including the fussy pedantry of the narrator, all squeam and arch quotation marks and italicizations, looks as if it has been ransacked piecemeal from the Nabokov shelf. Yet this novel, despite its trail of still-bloody umbilical cords, is Miss Murdoch's best for a very long time; an uneven haphazard book which never seems to be quite sure about where it is going, but which is so ambitious in its—rather too many—directions that it can afford its failures. It has a reassuringly old-fashioned lumpish density, resonant with atmospheric detail, strong on incident, and marvelously satirically observant of the society it embodies. . . .

As a book about evil, a devil's monologue, *The Black Prince* is superb. In Bradley Pearson, Miss Murdoch has found a persona in which she can satisfactorily sink the awkwardness of her own prose; in him that curious alternation between the tone of a tart philosophy seminar and that of a purple passage in Ouida sounds perfectly convincing. He is, one suspects, the writer whom Miss Murdoch fears herself to be, and by exposing him she has written a very fine, very black book. I have hardly mentioned the tricksy apparatus which surrounds it; it is just scaffolding—necessary, perhaps, for the novel's construction, but unsightly and distracting now it's finished. *The Black Prince* does not need to advertise its modernity so modishly; it is too good for that.

Jonathan Raban. Encounter. May, 1973,
pp. 84–85

It is not the matter of specific Irish writers which is finally of greatest importance in trying to assess Murdoch's debt to her Irish connection; it is, rather, in the less definable and demonstrable matters of her use of setting, her sense of the value of individual difference in characters, and her tolerance for and use of eccentricity as a way of achieving individual difference in a world of reductively dreary sameness. It is only sensible to acknowledge at once that any one of these aspects of Murdoch's work could have come to her from other sources, and, perhaps, ultimately did, but there is the inescapable fact that these aspects are strong indeed in the work and attitudes of those writers from Swift to Yeats who formed the modern Irish consciousness.

Murdoch uses setting for effect more unabashedly than most modern writers, except perhaps American Southern writers (who have their affinities with Irish writers), and while it is certainly true that a nineteenth-century English writer like Scott, whom Murdoch cites with approval in another context, could have provided her with her model for settings, it could have come as well out of the Irish literary tradition. In her penchant for the extremes of pastoral sunshine and gothic mists, for example, the influence could easily have been the Synge of *In the Shadow of the Glen, The Well of the Saints,* or *Deirdre of the Sorrows.* The perhaps overcareful emphasis upon the rain in *The Red and the Green* and the setting of Gaze Castle in *The Unicorn* are two cases which can be set beside the pastoral moment of the sunlit meadow in *The Sandcastle,* a moment which, insofar as versions of pastoral cannot be sustained, is quickly undercut by the weight of a real world in which expensive motor cars slowly but inexorably overturn to settle on their tops in crystal-clear rivers.

Equally difficult to establish with absolute certainty but coincidental enough to bear consideration is the insistence by Murdoch on eccentricity, the exaggeration of character and gesture which is everywhere in the Irish literary tradition. Again, it is clear that Murdoch's model might be elsewhere—in Dickens, perhaps, but in the use Murdoch makes of eccentricity for mounting an attack on the comfortable veneer of middle-class life the echoes are those of Synge or Yeats, O'Casey or Joyce. Yet there is in Murdoch none of the rage associated with such attacks in these writers. Although her mode is also comedy, an ironic detachment like that Murdoch so admires in certain nineteenth-century English writers is a fact that makes it difficult to push too hard an exclusive claim of Irish influence in the treatment of character. Murdoch's eclecticism makes it difficult to speak of her solely within the Irish context, and yet it virtually guarantees that the force of her Irish background is to be felt, if only indirectly.

Donna Gerstenberger. Iris Murdoch
(Lewisburg, Pennsylvania: Bucknell
University Press, 1975), pp. 77–79

In Murdoch's four most recent novels, *The Nice and the Good, Bruno's Dream, A Fairly Honorable Defeat,* and *An Accidental Man,* the ethical framework provides a fairly consistent structure, a central debate and resolution worked through the usual Murdoch world of bizarre incident and predictably unpredictable encounters. In two of these novels, *The Nice and the Good* and *A Fairly Honorable Defeat,* the debate contrasts a false morality with a genuine one by establishing a married couple who think their relationship a model for others. In one novel, Murdoch satirizes their hollowness; in the other, she introduces an agent of evil, impelled by his own isolation and pain, who destroys them. Often, in these novels, the false, the smug, and the self-righteous are articulate about their pretended virtues; they theorize and erect structures that delude themselves and others. But those posed against them, the genuinely good, are not the unconscious creatures of the earlier novels: rather, more quietly, less grandiosely, they both articulate and act out their ethics, their concern for others, their capacity to see and act in terms of the self and other selves and of individual human particularities. God figures, too, are not simply the deluding myths of the early novels, for God figures, given their supernatural powers and status only by themselves or other human beings, have the humanly ethical choice between involving themselves in human concerns and judgments and remaining remote in the enclosures of human fabrication. The unconscious characters, on the other hand, are, in the later fiction, likely to be characterized as "accidental," exercising no will, following random personal impulse, and living as harmful parasites.

James Gindin. In Alan Warren Friedman,
ed. Forms of Modern British Fiction
(Austin: University of Texas Press, 1975),
pp. 34–35

Iris Murdoch's novels continue to be interesting because the ideas that originally animated them still obsess her and because she resists simplifying them. It is no secret that her characters and situations have become stock. I would hazard that she turns out novel year after year not because the formula is perfect or the money pleasant but because the spiritual craving persists. How to convey one more time the opacity of persons and the mysteries of freedom? Viking's blurb quotes her revealingly: "I try to prolong the early stage of inventing as long as possible. Once it is written, it ceases to be flexible. I always work out the plot closely, making a very detailed synopsis of the whole thing before I write a word." A wordless period of exploration and evolving possibilities, followed and perhaps spoiled by an inflexible plot; no wonder she must always begin again.

It is remarkable how much of her latest, *Henry and Cato,* may be referred to Murdoch's essay "Against Dryness" (*Encounter,* January, 1961), where she cautioned against an art that offers consolation instead of truth. We console ourselves, she said in 1961, with myths and stories, fantasies and magic, assuming we are free to know the real world according to our own images. . . . Most of the characters in *Henry and Cato* suffer from this malady. Henry Marshalson fancies himself an art historian in America, then a stand-in for his late brother (inheriting a mistress as well as the family estate), then an idealistic social reformer (he will sell the estate and give away the money). Cato Forbes thinks he is free to become a Catholic priest, then free to lose his faith and become father-protector to Beautiful Joe of the slums. . . .

These self-deceptions might be comic if Murdoch had failed to give weight to their appeal. What she is best at, however, are moments when occasions of intense fantasy disclose something more real. In Henry's veritable orgy of possessing his brother's estate (just as it's an "orgy of will," later, to get rid of it), he falls prey to an inexplicable desolation: "Was there some ritual, some ceremony of possession, for which he was never to become worthy?" Still feeling excluded, "lacking the key to enchantment," he senses his need "to see man," as Murdoch wrote in 1961, "against a background of values, of realities, which transcend him." Richly figured in the family tapestry, in [his mother's] brocade robes, and in the natural world, Henry's background at last comes to possess him. . . .

What undercuts the complex moral design of this novel, and so many of Murdoch's others, is its crystalline plot. It caters to the reader's weakness for magic fantasy, and tends to cancel the mysteries and opacities of the real world. It schematizes experience even as it condemns characters who do the same. Trying to conceal the fact that her scheme is there, Murdoch clutters the story with details that fail to be mysterious. And once again, instead of the articulation of "the difficulty and complexity of the moral life," she offers mainly an intellectual entertainment.

Dean Flower. *Hudson Review.* Summer,
1977, pp. 307–8

A fifty-year vogue for "experimental" novels notwithstanding, Iris Murdoch continues, to all outward appearances, to write nineteenth century fiction. But if she avoids word play, unstructured plots, even the stream-of-consciousness, her novels are still experimental, but in Zola's sense, not Joyce's. Like her French predecessor, Murdoch believes that the novel can evaluate ideas; for her literature is "the most essential and fundamental aspect of culture . . . an education in how to picture and understand human situations." Thus, although she has written a number of philosophical essays, Murdoch seems uncomfortable with abstract pronouncements and repeatedly returns to the novel, where ideas about moral behavior can be acted out in recognizable psychologies and situations. To a great extent, the success of her novels depends on the rigor of the experiment; at best, they criticize, complicate, or even contradict her preconceptions, while at their worst, they serve as vehicles for expounding ideas they fail to dramatize. This link between successfully developed ideas and successful fiction can be seen if we look, for example, at Murdoch's critique of romantic suffering—and, by extension, of romantic love. Set forth in *The Sovereignty of Good,* a collection of essays published in 1970, it has subsequently become a major theme in two novels, *An Accidental Man,* published in 1971, and the 1974 novel *The Sacred and Profane Love Machine.* By tracing this theme from the essays through the two novels, we see how Murdoch challenges her own tenets, and we discover that the superiority of *The Sacred and Profane Love Machine* derives from the fact that, with its more complicated characters, it is able to test the implications of romantic suffering and romantic love more radically than either of the earlier works. . . .

In *The Sacred and Profane Love Machine* we sense a writer more profoundly concerned with experiment, more willing to dramatize all of the problems her views entail. This latest novel is far from comforting, either to Murdoch or to ourselves, but it confirms at least the negative vision of *The Sovereignty of Good,* in which Murdoch wrote that "Almost anything that consoles us is a fake." If she has not yet achieved the "austere . . . beauty" of great art, still the genuineness of psychology and the rigor of thought in *The Sacred and Profane Love Machine* augur well for the philosophical novel in our time.

Margaret Scanlan. *Renascence.* Winter,
1977, pp. 69, 85

The work of the philosophy don Iris Murdoch, born in Dublin and an unabashed francophile, is more plainly related to the French reflexive tradition. Her first published book was an examination of Jean-Paul Sartre, *Sartre: Romantic Rationalist* (1953). As could be expected, it devotes a chapter to that French author's self-begetting novel, *La Nausée.*

Iris Murdoch's own first novel, *Under the Net,* was published in the following year. Dedicated to the contemporary French novelist Raymond Queneau, the text of *Under the Net* sparkles with an abundance of italicized French expressions—*par exemple, mêlée, frisson, tour de force, tête à tête, bien renseigné, dérèglement de tous les sens, je m'en fichais* and *au fond.* Some important scenes in the novel are set in Paris, and its narrator and central protagonist, Jake Donaghue, is English translator of the fictive French novelist Jean Pierre Breteuil. A discussion of Marcel Proust with Hugo Belfounder has significant consequences for Jake, while Jake's description of "a suburb of southern London where contingency reaches the point of nausea" recalls Sartre's distinctive terminology. . . .

[But] Murdoch's reading of Sartre suggests a view of French fiction as aseptic. She regards it as her British, and human, duty to introduce microorganisms, "the *stuff* of human life," into the Petri dish furnished by her teachers on the Continent. . . .

In her essay "Against Dryness," Murdoch contrasts imagination with fantasy. According to her view, imagination, which respects the contingency of the world, is a reflexive, provisional faculty, whereas fantasy naïvely distorts reality by hypostatizing it in inflexible myths. Fantasy, rather than an emancipator, is a servile attempt to flee messy ambiguities for a realm of complacent artifice. Imagination, by plunging us into the complex mire of human existence, is thereby an exercise in free will. . . .

Literature, as evident in the example of Jake Donaghue, can be an effective means of accommodating the contingent world. Murdoch promises:"Through literature we can re-discover a sense of the density of our lives. Literature can arm us against consolation and fantasy and can help us to recover from the ailments of Romanticism." And *Under the Net* is a striking portrait of its central protagonist's moral progress.

Although its narrator confesses, "I'm not telling you the story of my life," *Under the Net* creates the illusion of an extended *Bildungsroman*. The narrative is defined by two visits to Mrs. Tinckham's. When he returns to her shop at the end, Jake receives the following greeting: "'Hello, dearie,' said Mrs. Tinck. 'You've been a long time.'" In terms of clock-time, it has not been especially long—a matter of days rather than the years usually encompassed by novels about the making of a novelist. However, much has happened. Jake's life has undergone a transformation, one that, presented in a novel, is made possible by his commitment to the complexities of novel-writing. Begetting itself and a new self for Jake, *Under the Net* avoids flight. It returns for a candid assessment of itself and the world in which it is enmeshed.

Steven G. Kellerman. *The Self-Begetting Novel* (New York: Columbia University Press, 1980), pp. 87, 92–93

A patient study of Murdoch's work reveals how deceptive the bourgeois surface in fact is, and how ironic her deployment of its materials. Although she operates structurally from situation and character, the process of her best books involves a subtle peeling-off of layers of bourgeois complacency and prejudice. Her primary tools are a devastating accuracy in the detail of human character and an enormous allusive frame which pushes the reader toward a willingness to see how large her intentions are. When the allusions fail, as they tend to in early novels like *A Severed Head* and *The Italian Girl,* the result is overplotted, tricksy books where the profound laws of causality central to Murdoch's thought are lost in clever satire. When these allusions to mythology, art and religion are functioning at a high level of imaginative power, however, their syncretic force is such that they become images assisting the novel towards profound and unnerving ends. These ends are religious in impact, but the novels never succumb to the warm fuzziness of consoling or salvational piety. Great mystics are invoked, especially Julian of Norwich and occasionally St. John of the Cross, and Christ actually makes a personal appearance in one novel, but the real direction of the fiction works through the characters of the workaday world which realism has always used as its basis: as a character in *Nuns and Soldiers* describes the process, the problem for Murdoch is "to try, to invent, to work through our nature against our nature." The goal is spiritual discernment; the enemy, debasement of the religious task.

The fact that ultimate reality, even the cosmos itself, lies behind the drifting and often frenetic bourgeois surface is the vast secret of Murdoch's best fiction, and the sheer nerve and ambition required in the projection of such a stage on which to place traditional realism make her fictions risky in the extreme. There can be no doubt, for example, that it is correct to read *A Fairly Honourable Defeat* as an oblique commentary on the combat of good and evil and the defeat of the Christian Trinity, and yet its psychological verisimilitude deflects the allegorical loftiness of its conception. Similarly, Murdoch's often studied references to sainthood are seen in her serious work as an ironic chimera, a product of bourgeois optimism and atavistic memory of a golden age long since past. As she studies the realms of ethics and spirituality in novel after novel, it becomes clear that such conceptions as sainthood are too sadly far from the realist world of our present, and the mediocrity of our response to her hard, cool moral discriminations can keep us from pursuing them in their final implications.

Elizabeth Dipple. *Iris Murdoch: Work for the Spirit* (Chicago: University of Chicago Press, 1982), pp. 3–4

It is always dangerous to impute a character's views to an author: but in Iris Murdoch's case there is a special hazard. Just because she does seem to hold that what makes utterances true or false is not the same as what makes statements true or false, so that a true statement can be uttered as a falsehood (but not, I take it, vice versa), Iris Murdoch's characters sometimes appear, for the moment at least, to deprive Iris Murdoch's philosophical views of credibility by the way in which they utter them. So in *The Time of the Angels* as the two brothers, Marcus and Carel, move unerringly and unintentionally toward disaster, what Marcus utters to himself as false consolation are pieces of Iris Murdoch's own philosophy. Marcus is writing a book called "Morality in a World Without God" in which he attacks those who have tried to understand judgments about goodness as expressions of will or choice in just the way that Iris Murdoch has done in more than one essay. Carel, an Anglican priest who no longer believes in God, and according to whom no one has as yet understood in a sufficiently radical way the consequences of not believing, embodies a view of which Iris Murdoch has said that she "is often half persuaded," but which she finally rejects: the view that if God is not credible, then God too is a superstition. Marcus after the disaster reflects: "Would he go on working on his book? Perhaps it was a book which only a genius could write, and he was not a genius. It might be that what he wanted to say about love and about humanity was true but simply could not be expressed as a theory."

What this suggests is not only that a truth may be uttered so that it is a lie, but that moral truth may be such as to evade *any* theoretical expression—perhaps with the consequence that all theoretical expression of it will be to some degree a lie. Iris Murdoch's novels are philosophy: but they are philosophy which casts doubts on all philosophy including her own. She is an author whose project involves an ironic distance not only from her characters but also from herself.

Alasdair MacIntyre. London Review of Books. June 3, 1982, p. 15

The Red and the Green is clearly an Irish historical novel in terms of its subject matter as well as many of the conventions it adopts. The Irish literary influences apparent in Murdoch's work are fellow travelers among the Ascendancy: [Sheridan] Le Fanu, [Standish] O'Grady, and Yeats. Her novel *The Unicorn* (1963) was a Gothic novel influenced by the work of Le Fanu. In *The Red and the Green,* the antiquarian Christopher Bellman expresses opinions remarkably like those of O'Grady: "Ireland's real past *is* the ascendancy. Ireland should turn back to the eighteenth century." Arguing that Anglo-Irish leaders of the eighteenth century would have worked with English leaders to relieve the Great Famine, Bellman calls the romantic Pearse an "idiot" and echoes O'Grady's nostalgia for the Anglo-Irish "Patriot Parliament" of Gratan and Flood. Similarly, throughout the novel there are echoes of Yeats, especially at the end, where the tone and even the language of the 1938 "Epilogue" to the Rising are very close to Yeats's pronouncement that the leaders of 1916 have been transformed, that "a terrible beauty is born."

As in [Walter] Macken's novels, a new sense of distance from history is evident in *The Red and the Green*. Writing in the 1960s, Murdoch has the detachment necessary to explore her main theme: the conflicts between energy and order, rebellion and law, eros and impotence, among an Anglo-Irish family fifty years earlier. But in contrast to Macken's chronologically sprawling novels, *The Red and the Green* is focused upon just a few days before and during the Rising in April 1916. This permits an interesting comparison of the novel to O'Flaherty's similarly focused *Insurrection*—a comparison which yields, for the most part, contrast more than semblance. . . .

Much of the criticism on *The Red and the Green* quite rightly focuses upon character conflicts in the novel; character is always Murdoch's prime concern. Weldon Thornton, for example, points out that the novel's characters seek an elusive balance between energy and order, passion and control, always desiring the qualities in others which they feel to be lacking in themselves. Pat Dumay's cousin Andrew Chase-White is jealous of Pat's resoluteness and courage—qualities we discover to be deceptive. Christopher Bellman seems to possess British restraint and good sense, but then he perishes on his way to join the rebels in the General Post Office. Barney Drumm seeks courage by participating in the Rising and then shoots himself in the foot. Aunt Millie seeks true individuality and discovers merely roles, a facade. These character conflicts possess a broader political, historical significance. The most important conflict is that between Andrew Chase-White and Pat Dumay, for they are really the Red and the Green of the novel, and they never understand each other.

James M. Cahalan. *Great Hatred, Little
Room: The Irish Historical Novel* (Syracuse,
New York: Syracuse University Press, 1983),
pp. 165–66, 168

To assert that Iris Murdoch is a major contemporary writer is to suggest something of the state of the post-war novel in Britain. In the period since the appearance of her first published novel *Under the Net* in 1954, she has emerged not only as one of the most productive and influential British novelists of her generation but, equally importantly, as a powerfully intellectual and original theorist of fiction. The increasingly evident liveliness and variety of British fiction since the war has contrasted very curiously with a sense of restraint about aesthetic discussion of the novel: Iris Murdoch is unusual in having consistently taken a clear view of the form she has explored. She has emphasized that she aims to write as a realist, in an identifiably nineteenth-century tradition of English and European fiction. At the same time, however, she has maintained that it is now practically impossible for novelists to do this, for good philosophical and epistemological reasons. In all this, she has indicated the difficulties and at the same time the potential of contemporary fiction, especially in the British tradition, and both her views and her practice are deeply revealing about the novel today. . . .

Murdoch's theoretical position is in fact a deeply examined one. It owes its development not simply to her "other" career as one of Britain's leading moral philosophers, but results, more generally, from a habit of reading and thought which displays a carefully cultivated, historically aware, and genuinely international literary sensibility (unlike that of other writers who have been associated with the revival of realism in post-war Britain). It arises from strong conceptions of the role of art in society and as an instrument of human knowledge. . . .

We have also to be able to read her novels less as examples of traditional realism than as manifestations of curiosity about the elements and assumptions which made the novel a serious form of art, insofar as they constitute an extended enquiry which has itself deepened and grown complex as time has gone by. In this way her career can be seen to have fallen into a number of phases and stages leading her from the influence of post-war existentialist fiction to a position now peculiarly her own.

Richard Todd. *Iris Murdoch* (London: Methuen, 1984), pp. 13–15

Iris Murdoch's novels pose in new and tantalizing ways the question of what it means to write as a woman, to read as a woman. They disconcert and fascinate both female and male readers by continually questioning gender identity and transgressing gender boundaries. At the same time they have notably not attracted the attention of feminist critics. . . .

In the most obvious sense of the phrase Iris Murdoch does not "write as a woman." Unlike so many of her sister-novelists, Doris Lessing and Margaret Drabble for example, she has not apparently been concerned to explore what Elaine Showalter has called the "wild zone" of female experience, that area where women's experience does not overlap with men's. On the contrary the fictionalized masculine perspective is everywhere apparent in her novels. She is a female writer who likes wearing male masks. In the seven novels where she employs a dramatized narrator, from her earliest novel, *Under the Net* (1954) to her latest but one, *The Philosopher's Pupil* (1983), that narrator is invariably male. These seven novels, which also include *A Severed Head* (1961), *The Italian Girl* (1964), *The Black Prince* (1973), *A Word Child* (1975) and *The Sea, The Sea* (1978), cover the thirty-odd years' span of Iris Murdoch's career to date; they constitute, it will readily be agreed, some of her most distinctive and thoughtful work. . . .

The male narration obviously de-centers the female point of view. As a woman writing, Iris Murdoch is clearly aware of what she is doing and can both seriously and playfully exaggerate this de-centering effect. . . .

Iris Murdoch shows all human beings, men and women alike, as subject to *eikasia* and particularly to that form of *eikasia* which renders other people invisible. But it is much more likely to be a woman than a man who exclaims in exasperation, as Georgie does to Martin in *A Severed Head,* "you've got to *see me.*" Part of the reason why Iris Murdoch's male narrators fail to "see" is precisely because they talk too much. Like Plato's bad art-object they cherish their volubility. . . .

In terms of the current psychoanalytically based theories of sexual difference, notably the work of Luce Irigaray, this "male mimicry" can be seen as a potential means of undoing the repressive (patriarchal) structures encoded in language itself (Lacan's "symbolic order"), as a way of "exposing through imitation." As such it can point the way forward to a possible recovery of the operation of the "feminine" in language.

Deborah Johnson. *Iris Murdoch.* (Brighton, England: Harvester, 1987), pp. 1–2, 8–9

There is little disagreement among critics that Iris Murdoch's fiction contains comic elements that are an important aspect of her work. Problems arise, however, in critical evaluations of her use of comedy, for although several critics praise what is usually described as her "wit," others believe that the humorous tone of her novels, coupled with the serious and sometimes tragic nature of the subject matter, creates an unresolved tension that undermines her achievement as a novelist. . . .

Murdoch's comic fiction attempts this presentation of "whole, impure humanity in action"; her comedy is generally one of acceptance and tolerance of contingency, human frailty, and eccentricity. She wants to create a realistic world that can do justice to the ludicrous, incomplete, and accidental "jumble" of everyday life, and by doing so, to express the density and importance of what she has called "transcendent reality." The comic dimension of this presentation of reality is heightened by the fact that the novelist must use words that distort the reality he is expressing. For Murdoch, then, the novel is comic both in its range of content and in the ironic quality of language itself; it now remains to look closely at three novels that best illustrate Iris Murdoch's talent as a comic writer.

Angela Hague. *Iris Murdoch's Comic Vision:* (Cranbury, New Jersey: Susquehanna University Press, 1989), pp. 42, 69

The idea of art as a means of changing consciousness is shown throughout her writings. Any art, including such expressions as painting, music, dance, theater, and literature, can illuminate if it is great enough. Literature, for example, conveys fundamental truths across cultures and through generations. Murdoch says in the essay "Existentialists and Mystics" that "we today have no great or essential difficulty in understanding plays written by Greeks in the fifth century B.C. We make, in many respects though not in all, the same kinds of moral judgments as the Greeks did, and we recognize good or decent people in times and literature remote from our own. . . .

Because of the truth-conveying properties of art, Murdoch believes artists have a messianic duty to present reality in their art. Thus her aesthetics emphasize the importance of realism in the novel, and she regrets the experimental nature of the modern novel and its lack of adequate and truthful characterization.

For Murdoch, the artist who truly apprehends the existence of others has virtue, and she would encourage the writer to attend carefully in order to reveal the greatest amount of truth possible. . . .

Murdoch's message has not changed considerably throughout forty years of writing. It has become more complex and highly textured by allusions, iconography, and comic irony, but the moral philosopher emerges from behind her realistic portrayal of unique individuals. And the Platonist in her concludes that individuals live in a world of illusion and will never know much. However, Murdoch maintains an optimism for the human race which belies her portrait of egoistic individuals who attend only to themselves and cling to the consolations of the world. The vision of truth is there, even if individuals can gain only intimations of it, and the artist who attends carefully in order to present a just and accurate vision will be an instrument of truth for the world.

Cheryl K. Bove. *Understanding Iris Murdoch* (Columbia: University of South Carolina Press, 1993), pp. 191–94

NAIDU, SAROJINI (INDIA) 1879–1949

Like Tagore and Aurobindo, Sarojini Naidu too was more than a poet; she was one of Mother India's most gifted children, readily sharing her burden of pain, fiercely articulating her agonies and hopes, and gallantly striving to redeem the Mother and redeem the time. It was as an English poet Sarojini Naidu first caught the attention of the public, but that was only the beginning. In course of time the patriot exceeded the poet, and Sarojini Naidu came to occupy some of the highest unofficial and official positions in the public life of India. . . .

The Golden Threshold, Sarojini Naidu's first collection of poems, came out in 1905. The papers were enthusiastic. "This little volume should silence for ever the scoffer who declares that women cannot write poetry," so wrote the *Review of Reviews;* "Her poetry seems to sing itself as if her swift thoughts and strong emotions sprang into lyrics of themselves," cooed *The Times;* and the *Glasgow Herald* made an important point: "The pictures are of the East it is true: but there is something fundamentally human in them that seems to prove that the best song knows nothing of East or West." As a poet, then, Sarojini Naidu had definitely arrived. In India she was hailed as the Nightingale of Indian song. . . .

Sarojini Naidu's second volume of poems, *The Bird of Time* came out in 1912. In his Foreword to the book, Edmund Gosse remarked that there was discernible in it "a graver music" than in the earlier volume. These are "songs of life and death"—life is often brightly painted, but death's shadows creep or linger. . . .

The change in note, however, is sharper in Sarojini Naidu's third and final collection, *The Broken Wing,* which was published in 1917. The memorial verses addressed to her father and to Gokhale are nobly articulate. . . . With the arrival of Mahatma Gandhi on the political scene, Sarojini Naidu found a new power to galvanize her to life. It was an age of heroic striving, an age of imperatives and absolutes. She looked into her bruised and broken heart once more and saw there a new Vision—the Vision of the chained Mother—and vowed to break the bonds. "My woman's intelligence," she once remarked, "cannot grapple with the transcendent details of politics." But love of the Mother was no abstruse science, and therefore for Sarojini Naidu politics was but a form of love, and sedition but a form of poetry. The new lover expressed herself in inspiring oratory and fearless action. . . .

While she usually preferred the calm of mind to the storm, the music of the flute to the tumult of the soul, she has sung of these too—the whirling eddies, the raging fevers—in several of her poems, notably in *The Broken*

Wing. She was, above all, sensitive to beauty, the beauty of living things, the beauty of holiness, the beauty of the Buddha's compassion, the beauty of Brindavan's Lord. She didn't specially seek out the bizarre, the exotic, the exceptional, but her poems lack neither variety nor the flavor of actuality. Children's poems, nature poems, patriotic poems, poems of love and death, even poems of mystical transcendence, Sarojini Naidu essayed them all; and with her unfailing verbal felicity and rhythmical dexterity, she generally succeeded as well. Seldom did she venture out of her depth; she wasn't interested in wild experimentation; she didn't cudgel herself towards explosive modernity. But she had genuine poetic talent, and she was a wholesome and authentic singer.

> K. R. Srinivasa Iyengar. *Indian Writing in*
> *English* (New York: Asia Publications,
> 1983), pp. 207, 215–17, 222, 226

Sarojini Naidu writes instant poetry where images and metaphors come rolling ready on the hotplates of imagination. Her poetry is intensely emotional, at times passionate to the point of eroticism and always has a spring-like lyricism. In her can be perceived the influence of the British Romantic poets, but what makes it interesting and relevant to the Indian tradition is the sustenance from the twin indigenous sources. More discerning critics have traced in her poetry the deep and pervasive classical Sanskrit aestheticians' tradition, the Sringarik verse. She combines in many of her poems the classical Sanskrit tradition with the voluptuousness of Persian poetry. The fascinating appeal of the *gazal* and the *thumri* is also ingrained in her lyrics.

In 1894 she met Mahatma Gandhi and since then she went on extending the frontiers of her political achievements. The poet in her was smothered, and the singer silenced but not before Mahatma Gandhi had given her the title—"The Nightingale of India."

> Hari Mohar Prasad and Chakradha Prasad
> Singh. *Indian Poetry in English* (New Delhi:
> Sterling, 1985), p. 22

Despite her great political prominence, Sarojini Naidu first entered the public realm as a poet, and was celebrated as such. She espoused a mellifluous if dated English diction: her images of private, pained women suffering emotional deprivation, even psychic imprisonment, stand as a direct foil to the public life she so fearlessly took to. In the cause of National freedom, she traveled countless miles, often in hardship, courting arrest, campaigning in her strong orator's voice all over India from as early as 1903. Was she indeed able to cauterize her private pain through her poems and then move outwards into the public sphere? Or did the poems with their sometimes cloying diction, their female figures trapped in an unredeemed sexuality, force her to leave them behind, the writer herself consumed more and more by the political struggle so that by 1917 she effectively stopped writing?

Naidu inherited something of the complex linguistic situation of India. Born in 1879 of Bengali parents in the city of Hyderabad, she spoke not Bengali but Urdu, the Islamic language of culture in Hyderabad. Living at the edge of Bengali and espousing Urdu, Naidu added to these English, the language of colonization. She used English both in her poetry and in her powerful orations.

Her first book of poetry, *The Golden Threshold*, was published in London in 1905. Its frontispiece was a pen and ink drawing by J. B. Yeats: "June 1896" appears under the clearly legible signature. Her image is instructive. The face of the young woman, her posture upright though not stiff, is grave, composed. Her eyes are dark, etched firmly under the straight brows. Her hair is tied back. The hands clasped above her chest form a graceful line to the chin. The shoulders are erect. It is clear from this line drawing that both the gravity and the innocence of this adolescent were visible. . . .

Indeed, Naidu's early poetry (and all her poetry was composed in English) establishes a theme never overcome in her career as a writer. The work is haunted by a voice telling of other female selves, resonances of subjectivity, that endure mutilation and are imprisoned psychically. . . .

[The year] 1917 saw the publication of Naidu's last volume of poetry, *The Broken Wing*. She was thirty-eight. After it, though she might have scribbled a few lines from time to time, she never seriously wrote poetry. Her life was consumed by the rigors of public campaigning, her years punctuated by imprisonment. Politically, she was known throughout India. This last volume culminates in a long poem called *The Temple*, a poem of undeniable eroticism that the epigram from Tagore ("My passion shall burn as the flame of Salvation") cannot quite mask. One gathers that the poem caused quite a stir when the volume first appeared. There were rumors of illicit love or a sexual passion the poet could not wholly fulfil in her life.

Meena Alexander. Ariel. 17, 1986,
pp. 51–52, 57

NALKOWSKA, ZOFIA (POLAND) 1884–1954

Specifically the story of Polish life, this very unusual book [*Kobiety (Women)*] reveals the secret springs of all human life. To read it after a long course of the mediocre, superficial writing through which a reviewer, in the course of his duty, must wade is like emerging from the subway and drawing pure air into the lungs.

The book is written in the first person and is really the diary of a young girl, physically beautiful, possessing an alert mind, who gazes on the confusing spectacle of life and "strives to find a meaning in it all." She is passionate and eager, as are all the characters with whom she comes in contact. . . .

The feminine soul, with its curious inconsistencies, its transports, its idealisms and its little meannesses, is relentlessly laid bare. Janka Dernowicz, the girl through whom the authoress chooses to speak, is naïve and unafraid. . . .

This is the first of Mme. Nalkowska's novels to be translated into English. It is to be hoped that it will not be the last.

The New York Times. October 24, 1920,

p. 25

The central theme of *Granica* [The Border] reminds the reader of Tolstoi's *Resurrection.* It is, as it were, an artistically different variation on the same theme. In a number of interesting ways, the fates of Zenon Ziembiewicz and Justyna Bogutowna parallel those of Dmitri Nekhludov and Katya Maslova; the differences are even more interesting.

Nalkowska's novel, unlike Tolstoi's, is suggestive mainly through its artistic value. There are some attempts at attaching philosophical formulas to the tragedy, but the novel's main value does not rest on them. Zenon is convinced, as we all are, that his experience differs from everything other people may experience and everything other people may think of it. The external plot is that he had a love affair with a girl from a lower social class, that through an unspoken, secret wish (which she nevertheless understood very well) he forced her into an abortion, that he later married an intelligent and loving woman, had a son with her, and should have been very happy.

So it looks from the outside, but from Zenon's subjective viewpoint it was very different. At first he felt everything was unique and imperative. Much later he comes to the conclusion that "we are as others think us to be, not as we think we are" . . . that there is a "borderline beyond which one should not go, beyond which one ceases to be oneself." These formulas, however, do not exhaust the ideological meaning of the novel. What follows, together with the events described here, cannot be reduced to a contradiction between the individual and the collective ethical criteria. This novel, like every true work of art, communicates something that cannot be expressed through logical categories. Behind the tragedy described here there is a sober and cruel truth about life, a truth that is in its essence inexpressible. It can be revealed for an infinitesimal moment, but it cannot be formulated in any kind of aphorism. The fact that such a moment can arise while reading *Granica* is the greatest and the most decisive value of this novel.

Leon Piwinski. *Rocznik literacki.* 1935,

pp. 75–76

Even [Nalkowska's] early short stories and novels, of which *Kobiety, Ksiaże* [Prince], and *Narecyza* [Narcyza] are good examples, reveal an original and mature talent well aware of its means and intentions, an unusual gift for penetrating analysis and well-planned structure, and a style fully harmonizing with the somewhat hot-house atmosphere of that world.

After the war that world changed, and new problems appeared. *Hrabia Emil* [Count Emil] showed war as "a terrible evil, regardless of what it is waged for"; *Romans Teresy Hennert* (The Romance of Teresa Hennert) presented "a picture of changes which took place in Poland in people and among people"; *Sciany swiata* (The Walls of the World), was a gloomy book about people in prison "who took evil upon themselves considering that evil as their duty, since the inevitable sum of all evil must be somehow distributed among people."

In connection with this, Nalkowska's style also underwent a thorough change. It began to be characterized by an ever-increasing simplicity, economy, and concentration, together with a striving for "authenticity" in grasping and elaborating her themes. The hunger for "authenticity" and "truth" which engrossed the minds of all post-war Europe, was reflected in the Polish novel as well. The slogan of "new objectivism" ("neue Sachlichkeit") was modified by Nalkowska to "written reality." This meant consciously foregoing many traditional means of intriguing the reader and of keeping him in suspense; sometimes it even meant breaking with the traditional novel form for the sake of an exact, dispassionate description of a seemingly simple and commonplace reality, which, however, contained profound problems. Consequently many of Nalkowska's works of that time lack the character of traditional novels with absorbing plots and conflicts; nevertheless, they are original and well-constructed works of art (*Dom nad lakami* [The House on the Meadows]; *Chaucas* [Chaucas]).

Nalkowska did not limit herself to this form, however. The force of the novel tradition is evidently so great that a true novelist must write novels in the proper sense of the word. Nalkowska's last work written before the Second World War, *Granica*, is just such a novel, in which a fascinating plot is combined with the style of "written reality" to make an original entity.

Manfred Kridl. *A Survey of Polish Literature and Culture* (New York: Columbia University Press, 1956), p. 496

One of the most important of Zofia Nalkowska's postwar works is *Medaliony* [The Medallions]. It is based on the materials with which Nalkowska became acquainted as a member of the International Commission for the Investigation of War Crimes. She visited the mass-extermination camps of the Fascists, studied acts of indictment, and attended trials.

Medaliony consists of eight brief episodes based on concrete facts. Nothing is fiction here. Facts, words, intonations—all is taken by the writer from the testimonies by the victims of the Fascists and other eyewitnesses. Nalkowska consciously tried to limit her intervention as a narrator, on the principle that any comment would obscure the authenticity of the picture. From one episode to the other, one thought is carried through and expressed in almost identical words: "She went through things no one would believe. And she herself would not have believed it if not for the fact that this was—the truth." "It was these people's lot to go through things it is impossible to go through."

Medaliony is laconic in the highest degree. In each of the accounts there are just a few authentic details, powerful and expressive. An example is the scene at the Institute of Anatomy of O. Spanner, where the human bodies are pedantically prepared for the production of soap. . . . But *Medaliony* is not only description; through concrete, authentic facts Nalkowska has created a generalized picture of the Nazi crimes, has shown their inhuman essence. . . . And the epigraph to *Medaliony*—"Men have conceived such a fate for men"—became a frightening alarm, a call for alertness that characterizes the whole postwar career of Nalkowska.

T. P. Agapkina. *Istoriya polskoi literatury*
(Moscow: Nauka, 1969), pp. 263–64

NARANJO, CARMEN (COSTA RICA) 1931–

The very poor distribution that books of poetry enjoy keeps many of the splendid poets who rise like the morning star in the firmament of Spanish American letters in obscurity. They are there, but almost nobody sees them. For this reason, the cultural endeavors of a country must entail circulating the work of its poets by promoting the scholarly study of the best of them so that readers and students can understand them more deeply.

Carmen Naranjo held the post of Minister of Culture, Youth and Sports in Costa Rica (until April 30, 1976, when she resigned) and her name stood out every day in newspapers and magazines. Politics thus provided her with an unusual publicity. Nonetheless, when, in 1964, this enterprising woman . . . published *La canción de la ternura* (The song of tenderness), tending the flame of the muses was such a lonely experience that only a few of her friends read it. . . .

Other books of poetry followed this one and the author has since successfully negotiated the labyrinths of the novel. In 1967, she won the Aquileo Echeverria Prize for *Los perros no ladraron* (The dogs will not bark), and she subsequently obtained other Costa Rican awards, as well as a Guatemalan one.

Going back in time, let us return to *La canción de la ternura* to identify her essential characteristics of universality, depth, and aesthetic value within the profoundly lyrical tonality that the poem configures. . . .

The verbal style that characterizes the author, in prose as in poetry, is that of an amazing abundance of words, images, concepts, metaphors, and enumerations, with which she is eager to arrive at "the full voice" "without orthography or syntax." . . .

The whole key to the poetic mystery of *La canción de la ternura* is thus concretized in this metaphorical order: first was the light and then the word. For this reason, in this poem and in all her literary work, Carmen Naranjo tries to turn back on her route to return to face the light through a heroic struggle with the word.

Victoria Urbano. *Kañina*. 1:2, 1977,
pp. 5, 28

Los perros no ladraron, by Carmen Naranjo, is a novel with a simple plot; rather than a theme, what it is is a sort of review or panorama of a life, as shown through the tasks and the little events of a Friday, the last work day of the week.

By its content, it is, as Alberto Canas insightfully defines it, "the novel of the Costa Rican bureaucracy," the novel of the middle class; however, from this point of view other social strata are also observed: that of the junk man, the good-natured madman, the professional, the domestic servant, and the entrepreneur. So the fact of selecting one sector of the population does not impede her ability to capture the community as a whole; in a sense, it would be impossible to cut off one social group from the rest, given that it has characteristics that proceed from the totality of the community and relations within the entire social system.

Through the bureaucratic lens, we encounter a hierarchical society divided into the man in the cellar, the man at ground level, and the man up above.

The first propositions are essentially of a social and economic order, circumscribed, of course, by the man of the middle-bureaucratic class, a man defined as a being without horizon who lives and "struggles" in his social milieu. Nonetheless, the human problem, the struggle of this man with himself, is identified by means of other aspects, and launches the narrative into much wider and comprehensive orbits, creating a totalizing vision. And in this sense, the value of the novel resides, among other things, in bringing the basic and characteristic elements of the social structure together with its direct impact on the individual.

It is a realistic novel in its narrative approach and style. It is, in the good sense of the word, a social novel, since it makes reference to the work life, the mode of being, and the circumstances of a sector of the population, through a representative case. . . .

As a social novel, it is concretely inscribed within what has been called critical-social realism. The criticism is implicit and the realism resides in the equally implicit acceptance of an objective reality that it documents by means of details or incidents that proceed from a social reality. In other words, the surrounding milieu, the kind of conflicts that the characters face, are related to a reality, a truth, that it attempts to represent in an objective fashion. It is a question, then, of immersing the reader in the life experiences of a social group, with the intention of showing him or her the problems of its members. . . .

Los perros no ladraron signals an innovation in the Costa Rican narrative as discourse: it is the first novel in our tradition that dispenses absolutely with the narrator. Furthermore, this form of exposition is perfectly consistent with the story that shows . . . the effect of that reality Barthes speaks of or what others call objectivity, verisimilitude.

Los perros no ladraron is the broad X ray of a human group born of the complex network of social relations in modern society: the ground-level man, for whom there is no fate but uniformity, statism, and negativity.

The ground-level man is denied everything: love, friendship, the possibility of fulfilling himself in his work.

Around him are lies, intrigue, injustice, and humiliation. But he seeks nothing more than renunciation of himself, his aspirations, and his integrity. For him there is no destiny beyond passivity and conformity, no remedy for his misery but death.

Maria Amoretti. Kañina. 3:1, 1979,
pp. 19–20, 32

Carmen Naranjo's first novel, *Los perros no ladraron,* appeared in 1966. . . . Her second novel is called *Memorias de un hombre palabra* (Memoirs of a word man) and received mention in Guatemala's Floral Games in 1968. . . . In 1968, a short novel, *Camino al Mediodía* (Road to noonday), reissued in 1977, appeared.

The fourth novel, *Responso por el niño Juan Manuel* (Requiem for the child Juan Manuel) was first published in 1971. Her last novel to come out, *Diario de una multitud* (Diary of a multitude), was published in 1974 and reissued in 1979. In addition, there exist unpublished novels.

None of the novels resembles any other as regards the organization of the text, but, despite the desire for technical variety, certain elements recur among the five. . . .

It can be stated that one of the most consistent elements in the work of Carmen Naranjo is the moralistic vision of a contemporary social milieu in Costa Rica: the petty bureaucracy in *Los perros no ladraron* and in *Memorias de un hombre palabra;* a new type of bourgeoisie . . . in *Camino al mediodia;* certain intellectual milieus in *Responso por el niño Juan Manuel;* the life of all urban classes in *Diario de una multitud.* . . . All the novels take a moralizing critical approach, whether towards a state of affairs or certain individual attitudes. Another important element in the novels of Carmen Naranjo is the absolute absence of the countryside—an important characteristic in a highly agricultural society, where literature arose and has continued by making reference to the countryside. Naranjo's invariable setting is the city. . . .

Finally, in relation—though not necessarily causally—to this urban character of Naranjo's novels is the fact that her prose fiction constitutes an innovative effort. Each and every one of the novels adopts and attempts different narrative means . . . and various techniques are also adopted: successive monologues, dialogues without spatial or temporal reference points, transformation of the classic omniscient narrator . . . multiplicity of foci, narrative in the form of an enigma, etc. However, it should be stated that the adoption of and experimentation with these techniques does not follow a parallel evolution of Costa Rican fiction. . . .

Carmen Naranjo imports the techniques of the evolution of the world and Latin American novel, and these are not the fruit of collective investigation, work, or exploration on the part of Costa Rican novelists. Carmen Naranjo's work can be better understood from this perspective, as an individual effort to put a given conception of the novel into practice.

> Alicia Miranda Hervia. *Cahiers du Monde*
> *Hispanique et Luso-Brésilien.* 36, 1981,
> pp. 122, 126–28

Her work is intellectual, original, linguistically innovative, psychological and compassionate. Her poetry is metrically free and structurally lyrical; her narrative exhibits a mixture of fantasy and reality, a preoccupation with the Spanish language, and a search for identity, both individual and cultural. Naranjo remains Costa Rican in her choice of common people as characters; and her use of regionalisms of language (e.g., "vos estés"). In highly metaphorical language, Naranjo is brutally frank and realistic. Her works take place in San José with constant references to its rain, streets, and lost, wandering people. In the narrative part of the poetry, her main characters are symbolic of herself.

> Arlene O. Schrade. In Diane E. Marting, ed.
> *Women Writers of Spanish America*
> (Westport, Connecticut: Greenwood Press,
> 1987), p. 267

Although it is a genre with great expressive variety that is structurally demanding because of its lack of length, the short story often fails to receive the attention it deserves, in comparison with other literary genres. This has been the case of the short story writer Carmen Naranjo, a writer usually better known for her poetry and her novels. However, it is interesting to note that in her three volumes of short stories, entitled *Hoy es un largo dia (Today is a long day)*, *Ondina* (Ondine), and *Nunca hubo alguna vez (There Never Was a Once upon a Time)*, certain themes and techniques from her novels may be identified. . . .

Although in some of Carmen Naranjo's short stories the traditional characteristics of the genre appear—unity of situation . . . reduced number of characters, and tight closure—the undeniable features of the modern short story, which has for some time been challenging the boundaries between the novel and the short story, also appear. . . . The dramatic action of Naranjo's stories serves as a point of departure to explore the psychology of a human being in relation to his or her environment. And . . . the experiences of a specific situation cross over the bounds of the traditional short story to become part of the great human existential fabric which, in narrative, used to be the exclusive province of the novel.

Evelyn Picon Garfield. Revista
Iberoamericana. 53, 1987, pp. 287, 289

The narrative of Carmen Naranjo has been favorably compared with the writing of not only the best women writers of Costa Rica and Central America, but with that of the best writers, women and men, of all of Spanish America. Her novels and short story collections have been honored with the most prestigious literary prizes of her nation and her region.

Naranjo . . . has written prolifically. *There Never Was a Once upon a Time* is her third collection of short fiction, published as *Nunca hubo alguna vez* in 1984 in Costa Rica. *Hoy es un largo día* (1974; Today is a long day) and *Ondina* (1983) preceded it. *Otro rumbo para la rumba* (1989) is her most recent collection. Her writing includes numerous volumes of poetry, among them *América* (1961), *Misa a oscuras* (1967; Brought to shadows) and *Mi guerrilla* (1984; My guerilla). She is probably best known for her novels, including *Los perros no ladraron* (1966), *Memorias de un hombre palabra* (1968), *Responso por el niño Juan Manuel* (1971), *Diario de una multitud* (1974) and *Sobrepunto* (1985; Overpoint).

There Never Was a Once upon a Time is a departure from her other writings in its use of child and adolescent narrators. The narrated events in these stories mark steps toward maturity for the children, many of whom are entering adolescence. . . .

For Naranjo, the child narrators of her stories in *There Never Was a Once upon a Time* offer a view of reality that is at times so magical that it becomes a new reality.

Linda Britt. Translator's introduction to
Carmen Naranjo. There Never Was a Once
upon a Time (Pittsburgh: Latin American
Literary Review Press, 1989), pp. 9–10

NASRALLAH, EMILY (LEBANON) 1938–

A number of other women have followed in Laylà Ba'labakkī's footsteps, choosing the theme of the revolt and search for identity of a female main character for their books. One of the best known in Lebanon is Amīlī Naṣrallā, who has published several novels and collections of short stories. In her first novel, which was awarded a prize, she attacks the traditional value-system of the Lebanese village as far as it concerns women, her special targets being arranged marriages and the age-old custom of killing any girl who has violated the code of honor and thus brought shame on her family. The savagery of this system of values is brought out all the more clearly because it is portrayed in the beautiful surroundings of the Lebanese mountains which Amīlī Naṣrallāh knows so well how to evoke. In her most recent works, however, she has turned her attention away from the theme of the position of women to concentrate on the war in Lebanon and what it means both to the ordinary citizens and to the Lebanese emigrants abroad, who must stand by impotently and watch.

> Hilary Kirkpatrick. In Mineke Schipper, ed.
> *Unheard Words: Women and Literature in*
> *Africa, the Arab World, Asia, the*
> *Caribbean, and Latin America* (London:
> Allyson and Busby, 1985), pp. 81–82

From the moment of her own rupture from a tradition-bound existence, Nasrallah seems to have been tormented by the anxiety that she had lost an essential part of herself when she abandoned the village. . . .

Nasrallah, like many others, has written of the uninformed image of the emigrant forever etched in the minds of those left behind. They do not know, or do not care to know, of the humiliations and loneliness endured. If the emigrant returns, usually in search of a bride, he is extravagantly welcomed. With the assumed change in economic and social status, the known weaknesses and liabilities are conveniently forgotten, or at least overlooked, as the girls vie for the attention of the frog/prince. . . .

Such were the successful emigrants—and they were all men. A careful reading of *September Birds* reveals that when a man is described as leaving the village, the departure is presented in positive terms even if it causes incalculable grief: he is going to school, or to make money to keep an old father. But when it is a woman who leaves, the action is anomalous and is invariably branded "escape." . . .

Escape is a negative form of protest, and in two of her later novels, *The Oleander Tree* (*Shajarat al-difla*, 1968) and *The Pawn* (*Al-rahina*, 1973), Nasrallah experiments with different forms of protest that may be termed positive. *The Oleander Tree* is the story of a rebellious girl who chooses a village wedding to stage her protest against the status quo, in this case, arranged marriage. . . .

Rania, in *The Pawn*, does not escape from the village, although the road to escape is opened wide during her studies in Beirut. She falls in love with a man but rejects him and returns to the village and the man to whom she had been betrothed at birth. Again, the novel does not continue, and we do not know the final outcome. But we do know that she has chosen to return and not to escape. Both of these heroines chose their destinies; they are not oppressed and passive, as has been claimed.

Nasrallah's female personae are the best-prepared to face the challenge that a transitional society throws out. They struggle against the strictures of their society whose roots are conservative—even feudal—and oriental, but whose surface and pretentions are liberal and occidental. True modernization is not the replacement of one order by another, but the melding of the two. Yet perception is not enough. In *Those Memories,* there is the recognition that women must be liberated from the self-imposed shroud of tradition that

> is worn like a garment. The women will not remove it and if they notice that it is torn they will add another patch."

Women must cease to be their own worst enemies in condoning traditions invidious to their well-being. . . .

It is not until the last story of *The Source,* entitled "The Miracle," that Nasrallah deals with the first days of the civil war. It is situated in Beirut and not in the country. There is a commotion on the other side of town which is compared to the jinns' welcome of the bride. When the children ask where all the people have gone, the mother tells them that they have gone to the jinns' wedding. Then, suddenly, a shell lands in the house, a shell that is dreamily dismissed in an image of a large bird. There follows a brief spell of action when someone escapes death from an explosion because she had been asleep. With this miracle the war is dismissed. The battle is happening elsewhere, and even when it does hit home, it is in a dream. . . .

Nasrallah is not writing so much about women, but about the feminine condition—staying and escaping—which, as shown above, may be shared by men. Her oeuvre illustrates the impact the war has had on this condition, and how the ramifications of its impact resolve questions of identity. . . .

Emily Nasrallah's writings are a cogent example of nascent patriotism. Before the war, when a woman chose to leave her home, she was condemned to alienation from her true identity. However, the war transformed this tragic exile. Nasrallah redefined Lebanon, the sick child, as a village. To have stayed in Lebanon, even if it was in the capital, was to have stayed and waited in the village. Hence, those who had left the village recovered through the war their lost identity, and with it their right to belong and to call themselves Lebanese. But who had stayed? The women. The women's enforced passivity was thus transformed into identity formation. Those who stayed were the only ones who deserved to call themselves Lebanese; the only ones who deserved to share in the country's reconstruction.

Miriam Cooke. *War's Other Voices: Womens' Writings on the Lebanese Civil War* (Cambridge: Cambridge University Press, 1986), pp. 7, 146, 149–50, 162, 166

Flight against Time, by Emily Nasrallah, involves an elderly couple, Radwan and Um-Nabeel abu-Yusuf, who leave their small village in southern Lebanon in 1975 to visit their children and grandchildren on Prince Edward Island in Canada. During the long flight across the world, Radwan reminisces about his early life and marriage. All of his children are now in Canada, and his oldest son has sent money for the trip. Before the couple leaves Lebanon, they receive many presents, the most touching of all from a crazy woman who gives Radwan a small packet of the earth of the village.

Radwan and Um-Nabeel are warmly received by their successful family. The only cloud is the fact they cannot communicate directly with their grandchildren, who speak only English. Yet, in spite of the efforts of the whole family to make him feel at home, Radwan misses his village. Even though it is now in a war zone, he returns, leaving his wife behind.

Not long after, he is kidnapped, tortured, and executed. His funeral is well attended, and the novel ends with: "The unknown kidnappers tortured his body, but his soul soars beyond their reach. It rises above hatred and revenge, it rises high with forgiveness and love." This is a moving and appropriate conclusion to a beautifully written and sensitive tale about first-generation immigrants and those they left behind.

Jean-Louise Thacher. Middle East Journal.
42, 1988, p. 485

NAYLOR, GLORIA (UNITED STATES) 1950–

In [*The Women of Brewster Place*], Gloria Naylor's fierce, loving group portrait of seven black women in one housing development . . . the bonds between women are the abiding ones. Most men are incalculable hunters who come and go. They are attractive—but weak and/or dangerous—representatives of nature and of violence who both fertilize and threaten the female core.

Gloria Naylor's *The Women of Brewster Place* is set in one of those vintage urban-housing developments that black people (who are, in truth, "nutmeg," "ebony," "saffron," cinnamon-red" or "gold") have inherited from a succession of other ethnic groups. The difference is that while the Irish and Italians used it as a jumping-off place for the suburbs, for most of its "colored daughters" Brewster Place is "the end of the line": "They came because they had no choice and would remain for the same reason." But the end of the line is not the end of life. With their backs literally to the wall—a brick barrier that has turned Brewster Place into a dead end—the women make their stand together, fighting a hostile world with love and humor. . . .

Despite Gloria Naylor's shrewd and lyrical portrayal of many of the realities of black life (her scene of services in the Canaan Baptist Church is brilliant), *The Women of Brewster Place* isn't realistic fiction—it is mythic. Nothing supernatural happens in it, yet its vivid, earthy characters (especially Mattie) seem constantly on the verge of breaking out into magical powers.

The book has two climaxes, one of healing and rebirth, one of destruction. In the first, Mattie magnificently wrestles Ciel, dying of grief, back to life. In the second, Lorraine, rejected by the others, is gang raped, a blood sacrifice brutally proving the sisterhood of all women. Miss Naylor bravely risks sentimentality and melodrama to write her compassion and outrage large, and she pulls it off triumphantly.

Annie Gottlieb. New York Times Book
Review. August 22, 1982, p. 11, 25

Gloria Naylor's first novel, *The Women of Brewster Place,* which won an American Book Award in 1983, chronicled the plight of eight black women living in an urban lower-class cul-de-sac. With few exceptions—most notably the portrayal of a ghastly gang rape, which took on mythic proportions—that book realistically portrayed the characters' efforts to overcome the poverty and anguish of their lives. *Linden Hills,* Miss Naylor's second novel, also uses a confined geographic setting to construct a tale about the interconnected lives of a group of black characters. It is, however, a much more ambitious work in which realism is subordinated to allegory. Although flawed, it tackles a controversial subject with boldness and originality.

Like Amiri Baraka in *The Systems of Dante's Hell* (1965), Miss Naylor has adapted Dante's *Inferno* to her own fictional purposes—in this instance a tale of lost black souls trapped in the American dream. . . .

Although Miss Naylor has not been completely successful in adapting the *Inferno* to the world of the black middle class, in *Linden Hills* she has shown a willingness to expand her fictional realm and to take risks. Its flaws notwithstanding, the novel's ominous atmosphere and inspired set pieces— such as the minister's drunken fundamentalist sermon before an incredulous Hills congregation—make it a fascinating departure for Miss Naylor, as well as a provocative, iconoclastic novel about a seldom-addressed subject.

Mel Watkins. New York Times Book Review.
March 3, 1985, p. 11

Gloria Naylor's second novel, *Linden Hills,* is a modern version of Dante's *Inferno* in which souls are damned not because they have offended God or have violated a religious system but because they have offended themselves. In their single-minded pursuit of upward mobility, the inhabitants of Linden Hills, a black, middle-class suburb, have turned away from their past and from their deepest sense of who they are. Naylor feels that the subject of who-we-are and what we are willing to give up of who-we-are where-we-want-to-go is a question of the highest seriousness—as serious as a Christian's concern over his salvation.

Naylor could not have chosen a more suitable framework for *Linden Hills* than Dante's *Inferno.* The Dantean model emphasizes the novel's serious moral tone and gives a universalizing mythic dimension to what otherwise might be considered a narrow subject, the price American blacks are paying for their economic and social "success."...

By basing the structure and the ethic of *Linden Hills* on the *Inferno,* Naylor places the novel at the heart of the American literary tradition; moreover, she forces all her readers, and not just the middle-class blacks who are the subject of *Linden Hills,* to apply to their own lives the hard questions the novel raises.

The novel also shows the influence of some of the best contemporary black writers without imitating any one of them. *Linden Hills* deals with men's oppression of women, a subject that Alice Walker has examined so forcefully in *The Third Life of Grange Copeland* and *The Color Purple.* Naylor's novel also emphasizes the important role a person's cultural history plays in his identity, a topic that has been explored by Paule Marshall in *Praisesong for the Widow* and by Toni Morrison in *Song of Solomon* and *Tar Baby.* Finally, the lyricism and imagery of *Linden Hills* recall the poetic style of both Morrison and the earlier Zora Neale Hurston. Naylor is a fresh, daring voice in American letters. . . .

Linden Hills is an uncomfortable and dangerous book which pricks the conscience. It takes the reader on a perilous pilgrimage and forces him to consider the hidden cost of his choices. It strips him of the ease of innocence. Naylor has risked much by writing such a disturbing tale. Her readers may view her subject too narrowly. If they do, she could lose a black audience that feels unjustly challenged and a white audience that thinks the novel's hard questions are not meant for them. Naylor also risks offending modern sensibilities that regard an allegory about moral accountability too medieval for their tastes. But because Naylor knows who she is, where she has been, and where she wants to go, she dares to tell her tale and dares the reader to reckon with it.

Catherine C. Ward. Contemporary Literature. 28, 1987, p. 67–68, 80–81

In *Linden Hills,* Naylor broadly transmogrifies Dante's *Inferno:* two young black men take on odd jobs in the affluent black suburb of the book's title. Willie (audaciously nicknamed Willie White because his skin is so black) is an oral poet, who grew up in the Putney Wayne Projects, a very different kind of community from its near neighbor, plush Linden Hills. Willie White has committed over 600 poems to memory and can cast the ingredients of a cereal box into heroic couplets at a single glance. Lesterfield Tilson (known as "Shit" because his skin is the color of a baby's stool), though born and raised in Linden Hills (in its more modest section) and a writer in the more formal sense, is maverick enough to prefer the education of the streets that he gets while hanging out with his partner. Together they embody the best of the oral and literate traditions in Afro-American experience.

At the bottom of Linden Hills where the most opulent homes are (Naylor plays on the black idiomatic sense of "down") is the seat of the successive generations of the dark-skinned "satanic" Luther Nedeed. The original Luther was a freedman who, having bought the land in the 1820s, rented shacks to blacks who were too poor to farm. The later Luther Nedeeds, prosperous morticians all, follow in the patriarch's footsteps—each acquires an "octoroon bride" to bear the next generation and presides over the increasingly wealthy Linden Hills of his particular day.

Naylor also revoices motifs and devices from the recent fiction of Toni Morrison and Alice Walker, often with remarkable effectiveness, as in the relationship between Willie and Lester which echoes, without imitating a similar one between the major characters in Morrison's *Song of Solomon*. Naylor is at her best, powerful and chilling, where the last Mrs. Nedeed unravels the stories of previous generations of Nedeed women. Letters (like Walker's Celie in *The Color Purple*, Mrs. Nedeed writes to herself), recipes, shopping lists, photographs are all a means of piecing together these women's histories, of excavating their buried lives.

Although *Linden Hills* has many compelling moments, the "sins" of this community—hypocrisy, loveless marriages and marital infidelities, idleness—seem too trivial to carry the weight of Naylor's expert literary attentions. Still, in this second novel, Naylor serves notice that she is a mature literary talent of formidable skill.

Sherley Anne Williams. *Ms.* June 1985,
p. 70

On a note card above my writing desk hang the words of the late American original, Liberace: "Too much of a good thing is simply wonderful."

Excess—of plots and subplots, of major characters and walk-ons, of political issues and literary allusions—is what Gloria Naylor's *Mama Day*, her third and most ambitious book, is blessed with. "There are just too many sides to the whole story," Cocoa, Mama Day's grandniece, explains at the end of this longish novel, and the story obviously feels urgent enough to both Cocoa and to Ms. Naylor that they present it to us whole.

If novels are viewed as having the power to save, then novelists are obliged, first, to relive the history of the errors of earlier chronicles and filling in the missing parts. Recent novels like *Mama Day*, Toni Morrison's *Beloved* and Louise Erdrich's *Love Medicine* resonate with the genuine excitement of authors discovering ways, for the first time it seems, to write down what had only been intuited or heard. These are novelists with an old-fashioned "calling" (to bear witness, to affirm public virtues) in a post-modernist world; their books are scaled down for today's microwavable taste, but still linked to the great public voice of nineteenth century storytelling.

Mama Day has its roots in *The Tempest*. The theme is reconciliation, the title character is Miranda (also the name of Prospero's daughter), and Willow Springs is an isolated island where, as on Prospero's isle, magical and mysterious events come to pass. As in *The Tempest*, one story line concerns the magician Miranda Day, nicknamed Mama Day, and her acquisition, exercise and relinquishment of magical powers. The other story line concerns a pair of "star-crossed" (Ms. Naylor's phrase, too) lovers: Ophelia Day, nicknamed Cocoa, and George Andrews. . . .

As long as the narrative confines itself to Mama Day and daily life on the bizarre island full of rogues, frauds, crazies, martyrs and clairvoyants, the novel moves quickly. Curiously, the slow sections are about the love story of twenty-seven-year-old Cocoa, who has relocated from Willow Springs to New York, and George Andrews, who is meant to be emblematic of the good-hearted, hard-driving but culturally orphaned Northern black man. The courtship occurs all over Manhattan—in greasy diners, in three-star restaurants, in midtown offices, on subways—giving Ms. Naylor a chance to accommodate several set pieces. But she is less proficient in . . . [representing] the familiar.

But I'd rather dwell on *Mama Day's* strengths. Gloria Naylor has written a big, strong, dense, admirable novel; spacious, sometimes a little drafty like all public monuments, designed to last and intended for many levels of use.

Bharati Mukherjee. *New York Times Book Review.* February 21, 1988, p. 7

Gloria Naylor is building a world. *Mama Day* is the third in a set of novels whose locales and characters are loosely interrelated. *The Women of Brewster Place* come to their ghetto street when hope and possibility run out; on the other side of a dividing wall their rich but equally desperate neighbors in *Linden Hills* live trapped in artifice and greed.

In search of yet another kind of destiny, *Mama Day* plays out a preoccupation of black writers in general, and black women in particular, with the gains and losses that have come with the move from rural to urban, from intuitive to rational, life. Alice Walker's mother's garden, Toni Morrison's faith in the *other* reality of hauntings and magical powers—all are related to the contest in *Mama Day* between two ways of knowledge. Naylor's book is a paean to the old mysteries of the irrational, and to the heroines who have, throughout history, wielded enormous powers of healing and wholeness. . . .

The schematic parts of *Mama Day* when the power of the old wisdom is at hand, are clearly what Naylor wants us to pay close attention to, and they are lively and specific enough to go down more easily than many literary lessons. But, heretical or not, I can't help but wish she felt less of a need to elevate by making symbolic, or by fitting everything into a larger scheme— *Linden Hills* used nothing less than the *Inferno* as an armature. Most black novelists, granted, might call it a white folks' luxury to write, in novelist Paula Fox's memorable phrase, "uncompromised by purpose." But when she is not didactically fostering our spiritual construction, Gloria Naylor serves another worthy purpose beautifully: she invites us to imagine the lives of complex characters at work and play, and gives us faithfully rendered community in all its seasons. I hope she'll choose to continue to move, in a loose and unconstrained stride, in that direction.

Rosellen Brown. Ms. February 1988, p. 74

The Women of Brewster Place is a novel where time and place (space) immediately collide. The first section, "Dawn," is an introduction to the history of Brewster Place, which Naylor characterizes as a "bastard child." The focus in the novel is on the women of this place, whose own histories are as bastardized as their contemporary locus. Mattie, Ciel, Etta Mae, "The Two," and Kiswana are all women separated from their familial sources and are left alone to become the communal "daughters" of the place. Such spiritual dislocation, complicated by the vapid air of Brewster Place, exacts its tragic due. In the last section of the novel, "Dusk," Brewster Place "wait[s] for death, which is a second behind the expiration of its spirit in the minds of its children . . . the colored daughters of Brewster, spread over the canvas of time, still wake up with their dreams misted on the edge of a yawn."

In this work, the metaphor of a place serves as an ancestral presence. Brewster Place exists both before the women who inherit it and afterwards. Its fundamental irony, and Naylor's bitter commentary on these spiritually dispossessing city spaces, is that Brewster Place is generatively inadequate and sterile. Over and over again African-American women's texts present characters poised between a spiritual place and a place that has been defined for them, assigned by some person, or extracted from some ritual they are unable to remember.

Karla F. C. Holloway. Black American
Literature Forum. 24, 1990, p. 622

Like Toni Morrison, Gloria Naylor is intrigued by the effect of place on character. Perhaps African-American writers have been particularly interested in setting, because displacement first from Africa and then through migrations from South to North, has been so much a part of our history. Because of the consistency of forced displacement in our collective experience, we know how critical our location is to the character of our social creations, how place helps to tell us a great deal about who we are, and who we can become. Perhaps place is even more critical to African-American women writers. For women within the African-American community have functioned both inside and outside the home, have been conservers of tradition (if only because we are mothers), while we have had to respond to the nuances of a changed environment. How we negotiate the relationship between the past, as it has helped to form us, and the present, as we must experience it, is often a grave dilemma for us.

The setting of Linden Hills, Naylor's second novel, makes it clear that she is creating a geographical fictional world similar to or in the manner of Faulkner's Yoknapatawpha county. Her first novel is set in Brewster Place, her second in Linden Hills. Brewster Place and Linden Hills are geographically in the same area; both are inhabited by blacks, and in both novels, characters refer to each of these places as proximate neighborhoods. . . .

The outside world perceives Linden Hills as a symbol of black achievement while Brewster Place is seen as a manifestation of failure. Ironically, through her two novels' respective characters and structure, Naylor portrays Brewster Place as a black community (though flawed and vulnerable) held together primarily by women, while Linden Hills is characterized as a group of houses that never becomes a community, a showplace precariously kept in place by the machinations of one wealthy black patriarchal family.

Barbara Christian. In Henry Louis Gates,
Jr., ed. *Reading Black, Reading Feminist*
(New York: Meridian-Penguin, 1990),
pp. 348–49

The dream sequence which appears at the end of Gloria Naylor's award winning novel *The Women of Brewster Place* not only recapitulates the female characters' collective experience of the male, it also reveals their subconscious desire for rebellion and revenge. The dream is filtered through the consciousness of Mattie Michael who, as principal female character, is both matriarch and chief ministrant to all of the women in the novel. The immediate source of the dream is a violent rape and murder that have occurred in Brewster Place, but the dream distills years of the suppressed longing and disappointment, the frustration and anger, the resentment and humiliation that all of these women have collectively experienced in their relationships with the men in their lives. . . .

In the dream sequence, the women of Brewster Place join to act out the rage and resentment at their collective experience of the male. By uniting in an exclusively female experience, they experience, in a broad sense, solidarity with all women. Like Lorraine and Theresa, they share a moment of communion, free of men, bound together by the recognition of their sexual common identity, which is, at once, the source of their unique identity, but also of their powerlessness and oppression in their male-dominated society.

Lori Duin Kelly. *Notes on Contemporary
Literature*. 21, 1991, pp. 8, 10

Gloria Naylor, in *Bailey's Cafe,* addresses female circumcision in Africa (in this case, Ethiopia) as part of a larger examination of the sexual mutilations inflicted on women in contemporary society. Like [Alice] Walker's Tashi [in *Possessing the Secret of Joy*], Naylor's characters are based on archetypes—mostly from the Bible—but, unlike Tashi, they are not universalized. The novel takes place in a blues cafe down a dead-end street at the tip of New York City. On this city block are Bailey's cafe, Eve's garden and boardinghouse and Gabe's pawnshop. The novel's fluid time-sequence culminates in New Year's Eve, 1949. As in her other novels, Naylor infuses day-to-day living with an alternate, magical reality.

Bailey and, at times, his wife Nadine orchestrate the story as a whole, introducing each character in turn. But the focus of the novel are the first-person blues narrations of the cafe's patrons—mostly women, always in some way abused. Eve tells us she is at least a thousand years old. She describes being raised and abused by "Godfather." He threw her out of his "paradise" in Louisiana because of her awakening sexuality, but not before leaving her "kneeling in a pool of vomit and shit" from a monumental purge "with jars of water and epsom salt." Eve then finds her own garden on this New York City block and sets about helping other lost and abused women. The women who end up at her boardinghouse choose their own men and find refuge from their abusive past. Some of them tell us their stories in Bailey's cafe; their lives are often revisions of biblical stories, now cast from a woman's perspective. . . .

Naylor ends *Bailey's Cafe* as she did her first novel, *The Women of Brewster Place,* with a kind of miracle; readers familiar with her most recent novel, *Mama Day,* will find a special surprise.

Bailey's Cafe is Naylor's finest novel to date. Her rendering of life in a New York alley reflects the city's magic, its jazz, its violent stories, its street-lamp sparks of hope. It examines a broad spectrum of black women's lives while dealing with the complexities of a multi-ethnic American society still caught up in restrictive notions of color, gender and culture. It is more literary than polemical, bridging ancient stories and modern problems to create a context for the mutilations women have suffered and a space for curing their (our) souls.

Gay Wilentz. *Women's Review of Books.* 10,
February 1993, p. 16

NEERA (pseud. ANNA RADIUS ZUCCARI) (ITALY) 1846–1918

Who would ever have thought of rereading Neera's work, if the opportunity had not arisen through the recent republication of one of her first novels, *Teresa? Teresa* was published in 1886, but it is surprising today and not only for exquisitely literary reasons. All it shows is the social and emotional education of a young girl of the provincial petty bourgeoisie; her life and the life of a woman who does not live in her own right because she has no right to it and has been from her tenderest youth socialized to accept this condition, along with the sole authority of the father, from which there is no appeal. She is the fated victim of a prefabricated destiny.

The violence that comes from these facts and that whirls around this little story (and increases and moves one more than any historical conscious-ness) cannot be isolated from the case. The author did not intend to do a sociological study à la Zola, remaining a witness separated from what she is writing; the working out of the narrative involves her in the first person in the very tumult of passions and renunciation. As Luigi Baldacci stressed in his introduction to the recent Einaudi reprint, the works of Neera and particularly *Teresa* "are revealed as the essential documents of the feminist spirit, to the extent to which woman is experienced as an (oppressed) class and not as the ideal complement of man." Consequently *Teresa* was revealed as one of the few (and the first) Italian feminist novels. The reader—the male one, but even more the female one—must wonder who Neera was, what else she wrote, what ideas she had about the society surrounding her, what was her background for womanhood and writing.

Starting from *Teresa,* then, and from the other novels of Neera that always represented women's fates signed and sealed by decisions and destinies coming from a masculine society and law to which there was no choice but to sacrifice oneself to go forward. (I am thinking particularly of *L'indomani* (Tomorrow) and *Duello d'anime* (Duel of souls), it occurred to me to read the long chapter "Confessioni letterari" (Literary confessions) prefacing the second edition of the novel *Il castigo* (The punishment) in 1891 and dedicated to Luigi Capuana; and "Le idee di una donna" (A woman's ideas), published in 1903. In a certain sense, I had before me the two poles of the problem: in "Confessioni letterarie" I came to know what house she had lived in, who her father and mother were, how she began to write and finally her intellectual position in the environment of Italian narrative at the turn of the century. "Le idee di una donna" were the ideological elaboration of her existential experience. . . .

To protect and love woman's own "private being" and point out the exploitation of woman in industrial society, thus in the world of work, were two positive goals. Society, women, and even women's literature, have passed along the road that Neera abhorred—identification with the masculine—and that was probably the only one possible for an ideological and economic enfranchisement. But times have changed. Contemporary feminism no longer looks to a masculine model, but rather rejects one. The father, ideal or god of Moloch, has been put on trial, can be understood to be heading for defeat. I do not know if it is yet time to begin to study, in literature, the victims of Moloch, who have experienced in contradictory manner, often only on an unconscious level, their role as women and women writers. If it is, Neera would deserve "a room of her own."

Francesca Sanvitale. Introduction to Neera.
*Le idee di una donna e Confessioni
letterarie.* (Florence: Vellecchi), 1977,
pp. v–vi, xv

[Anna Radius Zuccari] published her first novel in 1985, in the Milanese newspaper *Pungolo,* signing it with the pseudonym Neera, a name that, as she herself records, impressed itself on her in her youth while reading an ode of Horace's to Neera. In her early years as a writer, she also used other pseudonyms, but she then definitively returned to Neera. She published in *Fanfulla, Bersagliere, Corriere del mattino, Corriere di Napoli, Fanfulla della Domenica, Marzocco, Il Giorno, Corriere della sera* and many other newspapers and magazines. She also contributed two short stories to the volume, *Nell'azzurro, racconti di sei signore* (In the blue: stories by six ladies), edited by Roberto Sachetti to raise funds for orphans.

Neera had begun to write in a period in which debates on women's emancipation were growing hot. Influenced by the romantics and the first works of the realists, she published three novels in one volume, *Un romanzo* (1876; A Novel), *Addio!* (1877; Good-bye), and *Vecchie catene* (1878; Old chains), followed by *Novelle gaie* (1879; Gay stories), the novel *Un nido* (1880; A nest), which attracted the attention of Capuana, who . . . defined the art of the new author as "reveries" and recommended her to Italian readers. Neera herself wanted to reserve an analytical function for her novels, but not in the form used by the realists. She thus confessed that she was not in fact interested in form, but in spirit, coming in this way to a sort of confession, a private and emotional history. Her style is often rapid, without embellishments. Sometimes there is a monotonous list of consecutive facts that seems ugly and ill-written in the Crocean sense, but which gives an idea of the sad monotony of life deprived of joy and important events. Today this way of narrating appears more modern than that which is customarily defined as the "beautiful page."

Neera succeeded above all in representing with a delicacy of psychological penetration the world of woman (whatever her social condition), observed and analyzed in her emotions, her passions, her sacrifices, often within the limits of daily life. For this reason, we can very well define her as the author of poor isolated women, ladies and housewives (often victims of the dominating egotism allowed to the man), destined to dream a lot and renounce as much. Quite aware of the limitations of her heroines, the author does not contemplate a rivalry between man and woman, who still lives tied to family and home, but stands up for her protagonists through a sense of moral justice that makes her a feminist in her fashion, not of the suffragist type that wanted the same political and professional rights to compete with men, but of a more conservative type, that called for a woman's right to a life of her own, to love and passion, often negative to the family and the man, who impose submission and renunciation, denying the depth and moral nobility of the woman's character.

This point of view was elaborated by her in the moral studies *Battaglie per un'idea* (1898; Battles for an idea) and *Le idee di una donna* (1903; The ideas of a woman), where she asserts, among other things, that woman is neither inferior nor superior nor equal to man, but forms a whole with man. Her progress is tied to the man's progress, which is to say, to society's. The problem of the woman depends above all on her social status, but equality with the man does not necessarily give her nobility, but rather makes her a less fine being. Neera was aware that not all women are good and virtuous, but she did not blame society. She saw virtue as an innate and personal thing, which is found at all social levels, because money does not constitute a guarantee against vice. The author would not deny education and practice of the liberal professions to woman, but says simply that not all have the need of them because they find their happiness in the home and in motherhood, the most sacred of the mysteries of life. In *Le idee di una donna,* she defended the traditional position of women so much as to appear anti-feminist, perhaps because she was aware that practicing a profession multiplied the duties of a woman without the man's being able to assume all the female duties. But in her novels we find very happy wives and mothers. . . .

More than the stories of her protagonists, which unfold with a minimum of sentimentality not without their realistic shades, Neera's feminism is reflected in the thoughts of her heroines and in the descriptions of everyday family situations.

Natalia Costa-Zalessow. *Scrittrici italiane
dal XIII al XX secolo* (Ravenna: Longo),
1982, pp. 240–42

In Neera, we come into contact with even more contradictory female characters. Dissatisfied . . . within, externally Neera's women live a normal life. Resigned to the traditional moral code, which wills them to be quiet little faithful wives, however unhappy, they accept their fate without rebelling. In theory, Neera, like the majority of women of the time, is anti-feminist and anti-divorce, but, in practice, she felt and showed sympathy for women alienated in their marriages, for those new brides who lived incredulous and alone beside a husband who was alien to them, after the wedding night. . . . If it is true, as Croce says, that for Neera "the problem of woman and that of love take the form of the principal and almost the sole object of her study" it is also necessary to add that this love is not an end in itself, but becomes a metaphor for woman's life. It provides the lens through which the woman sees human relations clearly and becomes aware of the impossibility of attaining her own dreams.

Paola Blelloch. *Quel Mondo dei Guanti e
delle stoffe: Profili di scrittrici italiane del
'900* (Verona: essedue), 1987, pp. 61–63

NEMES NAGY, ÁGNES (HUNGARY) 1922–

Her poems are concerned with fundamental questions about man's place in life and universe, and are often criticized for their "closed world."

Vas, István. "Kettős világban," *Magyarok,* III (1947). [This is a] review stating that her poems are not easy to characterize, that her statements are puritanical both in outlook and poetic method, that all subjects fit into her puritanism, that her imagery is like John Donne's, and that the poems do not provide a clear basis for a prediction about the direction of her future development. . . .

Kardos, László. "Nemes Nagy Ágnes: Szárazvillám," *Kortárs,* I (October, 1957). Her work after ten years of silence [was] well received, [the reviewer] finding that it fulfills the promise of her great ability, that her artistic seriousness is very apparent in it, and that the antithesis between form and substance is reconciled by her deliberate artistic power and her impressive and highly refined calculation, that her poems are occasionally marred by obscurity at certain points, but they are enlivened by splendid plastic and animated pictures. Self-involvement in her people and country would considerably enlarge the horizons of her poetry. . . .

Rónay, György. "Nemes Nagy Ágnes: Szárazvillám," *Vigilia,* XXIII (1958). [This is a] review which maintains that the poems are strictly molded and surrealistic, and expresses the hope that she will not eliminate "the warmer, milder, looser voices and emotions" in her lyrics for which she has shown ability in her translations. . . .

Ila, Egon. "Agnes Nemes Nagy," *Arena,* November (1962). Considers her to be one of "the most significant and remarkable poets of today." Delineates her life and ideas, especially the problems of evil and faith, on the basis of translations of four of her poems: "To my ancestors," "To liberty," "Ice," and "Toward springtime."

Albert Tezla, selection from entry on
Nemes Nagy and summary of Hungarian
critical opinions in *Hungarian Authors: A
Bibliographical Handbook* (Cambridge:
Harvard University Press, 1970), pp. 668–69

Ágnes Nemes Nagy, one of her country's finest living poets, would probably not have a large readership even if Hungarians were in fact as receptive to the language of poetry as they are reputed to be. For one thing, her output is small, and that, to many of her countrymen, immediately suggests a difficult poet. What's more, her frame of reference is rarely the shared experience of a people (her allusions to historical events are few and oblique), but rather her private traumas and dreads which she conveys in images that are precise, tough and jarring. Even in poems that celebrate love, freedom, art (in this volume, "To a Poet," "To Freedom" and "To My Craft") there is a steady undercurrent of regret and despair. But what make Nemes Nagy's work really demanding and challenging are not her private symbols and somber moods, or her aloofness from more common Hungarian poetic themes: the difficulty lies in comprehending a view of the world that attributes eruptive, inexplicable power to physical matter and at the same time stoically accepts its soulless existence. Nemes Nagy pays close attention to the world of objects: she scrutinizes "the intersection of the animate and the inanimate." And because she does believe in a kind of cosmic consciousness, not even her starkest landscapes, her eeriest juxtapositions seem that alien to us. She doesn't exactly humanize nature: indeed, her greatest gift is to register phenomena with uncanny objectivity. In her poems, trees and stones and geysers may ultimately become emblems of human fears and passions, but they also remain unyieldingly real. The world Nemes Nagy creates is inhospitable, full of hard surfaces and strident echoes, though it is not impenetrable. This supposedly difficult poet can also communicate her messages unambiguously, instantly. Consider, for example, the moving parable "Lazarus," one of her best:

> Slowly as he rose, in the region of his shoulder
> every muscle of his whole life was torture.
> His death was flayed from him, torn off as gauze is torn.
> Because it is just that hard being reborn.

Bruce Berlind's translations of [*Selected Poems*, 1980] Nemes Nagy's poems are remarkably simple—and faithful. . . . In his introduction Berlind remarks on the historical and political pressures that shape the work of East European poets. Perhaps because Ágnes Nemes Nagy is a rather atypical East European literary artist, this pressure is felt only indirectly; it gives way to weightier, denser pressures, the responses to which are that much more stunning and disquieting.

Ivan Sanders. World Literature Today. 55,
1981, p. 354

In my introduction to Ágnes's *Selected Poems,* I referred to "Statues" as a

> terrible and bitter poem . . ., in which the products of creation, of a Creator, are seen as artifacts, sculptures, with just enough human consciousness to perceive their helpless condition but without the capacity to rectify it. The poem asks the same question that Blake seeks in "The Tyger," except that here the products of creation—or evolution—are impotent pieces of junk-sculpture with nothing of the power with which Blake endows his tiger.

That still seems to me true enough of the poem, but it is not enough of the truth. What I could not say in 1980—chiefly out of concern for Ágnes's safety, but also to protect myself from being blacklisted for subsequent visas—was that it is a deeply subversive poem, as direct a response to the totalitarian regime as the regime was likely to tolerate. . . .

Nemes Nagy's poetry is almost uniformly subversive, although it is often difficult to say why that is so, to pinpoint what specifically is subversive about it. . . .

I don't know of anything in American poetry, even in the poetry that we can justifiably term political, that is remotely like the poetry of Ágnes Nemes Nagy. Our political poetry, with rare exceptions, is protest poetry directed at specific social or historical events—not, as with Nemes Nagy's, at a social and historical *condition*. This is not caviling; there is a world of difference between protesting, and so trying to alter, a course of events which gives some hope of remediation and, on the other hand, confronting a way of life, a moral atmosphere, which appears unalterable. Political poetry in America is consequently more occasional, in the old sense of the term; it is an ad hoc sort of poetry. The great exception is the Blues tradition and some of the poetry by African-Americans that evolved from it, although most Black poetry continues to protest. And there are women poets whose work is closer in its political dimension to the sort of poetry that concerns me. Still, the generalization holds. Our most recent event that called forth a spate of protest poetry was of course the Vietnam War. As with all protest poetry, some of it was good; most of it was not. And what was good will probably survived because it managed to transcend the immediate event that gave rise to it. The political dimension of Nemes Nagy's poetry—and in this sense it is representative of the best poetry of Communist Europe—is more pervasive, more deeply ingrained, more inextricably embedded in the texture of its ostensible landscape. A frequently encountered remark in Hungarian criticism is that love poems very often have political overtones which it is impossible to disentangle from the love element. . . .

But the chief difference to keep in mind when thinking of our own protest poetry is that we *may* protest, we are free to do it with impunity; poets in Communist countries were not, and the fact that they were not forced upon them the necessity of developing strategies to speak the unspeakable. The richness and subtlety of Nemes Nagy's poetry seems to me a direct result of her insistence upon dealing with the conditions of her life (and of her part of the world) without, however, writing her own obituary. This does not mean that there weren't apparatchiks who knew what she was up to, who could read as carefully as anyone else. But in the relatively benign years of the Kádár regime a poet as revered and as difficult as Nemes Nagy could afford to be indulged. . . .

If the end of Nemes Nagy's poetry is not, as with protest poetry, to effect a change, what is its end? What is the end of any political poetry which is not protesting? I would answer that it provides a context for the poet's engagement with *any* subject matter, and thereby serves as witness to life beyond the immediate life of the poet: "like the personal poem," says Bly, "it moves to deepen awareness"—which I would modify by insisting that it may *be,* in precisely the sense Bly means, an intensely "personal poem." At its best, the political context may be the way a personal poem realizes itself.

Bruce Berlind. *American Poetry Review.*
22:1, January–February 1993, pp. 5, 7–8

NIN, ANAIS (UNITED STATES) 1903–77

One feels the effort of truth in the face of curious reticences and obscurities. The vast congeries of prose is lyrically expressive of certain feminine, in instances almost imperceptible, feelings connected with an aesthetic world mainly that of decadent Paris; expressive even more of a feminine self-consciousness strangely enamored of the very state of feeling, yet singularly perceptive of the subliminal and marvelous. The element of the irrational, germane to all lyricism, is included in the style: it is prevalently surrealistic. Audaciously it exploits the connotative power of language while presenting the unseen through wild, often far-flung analogies.

Paul Rosenfeld. *The Nation*. September 26,
1942, p. 276

The virtue of Miss Nin's writing, in a time of "human winter," is that by its exclusive preoccupation with the intimate problems of feminine psychology, it is concerned with an aspect of human values as such. Her style, moreover, in its use of fairly broad emotive language and in the expression it gives to feeling and sentiment, possesses a certain *Innerlichkeit,* an air of immediate reality, for lack of which so much modern American writing is dying such a hideous, choking death. But Miss Nin approaches the human by way of psychoanalysis. . . . The task she assigns to literature seems to be no more than to present and amplify the insights of psychoanalysis.

Isaac Rosenfeld. *The New Republic*.
December 17, 1945, pp. 844–45

She is fascinated in a simplified psychoanalytic way with waking fantasies, with ego-ideals, and our pictures of ourselves as they affect our relations with others. Except for occasional flashes into the past, she does not work out articulated case histories. She omits what can be directly observed and objectively reported. She does not look at scenes and faces like a photographer or even a painter. . . . What Miss Nin records are subjective states, configurations of character, the fields of electric tension, movement and resistance in human relationships. She defines these with elegance and insight in apothegmatic general statements of a sometimes pretentious sort. . . . The result is an abstract, psychic music, a dance of generalities and types, charming and suggestive in a narrowly romantic way.

Robert Gorham Davis. *The New York Times*.
November 23, 1947, p. 36

Miss Nin's flavorful words are as piquant and stimulating to one's mental taste as exotic, highly seasoned foods to one's palate. Her constant psycho-analyzing of characters never lags. In these two characteristics lie the fascination of her writing. The present book *(The Four-Chambered Heart)* considered man's dual nature, i.e., of construction and destruction as brought out by the two women in his life. The characterizations are fuller, less impressionistic and less sketchy than in her previous writings. The story is closer knit, attaining a wholeness, an entity absent from Miss Nin's other books. There is the same swiftness of rhythm and fluidity of movement—Miss Nin's artistic label.

Elizabeth P. Nichols. *Library Journal.*
December 1, 1949, p. 1818

To Miss Nin external events form only one side of true reality, in which two realms—the inward and the outward, the world of dream and of waking—are united.

Miss Nin has the gift of communicating directly. External action is deepened by being converted to inward experience; the visionary and hallucinatory become integral parts of reality. The River Seine and the flowing Seine of the psyche are thus presented as one stream of life.

Rene Fulop-Miller. *The New York Times.*
January 29, 1950, p. 4

Anais Ninis is, as Edmund Wilson has said, "a world of feminine perception and feminine fancy"; a world, too in which the iron curtain between the ego and the unconscious is continually pierced. . . . The effects achieved by Miss Nin's writing—poetic prose of singular vitality and beauty—reminded me, rather strongly, of the dance. *The Four-Chambered Heart* evokes the grace-in-motion and the elegant patterns, the emotional directness and dreamlike aura of a classical ballet.

Charles J. Rolo. *Atlantic Monthly.*
February, 1950, p. 87

A Spy in the House of Love is . . . a sensitive and discerning fable of a woman's love life, which manages to compress within a very brief compass some of the rewards and almost too many of the anguishes of passion for its own sake. . . . We begin to realize that Miss Nin is one of the few women writers in our literary tradition to affirm the centrality of the biological impulses for her own sex, and on the same terms as for men.

The point is also that she is prepared to describe these emotions from the feminine point of view with the same ruthless honesty that marked a D. H. Lawrence or a Dreiser.

Maxwell Geismar. *The Nation.* July 24,
1954, pp. 75–76

It would be hazardous to speculate on the relation of this fiction to Anais Nin's diary without the privilege of reading the diary; but it would be equally hazardous to attempt to assess the failure of the fiction without taking into account the effect of the diary-writing habit on her art. A diary is not a work of art, and the very qualities that make a diary most successful are largely antithetical to the aims of art. In "Un Etre Etoilique" *(The Cosmological Eye)* and "More about Anais Nin" *(Sunday After the War)* Henry Miller speaks of the devastating honesty and the complete lack of malice in her journal; of the gargantuan inclusiveness and the complete self-absorption of the reverie; and of the fluid, undersea sinking of the narrative personality, so that each time one thinks the personality has reached rock-bottom, it reveals deeper and darker vistas. Without the disciplined control that is synonymous with art, such honesty becomes vulgarity, the lack of malice seems a lack of standards, the inclusiveness looks flabby, and the self-absorption leaves the reader puzzled and uncertain, since he—by what must be one of the most elementary laws of epistemology—does not share the same self.

Frank Baldanza. Minnesota Review. Winter,
1962, pp. 270–71

Henry Miller, with understandable partiality and consistent exuberance, has described Miss Nin's diaries as destined to take their place beside the confessions of St. Augustine, Petronius, Abelard, Rousseau, and Proust. Whether this is true of the millions of unpublished words we cannot say; but the present "sampling" offers a modulated and low-pitched portrait of the early Depression years in Paris after most American expatriates had fled. The myth of D. H. Lawrence prevailed; and life in the Villa Seurat had not yet become the Miller-Durrell legend. Miss Nin is a child of the Lawrentian revolt and of the Surrealists, that phase of the movement which looked inwardly into the distortions of the dream. Literary history will probably place her with that last backwater of Romanticism before World War II.

Leon Edel. Saturday Review of Literature.
May 7, 1966, p. 91

She writes in her diary to establish that self lost by being a mirror to others; she writes also not only to save her own point of view but to project it. But when she keeps on arguing for the diary form, claiming it is more truthful than the novel, when she courts a kind of mirror intimacy, she falls into self-idealizings and self-justifications. . . .

In the first volume a larger design energized the parts: the explorations of psychoanalysis with Otto Rank (who reappears in the early section of this volume, as a close friend); the meeting with her father, Joaquin Nin, whom she had not seen since her early childhood; the new friendship with Henry Miller and the world he introduced her to. This section of the diary [volume two] is, as it were, midstream, and like many a middle section, it has its difficulties. A question of slackening pace or drive? The observations accumulate without that kind of economy that a good letter has, addressed as it is to another, who may become impatient if it goes on too long. The sense of the dialogue of the self with the self is often lost; she is carried away even from the realities of her most subjective experiences on a flight of language.

Jean Garrigue. *The New York Times.*
July 16, 1967, pp. 4–5

A few preliminary words need to be said about some of the typical character-istics of Miss Nin's novels and style. It may be observed that the unity which Miss Nin achieves is accomplished largely through three devices: (1) recur-ring characters, symbols, and motifs; (2) direct and indirect psychological analysis; and (3) the result of the first two: the definition of a single primary character. Curiously, each of these devices is used in Miss Nin's *Diary* also, but . . . with much more success than in her fiction.

Style, an amorphous subject at best, is conspicuously and consistently one of the attractive qualities of Miss Nin's art. The originality of her diction, imagery, and symbolism has led some to charge her with being too esoteric, but I think that one will find, upon close examination of her works, that she seldom introduces extraneous words and images into her writing, and that unity is a chief characteristic of nearly all her works. Miss Nin's rich vocabu-lary enables her, especially in the *Diary,* to make her pronouncements and descriptions clearly and precisely. In all of her writing she is sensitive to rhythm (and the idea of rhythm, movement, is a key symbol in her art), sensitive to rich and sensual images.

Duane Schneider. *Southern Review.*
Spring, 1970, pp. 506–7

Miss Anais Nin has acquired during the past thirty years a hothouse image, like some rare orchird—exotic, delicate, yet rich with voluptuous promise, a writer whose *Journals,* of which further volumes are promised, have become a literary legend to many who will never read a word of them. It's therefore likely to surprise anyone familiar with such an image to find that this slim . . . reissue of a novel [*A Spy in the House of Love*] which first appeared in 1954, is beneath the dreamlike imagery and modish, tentative exploration of emotional disturbance, an impassioned cry for Women's Lib. Not that Miss Nin would dream of wasting fine writing on blueprints for economic indepen-dence, the burdens of domesticity, or the recognition of a woman's capacity in a man's role; she is concerned here with the obsessive guilt and bewildered longings of a woman who cannot bear to be caged by one man, one home, one personality, who will lie and cheat to retain sexual independence and who, above all, recognizes and is appalled by her desire for passion without responsibility, sex without love, for the game of "defeating life's limitations" by "passing without passports and permits from one love to another."

(London) *Times Literary Supplement.*
January 29, 1971, p. 113

Miss Nin's diaries emphasize her resort to frequent bouts of psychoanalysis to rescue her from the desperate restrictions of an untrammeled life. Absorbed in narcissism, she flounders among the multitude of selves she perceives. Committed to fantasies of feminine power, she involves herself therefore in endless responsibilities to others. Her self-display requires an audience, her audience makes demands, her freedom eludes her. Her relationships lead her back only to herself. It seems a strangely symbolic fact that her husband has disappeared, apparently by his request, from her published diaries. The stillborn fetus might, for all we are told, be a virgin birth: the figure of Anaïs Nin, surrounded by others, exists nonetheless in a terrifying isolation of self-concern.

Patricia Meyer Spacks. Hudson Review.
Winter, 1971–72, p. 564

Anais Nin is one of the most extraordinary and unconventional writers of this century. Her vast diary, which encompasses some 50 years of human relationships, resembles no other in the history of letters, and as a novelist she has been distinctly catalytic. With her direct knowledge of the mechanics of psychoanalysis, she conveyed the even flow of uncensored speech in a series of prose writings which constitute one continuous novel. Collected under the title, *Cities of the Interior,* these writings in fiction are so detached from historical epoch, and the topography of her inner spaces so remote from the naturalistic landscapes of her fellow novelists of the 1940s and 1950s that they might well have been left untouched as a legacy for future generations, had not the publication of her diaries, beginning in 1966, brought her into full public view, earned her a sizable American audience, and a particularly remarkable popularity with younger readers. . . .

If conversation and letter writing project the psyche outward, a continuously flowing interior monologue provides the channel for self-analysis. The splicing of dialogue and monologue, and the determining of their relationship to each other, are important features of Anais Nin's artistry. As she reports people's confessions, as she reveals their letters to her, she manages to bypass the kind of gossip and anecdote that we have learned to expect from diarists. Imagine a conversation in which nothing unimportant is ever uttered, where each bit of dialogue is crucial, digs deep into vital issues, where each meeting occurs at times of heightened awareness!

Anna Balakian. The New York Times.
January 16, 1972, p. 28

Like Anaïs Nin's fiction, her Diary is also a collage composition. The assembled elements are the bits and pieces of her life: fragile evocations of her feelings; her victories over herself; her occasional moods of despair; richly detailed portraits of the people who moved her, inviting friendship and compassionate analysis, or provoking her disapproval and critical analysis; passages from books and letters; passionate declarations of her aspirations as a writer; passages brilliantly describing the psychological problems of the artist; sharp observations of the cultural patterns of America; and fascinating accounts of Nin's own repeated journeys into psychoanalysis. Selected from the mass of materials of the unpublished diary, the passages that comprise each published volume are themselves a collage composition presenting a phase in the life of their creator.

Nin's Diary, a work of art in itself, possesses special importance for those who are intrigued by the creative process. Because this Diary exists, we can see exactly how Nin's fiction was made. Even greater insights may someday be available to those who are able to study the unedited manuscripts. But a comparison of the present version of the Diary with the fiction reveals first, and perhaps most strikingly, Anaïs Nin's insistent need to preserve her experience, the stuff of her life, by recording it with astonishing dedication, even passion. The intensity and power of this need explains why Henry Miller and Otto Rank were unsuccessful in their attempts to free Nin of the diary. The diary *was* her life, her inner life, which the circumstances of her outer life prevented from receiving full expression. This need to preserve her experience, to protect it from alteration, change, or loss, proves the depth and strength of Anaïs Nin's creative will and inadvertently demonstrates one of the theories of her most famous analyst, Otto Rank. . . .

As she has repeatedly told her readers, Anaïs Nin's most valuable resource as an artist is her own complex self. Picking and choosing from the many and varied experiences of this self, she has created her ingenious books by combining elements that would not be found together in traditional fiction. She welds odds and ends of experience into collage compositions with the intensity of her personal vision of self and reality. As she has grown and changed, so have her books, reflecting the life that gave rise to them, just as the life has fed upon and been nourished by the books.

The quest that is traced again and again in Nin's writings actually involves a very radical concept: the abandonment of the idea of the self as a given fixed entity or essence. We create ourselves as we live. Nin explains poetically in her books and in the example of her own life that is revealed in the Diary. The idea of the self as a collage of experiences is central to Nin's psychological vision. Max Ernst, in writing of collage, quotes André Breton: "Who knows if we are not somehow preparing ourselves to escape from the principle of identity?"

Sharon Spencer. *Collage of Dreams: The Writings of Anaïs Nin* (Athens: Swallow/ Ohio University Press, 1977), pp. 6–7, 17

Approaching Nin's *Diary* is difficult; the fact that it consists of edited versions of her original entries places it somewhat in a category of its own. A curious blend of direct access to a younger psyche or self, but with elements deemed unimportant edited out by the same psyche grown older, Nin's *Diary* has as little affinity with the retrospective reminiscences of an older Benjamin

Franklin as it does with the daily entries of a Samuel Pepys. Indeed, one sometimes wonders whether Nin's *Diary* is not closer to fiction than autobiography, since in view of her deliberate omission of certain figures and aspects of her life, what we are really given here is the life of a "persona" rather than that of the author herself.

At the same time, however, one could argue that the editing only enhances the value of the *Diary* as a document of the growth of a psyche: as the teleology of inflation or regression is more apparent to the finished personality, so in the *Diary* we have only those aspects of her younger self that the older Nin found to be most strongly incorporated within herself. . . .

The most striking aspect of the first *Diary*, for example, is the larger-than-life quality and the numinous force of the individuals Nin presents. The clue to this exaggeration is to be found in the psychological theory of projection, but not, however, projection of the reaction formation variety—projections that are merely opposite to unconscious feelings. Rather it is a matter of the projection of archetypes, configurations which are intrinsic in one's psyche and which when projected onto individuals in one's life empower these individuals with sacred or divine forces for one's self. The "inflation" is "pathological" in the sense that it "naturally depends on some innate weakness of the personality against the autonomy of collective unconscious contents," but it is also part of the process whereby one is enabled "to annex the deeper layers of the unconscious." In the *Diary*, the constellation of projections is like a star, with the Self (Nin) at the center, radiating energy into the figures around her while at the same time she gradually incorporates their power; as she takes back into herself the energy she has previously projected outward, the Self begins to gain in confidence and ego strength.

Stephanie A. Demetrakopoulos. *Mosaic.*
Winter, 1978, pp. 121–22

For Nin, perhaps more so than with most writers, the significance of her achievement in twentieth-century literature is linked closely to her literary career. As a fiction writer she tried consistently to keep before her the same principles that she later sustained so effectively in the *Diary*, but the nature of her attempt to describe and simulate psychological reality was often not apparent to her readers during the late 1930s through the early 1960s and in fact was not made clear until she became one of her chief literary critics and analyzed her works in the *Diary* and in *The Novel of the Future*. . . . Only after she perceived that the *Diary* would be her most acclaimed contribution to letters did Nin seem to recognize that her mode of autobiography was as effective a vehicle for her ideas as the novels. It is not the first time that a writer has tenaciously subscribed to a particular approach or genre, only to find later that acceptance and literary success lay in quite a different direction. . . .

Her fiction, although kept in print, is, regrettably, generally not given great attention. Nin was too long neglected, and she has been praised to excess recently for the wrong reasons. Her greatest value is as a legitimate cicerone through the feminine psyche, as an author who shows both women and men that the pursuit of one's completeness is a difficult task that must be undertaken, even though it is unpleasant to do so and even though it might not be successful in the end. She was nonetheless an optimist in a landscape of psychological despair, and her vision was augmented by her dedication to moderation and understanding.

Benjamin Franklin V and Duane Schneider.
Anaïs Nin: An Introduction (Athens: Ohio
University Press, 1979), pp. 291, 294

Anaïs Nin's greatest achievement was her multi-faceted self-portrait, contained in both her Diary and her experimental fiction. The Diary is by far her more successful literary accomplishment, especially the first two volumes which are Nin's finest works of art. Throughout the Paris Diaries, there are passages of extraordinary brilliance and perception, descriptions of psychic states of confusion and duality, dramatic scenes which captivate and delight us with their candor and charm. The spectacle of Nin's continually changing masks and roles fascinates us, as does the subtle mating dance between Nin, June, and Henry Miller. In June Miller, Nin discovers her greatest subject, her most compelling alter ego, which she also makes the basis of her most effective work of fiction, *House of Incest*.

As the pages accumulate, however, the narcissism evident in Nin's Diary from the start becomes more problematic as the author grows increasingly preoccupied with convincing herself and her readers that she is worthy of such immense attention. The more she utilizes her Diary as a means of defense and persuasion, the less concerned she appears to be with the aesthetic merits of her text. In volumes V and VI this situation is reversed to some extent; Nin makes a determined effort to observe the surrounding world with a sharper eye, to offer skillful portraits of others. But her intention to make her book a "journal of others" is not altogether convincing when the others she summons into her text all appear to be witnesses for the defense, especially in the last volume where the testimonies to Nin's uniqueness overwhelm her book.

However, the two early Diaries published since Nin's death counterbalance this negative last impression, for they are full of a precocity and charming ingenuousness which engage us as the journals of the older Nin often do not. It remains to be seen how the two intermediate volumes yet to be published will effect the overall design and value of the Diary. Until these Diaries are in print and a few more years have passed, Nin's stature will not be decided. Nevertheless, it is clear that the greatest significance of Nin's Diary is in its universality. . . .

Nin's fiction is best appreciated in tandem with her Diary, since it is a variation on the autobiographical themes first set out in the journal. *House of Incest* is least in need of the Diary for support; it easily stands on its own as a fascinating surrealist descent into a woman's inner hell. The same is true for a handful of the stories in *Under a Glass Bell,* such as "The Labyrinth," "Birth," and "Hejda," which although derived from the Diary, have a highly wrought intensity and poetic condensation which are most effective. The first section of "Stella" is also extraordinarily compact and emotionally charged, but this novella does not fulfill the promise of the opening movement. The remainder of Nin's fiction subsequent to this point also disappoints as a whole. *Cities of the Interior* is an interesting experiment, but not a great work of art. Although it contains passages of subtlety and emotional power, overall the stylistic and structural problems detract significantly from the effectiveness of the work. Having removed the recognizable signposts from the outer world, clearly differentiated characters or fully elaborated metaphors or themes, Nin fails to substitute a stylistic perfection which might compensate for the unsubstantiality of her text. As a stylist, Nin is undeniably flawed, but as the author of a complex, enigmatic self-portrait of great richness and charm, Nin will continue to captivate readers of the future.

Nancy Scholar. *Anaïs Nin* (Boston: Twayne, 1984), pp. 131, 133

NJAU, REBECCA (KENYA) 1932–

The examples of Rebeka Njau's *Ripples in the Pool,* and Ngugi wa Thiong'o's *Petals of Blood* serve as excellent cases to elucidate this point.

Before probing into the way the sexes are depicted, and before suggesting reasons for this portrayal in both novels, I wish to risk being labeled a male chauvinist by clearly stating that, structurally, at least, *Ripples in the Pool* is much inferior to *Petals of Blood.* Firstly, unlike Ngugi who is able to effectively demonstrate the exploitation and oppression of the Kenyan people from the colonial period to the present era of black neo-colonialism as a major theme, Njau lacks the artistry to present even one clearly defined theme. One is often in doubt about what Njau is trying to say in *Ripples in the Pool,* not because of the writer's complex, or even "obscure," way of saying it, but rather because of the poor manner in which characters and events are presented. The reader is never sure whether Njau is dealing with the mother-fixation theme, or whether she wants to call attention to the abandonment of traditional values or, finally, whether she is just trying to make a comment on a general malaise in the society. There are elements of each of these themes in the text, but none of them is developed enough to form a thematic unit. Njau also demonstrates an astounding capacity for creating colorless and hazy characters: the heroine Selina's friend, Sophia, Kefa Munene, who is the local M.P., Munene's father-in-law, Maina, and the nurse in Munene's "home" for the disabled, Maria, are examples of characters who, in spite of snippets of conversation allotted to them, quickly vanish from the reader's mind. Finally, the depth of psychological penetration which charac-terizes Ngugi's *A Grain of Wheat,* and part of which we see in *Petals of Blood,* is, at best, only hinted at in *Ripples in the Pool.*

Some parallels in plot and theme nevertheless make an examination of Njau's and Ngugi's novels most significant in the context of the "woman question.". . .

Despite the seemingly close links between *Ripples in the Pool* and *Petals of Blood,* a closer examination of the sexual images in both texts reveals a basic difference between the two writers. The difference between Ngugi and Njau is most obvious when one looks at their portrayal of women: whereas Ngugi continues his tradition of representing "brave, resilient, resourceful and determined women," Njau reduces even her leading women characters to the traditional stereotypes found in all literatures. . . .

Despite isolated occurrences such as these which show Njau as a writer who obviously demonstrates sympathy and understanding for people in gen-eral, and for women in particular, one is generally repulsed by her main female characters, especially when their attributes are viewed in full perspec-tive and in context. Both Selina and her mother-in-law would certainly rank among the worst stereotyped women ever portrayed in the literatures of Af-rica. Selina comes out exhibiting the crudest type of neurosis imaginable.

The images of Selina as a "bitch" and of her mother-in-law as a witch are constantly hinted at or shown.

Abioseh M. Porter. Ariel. 12, 1981,
pp. 63–65, 67

Ripples in the Pool is a mystery story in which the author dramatizes various kinds of tragic relationships among people and the conflict of ideas which usually lead to such tragedies.

The most tragic of such relationships, one that is crucial to the central preoccupation of the novel, is the love affair between Gikere and Selina. The two are incompatible and cannot be expected to live a happy marital life. Gikere is a simple village lad, unused to the intricacies of life in the city. He is a humble hospital attendant, content with his position in life, but vaguely hoping that one day he may be of help to his people at Kamukwa by establish-ing a clinic there. Selina, on the other hand, is a prostitute who has become an expert in playing on men's passions. She is, we are told, "no ordinary girl: she was arrogant, self-centred, highly expensive and feared no man.". . .

All activities converge on the pool which is presented in this novel as the communal symbol of truth and purity. From it every event derives its character and authenticity. It is the touchstone against which everybody is judged. It embodies a mystery which needs to be unravelled by every individ-ual for himself. Its antiquity commands respect, and nobody can defy its laws with impunity. It is an inscrutable personality which remains forever to bring prosperity and happiness to those who do good and ruin to those who cheat their countrymen and indulge in city vices. The closer any character is to accepting the mystery connected with the pool, the better life is for him. That is why, when Karuga is uncertain of his future and is desperately looking for a spiritual anchor on which to rest his hopes of success, he is advised by Muthee to rely on the life-giving power of the pool. . . .

It would appear that many people in the novel commit sins "against the spirits of the pool" without knowing it. These spirits demand, among other things, honesty, hard work, respect for the truth, loyalty to indigenous culture and total commitment to individual liberty. Given this yardstick, it is easy to see why Selina's life ends in disaster.

Oladele Taiwo. *Female Novelists of Modern Africa* (New York: St. Martin's, 1984), pp. 29, 31–32

A writer like Grace Ogot (Kenya), for example, may seem more inclined to conform to certain norms than to condemn them, and she is sometimes harshly criticized by more progressive colleagues, who regret that one of the few women writers does not use her talent in a better cause.

The same can certainly not be said of someone like Rebecca Njau, who writes in both Swahili and English. Her novel *Ripples in the Pool* (1975) was well received inside and outside of Kenya. The book gives a balanced view of a number of contrasting ideas in which good, evil, the occult and other forces run counter to the often artificial lines of demarcation between tradition and Westernization, village and city, male and female. Njau's plays are a plea for more individual freedom. *The Scar* (1960) centers on the subordinate position of women in a rural Kikuyu society. The central character is Mariana, a prominent local figure with "revolutionary" ideas. She tries to persuade the other women to give up such senseless practices as the "circumcision" of girls, and to reject the fear and superstitions which are designed to keep them in their place. Not surprisingly, the older women are suspicious of her, but Mariana does have some success in awakening the women and girls of the village to the new opportunities awaiting them. In the end, however, she has to leave town when it becomes known that she was raped at the age of sixteen and gave birth to a child.

Mineke Schipper. *Unheard Words: Women and Literature in Africa, the Arab World, Asia, the Caribbean, and Latin America* (London: Allyson and Busby, 1985), pp. 46–47

NOAILLES, ANNA DE (FRANCE) 1876–1933

Anna de Noailles was one of the most admired writers of her era. Contemporary readers voted her their favorite woman poet next to Marceline Desbordes-Valmore, and along with Colette, her name dominates the pages of French literary history devoted to early twentieth-century women writers. In 1913 the London *Times* declared Anna de Noailles "the greatest poet that the twentieth century has produced in France—perhaps in Europe."

A prolific writer, Anna de Noailles produced over 1,900 pages of verse along with several novels during her thirty-year career. Her work appealed to a wide readership; she was frequently anthologized and included in popular series, and many of her books became best-sellers. The French Academy expressed its appreciation of Noailles's work by crowning her first collection of poetry, *Le Coeur innombrable* (The innumerable heart, 1901), with their annual Archon Despérouses Prize, and in 1921 she received the academy's Grand Prize for Literature. The following year she became the first woman ever accepted into the Royal Belgian Academy of French Language and Literature (Colette was accepted in 1933).

Noailles was more than a successful writer; she was also the star literary personality of her day. . . .

As a literary personality, Anna de Noailles is not forgotten—there is a recent biography, and the new wing of the Carnavalet Museum in Paris contains her bed and a reproduction of her bedroom—but as a poet, she has been sadly neglected. Her works are now out of print, rarely studied, and then usually examined only as typical examples of "feminine poetry." Fin-de-siècle critics defined feminine poetry as spontaneous and sensual lyricism deriving from woman's feminine nature. This biased, inaccurate, and restrictive categorization is largely responsible for marginalizing Noailles's work, and thus distracting modern readers from recognizing her influence on a whole generation of men and women writers. Noailles is neither typical nor representative; she is an original who dared to challenge convention and breathe new life into an art form that had become increasingly intellectualized by the end of the nineteenth century. . . .

As a child . . . Noailles began a love affair with nature that would eventually dominate her entire poetic oeuvre. Though some consider her a pantheist, Noailles was looking for herself, not God, in nature, which seems to exist solely for her sensual enjoyment. . . .

Noailles does not restrict her comparisons to flowers, but extends them to the entire vegetable kingdom, a practice that some critics ridiculed. Her use of many of its less poetic members earned her the title "Muse of the Kitchen Garden." . . .

Noailles felt that her writing was shaped by two opposing forces, which she called "the bacchante and the nun," but others have variously labeled these contrasts romantic/classic, northern/southern, and dionysian/apollonian. The poet's exuberance for life, for example, is frequently darkened by a melancholic contemplation of her mortality, nostalgic yearnings, and a fervent desire to be remembered. A materialist who rejected the possibility of an afterlife, Noailles believed only in the natural living world of sensation and envisioned death as cold, dark emptiness. . . .

From a thematic perspective, Noailles had much in common with the women poets of her generation, who also wrote of childhood, love, nature, and death, but Claude Mignot-Ogliastri, her biographer, notes that the extremely narcissistic nature of Noailles's poetry separates it from the work of other women. Maternal love, for example, is strikingly missing from her work. When Noailles strays from her major themes, she writes lovingly about her country and the French heroes, whom she calls "the affirmers of life." . . .

Critics engaged in reshaping our understanding of literary history, and particularly the role of gender, may yet revive interest in Anna de Noailles's poetry. Contemporary reaction to her work, for example, provides a fascinating example of how women writers were read. But Noailles is more than an interesting case history. Although she did not claim to be a feminist, she broke new ground for women writers through the example of her success, and, by defying poetic convention, produced some startlingly fresh images, with a passion for life and language that today's readers will still find moving.

Tama Lea Engelking. In Eva Sartori and
Dorothy Wynne Zimmerman, eds. French
Women Writers: A Bio-Bibliographical
Sourcebook (Westport, Connecticut:
Greenwood Press, 1991), pp. 335–36,
340–41, 343

When we read the most celebrated woman poet of the [turn of the century] period, Anna de Noailles, from our present viewpoint, we are confronted and dismayed by the sustained outpouring of a rich rhetorical language cast in an outdated verse form. In poem after poem, Anna de Noailles pours out her sense of herself as reflected in "nature," a nature that reflects back to her in turn only her own fervent infatuation with her image of herself as an inspired woman poet. In a self-indulgent society she is without doubt, and most unfortunately for her own talent, a kind of unadulterated Narcissus, living in her own closed world. She offers us a typical image of a feminine writer and feminine writing. It is true too that we are only now beginning more carefully to scrutinize the many women poets who achieved some celebrity in those years. More carefully—more favorably too; perhaps a changed attitude will bring about a changed evaluation of their work.

Germaine Brée. Women Writers in France:
Variations on a Theme (New Brunswick,
New Jersey: Rutgers University Press,
1973), pp. 43–44

Strongly influenced by romanticism, employing a still classic form (though sometimes a bit careless), Anna de Noailles makes an authentic, simple, and tender voice heard. Her poetry is highly lyrical, assigning itself the task of exalting the reality accessible to the sense with an extreme sensuality. . . . Her images evoke a whole world of odors, light, fruits, where summer takes a central place. . . . The Orient appears, most often, as a paradise of the senses, an extreme pole of summer. The ardent wish to "hold in one's arms the world and its desires" implies a pantheism and a mysticism of nature, a "pagan holiness." Images of fusion with sensory elements are very common.

On the horizon of such a passion for living, may be perceived, from the earliest collections on, a secret despair, a profound and moving melancholy; the urge to live intensely translates a struggle against death (which becomes an obsessive element in her work after 1913) and forgetting. As the exaltation of the living self, poetry perpetuates that exaltation beyond death and becomes a "shade laughing and full of clarity" to which readers will come to warm themselves up.

With her fervent voice, removed from all fussy intellectuality, Anna de Noailles knows how to plunge us back into the sensory and turn us towards the life "of men who will come to drink at the springs that I was."

A. Déchamps. In J-P de Beaumarchais, ed.
Dictionnaire des Littératures de Langue Française (Paris: Bordas, 1984), p. 1644

NOGAMI YAEKO (JAPAN) 1885–1985

In my opinion, the only literary writer among Sōseki's many students who proceeded like a cow—that is, kept writing slowly but steadily—was Nogami Yaeko, who probably has had the longest writing career of any author in Japan and is also one of the world's oldest living authors.

Nogami Yaeko made her literary debut in 1907 at the age of twenty-two with "Enishi" (The ties of love), a short story which was published with Sōseki's recommendation in the magazine *Hototogisu*. That was the fortieth year of Meiji, and in 1982, at the age of ninety-seven, she is still engaged in writing. Naturally, writing for many years does not mean that a person is a great writer. But in Yaeko's case, with each new work since her first story, she has steadily matured both in technique and insight. Her historical novel *Hideyoshi to Rikyū,* which was completed in 1963 when she was seventy-eight, is considered by such critics as Senuma Shigeki, Kōno Toshirō, and Ara Masato to be one of the masterpieces of modern Japanese literature. After the completion of *Hideyoshi to Rikyū,* Yaeko wrote several short stories, miscellanies, and numerous essays of a socially critical nature. Then at the surprisingly advanced age of eighty-seven, she published the first installment of her autobiographical novel *Mori* (The Forest). This has been published chapter by chapter in the literary magazine *Shinchō,* averaging one or two chapters a year since May 1972. The latest installment, chapter 14, appeared in the June 1982 issue. She intends to conclude this novel with the next chapter. . . .

Nogami Yaeko is sympathetic to the socially concerned youth, whose serious thinking often made them lean toward the left. Yet she does not approve of ultra-revolutionary ideas at the expense of human compassion. At the same time, she clearly despises the affectation and hypocrisy of the rich; yet she still approves of the upper-middle class, if they are equipped with good sense, fine sensibility, and human warmth. In short, in *Machiko* both extremes are rejected and common sense prevails at the end. This novel is not as forceful as some of her later works, but it is interesting enough to carry readers through the entire novel. The main characters, Machiko, Kawai, and Seki, are psychologically and physically well depicted. A few supporting characters such as Machiko's one sister, her husband, and several snobbish upper-middle-class women, are also quite well portrayed. The psychological realism with which the characters are depicted creates a story which is a skillful testimony to the foibles of human nature. . . .

Indeed, Nogami Yaeko seems to have followed Sōseki's golden rule for an author: she has proceeded like a cow. Since she first published *Enishi* in 1907, Yaeko has worked steadily and diligently, developing her skills with each new work. Even after the completion of her masterpiece *Hideyoshi to Rikyū* at the age of seventy-eight, she remained indefatigable in her effort to grow. Today at ninety-seven she still sustains this effort. As Sōseki predicted over sixty years ago, the world has forgotten many flashier writers, but it has admired and bowed to Nogami Yaeko for her ninety years of intellectual pursuit and continuous diligence, resulting in literary works of enduring value.

Yoko McClain. *Journal of the Association of Teachers of Japanese.* 17, 1982, pp. 159, 161, 169

In the summer of 1984, a big party was held in Tokyo to celebrate the one-hundredth birthday of Nogami Yaeko. Among the people attending were many major figures from the Japanese literary world. Shortly afterward, her autobiographical novel, *The Wood (Mori),* not yet completed, Yaeko died. She had been working on the novel for over ten years by then, at a pace that suited her—slowly and steadily. Yaeko's disciplined approach to her writing, sustained even while in her nineties, was the hallmark of her work. Her remarkably long and productive career spanned eight decades—her first published story appeared in 1911. Though she had neither a brilliant debut like that of her friend Miyamoto Yuriko, nor the financial success achieved by Hayashi Fumiko, Yaeko's accomplishments as a writer were equally impressive. Her critical mind and rigorous self-discipline helped her write fiction with a perspective far beyond her limited personal experiences, and she established an independence few other women writers of her time were able to achieve. Several of her novels stand today as masterpieces of modern Japanese fiction. . . .

Yaeko's literary themes were as wide-ranging as her personal interests. She was the first modern Japanese author to write stories from the perspective of a mother of young children. In *A New Life (Atarashiki Inochi)*, a collection of stories published in 1916, Yaeko portrayed children through the eyes of young mothers, using this point of view to critically view society. This innovation was very effective and demonstrated Yaeko's increasing skill as a fiction writer. She moved on to new themes in *The Neptune (Kaijinmaru,* 1922). Based on an actual event, this novella about a shipwreck and the ensuing cannibalism is a vividly gruesome human drama that poses profound questions about human nature. This work helped to silence critics who claimed that women were incapable of writing about events and themes outside the confines of their everyday existence. Yaeko surprised the literary establishment again a few years later with the publication of *Ōishi Yoshio,* a novel about an immensely popular historical figure of the eighteenth century. In her treatment, she challenged the accepted public image of this national hero by depicting him as a man unsure of himself, trapped by the events of history.

In 1928 Yaeko wrote *Machiko,* a novel based on her observations of the decade's political upheavals, especially their effect on young people. Machiko, the heroine of the novel, is a bright and sensitive young woman studying sociology. Concerned with her social responsibility, Machiko rejects her family's bourgeois conventions and sympathizes with leftist activists. She eventually comes to see, however, the hypocrisy in her leftist lover and his excuse that theory and practice are not the same. At the heart of the novel is the dilemma between rationality and passion, both of which were equally authentic to Yaeko.

Politics and power interested Yaeko greatly. Over a period extending from 1937 to 1956, Yaeko wrote *The Labyrinth (Meiro),* a novel in five volumes. It is an ambitious work that examines many layers of Japanese society—the upper-class politicians and businessmen, the working-class revolutionaries, the traditional artists and scholars. Seen through the eyes of a young man who has renounced his leftist beliefs, the novel portrays a civilization on the brink of self-destruction. *The Labyrinth* has a complex and a symphonic structure unparalleled by the work of any woman writer in modern Japanese literature.

Yaeko's recurring theme—and her own personal conviction—was that among all human endeavors, only art transcends time. She took up this idea once again in her historical novel *Hideyoshi and Rikyū,* published in 1962 and for which she received a prestigious literary prize. The novel deals with a conflict between Rikyu, a famous sixteenth-century artist and tea master, and Hideyoshi, a political genius who ruled Japan. By the time Yaeko wrote this novel she had been writing for over half a century.

Besides the many years it spanned and the wide range of topics addressed, what is striking about Yaeko's career is the continual development of her work—from short, often sketchy stories to full-length, complex novels of almost perfect form. Unlike many other women writers of her time, she did not write autobiographical fiction until the very end of her career.

Yukiko Tanaka. *To Live and to Write:
Selections from Japanese Women Writers
1913–1938* (Seattle: Seal Press, 1987),
pp. 147, 150–51

There are striking similarities between *Machiko* and *Pride and Prejudice.* Yet the two works give quite a different impression to the reader: while *Pride and Prejudice* is bright and light, *Machiko* is gloomy and serious. This difference may be partly caused by the characterization of the heroines. Though both of them are intelligent young women with "independent thoughts," they are very different in their disposition.

Elizabeth is a cheerful and playful woman who likes to "laugh at follies and nonsense, whims and inconsistencies." . . .

On the other hand, Machiko is an introspective and passionate woman. She is awakened to social problems, criticizes the leisure class to which she belongs, and tries to get out of it. She refuses Kawai's proposal of marriage because of her hatred toward the upper class and tries to devote herself to a new life with Seki, the revolutionary. Yet Yaeko, the author, makes her realize her mistake and choose a love based on sober reality, even as Elizabeth did.

The early Showa Era, in which the story of *Machiko* is set, was a time when the socialist revolutionary movement rapidly gained ground due to the economic world-wide depression. At the same time [the] deep-rooted concept of the feudal family still remained a powerful force in Japan. Yaeko created a young intelligent woman of the leisure class who groped for a meaningful way of life in these circumstances.

But why did she base her novel on Austen's work? In an essay entitled "Naru asamayama no fumoto kara" (From the Foot of the Thundering Mt. Asama; 1931), Yaeko admits that it is natural for young people who are awakened to the contradictions of their present social system to want to get out from under the exploiting class and to reform society. But she realizes and states strongly that everyone cannot join a revolutionary movement. She tells Tami, a young woman of the leisure class, that "If one engages in such a small duty as unperceivable by anyone in a post suitable to his ability, he cannot be a mere onlooker. This advice might be given to Machiko. . . . Though Yaeko watches her young heroine with kind, mature eyes, she criticizes the contradictions contained in the radical, revolutionary ideas. As Austen does she believes in good sense and moderation based on human reason.

Yoshiko Enimoto. *Comparative Literature
Studies.* 28, 1991, pp. 257–58

NORMAN, MARSHA (UNITED STATES) 1947–

Getting Out, the prizewinning play by Marsha Norman, has been acclaimed for its tightly crafted script, in which the two lives of the same white female convict are interwoven on the stage. The audience experiences the first day of Arlene's release from prison, during which time we respond with concern and maybe even trepidation to the simultaneous presence on stage of Arlie, her younger, violent, and self-destructive self who has just spent eight years in prison for the cold-blooded murder of a cabbie. This time in prison is but a minor and relatively static period of Arlie's life replete with prostitution, forgery, and hateful aggression toward her peers. Her crimes are the partial result of a rapist father [and] a seemingly uncaring mother. . . .

In the short space of the fiction's twenty-four hours, the audience sees Arlene fight off yet another rape, this time by Bennie, her sentimentally confused jailer, yet another confrontation with the uncaring, but present mother, and still another temptation to get out of poverty (but not, of course, out of bondage) by repeating the theatrical rituals of prostitution—Arlene again has the option to work with Carl, her previous pimp/lover. On the bright side, the audience hears her naive, but vehement desire to be reunited with her eight-year-old son, Joey (Carl's child whom she has not seen since his birth in prison). The spectators want her to join the ex-con cook upstairs, the tough but respectable Ruby, in a life without further crime. And the Christian viewers share Arlene's hopes in her new found lover, Jesus Christ. . . .

Getting Out (in theory) ends with the smiling sign that its spectators might not have to perform a tragedy after all. Arlie's laughter, especially if mimicked by the audience, suggests that while there are limits to patriarchal panopticism, that while authorities and audiences can always shit on their visual victims, they can in turn be pissed on in a diffusing manner, in the disguise of a bad joke. The libidinal economics of institutionality. The play's final gesture is not to join Arlene in *Getting Out* with the likes of Johnny Carson but to incite her playhouse spectators to represent the performance of power different from the exploitive, sexual-commercial world of paternal entertainment. The play closes with a seductive smile, asking its audience to join Arlene in her desires to be free of the macho world of control as it intertwines law, sex, and economics, as it prescribes production and subjection.

Timothy Murray. Theatre Journal. 35, 1983,
pp. 376–77, 388

Clearly the success of *'night, Mother* rests on the peculiar power of the play in performance; it works for audiences, when it does work, on a number of levels—the naturalistic illusion so carefully maintained that the play, like unmediated experience itself, appears open to multiple interpretation. However, I would like to suggest the possibility that male and female audience members "read," comprehend, and respond to the play in ways fundamentally different. While universal themes of death and desire, of human dignity and human pain, of hope and existential despair are accessible to all, these seem but "secondary elaborations" of the primary drama that women may cathartically experience in Norman's play. If we accept the psychoanalytic premise that given the specific pressures, complications, and resolutions offered the female child within the Oedipal situation, the process whereby men and women gain their sexual identity is not identical, then it stands to reason that a literary work in which such issues are represented should provide for the audience of each sex a different *kind* of experience. *'night, Mother* provides an interesting case since it both self-consciously addresses a female audience and subconsciously works upon the female psyche in powerful ways, positioning male and female viewers differently in the process. Indeed, because of the way in which the text foregrounds issues of female identity and feminine autonomy, focuses on the mother-daughter relationship, and controls the narrative movement, the relatively detached position available (however tentatively) to male viewers simply cannot (without great risk) be taken up by women. . . .

Whether or not Norman's *'night, Mother* is a "feminist" play is another question . . . but one not easily avoided. Clearly about and for women, the play offers women for identification unmediated by the gaze of men. The play also focuses on complicated issues of gender and female subjectivity, but does so without sacrificing traditional or conventional sources of pleasure through (Oedipal) narrative, closure, the illusion of reality, emotional catharsis. Much of the play's political effect (the area most closely associated with a feminist practice) lies in the theater event itself—how it is performed, what kind of discussion follows, what kind of reviews and critical commentary the play generates. If women were to see the actions and positions taken in the play as both recognizable and yet somehow untenable, then the play might offer the kind of dynamic contradiction that once brought to consciousness could generate radical change. In other words, this play allows women to perceive themselves as living in contradiction and to feel overwhelmingly uncomfortable about it. Norman herself, however, offers the audience no way of finally understanding that contradiction in social terms.

The danger . . . is that the play presents a mirror to reality in which women mis-recognize themselves in quite traditionally negative ways, the emotional catharsis serving a different therapeutic effect by reintegrating the spectator into her place within the dominant order, without challenging in any fundamental way the prevalent image of women in society—as those who reproduce, consume, and are consumed, who are powerless, inadequate, unworthy, and mutually destructive. After all, Jessie and Mama seem barely capable of handling the social dynamics of even their own limited lives. Norman's *'night, Mother* can perhaps best be understood as a profoundly naturalistic play in both intention and effect. It offers its audience images of women closely connected to a lived reality—characters neither idealized nor heroic, but shaped and determined here by the limited set, the limited options, and the tragic misapprehension of both themselves and the broader social dynamics of their specific situation.

Jenny S. Spencer. *Modern Drama.* 30, 1987,
pp. 364–65, 374–75

Despite its widespread critical acclaim, *Getting Out* is so infrequently described as a political play that a definition of the term becomes essential: political theater shows public policy, laws, or unquestioned social codes impinging unfairly and destructively upon private lives. Individual though the protagonist may be, what happens to this character is not an example of isolated fate but rather is the result of historically alterable conditions which are inherently unfair to a segment of society. What happens to Arlene Holsclaw could not happen to every woman, but it does happen to many, and because of our laws, policies, and social codes, it is much more likely to happen to women than to men.

Getting Out takes place in a prison within a prison, in a present that is surrounded by—and a reflection of—the past. The setting is a one-room apartment in the slum area of a large Kentucky city. It is bare and dingy, and there are bars on its single window. Its former occupant was a prostitute whose trade paid for her pimp's "green pants." Its present occupant, the prostitute's sister, Arlene Holsclaw, has just arrived from Alabama where she has been paroled after serving eight years for a second-degree murder committed during an escape from a prison where she was serving three years for forgery and prostitution.

On a catwalk above the apartment are the locales of a prison—sometimes literal and sometimes figurative—whose chief occupant is Arlie, Arlene as a teenager. . . .

What does it mean to "get out"? At the bitter moment when she discovers just how limited her options for the future are, Arlene tells Ruby, "outside's where you get to do what you want." By this, she primarily means being free of the constrictions placed upon her by her social and economic standing in the community. Arlene has come to believe that by eliminating that part of herself that society has always objected to, the rebellious, antiauthoritarian Arlie, by becoming "meek," she could "inherit the earth." The emphasis is on the tangible fulfillment of her desires. . . .

It is her final rejection of self that causes the prison to decide Arlie is rehabilitated. The shell she has developed to hostility and neglect is vulnerable to kindness and attention. In prison she comes to rely on the chaplain who renames her Arlene, teaching her that Arlie was her evil side that God would help her destroy. The destruction of Arlie was God's will, so that Arlene might join the meek that inherit the earth. Then, without telling Arlene before he left, the chaplain was transferred away. . . .

Arlene comes to trust Ruby's political analysis and accept her friendship because Ruby is able to validate Arlene's experience by showing its similarity to her own. The acceptance by another of her views is to Arlene in miniature the beginning of the end of her alienation, her awakening to a history of which she is a part, and the subsequent strengthening of her self-concept. When Arlene describes her suicide attempt, the "murder" of Arlie, it is Ruby who convinces her that "you can still love people that's gone." The play ends with Arlene and Arlie sharing a pleasant memory—an acceptance by Arlene of her past and of the qualities in Arlie without which the battle for the future will be lost.

Meanwhile, the bars on Arlene's window remain. Men have placed them there—Bennie insists—"to keep folks from breakin in." Perhaps—in some men's eyes—this is true. When will the bars be removed? Perhaps when men realize that keeping a caste in its place is as socially limiting to the confiner as to the confined. Perhaps when women recognize that they're there.

James Redmond. *Women in Theatre*
(Cambridge: Cambridge University Press,
1987), pp. 186, 191, 193–94

In Marsha Norman's *'night, Mother*, thirty-seven-year-old Jessie informs her mother Thelma that she will kill herself that evening, after having organized the details of her mother's life and her own death. After much argument, during which time the mother attempts to change the daughter's mind, the suicide happens anyway; the mother is left alone on stage, and the audience leaves the theater, some obviously in tears. Although touted by some critics as a feminist investigation of the hopelessness and degradation of women's lives in patriarchal society, the play ultimately reinscribes the dominant ideology in its realist form. It is indubitably a narrative built on enigmas and mysteries which are revealed gradually until the final scene of (dis)closure. It steadfastly maintains that illusion of reader-as-subject who shares with the absent narrator the position of knowingness and ultimate understanding; a coherent, unified text that renders up its pleasure in the satisfaction of catharsis, in the illusion of change without really changing anything. As Brecht noted, "The theater as we know it [he calls it illusionism] shows the structure of society (represented on stage) as incapable of being influenced by society (in the auditorium). Narrative closure reinstates the pre-existing order after instigating its temporary crisis. In what Roland Barthes would call a highly "readable" text, Jessie and her Mother are thus "known" fully; they are consumed characters, and the explanation for Jessie's suicide is perceived not within social relations (ideology) but in individual failure (or worse, as an heroic act, courageously ending a life that was indeed worthless).

Jeanie Forte. *Modern Drama*. 32, 1989,
p. 117

The power of the play *'night, Mother* lies in its relentless movement toward the final gunshot. No matter how much we do not want to believe it will come, we are forced to share with the mother a growing realization that the evening will end with Jessie's death. Death lends to all of human existence an urgency and poignancy, a sense of meaning that arises from the awareness that life will not last. In Jessie's case the knowledge and control over the timing of that end and its immediacy are themselves the source of meaning never before existent in her life. Her suicide arms her with a power, a sense of control over her life. It is the lens through which she offers a view of her existence, an existence so fraught with detachment and boredom that she chooses to continue meticulously in the tedious business of its day-to-day routine until that moment when she shuts it off. But when her life is compressed within the boundaries of that evening, what emerges are a few hours of honesty and intensity that burst like a meteoric glimpse of what this mother-daughter relationship is and what it might have been. . . .

As we are left to wonder how this daughter came to see all of the elements of her life as indicative of failure and alienation, and how this mother's experience contributes to this conclusion, we have only the evidence of this brief, private conversation. As Jessie says, "You're it, Mama. No more." The horrible bleakness of life, the emptiness Jessie experiences is not a peculiarity of female existence. But the significance of the mother-daughter relationship in the daughter's sense of powerlessness is unique to women. This play is not merely about the perils of parenthood or, more specifically, even the precariousness of motherhood in regard to daughters. It is about the problem and the elusiveness of autonomy, one of the stages on which the drama of human development unfolds.

Sally Browder. In Mickey Pearlman, ed.
*Mother Puzzles: Daughters and Mothers in
Contemporary American Literature*
(Westport, Connecticut: Greenwood Press,
1989), pp. 109–10

One way of approaching this drama [of mother-daughter doubling] is by looking at its banal surface in the context of the underlying mythic relationships of Demeter and Kore (Persephone), a relationship that offers clues to the mother-daughter relationship in the play. C. G. Jung and C. Kerényi, in their exploration of the Mysteries of Eleusis in *Essays On a Science of Mythology,* suggest an essential oneness of the Demeter and Kore figures in mythology, a oneness that is actually threefold, also embracing the third mythological figure, Hecate. Commenting on the identification of mother and daughter, Jung writes, "Demeter and Kore, mother and daughter, extend the feminine consciousness both upwards and downwards. They add an "older and younger," "stronger and weaker" dimension to it and widen out the narrowly limited conscious mind bound in space and time, giving it intimations of a greater and more comprehensive personality which has a share in the eternal course of things. Much of the power of Norman's play emerges from a mythical identification of mother and daughter that leaves Thelma bereft of the daughter she thought she had possessed but ironically at one with that daughter from whom she has derived new strength and life. More cathartic than depressing, the play reveals a bond between mother and daughter and a mythical sense of their oneness that allows for what Kerényi, commenting on Jung's ideas, calls *"being in death."* . . .

Marsha Norman surely did not attempt to make *'night, Mother* a modern version of the Demeter myth. The rhythms and resonance of that myth, however, give the play, despite its great sadness and sense of loss, its quickened sense of life. "Hades," it has been noted, "is the god presiding over our descents, investing the darkness in our lives, our depressions, our anxieties, our emotional upheavals and our grief with the power to bring illumination and renewal. Jessie embraces this god, and it is he that she introduces to her mother, who perhaps is able to see him more clearly through the image of Agnes's fires, a torch that burns to help one find what is lost. Mama learns from Jessie what it is that she used to whisper about after dinner with her withdrawn father—"His life, I guess," Jessie reveals. "His corn. His boots. Us. Things. You know." And now Mama does.

Katherine H. Burkman. In June Schlueter, ed. *Modern American Drama: The Female Canon* (Madison, New Jersey: Fairleigh Dickinson University Press, 1990), pp. 254–55, 262

In *The Holdup* (1980–83), Marsha Norman confronts the frontier West—long the focus of a male-centered mythology. While admitting that this play was not a typical "Norman play," that it has more fantasy than substance, and that it was not intended "to substantiate Western mythology" (all facts that might explain why some critics responded negatively to it), Norman also claimed that in *The Holdup* "there are serious things to be said about stories and how they operate on our minds." Indeed, the structure of this play's "story" suggests a transformation of the frontier myth. . . .

Inverting the traditional initiation rite, Norman presents a feminist version of the frontier myth that has general significance. Here, the frontier experience is the source of neither American uniqueness nor present day contradictions in American cultural life, but functions as a paradigm of a kind of maturation which was and remains relevant to American development. Other American women playwrights of the 1980s have written frontier plays taking a similar approach. In plays like *Going to See the Elephant* (1982), created by Karen Hensel, Patti Johns, Elana Kent, Sylvia Meredith, Elizabeth Lloyd Shaw, and Laura Toffenetti, and *Abundance* (1989), by Beth Henley, the categories of civilization and savagery, as they appear in the traditional frontier myth, are shown to be too simplistic to provide insight into the frontier experience. In these plays as well as in a musical like *Quilters* (1984), by Molly Newman and Barbara Damashek, the frontier experience is viewed less as an end in itself than as a gateway to "an experience of the majesty of cosmic law." Marsha Norman may or may not have paved the way for these other frontier plays, but she took steps toward reformulating the frontier myth, and her work along with that of these other playwrights may help to change the way in which the frontier Western past is viewed and (ab)used in the future.

Richard Wattenberg. Modern Drama. 33,
1990, pp. 507, 575

NOVAK, HELGA (GERMANY) 1935–

A somewhat more appropriate—albeit less original—title for the present collection of stories [*Palisaden*/Palisades] might be "The Best of Helga M. Novak." With the exception of four stories, everything offered here has already been published in the Federal Republic or, in the case of two pieces, the U.S., which is in contradiction to the assurance on the volume's back cover that countless (*zahlreiche*) texts are published here for the first time.

Novak's prose, grouped into seven vastly differentiated and yet often chillingly similar areas, reflects her personal experiences between 1967 (the year after she was stripped of her DDR citizenship) and 1975. Her style is powerful and personal. Frequently stalking her subject with tape recorder and microphone hidden in her purse, she does not merely interview night watchmen or the inhabitants of the "Building Across" in Frankfurt's dreary West End; she takes a resolute and active part in what goes on around her, at one point very nearly provoking a physical fight with a foreign worker.

Her gritty world includes work in an Icelandic fish-processing plant and a visit to a Portuguese farm co-op. Of lingering concern throughout her narratives is the conflict arising from the exploitation of working people by their superiors. An occasionally abstracted, even rudimentary syntax, coupled with a vivid vocabulary, makes that conflict come to life on the printed page. Helga Novak knows the power of language, and she rarely wastes words. The first, very short story in the volume, "Arbeitnehmer—Arbeitgeber" (Employer—Employee), is a forceful attempt at fundamental redefinition: *Arbeitgeber* literally means "work giver"; since the employee performs the work for the employer, Novak reasons, it follows that the employer, taking the fruits of that person's work, actually should be called *Arbeitnehmer* (work taker).

Simultaneously tough and tender, Helga M. Novak has emerged as one of the most outspoken women writing in the German language today. *Palisaden* is a welcome sampler of her craft.

Klaus Phillips. World Literature Today. 55,
1981, pp. 661–62

A poignant example of the struggle for autonomy is found in Helga Novak's novel *Die Eisheiligen*. With keen contemporary insight the narrator tries to come to terms with the powers that determine her life. Through the persona of the main character, she experiences her own childhood during World War II, and her battles against her mother's oppressive power, which severely hinders the development of the daughter's independence. It is true that in most mother-daughter constellations a dependence and an unequal distribution of power are inevitable. In this case, however, we witness how easily power can be misused and become a means of oppression. The mother brutally forces the daughter into a mode of behavior which benefits her, but causes an emotional deficit in the child, as well as deep psychological problems. A power struggle ensues, which both relentlessly pursue. . . .

Alone the nickname "Kaltesophie," which the mother receives from the daughter—a symbolic allusion to the namesday St. Sophie, which often brings frost in early spring—indicates that this woman could hardly personify the "ideal" mother. By displaying a cold attitude toward her daughter, she grossly neglects the child's natural need for security and warmth which are so necessary for the development of a positive self-image. . . .

Novak's insights coincide with those expressed by the German psychoanalyst Alice Miller. It can hardly be expected, Miller points out, that a very young and powerless child withstand the influence of her mother or distance herself through intellectual processes. Thus, Kaltesophie's "coldness" is transferred to the daughter and permeates her whole being. In the end, Novak's narrator confesses that she has also become one of the "Icy Saints," to which the novel's title refers. The continuous circle of influence which dominates the mother-daughter relationship becomes apparent. Her legacy is insecurity, melancholy and suicidal tendencies. . . .

The novel shows how an influential institution can take advantage of young people who are searching for a self because they have at one point in their lives been hindered from reaching autonomy. The communist regime in East Germany after the war was not interested in educating people to think for themselves, rather, it advocated a single, restrictive pattern of behavior. The daughter, who appears particularly susceptible to such indoctrination, suspects that she may not have found her salvation when she is asked to betray her parents, since they do not completely conform to the dictates of the state. Thus, her new environment reflects the dehumanizing treatment that she had experienced at home. Just as the mother does not have her well-being in mind, neither does the political institution.

Nevertheless, she "adopts" the state at the age of fifteen, and legally leaves her parents. The switch is not without forebodings: in the last sentence of the novel, she is met by a tall wall around her new "home," crowned with pieces of broken glass.

Helga W. Kraft and Barbara Kosta. German Quarterly. 56, 1983, pp. 74–75, 78

Helga Novak . . . for five years lived in Iceland, where for a time she worked preparing fish in a cold storage depot; experiences there are reflected in several of the short prose texts included in *Geselliges Beisammensein* (1968), a volume which already demonstrates Novak's characteristic strategy of subjecting the familiar to intense and alienating scrutiny. By the time that book appeared, Helga Novak was in West Germany, where an enthusiastic reception saw her awarded the Bremen Literature Prize. Two collections of poetry had already appeared, *Die Ballade von der reisenden Anna* (1965; The ballad of traveling Anna) and *Colloquium mit vier Häuten* (1967; Colloquium with four skins), both in the West, and it was the publication of the first of these which resulted in her East German citizenship being withdrawn in 1966, on her return to Leipzig from Iceland. Squibs and angry questions in the 1965 volume, such as could uncomfortably be tolerated in the late Brecht since his presence in the East was important, quickly ensured that Novak was non grata. . . .

The closing years of the 1960s were a prolific period for Novak, and the finest of her early prose pieces, "Palisaden oder Aufenthalt in einem irren Haus" and "Berenike ist weg," were written in 1968 and 1969 respectively, and published in *Aufenthalt in einem irren Haus* (1971; Living in the wrong house). The title fiction, a horrifyingly inhuman account of a season in a mad house, shows the early evolution of Novak's technique of juxtaposing prose passages of distinct rhetorical character, to create a cumulative effect of nihilistic irony. . . .

In 1973, after a hiatus of some years, Helga Novak returned to writing poetry and the results were published in *Balladen vom kurzen Prozeß* (1975; Ballad of a short trial) and *Margaret mit dem Schrank* (1978; Margaret with the cupboard)—a selection of her poetry written between 1955 and 1980 then followed under the title *Grünheide Grünheide* (1983), and the reader familiar with German will do best to begin reading her poetry in this volume. The contents of the 1970s collections are more emphatically committed to ballad writing and to commentary on social injustice: poems deal in robust, jaunty, unsmoothed rhythms with the history of the cold war, the proceedings of the police courts, and the thousand and one daily repressions of individual liberty. . . .

Novak's poetry in this vein has a raw, popular power, the power we associate with the lyrics of protest songs rather than with poetry on the page; its crudity usually disinclines us to rate it highly, but at times Novak's propagandist verse can stand beside Brecht's.

In prose, the stories Novak published at the start of the decade were followed in the mid-1970's by *Die Landnahme von Torre Bela* (1976; The annexation of Torre Bela), a journal recording the fortunes of a Portuguese workers' collective, and then, at the close of the decade, by the first, commanding volume of autobiography, *Die Eisheiligen* (1979; The Ice Saints), shortly followed by an equally authoritative second, *Vogel Federlos* (1982; Featherless bird). . . .

To call these two books autobiography is perhaps as inadequate as to imagine them fiction, as some commentators have done: a rhythm of distinctive strength is established in the prose by the alternation of different forms of prose narrative, by the interspersing of free verse passages, slogans, quotations, statistics, and so on, and by the subtle modulations in tone which the ironic distance between Novak and her first person narrator creates. Autobiography here is both tough and real, and fictionalized, indeed almost poeticized. Berlin dialect, acutely realized interrogation scenes, misty adolescent reverie, cool analytic passages, nature description, refrain effects: Novak employs so wide a variety of rhetorical strategies that it is difficult to imagine a childhood narrative of the period more excitingly written. The hindsight wisdom of the adult and the streetwise robustness of the teenager complement each other excellently, and the result is convincing, moving and instructive.

Helga Novak's position as a GDR exile is a familiar one: she has not abandoned her socialist commitment, but still is critical of both East Germany and her new West German home. Beyond political systems, she sees an ethical atrocity in any curtailment of the individual's right to choose his own life. If the tub-thumping crudity of some of her writing leaves us more persuaded of her propagandist skills than of her literary sensitivity, nonetheless her compassion and humanity are not in doubt.

Michael Hulse. Antigonish Review. 62–63, 1985, pp. 224–28

In "Märkische Feemorgana," (Markish Morgan le Fay) the title section of her new work, Helga Novak charts a lyric geography and archeology of personal experience. Her themes are the universal ones of human loss: the loss of hopes, love, and home. She seeks to reverse these losses by returning to a condition of vitalistic innocence and oneness with nature, in zones that lie beyond historical memory, in a mythicized landscape of her native Mark Brandenburg.

What makes Novak's path often difficult to follow is the uncommon terminology she sets along it: "Kalidophase," "Abschmelzfuge," "Lithozone," "Geschiebemergel," "Pontische Nadeltaiga," and the like. However, it is precisely this impeding device that underlies her poetic strategy. Blocking the way to unmediated comprehension, she compels us to repeated, concentrated readings; and this effort draws us as though by the power of incantation into the sphere of elemental imagery, sound, and rhythm from which her "Märkische Feemorgana" derives its remarkable vigor. At the same time, the admission that she has culled her technical lore from maps, charts, and tables ("kein Zufall daß ich hier gelandet bin"), along with the robust humor that frequently lightens her mythic trek, dispels any notion of poetic escapism or naïveté. Although poems that clearly evidence a political content, such as "als eine Diebin hereingeschlichen," are the exception, they show that Novak's deepest personal losses derive in good part from her nation's loss of historical identity in her own time.

As their title suggests, the "Epigramme für dich und mich" of the book's middle section are likewise deeply intimate. In the main, however, the longings and pain that they voice—with the help of sharply focused, powerfully emotive images and here and there a hard-edged humor—speak directly to both the aching questions of our private lives and the life of our times. The "Isländische Elegien" that conclude the volume sustain the poignant, melancholy thrust of the two previous sections, but the pensive, softer tone of the ninth and last, "Das Eis auf den Höhenzügen," in which spring returns to the wintry island, seems to presage an inner renewal.

Helga Novak has long since made her mark as a defiant, original, activist poet and prose writer, who has always planted her feet squarely on the firm ground of experience. *Märkische Feemorgana* shows her in full, concentrated control of her poetic strengths; it is a new peak in her work. One eagerly awaits the next, in expectation of challenge and reward.

Sidney Rosenfeld. *World Literature Today*.
64, 1990, pp. 304–5

NWAPA, FLORA (NIGERIA) 1931–93

In *Idu* the writer tries to dramatize the importance of children in an African marriage, or the value that Africans attach to children. To portray this theme we watch the dramas in the lives of two different women—these are Idu the heroine and Ojiugo who is described as Idu's great friend. . . .

On putting the book aside after reading it, there are hardly any memorable incidents one can recall, because the bulk of the story is made up of bits of gossip instead of interaction of characters. Even the few incidents one can recall such as Idu's death and Amarajeme's suicide suffer from serious flaws. The effect of Amarajeme's suicide is pathos, not tragedy. . . .

Considering her performances in both *Efuru* and *Idu* one cannot help wondering what motivates Miss Nwapa beyond the elementary wish of everyone to be a writer. In her novels there is a complete absence of that phenomenon that has been described by various writers as the impulse to write which "kicks you in the pit of your stomach." If this impulse is absent one expects, at least, to be compensated by other things such as beautiful narrative style, amusing and vividly described incidents and powerful characterization. All these are sadly missing in both *Efuru* and *Idu*.

Adeola A. James. *African Literature Today*.
5, 1971, pp. 150, 152

Flora Nwapa's *Idu*, like her previous novel, deals with the culture and lifeways of the Igbo and more specifically the fishing and farming residents of Oguta, who find occupation and pleasure in the Oguta Lake, and to whom the "fantasies" of the "woman of the lake" are a reality. These are the people about whom Flora Nwapa writes in these novels but this is not enough to make her an authentic Igbo novelist. An Igbo novel (or Igbo literature as a whole) emanates from Igbo life and language. It embraces the social, political, economic, and emotional forms under which Igbo life is manifest. The evaluation of an Igbo work of art is essentially an appreciation of the validity of content as well as the appropriateness of technique. What the writer says about the Igbo is as important as how he says it. Neither alone can constitute his success but the failure in both could mean his failure as an artist. Flora Nwapa's *Idu* is a successful Igbo novel by both standards. . . .

The realism of her themes and her ever increasing sensitive use of language are two of Flora Nwapa's most enduring qualities as a novelist. Of the former one might tend to say she is over-preoccupied with the concern for children in marriage in an age when the fear of over-population is acute and some ecologists are talking about "zero population growth," but then among the Igbo (and I fear most Africans) "what we are all praying for is children. What else do we want if we have children?" One might tend to find Flora Nwapa's characters too talkative and gossipy, and her Ajanupas and Onyemurus too boring by virtue of the same organ that gives them distinction— their tongue—but these novels are mostly about women by a woman, and one should not take lightly the line in which Nwapa says "You know women's conversation never ends.". . .

But when everything is considered, *Idu* remains a success in the Igbo literary tradition. In the appraisal of a work of art by an Igbo, the critic is looking for a number of things. He should identify the content, the traditional content in each case. He should show what the author has done with the traditional material, how he has changed traditional forms to fit modern conditions. A piece of oral literature (folktale, song, proverb, etc.) exists as long as it is being performed. The same performance will be different in the hands of different performers. When it is appreciated, the critic is really appreciating the art of the performer, rather than the performance itself. At the same time, in appreciating the art of the performer, the critic would be appreciating quite a lot of things which would be accepted as criteria for written literature—irony, the shape of the story, and a certain amount of simple but vivid characterization. Thus the critic of African literature has many things to explore beyond "what motivates" any particular author to write.

Ernest N. Emenyonu. African Literature
Today. 7, 1975, pp. 29, 32–33

While [AmaAta] Aidoo's short stories are based on the skillful manipulation of diverse narrative forms, Flora Nwapa's technique as short-story writer is more uniform. This uniformity is not really a shortcoming in the work of this Nigerian writer. *This Is Lagos and Other Stories* actually owes much of its undeniable power to a consistently spare and taut style skillfully adapted to the writer's intense irony and to a brooding sense of tragedy throughout the collection. . . .

Nwapa's personal life has . . . involved a certain degree of public service that has inevitably exposed her to the workings of public institutions in contemporary Nigeria. This exposure is fairly evident in her short stories which are set in modern, urban Nigeria—particularly Lagos—and which deal with the lives of civil servants, teachers, and students, as well as the marginally educated immigrants from the rural areas. The uniform style of the collection arises from the fact that this world is invariably the setting of her stories—and from the additional fact that the main theme remains the same throughout. That theme centers on the lives of women in Nigeria's modern urban life, especially the traumas and disorientation to which these women are subjected. In Nwapa's short stories, Lagos and other cities are invariably destructive for seasoned city-dweller and rural newcomer alike.

The life style in Nwapa's cities is dominated by the continuous round of vicious sexual intrigues, domestic squabbles, tribal conflict, and civil war. That most familiar of city symbols, automobile traffic, sums up the confusions and conflicts of urban life. The ceaseless traffic jams of Lagos become living extensions of the individual disorientation and of the cultural disorder which the stories explore. . . .

It appears that Nwapa's very choice of genre, as well as her choice of techniques within the selected genre, are interwoven with her most fundamental perspectives. Her perception of contemporary life in urban Nigeria demands a short-story format, one that does not depend to any significant degree on the kind of oral modes that are so integral to much of Aidoo's short fiction. It is a format which reflects that largely literate, Western middle-class world within which her women move (as in the case of Bisi or Amedi). That literate world's dominance in the lives of older, rural-oriented women like Mama Eze is emphasized by the uniformly literate method which describes *their* experiences. In Nwapa's hands the short story seems especially appropriate for brief, even deliberately unfinished glimpses of urban life. Thus many of the stories leave their protagonists in the middle of seemingly insoluble crises, or at best, in the face of disturbing and unanswerable questions. Taken together, these suggestively abbreviated vignettes suggest the fragmentary nature of the social experiences out of which they arise. In addition, the spare language which Nwapa sustains throughout suggests that thinness of spirit and that limited humaneness which the stories themselves attribute to the society as a whole.

The rural and largely traditional world of the older Nigeria, as it is envisaged by Nwapa, seems to require a different style—an expansive use of language reflecting the formal richness and ornate modes of traditional oral cultures. It seems to demand the detailed duplication of those social conventions intrinsic to everyday relationships in that milieu of elaborately defined roles. When Nwapa turns to that milieu she selects the genre that most easily accommodates an expansive language and elaborate design, for these features reflect the complexities of a society that is always more ambiguous (fulfilling in some respects, while limiting in others) than the general meagerness of urban life. She selects the novel.

The Nwapa novel is typical of the kind of African novel that resists purely Western-oriented approaches to the genre. . . .

The community's collective perception of Efuru, or of Idu, is as crucial in the novel's theme and structure as her reaction to the community and its traditions. Nwapa's "name" title therefore identifies the focal point of the community's attention as much as it pinpoints the individual's personal experience within the community. The community's attention and its relationship with the Nwapa protagonist are defined and communicated by a dialogue format which bears all the signs of the novelist's careful attention to oral forms that reinforce her communal themes. To read the Nwapa novel is to be immersed to a remarkable degree in a ceaseless flow of talk. . . .

Without rejecting the communal system, Idu manges to circumvent it in a way that satisfies her personal needs rather than the community's overriding criteria (marriage and motherhood). The community's value system remains intact—at least, they are not overtly challenged, and in the process Idu is able to have her own way. What we have is a balancing act by Nwapa. The communal system continues, but individuals like Idu are being allowed more room than even Efuru to exercise their own eccentric sense of need or choice—as long as that eccentricity does not outrage or disrupt the communal order. On balance, *Idu* falls somewhere between the frank espousal of the communal tradition in [Efua] Sutherland's drama and the Western-oriented sense of individualism in the novels of South Africa's Bessie Head.

Lloyd W. Brown. *Women Writers in Black Africa* (Westport, Connecticut: Greenwood Press, 1981), pp. 122–23, 134–35, 137, 157

The first African woman writer to gain international recognition was Flora Nwapa. Her first novel, *Efuru* (1966), was unique in that it provided a female view of the world of Eastern Nigeria, which a number of male writers, notably Chinua Achebe, had previously described in their novels. Efuru, the heroine of the book, is rich and beautiful, but not happy. Her first child dies, her husband leaves her and later she leaves her second husband. Efuru is intelligent, independent and capable of managing her own life. But childlessness is a disgrace, a "curse and a failure." A daughter-in-law without children is worthless. "She may be beautiful, but we cannot eat beauty. She may be rich, but we cannot send money on an errand." Efuru remains childless because, as we are told, she has been singled out by the water goddess to be her companion. This causes gossip and her narrow-minded and superstitious neighbors do not come off well in the book. Flora Nwapa's second novel *Idu* (1970) is about a woman's struggle to retain some measure of independence. Again the heroine finds herself in an uncommon situation, but this time she takes her fate into her own hands, instead of leaving everything to a goddess or "the others." Defying tradition, Idu refuses to marry her dead husband's brother, preferring to join her husband in the hereafter. Nwapa's volume of stories *This is Lagos* (1971) deals with a number of themes, and again there is a prominent role for the woman victimized by convention or by the rapidly changing, crowded and chaotic world of the Nigerian capital.

Mineke Schipper. *Unheard Words: Women and Literature in Africa, the Arab World, Asia, the Caribbean, and Latin America* (London: Allyson and Busby, 1985), pp. 41–42

Flora Nwapa has written three novels, *Efuru* (1966) and *Idu* (1970) and *One is Enough* (1984) which deal with motherhood. First of all, unlike Achebe and Nzekwu she often titles her works with the names of her heroines, indicating that she is telling strictly of the woman's experience. This is in striking contrast to the male writers who avoid names as titles altogether, even when telling essentially a woman's story as is the case of Nzekwu.

The first point to be made is that in *Efuru,* the author creates a world of women: men are shown to be intruders. Gossip, small talk, trading and selling, concern over each other's activities all have places in this women's world. In her first paragraph, Nwapa introduces her heroine simple as "the woman." It is only in subsequent paragraphs that she names Efuru. . . .

The Woman of the Lake and Efuru's adherence to her reaffirm her belief in herself and her contributions to society and provide a societal alternative to motherhood for women "who are not so blest." Her novel *Idu* shows a woman fulfilled in a marital relationship at first without and later in spite of her children. Idu and her husband are so close that when he dies after a troubling illness, she decides that she is not going to be the wife of his brother according to tradition. Instead she wills herself to join her husband in death and does so leaving her children alive. *One is Enough* deals with themes similar to *Efuru*: the childless wife who is otherwise successful but rejected by her husband. Here, Amaka, after she has achieved her financial goals, conceives twin boys miraculously. In a sense then, the novel plays with the "immaculate conception" motif because the children's father is a man of God (a Catholic priest). Amaka disdains marriage now, hence the title, and is satisfied with her business success and her two sons. The ending of *Efuru* which deals with "the joy of motherhood" sets the theme for Emecheta's classic novel on motherhood which [bears this title].

Carole Boyce Davies. In Carole Boyce Davies and Anne Adams Graves, eds. *Ngambika: Studies of Women in African Literature* (Trenton, New Jersey: Africa World Press, 1986), pp. 249, 252

Nwapa's Efuru is no paragon of female submissiveness. She demonstrates a marked sense of independence and a determination to lead a fulfilling life. From an early age she reveals a resolve to control her own life rather than to submit blindly to tradition. She is by no means a revolutionary because she does not completely abrogate tradition, but neither is she enslaved by it. Whenever traditional stipulations stifle her individuality, she steps out of them to adopt alternative means that best enable her to express her personality. For example, she contravenes the mores governing male-female relationships and declares herself married by moving in with her lover who is of low social status and too poor at the time to afford her dowry. But later, through her enterprising nature, she makes enough money with her husband to pay her dowry. Also when her first husband deserts her, she continues to live in his house for a considerable length of time—two years. She even goes in search of him. But after waiting long enough to avoid accusations of impropriety, she returns to her father's house, an indication that she is ready, among other things, to consider other possible suitors. She marries again, shortly after moving back to her father's house and enjoys a period of near total marital bliss with her new husband. Not only do they work together, they do every-thing together. She acts as his counselor, advising him on what projects are ripe for pursuit. In addition, they enjoy a closeness that is not quite usual in the rural setting within which they live. They even go to the stream together to swim and thereby attract a lot of gossip from envious women bound by unexciting lives and the values of their rural world. . . .

Above all, Nwapa's portrayal of her heroine presents an in-depth study of womanhood. Her novel is a study of the growth of Efuru, and both her physical and psychological development are brought to light as she searches for options for self-actualization. Efuru begins by accepting the traditional sexually-oriented prescriptions for defining a woman's identity, but she moves gradually towards a new definition of a sense of self, a better option for self-definition.

Naana Baryiwa Horne. In Carole Boyce
Davies and Anne Adams Graves, eds.
*Ngambika: Studies of Women in African
Literature* (Trenton, New Jersey: Africa
World Press, 1986), pp. 125–26

Amaka, the heroine of Flora Nwapa's latest novel, *One is Enough,* also starts off in a state of feminine submission and dependence. The novel opens with her groveling before her heartless mother-in-law, begging not to be "thrown away" because she has failed to produce a child in six years of marriage to Obiora. The tragedy of barrenness is a recurring theme in Nwapa's work, going all the way back to her first novel, *Efuru.* In African culture barrenness is perhaps the worst affliction [even crime] a couple can endure [or commit], and it is almost always attributed to the woman. In traditional society for a woman to lack reproductive power is to lack all power, indeed to be deprived of her very identity and "raison d'être" in life. So fundamental is female fertility to an African woman's social position and self-worth that out of the five radically feminist novels under discussion only two have childless heroines. (And to move parenthetically from art to life, though many contemporary women writers in Africa are unmarried, virtually all of them have children). Reflecting on her fate Amaka thinks, "God had deprived her of the greatest blessing bestowed on a woman, the joy of being a mother." And then she goes on to ask, "Was that really the end of the world? Was she useless to the world if she were unmarried?" Much of the novel involves her formulation of negative answers to these questions. . . .

For Nwapa the route to liberation is economic power. The novel is dedicated to Nwapa's mother-in-law "who believes that all women married or single must be economically independent." In an interview Nwapa has herself insisted on this point when she talks of women from her own background and their business acumen: "if it means selling oranges, then we sell oranges" to be financially autonomous. Where [Mariama] Bâ sees female solidarity and [Buchi] Emecheta education as the crucial factors underlying women's self-determination, Nwapa believes that unhampered financial prosperity is the key to happiness and success for women. . . .

Amaka . . . is a problematic and somewhat disconcerting heroine. On the one hand, she clearly articulates a radical feminist-separatist credo: "She would find fulfilment, she would find pleasure, even happiness in being a single woman. The erroneous belief that without a husband a woman was nothing must be disproved. But at the same time she has the materialistic, good-time, rather vulgar desires and values of a Jagua Nana: "she wanted peace to go about her business, look beautiful, wear good clothes and go to the hairdresser every week, in fact, enjoy life fully." Amaka . . . wants, . . . [to be] moved out from the shadows and in doing so has lost the feminine impotence or powerlessness of the traditional African woman she was at the start of the book.

Kathleen Frank. *African Literature Today.*
15, 1987, pp. 20–22

Despite its paradigmatic status, relatively little critical attention has been paid to *Efuru*. Critics have dismissed Nwapa's writing as trivial, useful only for an understanding of domestic Igbo village life. Curiously, many defenders of Nwapa argue that it is precisely *because* she offers such a narrative of domesticity that she deserves her place in the African canon. My interest here is neither in the authenticity nor the importance of Nwapa's representation of village life, but rather, on the tensions that the first woman-authored novel must confront when written in a colonial/neo-colonial situation. On the one hand, she manipulates the language and narrative form of the colonizer; on the other, she represents a dignified African female character against the backdrop of frequently perjorative representations of female characters by male authors. This (dialogic) tension is symptomatic of the choice between "tradition" and "modernity" that a first novel in a colonial context must make. *Efuru's* insistence on the virtue of its protagonist and on the importance of Igbo custom dictates Nwapa's privileging of the discourse of tradition over that of modernity. . . .

Nwapa's insight lies in her representation of an (economically) independent female character who determines her own life without denying her Igbo identity. Efuru's status as a "genuine" African female subject inserted into the male dominated discursive system of literature is established by the text's implicit rejection of the corruption that the city signifies and by its nostalgic resurrection of Igbo history. Nwapa locates her ideal representation of Igbo female power and independence at the turn of the century. This narrative strategy is especially telling when historically contextualized; at the time Nwapa was writing, Europe and the United States were witnessing the birth of the second wave of European feminism. That Efuru's life appears to have no contact with Europe, certainly none with European-style feminism, means that the narrative's prototype of female power is Igbo—a powerful statement in the face of a post-second-world-war feminism that implied the global liberation of women would begin in the "West." Efuru's life, that of a noble and dignified village woman, is the prototype of an idealized "traditional" woman under duress. She adheres to the role of the dutiful daughter and wife: she works hard, cooks well, respects her elders, behaves without condescension to the other inhabitants of Ogwuta, helps those in need—and eventually becomes a devout follower of the female/feminist deity, Uhamiri. Efuru's adherence to indigenous practices such as polygamy and cliterodectomy can be interpreted, among other ways, as a valorization of traditional Igbo custom.

Female solidarity and strong woman's friendships arise from the practices of Igbo life, and Nwapa makes her strongest feminist statement through the affirmation of a traditional women's community. Although she is generally considered an exceptional woman, no one appears to envy Efuru. Only one woman, the village gossip Omirima, speaks ill of her when she comments spitefully on Efuru's childlessness. Toward the end of the narrative, she is the one who initiates the rumor that Efuru is an adulterer. In both instances, however, Efuru's reputation is rescued by the efforts of the other women of the village.

Susan Z. Andrade. Research in African
Literatures. 21, 1990, pp. 97–99

Flora Nwapa was born in the East Central State of Nigeria, and during the [Biafra] war she returned from Lagos, where she had been working, to her home state, as did thousands of other Ibos in 1966. This pattern of movement appears repeatedly in Nwapa's collection of short stories *Wives at War and Other Stories.* Her Civil War novel *Never Again* captures the war in progress and emphasizes the psychic trauma of refugees in the process of fleeing from one town to the next, the federal troops at their heels. The oppressiveness of the state of paranoia existing among those in the Eastern Region within the boundaries of the shortlived Republic of Biafra takes shape within the narrative that unfolds. Like Nwapa's other works that are woman-centered, the narrative is told from the point of view of a woman who has already quietly accepted the idea of defeat although she embraces the idea of an independent Biafran state. The novel captures the simultaneous hysteria and the weariness of a people fleeing for their lives, leaving behind the security and memories of past lives. . . .

Nwapa's *Wives at War and Other Stories* additionally focuses on the displacement of the Eastern Nigerian seeking refuge at the outset of the war. In the early moments of the war Ibos were "called home" in response to the massacres, the brutalization they suffered in other parts of the country.

Maxine Sample. Modern Fiction Studies. 37,
1991, pp. 449, 451

Flora Nwapa, a Nigerian and the first African woman to publish a novel in English . . . was one of the earliest writers to emphasize the important role women play in the transmission of culture from one generation to the next in West African village communities. Ironically, her novels most often deal with childlessness, exploring how a woman functions in her community when she cannot serve as a mother in the biological sense. In *Efuru,* the protagonist, unable to have a child after her first daughter dies, suffers through bad marriages and the feelings of inadequacy that come from this loss, especially in a community which views a childless woman as one who "has failed an essential life goal." Efuru herself states, "It was a curse not to have children. Her people did not take it as one of the numerous accidents of nature. It was regarded as a failure." Yet, by the end of the novel, Efuru has dedicated herself to be a worshipper of the female deity Uhamiri and has become a community "mother" for the children around her. Nwapa's other two novels, the somber *Idu,* in which the pregnant protagonist wills herself to die rather than live without her husband, and the cynical *One is Enough,* which challenges the whole notion of women's role in the society, do not present the kind of reconciliation of woman and her community that *Efuru* does. Nonetheless, all of these works attest to women's prominent role in child socialization and maintaining the traditions. Even though the role of the biological mother is minimal in these first two novels, the role of community mother (although not an adequate substitute for fertility) reflects an extended family structure that is village-wide. . . . In a traditional setting, Nwapa's *Efuru* examines how women pass down and maintain traditions which are not only restrictive but sometimes harmful to women's lives. It is the older women who perform the clitoridectomies. Even though they try to pass on ways of dealing with this experience through proverbs like "The pain disappears like hunger," they still do not question this scarring and potentially dangerous act. Nwapa's latest novel, *One is Enough,* is an overt attack on both modern and traditional Nigeria's marital restrictions for women.

Gay Wilentz. College English. 54, 1992,
pp. 390, 393

Perhaps we could say . . . about Flora Nwapa herself: she compelled us to take a fresh look at women in Igbo society and West African culture in general. From her early work based in village life to her later works like *One is Enough* (Tana Press, 1981; Africa World Press, 1992) and *Women are Different* (Tana Press, 1986; Africa World Press, 1992), set in urban and rural Nigeria, Nwapa always invested her female protagonists with the strength she saw in the women who influenced her as she grew up. For those in her own culture, she presented a view of traditional and modern African society that focused on the place of women, unlike the portrayals proffered by her male contemporaries like Chinua Achebe and Wole Soyinka. For those outside her culture, she brought us into a matrifocal world, close to its precolonial roots, where women suffered from the constraints of society and their men, but where women were and are also the lifeblood of the community.

Like the Oguta women before her, Flora Nwapa was prominent not only in her writing but in her governmental work and publishing as well. She worked to help rebuild Nigeria after the Biafran war through her position on the East Central State Executive Council from 1970 to 1975, and she received the national honor of the Officer of the Order of Nigeria in 1982. Most important, in 1975, when she left her government position, Nwapa made the choice not to write in isolation but to begin her own publishing company, Tana Press. Today Tana Press publishes books by Nigerian authors, paying particular attention to women writers and children's books, and its work is one of the ways she will be remembered.

Although early critics often dismissed Nwapa's writings as a mere recording of her culture's life, today she is widely praised for her portrait of African womanhood and her ability to adapt the English language to capture the flavor of the Igbo idiom. Flora Nwapa's commitment to create literature from the oral heritage of her foremothers has placed her in a continuum in which she, too, is a foremother to a new generation of readers and writers. Well-known Nigerian novelist Buchi Emecheta, with a nod to Nwapa, took the last line of *Efuru* as the ironic title of her 1979 novel, *The Joys of Motherhood* (Braziller, 1979). To me, this is the true honor: Flora Nwapa will be missed by those of us who knew her personally, but she will also be celebrated through generational, cultural and literary continuity. She takes her place with the ancestors, and by reading her works we perform a libation for her.

Gay Wilentz. *Women's Review of Books*. 11, March, 1994, p. 8

When Nwapa died, Nigerian newspapers stressed that she published under her birth name "with her husband's permission," and Chinua Achebe—whose 1959 novel *Things Fall Apart* is the best-selling African novel ever—praised her for writing about women's issues without being a feminist. Typical, I thought bitterly: in death she loses her very identity, while in life she was criticized for her very focus on women.

I'm not an admirer of Nwapa's later work—the books written after her first two novels are poorly edited, if at all, and the style, no longer creatively indebted to Igbo oral traditions as in the first two, is flat-footed, sterile and at times incoherent. But I deeply regret the loss of what her career came to represent: a concern with the everyday lives of contemporary Nigerian women voiced, so to speak, from the trenches. Like very many so-called "Third World" women writers, Nwapa enjoyed personal privileges by no means typical of women in her country: university education, the leisure made possible by servants, international travel. Unlike most of her sister Nigerian writers, however, she did not live, work and publish in Britain or the US for extended periods of time, although her audience (predominantly Western feminists) was similar to theirs. This apparent paradox—that the African woman writer addresses a largely non-African audience and, indeed, owes her reputation to that audience—led me, over the past two summers, to visit Nigeria to investigate the factors that condition the emergence of a younger generation of women writers. . . .

In the end, my admiration for Flora Nwapa is not so much for her artistry but for her entrepreneurship and commitment to women: as her entire work reminds us, a girl is not a failure to have a boy; a woman need not be defined by marriage and, above all, motherhood; the woman who supports herself depends on men less. Her death is a loss not only for Nigeria but for all of us.

Susan Gardner. Women's Review of Books.
March 11, 1994, pp. 9–10

OATES, JOYCE CAROL (UNITED STATES) 1938–

Unlike many collections whose short stories have been gathered arbitrarily to manufacture a book, Miss Oates' book [*By the North Gate*] has emotional consistency and thematic unity that produce a single effective fictional experience. It is one that, at times, seems too painful to bear. Yet it is also too interesting to ignore, too perceptive to turn away from and too honest to reject.

R. D. Spector. *Book World.* November 17,
1963, p. 32

One of the excellent qualities of this novel [*With Shuddering Fall*] . . is an unswerving fidelity to its theme. The theme is violence, beginning with a minor automobile accident, then accelerating swiftly to a nearly mortal flight, an immolation, onward and downward into an ever faster and stronger whirlpool of violence, until the entire world of the novel is caught in a paroxysm of hate and destruction. . . . This material is not as garish as it sounds because of the clarity, grace and intelligence of the writing.

John Knowles. *The New York Times.*
October 25, 1964, p. 5

The question is no longer whether Miss Oates is a very good writer—she is, indeed—but just how far and high she can thrust the trajectory of brilliant accomplishment she has begun. It appears to me that her gifts are at least equal to Flannery O'Connor. If she is not absolutely more serious than Nabokov—whose *Lolita* this present novel [*Expensive People*] resembles in its virtuosity—she is more obviously "ours" and therefore to be taken more seriously by us. Everything she touches turns to such blistering gold that sometimes I suspect she must have had Rumpelstiltskin in to help her spirit in the night.

Expensive People contains and exploits a little of everything. It is satire, confession, dream, report on suburbia, gothic tale in contemporary dress, with even some touches of the pop novel thrown in to show that the author can find a valid use for the screech of that untuned fiddle, too. But though her technique is eclectic, parodistic, sheer magpie, her bits of everything are fused into a prophetic novel as singular in effect as the night cry of a hurt animal.

R. V. Cassill. *Book World.* November 3,
1968, p. 5

Even though all her technical faults remain untouched, *A Garden of Earthly Delights* not only fulfills her early promise, it makes her, for me, the second finest writer in America. Wright Morris is a better writer because I think aesthetic values are of more lasting importance. I am unable to explain in aesthetic terms the mystery of Miss Oates's genius for sustaining the intensity of her vision and for creating such totally alive characters and situations. I know of no other young novelist who succeeds in creating life with an apparent absence of art. She seems to make criticism irrelevant; it elucidates her work very little beyond offering an introduction. (The opposite is true of Wright Morris.) Joyce Carol Oates is a phenomenon, an original, a natural—not a mentor, as Joyce, Morris, Hemingway, and sometimes Fitzgerald and Faulkner are. She must be experienced, not analyzed—this is simply a brute observation, not praise. The young writer who cites Miss Oates's writing as justification for his own faults disguised as virtues can only suffer, and may not survive.

David Madden. *The Poetic Image in Six Genres* (Carbondale: Southern Illinois University Press, 1969), p. 46

At this hour in her career Miss Oates resembles, speaking harshly but I believe truly, a female James Jones donning and doffing, by turns, an unseductive doctoral hood. There is nothing mysterious about her emergence as writer or teacher, nor are the anti-elitist elements of contemporary culture responsible for that emergence without exception negative, regrettable influences. But seeing Miss Oates merely as part of a whole cultural configuration is, in the end, unjustifiable; hers is an individual human situation and, as such, deserves respect and understanding. The primary fact about that situation is, perhaps, that only an exceptional creature—someone combining in himself extraordinary will, intelligence, and humility—could, given its nature, win through to a significant literary achievement. There could be richer rewards than have ever been forthcoming from prodigies, publishing phenomena and the like if Miss Oates could find such resources within herself. Best, therefore not to quote odds; best simply to wish her well in what cannot fail to be a long and arduous search.

Benjamin DeMott. *Saturday Review of Literature.* November 22, 1969, p. 89

Heart is Miss Oates's part. Though she speaks of irony, she is skeptical of it. Fortunately there is in *them* itself no counterpart to the uneasy self-depreciation which warps her Author's Note, with its concluding curtesy about "the rather disdainful and timorous title *them*." Disdainful and timorous Miss Oates is not, and knows she is not. She has a proper dislike of self-depreciation, and pities those who have been unnerved out of confidence. One of her earlier stories, "Archways," speaks bitterly of how the young are "educated now into knowing their unworth"; this story has clear affinities with the end of *them* and a sense of "unworth" is Miss Oates's true and desolating concern. She would not adopt the old pompous ways of speaking of self-respect . . . but she has a staunchly old-fashioned, and salutary, sense of the relations between self-respect and respectability. The degradations of city life are so intense, and so intensely created by her, that respectability can be seen as vital to self-preservation; one remembers Steven Marcus's fine account in *The Other Victorians* of respectability and urban brutality, and of the amount that respectability made possible that was not just worth-while but a matter of life and death.

Christopher Ricks. New York Review of
Books. February 12, 1970, pp. 22–23

Miss Oates's work presents a mixture of two styles—one of them a large, earnest naturalism from which come detailed scenes of rural and urban desolation, the other a tendency to push beyond these life scenes toward transcendent meaning, an urge that expresses itself in the eruption of hallucinatory violence. . . .

There is an authentic feeling in her stories for the physical ambience of poverty, for the grease stains, the stale smells, the small pathetic decorative objects of plastic. . . . What seems less authentic, however, is the violence itself, and the rather programmatic way it is used to resolve every situation.

Elizabeth Dalton. Commentary.
June, 1970, p. 75

[Oates's] virtues aren't difficult to sum up: a native gift for "story telling"; a more or less clean narrative line, taking her from recognizable starting-points to conclusions very solidly on the same track; a passion for, amounting to an obsession with, what we like to call inner life; a good, almost photographic eye and ear for the minutiae of ordinary existence; a concern with some central human issues and conditions: the myths of love, the nature of female morale, the oppressions of family life, the aridity of urban and suburban existence; the quest for communion, the struggle against others.

In any conventional accounting for literary potentiality and achievement this cluster of attributes would rank high. And that in fact is the point about Miss Oates: in a time of uproar and uncertainty in literature, a period of violently shifting standards and aggressive new imaginative proposals together with a counteracting erosion of confidence about writing itself, she satisfies a longing for familiar ground, for what literature is supposed "to be about" for the appearance of stability, continuity and graspable seriousness. And she does this handsomely, with few blatantly false steps, no inept images or gross failures of rhetoric, and with just the right degree of "experimentation" to keep her from resting too complacently in the bosom of the familiar.

Richard Gilman. The New York Times.
October 25, 1970, p. 4

Wonderland reaches its peak early and sustains it for almost 400 pages; but it's as precarious as the fat girl's tower of numbers holding itself up by the force of its own motion and the novel finally collapses and ends in shambles. The book begins to fail when Oates tells us that her characters are emotionally shaken and their lives changed by JFK's assassination; as in her use of the Detroit riots in *them,* the reality the narrative has created is so strong that actual events we ourselves have witnessed seem bland in comparison, and we can't believe that they could affect the characters' lives. The savage personal vision is lost and not regained; and *Wonderland,* the most involving, the most poetic, the greatest of Oates's novels so far becomes the most deeply flawed of her long works, because it has reached a higher plane than her other books and therefore must fall through a longer distance. Its ultimate failure seems inevitable and even admirable, since anything that exists at this degree of heat must burn itself up if it keeps going, and Oates isn't one to quit when she's ahead.

John Alfred Avant. *Library Journal.*
August, 1971, p. 2545

Joyce Carol Oates doesn't pick at her characters' brains. Having escaped the fascination that motive and mental state have for other contemporary writers, she keeps the unfortunates who populate her novels so busy they have hardly a moment for introspection. Miss Oates tells what happens to her characters and what their experiences—usually terrible—do to them but she rarely explains what they are thinking about their plights. . . .

A number of the major themes of literature are recognizable in Miss Oates's work. She has Tolstoy's sense of history as it overwhelms the individual, and she reveals a classical affinity for fatalism and lost innocence. Her characters are afflicted with the anomie explored by the French existentialists. On a lesser scale, she shares James Agee's reverence for the terror and frailty of childhood and, like D. H. Lawrence, she scorns the life of the mind as ineffectual and irrelevant.

But, most of all, Miss Oates's ties are to the twentieth-century school of American naturalism, particularly Theodore Dreiser. Although she is less concerned with sociology than he was, Miss Oates's stories unfold in the same harsh settings, and her characters fight to survive with the same befuddled amorality of those in *An American Tragedy.*

Brian P. Hayes. *Saturday Review of
Literature.* October 9, 1971, p. 38

Wonderland is about a cluster of deeply related things—a cluster that seems to writhe frighteningly from a single source. It is about the spirit's hunger for strength and identity, its consequent need to possess others, its terror of the anonymity of flesh, of the blank nothingness of death. Oates seems uncannily up with all of us, the very young, the middle-aged, the old; and though her three "gook" titles sound tritely pretentious—"variations on an american hymn," "the finite passing of an infinite passion," "dreaming american" she is to my mind one of the most comprehensive and knowing American novelists now writing. . . .

The supreme attraction, the essential originality of *Wonderland*, as of *them*, is its dramatic unpeeled quality. Everything in it seems loaded, exposed, veined and vulnerable yet opaque, like a skinless plum. The scenes and characters (even the minor figures) are fully there without being contained. They are uncovered rather than delineated, broken into, never packaged. Oates's style, correspondingly, is inventive and continually fresh without being sharp or self-alerting—it is not a stylist's style. Seriously, steadily, it reveals; it is the perfect medium for her empathic imagination.

What a shame were *Wonderland* to be neglected or resisted because *them* made so recent an impact. In achievement it is more or less the equal of the earlier book, and the two together, like the gifted and enormous Pederson children, are distinct yet related wonders.

Calvin Bedient. *Partisan Review.* November 1, 1972, pp. 124, 127

Joyce Carol Oates has come out with another book of poetry, her first [*Anonymous Sins, and Other Poems*] having met in many quarters with gentle critical disapproval. It is often difficult for an artist to move from one *genre* to another. Miss Oates is a novelist and short story writer of enormous power and widespread recognition; her prose skillfully recreates for us the chaos of our lives, the empty sentimentality of our hopes. Though her second group of poems, *Love and Its Derangements,* is an improvement over the previous book, it is not as consistently satisfying as the prose works. The least skillful characteristics of her novels and stories appear in the poems; there is little remaining space for the dramatic virtues she does possess. There are stunning poems in the volume, but they appear all too infrequently.

The essence of Miss Oates's poetry is emotion—intense, but unattached, free-floating. Poetry, to be truly effective, must "organ-ize" emotion in two senses: it must give coherent organic form and direction to feeling and it must make that emotion felt in a direct, internal, and particular way. One of the worst criticisms one can make of a poem is to say that it abounds in vague emotion or empty verbiage. Unfortunately, a few of Miss Oates' poems do just that. Others employ stale or illogical metaphors. Some, however, probe deeply the moving themes of her novels—the psycho-sexual framework of love, the disappearance of concrete personal identity in our world, the need to achieve an existential relation between man and woman which forever lays the ghost of the old absolutist romantic notions which inevitably betray the hopeful beings who hold them. At these moments Miss Oates is at her poetic best.

Sally Andersen. *Spirit.* Fall, 1972, p. 24

Critics slight Joyce Carol Oates when they tag her as merely, or primarily, a "gothic novelist" (i.e., lurid, grotesque, grisly). Some have clucked suspiciously about how much she manages to write and publish . . . hinting quality must suffer. Some find her work repetitious in theme and content, even (somehow) more like refined but still sensational journalism rather than carefully crafted fiction. These demurrers shy from the most astute challenges posed by Oates in her lushly tense, often wounding novels and stories. She is no more "gothic" than today's headlines, no more violent than the nightly bloody canapes served up on the six o'clock news. But her focus and creative impulse tend to deinstitutionalize the blood-letting, causing the impact to bite deep, even in media-narcotized minds. If there is any "journalism" in her writing, it is in the crushing immediacy of contemporary atmospheres and details which coupled with her unabashed fictional virtuosity, makes the terrifying aspects of American life vivid for her readers. Certainly there has been no absence of acute high quality in anything she has recently undertaken in fiction. And rather than repetitions in her work (are Matisse's nudes or Picasso's satyrs repetitious?), I think one discovers Oates has a brazenly disciplined and audacious methodology for attacking metaphysical problems while integrating the real, or apparent, textures of modern life into the equation.

S. K. Oberbeck. *Book World.* September 17, 1972, p. 4

In the landscape of the contemporary American short story Miss Oates stands out as a master, occupying a preeminent category of her own.

It was as a writer of stories that she began her career in the early 1960s, and she has continued to write stories ever since, not as a diversion or spinoff from the writing of novels, but as a central concern in her work—a fortunate recognition that the shorter form is peculiarly suited to her. There is a sense of tension, of nerves stretched to the breaking point, of "the pitch that is close to madness" in much of what she writes. Sustained too long, it would lose its emotional effectiveness and intellectual credibility. As it is, a story such as "The Dead," which tells with the utmost conviction of a young woman writer going gradually to pieces, is not only harrowing to read but unfaltering in its control, written as close to the edge as possible without crossing over it.

William Abrahams. *Saturday Review of Literature.* September 23, 1972, p. 76

The life people live in the fiction of Joyce Carol Oates is both drab and electric, full of melodrama and yet curiously dull. Life is mysterious, a character thinks in her novel *them* . . . and then wonders why the mystery is cast in the forms of such diminished people. The suggestion is that melodrama is not nearly as unusual as we think, is hardly extraordinary at all. It is all too often merely a familiar instance of life's heavy hand as a scenarist. We live with it, lose our friends and children by it, but we acquire none of the glamour that seems our due, we are as diminished as ever.

Yet there is also the suggestion in much of Miss Oates's work that the glamour refused to us in reality can nevertheless come to us as an irrational promise, an exhilaration in the midst of mess and despair. We can tell large, important lies to ourselves even when we are at our most diminished, and they are not entirely lies, because they arise out of feelings we really have. Melodrama fuels these feelings, seems to confirm them, but stops short of making them come true, leaves us with a bright mood only, stranded this side of transfiguration.

Michael Wood. *The New York Times.*
October 1, 1972, p. 6

Much of the power of Joyce Carol Oates' fiction lies in her disturbing ability to identify and expose the fears we have deep within us. Through her art she touches these dark, personal fears: those we admit, those we deny, and those we dimly perceive—but perhaps refuse to confront.

Many of Oates' stories explore two major fears. One is the individual's fear of physical or emotional damage inflicted by another person. . . . The second is man's secret fear of the consequences of a sudden eruption of hidden psychic forces—forces which he suspects lie within him but which he can neither fully anticipate, understand, nor control. . . .

Most interesting of all, perhaps, is Oates' treatment of the fear of being the Outsider. No matter what else the story is about, nearly every one touches on this particular terror. The Outsider is a person who perceives himself as somehow cut off from, shut out of, the human race. He suffers from being uncontrollably different, an aberration. . . .

Given the horror of his situation, where does the Outsider in Oates' fiction look for comfort and solace? With genuine love unavailable, many of the characters look to art and the act of writing, desperately hoping to stave off disaster by fashioning pattern out of flux and sense out of absurdity.

Carolyn Walker. *Critique.* 15:1, 1973,
pp. 59–60

With her torrent of words, her absorption in feeling and her pitch of drama, why shouldn't [Oates] succeed as a poet too. Melville did; Hardy did; Lawrence did; Emily Brontë did; it is possible; it even, on the face of it, seems natural. . . .

These poems [*Angel Fire*] have an awkward gait and an ungainly structure, an incoherence of parts and a lack of conclusiveness in the whole. They are the poems of someone with ideas enough to make poems and with words enough to make poems but without the mysterious power to create the voluptuous surfaces, the original cadences, or the visual juxtapositions of words which alone convince us of the existence of a genuine new poet.

Helen Vendler. *The New York Times.*
April 1, 1973, pp. 7–8

Is Joyce Carol Oates, the only American woman writer of talent who has matched the industry of her British counterparts such as Doris Lessing, Muriel Spark and Margaret Drabble, to be cubbyholed as they have been? Is this remarkable novelist, a woman who is never afraid to take risks, a woman whose fictional works confront our contemporary scene, doomed to suffer the fate of Lessing, for example, and be seen only as an authority on the role of women? To do so would be to miss what she is all about.

In novel after novel, story after story, Oates gives us her own tragic America, a personal vision as perceptive as it is instructive and terrifying. She does not so much preach as show us ourselves on an exaggerated screen. Her damaged women, her haunted men are grotesques but always under her firm artistic control. They are as old fashioned as the wild, secretive loners who roamed the streets of Winesburg, Ohio at twilight. But, as with Sherwood Anderson's folk, Oates' swollen characters are relevant to and complement the horror and dangers of our American landscape. The truths of our lives are exhibited in the excesses. In no work of hers is this as evident as in her latest, lengthy novel, *Do With Me What You Will.*

Charles Shapiro. *The New Republic.*
October 27, 1973, p. 26

At first the novel [*The Assassins*] seems a murder mystery: who killed Andrew? But to develop that topic would require at least one well-meaning, rational investigator. Stephen means well but is helplessly irrational; no one else is rational, well-meaning, or even well. The novel therefore reaches only coarse conclusions. By its end one of the leading characters has been set wandering aimlessly; another is deaf, blind, dumb, and paralyzed as the result of a suicide attempt; the third has been shot; and the fourth has been shot and hacked to pieces with an ax. Why? What does it mean? Such questions are pointless. Motivation is unknowable and finally irrelevant in this world of paranoid neurosis: "they" make things happen, and these suspicious, isolated, hysterical victims merely flounder as their sickness bids.

J. D. O'Hara. *The New York Times.*
November 23, 1975, p. 18

In Joyce Carol Oates's works three themes—women, city, and community—merge into an all too real nightmare. Her cities are the settings for death, riots, and the violent wreckage of human lives. Her women are victims, raped physically and psychically by both men and the world. Not only is community an unrealizable dream, but few characters even aspire to it. . . .

Continuously, her fiction searches out and exposes the very root of violence: a sense of personal impotence. At the heart of violence in her world is the absolute and utter inability to affirm oneself—without which the person is unable to live fully as a human being, to define, affirm, and assert himself, and to enter satisfying relationships with other persons. . . .

One of Joyce Carol Oates's persistent concerns is to make the tragic vision real to the twentieth century. She seeks through her works to awaken contemporary society to its own destruction, to deepen the consciousness of her readers to the tragic dimensions of life. This task demands that her own perceptions of the times be sharply defined, that she confront—because resolution is impossible—the ambiguities of the day without trying to answer them, and that in so doing she offers to her readers something more than the sensationalism of the daily news. . . .

Oates's works are limited, and she pays a price for her lack of humor. The tragic burden of the lives of her characters at times becomes barely tolerable and excessively oppressive: unrelieved, catastrophic events strain, if not defy, the imagination. Oates's characters may be ordinary people in one sense, but they suffer an extraordinary number of misfortunes and endure unbelievable afflictions—factors which tend to limit the works.

Unless she can move away from the two-dimensional, often superficial characters to which she has thus far almost solely confined herself and more directly towards her announced stronger moral posture and affirmative, transcendent vision, Oates will be doomed to repeating herself—a criticism frequently leveled at her at present. She has richly exploited the resources of her thematic concerns and of her choice of characters and unless she moves on, she will become derivative of herself. Her tragically diminished people have told their tales, and their power to raise our consciousness is fast becoming exhausted. Her response to the complex phenomenon of urban life amounts to a deeply sensitive witness, but unless she is able to go beyond this, she fates herself to monotony and redundancy.

> Mary Kathryn Grant. *The Tragic Vision of
> Joyce Carol Oates* (Durham, North
> Carolina: Duke University Press, 1978),
> pp. 15, 32, 117, 140–41

As Oates's skills as a novelist have developed, her work has increasingly evoked the confusing experience of our time and, more importantly, related our chaotic and imperfectly apprehended experiences to wider patterns of significance. Her importance for us is seen partly in the seriousness with which she sees the writer's dual, and perhaps contradictory role of submerging herself in our age, and partly as well, in her struggle to achieve a transcendence of our time in her articulation of it. In Oates's most recent work one now discerns a movement, observable in her essays as well as her fiction, towards a fascination with Eastern renunciatory philosophical modes. It is as if the violence and egocentric destructiveness which have been such tragic outcomes of Western history and philosophy must somehow be transcended by embracing the opposite vision. Of course such a development in Oates's thinking is prefigured in Lawrence's own. Lawrence, too, came to despair at the cultivation of the uniqueness of the self which has been so fundamental to Western consciousness. His later vision is not unlike that of Oates in *The*

Assassins, where we first see, in her novels, her espousal of something akin to Eastern renunciation, a growing interest which seems to be entering all her work in the mid-1970s. On the surface, such a development is strange in writers like Oates and Lawrence, so imbued with the possibilities of transcendence achieved through the flesh, and it may be that the next stage in her career will show her developing in surprising, even more experimental, directions.

Possibly more than any American novelist now writing, Oates has shown herself sensitive to the eddying feelings of living in the 1960s and 1970s. But of course we look to writers to respond to more than the intellectual or social fashions of their age. Oates sees the cultural roles of the artist as that of struggling with and articulating the underlying, ongoing movements of feeling, not merely its glittering surface.

G. F. Waller. In Linda W. Wagner, ed.
Critical Essays on Joyce Carol Oates
(Boston: G. K. Hall, 1979), p. 17

Bellefleur is the most ambitious book to come so far from that alarming phenomenon Joyce Carol Oates. However one may carp, the novel is proof, if any seems needed, that she is one of the great writers of our time. *Bellefleur* is a symbolic summation of all this novelist has been doing for 20-some years, a magnificent piece of daring, a tour de force of imagination and intellect.

In *Bellefleur* Miss Oates makes a heroic attempt to transmute the almost inherently goofy tradition of the gothic (ghosts, shape-shifters, vampires and all that) into serious art. If any writer can bring it off (some will claim it's already been done), Joyce Carol Oates seems the writer to do it. . . .

Whatever its faults, *Bellefleur* is simply brilliant. What do we ask of a book except that it be wonderful to read? An interesting story with profound implications? The whole religious-philosophical view of Joyce Carol Oates is here cleanly and dramatically stated. She has been saying for years, in book after book (stories, poems, a play and literary criticism), that the world is Platonic. We are the expression of one life force, but once individuated we no longer know it, so that we recoil in horror from the expression of the same force in other living beings. "Don't *touch* me," Gideon Bellefleur keeps saying, as Yvonne Petrie said in *The Assassins,* Laney said in *Childworld* and a host of other characters said elsewhere. Blinded to our oneness, we all become assassins, vampires, ghosts. We are all unreflectable nonimages in mirrors, creatures of time, and time is an illusion; we are all sexual maniacs, lovers engaged in a violent struggle to become totally one with those we love (copulation and murder are all but indistinguishable); we are all crazily in love with the past—first our own Edenic childhood, second the whole past of the world. . . .

Joyce Carol Oates has always been, for those who look closely, a religious novelist, but this is the most openly religious of her books—not that she argues any one sectarian point of view. Here as in several of her earlier works the Angel of Death is an important figure, but here for the first time the Angel of Life (not simply resignation) is the winner. In the novel's final chapters Gideon Bellefleur turns his back on all he has been since birth, a sensualist; starves himself until we see him as a death figure; finally becomes his family's Angel of Death.

Joyce Carol Oates is a "popular" novelist because her stories are suspenseful (and the suspense is never fake: The horror will really come, as well as, sometimes, the triumph), because her sex scenes are steamy and because when she describes a place you think you're there. Pseudo-intellectuals seem to hate that popularity and complain, besides, that she "writes too much." (For pseudo-intellectuals there are always too many books.) To real intellectuals, Miss Oates's work tends to be appealing, partly because her vision is huge, well-informed and sound, and partly because they too like suspense, brilliant descriptions and sex. Though *Bellefleur* is not her best book, in my opinion, it's a wonderful book all the same. By one two-page thunderstorm she makes the rest of us novelists wonder why we left the farm. How strange the play of light and shadow in her graveyards! How splendid the Bellefleurs' decaying mansion! How convincing and individual the characters are—and so many of them! In one psychic moment, when the not-yet-two-year-old Germaine cries "Bird—bird—bird!" and points at the window a moment before a bird crashes into it, breaking its neck, we're forced to ask again how anyone can possibly write such books, such absolutely convincing scenes, rousing in us, again and again, the familiar Oates effect, the point of all her art: joyful terror gradually ebbing toward wonder.

John Gardner. The New York Times.
July 20, 1980, pp. 1, 21

Angel of Light demonstrates, perhaps better than any other Oates novel, what I think is the *real* reason for the critical unease surrounding her work: that she goes against the prevailing impulse in contemporary fiction toward the private and personal, a small-scale vision illustrated in the work of such a much-admired writer as Ann Beattie. As *Contraries,* Oates's thoughtful and illuminating collection of essays, makes clear, Oates's models are the nineteenth-century masters like Dostoevski and Conrad; like them, she is what I would call a "social" novelist, interested in creating microcosms of the world that reflect the moral and philosophical questions encountered by man as he is in conflict with society, nature, God, history. What she admires in those novelists is passion, energy, the courage to take artistic and emotional risks. . . .

Angel of Light is neither small nor tidy. It is a complex, dense, multilayered work that unfolds with all the profound implications of Greek tragedy—in fact, the story is a modern version of the fall of the House of Atreus. Yet Oates seems at last to have in control two of the weaknesses that have sometimes been the result of her considerable ambition and energy—a feverish, overwritten prose style and a heavy-handed use of symbolism.

Susan Wood. *Book World.* August 16, 1981,
p. 5

Even when Joyce Carol Oates is in a playful mood, her writing fails to provide patches of sunlit ease; she's too self-mesmerized to tune out the racket in her head and clear away a pool of summery calm, preferring instead to heap on the rubble, the noise, the piles of broken glass. She doesn't write books now, the books write her. She's like an obsessive pianist who even in her sleep practices arpeggio runs, her fingers rippling up and down a phantom keyboard. Snap to, Ms. Oates. It isn't too late. Wake up, wake up, wake up! . . .

Although *A Bloodsmoor Romance* has the fixings of a provocative anti-novel, Oates's inability to turn off the babble once again plunges her into the gumbo. In a typical Oates novel, the reader is treated—if that's the word—to a series of Big Scenes connected by a lot of flimsy, careless doodle. Her fans probably drum their fingers patiently during the drowsier passages, knowing that Oates will soon barbecue a new fright for their snacking pleasure. . . .

Perhaps the key to Joyce Carol Oates's fiction is her phantasmagorical fear of sex, her revulsion from the flesh's treacheries. Sex in her fiction is seldom a tender idyll, a bit of lingering play, or even a collision of will and temperament. . . . Sex is instead a ghoulish prank, a corporeal meltdown. . . . Oates's books . . . are wonders of reckless energy and dishevelment. Although Oates's poetry is hardly ringing or memorable, it's easier to take than her prose because in writing poetry she's compelled to choose this word, that. But in writing fiction she doesn't seem to spiff up her sentences before dispatching them into the world; ragtag and motley, her phrases are thrown into the breach like waves of ill-prepared soldiers, a doomed multitude. She ought to spend more time revising and paring down, but she seems incapable of trimming away her wordy flab, or unwilling. Perhaps she *prefers* to drift high and free in the transcendental ether.

What *A Bloodsmoor Romance* makes clear is that writing, for Oates, is not a vocation or a calling but a semidivine compulsion. To her, the writer is a shortwave set receiving and beaming messages into the far reaches of dreamland.

James Wolcott. *Harper's.* September, 1982,
pp. 68–69

Joyce Carol Oates's Manichean vision of contemporary America threatens to overwhelm any literary form she uses to try to encompass it. Emotions override reason; monologue buries meaning; individual characters dissolve beneath the full force of their feelings, insights, and omnivorous yearnings. Even her apparent method of creation suggests the power these characters and emotional forces have upon her: "When I'm with people I often fall into a kind of waking sleep, a day-dreaming about the people, the strangers, who are to be the 'characters' in the story or novel I will be writing. . . . At times my head seems crowded; there is a kind of pressure inside it, almost a frightening physical sense of confusion, fullness, dizziness. . . . 'My characters' really dictate themselves to me. I am not free of them, really. . . . They have the autonomy of characters in a dream." It is as if exorcism replaces fiction. Confession overpowers its literary container.

Dark dualistic design stalks Oates's haunted mind as starkly as it did Hawthorne's, but with more sheer emotional power and force: "In the novels I have written, I have tried to give a shape to certain obsessions of mid-century Americans—a confusion of love and money, of the categories of public and private experience, of demonic urge I sense all around me, an urge to violence as the answer to all problems, an urge to self-annihilation, suicide, the ultimate experience and the ultimate surrender." Dualism becomes a dominant demonic force that, if outrun, suggests both an ultimate freedom and ultimate self-destruction. As G. F. Waller suggests, Oates tears through that very American sensibility with its often uneasy alliance between the mystical and the material, "the dislocation between dream and materialism in America." In fact, "to assert the primacy of the unquantifiable seems necessarily to end in the Manicheism which has constantly characterized American experience." "All the books published under my name in the past ten years," Oates asserts, "have been formalized, complex propositions about the nature of personality and its relationship to a specific culture (contemporary America)." Obsessed with the Western myth of the self, the ego, Oates presses that fiction to its limits, seeking necessarily some wider space beyond, some other ultimate reality beyond the materialized, self-conscious self in contemporary America.

Violence alone seems capable of breaking through the boundaries of the Western ego. Only a palpable, forceful wrenching can shatter such historical self-images. "Violence is always an affirmation," Oates insists.

Samuel Chase Coale. In Hawthorne's
Shadow: American Romance from Melville
to Mailer (Lexington: University Press of
Kentucky, 1985), pp. 161–62

Joyce Carol Oates's versatility as a fiction writer relates directly to her overwhelming fascination with the phenomenon of contemporary America: its colliding social and economic forces, its philosophical contradictions, its wayward, often violent energies. Taken as a whole, Oates's fiction portrays America as a seething, vibrant "wonderland" in which individual lives are frequently subject to disorder, dislocation, and extreme psychological turmoil. Her protagonists range from inner-city dwellers and migrant workers to intellectuals and affluent suburbanites; but all her characters, regardless of background, suffer intensely the conflicts and contradictions at the heart of our culture—a suffering Oates conveys with both scrupulous accuracy and great compassion.

Her particular genius is her ability to convey psychological states with unerring fidelity, and to relate the intense private experiences of her characters to the larger realities of American life. "I think I have a vulnerability to a vibrating field of other people's experiences," she told an interviewer in 1972. "I lived through the '60s in the United States, I was aware of hatreds and powerful feelings all around me." Her frequently remarked tendency to focus upon psychological terror and imbalance thus relates directly to her vision of America, what Alfred Kazin has called "her sweetly brutal sense of what American experience is really like." Though she has been accused of using gratuitous or obsessive violence in her work, Oates has insisted that her violent materials accurately mirror the psychological and social convulsions of our time. In an acerbic essay titled "Why Is Your Writing So Violent?," she points out that "serious writers, as distinct from entertainers or propagandists, take for their natural subjects the complexity of the world, its evils as well as its goods. . . . The serious writer, after all, bears witness."

In responding to the "vibrating field of other people's experiences," Oates's imagination has created hundreds and possibly thousands of fictional characters: people coping with the phantasmagoric wonderland of American life and suffering various degrees of psychological and spiritual isolation. Her typical protagonist is tragically blinded to the possibility of the "communal consciousness" that Oates sees as a likely salvation for our culture. "In many of us the Renaissance ideal is still powerful," she has written. "It declares: *I will, I want, I demand, I think, I am.* This voice tells us that we are not quite omnipotent but must act as if we were, pushing out into a world of other people or of nature that will necessarily resist us, that will try to destroy us, and that we must conquer." Positing the hopeful idea that the violent conflicts in American culture represent not an "apocalyptic close" but a "transformation of being," Oates suggests that we are experiencing "a simple evolution into a higher humanism, perhaps a kind of intelligent pantheism, in which all substance in the universe (including the substance fortunate enough to perceive it) is there by equal right."

Because this epoch of cultural transcendence has not yet arrived, Oates has conceived her primary role as an artist who must dramatize the nightmarish conditions of the present, with all its anxiety, paranoia, dislocation, and explosive conflict. Her fiction has often focused particularly on the moment when a combined psychological and cultural malaise erupts into violence; and despite the notable variety of her character portrayals, there are several representative "types" that recur frequently and present distinctive facets of the turbulent American experience.

Greg Johnson. *Understanding Joyce Carol Oates* (Columbia: University of South Carolina Press), 1987, pp. 8–10

Pursuing the phenomenon of Joyce Carol Oates over three decades, we come back to our original questions, conscious that they must remain open-ended: How can we grasp her ambitious project, assess her significance, see her not only as an amazing American original, but in a broader context? How are we to make sense of her beyond the often-contradictory reigning estimates—not as eccentric, not as a kind of literary parodist, not as a staggeringly prolific producer of bestsellers, but as an artist who provides a new angle of vision about both our intellectual heritage and our contemporary cultural disarray?

Clearly, Oates has become an imposing presence on the public scene, in the critical press and classroom, and in the interpretive community. She continues to exhibit an insatiable appetite for ideas; a reverence for the sacred arts of poetry and fiction; and the deliberately profane intentions of the probing cultural critic. She has thus accepted her residential status in the fullest sense. She not only teaches, writes, and publishes, but is continually refreshing her work through a series of lively experimental projects of imaginative revision, drawing upon academic resources at the same time that she challenges the privileged status of the canon with new readings.

To paraphrase the title of one of her best-known short stories, "Where is she going? Where has she been?" She has already contributed a collection of criticism, poetry, and fiction which would fill several library shelves. Her early work reflects the cross-currents of American literature: homage to English forebears; reexamination of the strategies developed by the American realist and the philosophy of the naturalist and existentialist. Her later work (after *Wonderland*) is most centrally a refutation of the fabulational or postmodernist enterprise, a counterstatement to the fashionable fiction of "quanta," randomness, ellipsis, and contingency. Yet she shares with her avant-garde contemporaries the sense of being caught between the acts, groping for words in an Orwellian world, seeking a structure to honor reality in a time marked by discontinuity. Pushing beyond the superficial delights of fabulation (she is not entirely immune to its seductions), Oates directs her own powers of imaginative recreation at a multilayered and irreducibly real world. It is a world in which she continues to insist that poetry *does* make things happen. . . .

Joyce Carol Oates is more than an iconoclast or subversive reader. She also brings us news of an emerging aesthetic strikingly akin to the stylistic and mythic tendencies of contemporary women's art. . . .

Naming Joyce Carol Oates an "artist in residence" does not restrict her to conventional categories or relegate her to some elite and privileged sanctuary. Like Bellow, she has no patience for sassy academic con-men and noisy self-promoters; she even reinvents the minor genre of college fiction to expose her confreres and their hubristic pretensions. A moralist, she has more soberly registered the end of academic innocence and the invasion of the cloister. She has protested the abuses of looters and tricksters in her midst; she has testified to the predicament of young and vulnerable acolytes and prodigies, transformed into the terrorists of our own lost generation. More importantly, perhaps, she has unmasked the restrictions of our "symbolic code," questioning long-accepted dogmas and violating decorum.

In the largest sense, then, her position as artist in residence becomes a compelling metaphor for her past achievement and her future direction. Redefined on her terms, it also is a model for contemporary American writers. Sustained by the intellectual community at many levels, as critical commentator, as mentor, as student, as teacher, open to the play of multiple texts and the call of the world, Oates has recovered and reopened mythic space. She rejects the self-referential satisfactions of contemporary tabulation, what the late John Gardner labeled "literary gimcrackery." Her own imaginative realm resonates with literary and extraliterary influence, our culture's vital signs. In the face of the violent and explosive pressures of modern life, Joyce Carol Oates offers her creative and critical work as regenerative art; a process of revision and mediation; "a kind of massive, joyful experiment done with words . . . submitted to one's peers for judgement."

Eileen Teper Bender. *Joyce Carol Oates,*
Artist in Residence (Bloomington: Indiana
University Press, 1987), pp. 179–80, 183

In her two most recent novels, *American Appetites* and *Because It Is Bitter, and Because It Is My Heart* Oates is prototypically herself, using the realistic mode that has been her dominant style and focusing on the themes and situations that have preoccupied her throughout her career. Even the structures of these novels, which each begin with a scene of catastrophic violence, follow a pattern that has been Oatesian from her very first novel, *With Shuddering Fall* (1964). *American Appetites* might be seen as a nonsatiric version of *Expensive People,* recording a scene of family violence amid the affluent, privileged, upper-middle-class world. Ian McCullough is a character type that has been portrayed many times before in Oates's fiction. *Because It Is Bitter and Because It Is My Heart,* although it interjects a racial dimension into the conflict, recalls many other of Oates's novels, including *them,* with its portrayal of the survival tactics of a young girl and young man of the underclass, and *Childworld, Marya,* and *You Must Remember This,* with their depictions of adolescence and incipient intellectual awakening in the bleak cities and backcountry of Oates's Eden County.

Despite the imaginative richness of Oates's fictional world, in other words, there is an underlying repetitiveness. Oates is obsessed with the same subjects and situations, recast into new fictions. Her central obsession is with the search for authentic individuality. She recognizes that the old stable ego is a fiction; rather, the personality is a fragile, protean, passionate, mysterious entity, precariously balanced between conscious and unconscious contents. Oates respects the other within the self, other people, and the natural world. She depicts the need to get beyond the conflicts and contradictions in our culture that would deny authentic selfhood, and she portrays the enormous difficulty of that task.

The way toward fulfillment is not through a repudiation of one's culture. Oates's portrayals of characters who attempt radical alternatives, who attempt to cut themselves off from an engaged role in ordinary life—Stephen Petrie, Nathanael Vickery, Jedediah Bellefleur—are all tinged with irony. Neither can one choose not to play the games of the social masquerade, like Ian McCullough in *American Appetites*. While characters like Ian reach a despairing dead end in the quest for meaning, Oates does not. Her role is to catalogue his pain, not necessarily to share in it. In most of her novels, such as her most recent *Because It Is Bitter, and Because It Is My Heart,* she portrays characters who despite embittering experiences retain a tenacious will to endure and a restless human spirit.

Joanne V. Creighton. *Joyce Carol Oates: Novels of the Middle Years* (Boston: Twayne, 1992), pp. 117–18

ŌBA MINAKO (JAPAN) 1930–

Unlike Tomioka [Taeko], who has always been inside the literary arena as a modern poet and novelist, Ōba Minako had a long period of submergence as a housewife living in the United States, completely out of touch with Japanese literary circles. During those years, however, in the manner of Jane Austen, she stored observations of life as well as her own frustration, creating a rich reservoir of imagination on which her expression, once it was released, could draw heavily. "The Smile of a Mountain Witch" reveals a devastating perception of human psychology and the logic of people's inner world, presenting traditionally expressionless women as the actual centers of consciousness.

In her recent major novels she searches for the archetypal origins of life and of modern culture, exploring the nature of maternity. She has also written a series of autobiographical novels in which maternity and the search for female identity form the central theme, a theme pursued realistically as well as symbolically in the manner characteristic of her works.

Noriko Mizuta Lippit and Kyoko Iriye Selden. Introduction to *Stories by Contemporary Japanese Women* (Armonk, New York: M. E. Sharpe, 1982), p. xxii

Ōba Minako's female characters, most of them comfortably married, are at odds with the traditional view of feminine roles, just as [Yumiko] Kurahashi's are, and share a similar sense of dread at being a woman. In Ōba's "The Three Crabs," Yuri, a housewife and the central character of the story, recog-

nizes the self-hatred—poison, she calls it—that enables her to see the pettiness and shallowness in the other women gathered at her party. She looks
critically at middle-class sensibility and values and refuses to go along with
prescribed roles. She tries to escape a sense of meaninglessness—which she
expresses as the nausea of morning sickness, a uniquely female experience—
but she has no clearly conceived plan for doing this. She acts on impulse and
eventually returns home, defeated and undoubtedly filled with even more
self-disgust. Even though her attempt to escape was destined to fail, she has
tried something that women in earlier stories never thought of. Yuri represents a middle-class housewife whose discontent lies not in a specific situation
or relationship but in something more essential: being a woman who has
awakened to the discrepancy between her role and her sense of self.

> Yukiko Tanaka. Introduction to Yukiko
> Tanaka and Elizabeth Hanson, eds. *This
> Kind of Woman: Ten Stories by Japanese
> Women, 1960–76* (Stanford: Stanford
> University Press, 1982), pp. x–xi

The novella *Higusa* (1969; Fireweed, tr. 1981), by Ōba Minako, claims a
distinctive place in Alaskan literature. It may be the first story in which a
native Alaskan culture, in this case the Tlingit, was adapted as the milieu for
the telling of a modem tale in an Asian language.

Certainly, *Fireweed* is the only piece of Japanese Alaskan adult literature,
with the exception of a later work by Ōba, that has come to my knowledge
to date. I first happened upon *Fireweed* in Ōba's collection of short stories
titled *Yāreitachi no Fukkatsusai* (1970; Easter's ghosts), in Sitka, Alaska.
Fireweed is unique among Ōba's works by reason of the vehicle she used to
tell the story. Although the Sitka area appears in other of her works, most
notably in *Garakuta Hakubutsukan* (1975; The rubbish museum), which won
the fourteenth Women's Literary Prize in 1975, *Fireweed* is woven of strands
of Tlingit culture, many of which overlay similar strands of traditional Japanese culture. . . .

Why did Ōba choose this set of factors to unfold this story? Why did
she choose to write this kind of story at all? I think it just appealed to her
at the time. Most of her other works are very different in character and time
and place.

Fireweed was written and published while Ōba was still in Alaska and
within two years of her maiden work. It is very likely her stylistic attitude
was not firm yet, which may account for *Fireweed's* difference from her other
works and for its charm. And my guess is that her personal experiences in
Sitka were for her a kind of half-mythical dream. And that in that period of
her personal life, she reached some kind of turning point, some kind of fulfillment that she could not have reached outside of that semi-isolated, semi-
idyllic environment. I think this period represented a sorting out of all the

threads of various views of the world she had been gathering from the time of the A-bomb [when she worked in Hiroshima]. . . .

Sitka was a place that rounded out Ōba's world view. She had been placed by chance into a place of solitude where the only crowds were soaring gulls, spawning salmon, restless tides, and burgeoning, dense forests, and where every living thing was either copulating or dying and furnishing food for the endless regeneration of life in the natural rhythm of the earth. This was, for her, a first immersion in a nearly untouched world, and a whole different way of life opened for her. Where were those "wastelands" of Eliot now? She absorbed the life in Sitka like a thirsty sponge. Even though she was fully aware of the changes taking place in Sitka as elsewhere, the difference in life rhythm was staggering. The point is, Sitka, for her, was peopled with persons, not with blank faces doing anonymous things, and Ōba became one of those persons, doing things. I think this fulfilled her and deepened her perspective in a way that could not have been done before that point in time, nor in any other place in the world quite so well.

I think this is why she chose to write *Fireweed* as a kind of fairy tale. She calls it a *monogatari* (tale) in a taped interview with Takeda Katsuhiko, then professor of comparative literature at Waseda University.

It can hardly be denied that Ōba's sojourn in Alaska has had a bearing on all of her works by reason of the maturing she did there and the Alaskan experience that she absorbed. Alaska should be greatly honored by this tribute to its regenerative strength.

The fact that Ōba was placed by chance in both the desolation of man's worst folly, Hiroshima, and in the abundant fertility of Sitka is truly remarkable. I suggest that she has become Fireweed. Not the false symbol of the tale, but the true "woman of good fortune" who was rescued from the swamp and who is blooming out of the ashes of past fires.

Marian E. Chambers. Japan Quarterly. 38,
1991, pp. 474, 482–83

In Minako Ōba's story "Candle Fish," characters leave behind nationality to search for universal truths of women's experience. As in many of Ōba's stories, the protagonist of this story is a middle-aged woman who has left her native country, Japan. The women she encounters abroad are also exiles, at least in spirit. Olga, for instance, is a woman whose marriage to an egocentric musician has ended in bitter disappointment and estrangement from her true self. The narrator of "Candle Fish" forms a friendship with Olga as together they question their roles as wives and mothers. Many years after the two have ceased to see each other, Olga returns to the protagonist in her daydreams in the form of an ageless woman, the spirit of the moon. She both mocks and consoles the protagonist, who is transformed during these encounters into a *yamanba,* an imaginary folktale character who destroys men when they venture into her dwelling deep in the mountain.

The Japanese legend of the *yamanba,* or the old woman of the mountain, is used as the central motif in "Candle Fish" and in several other stories by Ōba. Although the *yamanba* commonly appears in legends as an old woman, Ōba sees her as ageless; she articulates repressed desires, and is the embodiment of all women who defy the constricting rules of society. Since her literary debut with the story "Three Crabs" (included in *This Kind of Woman*), which was awarded the prestigious Akutagawa Prize in 1969, Ōba has been exploring the tension contained in the figure of the *yamanba:* the dialectic between a woman's desire for independence and self-expression on the one hand, and the psychic pain resulting from her solitary existence on the other. Many of Ōba's stories are autobiographical, and Sitka, Alaska, where she lived for a while with her husband, provides the backdrop for "Candle Fish." Like the protagonist of this story, Ōba started writing seriously in her late thirties when she returned to Japan. She is a prolific writer still actively publishing, and is considered to be one of the most important Japanese women writers.

Yukiko Tanaka. Unmapped Territories: New
Women's Fiction from Japan (Seattle:
Women in Translation, 1991), pp. xii–xiii

When Ōba, a frustrated housewife, submitted "Sanbiki no kani" (1968; "The three crabs," 1978) to a literary magazine, she won immediate acclaim as recipient of the Gunzō New Writer Award and the 59th Akutagawa Prize for new talent in serious fiction. A repulsion for society's hypocrisy and the spiritual isolation of the individual are themes that form the basis of her later work. Rejecting the "coherence" of Western literature with its emphasis on structure and plot, Ōba has developed her own form, a kind of nonform, a spontaneous flow of thoughts and images permitting maximum freedom of time and space. Ōba's work is recognized for its intellectual and witty dialogues, graphic and sensuous imagery, sensitivity, and lyricism. Ōba is a master of simile and metaphor in which plant and animal imagery are used to strip humans of their artificial clothing and housing, to lay bare our physical and mental state. More important than individual images is the manner in which they symphonize. This may be said of Ōba's stories and novels, as well.

In *Garakuta hakubutsukan* (1975; The junk museum), recipient of the Prize for Women's Literature, Ōba focuses upon three women of diverse ethnicity, who, uprooted from their homeland, drift to a small Alaskan town. It is their individuality that is the key to their identity. They have attained their freedom, but at the cost of a certain loneliness.

Ōba's protagonists are often found in triangular relationships, with a focus on the female role. As in "Yamauba no bishō" (1976; "The smile of a mountain witch," 1982), traditionally expressionless women are depicted as the center of consciousness, as Ōba explores the price of suppressing fundamental thoughts and feelings to the point that one is anesthetized by social norms.

In *Katachi mo naku* (1982; formlessness and solitude), awarded the Tanizaki Prize for leading writers, Ōba seeks a state beyond the established "form" of marriage, dispelling the myths that have given shape to this institution. The fundamental nature of the relationship between heterosexual couples and the search for female identity is explored further in a series of autobiographical novels, *Kiri no tabi* (2 vols., 1980; Journey through the mist) and *Nakutori no* (1985; Of singing birds), which won the Noma Literary Prize (1986).

Umi ni yuragu ito (1989; Lines that drift through the sea) is a collection of stories which finds the protagonists of *Nakutori no* revisiting a small town in Alaska. The narrator follows the thread of life, not attempting to untangle or determine its course, relating tales in such a way that the past lives in the present, Japanese legends merge with Tlingit Indian myths of southeast Alaska, characters from literature are juxtaposed to "real life" acquaintances, and dreams and reality are intertwined. The title story, "Umi ni yuragu ito" (1988), was awarded the Kawabata Yasunari Literary Prize in 1989.

Ōba's feminist voice, sensitive cross-cultural comparisons, anecdotal style, and tendency to glide freely between different periods in time are seen in the biography *Tsuda Umeko* (1990), awarded the Yomiuri Literary Prize. After being raised and educated in the U.S., Umeko (1865–1929) returned to Japan and established Tsuda Women's College, creating the opportunity for students such as Ōba to acquire the education and self-confidence necessary to contribute to and find self-fulfillment in a society dominated by men.

Ōba's work is distinguished by its fresh and immediate perception of life, its uninhibited expression of ideas, and its treatment of all aspects of life as part of a continuum, in which past and present, hope and despair, humans, plants and animals, self and other, lose their distinction in an exploration of the possibility of a new state of freedom and harmonious existence beyond established social systems.

Karen Colligan-Taylor. In Steven R. Serafin
and Walter D. Glanze, eds. *Encyclopedia of
World Literature in the 20th Century* (New
York: Continuum, 1993), pp. 459–60

O'BRIEN, EDNA (IRELAND) 1932–

The Country Girls is a first novel of great charm by a natural writer. It is the story of two girls growing up in Ireland, first in a derelict village, then in a convent, then in Dublin. It is not a series of idylls nor a breathless account of hilarious adventures, though its tone is light and there are passages of comedy. In mood and manner Miss O'Brien's novel resembles *The Bachelor of Arts* by R. K. Narayan. Caithleen's mother dies shortly after the novel opens; her father is a drunkard who steadily impoverishes himself. Baba comes from a more ordered home, though her mother likes to spend the evenings on a high stool at the bar of the village hotel. Baba is adventurous and bullying, and where she leads Caithleen must follow. It is Baba who engineers their expulsion from the convent; and when they go to Dublin, it is Baba, innocently and pathetically rapacious, who takes Caithleen into hotel lounges to pick up elderly businessmen. Baba falls ill. Caithleen prepares to fly to Vienna with the elderly man with whom she is in love; but he does not turn up.

Neither of these events is explicitly tragic; both girls will recover. The true tragedy lies in the sense of time passing, of waste, decay, waiting, relationships that come to nothing. Yet Miss O'Brien never says so. She makes no comment, stages nothing. She simply offers her characters, and they come to us living. She does not appear to have to strive to establish anything; the novel, one feels, is so completely, so truly realized in the writer's mind that everything that comes out has a quality of life which no artifice could achieve. Miss O'Brien may write profounder books, but I doubt whether she will write another like *The Country Girls,* which is as fresh and lyrical and bursting with energy as only a first novel can be.

V. S. Naipaul. *The New Statesman.*
July 16, 1960, p. 97

In 1960 Hutchinson of London published a novel, *The Country Girls,* by an unknown Irish writer called Edna O'Brien. The critical reception was considerable and Miss O'Brien was hailed as an important new Irish writer with a fresh, unselfconscious charm, an acute observation of life and a fine, ribald sense of humor. Her second book, *The Lonely Girl,* had the same kind of success and Miss O'Brien was regarded as having passed the difficult hurdle of the second novel. She had become an established literary figure and the third novel of the trilogy was awaited with considerable expectation. When this novel, *Girls tn Their Married Bliss,* arrived, it proved to be so different from the first two books that readers were startled. The two girls, the heroines of these books, now married, had lost their girlish laughter. The book's title was seen to be bitterly ironic and the London life of Cáit and Baba was sordid. The writing tended to be slipshod in parts and a kind of humorous detachment that made the earlier adventures so enjoyable was missing. Miss O'Brien seemed in places to be writing a kind of neo-feminist propaganda. This committed writing was continued in *August Is a Wicked Month* and in *Casualties of Peace.* In this last novel there is perhaps evidence of further development, but it too is seriously clogged with a self-indulgent gloom. None of the later books has the deftness and tact of the Irish novels.

Miss O'Brien is still young and there is no reason to suppose that the present retardation is anything but temporary. Even these latest novels claim the same critical attention as those of her female contemporaries, Muriel Spark, Iris Murdoch, Brigid Brophy, Mary McCarthy and Doris Lessing. Though Iris Murdoch was born and educated in Ireland, and Brigid Brophy and Mary McCarthy can claim Irish descent, though Muriel Spark became a Catholic, Miss O'Brien is the only one of them all to be born, reared and educated Irish and Catholic. This may mean little or nothing at all in literary circles in London or New York but in Ireland there is considerable interest in such a writer. This interest is social rather than literary and Miss O'Brien shares with another Irish writer, Brendan Behan, the dubious fame of being better known than her works. It is peculiarly difficult to get past this public personality. All of her novels have been banned in Southern Ireland.

Sean McMahon, Éire-Ireland. Spring, 1967,
pp. 79–80

It is always hard to evaluate a literary work that provokes so many nonliterary judgments as this one by Edna O'Brien. But maybe literature only begins to matter when it carries us beyond the safe confines of literary criticism. D. H. Lawrence thought so, evidently Miss O'Brien does too.

Girls in Their Married Bliss is a sequel to *The Country Girls* and *The Lonely Girl* (filmed as *The Girl with Green Eyes*). Here again are those former convent schoolmates, Baba and Kate, less spirited now and more, to their horror, like their mothers. They are living in London, and have husbands, lovers, and plenty of trouble. Yet the novel is no bedroom or bedhopping farce. Each sexual skirmish in the girls' lives is both a calamity and a narrow escape from a worse one. Miss O'Brien's portrayal of the psychology of adulterous love is brilliant. She describes how lovers are more difficult than husbands; how, if marriage is boredom and compromise (but compromise with what?), then adultery is a cave of madness. The sensitive spot she probes is the knot of impulses that shape our basic needs and, therefore, our personalities.

The characters in *Girls in Their Married Bliss* are dreadfully alone. They are not interested in music, sports, or handicrafts; family, religion, and politics also exert small influence. Baba's and Kate's need to heal their broken, disconnected lives drives them to trade anything for a scrap of love. Here is where many readers will recoil. Do social institutions and ties matter as little as Miss O'Brien suggests? Are we so desperately detached from any living tradition or ideas? Conceding the difficulty of summoning moral principles in times of stress, do these stresses always take a sexual form?

If Miss O'Brien fails to answer these questions, she does examine them honestly and diligently. Her subject is sex, its dynamics and ethics, and she treats it as a many-sided problem. Where one character views a love affair as passionate, a second sees it as simply cheap, even boring. Either interpretation is as convincing as its opposite, and Miss O'Brien's narrative technique does not weight the scales.

This technique is the book's core. Miss O'Brien does not explain sex; she conveys its sensations—the excitements, the limits, the renewals. She wants us to react to her book as we would to a first-hand experience, and to achieve this purpose she alternates her narrative between voices, between dialogue and description, between epigram and summary. The suddenness of these changes jolts us; the off-key logic and rhythm communicate, probably better than conventional writing could do, the immediacy of the impact. . . . *Girls in Their Married Bliss* is a minor masterpiece. Though it lacks the range of major fiction, Miss O'Brien must be credited for inviting the comparison with it.

Peter Wolfe. Saturday Review of Literature.
February 17, 1968, pp. 38–39

When Edna O'Brien ceased to be a country girl and turned her fancy to thoughts of sex, some people complained. The freshness and charm of her first two novels, we were told, had been routed by bitterness: all that was left were the unholy passions of flesh. In this first collection of her short stories [*The Love Object*] the two faces of Miss O'Brien are laid down side by side and it is at once apparent that between them the difference is slight. Solitude has always been her subject, and it remains so. The sex, in her later novels and in some of these stories, is a single aspect of it: her girls' final effort, often wrought of desperation, to belong and to communicate. . . .

Miss O'Brien's stories rattle with an honesty that is as compelling as the style that shapes her lively prose. Her girls are frankly presented, without romance. . . . If you read Miss O'Brien's first three novels, one after another as parts of a single whole, you will find a perfect balance of comedy and tragedy and a pattern that begins and ends with loneness. This brief collection, eight stories in all, more swiftly exposes that same breadth of talent. From the whiff of fair-day dung outside the Commercial Hotel to the rich after-dinner figs, symbol of sex in a London restaurant, there is a ring of reality in every movement. One or two of the pieces are slight, but none is false, and taken together they confirm my impression that rarely has an Irish woman protested as eloquently as Edna O'Brien. In sorrow and compassion she keens over the living. More obviously now, despair is her province.

William Trevor. The New Statesman.
July 5, 1968, pp. 18–19

If a lesser author had written *Night,* one would never have bothered to read it through. But Miss O'Brien is a novelist of many gifts, including poetry and comedy and compassion: that is why the reader keeps the presumption of innocence alive by forced feeding to the very end, and why he then feels so frustrated and so cheated. The flash of poetry, of irony, of insight now and then is not enough to make a work of art out of a sentimental, predictably repetitious monologue of the kind that, at almost any hour, one can hardly escape in a certain category of Third Avenue bar. Even the pretentious malapropisms of those reduced sibyls are Mary's [the protagonist], too. But they serve no better than the lexicon of bed and bath to fashion drama or comedy.

The reasons for the book's failure may be indeed more interesting than the book. Is it conceivable that the vein has been mined out? Is it possible that virtually nothing new can be thought or said about the emptiness of lives that are just plain empty? Is it thinkable that there are really subjects that not even the finest writer can bring to life because there is simply nothing there? Apparently, yes.

In one of his essays on film and film criticism, René Clair has remarked on the fashionable fear of attacking vulgarity or tastelessness lest one be excommunicated as outmoded or prudish. The fact remains that much of *Night* is as gratuitous as those portentous examinations of nakedness, violence and real or simulated coupling that have become almost mandatory in films and novels—from the frankly commercial to the most solemnly "artistic."

Charles Lam Markmann. *The Nation.*
May 14, 1973, p. 631

"When I was young," Edna O'Brien said in an interview for *Hibernia* (December 3, 1971), "I always wanted to be a writer and since then I have realized this dream. It's some sort of ache or dissatisfaction which makes me go on. It's something terribly intangible—almost like seeing something superb in the sky, in behavior, or in the land, and seeing it is not enough. You have to somehow set it down for someone else to see, even though that sounds arrogant." What she sees, as her vision becomes apparent through her fiction, has remained consistent in regard to her commitments to Ireland, to the theme of love, and to writing as a dedication.

The style during these years has developed from the simple and barren naiveté of the young Caithleen with her revealing touches of ingenuousness ("I felt badly about being the cause of sending them solicitors' letters but Eugene said that it had to be") to the discursive ruminations of Mary Hooligan who reels off exhaustive lists like those of Samuel Beckett's Watt and converses with herself in a stream-of-consciousness-with-plot technique somewhat like that of Molly Bloom. Most of the fiction is written in the first person, which enhances both its verisimilitude and, one suspects, the critical tendency to treat it as autobiography. The best passages of the early novels are those scenes which reveal contrasting personalities—in *The Lonely Girl,* when Gaillard comes to tea with Joanna, when the deputation of virtuous god-fearing farmers call upon the agnostic Gaillard to retrieve Caithleen's honor, when the locals in the pub insult Gaillard and Caithleen—and these point to a successful career in drama. *Girls in Their Married Bliss,* the most discomforting of the novels, is blunt and direct in diction. The same attitudes on love, or the female condition, or religious friction may be phrased more subtly in the later works. The progression in style has permitted experimentation in technique, notably in *A Pagan Place,* which is written in the second person with the child-heroine identified only as "you," the father as "he," and the mother as "she." The two kinds of fiction—the Irish and the urbane—are produced from two life styles in Ireland and in England. Caithleen from County Clare is, in Baba's terms, a "right looking eejit" (a Clare expression), and a heroine may appear "streelish" in Ireland and "wanton" in England. The last novel, *Night,* marks a maturity not only in style and content but also in perception about the home land. Using real Irish names, Miss O'Brien has now created a territory as Faulkner did with Yoknapatawpha.

Grace Eckley. Edna O'Brien (Lewisburg,
Pennsylvania: Bucknell University Press,
1974), pp. 77–78

This collection [*Mrs. Reinhardt, and Other Stories*] has twelve stories by Edna O'Brien, three of which are of novella length. The settings of the stories are variously London, Vermont, Cambridge, the Italian Mediterranean, Brittany and, inevitably, Ireland: The Irish seaside, and the Irish countryside of Edna O'Brien's heart, mind and sensibility. The scenery is sketched vividly and briefly but its atmosphere pervades and illuminates; Vermont is crisp, cold and clear and Jane, who lives there, is fresh, open and clear-sighted, while Nell, her guest from Ireland, is alien in her introspection and self-doubts. Cambridge is evoked by contrast. We all know of its ambience but we imagine it the more by feeling Len's disappointment in "In the Hours of Darkness" when her night there is spent in an anonymous, contemporary hotel bedroom.

The subjects of the stories are women: the subject of the collection is Woman. Each story is a search for identity, a search which continues during sleep; dreams are frequently and revealingly recounted and much of the action of "Number Ten" takes place during "sleepwalking." Characters find themselves in their relationships with mothers, lovers, husbands and in their own loneliness. Many facets of personality are explored and there is often the sense that they are the facets of one personality (and that same personality has been explored in other books by Edna O'Brien). It is surely no coincidence that in two of the stories the women use one man to help erase the remembrance of another, that in three of the stories the women renounce the final consummation to retain their illusions, that many of the women put disproportionate faith in talismans—a pebble, a necklace, as ties to a loved one—and, more trivially, that two women press wild flowers under the hall carpet.

The Irish stories seem to be further incidents from the life described in the novel, *A Pagan Place,* and it is in these that the author reveals the heights of her talents for comic characterization. "A Rose in the Heart," explores the fierce, tender, suffocating and ultimately destructive love between mother and daughter—the same mother and daughter from the earlier novel (the mother in each uses a particularly primitive method of contraception).

The men of Edna O'Brien's stories are shadows, but shadows that, para-doxically, illuminate the women: they have life only in juxtaposition to the women. Even the male first person narrator of "Clara" becomes human only as his friendship and love for the girl from the asylum develops and he, finally, seems to be absorbed into her identity. The eponymous Mrs. Reinhardt's love for her husband is real and vivid but the recipient of that love is a vague figure until he briefly lives for the reader in his infatuation for a young girl. The closest the author comes to presenting a fully drawn male is in the story "Baby Blue" but. although an endearing and tender lover, he descends to weakness and vacillation and finally leaves his lover and returns to his emas-culating wife. Edna O'Brien recognizes that men are necessary to women but she does not seem to admire them.

Alice Harrison. Anglo-Welsh Review.
No. 63, 1978, pp. 170–71

The journey back to the state of being before knowledge, to reclaimed inno-cence, is one Edna O'Brien's heroines have tried to make in each of her eight novels. That the journey is a perilous one . . . earlier pilgrims attest. . . . But Miss O'Brien's heroines, pursuing an even course in the early novels, appear to have lost their way.

Reviewing the early novels in the pages of *Éire-Ireland,* Seán McMahon noted that the first novel, *The Country Girls* (1960), established Miss O'Brien "as an important new Irish writer with a fresh, unselfconscious charm, an acute observation of life, and a fine, ribald sense of humor"; the second novel, *Girls with Green Eyes* (1962), affirmed this reputation; and the third, *Girls in Their Married Bliss* (1964), proved startlingly disappointing. The trilogy, it is true, carries a pair of innocents, Caithleen Brady and Baba Brennan, from their school days in County Clare to divorce and adultery in London. Because the note of ironic disillusion first sounded in *Girls in Their Married Bliss* grows more strident with each succeeding novel, the reader asks why the journey, the quest for good love, so regularly fails for Miss O'Brien's heroines. . . .

The quest for "radical innocence" has taken a tortuous route for Miss O'Brien's heroines. Caithleen and Baba of the early trilogy looked for and failed to discover it in marriage. Disillusioned with marriage, Ellen of *August Is a Wicked Month* sought it in a festival of sex and found only boredom and despair. In *Casualties of Peace,* Willa's efforts to overcome her dread of sex, marital and extramarital, resulted in her death. And Mary Hooligan of *Night,* divorceé and many times mistress? Surely the murderess Nora of *Johnny I Hardly Knew You* . . . dissipates the theory that, in Mary Hooligan, the O'Brien heroine attained to maturity. In undertaking the journey to earned innocence, Miss O'Brien's heroines select one route only: sex. They never consider the professions, social service, art and music, politics, travel. Willa, it is true, works in glass, but less as a craft or art than as a defense: and Nora, who restores paintings, does so only for a livelihood. A monomaniacal lot, these women reject all of life but sex. Indeed, in greedily defying an incest taboo, Nora rejects life. Unless a future heroine plots the journey afresh, she must continue to record not, that trenchant childhood route . . . to one's original place," but a tedious sojourn in decadence and despair.

Lotus Snow. Éire-Ireland. Spring, 1979,
pp. 75, 82–83

Edna O'Brien left Ireland for London in 1960, taking her two young children with her and leaving a failed marriage behind. Filled with anger and self-pity, she left, she said, to separate herself from "family, religion, the land itself." But as her latest collection of stories, *Returning,* demonstrates, Ireland is still at the heart of her work. O'Brien has often gone public in her quarrel with her native land; in fiction, interviews, the autobiographical *Mother Ireland,* she has detailed the problems created by her personal and social history. With five novels banned in Ireland in the past, O'Brien has lashed out against the indoctrination of Irish Catholicism, claiming it produces sexual repression, guilt, terror and confusion. Although she once described herself as a gypsy, she also admits that "leaving is only conditional." Like the heroines in most of the stories in this collection, she keeps coming back.

Most of these stories were published in the *New Yorker* between 1979 and 1982 and are filled with landscapes and characters familiar since the Country Girls trilogy established O'Brien's reputation more than twenty years ago. Women seeking love and acceptance while challenging moral and sexual codes, young girls craving a mother's love or a nun's favor, men drunken and confused act out a tragic drama of the minute details of Irish village life. O'Brien's characters can be cruel, promiscuous, arrogant, naive, but they are all inevitably alone. The narrator of the lead story, "The Connor Girls," speaks for many of them when, explaining how her marriage to a non-Catholic has alienated her from her community, she concludes: "we gradually become exiles, until at last we are quite alone."

In the conflict between men and women, the most persistent and pervasive theme in O'Brien's fiction, females are often victims of male cruelty and indifference. That her own memories helped shape these stories is evident from O'Brien's comments about her childhood; she once told an interviewer that in Taumgraney, her home town, the men had a "cruelty and a crossness," the women were "tenderer and nicer." Such characteristics, appearing often in the stories in *Returning,* lead ultimately to suffering. Women are naive martyrs whose pursuit of unrealistic dreams pushes them into destructive action. Some are like Mabel in "Savages" who "died, as she had lived, a simpleton." Juxtaposed with such women are foolish males, like the three in "Tough Men" who negotiate a secret business deal only to be swindled by a con man cleverer than themselves. O'Brien's characters, though they try various methods of escape, never quite succeed. . . .

O'Brien has said in the past that she was not interested in literature "as such" but that she felt strongly about the "real expression of feeling." This is indeed her strong point: the feelings expressed by the female narrators of these stories range from anger to sadness, humor and confusion. The narrators return in memory or in actuality to their Irish village and try from a distance, with an enlightened perspective, to objectify their childhood experiences. Their inability to completely understand, however, creates a vulnerability and an ambiguity which is both realistic and appealing.

Patricia Boyle Haberstroh. Irish Literary
Supplement. Spring, 1983, p. 38

You see a country and a culture impressing itself deeply on this writer. The country is Ireland, and from the evidence available, she is more succubus than mother. The need to escape is visceral. There is a sense of protest in these stories [*A Fanatic Heart: Selected Stories of Edna O'Brien*], but it is often concealed or channeled into pain, perhaps because the author is a woman. When the background is rural—even barbaric—there is a rawness and earthiness in Edna O'Brien that some critics have compared with Colette. But she is not like Colette, because the stories are darker and full of conflict. In an essay about James Joyce, Frank Tuohy says that while Joyce, in *Dubliners* and *Portrait of the Artist,* was the first Irish Catholic to make his experience and surroundings recognizable, "the world of Nora Barnacle had to wait for the fiction of Edna O'Brien."

The stories set in the heartland of Ireland almost always depict women—with men, without men, on the make, on the loose, cracking up, women holding to reality by the skin of their teeth. Many are love stories, among them eerily intimate stories relating to sexual love, and these are what people chiefly associate with Edna O'Brien. But her range is wider than that and there is an acute, sometimes searing, social awareness. The worlds depicted are not just those of small farms full of lovelorn women and inebriate men, but also the larger world of cities, of resorts, of estrangement, the world of the very rich and careless. In a long story, a novella really, "Mrs. Reinhardt," there is an idyllic recapture of the countryside of Brittany that ends in disenchantment and havoc; in another story, "Paradise," the narrator says of the fashionable house guests, "All platinum . . . They have a canny sense of self-preservation; they know how much to eat, how much to drink . . . you would think they invented somebody like Shakespeare, so proprietary are they. . . . You could easily get filleted. Friends do it to friends."

The sensibility is on two levels and shuttles back and forth, combining the innocence of childhood with the scars of maturity. It is what gives these stories their wounded vigor. The words themselves are chiseled. The welter of emotion is rendered so sparsely that the effect is merciless, like an autopsy.

Philip Roth. Foreword to Edna O'Brien. A
Fanatic Heart: Selected Stories of Edna
O'Brien (New York: Farrar, Straus &
Giroux, 1984), n.p.

In this collection of old and new stories [*A Fanatic Heart: Selected Stories of Edna O'Brien*], Edna O'Brien adopts Yeats's diagnosis of the disease of the Irish spirit, but she does not share his view of its etiology. Her Ireland breeds a fanaticism of anguish and despair, and her characters, maimed by their unfulfilled longing, cry out, not in rage and hatred, but in pain and desperation. Though apt in its suggestion of emotional intensity, the Yeatsian allusion in the volume's title seems ill-suited to the passivity and victimization that characterize O'Brien's vision of Irish feminine sensibility.

Indeed, if *A Fanatic Heart* bears any relation to Irish masculine experience and expression, it is not to Yeats's poems but to Joyce's dispirited *Dubliners*. As an exile, looking back at the land that formed her, O'Brien traces female consciousness from the fragility of childhood, through the disquiet of maturity, to the loneliness of senescence. Although she does not pursue her portrait with Joyce's chronological exactitude, her stories convey the sense of unfulfilled movement and growth found in *Dubliners*.

Despite its evocation of Yeats and recollection of Joyce, *A Fanatic Heart* speaks with O'Brien's unmistakable voice, articulating her singular view of Ireland and Irish womanhood. This excellent selection of her short stories includes the whole of *Returning*, her most recent volume never published in the United States; the best work from her earlier collections, *The Love Object, A Scandalous Woman* and *A Rose in the Heart;* and four previously uncollected but interrelated pieces. In each of the volume's stories, the central character and narrator (in every case but one, a woman) is excruciatingly aware of the inadequacies of her existence. It is this awareness that typifies O'Brien's women. Clinging to the experience of pain and sorrow as a means of maintaining identity and preserving vitality, her characters never lose their searing self-knowledge. As the narrator in "The Love Object" explains, savoring the torment of her lost love, "If I let go of him now . . . all our happiness and my subsequent pain . . . will have been nothing and nothing is a dreadful thing to hold on to."

What makes many of these stories so wrenching and so distinctly O'Brien's is the double sense of loss they convey. Returning to the world of childhood, O'Brien explores its griefs in exquisite detail, yet she reveals how the loss of the troubled past is, in itself, a blow—another source of sorrow. Pursuing the pain of love, she portrays the agony when love's special torture is gone. As the stories move from childhood to maturity, and from Ireland to England and the continent, the vulnerability of the characters intensifies; their self-awareness heightens. New losses compound old anguish.

The fanaticism of O'Brien's heart is not Yeats's. One almost wishes that she had chosen for her title the other organ in Yeats's memorable lines.

Adele Dalsimer. *Irish Literary Supplement.*
Fall, 1985, p. 50

Edna O'Brien's *Mother Ireland* is a book filled with memories that move starkly between terror and pity as it explains, with the help of the haunting photographs of Fergus Bourke, why Ireland must be left and why Ireland can never be escaped. Her last statement is a remarkable admission of an entrapment at once willing and unwilling, a confession of both victory and defeat:

> I live out of Ireland because something in me warns me that I
> might stop there, that I might cease to feel what it has meant
> to have such a heritage, might grow placid when in fact I want
> yet again and for indefinable reasons to trace the same route,
> the trenchant childhood route, in the hope of finding some clue
> that will, or would, or could, make the leap that would restore
> one to one's original place and state of consciousness, to the
> radical innocence of the moment just before birth.

The entire book, short as it is, clearly demonstrates the extent to which O'Brien's own life has been transformed into the early novels (especially *The Country Girls Trilogy*) and a number of her short stories (many collected recently in *A Fanatic Heart*). What makes this autobiographical statement so unusual is that it is an admission that the only escape from the oppressive heritage of moral obligation and social responsibility lies not in death or in unconsciousness, but in *pre*-consciousness: a state prior to knowledge that can only be lost at birth, befuddled by life, and fixed forever in death. Her work is an attempt to return to this condition of stasis, of innumerable possibilities unencumbered by the mothering that is their ruin. . . .

It is mothering throughout O'Brien's work that condemns the women of Ireland to the support of a social and moral order that is hopelessly destructive.

In O'Brien's Ireland, this order is the product of a mediaeval repression that focuses on reproduction in general and motherhood in particular. Divorce, contraception and abortion are all proscribed, leaving women with no choice but to be "good." Thus Irish women fear men who will not care for them and whose dominance is supported by Church and State; they conceive new life long before they have even an elementary understanding of their own; they deliver children into a world that denies natural emotion and desire. The result is successive generations of women who associate the misery of life, not with the oppressor, but with the oppressed who support with resignation this obliteration of intelligence and identity. Mothers are, therefore, more feared and hated than loved by their daughters. The prospect of motherhood itself is so horrible to O'Brien's young women that it leads to emotional and physical deformity. Clearly, a woman's own birth and its replication in the birth of her daughter is, in Ireland, a tragedy of impossible proportions. This is the thematic center of O'Brien's stories and her novels.

James M. Haule. *Colby Library Quarterly.*
23, 1987, pp. 216–17

O'BRIEN, KATE (IRELAND) 1897–1974

Miss O'Brien has confessed to being a sentimentalist; and she certainly appears in the three novels [*The Ante-Room, Mary Lavelle,* and *The Land of Spices*] as a sentimental romantic human being. Mary Lavelle in Spain loses her heart and her virginity, returns to Ireland with tears in her eyes and the first seeds of experience sown in her soul. The young man in *The Ante-Room* loves his wife's sister with a hopeless love and ends it romantically and sentimentally by thinking of his childhood and looking down the barrel of a gun. . . . In *The Land of Spices* the memory of the fearful moment when her father's abnormality had been revealed to her could not black out in the nun's mind the many memories of a lovable civilized man savoring Trahearne and Herbert and Crashaw.

But in *That Lady* Miss O'Brien has deliberately sacrificed every human consolation, has seen her people and their sin against the background of the reality of God. Outside Mauriac I do not know of any modern novelist who has so carefully analyzed the motives and the results of a sin; and it would be possible to draw out a lengthy comparison between Ana in her dungeon and Thérèse Desqueyroux in the prolonged penance imposed on her by Mauriac in *La Fin de la Nuit*. The difference is that Kate O'Brien—and God—are a little closer than François Mauriac to the meaning of mercy and never in *That Lady* as in *Les Chemins de la Mer* do you feel that the novelist has condemned her people, has seen above everything the existence of hell, and is relentlessly driving the creatures of her imagination to a judgment already irrevocably given. . . . Kate O'Brien follows her own path, sees the attractiveness and the pity of the doomed passion, the doubt of the sinner, the complexities of repentance, the shakiness of the ground on which the king stands when he contrives judgment and punishment. Ana de Mendoza, with her lover in her arms and fearful scruples in her mind, thinks: "Is my poor scruple greater than what I give this man and take from him? Am I to set my little private sense of sin above his claim on me and his unhappiness? Am I cheating because I want him, and have grown tired of the unimportant fuss of my immortal soul? Am I pretending to be generous simply to escape again into his power?"

Those questions leave little room for romantic illusions but they open the door to pity—not the destructive pity outlined by Graham Greene in *The Ministry of Fear* or *The Heart of the Matter* but a tired welcoming pity that could be a faint shadow of the mercy of God. And when, towards the end of the book, Ana and her friend Cardinal Quiroga talk about her troubles, the novelist removes the last illusion by showing that even the mercy of God may be presumed upon.

Benedict Kiely. *Modern Irish Fiction: A Critique* (Dublin: Golden Eagle Books, 1950), pp. 139–41

Considering the success of *Without My Cloak,* the distinction of both *The Ante-Room* and *Mary Lavelle,* and the polemical force of *Pray for the Wanderer,* it seems correct to assess that the 1930s were a time of fulfillment for Kate O'Brien. Outward triumph, the making of new and lasting friendships and financial security helped bring about a temporary truce between those fractures of ritual and rite, sense and spirit, sexuality and intellect—all of which had wounded her deeply.

But the fractures still existed and the truce was not a treaty. And so with infinite courage she turned to explore the very source of her weaknesses as an artist, to vanquish or be vanquished by them. In three books, *The Land of Spices,* published in 1941, *That Lady* and *Teresa of Avila,* published in 1951, she confronted the quandaries of spirit versus sense. That she had the courage to attempt it indicates how bold was her imagination. That she failed to accomplish it is a measure of her honor, for she must have been aware of the odds; for after *That Lady*—with the exception of *Teresa of Avila,* which was not a novel—she never wrote well again, but degenerated into the repetitions and sentimentalities of writing which she herself would have been the first to scald with dismissal.

It is almost a critical consensus that after *That Lady* in 1946, Kate O'Brien's work never again had the attack, the flair, the perception it possessed before. It is also a critical consensus that in the novel which preceded it she achieved the highest perception into her world and made it accessible to others. This was called *The Land of Spices,* published in 1941, which Mary Lavin, the distinguished short story writer has called "an incredibly intricate piece of work, brilliantly brought off." It is, in fact, a study of convent life, and of a nun who in one passage remembers as a child having seen her father—and I quote—"in the embrace of love" with another man. For those five words the book was banned in one of the most ruthless acts of vandal censorship in an era which indulged in many of them.

In 1943 she published *The Last of Summer* but was already working on *That Lady,* a novel set in the Spain of Philip II, which was hailed in 1946 as "one of the finest historical European novels." She herself, that October night, told us that the scheme for the novel—the story itself had haunted her for years—came to her like a gift, after an air raid, in London. She had been writing letters, and after the all-clear set out to post them. And that simple journey clarified her plot, her vision and she set to work. It was a given moment, but the years of research were wearing. And yet curiously, the last part of the book was also something of a gift. She began the epilogue to it— some 7,000 words—as midnight lightened into a summer dawn in her sister's house in Currafin beside a lake. In three or four hours of writing, she had completed it and broke down when she told her sister.

Never again was she to write so well.

Eavan Boland. *The Critic.* Winter, 1975,
pp. 22–24

To say that [Kate O'Brien] produced work which was "a chronicle of her time" is perfectly true. The ambience and milieu created are authentic and accurate. These are brought to life and vitality by the women who people her stage and through Kate O'Brien's method of "interiorizing," or allowing herself the liberty of knowing their thoughts and feelings. The author concerns herself with the resources that these women can evoke in times of crisis, in order to transcend the bonds that bind them: "The strictures are those of manners and morality." Kate O'Brien has an unswerving faith in womankind, most of whom find themselves "imprisoned in a code of response, a minuet of programmed answers and expectations." Love is the pivot of their emotional lives. The author peels back the layers of their personalities in denying them that love; in placing it out of their reach in their particular situation, or she allows it to be snatched away by circumstances outside the self. This is the tragic situation of Kate O'Brien's female characters. . . .

While the women of *Without My Cloak* and *The Ante-Room* lived out their lives as mothers and spinsters, and while their social values were evident in their jewelry, their clothes, their snobbery, their chat, their musical events and games of whist, their horses, carriages and servants; these characteristics were not of a peculiarly Irish nature in the later part of the nineteenth century. The author's concern is with the interior world of the female mind. It is of these characters that the claim has been made: "Miss O'Brien is as fond of the case of conscience as any zealous Jesuit could be." However, in *Pray for the Wanderer* the heroines, Una and Nell, are very much of their time and context. Their dialogue speaks their reality, they are in tune with their world, and Kate O'Brien chooses to define their characters against the dynamism of Irish society of that day.

Una . . . can be considered as the stereotype wife and mother who runs the home with infinite patience, efficiency and love, living through others with no obvious impulses of her own. The author portrays her as a flawless woman, admired by her family, radiating happiness. However, there are a few gentle question marks inserted here and there in the course of Una's characterization, which make her more believable; less of a stereotype. Kate O'Brien, I believe, thoroughly approves of Una, approving through her of the traditional, domestic role of women, and Una's weaknesses are part of the predicament of human nature. . . .

Nell, Una's sister, is almost the antithesis of Una in all aspects of her existence. She is thirty-three years old and a spinster. . . . She shuns the personal and moral responsibility that comes with personal integrity. She must have law and order, guidelines and rules; without the values inherent in these, Nell knows that she is personally abandoned to chaos.

The moral code that Nell adheres to is not inherently Irish. In the post-Famine era in Ireland "the prudish values of Victorian middle class morality, which simultaneously idealized and repressed women," were superimposed on Catholicism in the European context. Prudery and morality became synonymous. Kate O'Brien has very deftly personified the attitudes of the time in Una and Nell, but she has also given them hearts. Love is the pivot on which Una's world revolves, and Nell, disappointed in love, having rejected Tom when she discovers that he has fathered a child out of wedlock, almost misses love altogether. Nell believes in emotion, as all Kate O'Brien's heroines do. . . .

Kate O'Brien leaves Una and Nell in . . . a land that she knew and interpreted at first hand and which she presents to us through the aesthetic integrity of the novel form. She does not moralize or comment, but the reader is actively involved in the predicament of these women whose characters are defined against such a social and religious climate. The following comment can, I feel, be the hallmark of Kate O'Brien's artistic integrity: "I offer here as nearly as I can my Ireland, in possession of which I am unique, as are you, and you, dear readers."

Joan Ryan. In Heinz Kosok, ed. *Studies in Anglo-Irish Literature* (Bonn: Bouvier, 1982), pp. 322–23, 325–26

Like many of O'Brien's other novels, such as *The Land of Spices* and *Mary Lovelle, The Ante-Room* is about the unworkability of love, the loneliness of people, and how, ultimately, the best we can hope for is "a quiet mind." In *The Ante-Room* she explores a series of love-relationships, more or less repugnant or hopeless. The relationships which she explores in depth are those which fall outside the realm of "unequal dependencies"; the love of Agnes for Vincent, her brother-in-law; and the love of William Curran for Agnes. These are central to the book's preoccupation with failed love. William Curran thinks that he has the measure of love: "emotional attachments . . . were only added things," the inessentials; and he considers that marriage is merely "a social and religious contract." But love is something that steals up on him. . . .

But as fate and the author's humor would have it, Agnes, the focus of this mad passion, is in love with someone else, Vincent. While Vincent, and also William, love what they *cannot* have, Agnes loves what she *must* not have: It is a question, for her, of morality. (O'Brien's concern for moral values makes for sober reading. There is nothing in her of the sentimental agony-aunt!) As in her other novels, sexual love cannot thrive.

Sisterly affection fares best in this novel. The relationship between Agnes and her sister Marie-Rose runs like a bright thread through the narrative. It is a real and exacting love that withstands the demands made of it. Through it Agnes finds the link with her past self: She needs Marie-Rose to affirm a vision of herself.

If sexual love is not the answer to human happiness, neither is the spirituality of Catholicism a final answer. As Eavan Boland points out in her fine introduction to this new edition of the novel, "The cold fears and aloneness of the characters in this book are not really warmed" by the rituals of Catholicism, which forms one of its strongest elements. In spite of the prosperity and sophistication of the domestic scene in Mellick, Kate O'Brien's novel concentrates on the inner life of the characters and on their grim struggle for peace of mind.

Louise Barry. Irish Literary Supplement.
Spring, 1984, p. 45

The subject of feminism is never openly raised in Kate O'Brien's work. But the theme of her novels is the necessity for woman to be as free as man. . . . None of Kate O'Brien's heroines shows the least tendency to imitate men in this way. None of them is what used to be called, when I was a child, a tomboy. They merely want the essential conditions of life that men enjoy, the freedom to educate themselves, to develop what gifts of mind they have been endowed with and to gain from this education the qualifications to earn their living; only then can they make the free gift of themselves in love. Education is necessary even to make a case for women. . . .

The world of Kate O'Brien's novels is a somber place, in the sense that men and women are shown as very rarely happy and when they are, but briefly. Her heroines, however, are the proof that she does not see happiness as the end of life. The end of life for women as for men is effort, achievement, the realization of potentialities: it is love, not sexual satisfaction, and love is a gift that only freedom allows one to bestow. Sometimes her heroines achieve spiritual freedom in an environment that limits physical freedom, as her nuns do; sometimes spiritual freedom involves the complete loss of physical freedom. . . .

Kate O'Brien's originality consists in using new material—the educated, middle-class of Ireland during the end of the last century and the beginning of this, and especially the girls and women of that class, as they struggle to escape from the lot of women everywhere—the condition of being the passive victims of the social mores of the time—as they endeavor to acquire an education which will enable them to earn their living, as they try to free themselves from the necessity of merely accepting love and, instead, attain to a position in which they can offer love. Kate O'Brien is never unaware of Christian Europe outside of Ireland, and how much Ireland has to learn from it. There was a common Europe of civilization and culture long before the Common Market of today. Kate O'Brien belonged to it: many of her heroines belong to it too. She detested the complacent self-regarding, Puritanic pietism of the 1930s and 1940s in Ireland and saw it as an aberration from the great European tradition of Catholicism. St. Patrick, she reminds her readers in the journal, *Hibernia,* was a "European gentleman." Catholicism as a formative influence on character, as a shaping of the inner life, she valued; even when she had ceased to believe in Catholic doctrines. She exploited the dramatic possibilities it afforded, as any system which imposes on human creatures a rigorous abstract training to meet the inevitable assaults of the senses and the emotions must do. Tension and conflict necessarily result and tension and conflict are the stuff of drama.

Kate O'Brien shows her women possessing a moral life as much as men, indeed more than most men. They rely on their own knowledge, intelligence and instinct. In this she is heir to Jane Austen and Henry James, but she is also in another sense heir to the nineteenth-century Irish novelists, in whose work human feelings had been largely determined by historic factors, and human happiness to be regarded as rendered impossible by economic pressures. It is the incompatibility between human expectations and the facts of existence, between human potentialities and the chances of their realization that mould the life of Kate O'Brien's characters, especially the life of her women characters. In short, she is a modern novelist.

Lorna Reynolds. *Kate O'Brien: A Literary Portrait* (Gerrard's Cross, Buckinghamshire: Colin Smythe, 1987), pp. 128–32

The bleak landscape upon which [Liam] O'Flaherty's characters so violently, if ineffectually, loom could hardly seem further removed from the world at the heart of Kate O'Brien's fiction—Catholic (and usually Irish Catholic), "Victorian" (as she often calls it), bourgeois (another of her favorite labels). The two writers, born within a year and within sixty miles of each other are, in all apparent ways, angry opposites. . . . But terms of simple contrast do not adequately place the two writers. O'Brien is anything but a sentimental defender of the Catholic middle class; it is the character of monasticism that interests her, as witness her study of St. Teresa. And she is every bit as much concerned with the work of individuation, of self-definition. . . .

Her fiction directly explores the complex interactions of obligation and independence, of home and escape. . . . What she calls . . . the necessary, even inevitable, "*locus standi* from which to view the world" in her work, and the source as well of the "innate passion by which to judge" . . . is the prosperous Catholic middle class, especially as it existed in Ireland in the period from about 1870 to 1914. It was a world of ironmongers, horse traders, vintners, and doctors, a world not far removed in time from its origins in the massive dislocation of the Irish peasantry during the Famine but far enough advanced in wealth and standards to sustain large country houses and the polite education of its children. . . .

Of all the difficulties that stand in the way of the desire for independence, the greatest is love—familial, sensual, religious. For the intelligent and passionate young women who are at the center of O'Brien's attention, the only immediately available paths (and neither is without its appeal) are marriage and the convent. To be, as the title character in *Mary Lavelle* wishes, "a free lance" without foregoing altogether the roles of wife, mother, sister, lover, is the complex and often unattainable goal of O'Brien's women. The battle is played out in enclosed spaces: the parlor and the dining room of bourgeois life, or the presentation parlor of a convent. And the alternative to these often airless rooms seems to be yet another enclosure; a room of one's own more like a monastic cell than a writer's workshop. Baldly put, the great conflict that generates O'Brien's fiction is that between intelligent detachment and passionate, sensual love; and thus, in broader terms, between separation and freedom of movement, on the one hand, and relationship and obligation, on the other.

John Hildebidle. *Five Irish Writers: The Errand of Keeping Alive* (Cambridge: Harvard University Press, 1989), pp. 51–52

The hysteric's refusal to become inured to deprivation reflects Mary Lavelle's dilemma, and both can be clearly traced in the poetics of Kate O'Brien's novel. Mary's desires harmonize little with the image she projects. Under the mask of tranquil satisfaction, Mary repeatedly breaks the rules. Like Mary, the hysteric is deeply unconventional in a society where convention touches upon everything. Society imagines the hysteric as paying for her sins, but she is instead being made to suffer for her virtues. . . .

The situations in *Mary Lavelle* (1936), and also *The Ante-Room* (1934), for example, are linked to the struggle between one's desires and the internal constrictions of one's conscience, in which Kate O'Brien attempts to unravel the skein of repression which was a result of her deeply rooted Roman Catholic education and her spiritual integrity. . . .

O'Brien rejects the rigid restrictions of Catholicism not by way of attack, but by seeking to portray characters who reside outside the locus of power and authority—characters who, although charged with ambivalence, refuse to capitulate to convention. Both Mary Lavelle and Agnes Mulqueen, the heroine of *The Ante-Room* who falls in love with her sister's husband, possess liberatory qualities which rival their constrained lives. . . .

One of Kate O'Brien's main themes in *Mary Lavelle* is that the urge for freedom comes into conflict with forces that constrict it. O'Brien's portrayal of women as powerless objects underscores their marginal position. Mary Lavelle is not free because she is caught between what she aspires to— that is, what she is permitted to accomplish—and what drags her down. Consequently, a "fall from grace" becomes the motto for Mary in her quest for transcendence.

Rose Quiello. *Éire-Ireland.* 25, 1990, pp. 46–48

OCAMPO, SILVINA (ARGENTINA) 1903–

Readers familiar with Silvina Ocampo's stories will immediately think of so many examples of imaginative murder in them that they may sympathize with the committee members for the Argentine National Prize for Literature which denied Ocampo its award in 1979 with the comment that her stories were "too cruel." Among Ocampo's narratives most noted for their violence and grotesque cruelty are several which involve an intense hatred between two women. Though not all of Ocampo's brutal doubles are female characters, the patterns of these admittedly unpleasant stories are so marked in Ocampo's work that they deserve closer examination. The stories involving female pairs are notable for the protagonists' animosity toward each other and also for their curious lack of motivation. One of Ocampo's characters, herself a short story writer, comments upon the process of developing a character who has decided to commit suicide: "What is it which motivates his resolve? I never managed to determine it because to me it seemed superfluous, irritating to write about." [¿Qué es lo que motiva su resolución? Nunca illegué a determinarlo, porque me parecía superfluo, fastidioso de escribir (*La furia*)]. Like her character, Ocampo as author works and reworks the theme of female hostility without seeming to examine its origins. That Ocampo's characters have no "reasons" for their extreme reactions makes the power of their emotions all the more perplexing and ominous. The reader reacts to these stories with a degree of horror which places them within the world of the grotesque.

It also seems clear that these stories represent a series of mad doubles. . . . The trajectory of Ocampo's treatment of the theme of the female double . . . [shows] a roughly chronological process by which this remarkably creative woman has fought to see beyond the images of monster and angel. At first she deals with these images in the traditionally male polarization of good woman versus evil woman. As her stories empower the creative monster, however, she discovers the hidden dangers of the passive-aggressive angel as well. Finally, in her conception of both parts of the woman myth as victims of their seething hatred, occasioned by a patriarchal system which pits women as competitors for male favor, Ocampo has at last exorcized these images for herself. . . .

The ability to see the admittedly disconcerting, hateful women protagonists of her stories as expressions of Ocampo's own "anxiety of authorship," her attempt to work through for herself the painful questions of self-definition, should serve only as the beginning of an exploration of other feminist issues presented by Ocampo's work. The raging, destructive female characters of Ocampo's stories should be viewed as part of her preoccupation with the victimization and revenge of women, children and "deviants" in her works. Ocampo recognizes the hidden power of the angel figure, just as more generally in her fiction, she acknowledges the power of the powerless; she validates the monstrous self, just as she recognizes the hidden worth of other of society's *lumpen*. To date, Blas Matamoro has seen most clearly the political meaning behind her violent, absurd and fantastic fictional world. He observed the subversion of oligarchical society in her stories, though he did not attribute this characteristic to a particularly female point of view. The "oddness" of Ocampo's works vis-à-vis her closest peers has prevented her from being more fully understood, but Gilbert and Gubar's theory of women's creativity provides the key which will unlock other of Ocampo's strategies for undermining not just the oligarchy, but more specifically, the patriarchal society and literature in which she has worked.

Patricia N. Klingenberg. *Latin American Literary Review.* 16:32, 1988, pp. 29, 38

This collection of stories [*Leopoldina's Dream*] is necessary reading for any critic of Borges, Adolfo Bioy Casares, and *Sur,* the magazine founded by Victoria Ocampo. Silvina Ocampo is the sister of Victoria; she is the wife of Bioy Casares; she is one of the editors of the significant anthology of fantastic literature published in 1940. (The other editors are Borges and Bioy Casares.)

Silvina must be more than a mere footnote in Spanish literature. Her bizarre, beautiful stories are perhaps as good as those written by Borges and Bioy Casares. She is, indeed, so extraordinary that her collection has received acclaim from Borges, Calvino, and Amado, who call her an incomparable artist, "the leading writer in Spanish."

This collection contains stories from earlier collections, but they are so similar in theme, imagery, and *vision* that we cannot see any process of development. The stories demonstrate an artist who is "eternal"—one who is beyond change.

The stories are short because they are revelations, epiphanies, visions; they recount an astounding flash of insight; they are mystical. . . .

After we read the wonderfully rendered stories, we are strangely moved. We understand that we cannot ever read—or write—the same realistic, earthbound fictions we have done in the past. We must somehow move beyond language to describe (see) "true faces." We must bow our heads as silent witnesses.

Irving Malin. *Hollins Critic.* 26:5, December, 1989, pp. 16–17

Of the trio known by some as "the holy trinity," Silvina Ocampo has been the least celebrated, whereas Jorge Luis Borges reached Nobel proportions (though never receiving the prize) and Adolfo Bioy Casares won international acclaim both for his own stories and for his mischievous collaboration with Borges under the pseudonym of H. Bustos Domecq. *Cornelia frente al espejo* reminds us once more, however, of Ocampo's place at center stage rather than in the wings, overshadowed by the public acknowledgment of her husband (Bioy Casares) and her dear friend (Borges).

The thirty-five selections (primarily prose but also some poetry) in the Tusquets collection echo several of the themes, motifs, and concerns of Ocampo's early stories, first published in *Sur* (Victoria Ocampo's literary magazine, the initial meeting ground for Victoria's younger sister, Bioy, and Borges). Now, again, she plucks at intimate chords exposing fragile private worlds (usually in the lives of children and of couples), not without discomfort to the reader who relies on the illusion of order and boundaries in life and who is comforted by the safety of home and the conviction of happiness. In Silvina Ocampo's fiction the perverse and the absurd are made everyday and the quotidian becomes magical. Dreams punch a hole in drudgery and predictability ("Del color de los vidrios"), while nightmares and mirrors ensnare victims like a spider web ("Cornelia frente al espejo"). Revelations are frustrated by the limitations of childhood—and adulthood ("Intenté salvar a Dios"). Animals and humans share intimate passions ("Miren cómo se aman," "El mi el si o el la"). Horror and innocence caress each other.

Still, *Cornelia frente al espejo* (Cornelia before the mirror) is entirely fresh, with narrative surprises and verbal delights that only a master storyteller and seasoned artist can offer in an unburdened refined language. Unlike the title story (some forty pages long), most of the other narratives are only one to five pages in length. Each of these is a little gem, some laced with humor and irony ("Los celosos"), others absurdly tender ("Amé dieciocho veces pero recuerdo solo tres"), some with elements of the Gothic ("Jardín de infierno"), and still others brutally obsessive ("Ocho alas"). All share one thing in common: they dig into the most guarded interstices of our emotional experiences. Silvina Ocampo's keen fables and frightening anecdotes unveil our secret desires, our hidden fears, our private curiosities. We are spared sentimentality and cowardice in her narrative, however, in exchange for honesty. That is why we keep reading.

Ana C. Cara. *World Literature Today*. 64,
1990, p. 78

OCAMPO, VICTORIA (ARGENTINA) 1893–1979

In a long lifetime of devotion to literature and the arts, Victoria Ocampo's name has become synonymous with two objectives: the pursuit of creative excellence and the nurturing of cultural dialogues between nations of all continents. Through her review and publishing house, both of which are named *Sur,* she has led what began as a personal crusade to export the finest examples of Argentine culture and, at the same time, import the highest quality of literary and artistic expression from abroad. Seeking out authors and works that represent the best aspects of contemporary culture, whatever their country or political affiliation, has been both her business and her pleasure.

If there is one quality that characterizes Victoria Ocampo today just as it did in her youth, it is her intellectual generosity, her eagerness to share her enthusiasms with others. Those who have known her personally, as well as those who know her only by the publications that carry her name, can testify to the bountiful nature of the woman whom her friend André Malraux once called "la superbe Argentine." . . .

The open letter she wrote to Virginia Woolf at the head of her first volume of *Testimonios* declared her intention to set new precedents. From now on, she said, women had to express their views more openly. "Whenever the occasion presents itself (and if it doesn't I seek it out), I declare my solidarity with the female sex." This was her earliest pledge as a writer in 1934, and it has continued to be one of the most powerful motives behind her testimony. If she is to be judged by posterity as a witness to her time, she wants to be held morally accountable not just as a writer, but as a woman writer. . . .

She once considered calling her volumes of testimonies "kaleidoscope," but rejected the title on the grounds that it could apply to the works of any author—Proust, Dante, Shakespeare: "In all of us, small colored objects are eternally moving around: thoughts, dreams, emotions, memories. In all of us a composite play of mirrors and day-to-day tumult *regroups* those small objects that don't change, giving us the illusion of an infinite variety subject to laws of inexorable symmetry." The colors and shapes of one author's kaleidoscope may vary from those of another; for each, however, the fundamental components remain the same and are therefore revealing. In Victoria's ten volumes of testimonies—each volume contains approximately twenty to thirty essays—the small colored objects of her life that regroup again and again include memories of her childhood, equal rights for women, the internationalism of artistic excellence, nonviolence, her love of music, nature, Argentina, France. The variety appears infinite, but an inexorable symmetry is nonetheless there. Whatever she writes has an unmistakable spiritual configuration, whether it is her early work, such as *De Francesca a Beatrice,* or her later study of the life of Lawrence of Arabia.

One of her works that few people have read because copies are difficult to find is a fairy-tale play for children called *La laguna de los nenúfares* (The water-lily pond).

> Doris Meyer. *Victoria Ocampo: Against the Wind and the Tide* (New York: George Braziller, 1979), pp. xvi–xvii, 177, 186

Among the stars that fill the literary firmament in Latin America, Victoria Ocampo will be perhaps less luminous than many others. Nonetheless, she became a legend in her own lifetime and has already drawn biographers and critics from Argentina and the United States for book-length studies.

She is certainly going to attract more scholarly attention in the coming years in the Western world, including Latin America, for her cultural mores, and in the Orient, especially India, for her association with Tagore, Nehru and Gandhi. It is fortunate that she left seven sets of manuscripts together constituting an autobiography which she started writing in 1952. Two of these have now been published in the last month of 1979 and in early 1980. The two volumes, subtitled "The Archipelago" and "The Insular Empire," recall her wealthy childhood and sensitive adolescence. The first stands out for its narrative coherence and fidelity as it unfolds a rare sensibility, especially in the context of her rejection of all forms of injustice, while the second takes us in a Proustian way through the many crises of her growing years, well-documented with letters.

Ocampo's style is a conversational tête-à-tête with no attempt at embellishment, which stands out with the strength and beauty of a rough-hewn rock. Renée María Cura, a close associate of Victoria Ocampo for many years and the moving spirit behind the Sur publishing house, is now busy working on the remaining manuscripts, which are scheduled to appear at the rate of two volumes a year. The photographs and the other illustrations from the rich and varied archive of Victoria Ocampo contribute to the impact of the publications.

Susnigdha Dey. World Literature Today. 55,
1981, p. 439

Ortega y Gasset, the Spanish philosopher, was . . . effusive in his epilogue to Victoria Ocampo's *De Francesca a Beatrice* (From Francesca to Beatrice) (1924), a long essay based on her reading of Dante's *Divina Commedia*: "You are, Madam, an exemplary apparition of femininity. The most unusual perfections converge in your person with radiant grace. How couldn't our curiosity be aroused seeing you descend to the imaginary cosmos of Dante where all forms of existence are found? The otherworldly trip that we made so many times takes on in this manner a new dramatism and becomes full of suggestive adventures." The condescension underlying their praise is undoubtedly more obvious to us today than it was to the men who wrote . . . [such] lines. . . .

Reading Ocampo's essays, one becomes witness to a personal journey of self-discovery, a psychological odyssey comparable to that of [Teresa de la] Parra's and [Maria Luisa] Bombal's narrators. Like them she writes to unburden herself, to make order out of chaos, to communicate—even if only with herself—in order to understand. For all three, writing about themselves was not an act of vanity; it was a form of surviving in an uncomprehending world. Where Ocampo differed from the others—even from Parra and Bombal—was in her willingness, indeed her need, to testify openly about herself. In the more visible European tradition of Mme de Sévigny, George Sand, and other women who wrote autobiographically, Ocampo showed her inclination toward European culture fostered by her education, her friendships, and her regular travel abroad. The intellectual distance this afforded her along with her own aggressive personality—the will to share her enthusiasm—made the first-person essay her natural choice.

Doris Meyer. In Doris Meyer and Margarita
Fernández Olmos, eds. Contemporary
Women Writers of Latin America:
Introductory Essays (Brooklyn: Brooklyn
College Press, 1983), pp. 6, 12

Victoria Ocampo's *Testimonios* (Testimonies) constitute a mosaic in many pieces, rigorously arranged by date, with few exceptions, in which more than a half century in the intelligent life of a South American woman of the traditional upper class is covered.

The topics dealt with there uncover the social aspect of a personality in such a way that the general tone that results in no way crosses the boundaries of a discreet vision of the writer's own intimacy and a no less careful respect for that of others.

A common territory remains to be signaled, in which communication with others is possible, leaving out that intimate "I" that she considered inviolable, both because of its lack of importance and the impossibility of transcending it for others.

This is the exemplary quality that makes it possible to see in this mosaic the sort of life shared by an intellectual sector of Buenos Aires during a great deal of the twentieth century. . . .

In her devotion to mastery of her tongue, Victoria Ocampo bears witness to her own integrity and her literary vocation. The work also shows that there is a spiritual origin to this linguistic dedication to the exercise of the craft of chronicler, a chronicler who, thereby, is witness to her epoch.

Marta Gallo. Revista Iberoamericana. 51,
1985, pp. 679, 686

Victoria Ocampo . . . was a wealthy Argentine feminist who defied cultural restrictions against women to assert herself as an influential publisher, editor, translator, and writer. She founded and underwrote the literary journal *Sur* (South), promoted the translation of European and North American literature into Spanish, and encouraged Latin American writers. Although she herself wrote hundreds of essays and some fiction, Victoria Ocampo more often is considered a patron of literature than a literary critic or writer. However, even a cursory reading of her critical work reveals another Victoria, whose approach repudiated traditional, patriarchal notions of appropriate literary criticism in order to express her experience as a woman reader.

Like many avid readers, Victoria Ocampo had a few particular writers of whom she wrote most frequently and after whom she modeled herself as a writer and critic. Among her favorite literary people were Rabindranath Tagore, T. E. Lawrence, Aldous Huxley, and Virginia Woolf. Ocampo's relationship to Woolf differed from her relationships to other writers, because she identified with Woolf both as a writer and as a woman. In her writings about Woolf and her work. Ocampo emphasizes Woolf's treatment of the feminine and of women's relationship to literature; she was one of Virginia Woolf's first feminist readers. As feminist documents, her critical essays chart the relationship between a woman writer and her feminist reader. Their relationship—a metaphorical room where they spoke to each other away from the company of men—exemplifies how two women writers may encounter each other and alter the terms of literary discourse. . . .

Ocampo consistently used Woolf's texts to identify and clarify her image of herself. Over and over she defined and differentiated: "In this we are the same, in that different." Since women always have defined themselves within a hierarchy that separates and judges according to masculine values, it has never been easy to say "I am this, she is that" and to leave the statement unfettered, plain, the two sides equal. While Ocampo acutely felt and expressed her differences from Woolf, the body of her work on Woolf is impressive in its insistent identification with text and author, its determined belief that Woolf's texts could lead to an understanding of the self as woman, and its sustained pursuit of the author through her text. Ocampo was able to gain access to Woolf by asserting her difference from the Englishwoman; instead of allowing patriarchal definitions to identify and hierarchize her difference, she used it as a powerful feminist tool to explore her relationship to writing and texts.

> Bernice L. Hausman. In Noël Valis and
> Carol Maier, eds. *In the Feminine Mode*
> (Lewisburg, Pennsylvania: Bucknell
> University Press, 1990), pp. 204–5

O'CONNOR, FLANNERY (UNITED STATES) 1926–64

There is in Flannery O'Connor a fierceness of literary gesture, an angriness of observation, a faculty for catching, as an animal eye in the wilderness, cunningly and at one sharp glance, the shape and detail and animal intention of enemy and foe. The world of *Wise Blood* is one of clashing in a wilderness. . . . Miss O'Connor's style is tight to choking and as direct and uncompounded as the order to a firing squad to shoot a man against a wall. One cannot take this book lightly or lightly turn away from it, because it is inflicted upon one in the same way its people take their lives: like an indefensible blow delivered in the dark.

> William Goyen. *The New York Times.*
> May 18, 1952, p. 4

Wise Blood is the first novel of a twenty-six-year-old Georgia woman. It is a reasonably accomplished, remarkably precocious beginning. Written in a taut, dry, economical and objective prose, it is an important addition to the grotesque literature of Southern decadence. It is also a kind of Southern Baptist version of "The Hound of Heaven.". . . The stifling world which emerges from these pages is an animalistic world. The author's predilection for zoological symbolism is more than a trick of style. . . . Nobody here is redeemed because there is no one to redeem.

> John H. Simons. *Commonweal.*
> June 27, 1952, pp. 297–98

The theme of *Wise Blood* is Christ the Pursuer, the Ineluctable, with a satire on Protestantism thrown in. . . . It is quite clear what Miss O'Connor means to say . . . is . . . there is no escaping Christ. But the author's style, in my opinion, is inconsistent with this statement. Everything she says through image and metaphor has the meaning only of degeneration, and she writes of an insane world, peopled by monsters and submen. . . . Let me say of *Wise Blood* that it does deal with one of the themes, and shows a variety of sensibility, out of which the kind of fiction that matters can be made.

Isaac Rosenfeld. *The New Republic.*
July 7, 1952, pp. 19–20

Miss O'Connor is a regionalist in the best sense of the word; that is, she understands her country and its people so well that in her hands they become all humanity. The stories in *A Good Man Is Hard to Find* take place in Georgia, but they are moving for their inescapable reality and not because of picturesque and local color. Such things, we recognize, could happen anywhere; some are grotesque and some terrible but we dare not say of any, "This only took place in the writer's imagination."

For she lays hold of the significant detail; her poetic awareness is constantly receiving, selecting the illustration which gives us a man or a woman or a certain kind of hot summer evening living and whole.

Sylvia Stallings. *New York Herald Tribune.*
June 5, 1955, p. 1

Miss O'Connor's works, like Maupassant's, are characterized by precision, density and an almost alarming circumspection. There are few landscapes in her stories. Her characters seem to move in the hard white glare of a searchlight—or perhaps it is more as if the author viewed her subjects through the knot-hole in a fence or wall. . . . Miss O'Connor for all her apparent preoccupation with the visible scene, is also fiercely concerned with moral, even theological problems. In these stories the rural South is, for the first time, viewed by a writer whose orthodoxy matches her talent. The results are revolutionary.

Caroline Gordon. *The New York Times.*
June 12, 1955, p. 5

Scarcely thirty years old, and a Georgian by birth and chance, Flannery O'Connor is not easily fitted into any identifiable group of Southern writers. She stands among, but is not of them. To be sure, her characters have certain traits linking them with the Southern tradition in fiction: for the most part they are poor and rural folk dominated by the old ancestral fears—of death, the unknown, the foreign, and all the shadows of evil. But they are strangers to despair, and this is their distinction. They hold their fears at bay with a rustic religiosity that is as functional as their speech or dress.

James Greene. *Commonweal.* July 22, 1955,
p. 404

A Good Man Is Hard to Find certainly presents an abundance of victims of grotesque fate and weird villains. . . . Beyond the grotesquery and the symbolism, this reviewer finds in these diamond-hard, diamond-brilliant stories a fiery rejection of Bible Beltism, of small, mean minds and small, mean ways. Interestingly enough, the critical touchstone is Catholicism.

Riley Hughes. *Catholic World.* October,
1955, pp. 66–67

Something about Miss O'Connor's work is reminiscent of the best work of another Georgia writer, Erskine Caldwell. Perhaps it is subject matter most of all. Though in no sense concerned with the pornography and lasciviousness to which Caldwell often resorts, she too goes in for the miseries of the poor whites. . . . Perhaps the similarities are enhanced, too, by the style of Miss O'Connor's stories—realistic, plain, literal. . . . Where Miss O'Connor's art differs—profoundly—from Caldwell's is not in language and subject matter as much as in the attitude of the author. Caldwell is the naturalist, out to make a social point. . . . More kin to the Bundrens of *As I Lay Dying,* her people confront spiritual and moral problems, not economics. There is in her characters a dignity, a human worthiness, that shows the real respect Miss O'Connor has for them.

Louis D. Rubin, Jr. *Sewanee Review.*
Autumn, 1955, pp. 678–79

There are few modern writers whose wit is more unexpected and brilliant, or whose satire is more scathing than Flannery O'Connor's—a sample of her when she *really* wants to be mean is her satire on the South and its nostalgia for the days of glory long-past-but-not-forgotten, in "A Late Encounter With the Enemy"—yet her greatest strength lies in another quality which is at a premium among satirists: compassion for those whom she satirizes. The current of irony runs deep throughout her stories, but rarely does it run as deep as her compassion. . . . Because of her genuine horror of sentimentality, at just the point where many writers would soften, Flannery O'Connor's wit appears to become more wry and her satire more scathing, the result being a quality of humor remarkably akin to that of Chaucer in which the author tells with apparent ease and gusto side-splitting stories, which, nonetheless, contain implicitly matter for some very sobering thought.

Robert McCown. *Catholic World.* January,
1959, p. 290

A Flannery O'Connor story or novel is always the slowly paced, leisurely uncovering of a series of unusual people and circumstances. She seems always intent on at first disenchanting us—mainly through a systematic puncturing of the myth of southern gallantry and gentility—and then restoring our confidence when she has forced us to view her world on her own terms. She forces us to go through a complete Cartesian purgation; our minds are cleansed of all previous notions. When we have forgotten the other books we have read, we can then allow for the existence of her Hazel Motes *(Wise Blood)*, her Rayber *(The Violent Bear It Away)*, and her "The Misfit" *(A Good Man Is Hard to Find)*. We almost willingly "suspend disbelief" in the face of impossible happenings to unlikely people. This is part of what we must go through when we read most fiction writers. But never have I felt the compulsion to reject everything and start over again that I feel with Flannery O'Connor.

Melvin J. Friedman. *The English Journal.*
April, 1962, p. 236

Her satire and irony, exuberance of ear and invention, are inseparable from the central knowledge that in varying degrees they serve. "Religious" is a poor word for this knowledge if it does not mean "knowledge of the world." She sees the South, it seems to me (who am no Southerner but no Northerner, either), as populated by displaced persons. Almost all her people are displaced and some are either aware of it or become so. But it is not a sectional or regional condition; it is a religious condition, common to North and South alike, common indeed to the world we live in.

The stories not only imply, they as good as state again and again, that estrangement from Christian plenitude is estrangement from the true country of man.

Robert Fitzgerald. *Sawanee Review.*
Summer, 1962, pp. 393–94

But if [Nathanael] West wrote less effectively whenever he attempted to take into account the presence or absence of God, while Flannery O'Connor would not write at all without what she calls the "attraction for the Holy"; or if it appears that Flannery O'Connor is writing about the spirit (the absurdity of disbelief), while Nathanael West was writing about the dream (the painful absurdity of sexual desire), at least I would say that the "pitch" of their comic fictions is very nearly the same. Both writers are demolishing "man's image of himself as a rational creature" (Flannery O'Connor, for instance, in her wonderfully unsympathetic portrait of the ridiculous school teacher, Rayber, in *The Violent Bear It Away,* and West in his creation of total and hapless dementia in *The Day of the Locust*). And both writers are reversing their artistic sympathies, West committing himself to the creative pleasures of a destructive sexuality, Flannery O'Connor committing herself creatively to the antics of soulless characters who leer, or bicker, or stare at obscenities on walls, or maim each other on a brilliant but barren earth. And finally both writers—one a Roman Catholic, the other a man of no particular religious drive—are remarkably similar in their exploitation of the "demolishing" syntax of the devil.

John Hawkes. *Sewanee Review.* Summer,
1962, pp. 397–98

The genius of Miss O'Connor's humor is that she nowhere appears the partisan of human fallibility. This is the initial requirement of the orthodox outlook: the Christian must realize that he is as liable to human weaknesses as any sinner or the unbeliever. She gives us an apt simile for this viewpoint in her story, "The River": where Mrs. Cronin stood, staring into the room, "with a skeleton's appearance of seeing everything." We have the feeling that the skeleton itself, with nowhere to hide anything, must be able to see through us with its own inner visibility. That sense of conscience, that nakedness before God, is the source of religious realism and the premise for Miss O'Connor's humor.

Brainard Cheney. Sewanee Review. Autumn,
1963, p. 646

Now and then, the fierce contempt for liberal humanist do-gooders on the one hand and hellfire Biblical sectarians on the other seemed to me to twist and bias her vision—as it does in "The Lame Shall Enter First," a story of enormous power, but power warped and cruel; pity, for once, is lost in anger and scorn. It is certainly a strange world her stories live in: I never cease to wonder (speaking as an alien) at the American South as its writers portray it.

Patrick Cruttwell. Hudson Review. Autumn,
1965, p. 445

A perusal of Miss O'Connor's fiction will reveal that Christ-haunted figures furnish the author her principal subject matter. Through the conflicts, often violent ones, of these protagonists who oscillate between belief and unbelief, between self-will and submission, the author presents her view of reality. This grotesque drama that she presents takes place in a discernible theological framework. . . . Thus, Miss O'Connor's fiction is primarily concerned with man's life-and-death spiritual struggle. The protagonist, rebelling against belief, forces a crisis that reveals to him his haughty and willful misconception of reality, at which time he experiences what Miss O'Connor has called his "moment of grace." Without exception this moment comes at great price.

Bob Dowell. College English. December,
1965, p. 236

Exploding upwards into God is the action in all Miss O'Connor's stories. It is always an explosion of violence, generally physical violence, and always resulting from the violent agitation is a revelation, a striking disclosure, sometimes to the characters, always to the reader. This revelation is actually more devastating than the physical violence which preceded it. In the wake of the revelation a sense of mystery lives on—*the mystery*—the mystery of human nature, its context and complexities. It is the ability to evoke this mystery that gives Miss O'Connor's stories their peculiar depth and power.

Always the mystery is in terms of the real. The violence is born of the clash of illusion with reality. This reality is not only that of perceptible fact;

it has a fourth dimension, a kind of space-time continuum, that reaches up to heaven and down to hell. The mystery gives Miss O'Connor's people a significance beyond what appears in the narrow Georgian groove and on the grimy exterior of their lives. The worst specimens of humanity communicate something of man's grandeur and misery. Her people are real, often the substratum sort, genuine in their perversity and in their comic antics, and they shock the reader by exposing the depths and the heights in man which the explosion opens up.

Jean Marie Kann. *Catholic World*.
December, 1966, pp. 158–59

Flannery's early stories met with . . . unreflective criticism. Why, people wanted to know, did she have to write about such unattractive characters? And why write only about the South? Were there no other parts of the country worth portraying? From the point of view of sales, however, her stories had one thing in their favor: violence. Ours is an age which may be said to specialize in violence. Flannery's characters live in a matrix of violence and some of them meet violent ends. People continued to wish that they could meet at least one "attractive" person in her stories, but they kept on reading. She began by writing stories which few people could understand. She ended by writing stories which everybody—or almost everybody—professed to "love."

This pattern seems to recur over and over in literary history. It usually signifies the emergence of a strong and original talent. In Flannery's case there is no question of the strength and originality of the talent.

Caroline Gordon. *Sewanne Review*. Spring,
1968, p. 267

In Miss O'Connor's fiction, the religious vision is markedly apocalyptic. According to this vision, everything in life leads to death, and death is revelation. It is exactly in the instant of passing out of time and life and into eternity that her characters seem to live most fully: they *begin* their humanity exactly when it is ended in time. She quietly insists on viewing death, however horrible and violent, from the perspective of eternity. If the reader resists this view, there will seem to be no moral or emotional resolutions to her stories: only the arbitrary, violent, and meaningless "resolution" of an equally arbitrary, violent, and meaningless death. If he accepts her view, he will be asked to see that the death of any character is supremely valuable as a means to his awakening to reality. . . .

The particular view of death that we find in Miss O'Connor's fiction is related to her presentation of the operation of grace. In this fiction, the effects of grace are rarely visible in the active and fruitful union of the human with the divine will, and redemption does not seem to happen *in the world*. Grace is usually seen to operate as a powerful but hidden force which is entirely separate from human will and intention. It seems as though God is out to accomplish His salvation in spite of the sinner's willful drive against Him.

Ruth M. Vande Kieft. *Sewanee Review.* Spring, 1968, pp. 345–46, 350–51

The work of Flannery O'Connor is remarkably free of morbidity because, like Greek tragedy or Christian myth, her attention is less on catharsis and loss than on transfiguration; less on the fact of death than on its attendant circumstance and aftermath—the apocalyptic vision of possibility. . . . The thrust of Flannery O'Connor's work . . . is into the heart of paradox, epitomized by serious consideration that man's mortality might be an act of grace and the occasion of death a prophetic sign. . . .

Flannery O'Connor undercuts the more sensational or melodramatic aspects of dying, because she is concerned less with documentary realism than with the aura of understanding effected in the agonist himself or in a bystander.

Leonard Casper. In Melvin J. Friedman and John B. Vickery, eds. *The Shaken Realist* (Baton Rouge: Louisiana State University Press, 1970), pp. 290–91, 293

Flannery O'Connor's Catholic celebration is unique in contemporary literature. Her literal, banal style disguises a sense of participation in the sacred action of the universe: the salvation of man. She remains firmly grounded in the physical scene, the rural, biblical South, but she shows us the mystery on which that scene is built. At times communal, more often personal, the hidden celebration in her work is perhaps the finest testament of her ability to connect fact and mystery.

Although Flannery O'Connor and Eudora Welty are both southern ladies (Miss O'Connor would be amused at the term) whose literary imagination is thoroughly grounded in the rural South, they are not really comparable. Eudora Welty's countryside is rich, historical, and mythical; her lyric style has its closest affinities with poetry; her essential subject is the incommunicable uniqueness of life. Flannery O'Connor's South is all red clay and pine-woods—often aflame in one way or another; she used ugliness, grotesquerie, suffering, and Old Testament violence to point up the need for a salvation greater than ourselves. To this end she was anti-humanist and conservative, fearing the false comforts of liberal compassion and urban civilization. Her closest affinities are not with southern literature at all, but with French literature. One hears in her work the tragic echoes of Pascal, the prophetic thunder of Leon Bloy, and the dying words of [George] Bernanos's country priest—"Does it matter? Grace is everywhere."

Richard H. Rupp. *Celebration in Postwar American Fiction* (Miami: University of Miami Press), 1970, p. 98

A major premise of O'Connor's thinking is that the realm of the Holy interpenetrates this world and affects it. It is the workings of this mystery that she was most concerned with demonstrating in her fiction. By her own explanation, the grotesquerie of her stories is directly related to her Christian perspective. This is a point that has bothered some critics, who feel that a Christian view of life ought to tend toward the reconciliation of opposites, toward wholeness and affirmation, whereas the grotesque is by definition distorted, incomplete, or incongruous. To these critics O'Connor might have responded that they were trying to claim what has not been fully achieved: while opposites might be reconciled in Christ, the world was not yet reconciled to Him; we may know of the existence of wholeness because of Christ, but we are not yet whole ourselves. O'Connor's Christian conception of wholeness gave her the background against which she saw man in his present condition as, at best, incomplete; even the good, she felt, has a grotesque face, because "in us the good is something under construction."

O'Connor found elements of her Christian vision of man in both the religion and history of her native region. The legacy of a revivalistic past has lingered longer in the South than in any other region of the country, and while O'Connor hesitated to describe the South as Christ-centered, she did feel it to be Christ-haunted. The South's history included a major experience—the loss of the Civil War—in which O'Connor found important theological implications. She saw the loss of the Civil War as the South's collective and personal experience of the biblical story of the Fall. . . .

While she was an artist of the highest caliber, she thought of herself as a prophet, and her art was the medium for her prophetic message. It was her intention that her stories should shock, that they should bring the reader to encounter a vision he could face only with difficulty or with outright repugnance. And she wanted her vision not only to be seen for what it was but to be taken seriously. She was confident enough of her artistic powers to believe this would happen, even if it took fifty or a hundred years.

Dorothy Tuck McFarland. *Flannery O'Connor* (New York: Frederick Ungar, 1976), pp. 1–2, 114

What *is* the serious religious writer to do in an age like ours? He cannot ignore his readers, nor can he bow before them. For Flannery O'Connor the solution was to shock them—to assault their modern rationalism and undermine it to the point where the readers themselves would have to admit its limitations. She wanted to make them *see*. . . . When she spoke of "ever more violent means," I think she was referring to the total structure of her works, not just to one set of characteristics, however important. The plots themselves were carefully and deliberately structured to shake the reader's confidence in his own rational abilities, and thus to make him see Christ's suffering and man's redemption as the basic fact of human life. . . .

Flannery O'Connor wrote the way she did because that was the only way she felt she could write to make her readers respond the way she thought they should. She wanted the actual experience of reading to be itself a process of reorientation, a refocusing of the mind's light toward what she once told Robert Fitzgerald was that great "sense of Mystery that cannot be accounted for by any human formula." Every element in the stories and novels had to be carefully constructed so that the reader would be sure to be affected by it. His eyes would finally, she hoped, be burned clean, so that like Tarwater's at the end of *The Violent Bear It Away,* "they would never be used for ordinary sights again."

It would be no easy job to reorient these mulish modern readers, Miss O'Connor knew. She must build her stories out of steel, so they would be tougher than the reader's will to resist. But at the same time she could not be too direct, or the readers might find out what she was up to and stop reading before the book had a chance to affect them. Her primary strategy, in this assault on modern skepticism, was to entice the reader into believing that he was seeing things from the author's point of view, only to pull the rug out from under him at the story's end. This shock—the realization that the author actually saw things from a wholly unexpected perspective—would, perhaps, demonstrate to the reader that his rationalistic twentieth-century vision, which he had thought so sophisticated, was wholly inadequate to deal with the mysteries of divine grace at work in the world. By showing him some manifestations of that "amazing grace" in her fiction, Miss O'Connor hoped to have prepared the reader to look for it, and to welcome it as it occurred in his own life.

Robert H. Brinkmeyer, Jr. Southern Review.
Spring, 1979, pp. 314–15

Flannery O'Connor never wrote a first-person narrative, nor did she ever completely surrender her third-person prose to the limitations of a subjective point of view. She undertook the offices of writer with all the freedoms of traditional storytelling, assuming the omniscient manipulation of fictional destinies with an unquestioning ease. One wonders if she could have written otherwise, for a subjective perspective in fiction writing narrows the authority of the given account; it implies that there can be another point of view, a different set of meanings to assigned events. In turn, this relativity suggests that one can live in doubt, that one can live, as Lionel Trilling has said, "by means of a question" instead of by an unassailable religious persuasion.

This was exactly what O'Connor did not want to do—to concede that there could be more than one viable interpretation of reality. In her opinion, conflicts between ways of being constituted a challenge to Christian truth that could not be brooked, and with this certainty of outlook, she reserved final narrative authority for herself. For the hard of hearing she would "shout," for the blind she would "draw large and startling figures." Yet with all this allusion to rhetoric, to bold and unambiguous fictional strategies,

O'Connor was curiously reluctant to exploit the potential of the omniscient voice. Rarely in all these tales of bizarre and violent experience does she reflect on the meaning of the grotesquery or give explicit value to fictional events. She infrequently enunciates in her fictional world what she had no trouble conveying in personal life—that Christian orthodoxy was the consistent measure of experience. This is usually left for the reader to infer, to come upon through the indirections of allusion, incongruities, and distorted hyperbole. . . .

To the extent that she called folly by its right name, she was a truth teller in both a doctrinally condoned and a more widely recognized sense. This is an accomplishment that remains unaffected by the limits of inference. Even when unembellished by revealed analogical implications, Flannery O'Connor's work retains a weight of human concern that makes the reading of the fiction a disturbing encounter, valuable to readers of any persuasion because its haunting truth rests on sharable experience rather than prohibitive religious allusion.

Carol Shloss. *Flannery O'Connor's Dark Comedies: The Limits of Inference* (Baton Rouge: Louisiana State University Press, 1980), pp. 102–3, 128

Flannery O'Connor . . . is acknowledged today as one of the greatest American post-war writers of short stories. Her writing is religious in nature and intent. In her fiction she seeks to explicate her characters and plots in terms of theological meaning. Her primary concern is the operation of grace in the world, that moment of gratuitous interaction between the divine and the human. She asserts that the action of grace marks the definitive event in each person's life. She holds that cooperation with God's grace is normative for the artist and that the reality of grace is especially suited for portrayal through the narrative form. Knowing that fiction is not capable of portraying the essence of grace, but that it is able successfully to depict the operations of grace, she explores a wide range of theological assertions concerning these encounters between God and human persons in her fiction.

Lorine M. Getz. *Nature and Grace in Flannery O'Connor's Fiction* (Lewiston, New York: Edwin Mellen Press, 1982), pp. 2–3

In an early press interview, Flannery O'Connor stated: "Mine is a comic art, but that does not detract from its seriousness." This is a typical example of her wry understatement. O'Connor's readers know that the comic tone of her works, and the art that produces that tone, adds greatly to the seriousness of her stories. Her comic art is the working out of a vision of reality which measures what is and what could be, and laughs at the infinite distance between them. This laugh is not one of disdain or despondency or superiority, but rather one of deep understanding. Within the limits of her vision, Flannery O'Connor "knew what was in man," and that knowledge made her hopeful that her stories would both amuse her readers and move their hearts. . . .

O'Connor's omniscient narrator voice, though not intrusive in the usual sense, is a complex aggregate: the comic and ironic voice of the *eiron;* the rational and moral voice of the chorus; the prophetic and apocalyptic voice of the oracle. These speak in turn of the comically distorted, the morally grotesque, and the mystically Terrible. The *eiron* creates; the chorus judges; and the oracle condemns, though sometimes it redeems. In plain words the voice is amused, engaged, and delighted; solid, stable, and reliable; arch, a little smug, perhaps a touch vindictive. To my ear the complex voice is incarnated in the witty but sardonic comment on the dedication of her first story collection to the Fitzgeralds: "Nine stories about original sin, with my compliments."

> Kathleen Feeley, S.S.N.D. In Karl-Heinz
> Westarp and Jan Nordby Gretkind, eds.
> *Realist of Distance: Flannery O'Connor*
> *Revisited* (Aarhus, Denmark: Aarhus
> University Press, 1987), pp. 66, 80–81

The family in O'Connor's stories bears no resemblance to most we associate with Southern fiction, although unquestionably they are of the Gothic, grotesque school. There is, as one critic states, "horror . . . at the core of family life," in the stories of O'Connor. In all her work, parents and children want and expect things of each other that can never be given. Either the parents are cold, calculating, selfish, or totally indifferent to the child, as in her stories of parents with small children; or the children are people who are grown up only chronologically, who remain adolescents, totally dependent, hostile, and filled with a sense of self-importance and superiority. In the smoldering atmosphere of anger, rejection, and repulsion, violence usually erupts. If the child does not kill himself or the parent directly, something he does leads to an act which is a type of violation. Fear and repression often bring about a displacement of anger. Sometimes, but this is rare, the result of the explosive act is the beginning of understanding. But more often, the reader is left to sort out the effects of the final deeds on the characters.

> Helen S. Garson. In Kerl-Heinz Westarp
> and Jen Nordby Gretkind, eds. *Realist of*
> *Distance: Flannery O'Connor Revisited*
> (Aarhaus, Denmark: Aarhaus University
> Press, 1987), p. 113

Love is . . . at the very core of Flannery O'Connor's fiction. The affection shrouded in Tarwater's personality seems still more inaccessible in the sensibility of his author, whose work has aroused even greater consternation than that stirred by the teenage murderer. Most readers come to terms with the perplexity surrounding O'Connor through familiar categories set forth by the grotesque or the romance or the allegory; some enthusiasts rely on regional and doctrinal explanations for violence in the writing of an orthodox Christian; and a few commentators take psychoanalytical approaches to the eccentricities of her characters. O'Connor's art warrants such varied tacks to clarify her startling dramas, and benefits from lively argument among her critics. . . . The initial assumption is that O'Connor depicts primarily the moral ruin that attends modern apostasy. That observation is so compelling that it doubles as the final comment on her art. The debate has taken as its central issue the ways in which O'Connor defines the peculiar notion of evil that brings about the spiritual waste she contemplates.

The focus of this controversy misses the Flannery O'Connor who wants to stop and greet each reader and who stands troubled, sometimes hurt, by the hostile response to her open hand. The ardor that readers find permeating her letters flows as well through her fiction. To recover this warmth of spirit we need a new perspective on her stories and novels. The question that cleaves to the bone is not the one constantly posed: What is the source of sin in her characters? It is exactly the opposite: How do sinners atone for sin? The result of sin is to destroy human nature by degrading the image of God that is the human person's glory, whereas the result of grace and retribution is to restore human nature to loving fullness. Read by the light of salvific possibilities, O'Connor's fiction can be seen as not only clarifying the idea of God for the unbelieving modern mind, but also as modifying our image of the human person.

> Richard Giannone. *Flannery O'Connor and the Mystery of Love* (Urbana: University of Illinois Press, 1989), pp. 2–3

After reading one of O'Connor's stories, one is often left most strongly with a visual image or the memory of a grotesque or violent plot. What sticks in the mind is the image of welts rising on a tattooed back or of a man preaching against Jesus from the hood of an old car. O'Connor's works are full of ideas. They are animated by Christian doctrines and address many of the issues that agitate modern culture. But they never show the least tendency to become tracts or essays instead of stories. (As her letters and lectures show, O'Connor could state her positions on both religious and cultural matters in plain prose when she chose to.) Her exploration of the mystery of the Incarnation is always the story of a tattooed man, never a précis of the Baltimore catechism; the vehicle for her attack on the American Adam figure is always the story of a man with a beat-up car, never an analysis of Emerson or Cooper.

By embodying the most lofty Christian doctrines in stories that seem grotesque and violent, O'Connor reclaimed a large region of literature for the religious writer. . . . Thanks in part to O'Connor's example, fiction writers who see the world in the light of the Christian mysteries can no longer be expected to observe any stifling decorum.

O'Connor's techniques have, of course, influenced writers who do not share her faith. The use of violence and the grotesque in much recent fiction seems heavily indebted to O'Connor's work. Violence has, of course, been one of the hallmarks of modern fiction throughout this century, but in O'Connor's work unexpected violence not only shocks the reader, it also marks those moments when a character is confronted with the offer of grace. Many recent writers use unexpected violence in a similar way, marking some epiphany for a character, often one that is in no way religious.

Brian Abel Ragan. *A Wreck on the Road to Damascus: Innocence, Guilt, and Conversion in Flannery O'Connor* (Chicago: Loyola University Press, 1989), pp. 197–98

ODIO, EUNICE (COSTA RICA–MEXICO) 1922–74

Woman, in all Central American and Caribbean cultures, has been the guardian, the symbolic unity of a centripetal desire to defend the identity threatened by empires that have been, that are, and that are to come.

The woman [like Julia de Burgos or Eunice Odio] who has refused to accept her role as passive transmitter of this reflexive and passive nostalgia has always been the object of finger-pointing scorn. . . .

Alfonso Reyes described Eunice Odio, in her time, as "the great poet of the Americas." Carlos Pellicer and other writers paid homage to her in a "Corona funebre para Eunice Odio" (Funeral wreath for Eunice Odio).

Juan Liscano, in his introduction to the *Antologia de Eunice Odio* (Eunice Odio Anthology) . . . decried the fact that "in Latin America the hardly credible phenomenon can occur of an exceptional poet, crushed, dying in poverty, without a platform, without readers, and without a publisher." Humberto Díaz Casanueva extends Liscano's denunciation, assuring us that, "impoverished, misunderstood, unpublished, she does not even have a page in the pompous, vulgar, and commercial anthologies of the last few years, which build up and repeat names and create reputations."

Eunice Odio's first book, *Los elementos terrestres* (The terrestrial elements), winner of the prestigious September 15th Central American Prize in Guatemala in 1947, provides a possible reading that hitherto has not been suggested, in which the rules of life chosen by Eunice Odio from her earliest childhood are given. . . . [Such a reading shows] the fact that Eunice Odio lived against the grain of the existential and social paradigms that her times imposed on her role of "good woman." . . .

In spite of personal dramas, which pass irreversibly into memory from anecdote and from memory to the forgotten and from the forgotten to nothingness, the daring of Eunice Odio in accepting that cursed role that [Octavio]

Paz [in "Mascaras Mexicanas"] depicts as marginal, in the face of a dominant machismo, was one of the cornerstones of a great body of work, which will undoubtedly take its place in our literature and translate that paradigmatic "opening" into what the ancient Aztecs called "flower and song" and that a great poet of our day expresses this way: "and the furrow opens between the flower and the lip."

Laureano Alban. *Revista Iberoamericano.*
53:138–39, 1987, pp. 325–27, 329–39

The main themes of her texts deal with creation, love, mankind's fate, the mystery of life, loneliness and the plurality of the creator/poet. Her poetry may be classified as *creacionismo,* especially that of *El transito de fuego* (The path of fire), her last book. Although recognized by well-known critics . . . as an outstanding poet, her lyrical texts have not been translated or reprinted. Her prose writings, which include essays, and short stories had been scattered in magazines all over the world until they were recently collected in *La obra en prosa de Eunice Odio* (Eunice Odio's prose work). . . .

The lyrical texts in . . . [*Antologia, Rescate de un gran poeta* (Anthology, redemption of a great poet), edited by Juan Liscano] allow the reader to follow, in poetry and in life, Odio's evolution towards a deep, fanatic Catholic faith. "Arcangel Miguel" (The Archangel Michael), considered a masterpiece of Spanish American poetry, is one example. Last but not least, it offers the interesting collection of letters sent by Odio to Liscano from 1965 to 1974. These letters not only give unusual insights into her poems, psychology, and life, but some are masterpieces in epistolary literature.

Los elementos terrestres (The elements of earth) is a collection of eight long poems written in free verse, with a mystical-erotic theme and a cosmic conception of reality. The connotative power of the lyric images suggests the cyclic course of nature, of love, and of poetic creation. Theme, tone, metaphors, key words, and rhythmic devices (i.e., repetition, alliteration, stress) are reminiscent of the *Song of Songs.* At the same time, they remind us of Saint John of the Cross's "Cantico espiritual." . . .

Written in free verse from 1948 to 1954, Odio's masterpiece [*El Transito del fuego*] is conceived in the form of a transcendental dialogue between the creator Ion (the poet), different mythical beings, and the chorus which transmits to the whole a dramatic and metaphysical quality. It is divided into four parts: "Integracion de los Padres" (Integration of the fathers); "Proyecto de Mi Mismo," (Design of myself); "Proyectos de los Frutos," (Designs of the fruits); and "Alegría de los Creadores," (Joy of the creators)," representing an allegory of the fate of mankind's Creator.

Rima R. de Vallbona. In Diane E. Marting,
ed. *Women Writers of Spanish America*
(Westport, Connecticut: Greenwood Press,
1987), pp. 283–85

One of the most remarkable Costa Rican poets of the twentieth century, Odio began to write very early in her life and started to publish her poems in 1945 in the journal *Repertorio Americano* of San José. She was awarded the prestigious "15th of September" prize for poetry for her volume *Los elementos terrestres* (The element of earth), which was published in Guatemala in 1948. Odio became a Guatemalan citizen, and continued to write poems, many of which were published only after her death in an anthology she edited herself, called *Territorio del alba y otros poemas* (1974; Territory of dawn and other poems). She wrote her second book, *Zona en territorio del alba* (Zone in the territory of dawn) between 1946 and 1948 and it was published in 1953 in Argentina, where it was much acclaimed. A year later, she completed a very long poem called *El tránsito de fuego* (1957; Path of fire), which was published in San Salvador. After her move to Mexico in 1955, she worked as a reporter for *El Diario de Hoy* and wrote articles for many different journals. Odio spent over two years in the U.S., and wrote extensively about the experience of exile. As well as poetry and essays, she wrote at least three stories in her later years, one of which, *El rastro de la mariposa* (1968; The trace of the butterfly), was published in booklet form.

Odio's poetry evolved over the course of her writing life from traditional verses in the early and mid-1940s to mystical-sensual-biblical allusion in *Los elementos terrestres* of 1948, to techniques of surrealism and other vanguard movements in *Zona en territorio del alba* of 1953, and finally to the lyric allegory of *El tránsito de fuego* of 1957 and subsequent poems and stories. Her early poems assimilate and use traditional lyric forms and often outspokenly advocate political activism, particularly in regard to the Spanish Civil War. *Los elementos terrestres,* a collection of eight long poems in free verse, derives its unity from the repeated lyrical insistence on natural cyclical process: night and day, the seasons, the rhythms of birth and death, love, and poetic creation. Allusions and interwoven paraphrases of the Song of Songs, Job, Genesis, and the Psalms intensify the fusion of mysticism and sensuality.

Zona en territorio del alba is far more experimental in form and in ideas. The book collects a varied series of poems in free verse about such themes as the importance of childhood, friendship, and the various artistic media: poetry, dance, and music. *El tránsito de fuego,* usually considered to be Odio's culminating masterwork, is an extensive poem, nearly five hundred pages long, in the form of an allegorical drama with many participant voices and choruses. The central plot revolves around the effort to understand Ion, the creator of the cosmos. Odio's passion for the creation and elaboration of myths culminated in her celebration of a cult to the Archangel Michael, dramatized in one of her best-known poems, "Arcangel Miguel" (Archangel Michael).

Odio has been widely recognized as a poet of extraordinary lyric intensity. Her poems celebrate creation, imagination, erotic love, and, above all, light. Her major poems have been interpreted in many different ways, but it is mainly the luminous harmony of her verse that impresses the reader.

Mary G. Berg. In Steven R. Serafin and
Walter D. Glanze, eds. *Encyclopedia of
World Literature in the 20th Century* (New
York: Continuum, 1993), pp. 460–61

O'FAOLAIN, JULIA (IRELAND) 1932–

If a significant proportion of the new Irish writing is concerned with the survival of human values under reductive economic pressure, Ireland also has, in Julia O'Faolain, an outstanding satirist of the affluent society. For a number of excellent reasons, her work is different in kind to that of other [contemporary Irish] writers. . . . Born and brought up in Ireland, the daughter of Sean O'Faolain, she is married to an American Renaissance specialist, has lived in France and Italy, and now lives in the United States. Consequently, she is, along with Francis Stuart and Aidan Higgins, among the very few Irish writers who are truly international in range. Sean O'Faolain and Mary Lavin have both set stories in Italy: Julia O'Faolain has been able to write, as it were, from inside Italian life. Where she differs most sharply, however, from other Irish writers is in choosing to work from within the contemporary flux of modes and passions. Her characters generally have comparative economic freedom. Not being pinned down in one situation, they escape that terminal haunting that gives most Irish fiction its metaphysical unease. They do not escape, though, essentially the same challenges: only in their case the pressure comes from within, generally as a conflict between the direction of their own vitality and the assumptions of the way they have been brought up. Sally Tyndal, in *Godded and Codded,* is as much an explorer after the true nature of herself as McGahern's Elizabeth Reegan; only where Elizabeth, dying of cancer in her mid-forties, searches for meaning through reflection, Sally, in her twenties and hungry for experience, searches through action. To call Julia O'Faolain a satirist, as I did a few lines back, is to do her work only partial justice: it suggests the incisiveness of her talent—for wit and verbal devastation she has few equals among her contemporaries— but not the strength nor the subtlety of her concern. There is a power of mind behind her work, as well as an irreverently perceptive eye, that catches the intensity of human drives, the essential seriousness of the effort to live, without swallowing any of the trends in self-deception. She is an acute observer, who is involved at a level of concern deeper than the substance or sum of her observations.

Immediately striking in Julia O'Faolain's first collection of short stories, *We Might See Sights!* (1968), is the use of surreal imagery, particularly of expressions: "the wrinkles in her face moved in the sun like the long-jointed legs of agonizing insects." Agonizing can have a transitive, as well as an intransitive use. Age, disappointment or lust, like medieval vices, become monsters that take over the flesh: "multimouthed animalities stirred beneath her skin." . . .

In her first novel, *Godded and Codded* (1970) this verbal skill is employed to show the contradictions involved in being young, awake and Irish. The first contradiction is that in Ireland it is the old who seem young: they had enough excitement in the Troubles to give them a perpetual lien on romance, despite the decades of stolid respectability since. The young are up-staged, and yet still bereft of advice, for an unspoken double-standard operates.

Roger Garfitt. In Douglas Dunn, ed. *Two Decades of Irish Writing* (Chester Springs, Pennsylvania: Dufour, 1975), pp. 239–40

Julia O'Faolain's distinguished novel [*No Country for Young Men*], with finely controlled time-shifts, involves three generations. Years ago, Judith had been shoved unwillingly into a convent, because she might have known too much about the death of an American fundraiser in dreadful 1922. She was later given electric shock treatment, in circumstances increasingly suspicious. The convent is now dispersed, Judith packed off to unwilling relatives bemused with their own troubles. Her memories, scattered, raddled, now committed to tape, may endanger a slice of heroic Republican history. Old muck conceals nasty matter. Too many reputations were ambiguously earned, a dead hero-patriot is vulnerable, likewise the murdered American. A scandal may emerge about lost party funds and the clandestine extremist associations of political respectables. . . .

The link with Yeats's ideal Byzantium observed in the novel's title is ironic. This Ireland more relates to the actual Byzantium, with its maimings, vendettas, hypocrisies, theological nonsense, and threatened dispensations. As with Imperial Rome, one senses a community with too little to do, a lack of the useful, with wounds left untreated, a coarsened imagination blocked by too much history, under-used strengths finding malice the easiest remedy for mediocrity. Now, the demagogic film will never be made, the escape from a hopeless marriage will fail, the young son will probably end in violence, shocked by the futility of his elders—the bottle, the maunderings over end-lessly lost chances, the cowardly ambushes enlarged into heroic battles, the spells woven by the dead, the imaginary and the contrived. . . .

The imagery derives from observation rather than the overblown gener-alizations that infect so many of the people, seen here with unusual propor-tions of sympathy and detachment.

Peter Vansittart. *London Magazine.* July, 1980, pp. 91–92

The contemporary Irish story seems to be to offer a paradigm of the condition of Ireland herself, both as she exists within herself and in relation to the world outside, and in the stories of Julia O'Faolain, the brilliant daughter of Sean, we see traditionally Irish themes merging into the Jamesean International Subject, though opening out beyond the mutual involvement of Britain and the United States.

Her range is wide. There is the story "It's a Long Way to Tipperary," which deals with the problems of the Irishman forced, in some sense, into Englishness. Cudahy enlists as a private in the British Army in 1914, rises to the rank of captain, and marries an English woman of better class than himself. He eventually comes back to Ireland a renegade twice over, a renegade Catholic through his wife's influence and a renegade Irishman.

"It's a Long Way to Tipperary" is at once funny almost to the point of farce, a hard-headed and moving story of a specifically Irish dilemma. Julia O'Faolain is a writer of great flexibility, reminiscent to some degree of Kipling in her diversity of scene. Thus, besides "It's a Long Way to Tipperary," *Man in the Cellar,* the volume in which it appears, contains two other brilliant stories in modes very different from it and from each other. One is "This Is My Body," which is set in a convent in sixth-century Gaul and is a dramatization of the impact of Christianity on people still pagan in feeling and impulse. The other is "Man in the Cellar" itself, and here the International Subject is subsumed in another subject, one we may call in rough shorthand Women's Lib. It is an index of the story's success that it will almost certainly recall Poe. The story is in the form of a long letter to her mother-in-law written by a young Englishwoman describing the revenge she has taken on her domineering and sadistic Italian husband. "Marriage," writes Miss O'Faolain in her last paragraph, "like topiary, distorts growth."

"Romantic Ireland's dead and gone." Certainly the Ireland of today is a different Ireland from Yeats's and Joyce's or even O'Connor's. But, as the short stories being written at the present time show, it is no less Ireland, for all that it has moved into the modern world. The Irish dimension in these stories of the 1960s and 1970s is as pronounced as it has been at any time in the history of Irish writing in English, and in this respect the contemporary Irish story may be held up as a model.

Walter Allen. *The Short Story in English*
(Oxford: Oxford University Press, 1981),
pp. 393–94

Julia O'Faolain often creates sexual encounters that are also encounters between cultures: Algerian and Irish in her first novel, *Godded and Codded;* Italian and Irish in many of her short stories: Californian and Irish in her recent *No Country for Young Men.* In doing so, she inevitably distances her lovers from one another, to throw into high relief the whole issue of differences between sexual partners—differences ignored or flattened in more conventional love stories—and therefore to focus our attention on the woman's apparent need to abandon or re-fashion her identity.

The protagonist of *No Country for Young Men*, a researcher from Los Angeles, finds a unique excitement in an affair with a Dublin woman who still takes sex—and sin—seriously. *The Obedient Wife* partly reverses this situation, and partly toys with it. Carla Verdi, from Rome and Milan, who is serious about her responsibilities as wife and mother, finds herself among the temptations of Los Angeles. Her obedience is to her absent husband's advice—orders—which are to explore the sexual freedom around her, to have an affair, acquire experience. His motives are not entirely clear, but are hinted with subtle ambiguity. . . .

Carla's choice is a Catholic priest, who is initially attracted by her dedication to marriage, her stability, even by her good cooking. For her there is no sense of supernatural risk in the affair. She comes of an old anti-clerical family. Nor does the priest seem much troubled by sin (I am probably too ingenious in imagining that Carla's last name puns on Graham Greene, who treats this sort of affair more portentously). His easy slide into sex is perhaps a further reminder of the easy morality along the Santa Monica littoral, as is the book's recurrence of casual and temporary matings, of infidelity impossible to condemn because fidelity itself can hardly be imagined. . . .

"Her life had been structured by rules as easily tested as a recipe for sauce," Carla muses, as she tries to decide whether to let her old personality "dissolve. . . . What did happen to a family when the mother gave these [rules] up? Surely it must collapse like an umbrella with a broken spine? Like a belly released from a corset or a stern old society robbed too suddenly of hierarchy and belief?" When she coolly appraises both her marriage and her affair, and recognizes her own commitment to "keeping things together," she has convincingly liberated herself to make a choice on her own terms, in response to her own needs. That it is a convincing choice is due to the care with which Julia O'Faolain has slowly developed her character, and placed her in a network of memories, affections, and desires that define and support her without stifling her, that paradoxically allow her independence.

Robert Tracy. *Irish Literary Supplement.*
Fall, 1983, p. 29

As the accomplished novelist Julia O'Faolain's sixth book [*The Obedient Wife*] begins, Carla Verdi—the Florentine wife of the title—waits in a rented Los Angeles house for her unfaithful husband's return from Italy. She and her 13-year-old son, Maurizio, have been waiting for three months, and the autumn rains have come, bringing a mud slide that destroys her neighbor's house. From the rain and mud appears Leo, a handsome young priest, who helps in the crisis. Carla is under orders from her husband to learn more about the world—by which he means she should have an affair—but she resists obeying until he reappears, ready to resume their marriage. Then she begins an affair with the priest. When husband and child return to Italy, she must decide if she will join them or start a new life with her lover, who has left the priesthood. Carla is an intelligent but unresponsive heroine, passive and judgmental. Even in matters of love, she is analytical and skeptical, just when the reader would like her to get carried away. The city and Carla's friends are slightly off kilter and unconvincing, seen in snatches through the eyes of a reclusive foreigner: the compound of an Arab family even more mistrustful of America than Carla is; the radio show of an opportunistic Briton; the messy love life of Carla's friend Jane, who gets breast cancer and loses her lover in one blow. Carla's disobedient son is the most convincing, passionate and sympathetic character in this distant novel, and he alone tries to deal with the contradictions his mother muses over. Significantly, Maurizio is the only character damaged by the social and marital problems the novel presents.

Laura Furman. *The New York Times*.
December 1, 1985, p. 24

A young woman, Anne, travels to Florence from her native Ireland after her mother's death, the better to understand her mother's life. The mother, at nearly the same age, served as *au pair* to an aristocratic Italian family and, discovered in a romantic adventure, was dismissed. Sweet memories sharpened by loss were to color the rest of her days, and the sensibilities of her young daughter as well. The father, also dead, never counted, never shared in the mother's erotic daydreams or the intimacies conveyed to the daughter. "Passion, in Mummy's book, excused all, but without a high, hot blaze of it sex was tawdry." "Mummy's reluctance to acknowledge disappointing truths had left Anne leery of fantasy—especially Mummy's." Anne comes, finally, to absorb "a horror of the unlived life."

In Julia O'Faolain's *Irish Signorina* the daughter must throw off the epic of the mother and create her own story. Ironically, she very nearly repeats the drama she meant to understand. Invention and deception are engendered in all family sagas, and Ms. O'Faolain's eighth book is full of these—plus a modest mystery that discretion dictates we preserve for her readers.

The premise of this novel is an interesting one, yet in this novelist's hands the characters and the story are strangely operatic (one scene is actually played with a character hidden "comically" behind a couch). The cast includes the Marchesa Cavalcanti, an ailing matriarch; the Marchese Bonaccorso, her aging suitor; Guido, the Marchesa's unhappy son, Neri, the passionate and political grandson; Ida, the loyal maid, and so forth. Further, to continue the comparison, the libretto seems to exist just to prop up the music—in this case, the writing—which is speculative, ruminative, descriptive and overly gorgeous, as if too much had been made of this writer's gift for nuance and detail.

Ms. O'Faolain is clearly a gifted and devout observer. She writes of "Olive groves and towers awash in . . . spinach-water light," a house like a "conch sour with the smells and echoes of dead tides," "a skin of wrinkled damp" clinging to windowpanes, and so on. But the descriptions get away from her. At an intense narrative moment, when the reader needs a no-nonsense answer from a character, we are obliged to observe that his "head bobbed in the dimness like a parsnip in simmering broth."

Superfatted descriptions, together with a surfeit of quotations and mythological references, finally topple the task at hand. The destruction is complete when the characters are betrayed. Just when you think they are about to speak, out comes the writer's voice. The result is that they all seem to have an uncanny literary sensibility, an epigram for every occasion, and the wisdom of the ages. It is not wise, perhaps, to bend credulity all out of shape just when you're bringing the ship home. Readers are so trusting, so grateful for dignified prose. But when they're been promised a mystery, told that lives are at stake and love is on the boil, it's more prudent to depict irony than to discourse upon it, sword in hand, so to speak.

Julia Whedon. New York Times Book Review. July 20, 1986, pp. 2–3

Julia O'Faolain is one of several contemporary Irish women writers who are attempting a revision of Irish myths, history, cultural and political attitudes. Apparently telling a tale of the sequence of Irish "Troubles" in No Country for Young Men, O'Faolain uncovers a destructive pattern that, despite its inevitable trail of personal and political disaster, persists through myth and history into the present time. O'Faolain's central character, Gráinne O'Malley, alerts the reader to O'Faolain's myth, when she tells the American filmmaker James Duffy that she is named after the central figure in the Diarmuid and Gráinne legend. According to Eóin Nesson's rendering of the legend, Fionn Mac Cumhal, the general of the Fianna warriors in Ireland, decided to assuage his loneliness by marrying Gráinne, the beautiful daughter of King Cormac. But Gráinne is reluctant to marry the aged Fionn because she loved Diarmuid, one of Fionn's young warriors, put geasa, similar to obligations of honor in an Arthurian legend, on Diarmuid, and he was obliged to flee with her. Furious, Fionn sent hosts of the Fianna after the runaway lovers, to battle the forces supporting Diarmuid and Gráinne. Much land was destroyed and many lives lost before Fionn, aided by magic, succeeded in killing Diarmuid. Still desiring Gráinne's favors, Fionn remained away from the Fianna pleading his cause. When, for the sake of her children, Gráinne finally consented to return with Fionn to the Fianna, Oisin, bitter at the destruction, blamed, not Fionn for what he had wrought, but Gráinne.

Order then is restored to the Fianna when Gráinne forgoes her own desires and accepts the principle of conquest. As a woman, Gráinne is related to Ireland. . . .

The madness that forces women to act against their best judgments and against their best interests is, in No Country for Young Men, associated with the political confusion that has affected Ireland for over sixty years. The possibility of immediate change is remote, but there are some optimistic glimmerings in O'Faolain's work. In a work that emphasizes the preservative power of the bog, we might expect . . . memories to be preserved, and we are given strong suggestions that she has taped and so preserved them. . . .

[As] O'Faolain's text preserves the truth about the fictional O'Malley family, so the myths and texts of history have preserved, albeit in scattered formations, the truths of the past. O'Faolain challenges her readers to a new beginning, then, not through the traditional Irish way of physical revolution, but through textual revolution. The "glowings" are uncertain; Gráinne stands alone, but male history itself *is*. O'Faolain shows . . . the consequences of following principle at the expense of community. A wider perspective in general leads to a wider level of tolerance; faint as they are, O'Faolain's "glowings" suggest the benefit to the Irish people in political leaders' abandoning the predominantly male model of human judgment and establishing instead a wider model, one that incorporates both male and female moral perspectives. Incorporating the vision of the Gráinnes and the Kathleens, this wider model might eventually incorporate the vision of the majority of the Irish people, north and south, Protestant and Catholic. But it is the women who will have to effect the change: being largely unaware of the injustice and danger inherent in a pattern which benefits them, men will act only when women place a compelling vision of human harmony before them—a vision which, if clearly seen, may finally prove as irresistible as and may, indeed, be Gráinne's ancient *geis*.

Ann Weekes. Eire-Ireland. 21, 1986,
pp. 90–91, 101–2

No Country for Young Men by Julia O'Faolain, "one of the most accomplished Irish writers of her generation" is, as Jay Halio has described, "a darkly comic stor[y] concerned with the position of women." Dark in that it certainly has its share of death and mystery, the novel nevertheless retains a twisted touch of comedy, which challenges the readers' emotions; we laugh sometimes only because otherwise we would cry. This sense of painful comedy is embodied by the women characters throughout the story. For, despite a title which might lead one to believe otherwise, *No Country for Young Men* is unavoidably about Irish women. In particular, it is about Judith Clancy, the old mad nun great-aunt of Gráinne and Michael. Through Judith we see how the lives of women in Ireland have been, are, and no doubt will continue to be affected by war, politics, men, and the Church. What sets Judith apart from other women is that she has dared act on her own initiative—refusing to be completely squelched by the limitations generally placed on women— and has suffered punishment for doing so for the rest of her life. Furthermore, Judith is symbolic of Ireland itself, bringing to mind the Caitlin Ni Houlihan/ Shan von Vocht myth. Although Ireland ultimately controls her behavior, Judith never loses her passionate love for it; indeed, she lets nothing stand between her and what she believes to be the good of Ireland and its people. . . .

Because of the construction of the novel, Judith, the dried up old hag, is simultaneously the dynamic young figure of Caitlin Ni Houlihan. As a vibrant, passionate young woman she symbolizes the "magic, irresistible lure" described in the old myth. Kathleen's statement "[Sparky]'s starry-eyed about Holy Ireland. Caitlin Ni Houlihan . . . has yer man's interest" is loaded with implications of Judith as Caitlin once we discover Sparky's attraction to the younger sister. This Caitlin Ni Houlihan, however, struggles against any attraction men may have for her, perhaps because of her superstitious fear of the luring power of a woman. Yet, intentionally or not, she does finally lead a young man to his death for the sake of the Ireland she loves.

Laura B. Van Dale. *Colby Quarterly.* 27,
1991, pp. 17, 25

OGOT, GRACE (KENYA) 1930–

Grace Ogot . . . treats of both traditional rural (even pre-colonial) themes, and others developed amid the paraphernalia of the modern city. In her collection of short stories *Land without Thunder* (1968) these themes are juxtaposed and we may study what modification of her earlier Luo style Mrs. Ogot makes when she comes to treat of the problems of a young African secretary in Nairobi fending off her lecherus employers. . . .

In a passage from the very effective title story about a haunted fisherman whose cousins have drowned in the Kavironedo Gulf, his anxious young wife goes to draw water at dawn:

That morning when Apiyo went to fetch water she studied the pond carefully before dipping her pan in the water to fill it. The reflection of her face stared back at her, moving rhythmically with the gentle tide. She drew water with the little calabash, filled her mouth and then spat it towards the sunrise.

"Thu! may we have peace in the family, today and forever, may Owila's health be assured."
She filled her waterpot and hurried home.

Perhaps the only obvious "vernacular" feature here is the single word "Thu." The whole scene is described in a bare, simple straightforward English, but *what* is described locates the action for us in a very distinctive way. The whole passage is charged with the sense of a traditional world in which every act or object has potentialities for good or evil; nothing happens by chance and much misfortune can be avoided by knowledge and care. Hence Apiyo, already acutely worried about her husband, studies the pond carefully before deciding where and how to break its surface. The reflection of her face is a reassurance and so is the gentle movement of the pond, in implied contrast to the angry lake that has just swallowed three men of the clan. Then comes the more specifically ritual act of spitting towards the rising sun and breathing a prayer for communal well-being. All these acts precede the drawing of the water, ostensibly the sole purpose of her expedition.

Because Grace Ogot's style is, at its best, a clear glass through which we look at different kinds of action and different worlds of experience, she can apply it likewise to a scene of more acute loneliness and disorientation in the city, where another young girl, recently raped by her employer, seeks to hide her misery from the world:

> Elizabeth drew the curtains to shut out the city and its people from her. She felt out of step with the sophisticated life in towns. She wondered whether she would ever get used to it. A sudden aching longing for her home in the country, the close-knit family life she had shared there, and the security she had felt, gripped her. She took her toilet bag and walked slowly to the washroom—She entered the incinerator room, pulled out her blood-stained nylon pants that Ochola had sent her for Easter, and wrapped them tightly in a brown paper bag. She pressed the incinerator open, and dropped the pants in the fire and let it close. She stood there sobbing quietly as the pale smoke reluctantly curled up towards the sky.

Here too is a kind of ritual, however desolate and sad. the pants are almost a burnt offering to a god who will not be appeased. And the very surroundings—the hard impersonality of the apartment-block, the washroom, the incinerator—speak of that implacability which leads eventually to the girl's suicide.

Gerald Moore. *Dalhousie Review.* 53,
1973–74, pp. 692–93

Lauretta Ngcobo summarizes Kenyan women's writing this way:

> When women write about other women, they often create full-bodied characters who become their mouthpieces. They write to highlight the fears that African women suffer in silence: fears about childlessness, about inadequacies that arise out of sharing husbands, and about pangs of jealousy and loneliness growing from relationships with men whose loyalty is spread too thinly among several women. These writers admit to women's deep need for love and gentle care, not only before marriage, but throughout married life.

Such is the story of Achieng in Ogot's "Bamboo Hut." In her pursuit to maintain her marriage and family, Achieng, the second of nine wives, abandons the girl of a set of twins so that a son heir might bring happiness to the chief. Abandoning the baby of a sex already overrepresented in Mboga's homestead (he has sixteen daughters) proves Achieng's love and devotion for her husband, her devotion to him. Achieng realizes that her husband cannot feel that his chieftancy has been ordained by God and cannot feel that God loves him and the people of Kabido until he has a son. Not only is Achieng concerned with the chief's happiness, but she is also concerned for her own happiness and her daughter's happiness. The daughter wants to move into the bamboo hut where the headed stool is and perhaps where there are a few more creature comforts than in the regular hut. The wife who produces a male heir can move into the chief's bamboo hut. Because Achieng's actions are for the purpose of maintaining love, marriage and family, Mwanzi believes that "Ogot does not seem to hold this kind of acceptance of servility on the part of women as morally wrong."

This pursuit of happiness is most often related to having children, especially male children who hold an important place in African society.

Ogot's characters fare better when they are in tune and more in keeping with their traditional values. Although Elizabeth [in the story of that title] is the exception, Elizabeth commits suicide, because of pregnancy. She feels that her pregnancy as an unwed mother, albeit from rape, is a violation of traditional belief. . . . [She resists her oppression in that] her suicide in Mr. Jimbo's house sends a message to his wife and his family. It shames him, exposes his hypocrisy, his rudeness, which had been hidden under a false dignity. Mwanzi believes that the suicide also averts the shame and misery that come from watching a fatherless child suffer. Thus, her suicide is strength. . . . [Many of Ogot's other women characters] are victims of circumstances and, therefore, can be viewed as strong and positive women, but most of all, keepers of the norm: the nurses in "Old White Witch," Achola in "White Veil," and Achieng in "Bamboo Hut." They are workers; some, like Dora Ayonga, till the fields; some have been educated and have desk jobs. They are mothers or are in search of love, marriage and family. As with all peoples in changing society, there are conflicts—changes in values and, consequently changes in behavior. And, with change, there is conflict. Ogot and [Rebeka] Njau unite as one voice to urge their women to maintain their traditional beliefs. But, if there is change, they are not to change at the risk of destroying values. They are to be in the world, but not of the world.

Margaret A. Reid. *MAWA Review.* 5:2, 1990,
pp. 52, 54

Questions of social morality and the quest for nationhood have preoccupied African writers dealing with post-colonial society. Novelists like Kofi Awoonor, Ayi Kewi Armah, Chinua Achebe, Wole Soyinka, Ngugi wa Thiong'o, and Meja Mwangi have all examined these two dimensions of Africa's post-colonial reality. So has Grace Ogot. The novelists may differ in their ideologies, hence in their social visions. . . .

A study of Grace Ogot's fiction reveals that whereas problems of nationhood loom large in her short novel, *The Graduate,* problems of morality are more central in her short stories, especially such short stories as "The Middle Door," "The Honorable Minister," "Elizabeth," "The Professor," and "Pay Day." Nevertheless, her treatment of moral problems also suggests that post-colonial society's moral problems pose a deadly threat to its quest for national authenticity.

The Graduate deals with three major and intertwined issues all connected with Kenya's quest to overcome her colonial legacy of underdevelopment and sham independence. Ogot identifies problems of getting indigenous manpower, problems of foreign conspiracy against the new nation, and problems of woman's status in the post-colonial scheme of things. . . .

Grace Ogot's short novel *The Graduate* has raised a number of problems facing African states in their quest for an authentic nationhood. . . . [But] because most of Ogot's themes center on women, women issues have also formed the matrix within which socio-historical or socio-political phenomena are discussed. This applies naturally to her exploration of Kenya's quest for authentic nationhood.

Ify Achufusi. *Journal of Commonwealth Literature.* 23, 1992, pp. 179–80, 186–87

OKAMOTO KANOKO (JAPAN) 1889–1959

Kanoko Okamoto does not hesitate to rely on a detailed description of the places where the dramas take place or the clothes characters wear. But all of these descriptions are necessary in terms of her fictional structure. While she is seemingly dwelling upon straightforward descriptions of a town or mountains, she is preparing the reader, by creating sense images of shape, color, smell or sound, for the inner emotional drama that is to come.

When Henry Miller read my translation of "The Story of an Old Geisha," he said rather disappointed, "But nothing actually happens in the story. . . ." I was a little baffled by this comment, because I had felt that the story had such a strong appeal. I thought that an extremely poignant drama was enacted in the inner self of the old geisha. But of course, Henry Miller is right in a sense, for there is no exterior conflict or struggle taking place among the characters. No one passionately falls in love, no one dies a tragic death.

The old geisha's calm face is presented rather casually. Yet if we can see through it, we realize that behind this mask are hidden her deepest emotional dramas. Behind the facade of an understanding, mature old woman, we see her sadness at becoming old, her enormous sense of loss for not living a full life, her strong will trying tenaciously to hold onto the life-force of youth to bloom once again. She may well be a *shite* with a serene female mask in Mugen Noh, who is just an anonymous village woman in the first act, and in the second, reveals her true identity in the dream of a bystander. She is the spirit of a woman, long dead, whose deep-rooted delusions for unfulfilled love give her soul no rest, but force her to linger in the twilight world where the souls of others, perhaps more courageous than hers, can at last fulfill her dreams.

Kazuku Sugisaki. Foreword to Kanoko Okamoto. "The Tale of an Old Geisha." In Anaïs Nin, ed. *The White Bird and Other Stories* (Santa Barbara: Capra Press, 1985), pp. 11–12

In striking contrast to Nin's hyperbolic self-absorption are Okamoto's reticent, observant stories of men and women coping with the changing life of Japan in the 1930s. The title story in particular, with its fond, sad study of older and younger women finding grounds for mutual understanding, recalls some of the great Japanese films.

Sally Lodge. *Publishers Weekly.* March 15, 1985, p. 114

Kanoko began writing *waka,* traditional Japanese poetry, when she was in her teens; her first collection was published when she was twenty-three. . . .

Kanoko's interest in fiction writing and her resolve to learn its art paralleled her dedication to the study of Buddhism. Although she had been writing *waka,* she felt constricted by the brevity of its thirty-one syllables and decided that fiction could more adequately express the complexity of her soul. She spent ten diligent years studying the art of fiction, which included the extended trip to Europe (with stays in Paris, London and Berlin) that was undertaken for her education as well as for her son Taro, an aspiring painter.

Kanoko's first published story, "The Crane was Frail" *(Tsuru wa Yamiki),* is based on her encounters with Akutagawa Ryūnosuke, a writer who killed himself over his irreconcilable conflict between his life and art. It wasn't widely hailed but did receive excellent reviews in *Literary World (Bungakkai),* a journal published by the young writers who started the literary trend of Neo-Sensualism. Her second work, entitled "Mother's Love" *(Boshi Jojō,* 1937; tr. 1982), established Kanoko as a fiction writer. . . .

The images of women in Kanoko's fiction are always very powerful. Her female characters are strong and vital, beautiful and passionate, and they very often overpower the men who are drawn to them. Kanoko was often compared with the male writer Tanizaki Junichiro because of her aestheticism, particularly her elevation of physical beauty to the metaphysical level. The beauty Kanoko worshipped, however, was not abstract but concrete and earthly. Unlike Tanizaki's female protagonists, who were often the reflection

of the author's obsessive adoration, Kanoko's central characters were women
conscious of their strength; they are heroines in a true sense.

Yukiko Tanaka. In *To Live and to Write:
Selections by Japanese Women Writers
1913–1938* (Seattle: Seal Press, 1987),
pp. 199, 201–2

OLDENBOURG, ZOE (FRANCE) 1916–

Apart from diving here and there into stream of consciousness, Oldenbourg
is happy with the methods of nineteenth-century novelists. She has prowled
Paris streets with the eagerness of a Balzac, studied the interiors of homes
with the avidity of an Edith Wharton, investigated documents with the faith-
fulness of a De Goncourt, a Zola or a Daudet, and accepted with Charlotte
Brontë that differences in age are no bar to passionate and enduring love.

Reaching back even farther for inspiration, she sees a reincarnation of
Romeo in protagonist Vladimir Thal. Vladimir, a graying father, is a handsome, gifted Russian émigré who fled the Revolution, settled in a Paris suburb, wrote poetry, earned a meager livelihood and, after owning up to a
secret passion, left his family for sixteen-year-old Victoria Klimentiev. His
Juliet had lost her mother and had no compunction over deserting her hard-
drinking father. Klimentiev, however, fancied and even reveled in the role of
injured father and deprived Vladimir of his job, his health and ultimately his
life. Almost satanic in his righteousness and hypocrisy, Klimentiev is a whin-
ing parasite who succeeds through self-deception. He is almost worthy of
Dostoevsky.

Oldenbourg, the author of epic historical novels and an admired biography of Catherine the Great, attends throughout her novel [*La Joie-Souf-
france,* Joy-suffering; The Heirs of the Kingdom] to a tragedy more subtle
than the exquisite sufferings of her lovers: the spiritual displacement and
economic distresses of involuntary immigrants. A leisurely book that
achieves moments of suspense and illumination.

J. Walt. *World Literature Today.* 55, 1981,
p. 279

The Heirs of the Kingdom is an effective and powerful historical novel. Our
juvenile daydreams about the Middle Ages may resemble the world described
by Duggan; but in Oldenbourg's novel, living there as we do among the
medieval poor for almost six hundred pages, we may well feel that we are
getting an accurate picture of one aspect of the Middle Ages. And Oldenbourg
does not make another error cited by Lukács: she does not, as far as possible,
modernize the psychology of her characters. Again, these are not twentieth-

century people dressed in medieval clothing. Yet at the same time she uses her medieval characters and situations to illuminate our understanding not only of the Middle Ages but also of our time. It looks like the poor always will be with us, and by understanding the medieval poor in their context, perhaps we can better understand the modern poor in our context. And when we see a priest like Brother Barnabe, who ministers to the poor, who berates and defends them as appropriate, we can imagine how the Church—or any church—should function in a society. Similarly, Oldenbourg's careful depiction of the role—and special suffering—of the female poor (and even the female rich) should be of immediate concern to us, and it is significant that her novel ends not with the conquest of Jerusalem but with the capture and enslavement of Marie and her friends by the infidels.

Oldenbourg, then, has done an admirable job in her novel about the First Crusade. It is an exciting, interesting account, and as a historical novel, in the sense that Lukács uses the term, it succeeds quite well. It views the Crusade as basically a good movement, but a movement in which the plight of the lower classes can be clearly seen and analogized to our time.

Theodore L. Steinberg. *Studies in Medievalism*. 2, 1982, p. 84

"P.S. ou Les dix ou onze morts de Pentheisilea Singingbells," the first of the three novellas in *Déguisements* (Disguises), opens in the manner of a detective novel of the Golden Age, as Sir Bartholomew Hardcastle, lord of an English manor, discovers the body of an unknown woman in his library. However, since the novella is a spoof of the detective novel, it does not follow the rules. It is not the detective who rounds up all the suspects, discovers their motives for committing the crime, and then identifies and arrests the perpetrator; rather, each of the suspects writes a different scenario in which he or she is the murderer. Although the conceit is clever, the execution is labored, and Zoë Oldenbourg's first attempt at humor in her distinguished literary career fails.

The second selection, "Cassandre," is more successful. Cassandre is the name given to a clairvoyant accused of having predicted misfortunes that subsequently took place. She is tried and exonerated. During the trial the prosecuting attorney notes the fleeting horror and pity in her eyes when she looks at him. As he attempts to find out what prompted her reaction, he gets caught in his own trap and plunges headlong into the very catastrophe he fears.

"Déguisements," the third novella, centers on an amateur theatrical that is to be staged in a château. The play, *Le bal des ardents,* portrays a famous historical episode during the reign of the mad Charles VI, whose kingdom, torn by feudal rivalry between the Burgundians and the Armagnacs and governed by Queen Isabeau de Bavière and the bloody butcher Caboche, fell almost completely into the hands of the English in 1420. The action of the play is paralleled by a drama that is taking place among the actors. At the end the two story lines join, and the social diversion turns into a nightmare.

Lucille F. Becker. *World Literature Today.*
64, 1990, p. 606

OLSEN, TILLIE (UNITED STATES) 1913–

About Mrs. Olsen one is not inclined to say, as might have been said about Bernard Malamud or Philip Roth on their first appearance, that here, no matter what comes of it, is a rich outpouring of talent. Mrs. Olsen's stories [in *Tell Me a Riddle*] depend heavily on her own experience, and that experience seems to be narrow. But, to judge from the stories, it is also one that she has felt very deeply and pondered and imaginatively absorbed. The one remarkable story in her book, "Tell Me a Riddle," is a *tour de force* which pits aging and dying immigrant Jews against their native-born children, prosperous, troubled and helpless. Mrs. Olsen treats this familiar subject with balance, a cool humaneness, as if she were trying to see through the eyes of both generations and accept the self-pity of neither. . . .

Mrs. Olsen writes with steady hardness of tone, clinging to the one perception—the perception of loss and forgetting—which controls her story. In some passages she presses too hard, trying for verbal effects, intensities upon intensities, she cannot quite control, and not allowing her fable to move freely on its own. Nevertheless, the story is a remarkable piece of work, and one can only hope that Mrs. Olsen, having been possessed by the powers of memory, may now move ahead to fiction in which everything depends on the powers of invention.

Irving Howe. *The New Republic.* November
13, 1961, p. 22

Four stories make up this first book by a gifted, mature artist with an uncanny sense of compassion. Rarely, at least in recent years, has the literature of alienation been engaged in such devout service of the imagination. In writing which is individualized but not eccentric, experimental but not obscure, Mrs. Olsen has created imagined experience which has the authenticity of autobiography or memoir. With a faultless accuracy, her stories treat the very young, the mature, the dying—poor people without the means to buy or invent lies about their situations—and yet her writing never succumbs to mere naturalism.

Some critics will persist in finding analogies to Mrs. Olsen's work in the socially conscious literature of the 1930s. They are there, if one wishes to be blind to everything else, but the truth is that Mrs. Olsen has been more daring. Sometimes she is able to compress within the space of a single sentence or a brief paragraph the peculiar density of a career, a lifetime, in the manner of lyric poetry. It follows that the poverty which she describes never strikes one as formulary or anachronistic, but as an image for contemporary experience. Although addicted to metaphorical language, she uses it flexibly and unself-consciously to record, to analyze, and then to judge, fusing it with thought and feeling in such a way that the prose becomes the central intelligence of these dramas. . . .

Some of these stories have their faults, but they are faults of enthusiasm. Occasionally the prose will get out of hand, or, in choosing to be on such intimate terms with her characters, Mrs. Olsen will descend to a literal-mindedness which is her humanity unrestrained. Even so, there are stories in this collection which are perfectly realized works of art.

The foremost of these is a dramatic monologue entitled "I Stand Here Ironing," in which an unnamed and physically nondescript woman (a voice really), after a lifetime of deprivation, explains as she does the day's ironing the growth of her estrangement from her homely, first-born daughter. As she describes the early slights and disasters which brought such a relationship about, one has revealed the many human forms which loss can take. Mrs. Olsen's woman is burdened with exhaustion, a victim of a world in which all the panaceas have been discredited. To say that she seems ordinary or without stature indicates only the costume she may be wearing, for her suffering is made extraordinarily vivid and historic. . . .

Although she had explored the possibility of multiple consciousnesses functioning within the same dramatic situation in the earlier "Hey Sailor What Ship," one feels that in the final story she has actually fleshed two protagonists of equal vigor, enmeshing them in a marriage which seems as real and as permanent as any one will encounter in recent fiction. "Tell Me A Riddle" is a modern day "Ivan Illych." The death of Mrs. Olsen's heroine is the death of social consciousness itself, gruesome, alienated, and without consolation. In the death-struggle of this old activist and her mate (with both continually pitting their dignities against the other), Mrs. Olsen has envisaged a true tragedy of human mortality. In the last grim acts of a social protest which sprang from love, not cant, she puts it more eloquently than I can, in the words of the desolated old man who has been left behind, when he says: "Aaah, children . . . how we believed, how we belonged."

Richard M. Elman. Commonweal. December
8, 1961, pp. 295–96

Tillie Olsen's *Yonnondio* is unfinished, but what we have is an extraordinary achievement. The book was begun in the early 1930s, and worked on intermittently until 1936 or 1937. A few sketches appeared in print during this period, and then nothing. The manuscript of *Yonnondio* was set aside while Mrs. Olsen began to take on "everyday jobs" and raise a family. . . .

Yonnondio clearly must take its place as the best novel to come out of the so-called proletarian movement of the 1930s. The dogma and stilted characterizations that deform so many of the novels of that period have no place in Tillie Olsen's writing. She is a consummate artist who, in a paragraph such as the following one about the life of a miner, demonstrates just how searingly successful "protest" writing can be: "Someday the bowels (of the earth) will grow monstrous and swollen with these old tired dreams, swell and break, and strong fists batter the fat bellies, and skeletons of starved children batter them, and perhaps you will be slugged by a thug hired by the fat bellies, Andy Kvaternick. Or death will take you to bed at last, or you will strangle with the old crony of miners, the asthma. "I know of no work that "bespeaks the consciousness and roots" of the 1930s as brilliantly as *Yonnondio*.

But it would be a terrible mistake to see *Yonnondio* as a work limited to, and bound by, the 1930s. Mrs. Olsen's richness of style, her depth of characterization, and her enormous compassion make *Yonnondio* a work which must not—cannot—be restricted by any particular time or period. Its publication simply reinforces what we already know from *Tell Me a Riddle*: Tillie Olsen is one of the greatest prose stylists now writing. One can only think ruefully of what might have been had she not been "denied full writing life"—had those 40 years been hers, and so ours, not 40 years of "unnatural thwarting of what struggles to come into being, but cannot." Mrs. Olsen is quite right when she says (again, in "Death of the Creative Process") that a writer cannot be reconciled "for what is lost by unnatural silences." "*Yonnondio! Yonnondio!* The word itself a dirge," wrote Whitman. "Then blank and gone and still, and utterly lost." But now, with the publication of the found manuscript—unfinished as it may be—we can say: At least not that—not utterly lost. *Yonnondio* is a magnificent novel, one to be all the more cherished for the disruption it makes into the unnatural silence of Tillie Olsen.

Jack Salzman. *Book World*. April 7, 1974,
p. 1

There is no more powerfully moving a piece of fiction in recent years than Tillie Olsen's long story "Tell Me a Riddle." . . . All of the stories of *Tell Me a Riddle* are superb but the title story is the one that remains most vividly in the mind. It will withstand repeated readings—and the sort of close, scrupulous attention ordinarily reserved for poetry. . . .

[*Silences*'s] strengths lie . . . in its polemical passages. Olsen asks why so many more women are silenced than men; she asks why there is only one woman writer "of achievement" for every 12 men writers; why our culture continues to reflect a masculine point of view almost exclusively. . . .

One feels the author's passion, and cannot help but sympathize with it. Certainly women have been more generally "silenced" than men, in all the arts. But the book is marred by numerous inconsistencies and questionable statements offered as facts. . . .

Tillie Olsen must have felt justified in subordinating—or silencing—her own considerable artistic instincts during the composition of *Silences*, and I would not quarrel with her decision. It was a generous one: she wanted to reach out to others, to the living and the dead, who have, evidently, shared her own agony. One must respect such an impulse. But the thinking that underlies *Silences* is simply glib and superficial if set in contrast to the imagination that created *Tell Me a Riddle* and *Yonnondio,* Olsen's novel.

Joyce Carol Oates. *The New Republic.* July 29, 1978, pp. 32–34

Tillie Olsen's remarkable power comes from having almost never written at all. A working-class woman who grew up in America in the 1930s, had children, and did "someone else's work" for years to support her family, Olsen was likely to have been silenced by daily struggle until, like the dying grandmother of her story "Tell Me A Riddle," she would want only the "reconciled peace" of a small, clean, empty house. Instead, through an incredible effort of will, Olsen, like Walt Whitman, used her enforced "long foreground" not only to write but to do so with extraordinary empathy. Part of Olsen's present high reputation in America admittedly springs from her role as heroine of her own life. The sheer grit that she needed in order to find the strength and time to write—and to believe she *could* write—has meant that she (usually implicitly) adds the argument of her experience to her discussion in *Silences* of the conditions of creative work: I am the woman, I suffered, I was there.

Olsen is far more than the token working-class writer whose presence soothes the middle-class American women's movement (though she is certainly also being used as that). First a silent, then a vocal conscience for American women's writing, Olsen writes with an elegance, compassion and directness rare in any period. Though her politicized recognitions form a unique link between 1930s radicalism and the women's movement of the 1980s, Olsen has published little. . . . Olsen's great subject, the emotional life of the working-class family, has been so buried in American culture since the 1930s, that it looks completely new. . . . Unlike Whitman, Olsen does not sublimate private despair into cosmic affirmation. The external circumstances of her characters generate ironies characteristic of nineteenth-century realism: poverty, dirt, tired bodies, heat, smells, drink, labor, recalcitrant objects and a toxic failure of will that manifests itself in violence or withdrawal. Only sex is left out; as Cora Kaplan remarks in her introduction to *Yonnondio,* Olsen sees neither fulfillment nor release there. Within such limits, family love (maternal passion in particular) is peculiarly generous, since it is felt in full knowledge of inevitable separation and probable crushing of hope. All of Olsen's narratives deal with two generations. . . .

In Olsen's subjective essays motherhood looms large as a cause of silence precisely because it does engage one's deepest emotions: "There is no one else responsible" for children's needs. "It is distraction, not meditation, that becomes habitual; interruption, not continuity; spasmodic, not constant toil." In her more objective fiction she sees motherhood as the experience which expresses continuity and separation simultaneously, a paradox which politicizes it: the mother, cut off from experience of the world by sexual division of labor, must nevertheless impart values to her children or see them fall.

Helen McNeil. (London) Times Literary
Supplement. November 14, 1980, p. 1294

Olsen's importance to contemporary women who read and write or who write about literature is widely acknowledged. Yet although her work has been vital for feminists today, and although one article does discuss her background in some depth, few of Olsen's contemporary admirers realize the extent to which her consciousness, vision, and choice of subject are rooted in an earlier heritage of social struggle—the communist Old Left of the 1930s and the tradition of radical political thought and action, mostly socialist and anarchist, that dominated the Left in the 1910s and 1920s. Not that we can explain the eloquence of her work in terms of its sociopolitical origins, not even that left-wing politics and culture were the single most important influences on it, but that its informing consciousness, its profound understanding of class and sex and race as shaping influences on people's lives, owes much to that earlier tradition. Olsen's work, in fact, may be seen as part of a literary lineage so far unacknowledged by most contemporary critics: a socialist feminist literary tradition. . . .

On the whole, in spite of the Left's demands on her time and energies, the prescriptiveness of its more dogmatic criticism, and the androcentrism or outright sexism of many of its spokesmen, there is no doubt but that Olsen's Marxian perspective and experience ultimately enriched her literature. . . .

In the 1950s, partly out of a spirit of opposition to the McCarthy era, and blessed with increased time as the children grew up and there were temporary respites from financial need, Olsen began to do the work that gave us the serenely beautiful but still politically impassioned stories of the *Tell Me a Riddle* volume. Olsen's enduring insistence that literature must confront the material realities of people's lives as shaping circumstances, that the very categories of class and race and sex constitute the fabric of reality as we live it, and that literature has an obligation to deepen consciousness and facilitate social change are part of her—and our—inheritance from the radical tradition.

Deborah Rosenfelt. Feminist Studies. Fall,
1981, pp. 373–74, 403–4

No one has written so eloquently about silences as Tillie Olsen, or shown as poignantly that a writer can recover her voice. In her most recent fiction, a long story called "Requa," Tillie Olsen reclaims once more a power of speech that has proved at times extremely difficult to exercise. . . . In 1970 "Requa" appeared, an impressive work which received immediate recognition and was reprinted as one of the year's best stories. For apparently fortuitous reasons, it is now little known, though as Olsen's most innovative and complex work of fiction, it deserves critical attention. Complete but unfinished, "Requa I" is a still-to-be continued story that develops the theme of human continuity in ways which seem almost subversive. Its form is discontinuous, as though to challenge its theme; the text broken visibly into fragments separated from each other by conspicuous blank spaces—gaps the eye must jump over and the mind fill with meaning. However, the story repudiates the meanings that might be inferred from its disintegrated form, and from its imagery and setting, both influenced by literary traditions of the past that Olsen continues only to subvert. "Requa I" evokes the poetry of the 1920s in its wasteland motifs, and novels of the 1930s in its realistic portrayal of America's Great Depression. Waste and depression are Olsen's subjects in "Requa," but Olsen's voice, resonant after long silence, is attuned to her vision of recovery—a vision central to this essay, which hopes to show how the process of recovery, described and enacted in "Requa," produces a work of art. . . .

Olsen's style in "Requa" is conspicuously varied. Lyrical passages are juxtaposed to crude dialectic speech, and stream-of-consciousness passages to objectively seen realistic details. Numerous lists of things represent a world of objects proliferating outside the self; but a mind encompasses these objects and tries to find in their disorder a way of ordering an inner tumult expressed by the story's roiling fragments. Like the junkyard, the story is the repository of bits and pieces: sentences broken into phrases, phrases separated into words, words isolated by blank spaces. Single words on a line or simply sounds—"aaagh/aaagh"—mark the end of narrative sections, some introduced by titles such as *"Rifts"* and *"Terrible Pumps."* Even the typography is discontinuous, so that the text seems a mosaic of oddly assorted fragments. In creating a visibly discontinuous text, in effect, turning "Requa" into a design upon the page, Olsen attracts attention to her form which, however, always refers the reader to a social world that "Requa" presents as real, recognizable, and outside the fiction. Still, "Requa" exists as an object: its varied typography creates truncated patterns of print that catch the eye; words placed together as lists or as fragmentary refrains form distinct visual units; blocks of nouns separated from the text produce concrete poems; intervening spaces turn into aesthetic entities. Mimetic of her theme, Olsen's form is enacting the story's crucial phrase: *"Broken existences that yet continue."* As a text, "Requa" is broken and yet continuous, its action extending beyond its open-ended ending. The story transforms a paradox into a promise as it turns the polarities of fragmentation and continuity into obverse aspects of each other. Merged together, the broken pieces of "Requa" create an integrated self as well as an aesthetic entity. The story enacts a process of composition to show broken existences continuing, order emerging from disorder, art from images of waste, and speech from the void of silence. . . .

In "Requa," Olsen has said nothing about art. Her speech, resumed after ten years of silence, simply *is* art. This is the secret inherent in Tillie Olsen's story of recovery in which a child's renewed will to live becomes inseparable from an artist's recovered power to write.

Blanche Gelfant. *Women Writing in America*
(Hanover: Dartmouth/University Press of
New England, 1984), pp. 61, 69–70

[Olsen] has a place in the Western Writers Series, because in a figurative sense she has always faced west, always placed herself on some kind of frontier. She has been—and is—ardent in the cause of change in the thinking and attitudes of men and women. She wants to see life for everyone freer, more laden with opportunity, with a chance for growth. She is Western in that she looks to the future for a better world.

Olsen is Western not only in attitude, but also in what she writes. Many of her characters are Westerners who live in towns and cities; and from its beginnings as a region, the West has had mostly a population of town and city dwellers. She also writes about miners and sailors; and such workers are as much a part of the West as its cowboys. The "invisible Wests"—women and minorities—gain visibility in Olsen's work. She has not tried to write another *Riders of the Purple Sage*, nor is she a regionalist in the derogatory sense in which that term is often used; but to say that she is not Western because she fits into neither of these narrow categories is to deny to Westerners—especially to those who are women, workers, and minorities—an understanding of the full richness of their regional culture. Olsen's work transcends the regional, but it is written from the American West and about the West.

Abigail Mouton. *Tillie Olsen*, Western
Writers Series (Boise: Boise State
University Press, 1984), pp. 5–6

Coherent and serious works of literature invite conversation about being human and possibilities for transcendence. Some texts, more than others, evoke such conversation. These texts bring us into an awareness of healing and perhaps transcending presence in human experience, or they compel us toward moral contemplation in their presentation of a way or mode of being in the world. Olsen's literature invites a religious engagement in both of these senses. In our reading of her fiction, we sense longings and dreams that give rise to an envisioned world of harmony, nurturance, and fulfillment. The human infant as well as the exhausted mother of children is emblematic in Olsen's world of the hoped for and healing experience of human to human unfolding and becoming. When, in her last published fiction ["Requa I"], Olsen describes an orphaned boy's emotional resurrection, she points vividly to this vision through its beginnings in concrete experience: The miracle of life, of renaissance and transformation, is rooted in the human necessities of caretaking, nurturance, and encouragement. Knit of broken and abused lives, the hoped-for world this literature evokes is apocalyptic. It is a transformed world, celebrant of child and of the sacred powers of life and creativity. This vision is Olsen's transcending message, transcending because it offers deep connection and hope. In her world, we as readers begin to comprehend ourselves as moral beings whose destinies are connected with the characters'. We see our own history and future in light of theirs.

Elaine Neil Orr. Tillie Olsen and a Feminist
Spiritual Vision (Jackson: University Press
of Mississippi, 1987), p. xv

Olsen's career includes two periods: All of her 1930s publications appeared in 1934, when she was only twenty-one; her "second period" dates from 1953, when the youngest of her four children entered school. Olsen's writing from the 1930s, like [Meridel] Le Sueur's, is marked by a tension between official and unofficial views of proletarian literature.

Olsen's writing from her two "periods" also represents two distinct types of oppositional form. Whereas the content of her 1930s literature is culturally and politically agitational, the discursive model has been borrowed, unmodified, from dominant modes of representation, taking the processes of signification for granted. These texts foreground the "message" rather than the production of meaning. Openly tendentious, Olsen's published 1930s writing is marked by an uncontested authorial voice and a completion and closure of meaning. In what Bakhtin terms monological discourse, these texts directly address the reader, anticipating responses and deflecting objections; meanings are seen as delivered, unchanged, from source to recipient. In the tradition of muckraking, social journalism, and reportage, Olsen's writing during this period, like Le Sueur's "Women on the Breadlines" and "I Was Marching," was intended to spark political resistance. At the same time, however, its didacticism, like that of Le Sueur's more tendentious writing, actually limits involvement by undercutting the reader's role as an active producer of meaning. As we will see, Olsen's *Silences* (1978), on the other hand, challenges the ideological character of the signification process itself. The production of meaning, as much as the message, becomes a site for dissent. . . .

While Olsen's "message" continues to be oppositional in her more recent writing, the rhetorical model is more dialogic than that of her 1930s publications, challenging the signification process itself. Culturally mainstream modes of representation lend themselves to forms of domination that can be countered by alternative modes of representation such as those prefigured in *Silences* (1978), a nonfiction book that catalogues impediments to a writer's productivity. By now a classic of American feminism, *Silences* employs the strategy of a pluralized text, suggesting one form that a literature of resistance might take.

Constance Coiner. In M. Bella Mirabella and
Lennard Davis, eds. Left Politics and the
Literary Profession (New York: Columbia
University Press, 1990), pp. 172–73, 179

At first glance, Tillie Olsen's book *Silences,* published in 1978, would seem to inhabit that readily identifiable universe of discourse known as literary criticism. But ponder the significance of the term *literary criticism* for a moment. It refers to the practice of writing thoughtfully about an existing body of texts: it presumes a body of "literature" about which one can wax "critical." In this remarkable volume, however, Tillie Olsen is only partially concerned with writing critically about a body of existing literature. Her larger concern is with the books that never got written and with the people who never wrote them. Like [W. E. B.] Du Bois and [James] Agee before her—both of whom were very much on her mind as she wrote *Silences*—Olsen cares passionately about documenting the experiences of those who cannot tell their own stories. Bearing witness to realities that have heretofore eluded the printed page, she wants to issue a cultural report from the realm of the silent and the silenced. Olsen also wants to understand patterns of silencing that persist into the present. She wants to write not only about the books that have never been written, but about the difficulty—for many would-be writers—of writing books even now.

How do you write literary criticism about the lack of a body of literature to criticize? And how do you effectively address the nearly insurmountable obstacles facing, say, working class women writers, without creating a book that is, by its very existence, close to being self-refuting? . . .

What is the relationship of a writer with Olsen's agenda to the traditions of discourse into which her book of necessity enters? In a word, complex. In this essay there is space to focus on only one of the techniques Olsen employs to achieve her end. I would argue, however, that the entire catalog of innovative and creative strategies she uses in the book are designed to teach her readers to allow voices previously faint or silent (including, one might add, the reader's own) to be heard. She is remarkably successful in this endeavor.

How does one learn to "hear" silence? Explicating this apparent oxymoron is indeed the principal technical challenge Olsen faces. It might help to remember that the word *silence,* for Olsen, is itself, for the most part, a metaphor for the absence of written texts. The direct analogue to *silence* in a visual context is *blankness.* Olsen sagely recognizes that the auditory concept of *silence* is more powerful and allusive than the visual concept of *blankness* for a variety of reasons, not least of which is the convenient link with the familiar silencing of women's real voices in family conversations, as in the larger cultural conversations that have gone on throughout history. But hearing silence—indeed investigating silence—is by definition problematical.

Shelley Fisher Fishkin. In Norman Sims, ed.
*Literary Journalism in the Twentieth
Century* (New York: Oxford University
Press, 1990), pp. 151–54

What does Olsen suggest to change the crippling circumstances of gender, race, class, nationality, age? I see two answers, both of them based on Olsen's strong sense of community and her view of history. The first is the simple but fundamental idea that change is possible if people gather together, with all their differences intact, to create it. Olsen is true to what she calls "the lessons [of] the 'thirties"—"that so-called ordinary people can in their own time make changes with their pool of strength, that people resist, that they make as much of life as they can. The second answer Olsen offers is the experience of joy as a source of community and power. These two beliefs, while they do not provide a blueprint for the "revolutionary, subversive movement in our time" that Olsen calls for, do provide an impetus toward it.

While Olsen rejects a cyclical interpretation of history and the sense of isolation and impotence it breeds, the alternative she offers is by no means a simplistic faith in human progress. Olsen was not deluded by the material prosperity of the 1950s and 1960s, for example, into thinking that the Great Depression was over. It is significant that "Requa," completed in 1970, is set during the depression, allowing Olsen to reveal to the current generation of readers the endurance of the people of the 1930s. But more important, situating the story in the depression expresses Olsen's view that the poverty and terror of that time continue into the present for many people in the United States, whose lives are still invisible and who are unemployed or working at jobs that do not pay them a living wage, much less the honor she accords them, their work, and their tools. The depression setting also reveals Olsen's understanding of the extent to which women's position in the United States, as elsewhere, is determined by economic fluctuations and inequities. The gains won for some women by the most recent feminist movement did not even touch the lives of many others.

Mara Faulkner, O.S.B. *Protest & Possibility*
in the Writing of Tillie Olsen
(Charlottesville: University Press of
Virginia, 1993), pp. 146–47

Olsen's lifelong commitment to working-class, racial-justice, and peace movements informs her literary work, but, along with the effort of rearing four children and doing paid labor as well, it cut severely into the time and inner space she had available for writing. Her literary career is thus divided into two parts, separated by twenty years devoted almost exclusively to family, "everyday" jobs, and political life. In the earlier period, the 1930s, she published journalism, poetic prose drawn from her activist experience, and, in the 1934 *Partisan Review,* a short story that was the beginning of the novel *Yonnondio: From the Thirties* (1974) that she was to publish, still incomplete, some forty years later. It was not until the mid-1950s that Olsen began to write fiction again. Her three short stories from those years, "I Stand Here Ironing," "Hey Sailor, What Ship?," and "O Yes," offer realistic glimpses into the experience of working-class women, men, and children through use of experimental modernist techniques of narration. These three loosely connected stories are collected in a volume, *Tell Me a Riddle* (1961), along with Olsen's novella of that title.

The novella "Tell Me a Riddle," which won the O. Henry Award for the best American short story of 1961, focuses on the last months in the life of an elderly Russian Jewish immigrant woman, a political activist who survived the revolution of 1905 only to witness the erosion of her own possibilities for a full life into the stifling experience of American working-class wife and motherhood. Embittered by the demands her experience has made on her, the dying woman's stream-of-consciousness . . . is studded with the texts of suppressed idealism, the socialist humanism of her youth, in which she has never ceased to believe; these are words that make a vivid, ironic contrast with the ugly, self-satisfied world of America in the 1950s by which she is surrounded.

Olsen's other fictional works include "Requa-I" (1971)—another long story—and *Yonnondio,* the novel begun in the 1930s and revised—though not completed—by the author in her maturity. *Yonnondio* is a narrative of the migrations of a working-class Midwestern family, with special attention to the way that the job and joblessness shape relationships between the sexes and the generations, as the violence of the workplace and the economy of which it is a part translates into domestic violence, marital rape, and child neglect.

As a critic, Olsen concentrates on the power of "circumstances," particularly race, class, and gender, to cut off creativity. *Silences* (1978) starts from her own experience as a "first generation" working-class writer and a woman and proceeds to elaborate a theory about the relation of material conditions to culture. Olsen's efforts to make the work of such nearly forgotten authors as Rebecca Harding Davis (1831–1910) and Agnes Smedley (1890–1950) available to a new generation of feminist readers derives from this same sense of the social obstacles to creation and the great value of what is accomplished in spite of those obstacles.

> Lillian S. Robinson. In Steven R. Serafin
> and Walter D. Glanze, eds. *Encyclopedia of*
> *World Literature in the 20th Century* (New
> York: Continuum, 1993), pp. 461–62

ONWUEME, TESS (NIGERIA) 1954–

What is important for Tess is the writing: "the communion between myself and paper." So she doesn't necessarily feel disappointed when she doesn't receive royalties. "I understand the problems of these smaller publishing companies like Heins (who published *The Desert Encroaches*). They need to be sympathized with. I don't write to get money. It would be retarding until you have delivered it (written what you have in you)."

Tess first attempted writing in 1978 when the Nigerian universities were shut for three months. She received her first rejection slip that same year. Since then she has had more success and at thirty is emerging as one of the country's best political satirists. Her other works include: *Broken Calabash*, published by Total (1984), the film of which was featured by Nigeria's National Television Network (during the country's silver jubilee celebration), *A Hen Too Soon* (Heins 1983), *A Scent of Onions, Faces of a Coin, Our Son, Tom* and *De Governor.*

Emmanuel Ibeleme. New African.
March, 1986, p. 49

Tess Onwueme, whose first play, *A Hen Too Soon,* appeared in 1983, caught the attention of Nigerian literary critics in 1985 when her third published play, *The Desert Encroaches,* won that year's Association of Nigerian Authors drama contest. Since then, four more works *(Ban Empty Barn, The Artist's Homecoming, Cattle Egret Versus Nama, Mirror for Campus)* have appeared in quick succession, signifying the fertility of her artistic mind. She has also presented *A Scent of Onions, Faces of a Coin, Our Son, Tom, De Governor,* and *In Search of a Theme—All of Us* to large audiences.

The Reign of Wazobia is incidentally Onwueme's first feminist play. Although women and their predicament have been a major focus in her work, it is in her latest piece that she gives fangs to her female characters; for the first time her women organize a resistance against male domination of tradition. Wazobia is a young educated female who is appointed a regent after the death of Ogiso, the king of Ilaaa. The choice of a female king-surrogate is of course in consonance with tradition. However, when Wazobia is asked to leave the throne after three seasons, as custom demands, she refuses. This is the main conflict of the play, which is constructed in six "movements."

Both men and women versed in Ilaaa tradition are piqued by Wazobia's rebelliousness, and they are determined to remove her. Through a series of addresses directed at the women, Wazobia wins their confidence and respect and is able to raise their level of consciousness. In one of her emotionally charged entreaties she screams at the women, "For ages you have been dancing to feast the eyes of licentious men and visiting generals. Dance no more!" The women, naked, build a fence around her as the men, led by the priest of the land, come to chase her away from the throne. The men "are so shocked that they retreat, stagger and freeze in their stupefaction." As the play ends, Wazobia urges the war-mongering women not to spill blood, because "ours is to plant seedyams. Not blood to feed worms." In other words, her revolution is a bloodless one, and this is probably the playwright's own artistic disposition toward the fate of women in Nigeria. (The name "Wazobia" is coined from the three major ethnic languages in the country: *wa* is Yoruba, *zo* is Hausa, and *bia* is Igbo, each meaning "come." Wazobia is thus a personi-fication of unity among the womenfolk in a patriarchal society.)

Stylistically *Wazobia* is one of Onwueme's most satisfying plays. The language has heave, full of the cadence of typical Nigerian speech idiosyncra-sies. The imagery and metaphors are taken from the flora and fauna of the play's physical setting. The characters frequently resort to the use of prov-erbs in order to drive home their points, and this is done with esthetic pleasur-ability. Omu, slighted in the rites of cleansing the late king's wives, asks the priest of Ani, "How do you think you can snap the finger without the right thumb?" She reminds Wazobia that she is older and wiser: "She who has cooked longer can boast of more broken pots." Because of the appropriate deployment of theme and style, I am sure that *The Reign of Wazobia* will "reign" for a long time in African dramaturgy.

J. O. J. Nwachukwu-Agbada. *World Literature Today.* 63, 1989, pp. 729–30

Tess Onwueme's victory at the Association of Nigerian Authors (ANA) drama contest in 1985 called attention to the artistic potential of her drama-turgy. Until then she had had only two published plays, *A Hen Too Soon* (1983) and *The Broken Calabash* (1984). Like most artistic debuts, *A Hen* was an amateurish work. The play revealed two basic problems: the conception of artistic verisimilitude was poor, and the linguistic facets fell short of the level for which accomplished African dramas are now recognized. In a short critique of Onwueme's first play entitled "A Writer Too Soon," Afam Ebeogu, despite awarding the work an overall passing grade, finds weak points in its "hackneyed" theme and in the nonsustenance of the feminist undertone. . . .

The Desert Encroaches (1985), described by Olu Obafemi as "positively ambitious," is a clarion call for change in a world dominated by the arms race, by the covetous lust for others' resources, by oppression and repression, by ideological rigidity and similar lethal maladies. The work is Onwueme's "large" play because of its scope and the range of its concerns. As the world faces a possible nuclear war, the playwright calls for peace, for a new attitude which will supplant the present struggle of "shooting the stars, scuffling for ascendancy, daring each other, while we burn below." Her tangent is largely African and Third World. . . .

Ban Empty Barn (1986) is another of Onwueme's experimental plays in which [as in *The Desert Encroaches*], animals are characters. The scope here is less global; the focus of interest is Nigeria with her deep-rooted hierarchical structure of oppression. . . .

In *The Broken Calabash* (1984) the world of the play is no longer fabular. The work seems to be an attempt to return to the thesis of *A Hen Too Soon*, which the dramatist might have realized was poorly handled in the earlier play. Here both the theme and the language are better implemented. The play is not a feminist work in the vulgar sense of the term; it is instead an effort to assert the individual self and, in that way, earn some self-actualization. . . .

Tess Onwueme has also published *The Artist's Homecoming* (1986), *Cattle Egret versus Nama* (1986), *Mirror for Campus* (1987), and *The Reign of Wazobia* (1988). In each of these plays she attacks the forces of backwardness and in that way calls for new social forms and values in order to create and forge a new personal and social understanding. . . .

Each of Tess Onwueme's published plays so far, it would seem, is a clarion call for social change, the cultivation of new attitude and new hopes. The society she targets in her works for the stage is both national and international, and at each level her position seems to be that the old order of traditional, social, and economic oppression must give way to a new and more healthful one. Her quest for social change goes beyond the raising of feminist consciousness in society to include a swipe at the diminishing status of supposedly independent African countries as a result of the powerful gains of neocolonialism. In her plays there is the consistent vision that, at both the social and the personal level, a clear disparity exists in the quality of people's lives, a situation which has been promoted by the oppressive tendencies immanent in our kind of polity. In the end we observe in Onwueme's dramatic corpus an artistic desire to change the status quo through the ridiculing of the obnoxious in our tradition as well as by exposing the political and economic conditions in the society depicted in her drama.

J. O. J. Nwachukwu-Agbada. *World Literature Today*. 66, 1992, pp. 464–67

OREAMUNO, YOLANDA (COSTA RICA–GUATEMALA) 1916–56

On a number of occasions, Yolanda Oreamuno has protested that critics have a tendency to make inappropriate comparisons between her work and that of others and to point out nonexistent influences on her. More particularly, in a letter to Victoria Urbano, she states: "I haven't read Maria Luisa Bombal (with whom I've been compared), nor Joyce (with whom they've also compared me); much less Jean Paul Sartre or the existentialists (to which group I've been accused of belonging)."

By contrast, she herself openly acknowledges her taste for certain authors and books. From repeated references throughout her work, we may conclude that among these are the Golden Age writers, especially [Lorenzo] Gracián; *Miau* by [Benito Pérez] Galdos, a work that she has reread many times; Eduardo Mallea, especially *La bahia del silencio* (The bay of silence) and *El sayal y la purpura* (Sackcloth and royal purple); Thomas Mann's *The Magic Mountain,* and finally Faulkner's *Wild Palms.*

Despite her enthusiasm for the above-mentioned authors and books, Yolanda Oreamuno's admitted literary obsession is Proust. . . .

It is generally recognized that Yolanda Oreamuno draws upon Proust for her ability to penetrate into the depths of the unconscious and to draw subtle psychological shadings of characters, starting from acute observation of situations, attitudes, emotions, and relationships. Furthermore, like Proust, she delights in details that her narrative communicates in a *tempo lento*. . . .

A study of . . . *La ruta de su evasion* (The escape route) could show a significant point of contact between the two writers and reveal whether she produces a mere imitation of Proust's work or [as I believe] what Jacques Derrida describes as a supplement. . . .

La ruta de su evasion is a novel inhabited by anguish, loneliness, hatred, silence, emptiness, and death. . . .

The characters of the novel all live with compromise of one sort or another—be it through their own temperaments, family circumstances, or the external world—and attempt to escape. . . .

One important way in which Yolanda Oreamuno's writing may be distinguished from that of Proust is through the constant presence of the man (father)/woman (mother) theme, which is not a great concern of the French writer. The relations between and among the female and male characters in *La ruta* illustrate and represent, on the thematic level, a censure of traditional patterns of behavior as a system in Latin American and also in universal culture. The reader encounters a text in which there is an intense and constant protest against the socially constructed differences between the sexes.

Rima de Vallbona. *Revista Iberoamericana.*
53, 1987, pp. 193–95, 198–99, 216–17

The protagonist of Yolanda Oreamuno's "Valle alto" (High valley) is an unnamed woman traveling alone in a foreign country. She begins this episode of her journey at the bus station of an anonymous city. Her intended destination, her motives for traveling, her origins? We know only that she is alone, that she feels she must arrive at her destination before nightfall, and that she is preoccupied with some unarticulated concern.

The opening paragraphs begin with physical descriptions that correspond to inner realities as much as to external conditions. The city is sterile, dry, and unbearably bright. Its lines are angular, there is no wind, and the clouds, pregnant with water, are painfully close to the city, yet it doesn't rain. The air is full of a disquieting vibration. In this city, the woman is estranged and desperate: the elements are all wrong. We sense that she has been traveling for a long time, searching for a way to break out of loneliness. The next morning, the woman wakes up and discovers she is in a narrow bed in a country inn, alone, unable to recall how she got there. She begins and ends in loneliness and emptiness, but what is significant is what happens on the way to her destination.

Between loneliness and loneliness lies temporary union. The woman experiences respite from solitude, breaking through her loneliness and her existential aridity by creating (or living) a beautiful and sensual erotic fantasy. . . .

If the story opens and closes with sterile alienation and disorientation, then the body of the text is just that—an actual physical presence, a fertility rite in the woman space. Her fantasy satisfies her desire for union, if only temporarily, because it is her creation and therefore her union with her dark silences. The woman exhibits two very different personalities during the story. In the city, and again at the inn the next morning, she is passive, disoriented, and somehow one-dimensional. During her adventure/fantasy, on the other hand, she becomes increasingly assertive, creative, poetic, and at peace. Her erotic fantasy is a breathing space, a stop along the road of her lonely life's search or journey, that integrates her with herself, with man, and with all of nature.

> Janet Gold. In Noël Valis and Carol Maier,
> eds. *In the Feminine Mode: Essays on*
> *Hispanic Women Writers* (Lewisburg,
> Pennsylvania: Bucknell University Press,
> 1991), pp. 196–98

Best known for her short stories and for her novel *La ruta de su evasión* (1948; The route of their escape), Oreamuno is one of the most prominent Costa Rican writers of the twentieth century. Born in San José, Oreamuno was twenty when she published her first stories. Many of her stories and essays appeared in *Repertorio Americano*, of San José, a journal edited by Oreamuno's mentor and friend Joaquín García Monge (1881–1958). In 1940, Oreamuno's novel *Por tierra firma* (For native land) won the novel prize of the Congress of Spanish American writers sponsored by Farrar and Rinehart, but the manuscript was lost and never published. A second novel, *Casta sombría* (Dark race), was also lost, but several fragments of it were printed in *Repertorio Americano*. After a bitter divorce and loss of custody of her son, Oreamuno's health declined, and she was ill for much of the remainder of her life. "México es mío" (Mexico is mine), one of her most remarkable texts, appeared in 1945, "Valle alto" ("High Valley," 1978) was published in 1946, and in 1947 Oreamuno sent two novels to a literary contest in Guatemala. In 1948 she won the prestigious "15th of September" prize for the best novel of the year in Guatemala for *La ruta de su evasión;* the other novel manuscript, *De ahora en adelante* (From now on) was lost. Oreamuno, who had left Costa Rica in 1943, became a Guatemalan citizen. She lived in Guatemala and later in Mexico, where she continued to write novels and stories, many of which were still unpublished at the time of her death in 1956.

Since her death, the publication of several volumes of her collected stories, essays, letters, and novel chapters has brought her wider recognition and admiration than she enjoyed during her lifetime. A new edition in 1984 of Oreamuno's only extant complete novel, *La Ruta de su evasión*, has met with extensive praise for the skill with which Oreamuno combines interior monologues, realistic description, and fantasy. The novel explores the inter-dynamics of the Vasco family through analysis of the motives of the women characters, their dreams and their aspirations. Many of Oreamuno's better-known stories, such as "Las mareas vuelven de noche" ("The Tide Returns at Night," 1978) and "Valle alto," are also written in surreal, powerful prose, the images stacked against each other, sensuous and poetic, bypassing ratio-nal logic of cause and effect.

Much of Oreamuno's fiction is fragmentary and poetic, obsessed with time and with the definition of identity. Although her stories are set around the world, in Bogotá and Carthage and Hong Kong as well as in a mythic, mysterious Mexico or generic Central America, autobiographical elements are woven throughout Oreamuno's fiction, and her tone of personal passion is convincing. She writes with hallucinatory intensity of the complexity of male-female relationships and of the simultaneous multiplicity of motives behind even the simplest of social acts. Oreamuno's published work is not extensive, but it is highly accomplished and varied, ranging from humorous satire to poetic allegory. As her work has become more available to a reading public, she has become one of the most highly esteemed Costan Rican writers of the century.

> Mary G. Berg. In Steven R. Serafin and
> Walter D. Glanze, eds. *Encyclopedia of
> World Literature in the 20th Century* (New
> York: Continuum, 1993), p. 463

ORTESE, ANNA MARIA (ITALY) 1915–

First published in 1965, *The Iguana* belongs to a long and uproarious Mediter-ranean tradition of philosophical fables. In these tales, the natural world doesn't behave quite properly, perhaps because the human world misbehaves toward it. Sexual urges, the class structure, the imponderability of weather, the disturbing texture of the dinner set before you on the table—all come into question through some fantastic, alluring break in the animal world's order. . . . It's the novel that might have come about had Jane Austen sat down to rewrite *The Good Soldier* and got the pages mixed up with *The Metamorphosis*. . . .

Anna Maria Ortese has called up the myths of the tortured aristocrat; the abused brute; the false innocent who cannot admit his desires; the blame-less sinner caught helplessly in her sins; and, above all, the myth of the human soul. As Daddo guessed before he set out on his voyage, these are the demented stories we like to tell ourselves, and which we easily enter. There are a lot more of them, too. As Ortese spins them out, she sometimes drops her mask of genial satire, but never falls into the routine or the expected. Her tone and timing are often disconcerting, but they're unfailingly sure—much like the instincts we so admire in soulless Nature.

Stuart Klawans. *The Nation.* December 5, 1987, pp. 688–89

Ortese's first publication was a poem, "Manuele" (1933; Manuele), written at the death of her twenty-year-old brother, killed in a naval accident. It created such enthusiasm among young poets that Alfonso Gatto . . . said: "[The] poem makes her a new Ungaretti . . . the man of sorrows."

A few years later Ortese started writing short stories for the prestigious journal *L'Italia letteraria.* These stories—lyrical visions and private dreams—captured the attention of many writers, particularly of Massimo Bontempelli . . . the father of "magic realism" . . . who collected and published them under the title *Angelici dolori* (1937; Angelic sorrows). In this book, which is the history of a life of "solitude," Ortese intertwines her life and her family's with the lives of such characters as American Indians or with fantastic adventures and dreams. These stories are a poetic amalgam of reality and fabulation. *Angelici dolori* is fundamental to the understanding of the rest of Ortese's work.

Il mare non bagna Napoli (1953; *The Bay Is Not Naples,* 1955) received both national and international recognition. Translated into many languages, it contains touching stories of Neapolitan poverty. For example, "La città involontaria" (Involuntary city) is a description, realistic yet compassionate, of a decrepit military barracks in which homeless people—like Ortese herself—live in subhuman conditions. She has been accused of "desecrating Naples," but it is truer to say that, as in the story "Il silenzio della ragione" (Silence of reason), Ortese—together with a group of younger writers around the Neapolitan journal *Sud*—participates in the sorrows of her people and dreams of a better future for them.

In his remarks written for the jacket of *Il mare non bagna Napoli,* Elio Vittorini called Ortese "a gypsy absorbed in a dream." The "gypsy" (who had moved, and would move until 1975, from city to city in search of the financial stability she never had) always felt "poor and simple." It may be indicative of her lifelong "solitude" that in her fascinating fable-novel *L'iguana* (1965; The iguana) the "iguana"—Estrellita, the poor little faithful servant—works all her life for a rich family (who pay her not with money but with little stones) and lives otherwise isolated in the "absolute darkness" of a cellar.

Although Ortese's works have been acclaimed by many critics and although several were translated into a number of languages, writing has not made her financially comfortable. Her major novel *Il porto di Toledo* (1975; The port of Toledo) cost her five years of strenuous effort. A profound reworking of nine stories in *Angelici dolori,* it is a lyrical work of mythopoeic power. Toledo is a metaphor for Naples, and Ortese incorporates her life and times from childhood to the end of World War II in a synthesis of reality and dreamlike transformation, hope and disappointment.

Ortese emphasizes these same ideas in her latest novel, *Il cappello piu-mato* (1979; The feathered hat), which is set in Milan in the aftermath of World War II. The narrator scrutinizes the interior lives of a "poor and simple" group of young intellectuals, whose efforts to preserve their belief in love and politics end in the complete failure of their dreams.

M. Ricciardelli. In Leonard S. Klein, ed.
Encyclopedia of World Literature in the 20th Century (New York: Continuum, 1983),
pp. 438–39

OWENS, ROCHELLE (UNITED STATES) 1936–

Bestiality—oh final horror—has come to Off Broadway. It came last night at the Theater de Lys in a play called *Futz!* The strange thing is—and is this a sign of the corruption of our society?—the crime, act, fact, or whatever you want to call it, of bestiality would have come to sacred Broadway itself if another show *Leda Had a Little Swan,* had not been beastly enough, and sadly, boring enough, to collapse during previews before the scheduled opening. However, Rochelle Owens's *Futz!,* which I saw at one of its final previews, has beaten its controversial path into our ken. And I must say I am glad it did.

Miss Owens's play was first given for one performance nearly three years ago at the Tyrone Guthrie Workshop of the Minnesota Theater Company. In March of last year it was offered, in decent obscurity, off off Broadway at the Café La Mama. But then last fall, the La Mama Troupe ventured to the Edinburgh Festival, and incurred some charming legal judgments and journalistic opinions from the worthy Edinburgh burghers. Indeed, probably at this very moment some earnest German playwright, an adherent of Hochhuth's Theater of Fact, is researching an original play totally based upon the relevant documents.

I suppose you might call *Futz!* nothing more than *Tobacco Road* gone to pot, but although it certainly is full of a rude and rustic gusto, Miss Owens's play presumably has a moral purpose.

What denigrators of the play's subject matter neglect is the strong possibility that Miss Owens is not in actual fact recommending bestiality as a way of life—any more than Jonathan Swift in his pamphlet "A Modest Proposal" was really in favor of cooking and eating tiny babies. Perhaps Miss Owens is an advocate of animal as opposed to vegetable love, and for all I know the venerable Dr. Swift really was in favor of cannibalism (certainly he makes young babies sound extraordinarily succulent). But I think it more likely that both authors used shocking precepts to further a moral cause.

Cyrus Futz is a simple farm boy who happens to be in love with his pig, Amanda. Indeed he regards Amanda as his wife. As he tells his pig: "We tried to go to church but they wouldn't let us in—so I read you the Bible at home." However, Cy and Amanda are no normal couple, and the seedy normality of the village turns upon them, and Cy is murdered by vengeful villagers.

Miss Owens's little parable of nonconformity is as plain as a pikestaff—indeed, this simple moral exemplum is scarcely enough to support an evening. Yet she is a baroque artist, she embroiders wildly on fevered fantasies, and suggests a mad world comically replete with mud and lust, yet a mad world rather less comically reminiscent of our own.

In *Futz!* Miss Owens is surveying man "the naked ape," looking at our animal impulses, and satirically pinpointing them at their most obviously animal.

Clive Barnes. The New York Times. June 14,
1968, p. 39

Some people have been scandalized by *Futz!* because its hero marries a pig and the play proposes that it is the right match for him. I am going to have to pass this one. The pig—sow, I should say—does not appear in the play, and since I never got to see her I feel I am in no position to judge. I am scandalized by *Futz!* nonetheless. I am scandalized that such slovenliness should be permitted to masquerade as new art.

In the process of welcoming experiment and ruthlessly breaking old habits of thought, we should be just a bit careful not to lose our eyes and ears; indeed it is urgent that our eyes and ears be in better working order than ever. The one thing we must do with a play that abandons an old-fashioned logical sequence for a poetry of discontinuity is *listen* to it. How are we to tell whether the colliding fragments that bombard us really connect—connect in our viscera or in our brains—unless we can hear them? The one thing we must do with a visual image that means to explain reality by contorting it—a man is hanged, say, and the entire stage erupts into a dance of jerked heads and clucked tongues—is *see* it, see it plainly and cleanly so that we can inhale its intention. . . .

The play takes our sympathies for granted, it does not earn them; and unearned sympathies are sentimental sympathies. The play's language would seem unsure of its footing. A backwoods cretin turns to Futz, who is very, very proud that his bride has twelve teats or exactly ten more than any stupid woman has, and says of the community that "anyways they would like the full freedom to do what you done." I don't think "the full freedom" is a cretin's phrase. I think it is Miss Owens's phrase, insensitively and tendentiously dropped in from the outside; it makes me disbelieve in her cretins. The play's structure—if one may use such a conventional term in these outlands—is aimlessly disproportioned, spending far more time on a mother's boy who has slaughtered his sweetheart than is ever helpful to our presumed concern for Futz.

Walter Kerr. *The New York Times*. June 30, 1968, II, p. 1

Rochelle Owens's play *Futz!* is surprising enough a work to find yourself reviewing once, let alone twice. And yet this domestic idyl of the pleasures and dangers of nonconformity in a conforming society has not only run off Broadway for a surprising length of time—after all how many pig lovers are there?—But it has now had a complete change of cast. . . .

It is a curious and wryly compassionate piece. Miss Owens writes with a kind of gospel-thumping vigor. Her words bounce out with the accuracy of an old-time sheriff hitting his old-time spittoon. The theme itself, of a man enamored of his pig, is satiric fantasy, but the moral purpose of people being allowed to do their own thing in all circumstances is not bad. And best of all, the play Miss Owens has developed is in its strange, rambustious way, fun.

This is not, by any means, an avant-garde play—rather it is a conventional play about an unconventional subject.

Clive Barnes. *The New York Times*. October 22, 1968, p. 37

If you hated *Futz!* I should imagine that you would positively detest *Beclch*, Rochelle Owens's latest play to reach New York, which last night slithered into the Gate Theater, belching fire, brimstone and bad taste.

To the printed text of *Beclch*—and before we go on I had better break the news that it is pronounced "Bek-lek" as if you didn't know all the time—Miss Owens has appended a long quotation from Arnold Toynbee regarding "schism in the souls of members of a disintegrating society." In this, Mr. Toynbee suggests that such a soul is polarized into a diminishing choice between active or passive action, neither of which offers the opportunity for creativity. It is an extraordinarily interesting idea, and Miss Owens has written a play about it.

About that and about many other things. *Beclch* seems to be about kingship and society in a world where natural order has been replaced by natural instinct, where the ritual of action has displaced the processes of thought—a world nearer to the Old Testament than the New Testament, and nearer to *The Golden Bough* and the Greek tragedies than either.

What *Beclch* is about is one thing, but what emerges is another. Miss Owens favors plays knee-deep in filth and metaphor, which given the human condition is not unlikely. It is a stinking place where Hieronymus Bosch would feel at home, and even the famous Krafft-Ebbing would scarce feel uneasy. Yet where in *Futz!* her dirty-black humor found a joyous imagery in the nonconformist pig lover, her story of Queen Beclch is more obscure, more obscene, and more tantalizing.

To put no finer point on it this play, conventionally, in many ways is absolutely disgusting. . . .

But where Miss Owens disappoints is not in her ideas—however raw and rough these may be on tender sensibilities—but in their execution. The play is badly written—or at least this production made it seem so, for it reads better than it was played here.

The symbolic story of the great white African queen exerting her power over kings and subjects, until at last her time for ritual destruction arrives, might have been engrossing. But Miss Owens can never decide satisfactorily whether she wants to emphasize the darkness of her human sacrifices, the grim terror of a world without conscience, and the insensitivity of the new human jungle, or whether she wants to play intellectual footsie with us. Thus at one moment she is all blood-serious, and the next she is sliding wildly into bathos with a feeble joke or a careless idiomatic anachronism.

And her central theme, beneath the human mess she revels in, is glimpsed only sporadically. At times you want to grab the playwright by the throat and say: "Lady, it is not only an interesting thing you are trying to say, it would be even more interesting if you were saying it."

Clive Barnes. *The New York Times.*
December 17, 1968, p. 59

The bestiary of Rochelle Owens, who unleashed *Futz!* and *Beclch* off Broadway last year, opened again last night to disgorge a new cargo of grotesques into the Cafe Le Mama Theater in two one-act plays, *The Queen of Greece* and *Homo.*

A naturalist who culls her specimens in the jungle of human degradation, Miss Owens works for the most part with primordial types, deformed in intellect or physique, who infect the planet with lingering coarseness, greed, racism and war while lusting after the meretricious.

Their distinguishing mode of expression—their primitive poetry—is the grunt, the moan, the obscene gesture, the gross insult or open brutality. The symbol of their misguided lust—in both the brief curtain raiser, *The Queen of Greece,* and *Homo*—is the blonde bitch, forever luring, forever humiliating her blindly devoted subjects into uncivilization.

Miss Owens is having fun with the myth of Nordic superiority; she is raging at the inching, haphazard pace of mankind toward betterment; and despite the bleakness of her vision, the fact that she cares enough to express it conveys its own optimism.

But it is easier to admire her darkly durable faith than it is to praise her technique as a playwright. Like her primitives, she is unrefined, dealing in suggestion and shadow rather than striking sharply to illuminate. What little there is of language is scarcely memorable and never sustained and much or the fleshing out of scenes appears left to the director. One carries away the recollection of isolated moments of involvement with anguish, but little sensation of cumulative force.

Lawrence van Gelder. The New York Times.
April 12, 1969, p. 40

Her ground-breaking play, *Futz!*, written in 1958 and first produced in 1965, relates in expressionistic fashion the barnyard love of farmer Cyrus Futz for his sow, Amanda, and the destructive effects their amour has on the local villagers. *He Wants Shih*, written in 1967 and produced in 1975, tells of the mythical Chinese Emperor Lan, who sheds his own cultural definitions of masculinity and patriarchy to discover the "shih"—the everything—in himself.

Owens is also the author of *Beclch, Homo, Istanboul, The Karl Marx Play, Contraption, Emma Instigated Me, Chucky's Hunch,* and *What Do You Want Piere Vidal?* Her latest play, *Three Front,* was recently given a workshop production at The Omaha Magic Theater.

Although best known as a playwright, Owens is an equally prolific poet, having written nine collections of poetry, including *The Joe Chronicles* (1979), and *Shemuel* (1979). Recently Owens has also worked in video. She directed an autobiographical work which merges video art with paintings, sculpture, and photographs in a fractured narrative based on her most recent collection of poetry, *How Much Paint Does the Painting Need* (1988).

Critic Len Berkman notes that Owens's poetry informs her dramatic aesthetic, albeit not in the hackneyed sense of the naturalistically "poetic" language enshrined by writers like Tennessee Williams. Owens's dramatic poetry is predicated on a visceral and semiotic transformation rather than an emotional lyricism.

Speaking of Owens's *The Karl Marx Play* (1974), which juxtaposes the historical Marx, literally entangled with his intestinal bourgeois aspirations, with a messianic Marxist Leadbelly of Blues fame, Berkman remarks that:

> She achieves here a depth-by-juxtaposition (as opposed to depth-through-exploration); she carefully arranges and repeats in varied patterns the primary influences and absorptions of Marx's career. (This method is also a trait of her poetry.)

Chucky's Hunch (1981) is one of Owens's more accessible works; it ostensibly addresses more mundane and contemporary feminist concerns such as empowerment and victimization. Written in the form of an epistolary monologue, the alcoholic Charles "Chucky" Craydon composes unanswered letters to his ex-wife who has just won the New York State Lottery. Woven into this narrative is a grotesque parody of an Oedipal nightmare, as Chucky witnesses the sexual ascent of his eighty-five-year-old mother.

Whether it be Cyrus Futz, Emperor Lan or Chucky Craydon, Owens's characters challenge our cultural perceptions of gender and sexual identity. If we usually understand the term *gender* as a purely cultural definition of sexuality . . . it can be said that many of her plays explore gender and cultural perceptions of sexuality in ways that allow for an expanded consciousness and redefinition of these terms.

G. B. Coleman. *Theater.* 20:2, 1989,
pp. 19–20

A curious and contradictory writing strategy motivates the "play" *Chucky's Hunch.* Rochelle Owens pens a compelling and disturbing contemporary performance by silencing dramatic dialogue and minimizing theatrical action, those two very tangible attributes of occidental drama that lend shape to heroic characters and theater's many primal scenes. Although Chucky himself enunciates the terrors of sexual trauma and what he calls "reptile age fears," his author limits his theatrical properties to the echoed monologue of twelve letters already written to Elly, the second of Chucky's three wives. These epistles are supplemented in performance by two other texts. First, a taped narration of "primal scene" in which a copulating bestial couple, a snake and a porcupine, devours Chucky's dog in the course of a love ritual. Second, a supplementary epistle from Chucky's mother to Elly. This letter recalls Elly's earlier "loss" of Chucky's unborn baby and confirms the death of the dog Chucky had grown to cherish "just like a little child, my son, and Ma's grandchild." Similar accounts of loss doubled by the wounds of representation surface throughout this spoken performance. Reliving the broken memories of the unfulfilled American dream, Chucky's letters recount the disruption of his fragile life brought about not only by the unnatural death of his dog but also by an added instance of Oedipal displacement—the erotic love affair of Chucky's eighty-five-year-old mother with the eighty-two-year-old Chester Nickerson. The complex memory of doubled Oedipal threat prompts Chucky to recount his subsequent epic journey into upstate New York's "forest primeval" to avenge the ritualistic slaughter of Freddy. This scenario is accompanied by other graphically violent tableaux inscribed throughout the play's primary scene of textuality, the series of Chucky's misogynistic love letters, replete with the best of the epistolary genre's incompatible narrative impulses—vengeance and nostalgia, defiance and desire. . . .

Clearly, Rochelle Owens presents her audience with only a slight degree of any feminine force; still, the degree itself could be argued to be almost inconsequential. For it is the symbolic value of measure, the Law-of-the-Father, that is here under review. Marked by a tone different from the "awful" judgment of the "old American father," this marginal letter [from his mother] so out of place among Chucky's angry communications, equates the experience of writing with primal reflections on the female scene of creation. This is the enigmatic scene that stands aside—in-difference—from the dangerous inheritances of fathers and their maddening dramas. This is the scene "of woman's style" that Owens' anxious readers might want to remember amid the maddening spectacle of Chucky's phallic play of letters.

Timothy Murray. In Enoch Brater, ed.
*Feminine Focus: The New Women
Playwrights* (New York: Oxford University
Press, 1989), pp. 186–87, 207

There's a celebration going on this fall at La Mama to fête the theater's thirtieth anniversary, and the party girl of the moment is an invisible sow named Amanda. Amanda is the star of *Futz!*, . . . by Rochelle Owens, that's being revived with much of its original cast (through November 3). The pig may be imaginary, but that doesn't matter to Farmer Futz (John Bakos), who looks at her from across the barnyard with an affection not seen since Tom Ewell serenaded his hog in the 1962 version of *State Fair*. Bakos's attachment, unlike Ewell's, is carnal, and it meets with widespread scorn. The town tramp (Penny Arcade) thinks the love unnatural; when Futz spurns her, she riles up the townspeople. Local fellers, led by Sheriff Sluck (Peter Craig), conduct an inquisition. . . .

When Tom O'Horgan (*Hair*, etc.) directed *Futz!* twenty-four years ago, it was thought daring and dirty: a parable about sexual repression. This time around, his production comes off as pure corn pone—ritualistic hokum.

The New Yorker. November 4, 1991, p. 4

OZICK, CYNTHIA (UNITED STATES) 1928–

When Cynthia Ozick clears the Jamesian hurdles she has set up for herself in her large first novel, *Trust*, we realize that she has a voice of her own, and that it is direct, poetic, inventive, playful, and, more often than not, full of wisdom. But first we must dismiss, as a dismal bore, a great part of the pseudo-Jamesian concerns of her book. Mrs. Ozick offers a world of high finance and policy-making, a world not entirely supported by the author's craft despite her verbal skill. . . . In this densely populated book filled with characters and caricatures who insist upon their right to be endlessly clever with each other, only the heroine and her stepfather, Enoch Vand, achieve real life. His odyssey from ambition to theology is worldly but personal, and Mrs. Ozick handles it movingly. For she is a committed, serious writer, concerned with the world but also with the word. She has written an interesting and sometimes brilliant first novel.

Elinor Baumbach. *Saturday Review of
Literature*. July 9, 1966, p. 34

The sense of gratuitousness [in *Trust*] extends to the very existence of the characters. For instance, for all the detail in the rendering and the energy with which she is invested, the heroine's mother seems more like an hallucinated projection of the heroine's resentment than a credible mother or wife or woman. Mrs. Ozick, on the other hand, is successful in creating her arch-conservative first stepfather, particularly in the long episode in which he reveals to the heroine the truth of her past.

One wants to mitigate the harshness of the judgment of the novel, because the novel shows symptoms of power and talent. But the inescapable impression that the novel makes, despite every desire to wish it well, is that the book is a performance from ambition, that if Mrs. Ozick is to write a successful novel she must achieve a more authentic accommodation between her language and her feeling.

Eugene Goodheart. Critique. 9:2, 1967,
p. 102

There is now in this country a generally unrecognized renaissance of the short story, and for one writer to put three of the best into her first collection [*The Pagan Rabbi, and Other Stories*] is extraordinary. Cynthia Ozick works with fantasy, or with engaging conceits. Her stories, nudged on to the track, accelerate, change gears, turn at alarming angles from their predicted courses. . . . Living fraudulently, whether by ignorance or design, is one of [her] major themes. . . . Nothing happens in her stories that is not bound up into the whole. Nearly all of them, for all their wit and their absurdities, turn out to be both funnier and sadder than we expected at the start. She builds her stories carefully and she writes them very well. They will be with us, I think, for some time.

Peter S. Prescott. Newsweek. May 10, 1971,
p. 112B

Miss Ozick's first book, the novel *Trust*—rich, convoluted, even virtuosic—revealed a rare quality of mind and a joy and a facility in language that was almost literally staggering but, because of its very complexity, tended at times to be opaque. In [*The Pagan Rabbi, and Other Stories*] . . . all that was best in the novel—that relentless, passionate, discovering and uncovering intelligence—is present and instantly recognizable, but there is now a difference in the prose. It is sharpened, clarified, controlled and above all beautifully, unceasingly welcoming. . . . Cynthia Ozick is a kind of narrative hypnotist. Her range is extraordinary; there is seemingly nothing she cannot do. Her stories contain passages of intense lyricism and brilliant, hilarious, uncontrollable inventiveness—jokes, lists, letters, poems, parodies, satires.

Johanna Kaplan. The New York Times.
June 13, 1971, p. 7

Cynthia Ozick comes forward in [*The Pagan Rabbi, and Other Stories*], not as a Jewish writer, but as a Jewish visionary—something more. All of her characters are, to begin with, distraught, distended by the world, trapped by misunderstanding, incommunicativeness, loneliness, exhaustion. But their distraction is only a starting-point. The stories are never simply descriptive or evocative. . . .

Cynthia Ozick is always refining and winnowing obsessions and for the projection and substantiation of obsessions, thought is indispensable. A writer has to mind the language when obsession is at stake. It isn't enough to record the experience, because the experience is not given. It is wrested from the encumbrance of normal perception and wrenched apart, examined like the entrails of a haruspex and sewn up again differently. For this work all of the literature, philosophic, moral, mythological, and all of the language, its unfamiliar words and its delicious words have to be used. And Cynthia Ozick does all this, the language textured by a network of associations, reminiscences, allusions to the vast intellectual tradition of the West which has tried to crack the hard nut of thought with its bare teeth.

Arthur A. Cohen. Commonweal.
September 3, 1971, p. 462

Cynthia Ozick is a writer with a lot on her mind. Being American she worries about it and claims at one point that she is as ignorant as a writer must be and reads nothing but sensational newspaper accounts. Being Jewish and intellectual she doesn't push that pose very far and actually gives us [in *Bloodshed, and Three Novellas*] a thoughtful preface along with four substantial stories that contain or point at serious ideas without precisely succumbing to viewiness. What does she think about? About the conflict of cultures taking place in the minds and hearts of young Jews living just a generation past the time of the Holocaust; problems of conduct and belief for those who may want access to Jewish tradition yet who cannot accept the cultic aspect of the religion. . . .

Ozick's thoughts remain interesting even when the reader finds flaws in their logical process or finds them suffused with a sort of parochialism. . . .

All these stories have puzzling endings. That's because Ozick's imagination is adventurous, with a feeling for life as mystery and riddle. When she uses complex forms, as in "Usurpation," it's not for show but because the relationships to be defined between tradition and the individual talent are themselves complicated and morally perplexing. Her prose is often richly colored and nuanced, owing something to Woolf and Lawrence, and she also has an acute ear for the way the varieties of American character betray themselves in the many variations of American vernacular speech, including such "foreign" American vernaculars as that of the worker-rabbi in "Bloodshed" and the Bulgarian-American doctor in "An Education." Wherever

American writing is going now, Cynthia Ozick is a distinctive and bright part of that movement into the future.

Julian Moynahan. *The New York Times.*
April 11, 1976, p. 8

Cynthia Ozick could have been a scholar; a generation younger and she might have been a rabbi. What she has become, luckily for us, is a unique and challenging writer whose intellect is vivified by all the lively juices of a story-teller and a reveller in language. Most of Ozick's work is fraught with the tension between rationalist and holy thinker on the one hand, and talemaker, invoker of magic and miracle on the other. . . . So the action of fiction and the action of magic are identical for her—both proceed by a confounding of instances, a perception of the hidden symmetry in creation's parts. . . .

Ozick has no trouble finding ideas for her stories, it's her inventive powers that are less reliable, the inhibition against tale-telling has taken its toll. What she sometimes lacks is the insane, trusting, necessary willingness of the truly relaxed natural tale-teller to let her characters walk off just out of hearing of her commands and live lives that might surprise her, almost as though she were one of her own readers. Her desires for these stories and her overwhelming delight in conundra, at times overwhelm and inhibit them; then they move like Talmudic argument, not like stories on their way to a destination.

Rosellen Brown. *The New Republic.*
June 5, 1976, p. 30

Self-consciousness about writing fiction can lead to overindulgent prose and the substitution of egoism for ideas. Cynthia Ozick is the most self-conscious writer I know of. Yet she steadfastly shuns overindulgence of any sort, and instead does what too few contemporary fiction writers do on a regular basis—think. Ozick is obsessed with the words she puts on paper, with what it means to imagine a story and to tell it, with what fiction is. The result is a body of work at once as rich as Grace Paley's stories, as deeply rooted in Jewish folklore as Isaac Bashevis Singer's tales, as comically ironic as Franz Kafka's nightmares. . . .

A perfectionist, she has written just one novel, *Trust,* and three collections of short works: *The Pagan Rabbi, and Other Stories, Bloodshed, and Three Novellas,* and now *Levitation: Five Fictions.* Yet she is one of the best. Because she deals with ideas—many of them steeped in Jewish law and history—her stories are "difficult." But by difficult I mean only that they are not in the least bit fluffy. No word, emotion, or idea is wasted. They are weighty, consequential tales, lightened and at the same time heightened by their visionary aspects.

Ozick writes magically about magical events. But she distrusts sorcery, the stock in trade of fiction writing. This irony gives her work a thought-provoking dialectical quality. Her stories are elusive, mysterious, and disturbing. They shimmer with intelligence, they glory in language, and they puzzle.

In "Puttermesser: Her Work History, Her Ancestry, Her Afterlife" [in *Levitation*], we first meet Ruth Puttermesser—thirty-four, an unmarried lawyer, something of a feminist—while she is living in her family's apartment in the Bronx. . . .

"Puttermesser and Xanthippe," the longest of the five fictions, is an almost perfect novella. Ozick's character, Puttermesser, now forty-six, is still single. She is still working for the city government. . . . When the mayor ousts her boss, political appointees take over. And "in their presence the work instantly held its breath and came to a halt as if it were a horse reined in for examination." Patronage is in; Puttermesser is out; the city is falling apart.

Puttermesser, pushed beyond fantasy, creates a golem—an artificial creature of cabalist lore—out of the earth in her potted plants. When Puttermesser is fired, the golem, who insists on being called Xanthippe after Socrates's shrewish wife, gets her elected mayor of New York.

Under Puttermesser's rule, the city is transformed: Gangs of youths invade the subway yards and wash the cars; lost wallets are returned; muggers form dancing troupes, traffic grids unlock; out-of-work corrections officers take gardening jobs; litter vanishes; New York extends interest-free loans to the federal government. . . .

Like Ozick, Puttermesser is an intelligent rationalist. Puttermesser makes a golem; Ozick makes up stories. Ozick equates the magic in her stories with the magical process of writing fiction. So writing about rooms levitating and golems becomes writing about writing, about making magic. For Ozick, fiction *is* magic.

Robert R. Harris. *Saturday Review of Literature.* February, 1982, pp. 58–59

Once there was a "near-sighted, twenty-two-year-old young woman infected with the commonplace intention of writing a novel." In pursuit of this intention, she "became" Henry James. She exulted in his work, anguished over her own, and worshiped at literature's altar. . . .

Having been James, Cynthia Ozick knew his struggles with Europe and with his Americanness quite well, and this knowledge was of use when she set out to establish herself as a religious Jew amid and in opposition to Christian culture. We are not speaking of religion as metaphor—like that rigorous Catholic Flannery O'Connor, Ozick refuses atheist and agnostic readers such an escape hatch. The characters of both are filled with anxiety about their place and privileges in the world; the writers then put them through their social and spiritual (add intellectual for Ozick, social for O'Connor) paces with high seriousness, low vaudevillianism, and assorted shades of irony. . . .

Cynthia Ozick's new novel, *The Cannibal Galaxy* . . . in a series of As Ifs that are bold, cunning, and wholly her own, examines motherhood, pedagogy, the premises of cultural and biological reproduction, assimilation, exile, ambition, idolatry, and immortality. . . .

Like a murder mystery, the book's title suggests the ferocity and tension that run through its story. The literal murders are history's province. Culture makes a place for the subtler ones in families and in schools; between parents, teachers, children, patriots, exiles, the privileged, and the dispossessed. All take their chosen or allotted place, drawing what they can from tradition, belief, and need. Those with more predatory urges join the cannibal galaxies, "megalosaurian colonies of primordial gases that devour smaller brother-galaxies—and when the meal is made, the victim continues to rotate like a Jonah-dervish inside the cannibal, while the sated ogre-galaxy, its gaseous belly stretched, soporific, never spins at all—motionless as digesting Death."

This is Ozick's first novel in fifteen years, and its length allows her to draw out her themes and her language—to portray and parody the repetition of school years, school lessons, habits, ideas; to show children as prosaic as they are precocious and a Paris as full of detail as of tragedy. "The novel is long," Ozick wrote in her introduction to *Bloodshed's* novellas, "because it is a process, like chewing the apple of the Tree of Knowledge: it takes the novel a while before it discovers its human nakedness." In that process, her gifts—a series of Dual Curriculums containing drama and didacticism, humor and passion, plain and highly enameled prose—are laid fully bare as well.

Margo Jefferson. *Voice Literary Supplement.* September, 1983, pp. 1, 12–13

No doubt many of the affinities I've already suggested account for the reviewers' habit, by now well-established, of linking Ozick with Flannery O'Connor. For one thing, both are women and, more important, both write within, and about, definable religious traditions. To be sure, mainstream Catholics had as much difficulty with O'Connor's grotesquery, with her darkly comic vision, with her powerful sense of original sin and her slippery sense of grace as Orthodox Jewry has had with the writing of Ozick. Indeed, Ozick—herself an observant Jew—is uncomfortable with the very notion of "orthodoxy." And despite those who would glibly equate her uncompromising stands with the God of "Old Testament vengeance" (a phrase, by the way, that betrays ignorance at every turn and most assuredly would lead Ozick to conduct an impromptu history lesson), or those well-meaning souls who think they honor her by calling her "rabbi" (something she is clearly not), Ozick simply (simply?) concerns herself with things *Jewish*.

And here, I think, is where important distinctions between Ozick and O'Connor need to be made. It is possible (some would even say "preferable") to read O'Connor's stories *without* recourse to her Catholic commentaries, but one is less sure that the same thing holds true for Ozick. A self-confessed "autodidact," Ozick forces her readers to become something of the same thing, lest they miss the enormous cultural forces that bubble just beneath the surface of even her most "realistic" fictions. . . .

To put the matter bluntly, future Jewish-American writers—to say nothing of readers, Jewish and non-Jewish alike—will ignore Ozick at their peril. She has changed radically the expectations that we bring to "stories." But, that much said, if there is any certainty about Ozick, it is the certainty of exploration, of development, in a word, of *change*. Hers is a restless mind, and an equally restless imagination. That she has been one of the dominant voices in Jewish-American letters for the last fifteen years will assure her an important place in the literary histories of post-World War II literature. At the same time, however, no one would want to "write Ozick down" at this stage of her career; she has many books and many essays ahead of her.

My hunch is that, as her novellas grow ever longer and more ambitious, she may yet write the important thick novel that eluded her when she was young. And I am also convinced that, whatever shape this as-yet-unwritten novel will take, it will *not* be a sustained exercise in Jamesian imitation. Rather, it will have Ozick's thumbprint on each delicious page. In short, I can think of no contemporary American fictionist who is better positioned to write the sort of novel that American literature used to produce with great regularity—namely, one in which "style" is commensurate with significant issues. I am hardly alone either in my confidence about Ozick's ability or in my anticipation about what she will produce next.

Sanford Pinsker. *The Uncompromising*
Fiction of Cynthia Ozick (Columbia:
University of Missouri Press, 1987),
pp. 4–5, 114–15

"I believe that stories ought to judge and interpret the world," Cynthia Ozick wrote in the *Bloodshed* preface. Hers is therefore a moral fiction, set in a world in which human actions matter. A passionate advocate of an essentially Jewish literature which, although written in English, she calls "liturgical," Ozick observes the world through the eyes of a deeply committed Jew. Opposing ideologies clash on the moral battleground of fictions peopled largely by contemporary Jews. On one side is convenantal Judaism; on the other, whatever is not: paganism, Christianity, secularism. A quintessential Ozick story, "The Pagan Rabbi" forces the title character, Isaac Kornfeld, to choose between Jewish and pagan values embodied respectively in his first and last names. Although it is Hellenism that here constitutes the opposing ideology, it might just as well be any system that inculcates multiplicity. Because Judaism is above all monotheistic, the Jew must shun idolatry in all its many forms and hew steadfastly to the Second Commandment. In a typical Ozick story idol worship signifies moral transgression. And if one of her Jews strays from the path of righteousness, his apostasy generally consists of abandoning one God for many gods. Uncompromisingly monotheistic, Judaism (and Ozick) refuses to countenance divided allegiance. What initially appear to be arbitrary or misconceived antitheses to Jewishness—nature in "The Pagan Rabbi"; art in "Usurpation (Other People's Stories)"; Christianity in "Levitation"—invariably turn into idolatrous systems rooted in polytheism and thus radically opposed to the Jewish idea. So pure for Ozick is this idea that it threatens to undermine its artistic expression. Since art itself can be the locus of competing ideologies, the Jewish writer must endlessly confront the dilemma not only of what to write but of whether to write at all. In the same preface to *Bloodshed*—one of her most important aesthetic statements—that reveals her moral intentions, Ozick also expresses her anxieties as a Jewish writer. As she wrestles to overcome her fear that fiction is at best frivolous, at worst idolatrous, she is uncertain even about the language in which she writes. Because "English is a Christian language," it may prove inadequate to communicate Jewish experience. The moral struggle at the heart of Ozick's art reflects her struggle to embody the Jewish idea in fictional form.

Lawrence S. Friedman. *Understanding Cynthia Ozick* (Columbia: University of South Carolina Press, 1991), pp. 7–9

God's exchange of human immortality for "Life Permanent" can have rather startling consequences for humanity, as "Urn-Burial," a poem Ozick published in 1982, reveals; for as soon as life becomes permanent, "The hinge of generation would not move" and the world grows static. Those "hinges of life"—the mysteries of transition, the evanescence of transformation—are what Ozick declares writers are drawn to. In a commencement address, an occasion she called an instant of "germination," she defined that moment as the one when human beings cease being "receivers" and become "transmitters." And that idea of transmittal, the capacity to inherit a culture, which she deems critical to the energy to send a culture on and to nurture the inventive force necessary to supplement and adorn culture, informs her art. Again and again she returns to the power of historical understanding, the nurturings of a heritage; for without them, the past, as well as the present, is forfeited. For Cynthia Ozick, not to receive the achievements of a tradition is tantamount to rejecting continuity: it is to renounce the claim to culture and influence.

A cultural patrimony, the "hinge of generation"—these are convictions vital to her texts and they are embodied in that complex and multiform figure, the father who threads his way through all of Ozick's fiction. In *Trust,* the novel to which *The Messiah of Stockholm* is so closely tied, the narrator's search for a father yields up the "secrets of inheritance" the mother has denied her daughter by attempting to re-father her. To the figure of the father in her first novel Ozick attaches cosmic knowledge, comprehension of the shaping cultural forces of history, the tradition necessary for "being and becoming." The strife against that tradition obsesses the tales she published five years after *Trust.* The generations are embattled in *The Pagan Rabbi;* fathers disapprove of their children and they, in turn, endeavor either to divest themselves of their fathers' heritage or to quiet the inner roil such a desire arouses. In Ozick's first collection of stories, the lure of a pagan world challenges the demands of Mosaic law. The abandonment of it lies at the heart of *Bloodshed*. To become a secularist or an impersonator, a person who desires a father other than the natural one, is to abdicate one's cultural roots and to usurp another's identity. The "dread of imagination," of "fantasy and fancy," of idolatry is the idea toward which the tales in Ozick's second collection of stories drive. That the Supreme Patriarch must not be disobeyed; that the father's gift of transmission is crucial, a link in the unbroken chain of tradition; that discontinuity brings on competition with God—these ideas inhere in "Usurpation," a tale that adds a further dimension to the figure of the patriarch, that of literary predecessor. . . .

The boldness of her originality lies in her intricate transformation of tradition, in her dialectical apprehension of it, in her strong writing in the Bloomian sense. Her essays and stories balance two meanings and are frequently irreconcilable. Individual stories are double-natured within the same tale and often assume shifting implications, for she is concerned to show the doubling involved in all identity. Hers is a consciousness that apprehends ideas through a prism of its own, which splits into many colors the rather austere light others glimpse. To view her art in that light is to miss her lavishing imagination, to misconstrue the laws that govern her fiction; it is to be blind to what is uniquely and supremely Cynthia Ozick.

Elaine M. Kauvar. *Cynthia Ozick's Fiction: Tradition and Invention* (Bloomington: Indiana University Press, 1993), pp. 237–38, 240–41

PALEY, GRACE (UNITED STATES) 1922–

Eleven short stories [*The Little Disturbances of Man*]. Mrs. Paley's writing is fresh and vigorous, and her view of life is her own, but she juggles her phrases at such a dizzy speed, executes so many sleights of hand and quick reshuffles, and generally presents her reader with such a variety of little surprises that it is not always easy to see whether she is telling a story or merely performing tricks with words. Most of the stories are told in the first person singular, and most of them deal, in a wry, half-compassionate, half-tough tone, with the predicament of being a woman, young, old, or middle-aged, in the world today.

The New Yorker. June 27, 1959, p. 90

Grace Paley . . . is a *regional* writer, the scribe of a local moral and psychological dialect. She writes about New York City in the way that Giono wrote about Provence or George Borrow wrote about gypsies, quietly maps out a whole small country of damaged, fragile, haunted citizens. This would seem to suggest some sort of order and stability and continuity—at least a world which stays put long enough to be fixed in fiction by a writer who publishes a book only once every fifteen years (Grace Paley's previous volume *The Little Disturbances of Man* appeared in 1959). But the suggestion is deceptive. This country is veined with cracks just waiting to open, as the language of these books is strewn with almost invisible landmines. . . .

What happens in these seventeen new stories [*Enormous Changes at the Last Minute*]? A woman watches her children play in a park. She visits her mother and father in the Children of Judea. Another woman has a brief affair with a young song-composing taxi-driver; another returns two library books that are eighteen years overdue. Children die; friends die. A mother takes to long-distance running. Blacks, Jews, Italians, Puerto Ricans, the Irish all appear and speak: the melting pot, romantic New York, a meeting place only in print now for modes of life fiercely at odds in reality. . . .

Grace Paley is occasionally a bit defensive about the breeziness of her writing manner; seems tempted to apologize for it. If you're *not* blind or cockeyed, she implies, you need jokes in order to be able to look out at the cold street. But then if the jokes don't come off, you're left with your thin skin. If they come off too well, you've hidden the street away altogether. And the nagging question keeps returning: what if the world after all could be looked at without the filter of fun?

In a remarkable story printed here Grace Paley has a writer visit her very old father, who asks her to write a simple story, "the kind de Maupassant wrote, or Chekhov, the kind you used to write." The writer thinks, and comes up with a bald, ironic tale about a woman who becomes a junkie in order to remain close to her junkie son. The son then gives up dope and leaves the city. His mother stays, hooked for good, hopeless. "We all visit her," the story ends. The writer's father says that's not it at all, she's left everything out, but when she tries again, she puts in all kinds of quiet eccentricities and odd details, writes a Grace Paley story, in fact. The father concludes that jokes are her trouble, because she won't confront tragedy and despair.

Grace Paley's jokes are an expression of her hope, then, a personal, human cancellation of life's mournful lack of a sense of humor.

Michael Wood. New York Review of Books.
March 21, 1974, pp. 17–18

Grace Paley's first collection of stories, *The Little Disturbances of Man*, appeared in 1959, when Paley was thirty-seven years old. In 1974, she published a second volume of stories entitled *Enormous Changes at the Last Minute*. These two collections have established her considerable reputation as a writer—an extraordinarily strong reputation considering that her early stories consistently met rejection, her first book disappeared from print for several years, and her style, which does not appeal to everyone, stuns responsive readers in ways they find elusive. She achieves an almost inexplicable compression in her fiction. Even her short short stories, like "Love," produce the effect of totality: they tell of life, the whole of life, and not of incidents; and the art of their telling is so consummate and yet so neatly concealed—her stories are in their own way as seamless as Katherine Anne Porter's—that she has become, like Porter, a writer's writer. Her peers have praised her publicly. Philip Roth called her a "genuine writer of prose," and Herbert Gold, "an exciting writer." Susan Sontag, perhaps selling short Paley's deliberate artistry, called her "a rare kind of writer"—a "natural." Donald Barthelme said simply she was "wonderful." For many years during the 1960s, Paley was an underground favorite, one whose book was passed from hand to hand from one reader to the next, especially when *Little Disturbances* was out of print. Now she appears in such chic magazines as *Esquire* and *The New Yorker*. The Bronx is not out of her system, but like blue jean cloth and corduroy, used originally for workingmen's trousers, it has been accepted as fashionable material by the arbiters of style.

Blanche Gelfant. New England Review. 3,
1980, pp. 284–85

In contemporary fiction, the impulse to recreate form is at loggerheads with the impulse to tell about everyday life. Grace Paley is a rare contemporary who feels both impulses, and in her work they cohere. It would be easy to read her stories without recognizing that they give two very different kinds of pleasure—the intellectual, aesthetic pleasure of inventive language and form, and the emotional, moral pleasure of deftly handled, poignant theme—

without realizing that one was having the best of two historically sundered fictional modes.

Though Paley has published only two collections of stories, *The Little Disturbances of Man* and *Enormous Changes at the Last Minute,* she is nonetheless an important writer—important in the significance of the fictional possibilities she realizes rather than in the uniform merit of her published work. She is not always at her best. But when she is, Paley reconciles the demands of avant-garde or postmodern form for structural openness and the primacy of the surface with the seemingly incompatible demands of traditional realist material for orchestrated meaning and cathartic emotion: . . .

The tragic subject matter of Paley's work reaches the reader emotionally as pathos, a tricky entity because it so easily becomes sentimental. However, pathos remains pathos in Paley's work: she jerks no tears but neither does she freeze them. Instead, she distracts the reader from pathos at dangerous moments, when sentimentality threatens, by calling attention to her wildly inventive, comic language and imagery. In those moments when her language takes on the burden of simultaneously communicating and distracting from pathos, Paley creates a unique and fascinating literary object. . . .

At the heart of Paley's engagement with everyday life is her deep empathy with her characters. Even the deserters and betrayers she allows their "reasons," as she might say, and the rest she actively likes—a stance even more unusual in serious postmodern fiction than her assertions of hope in the face of our despair. It is not surprising that this uncommon empathy, which is really the condition of adherence to subjects of everyday life, is the province of a woman. Empathy and compassion are legacies of sexism that women do well to assert as privileged values rather than reject as stigmata of oppression. Uncomfortable as it makes her to write in such a predominantly male tradition, as a woman in the avant-garde, Paley is in an especially propitious position to unite interesting forms with important themes. She uses innovative form much as she uses innovative activism, to make new the endlessly dreary and shameful moral-political world we inhabit.

Marianne De Koven. Partisan Review. 48,
1981, pp. 217, 220, 222–23

Unsuccessful daughter, twice-abandoned wife, struggling single mother, Faith Darwin embosses Grace Paley's fiction as an emblem of hope in a hopeless world. Despite hardships, both real and self-perpetuated, Faith Darwin, the protagonist of eight of Paley's short stories collected in two volumes and in the *New Yorker,* has willfully chosen her crusty life and is sustained by a rosy, secular creed. Faith's averred bohemianism, her marginal existence, her commitment to urban life, her adoration of her children, her love of her family, her devotion to friends and neighbors, comprise the ever-expanding nucleus of her alternative faith. Paley does more than yearn for a time when her heroine's heart will find its "ultimate need." For Faith envisions a redeeming and happier future as naturally evolving out of historical process which improves upon the past. For most of Paley's other characters who cohabit Faith's imaginative world, such faith in the future is often questioned, and more often rejected. But Faith, sturdy American Jewess, is a persistent optimist.

Dena Mandel. Studies in American Jewish
Literature. 3, 1983, p. 85

American short-story writers are a tough breed in any event—standing firm in a country where the average reader prefers a novel—but Grace Paley must be one of the toughest. Not only does she continue to produce stories, and usually very brief ones; she continues to speak in a voice so absolutely her own that a single line, one suspects, could be identified as hers among a hundred other lines. She is resolute, stalwart, vigorous. She is urban to an unusual degree, cataloging both the horrors and the surprising pockets of green in her native New York City. And she is unique, or very nearly unique, in her ability to fit large-scale political concerns both seamlessly and effectively onto very small canvases.

When characters meet on these pages, it's at the National Meeting of Town Meetings or the League for Revolutionary Youth. When they travel, it's to observe socialist societies. When they start a conversation with an attractive man, their subject is the ecological damage in Vietnam. Yet they avoid self-righteousness; they're not offensive. The reason, I believe, is that Grace Paley never loses sight of the personal. She is in touch with those individual lives affected by the larger issues; she can tally the cost of what she calls the "expensive moment," the private sacrifice that historical considerations may demand. . . .

There is humor, too; that always helps—a kind of running thread of humor underlying nearly every passage. And there's an earthy, angular style of speech. If I had to summarize this book's best feature, though, I would quote a single sentence. It's a line referring to Faith and her friends, but it describes Grace Paley's stories equally well: "They were all, even Edie, ideologically, spiritually, and on puritanical principle against despair."

The stories collected in *The Little Disturbances of Man* (1959) and *Enormous Changes of the Last Minute* (1974) brought to our attention a particular kind of heroine: the gritty, embattled urban mother. Sometimes on welfare, sometimes not, generally between husbands, fiercely protective of her children but often a little sloppy with her housekeeping, this woman had different names but always the same amused, ironic voice—a sort of "Oh, well" tone, accompanied by a shrug of the shoulders. In the case of Faith, the most endearing of these women, the shrug was meant solely for her own messy life, never for the messy state of the world, which she was constantly hoping (and picketing, and petitioning) to alter.

Faith is the character who emerges most clearly from this new collection [*Later the Same Day*], and she's the one who gives special meaning to the title. It is, indeed, later the same day: the woman we observed rearing her two little boys alone and dealing with the middle age of her parents is now middle-aged herself. Now she is coping with her parents' old age and with the eventual death of her mother. She is facing the fact that even though romantic love continues to interest her, it will have to be weighted with a history of past loves. And when she worries about her sons, it is because they are beyond her reach, out in that very world she's been trying to change all these years. . . .

Faith has hung on to her political fervor, as have the other characters in this collection. In "Anxiety" a woman leans out her apartment window to harangue a young father. "Son," she says, "I must tell you that madmen intend to destroy this beautifully made planet. That the murder of our children by these men has got to become a terror and a sorrow to you, and starting now, it had better interfere with any daily pleasure." In the old days, she reflects, these windows were full of various women issuing their orders and instructions. It's a thought that calls up an instant image of the Paley heroine: arms akimbo, jaw set pugnaciously, but her head now grayer and body thicker.

Anne Tyler. The New Republic. April 29, 1985, pp. 38–39

It's no accident that . . . [Paley's] third collection of short stories in twenty-six years is titled *Later the Same Day.* The same voices, older now, speak from its pages; the same characters, despite years of knowing "that madmen intend to destroy this beautifully made planet," remain "ideologically, spiritually, and on puritanical principle against despair"; the same eyes, unmistakable eyes—humorously or fiercely survey their world.

In a sense, Paley's three slim volumes of stories can be read as one continuous novel, a Jewish Greek chorus of witnesses and survivors, "revisionist Communists and revisionist Trotskyite and revisionist Zionist registered Democrats" . . . talking and talking and talking. More than any writer I can think of, Paley delights in voices. . . .

Paley's tales don't offer resolution, closure; characters age, wars are fought and children disappear, but in a sense the stories are fragments, portraits, selections from the human chorus. . . . Instead of plot, she gives us dialogue; instead of endings, possibilities; instead of conflicts resolved, conversations overheard. Most of all, Paley, refusing despair, insists on giving us hope.

Carol Sternhell. The Nation. June 16, 1985, p. 739

I don't want to pretend that these two poets—one of whom is also of course one of the finest prose writers of our time—are exactly twins or even basically share the same concerns. However, the congruencies in these books are striking, especially so since the younger, Laura Jensen, has broadened her subject matter in *Shelter* and become in part a citizen-poet, able to take her place beside Grace Paley, who in *Leaning Forward* once again takes "to the streets" with her just causes. On issues such as black-white relations, war (in Vietnam and elsewhere), money, power, how we treat old people (especially our parents), both poets don't fool around making nice images and wagging an admonishing finger. It's especially instructive to see both make valid and vital use of the facts of our public and private lives, and through their interrelationships ask the right questions—questions that poems perhaps raise best. In so doing, both writers replay Rilke's "you must change your life" (for having witnessed certain things), and both find fresh and sturdy forms for the texts they offer up.

As we know from her wonderful prose pieces, Grace Paley has been doing similar work in fiction for some time, but in this moving collection she shows how poetry can catch us off guard too.

Stuart Friebert. Field: Contemporary Poetry
and Poetics. 34, Spring, 1986, p. 93

The form of Grace Paley's stories is innovative, avant-garde, some say. The technique of her conversational stories drives them by means different from the narrative of Henry James, the epiphanies of James Joyce, the drama of Ernest Hemingway, or the severe irony of Flannery O'Connor. Her omission of quotation marks is more than an incidental choice. The absence of quotation marks draws dialogue together with details of thought, character, and place. All are one with conversation, and conversation is the form of Paley's stories. Conversation creates a community that defies the kind of alienation which inhabits much twentieth-century fiction, especially that from the United States, and that eschews the accompanying romantic self misunderstood by a hostile world. Paley's community does exist within a hostile world where characters are sometimes alone, sometimes misunderstood, but their thoughts, their tables and chairs, their very selves are a part of an ongoing conversation which is necessary, evolving life. Often conversation is with the reader made confidante. But even when the characters share their stories among themselves, the reader is not the observer of drama—as in the conversations of Hemingway, or even James. Paley's reader is not a guest in the house.

The form of Paley's stories resists alienation, romantic self-absorption, and a sense of epiphanic change. Over the course of her thirty-year career as a writer of short fiction, her stories demonstrate a consistent distrust of the wounded, alienated self and develop an understanding of the evolutionary nature of change. Change often recognized in a moment happens in a lifetime or lifetimes of days: a Paley character occasionally finds herself changed one day, but she is never in a moment devastated or reborn. This evolutionary change has a domestic quality usually considered feminine. It is, for example, a sense of change born of housework always undone simultaneous to its doing. Housework requires patience, persistence, modest expectations, but a vision of some tangible improvement. A sense of gradual change also arises from child-rearing. Only if a parent persists in certain daily repetitions will

a child's inevitable change be in a direction the parent desires. The evolutionary change evident in nature and domesticity is not the change usually associated with politics. But in Paley's fiction personal and public survival
come to depend on the persistence and patience inherent in this sense of
gradual change.

Barbara Eckstein. In Adam Sorkin, ed.
Politics and the Muse (Bowling Green,
Ohio: Popular Press, 1989), pp. 124–25

In a world where women's voices have been routinely silenced, Grace Paley
dares to create a voice that is boldly female. In her three volumes of short
stories, Paley manifests a willingness to speak the unspeakable: she is irreverent, comic, compassionate, and wise. Critics have regularly remarked on the
distinctiveness of this voice; Paley is an innovator, and her innovations often
occur in relationship to the particularly female consciousness she articulates.

Paley reports that she began writing fiction because she was "thinking
an awful lot about women's lives" and "wasn't able to get it into poems."
Convinced that women's lives were "common and important," she created
her first stories out of a desire to understand and record the lives of the
women around her. Her first short story collection, *The Little Disturbances
of Man: Stories of Women and Men at Love* (1959), reveals a sensitivity to
women and a woman-centered consciousness remarkable for the tradition-
bound decade of the 1950s. *Enormous Changes at the Last Minute* (1974)
and *Later the Same Day* (1985) continue this concern with the lives of ordinary women, while adding to Paley's achievement as an innovator in language
and subject matter.

On the strength of three slim volumes of short stories containing only
forty-five stories, Paley has earned a reputation as a writer's writer. Written
in colloquial language, her stories are deceptively simple; they can seem at
first glance to be uncomplicated and even unadorned tales, but closer inspection reveals their careful craft. Again and again reviewers and other authors
describe her as one of a kind, an original, unique. . . .

Paley's language has attracted attention as the chief source of her originality. Her stories make brilliantly inventive use of semantic and narrative
structure. Reviewers consistently remark on a language that is "uniquely her
own" and a voice that is "the defining characteristic of her art." She writes
in dialogue with and often in defiance of the semantic and narrative conventions that constrain all writers.

Jacqueline Taylor. *Grace Paley: Illuminating
the Dark Lives* (Austin: University of Texas
Press), 1990, pp. 1–3

[Her] craft, invisible as we read—carried along by the story—appears under
the light of analysis. For instance, Grace Paley's stories produce the effect
of "reality" while they call traditional literary definitions and categories into

question. They often lack conventional literary direction, so that readers must follow a story's movement from one voice, one year, or one scene to another, out of order and without the usual markers—those hints and guides that literature used to offer before the radical postmodern rulebreakers got our attention. In Grace Paley's texts, there is no apparent line, no formal, defined separation between fictions, between fiction and nonfiction—or between life and art.

Certainly her frequent use of the I-narrator and the style of her dialogue—now almost always without quotation marks—produce a spoken quality in tone and language, encouraging readers to feel they are being addressed directly and personally or are overhearing an actual exchange. The occasional direct address of earlier writers, such as the nineteenth century's classic "Reader, . . . ," was suddenly and strikingly at odds with its surrounding text, but Grace Paley's conversational engagement of her reader is wholly integrated with her narrative. One of the principal devices she employs— producing the immediacy of an apparently live presence—is the *overheard narrator*: characters respond in dialogue to what narrators say—as if they had been reading along with us and have "heard" the narrative voice.

Moreover, in her most apparently autobiographical work, characters reflect her well-known political stance, including her struggle to be responsible for her own consciousness: what she learns is learned by those characters. . . .

Scholars have begun to analyze the intimate and overtly personal translation of the family life of women and children into art, and they have defined autobiography as a frequent and major subject—acting as both cause and effect of sociopolitical consciousness—in the literature of women and (other) despised groups. Autobiography in fiction offers a telling of stories that have been untold or ghettoized, stories that have been buried, warped, or shunted aside. Ironically, their telling *realizes* them in a world that has defined them as fantasy or denied them into nonexistence. Grace Paley's stories constitute and provide such realization. Indeed, her life's work is defined by its internal coalition of political action and literary production.

Judith Arcana. *Grace Paley's Life Stories: A Literary Biography* (Urbana: University of Illinois Press, 1993), pp. 5–7

PANÓVA, VERA (RUSSIA) 1903–73

Fellow-Travellers [*Sputniki*], though a work of great merit is not without shortcomings. While following the two principal lines along which the writer's concept develops ("not to explain that which is perfectly clear" and "to avoid stereotypes") the reader will find in each some features with which he may rightfully disagree. . . .

What has led to the confusion is obviously Panova's dread to impose "explanations."

Neither the critic nor the reader demand didacticism from the writer. There is no need for the writer to assume the solemn pose of the preacher and judge and read sermons or sit in judgment upon his characters. In her portrait of Danilov, the authoress without in the least digressing from the principle of her method and without resorting to long-winded elucidations might have solved her problem. She could have done it in many ways without direct imposition of her thoughts, by shades of intonation, by the very method of representation.

Though not all the ideas of the novel nor all the artistic lines along which it develops have been consummated and answers have not been given to all the questions posed in its pages, *Fellow-Travellers* is, nonetheless, a talented piece of writing which deals with the recent war, the men and women who won the victory and the new ethical values born out of the moral and political unity of the Soviet people and as such has earned wide popularity among the Soviet reading public.

Vladimir Aleksandrov. *Soviet Literature.*
August, 1947, pp. 58–59, 61

[*Sputniki (The Train)*] is a remarkable first novel. You have not read half a page before you realize that you are in the grip of a masterly and masterful craftsman, who knows exactly, to a hair's breadth, where she wants to put you, and who can and does, put you right there on the dot every time. . . . Miss Panova's canvas has a Russian largeness, and she carries on, too, the old Russian classical tradition of writing with a cold objectiveness. . . . But what pleases, particularly, is the never-forgotten contrast between the hopes of the individual and the totally unexpected impact of circumstance upon him.

Julia Strachey. *New Statesman and Nation.*
January 22, 1949, p. 85

Panova's . . . *Kruzhilikha* (1948; the title is the name of a factory) dealt with some problems of transition from wartime to peacetime conditions in Soviet industry, but Panova's chief concern was again with human beings and their relationships. Though not as good as the earlier work [*Sputniki*], it had the same quality of detachment and understatement. *Kruzhilikha* led to a curious and typical controversy, during which some critics blamed Panova for this very quality. One of them complained, with naïve earnestness, that Panova did not "decipher" her characters enough, that no sooner did the reader come to like a character than he discovered that the author meant that character to be a "negative" one, and vice versa, thus "shouldering upon the reader the responsibility for appraising her characters.". . .

The Literary Gazette complained that at a critical discussion of *Kruzhili-kha* the novel was used by some [Russian] critics "to preach non-Party spirit in literature." The critic Munblit was quoted as saying that the principal charm of Panova's novel lay in the fact that "one cannot tell which character is positive and which negative. . . . I find it interesting to meet such imperfect people who change and toward whom my attitude changes." This, said *The Literary Gazette,* was the statement of an aesthete, "aimed at the principle of Party-mindedness in our literature." Although both of Panova's novels were singled out for Stalin awards, several critics maintained that her "detachment" was incompatible with Socialist realism.

Gleb Struve. *Soviet Russian Literature
1917–1950* (Norman: University of
Oklahoma Press, 1951), pp. 362–63

Vera Panova is one of the more gifted and prolific Soviet writers to have appeared since the last war. She was never a Party writer, nor did she directly concern herself with major political or social themes. Since the thaw, she has become increasingly absorbed with the hum-drum, the ordinary, the seemingly trivial and indisputably private events of every day. This is not easy. Pressure by official critics and state publishing houses need hardly be described here. But there is another, perhaps new, probably from the point of view of what it can do to a writer, more dangerous and more subtle pressure. Now that small areas and islands of private life have been opened for possible habitation, they swarm with the most intense and sanguine of hopes. There is a large and sympathetic Soviet reading audience prepared to accept writers who attempt to convey the personal tragedy of a public destiny; but to accept a private life not directly touched by public affairs as in itself inherently tragic would be almost more than a Soviet audience could bear. It is an optimism born of terror, a sincere but distorting necessity, to which Panova unfortunately cannot resist submitting her judgment as a writer, and which mars the otherwise excellent little novel *Seriozha* recently translated under the inappropriately poetic title *Time Walked.*

The book itself (not so much Russian as it is feminine) is presented in terms of the sensibility of an ordinary, sympathetic six year old boy. Delicately, it hangs by a hair. Panova conveys the essential helplessness of a child, and the painful, humorous, touchingly beautiful inner tricks and devices by means of which he tries to make the formidable, incomprehensible world into a world he can manage. Unfortunately, what might otherwise have been a small but flawless jewel is marred by a sentimental, or at least unrealistic ending, in which too much depends on the wisdom, insight, and character of a well-meaning adult, and which shifts attention from the tragic helplessness of the child to the strength of the adult in order to project a falsely optimistic future.

Sidney Monas. *Hudson Review.* Autumn,
1959, pp. 449–50

The novelist Panova is a sensitive woman, whose interests are those of a woman, and whose comments on life have feminine gentleness and tact. She is a "Party writer," but one with sentiment. She wears the "leather jacket," but hers has yellow ribbons on it. Her work is important because she must be credited with having introduced and insisted upon some of the most important themes of the immediate post-Stalin "thaw." Her chief themes are those that have special interest for women: love, the need for human tenderness and consideration, the reality of private emotion, the family, the education of children.

Edward J. Brown. *Russian Literature since the Revolution* (New York: Crowell-Collier, 1963), p. 245

Panova . . . expressed her ideas about the importance of truthfulness in art, both in big and small things, in the general conception and the details.

"Sometimes," said Panova, "you read a novel, and you don't believe the author on the second page, on the tenth, on the seventeenth. And if there is suddenly a flash of truth on the hundredth page, you suspect even that, for it is buried under all that falsehood. Nothing that compromises artistic truth can be tolerated in art."

Among the new writers who came upon the scene after the war there are some who are more talented than Panova. Her voice is not loud, but she wins the hearts of her readers, not by sharp postulation of contemporary problems, and not even by beauty of style, but by the special warmth of her intonation. Her literary voice is very much like herself, as she appears in numerous photographs. In these portraits we see a woman in her middle years looking at us with small, transparent, very animated eyes. The mobility and even nervousness of the face is revealed by the asymmetry of the eyebrows. The attractive lines of the mouth are enhanced by the soft oval of the chin. But best of all in the face is the smile—a smile kind to the point of shyness. This smile is felt in her work as well, and it endears Panova to her readers.

Vera Alexandrova. *A History of Soviet Literature* (New York: Doubleday, 1963), p. 283

Every new theme, image, aesthetic idea, new angle on reality has been pioneered by someone. It need not be the most powerful book in the succession of books that follow. At times people even tend to forget it when they read later and better books.

But it is the first all the same.

One thinks of this reading *My Life, Books and Readers,* on which Panova was working before she died. Just as all her earlier books addressed themselves to the present, often discovering new themes, so her last book—in which she reflects on life, literary skill and the destiny of her books—has occupied a place all its own in the new kind of literature that has emerged in recent years and is undoubtedly popular with readers.

It is neither a memoir taking a personal look at the times in which the writer lived, nor a diary meticulously recording events day by day. It is a series of stories about the artist's journey in search of himself, his own manner, approach to writing and his own view of the world.

Panova's book is a professional's reflections on the impulses that give birth to an idea, how the plot takes shape, how the material dictates the form or vice versa and how the material often resists the treatment that has been selected, upsetting the original idea, of the impressions that come together to shape the image of the main character. These and numerous other tricks of the writer's trade are not ends in themselves. In accordance with the inexorable law of all art, every line characterizes the author like a cardiogram, you see the ups and downs, the strengths and weaknesses of his talent. This kind of literature hinges on the author's personality. . . .

We are given a generous and frank account of the background to *The Train* in Panova's last book. Her own experience of grief and courage, the deeply felt philosophy of the heroic plus the experience of the people who manned the hospital train revealed to Panova the larger meaning of what was taking place and brought her closer to understanding the nation's destiny.

The Train broke new ground in the literature of the time. Like all literature about the war, it shows heroism but it shows it in the ordinary, almost humdrum life of a hospital train through "personal," "peacetime" feelings and experiences, an approach that was unusual in the prose of the time.

The author tells us more and more about the lives of the characters, both in the present and in happier times before the war. She chronicles their little triumphs and setbacks and in the process presents us with a canvas of a great war which cannot be lost because the whole people is taking part in it.

Her studied attention to the trivia of daily life and the deliberate choice of unexceptional characters lends authenticity, psychological realism and high drama to the life she portrays. The prose is hauntingly emotional. All this bespeaks an aesthetics of writing that builds on the Chekhovian tradition and has a considerable following in Soviet literature to this day. The important thing is that everything she writes is the truth, not just the truth of fact, but a panoramic and truthful portrayal of life as it is.

Telling us the story of almost all her books, Vera Panova keeps returning to how she conceived every new book, how a trivial incident sometimes gave an impulse and provided a pretext for a new work. Trivia, details, visual impressions. The chapter on how she got ideas for her books is entitled *How to Build from Blocks*. The whole structure of her work serves to bring home the point that there are no trifles in art. Often a thoroughly mundane unpoetic trifle may give a powerful creative impulse. She quotes Anna Akhmatova: "If only you knew from what litter poetry grows shamelessly."

Diana Tevekelyen. *Soviet Literature*. 10,
1986, pp. 142, 144–45

The earliest novel [of the post-Stalin years] to voice formerly taboo sentiments was *Vremena goda* (1953; *The Span of the Year*, 1957), by Vera Panova (1905–73). Less obviously civic-minded than many other works of the period, *The Span of the Year* nevertheless touches on many of the themes that rapidly became associated with de-Stalinization in literature. In striving for an objective portrait of Soviet life, the novel reveals corruption in high places and discontent among the younger generation. In addition, Panova insists on the reality and relevance of family life and private experience. Ultimately, *The Span of the Year* projects a more complex, less black-and-white vision of the world than the Stalinist classics had ever proposed. Panova's distinctive voice, compassionate tone, and avoidance of didacticism make this novel one of the best of its kind.

David Lowe. *Russian Writing since 1953: A
Critical Survey* (New York: Ungar
Publishing, 1987), pp. 78–79

PARDO BAZÁN, EMILIA (SPAIN) 1852–1921

[Her earliest work reflects] the formative influences that developed the author: an innate tendency to direct and faithful artistic interpretation, a substantial foundation of the best literary traditions of Spain, and an ephemeral ingredient of romanticism, destined to speedy dissipation in the powerful solvent of the author's true nature. The remarkable erudition of Señora Pardo Bazán, her well grounded knowledge of science and philosophy, was manifest . . . in her first novel. . . . She comprehended more and more the tendency of the modern novel, its leading place in contemporary letters, its obligation to reflect nature and society in their vitality, without juggling the truth to give place to literary fictions more or less beautiful. She concluded that every country must cultivate its own literary traditions, particularly when they were so illustrious as those of Spain, but must do this without prejudice against the acceptance of modern methods. . . . With these ideas fresh in mind, [she provided] one of the first echoes in Spain of French Naturalism, with which she contrasted, and gave preference to, a national realism.

Sylvester Baxter. *Cosmopolitan*. June, 1893,
p. 232

Although credited by some writers with having founded the realist school in Spain, the authoress herself always denied it, affirming that Pereda had been before her. However that may be, there is no doubt that her novels, and still more her polemical writings, in which she showed herself a fearless champion of the New School, had a great and permanent influence on the literature of her country. It is the position taken up by this intrepid woman writer at a critical stage of literature, as well as her gallant struggle against sex disabilities, more marked in Spain than in other lands, that make her story so interesting. Regardless of criticism, she deliberately threw herself across the strong current of contemporary national production, taking what she required from French sources—from Daudet rather than from Zola—and grafting it on to the sturdy tree of the old Spanish tradition, [and] started that series of novels that have since made her famous.

Beatrice Erskine. Contemporary Review.
August, 1921, p. 241

Doña Emilia discreetly calls those books that aspire to reform while they divert hybrids, and she considers it less evil not to pay attention to morals than to falsify morals, and she regards as deadly and pernicious almost all novels that sustain theses or theories, granted that they are taken seriously. . . . After affirming such things . . ., for this lady to persist in telling us that she is a naturalist is as if, after expounding the Christian doctrine in as Catholic a fashion as Father Ripalda, she should say to us that she is a Quaker or an Anabaptist. . . . When Zola learned that there was in Spain a militant Catholic woman who defended his system he hardy believed it; he was astonished. . . . It is evident that Spanish naturalism is of another sort and not Zola's. . . . Doña Emilia strives to reform naturalism in order that she and other Spanish authors may be comfortably embraced in the movement.

Juan Valera. University of Texas Bulletin.
July 1, 1926, p. 14

For her contemporaries, Pardo Bazán was a writer of surprisingly virile temperament. She was considered very much as the next generation regarded Unamuno, as an aggressive polemicist brought up in the stale odor of tradition yet inwardly craving for life-giving breezes from distant horizons. . . . This polemical activity, incompatible with traditional domesticity of Spanish womanhood, seemed most unusual to critics; they adopted the practice of referring to the "masculinity" of Pardo Bazán. . . . What Pardo Bazán lacked in originality was offset by her understanding and breadth of vision. No side of human activity failed to awaken vibrations in her mind, and in every sphere of knowledge she displayed an understanding superior to that of, say, Unamuno. . . . These qualities make her much more typical of her period than Unamuno. . . . [She is] the most enlightened, if not the most illustrious representative of her age.

Ronald Hilton. Books Abroad. Autumn,
1952, pp. 345, 347

Doña Emilia was essentially a truth-worshipper. This is what undoubtedly first attracted her to Zola's naturalism. It was a school that made of the novel a study, something more than a mere piece of entertainment. And she has a gift for seeing the truth. . . . A firm equilibrium and a clear penetration are her two outstanding qualities. . . . She could appreciate Zola's epic genius and lyricism, although in attempting to imitate them she was unsuccessful. Her pictures always came out as clear and real as her own matter-of-fact way of seeing the world around her. And this is the inevitable realism of her temperament that gives unity to her work.

The influence of Zola upon Pardo Bazán was great, long-continued, and entirely beneficial. Under it she wrote her best novels. Ostensibly regional many of them, yet they have a cosmopolitan, modern spirit which will make them last and which makes them intensely readable.

Donald Fowler Brown. *The Catholic
Naturalism of Pardo Bazán* (Chapel Hill:
University of North Carolina Press, 1957),
pp. 154–55

Pardo Bazán was similar to Zola in her sensitivity to the momentary effects of light on objects and to the varying nuances of color. . . . In the novels which best represent her modified Naturalism . . . Pardo Bazán has recourse to Impressionist techniques in her descriptions of landscapes and characters, and examples of these techniques occur often enough to affirm that they were the result of a conscious effort to effect Impressionist verbal imagery. . . . Like the Impressionist artist who seeks to capture the everchanging colors of the landscape, Pardo Bazán, through vigorous expressions of shades and colors, endeavors to convey the kaleidoscopical nature of the landscape. . . . [After a period of] near disregard for Impressionist techniques . . . she [then] reverts to those methods impelled by a new interest, awakened by the influence of Modernism, in the procedures of the painters of the Impressionist school.

Mary E. Giles. *Hispanic Review.* October,
1962, pp. 306–15

Emilia Pardo Bazán . . . one of the giants of nineteenth-century realism and naturalism, ranks on a par with Galdós, Clarin, and Valera, and clearly above other male writers. Spain's most significant feminist in the past century, she is also that country's greatest woman writer, rightly credited with introducing naturalism to Spain. Influential both in her theory and practice of the novel, she defended higher education for women and advocated better treatment of illegitimate children. Her presentation of female sexuality as natural rather than reprehensible, criticism of the double standard, and impersonal presentations of many instances of abuse of women and children are but a fraction of the necessary and significant foundations she constructed for the benefit of future writers. More important than her ideas, perhaps, was her example, and the tenacity with which she defended women's rights to areas previously reserved for men. Pardo Bazán, Monserdà, and several lesser contemporaries lived until well into the present century, so that new feminine writers appearing on the scene after 1900 were not alone, bereft of tradition and preceptors, as had been essentially the case a hundred years before. Their establishment of an initial feminist canon helps to explain the surprising quantity, quality, and visibility of women writers in Spain today.

Janet Pérez. *Contemporary Women Writers of Spain.* (Boston: Twayne, 1988), pp. 13–14

When Emilia Pardo Bazán published *Los Pazos de Ulloa* (The manor house of Ulloa) in 1886, the diversity of competing genre models placed contradictory demands on the shape of the narrative. The writer whose work would emerge as the seminal novelistic presence in late nineteenth-century Spain, Benito Pérez Galdós, had already begun to define the contours of Spanish realism in his own novels, while the theories and novels of Emile Zola were being debated in literary circles in a polemic to which Pardo Bazán herself added no little fuel with her reasoned but unflinching presentation in *La cuestión palpitante* (The critical question) (1883). Against these two emergent models stood the tradition of the prevailing genres that had given shape to the Spanish narrative throughout the nineteenth century: romanticism, *costumbrismo* or regional sketches, the sentimental novel, and such enduring genres as hagiology. Pardo Bazán stands at the confluence of these literary impulses, some in ascendancy, others on the wane, and charts the path of her novel through the largely male-defined and male-dominated waters. In adopting the realist-naturalist mode, she also positions herself within a male genre tradition without entirely disengaging her fiction from the influences of either male-voiced *costumbrismo* or the female-voiced sentimental novel.

Pardo Bazán forges her novel from the conjunction of *costumbrista* set pieces, realistic portrayal and plotting, sentimental exaltation of motherhood, and naturalist observation of man and nature. Fashioning her response to the claims of competing genre traditions, she builds a synthesis of referential representation (realism), detached observation (naturalism), and moral suasion (sentimental novel). Within this resolution of conflicting genre imperatives, *Los Pazos de Ulloa* manifests an underlying gender-linked tension. This tension arises from Pardo Bazán's subversion of the boundaries of gender differentiation marked out in the varying modes on which her novel draws. . . .

As a female novelist writing predominantly within genre traditions established by male writers, Pardo Bazán might be expected to mark her difference by expressing her fictional world through a female narrator or privileging female experience. Instead, in *Los Pazos de Ulloa* she appears to work consistently within the conventions already shaped by her male contemporaries. And yet, beneath the ostensibly male narrative voice and the male-dominated vision there is a discernible female presence and, more significantly, a female voice that subverts the boundaries of male and female experience and vision. The female presence is secondary and subordinate in the novel, the female world is interior and enclosed, the female voice is silenced, the female is externally defined and dependent—it is precisely these features constituting the vision of the feminine that Pardo Bazán incorporates into the novel. Julián's insistent comparison of Nucha with artistic representations of the Virgin underscores this view of woman: she is pre-viewed, pre-read, predetermined. Her essence is imposed essence, her identity responds to external definition. That is, the process of reading is in itself a preshaped experience, prepared by our expectations and knowledge of genres and readers. Pardo Bazán utilizes reader expectations not only in her reworking of familiar thematic material but in challenging the boundaries of male and female spheres while appearing to retain the conventions of the male narrative voice and shared male world.

> Mary Ellen Bieder. In Noël Valis and Carol
> Maier, eds. *In the Feminine Mode: Essays
> on Hispanic Women Writers* (Lewisburg,
> Pennsylvania: Bucknell University Press,
> 1990), pp. 131, 142

By the time Emilia Pardo Bazán published *Memorias de un solterón* [The memoirs of a confirmed bachelor] in 1896, she could have become a very discouraged woman. Long committed to the instruction and enlightenment of Spanish women by means of her fiction, numerous publishing projects—including Spanish translations of works by Mill and Bebel—and the example of her own experience, Pardo Bazán's efforts were met repeatedly with indifference at best, hostility at worst. Considering this plight toward the end of her career, she quipped: "I have proof that if there were to be a plebiscite for the purpose of deciding whether to hang me or not, the majority of Spanish women would vote yes!" ["Tengo la evidencia de que si se hiciese un plebiscito para decidir ahorcarme o no, la mayoría de las mujeres españolas votarían ¡sí!"] But Pardo Bazán remained undaunted; although chastened by the trying consequences of her feminism, this tenacious reformer made yet another attempt through *Memorias* to sell her message. Continuing the family saga of *Doña Milagros* in this novel, the author directs her attention to the everyday struggles of the novel's female characters. . . . [T]he novelist hoped that by means of another engaging tale, she could sweeten her lesson and finally insinuate it into the hearts of her female readers.

> Elizabeth J. Ordóñez. In Noël Valis and
> Carol Maier, eds. *In the Feminine Mode:
> Essays on Hispanic Women Writers*
> (Lewisburg, Pennsylvania: Bucknell
> University Press, 1990), p. 146

Un viaje de novios (A wedding journey), published in 1881, is Emilia Pardo Bazán's second novel. The scant critical attention which it has been accorded condemns it as a failed realist-naturalist novel, and in one case it is dismissed as being no more than a "feeble romantic novelette." The common perception of critics from Alas onwards who have dealt with *Un viaje de novios* in terms of genre and structure is that it is an experimental work, lacking in the proper balance of narrative elements; that it is ridden with "inhibiciones" of a moral, social or aesthetic nature which vitiate its standing as a realist novel; and that it is marked by "a gap between theory and practice" which [David Hern sees], characteristic of Pardo Bazán's literary output in the decade 1879–1889.

In general, it would be fair to say that such critics are uneasy about the degree of control, or lack of it, which the author exerts over her text. They are particularly dismissive of the novel insofar as it demonstrates a residue of Romanticism, which they perceive as inappropriate in a work which Pardo Bazán herself claims in the Prologue to be an "estudio social, psicológico, histórico" in true realist tradition. Always implicit in this criticism is the assumption that this resort to the Romantic is a tendency peculiar to the female writer, to which she turns despite herself and in spite of her professed intent to adhere to the objective, scientific doctrines of realism. . . .

Pardo Bazán's recourse to the romantic mode in *Un viaje de novios* is not due to defective narrative technique, nor to unconscious impulse, but it marks the first step on the path to the denunciation of the condition of women in Spain which Pardo Bazán later states plainly in her essays on women in Spanish society.

Judith Drinkwater. In L. P. Condé and S. M.
Hart, eds. *Feminist Readings on Spanish
and Latin-American Literature* (Lewiston,
New York: Edwin Mellen Press, 1991),
pp. 63, 74

PARKER, DOROTHY (UNITED STATES) 1893–1967

Dorothy Parker runs her little show as if it were a circus; she cracks her whip and the big elephant joke pounds his four legs in glee and the pink ladies of fantastic behavior begin to float in the air like lozenges. . . . Mrs. Parker has begun in the thoroughly familiar Millay manner and worked into something quite her own. . . . Miss Millay remains lyrically, of course, far superior to Mrs. Parker. . . . But there are moods when Dorothy Parker is more acceptable, whiskey straight, not champagne.

Genevieve Taggard. *New York Herald
Tribune.* March 27, 1927, p. 7

Here is poetry that is "smart" in the fashion designer's sense of the word. Mrs. Parker need not hide her head in shame, as the average poet must, when she admits the authorship of this book. For in its lightness, its cynicism, its pose, she has done the right thing; she is in a class with the Prince of Wales, the Theatre Guild, Gramercy Park, and H. L. Mencken. And these somewhat facetious remarks are not intended as disparagement. It is high time that a poet with a monocle looked at the populace, instead of the populace looking at the poet through a lorgnette.

Marie Luhrs. *Poetry.* April, 1927, p. 52

In verse of a Horatian lightness, with an exquisite certainty of technique, which, like the luster on a Persian bowl, is proof that civilization is itself a philosophy, Dorothy Parker is writing poetry deserving high praise. . . . I suspect that one should quote Latin rather than English to parallel the edged fineness of Dorothy Parker's verse. This belle dame sans merci has the ruthlessness of the great tragic lyricists whose work was allegorized in the fable of the nightingale singing with her breast against a thorn. It is disillusion recollected in tranquillity where the imagination has at last controlled the emotions. It comes out clear, and with the authentic sparkle of a great vintage.

Henry Seidel Canby. *Saturday Review of
Literature.* June 13, 1931, p. 891

More certain than either death or taxes is the high and shining art of Dorothy Parker. . . . Bitterness, humor, wit, yearning for beauty and love, and a foreknowledge of their futility—with rue her heart is laden, but her lads are gold-plated—these, you might say, are the elements of the Parkerian formula; these, and the divine talent to find the right word and reject the wrong one. The result is a simplicity that almost startles.

Franklin P. Adams. *New York Herald
Tribune.* June 14, 1931, p. 7

To say that Mrs. Parker writes well is as fatuous, I'm afraid, as proclaiming that Cellini was clever with his hands. But it's fun to see the lamented English language rise from the Parisian boneyard and race out front with the right jockey in the saddle, and I cannot help attempting to communicate to others my pleasure in the performance. . . . The trick about her writing is the trick about Ring Lardner's writing or Ernest Hemingway's writing. It isn't a trick.

Ogden Nash. *Saturday Review of Literature.*
November 4, 1933, p. 231

Drunk or sober, angry or affectionate, stupid or inspired, these people of Mrs. Parker's speak with an accent we immediately recognize and relish. Mrs. Parker has listened to her contemporaries with as sharp a pair of ears as anyone has had in the present century, unless, to be sure, Lardner is to be considered, as he probably is, without a rival in this field. Mrs. Parker is more limited than Lardner; she is expert only with sophisticates. . . . But she does her lesser job quite perfectly, achieving as she does it a tone halfway between sympathy and satire. . . . Again it is only Ring Lardner who can be compared with her in the matter of hatred for stupidity, cruelty, and weakness.

Mark Van Doren. *The English Journal.*
September, 1934, pp. 541–42

One comes back to Mrs. Parker's light verse with the greatest pleasure; with its sharp wit, its clean bite, its perfectly conscious—and hence delightful—archness, it stands re-reading amply. Here her high technical polish has great virtue. . . . But what, of course, is more important is the sense of personality that converts what might otherwise be merely a witty idea into a dramatic, however cockeyed, situation; a sense of personality that gives us not cynicism in the abstract but laughter applied to an objective. There is no one else in Mrs. Parker's special field who can do half as much.

Louis Kronenberger. *The New York Times.*
December 13, 1936, p. 28

Men have liked her poems because of the half-bitter, half-wistful tribute to their indispensability and their irresistible, fatal charms. A different kind of lover, the lover of light verse, has admired her extraordinary technical competence and the way in which her verse constantly veers over into the domain of genuinely lyric poetry. The wits of the town have been delighted to see a Sappho who could combine a heart-break with a wisecrack.

Irwin Edman. *The Nation.* December 19,
1936, p. 737

The urbanity of these stories is that of a worldly, witty person with a place in a complex and highly-developed society, their ruthlessness that of an expert critical intelligence, about which there is something clinical, something of the probing adroitness of a dentist: the fine-pointed instrument unerringly discovers the carious cavity behind the smile. . . . Mrs. Parker may appear amused, but it is plain that she is really horrified. Her bantering revelations are inspired by a respect for decency, and her pity and sympathy are ready when needed.

William Plomer. *The Spectator.* November
17, 1939, p. 708

Mrs. Parker's published work does not bulk large. But most of it has been pure gold and the five winnowed volumes of her shelf—three of poetry, two of prose—are so potent a distillation of nectar and wormwood, of ambrosia and deadly nightshade, as might suggest to the rest of us that we all write far too much. Even though I am one who does not profess to be privy to the intentions of posterity, I do suspect that another generation will not share the confusion into which Mrs. Parker's poetry throws so many of her contemporaries, who, seeing that much of it is witty, dismiss it patronizingly as "light" verse, and do not see that some of it is thrilling poetry of a piercing and rueful beauty.

Alexander Woollcott. *The Portable*
Woollcott (New York: Viking, 1946),
pp. 181–82

In her own stories her acidity bit most often into the gilt and brass of a certain type of American personality, the self-absorbed female snob. This happened to be a type she knew best in its middle-class manifestations. . . . Miss Parker invites comparison with [Ring] Lardner in her focus on the female companion of Lardner's idle middle-class man, also in her frequent use of the diary form, the monologue, and trivial dialogue. Sometimes her idle, middle-class females are smug and aggressive; sometimes they are pathetic like Lardner's "victims"; sometimes both. Occasionally they are more amusing than anything else.

Norris W. Yates. *The American Humorist*
(Ames: Iowa State University Press, 1964)
p. 266

In print and in person, Miss Parker sparkled with a word or a phrase, for she honed her humor to its most economical size. Her rapier wit, much of it spontaneous, gained its early renown from her membership in the Algonquin Round Table, an informal luncheon club at the Algonquin Hotel in the nineteen-twenties, where some of the city's most sedulous framers of bon mots gathered. . . .

Her lifelong reputation as a glittering, annihilating humorist in poetry, essays, short stories and in conversation was compiled and sustained brickbat by brickbat. One of her quips could make a fool a celebrity, and vice versa. She was, however, at bottom a disillusioned romantic, all the fiercer because the world spun against her sentimental nature. She truly loved flowers, dogs and a good cry; and it was this fundamental sadness and shyness that gave her humor its extraordinary bite and intensity.

Alden Whitman. *The New York Times.*
June 8, 1967, pp. 1, 38

"Mrs. Parker's published work does not bulk large," [Alexander] Woollcott wrote. "But most of it has been pure gold and the five winnowed volumes on her shelf—three of poetry, two of prose—are so potent a distillation of nectar and wormwood, of ambrosia and deadly nightshade, as might suggest to the rest of us that we all write far too much." Even so, he—and we—have misjudged her. We are still amused at the surfaces of her work but neglect to consider their sardonic depths. We have praised her fiction beyond her poetry and her criticism beyond either, yet her earlier criticism can be cloying, her fiction until the mid-1930s repetitive, formulaic, mannered, emphasizing her "obsession [with the rich]—all of those mousy ladies who live in drab two-room apartments and visit their 'betters' for a charitable cocktail, all of those black or Irish servants who suffer in silence and *endure*." Still she had, in the end, unerring taste and leaves in the pages of *Esquire* some of the very best personal literary criticism of the modern and postmodern periods. But her greatest success remains the epigram, a form always more European than American. Here is her chief triumph: she is the best epigrammatic poet in our country, in this century. It is not much; it is a great deal; had she been willing to believe it, she might have stopped her searching. Fortunately, she did not, and so no matter where we come upon her, she leads us back to the best of her poetry, fiction, and criticism and outward to the rest. Each still has its proportionate rewards.

Arthur F. Kinney. *Dorothy Parker* (Boston:
Twayne, 1978), p. 167

"Edie was a lady," Dorothy Parker said of Edith Wharton—but Dorothy Parker was not. She was perhaps the first woman writer since Marietta Holley who could truly be called a humorist—that is, a writer whose main focus was on humor, rather than a writer who used humor as one of many literary techniques. Parker is, of course, best-known for her withering one-liners. "You know that woman speaks eighteen languages?" she said about one acquaintance. "And she can't say 'No' in any of them." To a man nervous about his first extramarital affair, Dorothy Parker said soothingly, "Oh, don't worry. I'm sure it won't be the last." And of *The House at Pooh Corner,* a book she reviewed for the *New Yorker*'s "Constant Reader" column, Parker summarized her disgust: "Tonstant Weader Fwowed Up."

Parker's funny-but-deadly poems include meditations on suicide: "Razors pain you . . . Nooses give . . . Gas smells awful . . . You might as well live." Her voice is breezy, worldly, and very cynical: "I shudder at the thought of men . . . I'm due to fall in love again." Her poems expect deception out of love, and her clever turns of phrase offer satire, not hope. . . .

Similarly, Parker's short stories suggest that woman's lot is not a particularly happy one. Unlike nineteenth-century heroines, her characters are not made contented through creating well-ordered solitary lives. In fact they are quite incompetent in the household: one husband, surveying the bed his wife has just made, demands: "What is this? Some undergraduate prank?"

Some Parker short stories have a unique blending of humor and resentment that no other writer has ever managed—particularly in such soliloquies as "The Waltz," a young woman's cynical musings while dancing with a young man. . . .

Dorothy Parker emancipated women writers from the need to be nice, to hide their anger. Though her wit was often at her own expense she nevertheless said what she thought. In fact, she paved the way for a new openness in humor—for housewives, for feminists, and for women who are both.

Emily Toth. In William Bedford Clark and
W. Craig Turner, eds. *Critical Essays on
American Humor* (Boston: G. K. Hall,
1984), pp. 206–7

As one of a handful of national exemplars, the Dorothy Parker persona was desirable to the extent that she was indeed modern and reassuring to the extent that she left certain basic femininities intact. Parker's rhetorical modernness lay in her daring sexuality (for which she paid by having her heart routinely broken) and in her sophisticated tone (which was feminine bitchiness revealed). And yet she successfully projected beauty and style, a near-total preoccupation with love and men, and a ladylike suppression of hostility (expressed only in "confidence" to her audience). The discursive space that she was able to create for herself depended partly on the gendered character of sophistication, and partly on the distinction between mass femininity—as represented by the *Vanity Fair* debutantes—and individual women. While the one was the very embodiment of female threat, the other concentrated the characteristics of "new womanhood" in iconic self-presentation, without any suggestion of alliance with the feminine horde—and indeed, with the strong suggestion of abhorrence of such alliance. In particular, the Dorothy Parker "personality" held out the promise that the New Woman's aggression would be titillatingly invested in the new heterosociality. . . .

To varying degrees of success, Parker's work managed a central contradiction: that of *speaking* to a public and *appearing* as a woman. Widespread commodification of femininity and love in the period of Parker's greatest prominence put her at increased risk of becoming a public spectacle in her own person; yet it also offered her greater capacity for manipulating the form and meaning of her persona as a love poet. Her writing as a whole worked actively to transform the conventionally private experience of love and its privatizing effects on the female lover into a social identity within an arena of public discursive exchange. More than simply releasing her from heterosexual claustrophobia, Parker's "public love" offered her *female citizenship* as a horizon of possibility rather than a contradiction in terms.

Nina Miller. *American Literature.* 64, 1992,
pp. 767, 782

PARRA, TERESA DE LA (VENEZUELA) 1891–1936

Teresa de la Parra was one of the first of the Latin American women writers to deal with the problem of a career versus marriage, and the conflict between personal choice and social convention. In clarifying her position concerning her novel *Ifigenia,* which had appeared a few years before, she said:

> The diary of María Eugenia Alonso is not a book of revolutionary propaganda, as some have tried to say; no, on the contrary, it is an exposition of a current contemporary sickness. . . . In order that the woman be strong, whole, and truly free from

hypocrisy, she should not bow before others' rules but, on the contrary, she needs to be free with herself, aware of dangers and responsibilities of her lifestyle, useful to society even if she is not a mother, and monetarily independent—not an owner, enemy or exploitable person, but a companion and friend to man. The true enemies of feminine virtue are not the dangers which wholesome activities may bring, not books, universities, laboratories, offices, nor hospitals—it is frivolity, the empty fluttering of butterflies with which the young married woman, or the lady with a poor marriage, educated in the old way and sick with scepticism, tries to distract herself, an activity which had it been channeled toward study and work would have had a much more noble and holy end.

In her own life she was able to evaluate marriage with a balanced attitude, and turned down many proposals, preferring to remain single. On the other hand, María Eugenia, the heroine of *Ifigenia* is driven to marry a man she detests by her fear of becoming a spinster. María Eugenia is forced for years to stifle her spirit, an artistic spirit, free and vital. She has become obsessed with escaping the tragic destiny that had befallen her spinster aunt, a shadow of her former self. Teresa de la Parra took her inspiration for *Ifigenia* and *Las memorias de Mamá Blanca* (The memoirs of Mama Blanca) from respectively, two of her intimate friends and her grandmother. They died before the books were published, upon which Teresa reflected, "Situated at the extreme ends of a lifetime, they stayed with me for a while, they told me of their desires for life, the sadness at having lived and when they had finished their confidential stories they discreetly went away when it came time to edit the books."

Lucía Fox-Lockert. *Women Novelists of Spain and Spanish America* (Metuchen, New Jersey: Scarecrow, 1979), pp. 13–14

Predictably . . . the male critics who praised [women's] work were more given to hyperbolic admiration of the women themselves than of their literary efforts—a custom Elaine Showalter has labeled "*ad feminam* criticism." Of Teresa de la Parra's *Ifigenia,* the French author Francis de Miomandre wrote in his prologue to the first edition: "Teresa de la Parra says everything that goes through her head, that pretty head so well made without and within, and we never feel shocked, because even in the very moments when she is most carried away by the whims of fancy or by the logical conclusions of her liberal convictions, she always observes a kind of inner law, so to speak, that prevents her from going farther than she should." . . .

Teresa de la Parra [in *Ifigenia*] instinctively portrayed the complex journey of an ego-conscious personality in search of self-understanding. That her protagonist should be a woman like herself, and one who is tormented by the paradoxes of a modern woman's condition (image vs. self, duty vs. desire, etc.), makes this a particularly contemporary and dramatic work of literature. Just as María Eugenia Alonso looks in her mirror and feels herself "in the presence of a very familiar and beloved person who was not myself" (her alter-ego judging and restraining her impulse to rebel?), the reader of this book experiences a similar feeling—especially if she is female—seeing her own other self in the mirror of the book. María Eugenia's story is not one of triumph, however, except in the sense that she confronts the perils of self-knowledge and dares to come face to face with her weaknesses.

When this book was published in Venezuela after being a success in Paris, it was met with hostility and resentment and was branded as a pernicious, Voltarian influence on young women readers. Parra's response was the following: "María Eugenia Alonso's diary is not a book of revolutionary propaganda but rather the portrayal of a typical case of our contemporary illness, that of Hispanic American Bovarism, that of severe reaction against sudden changes of temperature, and the lack of fresh air in our midst."

Doris Meyer. In Doris Meyer and Margarita
Fernández Olmos, eds. Contemporary
Women Writers of Latin America (Brooklyn:
Brooklyn College Press, 1983),
pp. 5, 9

The chronicle of the failed *Bildung* of Maria Eugenia Alonso, the measure of the tension between her potential and her actuality . . . is reflected in discursive practices: reading and writing. This type of self-reflexive, imaginative activity is central to novels of apprenticeship, where the essence of the genre is the dialectic that is established between the poetry of imagination and the prose of reality. This explains why many novels of initiation are simultaneously *Kunstlerromane*, narratives of the development of an artistic talent—poet, writer, actor—for whom the enterprise is a means for exploring the I and investigating how this can manifest its own fictionality—and in this sense the genre is very modern—precisely because the discursive work is so central that we clearly understand that we are in the realm of the narratable while we join the protagonist in the voyage of exploration. . . .

Throughout the book, literature effectively becomes the instrument that the young woman makes use of to explore herself in relation to her circumstances and find a meaningful role in society. . . . Maria Eugenia bears witness to her life as a way of coming to know herself. She reveals the disjunction between *her* concept of *Bildung* and the societal concern of female *Bildung;* she exposes the mechanisms she makes us of to bridge this painful disjunction, and confesses her ever greater recognition that she lacks the force of will to put her liberatory convictions into practice.

Edna Aizenberg. Revista Iberoamericana.
51, 1985, p. 543

In the work of Teresa de la Parra—let us take *Ifigenia* for example—the protagonist leaves Paris after the death of her father to go to Caracas and live with her cousins and her grandmother. Her new life is so uncomfortable for her that she begins to submerge herself in fantasies that cut her off from everyday reality. It is interesting to note that in this novel *all* the women are disinherited from their property and all the men in the novel show as clearly as possible that they are incapable of defending what belongs to them. In this way, the novel forces one to reflect on the social marginality of woman, who remains excluded from privileges of the civil code and the rights of the family code. . . .

The case of *La memorias de la Mamá Blanca* is interesting because, although the novel depicts a family run by the authoritarian father, the most forceful dialogue, which shapes the book itself, is the one established between Mamá Blanca and the young female narrator. A new unity is established between the two women, which encompasses spirit and letter, authority and imagination.

Francine Masiello. *Revista Iberoamericana.*
51, 1985, pp. 810–11, 816

To say that Teresa de la Parra's writing is "amiable" is the same as indicating that the texture of her literary works lacks edges, that "good taste" is imposed and that the author would be incapable of letting slip the slightest boldness in a world presented as harmonious and with that "style" that is proportioned by being raised in good society. . . .

It was in *Ifigenia* that the theme of feminism encounters its dialectical expression through a process . . . that leads to the acceptance of a conservative ideology opposed to the demands of so-called feminist movements, considering as such not only the present ones but also those that were already established at the beginning of the century. The relationship between *Ifigenia* and *Las Memorias* as regards the theme of feminism is great, although at first glance it may appear that the theme is absent from Teresa's second novel. What actually happens is that in *Las Memorias* we start from the assumption that the theme is not yet discussable, an attitude that makes us connect the ending of *Ifigenia* directly with the ideological framework of *Las Memorias*. By Maria Eugenia's renouncing her rebellious attitude, although by means of sacrifice, the woman's role within the family, submissive to a society dominated by the patriarch is reestablished. This ideological schema is the one that *Las Memorias* presents throughout. . . .

Since *Las Memorias* is an ideologically conservative work, its feminism corresponds to the modified and moderated vision that Teresa de la Parra consciously adopted. At the same time, we have the impression that the women's liberationist stance that Teresa defends in her lectures, although limited by the restrictions of her own conservative thinking, appears at a subconscious level in *Las Memorias*. In this way, the internal debate within

Teresa de la Parra, caught between a conservative past and the modernity of her European life, is transmitted to the novel itself.

Jose Carlos González Boixó. In Velia
Bosch, ed. *Memorias de la Mamá Blanca,*
Section 4, "Lecturas del Texto" (Nanterre,
France: Archivos, 1988), pp. 227–28, 235

There is in this work a permanent confrontation, usually implicit but sometimes explicit, between two moments: an *ideal* moment which is the past and a *real* moment which is the present. But in order for the past time to acquire its character as an "ideal," thus validating itself as an ideological alternative to the present world, it has to be idealized, that is, mythified. Whence the fact that the past that is shown to us in *Las Memorias* is that of a fictitious world, in the double sense of the term, since it belongs to a work of literary fiction and also that it is further mythified. . . .

This idealization and mythification of the past (colony/childhood) arises as a necessary condition to support the ideological hypothesis that informs Teresa de la Parra's vision of the world. In counterposing to a degraded present an idyllic and mythic past, valid only as a fiction and as an illusion to compensate for reality, the historical invalidity of such an ideological project is apparent. And it is this that, in the last analysis and without denying the strictly literary value of the work, permeates it with an "intimately reactionary sadness."

Nelson T. Osorio. In Velia Bosch, ed.
Memorias de la Mamá Blanca, Section 4,
"Lecturas del Texto" (Nanterre, France:
Archivos, 1988), p. 249

The unexpected popularity of the work of Teresa de la Parra . . . provoked a critical exuberance characterized by both excessive adulation and censure. A profusion of "critics without criticism," impelled at times by literary fashion and at times by the desire to "put in their two cents worth" about every book, showered the work of the Venezuelan author with, in the words of the creator of Mamá Blanca, "a white shower" (aguacerito blanco) of trivial essays of no substance. In 1980, Velia Bosch selected and published some of the more thoughtful critical essays, choosing an average of three writers to represent each decade. The selection offers an interesting chronological panorama of "la crítica teresiana," revealing changes in tone and taste, as well as certain uniformities in the critical reading of her work. The critics comment on the author's life and work, or they respond to previous criticism, either to corroborate it or to disagree and correct it. . . .

The most significant aspect of the criticism of Teresa de la Parra is how it unconsciously problematizes the feminine. The male critic confronts the difficult problem of how to locate himself before what culture has construed as otherness. . . . She (text and author) becomes the projection of an imago (cultural construction of the feminine) that in fact does not truly exist.

What does exist is the feminine subject who writes in all her complexity; it is the feminine text that speaks with all its ambiguity. The critic, however, addresses a less problematic figure: the feminine enveloped by patriarchal constriction, where the feminine responds to an imaginary configuration. The critic stands in a mirror relation to the feminine text, which functions as a slave serving his desires, particularly his desire for recognition. He exercises authority over the feminine text with a dominating, magisterial discourse that seeks its own satisfaction above all else. In other words, the (male) critic reads in Teresa's work that which Barthes has named the *texte lisible,* a fundamentally univocal aspect of the text that the reader understands and assimilates. The *texte lisible* represents that aspect of the text that is significant because it is recognizable; because, in effect, the reader has already read it. . . .

With the advantage of time since *Ifigenia's* publication, Araujo points out that it was de la Parra's irreverence and irony toward the official position, toward the cultural canon consecrated by custom, that was then so objectionable. That the irreverent words and attitudes might spring from the lips of one of the best families in Caracas, from the lips of a well-to-do "señorita," envied for her refinement and intelligence, was intolerable to her contemporaries. Araujo's reading answers those who gave the first critical response to *Ifigenia*—or, better said, those who orchestrated a chorus against the novel. The earlier criticism that read with condescension, a moralistic and censorious attitude, and an explicit ambivalence or insult, is deconstructed by this new appreciative reading. What actually undoes the earlier reading is the presumption that the Imaginary mode of signification would dominate unequivocally and would impede the possibilities of different modes of signification. . . .

There exists a level of critical discourse that does not acknowledge the feminine subject who writes in all her complexity nor the feminine text that speaks with all its ambiguity, but knows only an imago, a cultural construction of the feminine. This constitutes the recognizable text within the critical text. The recognizable text repeated itself each decade but with certain differences: what is constant is the ambivalence and the devaluation of the feminine.

Elsa Krieger Gambarini. In Noël Valis and
Carol Maier, eds. *In the Feminine Mode:
Essays on Hispanic Women Writers*
(Lewisburg, Pennsylvania: Bucknell
University Press, 1990), pp. 177–78, 191

PARRA, VIOLETA (CHILE) 1917–67

It's not easy to speak of Violeta Parra, the expressive symbiosis of the city and the country, the weaver of connections between popular poetry and high-culture elements. How can I speak of this humble peasant woman who revolutionized Chilean popular music and, by extension, the new Latin American song; who traveled through countryside, plains, and docks collecting a very old art that, however, is always renewing itself: folklore? How can I sing the life of this woman who was a singer, a composer, a painter, ceramicist, a weaver, a researcher; which is to say, the integral voice of her people?

We will not be speaking of Violeta Parra from an academic perspective. Viola wouldn't have liked that. Moreover, the libraries still neglect her and she never held university chairs; she was always suspect as this strange women without formal academic background, and this strange woman was always suspicious of the scholar who looked at art from a certain distance. . . . At least, the folklore collected by Violeta Parra does not remain locked up in lost memories and archives; rather, Violeta gave it back to her people.

To return to the initial question: how to speak of Violeta—we can do it by way of her own voice and the story that she tells in her *Decimas—autobiografia en versos chilenos* (*Decimas*—autobiography in Chilean verse meters). In these *decimas*, personal and collective history develop simultaneously. Thus, the view of the world is defined from a personal and popular experience in which various elements are incorporated: folklore, along with her own notions of a primitive Christianity, whose irrational force creates a fascinating and complex vision. In this way, the author's private "I" also belongs to a collective class consciousness. . . .

Violeta Parra compiled more than three thousand songs, refrains, and legends, exploring in that rich and hidden terrain where few have traveled. In *Gracias a la vida* (Thanks to life), Gaston Soublette claims that the hardest part was to reconstruct the text of the songs that are often found incomplete or mixed up with other songs. Violeta had to separate them and continue to seek them out, town by town and farm by farm, to put the lost fragments together.

It should be noted that the verses that Violeta compiled have links with the Spanish *romancero* as well as with the rhythm of Andean music. Various unknown instruments are also reincorporated with this music. . . . But the most important thing is the fact that Violeta facilitated the awakening and the artistic consciousness of the people.

Marjorie Agosin. *Plaza*. 5/6, 1981–82,
pp. 158–59, 162

As a movement within Chilean popular music, *La Nueva Canción* has attempted with considerable success to establish an alternative mode of popular music that builds upon indigenous folk music as opposed to imported forms while being motivated by a preoccupation with social justice rather than the commercial concerns we normally associate with popular music. Because of its intimate relationship with Chilean social life over the past thirty years, it is possible to trace the recent political history of Chile via *La Nueva Canción* as it has evolved through four distinct stages from what Paulo Freire calls *"conscientização"* (awareness) to protest, to militancy, and finally to the resistance movement that has developed since the military coup d'etat of 1973.

Violeta Parra's significance stems from her part in forming the foundation of this cultural movement and infusing it from the very outset with those qualities which have shaped its evolution. At a time when Chilean culture was gradually becoming dominated by foreign and commercial interests, Violeta's work emphasized traditional folk styles while raising pertinent questions concerning the nature and future of Chilean society. Violeta's art—which included embroidery, painting, acting, sculpture, and poetry as well as musical performance and composition—was of such uncompromising honesty and delicate beauty that it has served as an example to younger generations and even now, nearly twenty years after her death, it remains unequaled in the power of its expression and its ability to shake whole sections of the population. . . .

By bringing forth into the national consciousness the folklore of Chile, Violeta Parra was actually opening the door through which the entire *Nueva Canción* would pass. What at this time appears to be a relatively modest step, eventually grew into a full scale movement of revolutionary dimensions. For by entering into this dialogue with her people, both Violeta and the public were commencing the process of *conscientização* which . . . is "learning to perceive social, political, and economic contradictions, and to take action against the oppressive elements of reality." . . .

Patricio Manns argues quite correctly that Violeta Parra did not create a "new song" movement since the impetus behind her music was something that already existed in the creations of hundreds of anonymous poets and singers, both living and dead. What is significant in the work of Violeta was that she was able to construct a bridge over which the traditional culture of Chile could pass into the age of mass media. . . .

In the 1960s, Violeta confronted the economic and political exploitation of Chile by composing a number of effective protest songs that were to become a permanent part of Chilean culture. She also broadened the appeal and effectiveness of folk music by combining modern lyrics to the traditional forms she had cultivated in the countryside. Gradually, she began to fuse contemporary sentiments, usually of a highly personal and intense nature, into her music with profoundly successful results. Indeed, it was this musical hybrid of the past with the present that was the true genius of her work and a primary factor that set in motion this second stage of *La Nueva Canción*. . . .

The popularity and influence of Violeta Parra, rather than diminish with her absence from the scene was actually becoming more widespread than ever before. During [the Allende] period, streets and whole neighborhoods were renamed in her honor while nearly every singer and group of *La Neuva Canción*—whether professional or amateur—included at least one of her songs in their repertoire. Violeta had always been recognized by the artists themselves as the principal figure in their movement to reconceptualize the nature and function of popular music in Chile but now, as the appeal of *La Nueva Canción* expanded, so did the importance of Violeta. . . .

"The poor ask for bread," Violeta once sang, "and they answer them with lead." In the voice of Violeta, Chileans [under Pinochet's military dictators] hear their own voice. In her defiance and persistence, they find their own defiance and persistence. Everywhere one hears the voice, sees the face, and reads the words of Violeta Parra. . . .

I have no doubt that on the day that Pinochet falls, the New Song movement will flower once more, that Chileans will dance and *La Nueva Canción* will supply the music. And soaring above all this jubilation, like a dove joyfully returning to her nest, will be the tender voice of Violeta Parra.

Albrecht Moreno. *Studies in Latin American Popular Culture.* 5, 1986, pp. 108–9, 111–112, 120, 123–24

Twenty-two years after Violeta Parra's 1967 suicide, the study of her work continues to increase. She was a sculptor, ceramist, painter, fabric artist, composer, interpreter, poet, and compiler of Hispanic poetic folklore; as publications on her life and her genius multiply and her memory is enhanced, the dimensions of her magnificent work, particularly in poetry, become clear. . . .

Of the innumerable facets of Violeta's artistic life, her poetic work is one of the most outstanding. Its principal themes are love, politics—in the expression of her social conscience—death, nature, and time. . . .

Two aspects of her poetic creation are notable: her work as compiler and her work as creator. As compiler, she collected some three thousand poems, many of which have their roots in the Spanish Middle Ages. With guitar in hand, fountain pen and notebook at her side, indefatigable, she made incursions into the most isolated parts of the Chilean countryside, won the confidence of peasants old and young and obtained from their lips material that otherwise would have been lost. From this research, she reworked, adapted, or composed her own poems.

Ignored, despised, crushed in her lifetime by poverty and her condition as a woman who wanted to struggle on a basis of equality with men, frustrated by lack of understanding, failure in love, and an internal solitude that always accompanied her, today her name crosses national borders and the enormous contribution she made to national and Hispanoamerican culture is recognized. . . .

In the enormous body of Violeta Parra's love poems—whether compilation, adaptation, or creation—her poet genius appears to operate without admitting mediating terms: either it operates in an intense and active form with the best elements of traditional folk poetry or it repeats almost verbatim what it has collected. In other words, we may observe in Parra with greater or lesser frequency, condensation, simplicity, elimination of introductory words, dramatization, variety in verb tenses, dynamism, suggestions, allusion, elisions, etc. . . . In general, analysis of her work, especially the folklore work, presents Violeta as a minstrel of the twentieth century.

> Ines Dölz-Blackburn. *Literatura chilena,*
> *creación y critica.* 13, 1989,
> pp. 159–60, 167–68

The Chilean Violeta Parra's "sung poetry" is true evidence of the continued practice of the oral tradition.

Both as a poet and a singer Violeta Parra, celebrating or condemning life as a kind of metaphysical revenge (for example in "Here's to Life" and "God Damn the Empty Sky"), criticizing society from the viewpoint of "the people" with an authentic working-class concern, or scanning the triumphs and defeats in her own life (in her "Décimas"), represents a significant part of our collective unconscious "return" to the origins of our culture. And somehow she embodies part of the twentieth-century "social imagery" of the Latin American woman poet.

> Miriam Díaz Diocaretz. In Susan Bassnett,
> ed. *Knives and Angels: Women Writers in*
> *Latin America* (London: Zed, 1990), p. 87

The structuring of the book [*Violeta del Pueblo,* 1976] in four sections— "Canciones Amorosas," "Canciones Políticas," "Canciones de Aire Popular," and "Décimas"—illustrates the trajectory of Parra's work as a poet, musician, and folklorist. Especially significant are the political compositions which demonstrate a committed voice denouncing colonialization, imperialism, and urbanization, and exalting revolutionary heroes. In several works, the ironic treatment of the contradiction between the teachings of the Gospel and the practices of the Church exemplifies the didactic goal of her political poetry. In the introduction Martínez nicely points out the relationship between folklore and politics in Parra's work, and discusses this tradition in Chilean folklore.

> Catharine Wall. In Diane E. Marting, ed.
> *Women Writers of Spanish America*
> (Westport, Connecticut: Greenwood Press,
> 1986), p. 294

The exultant expression of the effects of love, product of a reciprocal relation between lovers, is not as frequent in folk poetry as the stance that presents the devastating effects of unrequited love or abandonment.

The same imbalance may be observed in the love poetry of Violeta Parra. Her poems, whether reworkings of tradition or personal creation, are better concentrated in chaos, in the disharmony caused by the pain of love than in the expression of the feeling's all-embracing effects. . . .

The intense spirituality that breathes through these poems is not expressed in esoteric and abstract tones, but rather in concrete and everyday terms. . . .

Parra's voice emerges vibrant and powerful with the use of traditional folk themes and techniques that she molds and adapts to her own style with a clear understanding. . . .

Pessimism, attraction to and fascination with death, darkness, and sadness are expressed in the unhappy love poems. Finally, there are no ambiguities in Parra's poetry. It is either white or black, smiles or tears, spoken or broken, good or evil. These alternatives, which are constants in her poetry, are ultimately resolved with a decisive inclination toward the negative pole, empty, annihilating, somber, shadowed, and weakening.

Ines Dölz-Blackburn. Confluencia. 5:2,
Spring, 1990, pp. 39, 44

PARUN, VESNA (CROATIA) 1922–

The publication of the poetry of Vesna Parun is one of the greatest events in contemporary Croatian literature. That can already be said with certainty. . . . At its best, Parun's poetry has represented, and continues to represent, a significant synthesis of Croatian poetry of the first half of the twentieth century. . . .

Aside from achieving a synthesis of earlier Croatian poetry in her own poems, she has refreshed her own expression as well as that of our poetry in general through French poetry (Apollinaire, Lautréamont), which she has read much of and in the original language. Her expression is stimulating, strong, and unerring. It is distinctly extroverted, but almost always accompanied by strong inner intensity and created through an unusual and complex intuitive process.

Zlatko Tomičić. Republika. September, 1955,
pp. 726, 733

[Vesna Parun] reveals in [her poetry] not only that she is not always a consistent poet (that, unfortunately, is a characteristic feature of her work) but also that the vital, virile, revolutionary power that was once hers has broken down or, rather, has lost its edge, that political affairs and the reality of life have withdrawn to the background, and that the woman in her has taken control. While in the fourth part of her first collection, *Zemlja* [The Earth], the political element is predominant, in her last three books there is no mention at all of the land in which she writes; her experiences and her sorrows in love might just as well have taken place on the beaches of Lebanon or California as on those of the blue Adriatic. I think it can be maintained that purely political subject matter, as also would be true of extravagant sentimentalism and sensibility, does not suit her. She is most effective when she interweaves her own personal feelings into a description of external events or when her feelings are aroused by external factors and are not just the fruit of free fantasy.

Ante Kadić. *American Slavic and East European Review.* December, 1958, p. 517

Vesna Parun feels at home in the temple of Eros, and here she is least likely to miss the mark. Different from many masculine women poets who think that they are the more poetic the more they conceal their nature and mimic others, Parun does not hide her nature but, on the contrary, emphasizes her femininity, even when she writes that she "was a boy." There is also in such poems, to be sure, a semibiblical eroticism. Just the same, she is at her best when she harnesses to her poetic coach the "agitated stallions of love," especially sensual love. . . .

Her poems could have been written only by a woman, and in our literature no one has written such poems better. In them, woman is identified with all of nature, borrowing from it the wealth of metamorphoses and forms and offering in exchange the feminine powers of surrender, tolerance, and fertility. Here Parun is a poet of basic experiences, of a powerful drive expressed either through the thin thread of foreboding or through the breakthrough of passion. Often from under the simple adornment of scenery there surfaces an animalistic sadness of *sexus.* The poet follows the entire love game: from the trepidation of expectation, through the passion of first touches, to the burden of habit and gloomy parting.

Tomislav Ladan. *Večernji list.* March 30, 1963, p. 7

Vesna Parun is, through the range of her poetic register and the forcefulness of her elemental and sensual paeans of emotionality, unique in her postwar generation in the invariable excitement generated by the luxuriant metaphors of her verse. Indeed, she is the best poetess in Croatian literature so far. Her best patriotic and social poems of the age are so powerfully charged with the individual optimism of trust in the reality of protest at the paroxysm of pain and black vision of life in an age when the knife ruled, others so replete with the individual optimism of trust in the reality of socialism, that the excellence and vigor of these poems sets them apart from the average declarative, committed poetry in Croatia after the war. . . .

Later books of poems . . . introduce new, more refined personal accents, and an individual, irrepressible, sensual, and subtle aroma for the external subjects of lyrical poetry: love. Sophisticated confessions, reveries about the most intimate textures of the human soul, fluid spiritual longing, the impulsive, erotic desires of woman had never before the appearance of the poetry run so suggestively in Serbo-Croatian. Her more recent books of verse were more a supplementation than an expansion of these basic preoccupations, except for the addition of homage to Nature and her "glorious charms."

Miroslav Vaupotić. *Contemporary Croatian Literature* (Zagreb: Croatian P.E.N. Club, 1966), pp. 65, 67

[In *Ukleti dažd* (The accursed rain)] Vesna Parun moves consistently within the traditional framework of intimate lyricism. Her poetry almost always bears the stamp of a confession and offers a very immediate communication of emotional experiences. The world about which Parun writes is sometimes the irretrievably lost world of late childhood and early adolescence; sometimes it is the moment in which, and for which, we live.

In Parun's world, poetry and love go hand in hand. Love is the highest level of poetry; poetry is the fullest expression of love. Moving within this circle Parun, with an unusual linguistic inventiveness, succeeds by constantly imparting fresh tones to her material, so that her thought, as well as the manner in which it is conveyed, never sounds banal, no matter how usual its essence may be. When I say linguistic inventiveness I do not mean innovation. On the contrary, Parun's efforts are directed toward an entirely different direction: to find within the traditional framework of poetic expression new, undiscovered possibilities. Her poetry sometimes sounds like the poetry written during the interwar years. At times one perceives echoes of poetry of even earlier periods. But she knows how to make this traditional experience contemporary and, as is the case with good poets, to give old poetic expressions new charm and beauty.

Predrag Protić. *Književnost*. May, 1970, p. 508

PAWLIKOWSKA-JASNORZEWSKA, MARIA (POLAND)
1894–1945

After all the many beautiful and surprising books we have had from Pawlikowska-Jasnorzewska, in *Cisza leśna* (Wooded silence) her tones seem diminished. We have here all the strings of her astonishing instrument, but they produce a thin sound. Her mastery has turned into virtuosity, and virtuosity turns naturally into nonchalance. In the fragile imaginary world of Pawlikowska-Jasnorzewska the flame has become extinguished. . . . The shape remains, the sad beauty of form at the service of the author's whim.

Sensual, sophisticated, ironic, and melancholy intelligence vibrates on strings that are overstrung. Stars turn to starlets, clouds acquire picturesque hair-dos. Little cataclysms or sentiments are arranged like colorful stones. . . . Perhaps one should call this kind of poetry "hidden," since the mysterious suggestiveness is achieved through a mere arrangement of syllables, a mosaiclike selection of words. Yet in this volume words have the lifeless glitter of dying jewels. . . .

Stefan Napierski. *Wiadomości literackie.*
July 29, 1928, p. 3

The filigreed, caressing, precious little poems of Maria Pawlikowska-Jasnorzewska (née Kossak), which are collected in a pocket edition entitled *Niebieskie migdaly* [Blue Almonds], are so frail, thin, fragile, so much like Batavian glass beads, that many a pedantic old Zoilus, many a shrewd connoisseur of poetic delicacies would probably be afraid to handle them with his brutal paw, or to place them with tweezers under a magnifying glass, for fear that these shiny knickknacks might break like Christmas toys. . . .

This would not be such a disaster for literature, and I would hardly shed a tear. . . . But simple courtesy makes it rude for one to disturb a game of amorous intrigue conducted in the chic blue doll's boudoir filled with the twitter of birds. Taking care, then, not to blow away the lacy illusions of the voile and the tulle, let us gallantly pretend that we, too, are amused by this discreet flirtation with the poetic Nymph and that, at least as a momentary *dolce far niente,* we are glad to listen to her confidences about her playful liaison. But the secrets must be caught with a fine net of muslin so as not to brush the butterfly make-up and powder off the frivolous wings. Clearly, we shall not find many kernels in the shells of these little nuts ornamented with golden leaves. . . . [1923]

Ostap Ortwin. *Pròby przekrojów* (Lvov:
Księgarnia Polska, 1936), p. 259

Pawlikowska-Jasnorzewska has won a distinguished literary position in Polish literature because, unlike many other women poets, she was not afraid to write of herself as she really was, to utilize the qualities of womanhood to the full. In her earliest poems she freed herself from the two most glaring faults of female poetry—prolixity and emotionality—by adopting a rigorous form of expression and an ironic point of view. . . . Pawlikowska-Jasnorzewska moved in the world of ballads and romances, of mysterious lovers, Pekinese dogs, and *fin de siècle* exaltations. It was a world of sophisticated feelings and delicate dreams originating in literature. In spite of the dazzling charms of these precious phantoms, Pawlikowska-Jasnorzewska was capable of seeing them with the eyes of an uncommitted observer. It is for this reason that her poetry can claim distinction. . . .

Perhaps it is not surprising, then, that, faced with the cataclysm of war, Pawlikowska-Jasnorzewska found herself helpless. Her attempts to treat war as if it were a love of a lady from high society seem grotesque.

Adam Czerniawski. *Kultura* (Paris).
September, 1956, pp. 134–35

In her later, more mature period, Pawlikowska-Jasnorzewska freed herself both of the coyness typical of her earlier work and of the mystical overtones of her middle period. . . . She became a classicist. This has been hardly noticed by such critics as Jerzy Kwiatkowski, Michal Glowiński, or Janusz Slawiński, who have allowed themselves to be sidetracked by the flirtatious charms of her youthful *Pocalunki* [Kisses] and have searched for her best work in her early period. They have failed to notice that it is only in her later volumes—in *Śpiąca zaloga* [The sleeping crew], *Balet powojów* [Ballet of ivy], and *Krystalizacje* [Crystallizations]—that she achieves not only her own finest work but a greatness that makes this poetry one of the finest accomplishments of the interwar period [in Poland].

The poems contained in these volumes are sensual, but the sensuality is no longer coquettish: it is profound; its dimensions are no longer miniature but cosmic. Instead of the playful face of a nymph, these poems reveal an intense passion, almost to the point of impersonality. They reveal the face of a mature woman. . . . Pawlikowska-Jasnorzewska's eroticism loses what hitherto had been too personal in it; it becomes objective and broad enough to include all nature, to become transformed into paneroticism. Her love, freed from personal details, becomes identified with the ineluctable cosmic love that draws mosquitoes and the constellations into its orbit. Her tenderness concentrates less on men, or on human beings in general, more on life in all its forms, on the life of jellyfish, of earthworms, of nettles.

Artur Sandauer. *Przegląd humanistyczny.*
June, 1962, p. 69

Whenever I read a new volume of Pawlikowska-Jasnorzewska's poems . . . and try to formulate my impressions, I always realize the need to repeat what I have frequently said before about her unmistakable and homogenous "manner" of writing. At the same time, I realize the imprecision and inadequacy of all these formulas. . . . The originality of Pawlikowska-Jasnorzewska's poetry is striking, no matter where we begin our analysis. Her themes arise from her myopic vision of the world, which for her is an inexhaustible object of rapturous observation, a veritable "forest of symbols." . . . Philosophically and emotionally, her poems reveal the melancholy hedonism of a person who, while concentrating on earthliness, is conscious of the transitory nature of what delights her: hence the frequent celebrations of the passing beauty of the world, of the ephemeral, of the blossoming flower and the tragedy of its death. . . . She is always ready to intercede on behalf of everything that is beautiful, that delights, everything whose beauty and delight is an aim in itself. She disregards utility and the norms of any absolute or general ethics that goes beyond the world of nature. . . .

An even more astonishing artistry of her technique [than her ability to create pictorial imagery, or combinations of images drawn from various senses] is revealed in the use of puns and word play, of proverbs and common-place expressions. . . .

The immutability of the poet—notwithstanding all its variety—can lead to malicious attack and can become wearisome to the poetic mistress herself. "I wish I weren't Valeri Bryusov," said the excellent Russian symbolist in a moment of depression. One can also sense this desire to transcend oneself in Pawlikowska-Jasnorzewska, and it leads her to attempts to go beyond her style, which are, fortunately, unsuccessful.

Karol W. Zawodziński. *Wśród poetów*
(Cracow: Wydawnictwo Literackie, 1964),
pp. 287–89

[Pawlikowska-Jasnorzewska] is a popular poet. Her poetic miniatures, which combine wit, nice sentiments, and subtle observations, are really charming. But they deal with a small, drawing-room fragment of life. They display the ready-made elegance of a lady who goes to a ball to be admired. They are Sybaritic and lack even a modicum of inner conflict: at the most they present trifling griefs and little acts of compassion. No doubt the poems express a true and original life, formally so strong that they can withstand the competition of many a "proletarian" poem.

But it is not so easy with drama. Although drama is an objective form of writing, one must be a "somebody" to be able to measure up to it; one must inevitably reveal one's tastes and aims (willingly or unwillingly) and prove their value in the world. Not every lyric poet, or even a novelist, is equal to the demands of drama.

Pawlikowska-Jasnorzewska's first play, the comedy *Szofer Archibald* [Archibald the driver] struck me as snobbish: the second *Egipska pszenica* [Egyptian wheat] was trivial. The latest one, *Zalotnicy niebiescy* [The blue sky suitors], is ten times better than the other two. There is in it [at least] some attempt to examine life and its forms.

Karol Irzykowski. *Recenzje teatralne*
(Warsaw: PIW, 1965), p. 406

Pawlikowska, whose poetry in the eyes of her critics was the essence of "femininity," did not view or explicitly declare herself to be a feminist. Yet, she was both claimed by the feminists and attacked by them for precisely the same reason: her poetry's femininity. Furthermore, some of her male critical detractors felt that she had gotten "dangerously close to the vulgar feminists," while others had praise for her "emancipated and daring" expressions of femininity.

The formal features of Pawlikowska's poetry, however, were highly acclaimed by her friends and foes alike. Her poems were most frequently described as charming, elegant, delicate, subtle, and pointed. . . .

Even though some critics think that Pawlikowska's plays are of a secondary importance in her literary output, these plays, more directly than her lyrics, give evidence of her feminist convictions. Two plays in particular need to be brought to light. Both *Zalotnicy niebiescy* and *Egipska pszenica* were written and staged in 1934, and both were as successful as they were controversial. . . .

Clearly, Pawlikowska escapes an easy classification. There can be no doubt, however, that the ideas she expressed in her poems and plays are as relevant today as they were in the 1920s and 1930s. Woman's right to be a human being, free to love and be loved, free to be honest with herself and with a man, and her right not to be bounded by society's rules and conventions that set different standards for men and women are concepts almost taken for granted by contemporary western society. Yet, even today, the theory and practice are far apart. Woman's refusal to accept that "biology is destiny," and her refusal to play a conventional "feminine" role and to accept the conventional myth of "masculinity" are as much an issue to a thinking woman today as they were to Pawlikowska.

Malgorzata Pruska-Carroll. Polish Review.
26:2, 1981, pp. 36, 48–49

PERI ROSSI, CRISTINA (URUGUAY) 1941–

Cristina Peri Rossi is the author of four books of poetry and six collections of short stories, the last of which has just appeared in Spain with a rather strange title—*The Museum of Useless Efforts*. The title story introduces us into a fascinating universe, which, by its very absurdity, casts doubt on those activities of ours that have always been consecrated by tradition. The traveler who has walked through an infinity of labyrinthine museums in his informed wanderings from city to city, and seen so many Greek vases, Egyptian mummies, Aztec statuettes, medieval suits of armor and countless other artifacts, that he has given up trying to remember what he has seen in which anonymous hall, is suddenly confronted by another museum of a very different nature—or is it really so different?—a museum of "useless efforts." Descriptions of the senseless endeavors of humanity are painstakingly catalogued—children who tried to fly, men in search of riches, unhappy couples, prostitutes who wanted to change their profession, a woman with artistic aspirations. Only an infinitesimal part of mankind's useless efforts can be stored in the museum, since there is such an exorbitant number of them. The protagonist, who spends every day in the reading room, finds accounts of people trying to teach their dogs how to speak, of a man wanting to conquer a woman for twenty years. Others have wasted their lives in the reconstruction of their family tree, the search for gold, the desire to win the lottery, the vain hope of avoiding war, or the attempt to regain a boxing title. The most extensive section of the museum is devoted to travelers. . . .

Through the fantastic world of Cristina Peri Rossi, we get a different insight into our own experiences and the world around us. Her imagination amplifies and distorts reality in such a way that the commonplace becomes noteworthy and the remarkable becomes common. The improbability of the situations in her stories does not lead us away from our own world. As Lord Haldane once remarked, "The universe is not only queerer than we suppose, but queerer than we can suppose."

Amaryll B. Chanady. *Antigonish Review*. 54,
1983, p. 45–48

[A virtuoso] display of vocabulary illustrates Peri Rossi's concern and preoccupation with language; that sense of its inadequacy felt by many authors, but perhaps more strongly in Latin America where the language in use, originating from another continent, is not only insufficient to express a reality infinitely richer, but also bears the mark of the dominion of which it has been instrument over several centuries (as Rosario Castellanos said in *Mujer que sabe Latin . . .*). Hence, the author feels that writing not only involves a constant fight between her creative force and the restriction which language imposes . . . but also an endless attempt to liberate oneself from these restrictions, renew the language and impress upon it the identity of the new continent. This condition forms the inspiration of several of Cristina Peri Rossi's poems, some of which appear in *Diáspora*. If only speech were allowed to flow unhampered by rules! *"Amabas a las niñas/ porque su lenguaje/ volaba libre/ . . . desconociendo las leyes fundamentales."* (You loved children because their language flies freely, ignoring the fundamental laws). If it could be as instinctive and spontaneous as the manifestations of our emotions *"Si el lenguaje . . . fuera el modo/ de hacer el amor . . ./ de meterme entro tu pelo"* (If only language were the way of making love, wrapping myself in your hair). The frustrations which language entails and the desire to rebel against its laws, are often manifested in Peri Rossi by outbursts of poetry within prose narrative. . . .

The stories from Peri Rossi's latest collection, *El museo de los esfuerzos inútiles*, reveal a newly found control of language and the ability to handle a variety of themes with directness and clarity without losing the power of images nor stopping the flow of a poetic vision. The author challenges sexual conventions and the traditional distinction of roles; a startling statement like: "We have the sex they impose on us—at most we accept it," appears in the middle of a story, and opens up a totally ambiguous set of meanings adding new facets to the situation described. Men's and women's inability to break up a deteriorated amorous situation, the destructive parasitical function of those who "give themselves for life" demanding at the same time a life in return, these are some of the myths of love which she attacks with caustic sarcasm and convincingly destroys without the hint of a polemic accent or the use of rhetoric images.

Psiche Hughes. In Mineke Schipper, ed.
*Unheard Words: Women and Literature in
Africa, the Arab World, Asia, the
Caribbean, and Latin America* (London:
Allyson and Busby, 1985), pp. 250–52

Cristina Peri Rossi hails from Uruguay, but in 1971 she moved to Spain as an exile and for the last few years has been residing in Sweden. She has published at least seven books, including poems, short stories, and a novel. She worked first as a teacher and then as a political journalist, collaborating with such writers as Eduardo Galeano, Juan Carlos Onetti, and Angel Rama. Feminist concerns have also informed her work.

The stories contained in *La rebelión de los niños* (The children's revolt) are fantastic tales which draw from surrealism, science fiction, and political satire, with the occasional incorporation of a silent monologue. Peri Rossi has a masterly capacity for depicting exceptional psychological states and for imbuing such descriptions with metaphysical overtones. In a way her work is closely related to that of Julio Cortázar while remaining essentially independent from it; when a volume of her stories was published in Stockholm, for example, it included an enthusiastic introduction by Cortázar in which he emphasized the fact that she is a woman who has experienced both the hell of our world and the hell of writing about the times in which we live. He also found in her works a commendable intent to transfigure the actual and historical—however tragic—into something fantastic, both conserving its most exact meaning and manifesting its power on a new, higher level.

In some of her stories Peri Rossi paints a gruesome picture of a society in which tyranny reigns and secret police and soldiers carry out their terrifying duties as servants of repression and torture. In this appalling world children play a significant role, and the author is always concerned with their destinies. Peri Rossi is a master of style, even if her sentences are sometimes quite long and complicated and their content rather abstract. There is always a deeper meaning within her work, a message for all her readers.

Jöran Mjöberg. *World Literature Today.* 64,
1990, p. 79

La nave de los locos (1984) by Cristina Peri Rossi . . . is a playful, postmodern text which describes the (mis)adventures of a character whose name is simply a letter of the alphabet, Equis, in a variety of urban settings; the novel includes episodes describing sordid sexual encounters, far-fetched dream-sequences, and Equis's philosophizing about life and the universe with his companions, Vercingetorix and Graciela. The novel has little narrative structure and is furthermore punctuated by a backdrop-discourse which describes in meticulous, and indeed factual, detail the celebrated, eleventh-century tapestry depicting the creation of the world which is held in Gerona Cathedral, Spain.

The above brief description of *La nave de los locos,* in its emphasis upon playfulness and the rejection of plot strategies, tends to confirm its identity as a postmodern text. But there are other ways in which Peri Rossi's novel is postmodern. In the epilogue to *The Name of the Rose,* Umberto Eco underlines that the postmodern stance "consists in recognizing that the past, since it cannot really be destroyed, because its destruction leads to silence, must be revisited: but with irony, not innocently." Thus, the "already said," following the postmodern move, will be acknowledged, albeit playfully, ironically or parodically. Indeed, the consciousness of being "somehow or other belated, *nachträglich, après coup,*" a central motif of the postmodern text, is at the core of Peri Rossi's *La nave de los locos,* which situates itself in an epigonic relationship to a variety of other texts such as Sebastian Brant's *Narrenschiff* (1494), Pío Baroja's *La nave de los locos* (1925), and Katherine Anna Porter's *Ship of Fools* (1959). . . .

Cross-dressing, on a primary level, tends to deconstruct the notion of a fixed sexual identity and, in this, Peri Rossi's text seems to advocate a utopian love which is unisex, encompassing hetero- and homosexual love. In its search for sexual "in-difference," however, *La nave de los locos* runs the risk of *appearing* to go beyond the phallic order but being in fact simply a confirmation of the existing phallocratic order, thereby running a risk that critics have pointed to as existing in a paradigmatic work on the text/sex relationship, namely, Roland Barthes's *Le Plaisir du texte.* As Jane Gallop suggests, á propos Barthes's text, with words which are potentially applicable to *La nave de los locos,* the "wish to escape sexual difference might be but another mode of denying women." Ultimately, the decision will be the reader's. The message on the billboard, DECIDA USTED MISMO, is thus to be seen as implicating the reader directly in the process of gender discovery, a decision which the text leaves open. Since the novel ends with a cross-dressing scene, however, one thing at least is clear: *La nave de los locos* projects the (rhetorical) question "What is the greatest tribute and homage a man can give to the woman he loves?" as not unanswerable, but simply a misguided question to ask in the first place.

Stephen M. Hart. *White Ink: Essays on
Twentieth-Century Feminine Fiction in Spain
and Latin America* (London: Tamesis, 1993),
pp. 124–25, 131

PETRUSHEVSKAYA, LUDMILA (RUSSIA) 1938–

Ludmila Petrushevskaya's *Moscow Chorus* at the Moscow Art Theater echoes the indictment. The bitter internal struggles of a Moscow family, and the solemn choral music sung onstage by students of the Nemirovich-Danchenko Studio, convey the Stalinist schizophrenia of repressed realities beneath a surface harmony. The family of Lika, matriarch and survivor, is torn by her son Sasha's philandering and alcoholism, by the presence of her sister Neta and her niece Liuba newly arrived from exile, and by the cynicism and lack of direction of the younger generation, represented by her granddaughter Olya and niece Laura. Neta's Communist ideals appear silly and dangerous because of her parasitical attachment to the living space provided by Lika; at the end of the play Neta, herself a victim of Soviet mores, writes a letter denouncing her sister's family; the young girls discover sex amid the coarse intimacies of communal apartment life; and as the chorus sings on, Sasha abandons the family for a woman carrying his illegitimate child. The play is set during the years immediately following Stalin's death, in overt criticism of his legacy.

Nicholas Rzhevsky. *The Nation.* August
7–14, 1989, p. 180

Ludmila Petrushevskaya is part of a "new wave" of Soviet playwrights, as her wonderfully adept German translator introduces her with German versions of two early one-act plays. The title piece [*Cinzano*] (1973) long went unperformed, then was staged only unofficially in studios and workshops and is still unpublished in Russian collections of her plays. After World War II successive waves of USSR playwrights depicted not positive heroes of "socialist realism" but people. One member of the first wave of the 1950s, Aleksei Arbuzov, was Petrushevskaya's teacher in his playwriting course. The portraitist of the dropout hero, Alexander Vampilov, though born in the same year as she, is her immediate ancestor from the wave of the 1960s; she read his work only in the year of his premature death (1972), whereupon in enthusiastic confrontation she wrote her first one-act and then a year later *Cinzano*.

Communist goals concern the three heroes of *Cinzano* only insofar as the three default from them. They duck out on work to drink Cinzano vermouth together, sitting in an empty apartment on a packing box and junk-pile chairs. Petrushevskaya explains, "I had shortly before heard the story of a man's asking the return of a sum of money he owed and had almost all paid back, so as to use it for the burial of his mother, but had then spent it all on Cinzano." Nothing happens in the play except that the three nonheroes' venality and meanness become ever clearer in their increasingly drunken conversation, until in a total stupor Pasha fails to go to his mother's funeral.

Smirnovas Geburtstag (Smirnova's birthday), the second playlet in the volume, was written to round out the evening which in 1977 Oleg Efremov, director of the Moscow Art Theater, hoped to make of *Cinzano* in performance; unfortunately he never received permission to stage it. When the Actors' Theater of Louisville invited the Moscow studio-theater group "Chelovek" to perform *Cinzano* in Russian at the "Classics in Context Festival, 1989," Elise Thoron provided an English translation of the work, which was published in the festival monograph. She summarizes "Smirnova's Birthday" thus: "Three women tangentially related to the three men of part one accidentally gather and end up around a kitchen table drinking Cinzano." Actually the women are intricately involved with the men, as they reveal in their increasing intoxication. One deeply loves Kostia despite his alcoholism and infidelities, and his two children fill her life. Another juggles her career with educating her and Pasha's daughter also for a profession. The title heroine, who pretends scorn for children and casualness toward men, later tearfully confesses the abortion by which for a man's sake she lost her only son. Humanity, then, lies beneath the often aggressively mean, vulgar talk, which Rosemarie Tietze defends as follows: "She [Petrushevskaya] has discovered that this language," which sounds like kitchen quarrels and backstairs gossip, "reveals truth, that it has its own poetry."

Will Petrushevskaya, as quintessentially represented in *Cinzano,* survive the removal of the communist wall to which her characters devote their escapism? Presumably the wave of her plays about all-too-human human nature will now unhindered glide up on the shore of *perestroïka.*

Marjorie L. Hoover. *World Literature Today.*
64, 1990, p. 326

Until the mid-1980s only a handful of Petrushevskaya's more than forty stories and plays saw the light of day. Efforts to stage her works met with continued official resistance. The theaters that succeeded in presenting her plays tended to be experimental, amateur, or provincial. The two-act *Uroki muzyki* (1973; Music lessons) was performed briefly at Moscow University in 1979; the diptych *Chinzano* (1973; Cinzano, 1989) and *Den' rozhdeniia Smirnovoi* (1977; Smirnova's birthday) premiered in 1978 in Estonian translation in Estonia. Only her one-act play *Liubov'* (1974; Love) enjoyed a long, successful run in Moscow after its inclusion in the 1979–1980 season. . . . Owing to the pendulum swing in her fortunes, Petrushevskaya has become the most popular dramatist in Moscow, with several plays simultaneously enjoying extended runs in major theaters. Her stories likewise have become staple fare in mainstream journals and newspapers. Under glasnost both Petrushevskaya and her plays travel abroad, to Europe and the U.S.

Petrushevskaya has provoked heated controversy as both prosaist and dramatist partly because her oeuvre portrays a nightmarish life on the edge of existence, devoid of palliative reassurances. Permeated with morbid humor and grotesquerie, her harshly unidealizing works deal with the underbelly of human relations—the nasty traffic in human desires and fears, where everything carries a literal and metaphorical price. Life for Petrushevskaya is the penalty we pay for having been born. Everyone in her grim universe tends to be cut adrift from a reliable mooring; is ruled by appetite and self-interest; falls into seemingly irreversible patterns of (self-)destructive behavior; abrogates moral responsibility; inflicts and experiences pain in an unbroken chain of universal abuse. Suicide, alcoholism, child abuse, fictitious marriages, one-night stands, prostitution, unwanted pregnancies, abortions, crushing poverty, theft, and physical and psychological violence constitute the stuff of Petrushevskaya's fiction and drama.

Petrushevskaya's stories, like her plays, concentrate on the middle class, largely the urban technical intelligentsia. The majority of her protagonists and narrators tend to be women whose lives are maimed through personal weakness, uncontrollable circumstances, male mistreatment, and relatives' interference or overbearing demands—numerous female protagonists must tend simultaneously to dependent children and needy, frequently hospitalized, mothers. Alienation, betrayal, and humiliation comprise the lot of these beasts of burden, because pragmatic calculation fuels relations between family members, spouses, and lovers. . . .

Petrushevskaya's plays mirror essentially the concerns of her prose and contain analogous types. Family as a synecdoche for society dominates Petrushevskaya's drama, its microcosm reflecting the dissolution of human bonds—of kinship, support, and responsibilities—whereby relatives and husbands are estranged and instrumentalized. In *Syraia noga, ili vstrecha druzei* (1977; A raw leg, or a gathering of friends), Serezha the boxer steals money from his old mother's savings and beats his wife Natasha senseless; in *Liubov'* Evgeniia Ivanovna's selfish hostility to her son-in-law Tolia drives him and his new bride Sveta out onto the street on their wedding night; in *Moskovskii khor* (n.d.; Moscow chorus) savage family feuds, rife with vilification, erupt when members victimized by the purges return from the camps.

As setting Petrushevskaya favors kitchens and overcrowded rundown apartments whose spatial limitations symptomatize the psychological claustrophobia of its occupants, their entrapment in their situation. Lack of adequate space or a roof over one's head signals an absence of psychological refuge, of belonging, exemplified by Ira's dilemma in *Tri devushki v golubom* (1980; *Three Girls in Blue,* 1988). Spatial and temporal boundaries, however, are extended through Petrushevskaya's technique of reminiscence and reference, whereby hearsay characters, their words and actions, become incorporated into a play when those present quote them or refer to incidents in which they participated. In *Syraia noga, ili vstrecha druzei* Volodia suggests to Sonia that they renew their former sexual intimacy, while blithely volunteering the information that one of his students in Kalinin supplies him with sex three times a week. While lying with his head in Ira's lap, he confesses that he cannot do without a woman for three days maximum, and recalls once propositioning ten women at a train station until one agreed to oblige him. By indirectly revealing the behavior of multiple hearsay characters, Petrushevskaya universalizes the moral dissoluteness of those we actually see.

Fewer than twenty individuals inhabit the stage in *Tri devushki v golubom,* but over a hundred are mentioned, and the sheer volume depersonalizes people into a mass. When that technique resurrects relatives from the past, it also underscores the themes of heredity and continuity. Errors, vices, and weaknesses are one generation's legacy to the next. In *Uroki muzyki* eighteen-year-old Nina's mother, Grania, throws her parental duties, including the care of her baby, onto Nina's shoulders so as to concentrate on the violent, alcoholic ex-convict who fathered the child. When he returns uninvited to their apartment, revulsion and insufficient room force Nina to seek asylum at a neighbor's. Yet Grania's sole worry is her loss of a baby-sitter, especially when she has to check into a hospital for an abortion and fears leaving the baby with her unpredictable brute of a husband. Maternity, which serves as a key moral gauge in Petrushevskaya's system of values, suffers endless violations, exemplified by Galia in *Lestnichnaia kletka* (1974; The stairwell), who plans to conceive a child with a stranger, only so as to mollify her hysterical mother. . . .

Critics have commented on Chekhovian elements in Petrushevskaya's drama, whereas the only common features are dialogues that are essentially sequentialized monologues and the habit of calling "comedies" works that audiences perceive as devastatingly somber. Others have remarked on Petrushevskaya's debt to Aleksandr Vampilov (1937–72), whose antiheroes, indeed, do prefigure the decidedly unadmirable types that predominate in Petrushevskaya's plays. In response to queries about her unremittingly gloomy vision of life, Petrushevskaya claims to pose problems that invite [the] audience's self-confrontation. Optimally, that process will catalyze one's humane impulses. Petrushevskaya scrupulously excludes all explicit judgment, sermonizing, and hope for moral progress from her fiction and drama. In fact, it would be difficult to imagine a world more desolate and bereft of hope than that portrayed by Petrushevskaya which may be summarized by the famous Sartrean formula "Hell is other people."

Helena Goscilo. In Steven R. Serafin and
Walter D. Glanze, eds. *Encyclopedia of
World Literature in the 20th Century* (New
York: Continuum, 1993), pp. 483–85

PETRY, ANN (UNITED STATES) 1911–

An oppressive but moving account (*The Street*) of a young Negro mother's struggle to support herself and her child and retain her self-respect in Harlem. Decency, she finds, is a luxury not everybody can manage to cling to, especially when pursued by some of the most repulsive characters ever to appear in print. Miss Petry has a tendency to overwrite, but her integrity and her forthright and knowledgeable presentation of Harlem's shocking plight—a subject too many people are inclined to shy away from—make this a book well worth reading.

The New Yorker. February 9, 1946

[In *The Street*], Mrs. Petry tells us the story of a young colored woman who, having lost her husband when the depression forced her to "live in" in domestic service, tries to make a decent life for herself and her small son in Harlem. Lutie is not only very pretty and energetic; she also has had a high-school education. The degradation she must suffer despite these advantages is symbolized by the dreadful apartment in which she must live, just as the whole of the Negro degradation is symbolized by the dirt and wretchedness of Harlem's 116th Street.

In her period of domestic service Lutie worked for a white family in Connecticut. By her own experience, her employers were a miserable family group—Mr. and Mrs. Chandler were unhappily married, Mr. Chandler drank, Mr. Chandler's brother shot himself before their eyes, the Chandler baby was a sad little youngster. But the Chandlers already had a lot of money and they were on their way to having a lot more; and Lutie had seen what a pleasant surface money can put on suffering. Her only complaint against being colored is that it denies her the opportunity to live with the cleanliness and financial ease of a Mrs. Chandler. No matter how hard she is willing to work, no matter what her talents, she is unable to rise above the Harlem ghetto. . . .

To Mrs. Petry, equality of opportunity means a free capitalist economy in which the Negro individual, no less than the white, can gain as much as he desires and is capable of gaining. . . .

[T]he fact that is so frankly and unself-consciously addressed by *The Street*. . . [is] that class feelings are as fully ingrained in the colored population of this country as in the white; that there is nothing inherently virtuous, from a political point of view or from any other point of view, about being a member of a mistreated minority.

Diana Trilling. *The Nation.* March 9, 1946, p. 291

Ann Petry's writing in this second novel shows much of the improvement one was led to anticipate on reading her first. *Country Place* is a fast-moving, somewhat melodramatic tale of a small New England town as seen through the eyes of its druggist, Mr. Fraser.

Johnny Roane, a veteran of the recent war, returns home after a four-year absence, to find his home town a bit strange and his beautiful young wife, Glory, more than a little estranged from him; yearning, in fact, after the affections of the town's chief seducer. Glory's mother, having artfully achieved marriage with the not very manly son of one of the town's first families, broods over her failure to achieve status among the citizenry as well as over her complete frustration in attempting to become the recognized mistress of the Gramby estate, a park sternly and jealously presided over by her aged and ailing mother-in-law. Bits and pieces of unassembled gossip flit tentatively and covertly about the town, but The Weasel, a taxi-driver, is impatient with the normal speed of gossip and he frequently finds ways of helping it to take a jump or two ahead of schedule so that it will land in the places where it will do the most damage.

There is a hurricane, too, and the story is geared to its onset, climax, and departure. At the height of the storm, the smoldering hates, loves, and confusions of the main characters are whipped up into swift, decisive action; and in the wake of the big wind, the uncovered emotions of our main characters lead them into areas that might have, otherwise, taken years to reach.

Most of the characters are well done, but, curiously enough, Johnny Roane, the hero, is not; for he is not filled out to real-life, believable proportions. It is hard to believe, for instance, that a young man, just home from four years of war, would not relate a great deal of that most recent experience to the events in his new existence as a civilian, especially when slogging about on a rainy night in a muddy forest; and a fight with a soft, middle-aged civilian—a cardiac patient at that—would have been a much more business-like piece of action than Johnny displays.

Taken as a whole, though, *Country Place* is a good story, worthy of the telling. It preaches no sermons, waves no flags. It tells a plausible narrative of, for the most part, some very human people in an earthy situation. It need not have been told through the eyes and perceptions of the druggist, and it might even be that this technique detracts from its readability; for you may find yourself wondering, on occasion, where in the world even so wise a person as Mr. Fraser could have found out so much about the thoughts and behavior of his fellow citizens.

John Caswell Smith, Jr. *Atlantic Monthly.*
November, 1947, pp. 178–79

An anguished book, [*The Narrows* is] written with an enormous amount of emotion and some thought; [it] does not quite succeed because there is far too much of it. It seems to choke on itself, with so many people trying to tell everything about themselves all at once. The voices are plain, but the people remain in darkness, although there are moments when one or two of them seem about to come clear of the rest and stand alone in full view. This is particularly true of Powther, the butler, a beautifully constructed character who should not have been allowed to be lost in the general melee. The locale of this novel is a small New England town, and the activities of the people described eddy around the doomed love affair between Link, a poor, bitter young man, and Camilo, the attractive daughter of the richest family in town. Link is a Negro and Camilo is not, but their story is actually based on the impossibility of there being a reasonable understanding between two people who, no matter what their color, are equally resentful, equally weak, and equally flamboyant. Mrs. Petry's ending is foolishly melodramatic, but she is chiefly to be reproached for devoting herself to examining a poor sort of love, instead of doing more with the gift for writing about ordinary, very human beings that she shows in some sections of this book.

The New Yorker. August 29, 1953, p. 78

This [*The Narrows*] is a long, sprawling, eclectic, and melodramatic novel primarily about a violent and passionate love affair between a young intellectual Negro, who is lost, and the white heiress of a munitions fortune, who is even more lost. The setting is in a typical Connecticut river town, with touches of New York and Harlem. Mrs. Petry adds innumerable minor stories and characters to the whole panorama of both Negro and white society. She means well; she tries hard. But one gets the impression of a hodge-podge of styles, structures, ideas. Through attempting to view her literary figures from every point of view, she never quite succeeds in seeing them at all. Her theme is bold, her purpose is serious, but her technique (horrid word) is faulty.

The Nation. August 29, 1953, p. 177

By contrast with the majority of black novelists, Ann Petry seems old-fashioned, so surprisingly "slow" in her narrative rhythm that you wonder if the title story in *Miss Muriel and Other Stories* took place in another century. Mrs. Petry's timing is as different from most contemporary black writing as is her locale, which in the best of these leisurely paced stories is a small upstate New York town where a pharmacist and his family are the only Negroes. Their life centers entirely around the drugstore itself. The longest and most successful of these stories, "Miss Muriel," tells of an eccentric elderly white shoemaker in the town, Mr. Bemish, who, to the astonishment and terror of the Negro family, falls in love with Aunt Sophronia. There is no "Muriel" in the story; the title is a sad joke about an old Negro who asked for "Muriel" cigars and was sternly told that *he* would have to ask for them as "Miss Muriel." But the feeling behind the "joke" is so strong in the small, isolated black family that poor Mr. Bemish not only doesn't get Aunt Sophronia, but is driven out of town for falling in love with a black lady.

This reversal of roles is typical of Mrs. Petry's quiet, always underplayed but deeply felt sense of situation. The other stories aren't as lovingly worked out as "Miss Muriel"—which is an artful period piece that brings back a now legendary age of innocence in white-black relationships. Several stories are just tragic situations that are meant to touch you by that quality alone. A famous black drummer loses his adored wife to a pianist in his band, but the drumming must go on; a Harlem old-clothes man falls in love with the oversized statue of a dark woman he calls "Mother Africa"; a Negro teacher is unable to stand up to a gang of young students and flees town, ashamed of not having played a more heroic part; a Negro woman at a convention is insulted by a white woman, and realizes in the morning, on learning that the other woman died of a heart attack during the night, that she might have saved her. These delicate points are characteristic of Mrs. Petry's quietly firm interest in fiction as moral dilemma. Clearly, her sense of the Negro situation is still "tragic." Her stories are very far from contemporary black nationalist writing, and by no means necessarily more interesting. But they are certainly different.

Saturday Review of Literature. October 2, 1971, pp. 34–35

The novels of Ann Petry have been overshadowed and her talent misrepresented by their frequent comparison to the fiction and achievement of Richard Wright and Chester Himes. Robert Bone, for example, claims that *The Street* (1946), her first novel, suffers by comparison to Wright's *Native Son* because "it is an attempt to interpret slum life in terms of *Negro* experience, when a larger frame of reference is required." In contrast, he considers *Country Place* (1947), her second novel, "one of the finest . . . of the period" because it is "a manifestation not so much of assimilation as of versatility." He does not mention *The Narrows* (1953), the best of her three novels, in either edition of his *The Negro Novel in America*. Neither does critic Addison Gayle, Jr., who discusses only *The Street* in his more recent book, *The Way of the New World*. For Gayle, Petry is similar to Himes in that she develops characters with some status and education, and to Wright in that "both were interested in the effects of environment upon the psychological makeup of characters." Unlike Wright, however, Gayle concludes, "Miss Petry is more interested in the effects of the environment upon her characters than she is in the characters themselves." Whether valid or not, these critical views do not adequately express the complexity and distinctiveness of Ann Petry's aesthetic vision and achievement.

Ann Petry actually moves beyond the naturalistic vision of Wright and Himes in her realistic delineation of cultural myths, especially those of the American Dream, the city and small town, and black character. In exploring the black community's place in time and space, its relationship to the American past and future, she effectively debunks the myths of urban success and progress, of rural innocence and virtue, and of pathological black women and men. Embodying the values and beliefs of a community, *myths*, as we are using the term here, are stories people in a particular society tell to organize, explain, and understand the realities and metaphysics of their world. . . .

Petry, like Himes and Wright, is adept at character delineation, but her protagonists are cut from a different cloth than those of her major contemporaries. Rather than sharing the pathology of a Bigger Thomas or Bob Jones or Lee Gordon, Lutie Johnson and Link Williams are intelligent, commonplace, middle-class aspiring blacks, who, despite the socialized ambivalence resulting from racism and economic exploitation, are not consumed by fear and hatred and rage. Petry's vision of black personality is not only different from that of Himes and Wright, but it is also more faithful to the complexities and varieties of black women, whether they are big-city characters like Mrs.

Hedges in *The Street* or small-town characters like Abbie Crunch in *The Narrows*.

Bernard W. Bell. In Marjorie Pryse and
Hortense J. Spillers, eds. *Conjuring: Black
Women, Fiction, and Literary Tradition*
(Bloomington: Indiana University Press,
1985), pp. 105–6, 114

Ironically, then, the only "pattern against the sky" which the novel [*The Street*] creates is, after all, motherhood—but a motherhood not of biology but of human connection, in which the Prophet David becomes the symbol of nurturing power in the black community, the force capable of countering the perverted indifference of feeling represented by Petry's portrait of Mrs. Hedges. Like the snow at the end of the novel, which "gently" obscures "the grime and the garbage and the ugliness," *The Street* does offer its readers an alternative in the vision of a black community which might embrace its grandmothers, its folklore, and the survival of human feeling, a street which might become, and thereby transform, "any street in the city"—even the street in Lyme, Connecticut, on which Petry shows us white people, like Mr. Chandler's brother, blowing their brains out.

In so doing, *The Street* stands as a connecting link in a fictional tradition that looks back to Zora Neale Hurston's portraits of black community and folklore and looks ahead to those contemporary novels by Marshall, Alice Walker, Morrison, and Bambara (and Ralph Ellison and James Baldwin and Al Young) which have taught readers to rediscover, reassess, and reclaim the human values signified by folk community in black fiction. Such fiction really proclaims our declaration of independence—our refusal to be any longer enslaved by human indifference in any form, in any culture.

Marjorie Pryse. In Marjorie Pryse and
Hortense J. Spillers, eds. *Conjuring: Black
Women, Fiction, and Literary Tradition*
(Bloomington: Indiana University Press,
1985), p. 129

Lutie Johnson of *The Street* resembles the mulatto heroines of the preceding literary era only in her creator's insistence on the maleficence of background as the primary and controlling agency of human action. But this single basis of a structural alignment is enough to juxtapose Petry and the past, except that the voice of Hurston intrudes itself forcefully enough to create a break whose particular features demolish any notions of immediate linear continuity or "influence." Furthermore, Petry's ideology of the environment—one of the strains of a materialist philosophy—is so sharply divergent from Larsen and Fauset's genetic determinism that these apparently comparable philosophies of ascription occupy, in fact, quite different orbits of the literary universe.

Lutie Johnson, in short, has been stripped of the decorative object, or the ornament of fashion, that constitutes an entire repertoire of traits in the work of the earlier generation of writers. Lutie's new class affiliation for literary character appears to be an effect of an altered perspective rather than a cause, as Bigger Thomas's impoverishment is a physical sign of his spiritual and psychic degradation. These elements of *lumpen proletariat,* the urban dispossessed, are mobilized on the literary landscape with a specificity that rivals the concretely delineated products of a new civic order—Norris's and Faulkner's trains; Dreiser's cities and hotels; Wright's skyscrapers and airplanes. These powerful signs of plenitude assume the character of a prohibition, mark off a territory of the sacred, which the pariah, coexistent with it, can either not approach at all or only inchoately understand. To Lutie's mind, the "street," for instance, becomes an undifferentiated spatial progression that oppresses her as in an endless nightmare, retrogressively involving into itself. This horrible absence of closure for the naturalistic agent identifies precisely the vacuum the action would fill up, since the character is impeded by an antagonism infinitely more potent than itself and is anaesthetized by it. To be stripped on such a background is not only degradation. It is death to the agent. The naturalized scene, as a result, is a proliferation of antinomous meanings—ruined bare rooms over and against the tangible manifestations of power. Their binary evocation is meant to seal the exacting rule of destiny, whose latest disguise calls itself "environment."

> Hortense J. Spillers. In Marjorie Pryse and
> Hortense J. Spillers, eds. *Conjuring: Black
> Women, Fiction, and Literary Tradition*
> (Bloomington: Indiana University Press,
> 1985), pp. 254–55

PIERCY, MARGE (UNITED STATES) 1936–

Dance the Eagle [to Sleep] is a novel deeply informed by experience with revolt and revelation during the past decade, but . . . it is not a happy, idyllic romp, a lyrical reassurance that the Generation Gap has opened into Happy Hollow. . . .

The classics that Marge Piercy has chosen as models are those dark fantasies, like *Lord of the Flies* and *Lord of the Rings,* lord-books heavy with pessimism and persecution, and animated by the age-old Manichean struggle between Good and Evil in which winners are somehow always losers. *Dance the Eagle [to Sleep]* tells the story of some not-too-distant time in which a small army of youth, drawn together by mutual feelings of alienation and hostility towards an oppressive, dehumanized system, declare themselves a nation apart. Secession first takes the form of an armed takeover of a New

York City high school and the establishment of a communal lifestyle during the ensuing siege. Though the initial revolt is put down, the rebels retreat to the New Jersey countryside for a prolonged period of communal experience, self-imposed and underground exile which is followed by a suicidal episode of guerrilla counter-attack. The resulting holocaust of repression by "them" scatters and decimates the rebels, but like an earlier Civil War, does not diminish the spirit of secession. The firestorm passes, leaving smoldering embers that are carefully nurtured by the surviving few. . . .

Dance the Eagle [to Sleep] is a frightening book, which will reassure only those who can take solace from the fact that it is cast as a futuristic novel. This is no real solace, since Marge Piercy has used the future only as a parabolic mirror of the recent past; her novel is indirectly about the Movement, more specifically about the rise, fragmentation, and fall of the Students for a Democratic Society. The future setting allows her a certain freedom of exaggeration and abstraction, so that she may elevate the rise and fall of Reich III into a Götterdämmerung of symbolic and tragic proportions, and by so doing extrapolate and give fabulous substance to the essential Myth of the Movement.

Seen from this angle, the novel leaves the reader with a devastating sense of how far apart the generations have indeed moved, that the Gap has become an abyss. It is obvious that Piercy feels that her compatriots have passed through a trial by fire, that they are scattered and diminished but that the encounter has been a confrontation of massive proportions and implication. They have gained more than they have lost, and what they have gained is the solidarity of identity, a new consciousness far more sombre in implication than a sappy love of bell-bottoms and peanut butter.

John Seelye. The New Republic. December 12, 1970, pp. 24–25

At the very beginning and the very end of this rambling novel [*Small Changes*] Marge Piercy powerfully covers that particular quality of lost identity and desperation which, once recognized as common experience, has sparked the rage and solidarity of the women's liberation movement and created the concept of women's consciousness. The novel spans the 1960s in the lives of two women: Beth, the provincial working-class girl who discovers that the ideal marriage she's always dreamed of is a living hell and gathers her strength to escape it; and Miriam, the brilliant, "independent" mathematician, who is caught, blinded and thoroughly trapped—at least for the moment—by a middle-class version of the same nightmare.

In exploring both of their lives against a blurry background of late 1960s youth culture and radical politics, Piercy means to show the cross-class experience of women's oppression, to demonstrate the situations in which it occurs and to show some of the ways in which it is confronted. She succeeds in the first, and that success is the novel's strength; but it cannot compensate for the wordy, rhetorical and often monotonous quality of much of the narrative, nor for the fact that its author forces highly unconvincing resolutions to situations that are described at such length that they deserve at least open-ended fates. . . .

A final problem. Many women radicals will understand this novel's hostility to political "heaviness" on the American left, and how one of its functions was to celebrate machismo at the same time it relegated women activists to the kind of subservient roles that a real revolution must banish. But I wonder if most non-movement readers of the book won't assume that the hostility is directed toward the general priorities of the 1960s left. Piercy has been careless about her targets, and her failure to integrate and unify the issues that float through the novel—feminism, the antiwar movement, the oppression of the working class, the Government's outrageous (and continuing) use of grand juries to harass and jail radicals—implies that most of these concerns should be discarded in favor of the more important struggle, sexual equality and freedom. On the basis of Piercy's first two novels, and her often eloquent poetry, I find it hard to believe that she means this; yet it's disturbing that, in a novel of this length, set among highly politicized people, almost all of the characters are obsessively self-concerned: with alternate life-styles, aspects of communal living, their own emotions. Neither poverty nor racism, for example, is more than casually mentioned.

The problem of how to transform the cultural conditioning of women, which is inseparable from transforming the lives of all the exploited and the structure of the society that keeps them that way, is a profound one. Piercy shows what happens when women struggle for themselves (Beth) and what happens when they give up (Miriam). But the context in which the author allows their lives to evolve is too rigid, too blurry and sometimes too downright confused to grant the characters she has created the reality and the strength they deserve.

Sara Blackburn. *The New York Times.*
August 12, 1973, pp. 2–3

Piercy's desire is for a world of wholeness and completeness, where natural growth and development can lead to a satisfying participation in the fullness of life. As individual poems recount instances in which a sense of wholeness is attempted or gained or lost, they also explore the attitudes and actions necessary for a state of sustained community. . . .

As a woman, Piercy is particularly concerned about women and their ability to participate with integrity in a fully-realized life. In a number of poems, she examines the female growing-up process in America; in each case, the young girl is shown to possess great potential strength and individuality which is slowly but surely diverted or covered over. . . . Traditionally, a male/female dichotomy has been assumed in which the male has been viewed primarily as an objective, rational, abstract theorizer, too busy with the important intellectual progress of the world to be bothered by daily problems. The female, on the other hand, has been viewed primarily as an emotional, subjective, grubby doer of ordinary tasks. Man equals mind equals significant mode of knowing and being; women equals body equals lesser mode of knowing and being. What Piercy wants to do is to change the value assigned to these two modes; and, in addition, she wants to synthesize and unify the separate parts to form whole people: thinking, feeling men and women, confident in mind and body. . . .

Piercy views contemporary America as a dream turned nightmare. The fertile land which once offered a place of freedom and tolerance—a place of growth—has now become full of death and destruction. Possession, subjugation, and selfishness have violated the land itself and the people who live in this society.

Jean Rosenbaum. *Modern Poetry Studies.*
Winter, 1977, pp. 193–94, 201–2, 204

Marge Piercy is a prolific novelist and poet, a one-time organizer for SDS, who has become a spokesman for radical feminism. Though she presents herself as a revolutionary, battling against orthodoxies of every kind—political, cultural, sexual—her novels are surprisingly conventional. In conception and style, in the grim determination of her didactic intentions, her work is reminiscent of the radical-proletarian fiction of the 1930s, in which the message outweighed the manner of its telling. In each of her six novels, Miss Piercy seizes upon a problem that she regards as symptomatic of a sick, unjust, patriarchal society, and builds a heavily documented narrative around that problem to drive her moral home.

In *Woman at the Edge of Time* she concentrated on mistreatment of the insane; in *Small Changes* on women trapped in repressive marriages; in *Dance the Eagle to Sleep* on the exploitation of radical women by their sexist comrades; in *The High Cost of Living* on the high cost of being a lesbian in a bigoted academic milieu. Through the exhaustive detailing of social and sexual atrocities, Miss Piercy turns her novels into indictments crackling with outrage. Now and then she has tried to leaven the heavy freight of actuality that is her stock in trade with utopian imaginings, in the spirit of Doris Lessing's more elaborate science fiction, as in the futuristic dream world envisioned in *Woman at the Edge of Time.* But these fantasies are just as programmatic as her realistic novels. . . .

In her most recent novel, *Vida,* Marge Piercy looks back with elegiac nostalgia to the 1960s and the exhilarations of the anti-war movement as remembered by Vida Asch, a Weatherman fugitive. . . .

What is in some ways most bewildering about *Vida* is the way Marge Piercy's ideological severity toward bourgeois values—"We can't make a new society in the shell of the old if we're living a middle-class existence"—is insidiously overwhelmed by her rather girlish enthusiasm for the good things of that life. . . .

Vida is crammed with . . . arcane trivia, the sort of padding that was left out of an earlier and far more affecting fictional account of the antiwar apostles of violence, M. F. Beal's *Amazon One,* published in 1975. In that powerful novel, Miss Beal captured the derangement, the complacency, the resentful and terrified confusion of the Weatherman mentality in fiercely compressed prose that had the authentic ring of imaginative and historical truth. Next to M. F. Beal's radical activists, Marge Piercy's pale into ideological cartoons. *Vida,* almost twice as long as *Amazon One,* is stale and self-indulgent, leaving no breathing space or room for thought between writer and protagonist. At the end of this revolutionary soap opera, our heroine is still free, still running, and charged with unfounded confidence, as she walks into the sunset, that "What swept through us and cast us forward is a force that will gather and rise again." Those who have no sense of history can believe anything.

Pearl K. Bell. *Commentary.* July, 1980,
pp. 59–60

Marge Piercy is known in England mainly as a novelist. That the author of *Vida* and *Women on the Edge of Time* is also a powerful, distinctively American poet may come as a surprise, even to her admirers. As might be expected, *The Moon Is Always Female* reflects the uncompromising bias of the committed feminist, of which some of us by now are weary. But Marge Piercy's poems are so energetic and so intelligent that weariness is out of the question. This is, in fact, her sixth book of poems, and it is an excellent one. A tough, often humorous, sometimes angry view of herself emerges from the poems, yet they are free of embitterment. They lack that harsh edge of hysterial accusation—as if with a few nasty words one could instantly abolish half the human race—which spoils so many poems by women these days. Here finally is a feminist artist for whom one need rarely blush.

The Moon Is Always Female is gratifyingly longer than most poetry volumes, and absorbing throughout. In effect, Ms. Piercy is still a novelist in her poems; she has perfected an easy flowing unrhymed line in which she says what she means with few frills. If you object to poems that tell you things, then you will not like this book. . . . It is possible, of course, to find all this feminist rabble-rousing annoying. However good the advice, poetry may not be the best vehicle for it. Indeed, if Marge Piercy were only a rabble-rouser she would not be a poet. The fact is, she can be as subtle as anyone writing today. . . . "At the Well" alone would convince me that Marge Piercy is one of America's major writers. . . . The strength of Piercy's work is its outwardness, its frankness. Even if you do not agree with her, you have to meet Marge Piercy halfway.

Anne Stevenson. (London) *Times Literary
Supplement.* January 23, 1981, p. 81

Perhaps no other poet of this generation has more consistently identified herself with the political and social movements of her own times. Her earlier involvements were with the civil rights and antiwar movements of the 1960s, which generated in turn the women's-rights and antiwar movements of the 1970s. For anyone interested in what's been happening on the cutting edge during the past two decades, she's clearly essential reading.

Miss Piercy has the double vision of the utopian: a view of human possibility—harmony between the sexes, among races and between humankind and nature—that makes the present state of affairs clearly unacceptable by comparison. The huge discrepancy between what is and what could be generates anger, and many of these are angry poems—which, for those who want poetry to be nothing but beautiful, will mean points off. Because her poetry is so deliberately "political"—which, for some, means anything not about ghosts and roses—how you feel about it will depend on how you feel about subjects such as male-female relations, abortion, war and poverty. Those who don't like these subjects will use adjectives like "shrill" to describe the poems. . . .

Taken as a whole—and I recommend you do so only slowly, as this is rich fare—this collection [*Circles on the Water*] presents the spectacle of an agile and passionate mind rooted firmly in time and place and engaging itself with the central dilemmas of its situation. . . .

If poets could be divided into Prioresses and Wives of Bath, Miss Piercy would very definitely be a Wife of Bath. Low on fastidiousness and high on what Hazlitt called "gusto," earthy, bawdy, interested in the dailiness of life rather than in metaphysics, highly conscious of the power relationships between men and women but seeing herself by no means as a passive victim, she is ready to enter the fray with every weapon at her command. She is, in sum, a celebrant of the body in all its phases, including those that used to be thought of as vulgar. Surprisingly, her poetry is more humorous than her novels, although not all of it is what you'd call funny. The Wife of Bath was sometimes a savage ironist, and so is Miss Piercy. Neither has much interest in being ladylike. . . .

Tidiness is not her virtue, but then in the hierarchy of virtues this is surely not at the top. Essentially her poetry is a poetry of statement and story, and metaphor and simile are, characteristically, used by her as illustration rather than as structural principle. This does not bother me very much, since it's a mistake for a reader to look for the same qualities in every poet.

Miss Piercy's emotional range is great, and at her best she can make you laugh, cry, get angry; she can inspire you with social purpose and open doors through which you may walk into lived reality. One effect she almost never achieves, because she almost never tries for it, is that touch of the cold hand at the back of the neck, that glimpse into the borderlands. The darkness she sees is human-created and therefore potentially correctable. . . .

Margaret Atwood. *The New York Times*.
August 8, 1982, pp. 10–11, 22

Piercy in her 1970s utopias fully articulates a dynamic of the group's concern for its members' welfare. Piercy—poet, essayist, and novelist—requires little introduction. To date, she has published one volume of essays, eleven volumes of poetry, one play, and eight novels. Each novel attacks a different social problem, so that, like Phelps's utopias, Piercy's works exist in a context of fictional social criticism. Her first novel, *Going Down Fast* (1969), shows that urban renewal penalizes the powerless working classes. Both *Small Changes* (1972) and *High Cost of Living* (1978) explore the theme of the individual growth that occurs with the support of trusted small groups. *Vida* (1979) returns to considering efforts to effect institutional change. Finally, *Braided Lives* (1982) and *Fly Away Home* (1984) show women's need to control their lives, whether against life-threatening abortions, or against enervating relationships. In all of Piercy's social fiction, a nurturing community, either implicitly or explicitly, is necessary for the emergence of what she considers to be the best in human potential—behavior both responsive to group needs and assertive of individual rights. Her two utopias move from a "dream-nightmare" to a dream-vision of the same social goal. . . .

Piercy claims that *Woman on the Edge of Time* is not a utopia, "because it's accessible," but she does admit that it is a "vision of a reasonable society . . . in which it might be a rather nice place to live." In writing the book, she explains, her aim was to depict a society "not sexist, racist, or imperialist: one that was cooperative, respectful of all living beings, gentle, responsible, loving, and playful. The results of a full feminist revolution." Her utopia depicts these values more successfully than most—perhaps because she is a self-proclaimed pluralist who wants "people to make many different choices and flourish in them, and to respect the choices they don't make in their own lives as well as those they do."

The program set before readers in *Woman on the Edge of Time,* like that in other recent feminist utopias, involves communitarian, ecological, and spiritual values. Piercy sets this eutopia, which is called Mouth-of-Mattapoisett, Massachusetts, five generations into the future, in 2137. She then juxtaposes eutopian Mattapoisett with repressive dystopias, specifically with New York City's mental hospitals in the 1970s. We see both dystopia and eutopia through the eyes of a time-travelling protagonist, Consuelo Ramos (Connie), a Chicana who is prevented from pursuing her happiness by incarceration in such a hospital. Her name, translated, suggests a "branching consolation or cheer," for Connie is the one who can comfort us with hope for the future.

Carol Farley Kessler. *Journal of General Education.* 37, 1985, pp. 196–97

Piercy, in *Small Changes,* as did [Virginia Woolf,] insists that we question our standards of taste, our fastidious assumptions about stylistic decency, that we see the political *in*decency of "very very literary literature," and that we recognize Piercy's effort to communicate with a "popular" audience, specifically one that includes men and women "who don't go into bookstores," as she puts it. There are dangers, of course, in this insistence and this effort. There is a danger, for instance, that Piercy will go unread, or unappreciated, by people who do go into bookstores—people whom she also wants to reach, or so she says. And there is the more serious danger, perhaps, that Piercy's mistrust of language and literature can radically undercut the political message of the novel for any reader. If literature falsifies experience, why should anyone believe what *Small Changes* says about women's lives? If words change nothing, can a novel be "of use," as Piercy wants hers to be?

Such are the questions raised in *Small Changes,* crucial questions for many women writers today, and to my mind they make this novel a particularly exciting document for both the feminist critic and the student of contemporary narrative. This is not the conventional novel or the "merely" popular work that so many critics have plumed themselves on criticizing. Whether it succeeds or fails in the attempt to set new standards and say new things, it raises questions that are on the cutting edge of feminist aesthetics and feminist theory, and it repays critical analysis. One type of analysis, to which some of Piercy's other novels—especially *Woman on the Edge of Time*—might more obviously give occasion, is examination of her narrative technique as a kind of literary manifesto for contemporary women writers. From this perspective, *Small Changes* suggests several by now almost commonplace strategies and principles, including the subversion of conventional narrative openings and closings; the intentionally didactic, oversimplified, even allegorical nature of the work and its characters; the use of what [Rachel Blau] Du Plessis has called "mutipersoned or cluster protagonists" to affirm the "feminine" values of "collectivity" and "interdependence"; the rich (even "exhaustive" and "obsessively observed"—details, often associated with stereotypically female interests such as the way space is arranged in various domiciles, or the way "life support" activities are managed.

Along these lines, I want to suggest that the narrative structure of *Small Changes,* built on the stories of two women, can be seen as an experiment, not in "the variety of lifestyles that women in our time are adopting," but in two alternative ways in which the woman writer can write, can represent the experience of women while using the only language available and the traditional forms and myths available to any writer. I want to suggest, that is, that Piercy, wary like Beth of language, investigates the possibilities and the limitations of two prominent ways in which the woman writer can appropriate the dominant discourse: either by inverting the classic male plot, as in Beth's story; or by revitalizing and perhaps "legitimating" a conventional female form of narrative, as in "the ongoing soap opera" of Miriam's life. *Small Changes* is in this regard not an optimistic novel; it reveals in both modes the difficulties as well as the possibilities of appropriation, the price that women pay, the resistance of the dominant discourse—a system that is not user-friendly, as Miriam might put it, when the user is a woman writing for women and hoping to "do" something with words. . . .

Piercy thus uses the double narrative in *Small Changes* to explore both the possibilities and the limitations of two available narrative structures, one male and one female, for speaking the unspoken and perhaps unspeakable story of women's lives. The feminist *Bildungroman,* built on a culturally male model, facilitates the representation of a certain kind of revolutionary change, of individual growth and development in a woman's life; the soap opera more accurately presents and records ordinary women's experience. Each genre, as used in *Small Changes,* can be deployed to expose the oppression of women and to write stories that diminish the gap, for women, between reality and fiction, stories that do not betray the woman reader as Beth was betrayed by the fiction she once devoured, and stories that enable women to play the verbal game without turning into the oppressors. But neither mode is yet adequate to communicate a truly satisfactory vision of the as yet unrealized future in which no one is oppressed. *Small Changes* does not ask us to trust language and its present forms fully, but to remain wary of the ways in which literary conventions, like the world that produces and is shaped by them, "push women around"; and so from a late-twentieth-century feminist point of view each of the two characters and her story serves as a critique of the other.

> Elaine Tuttle Hansen. In Catherine
> Rainwater and William J. Scheick, eds.
> *Contemporary American Women Writers:*
> *Narrative Strategies* (Lexington: University
> Press of Kentucky, 1985), pp. 214–15, 220

PIÑON, NÉLIDA (BRAZIL) 1937–

Nélida Piñon challenges the imagination and interpretive skills of her readers. Her prose is rich with poetic devices. Narratives eschew linearity, and point of view often belongs to several different participants. Exposition of background information occurs gradually and sparingly. Shifts between interior monologue, dialogue, and narrated action are tenuously marked. Visual imagery is minimal. Lexical, syntactic, and logical combinations tend to be unconventional. Piñon has stated that part of her project is to act "against official syntax."

   Like most of her compatriots, Piñon decries social ills. Perhaps her best example of this commitment is the short-story collection *O calor das coisas* (1980; The heat of things). However, her focal point is not the streets, the fields, the factories, or the homes, but primarily the individual's consciousness. She specializes in the profound analysis of isolated characters—forceful, eccentric, and self-conscious—and causes the social dimension gradually to unfold around such interior dramas. Piñon's writings show also a fascination with religiosity, or more precisely, mysticism, since the stresses the individual experience over the institutional. For example, her first novel, *Guia-*

mapa de Gabriel Arcanjo (1961; Guide map of archangel Gabriel) features an extended dialogue between the female protagonist and her alter ego/guardian angel, regarding guilt, expiation, and one's relationship with deity. Another salient mark of Piñon's fiction is eroticism, which is exemplified by *A casa da paixão* (1972; The house of passion). The novel is a lyrical treatment of a young woman's sexual initiation, which presents interior monologues of the woman herself, as well as of her partner and other members of her household.

Piñon shows a profound interest in the myths that underlie human enterprises. In particular, she seems fascinated with the myth of origination. *Fundador* (1969; Founder) explores the establishment of a new society, which in some sense repeats itself through several generations of individuals. A related concern in Piñon's fiction is the experience of the immigrant. *A república dos sonhos* (1984; *The Republic of Dreams,* 1989), a semiautobiographical novel, explores this experience by means of succeeding generations of a Galician family that immigrates to Brazil. The story is primarily told by the patriarch-founder of this new Brazilian family, and by his granddaughter, a writer, who pays a return visit to her ancestral home. The structure of the work is rather like William Faulkner's *As I Lay Dying* (1930) in that the narrative content is developed as a series of flashbacks during the week in which the grandmother lies on her deathbed. This lengthy novel is generally considered to be Piñon's most important work to date, as well as her most accessible to the general reader.

Because of her careful sculpting of language, her strong individualistic characters, and her orientation toward interior consciousness, critics often point out similarities between Piñon and Brazil's greatest female fiction writer, Clarice Lispector. Feminist critics point to Piñon's decentered narrations as examples of *écriture féminine* (feminine writing).

Paul B. Dixon. In Steven R. Serafin and
Walter D. Glanze, eds. *Encyclopedia of
World Literature in the 20th Century* (New
York: Continuum, 1993), pp. 487–88

Epic novels of the last century created histories in which events encircled individuals. Those of the modernist type prefer instead to wrap individuals around the external occurrences of their times. *The Republic of Dreams* is the story of an émigré Galician named Madruga who arrives in Brazil in 1913 to escape the poverty of Europe, and to accept what he sees as his destiny to participate in the arduous life of settling a rugged new world. Brazil at that time represented to southern Europeans what the United States did to northerners a half century earlier. Transatlantic pilgrims found either reward or tragedy. If they prospered, they never came home. If they failed, they would return broken and disillusioned to resume a life which, by leaving it in the first place, they had deemed arid and meaningless.

Nélida Piñon's story turns on the reminiscences of Madruga in old age and those of his wife Eulalia near the time of her death. Their separate retrospections both complement and contradict one another. Madruga recalls his early days and that "Earning a living in a foreign country was the equivalent in the beginning of undergoing a series of painful amputations." He made his fortune and lived to see his children and grandchildren take their places in a country where a veneer of hypocrisy was sometimes the best suit of armor to wear for self-preservation. Eulalia's memories are more colored by her religious beliefs and the traditional role she assumed as a silent, spiritual force behind the family.

This novel does not have a single plot with rising and falling action that allows the reader to absorb information for some future dramatic moment. It is rather like having a thousand photographs spread out in front of us; we are given anecdotes, memories, and abstractions that occur in, and make up the lives of the characters. Only in an assemblage of the numerous impressions do we grasp overall significance.

The length of this work and the array of so many independent scenes might deter a reader impatient for a more focused narrative, but for that reason it is a volume that could be kept on one's table to be read passages at a time, like a book of meditations. *The Republic of Dreams* contemplates modern history and individual consciousness in the searching language of a gifted and contemplative writer.

Thomas Filbin. Review of Contemporary
Fiction. 12:2, 1992, pp. 205–6

Nélida Piñon's *The Republic of Dreams* has received a great deal of praise; this report, then, is a minority one. *The Republic of Dreams* is, in a curious way, an unfortunate contrast to Olga Masters's modest but impressive work. There's no modesty in *The Republic of Dreams;* Nélida Piñon repeatedly reminds us that she is writing of an exciting land in an exciting time—the Brazilian jungles and ports and frontier towns during the period when heroically avaricious settlers bargained and cheated and brawled their way to fortunes.

The structure of Piñon's novel—the recall of family stories—isn't new, but can be used quite effectively. Again, Piñon makes her task more difficult than it might be otherwise by telling us that the stories will be told by a master storyteller. Unfortunately, despite the promises of excitement and vitality, we are given a family saga that seems longer than it should, filled with events that seem duller than they need be.

Lee Lemon. Prairie Schooner. 64:2, 1990,
p. 131

PITTER, RUTH (GREAT BRITAIN) 1897–

In poetry, some of the best work has been done by Miss Ruth Pitter. A few poems are really first-rate. I recommend particularly "A Trophy of Arms" . . . and "The Spirit Watches." Here we have no jagged ends, no bleeding words; emotion and experience, like seed and soil, combine to produce new unities as natural as misted leaves and dewy flowers. But some inner reserve, some secret strength, perhaps saves Miss Pitter from the curse of finality. We always feel that the inward principle of growth is working in her. What she gives us is a dream, a vision, an apprehension woven round a chime of words. More is to come, she seems to be saying, while scattering jewels.

Ranjee G. Shahani. *Poetry Review.*
January-February, 1942, pp. 27–28

There is a spinsterish book of verses called *The Rude Potato* by Miss Ruth Pitter: these things will out even in the best Anglo-Catholic circles; Miss Pitter conceived the thought of a tuber of irregular shape, and a book of irregular verses is the result. The readers of her more religious poems will be left, no doubt, piously hoping that she will now weave this erotic imagery into harmony with her devouter work, as other mystics before her have done.

Stephen Spender. *Horizon.* February, 1942, p. 102

Miss Pitter rejoices some; those, I suspect, who need a chapel to go to, where they can examine the stained glass; no light, however, comes through the windows. The craftsmanship is there, that would ravish in a poem by Mr. Blunden or Mr. Andrew Young: no light, though. Not at any rate for me.

G. W. Stonier. *New Statesman and Nation.*
April 28, 1945, p. 276

She is "traditional" in the bad sense of the word, but her own sensibility and formal intelligence interrupt and occasionally transfigure her delicate, orthodox, and reasonably interesting exercises in what one might call Attic modes. What Miss Pitter is herself is sympathetic and valuable; but this no more than colors the aggregations of attitudes and techniques of which she is the unquestioning inheritor. She does not fully comprehend that these, like the linens in a tomb, vanish to the digger's "Ah!"—that the lives and possessions of the dead are inaccessible to us until we ourselves have lived and repossessed them.

Randall Jarrell. *The Nation.* May 25, 1946,
p. 633

Ruth Pitter had scarcely emerged from her teens when she produced her *First Poems* (1920). A second volume, *First and Second Poems*, appeared in 1927. But it was *A Mad Lady's Garland* (1934) which convinced attentive critics that the writer was a lyrical poet deserving much more than a word of passing praise. The impression was confirmed by *A Trophy of Arms* (1936), *The Spirit Watches* (1939), *The Rude Potato* (1941, among the most gracious humorous poems known to me) and *The Bridge Poems* (1939–44). There is a beauty moving between the troubled and the serene in *The Spirit Watches*—the piece entitled "The Downward-Pointing Muse" would hold its own in any anthology. But some of *The Bridge Poems* showed further advance, not indeed in sensibility or percipience or metrical aptness, present in all her poetry, but in range and depth of vision.

She is not, in the sense in which the word has been used, a "modern" poet. She belongs to no clique. She follows no modern fashion. Some of her poems assume a form that was within the reach of poetry long ago, but of these many have a significance which differentiates them from poetry of the past. She is intensely alive in the contemporary world, and sees it through its own eyes. But she is not quite of it. She stands apart, inhabiting a region of her own; and if it has not been as extensively communicated to the reading public as it might have been, that is perhaps because she belongs to no recognizable school, has no trumpeter, and has not been at pains to assert herself.

She has written some lovely poetry, authentic, unmistakable, which in her later work is distilled in experience and projected in language fashioned with fine tact and metrical skill. It has substance, and form; hardness, and fragility; grit, with tenderness.

R. A. Scott-James. *Fifty Years of English Literature: 1900–1950* (London: Longmans, 1951), p. 231

While reading the work of Ruth Pitter, written over more than half a century, I was immediately stuck by her acute sensibility and deep integrity. It does therefore seem important to say here something about the place of morality in poetry; by morality I mean a profoundly humane attitude towards the world in general and an honesty so large that it becomes a celebration of truth itself. I also mean a humility which, like Eliot's simplicity, costs "not less than everything." A poet must, too, possess a sense of vocation which entails a willingness to face arid times when no poems are written. These have to be endured if one is ever to know those rare moments when a poem really seems to succeed. Lastly, a fastidious commitment is vital to artists in any medium.

The poems of Ruth Pitter are informed with a sweetness which is also bracing, and a generosity which is blind to nothing, neither the sufferings in this world nor the quirky behavior of human beings; indeed, she rather enjoys the latter. Her introduction to her *Poems 1926–66* is a marvelously illuminating essay which tells us most lucidly her own views on the art of writing poems. . . .

Ruth Pitter . . . tells us of her lofty view of poetry. For her, it has been a life-long passion and she was ready to sacrifice money, security, luxury and all "consolations" in fact, to attain "the ineffable communion with the earth itself." She has, however, a highly developed sense of humor and admits ruefully that, though she has always tried to be "kind" to others, she has often felt her gift "privately boiling with these disgraceful rancouirs which are the exhaust-fumes of ruling passions.". . .

In short, poems spring from "beatitude and anguish" but Ruth Pitter finds that the comic spirit is also of great importance. As we know, lack of humor can betray a poet in to writing verse which is unwittingly funny. Wordsworth is the obvious example of this. A sense of the comic can be a harmonizing factor; it eschews egotism and insists on objectivity.

From her earliest published work, Ruth Pitter has shown herself to be a fine botanist and ornithologist and her Nature poetry has become, with each new book, more detailed, precise and vivid.

In the early work we never find faulty craftsmanship but there is at times a tendency to generalize and a use of archaisms which disappears fairly rapidly with each new book. Ruth Pitter's skill with a variety of verse forms, rhymed and rhythms, is always evident. As she become more adept at making her subjects and themes inseparable from form and music, so her observations of Nature appear more exact and more simple. . . .

Ruth Pitter's style may often appear simple but this is a hard-won simplicity of tone, of form, a simplicity which leads to the profound. . . .

Over years of dedicated craftsmanship Ruth Pitter has increased her formal dexterity and varied her ways of turning that "silent music," which she has spoken of so eloquently, into lucid and memorable sound informed by original thought. She is a very difficult poet to paraphrase because her meaning and music are so perfectly married. She is, I think, at her best with the short lyrical poem or the song because in them the intensity of her ideas and feelings are expressed with most immediacy.

Elizabeth Jennings. Introduction to Ruth Pitter. *Collected Poems* (London: Enitharmon Press, 1990), pp. 15–18

PIZARNIK, ALEJANDRA (ARGENTINA) 1936–72

For various reasons—among them the oneirism of her images and her search for a transcendental poetic experience—the poetry of Alejandra Pizarnik suggests a relationship with surrealism. Such a connection, however, is superficial. Essentially, Pizarnik betrays a profound discomfort with respect to her own poetic discourse, and this radically distinguishes her from the surrealist poets. Her criticism of the word is absolute. It keeps her on the edge of silence, striving for the security that any poet—even the most skeptical—needs to continue writing. If the surrealists (and other "modern" poets) question the language of poetry, they do it to impose in its place "other" language, more valid and innovative. . . . The critical attitude of these poets very rarely threatens the creative process. Quite the contrary: the formulation of a "new" discourse vindicates poetry and the work of the innovators. Pizarnik, by contrast, does not allow herself this satisfaction. She does not succeed in convincing herself that her words can endow the poetic enterprise with validity. This terrible doubt has followed her since her first poems and, with increasing effect, has been assuming power over her to the point of imposing itself as the central theme of her poetry. A vindication in "other" discourse eludes her to the end, so that the questioning of language intervenes in the best of her work. And then silence becomes the unique and seductive alternative for Alejandra Pizarnik, alone and disarmed before the ceremonious treachery of words.

Francisco Lasarte. *Revista Iberoamericana.*
49, 1983, p. 877

Starting with the very title of the book *El deseo de la palabra* (The desire for the word), Alejandra Pizarnik prepares us for the reading of a poetic text that incessantly names and reflects upon itself. The text unfolds a complicated fabric of echoes that simultaneously reveals and covers up the poetic sign. By means of the tale/manifesto "El hombre del antifaz azul" (The man with the blue mask), Alejandra Pizarnik will articulate a nostalgia and a passion whose maximum expression will develop in the poem.

The reading of the story inevitably sends us to another story, another very well known text, *Alice's Adventures in Wonderland.* By diverting the reader's attention to Lewis Carroll's text, Pizarnik succeeds in hiding her own text, camouflaging it with unusual skill within a structure of subtly interwoven differences or dissimilarities. The result of this maneuver is a double writing and hence a double reading. Carroll's text imprints a noisy diversion, an interference that silences or hides the interwoven text, such that reading becomes a task of excavating a sign hidden in another.

Isabel Camara. *Revista Iberoamericana.*
51, 1985, p. 580

[Pizarnik's] poems . . . are usually very short, sometimes only consisting of two or three lines, which, in turn, are often brief and truncated. In addition, an identifiably surrealist cast helps to give these poems an unfinished and indefinite appearance.

Two central preoccupations, death and absence, run through these poems. But, even though these ideas provide a unifying factor to the fragmentary verses, they create difficulties as well, since, as they are used here, they are concepts that are hard to grasp. In Pizarnik's texts both death and absence are treated as necessary and desirable factors for poetry, and, indeed for language itself. . . .

The interaction between the two facets of her self, between life and death, determines the unique poetic voice of her texts. . . .

Pizarnik's poems themselves . . . are formed on, around, and because of, absence. As a . . . summary of that semiotic framework centered on absence, it seems especially convenient and convincing to be able to let. . . . Pizarnik's own brief texts demonstrate how definitely stated and cohesive are the elements central to the poetry's structure. The first of these poems is essentially an outline or list of the most basic concerns of her poetry:

sólo palabras	[only words
las de la infancia	those of infancy
las de la muerte	those of death
las de la noche de los cuerpos	those of the bodies' night]

Childhood, death and night together form the region of absence, of non-existence. And this is where her poetry is born, thanks to the dialogue between her self and its "double." . . .

That interplay between duplicated selves takes place against an insistent background of absence. . . . and it is because of an awareness of that absence that this entire poetic process can happen, a point driven home by this final, purposely repetitious text:

el centro	[the center
de un poema	of a poem
es otro poema	is another poem
el centro del centro	the center of the center
es la ausencia	is absence
en el centro de la ausencia	in the center of absence
mi sombra es el centro	my shadow is the center
del centro del poema	of the center of the poem]

This almost magically concise text, which is itself the center of all of Pizarnik's poetry, opposes an explicit equivalency: the center is a poem is absence is herself. The poem forms itself against an awareness of the absence which engulfs it, and in the process opposes the effects of that assertive absence. The stark and haunting metaphysical imagery wrenched from only four repeated nouns gives these words an expressive power that comes near to reaching Alejandra Pizarnik's goal of "a language without limits."

Thorpe Running. *Chasquí.* 14:2–3, 1985,
pp. 45, 50, 54–55

In the case of Alejandra Pizarnik, who died tragically young in 1972, the process of resurrection entails bringing to light a great poet whose work has been so neglected that it is difficult to obtain. . . .

Alejandra Pizarnik was first pointed out to me as a parallel case to Sylvia Plath—a woman writer who committed suicide, a woman with a sense of cultural displacement (she was Argentinian, of Russian parentage) whose distressed self-image provided her with a central theme and who was fascinated by images of death and silence. Like Plath, she had a strong pictorial sense (she studied painting for some time in Paris) and used key words throughout her writing. Like Plath's poetry, her works—her seven collections of poems, her essays, her short fiction and her diaries—can be seen, indeed need to be seen, as a unified whole rather than as a series of separate entities. Ted Hughes pointed out that Sylvia Plath effectively wrote a single poem in many fragments, and the same argument can be made for Pizarnik's work. This is not to deny her poetic development, rather to emphasize the consistency of her poetic craftsmanship. . . . Reading Alejandra Pizarnik's work is a voyage of discovery fraught with difficulties. A voyage of discovery, even though Octavio Paz wrote the preface for her 1962 collection *Arbol de Diana,* which ought to have ensured her greater public recognition. In that preface, Paz wrote lyrically about the magic tree, the tree that is "transparent and gives no shade . . . that gives off its own brief, sparkling light, that is born in the dry lands of America, that has no roots . . . whose trunk was considered by the ancients to be the (female) sex organ of the entire cosmos . . . that is both masculine and feminine." Here Paz, in his usual blend of the real and the marvelous, was writing about a fusion of elements in the poems but most of all about Alejandra herself, the writer. . . . Reading Pizarnik's poetry today, in a post-feminist period, it is possible to see that she was wrestling with what have come to be perceived as some of the fundamental concerns of feminist aesthetics. She refused to own her poems, claiming that the many voices within them were just part of what she described as the triangular relationship involving writer, poem and reader, and she also refused to write specifically for any particular reader, hoping in this way to encounter readers who would understand her writing instinctively. . . .

The themes of loss and of hope betrayed are, however, only a part of Pizarnik's writing. There is another side to her work, one which is described by Ines Malinow in an introduction to a collection of Pizarnik's poems. Noting that Pizarnik felt, shortly before her death, that she was writing her best poetry (another extraordinary parallel with Plath), Malinow discusses her sense of humor, her irony and self-deprecatory wit, her fighting spirit and her refusal to give in. "Poetry like Alejandra's was not meant to communicate but to not-communicate [*incomunicar*]," she says, reinforcing Pizarnik's own statement about the life of the poem and its relationship with subsequent readers. Pizarnik may have written in *Arbol de Diana* about letting life fall and suffer, be bound with fire in the house of the night but she could also write, as in the little poem "Undoing":

Someone wants to open a door somewhere. Her hands
hurt as she grips her ill-omened prison of bones.

Susan Bassnett. *Knives and Angels: Women
Writers in Latin America* (London: Zed,
1990), pp. 36–37, 41, 44

PLATH, SYLVIA (UNITED STATES) 1932–63

Sylvia Plath [in *The Colossus*] writes clever, vivacious poetry, which will be
enjoyed most by intelligent people capable of having fun with poetry and not
just being holy about it. Miss Plath writes from phrase to phrase as well as
with an eye on the larger architecture of the poem; each line, each sentence,
is put together with a good deal of care for the springy rhythm, the arresting
image and—most of all, perhaps—the unusual word. This policy ought to
produce quaint, over-gnarled writing, but in fact Miss Plath has a firm enough
touch to keep clear of these faults. Here and there one finds traces of "influences" not yet completely assimilated ("Snakecharmer," for instance, is too
like Wallace Stevens for comfort, and the sequence "Poem for a Birthday"
testifies too flatly to an admiration for Theodore Roethke), but after all, this
is a first book, and the surprising thing is how successful Miss Plath has
already been in finding an individual manner.

John Wain. *The Spectator*. January 13, 1961,
p. 50

These last poems of Sylvia Plath's [*Ariel*], once read, hang around one like
the smell of morphia, impregnating everything. As the expression, or rather
unmodified articulation, of raw pain, with its precommittal intensification of
vision and its heightened sharp-edged clarity, they are unique in contemporary poetry. There is little regret or bitterness in them, certainly there is no
hope. They are of the moment, looking neither back nor forward, last-gasp
cries that long since lost any note of tenderness, or even ironic, self-directed
amusement. They are poems for the most part beyond art, as they are also
beyond consolation or compassion. Their tone and manner are almost
brusquely objective, gestures of vivid dismissal made by someone immune
from rescue and without either the mood or the time to modulate or concili-
ate. Acceptance of conventional, meaningful reality is token, the references
to continuing, ordinary life scant. . . .

This is not the sort of book discussable, at this stage anyway, in normal
critical terms. It belongs, ironically, to life rather than to literature, its nerve-
ends still squirming. In any poetry of such swerving trajectories and imbalance it is easy to lose track: the horrors flap off the walls like vultures,
awareness breaks and recedes in hypnotic waves of semi-consciousness. Each

of these poems stands recognizable as an act of courage, as a cleanly-struck blow against a superior adversary. But the nature of the conflict is never clearly defined nor the wounded areas properly probed. The ambulance bells are still ringing.

Alan Ross. London Magazine. May, 1965,
pp. 99, 101

Are these final poems [*Ariel*] entirely legitimate? In what sense does anyone, himself uninvolved and long after the event, commit a subtle larceny when he invokes the echoes and trappings of Auschwitz and appropriates an enormity of ready emotion to his own private design? Was there latent in Sylvia Plath's sensibility, as in that of many of us who remember only by fiat of imagination, a fearful envy, a dim resentment at not having been there, of having missed the rendezvous with hell? In "Lady Lazarus" and "Daddy" the realization seems to me so complete, the sheer fineness and control so great, that only irresistible need could have brought it off. These poems take tremendous risks, extending Sylvia Plath's essentially austere manner to the very limit. They are a bitter triumph, proof of the capacity of poetry to give to reality the greater permanence of the imagined. She could not return from them.

Already there are poets writing like Sylvia Plath. Certain of her angular mannerisms, her elisions and monotonies of deepening rhyme, can be caught and will undoubtedly have their fashion. But minor poets even of a great intensity—and that is what she was—tend to prove bad models. Sylvia Plath's tricks of voice can be imitated. Not her desperate integrity.

George Steiner. The Reporter. October 7,
1965, p. 54

In these poems [in *Ariel*], written in the last months of her life and often rushed out at the rate of two or three a day, Sylvia Plath becomes herself, something imaginary, newly, wildly and subtly created—hardly a person at all, or a woman, certainly not another "poetess," but one of those super-real, hypnotic, great classical heroines. This character is feminine, rather than female, though almost everything we customarily think of as feminine is turned on its head. The voice is now coolly amused, witty, now sour, now fanciful, girlish, charming, now sinking to the strident rasp of the vampire— a Dido, Phaedra, or Medea, who can laugh at herself as "cow-heavy and floral in my Victorian nightgown." Though lines get repeated, and sometimes the plot is lost, language never dies in her mouth.

Everything in these poems is personal, confessional, felt, but the manner of feeling is controlled hallucination, the autobiography of a fever.

Robert Lowell. Foreword to Sylvia Plath.
Ariel (New York: Harper and Row, 1966),
p. vii

Often, very often, Sylvia and I would talk at length about our first suicides; at length, in detail and in depth. . . . Suicide is, after all, the opposite of the poem. Sylvia and I often talked opposites. We talked death with burned-up intensity, both of us drawn to it like moths to an electric light bulb. Sucking on it! She told of her first suicide in sweet and loving detail and her description in *The Bell Jar* is just the same story. It is a wonder that we didn't depress George [Starbuck] with our egocentricity. Instead, I think, we three were stimulated by it, even George, as if death made each of us a little more real at the moment. Thus we went on, in our fashion, ignoring Lowell and the poems left behind. Poems left behind were technique—lasting but, actually, over. We talked death and this was life for us, or better, because of us, our intent eyes, our fingers clutching the glass, three pairs of eyes fixed on someone's—each one's gossip.

> Anne Sexton. In Charles Newman, ed. *The
> Art of Sylvia Plath* (Bloomington: Indiana
> University Press, 1970), p. 175

In [Sylvia Plath], as with perhaps few poets ever, the nature, the poetic genius and the active self, were the same. Maybe we don't need psychological explanations to understand what a difficult and peculiar destiny that means. She had none of the usual guards and remote controls to protect herself from her own reality. She lived right in it, especially during the last two years of her life. Perhaps that is one of the privileges, or prices, of being a woman and at the same time an initiate into the poetic order of events. Though the brains, the strength, the abundance and vivacity of spirits, the artistic virtuosity, the thousand incidental gifts that can turn it into such poetry as hers are another matter.

> Ted Hughes. In Charles Newman, ed. *The
> Art of Sylvia Plath* (Bloomington: Indiana
> University Press, 1970), pp. 187–88

If Sylvia Plath's performance [in *Ariel*] were not so securely knowledgeable, so cannily devised, so richly inventive and so meticulously reined, it would be intolerable. Many of these poems are magnificent; a whole book of them is top-heavy, teetering on that point where the self-created figure threatens to topple over into self-expression and the diversions of psychopathology. Reaching for a poet with whom to compare her, or in whose sphere of influence to "place" her—and only the illustrious will do—one hesitates before Blake (too "big," too masculine, too mythopoeic), before Baudelaire (too much the *poseur,* too *raffiné,* perhaps too comfortable in his rancor), and stops at Emily Dickinson. But anguish in Emily Dickinson is a consequence; it partakes of a classical notion of anguish: the great heart victimized by its own humanity. In Sylvia Plath, by contrast, anguish is not a consequence but the whole relentless subject itself. . . . Anything pursued far enough is likely to turn into its opposite: a shriek maintained for eighty-five pages becomes, to say the least, a bore. Nevertheless, what we have here is not, as some bewildered critics have claimed, the death rattle of a sick girl, but the defiantly fulfilling measures of a poet. Taken in small—one is almost forced to say, medicinal—doses, she is a marvel.

John Malcolm Brinnin. *Partisan Review.*
Winter, 1967, pp. 156–57

The poetry of Sylvia Plath's *Ariel* is a poetry of surrender, surrender to an imagination that destroys life instead of enhancing it. Nowhere in our literature has a finely wrought art proven so subversive as hers, so utterly at odds with those designs, those structures within which we customarily enclose ourselves to hold experience off at a distance. Emerging from encounter with her poems, as from the murky, subterranean depths of a well, one feels not so much emotionally raped as simply breathless into weariness and confusion. It is as though we had been flung into hideous contact with another order of being, suffocated by a presence too driven and hungry to be supported by the thinness of the air we breathe, a presence thrashing about, taking no notice of us, poor mortal creatures, a presence, finally, reaching, touching, shrieking on a scale that dwarfs into insignificance the familiar scale of our activities. It is with caution and humility that we must approach her art, for it is vaporous with potions that do not intoxicate, but depress and confound. If we listen humbly, there are insistent voices trembling beneath the surface of the poetry, voices which beckon to us, suggesting that we lift our heads from the page and answer the poet in kind, assenting to manipulation by that imagination which has taken everything around it for its own, wringing experience to satisfy its hungers.

Robert Boyers. *The Centennial Review.*
Spring, 1969, p. 138

Passions of hate and horror prevail in the poetry of Sylvia Plath, running strongly counter to the affirmative and life-enhancing quality of most great English poetry, even in this century. We cannot reconcile her despairing and painful protest with the usual ideological demands of Christian, Marxist, and humanist writers, whether nobly or sympathetically eloquent, like Wordsworth, breezily simplified, like Dylan Thomas, or cunning in ethical and psychological argument, like W. H. Auden or F. R. Leavis. Her poetry rejects instead of accepting, despairs instead of glorying, turns its face with steady consistency towards death, not life. But hating and horrified passions are rooted in love, are rational as well as irrational, lucid as well as bewildered, so humane and honorable that they are constantly enlarged and expanded. We are never enclosed in a private sickness here, and if derangement is a feature of the poetry, it works to enlarge and generalize, not to create an enclosure. Moreover, its enlargement works through passionate reasoning, argument and wit. Its judgment is equal to its genius.

Barbara Hardy. In Martin Dodsworth, ed.
The Survival of Poetry (London: Faber,
1970), p. 164

Little enough has been said of Sylvia Plath—but perhaps Robert Lowell's description of her poetry as "controlled hallucination" (in the introduction to *Ariel,* 1966) is worth volumes. Hers is a sensibility disturbed, which sees reflected in the exterior world the very tensions, conflicts, and fears that haunt the inner spirit. Her power as a poet derives from her capacity to express this state of mind through the evocation of profound horror. The sense of horror springs from many sources: from her habit of dredging up historical atrocities, from the violent intensity of her expression, from the accuracy and hardness of her language, and most significantly, from the nature of her perception. Always she is aware of the doubleness of things, the shark beneath the surface, the tumult beneath the calm, the glitter beneath the veil. The gaze which she turns outward upon the world is schizophrenic; of the things she perceives, her mind asserts, with the speaker in "Death & Co.," "Two, of course there are two."

This perception leads first to fear and eventually to despair, for it forces upon one the recognition that the world is disjointed, that things are not what they seem. Among Sylvia Plath's works run two rather different ways of expressing poetically the theme of doubleness. One method—the more obvious of the two—proceeds by revealing horror amid an atmosphere of apparent security. This is a somewhat traditional device, certainly not unique with Miss Plath, although in her hands it is capable of vivid effects. A second and somewhat more subtle method illustrates the validity of Lowell's comment: doubleness is conveyed by a sort of hallucinatory vision, a way of seeing simultaneously, the opposing qualities of a thing.

Lynda B. Salamon. *Spirit.* Summer, 1970,
p. 34

Sylvia Plath's only novel, the autobiographical *The Bell Jar,* is a deceptively modest, uncommonly fine piece of work. First published in England under the pseudonym Victoria Lucas . . . the book is more than a posthumous footnote to her career as a poet. . . . The novel is in its own right a considerable achievement. It is written to a small scale, but flawlessly—an artistically uncompromising, witty account of the experiences, inner and outer, that led to Miss Plath's earlier breakdown and recovery.

The book is humorous and dramatic, the prose for the most part lean but sometimes, suddenly, full of a transforming imagery. . . .

Miss Plath doesn't claim to "speak for" any time or anyone—and yet she does, because she speaks so accurately. . . .

The novel has a sharp and memorable poignancy. With her classical restraint and purity of form, Sylvia Plath is always refusing to break your heart, though in the end she breaks it anyway.

Lucy Rosenthal. *Saturday Review of
Literature.* April 24, 1971, p. 42

The novel itself [*The Bell Jar*] is no firebrand. It's a slight, charming, sometimes funny and mildly witty, at moments tolerably harrowing "first" novel, just the sort of clever book a Smith summa cum laude (which she was) might have written if she weren't given to literary airs. From the beginning our expectations of scandal and startling revelation are disappointed by a modesty of scale and ambition and a jaunty temperateness of tone. The voice is straight out of the 1950s: politely disenchanted, wholesome, yes, wholesome, but never cloying, immediately attractive, nicely confused by it all, incorrigibly truthful; in short, the kind of kid we liked then, the best product of our best schools. The hand of Salinger lay heavy on her.

But this is 1971 and we read [as] her analyst, too wily to be deceived by that decent, smiling, well-scrubbed coed who so wants to be liked and admired. We look for the slips and wait for the voice to crack. We want the bad, the worst news; that's what we're here for, to be made happy by horror, not to be amused by girlish chatter. Our interests are clinical and prurient. A hard case, she confounds us. She never raises her voice.

Saul Maloff. *The New Republic.* May 8,
1971, p. 34

For all the drama of her biography, there is a peculiar remoteness about Sylvia Plath. A destiny of such violent self-destruction does not always bring the real person nearer; it tends, rather, to freeze our asssumptions and responses. She is spoken of as a "legend" or a "myth"—but what does that mean?

Sylvia Plath was a luminous talent, self-destroyed at the age of thirty, likely to remain, it seems, one of the most interesting poets in American literature. As an *event* she stands with Hart Crane, Scott Fitzgerald, and Poe rather than with Emily Dickinson, Marianne Moore, or Elizabeth Bishop.

Elizabeth Hardwick. *New York Review of
Books.* August 12, 1971, p. 3

In some strange way, I suspect [Plath] thought of herself as a realist: the deaths and resurrections of "Lady Lazarus," the nightmares of "Daddy" and the rest had all been proved on her pulses. That she brought to them an extraordinary inner wealth of imagery and associations was almost beside the point, however essential it is for the poetry itself. Because she felt she was simply describing the facts as they had happened, she was able to tap in the coolest possible way all her large reserves of skill: those subtle rhymes and half-rhymes, the flexible, echoing rhythms and offhand colloquialism by which she preserved, even in her most anguishing probing, complete artistic control. Her internal horrors were as factual and precisely sensed as the barely controllable stallion on which she was learning to ride or the car she had tried to smash up.

So she spoke of suicide with a wry detachment, and without any mention of the suffering or the drama of the act.

A. Alvarez. The Savage God
(New York: Random House, 1972), p. 20

"Such a dark funnel, my father," Sylvia Plath cries out in her "Little Fugue." And Otto Plath is a funnel indeed, leading her psyche from the openness of youth down toward the small dark point of death. . . . To date no one has traced the trajectory of her father's memory in the body of Plath's work. We suggest that a pattern of guilt over imagined incest informs all of Plath's prose and poetry. When Otto Plath dies of natural causes in a hospital on November 2, 1940, he might just as well have been a lover jilting his beloved. Indeed, in all her poems Plath makes of this separation a deliberate desertion. In poem after poem the father drowns himself.

This is the central myth of Plath's imagination. Critics have called hers a poetry of annihilation, poetry in which her own suicidal impulses are set against the larger framework of a world which deliberately destroys—the Nazi genocide of the Jews, the Kamikazes, Hiroshima. Even a train is said to eat its track. A favorite Plath image is that of the hook: from the bend in a road, to the corner of her son's smile—both traps for the unsuspecting. Plath's is a terrible, unforgiving nature; in feeling victimized by her father's early death, and later by an unsatisfactory compensatory marriage, she makes no distinction between her tragedy and those of Auschwitz or Nagasaki.

Robert Philips. The Confessional Poets
(Carbondale: Southern Illinois University
Press, 1973), p. 128

Given the fact that in a few poems Sylvia Plath illustrates an extreme state of existence, one at the very boundary of nonexistence, what illumination—moral, psychological, social—can be provided of either this state or the general human condition by a writer so deeply rooted in the extremity of her plight? Suicide is an eternal possibility of our life and therefore always interesting; but what is the relation between a sensibility so deeply captive to the idea of suicide and the claims and possibilities of human existence in general? That her story is intensely moving, that her talent was notable, that her final breakthrough arouses admiration—of course! Yet in none of the essays devoted to praising Sylvia Plath have I found a coherent statement as to the nature, let alone the value, of her vision. Perhaps it is assumed that to enter the state of mind in which she found herself at the end of her life is its own ground for high valuation; but what will her admirers say to those who reply that precisely this assumption is what needs to be questioned?

Irving Howe. Harper's. January, 1972, p. 91

Winter Trees is the slimmest as well as the last of Sylvia Plath's collections; there are nineteen poems here on forty printed pages. But there is ample further evidence of her endless imaginative resource in the restatement of her familiar themes; all proceeding, ultimately, from the "divided self," the self which is alienated, oppressed, disembodied, dissolved. We meet again the familiar images, particularly the (characteristically schizoid) image of the mirror, which appears in all but two of these poems and seems to haunt them with its inevitability and its destructiveness. . . . We are dazed again by the complicated use of colors, almost as a symbolism, to signify states of mind, attitudes; the alienating absolutes of black and white, the terrifying violence red almost always means, the uncertainty of blue, which can signify the cold night-blue of the moon ("What blue, moony ray ices their dreams?"), blue angels—"the cold angels, the abstractions," or the sky-blue of a child's eyes; and the occasional consolation of the organic colors, brown and green.

Damian Grant. *Critical Quarterly.* 49,
Spring, 1972, pp. 92–93

The poems we write are the only poems we can. We pretend they are choices when, in fact, they may be so only in the obverse sense: that we are the chosen. Many times we may not even be free to leave them unwritten. This is especially true in a poet as obsessive and emblematic as Sylvia Plath, whose most noteworthy book was produced in something equivalent to Keats's "great year" which preceded, like his, a premature death.

Now, ten years later, surely enough time has passed that we can dispense with the "Plath myth," an obscuring glitter around *Ariel* and *The Bell Jar* which wraps them in biographical data. After all, the novel is little more than a psychologically meager but socially accurate portrait of the 1950s. Plath's last poems, however, project a mythic world which is not "confessional" in an autobiographical but a sacramental sense. What they achieve, finally, is even beyond their treatment of the persona as "woman"—a combination saint and witch in Ariel's speaker—a new dimension for the contemporary lyric in which tragedy is again possible because seen from a perspective both comic and magic.

Peter Cooley. *The Hollins Critic.* February,
1973, pp. 1–2

Tragedy is not a woman, however gifted, dragging her shadow around in a circle or analyzing with dazzling scrupulosity the stale, boring inertia of the circle; tragedy is cultural, mysteriously enlarging the individual so that what he has experienced is both what we have experienced and what we need not experience—because of his, or her, private agony. It is proper to say that Sylvia Plath represents for us a tragic figure involved in a tragic action, and that her tragedy is offered to us as a near-perfect work of art in her books *The Colossus* (1960), *The Bell Jar* (1963), *Ariel* (1965), and the posthumous volumes published in 1971, *Crossing the Water* and *Winter Trees*. This essay is an attempt to analyze Miss Plath in terms of her cultural significance, to diagnose through her poetry the pathological aspects of our era which make a death of the spirit inevitable—for that era and for all who believe in its assumptions. It is also based upon the certainty that Miss Plath's era is concluded and that we may consider it with the sympathetic detachment with which we consider any era that has gone before us and makes our own possible: the cult of Sylvia Plath insists that she is a saintly martyr, but of course she is something less dramatic than that, though more valuable. The "I" of the poems is an artful construction, a tragic figure whose tragedy is classical, the result of a limited vision that believed itself the mirror held up to nature—as in the poem "Mirror," the eye of a little god that imagines itself without preconceptions, "unmisted by love or dislike." This is the audacious hubris of tragedy, the inevitable reality-challenging statement of the participant in a dramatic action which he does not know is "tragic." He dies, and only we can see the purpose of his death—to illustrate the error of a personality that believed itself godlike.

Joyce Carol Oates. *Southern Review.*
Summer, 1973, pp. 501–2

For Plath, poetry had always been symbolic action. In *The Colossus,* she had used language to impose an order upon experience, but the order in her poems contradicted her vision of reality as fragmented and perpetually disintegrating. Only in a poem could the world be composed and controlled, and so poetry was artificial; it lied. In the later poetry, she begins to tell the truth. When she comes to see that reality resides in her own mind, words and poems become as real as anything else. The expression of her vision in words unleashes reality, for her poems describe what is real: her own consciousness. The action that is poetry is recognized as symbolic action (she never ceases to know the *difference* between art and life), but the symbols now reflect rather than counteract her own life. . . .

There remains a gap between woman and poet.

As poet, Plath sees with increasing clarity this gap. She sees as well the existence of life and its inevitable corruption into death. The forces in her that gave rise to her awareness of and fascination with death are surely complex; but surely the fact that she existed for so long with a sense of her own self as disparate, bifurcated, contributed to a desire for wholeness that she could equate only with death. The pulse of life was the movement towards disintegration: the stasis of death brought integration. And perfection. For Plath had viewed perfection as a solution to her problem, a perfection that she had been led to believe was achievable through talent and sheer willpower. She needed to be good at everything because in that way she could *be* everything: woman and poet. Although this program proved impossible, she was left with a belief in, and a desire to achieve, perfection. There was perfection in death.

Suzanne Juhasz. *Naked and Fiery Forms:
Modern American Poetry by Women—A
New Tradition* (New York: Octagon Books,
1976), pp. 102–3

If her poetry is understood as constituting a system of symbols that expresses a unified mythic vision, her images may be seen to be emblems of that myth. Red, white, and black, for example, the characteristic colors in her late poetry, function as mythic emblems of her state of being much as they do in the mythologies which she drew upon. A great many other particulars of her poetry are similarly determined by her system, and personal and historical details as well are subordinate to it. While a confessional poet might alter certain details to make them more fitting . . . Plath's alteration of details has a deeper significance. Her protagonist in "Daddy" says, "I was ten when they buried you," but Plath was only eight when her father died. A magical "one year in every ten" cycle, however, conveys the mythic inevitability necessary to define her state of being. It is precisely such details of confessional literalness that Plath most frequently alters or eliminates, when they are not sufficiently mythic. . . .

Without [the awareness of a mythic dimension in Plath's poetry], the elements of suffering, violence, death, and decay will generally be seen as aspects of a self-indulgent stance that is merely—albeit brilliantly—nasty, morbid, and decadent, the extremist exhibitionism. Were she a "confessional" poet, this might be the case. But her poetry is of a different order, and these details are absorbed into a broader system of concerns. To see the autobiographical details only as such is to regard Plath's vision of suffering and death as morbid, but to appreciate the deeper significance of her poetry is to understand her fascination with death as connected with and transformed into a broader concern with the themes of rebirth and transcendence.

To deal with the structure of Plath's poetry is primarily to deal with the voices, landscape, characters, images, emblems, and motifs which articulate a mythic drama having something of the eternal necessity of Greek tragedy. The myth has its basis in her biography, but it in turn exercises a selective function on her biography and determines within it an increasingly restricted context of relevance as her work becomes more symbolic and archetypal. . . .

Had Plath survived, it seems likely, given the nature of her concerns at the end of her life, that she would have further developed and further explored the overtly religious themes of some of the last poems, coming more and more to realize her power of what Ted Hughes calls her "free and controlled access to depths formerly reserved to the primitive ecstatic priests, shamans and Holy men. . ."; and, as in the case of her mythology, evolving a sensibility shaped by several traditions, but with a voice unmistakably her own. The unflinchingness of her gaze, her refusal to compromise the truth, her precision, her intelligence, and her passion—all of these would have qualified her uniquely in the discovery of her wholeness, to convince us that the achievement is possible.

Judith Kroll. *Chapters in a Mythology: The Poetry of Sylvia Plath* (New York: Harper & Row, 1976), pp. 4–6, 210–11

Romantic in its immediacy, her sharpened poetic was not quite typical of the 1960s, and precisely to the extent that it was Poundian. Poundian in the first place as to eye. Her work unfolds perhaps for the first time the full dramatic potential of what T. E. Hulme called "the new visual art," an art depending "for its effect not on a kind of half sleep produced by meter, but on arresting the attention, so much so that the succession of visual images should exhaust one." (This rapid piling up of "distinct images" produces "the poet's state in the reader." Now, despite the avowed classicism of Hulme and Pound, Imagism was actually a centaur poetic of which the basic and stronger half was romantic sensation. To induce the poet's state in the reader when that state is visual ecstasy, a state in which the magic breath of metaphor ripples the dull surface of life, is to write romantically.) But though the new visual art set itself off from leisured traditional description by rapid-fire figuration, it was notorious for being static, limitedly pictorial. The instant fixing of a single impression, as by a jeweled pin, was its convention. Still, there was nothing to prevent its being thickcoming and developmental; it could be galvanized.

Or so Plath, more than any other, was to prove. She made images burst forth and succeed one another under acute psychological pressure, the dramatic crisis of the poem a generating furor. In violent import, color, solidity, and velocity her images are unsurpassed. Even when her spirit ebbs, her imagery ferments. In "Words," for instance, one metaphor instantly gives rise to two others, which are then elaborated in quick succession, each giving way and coming in again, but without any effect of haste. Proliferation has perhaps never been more subtle and vigorous, more constantly deepening.

But the most "delicate and difficult" part of the new art, so Hulme implies, is "fitting the rhythm" to the image—fitting *all* the sound, I might amend. And Plath's ear is no less gifted than her imaginative eye. For instance, she rivals Pound's hearkening ear for the calling back and forth and expressive rightness of sounds. . . .

With Pound, Plath also shared the decidedly modern ear for what she called the "straight out" rhythms and words of prose and colloquial speech; like Pound, if less ambitiously and more evenly, she assimilated them into poetry, creating new verse rhythms. . . .

Plath's poetic, then, is Poundian—romantic. True, classical simplicity shows up in passages, and classical grace and proportion sometimes govern whole poems. Then, too, her persistent use of stanzas reflects the same orderly habit of mind that made her list each morning what she wanted to accomplish during the day. Undeniably, moreover, certain associations of the word *romantic* shrivel when held up to her flame. The shriek of her ego, the sound of a tense holding on to little, drove off every softness. She maximized horror as if she lived on menace. All the same, her poetic is full of romantic presence. No retreat, no passivity, can harbor in it; it is the aggressive poetic of one buried alive but not ready to die. (Even in expressing revulsion from reality she reached obsessively and inconsistently for visual analogy, a language of rapport.) What is her struggle against fear, pain, isolation, if not romantic? Perhaps we would deny her reasons for writing at all to think of it as anything else or anything less.

Calvin Bedient. In Gary Lane, ed. *Sylvia Plath: New Views on the Poetry* (Baltimore: Johns Hopkins University Press, 1979), pp. 15–18

Plath uses many devices, not all of them subtle, to achieve the artistic effect of a world in violent motion. For one thing, many of the late poems make use of the motif of journeying: "Blackberrying," "On Deck," "Crossing the Water," "Ariel," "Getting There," "The Bee Meeting," "Totem," and perhaps "Words" as well. There are also poems like "Black Rook in Rainy Weather" and "Letter in November" that seem to indicate that the shapes of her thoughts, her intuitions, come to her in motion rather than when she is standing still. Another of her devices is the beginning *in medias res*. No one is better than Plath at giving her reader the experience of being swept up in an action that has been gathering momentum for some time. . . . Two devices seem to me a part of her medium not always sufficiently considered when critics have sought to unravel her message. One of them is the deliberate use of ambiguity, of elaborate puns, . . . and the other is a manipulation of images that, in some of her better poems, makes her the poetic daughter of Wallace Stevens.

Richard Allen Blessing. In Gary Lane, ed. *Sylvia Plath: New Views on the Poetry* (Baltimore: Johns Hopkins University Press, 1979), pp. 59–61

Plath appears as a unique and disturbing figure in American poetry. She is a poet of enormous talent, who pushes toward a vitalistic account of human existence in its relation to a hostile external reality. Yet she fails to believe in her own theoretical and positive program sufficiently to overcome the corrosive effects of death-fear and death-longing. She enacts repeatedly a drama that can terminate in either life or death, using poetry as a means of playing out the alternate fates reserved for her by existence. The discrete moments of unity and ecstasy in her work anticipate a greater unity of thought and sensation, but that unification of diversity never emerges. As she returns again and again to the same symbolically charged landscapes and the same figures of death and suffering, she seems to lose faith in the ultimate triumph of the life force over the forces of negation. The process of self-transformation winds down into self-annihilation.

Yet it is perhaps absurd to expect that Plath by herself could present an integrated vision of body and mind, of life and death. Our culture has been riddled since Puritan times with intense divisions within its system of ideals and its versions of human purpose. Plath reflects a gigantic split within American culture between its positive valuation of a fierce selfhood and its radical denial of the body's sufficiency. Plath is unusual in the extremity of her rejection of the body, but her search for self-expansion through a denial of the surrounding physical reality—of the body, of the social system, of the limitations of time and space—is the essential American story. . . .

Plath's quest for initiatory change fails because the other cannot be brought under the domination of the self, even when the self wills its own destruction so as to merge with the world. Her fierce and brilliant language is all directed at the other whom she wishes to overcome, but the giants and colossi of her poetry fall down only to rise again; the body immolates itself only to return to its old, guilt-ridden shape. As Kafka says, the suffering the artist undergoes releases him—for more suffering. Plath's initiatory dramas release her from one state of suffering so that she may endure a new agony. For the briefest moment, though, she is set free from the imprisonment of selfhood; and it is this moment that her best poems, "Ariel," "Fever 103°," "Lady Lazarus," and "The Couriers," celebrate. If she could not sustain her liberation beyond the moment, she still provides an intense vision of the irreducible, entwined core of life and death.

Jon Rosenblatt. Sylvia Plath: The Poetry of Initiation (Chapel Hill: University of North Carolina Press, 1979), pp. 161–63

In *The Colossus* Plath failed to incorporate a perfect, unitive, imaginative vision into the functioning of her poetic sensibility. By using the most intimate subject matter available to her—women's blood and birth myths, voluntary and involuntary creation—she evaluates her old poetic, its failures and its promises in *Crossing the Water*. While Plath is exploring a new freedom in form, rhythm, and sound, she is also revising inherited stereotypes about women. These simultaneous functions form a more intimate commentary on—and guideline for—her future development than the distanced world of art provided her in *The Colossus*. . . .

Thematically and technically, the last poems, defying both critical and psychological labels, argue for a positive, creative space for ambivalence. Plath demonstrates her mobility between the contradictory extremes of self-effacement and the diminished life on the one hand, and theatrical energy on the other. The speaker reminds us that her enlarged sensibility is always at work weighing, balancing, and combining. Her expansiveness is not a matter of diffused emotions out of control or schizophrenic inattention. Rather, it is a conscious love of motion. . . .

Certain themes are present in slightly altered forms throughout her writings: she counsels physical limitations, warns against the hazards of an exclusive imaginative life, mocks romantic illusions and later marital-love delusions, recognizes the failure of a simple identity. Yet these themes seem less important, less defining, than Plath's consciousness of her changing poetic and her explorations of the startling gamut of emotional options for the speaking voice. By *Ariel* and *Winter Trees,* she has turned "fatal equilibrium" into creative ambivalence, giving a dual artistic authority to passivity and motion in her final poems.

Mary Lynn Broe. *Protean Poetic: The Poetry of Sylvia Plath* (Columbia: University of Missouri Press, 1980), pp. 180–81, 187–91

It has often been remarked that commentary on Plath tends to split into two antagonistic camps. There are those who pathologize Plath, freely diagnose her as schizophrenic or psychotic, read her writings as symptom or warning, something we should both admire and avoid. Diagnosis of Plath tends to make her culpable—guilt by association with the troubles of the unconscious mind. The spectre of psychic life rises up in her person as a monumental affront for which she is punished. Feminism has rightly responded to this form of criticism by stressing the representative nature of Plath's inner drama, the extent to which it focuses the inequities (the pathology) of a patriarchal world. But in so doing, it has tended to inherit the framework of the critical language it seeks to reject. Plath becomes innocent—man and patriarchy are to blame. More important, psychic life is stripped of its own logic; it becomes the pure effect of social injustice, wholly subservient to the outside world which it unfailingly reflects. Anything negative or violent in her writing is then read as a stage in a myth of self-emergence, something which Plath achieved in her poetry, if not in her life—an allegory of selfhood which settles the unconscious and ideally leaves its troubles behind.

It is, however, hardly surprising that the unconscious and its difficulty has had to be jettisoned by feminist criticism, when we see, in relation to Plath, the extent to which it has been abused. In fact, despite first appearances, those diagnoses of Plath remove the problem of the unconscious even more than the criticism that has come in reply. There is nothing like the concept of a purely individual pathology for allowing us, with immense comfort, to conjure it all away (her problem, not mine; or, talking about danger as a way of feeling safe). For me one of the central challenges presented by Plath's writing has been to find a way of looking at the most unsettling and irreducible dimensions of psychic processes which she figures in her writing without turning them against her—without, therefore, turning her into a case.

Jacqueline Rose. *The Haunting of Sylvia Plath* (Cambridge: Harvard University Press, 1992), pp. 3–4

In reading the Ariel poems, I try to account for the reciprocal relation between gender and representation implicit in Plath's texts, to "discover," as Nancy Miller has described feminist critical practice, "the embodiment in writing of a gendered subjectivity; to recover within representation the emblems of its construction." I see Plath's creative choices in the poems as at once symptomatic and strategic, symptomatic in that they suggest her culture's powerful shaping influence on her imagination, yet strategic in that they represent her effort to rewrite her lived experience in a poetics of survival. In her poetry Plath's goal was to rewrite her life; in her practice . . . we can understand how she also revised the very notion of "woman."

Plath's rage in her late poems was Vesuvian, to adapt Dickinson's metaphor of the woman poet's dissembling restraint and her potentially destructive expressive power. Plath constructs a highly theatricalized performance of the feminine victim in order to justify the retaliatory script of her consuming homicidal rage. But the feminine victim—mute, confined, tortured, dismembered—represents Plath's fear of poetic silencing as much as it does her erotic dependency. The extravagantly oppositional stance of these poems, driven by desire and defiance alike, provides the dialectic that defines Plath's sense of self and power.

In the poems in which she confronts the meanings of the female body, Plath resituates the female subject in a refigured body no longer defined by opposition but by appropriation. As she dismantles her earlier poetics in which she was fertile partner to Hughes's inspiring genius, Plath's scenarios move from victimization, through retaliation, and toward dangerous incarnations of female sexuality. She reinvests the male potency and authority that the rage poems protest in a new poetics of singularity. Creative primacy in these poems is asserted as a pleasurable repossession of a body endowed with incandescent energy, unconstrained liberty, and inviolable self-sufficiency.

In Plath's poetry, making babies and making poems are persistent metaphors for each other. As a mother who writes the Ariel poems, Plath explores the dissonance and ambivalence that arise when the conceit becomes a consuming reality. Plath was determined to prove that writing and maternity were both inherent expressive needs of female sexual identity. She depended on both to confirm her generativity and autonomy, yet her journals and her poems alike reveal that she conceived of them as fearful ordeals with uncertain outcomes.

Susan R. Van Dyne. *Revising Life: Sylvia
Plath's Ariel Poems* (Chapel Hill: University
of North Carolina Press, 1993), pp. 5–6

PLESSEN, ELISABETH (GERMANY) 1944–

Elisabeth Plessen's *Mitteilung an den Adel* (Information for the gentry) (1976) appeared relatively early in this [autobiographical] trend and is in many respects the most interesting of the group, for it illustrates both problems of reception and potential complexity for such autobiographical accounts of the 1970s; and, as an analysis of the work will demonstrate, *Mitteilung* presents the parent/child identity problem of the 1970s in a formal and thematic combination which may help us to understand the nature of these "shattered selves.". . .

Reviewers of Plessen's book have generally praised her stylistic sophistication, her thematization of language itself, and her portrayal of post-war nobility, lost in a time that seems to have no place for it. The two chief adverse reactions to the book, however, are interesting because of the critical assumptions they betray and the assessment to which these assumptions lead. Proceeding from references to the autobiographical correspondences in the work—"Augusta" is one of Plessen's several given names; dates and places parallel those in Plessen's life; and her own background is indeed that of "Gräfin von Plessen"—some critics then allow their own attitude toward the historical personage of the author to dominate their response to the figure of Augusta. . . .

They reduce Plessen's account to the petty, private, and psychoanalytically disposable saga of a "poor little rich girl"—and demonstrate in so doing the typically problematic reception of autobiographical writing. These reviewers so thoroughly project the historical author into the narration that they, in a sense, personalize the book: they lose sight of literary criteria and respond instead to the book's autobiographical reality-statement, concentrating on criticizing the author's personal beliefs, rather than examining the book for its literary merit. . . .

[T]he other source of critical disfavor toward the book is a mistaken judgment about the over-simplicity of the structure—a structure which, in these critics' descriptions, is limited to the plot-frame utilized by Plessen to propel the minimal action of the novel forward and to provide a concrete setting for eliciting the figure's recollections. What is overlooked within this approach is the subtle complexity of Plessen's narrative structure, an intricacy of thematic and formal levels which emerges from the establishment of parallels between Augusta and her father, and, by means of signaled commentary, between the narrated figure and the narrating voice.

To make the leap, then . . . from the autobiographical dimension to the author herself, we may indeed receive the message sent by the author through the medium of the literary speech-act, and see *Mitteilung an den Adel* as Plessen's address to herself, her own "Selbstgespräch." She presents a narrative which purports to be a third-person account of a young woman's internal struggle to reconcile her sense of self with her historical inheritance, and to forge her own identity from the debris left behind in the political and psychological wake of this century. In actuality, however—by means of the manifestly autobiographical nature of the book and the creation of a level of understanding which includes the book itself as an object of interpretation—Plessen's intricately complex novel illustrates by example the sources of crisis for many of her contemporaries: the weight of the past upon the children of the present, and the impossibility of an identity search which would begin with a rejection of all that has come before.

Sandra Frieden. *Seminar.* 18, 1982,
pp. 274–76, 285–86

The father's death also creates a condition for the daughter to be able to produce, by writing, the fiction of a closeness to him. In this, the daughter's writing is represented, like in Plessen's book, [*Mitteilung an den Adel*] as an attempt to revoke the father's absence. There, a passage about the father reads: "C.A.—die ewige Gegenwart?" (C.A.—the eternal present?) Schwaiger's father is also excessively present in his absence. Strictly speaking, her monolog is about the presence of the father's absence, a presence that has the character of a godly omnipresence and omnipotence. . . .

Above all, her father remains omnipresent in her love relationship to Birer . . . with whom she reproduces her dependence on her father and the structure of inaccessibility and the closeness/distance ambivalence. . . .

Although Birer is the expression of her opposition to her father, it is also true that:

She "has permission" to enter into a sexual relationship with Birer *because* he is a substitute for her father. And in the same way:

Although the book is a "settling of accounts" with her father, it is also true that:

Because she is writing about her father, she has permission to write—about herself. For that is what the text is really about.

Regula Venske. *Women in German*
Yearbook. 2, 1986, pp. 85–86

Augusta's car journey, in *Mitteilung an den Adel,* from Munich to Schleswig-Holstein lasts four days. The drive from the south to the north of West Germany is sufficiently long for the memories to unfold and the imagination to play havoc. Her inability, however, actually to face the reality of the death of her father is evident from her last minute decision not to attend the funeral even though she has reached her destination. . . .

Owing to the autobiographical nature of these father-daughter portrayals, the writing process per se may be regarded as a form of therapy for the writer. . . . It becomes clear that the narrator figure/the heroine is closely identified with the authoress herself, thus a personal conflict pervades . . . [the] narrative. The finished literary product provides the bereaved writer with the final word on the death of her father. . . .

Tradition and a set of values can no longer be enforced by the man in authority. In this way death has a belittling effect. It removes him from the world of which he was once in control. It is a sad fact that, after his death, when it is too late, there is the realization by the daughter that her father is not different. Thus, for the daughter, the death of her father is instructive; the recognition of his mortality enables the writer to discover the freedom to approach her father in literary form, thereby bridging the gap between them and forcing him to be part of her life, no longer a stranger, occupying a position of distance.

G. Bayley. *New German Studies.* 16,
1990–91, pp. 28, 34, 36

POLLOCK, SHARON (CANADA) 1936–

Let us consider Sharon Pollock's *Komagata Maru Incident.* While not literally a documentary in that no primary source material is identified as such in the play, it is in the spirit of documentary because it is based on documented facts, and because it effects a significant meeting of the actual event and the theatrical event. The play chronicles an incident in 1914 when the Canadian Immigration Department refused entry to all but twenty of three hundred and seventy-six British subjects of East Indian origin. The truth that the play conveys, however, is not primarily the truth about that incident. It is the truth that is immediately apparent to any member of an average Canadian audience who looks around him when the houselights go up. The audience is a component of the theatrical event that is rarely singled out as an object of attention. When this normal, automatic state of affairs is interrupted, as it is in *The Balcony* by Genet or Handke's *Offending the Audience,* an audience becomes sharply aware of itself. This is what happens in *The Komagata Maru Incident.* From the beginning, the audience is reflected back to itself in the role of an idly curious crowd at a carnival sideshow, by a character who functions as Master of Ceremonies. . . .

How can a Canadian audience reject the proffered role of idly curious uninvolved passersby without having to consider the predominance of caucasians in its own composition? As an audience we are alienated from our automatic acceptance of the predominance of "the White Race" in our country: it didn't just happen; choices were made and continue to be made to maintain it. The play forces us to either criticize or justify this state of affairs: we cannot take it for granted.

Sharon Pollock says something very illuminating in her "playwright's note": "As a Canadian, I feel that much of our history has been misrepresented and even hidden from us. Until we recognize our past, we cannot change our future." She is describing the function of the type of documentary play we are discussing now, which is to bring to our attention the hidden or ignored events that have created our present reality and to use them to bring that reality to our consciousness in the immediate present time of the performance.

Robert C. Nieman. *Canadian Literature.*
103, 1984, pp. 55–56

Sharon Pollock's play, *Blood Relations* (1980), initiates . . . an exploration. This play reproduces the patriarchal family's typical limitation of female roles to victim and victimizer, and then harshly denounces the bi-polar oscillation that this duality necessarily produces in female characters. Unlike much early feminist drama, which assumed that women eventually might trade the role of victim for a role of power and independence, *Blood Relations* insists that *under patriarchy* the woman who trades in her "victim script" will find herself just as fiercely trapped in the script of "victimizer." Further, whereas much early feminist drama attempted to slot women into the position of subject (formerly occupied exclusively by men), *Blood Relations* challenges the possibility of this position. Rather than valorize one woman's killing another to achieve "freedom" and "autonomy" promised to agentive subjects in an ideology of liberal humanism, *Blood Relations* deconstructs this ideology, offering characters who do *not* author their own meanings and actions, who do *not* originate their own histories.

In a Production Note preceding *Blood Relations* Pollock directs: "Action must be free-flowing. There can be no division of the script into scenes." Despite Pollock's injunction, we might divide the play into two modalities for purposes of analysis. The first takes place in "the present" of the play—a Sunday afternoon in late autumn, 1902—and includes action among three characters: Lizzie Borden, Lizzie's older sister, Emma, and an unnamed actress who comes to Fall River to visit her "friend" Lizzie. This "present time" brackets and occasionally interrupts the play's second modality, what Pollock calls its "dream thesis." In the dream thesis, we watch as the Actress (playing Lizzie), Lizzie (playing Bridget, the maid), and various other characters reenact events occurring in 1892, the year Andrew and Abigail Borden were murdered, and Lizzie was tried for and acquitted of the murders.

I want to begin consideration of *Blood Relations* with analysis of this re-enactment. As the Actress "plays"/re-plays Lizzie, both the participants and the spectators realize that first, daughters in nineteenth-century patriarchal households read from scripts that allow them only two options—to be killed or to kill; second, if daughters elect the second option, their initial victims, almost inevitably, will be mothers (the relative powerlessness of a mother makes her more attractive as a target than a father); and finally, this option does not produce the results—autonomy, integrity, self-coherence—that it promises. Focusing on a woman whose own mother dies in giving birth to her, a woman accused of murdering her stepmother, *Blood Relations* affords us the opportunity of laying out these oppositions in decidedly bold terms.

Ultimately, however, *Blood Relations* is concerned not only with extremes, but also with the range of little murders and little deceits occurring daily in patriarchal households.

Madonne Miner. *Literature in Performance.*
6:2, 1986, pp. 11–12

At a summer 1985 conference in Toronto on women's issues in the theater, Rina Fraticelli cited playwright Sharon Pollock (along with the American Joanne Akalaitis and British Caryl Churchill) as representing "the distinct female viewpoint" that in her estimation would eventually "transform the (male) esthetic code that has dominated Western Culture." Pollock herself resists the ideological label of "feminist" along with any other that restricts her artistic independence. However, since her plays from *Blood Relations* (1980) to the present show increasing attention to feminine individuality, Fraticelli's appropriation of Pollock as a feminist playwright might bear closer examination. Perhaps a feminist *manqué* is emerging from the wings, or more to the point what is taken for feminism is an aspect of this playwright's ongoing response to new dramaturgical challenges: what critic Malcolm Page regarded in 1979 as Pollock's "restless determination to avoid obvious approaches and search for angles which are effective and unusual."

While her continuing experimentation with dramatic styles and structures may seem to fit Fraticelli's conception of radical feminist dramaturgy, in this regard Sharon Pollock should also be numbered among the several new playwrights and playmakers beginning to write in the early 1970s, all of whom were challenging the conventions of theatrical aesthetics in their determination to establish a native drama. In her earlier plays of commitment to public and social concerns, Pollock in her Canadian context was actually closer to what British feminist critic Michelene Wandor has identified as the male-oriented stream of radical social theater in the Britain of the period as opposed to the personal focus of the feminist. Thus what makes Pollock's plays of the 1980s attractive to feminists should be examined in relation to her whole growth as a playwright, a growth that can indeed be explored through her approach to female characterization and feminine themes, but within the broader range of her thematic intentions and structural explorations.

In her first plays Pollock is offering perspectives on historical events that she finds directly related to contemporary problems: *Walsh* (1973) locates abuse of indigenous peoples in the expedient policies of the Macdonald government of the 1870s; *The Komagata Maru Incident* (1976) identifies contemporary racism against Asians in the self-protective legislation of the era before World War I. Canadians, she asserts, "have this view of themselves as nice civilized people who have never participated in historical crimes and atrocities. . . . But that view is false. Our history is dull only because it has been dishonestly expurgated." During this period she is also a confrontational voice on contemporary issues: in the comic handling of a housing expropriation incident, her political satire *Out Goes You* (1975) explores the failure of the modern political Left to distinguish itself from the Right; *One Tiger to a Hill* (1979) speaks of the injustice and cruelty of penal institutions. The political and social anger are strong in these plays, each with its different mode of expressive theatricality.

The women of *Walsh* and *The Komagata Maru Incident* function largely as devices to reveal the public conflicts of central male characters, to the minor degree of their slight appearance in the former, more pointedly in the latter. The two women characters of *One Tiger to a Hill,* although more firmly grounded within the conflict of the play, essentially are intended as two of several points of view within the play's ethical argument. There is a turning point in this regard with *Blood Relations,* Pollock's Lizzie Borden play, with its entirely feminine point of view, the one that the playwright concedes to be "feminist." Further, through its unusual manipulation of a play-within-a-play structure, this work subsumes its issues entirely within personal character conflicts. *Blood Relations,* therefore, may be judged both the culmination of Pollock's polemical phase and the anticipation of her later directions: a shift noted by Robert Nunn "from big issues to the characters on whom . . . these issues have their impact." With the changed emphasis from public to domestic worlds in the plays of the 1980s—*Generations* (1981), *Whiskey Six* (1983), *Doc* (1984)—women play crucial although still not necessarily central roles. . . .

Through *Blood Relations*' playful structure, then, the historical situation becomes "a metaphor for a more contemporary women's theme." The contemporary theme is the identity question that interpenetrates the outer and inner play by means of the romantic relationship played out between the two women in the process of the performance: one is inviting intimacy while the other is trying to respond. The climax of that performance and its aftermath, noted above, has the additional and perhaps more important effect of revealing the feminist politic of the play. This is to say, in the playwright's own comment, that "all of us are capable of murder given the right situation." In the context of the play as a whole, this is a feminist point.

Diane Bessai. In Shirley Neuman and Smaro
Kamboureli, eds. *A Mazing Space*
(Edmonton: Longspoon, 1989),
pp. 126–27, 131

PONIATOWSKA, ELENA (MEXICO) 1933–

In a documentary novel [such as *Hasta no verte, Jesús mío*; Until I see you, dear Jesus] it is necessary to emphasize a particular purpose. The novelist went to great pains to make recordings. She put much time and patience into each episode and then into the whole composition because she recognized that Jesusa offered a life so interesting that it would be hard to neglect. A very poor woman rarely writes her memoirs because she does not have the confidence, time, support or education. This does not mean, however, that this same woman does not have an extraordinary command of the language which would show the many variations of her spirit and her emotions. Such is Jesusa's case; the richness of her expression is such that we could say that she has a cinematographic language. While each reader may find interest in different facets of Jesusa's character, it is the attitude of a woman face-to-face with a male-dominated society that interests me here. In her evolution towards a transcendent reality Jesusa offers us the biography of a rebel, a non-conformist. If Margaret Mead were to have studied her, she would have come to the conclusion that Jesusa is more intelligent, more alive and full of resources than most of the rest of the women around her. Many episodes prove it. To prove it we have only to observe her curiosity, her character as a vagabond among her father's women, and later on her declaration of independence. Since she is very young she begins to show certain characteristics that she believes will help her overcome male dominance. Later, the Revolution is the perfect atmosphere in which to give free rein to her aggressive inclinations. The open challenge she offers to her husband when he beats her is one point in the affirmation of her equality. From that time on she will never allow any man, no matter how strong or important he may be, to abuse or mistreat her or any of those in her care and keeping. Of course as she explains, when she fights she does use "some" help—a beam, a pole or surprise. But Jesusa is not merely a fighter, she has a clear sense of justice and she soon becomes the spokeswoman who shows others that they can live alone, and need be neither exploited nor mistreated. Jesusa believes in work and as she has always been poor she does not hesitate to change jobs, to move without accounting to anyone. When she is widowed she refuses to marry again because she realizes that she can no longer pretend nor adapt to the tyranny of a husband. Also, she believes that if other women would be more courageous, the situation would be better for all. Of course she can never convince other women that she is right because no Mexican woman wants to end up as she does: alone, without children and a little fanatical about her parapsychological ideas. . . .

Jesusa . . . is different from the other women of her group [because] she is free to choose the style of life and beliefs that suit her rather than having to follow the Catholic teachings of her country. When she joins La Obra she belongs to a religious minority, since the idea of reincarnation is foreign to the doctrine of the Catholic Church. Because she is anticlerical it is easier for her to assimilate new ideas which help her to understand social injustices, misery, pain and the destiny of mankind. . . .

Jesusa is a living testimony of the changes that can occur in a woman in spite of her poverty, ignorance and humble origins. In reality Jesusa partakes of none of these; she is a woman in search of an identity that goes beyond the barriers of class distinctions. She is neither Indian, Mexican, lower class, *Adelita,* soldier, or laundress, these are only facets of her life. She is above all a woman who attains her human and spiritual dignity through her own efforts.

> Lucía Fox-Lockert. *Women Writers of Spain and Spanish America* (Metuchen, New Jersey: Scarecrow Press, 1979), pp. 274–77

The choice of Jesusa Palancares as protagonist speaks to a conscious effort on Poniatowska's part to incorporate a new female voice within the corpus of Latin American literature. Very few poor and working-class women have figured among the protagonists of patriarchal Hispanic literature, and even more rarely outside of stereotypical models. Jesusa reveals herself to us as a total being who works, struggles, makes mistakes, grows, changes, is eloquent at times and incoherent at others—in short, a human being.

> Margarite Fernández Olmos. *Revista/Review Interamericana.* 11, 1981, p. 72

Poniatowska's work is deeply committed to the Mexican circumstance. Thus she parallels her male colleagues whose writings reflect their desire to display and describe that which has been heretofore unknown: the Latin American experience. Poniatowska's production, however, is also a quest for roots. . . .

Along with her newspaper articles, Poniatowska has written poetry, plays, short stories, and novels. Always her world is Mexico. Her choice of topics, real and fictional, brings her closer to the country that she cares so much about. "I love Mexico with a passion," she has said. How could she then ignore the events of Tlatelolco in 1968, a moment which marks a crucial point in Mexican history. For in the massacre that occurred on the square in front of the church in Mexico City, Elena Poniatowska, as well as many other Mexicans, lost a loved one. In her case, it was her brother Jan who was only twenty-one years old. *La noche de Tlatelolco* (Massacre in Mexico) sprang from her professional and personal need to bear witness to this historically painful occasion. A literary reportage in which the author is barely visible, the book "presents the background, scene, and aftermath of the 1968 slaughter of some three hundred people while gathered on the square of Tlatelolco in Mexico City to hear student leaders protest political conditions." . . .

The reader is carried along by the gaiety and enthusiasm of the peaceful crowds into the horrifying and unexpected slaughter in the plaza, from which there is no escape, and finally to the prisons where many still languish even though several years have gone by.

As a testimonial to a personal loss, *Massacre in Mexico* gives us only brief visions of the author and the brother she lost. Instead we find an offering to the country that she loves. She bears witness to the evil that has been committed, and in recording it seeks to avoid its repetition. Her love for her brother is encompassed in her sense of responsibility toward her nation. It is important to note that Poniatowska continues to see herself in the role of both witness and public voice for those whose voices go unheard. . . .

If Tlatelolco can be seen as a clearly politicizing event in the life of the author, and *Massacre in Mexico* as her vehicle for bearing witness to the moment, it is interesting to look at the way in which Poniatowska chooses to "give voice" in her selection of another figure who also participated in a crucial moment in Mexico's history. The work is the first-person narrative based on a series of interviews with the author.

Jesusa Palancares, in *Hasta no verte, Jesús mío,* is the granddaughter of an Indian woman and a Frenchman. As such, she unifies several of the threads in Mexico's racial background while her adventures permit Poniatowska to become entwined in Mexico's evolution since the beginning of the twentieth century. . . .

Jesusa's life shows us the development of Mexico in the rages and hopes of its revolution, the land distributions and expansions of Mexico City, and the eventual betrayal of the revolution as seen in Jesusa's own disenfranchisement and resultant cynicism. Jesusa's end, bitter and alone, forces us to conclude that struggle, pride in work, and joy in play may nonetheless result in punishment and the need for atonement. . . .

What we find most often in Poniatowska's work are characters in conflict. They, like their author, are seeking a place in their world. Sometimes they struggle against the roles that their sex or social class has laid out for them. The conflicts permit the author to both describe a world and to criticize it. This allows her to speak out on problematic topics: male-female relations, class conflicts, physical handicaps, racism, alienation, poverty, work, and love.

Poniatowska offers us a rich and passionate vision of Mexico in the twentieth century. Her struggle to belong to that country, to find roots, to be its voice can be seen in many of her works. Through her testimony and that of her characters, the reader is challenged to see reality in a new light.

Elizabeth Starcević. In Doris Meyer and
Margarita Fernández Olmos, eds.
*Contemporary Women Writers of Latin
America* (Brooklyn: Brooklyn College
Press, 1983), pp. 72–74, 77

Women like Jesusa Palancares are not frequently represented in literature. In *Hasta no verte Jesús mío,* Elena Poniatowska portrays a female character whose life, attitudes, and expression invalidate the erroneous and offensive stereotypes of women that have been perpetuated. Unlike many others depicted in fiction, Jesusa is a hard-working individual who survives situations with dignity. She has a keen sense of justice that compels her to censure whatever she judges to be a social injustice. Thus, a new alternative has been

established: a liberated female hero; a positive role model who is independent, self-reliant, and physically, as well as emotionally, strong.

Joel Hancock. Hispania. 66, 1983, p. 357

It is arguable that Poniatowska's [1970] rejection of the Villaurrutia Prize was
an aesthetic as well as a political gesture; in refusing closure with the massacred subjects of her book, she acknowledges the sources of her art. . . . The
particular force of Poniatowska's work derives from the emptiness she found
in her position as a woman of privilege and from her using that position to
cultivate a readiness of imagination and spirit; when this readiness met with
vivid exposure to the dispossessed, she converted equivocal privilege into
real strength. Such an evolution would make her links to the dispossessed a
continuing necessity.

Bell Gale Chevigny. In Alice Kessler-Harris
and William McBrien, eds. Faith of a
(Woman) Writer (1984; Westport,
Connecticut: Greenwood Press, 1988), p. 210

To talk about the testimonial novel, and the activity or identity of its authors,
is to talk about a variety of testimonies that would aim to establish such a
text's truth. That testimony is given not only within the novel itself but also
around it and in its borders. However, we are also aware that, inasmuch as
the *novela testimonial* seems to testify to the truth of what it tells through
the language of literature, a good many questions may be raised about how
such a text may become accepted (or not) as truthful, and about how the
figure of the author associated with it may come to exercise any authority
at all.

Elena Poniatowska's *Hasta no verte, Jesús mío* addresses this kind of
question not only through what its author says about and does with the
documentary materials that comprise the text. Its narrator-protagonist also
problematizes such matters (unwittingly, it seems) within the narrative itself.
Poniatowska's novel may well serve as an instructive example of how the
route to a verifiable referent or to demonstrable veracity (apparently plotted
out by the testimonial novel) is also a reflexive route that turns our reading
away from as much as toward so-called reality. It also suggests ways in which
the figure of the author associated with such a work becomes visible (while
also appearing to efface itself) as a figure of renewed authority. . . .

The gestures of authorship inherent in Poniatowska's roles take the figure
of the author to a place in which it seems to have appeared before and yet
in which we seem to see it for the first time. The testimonial novel thus gives
testimony to the authority assumed by contemporary figures of the author
as much as it seems to testify to that figure's demise. *Hasta no verte, Jesús
mío* would therefore seem ready to tell us a good deal more about itself,
about some of the issues raised by the genre with which it is associated and
about the critical figures through which we read a variety of texts—even

when it would appear that, as a *novela testimonial,* it has already told us everything there is to tell.

Lucille Kerr. *MLN.* 106, 1991, pp. 371–72, 392

Elena Poniatowska, French-born Mexican journalist and author, is widely recognized for her substantial contributions to the growing body of Latin American testimonial and documentary narrative. Her many published works include short stories, novels, hundreds of interviews, chronicles of contemporary life and book-length nonfiction texts. Characteristic of her writing is the imprint it bears of the dialogue which Poniatowska has actively sought out and sustained with all sectors of Mexican society throughout her more than thirty year career as a journalist. This dialogue with the other is both the point of departure for her investigation and a structuring device which informs the text. As a journalist she has had ample access to the most prominent figures of Mexican culture and politics. *Palabras cruzadas* (1961; Cross words), a selection of her interviews done between 1954 and 1961, includes pieces based on conversations with Lázaro Cárdenas, Diego Rivera, Alfonso Reyes and Juan Rulfo. In the summer of 1982 she interviewed all seven candidates in the presidential election campaign, and those interviews have been published under the title of *Domingo siete* (1982; Sunday seven). But it is her particular dedication to recouping the silenced voices of the marginalized and oppressed which has defined her position as a writer and her critical stance toward the institutions of political, economic, and cultural authority in Mexico. In works such as *Hasta no verte, Jesús mío* (1969), *La noche de Tlatelolco* (1971; The night of Tlatelolco; Massacre in Mexico), *Gaby Brimmer* (Brimmer and Poniatowska, 1979), *Fuerte es el silencio* (1980; Strong is silence), and *Nada, nadie: Las voces del temblor* (1988; Nothing, no one; Voices of the earthquake), Poniatowska has opened up public discourse to members of oppressed communities. . . .

The editor of *La noche de Tlatelolco* is . . . an eminently parergonal figure. She participates actively in the production of the work, but is careful to hide the evidence of her transforming labor. She exercises control over the material at the same time that she allows the individual voices to claim their own authority as witnesses and participants in the history told. Narrative authority is a power which the editor constantly wields and abdicates, and which has no single origin or destination. The authority to speak and to be heard rests neither solely with the students nor with the writer-journalist, but rather in the relationship among the testimonies and between these and the editor. Poniatowska, a nonparticipant in the 1968 student movement, in her role as "E.P.," the editor-parergon who positions herself outside of the ergon, becomes an integral part of it, the essential extra who recuperates a silenced past and projects it into a possible future.

If one considers now Elena Poniatowska's other published works, it becomes clear that the figure of the editor as I have described it is emblematic of her stance as a writer in her adopted country. Once an outsider, a foreigner, through a constant and active searching out of the Other she has created for herself a Mexican identity. Mexico has supplied a lack she felt in herself, and in her work, she has recuperated for Mexico a part of itself, a part it may consider extra, secondary, or subordinate: the silenced voices, the anonymous faces, the darkened pages of history; all are on society's margins, another kind of framing figure which in fact penetrates to the center of her nation's collective life.

Beth E. Jörgensen. Latin American
Perspectives. 18, 1991, pp. 80, 88

Almost two decades later Poniatowska utilized a similar [testimonial] technique to dramatize the earthquake that killed thousands of people in Mexico City on September 19, 1985. *Nada, nadie: Las voces del temblor* thrusts its readers into the center of the tragedy that, like the massacre of Tlatelolco, will remain embedded in the Mexican subconscious for generations. The searing descriptions of the terrible first-person experiences both during and after the quake are impossible to forget. Also memorable are the references to fraud on the part of contractors who had ignored building codes for personal gain, and the instances in which army and police personnel placed public order before rescue efforts. As in *La noche de Tlatelolco*, Poniatowska remains objective, allowing those she has interviewed to describe one of the major occurrences in recent Mexican history. *Nada, nadie: Las voces del temblor* reads almost like a novel, juxtaposing moments of suspense, heroism, and suffering. It is one of the most moving works ever published by a Mexican author. . . .

Poniatowska's two other novels are *Querido Diego, te abraza Quiela* (1976; *Dear Diego*, 1986), in epistolary format, and *La "Flor de Lis"* (1988; The "Flor de Lis"), an autobiographical novel and a kind of Bildungsroman about a girl who leaves France for Mexico with her mother and sister during World War II. Poniatowska's best collection of short fiction is *De noches vienes* (1979; You come by night), which contains sixteen stories ranging in subject matter from social protest to the complex relations between social classes and the sexes.

Poniatowska is one of today's major practitioners of documentary fiction, a genre that has become increasingly important in Spanish America. Her popularity as a writer stems from her dramatic presentations of contemporary issues, her sympathy for the downtrodden, and her emphasis on colloquial language, which makes her writings accessible to most readers. For those seeking a better understanding of modern Mexico, Poniatowska's oeuvre provides an excellent resource.

George R. McMurray. In Steven R. Serafin
and Walter D. Glanze, eds. Encyclopedia of
World Literature in the 20th Century (New
York: Continuum, 1993), pp. 494–95

PORTER, KATHERINE ANNE (UNITED STATES) 1890–1980

Miss Porter's mind is one of those highly civilized instruments of perception that seems to have come out of old societies, where the "social trend" is fixed and assumed. The individual character as the product of such a background also has a certain constancy of behavior which permits the writer to ignore the now common practice of relating individual conduct to some abstract social or psychological law; the character is taken as a fixed and inviolable entity, predictable only insofar as a familiarity may be said to make him so, and finally unique as the center of inexhaustible depths of feeling and action. In this manner Miss Porter approaches her characters, and it is this that probably underlies many of the very specific virtues of her writing.

> Allen Tate. *The Nation.* October 1, 1930,
> pp. 352–53

It is to Miss Porter's high credit that, having fixed upon the exceptional background and event, she has not yielded, in her treatment of them, to queerness and forced originality of form. . . . Miss Porter has a range of effects, but each comes through in its place, and only at the demand of her material. She rejects the exclamatory tricks that wind up style to a spurious intensity, and trusts for the most part, to straightforward writing, to patience in detail and to a thorough imaginative grasp on cause and character.

> Louise Bogan. *The New Republic.*
> October 22, 1930, p. 277

Katherine Anne Porter moves in the illustrious company headed by Hawthorne, Flaubert, and Henry James. It is the company of story-tellers whose fiction possesses distinct esthetic quality, whose feelings have attained harmonious expression in the work. . . . Each of the narratives maintains its own tone—in the sense of effects of color and modulation and accents appropriate to the expression of its individual sentiment. And each of the poignant little dramas represented by them unfolds continually and unpredictably, never betraying its ultimate turns, which arrive as shocks and surprises. Ideal beauty, a fugitive poetry, again and again flashes through the substance of the narrative. But the tone, too, invariably is unemphatic and quiet.

> Paul Rosenfeld. *Saturday Review of*
> *Literature.* April 1, 1939, p. 7

Emphasis on her style should not obscure the fact that Miss Porter has other attributes of a good fiction writer. At her best she has mastered narrative pace and narrative construction; her dialogue is colloquial and at the same time graceful and dignified: she has observed with minuteness a variety of locales and ways of living; her people are speaking likenesses; she has wit;

and there is a shrewd modern intelligence, if not an extremely original or forceful one, dominating the story from some little distance.

Philip Blair Rice. *The Nation.*
April 15, 1939, p. 442

Miss Porter has no genius but much talent. Her average level is high, and she doesn't let you down. She is more fundamentally serious than Katherine Mansfield, less neurotic, closer to the earth. She is dry-eyed, even in tragedy: when she jokes, she does not smile. You feel you can trust her. . . . Having praised so much, I pause and wonder just what it is that prevents me from uttering the final, whole-hearted hurrah. . . . She is grave, she is delicate, she is just—but she lacks altogether, for me personally, the vulgar appeal. I cannot imagine that she would ever make me cry, or laugh aloud.

Christopher Isherwood. *The New Republic.*
April 19, 1929, pp. 312–13

Both in conception and execution her work seems to me to bear the relation to prose that the lyric bears to poetry. Her intelligence is extraordinary, but it is akin to that of a poet rather than that, say, of a novelist like Henry James, who was also interested in the thumb-print but had both the strong desire and the capacity for broad formulation which the long flight requires.

Margaret Marshall. *The Nation.* April 13,
1940, p. 474

The exquisite rightness of this author's art has been commented upon by many; and these sketches and tales reveal to the vague tribe, the discriminating reader, what fundamental brainwork goes into the creating of episodes that, on the surface, seem hastily thrown together. To be sure, this deftness is bought at a price, and the careful casualness of Miss Porter's approach sometimes reminds one of a cat stalking its prey with unnecessary caution. If some of these narratives were told in the straightforward narrative manner formerly characteristic of the short story, they might not lose in delicacy and might gain in dramatic power.

Howard Mumford Jones. *Saturday Review of
Literature.* September 30, 1944, p. 15

Miss Porter's thematic statements are given their extraordinary power through a rich and complex characterization. Four or five outstanding personality traits are usually boldly established, and these are used as reference points from which to thrust with the quick image and the loaded phrase into the spaces of modifying qualification. The qualification made, she retires for a moment to the center, waits calmly, and then stabs again—this time either farther in the same direction or in a new direction. In the end, though the characters are typical, recognizable types, they are also particular flesh and bones—somewhat fluid, unpredictable, elusive, contradictory.

Charles Allen. *American Quarterly.*
Summer, 1946, p. 93

The important thing to notice is that in all cases Katherine Anne Porter's characters possess qualities which have some point of similarity with her own experience. If they are Irish or Mexican, they are also Roman Catholic— or they are political liberals. They are usually Southerners. I don't mean to suggest this as a serious limitation, but it may help to account for the consistently high level which her work represents, a level probably unsurpassed by any writer of her time.

Ray B. West, Jr. *Hopkins Review.* Fall, 1952,
p. 19

Katherine Anne Porter is conventionally praised for her humanity and warmth and for the stoic virtues which her people show in the face of life's hardships. It is true that she sets up the stoic as the best of behavior. It is also true that the dignity and compassion of her characters are strikingly apparent. But Miss Porter's world is a black and tragic one, filled with disaster, heartbreak, and soul-wrecking disillusionment. The most noble of her characters . . . must submit in the nature of things to sorrows which are not ennobling but destructively abrasive of joy, love, and hope; all of them end with a bleak realization of the Everlasting Nay. They are confronted by the thing "most cruel of all," which in its enormity transcends all other sorrows— the obliteration of hope. The tiny particle of light must always be snuffed out in the depths of the whirlpool.

James William Johnson. *Virginia Quarterly*
Review. Autumn, 1960, p. 611

[*Ship of Fools*] is a vast portrait gallery, with portraits of all sizes hung here and there on the wall, high and low; and some of the portrayed ones seem to dance down out of their frames; some tumble out, some fight their way out, with fearful vitality. I can think of only one possible reason for anyone's not liking this book: just at the start the characters are almost too strong, one shrinks from them a little. No, you may say, I do not wish to spend another page with this smug glutton, or this hypochondriac drunkard, or this lachrymose widow; no, not another word out of that girl in the green dress! But presently, having read a certain number of pages, you feel a grudging sympathy with one and all, or a rueful empathy, or at least solidarity, as a human being.

Glenway Wescott. *Atlantic Monthly.* April,
1962, p. 48

Her contemptuous and morbid attitude toward human sexuality plays a large part in deflecting her sensibility to its incessant quarrel with human nature and in leading it by inevitable stages to a vision of life that is less vice and folly than a hideously choking slow death. For Miss Porter's versions of political action, artistic creation, religious belief, teaching, and so forth are no less skewed and embittered than her versions of copulation. Further, this clammy connection between sex and evil appears to rule out any feeling toward her characters other than a nagging exasperated irony, and to remove the possibility of any struggle toward deeper insight. As a result, the consciousness that is operating in the book, for all its range of view, is standing, so to speak, on a dime, and has little contact with the sources of imaginative vitality and moral power that renew a long work of fiction.

Theodore Solotaroff. *Commentary.* October, 1962, p. 286

Life—which to Miss Porter means personal relationships—is a hazardous affair, however cautiously we try to live it. We walk a tightrope, never more than a step away from possible disaster, so strong and so intimately connected with our need for other people are the primitive impulses of violence and egoism and so thin is the net of civilized behavior that is between us and the pit. Indeed if in trying to civilize ourselves we have been trying to make order out of chaos, Miss Porter seems to be saying that we have succeeded only in becoming more systematically and efficiently, though less directly violent; the more definite and clear-cut the code by which we live and expect others to live, the more clearly even our ordinary actions reflect the violence that is only imperfectly submerged and that may erupt savagely and nakedly at any time.

Marjorie Ryan. *Critique.* Fall, 1962, p. 94

Innovation in the modern novel is often mere trickiness: to eliminate plot, to eliminate time, even, as in some recent French fiction, to eliminate characters, Katherine Anne Porter in *Ship of Fools* has used no tricks that were not contained in the workbag of George Eliot. Her innovations, however, are still fundamental. Her book not only contains no hero or heroine; it contains no character who is either the reader or the author, no character with whom the reader can "identify." Nor is there anywhere in the book any affirmation of the basic striving upwards or even courage of mankind, always considered essential to a "great" novel. To have put it in would have begged the very question the novel asks. And, finally, despite all of Henry James's warnings, Miss Porter has eschewed her "native pastures." Not only does the action take place at sea, between the ports of countries other than the United States, on a German boat, but the American characters are less vivid than the German and Spanish, are even a bit pale beside them. Mrs. Treadwell seems less of a born New Yorker than the Captain seems a Berliner.

Yet the experience of reading *Ship of Fools* is still an exhilarating rather than a somber or depressing one, because Miss Porter has reproduced the very stuff of life in reproducing those twenty-seven days on the *Vera,* and her novel sparkles with vitality and humor.

Louis Auchincloss. *Pioneers and Caretakers*
(Minneapolis: University of Minnesota
Press, 1965), p. 151

She has constantly dealt with the chaos of the universe and with the forces within man and within society which have led to man's alienation. Her probings of the human condition are deeply personal and yet, because of the constant play of irony in everything she writes, impersonal also.

Her often and justly praised style is never mannered, is perfectly adaptable to her material, and is characterized by clarity. She has consciously avoided stylistic characteristics or peculiarities which would make it instantly recognizable. No skeleton keys are needed to unlock her stories or her style. She learned from Sterne, Mrs. Woolf, Joyce, James, and others; but she set out not to imitate them but to write simply and clearly, flowingly and flawlessly. She used her admirable style to create characters of complexity, characters which grip the imagination: María Concepción, Braggioni, Miranda, Stephen, Homer T. Hatch, Papa Müller, to name only a few. She also recreated with authority the social backgrounds of Mexico, of turn-of-the-century Texas, of Denver during wartime, of immigrant Irish in the slums.

George Hendrick. *Katherine Anne Porter*
(New York: Twayne, 1965), p. 154

Miss Porter's imagination is statuesque, not dynamic: it does not see life in dramatic terms as the grinding of past and present. She does not think at all in terms of action. In her best stories, to exist is to remember: this is the source of their identity, their stability. (Unamuno says somewhere: "Intelligence is a terrible thing, it tends to death as memory tends to stability.") When Miss Porter cares about her characters, she gives them a past dense enough and a memory searching enough to ensure their stability. But she feels a force only when it has fixed its object in position in its frame; and then she probes it by retrospection. A dynamic imagination works differently; as in John Crowe Ransom's poems, for instance, where actions speak louder than words or pictures.

Denis Donoghue. *New York Review of
Books.* November 11, 1965, p. 18

She knows, we are forced to believe, that if one is to try to see "all," one must be willing to see the dark side of the moon. She has a will, a ferocious will, to face, but face in its full context, what Herman Melville called the great "NO" of life. If stoicism is the underlying attitude in this fiction, it is a stoicism without grimness or arrogance, capable of gaiety, tenderness, and sympathy, and its ethical point of reference is found in those characters who, like Granny Weatherall, have the toughness to survive but who survive by a loving sense of obligation to others, this sense being, in the end, only a full affirmation of the life-sense, a joy in strength.

Robert Penn Warren. *Yale Review.* Winter, 1966, p. 290

The anger that speaks everywhere in the stories would trouble the heart for their author whom we love except that her anger is pure, the reason for it evident and clear, and the effect exhilarating. She has made it the tool of her work; what we do is rejoice in it. We are aware of the compassion that guides it, as well. Only compassion could have looked where she looks, could have seen and probed what she sees. Real compassion is perhaps always in the end unsparing; it must make itself a part of knowing. Self-pity does not exist here; these stories come out trenchant, bold, defying; they are tough as sanity, unrelinquished sanity, is tough.

Despair is here, as well described as if it were Mexico. It is a despair, however, that is robust and sane, open to negotiation by the light of day. Life seen as a savage ordeal has been investigated by a straightforward courage, unshaken nerve, a rescuing wit, and above all with the searching intelligence that is quite plainly not to be daunted. In the end the stories move us not to despair ourselves but to an emotion quite opposite because they are so seriously and clear-sightedly pointing out what they have been formed to show: that which is true under the skin, that which will remain a fact of the spirit.

Eudora Welty. *Yale Review.* Winter, 1966, p. 269

What is most striking about all her stories is their air of indestructible composure. Their elements seem admirably balanced and fitted, like parts of a machine. No energy is wasted here; and it is true that when, in stories like *Noon Wine,* the characters confront each other head-on, there is sudden power in the encounter. (Mr. Hatch and Mr. Thompson remain vivid because they are singular; the power of the representation derives from its incisive, unrelenting specificity.) More often, however, the author does not succeed in perceiving particulars with an intensity which would lend them the force and weight of general statement; instead, inventing circumstances which contain foregone conclusions, she elaborates general statements with appropriate details. . . .

. . . if one excludes *Noon Wine* and "The Jilting of Granny Weatherall" (a nicely executed *tour de force* of less than major interest), her most memorable stories—"Flowering Judas," *Pale Horse, Pale Rider,* and *The Leaning Tower*—are those in which the central characters are forced to test themselves against "other minds and other opinions and other feelings." In general, these stories deal with the attempts of individuals to resist everything in their experience which does not fit their own sense of themselves, to protect and preserve the secret myths enabling them to keep their lives in order.

Stephen Donadio. *Partisan Review.* Spring,
1966, pp. 279, 281

For years, [Katherine Anne Porter] was praised by discerning critics as the cleanest, clearest, and as they say of vines, most shy-bearing of the writers of our times: which in my opinion she probably is. Then, after writing the best seller *Ship of Fools,* she came to be regarded in wider circles with a certain uneasiness, as being negative, skeptical, prejudiced, formalistic: which in my opinion she is not. She is no more negative, I must argue, no more skeptical, et cetera, than it is very good to be. . . .

Miss Porter is a Modern, a beneficiary of a discipline which has been known as Modernism, just as surely as any of a number of writers who can be grouped together because of their affinities with James and Proust and Joyce. She is akin to Ezra Pound and Pablo Picasso. She grew up in a period in which the mastery of an art was held to be a lifelong, exacting discipline. It was a period, we can say from this distance, which accepted constraints and past history, as well as freedom and modernity.

Howard Baker. In Brom Weber, ed. *Sense
and Sensibility in Twentieth-Century Writing*
(Carbondale: Southern Illinois University
Press, 1970), p. 76

In the stories that have usually been considered Miss Porter's finest work, the central figures are people whose desperate preoccupation with themselves cuts them off from effective communication with all other human beings. In some instances, a family situation, present or remembered, may be responsible for the protagonist's alienation or provide its particular dramatic circumstances. But whether the setting is a New York rooming house, where the protagonist is a long way from home and alone for most of the time of the story's action, or a Texas farmhouse, with the family present most of the time, the reader's attention is fixed upon a totally private agony.

In all but one of these stories, the protagonist is a woman. . . . Especially in the stories about women, it may be in the failure of a sexual union that the fatal pride chiefly shows itself. But sex is ultimately of no greater importance than social class or occupation or level of literacy. What all these characters have in common, from the Miranda of "Pale Horse, Pale Rider" to Royal Earle Thompson of "Noon Wine," is a consuming devotion to some idea of themselves—of their own inestimable worth and privilege—which the circumstances of their lives do not permit them to realize in actuality but which they are powerless to abandon. The idea lives in them like a demon, directing all their thoughts and actions. Whatever it may be in which they invest that most precious and indefinable sense of self—a cherished grievance, a need to justify a fatal action, an ideal of order and mental discipline—

they pursue it relentlessly, through all discomforts and deprivations, even to death—and if not to the death of the body then of the spirit, incapacitating themselves not only for love but for the enjoyment of any common good of life, to walk forever among strangers.

John Edward Hardy. *Katherine Anne Porter*
(New York: Frederick Ungar, 1973),
pp. 62–63

The most powerful tension in her work is between the emotional involvements and the detachment, the will to shape and assess relations in experience; and the effect of this is sometimes to make a story look and feel strangely different, unanalyzably different, from the ordinary practice. But there is a more significant difference. A great deal of the current handling of the psychology of motive is a kind of clinical reportage. In two respects the work of Katherine Anne Porter is to be distinguished from this. First, she presumably believes that there is not merely pathology in the world, but evil—Evil with a capital *E,* if you will. Along with the pity and humor of her fiction, there is the rigorous, almost puritanical attempt to make an assessment of experience. Second, she presumably believes in the sanctity of what used to be called the individual soul. . . .

It has been said that the work of a major poet, in contrast to that of a minor poet, possesses, among other things, a centrality of coherence—or even obsession. The more we steadily inspect the work of Katherine Anne Porter, the more we see the inner coherence—the work as a deeply imaginative confrontation of a sensibility of genius with the *chiaroscuro* of modern civilization, in which it is often hard to tell light from dark. It becomes clearer and clearer what she meant when she said that she had been working on one central plan "to understand the logic of this majestic and terrible failure of the life of man in the Western World." . . .

What we find in the fiction is a hatred of all things that would prize anything above the awareness of human virtue: that is the essence of the author's dissent and the core of the despair that sometimes appears for our future—a future in which the responsible individual disappears into a "nothing," a mere member of what Kierkegaard called a "public," a "kind of gigantic something, an abstract and deserted void which is everything but nothing."

Robert Penn Warren. *Katherine Anne
Porter: A Collection of Critical Essays*
(Englewood Cliffs, New Jersey: Prentice-
Hall, 1979), pp. 9–10, 14–15

Ship of Fools is a brilliant book. Porter herself was fond of it, and she pointed out to carping critics that it developed a major theme present in most of her work—the theme of the life of illusion, of self-deception. But it is not a great novel. The structure is loosely episodic and the crowded cast of characters is far too large. Porter apparently did not have the ability to construct a satisfactory plot of novel length that would bring into a significant relationship a few fully developed characters. *Ship of Fools* cannot stand comparison with the great Victorian novels nor with the major work of Henry James (whom, incidentally, Porter greatly admired). Her true genre was the short story and the novella (or long short story), and her accomplishments in those forms can stand any comparison. Porter once said, "I don't believe in style: The style is you," and she didn't like being called a stylist. Nevertheless, she may be, in fact, the greatest stylist in prose fiction in English of this century. There is of course the aforementioned Henry James, but a comparison, for example, of the opening pages of her "Hacienda" with the opening pages of *The Ambassadors* would be instructive to a young writer learning his craft. Sentence by sentence, paragraph by paragraph, Porter is better. Compared to her precise perceptions and carefully modulated rhythms, James's prose is somewhat slow-moving, ponderous, and diffuse. . . .

As time goes by, the accomplishments in American fiction, poetry, and criticism between the wars take on more and more significance. Katherine Anne Porter's stories, especially those written during this period, will be given an increasingly high position in our literary heritage.

Donald E. Stanford. Southern Review.
Winter, 1981, pp. 1–2

The women in Katherine Anne Porter's fiction deserve to be studied first of all for the richness of characterization in them and for what they reveal about the psychic experience of womanhood. But they also deserve to be studied because in the largest sense they are feminine figures of the typical American hero: independent, isolated wanderers who choose rebellion (sometimes in the form of art) rather than love, marriage, or integration into civilization. They are also members of modern society, whatever their roots, and as much as the characters of Hemingway or Fitzgerald they chronicle what the advent of the twentieth century meant to the human race. Over and over, in the early stories as well as those focusing on Miranda, Porter's women must discover that love is usually attended by death and that independence is almost always lonely. They may have love or work, but not both. In that psychic reality, all these women—and their stories—come together. Whether the setting is Mexico, New York, a rural farm, or even the oceanbound *Vera* in *Ship of Fools*, Porter's women struggle with the tension between a desire to be feminine (in fairly traditional terms) and a desire—not to be alone—but to be free.

Jane Krause De Mouy. Katherine Anne Porter's Women: The Eye of her Vision
(Austin: University of Texas Press, 1983),
p. 206

Porter's concept of truth leads to her world view and eventually to the thematic unity of her fiction. Her concept begins with the premise that truth can be both subjective and elusive. . . .

She regarded the movement toward truth as arduous and never complete, and it moreover was filled with illusion. In fact, she saw some elements of truth to be beyond human understanding and simply to be accepted as unfathomable. . . .

Porter saw [the] illusions to which persons cling. Often these are ideals that seem in themselves to be truths, and they are clutched as obsessively as if they were the end-all of human life. For some, it is the illusion of romantic love or the illusion of the perfect past, ideals, Porter assures us, not grounded in the reality of chaotic human life.

Each of Katherine Anne Porter's stories and her novel fall within this design, which Robert Penn Warren summarized precisely as simply two propositions: "the necessity for moral definition, and the difficulty of moral definition." Each of her stories and her novel are about confronting and accepting the totality of life, including one's own nature and the Unknowable, or the bewilderment and suffering that come from failing to do so; or about the deception of systems and the illusion of ideals which we embrace as we attempt to find truth.

Darlene Harbour Unrue. *Truth and Vision in Katherine Anne Porter's Fiction*. (Athens: University of Georgia Press, 1985), pp. 6–7, 10

PORTILLO DEL TRAMBLEY, ESTELA (UNITED STATES) n.d.

According to Judy Salinas in her article, "The Image of Woman in Chicano Literature,"

> The Chicana woman, being a participant in both Hispanic and Anglo cultures and a product of both, enjoys the advantages and disadvantages of the restrictive traditions of the Hispanic female role as well as the freer, more liberated responsibilities thrust upon her by Anglo influences.

Although her position might need further elaboration and clarification, it is still a dialectic that might easily apply to the formation of the world-view of the Chicana writer Estela Portillo. In fact, in her short story collection, *Rain of Scorpions* (1975), and her play, *The Day of the Swallows* (1971), the specific dialectic is embodied in the theme of the oppression of women versus their attempts at achieving liberation. The archetypical conflict is between woman and the source of oppression, social conditions, restrictive cultural traditions, environmental patterns, or, more concretely, man. There is an ensuing struggle which is at times successful, or, if it is not, it may end in death, specifically suicide.

Indeed, one critic's summary of Portillo's first book points to this basic struggle: "*Rain of Scorpions* is composed of nine short stories and a novelette and in the majority of these selections the female protagonists are out to affirm themselves. They are presented as being isolated, oppressed to a certain degree, and constantly fighting against hostile surroundings."

It must be understood from the outset that Portillo's characters and settings are not usually Chicano. The setting more often is Mexico, one story is set in Paris, but other stories take place in the barrio or in tenement districts. The characters come from a number of nationalities: Mexican, Chicano, Anglo-American, Spanish Andalusian gypsy, and German.

Although her Chicana-ness has been challenged, there is no doubt that Portillo does specifically concern herself with a Chicano reality on a number of occasions. Her Mexican characters and settings certainly relate to the heritage of Chicanos. In any case, although she does deal with varied backgrounds and experiences, her vision is filtered through the sensibility of a Chicana, one whose women characters are almost constantly struggling against a male-dominated society. Portillo is, in this sense, a Chicana feminist. In her fictional world, "equality, liberation, and rebellion against the established order seem to be the issues. Females are portrayed as taking their destinies into their own hands. The fact that these works are narrated from a feminine perspective allows greater penetration into their psyches and modes of behavior." . . .

In most of the other stories in Portillo's *Rain of Scorpions,* women are also at the center, or at the very least function as significant catalysts. Stories such as "Recast," "The Secret Room," and "The Burning," as diverse as they may be, at some point emphasize the importance of female characters in the outcome of events. Docility is not an overbearing characteristic in Estela Portillo's fictional world.

The same is also true of Portillo's dramas, particularly *The Day of the Swallows.* . . .

In both *The Day of the Swallows* and *Rain of Scorpions,* Portillo has traced an intricate pattern. At the heart of it is a view of both the chaos and the tradition against which the assertive woman acts and reacts, sometimes with success, sometimes not. The stakes are high; the battle lines are drawn. The struggle from oppression on the way to liberation is an arduous one, but one, Portillo seems to be saying, that must be attempted.

Arthur Ramírez. *Revista Chicana-Riqueña.*
8, 1980, pp. 106–7, 110, 113

If most texts derive in some way from the central patriarchal text, the Bible, as Edward Said has suggested, and if the texts of women strain to break out of the boundaries of male-inscribed discourse, then an impulse to displace the authority of the Biblical text, and other sacred or mythical texts as they traditionally affect women, should emerge from a reading of our models. In the textual space left vacant, matrilineal myths may take the place of those patriarchal ones which are pushed aside. This is what occurs in a pair of Portillo's stories, "The Trees" and "If It Weren't for the Honeysuckles": in the former the protagonist is called "an Eve in a Garden of Eden," but some crucial distinctions are established between this Eve and her Biblical predecessor. The latter story fills the void left by the fatal hubris of "The Trees" protagonist. . . .

Beatriz of "If It Weren't for the Honeysuckles" replaces the patriarchal text displaced by Nina with a matrilineal paradigm of her own. Beatriz cultivates her own "thriving" garden; she has built her own house: Beatriz has created and defined her own space. Another survivor of male harshness—of the brutish ways of Robles, her intermittent male companion—Beatriz has learned to give order to things, as bad as they may be. Welcoming Robles's subsequent conquests as companions and allies, Beatriz forges matrilineal links between herself and the younger women, Sofa and Lucretia. The three women together form a stronger line of defense against Robles than could one woman alone. (The three women also suggest a noteworthy inversion of the Christian Holy Trinity.)

One day, while cultivating her honeysuckles, Beatriz discovers three deadly Amanitas mushrooms and decides to use them to acquire freedom for herself and her female companions. Robles is eliminated in a Dionysian ritual—another reversal of Christian symbolism—the women's garden is rid of its serpent, and what we might call a "working matriarchal order" is established. The myth of Eve is inverted; the patriarch alone—not woman—is displaced from the garden. Thus the garden becomes wholly woman's space, its reappropriation signifying a displacement of Biblical myth with a plot shaped and defined by woman herself.

Elizabeth J. Ordoñez. MELUS. 9, 1982,
pp. 22–23

Estela Portillo de Trambley's short story, "The Paris Gown," is a crafted fiction which develops its theme through masterful manipulation of traditional literary devices. The work is, certainly, other things as well. Charles M. Tatum has called attention to the story's liberation theme and declared its sensitive, feminine thrust. Judy Salinas has suggested that the piece emphasizes the "humanness" of woman "through an understanding of her role in Chicano society and in all society and how it restricts or frees her." Finally, Bruce-Novoa writes:

> "The Paris Gown" offers a less violent, but certainly equally positive tale of female liberation. Besides the open attack on anachronistic machismo and the creation of a strong, interesting female protagonist, the story proposes the need to shift from a rigidly defined, intellectualized aesthetic to a fluid, sensual one,

what Susan Sontag calls the movement from the hermeneutics to the erotics of art, or what Portillo would call the victory of the Dionysian principle over the Apollonian. When the metaphor of aesthetics is expanded to its cosmic significance, we understand that Portillo advocates a radical social revolution.

Comments like these have tended to classify Estela Portillo as a Chicano feminist. Admittedly, the classification is just, but we err if we do not look beyond the classification, if we do not see more than the feminist, if we do not try to discover the writer as artist. Portillo, herself, has said "It's going to take a lot of conditioning before men say that I am a Chicano writer and that I write just as well as the men." *Not so,* and "The Paris Gown," ostensibly Portillo's first short story (by virtue of its position in *Rain of Scorpions*), is the proof. In fact, in "The Paris Gown," one finds a tightly unified artifact that is fully capable of supporting a hermeneutic reading. When so read, Portillo's theme unfolds in such a way as to reveal that it has been developed through a skillful combination of image, metaphor, and symbol.

Phillip Parotti. *Studies in Short Fiction.* 24,
1987, p. 417

Portillo Trambley's outcry is a complaint against the subjugation of women in a male-dominated society. It is a plea for women to be self-determined, responsible individuals. It is a constant objection to the enslavement of any woman, from any place, at any time. When the writer was asked the question, "How do you perceive your role as a writer vis-a-vis literature itself?" she answered, "I would like to extend myself as a writer and find a U.S. audience. Not so much to be read because I am a minority writer, but because people can find themselves in what I write . . . all people. To be the kind of a writer to go beyond the local and contemporary, to find a common denominator in unifying people." It is not difficult to perceive that she has been successful in extending her outcry for liberation toward all women regardless of nationality. . . .

There is an assertiveness and uniqueness in each of Portillo Trambley's female protagonists which portrays them as strong, decisive people who will go to any lengths to pursue personal freedom. . . .

Portillo Trambley's penchant for dialectical structure is evidenced in her short stories. It is a skillful device for emphasizing the importance of decision-making in the lives of each of the women protagonists. It underscores a response to the author's voice of outcry as each woman reacts to the restrictions being placed upon her individuality and freedom. In "The Paris Gown" Clotilde represents freedom, liberty, and her father is the epitome of restriction and oppression. "Duende" portrays Marusha as the symbol of design and deliberation and Triano as chance and instinct. Each of Portillo Trambley's stories utilizes the stylistic device of conflictual opposites to provide a dramatic conclusion. In each case, the women protagonists take whatever action, pay whatever price, go to whatever lengths, to accomplish their goals. Portillo Trambley's women protagonists are self-determining, prototypical images of the females. They affirm their manhood while struggling against a hostile environment.

Sister James David Schiavone. *Americas Review*. 16, 1988, pp. 68–69, 75–76

POTTER, BEATRIX (GREAT BRITAIN) 1866–1943

This tiny Christmas book [*Wag-by-Wall*] is a legacy from Beatrix Potter to the countless children who have loved *The Tale of Peter Rabbit* and the other Potter classics. It tells the poignant story of old Sally Benson, who lived alone in poverty in her thatched cottage with only her clock and a nest of owlets for company. All day long the clock said "Tic:toc:gold:toes" until something happened on Christmas Eve to change its chant and bring happiness to Sally's old age. Since the author had not made illustrations for the book before her death, the publishers have been wise to leave it unillustrated except for a few fine woodcut decorations by [J. J.] Lankes.

The New Yorker. December 16, 1944, p. 86

Beatrix Potter first wrote *The Sly Old Cat* in 1906. Publication was initially postponed, then dropped. Appearing now for the first time, the book is simple, slight, and ingenuous, but amiable in its good-versus-evil appeal. Invited to dine by Cat, Mr. Rat watches his host's every move, preferring not to be consumed. Rat traps Cat's head in a jug, has a hearty tea, and disappears jauntily. No moral, but a satisfying finish.

Zena Sutherland. *Saturday Review of Literature*. May 20, 1972, p. 80

In her lifetime Beatrix Potter dismissed attempts to connect her work with artists and writers who had come before her. "Great rubbish, absolute bosh!" she declared about one appreciation, and to Graham Greene, who had done her the honor of comparing her to no one less than Shakespeare, she wrote "a somewhat acid letter" correcting his speculations on the emotional origin and inspiration of certain of her works. It is, therefore, with some trepidation that a scholar investigates the possible literary or personal influences which went into the making of her highly original tales. As her stories so successfully synthesize numerous literary and folk traditions, however, the attempt should be made.

Two interesting examples of her ability to combine and transcend a variety of sources are the books that feature the fox as villain—*The Tale of Jemima Puddle-Duck* (1908) and *The Tale of Mr. Tod* (1912). These contain elements from fairy tales, Aesop, Uncle Remus, and, as I hope to demonstrate, the old tradition of fox stories brought together in the medieval Reynard cycle.

How deliberately she made use of these traditions is an open question, but Beatrix Potter did seem aware, for instance, of the fairy-tale ingredients in her work. . . .

Consciously or not, Beatrix Potter brought together many traditions in these fox stories, and, illuminated by the accurate observations she recorded in both her drawing and her writing, the tales transcend their sources. Jemima stays in our minds as the type of foolishness and the eternal duck; Mr. Tod and Tommy Brock, as their names indicate, become the essential fox and badger. When Benjamin and Peter return the seven babies to Flopsie, "they had not waited long enough to be able to tell the end of the battle between Tommy Brock and Mr. Tod." As Beatrix Potter knew, the battle has no end. It is part of an enduring relationship that stretches from dim past to all future times that contain foxes, badgers, prey, and parables.

> Celia Catlett Anderson. *Proceedings of the*
> *Seventh Annual Conference of the*
> *Children's Literature Association* [1980]
> (West Lafayette, Indiana: Children's
> Literature Association, 1982), pp. 85, 87

The book is not a great moral treatise, touching on ideas of high spiritual and artistic importance in children's literature; when one considers its size, the book seems even less substantial and less likely a candidate for canonization. But no canon of children's literature can ignore *Peter Rabbit,* and the book remains a best-seller. It is my contention that Potter deliberately sets the book in no particular time, and yet in everytime, both in the narrative and in the illustration, and that the setting contributes to the book's popularity. Why Peter is everychild's everyrabbit is an important consideration for scholars interested in the issue of what makes a classic. . . .

Perhaps the major reason that *The Tale of Peter Rabbit* endures is the sense of the world that Potter created as ongoing, Potter's own explanation for the book's popularity: Mr. McGregor returns to his gardening when he fails to catch Peter; Peter returns home and is nursed back to health, to raid and raze another day. The ending may be a closed one, but neither Peter's life nor Mr. McGregor's garden is irrevocably altered by the adventure, and modern technology and urbanization seem to have little influence on the relationships between gardeners and rabbits. Though publishing practices and popular tastes in children's literature change, the story of the rabbit and the farmer do not, except in bowdlerized and cheap reissues. The text and illustrations are reliable and enduring, and if the Easter Bunny is also named Peter, it is because his predecessor set the pattern for all bunny rabbits to follow.

> Ruth K. MacDonald. *Children's Literature*
> *Association Quarterly.* 10, 1986, pp. 185, 187

Why does *The Tale of Peter Rabbit,* more surely than any other of Beatrix Potter's classics, deserve "touchstone" status? Three elements explain the extraordinary popular and critical success of this work: a unity of proportion, a perfectly constructed plot, and a protagonist both heroic and childlike. While Potter's other works may reveal one or more of these elements, none except *Peter Rabbit* unites all three. . . .

Potter's works typically transpire within relatively narrow boundaries. *The Tailor of Gloucester* takes place in the tailor's shop and his home in the cathedral courtyard just on the other side of the archway. *Jemima Puddle-Duck* moves from farmyard to woods nearby. *Two Bad Mice* is essentially set within one room, while *Samuel Whiskers* takes place primarily within Potter's own farmhouse, Hill Top. The parameters of the "core" of Peter Rabbit's world are his snug home beneath the pine tree at one end and Mr. McGregor's garden at the other. Mother goes outside of this setting—through the woods and to the baker—but her departure from the scene of our drama only serves to underscore the fact that she is going "there" and we are "here." All of this suggests what the child already knows: that his home and the surroundings into which he can walk can be the site of fascinating adventure.

In work after work, Potter expands our sense of this limited space by finding a number of smaller spaces within it. In works which take place indoors, she delights in secret passageways and hidden areas. . . .

In *Peter Rabbit,* as in many of Potter's other works, the story told covers a relatively short period of time. *Two Bad Mice* occupies only the length of time that Lucinda and Jane are out for a stroll. In *Samuel Whiskers* we know that Anna Maria and Samuel Whiskers do not have time enough to make Tom Kitten into a pie before his mother finds him again. *The Tailor of Gloucester* takes place over Christmas weekend; *Mr. Jeremy Fisher* in the course of a day; *Jemima Puddle-Duck* in about two weeks. Two actions occur by which we can gauge the duration of *Peter Rabbit:* the first is Mrs. Rabbit's round-trip to the bakery and the fact that she is back in time to fix dinner; the second is Peter's adventure in the garden, which begins as soon as Mrs. Rabbit leaves and results in a rapid succession of events. Only two periods of uncertain length transpire in the story. The first is the lull during which Peter wanders through the garden looking for a way out. The second is the length of time between his arrival home and dinner, but the fact that he lies prostrate in the background as Mrs. Rabbit prepares the meal suggests that his arrival home is recent. Thus the whole cannot have taken long. . . .

The simple plot of *Peter Rabbit* is predictable but exciting. In a story which manifests perfect circularity of form, Peter moves from the security of home to the danger of the unfamiliar, before arriving home again. The words are no sooner out of Mrs. Rabbit's mouth than we look at Peter— Peter with his unrabbitlike name, Peter the boy among sisters, Peter standing apart in blue as his sisters are laced up in their red shawls, Peter being choked into his jacket—and we know positively that he has no intention whatever of obeying, that he is headed straight for the forbidden garden. Indeed, the next time we see Peter, he is forcing his way under the garden gate; and, on the page after that, he is blissfully enjoying what he came for. So far, Mrs. Rabbit's prediction about Mr. McGregor has not come true; but it hangs over our heads with a delightfully ominous quality. Trouble is coming! And when it does, it occupies the next twenty-eight pages. For over half of the book's fifty-two pages, in other words, Potter uses the simple device of putting Peter into trouble and getting him out of it again. . . .

This brings us to the third reason why *The Tale of Peter Rabbit* is a touchstone—the unequaled appeal of its protagonist. Unlike Potter's other characters, Peter is at once childlike and heroic, or, in Ethel Heins's words, "naive but stalwart."

Jackie F. Eastman. In Perry Nodelman, ed.
*Touchstones: Reflections on the Best in
Children's Literature,* vol. 3 (West Lafayette,
Indiana: Children's Literature Association,
1987), pp. 100–104

The theme she had chosen to tackle in her earliest story, *The Tale of Peter Rabbit,* is one that recurs throughout her work, until it comes to final resolution in *The Tale of Pigling Bland:* Jack in the Giant's castle, the little fellow, the folktale hero who has nothing but his courage and his wits, struggling against an opponent of far superior physical strength. That she should choose such a theme is not very surprising—it predominates in Grimms' fairy tales and many of the other classic folktale collections, and it was perhaps a natural subject for someone congenitally shy, who viewed the prospect of any encounter with a stranger with considerable anxiety. Is it perhaps too fanciful to suppose that the oppressors in her stories—Mr. MacGregor, Old Brown the owl in *Squirrel Nutkin,* Samuel Whiskers, and the others—unconsciously stood in her mind for her own parents? It was in their home that she was trapped for much of her life, like Peter Rabbit caught by the buttons of his own jacket; and certainly the flight of Pigling Bland and Pigwig from Mr. Thomas Piperson in her 1913 book seems to refer to her own final escape that very year from the family fold—1913 was when she married William Heelis and at last became independent, at the age of forty-seven.

Humphrey Carpenter. In Penelope Avery
and Julia Briggs, eds. *Children and Their
Books: a Celebration of the Work of Ione
and Peter Opie* (Oxford: Clarendon Press
1989), p. 286

When we ask why Peter Rabbit has captivated reader attention for almost a century, we must perforce return to the ambiguous nature of rabbits—as being both sentimental and vulgar—and to Barthes's essay on female writers. Inherent to both is the tension between convention and independence. Potter captures the Barthesian paradox: Peter Rabbit *is* the projection of this inner state of tension indicative of women caught between the confines of the home and the lure of unrestricted freedom. Peter Rabbit's appeal, consequently, is strong in the nursery because as fantasy it offers an escape from the inevitability of social bondage. In the long run, however, the underlying message is compensatory—not liberating—as Potter fails to provide us with a new vision of society.

W. Nikola-Lisa. *The Lion and the Unicorn.*
15, 1991, p. 65

POULIN, GABRIELLE (CANADA) n.d.

The moment is well known where Gabrielle Poulin's heroines find themselves at the crossroads where two divergent routes meet: the way that, if it is followed without thinking too much about it, leads to some essentialist role, a life typical of all existence of this sort, and the other, along which only those beings can enter who are determined to reject stereotypes so as to choice an existential independence. The situation is summed up in *Cogne la caboche* in function of certain literary predecessors. Thus, Sister Anna evokes Claudel's *L'Annonce faite à Marie* only in order to refuse Violaine's example and declare herself in favor of Mara. Violaine is presented in the play as a sort of saint, but her example is rejected by Sister Anna nonetheless, for Violaine accepted a hagiographic essence: she realized her role. As for Mara (depicted in the play as a reprehensible character), to the extent that she escapes conformity and affirms her individuality, she constitutes a positive example.

For Gabrielle Poulin, her heroines' drama is played out against the background of a rigidly structured social system. In such a context, the essentialist role predominates, and everyone knows the recipe that determines every social function. . . .

To create one's world is to create oneself. This formula summarizes the problem of identity among [Poulin's] characters. . . . By having recourse to the terms "essentialism" and "existentialism," we hope that we have brought out the search for freedom that characterizes all Gabrielle Poulin's heroines.

Grahame C. Jones. *Revue d'Histoire
Littéraire du Québec et du Canada
Français.* 12, 1986, pp. 266, 277–78

One of the virtues of literary modernism, that "era of suspicion" of which Nathalie Sarraute speaks, is having acclimated us to reading on two levels: while recording the unfolding of a "story" with multiple facets, we pay attention to the novelistic "discourse" (especially to the point of view from which this story is narrated), that level of the literary work where the transformation from story to narrative occurs and where the reader him or herself becomes a creator in taking part in this transformation.

Considered in a typological range, going from the novel strongly dominated by the story itself that is narrated to the kind dominated by the narrative means. . . . *La couronne d'oubli* (The crown of forgetting) occupies one of the poles. . . . It tells a rather banal story, but one that is transformed by a very original discourse that makes it a compelling narrative. . . .

However, although banal, the story that Gabrielle Poulin tells us in *La couronne d'oubli* is hardly without interest, and what strikes a foreign reader, following the development of Québécois society from a distance, is that it seems well rooted in the socio-cultural history of the country. . . .

The fascination of this big little novel comes above all from the discovery that it forces its readers to make of that other woman who gradually relegates the woman-mother to the background. For this experience is not presented to us in a very regimented fashion. Unlike quite a few of the great modern novels that break with the logical-psychological tradition, *La couronne d'oubli* is addressed to a reader who desires to take an active part in the hesitant birth of this new being. Gabrielle Poulin proceeds by the difficult art of associations, spontaneous images, little touches, a method that seems to us perfectly in accord with the nature of Florence's experience; it is by putting together little bits of reality, pieces of memory, that she herself arrives at her own emancipation.

Canadian Literature. 131, 1991, pp. 208–9

POZZI, CATHERINE (FRANCE) 1882–1934

In 1920, Catherine Pozzi was thirty-eight years old. . . . All the salons of Paris were open to her, Proust's world, in short, which didn't interest her. . . . Despite the contempt in which she held social life, she owes to the salons the major encounter of her life, that with Paul Valéry.

The *Journal* just published by Claire Paulhan with a very illuminating introduction by Lawrence Joseph, begins in January of 1913 and ends four days before Catherine's death, in November 1934. Of the 661 pages of text, 388, which are the chronicle of a marvelous and terrible passion, occupy the center of the volume, as this dreadful love, however brief in time, occupied the center of her life. Its echoes can probably be, however masked, found in Paul Valéry's famous notebooks. . . .

Two years before her 1928 break with Valéry, Catherine had given Jean Paulhan a story entitled *Agnes,* a disguised autobiography signed only with initials. It appeared in the *Nouvelle Revue Française* in February of 1927. Paul Valéry did not wish to write a preface for it. She did not forgive him for this. . . . Admiration, tenderness, passion for Valéry nurtured in Catherine Pozzi and brought out from her, above and beyond the mere fact of their separation, several pure and ardent poems that are among the most beautiful in the French language. . . .

In eight pages, there are six of them. There were published by Jean Paulhan after her death in a 1935 issue of *Mesures*. He reprinted them in his collection *Metamorphoses* in 1959. They are going to reappear this year. Early versions may be found once or twice in the last sections of the *Journal* and it is very moving to see the certainty of ear and hand with which Catherine Pozzi slides her text towards a sort of absolute, a contradictory radiance of living water and flames. What did the author of *La Jeune Parque* (The young fate) and *Cimetière Marin* (Seaside cemetery), Valéry, think of them? At the first exhibit after his death at the Bibliothèque Doucet, Marie Dormoy, who organized it, had invited Mme. Paul Valéry to come to see the exhibit privately, the day before the opening. Mme. Paul Valéry looked at all the exhibits. She stopped a long time before the display dedicated to Catherine Pozzi, then, turning to Marie, murmured, "My husband said that she had a great deal of talent." But isn't the ardor of these poems, with its ashes and silence and peace, rather more like a lightning-stroke of genius?

Dominique Aury. *Nouvelle Revue Française.*
423, 1988, pp. 58–60

Thanks to the pioneer efforts of Lawrence Joseph, we are now becoming better acquainted with the life and work of Catherine Pozzi. . . . In the past she was known to the Paris literary elite as the author of a brief autobiographical nouvelle titled *Agnès,* a philosophical essay called *Peau d'âme,* and a few striking poems, but principally as the mistress and intellectual consort of Paul Valéry, who found in her "la grande réalité" of his life. Joseph's masterly biography is an indispensable guide to her works, especially to *Agnès,* the *Œuvre poétique,* and her *Journal* (1913–34), all of which he has edited.

Agnès, dedicated to Audrey Deacon, a young American lover of Pozzi, appeared in the *NRF* in 1927, signed only "C.K." (Catherine-Karin). It is an autobiographical portrait of herself as an adolescent romantically in search of "perfect love." Still a young girl, she had addressed to her imaginary lover the letters (some in English) which she rehandles in the nouvelle. She speaks of her family background, especially of her father, the famous surgeon Dr. Samuel Pozzi, a man of the world who had little contact with his wife and children. Feeling unloved, afraid of being unworthy of her ideal lover, Agnes (who, as Joseph observes, is finally an androgynous projection of Catherine herself) embarks, as Catherine did, on a strenuous program of physical and intellectual self-improvement. In the course of her studies she is assailed by religious doubts. *Agnès* concludes when the girl's pious grandmother takes her to Lourdes in the hope that her faith may be restored. As she drinks the waters of Lourdes, she prays: "Donnez-moi l'amour ou faites-moi mourir." In 1931 Pozzi added a few pages (included in the present edition) concerning the bitter . . . [disappointment] of Agnès's wedding night—which apparently resembled her own. Paulhan hailed the little work as a "fraîche merveille," and it was translated into German in 1928.

Pozzi grew up surrounded by poets. Hérédia, Leconte de Lisle, and especially Henri de Régnier were all friends of her father, who encouraged her to read, not only French poetry but also English and German poetry in the original. She began writing verse as an adolescent, but during her lifetime she published (in 1927, in the *NRF*) only one poem, "Vale." A group of six appeared in *Mesures* in 1935, followed by her translations of Stefan George in 1936. Gallimard brought out her *Poèmes* in 1959 (new edition, 1987), but it is only in Joseph's edition of the *Œuvre poétique* that her entire production has become available. The earlier poems may be useful in following her poetic evolution but essentially are of interest to specialists. They do serve, however, to pad a volume which would have been slim without them—and without the passages from the journals, sometimes more interesting than Pozzi's youthful exercises. The six poems which she personally wished to preserve were born of emotional and physical suffering: of the pain of her relationship with Valéry (clearly referred to in "Vale") and of her worsening health, which led to an increasing dependence on drugs and produced in her a state of mystical illumination. The poems also reflect Pozzi's studies in science and philosophy. "Nova," which refers to the astronomical phenomenon of a star that suddenly flares into incredible brightness, only swiftly to darken, may be interpreted as a metaphor for the soul of the poet. "Maya" expresses her belief that all cultures are interrelated, that the human soul, *her* soul, has inherited its sensibility from an immemorial past—not only Greek and Roman, but pre-Columbian as well. "Nyx" (Night), written shortly before her death, evokes a mystical trance in which she identifies with Louise Labé, "aussi de Lyon de l'Italie," and is related, in form and spirit, to Labé's sonnet "O beaux yeux bruns." In the Lyonnaise, Pozzi had found "une âme sœur" who could share her love and her pain.

John L. Brown. World Literature Today. 63, 1989, pp. 450–51

Lawrence Joseph's fine 1988 biography . . . has revived interest in the tormented career of Catherine Pozzi . . . whose sparse literary production—a *nouvelle* titled *Agnès*, a handful of poems, and an essay, *La peau d'âme*—has recently been reprinted. Those works leave us with the impression that Pozzi's major creation may have been her tumultuous life. Married briefly to the playwright Edouard Bourdet, whom she found too frivolous for her more serious intellectual tastes, she maintained a storm-tossed liaison of over a decade with Paul Valéry, with whom she shared a common passion for poetry and science.

Agnès and Pozzi's poems are relatively "reader friendly," but *La peau d'âme*, eccentric, often irritating, full of unfamiliar scientific allusions, yet occasionally illuminated by flashes of intuitive brilliance, can puzzle even the most attentive. Presented in six repetitive sections, the text resembles a series of notes not yet organized into a coherent whole. (Perhaps Pozzi desired precisely such an effect rather than conventional "structure.") She had already begun to write it in 1915, under the title "De Libertate," in which she confronts a philosophical problem that would occupy her, indeed obsess her, for the rest of her life: the relation of mind and matter, of body and spirit, the connection between the individual consciousness and an "alien" universe. Of course, as Joseph points out in his helpful preface, a number of contemporary thinkers, including William James and Bergson, were engaged in comparable enterprises. However, Pozzi, despite her extensive scientific studies (for several years she contributed a *chronique scientifique* to *Le Figaro*), refused to accept an exclusively "scientific" approach. Instead she dreamed of arriving at a synthesis of poetry and science, of subjectivity and objectivity, of "mysticism and positivism": "Je me conduis en positiviste, mais je sens en mystique." (Joseph well describes *La peau d'âme* as both a "document intime" and an "exposé scientifique.")

The title, as enigmatic as the contents, refers to an ancient Egyptian religious text, and also (in a spirit of self-deprecation?) to "La peau d'âme" of Perrault. Pozzi conceives of the soul as a complex network (*réseau*), as a "skin" which covers the body and produces the sensation she identifies with the individual's sensibility and intelligence. She replaces the Cartesian "Cogito ergo sum" with "Je sens, donc je suis." Up until her death, she continued her scientific studies, hailing L. de Broglie's work in quantum physics as a confirmation of her belief that there was no barrier between mind and matter. She revels in the deliberate unconventionality of her language (so different from the sober prose of her *Figaro* articles), using popular expressions, puns, made-up words, child talk, and bitingly ironic epithets directed against "the professors": "Ecoute, faisons l'idiot, ils diront ce qu'ils voudront." She has the poet's delight in linguistic play, for in spite of (or because of?) her philosophical and scientific studies she remains essentially a poet, one who produced some half-dozen lyrics (like "Maya" and "Nova") of a compelling emotional intensity in which her lifelong meditations on the relation of mind and body, of the spirit and the senses, find their most memorable expression.

John L. Brown. *World Literature Today.* 64,
1990, p. 442

PRICHARD, KATHARINE SUSANNAH (AUSTRALIA)
1883–1969

Here is a novel [*Working Bullocks*] that demands respectful attention. It does for the remote timberlands of Western Australia what *Maria Chapdelaine* did for the lonely homesteads of Canada. Grimly in contact with reality, *Working Bullocks* is a novel that no imaginative American can forget, once he has turned the first page. There are two definite appeals, either one of which is of sufficient vigor to make the book important: first, the general excellence of the narrative; and second, the fascination of the setting that is so unfamiliar to most of us. In judicious adjustment, these two interests combine to make *Working Bullocks* a rare pleasure. . . .

But if certain externals make Western Australia different from New England or North Dakota, the fundamentals of human living are not changed. Miss Prichard shows us the common ambitions, and loves, and stupidities living on in their eternal persistence. These poor swampers and bullockies are not far removed from the beasts they drive; just a little conventional relaxation, an unbelievable amount of work, and so each day. Working bullocks, unable to throw off the burden of their lives. Against a background of such a type the author tells her story of two girls and a man, of a mother and her "sixteen living and two dead," of primitive contacts with nature—tells it simply, honestly, and with power.

Saturday Review of Literature. July 30, 1927, p. 6

Miss Prichard's book [*Coonardoo*], which won the 1928 Best Australian Novel prize, tells a very old story. We have read over and over again of white men succumbing to the charms of native women and of their wives' discovery of these indiscretions. Here we have the same theme with a difference. We are led by some marvelous descriptions of native ceremonies to an understanding of aboriginal sex-consciousness, until we (like Mrs. Bessie, the hero's mother) find in it "something impersonal, universal and of a religious mysticism," and can sympathize with Coonardo, who bore her lover one son, as much as with the white wife, who gave him four daughters. . . .

This very tragic novel has great worth, not only as a story but as a commentary on two opposed moralities: as either it was worth reading. Miss Prichard writes very directly and has no mannerisms: she has given us, too, the words of many very lovely native songs, which have not been translated before.

The Spectator. August 31, 1929, p. 285

There is much that is fine and memorable in the collection [*Kiss on the Lips*]. It would seem to be the slow distillation of years and to recognize fully the difficult and intricate art of the short story. There is nothing casual or haphazard about the stories. Each one is finely bred, made and shaped, sometimes to the point of artificiality, but always by the hand of an artist. They are etched, bitten into copper with acid, finished and permanent, hard, clear, distinct. There is understanding but no softness in them. Their subject-matter is what is, not what might be. . . .

Each story is separate and stands on its own merits and yet there are strong links of unity making the book a whole. There is the author's style, which is so mature and so strongly individual as to give to each story a color in common that outweighs differences of subject-matter, like a family likeness binding together individuals however divergent they may be on the surface. Behind this is the preoccupation with one theme which holds good for the majority of the stories. Lastly, they are all cut out of the same attitude of mind—poetic realism.

The style is terse and brilliant. The expression sometimes has a dramatic roughness and verisimilitude which is not naturalism but an aesthetic adaptation of natural rhythms. . . .

The theme with which so many of the stories are preoccupied, the book's second source of unity, is happiness. This on the surface may seem paradoxical, but it is true. Perhaps happiness is too paltry a word, but I can find no other to fit it better. The author conceives happiness as a mystery, the flowering of the spirit, the search for a spiritual well-being that has little to do with outward circumstance. Here the pursuit of happiness is shown in its negative as well as its positive phase, but it is there at the core of almost every story.

M. Barnard Eldershaw. *Essays in Australian Fiction* (Melbourne: Melbourne University Press, 1938), pp. 34–36

In a long literary life extending over roughly thirty-five intensely active years, and encompassing the production of twelve novels, two volumes of short-stories, two of verse and a book of essays on life in the Soviet Union, Katharine Prichard has opened up vast tracts of Australia for literary visitation. Lawson and Furphy had dug deeply on small selections, Sydney, the Turon-Cudgegong goldfields, the Western plains, the Riverina. Katharine Prichard has moved from the coastal cities to the opal fields of Lightning Ridge, to the far North-West of Western Australia, to the karri forests of the South-West and the goldfields of Kalgoorlie and Boulder. . . .

Her approach in all her major books, when beginning to write about a "new" area (unlike that of some regional novelists who simply give an unusual, local setting to a story that might as well have happened in half a dozen places) is rather to reveal the threefold aspects of life—people and environment, with work as the nexus; for she is concerned to show how human character and behavior are molded by day to day surroundings and occupations.

Muir Holborn. *Meanjin.* 3, 1951, pp. 234–35

One of [Prichard's] most revealing themes is of the denial of a strong physical and spiritual affinity between a man and a woman because it cuts across social loyalties. This theme, like the similar one of the conflict between social loyalty and the desire to develop a musical talent, runs through nearly all the novels, forming one of the major threads in *Black Opal, Coonardoo, Intimate Strangers* and the goldfields trilogy. These two themes, which involve a struggle between the values of the simple life and the desire for something beyond it, give rise to the only real conflicts in Prichard's characters. She never arrives at a satisfactory resolution of the problem because for her it involves an opposition of two equally important absolutes, natural instinct and social being. . . .

Her work seems to me to show her romantic naturalism and her Marxism struggling for mastery. She is torn between nature and society just as her characters are. Their natural instincts and emotions struggle against the social ties that bind them. Although the poetic weight is given to the natural instincts, these nearly succumb before the recognition of social necessity. Her failure to resolve this conflict leads ultimately, in the trilogy especially, to a separation of the very conscious and unconscious being which she was striving to unite.

Ellen Malos. *Australian Literary Studies.* 1,
1963, pp. 36, 39

Fundamentally, Katharine Susannah Prichard is an artist of pagan sensibility. It could be her personal voice speaking through the thoughts of Elodie Blackwood in *Intimate Strangers*. "To live was to suffer: but to take the storms of life with exultation, defying the gods with joy of it all, that was the great achievement." Appreciation of color, form, sound, movement, the sensuous awareness of people and places, of delight and agony, of action and skill, permeates her writing. Her people sing a snatch or snatch a wildflower, gallop with expert abandon, rejoice in sun and shadow, thunder and rain, scents of the earth and the bush. In youth they revel in being young. "Gay" is a word that peeps up throughout the novels like one of the starry wildflowers, a challenge to the inexorable pressures of living, intentionally a badge of courage, unintentionally a comment on her own subconscious inclination towards a lightness of spirit, an illumination of the senses. . . .

Intimate Strangers is unique amongst the novels in that the true action occurs in the minds of the characters, and natural events (such as a storm in which Jerome displays qualities of leadership and prowess) are valued most for the mental changes they beget. The story moves on many levels: the daily round; the "hidden life"; through several layers of an urban community aware, or apprehensive, or ignorant, of changes in world economics that are stretching tentacles towards Australia. A revelation of Australian beach life at times even suggests a mystical link between the people and the sea.

Henrietta Drake-Brockman. *Katharine
Susannah Prichard* (Melbourne: Oxford
University Press, 1967), pp. 8–9, 43

It is Katharine Prichard's tragedy that she began to develop at a time when she could not hope to gain real sustenance in Australia for her peculiar metaphysical vision of earth and man. The themes were there to her hand in a community not yet alienated from its pioneering phase, but the climate of ideas and opinions was limited and limiting. Her roots dried for lack of sap, her ideas hardened into a mold that could only destroy her as an artist. Sometimes her lack of understanding of her own sensibility seems to have had something almost perverse about it, as if, after the suicide of her husband, Hugo Throssell, she willed her own creative death. The sensuousness of her imagery dries up, her style becomes arid and blind. . . .

Hers is a matriarchal universe dominated by passionately material figures. . . . The central male characters tend to divide into two roles, the sacred and the profane; the first based on a Marxist abstraction, the working-class intellectual who leads men, the other based on an animal sexuality. Beyond these personae is a simplified proletarian male chorus whose rhythm is man, earth, work. . . .

It is only when she is still able to create her figures against the landscape with a kind of Promethean paganism that we are caught up in her vision and accept it almost as a religious and metaphysical experience. The traps in this kind of writing are sentimentality, melodrama and unconscious comedy. When the climactic moment does not come off we are left with embarrassing lapses in taste, often not far removed from a *Woman's Weekly* love story.

Dorothy Hewett. *Overland.* 43, 1969,
pp. 28–30

Katharine Prichard's position as a writer in the Communist Party was double-edged. In many ways she was regarded as an asset: she was well known and respected in many parts of Australia, her novels were successful and *Working Bullocks* had been translated into Russian. She was applauded, yet she was subtly denigrated. She was considered an asset by people who did not always understand her literature or appreciate her literary importance, though aware of the prestige she reflected onto the Communist Party; yet, by the same token, she was often taken more seriously as a novelist than as a Communist. There was a constant tension between her two roles. . . .

In 1961 Jack Lindsay wrote an article on Katharine Prichard's fiction which is still a leading critical assessment of her work. In it he established the importance of her writing to the development of a social commitment in Australian literature and indeed this is a point that still needs to be made. . . .

For Lindsay, themes which culminate in her goldfields trilogy, *The Roaring Nineties* (1946), *Golden Miles* (1948) and *Winged Seeds* (1950), run through all her work. There is her preoccupation with the early pioneering community and the effects of capitalism on an Australian mateship tradition. The interrelations of man, work and nature are, he concludes, central to all her novels. In this schema, *Intimate Strangers* is seen as a failure to achieve her usual synthesis of these themes. While I would agree with Jack Lindsay that these themes do indeed appear throughout her work from her first to her last novel, I would disagree with his view of her work as a progression marred only by a certain weakness in *Intimate Strangers*. I would argue instead for a more central positioning of *Intimate Strangers* as a hesitation, a point of crisis in her fiction. For me there are two clear points of rupture, of change and movement in Prichard's writing. The first, with which Lindsay would agree, comes between *Black Opal* in 1921 and *Working Bullocks* in 1926. The second, with which he would not agree, occurs between *Intimate Strangers,* published in 1937 but written before 1933, and the goldfields trilogy (1946, 1948, 1950). The first change, which had excited Nettie Palmer with the publication of *Working Bullocks,* is related to a period of political confidence and personal happiness and to an experience and understanding of the West Australian bush. The second change, which occurred in the mid-1930s, is more complex and less easily defined. There is a quality to the earlier novels which, in my estimation, is missing in the novels of the 1940s and 1950s. There is no doubt that the trilogy is an important contribution to the school of socialist realism of that later period, but it lacks the vibrancy and tension that had marked her writing with *Working Bullocks* (1926), *Coonardoo* (1929) and *Intimate Strangers* (1937). . . .

Coonardoo is a novel of doomed love between a white man and a black woman. This love is fated not only because of racial attitudes but because of much deeper barriers. While Coonardoo is in tune with her instinctual life, with the environment, with her passions, Hugh is divorced as a White man from his colonized environment, the victim of convention, unable to follow his own perceptions. Hugh is destroyed because he has lost intuition, does not dare risk passion. Coonardoo, the romantic figure, is destroyed because she is the colonized Black woman, her death the ugly fate imposed on a fine people by colonial brutality. But her power remains through her tie with the land, with her people, with ritual.

Katharine Prichard's writing about Aboriginal culture was based on research and informed by a respectful curiosity that was rare in the late 1920s. Despite its romanticism the political significance of her writing about racism and the Aboriginal experience cannot be overemphasized in a tradition of literary neglect, disparagement or sentimentalization. For all the prominence of the bush in Australian literature, it was a bush that had rarely been populated with Aborigines. Aborigines had been portrayed for years in Australian fiction largely as part of an exotic background, as shadowy bystanders with bit parts, or as sentimental figures for White children to weep over. Katharine Prichard broke with these inadequacies in a novel that demanded Aborigines be recognized as an integral and important part of Australian life; that they be recognized as sexual, moral, intellectual beings. What is more, her realism made such statements inescapable.

Drusilla Modjeska. *Exiles at Home:*
Australian Women Writers 1925–1945
(Australia: Sirius, 1981), pp. 131, 133–34,
137–38

The uncertainty of the relationship between the traditional Australian Left and the expected world revolution is reflected in the novel [*Working Bullocks*] by the vexed relationship between the Australian working class ideals of mateship and fair play and the ideas of the internationally experienced agitator Mark Smith. More importantly, though, *Working Bullocks* reveals its historical moment in its relative paucity of directly political ideas and in its powerful valorizing, at the stylistic level, of political and other forms of human energy over ideological orthodoxy or organizational efficiency. In what could be seen as a first wave of cultural assimilation, Prichard's commitment as a novelist made up in enthusiasm what she and others in her position lacked in detailed knowledge. What she did know—and it became the structural cornerstone and stylistic keynote of the novel she wrote at this time—was that for the first time in history the working class really had appropriated the means of production. For that reason, the most inclusive metonymy of direct appropriation that appears in the novel is Red Burke's "smoldering desire to be admitted to [Mark Smith's] consciousness," for it signifies a desire to appropriate history itself in its current state of revolutionary momentum.

Pat Buckridge. In Carole Ferrier, ed.
Gender, Politics, and Fiction: Twentieth-Century Australian Women's Novels (St.
Lucia, Queensland, Australia: Queensland
University Press, 1985), p. 100

In *Coonardoo* (1929; serialized 1928) Katharine Susannah Prichard records fictionalized responses to her own interracial encounter with aboriginal culture and to the character of interracial encounters she observed on a 1926 visit to a cattle station in the northwest of Western Australia, a frontier of white settlement. She problematizes white sexual exploitation of black women and the qualities of character which suit white women for life on the frontiers of settlement and of interracial contact. For her original complicitly racist perspective audience, readers of *The Bulletin,* a magazine bearing the motto "Australia for the White Man," Prichard provides, for her day, an anthropologically accurate evocation of aboriginal culture, and partially challenges what Abdul JanMohamed suggests is the standard self-justifying manichean allegory of the colonial mentality: white is to black Other as light is to dark, as good is to evil, as superiority is to inferiority, as civilization is to savagery, as sophistication is to the primitive, as complexity is to simplicity, as intelligence is to emotion and superstition, as rationality is to sensuality and sexuality. This allegory provides the implicit or explicit foundation of white cultural hegemony in dealing with blacks and black cultures. Prichard's treatment of interracial sexual encounters and racial miscegenation was considered in 1928 a sensitive enough public issue for the editor of *The Bulletin* to censor every reference to the actual sexual touch of white man and black woman and for a paternalistic white government to prosecute the historical person on whom Prichard based Sam Geary, a shameless sexual exploiter of black women, and to outlaw white men bringing their interracial sexual relationships into "civilized" white public space by booking rooms for their conduct in hotels.

Prichard sees hope of improvement in the moral quality of typical white interracial contact to lie in the egalitarian, democratizing value of work done in common by black and white, in a growing mutuality of love for the land as a basis for cross-cultural respect, and in discouraging aboriginals for their own protection from contact with the corruptions of white towns—loss of tribal traditions, venereal diseases, alcohol, and vigorous, stubbornly unreflective racism. . . .

Part of Prichard's implicit project in *Coonardoo* is to present what anthropologists today would consider an "emic" view of aboriginal culture, that is, a view in which the observer attempts to comprehend the social realities of an "alien" culture through its own eyes. The emic anthropological approach seeks to minimize the influence of cultural imperialism, seeks to decenter the observing self and her/his internalized cultural baggage (potentially including the colonialist manichean allegory) in the presence of the cultural Other.

Sue Thomas. World Literature Written in English. 27, 1987, pp. 234–35

From the time when she wrote of the opal miners' fierce defense of their independence against the intrusion of the New York dealers in *Black Opal* (London: 1921), Katharine Susannah Prichard's novels had recorded the struggles of Australian working people wherever she found them. There was little opportunity for such reflections on the workers' political ambitions in her short stories. Not until the 1950s, her literary reputation established, the relationship with her publishers secure and her political stance in the final volumes of the goldfields trilogy already challenged as mere Communist propaganda, could she feel as though she could write as she pleased.

True to her own literary standards, the stories where for the first time she wrote of her own Party comrades are as authentic as the prospectors' yarns and the lyrical celebrations of the bush and the farmlands which Katharine wrote in the spring of her first ten years in Greenmount. The political stories tell of the experiences and ideals of the Communists she knew, worked with and admired. They remain among the very few examples of Australian writing about the lives and aspirations of the Communists, for all the preoccupation of the press and politicians with the "red menace," since Billy Hughes first raised the hue and cry against the Bolsheviks and "red rats" during the Conscription campaign in 1917. . . .

Critics have often lost sight of the strong vein of humor running through many of Katharine Susannah Prichard's short stories. By comparison with the novels and the more somber stories, her comic yarns are easily forgotten. They were written to amuse: anecdotes and yarns which tell of some of life's comedies, to be laughed at, retold for the fun shared, or forgotten. At their best, the stories written for a laugh rank with the traditional Aussie con aiming to knock the stuffing out of pretentious smart alecs and up-jumped authority. The three stories retold here are almost folktales in their simplicity. There is a pathos in many of them, true to the tradition of Chaplin's little tramp; but Katharine's sympathy for the underdog shows, even when she is joining in a laugh at the expense of their eccentricities. They reflect her own great joy in life, and her confidence that, given half a chance, it can be good to be alive.

Ric Throssell. Introduction to Katharine
Susannah Prichard. *Tribute: Selected Stories
of Katharine Susannah Prichard* (St. Lucia,
Queensland, Australia: University of
Queensland Press, 1988), pp. xix–xx

PRITAM, AMRITA (INDIA) 1919–

[An] event that had tremendous impact on the Indian, specially Urdu, Hindi and Punjabi, literatures was the partition of the country, the transfer of populations, and the resultant carnage of the communal riots in the Punjab. Responding to the challenge of the holocaust, the writers took up their pens to stem the tide of blood and hatred, and to uphold the banner of Humanity and Peace. The moment was too grim for them to care that they would be labelled as propagandists. The most beautifully haunting poem that came out of the partition riots was written by Amrita Pritam whose "New Heer" or "Aankhaan Waris Shah Nu. . . " (I say to Waris Shah), addressed to the author of the Punjabi romantic epic of immortal love, recounted the tales of inhumanity, horror and hate that besmirched the fair name of the Punjab, on either side of the newly-created border.

K. A. Abbas. In Surresh Kohli, ed. *Aspects
of Indian Literature* (Delhi: Vikas, 1975),
p. 150

The English-educated Indian middle class finds contemporary Punjabi literature obscene. Anything dealing with sex in the Punjab appears vulgar. To whom? Not to the peasant who freely uses four-letter words in his speech. Not to the bus driver speeding his vehicle, the farmer twisting the tail of his bullock, the mason laying bricks in midday heat—all spouting foul curses. Working women giggle over bawdy jokes. Their children raised in dusty streets are exposed to a rich sexual vocabulary. A writer cannot help reflecting all this in his work.

Smug officials champion the propagation of Punjabi, but deep in their souls perhaps they hate their mother tongue. A conversation or thought valid in their English becomes vulgar the moment it is uttered in Punjabi. Their grown-up daughters use obscene slang and discuss the latest bra fashions in the presence of their parents. The same conversation in Punjabi makes their parents squirm. While in the West even the four-letter word has ceased to shock readers, in Punjabi the mere theme of a neurotic relationship creates a furor. Addicted to trite expressions, harmless clichés and banal pleasantries, the anglicized middle class judges literature by a hypocritical moral yardstick. . . .

Amrita Pritam writes openly about sex, such as in her novel *Chak No. 36* in which a good girl who wants to go to bed with a certain man points out that she can play the role of a prostitute or a wife with equal ease because she loves him. Amrita's opinions about obscenity are less earthy because she is concerned with moral and ethical values. She feels that "Where values end, obscenity begins."

> Balwant Gargi. In Surresh Kohli, ed.
> *Aspects of Indian Literature* (Delhi: Vikas,
> 1975), pp. 62–63

Amrita Pritam has made a very extensive use of the symbol in her poetry—perhaps because she is a woman. And a woman in our present-day society may not say all that she chooses to say. The woman in her grows indignant at the injustices in our life and with the help of the symbol she registers her protest. Amrita Pritam is preoccupied with the basic problems of life. She talks about everyday happenings, the everyday wants and denials of common men and women. And this is, perhaps the secret of her popularity and also of her success as a poet. Her symbols are those of a woman sensitive and eternally young. Whereas Mohan Singh calls a woman property in his famous poem "Jaidad," Amrita Pritam has likened her to a cow, and she expands the symbol in a manner typical of her art.

Amrita Pritam has drawn frequently on the folk songs of the Punjab and there is the simplicity, the naive beauty of a folk song in her work. For her symbols also, she does not have to delve deep into literature or go far in search of them. She is a people's poet and sings in a manner which comes naturally to them. . . .

Amrita Pritam started writing as a sissy. In her search for freedom, she warbled love lyrics for a long time and gained popularity. She, however, seems to confuse woman's emancipation, of which there is a lot of talk these days, with contempt for social norms. She must smoke if smoking is prohibited in Sikhism, the religion in which she was born. She must drink if drinking by ladies in Indian society is not looked upon with favor. She must leave her husband after decades of married life with children and live with someone out of wedlock and yet continue to love a third man. Of late, she seems to revel, as it were, in the idiom of a rake. . . .

It was Amrita Pritam's heart of a mother that shed tears of blood immediately after the partition at the insensate massacre of innocent men and women on both sides of the border. I have it on the testimony of the poetess: A refugee from Lahore, she was heading for Dehradun in search of an asylum. Those days, as it was, you had to wade through blood and walk over dead bodies to reach the railway station. And you needed all the luck for the train to take you to your destination without bloodshed or rape at the intermediate stations. The night was dark, says the poetess. She was all alone in an over-crowded compartment full of homeless people who had walked through the shadow of death. The Muslims massacring the Hindus and the Hindus hungry for Muslim heads. It was like all decency, all good-neighborliness sinking around her. Suddenly the poetess found her lips moving, tears gushing in her eyes, she invoked Waris Shah, the great bard of the Punjab. . . .

K. S. Daggal. *Literary Encounters* (New
Delhi: Marwah, 1980), pp. 40–41, 48, 116

Amrita Pritam began her literary career as a poet and her novels and short stories also have a poetic quality. Her early work focuses on the inner life of her characters, many of whom seem to be projections of the author herself. Pritam's mature work is characterized by a search for harmony and truth. She is strongly influenced by Freud and intrigued by the way in which senti-mental young girls always seem to be in search of unselfish mother love. Her story "The Ghost" is narrated by a young girl. She has always been closer to her mother than her father, and feels the need to be loved by other mother figures too. She is crushed by her grandmother's rejection. Then suddenly she is told that her mother is actually her foster-mother, and that the lonely, sad but loving aunt who lives behind their house is her real mother. She cannot accept the truth; shaken and confused, she finally falls ill. Eventually she recovers, only to discover than she has lost both mothers.

The sorrow and loss felt by the little girl and the manner in which she deals with these emotions have autobiographical overtones. Amrita Pritam lost her mother when she was eleven, and with the encouragement of her father, she managed to cope with her loss by writing poetry. In a sense Pritam represents the modern progressive female. Her view of life was radically altered by the political partition of Punjab and the accompanying chaos and cruelty. Much later when she settled in Delhi, she felt strongly attracted to a more radical modernism. In her autobiography she focuses on these events as they have influenced her work.

Susujura Gupta. In Mineke Schipper, ed.
*Unheard Words: Women and Literature in
Africa, the Arab World, Asia, the
Caribbean, and Latin America* (London:
Allyson and Busby, 1985), pp. 137–38

Amrita Pritam's poetry depicts the feelings of a woman in love. She has loved dearly and suffered terribly. Her attitude towards love, in her early poems, is devotional, mainly because of her religious background. She loves with her whole being and considers her personality incomplete unless the man condescends to transform it into some thing, pure and sublime. . . .

Amrita's poetry is full of ardors, hungers, derelictions. She makes an admirable attempt to transcend her intense sexual impulse into poetic images of rare beauty. The excellence of her art lies in its intensity.

Amrita Pritam, in her masterpiece *Sunehre,* unfolds a beauty at once sensitive, sincere and wistful. She is totally absorbed in her personal grief and all that is around her fades into nothingness. What matters is he who has filled her dreams since adolescence and being a victim of social and religious convictions, has failed to reciprocate her love with the intensity and ardor it demanded. She rises from his dreams, goes to bed with his dreams, and is subtly content to imagine him grieving for her too. She is, however, hopeful of finding deliverance from the throes of her lost love. She is eagerly expectant of the day when her love will be reciprocated and thus mellowed.

N. S. Tasneem. *Indian Literature.* 28:4,
July–August, 1985, pp. 129–31

Amrita Pritam (born on August 31, 1919) is one of the finest writers in Punjabi. She has published twenty-eight novels, eighteen volumes of verse, five of short stories, and sixteen of miscellaneous prose. She was the first woman poet to be awarded the Sahitya Akademi Prize in 1956 for her volume of poems entitled *Sunehre* (Messages). She was awarded the Padma Shri in 1969, an honorary doctor of literature by Delhi University in 1973, and the Vaptsarov Award (International) from Bulgaria in 1980. Her volume of poems entitled *Kagaz te Canvas* won the Bharatiya Jnanpith Award for 1981.

Amrita Pritam's poetry achieves "a transcendent view of humanity in a broad sweep of concern for man's survival in a fast dehumanizing epoch." Her writings, in their totality, "reflect the human predicament, particularly as seen through the eyes of a woman, and are full of passages which have "a terrible beauty, and ecstasy which haunt us."

Her central theme of romantic love between man and woman is bound up with a repudiation of "the repeated curse of convention." No wonder, then, a sense of suffering and illegitimacy characterizes her concept of love and of the creative process. In her autobiography *The Revenue Stamp (Rasidi Tickat),* she speaks of her writing "as an illegitimate child" born out of the "forbidden consummation" of "an affair" between "the reality of my life" and "the dream of my heart." However, she insists that "my writing is personal but not about myself."

Indian Literary Review. 3:3, October,
1985, p. 3

PROU, SUZANNE (FRANCE) n.d.

Among the various writers who make up the contemporary literary panorama, Suzanne Prou occupies a preeminent place because of her originality
and the interest that her work has aroused in both readers and critics. . . .

This originality is owing, among other factors, to her not belonging to
any particular literary current, even though the influence of earlier French
and foreign literature—especially such writers as Proust, Butor, Kafka, and
above all Mauriac—can of course be found in her work. . . .

Although she had always written short stories and tales for children,
Suzanne Prou became known rather late to the general public, specifically in
1966 with her first novel, *Les Pataphoris,* followed by *Les demoiselles sous
les ebeniers* (The damsels under the ebony trees) in 1967, *L'été jaune* (Yellow
summer) in 1968, *La ville sur la mer* (The town on the sea) in 1970. *Mecham-
ment les oiseaux* (1971; Naughtily the birds) won the Cazes Prize in 1972 and
the author's success was confirmed by the Renaudot Prize for *La terrasse
des Bernardini* (The Bernardinis' terrace) in 1973. Five years later, in 1978
to be exact, Prou won the Provence Grand Literary Prize for the entirety of
her work.

If we were now to ask what is the interior and poetic world of this work,
we should reply that a constant concern for human beings is at the basis of
Suzanne Prou's entire literary output. Her tendency toward psychological
analysis allows her to penetrate into the vagaries of human consciousness
and find its most unusual feelings, its most secret dreams. In this way, the
writer succeeds in showing us "real" beings with their problems, their sufferings, and their uncertainties.

It is important, moreover, to underline the fact that Prou's inventive
capacity always takes off from real facts. . . .

This writer's genius, in our opinion, consists in uncovering that which
is not said, that which one hardly dares to think, that abyss of subtexts
masked by the most innocuous phrases. . . .

One of the most representative novels of Suzanne Prou's literary world
is *La terrasse des Bernardini* in that it includes a great many of the themes
and issues so dear to the author, like the inability to communicate, loneliness,
flight into the past. The characters of this novel, although living together,
really live in a world of their own, without establishing constructive relations
with one another. They are thus solitary beings, fearful of time that passes
and ready to flee the present reality by anchoring themselves to the past.

The book is pervaded, from the beginning, by a climate of ambiguity and
mystery which transpires through beings and things. . . . The novel opens,
in fact, with the description of the first "character," which is not a character
but a place, specifically the terrace of the Bernardini house, a luxurious old
residence that imposes its prestige over the entire city. . . .

Suzanne Prou certainly possesses all the qualities of a fine stylist; her knowledge of the French language allows her to make use of it in a way that is always appropriate and measured. . . . The writer has succeeded, in sum, in expressing herself through a means and a technique that are unified with her thought and her themes. It is perhaps precisely because of these qualities of hers that Suzanne Prou is without a doubt one of the most interesting figures in French literature today.

> Gabriella Gasparoni. *Quaderni di Filologia e Lingue Romanze.* 1985, pp. 263–66, 269–70

Suzanne Prou's latest novel, *Le temps des innocents,* centers on the loss of sexual, intellectual, and political innocence in the main character's passage from adolescence to adulthood. Divided into sections corresponding to academic years, the story commences when Julien enters the university at the beginning of the war in 1939 and ends with his departure for forced labor in Germany with the STO at the end of 1943.

Julien's entrance to college in September 1939 marks an awakening at all levels. New horizons of intellectual, social, and cultural awareness, which distance him more and more from his working-class parents, open up for him. At the same time, he experiences a more intense emotional life with a wider range of feelings. He falls in love for the first time with a girl who remains, in his eyes, the ideal he can dream about yet never attain. He finds in David, an artistically inclined Jewish boy, the friend with whom he can meaningfully share his literary aspirations. They try to fight anti-Semitism by founding a journal called "Hope," a name that holds the same sort of symbolism as did Malraux's great novel on the Spanish Civil War. The venture soon founders, and Julien discovers unsuspected truths about political facts and racial antagonisms.

As he completes his degree, Julien begins his first assignment as a substitute teacher full of illusions as to what he can achieve with his students. He is awed by some of his colleagues, one in particular whom he greatly admires but who will deeply disappoint him. The road to maturity, however, is replete with a multiplicity of deceptions and sorrows. The loss of the girl he loves to an older friend he fully trusted brings sadness and a sense of betrayal. The political murder of an esteemed professor and, most of all, David's suicide to avoid arrest as a Jew bring home the bitter realities of despair and death in wartime.

Set in a university town in southern France, not named but easily identifiable as Aix-en-Provence, *Le temps des innocents* returns to the area that was also the setting of *Le dit de Marguerite* (What Daisy said) . . . a region that Prou seems to know well. For those who shared some of the recounted experiences in the same locale during the difficult years of the war, the book is all the more realistic and enjoyable. The precision and accurateness with which Prou describes details of everyday life, as well as the psychological

states of mind of Julien and his girlfriend, are praiseworthy, as are the clarity
of her style and the keenness of her observations.

Yvonne Guers-Villate. *World Literature
Today.* 63, 1989, p. 652

Imagination shapes the lives of Suzanne Prou's characters. It colors memory,
constructs the present through interpretations more persuasive than reality,
and, for the truly adventurous, it anticipates a brighter future, which generally turns out as rehearsal for disaster. Her provincial world, guarded by the
unseen chorus of village opinion, is constrained by limited choices. A modest
rise in prosperity or rank leads mainly to new constraint. Some in *La demoiselle de grande vertu,* Prou's twenty-third book, find a safer way to break
free of convention: through fantasy. One such individual, a nameless old lady,
concocts a sympathetic past for the white-haired conductor who performs
every afternoon in a local tea room. Not dissuaded by an abrupt revelation
of his dissolute life, she tucks away the cherished memory, safe from ridicule,
as the solace of a last love. Those who misplace the boundaries of reality,
however, can pay a heavy price, like the fussy old woman who strays into
the wrong village and becomes permanently disoriented when she cannot
locate a familiar house in what seem like strangely altered streets, or like
the little boy who is horrified when he breaks his grandmother's Chinese vase
and cannot see why he is not also held responsible for the old lady's death.

Like several other vignettes in *La demoiselle,* the title story sketches
out a situation that recurs in one of the author's novels: Solange, scorned by
her only true love, finds a perverse sort of fulfillment in lifetime service to
his wife and family. In a longer version of this triangle in *La terrasse des
Bernadini* (winner of the Prix Renaudot in 1973 . . .) Paul's once-scorned
wife and his mean-minded former mistress endure a bickering old age together in the fine house where village opinion believes they killed him. Prou
seldom writes of complete or happy families. Men are weak or absent, and
love is a long-suffering emotion, private as disgrace. With few exceptions,
there are glimpses of old people saturated in memory, of amiable aunts and
shadowy children, the small events of life and death around a scarcely
changing village, bathed in the hazy shadows and baked-earth smells of southern France, where the author grew up.

In perfect keeping with her theme, Prou's tales open on a tight focus,
an object or small setting weighted as a sensuous representation of place and
situation. At the opening, people—a group of old women around a tea table—
can be treated as "object" more than "person." When a protagonist is revealed, outward appearances or apparent motives are often suggested
through a given nickname or a hovering viewpoint informed by collective
opinion. The stories are generated and usually seen from within, through
partly conscious attitudes and consuming concerns. The scene opens just
wide enough to encompass an incident drawn in spare detail, which moves
to a swift, sure denouement.

Prou's light, ironic portrayal of provincial minds and values is delightful; but in a sense her subject is also her undoing. Though microcosm can represent the world, the reader ultimately yearns for characters with the vision and ability to break through determinism without causing misery.

Lee Fahnestock. *World Literature Today*. 65,
1991, pp. 265–66

PUJMANOVÁ, MARIE (CZECH REPUBLIC) 1895–1958

After a period of painful upheaval . . . after a period of intensive searching for balance in life and outlook, the whole being of [Pujmanová] now burns with a new fire. A ripe wisdom and a love of life in all its breadth and dynamism have brought her a new, complex balance, enabling her to grasp wide expanses of life through emotion and understanding. What had remained hidden beneath the surface since her first book has now reemerged, rising from the deepest springs of her humanity and artistry.

In *Lidé na křižovatce* [People at the Crossroads] Pujmanová has made a bold attempt to seize the truth, and the result is a truly poetic work. Her balanced view of today's world in all its complexity gives her book stability, allowing her to bypass subjectivity. . . . And her honesty in facing up to reality has given her work an inevitable, pure, and transparent form, uncompromised by anything superfluous, arbitrary, or atypical.

Despite the fact that her work is a typification, the characters and their stories are presented with a lively, fresh individuality. Each has a specific atmosphere and mood, and they are arranged in sequence and placed in the correct proportion to the whole. All this gives Pujmanová's novel a stable yet fluid objectivity. Moreover, she now avoids oversimplification. She does not, for example, paint the capitalist world all black and the proletarian world white. She reflects their complexity, their internal differentiation and flux. And while the capitalist world comes out the loser, it is nevertheless portrayed in rich, full, and vibrant colors.

Thus, *Lidé na křižovatce* is one of our most successful novels. . . . The recording of the totality of the modern world through evocative condensation, which Pujmanová has largely succeeded in doing, marks an advance toward the great synthesizing novel we have yet to see.

Bedřich Václavek. *Literárni studie a
podobizny* (Prague: Československý
spisovatel, 1962), pp. 131–32

Pujmanová's major work of fiction derives from both a warm sympathy for people and a determination to reveal the truth. Only when she had discerned the direction in which society was moving was she able to write *Lidé na křižovatce* (1937), a masterly work of Czech fiction that can well compete internationally. Šalda recognized her great talent as early as her first book, but it was Neumann who perceived, in the novel *Lidé na křižovatce,* the profundity and breadth of her fiction and its social function.

In this work the characters are drawn with masterly touch. The world is shown both objectively and through the remarkable perspective provided by the viewpoints of the characters. The confrontation and interweaving of these viewpoints presents a picture of reality in motion, which sweeps up the reader. Pujmanová's narration is precise, yet fresh and unconventional. The language draws copiously on popular speech, while also displaying the most polished literary style.

This novel presents a broad picture. There are many characters, representing entire social groups. The *period* is used not merely as an atmosphere or background as was true of Pujmanová's first books—but as the object of interest, the very heart of the work. From the lives of individuals she creates a picture of an epoch. Their lives reflect the complexities and the tensions of a society marked by growing class conflict. The fates of individuals gives us indications of the choices to be made on the crossroads of history. The course is indicated by the young Ondřej, through the awakening of his proletarian class consciousness and his decision to visit the Soviet Union.

In any attempt to define socialist realism in our literature, this novel by Marie Pujmanová provides an outstanding guideline. This accounts for her front-ranking position in contemporary Czech fiction. With this novel, which was the culmination of her struggle to break away from the confines of her early subjective humanism and to achieve a broader view of society, Pujmanová entered the most progressive stream of Czech literature. Now she is beginning to shape its course—the course taken by the working class on its advance to socialism.

František Buriánek. *O české literatuře našeho věku* (Prague: Československý spisovatel, 1972), pp. 144–45

Marie Pujmanová's most ambitious work is a trilogy, in which the first two volumes present a panoramic view of Czech society from the 1920s to the end of World War II. All that is happening is seen from the point of view of a political radical. *Lidé na křižovatce* (Vol. I, 1937) focuses on two classes in prewar Prague society—the left-wing intellectuals, and the workers with their emerging socialist and communist sympathies. . . . *Hra s ohněm* (Playing with fire) (Vol. II, 1948), which is based on the Reichstag fire trial (especially insofar as the actions of J. Dimitrov are concerned), describes the anti-fascist activity of Czechoslovakia. These two novels established Marie Pujmanová as a gifted writer of the contemporary social novel.

Marie Pujmanová analyzed the Czech society of the first half of the twentieth century with considerable accuracy and psychological insight. She is to be credited with a sense of finely balanced composition, a talent for taut plotting, and skillful characterization and dialogue. In her handling of the interior monologue, she experimented with the vocabulary and the speech rhythms of popular language.

In the 1950s Marie Pujmanová came to prominence as a committed communist writer, propagating the doctrine of socialist realism that she willingly practiced. The result was that the third volume of her trilogy, *Život proti smrti* (Life against death) (1952), is a curious compound of naïve tendentiousness and starkly modern realism. Even her sympathetic critics balk at the lapses into didacticism and the frequent failures of taste and artistic tact that appear in her writings of the 1950s.

> Helena Kosek. In Wolfgang Bernard
> Fleischmann, ed. *Encyclopedia of World*
> *Literature in the 20th Century* (New York:
> Frederick Ungar, 1971), pp. 131–32

The subject of [Pujmanová's] first novel, her home and family world, to which she returned again and again, survived in her socialist period and in her major works. All Pujmanová's young people were created from one easily recognized mold: the world of her childhood and adolescence as she portrayed it first in *Pod křídly* (Under the wings, 1917). The adults of the outside world, on the other hand, were created from observation and reasoning. . . . Other early writings of Pujmanová show her unusual talent but do not predict her later socialist-realist orientation. It did not come overnight. . . .

In a way communism and its literary theory helped Pujmanová overcome a creative crisis which followed her first success. She had an exceptional gift of observation and sensitivity; yet her talent was not of the caliber to create an independent vision of the world. Socialist realism offered her a solution, a backbone for her fiction. In the collection of poetry *Praha* (Prague) (1954), she confessed her dependence on the party: "I was an unhappy and unstable creature . . . before I met you my comrades. . . . What would I be without you?—an aging woman."

> Milada Součková. *A Literary Satellite*
> (Chicago: University of Chicago Press,
> 1970), pp. 81–83

Marie Pujmanová . . . came from a patrician family and in her first books focused on her own class, however critically. But in *Lidé na křižovatce* (1937; People at the crossroads), the first part of a trilogy, she attempted a complex picture of Czech society from the first postwar years to the Depression, with her sympathies reserved for the left-wing intellectual and the worker. The second part, *Hra s ohněm*— (1948; Playing with fire) did not equal the first, and the third, *Život proti smrti* (1952; Life against death), combining fiction and journalism, is little more than proof of the sterility of Stalinist dogma in literature.

Igor Hájek. In Leonard S. Klein, ed.
Encyclopedia of World Literature in the 20th Century (New York: Frederick Ungar, 1983),
p. 522

PYM, BARBARA (GREAT BRITAIN) 1913–80

Barbara Pym, who makes her American debut with *Less than Angels,* is a Londoner with a nice sense of the ridiculous and some acquaintance with anthropology. In writing her second novel she has employed a kind of triple exposure. Tribal customs of the British middle classes—urban and suburban, bourgeois and bohemian—are presented direct. They are also observed through the bemused eyes of certain learned gentlemen accustomed to studying the African variety. By slyly poking fun, in turn, at the curious folkways of the anthropologists themselves, Miss Pym has given an extra fillip to a gently diverting comedy.

Much of her study concerns a triangle that develops into something more complicated. When he isn't out in the field, Tom Mallow has been too complacently living with Catherine Oliphant, a charming if mildly fey contributor to the woman's magazines, who sometimes wishes that Tom, like the heroes of the stories she writes, would propose marriage. But along comes Deirdre Swan, pretty and diffident, an earnest young student with worship in her eyes; and Catherine relinquishes Tom with rueful grace.

Tom, in any case, must soon return to Africa and his chosen tribe. And there are other men in Deirdre's life: Bernard Springe, for instance, a dull but worthy friend of her brother's, and Mark Penfold and Digby Fox, fellow students in anthropology. As for Catherine, she turns a speculative eye on Alaric Lydgate, a colonial administrator retired to a London suburb.

Numerous other figures, widely and amusingly assorted, disport themselves in this or in the more specifically anthropological aspect of the narrative, and Miss Pym finds grounds for laughter in all of them. She introduces sudden death as casually as E. M. Forster, and from Jane Austen by way of Angela Thirkell she inherits a faculty for extracting comedy from the fatuities of the dull or foolish or pompous.

Dan Wickenden. *New York Herald Tribune.*
May 5, 1957, p. 3

Between 1950 and 1961 Barbara Pym published six novels. All enjoyed a mild success with reviewers and the public. But for nine years now no book by this writer has appeared, and the time seems suitable for a provisional assessment of her small but consistent body of work. . . . When an assessment of Miss Pym is to be embarked upon, a greater name is usually invoked (sometimes apologetically, but apparently irresistibly)—that of Jane Austen. Can Miss Pym be claimed as the Jane Austen of our times? In some ways, of course, this seems presumptuous, but in other ways it is too modest since, though her canvas is small, her range and scope are considerably wider than those of Jane Austen. But the comparison remains valid. There is the same woman's view, dealing sharply but on the whole good-humoredly with the closely observed minutiae of middle-class daily life, always enlivened by the needle of wit. Barbara Pym's novels are indeed, as a reviewer once wrote, "small beer," but as the reviewer added, it is beer from an Oxford brewery. . . .

Barbara Pym's world, and this is in charm, is a closed one: an enchanted world of small felicities and small mishaps. Yet it is also real and varied in theme and setting. In *Some Tame Gazelle* we are immersed in the society of a village or small provincial town; *Excellent Women* is set mainly in the inner residential parts of London—Pimlico, perhaps—and one form of middle-class society is confronted by another, the Bohemian-academic; much the same sort of confrontation occurs in *Jane and Prudence,* which combines London and the country; *Less than Angels* centers round that academic life which goes on in the heart of London unsuspected by those who do not penetrate the mysteries of Bloomsbury or the Inns of Court; *A Glass of Blessings* is London and the country again; the last, *No Fond Return of Love,* observes with an anthropological eye the ways of a cheerful Thames-side suburb. The themes are universal: love thwarted or satisfied (even fashionable homosexuality is here, just under the surface in several of the books); worldly ambition, nearly always academic ambition, and the complications which ensue; the challenge of the daily routine—and Miss Pym was first in the field in the pre-occupation with the kitchen sink, over which her female characters so often come into their own. . . .

These novels are something more than simply books for bad days. Their acute observation of a limited social scene makes them a valuable record of their time, perhaps more valuable than anything an anthropological research team set to work in Surbiton could produce. As to art, Barbara Pym has evolved and remained close to a formula which has won her devoted readers, a small but select band, and she has made one area of life her own domain. Her works are miniatures, exquisitely, nearly perfectly, done. But beyond this, it is her wit and her sense of the ridiculous which makes her books both delicious and distinguished.

Robert Smith. Ariel. October, 1971,
pp. 63–64, 67

Barbara Pym's four elderly office-workers [in *Quartet in Autumn*] are bad mixers. Outside office-hours, each goes his or her solitary way. Against the intimations of mortality each has a private defense: resignation, religion, anger, and obsession to the point of madness. . . .

Quartet in Autumn is Barbara Pym's first novel for sixteen years, and one can only hope that it does for her what *Wide Sargasso Sea* did for Jean Rhys. Sixty-year-old Letty, one of the quartet, has changed her reading habit from novels to biographies, having come to realize "that the position of an unmarried, unattached, ageing woman is of no interest whatsoever to the writer of modern fiction." This is the author's joke against herself, since several of the protagonists and many of the minor characters in her seven novels are spinsters conscious of being left on the shelf; they find solace in High Church Anglicanism and in mothering—even, sometimes, in flirting with—the priests of the parish. The books are drily witty comedies about "the small unpleasantnesses rather than the great tragedies; the little useless longings rather than the great renunciations."

Although Letty, Marcia, Norman and Edwin work in the same file-cluttered room, they are not friends. Letty, "fluffy and faded, a Home Counties type," makes kind remarks to Marcia, but Marcia's "marmoset eyes" show no response. Edwin "collects" churches and church-services. Norman hates cars; he kicks those parked in the square where he lives, muttering: "Bugger, bugger, bugger." Marcia hoards tins of food, fearing another national emergency or war; she eats hardly anything. Letty and Marcia retire, and retirement is too much for Marcia. When she dies, the others go to her funeral and afterwards have lunch together. Diffident Letty thinks her own choice of food, *oeufs Florentine,* "frivolous and unfeeling, on a par with wearing something in 'French navy' to the funeral." Letty, Norman and Edwin decide to go on living in independent loneliness, and the book ends with Letty's reflection that "life still held infinite possibilities for change."

John Mellors. The Listener. October 27,
1977, p. 550

Misprision, ignorance, prejudice, all are matters for joyous confusion concerning the subject of anthropology, which, along with the church, is one of the staples of the novels of Barbara Pym.

After Oxford, where she read English literature, after the Wrens, where she served in Italy, Barbara Pym worked for nearly thirty years, from 1946 to 1974, as an editor for *Africa,* the esteemed journal of the International African Institute. Her notebooks of the late 1940s (now deposited, along with innumerable other treasures of her writing career, at the Bodleian) show from the beginning an amused and bemused tolerance of this new world: "Anthropology—I just let it *flow* over me." A little later, in the same notebook: "Essays presented to Professor ——, an anthropologist. Why are they all so obscene?" How detached she sounds, as detached as if she herself was an anthropologist. She became one; or at least brought a similar quality of objectivity to the ten novels which began to be published in 1950, four years after the beginning of her career with *Africa.*

Objective; but all-observant. Already there are other random entries in the notebooks which show her seizing upon this new life, the anthropological life, for part of the raw material—the field notes—of her novels. Here is one of her inspirations, in a notebook of the early 1950s: "An anthropologist who had been among the head-shrinkers of the Amazon and whose own head was already beginning to look a little shrunken."

Anthropology is everywhere in the novels, specifically African anthropology, which was the kind she knew most about. If ever any novelist wrote directly out of her life—her job, her friends, her lovers, her church—it was Barbara Pym. And yet, it must be asked at once, has any novelist treated the personal more impersonally, has anyone more elegantly refined the raw material? Of the ten novels, anthropology is central in *Excellent Woman, Less than Angels, An Unsuitable Attachment,* and *A Few Green Leaves.* The detachment of anthropology becomes the detachment of archaeology in one of the novels, *A Glass of Blessings,* where it preoccupies the heroine Wilmet's sprightly mother-in-law Sybil and Sybil's friend Professor Root. Africa disappears in *The Sweet Dove Died,* the most brittle and I often think the most brilliant of her London novels, surfacing only in an incidental remark of its snobbish heroine Leonora who, speaking of her upstairs tenant, an impoverished gentlewoman, says, "One feels that using paraffin at all is somehow degrading—the sort of thing black people do, upsetting oil heaters, and setting the place on fire." Elsewhere Africa surfaces ubiquitously, in comic images, similes, titles of pedantic articles, jargon, incidental sly descriptions, names for anthropologists, and most of all in the confrontations between English and African, two worlds and their ways. . . .

What were the dimensions of Barbara Pym's world? The geography of Barbara Pym consists of Oxfordshire villages and London, especially London suburbia, and, in the other geography of the mind, religion and anthropology were her studious concerns. One of the great richnesses of her novels derives from the contrast between the rites of anthropological Africa and the ceremonies of the world her characters, and we ourselves, think of as civilized, a churchy world of flower festival and rummage sale. How basic this contrast is in her books! It is a contrast between the raw and the refined, between the Congo and the Cotswolds, between the anthropophagist, if such there be, and the anthropologist, who bravely attempts to bridge the two worlds. This juxtaposition is the comic staple of the novels.

Charles Burkhart. Twentieth Century Literature. Spring, 1983, pp. 47–49

As one reads Barbara Pym's ten novels for the first time, one is apt to experience them as a curious mixture of the familiar and the strange. The reader will certainly be reminded of Jane Austen by their quiet but often hilarious comedy, avoidance of dramatic and startling events, unerring eye for social detail, focus upon the everyday lives of rather well-off English people, modest, lucid language, and firm, though often unstressed, reliance on a Christian scheme of moral values. And Pym's novels also have some obvious similarities to Anthony Trollope's: their use of the chronicle form, interest in the lives and loves of middle-aged people, skeptical attitude toward marriage, and recurring concern with the varieties of Anglicanism. Clearly, then, Pym's novels revive a great and familiar literary tradition.

But the mere act of transferring the realistic tradition of Austen and Trollope to a mid- or late twentieth-century setting has the effect of radically altering its impact upon readers. We are willing enough, for example, to accept the reality of an early nineteenth-century spinster, like Miss Bates in *Emma,* who contents herself with a quiet life spent in the bosom of her family, but similar characters from Pym's novels, such as Belinda and Harriet Bede in *Some Tame Gazelle* or Rhoda Wellcome in *Less than Angels,* tend to strike us as anachronisms, in need of special explanation. If they don't marry, why don't they work? If they neither marry nor work, how can they be happy? These days this is the sort of attitude toward the female psyche that we almost automatically espouse. Because she is a twentieth-century novelist Pym's failure to share these attitudes seems somewhat startling. . . .

Perhaps the most unusual features of Pym's novels are the sort of people she chooses to write about and the unfailing respect and sympathy with which she treats them. As one of the characters in *Quartet in Autumn* complains, "the position of an unmarried, unattached, ageing woman is of no interest whatsoever to the writer of modern fiction." And not of all that much interest to the writer of earlier fiction, either, she might have added, though there are exceptions of whom Trollope is perhaps the most notable. Pym sets out to redress this injustice.

Jane Nordin. *Barbara Pym* (Boston: Twayne, 1985), p. 8, 10

Barbara Pym's novels center on one great subject. "Some tame gazelle or some gentle dove or even a poodle dog: something to *love,* that was the point." This paraphrase of some lines from a half-remembered poem, which appears in Pym's first novel, is the perfect epigraph for her work as a whole. Although the near-quotation comes from a refinedly repressed spinster given to sighing over the unattainable man of her chaste dreams, she identifies the need whose expression or denial moves, shapes, or disfigures all of Pym's major characters: a glamorous young woman, an inelegant gay man, a retired woman losing her mind, or a country rector—women and men with radically different lives and personalities—all explore, in their individual ways, the guises of love, sought, attained, or frustrated.

Pym looks with a compassionate but penetrating eye at love in its different aspects. Every variety finds a place in her work; the heterosexual and homosexual types—even if we break them down into requited, unrequited, and, somewhere between these, the comfortable ardors of pure fantasy—are only its more obvious kinds. Especially when romantic love fails them or is not an option, for one reason or another, Pym's characters seek to find emotional sustenance in the affections of friendship or family ties; in the Christian love that asks "who is my neighbor?"; in the fondness for "child substitutes," human or not; and in the asexual "unsentimental tenderness . . . expressed in small gestures of solicitude" that one solidary soul might extend to another. *Extend* is the key word in Pym's universe, the heart and mind require an object as the bridge from their fearful isolation to the world of feeling and caring. . . .

In addition to treating the need and expression of love in its romantic or other manifestations, Pym eventually treats its total absence or failure. Characteristically, her forte is comedy. . . .

Barbara Pym published ten novels, and an eleventh was published in 1985 after her death. Her work was "discovered" recently in this country, and hailed as a comic masterpiece. This is praise, indeed, and accurate—in part: it fails to take into account the development of the author's vision on two fronts, from a feminine to a universal perspective and from the comic to the tragic mode. Pym's novels tell us a great deal about the lives of women and the problems peculiar to them, but her achievement was to become an astute chronicler of concerns and issues fundamental to both sexes. Her early novels suggest that she considers the inner lives of women her particular province; however, as her confidence in the universality of her vision grows, men become more prominent citizens of that province.

Diana Benet. *Something to Love: Barbara Pym's Novels* (Columbia: University of Missouri Press, 1986), pp. 1–2

Pym's commentators . . . have not been unanimous in finding her a modern-day Jane Austen. John Updike has remarked that "Miss Pym has been compared to Jane Austen, yet there is a virile country health in the Austen novels [not found in Pym's], and some vivid marital prospects for her blooming heroines." Other reviewers have noted that while Austen's characters stand firmly at the center of their imagined world, Pym's occupy a merely peripheral place in theirs. Nicholas Shrimpton, with this contrast in mind, has noted that "strict social and geographical limitation has at times prompted comparison with Jane Austen. But Pym's characteristic exiguity is far more than mere effect of setting. Where Austen was a Romantic miniaturist, Pym is a twentieth century minimalist. . . .

It is not as much that Pym's fiction is a twentieth-century version of Austen's as that while having certain affinities with her she is also distinctly different. What is conspicuous in Pym's novels . . . is her allegiance to classical form. With their clarity of theme, conscious restriction of scope, and elaborate symmetries of plot and characterization, Pym's novels belong to a tradition established by Austen in the early nineteenth century—so much so that they make Pym's disavowal of any possible influence seem disingenuous. Other similarities have been pointed out by reviewers—their absorption with domestic life, courtship, and marriage; their detachment, wit, and feminine point of view. But at a certain point the similarities end. Austen's characters have a solidity that comes from their belonging confidently to a social order that has tremendous reality in her imagination. It is an order that, if presumptuous perhaps in its consciousness of itself as the *great* reality, is nevertheless coherent and vibrant. The energies of Pym's world, on the other hand, are running down, and her characters are less certain of their place in society or of their connections with other people. If Austen is able to resolve the discordant relation of her characters into harmony, Pym can do so only apparently, for the isolation of her heroines is irremediable.

Robert Emmet Long. *Barbara Pym* (New York: Ungar Publishing, 1986), pp. 202, 204

The bachelor figure in Pym's novels is a curiously emasculated individual with many of the characteristics usually associated with spinsters. . . . Pym's bachelor character is separated from other men singled out for special treatment. He is the least sympathetic of Pym's characters: embittered, disgruntled, vulnerable, pathetic, petty, cynical, ambitious and selfish. While other characters may embody some of these traits from time to time, the bachelor is far more likely to possess an inordinate number of unpleasant qualities. Why? In Pym's view the bachelor possesses too much freedom. This total lack of responsibility to anyone other than himself is, in a sense, his downfall. The bachelor is under no obligation to alter his behavior for anyone, particularly for any woman. Married men, on the other hand, must defer on occasion to the needs of others, even if it is only to their wives. Because bachelors are absolutely free of the constraints and restrictions imposed by marriage, they constitute a special category of males in Pym's fiction.

While the dominant social order privileges the bachelor, on the deepest level of the narrative Pym exempts the bachelor from normal social obligations and relegates him to a marginal position. . . .

The bachelor's autonomy is shown as a burden rather than as enviable, because he is lonely and unfulfilled. This contrasts sharply with Pym's depiction of the joyous autonomy of the spinster, who is not tied to serving a man; the bachelor is only free from the responsibilities that come from being attached to a female. The wide and wild speculation that Sophia in *An Unsuitable Attachment* believes to be engendered by the bachelor is emblematic of Pym's subversive narrative strategy. By exempting the bachelor from the dual-voiced narrative, Pym invents a wide and wild strategy that undermines the patriarchy.

Laura L. Doan. In Janice Rossen, ed. *Independent Women: The Function of Gender in the Novels of Barbara Pym* (Brighton: Harvester; New York: St. Martin's, 1988), pp. 64, 80

For those not gently obsessed by Barbara Pym's fiction, it may sound odd to speak of her heroines as subversive, since they are hardly radicals who protest loudly against the dominant culture's expectations. Still, I maintain that on the miniaturized scale of the novel of manners, which examines the intricacies of how men and women think and act, such a protest is indeed taking place. . . .

Pym's heroines and narrators are not overtly feminist in the sense that they set out to overthrow male domination, but they do dramatize the heroine's perception of the discrepancy between her own and the dominant culture's assumptions, whether the dominant culture is represented by a male or by a group of men and women. . . .

The subversiveness of the heroines and of the narrators allows them to challenge the complacency of the male and female characters around them who conform to the dominant culture. But these challenges promote private laughter and a critical examination of their own assumptions too. They take place in an inner private space shared by narrator, heroine and reader rather than in the public space of the interaction between characters.

Barbara Bowen. In Janice Rossen, ed.
*Independent Women: The Function of
Gender in the Novels of Barbara Pym*
(Brighton: Harvester; New York: St.
Martin's, 1988), pp. 84–85, 92

To illustrate the central role homosexuality plays in Barbara Pym's novels is less to define it than to reveal her large-scaled impartial tolerance, and this intrinsic morality is one of the best reasons we have for liking and admiring her books. Our notion that she is a conventional writer evanesces, to be replaced by the recognition that her range is bolder than we might have thought.

Whatever homosexuality is, it is widely there, and it appears in all twelve novels by Barbara Pym which have so far been published. . . . Throughout the twelve novels, straight men are most of the time rather terrible creatures. She once protested that she *"loved"* men, but her novels do not show that she did. How often are her men preposterously vain, selfish, self-pitying and self-indulgent: men who use women, women who too often acquiesce because they have to. Anyone who has read Barbara Pym's work has noticed it. From the asperities of Archdeacon Hoccleve in *Some Tame Gazelle* to the flabby vanities of Graham Pettifer in *A Few Green Leaves*, straight men are out for what they can get, and the way the world is, they usually succeed. In a sense the homosexual men, or some of them, are a solace, though by no means a solution. For every pale and ineffectual curate there is a Wilf Bason; she had met him and knew him, and her experience and knowledge can enlarge and instruct our own. Her world is not so narrow after all.

Charles Burkhart. In Janice Rossen, ed.
*Independent Women: The Function of
Gender in the Novels of Barbara Pym*
(Brighton: Harvester; New York: St.
Martin's, 1988), pp. 95, 104–5

The relationship between men and women is central to Barbara Pym's novels, the intricacies of plot and subplot revolving around potential matches and mismatches between any number of pairs of males and females. Although many of her characters want very much to be loved and married, Pym's portrayal of such relationships makes one wonder why they bother. "Love" is a word Pym frequently uses to describe how men and women feel about one another, but it is a passionless emotion, seldom emerging in any of the characters as a genuinely felt experience. Marriages are often slightly antagonistic arrangements whereby each spouse has learned to tolerate the other's idiosyncrasies. Men are ineffectual, childish creatures who want women to be little more than domestic servants and clerical help, believing such services are their due and taking for granted that women should devote themselves exclusively to their needs. Women are defined in relationship to men and most have accepted the prevailing social belief that a woman is not fulfilled until she has married. . . .

By and large, most of Pym's characters, male or female, want love and marriage. Pym's particular comic stance points out the often ridiculous lengths men and women go to in order to attain those things by portraying the tremendous burden social attitudes and expectations surrounding romance and marriage place on women in a society where there are far too many women for the number of available men. With supreme irony, she also demonstrates how that social attitude toward women results in wonderful perquisites for men. Thus, when Beatrix Howick tells her daughter in Pym's final novel that the relationship between men and women is ridiculous, she is voicing a sentiment that Pym has illustrated throughout her canon.

Katherine Anne Ackley. The Novels of
Barbara Pym (New York: Garland, 1989),
pp. 33, 71

Pym's account of female experience, though often amusing, is by no means simply comfortable. Her fiction, it has been widely observed, has as a central focus the shock of disappointment and rejection. Her heroines have repeatedly to cope with feelings of neglect, desolation and loneliness. The theme of disappointment and the perception of underlying futility suggest the potential crisis with which her characters and their author have to deal. Where Pym fundamentally differs from the braggadocio of some male modernist writers (hard-riding existentialists, profuse Joyceans, insistent nihilists) is in her refusal to identify with meaninglessness—which is also a refusal to separate art from our human need to make meaning in our lives. Meaning must be sustained amongst us by good humor, a delight in the absurd, recurrent small gestures, taking an interest, loving anyway. Life delivers disappointments but if those disappointments are accepted—the virtue is humility—small joys and satisfactions still await us. Art is a way of sustaining a humorous and hopeful engagement with life. One of the attractions of Pym's novels is that we sense in them the author's own repeated commitment to hopefulness, the repeated act of imagining possibility. If we sometimes detect in her what she explores in some of her characters, a refusal at some level of life and relationship, we can also admire the candor of her exploration and her delight in the range of experience she does allow herself.

Michael Cotsell. *Barbara Pym* (New York:
St. Martin's, 1989), p. 5

Despite the originality and incisiveness of her fiction, Pym has been dismissed by many academics and serious literary critics. Her conservative views and extremely accessible style made her an outsider in the literary circles to which she aspired. Scholars lavish praise upon the works of Margaret Drabble, Doris Lessing, and Irish Murdoch with critical studies but practically ignore Barbara Pym. Their denser prose and more complex plots establish them clearly as writers of import, whereas Pym's emphasis on the domestic and the personal, rather than on feminist, psychological, and philosophical issues, has led to a mistaken condescension toward her work. For example, the novelist A. S. Byatt claims that Pym appeals to "fogies of various ages." In her view, "the new philistinism and the old" together have created a spurious academic interest in Pym.

Yet Pym's novels are important. . . . Pym's novels present a very significant, if minority opinion about social attitudes. They are not overtly feminist. Indeed the novelist herself defined success as having a husband. Nonetheless, being a female was central to her experience. She shared the perspective of marginal women of her generation, who, despite education and cultivation, felt they had no recognizable role left in the modern world. She observed that social changes had undermined their inherited status. Yet Pym presents this alienation with comic good humor. Her novels have a subversive flavor, rather like the wry stories mothers and daughters have traditionally exchanged about male absurdities and female forbearance.

Pym's novels have shown considerable popular appeal. Readers have appreciated her sympathetic wit, comic flair, and gift of expression. But no critic has hitherto attempted to unwind the many strands that created the texture of her life and work. Read from a life-cycle perspective, her novels contribute to the understanding of gender specialists, gerontologists, writing and reading theorists, and psychoanalysts, as well as to any dispassionate person interested in the careers of talented women. To grasp the unique contribution of her work, however, one must view her novels in all their quirky particularity.

Anne M. Wyatt-Brown. *Barbara Pym: A
Critical Biography* (Columbia: University of
Missouri Press, 1992), pp. 1–2

QUEIROZ, RACHEL DE (BRAZIL) 1910–

Rachel's independence of thought should not be considered as aimed at the destruction of the social order or as an attack upon marriage, religion, or morals. The course followed by Noemi [in *Road of Stones*] and by Guta [in *The Three Marias*] is not for ordinary persons but for those few with the absolute courage of their convictions, who stand outside the bounds of society, where only grief and pain await them. As the critic Almir de Andrade has expressed it, "Rachel de Queiroz manages to reach—quietly, without emotionalism—an inner plane of life which few can boast of having been able to attain, or rather, of having been able to discover; a plane of absolute and paradoxical sincerity, which lies beyond all our conventions, all our actions motivated by hypocrisy and sham, all our prejudices and submission to routine. A plane which lies beyond good and evil." Rachel de Queiroz, like her protagonists, has had the courage to invade this realm, not as an iconoclast, but as a searcher after truth. And as an artist, one of the most gifted of the present generation, she has been able to give beautiful form to her tragic but inspiring vision. . . .

The unit of composition of all her novels (three of which are objectively related, the fourth, *The Three Marias,* being narrated in the first person) is the short, carefully balanced chapter, often with the unity and completeness of a good short story. Rachel constructs her novels somewhat loosely, concentrating on significant moments in the lives of her characters. She avoids any pretense of a rightly woven plot. Thanks to her sense of the dramatic and her grasp of meaningful detail, monotony is rare in her novels.

The unity in the technique and construction of Rachel de Queiroz's novels is also to be found in their language. When *The Year Fifteen* was published, in 1930, the revolutionary gains made by the modernists were far from being consolidated. . . . In Brazil today it would be more appropriate, perhaps, to apologize for a literary idiom that failed to incorporate a good many elements of the popular spoken language. This has come about precisely because of the success of such books as *The Year Fifteen* and the rest of Rachel's works, which not only in the dialogue but also in the narrative remain faithful to the Portuguese spoken by Brazilians. . . .

Simplicity, sobriety, and directness are characteristic of all her writing, but are most highly refined in *The Three Marias*. Rachel is fond of using figurative language, but probably does so no more often than do people in ordinary conversation.

Fred P. Ellison. *Brazil's New Novel*
(Berkeley: University of California Press,
1954), pp. 152–53

The novelist who is a true artist will endeavor to get close to his characters, to penetrate within their souls, to understand them, not to pass judgment on them. While Amado rarely achieves this, Ramos and Rachel de Queiroz do, and with remarkable skill. Probing deeply within her characters, Rachel de Queiroz roves at large in their intimate realms of feeling, sympathetic and understanding, never condemning. Her heart wells over with pity for suffering humanity, especially for women, who so long have held a subordinate place in Brazilian society. Yet this compassion is not reserved for her sex alone. Raúl, an aging painter and libertine, fond of seducing young girls, is portrayed as a human being with human frailties. In the flirtation between him and Guta, the heroine of *The Three Marias,* she who leads him on in her innocence and then refuses to satisfy his desires appears just as guilty as he, if not more so.

Dexterously Rachel de Queiroz portrays the pathos of the family and its genteel heartlessness. This is perhaps best exemplified in the character of Guta's stepmother, a stodgy woman utterly lacking in imagination and warmth, who tried to be kind and do the proper thing by her stepdaughter. . . .

Rachel de Queiroz's warm mother-attitude towards her fellow men never gushes over into soppy sentimentalism. Her sharply intuitive sensibilities are balanced by a keen and clear mind. When Aluizio, a foolish romantic youth who pines away with love for Guta but never tells her of it, takes poison and then on his deathbed blurts out his passion before all the neighbors and relatives, Guta's reaction is perfectly logical: unstung by remorse, she feels only resentment that Aluizio should have betrayed her thus, placing her in such an uncomfortable position.

Employing a similar technique to that of Ramos in *Anguish,* Rachel de Queiroz occasionally delves into the past of her characters by means of flashbacks; however, they do not disturb the smooth flow of her narrative. Both writers thoroughly grasp the sense of time and its undertow forever dragging us back into the past which we regret or blame. But whereas in *Anguish* the protagonist's mind travels back and forth, mingling past and present continuously in an abstract perspective, in *The Three Marias* the shifting of time is more conscious and clear-cut.

George D. Schade. *Hispania.* 39, December,
1956, pp. 393–94

[Queiroz] conceives all her characters as sensitive human beings, and she conveys her interest in them by singling out the humble details of day-to-day life that affect them sentimentally. There is the scene [in *João Miguel*] where a refugee, fleeing on foot from the drought and harassed by his children's hunger, sees a man milking a cow. Automatically he extends his hand, but suddenly he realizes that he is begging for the first time in his life, and he runs away in shame without saying a word. Or one could cite the Sunday that João Miguel, still a prisoner, swallows glass upon glass of smuggled rum. The usually quiet man becomes a braggadocio, threatens to kill the soldier who stole his woman, behaves rowdily toward the sweet girl who has come to see her father. The next day he apologizes in humiliation. And so it goes; scene after scene expresses the author's vision of her characters through their reactions to ordinary experiences of their daily lives. She does not need external drama; incidents like these take on the proportions of drama for those involved.

For all her creations she feels a real sympathy. She understands why one hates or loves another, but she never takes sides with any of them. Her impartiality is particularly notable in *Road of Stones,* where the story of the Communist group would have given another writer a pretext for weighting his treatment heavily. Rachel de Queiroz transmits to her reader the enthusiasm of some for the work, the disillusion and caution of others. What her own attitude toward the cause may be, we cannot infer from her book; her interest centers not in the idea, but in the problems, the decisions, the joys, the heartaches of the individuals affected by it. Her wide range of sympathy protects her from impassive objectivity; she can understand differing points of view, and she presents them all sympathetically. . . .

The deceptive simplicity of expression . . . distinguishes her among her famous compatriots of the Brazilian Northeast. We have only to read a novel that she wrote in collaboration with them, *Brandão between the Sea and Love,* to gain a clear notion of the distinctive manner of each of them. In the lyrical prose of Jorge Amado, in the nervous writing of José Lins do Rêgo, even in the spare style of Graciliano Ramos, the reader feels the effort to create a given mood. Rachel de Queiroz achieves a deeper emotion, a more telling effect with a simplicity that seems effortless; in point of fact, however, it is a simplicity that she can have attained only through constant and stern self-criticism and self-discipline. It seems artless, but is in reality an art so polished that it conceals its art.

Benjamin M. Woodbridge. Hispania. 40,
May, 1957, pp. 145, 147

Accepting nativism as capable of forming the basis for a tragedy, Rachel de Queiroz [in *Lampião*] has opened up new perspectives in the renovation of literature, using the national condition as the raw material for noble artistic expression. Her first drama, a play in five scenes, based on one of the most legendary episodes in the heroic saga of Brazil, seems to me to be chiefly of value as literature, but it is also a sensitive theatrical experience.

She focuses on the Northeast landscape, which serves as background and underlines the scenes, and she singles out what is perhaps the region's most characteristic type, the *cangaceiro* [bandit]. She could have transformed him, if she had wanted to. . . . But, faithful to her material, she preferred to re-create an episode from his life.

Adonias [Aguiar] Filho. Modernos
ficcionistas brasileiros (Rio de Janeiro:
Edições O Cruzeiro, 1958), p. 222

Lampião, Rachel de Queiroz's first theatrical work, which enchanted so many readers and spectators, left me, I must confess, with rather mixed feelings. In it, Queiroz, although already in command of the requisite art of creating characters, putting them on the stage, and making them speak, still was looking for dramatic confrontation in skirmishes. It is as if someone were to see the heart of classical tragedy not in the intimate lacerating conflict of Phaedra but in the horrible duel of the dragon and Hippolytus.

Blessed Mary of Egypt, which has just been published, dispels any impression that Queiroz is a tentative or insecure dramatist. After having conquered the novel and the chronicle, she has now taken control of one more domain. More accustomed to reading plays than to seeing them on the stage, I am not quite able to evaluate the theatrical possibilities of the work; but I think it would offer an extraordinary opportunity for a company that possessed four first-rate actors. In any case, the book, enhanced with the powerful illustrations of Luís Jardim, is addressed to the reader—and it wins him over.

The play re-creates the life of a well-known saint, Mary of Egypt, who, when she lacked the money to pay the price of a river crossing, arranged transportation by giving herself to the boatman. In the vast corpus of Christian legends, there are few narratives that are so surprising, so capable of causing one to reflect, so full of romantic overtones. Among our writers, it had already inspired a ballad by Manuel Bandeira. . . .

The play is not, however, as one might suppose, a reconstruction of the legend in a dated exotic setting. Rather, Queiroz found in the story eternal dramatic situations applicable to any setting in which there are souls inclined to be strongly passionate, submissive to superstition, and susceptible to fanaticism.

Paulo Rónai. *Encontros com o Brasil* (Rio de Janeiro: Ministério da Educação e Cultura, 1958), pp. 191–92

[*The Year Fifteen*], Queiroz's first work, published when she was twenty, was a continuation of the Brazilian genre of the novel about the drought cycles [in the Northeast]. The novel revealed a gifted writer, whose qualities would reach their full flowering in her later works. If her first work shows her to be a natural, direct, colloquial, and sober writer, one conditioned by her environment . . . it also does not conceal serious defects in structure and psychology, in development and narration. After three third-person novels— *The Year Fifteen, João Miguel,* and *Road of Stones*—she shifted to the first-person point of view in *The Three Marias;* and although the subject matter in all these novels was equally biographical, she gained immediacy and authenticity by employing the first-person point of view.

Within the context of the geographical and social problems of the Northeast, Queiroz's central theme is the position of woman in the modern world, with its moral and social preconceptions. The female characters in her books, drawn with psychological subtlety, react against the dependent and inferior state of woman. These novels chronicle the rebellion of individuals against the domestic and social order, which has reduced woman to the condition of prisoner of an archaic tradition.

Nevertheless, despite her stance and her documentary, sociological subject matter, Rachel de Queiroz's novels do not have the markings of political, revolutionary, or propagandistic literature. She exposes problems without suggesting solutions.

Afrânio Coutinho. *A literatura no Brasil*
(Rio de Janeiro: Editorial Sul Americana,
1970), Vol. 5, pp. 219–20

In 1930 [Queiroz] made a sensational debut as a novelist with *The Year Fifteen,* which was received with enthusiastic critical acclaim throughout Brazil. The fact of her youth contributed to this success, but more important was the fact that the novel was one of the first, after *Sugar Mill* by José Américo de Almeida, to introduce to Brazil a new social-minded literature of the 1930s. Though the periodical droughts in northeastern Brazil had been the theme of a few earlier novels, the literary school initiated with the books of Américo de Almeida and Rachel de Queiroz substituted social and even socialist intentions and preoccupations for the traditional sentimental approach to that tragedy. The novel's title refers to the year of 1915, in which one of the most catastrophic droughts occurred. All these circumstances explain the immense interest awakened by *The Year Fifteen,* which was awarded the Graça Aranha Foundation literary prize in 1931.

In 1932, Rachel de Queiroz's second novel, *João Miguel,* was a tentative effort toward a proletarian novel. Its hero is in fact an antihero, the common man of northeast Brazil. In terms of Rachel de Queiroz's development as a novelist, it marks a transition from the social to the psychological approach. . . .

In the 1940s Rachel de Queiroz began to write columns for several newspapers and particularly for the periodical *O cruzeiro*. Her chronicles gained widespread popularity in Brazil and assured her reputation as one of Brazil's outstanding writers. Many of these chronicles were subsequently collected into books.

Wilson Martins. In Wolfgang Bernard
Fleischmann, ed. *Encyclopedia of World
Literature in the 20th Century,* (New York:
Frederick Ungar, 1971), p. 136

A prominent member of the Northeastern group of Brazilian writers, Rachel de Queiroz has distinguished herself for her quiet, unobtrusive style and her unabating insistence on presenting the familiar, everyday scenes, mostly of Northeastern Brazil, which constitute the basic scenario of a woman's life.

The main theme of Rachel de Queiroz's fiction is the Brazilian woman of the Northeast, her life, her character, and her role in society. While critics agree that the theme of woman is central to her novels, they have differing views regarding the specific adaptation and focus of this theme. . . .

In her novels, Rachel de Queiroz reveals her view of the condition of woman through the various stages of feminine problematic inherent in the seemingly common heroine stereotypes: Conceição, the avowed spinster; Santa, the martyred whore; Noemi, the liberated woman; Guta, the woman in search of herself; even the stage of resolution represented by Dora, Doralina, the woman-come-home. Dora, the heroine of the last novel, having gone through all the problematic stages presented in the earlier novels, is able to overcome them all to become the prototype of a free woman, alone and sufficient unto herself. Beyond containing universal and stereotypical elements, Rachel's heroines always remain profoundly human individuals with a problematic, which while being universal remains at the same time uniquely their own.

Joanna Courteau. Luso-Brazilian Review. 22,
1985, pp. 123–25

QUIROGA, ELENA (SPAIN) 1919–

I have in my hands a rich and beautiful book [*North Wind*], which won the Nadal Prize in 1950.

You can spend a long time with this book in your hands because although its reading holds your attention throughout the narration and the perfectly achieved dramatic atmosphere reaches a high point at the end of the novel, there are in this book passages and calm spots and beautiful sections that ought to be savored slowly, as one savors the colors of the earth and fragrances and the sparkling of water during a slow walk through the country. As in a walk in the countryside of Galicia—described so magnificently— when one reads this book the senses are drenched with the clean and delicate surrounding moisture, with the softness of mud, with the greenness of groves, and with old legends. A great restfulness, a serenity, a sweetness of life with a sense of continuity, of quietude, of peace, comes upon you. I, the reader, feel profoundly moved and thank the author of this novel for the presence of eternal roots deeply implanted into the soul of the land.

This book is without time. In the anguish of time that surrounds us, the anguish of the hours that pursue us, of the intense and burning problems, which although we may not wish them to, grab us by their claws, I do not know if this lack of obsession about time is a defect or perhaps the most accomplished mark of intuition that the great writer has had and has revealed to us in *North Wind*.

The characters from the patriarchal life of the Galician estates do not live in our age. Respected and beloved masters, servants content with their lot, united by a mysterious respect and love in the obedience to a kind but firm gesture of their master. They are not from our anguish-filled times—these people for whom life flows slowly and ponderously. Elena Quiroga has not wished them to be, but by leaving open the period to which they belong, perhaps secretly, she has wished that they were our contemporaries. Upon reading her novel, we wish they were too. . . . Elena Quiroga, youthful, full of creative energy, impulsiveness and love for her craft enters the front ranks of contemporary Spanish novelists with *North Wind*.

Carmen Laforet. *Destino.* May 12, 1951, p. 7

Among the many young novelists writing in Spain today, Elena Quiroga is unquestionably one of the most able and interesting. . . .

Notably manifest in the novels of Elena Quiroga are the qualities most essential in a writer of fiction: imagination, creative ability, and command of subject matter. Perhaps the highest compliment that can be offered this author is to say that interest in her stories rarely ever flags. Her novels possess that power of sustained attraction, which Ortega y Gasset calls "imperviousness," whereby the reader is held engrossed in a novelistic world from which he has little desire to withdraw. Part of Elena Quiroga's success in this regard can be attributed to her faculty for producing and maintaining a captivating mood or compelling atmosphere into which the reader is readily drawn. Interest in her fiction, however, derives chiefly from character portrayal, for which she has a superb capacity. Although her primary concern is the depiction of the inner lives of her character, she knows how to effect a proper balance between the purely psychological and external reality. Her novels, free of transcendental intent except as the reader may choose to infer, are penetrating studies of human nature in which the problems and conflicts presented are of a kind to give the reader a deepened understanding of human experience and a sense of personal enrichment.

Albert Brent. *Hispania.* May, 1959, pp. 210, 213

We believe that [*The Mask*] is a fine and perfect example of harmony between novelistic technique and the level of consciousness that is communicated to the reader. Elena Quiroga's *The Mask* has not had all the critical fortune it deserves. For some critics it is no more than a *tour de force* of technique, difficult to read, and therefore, something less than satisfactory as a novelistic creation. In accordance with what is already a tradition in stream-of-consciousness novels, when the key or structuring motif is grasped, the problem of comprehension is eliminated, and all the elements that make up this strange world are justified—a world that forms itself according to how the protagonist is stimulated by memories that come bubbling up from his past. . . .

A great number of contemporary Spanish novels are touched by the theme of the civil war and its social and personal consequences. Moisés is, in a certain way, a product of that Spanish experience. *The Mask* is part and parcel of this tradition, not on a sociological level but on a psychological one. Moisés is a social failure, an alcoholic and without hope. As a human being he is complex, apathetic, and totally frustrated. Elena Quiroga does not focus on her character as a social entity. Consequently, she does not censure him. She creates an individual for us who is naked on the inside and whose raw and painful truth evokes contradictory feelings in the reader. He is annoying because he lacks vital energy in order to emerge from his psychological morass. Compassion for the child Moisés! The novel transports us to his world, and seeing him flee into cowardice and into an inability to overcome his personal mode of being, angers us. His egotism is terrifying. Nevertheless, he is a man who has suffered since childhood and is now in need of salvation. The possibility of his enjoying life without bitterness, without disgust, escapes him when he leaves Augustín wounded or dead (we do not know exactly). The blood that he spills and that stains his hands anew does not redeem him from the nauseating smell of blood that has been with him since his childhood.

> Juan Villegas. *Cuadernos Hispano-*
> *americanos.* August–September, 1968,
> pp. 638–39, 648

Something's Happening in the Street is a good, well-modulated novel, poetic, simple in its structure and plot but complex in its psychological implications. It describes fairly well the society of Madrid of the 1950s. Although it is decidedly *not* a mystery novel, we still have no clear answer as to whether Ventura fell accidentally or committed suicide. Of major concern to us is Ventura's revelations through the thoughts of his family about the society in which he lives and the people he dealt with on a daily basis. . . .

One . . . notes Quiroga's tendency towards poetic lyricism, which diffuses the action of the novel, as well as the lack of psychological analysis of the motivations, conduct and beliefs despite the heavy reliance upon interior monologue to reveal the realities of her protagonists. We never have a *clear* idea of how the characters look or what they do. Nevertheless, *Something's Happening in the Street* is definitely a New Wave novel and Quiroga is firmly entrenched in this group precisely because of her efforts to renew the novel genre, inject it with poetic lyricism, deal with contemporary problems and probe her protagonists' psyches through the use of interior monologue. In this way, Quiroga definitely departs from nineteenth-century Realism. . . .

Quiroga's character creations do speak frankly. . . She is concerned with Spanish society as it is, implicit with its moral and social implications. Although some of her characters do not reach a level of reality for me because they seem more imaginary than real and because at times she refuses to concretize their feelings, heavily insisting upon poetic lyricism, Quiroga is still one of the few novelists, in keeping with the New Wave, who has tried to give new directions to the Spanish novel. Although we may consider her use of interior monologue, flashback, dichotomies between what is thought and said rather stylistically archaic now, we must have thought Eugene O'Neill mad in the 1920s when *Strange Interlude* was first presented on Broadway and his characters stepped out of their roles to talk to the audience and directly reveal their thoughts to us. In similar fashion, Quiroga does this in her novels of the early 1950s, but her insistence on writing about contemporary themes combined with an easy facility with words and a marvelous creative sense make her one of the leading novelists of modern Spain today.

> Ronald Schwartz. *Spain's New Wave Novelists* (Metuchen, New Jersey, Scarecrow, 1976), pp. 70–72

Throughout her novelistic development, Quiroga has articulated themes of freedom and solitude, concepts that relate both to her growing disillusionment with institutionalized religion and to her increasing emphasis on existential philosophy. Her characters are often solitary, even alienated individuals who know that they must seek the meaning of their lives within themselves; like Tadea [in *Sadness*] they insist upon the liberty to do so. Such a viewpoint is closely related to that of existentialism. . . . The individual has the freedom to shape his or her own identity, but with that freedom goes responsibility. Quiroga goes beyond merely symbolizing freedom through such images as the sea *(Blood)*, bulls *(The Last Bullfight)*, and wild horses *Sadness)* to insist upon responsibility in a Sartrean sense. Felisa in *The Mask* accuses the older generation of using the "senseless circumstances" of the Civil War as an excuse for failing to take positive action. For her even Moisés is to blame for his own destiny. The progressive priest in *I Write Your Name* thus rejects Ortega's formula "I am I and my circumstance" because the individual should transcend and indeed mold that circumstance as part of himself. Among Quiroga's characters there are at least two who behave as existential heroines, willing not only to accept their freedom and act but also to assume full responsibility for those acts. Presencia in *Something's Happening in the Street* has been faithful to her own conscience and is able to withstand society's ostracism for the choices that she has made. Carola in *I Write Your Name* expresses what she believes and with the dignity accepts her punishment— expulsion from the convent school—assuming responsibility for the group even though her classmates are too cowardly to stand with her.

> Phyllis Zatlin Boring. *Elena Quiroga* (Boston: Twayne, 1977), pp. 127–28

Elena Quiroga stands in a variety of positions in relation to the characters in her works. In many novels she steps back completely and allows the "implied author" to assume control of the narrative, often taking advantage of his omniscience to peer at random into the minds of several characters in order to relate the story from a variety of perspectives. Yet Quiroga's most poignant protagonists are undoubtedly those who speak directly in the first person. These dramatized narrators lend an extremely personal tone to the novels in which they appear and emphasize the semi-autobiographical nature of much of Quiroga's writing. More importantly, they build a foundation for the ironical undertones which abound in her works and are inseparably interwoven with the presentation of one of her major themes: The schism between reality and illusion. . . .

There are a number of general observations which can be made regarding the narrators which Quiroga uses to tell her tales. Three of these first-person voices are so closely similar to her own as to appear semi-autobiographical, and these novels are, in fact, based to some degree on her own experiences. Only *La sangre* offers a dramatized narrator who could not be mistaken for Quiroga herself. There is no reason why this should be surprising, for "the narrator is often radically different from the implied author who creates him," yet the preponderance of Quiroga-like women narrators makes the *castaño* notable for his variance from the norm. Since a non-human narrator enjoys the greatest ability to comment dispassionately on man's habit of self-delusion, Quiroga's creativity is of great thematic advantage in this novel. . . .

Quiroga's dramatized narrators appear to be searching for various things. Some must fight feelings of guilt and inadequacy; other battle hostility and bewilderment at what befalls them; still others seek only love. Yet there is an underlying quest which dominates the lives of all these *yo* voices: A desire to understand the meaning of their own existence and to ferret out the truth about the world around them. Reality in Quiroga's novels is never a constant, attainable thing, but the quest for truth is seen everywhere. Even in *Plácida, la joven,* where there is little overt attention paid to the theme, the novelist manages to tease the reader with the multiple planes of reality which she has built into this short work. In the other novels, it is the first-person narrator who offers most of the thematic insights. Nevertheless, throughout all five works, the give-and-take relationship between the author, the narrator, and the reader heightens this sense of mutual quest for an elusive reality in a world of illusions.

Martha Alford Marks. ALEC. 5, 1980,
pp. 39, 53–54

Elena Quiroga has been one of the first Spanish writers of the post-war literary generation to experiment creatively with time, and her novels reveal an extremely varied approach to this subject. Two novels in the traditional vein proceed chronologically from start to finish according to cosmic time, with no mental digressions. Others maintain a similar objective chronology, but are interrupted subjectively to a greater or lesser extent by flashbacks or thought projections into the future. There are some works which take place chronologically within a relatively brief period of clock time, yet mental time intrudes to flesh out the psychology of the characters. Finally, in some novels the chronological events are extremely limited in time and take place within a single afternoon or evening, yet the past is evoked so frequently and so abruptly that it fuses with the present to create a simultaneous narration on two temporal planes. It is in this last category that one finds Quiroga's most experimental novels. . . .

Whatever her ultimate place in the history of twentieth-century Spanish literature may be, Elena Quiroga has played an important role by experimenting with time in her novels. Although occasionally she has been faulted by the critics, who often prefer the less-demanding structures of more conventional writers, Quiroga has evolved into a novelist in full control of the manipulation of temporal shifts and internal narrative rhythm.

Martha Alford Marks. *Hispania*. 64, 1981,
pp. 376, 381

Presente profundo (1973; Profound present) is one of Quiroga's most philosophical works, influenced by ideas of all time as present, and Hegel's concept of reality (as seen by the readings of Rubén, sometimes narrator). Juxtaposing the stories of the suicides of two very different women, the novel provides a significant and probing analysis of their lives and of the feminine condition. So different are the women involved that it may well be that they were intended to be seen as a composite symbol of all women. Daría is an older Galician woman, a baker's wife neglected emotionally and physically and finally cast aside for a younger female, who one day simply walks into the sea when her children, too, forget her. Blanca, a cosmopolitan young divorcée, the daughter of international millionaires from Brazil, is separated from the child she loves, lives for a while in Madrid, and drifts into the drug culture, eventually dying from an overdose while staying in a hippie commune in Holland. These two extreme examples of the feminine condition are linked by the personality of a young doctor who happened to have contact with both of them. As an existentialist, he points out the vital significance of death, and meditates upon the complexity of time, the spirit, and the eternal scheme of things, relating them to the reality of the two women. Another philosophical element introduced by Quiroga comes from Oriental religions and the concepts of transmigration of souls or reincarnation. Daría's daughter-in-law, Amelia, is her continuation to such a extent that she seems to undergo a personality change after Daría's suicide and is taken over by her spirit, even taking on her physical appearance. Blanca's hippie lover is her continuation, as he carries out the plans she had made with him. Quiroga develops a narrative counterpoint between the two women, between Galicia and the urban world beyond, between present and eternity, that subtly underscores the all-inclusive nature of the symbolic extremes.

Janet Pérez. *Contemporary Woman Writers*
of Spain (Boston: Twayne, 1988), p. 131

Throughout her narrative works, Quiroga skillfully probes the inner worlds of her characters, uncovering their psychological reality. Her search often reveals an alienated individual a Moisés, a Tadea, or a Daría, who cannot communicate with the dominant society and who therefore retreats to silence, perhaps even to a path of self-destruction. Themes of orphanhood, alienation, and class prejudice persist throughout Quiroga's fiction.

Quiroga's novels do not belong to the category of objective realism; rather, they are characterized by a poetic style and innovative, Faulknerian narrative structures. Nevertheless, they are allied with objective realism in their presentation of a strong but subtle criticism of the sociopolitical background that gives rise to the individual situations that are examined in depth. There is no related criticism of the characters because the narrative structure forces the reader to reach conclusions without a narrator-guide and because Quiroga creates no villains. Perhaps her greatest strength as a psychological novelist is her ability to help the reader understand all of the characters in her novelistic world and see them all, in Ortega's terms, as themselves and their circumstances.

Phyllis Zatlin. In Joan L. Brown, ed. *Women Writers of Contemporary Spain: Exiles in the Homeland* (Newark, Delaware: University of Delaware Press, 1991), pp. 55–56

In *La enferma* the absence of woman's own voice is centered on Liberata, the maturing village woman who slipped out of verbal intercourse and into mutism when her beloved, Telmo, failed to return to her many years before. The visiting protagonist becomes a listener of varied tales told about Liberata, of contrasting points of view representing the particular positions of various citizens of the village. As critic Juan Luis Alborg has observed: "Los hechos se repiten, a veces, como si un mismo cuerpo se nos mostrara desde disintos ángulos, pero al final hemos recorrido toda su piel" (The facts repeat themselves, at times as if the same body were to reveal itself from different angles, but in the end we have traversed its entire skin). Those perspectives or points of view differ one from the other in their details, but all constitute articulations external to the subject and imposed upon her by others. Liberata, in this situation, embodies the Lacanian subject who "is spoken rather than speaking." And as the aging protagonist of *La enferma* ultimately identifies with the mute woman, she, too, comes to signify woman who is spoken—inherently with error and distortion—rather than able to speak herself. . . .

And so Liberata is that which the Other chooses to make of her. Nothing in herself, she is doubly fictional: ontologically and textually. . . .

Somehow the problems of aging, madness (or psychological alienation), and self-definition or its lack are all mirrored in Liberata for *La enferma*'s protagonist. In fact, the mirroring technique is multiple, for the narrator, in her passive reception of the villagers' stories about Liberata, reflects back upon herself the loss and lack of the madwoman. Both are dispossesed of youth, passion, psychic equilibrium, and most importantly, the opportunity to voice the content of their own desire. Caught in a metaphorical hall of distorting mirrors, the mature woman sees images that forebode little more than narrowing options and possibilities; the mirrors cloud up and darken, and around the refracted images there rises a wall of diminished possibility. *La enferma*'s narrator can only conclude with an obsessive image recollected from the past: a wall rising up and encircling her with fear and solitude. Others, too, seem to construct walls of words around her, making the way out—if any—seem more and more remote. So encircled, the protagonist of *La enferma* drowns out her ephemeral words and tears. Like *La Playa*'s narrator, who concludes her narrative epistle with the knowledge of her former lover's death, thereupon tossing her useless words into the sea, this second maturing narrator also withdraws into voicelessness. From ambivalence to anguish, the ontological and discursive options of these two narrators dissipate into reluctant resignation and silence.

Elizabeth S. Ordoñez. *Voices of Their Own:*
Contemporary Spanish Narratives by
Women (Lewisburg, Pennsylvania: Bucknell
University Press, 1991), pp. 64–65, 68–69

RAAB, ESTHER (ISRAEL) 1894–1981

Among the earliest Israeli writers, Esther Raab is unique in her ability to wed word to thought, both in her poetry and in her lyrical short stories. In her hands, the implement of the reborn Hebrew language is supple, plastic, infinitely varied, resonant. . . .

Unburdened by the dual loyalties of her contemporaries of the Second Aliyah who still longed for the green fields and forests of Eastern Europe, she loved the harsh landscape around her without reservations, and even found the thorny earth erotic and caressing. Her poetry celebrates the fierce soil as the matrix of a sensuous meeting between masculine white moonlight and the rounded breasts of bare hills. . . .

Severely self-critical, Esther Raab published barely a score of brief prose vignettes in literary journals, and only four small volumes of verse during her long career as a poet: *Thorns* (1930); *The Collected Poems of Esther Raab* (1963); *Last Prayer* (1972); and *Surging of Roots* (1976). Ehud ben Ezer and Reuven Shoham have now presented us with *Esther Raab: Anthology of Poems* (1982), a generous sampling that spans her entire *oeuvre* from 1922 to 1981. Shoham's fine critical introduction, notes and bibliography are a genuine contribution to appreciation. Here we can follow the poet's development, in form and theme, from early rhapsodies to nature and love, sensitive limnings of places and people, through deepening sadness and isolation, to supplication and requiem.

Edna Sharoni. *Modern Hebrew Literature.*
8, Spring–Summer 1983, pp. 62–64

A heartening contribution to the literary preservation of Israel's past, its fragrance and ways of life, is found in this collection of stories, *The Ruined Garden,* written by "the first *Sabra* poetess," Esther Raab. The stories were chosen and prepared for publication by her nephew, the author Ehud Ben-Ezer, who is responsible for her literary estate. The main body of the collection consists of stories of her childhood and youth and the experiences of a unique figure—not only in her creative world but also in her colorful personal life. . . . Her stories . . . [have received] less notice [than her poetry]. She began publishing them in the early thirties in *Bustenai,* and in *Gilyonot,* and she wrote others in the late forties. Her short stories are imbued with the same love and feelings as her poetry, with her pictorial talent, her rare attentiveness to people and vegetation alike, to the moshava and its daily life. Reading them takes one back to distant days, which seem to us, members of the video and stock exchange generation, like imaginary descriptions of prehistoric times.

All the stories are interwoven with echoes of Esther Raab's eventful life, for she might also well be termed "the first Bohemian in Hebrew literature.". . .

The stories in *The Ruined Garden* are not really stories in the common sense of the term. They have no poignant plot, philoshophical profundities, or innovative literary sophistication, but as part of the effort to preserve the life of the beginning of this century, her stories have a living, visual charm. They are authentic and savory, and through them members of the video generation can learn about ways of life, human and natural landscapes, which no longer exist. These stories are a requiem for a landscape, to use the title of the poem that closes the volume, and a requiem for a writer and poet.

David Melamed. *Modern Hebrew Literature.*
9, Spring–Summer 1984, pp. 69–70, 72

RAINE, KATHLEEN (GREAT BRITAIN) 1908–

Only the greatest pantheistic verse is able to resolve discordant forms within the magic retorts of art. This caliber the work of Kathleen Raine does not possess.

In a somewhat like fashion her mystical poems too often appear to lack that double discipline—that twin concentration—of thought and speech. Her subject swallows her up, and then her verse loses shape; is engulfed in waves of feeling. But now and again Kathleen Raine has her triumphs: poetic statements that seem to appeal as much by their poignant naturalness as by any earnestly labored art.

Derek Stanford. *The Freedom of Poetry*
(n.p.: Falcon Press, 1947), p. 223

Kathleen Raine is precise even in her mysticism, delicate in her choice of words. In her little book, *The Year One,* she showed signs of escaping from a quasi-mysticism which seemed likely to sterilize her poetry, and in coming down to earth she gained in force and attractiveness.

R. A. Scott-James. *Fifty Years of English
Literature: 1900–1950* (London: Longmans,
1951), p. 252

There is only one cause for regret at the appearance of Kathleen Raine's *Collected Poems*—that it is given to us after three or four years' silence instead of a book of new work. . . .

To reread the poetry in its chronological sequence as here presented, is to be confirmed in admiration at its integrity, purity, and musical beauty. Essentially, it has not changed: the symbols drawn from Nature ("who is always in the Year One") appear throughout—only the symbol of the angel, which was once powerful, practically disappears, presumably because it is the product of "fallen man," whom Miss Raine has somewhat scornfully discarded as a subject for her poetry. More superficial differences can be traced to the influence of her reading at one time or another—Jung perhaps giving place to Graves, Blake recurring throughout, with sometimes too plain an influence on the style. The latest work does not surpass the best of *Stone and Flower*—perhaps indeed there are now fewer of the pregnant single lines for which she is remarkable, such as, "It is not birds that speak, but men learn silence—" but the work is of more even quality. There were times in the earlier books when her use of words like *eternity* in an emotive rather than an intellectual way, and her reliance on much-worn symbols, such as that of the rose, without revivifying them, led to vagueness, even to sentimentality. It is still occasionally true that the actual words do not carry all that they are meant to convey. . . . Yet as always with the language of true vision, it seems that no conscious attention to technique could have produced better workmanship: her ear is impeccable, and the form of each poem seems unobtrusively right. She uses the blank verse line with a sure instinct.

Anne Ridler. *The London Magazine.*
June, 1956, pp. 83–84

It is quite obvious from even a casual perusal of her poetry that Kathleen Raine has allied herself through the most fundamental spiritual and artistic inclination with the literary tradition and its practice of which she speaks. That tradition in English literature is the Romantic one, and Miss Raine has remarked that her "idea of what poetry was derived from the English Romantic poets"; but it also, in its emphasis on correspondences to be opened between earthly and spiritual reality by means of poetic images, and in its conception of the poet as medium as well as maker, has affinities with the line of French Symbolist poets from Baudelaire through Rimbaud and Mallarmé. Yet in choosing to work in the tradition she so strongly admires, Miss Raine has never overstepped the bounds of the most becoming modesty. While it would be inaccurate to rank her with the major poets of her tradition, such as Yeats or Shelley, the collected edition of her poetry (1956), with its careful pruning away of weak and, unfortunately, some good poems, and her new book, *The Hollow Hill* (1965), reserve a unique place for her in contemporary British poetry and in the small group of fine English women poets of our century, which includes Edith Sitwell, Ruth Pitter, Anne Ridler, and Elizabeth Jennings. The unrelenting manner in which she has committed herself to a vision of reality and the labor she has exacted of herself in shaping that vision poetically deserve closer attention and wider appreciaiton than they have usually received.

Ralph J. Mills, Jr. Kathleen Raine: A
Critical Essay (Grand Rapids, Michigan:
Eerdmans, 1967), p. 8

Kathleen Raine is not interested in charm, though she is indeed charming, by the way. She has a marvelous thing to say, and the saying is urgent. She is a Platonist by conviction, perhaps indeed a Christian Platonist, and she is a poet. . . . *Defending Ancient Springs* is a collection of essays on certain choice spirits in the Neoplatonic tradition, with three expository chapters on myth and symbol. The poets described are Blake, Shelley, Coleridge, Yeats, St. John Perse, David Gascoyne, Edwin Muir, and Vernon Watkins. These are the adepts, initiates. The essays are always appreciative, as one would speak of one's friends; appropriately and warmly. But it is an exclusive club. Here, indeed, is the weakness of the book. Miss Raine assumes that if you are not a Christian Platonist you must be a positivist. The argument will not hold. . . .

Miss Raine's heroes are all poets; she writes of their work, very often, in accents which we can hear in, say, Yeats's essay on Shelley. She does not number the novelists or the dramatists among her friends. She tries to draw Shakespeare in, but the attempt is awkward. Novels and plays traffic with time, or they hardly live at all. History and fact constitute their element. Miss Raine writes of Vernon Watkins, but not of George Eliot or Henry James. She is free to choose; but a limitation of this kind casts a certain shadow upon the whole enterprise. It makes one wonder whether, in the nature of the case, her rhetoric has much to do with literature at all. *Defending Ancient Springs* may be read as chapters in Miss Raine's autobiography. Read in that way, the book is fascinating. But read as literary criticism, it is not convincing: it could not well convince, after all, since it argues that the world of imagination is outside history. Drama, fiction, and a thousand poems deny the claim.

Denis Donoghue. Southern Review. Autumn,
1969, pp. 1245–49

Although Raine is far from proud of many of the ways in which she handled incidents in her own life, she recently decided to publish her autobiography. With a characteristic compassion, she refused to release the major portion of the material while her parents were still alive, for "I did not want them to know how much I had suffered. . . . My own children," she added somewhat sadly, "have inherited all of my capacity for suffering without the ability to make it into poetry."

The first two volumes of the autobiography, *Farewell Happy Fields* and *The Land Unknown,* are currently available in the United States. The third, and perhaps most moving volume, *The Lion's Mouth,* has been published in

England and will be released here soon. Because of the enormity of aspiration contained in their pages, contrasted against the sorrow that her actual life so often held, they become elegies of hope for all of us and give us courage to try to live fully even if we must risk getting hurt. . . .

Each of the volumes of Kathleen Raine's autobiography contains its own "great love." And each of the three loves explored is representative of a different stage in the passage towards self-realization. . . .

But perhaps the most beautiful love story of all occurs in Volume Three, *The Lion's Mouth,* the tale of her fated meeting with Gavin Maxwell. Because Maxwell was a homosexual, their love remained unrealized in the carnal sense, giving the spiritual and emotional components far more vividness than they would normally take on. Here, through the very lack of actualization intrinsic to the relationship, we are given a rare glimpse of how intense the act of being in love can be.

Erika Duncan. *Book Forum.* 5, 1981,
pp. 514, 520–21

These are poems [*The Presence Poems 1984–87*] of vision and valediction.

"A Departure," which deals with the poet giving up her cottage in Cumbria and at the same time facing the ultimate loss, opens with Eliotesque solemnity:

> Always and only in the present, the garden,
> Always today of past and present, the sum.

This is the original, innocent world, where, as Rilke wrote, the angel first appears. In the clear sight of age, it must, nevertheless, be left behind.

> Break all bonds, old woman, while you may,
> Enter your own eternity.

Familiar articles of childhood are held as talismans against Pascal's *silence éternelle,* but cannot be preserved. What, the poet asks, do they gain

> Who follow an invisible master,
> Leave home, wife, father and mother?
> Nothing. Who can bargain
> With that giver who takes all?

The veil between nature and Kathleen Raine has always been thin. In "In Paralda's Kingdom," one of the most beautiful poems in this book, the poet remembers herself as a child hearing the "elemental host" on the wings of the wind. . . .

The Presence which the poet acknowledges throughout these poems is the underlying reality. As a very different writer, Sartre, said in one of his last conversations with Simone de Beauvoir:

"Everyone possesses within himself, in his body, in his person, in his consciousness, what is necessary to be, if not a genius, then at all events a real man, a man with the qualities of a man. But that is something that most people do not want. They stop at some level or other."

Kathleen Raines's achievement is to have continued.

Jean MacVean. *Agenda*. 26:1, Spring, 1988,
pp. 54–55, 57

There is a natural development detectable throughout Kathleen Raine's poetical career, from her first volume *Stone and Flower* (1943) to this present collection [*The Presence*] that one could summarize (if that were not too brutal a word to describe the least deterministic of poets) as a concentration on the tenets of the Imagination. . . .

The volume is taken up with the belief (stated in the Introduction to her *Collected Poems*) that "The ever-recurring forms of nature mirror eternal reality," but in a new synthesis. As with the Transcendentalists, Raine believes that memorable days vibrate to the imagination (most vividly caught in the poems on her mother) and that imagination respects the similarities between things, even across wide distances of time ("present, ever-present presence"). This belief shapes her forms also, which are based on a resolution of repeated phrases across pages, and her bold borrowings of tones from other poets whom she obviously admires (Eliot, Hopkins, Wordsworth, Bunting). Unlike most poems of recollection, there is no mawkish dwelling on the past here, but rather an enrichening placement of it in a universal context: Imagination is no mad boarder—the Possible's slow fuse burns fierce in Raine's mind. "This inexhaustible/Treasury of seeming." It is a book that should be read and re-read, to catch every nuance of feeling.

W. S. Milne. *Agenda*. 26:1,
Spring, 1988, pp. 58–59

RAMA RAU, SANTHA (INDIA) 1923–

In the course of bringing to the stage E. M. Forster's celebrated novel *A Passage to India*, adapter Santha Rama Rau has done one most difficult and interesting thing. While talking a great deal about the mystery of India, she has almost surreptitiously dramatized the mystery of character.

Over and over again during this delicate and bitter dance across the shifting sands of British-Indian relations, you find yourself frankly puzzled as to what a given figure—dark-skinned or light—may do next. You examine the possible alternatives, but warily—for there always seems to be a door open somewhere. Suddenly the door is opened, and the almost familiar figure is doing something that was not among your alternatives and could not have been anticipated. And the moment the act is done, it is all right. One more elusive and tantalizing thread has been since woven into what turns out to be an infinitely complex but none-the-less intelligible pattern. . . .

So much for the character-victory Miss Rau has wrung from her elusive materials. In terms of satisfying theater, it is a partial victory. For in the course of extending these supple lines of personality across two and a half hours, without being willing at any one point to give too much of any one secret away, the dramatist has permitted her life-lines to fray. . . .

The determination to be both complex and oblique drains body from the story-line and tension from portions of its telling. At the same time it builds elusive shadows into people and surprise into conviction. How much you will like the play will depend upon your willingness to pursue several provocative portraits across attenuated terrain. I found the journey interesting.

Walter Kerr. New York Herald Tribune.
February 1, 1962, p. 16

East–West encounter forms an important area of concern in the works of Kamala Markandaya, Santha Rama Rau and Ruth Prawer Jhabvala. There is an attempt to exploit the possibilities of the theme to portray the human situation. A major preoccupation seems to be the exploration of factors that hamper harmonious relations between diverse races and cultures. . . .

Santha Rama Rau treats the problem in its more fundamental aspect in *Remember the House.* Something that goes beyond political differences seems to stand for ever between East and West. There is a disparity between the two patterns of life, modes of thinking and feeling and in the objectives that each society sets before it. These differences are reflected in the breaking-up of the friendship between Alix and Baba, products of different cultures. Even at their closest, Baba is conscious of how different Alix's intonation is from hers when she talks of ambition, success, love and happiness—all interconnected in a restless pursuit. . . .

The breakdown of communication in human relations suggested in *Remember the House* is developed remarkably well in Miss Rau's dramatization of Forster's novel *A Passage to India.* Though it doesn't strictly fall within the scope of a study of fiction it might not be out of place to consider the handling of the dialogue, especially since it stresses an awareness of the basic factors underlying East-West encounter. It is the inadequacy of the means of communication which results in queer entanglements. The Indians and the English speak different languages so to say, and it is rarely they meet across the barrier of language. Underlying their different usages is the incompatibility of racial traits and social ethos.

N. Meena Belliappa. The Literary Criterion.
Winter, 1966, pp. 18–19

Starting in pre-war Tokyo and moving to Manila and then Shanghai during the years 1947–49, *The Adventuress* attempts to portray the devious methods employed by Kay for survival. To her, the biggest favor anyone can ask of life is to be alive. She is not worried about her life. She's constantly and continuously worried about her living, which is spelled m-o-n-e-y. . . .

Does the author of *The Adventuress* tell a story? Not really, for Kay's adventures are not that interesting! Show us a slice of Eastern life? Not really, for none of the characters really stand out, none of them concerns us, not even Kay—for whom we might feel occasional sympathy or interest but not deep involvement. The story doesn't go anywhere. It attempts to move, but most of the time it is stagnant.

K. Bhaskara Rao. Books Abroad.
Autumn, 1971, p. 738

With this book [*Children of God*] Shanta Rama Rao has made her debut in the field of novel-writing. Having half a dozen works of short stories, myths and legends to her credit, she has stepped in the arena of Indo-English novel with the very bold and challenging theme of untouchability, an offshoot of the major Indian theme of tradition *v.* modernity. Though the credit of blazing the trail of the theme of untouchability goes to Mulk Raj Anand who wrote *Untouchable* (1935) and *The Road* (1961) and though certain other novelists like Venkataramani and Raja Rao have grappled with it, Shanta Rama Rao's attempt to probe into this sensitive theme in an unconventional manner compels our admiration. . . .

It is a well-known fact that most of the low caste protagonists in Indian novels are depicted as victim-heroes (barring some exceptional heroes like the copper-smith Ananta in Anand's *The Big Heart*). In the present novel too we come across the usual weak, meek and helpless low caste people; but we also come across the rebellious brothers of the victim hero, who register their protest not by physically retaliating the caste people's action but by preferring to relinquish the Hindu religion and accepting Christian religion.

There is every danger of such a novel with a social theme taking the garb of a thesis, but the novelist has been successful in overbearing it with her graphic characterization, narrative technique, dramatic irony, sardonic wit and poetic vision. The use of Indianisms is moderate, the imagery is apt and the heartrending reminiscences of the mother-narrator have lent the novel an artistic touch.

V. D. Katamble. Indian Literature. 24:1–2,
1981, pp. 137, 139

Santha Rama Rau's works are difficult to find and many of them are out of print. This is a disservice towards an interesting South Asian woman writer. She writes well, but not brilliantly, and much of her work may feel dated. But at a time when most of Asia was still overtly under Western domination, she tried to understand and write about the complex ties and tensions between South Asians and Westerners as well as those between India and the rest of Asia. . . .

Home to India (1944) is an autobiographical account of Rama Rau's return to her Brahmin family at the age of sixteen, after years of education in the West. It is the story of a woman returning to her motherland when that land is living through the last years of the struggle for independence from Britain.

East of Home (1950), another autobiographical work, begins with the author's experiences in post-war Japan where her father was free India's first ambassador. From Japan she travels through the cities and villages—some well known and some not even on traditional maps—of China, Indo-China, Siam, and Indonesia. Anyone interested in studying the Chinese revolution and the Vietnam war will find this book both fascinating and worthwhile. *East of Home* is an unusual chronicle of an Indian woman's adventures and education in post-World War II Asia. Rama Rau's gradual realization of herself and her country as integral parts of greater Asia give this book much of its poignancy.

Remember the House (1956) presents a fictionalized character, Baba, a young woman disssatisfied by her high-society life within the confines of a traditional Hindu family. . . .

[M]ost of her works unfortunately read like an irritating travelogue, as though they were attempts to present an "exotic" culture to a Western audience. But when she begins to explore the inner landscapes of the relation within these houses—and even between houses—she ceases to be the correct, rather stilted tour guide. The return to familiar homes is presented as an attempt to go back to and settle down into traditional appointed places in the larger context of the family of India.

Roshni Rustomji-Kerns. *Massachusetts Review*. 29, 1988–89, pp. 655–56, 664

Something of the urbanity and enthusiasm—an unusual pairing—of Santha Rama Rau's travel books infuses her novel *Remember the House* (1956), the story of a young woman's development from immaturity to a sense of reality. Santha Rama Rau shows herself to be a new kind of artist on the Indian scene. Born and brought up in India, she lives in the United States, writes a very English form of English, travels extensively and draws the subject matter of this novel, which is wholly freed from any Indian connections, from Japan, the Phillipines and China. The heroine, Kay, is a notable creation who joins a child's innocent intensity of will to an unscrupulous finesse in maneuvering her way into other people's lives, that of an Arabian bureaucrat in Japan, an aristocratic old lady in Manila, a former airforce officer and then the wealthy, enigmatic David Marins in Shanghai. This pacy, spirited tale is organized on a system of surprises and reversals. Small, concealed, explosive devices hurl the narrative along. But more impressive than her technical dexterity is the author's genuine sympathy for and creative ability to realize the truth of alien cultures, strange people, the transient world of travel and difference.

William Walsh. *Indian Literature in English*
(London: Longmans, 1990), p. 103

RATUSHINSKAYA, IRINA (RUSSIA) 1954–

Irina Ratushinskaya's growing reputation in Western literary circles owes as much to the publicity surrounding her trial on charges of anti-Soviet political and intellectual activism, her confinement from 1983 to 1986 in a special "strict-regime" labor camp for Soviet women political prisoners, and her eventual release as it does to her achievements as a poet. Previously her poems had appeared only in *samizdat* publications in the Soviet Union and in certain émigré journals abroad. Northwestern's attractively formatted bilingual edition of forty-seven poems [*Beyond the Limit/ Vne limita*] is the first collection of her work to be published in the United States. . . .

Many of the poems reflect the unbearable conditions endured by the poet and her fellow inmates at Barashevo. Still, in spite of the frustration and suffering, the cruelty and inhumanity of life there, Ratushinskaya did not yield completely to despair. In her poem, "Well, We'll Live" the poet shares her joys and sorrows, her morsels of food, and her hopes for a better life with her only companion, a tiny gray mouse. Some other poems are dedicated to people she met in the camp and with whom she shares the same destiny and friendship, ideas, love, and hope. "Leaving Neither Son nor Home" is dedicated to Osip Mandelstam, the great Russian poet who perished in 1938 in one of Stalin's camps. (His work inspires her to create, and his fate reminds her that other Soviet poets before her have suffered captivity.) "Like Mandelstam's Swallow" alludes to other famous poets—Pasternak, Tsvetaeva, Tiutchev—and to all the Russian poets whose voice has not reached freedom. Other poems reveal Ratushinskaya's belief in the recurrence of human lives and historical catastrophes, her visions of the future, and her remembrance of the mythical and classical past.

Basically, Ratushinskaya adheres to classical traditions of Russian versification. Her poems are rhymed and quite rich in instrumentation. The syntax blends the diction of old Russian epic songs with modern Russian lexicology. It is a mixture of the language of fairy tales with labor-camp jargon. Words like *tiur'ma* (prison), *ètap* (prisoners' convoy), *matershchina* (swear words), *zeka* (convict), and *ssylka* (banishment) are ubiquitous. The translators compare Ratushinskaya to such giants of twentieth-century Russian poetry as Anna Akhmatova, Boris Pasternak, Mandelstam, and, above all, Marina Tsvetaeva. At this stage of her poetic development, though, such comparisons are not easily sustained. Her work thus far does not exhibit the depth or the scope of those masters. In fact, her tone and treatment of subjects have much more in common with the early work of Joseph Brodsky. . . . However, Ratushinskaya is still young—she was born in 1954—and further growth and maturation of her considerable gifts and spirit can be expected, especially now that she has been allowed to leave the Soviet Union with her husband.

Victoria A. Woodbury. World Literature
Today. 62, 1988, p. 299

Poems that were written in a forced labor camp on a bar of soap with a sharpened matchstick, to be washed away as soon as they were committed to memory, naturally raise the question of the poet's audience. Arrested in September 1982 and sentenced to seven years' imprisonment for alleged political crimes, what hope did Irina Ratushinskaya have for ever getting through to a readership? She barely had the means to let her husband know that she was alive. Under such circumstances poetry could serve not as a means of communication among people but as an escape from reality or as a private exercise in self-definition.

Some of Ratushinskaya's poems do indeed indulge in flights of comforting fantasy, but these take up only a small part of this volume. Self-definition, on the other hand, can hardly be private for a political prisoner: it almost inevitably involves defining one's group affiliations. One of Ratushinskaya's central concerns as an artist is to be able to state in aesthetically satisfying terms who she is, as she lies beaten on a damp prison floor, in relation to Soviet society. . . .

Beyond the Limit itself testifies to the fact that such oblivion was not in store for Ratushinskaya. Indeed, she was still in prison when her friends smuggled out of the Soviet Union the cycle of poems that had caused her arrest: these were published by Hermitage in 1984 as *Poems,* a trilingual Russian-French-English edition sponsored by International PEN. Subsequently Hermitage—which has become the major publisher of Russian underground and emigré literature—brought out a bilingual volume of her short stories, *A Tale of Three Heads,* as well (1986). Many of the poems she wrote in prison also reached her friends through channels which, as she said in an interview in *The New York Review of Books* (May 7, 1987), she would rather not reveal. These prison poems were just being shaped into *Beyond the Limit* when she was set free and eventually allowed to emigrate in the fall of 1986. As we become acquainted with more and more of her work, we realize that a major new poet has emerged from that fertile ground for literature, the torment of Soviet life. The bilingual *Beyond the Limit* shows the maturing of her art and offers the best translations so far, but as Avins says in the introduction, "The voice heard by readers of the English is inevitably in a different cadence, a different pitch, than that of the poet herself." One wishes that more American poets would come forward to attempt other approximations to the original.

Ratushinskaya herself has gotten out, but the main concerns of her poetry—isolation, falsification, and oblivion—remain gnawing problems for the intellectual elite to which she belonged back home. The worst temptation a Soviet citizen can succumb to, as she puts it, is to "choke on sleep," not even realizing that one has lived. She promises her fellow inmates that as she passes through in a convoy she will "commit it all— / to memory—they won't take it away!" Carrying a volume of poetry imprinted on her brain is tantamount to bearing witness to Soviet life. What she fears is that after she has pressed her confused hands to the hole where her heart used to be, "they'll sew me a white legend, fitting it, / to array me," and they will "fling blame at the murdered— / Deny it, weasel out with lies." Her worst nightmare in this regard is that (in my translation) "over the place of execution time itself has had a weight loss and a hemorrhage."

Preserving memory is vital to Ratushinskaya, even if it is a recollection only of horrors. . . .

The reasons why the Lost Generation grew suspicious of big words in the West were enhanced manifold under Russian conditions. One of the lessons Ratushinskaya has learned from her great predecessors is how to circumvent direct statement by allusion or association.

Paul Debreczeny. Partisan Review. 55, 1988,
pp. 497–500

Ratushinskaya tells most of her brutal facts with tremendous gaiety, even chirpiness; she might be describing life in a girls' school, full of games (Hide the Bible) and jokes ("A real lady never eats heavy food after six o'clock," the inmates pronounce, laughing, over their tiny meal). On Ratushinskaya's birthday, she is presented with a ruffled shirt made out of a bed sheet and, in recognition of her art (she has continued secretly writing poems), a laurel wreath: "The bay leaves have been carefully fished out when we chanced to get them in our skilly during the past months." To cheer themselves up during a holiday while they are on hunger strike, Ratushinskaya and her friend draw a Christmas tree with a paste made of water and contraband tooth powder. "I did the top and middle part and Natasha, lying on the floor (she was unable to get up by that time), drew the trunk."

Ratushinskaya does not leach away her own or her companions' strength with pity, but her heart goes out to the nonpolitical prisoners, who cringe before their guards and who, instead of friendships, have self-destructive lesbian passions. One woman refused to see her husband and two-year-old son, who had been allowed a rare visit, because she wanted to be faithful to her lover. Ratushinskaya learns that the criminal prisoners will inhale powdered sugar, risking tuberculosis, in order to be sent to the hospital, "where you get issued with milk." But in the hospital, there is no release from labor: The patients must clean the floors and carry coal to the boiler room. Those in the Small Zone, Ratushinskaya says, have PEN and other organizations to speak for them. Who will speak for the prisoners with no political convictions or artistic talent? . . . [S]he considers herself lucky: "I survived, I did not betray my conscience, and the man I love was waiting for me when I got out . . . What else can one ask for?"

Rhoda Koenig. New York. October 3, 1988,
pp. 69–70

In March of 1983, the day after her twenty-ninth birthday, Irina Ratushinskaya was sentenced to seven years of hard labor followed by five years of internal exile. The pretext for such harsh punishment, the harshest meted out to a woman since Stalin's time, was the charge that her poetry constituted "anti-Soviet agitation and propaganda." The poet was spirited off to a camp for women political prisoners at Barashevo in Mordovia without the benefit of a proper trial. The women at Barashevo suffered torture and deprivation until Gorbachev finally released them. Ratushinskaya was released in October of 1986 and left the Soviet Union for England in December of that same year. In 1987 she toured the United States giving readings and relating her camp experiences. She is at present living in London with her husband Igor Gerashchenko.

A diary kept by Ratushinskaya and her fellow prisoners was smuggled to the West and was published in 1986 under the title *A Chronicle of the Women's Political Prison Camp at Barashevo*. The autobiography *Grey Is the Color of Hope* is based on the events recounted in that diary and elaborates upon its stark entries. Ratushinskaya adds character sketches, motivation, commentary, and a philosophical viewpoint. Solzhenitsyn's depiction of the camps as representing the various levels of hell serves as an apt metaphor for Ratushinskaya's nightmarish world of punishments that are out of all proportion to the offense, of sadistic supervisors, of beatings, starvation, untreated illnesses, torture, solitary confinement (*shizo*), and repeated attempts to undermine the physical and mental health of the prisoners. With letters of protest, a secret pipeline to the West, hunger strikes, stoicism, faith, and indomitable wills, these courageous women outwit their persecutors and mange to survive. They survive because they are morally superior to their tormentors. Despite the advantages enjoyed by the KGB in its sadistic cat-and-mouse game, paucity of spirit assures its defeat.

Grey is the color of Ratushinskaya's zek uniform, which she has kept and treasures to this day. Criminal zeks wore black. Grey, then, *is* the color of hope, because in Ratushinskaya's inspiring autobiography it represents the political prisoners, whose inner resources provide them with a means of survival and triumph.

Bonnie Marshall. World Literature Today.
64, 1990, pp. 146–47

In *Grey Is the Color of Hope,* her camp memoir, Ratushinskaya confines herself with a deliberate strictness to the account of her experience of incarceration. The narration starts with the moment of the author's release (or, rather, her enigmatic ride under escort in a KGB car, which only after some tense moments turns out to be a ride to freedom). The rest is a 350-page-long flashback recounting, with an almost pain-inducing vividness, the details of her stay in the Small Zone, a special section for female political prisoners in a camp in Mordovia.

This exclusive focus on the camp theme may leave the unprepared reader in a fog. Ratushinskaya says next to nothing about her life up to the moment of her arrest, nor does she say much about what happened to her after her release. But then, it would be difficult to find a Western reader today who could claim total ignorance of this brave woman's life story. . . .

This book is not supposed to be a record of personal suffering, a settling of accounts with former persecutors, or a document of the author's own grace under pressure; or rather, it does perform all these functions on the side of the author's intent, while being primarily a study of what happens to our humanity under inhuman conditions. . . .

But can a prisoner deprived of virtually everything put up any successful resistance at all? Ratushinskaya's book, in fact not so much a memoir as a shrewd treatise on human deprivation and resistance, offers as many as three variants of an affirmative answer. First, you may beat your persecutors with their own weapon: if they threaten you with deprivation, you may adopt self-deprivation as your defensive strategy. This is the case of the hunger strike, which, ironically, may well be the most effective method of presenting your demands or protests to the authorities who put you on a starvation diet anyway. Personally, they don't give a damn about you and your health, of course, but a prisoner's having starved himself to death would be a major blemish on their professional records, so they may sometimes go to great lengths to avoid that (that is, unless they choose to resort to the brutal method of force-feeding). Second, even under the strictest regime there must be some leaks in the prison wall: your contact with the outside world can never be completely cut off, and any echo that your resistance provokes helps your cause. Third, and most important, the utmost deprivation may always be countered by your act of creating something. It may be a miniature vegetable garden that you grow and tend secretly on a patch of ground in your camp zone. It may be a window whose broken pane you fix with a lump of chewed-up bread. It may be a poem you compose in your memory, read to the audience of your inmates, and then try to smuggle out of the camp, sometimes succeeding in reaching the world at large. All these things, insignificant as they may seem, give you exactly what the enforcers of the camp "re-education" program try most fiercely to take away from you: your human identity and sense of purpose, the meaning of your own individual existence.

Stanislaw Baranczak. *Partisan Review.* 58,
1991, pp. 153, 156

RAVIKOVITCH, DALIA (ISRAEL) 1936–

This selection [*Windows*] from the 30-year career of a noted Israeli writer is a welcome addition to the growing body of contemporary Hebrew poetry available in English translation. Sensitive renditions by Chana and Ariel Bloch capture both the cadence of the original Hebrew and its rich allusiveness. Erotic yearning permeates much of the poet's early work: "I sank in a cloud of pleasure, / I sank, / I melted away. / No, I was drowned in the ocean, / there a man loved me." Later poems are replete with biblical imagery and with references to the history and geography of Israel. In the past decade, and especially since Israel's 1982 Lebanon War, Ravikovitch has become more politically engaged. Poignant protests against the conduct of that war are informed by moral outrage: "By the sewage puddles of Sabra and Shatila, / there you transported human beings / in impressive quantities / from the world of the living to the world / of eternal light." And the wish to escape the prospect of war and its horrors is evoked in the pastoral poem "New Zealand": "As for me, / He maketh me to lie down in green pastures / in New Zealand. / Sheep with soft wool, softer / than any wool, / graze there in the meadow."

Penny Kaganoff. *Publishers Weekly.*
March 24, 1989, pp. 63–64

[A] moral crisis came when the Christian Lebanese Army massacred women and children in the Palestinian camps of Sabra and Shatila, and Israeli soldiers, guarding the camps, refrained from intervention. The Israeli public was outraged, not only because of the terrible murder of women and children, but also because of the morally equivocal position of the soldiers. Dahlia Ravikovitch published two poems in the most popular literary journal, *Moznaim*. Both poems take their stand on the war on the basis of the simple humanity Ravikovitch felt was being lost in the rhetoric of politicians. "A Baby Can't Be Killed Twice," for example, pairs the young Israeli soldiers with the children they did not allow to escape from the massacre.

> "Back to camp, march!" the soldier ordered
> the shrieking women of Sabra and Shatila.
> He had his orders to fulfill.
> And the children were already lying in the puddles of sewage,
> mouths gaping,
> calm.
> No one will hurt them.
> A baby can't be killed twice
>
> . . . .
> Our sweet soldiers—
> they asked nothing for themselves.

How strong their wish
to come home in peace.

The effect of Ravikovitch's subsequent public appearances at antiwar rallies, where she was interviewed for the evening news and quoted in the daily papers, can only begin to be measured if one imagines Sylvia Plath at a sit-in. If someone who has been the emblem of self-involvement could now conceive it her duty to protest the war, who could remain silent?

These poets were widely discussed, their poetry published in newspapers and newsstand magazines and debated in panels at the university. They have been anthologized, published in book form, and—most significantly—read and talked about. Other voices also began to be heard, some more stridently than others, and all of them—in a country that thrives on controversy—welcomed by magazines, weekly literary supplements of daily newspapers, and feminist journals. Maya Bejerano, whose intellectual poetry, influenced by Eliot and Stevens, has been concerned with the role of women, took on the subjects of Lebanon and the destruction of the country. The "good fence," the open border between Israel and Lebanon, considered in 1980 a great step forward in Israel because it indicated improved relations between the two countries, was reconsidered by Bejerano three years later: "Child's play makes it possible to understand the 'Good Fence.' / The high railing is the good fence to children on the balcony / Who know that it is possible to fly off it, and do not fly, / See the distance and covet it, / for hours look through its bars as their desire grows."

Karen Alkalay-Gut. World Literature Today.
63, 1989, p. 23

Ariel Bloch and I just translated and edited a collection of Dahlia Ravikovitch's *The Window: New and Selected Poems,* drawing upon five volumes of poems published between 1959 and 1986. In the 1986 volume, *Real Love,* there's a section of overtly political poems, under the heading "Sugyot be-Yahadut bat Zmanenu" ("Issues in Contemporary Judaism"). At first we omitted all but one of these poems—on aesthetic grounds, we told ourselves: they seemed to us declamatory and shrill (as is often the case with political poetry), far less complex and subtle than most of Ravikovitch's work. This view was supported by Ravikovitch herself, who said in a phone conversation that many of these poems were "newspaper verse." "They were good when they were written, at the time of the war in Lebanon," she told us. "But now, six years later, some of them seem outdated, too sharp; they don't all hold up as poems." She left the editorial decision to us, with the understanding that we would make the decision on aesthetic grounds.

We had decided to include only a token sample of these political poems when our good friend and colleague Chana Kronfeld made us rethink the whole question. To omit these poems, Chana suggested, would be tantamount to censorship. . . .

At the kitchen table, Ariel and I wrestled with the issues. *The Window,* we told ourselves, is a collection of *New and Selected Poems,* its purpose is to give the reader a notion of Ravikovitch's best work. Many readers will be drawn to the political poems because they are so shocking, perhaps to the neglect of the other poems. We imagined the reviewer who would fasten on a line like *Tinok lo horgim pa'amayim,* "You can't kill a baby twice," as an occasion to talk politics, instead of attending to a body of work written over a period of thirty years.

On the other hand, these poems represent a real turning in Ravikovitch's career as a poet. Much of her earlier work is about her personal suffering and has been faulted for solipsism; in these more recent poems, she brings her sensibility and power of expression to new subjects: the suffering of women, the anguish caused by war, the resemblances between the plight of the Palestinians and that of the Jews, the moral dilemma of the Israelis. Such a dramatic turn in her work cannot be glossed over without seriously distorting the picture. Precisely because we were putting together a representative collection, we had an obligation, a responsiblity, to include the political poems. . . .

Our final decision about what to include was in some way influenced by the poems themselves. In the most haunting of Ravikovitch's new poems, "Hovering at a Low Altitude," the speaker presents herself as a witness to the rape of a young Arab girl, and describes herself satirically as watching from a distance and doing nothing:

> Makhshevotai ripduni bi-rfida shel mokh.
> Matsati li shita pshuta me'od,
> lo midrakh regel ve-lo ma'of—
> rekhifa be-gova namukh.

> My thoughts cushion me gently, comfortably.
> I've found a very simple method,
> not with my feet on the ground, and not flying—
> hovering
> at a low altitude.

"My thoughts cushion me gently, comfortably"—the irony of these lines was painful to us. In deciding about which poems to include, we didn't want to "hover at a low altitude"; we didn't want to make a "comfortable" choice. The decision not to be political would have been after all, a political decision.

Chana Bloch. Tikkun. 4, 1989, pp. 72–74

The Window offers a good representative collection of poems by Dahlia Ravikovitch (b. 1936), undoubtedly the most prominent female figure in modern Israeli poetry. . . . The poems are taken from five earlier volumes and are arranged according to chronological order: *The Love of an Orange* (1959), *A*

Hard Winter (1964), *The Third Book* (1969), *Deep Calleth unto Deep* (1976), and *Real Love* (1986).

Most of the poems in focus seem plausibly to represent prevailing tendencies in Ravikovitch's poetics. A female narrator dominates the poems' rhetorical layer while portraying herself as a deprived, deserted, and even chastised woman trapped and exploited by a hostile, humiliating society of notably male characteristics. The soft, sometimes childlike tone adopted by the narrator fortifies her iconic stance as a shy, weak woman, a Cinderella besieged by an oppressive, subjugating reality. In light of this, the pining for distant, enchanting, even spellbinding realms in many of the poems is cogently reasoned: the narrator seeks to free herself from her castigating deprivation and to extricate herself from her deteriorating misery. Hence also the many references to different kinds of birds, to flying, to hovering: these function as metonyms for the narrator's desire to leave behind her the admonishing dominions in which she is painfully anchored.

The opening of "The Marionette" radiates Ravikovitch's very poetic essence: "To be a marionette / in a gray, darling, dawn." A sense of deprivation is interwoven her with a sense of a shrouded, distant enchantment. The fact that some of Ravikovitch's recent poems report the agony resulting from war echoes her everlasting inclination to touch the cry in the dark. Robert Alter's foreword is informative and sensitive, and the Blochs' translation successfully preserves the original verbal tone.

Yair Mazor. *World Literature Today.* 64,
1990, p. 357

RAWLINGS, MARJORIE KINNAN (UNITED STATES)
1896–1953

South Moon Under is laid in a country far removed from the violences of the depression, the Florida scrub. It is a slow, old-fashioned novel, carefully and sometimes beautifully written, beginning with the coming of the Lantrys to the wilderness and ending with the flight of the lost generation to wilderness still deeper. There is a great deal of factual information packed away unobtrusively in the novel, information on such unfamiliar subjects as the making of corn liquor, on the ways of hunting wildcats, or the methods of rafting logs down the river. . . . And if the characters are sometimes a little misty, and seem mere passive agents for observing the multiple details of wild life, they at least always observe clearly.

Robert Cantwell. *The New Republic.*
March 8, 1933, p. 108

There comes a moment everywhere when ceasing to be a boy may be a tragedy like dying. But the story of that moment has never been more tenderly written than by Marjorie Kinnan Rawlings in this novel [*The Yearling*] of Jody, the boy of the Florida hammock country, and Flag, the fawn, who grew together out of a frolicking youngness to the bitter realities of maturity.

It is a story sad enough; one, indeed, which might easily fall into the bathos of youth's own humorless seeing of its incomparable despair. But Mrs. Rawlings wisely has not written in the solemn terms of tragedy. Rather her book of the Baxter family is crowded with comedy of character, with full-bodied folk wisdom, and with the silence and the excitement, the ultimate noise and accumulated natural history of the backwoods hunt.

Jonathan Daniels. *Saturday Review of Literature*. April 2, 1938, p. 5

Although she was born in Washington, D.C., was educated at the University of Wisconsin, worked on newspapers in the North, blue-eyed, 42-year-old Marjorie Kinnan Rawlings is pure Southerner in her literary career. Both her novels *(South Moon Under, Golden Apples)* and her short stories have dealt with the poor whites who live in the Florida scrub where she and her journalist husband went to live in 1928.

The Yearling tells the story of one year in the life of a towheaded, lively twelve-year-old named Jody Baxter. The Baxter clearing is even more remote than that of most crackers, but in his own eyes Jody lives an uneventful life. There is no school within reach. His days are spent mostly roaming the game-filled woods, hunting bear and deer with his kindhearted pa and a clan of big, bearded, hell-raising moonshiners and horse traders. Occasionally his pa takes him to visit a hearty old woman who lives in a village on the St. Johns River. He sees a flood, afterward goes hunting where stranded wild animals are thicker than flies. Jody's pal is a pet fawn. He takes it on hunting trips, even sleeps with it when he can get around his fussy, practical ma. The idyl ends when hard scrub reality forces him to kill his fawn because it cannot be kept out of the corn patch.

With its excellent descriptions of Florida scrub landscapes, its skillful use of native vernacular, its tender relation between Jody and his pet fawn, *The Yearling* is a simply written, picturesque story of boyhood that stands a good chance, when adults have finished with it, of finding a permanent place in adolescent libraries.

Time. April 4, 1938, p. 39

If the reader can survive the many "fragile clusters of lavender bloom," "white tufted sky," "pale green earth," "golden sunlight," and finally an "arched rainbow" of the first chapter [of *The Yearling*], he has a real treat in store for him, for Mrs. Rawlings writes with a sincere and unusual beauty. Her Cracker dialect is interesting and never becomes tiresome; her characterization is excellent; and her leisurely method of unfolding her plot fascinates the reader to the end of the book.

Philip Hartung. *Commonweal.*
April 29, 1938, p. 24

Writing fiction for adults about a child in a child's world is a delicately difficult literary undertaking. . . . Marjorie Kinnan Rawlings has succeeded where so many have failed, and *The Yearling* is a distinguished book. Her Jody Baxter lives, a person in himself, within the boundaries of his own years and his own world. One-third intuition, one-third knowledge, one-third perception, the boy moves through the Florida river country, and the chronicle of his year is unforgettably written. . . . Even a Thoreau cannot report on the world outdoors as a child might. The naturalist sees only those things which concern his informed eye. To a child the barn and the woodshed are as much a part of the natural workable landscape as the lizard under the log. Mrs. Rawlings has done a small miracle in that she knows this, never stops to interpret, never once steps outside Jody's perceptions, never mars her great skill by pausing to explain. She has captured a child's time sense, in which everything lasts forever and the change of season takes him always unawares.

Frances Woodward. *The Atlantic Monthly.*
June, 1938, n.p.

Few other contemporary American novelists exhibit so marked a detachment from the problems, the currents of opinion, the pressures and tensions which characterize American life today. So complete is her detachment from the specifically contemporary and the transient as, occasionally, to perplex her readers. . . . In the case of so intelligent and meticulous a craftsman as Mrs. Rawlings, it is absurd to suppose that this detachment, and the rigorous exclusions which it imposes, are purely accidental. They are obviously dictated by a personal perception of life, by a concern for ultimate rather than relative values, and by an intention to present experience in its most simple and enduring forms.

To make this point is merely to suggest that Mrs. Rawlings is essentially a classicist, writing at a moment when the dominant accent of our fiction is romantic. Her work more closely resembles Miss Cather's *My Antonia,* or Mrs. Wharton's *Ethan Frome,* than it does the novels of Ernest Hemingway or Erskine Caldwell. But, although a classicist in her perception of life, she is a romantic in her literary endowment. Sensibility is its most impressive element, and imparts to Mrs. Rawlings's writings certain qualities more familiar in poetry than prose fiction.

Lloyd Morris. *North American Review.*
Autumn, 1938, p. 180

This novel [*The Yearling*] has had this past summer a considerable American success, but it seems at first so localized in interest, and so slow in movement, that one wonders for some while whether and how it will survive transplantation. The scene is the, even in literature, unfamiliar "hammock" country of inland Florida half a century ago or more, covered by thick forests still plentifully inhabited by dangerous and other wild animals. The people of the story are the three Baxters—the small but tireless Penny, the practical and hard because hard-driven Ma, and their only surviving child, the twelve-year-old Jody, already done with schooling and (if with boyish lapses) his father's right-hand man on the crops or out hunting. The two go out together after bear, panther, deer, and even wolf and alligator; they visit and fight with their rough neighbors the Forresters; they go to the village and call in more friendly fashion on Grandma Hutto. Jody has fever, Penny is bitten by a rattler, rain and flood destroy the crops, and plague kills the animals which are no less a source of food.

So life goes on from day to day, yet as one reads one finds that out of these incidents a very solid sense of both place and character is built up in one's mind, and against the harder, harsher background the story of Jody's love for his pet fawn Flag, rescued from the forest after Penny had killed the mother, runs like a thread of bright and delicate beauty, cool and innocent as Jody's own clear outlook on the world. Through Flag, Jody is destined to learn how hard and harsh the world can be. This concluding episode is tenderly and deeply moving, holding something of the tragedy of the breaking of all childhood dreams, but if it is here that Miss Rawlings moves most surely from localism to universality, her earlier pages also provide some moments of authentic and appealing loveliness—glimpses of wild animals, of scenes in the forest, of father and son in happy, unperturbed companionship.

Times Literary Supplement. December 24,
1938, p. 813

Books about the country—even Thoreau's, for example—often exude a thin gas of disdain for the non-rural that suffices to fill the poor towny with a sense of guilt. And so, when he comes upon a writer quite free of this country-mouse snobbery, he crooks the knee of gratitude, as I do before the work of Marjorie Kinnan Rawlings. I can read her books about the incomparable advantages of living in a Florida semi-jungle, surrounded by all the benefits of quick-change weather, insect pests, and mildly homicidal neighbors—I can, I say, read these books with true pleasure and without any feeling that I am necessarily beyond the pale merely because my character is built along lines far less rugged and sterling than those of the people Mrs. Rawlings admires.

Cross Creek, which is also the title of her new volume, "is a bend in a country road, by land, and the flowing of Lochloosa Lake into Orange Lake, by water." It is where Mrs. Rawlings lives, and likes to live, and where *The Yearling* and her other books were composed. Cross Creek consists of five white and two colored families, great poverty, much nobility of soul, orange groves, more animal and vegetable life than any one hamlet can possibly use, spells of beautiful weather, spells of dreadful weather, and a stiff, local pride. The things that make up Cross Creek also make up what is surely one of the most fetching of Mrs. Rawlings' books.

The central fact about her is that she is a mystic. Beneath the pawky and tender humor, the sharp, almost New Englandish eye for character, the sturdy common sense, the womanly interest in the baking of a pie, the highly agreeable Rabelaisian vein revealed in *Cross Creek*—beneath all this is a deep-rooted love of earth, without which her books would be merely little masterpieces of local color and nothing more. "The earth may be borrowed but not bought. It may be used but not owned," writes Mrs. Rawlings. It is this sense of herself as a sort of worshipping tenant that gives to all her tales and people their quality.

Cross Creek is about the author's neighbors, and her troubles with maids, and her outhouse, and the odd, by no means always friendly animals amid which she amiably lives, and the food she cooks (some of it a little subtropical for one queasy, puritanic Northern stomach), and the four seasons, and the art of growing oranges, and such country matters. There's a three-page story about a man named Marsh Turner that is as beautifully turned as any brief tragic tale I can remember off hand, and there is a long anecdote called "A Pig Is Paid For" that confronts us sharply with the unassailable fact that Mrs. Rawlings is one of the funniest writers now operating in these states. All of her sketches and ruminations and local bits and pieces are firmly mortised with the cement of her even temperament, clear-eyed, humorous and reverent.

Clifton Fadiman. The New Yorker.
March 21, 1942, p. 68

There is a deceiving simplicity about *Cross Creek,* a book of pleasant reminiscences of "a bend in a country road" by the sharply perceptive author of *The Yearling.* By the time you finish it you realize that it is more than the story of the people and flora and fauna of a backwoods community: it is a way of life—a way that smacks of Thoreau, without Thoreau's asceticism, for the author, while believing that nature possesses the secret of happiness, loves all sorts of people, and records their peculiarities of temper and dialect with zest and humor.

"I do not understand," she writes, "how anyone can live without some small place of enchantment to turn to." She herself has found her small place among the colored folk, the white folk, the magnolia trees, the hogs, and the waters of the "Yearling" country, and in this narrative of her sojourn there she reveals herself again as an extremely sensitive observer, who sees much that others do not and feels keenly about everything. It is as if color and sound and happiness and sorrow were all heightened for her, and she translates this brightness and sharpness for the reader.

Louis B. Salomon. The Nation.
March 21, 1942, p. 346

Cross Creek is in a sense an unclassifiable book. It is not a "local color" book. Nor would it fit into, although it might nudge, the category of "Florida, Flora, and Fauna." It is not even a good sociological report. The Floyd family negate that possibility. No competent sociologist would admit into his records the fact that the Floyds thoroughly enjoyed belonging to the underprivileged class. Rather, and for the lack of anything better, Cross Creek would seem to be pure Marjorie Kinnan Rawlings. It's an autobiography. And for the sake of the record, it is necessary to add that Mrs. Rawlings does not make herself out either quaint, or amusing, or gay, or tragic. In *Cross Creek* she reveals herself as a good cook and an artist. That is an accomplishment, indeed, for one woman.

> Carroll Munro. *Saturday Review of*
> *Literature.* April 4, 1942, p. 6

One does miss the lift of *The Yearling*. It was as if the earlier book were written out of the heart because the author *had* to write it. There are moments in *The Sojourner* which read like so many novels that appear today— as if the author felt that he must go ahead and finish it. Do not let me mislead you. Mrs. Rawlings is a skilled and able writer, and she has a good story to tell. The characters are, as they say, "well drawn," although at times one feels that she is laying on the whimsy a bit thick.

> Louis Bromfield. *Saturday Review of*
> *Literature.* January 3, 1953, p. 10

It is perhaps the author's joy in her work which carries through to the reader so strongly the vitality of the characters and the gusto one feels in their hard and dangerous lives. There is much hardship and sorrow and tragedy in the book [*The Yearling*], but here, possibly more than in any other of her books, Marjorie Rawlings has conveyed the quality of these people who drew her sympathy—their gallantry, their grace of spirit and the joy in living that they find in lives which appear, in the facts, to be merely bitter struggles for survival. . . .

It is clear that the scrub and the hammock and, above all, their inhabitants, the Florida Crackers, were the well-spring of Marjorie Rawlings' inspiration and the lodestone of her writing talent. The best of her writing is that which is close to this land and to these people whom she understood so deeply because of her love for them. Through her they have gained a place in the literature of their country, and through them that literature has been enriched by the achievement of an outstanding writer.

> Julia Scribner Bigham. Introduction to
> Marjorie Kinnan Rawlings. *The Marjorie*
> *Rawlings Reader* (New York: Scribner,
> 1956), pp. xviii–xix

There is no easy way to sum up Mrs. Rawlings's life and work of the 1930s to the early 1950s. Unfair as it would be to average the literary quality of her output, it would also be unfair to draw hasty conclusions about her permanent contribution to American literature. But the question arises, was she, at least, an important minor Regionalist of the middle period of the twentieth century? Her own serious reservations about regional literature are recorded in a "position paper" of 1940, "Regional Literature of the South"; and academic commentary about her views has been provided by Bigelow in *Frontier Eden* and also by me in *Kansas Quarterly,* a quite different approach to Mrs. Rawlings being taken by each of us. What seems to be of greater significance than her so-called regionalism is her peculiar set of sensitivities, her distinctiveness as a suffering (and sometimes rejoicing) literary person who, in the final analysis, defies all labels and attempts at evaluation.

Mrs. Rawlings responded to rhythms that most people are unaware of or tend to misinterpret: the distant drum to whose beat she moved was often beyond the range of common hearing. Her soul selected its own society and the society of others with rare discrimination. Indicative as Mrs. Rawlings's personal writings are, her other writings also reveal something of her strange sensitivity, the distinctive cadence of "vibrations" that make her worth studying. It is easy enough, but hardly worth the doing, to give her credit for one Pulitzer Prize novel, a good autobiography, and a host of less significant works, mostly about the Florida backwoods. What deserves closer attention is the "line" that her fiction took.

If we look again at her four novels, and certain of her short stories, we find that the human struggle, as she depicts it in her fiction, has the effect of a spinal column in being a flexible source of strength that is supportive of the solitary sojourner on earth. But sooner or later something goes wrong— an intervertebral cartilage becomes displaced, so to speak—and the crippling force resulting from this mischance is felt throughout the rest of the story. This "slipped disk" picture of things is entirely different from Thomas Hardy's tragic view of life, in which an *ironic* Fate constantly frustrates poor God-forgotten earthlings struggling vainly on a blighted star.

Hardy's characters and their author constantly complain about the injustices of life, the ironic miseries that make a wretched human existence so hard to endure, but Mrs. Rawlings's characters (and their author) incline more to a stoic acceptance. In the words of Penny Baxter, they "take it for their share and go on.". . .

What do Mrs. Rawlings's stories seem to be saying? Man, the frail, struggling sojourner on this inhospitable planet, will *not* realize his fondest hopes and wishes—he will get knocked down by life, as Penny Baxter puts it—yet will have no choice but to get up again and keep on going every time the blow falls. Like Penny, again, he will be hurt at least "once too often" by his fellow humans. In this elemental story pattern (seen very clearly in "Jacob's Ladder," for example), with its overtones of the great folktales, there appears to be a deeply personal feature that characterizes Mrs. Rawlings's own life: the failure of the romantic dream.

Samuel I. Bellman. *Marjorie Kinnan Rawlings* (New York: Twayne, 1974), pp. 138–39, 141–42

Admirers of Rawlings's Pulitzer Prize-winning *The Yearling* and her other novels should welcome this first collection [*Short Stories by Marjorie Kinnan Rawlings*] of all but two of her short works, most originally published in the *New Yorker,* the *Saturday Evening Post* and *Scribner's Magazine* between 1928 and 1953. The stories, some only a couple of pages long, are presented in order of publication and come together piece by piece like the blocks of a simple homespun quilt. From the early "Jacob's Ladder" to "A Mother in Manville" and "Fish Fry and Fireworks," Rawlings sharpened her storytelling skills and deepened her understanding of the backwoods world of her Florida neighbors and the African Americans who worked for them. She had a knack for setting each scene with a few homey details, putting the reader right inside the story. Dialect, colorful but always intelligible, was used to great effect. In "Cracker Chidlings" Fatty Blake critiques his neighbor's Brunswick Stew: "I was born and raised in Floridy and I'm pertickler. I don't want no squirrel eyes lookin' at me out o' my rations!" [The] introduction provides essential background to set these stories in the context of the time and Rawlings's efforts to face her own feelings about race. "Black Secret," her last work on the subject, won an O. Henry Prize, as did "Gal Young Un."

Maria Simson. *Publishers Weekly.* March 14, 1994, p. 68

REDMON, ANNE (GREAT BRITAIN) 1943–

Memory and the past figure importantly in Anne Redmon's novels. Like [Shirley] Hazzard and [Cynthia] Ozick, Redmon recalls in her fiction precedent literary works. *Emily Stone* revises the legend of Tristan and Isolde, and *Music and Silence* appears to reconstruct Dante's *Inferno.* Both novels allude to and recast fairy tales. For example, in *Emily Stone* the narrator draws images and analogies from fairy-tale and magical lore, and in *Music and Silence* the powerful Ilse Alba is portrayed as a witch, whose garden mysteriously produces roses and vegetables out of season. Moreover, if Hazzard's characters are haunted by an unredeemable, blighted past and if Ozick's characters are circumscribed by a redeeming, unitive pattern of the past, Redmon's characters live somewhat in between these two states. They are caught within the web of their past, but sometimes this very entrapment can occasion a ritualistic action reminiscent of the redemptive rituals which are the heritage of Christianity. . . .

Fate for Redmon is a humanly perceived pattern encouraged by art. . . . Between Hazzard's stoical pessimism and Ozick's qualified optimism lies Redmon's point of view which, like the works of Michelangelo and Botticelli in *Emily Stone,* suggests the "indomitable spirit" of humanity without resolving the question of human destiny in terms of any Absolute.

The dialectic of fate and free will in *Emily Stone* makes up the central crisis in Emily's life, just as it does Maud's in *Music and Silence.* However, in Redmon's earlier novel, fate prevails, while *Music and Silence* more optimistically affirms the power of free will.

Catherine Rainwater and William J. Scheick.
Texas Studies in Literature and Language.
25, 1983, pp. 186, 202

Music and Silence is a baroque book. It is elaborate, highly ornamented, even overwrought. Some reviewers have wished for a simpler, more streamlined novel, missing the fact, I think, that Redmon is trying, and with considerable success, to offer fiction as layered and as emotionally sensational (and yet in some odd way flattened) as contemporary Western experience. Obvious symbols and almost stagey images—the drowned woman, the hanged mother, the leaf-burrowing Evangelical demon—decorate Redmon's landscape as abundantly and surreally as Dante's grotesques do the Inferno. Rhetorical simplicity is not Redmon's interest. Yet the controlling architecture of *Music and Silence* is very clean and simple, like Dante's; and the number three is Redmon's basic unit as well. . . .

As the story of a woman artist, *Music and Silence* links maternity with both destruction and creation.

Elizabeth Ammons. *Texas Studies in
Literature and Language.*
25, 1983, pp. 361–62

Through the managed relations among voices, Anne Redmon's *Music and Silence* organizes the chaotic "textures" of human experience fugally into an aesthetic unity; such unity is either imposed or discovered by the "sacred consciousness" of the individual, particularly the artist. Like fugue, *Music and Silence,* through its alternating narrative voices, both pursues and flees this ordering impulse that governs the text overall. Furthermore, Redmon's text is emphatically a searching out: not only do the characters themselves search out the patterns of their fate (cosmological formal design) or willed freedom (individual free-form variation), the narrative also develops a momentum of gradual discovery. Employing silence as well as statement, the narrative seems engaged in a process of searching out some immanent pattern and meaning in and between the voices. Such a discovery is not made completely by any one of the characters, or even by the omniscient narrator. . . .

[D]espite its omniscience, this third-person narrative voice is also a searcher, not in complete possession of any final truth but subject to changes introduced by Maud's exploring, inventing voice in flight from the narrator's more unified, deterministic vision. The fullest discovery becomes available perhaps only to the reader, to whom alone are available all the voices of the text as well as the interstices between the voices—the silences between the music. The narrative procedure of *Music and Silence* thus leads ultimately to the reader's heightened awareness of immanent meaning arising from the "music" (mere human communication or an aesthetic vehicle) and the silence uniquely shaped by such music.

Catherine Rainwater. In Catherine
Rainwater and William J. Scheick, eds.
Contemporary American Women Writers
(Lexington: University Press of Kentucky,
1985), pp. 71–72

Redmon, who was born in Stamford, Connecticut, but has spent most of her adult life in London, is especially known for *Music and Silence* (1979), a memorable account of the search for a faith in something enduring in a world characterized by human coldness and mortality. . . .

The reader of Redmon's novel is . . . denied exact answers for, like [Brian] Moore's book, [*The Color of Blood*] it abounds in plot twists and a final deliberate evasion of any clear revelation of the origin of the bizarre events undergone by the protagonist. However, in contrast to the inability of Moore's cardinal to close the gap between the material and the spiritual worlds, Redmon's narrator, Irene Ward, experiences, as a result of her epileptic fits, a total destabilizing of her sense of the phenomenal realm, a decentering that apparently amounts to a glimpse of the eternal informing the temporal world. . . .

Like Moore's novel, Redmon's book borrows from the convention of suspense fiction—the idea that it is a mystery is insisted upon—but, like Moore's narrative, it is more specifically a metaphysical thriller. Similar to the fiction of Graham Greene's middle period, both raise profound theological questions about the origin of the bizarre Kafkaesque *plot* informing human religious and secular actions in an ambiguous and paradoxical fallen world rife with ecclesiastical, political, and psychological strife. . . .

Redmon's novel hints that her narrator, unwittingly, *probably* has genuine mystical encounters during her epileptic fits that penetrate God's apparent silence in the world. Irene's seemingly deranged visions intimate the integration of the sacral and the secular, an integration expressed in her capacity to find fulfillment in love as an expression of the divine love informing creation. And her involuntary visions and their results suggest the Thomistic sense that in some ultimate sense all acts of human volition are "unfreely" grounded on the extrinsic causality of the deity.

William J. Scheick. *Religion and Literature.*
21:3, Autumn, 1989, pp. 43, 52, 57–58

REINIG, CHRISTA (GERMANY) 1926–

I assume Christa Reinig is in all consistency a socialist without wholly identifying herself with the political and social system of her country. Bringing
up this point would hardly matter if it did not contribute largely to explaining
the nature and source of her poetry. . . .

These poems are deserving of attention in West Germany because of the
genre to which they belong, because of the objective and critical approach
to contemporary events combined with an unbroken poetic quality. And they
have been published in a country where poetry on contemporary subjects
has faced many obstacles. . . .

Almost all Christa Reinig's poems contain a balladlike core. Perhaps this
characterization falls somewhat outside the limits of a strict history of the
genre. Yet, she describes the occasions that give rise to her poems, describes
the arena in which they move. Most of the time it is a factual, social, and
demonstrable event that sparks the poem. It does not grow out of an inner
movement by which the facts of experience are transformed and become
unrecognizable. Rather, acts and occurrences produce an emotionally critical
response. Naturally, the consequence is a strong mutual interaction between
world and brooding self, a direct and visible relationship, one we are familiar
with in our Western tradition of subjectivity and one that we frequently
demand.

> Wolfgang Maier. In Klaus Nonnenmann, ed.
> *Schriftsteller der Gegenwart* (Freiburg and
> Olten: Walter, 1963), pp. 244–45

Much of Christa Reinig's early work is poetry, none of which was ever published in book form in the German Democratic Republic. Her first book of
lyric poems, *The Stones of Land's End (Die Steine von Finisterre)*, was published in the West in 1960. It was followed by *Poems (Gedichte)* in 1963. They
are filled with the nightmarish visions and cruel detail of war. In 1968, a third
volume of verse appeared, entitled *Memorial Tablets of Schwabing
(Schwabinger Marteln)*. (Schwabing is the artists' section of Munich.) Her
ballads and songs contain Brechtian elements. Among her prose works, there
are the collection of stories *The Three Ships (Die drei Schiffe)*, 1961, and the
short sketches *Orion (Orion tritt aus dem Haus)*, 1968, with the subtitle:
New Signs of the Zodiac. The latter are brief, almost whimsical reflections
of contemporary life and human nature. *Papantscha Miscellany (Papantscha
Vierlerei)*, 1970, is a satire in verse about the shortcomings of our times; its
Indian and Persian settings give it an exotic flavor. *Heavenly and Earthly
Geometry (Die himmlische und die irdische Geometrie)*, 1975, is an autobio-
graphical novel that points out some of the discrepancies between the au-
thor's views and the expectations of the "State of the Workers and Peasants."
It testifies to her earthy, often irreverent, but not inordinately cynical sense

of humor. An all-pervasive philosophical strain underlies the author's delight with the surrealist and the supernatural. Her most recent work *Emasculation (Entmannung)* 1976, is the story of Otto and his four women, containing decidedly feminist elements. Many of Christa Reinig's writings reflect her proletarian background. Her earlier works, in particular, also suggest the air of the ghetto, loneliness, and despair, even thoughts of suicide, subject matter that inevitably led to conflict with the state in the East.

"Vocational Counseling" was published in *Motiv,* a collection of essays by seventy authors, written in reply to the question, "Why do you write?" Christa Reinig's contribution satirizes the automated selection process used for students and people entering the work force. The computer, only a part of a much larger "machine," the State, is totally incapable of counseling an individual, who is left-handed, nonconformist in her tastes and who has, at best, a sketchy and unorthodox education. This uniform, robotlike, and impersonal way of dealing with human beings will net equally self-defeating results when applied to a confused teenager whose ideas about unemployment have not yet been shaped by the party line or to the person who has become a loyal member of the group in power.

Elizabeth Rutschli Herrmann and Edna
Huttenmaier Spitz. German Women Writers
of the Twentieth Century (Elmsford,
New York: Pergamon, 1978), p. 87

In her autobiographical novel, *The Geometry of Heaven and Earth* (1975), and in her novel, *Castration: The Story of Otto and his Four Wives* (1976), Christa Reinig succeeds in telling stories . . . in "another" way, or at least in making visible a potential variant of feminist narration. . . .

Even more surprising is the utterly unique tone of her autobiographical novel. It is almost as if an image of the world imposes itself on everything, an image that comes straight from the "touch organ," uncorrected and "true to the lens;" an image in which it appears as though "up is down, and down is up." It is the lack of an ordering system, a system that would divide objects and events into "the null and void, and the important," that lends both novels their almost too sharply drawn sense of reality. . . . Reinig indeed has "her own principles," but they "are decentralized, and disconnected from one another." She colorfully throws together a multitude of world views, ranging from vegetarianism and Buddhism, to an esoteric interpretation of the Icelandic sagas and Dänikens' theories of outer space travelers, to the I-Ching and astrology; yet a biological conception of the relationship between men and women, combined with a rather vague interpretation of psychological terminology (phallocentrism), together assume the function of a sort of crystallization point. And though they do not bring unity to her pluralistic concept of the world, they nonetheless provide a central point of reference. . . .

Radical subjectivity—the need to share subjective experiences—sneaks up on men's control over thought and language as well as over women's silence, stammeringly assembling its utopia. She can not speak, for that which she is striving for—the asymbolic—is only possible outside of language. . . . Language is not only murder of the body, a bloody sacrifice of substance so that it can acquire meaning, but language is also a banishment of pleasure: torn apart and destroyed by the symbolic phallus itself, all that remains is the reflected image in which the subject recognizes itself again.

Peter Horn. In Manfred Jurgensen, ed.
Frauenliteratur: Autorinnen, Perspektiven,
und Konzepte (New York: Peter Lang, 1983),
pp. 101–3, 121

RENAULT, MARY (GREAT BRITAIN) 1905–83

As a story of high-keyed passion, *Promise of Love* is both complex and intense, yet it never loses touch with the solider kind of reality. The world—in this case the world of a great hospital—presses very closely upon Miss Renault's two lovers, conditions their moods, their problems, the ways in which they fail one another. A nurse, and a humble research worker, they are at the mercy of hard, driving, severely disciplined forces which do much to thwart and dissipate their love. They are governed, in short, as most of us are, by financial stress and the kind of job they hold. Therefore their predicament is acute and human. Even if Miss Renault's novel were not an extraordinarily moving love story, it still would be notable as a picture of hospital life. . . .

On a double count . . . *Promise of Love* strikes me as an unusually excellent first novel. There is a fusion here between background and personal drama, between inner and outer reality, which enriches and dignifies both. The story of Mic and Vivian would not be nearly so arresting as it is if one were not so sharply aware of the pressure of their environment. One sees them at work as well as in love—an important dualism which too many novelists neglect. When one adds to this that Mary Renault's style has a sure, fluid quality, that she possesses humor as well as sensitiveness, that even her minor characters are shrewdly drawn—the sum total is quite impressive. *Promise of Love* is a good novel. It deserves success and very probably may have it.

Edith Walton. The New York Times.
March 12, 1939, p. 24

In *The Friendly Young Ladies*, Miss Renault . . . uses the technique of the "point of view," and gives us that of the adults as well. When the point of view is that of the girl, Elsie, she is wholly and admirably successful. The opening chapters in Cornwall are amusing, sensitive and well written; the ridiculous middle-class parents and the atmosphere of the middle-class home are perfect. In Elsie's family there is a skeleton, tightly cupboarded: years earlier Elsie's sister, Leonora, has run away. Liberally over-interpreting the advice of a young doctor acting as a *locum tenens* in the neighborhood, Elsie runs away and joins her sister. As soon as Elsie gets into the world of the friendly young ladies, Miss Renault's troubles begin. Thenceforward, whenever things are seen from Elsie's angle, the book is lovely and real; her misunderstanding of the personal relationships around her is well done, and so are the few later actions to which her author commits her, including the final one. Unfortunately, a fog descends whenever Miss Renault tries to get inside her grown-ups, and a most promising book gets lost.

The book aims at depths which are impenetrable because Miss Renault has ignored the preliminary necessities of organization on the surface. It is a real lack of invention that makes Leonora and Joe seem so unreal and so nebulously conceived: both have pasts which are left too much to conjecture for their pressure on the present to be comprehensible to the reader; and the love scenes between these and other characters which mark the progress of such story as there is do not bring the characters any more clearly before us. One cannot even tell precisely *how* friendly the young ladies have been to each other. Miss Renault is at the difficult stage of being able to express subtle thoughts and truths about personality without being able always to attach them to personalities whom they fit; but she is a very able writer, and her younger heroine alone makes her book worth reading.

Henry Reed. *New Statesman and Nation.*
October 14, 1944, p. 256

The basic line of *The King Must Die* is uncomplicated and horizontal—one exploit after another, with each of which the hero's strength and self-knowledge increase. It ends, thus, with a round, full picture of the real beginning of King Theseus's manhood soon after a climactic, shuddery version of the story of Ariadne on Naxos, a scene of Dionysian celebrations, obliquely rendered and awful. . . .

Miss Renault has a vigorous sense of the life and variety of the cities and personalities of the era, and renders them without a trace of effort or monotony. The language in which she has Theseus tell his story is not elaborate, but it has elegance and pace; consistently clear, this story does not have such complicated passages on politics and philosophies as sometimes blur *The Last of the Wine,* her very interesting novel of a later Greece. Theseus is a bold and shrewd young man, much attracted to women and much endowed with a quickness of decision and dramatic sense of gesture that enable him to lead men successfully. Miss Renault, from her modern vantage point of psychological sophistication, gives him a simple but sure insight into human behavior.

At Knossos, having volunteered to go along with the other youths and maidens demanded as a tribute from Athens by King Minos, Theseus becomes part of the band of prisoners dedicated as "sacrifices" to the Bull God. Instead of their being killed and offered, the practice is that they become teams who perform dangerous acrobatic feats with bulls in an arena for the mere amusement of the spectators. Miss Renault's reconstruction, through her narrator, of the psychology of the teams, each member depending for his life on the skill and courage of the others, is a remarkable blend of research, style, and imagination—as, indeed, is the entire story.

Edwin Kennebeck. *Commonweal.*
August 1, 1958, p. 454

The Last of the Wine, The King Must Die, and *The Bull from the Sea* are set in eras far different from our own, yet even in the legendary world of Theseus, we recognize men who, like ourselves, are only men. As men they cannot escape the condition to which all men are born—the hardship and perplexity of a world which all too often is alien and evil. Alexias and Theseus, however, because they come to know themselves, are "ready" to do battle in that world for the values of truth, freedom, justice, and love which they hold dear. The battle has always been, and will always be, unequal; grief and loss are inevitable. But these men accept their *moira,* and by the end of their respective lives consent to give themselves completely in meeting that appointed end.

These three novels by Mary Renault will not begin a great movement back to the writing of historical fiction. The temper of our time seems to demand novels of social conscience in the world of atom bombs, labor unions, and committee meetings. Moreover, good as they are, Miss Renault's books have flaws. *The Bull from the Sea* is too episodic, partly because Miss Renault has been less skillful in reshaping the plot than she was in *The King Must Die.* In both of these books, the presentation of Theseus as a tragic figure suffers at the expense of action (interesting as that action may be for its own sake). Despite the surface restraint of *The Last of the Wine,* there are sections which appeal to the prurient.

But these are relatively minor faults to find in novels which have so many obvious virtues. The reconstruction of the historical era is achieved with such vitality and authenticity that setting and atmosphere play a major part in the shaping of character and theme. The prose style is flexible and at times capable of great force and poetic intensity. The structure of the books is carefully molded to define and reinforce theme. Thus, Miss Renault's novels are not merely good historical novels, they are good novels. And they should do much to alleviate the anomalous plight into which historical fiction has fallen.

Landon D. Burns, Jr. *Critique.*
6:3, 1963, pp. 120–21

Fire from Heaven covers only the first two-thirds of Alexander's life, from his fifth to his twentieth year. It is the perfection of a technique that appeared inchoatively in *The Middle Mist* and has been the author's trademark since

The Charioteer—tracing an adult's failure or success to his childhood environment. That Mary Renault should make Alexander's boyhood the key to his personality is not surprising, since she has been approaching characterization in this way since 1944. That she has succeeded in spite of odds that were almost self-defeating is another tribute to her talent for "wringing lilies from the acorn."

Alexander made a brief appearance at the end of *The Mask of Apollo*. Niko gazed at his piercing blue eyes and knew instinctively, as only an actor could, that he was destined for glory and suffering. Mary Renault has isolated that suffering in a childhood where a son was forced to choose between a bisexual father whose ambition he admired and a possessive mother whose affection he craved. The critic who might feel the novelist is repeating what is now a typical Renault boyhood would be correct; Alexander's youth could easily constitute a case history of parental polarization, but with one essential difference: most children facing the dilemma of divided allegiance would acquire a lasting neurosis; Alexander was a world conqueror when he died at thirty-three.

Mary Renault did not invent the facts of Alexander's scarred boyhood; history provided them, however obliquely, and the author interpreted them according to the canons of fiction. *Fire from Heaven* is her most Plutarchan novel.

> Bernard F. Dick. *The Hellenism of Mary
> Renault* (Carbondale: Southern Illinois
> University Press, 1972), pp. 101–2

I am particularly puzzled (and pleased) by the success of Mary Renault. Americans have always disliked history (of some fifty subjects offered in high school the students recently listed history fiftieth and least popular) and know nothing at all of the classical world. Yet in a dozen popular books Mary Renault has made the classical era alive, forcing even the dullest of bookchat writers to recognize that bisexuality was once our culture's norm and that Christianity's perversion of this human fact is the aberration and not the other way around. I cannot think how Miss Renault has managed to do what she has done, but the culture is the better for her work. . . .

In *The Persian Boy* Miss Renault presents us with Alexander at the height of his glory as seen through the eyes of the young eunuch Bagoas. Miss Renault is good at projecting herself and us into strange cultures. With ease she becomes her narrator Bagoas; the book is told in the first person. . . .

The device of observing the conqueror entirely through the eyes of an Oriental is excellent and rather novel. We are able to see the Macedonian troops as they appeared to the Persians; crude gangsters smashing to bits an old and subtle culture they cannot understand, rather like Americans in Asia. But, finally, hubris is the theme; and the fire returns to heaven. I am not at all certain that what we have here is the "right" Alexander but right or not,

Miss Renault has drawn the portrait of someone who seems real yet unlike anyone else, and that divinity the commercialites are forever trying for in their leaden works really does gleam from time to time in the pages of this nice invention.

Gore Vidal. *New York Review of Books.*
May 31, 1973, p. 15

Mary Renault sharply delineates Mediterranean paganism, in which the soul was a live tissue, to be felt, shared, occasionally exchanged, a short cut to the gleaming invisible. A world of omens, oracles, dramatic gestures, sonorous utterances, civic feuds and passions, horrible cruelty, and stubborn, thrusting individualism, austere, sybaritic, or smug. The divine is pervasive, a mouse may contain a morsel of radiant, jealous Apollo, a jug or statue hold latent supernatural powers, a song be chipped off from ideal, celestial Song. Sport and drama have religious magnetism, the gods themselves are accessible through harsh effort.

Renault novels rely more on this numinous atmosphere than on subtlety of narrative or characterization. Usually they depict a god-smitten boy of exceptional promise, maturing into his destiny as actor, warrior, savior of society, whose ambitions can win friendship with the famous—Socrates, Alcibiades, Plato. To introduce such figures is audacious, though the author is not one of those novelists who think it sufficient to clap some Fabian into wig and silk stockings and pass him off as Robespierre. Critics may complain that her heroes are rather too neatly packaged, within the conventions of the familiar adventure story, but in such a work as *The Last of the Wine,* her observation of landscapes, her personal slant on the nature of love, loyalty, vocation, infuses a distinct individuality. She has Murdochian relish in precise physical or technical description—a bronze statue being cast, a lyre being tuned, a chariot or galley in motion. Her dazzling young men can be robustly bisexual, but seldom split by dark, self-destructive cravings; Theseus in *The King Must Die* is the most complex, vulnerable to the evil eye of the universe. Her latest, *The Praise Singer,* is the poet Simonides (556–468 B.C.). Poetry was a further symptom of the divine: the severest critic would not be a Dr. Leavis, but a rival poet, educated public opinion, or that ambiguous area where Olympian symmetries were swiftly affronted by technical or emotional falsity. Simonides grows to be accepted by Anacreon, Pythagoras, the young Aeschylus, and the tyrant Pisistratus. Faction is rampant in rival Greek cities, the Persians threaten, Marathon is at hand. Simonides is shown very plausibly, despite occasional lapses of conversational tone. "Theas used to say he learned enough good stories to dine out for the rest of his life." "People say my curiosity will be the death of me."

The surfaces of Athenian life may seem somewhat over-polished for a slave society often romanticized, the sentiments occasionally too noble, from the school of Thucydides and Plutarch, though I myself have been stimulated to explore an area of history scarcely known to me, and I imagine, to many others.

Peter Vansittart. *London Magazine*.
April–May, 1979, p. 144

Power was the problem when Alexander met his shade. Like any god, he thought he was immune to shades. His lovely Mediterranean empire had to be divided up. Two pregnant queens were on their way to Babylon. After the usual intrigue and poisoning, one gave birth to a boy. Meanwhile, Alexander's idiot brother enjoyed the idea of kingship, and various generals grabbed Egypt, Persia and Macedon. Miss Renault enjoys the idea of this strange Philip as Robert Graves enjoyed the idea of Claudius. All kings are fools who want to be gods. The "mystery" of Alexander is that he almost got away with it.

Funeral Games is the third novel in Miss Renault's trilogy about a bisexual Alexander. His silent departure leaves a shambles. We might as well be in the Nixon White House, in which a Haig takes over. Perdikkas always occupies a vacuum. Who has the edge? Who wants it? Who holds and secures it? Nobody—although Ptolemy did a reasonably good job along the Nile. Miss Renault rather likes Ptolemy, who diverted Alexander's golden bier from Macedon to his own neighborhood, as she rather likes Eurydike, who more or less married Alexander's idiot brother. But most of all she likes Bagoas, who was a sexual threat to everybody.

From the Miss Renault who wrote *The King Must Die* and *The Bull from the Sea* we have come to expect certain virtues: her humor is sly. She will not knowingly lie to us. She has read more history than we are likely to have wondered about. She will dazzle with expertise—emblazoned leather tents, cuirasses and greaves, sword belts set with plaques of Persian cloisonné—and homoerotic innuendo. She seems to have been there, like Walter Cronkite, although Mr. Cronkite would not delight as much in the cruelty that being there presumed.

We have also come to expect certain deficiencies. She is all sex and no philosophy. (Gore Vidal, who admires her, can afford to: fierce thought has occurred to him; antiquity inspires in him the skeptical giggle more often than the blank swoon.) She licks her chops too much. (The politics of the harem are trivial; the desolation of the Persian boy is exquisite.) And her prose leaves too much to be desired. . . .

Miss Renault seeks a vernacular appropriate to myth, and fails to find it: "Trusting almost no one, he had trusted her and told her everything. Intrigue, revenge and treachery had been daily weather." The result is a kind of comic-bookishness, a mock epic with too many elbows in the ribs. Whatever else he might have been, Alexander wasn't funny.

John Leonard. *The New York Times*.
December 3, 1981, p. 23

In the first chapter of this third and final volume [*Funeral Games*] of Mary Renault's Alexandriad, poison has rendered Alexander comatose in Babylon. It is only a matter of time before the reader is comatose, too. Miss Renault lingers for a hundred and thirty pages in 323 B.C., rattles through the next dozen years (practically one per chapter), and then hops forward to 286, to portray Ptolemy, now King of Egypt, putting the final touches on *his* history of Alexander. The intervening pages are littered with Greek generals, Persian and Macedonian soldiers, and nests of venomous mothers and wives, not to mention mules in harness (sixty-four just to haul Alexander's sarcophagus from Babylon to Alexandria), dromedaries under saddle ("On the Royal Road to Susa, a courier traveled, his racing dromedary eating the miles with its smooth loping stride"), and royal elephants on parade (a phalanx of them tramples, on command, a crew of insurgents). There are also cinematic sound effects (extras rhubarbing in Babylonian and Greek), poetic similes ("The broken nose in Ptolemy's craggy face pointed like a hound's at a breast-high scent"), and dramatic dialogue ("Raising his large dark disillusioned eyes, Bagoas said with a vicious quiet, 'Since the day of the elephants'"). Only the most optimistic reader will hope that a historical novel so dull must at least be educational.

The New Yorker. December 28, 1981, p. 73

The *New York Herald Tribune* devoted the entire cover of its Book Review section to an article by Moses Hadas, Professor of Greek and Latin at Columbia University:

> All of Miss Renault's reconstructions carry conviction because her imagination is informed by careful study, as a minor detail may show. Medea in her short scene calls Theseus "Theseuss." Euripides too made Medea hiss by making the s-sound prominent in her speeches. Miss Renault must therefore either be credited with remarkably careful reading or with even more remarkable imaginative power. Theseus' desertion of Ariadne and his failure to raise the white sail are puzzling blots on his chivalry; Miss Renault's rational explanation of both these derelictions as part of his campaign against the old order gives cogency to her entire reconstruction. Her narrative is not, nor does it claim to be, history; but it is a well-considered suggestion of how things may have happened, and for the personality and culture with which she deals we have nothing more plausible. Books from which we learn so much so agreeably are rare.

Moses Hadas, 1958. In David Sweetman.
Mary Renault: a Biography (New York:
Harcourt, Brace, 1993), p. 189

When she died in 1983, Mary Renault was one of the most popular historical novelists in the English language, with her books translated into every major tongue, yet there was always something odd about this success. She told a good story, with enough adventure to satisfy the common reader, and her fastidious attention to historical detail made classical scholars some of her greatest fans, but it was also true that several of her leading characters were unashamedly homosexual at a time when many of those same readers would, under other circumstances, have considered the subject repellent.

A great deal about her life and work seems contradictory. While she is famous for books set in the ancient world, few remember that her earliest reputation came from a series of contemporary novels, published before and during World War II, which touched on the then forbidden subject of lesbianism. . . .

The Charioteer, the last of her six contemporary novels, was the first to deal openly with deviant sexuality, and the following eight novels, set in ancient Greece, made her the first author to reach a worldwide audience with books whose principal characters might be—though they were not always— male homosexuals.

Between her first historical novel and her death in 1983, the Western world underwent a revolution in thinking about human sexuality and an equally extraordinary revolution in sexual behavior. During this period Mary Renault's novels helped millions of people come to terms with their sexuality, people who had never "come out" or protested in public, but who, without her work, would have considered themselves alone and unnatural. One of her greatest achievements was to give homosexuals a place in history while offering non-homosexuals a sympathetic world where heterosexuality was neither the only nor the dominant sexual type.

David Sweetman. *Mary Renault: A
Biography* (New York: Harcourt, Brace,
1993), pp. xi–xii

In her . . . books she disdained preaching the case for a more liberal attitude toward homosexual love, but it was implicit in the novels she now began to weave from her study of ancient Greece. In her final "English" novel, *The Charioteer* (1953), she had depicted the homosexual love of a young man in a manner so audacious that her American publisher, William Morrow, refused to bring it out for fear that it would expose the company to the risk of prosecution for indecency (Pantheon published it six years later). But she had written so sympathetically that the novel, copies of which were brought into the United States by enthusiasts, did much to counterblast the wave of anti-gay phobia that swept Britain and the United States in the 1950s.

When she turned to classical Greece, her problem was lessened. The scene and the era were remote. In three novels and one biography she developed the history of Alexander the Great, the most admirable of youths, handsome, courageous, charismatic and bisexual. Renault's Alexander is an enhanced version of the young actors of her circle in South Africa.

In the best known of these books, *The Persian Boy* (1972), she tells the story of Bagoas, who is a eunuch of extraordinary beauty, castrated by his master and lover, the Persian king Darius, for fear that he might desert him for the love of a woman, and who, after Darius's death, becomes the lover of his conqueror, Alexander. The book is written in a singsong romantic style that perfectly bridges the enormous gap in years. It remains one of the most successful historical novels ever published, and one of the most expertly researched. To most writers and readers it would matter little whether the walls of Babylon were 50 or 75 feet high. To her it mattered a great deal.

The night before her death she heard from a friend that one of Gilbert Murray's successors as Regius Professor of Greek at Oxford, asked what to read to gain an insight into the Hellenic world, had replied, "Oh Mary Renault every time—perfect for historical accuracy, perfect for atmosphere." It was the last letter that she read. "That really bucks me up," she said, and died.

Nigel Nicholson. *The New York Times.*
June 27, 1993, p. 13

RHYS, JEAN (DOMINICA–GREAT BRITAIN) 1894–1979

Setting aside for a moment the matter of [Miss Rhys's] very remarkable technical gifts, I should like to call attention to her profound knowledge of the life of the Left Bank—of many of the Left Banks of the world. For something mournful—and certainly hard-up!—attaches to almost all uses of the word *left*. The left hand has not the cunning of the right: and every great city has its left bank. London has, round Bloomsbury, New York has, about Greenwich Village, so has Vienna—but Vienna is a little ruined everywhere since the glory of Austria, to the discredit of European civilization, has departed! Miss Rhys does not, I believe, know Greenwich Village, but so many of its products are to be found on the Left Bank of Paris that she may be said to know its products. And coming from the Antilles, with a terrifying insight and a terrific—and almost lurid!—passion for stating the case of the underdog, she has let her pen loose on the Left Banks of the Old World— on its jails, its studios, its salons, its cafés, its criminals, its midinettes—with a bias of admiration for its midinettes and of sympathy for its law-breakers. It is a note, a sympathy of which we do not have too much in Occidental literature with its perennial bias towards satisfaction with things as they are. But it is a note that needs sounding—that badly needs sounding, since the real activities of the world are seldom carried much forward by the accepted, or even by the Hautes Bourgeoisies!

When I, lately, edited a periodical, Miss Rhys sent in several communications with which I was immensely struck, and of which I published as many as I could. What struck me on the technical side—which does not much interest the Anglo-Saxon reader, but which is almost the only thing that interests me—was the singular instinct for form possessed by this young lady, an instinct for form being possessed by singularly few writers of English and by almost no English women writers. I say "instinct," for that is what it appears to me to be: these sketches begin exactly where they should and end exactly when their job is done. No doubt the almost exclusive reading of French writers of a recent, but not most recent, date has helped.

Ford Madox Ford. Preface to Jean Rhys.
The Left Bank (New York: Harper, 1927),
pp. 23–25

After *Good Morning, Midnight,* Jean Rhys disappeared and her five books went out of print. Although these had enjoyed a critical success, their true quality had never been appreciated. The reason for this is simple: they were ahead of their age, both in spirit and in style. One has only to compare Miss Rhys's early books, written during the 1920s, with contemporary work by Katherine Mansfield, Aldous Huxley, Jean Cocteau, and other celebrated writers of the period, to be struck by how little the actual text has "dated": the style belongs to today. More important, the novels of the 1930s are much closer in *feeling* to life as it is lived and understood in the 1960s than to the accepted attitudes of their time. The elegant surface and the paranoid content, the brutal honesty of the feminine psychology and the muted nostalgia for lost beauty, all create an effect which is peculiarly modern.

The few people who remembered their admiration for these books, and those even fewer who (like myself) were introduced to them later and with great difficulty managed to obtain second-hand copies, for a while formed a small but passionate band. But nobody could find her; and nobody would reprint the novels. Then, as the result of a dramatized version of *Good Morning, Midnight* broadcast on the Third Programme in 1958, she was finally traced to an address in Cornwall. She had a collection of unpublished stories, written during and immediately after the Second World War, and she was at work on a novel.

Francis Wyndham. Introduction to Jean
Rhys, *Wide Sargasso Sea* (London: André
Deutsch, 1966), pp. 10–11

Readers of Charlotte Brontë will recall Jane Eyre's first glimpse of the mysterious prisoner in the garret of Thornfield. . . . It is the Creole Bertha Mason, of course, the first Mrs. Rochester, the announcement of whose existence, just as the wedding ceremony is about to be performed, prevents Mr. Rochester's marriage to Jane. It is Bertha Mason who is the heroine and, for the greater part of the novel, the narrator of *Wide Sargasso Sea;* and she is indeed a plausible re-creation and interpretation of the one character in *Jane Eyre* that Charlotte Brontë tells us next to nothing about, presumably because she knew next to nothing about her. Jean Rhys, who herself comes from the Caribbean, convinces us that she does, and she does so because of her extraordinarily vivid rendering of life in Jamaica in the early 19th century, immediately after the emancipation of the slaves.

The novel is a triumph of atmosphere—of what one is tempted to call Caribbean Gothic atmosphere—brooding, sinister, compounded of heat and rain and intensely colored flowers, of racial antagonisms and all-pervasive superstition. It has an almost hallucinatory quality—and this is Bertha Mason's contribution, for it is through her mind, from childhood to her incarceration at Thornfield and her dreams of firing the house, that we view the action.

From the beginning she reveals herself as beautiful, pathetic and doomed, doomed both by heredity and environment. She is the child of generations of slave-owners who have suddenly been plunged in poverty by the emancipation and become objects of contempt for the freed Negroes, who call them "white niggers," and of the English alike. Her younger brother is dumb and bed-ridden, her mother distraught by circumstances to the point finally of madness.

What I find especially interesting in *Wide Sargasso Sea,* apart from the relationship with *Jane Eyre,* is that Bertha Mason seems to sum up in herself, more closely than ever before, the nature of the heroine who appears under various names throughout Jean Rhys's fiction. She is a young woman, generally Creole in origin and artistic in leanings, who is hopelessly and helplessly at sea in her relations with men, a passive victim, doomed to destruction. It is remarkable that after so many years Miss Rhys should have pinned her down in a character, however sketchily presented, from another novelist.

It is here that the critical problem arises. Francis Wyndham rightly says that Miss Rhys's book is in no sense a pastiche of Charlotte Brontë. But does it exist in its own right? I think not, for the reason that her Mr. Rochester is almost as shadowy a figure as Charlotte Brontë's Bertha Mason. One still, in other words, needs *Jane Eyre* to complement it, to supply its full meaning.

Walter Allen. *The New York Times.*
June 18, 1967, p. 5

It is perhaps too soon to assign Jean Rhys a definite place in literary history, although we can notice her relationship to her contemporaries. The story of her life inevitably makes us compare her to Katherine Mansfield. Both women were ex-colonials who never forgot the islands where they were born. Both of them—like many another colonial newly come to London or Paris—discovered a madder music in a bohemian life morally more lax than that which the natives of Swiss Cottage or the Boul' Mich ever enjoy. And although both Mansfield and Rhys frequently wrote about the helpless woman who needs the love and protection of a man, they were themselves solitary artists who knew their true life best when they were seated at the lonely writing desk.

Yet the differences in their personal attitudes make their writings quite different. Katherine Mansfield, in spite of her labors to master the Continental tradition of writing *contes* and her desire to be like a Chekhov or a de Maupassant who could fleetingly turn the brilliance of his genius upon prosaic events, illuminating and fixing them forever as he saw them, never departs from the traditional moral stance of the British novelist, except, from time to time, to slip from it into sentimentality. Jean Rhys, in contrast, employed not only the *mise en scène* of the Continent, but also the European *Zeitgeist*—its new ideas in psychology, its aesthetic application of certain philosophical ideas, and, most of all, its between-the-wars appreciation of the plight of the individual, the isolation of existentialism. Caught up in such ideas, she quickly leaves behind her the traditions of realism as practiced by earlier British novelists and, neither commenting upon nor manipulating her characters according to any moral pattern, allows them (or more accurately, the single character) to express what is. Relentlessly she develops her single vision of a world in which free will is a myth and the individual has no power to control his destiny. She pays little or no heed to the reader's resulting depression or occasional mystification and never, like Mansfield, utilizes an irony to exalt the reader. Katherine Mansfield often puts him on the side of the gods where he can feel superior to the self-deluding Miss Brills who flounder before him; Jean Rhys does not salve our pride, but aims through her various technical devices to make us experience the degradation and humiliation of her characters. In the Rhys world there is no superior vantage point for anyone.

Elgin W. Mellown. Contemporary Literature. Autumn, 1972, pp. 473–74

To my mind, [Jean Rhys] is, quite simply, the best living English novelist. Although her range is narrow, sometimes to the point of obsession, there is no one else now writing who combines such emotional penetration and formal artistry or approaches her unemphatic, unblinking truthfulness. Even the narrowness works to her advantage. She knows every detail of the shabby world she creates, knows precisely how much to leave out—surprisingly much—and precisely how to modulate the utterly personal speaking voice which controls it all, at once casual and poignant, the voice of the loser who refuses, though neither she nor God knows why, to go down. Because of this voice, the first four novels read as a single, continuing work. They have the same heroine—although she goes by different names—the same background of seedy hotels and bedsitters for transients in Montparnasse and Bloomsbury, and they recount the single, persistent, disconnected disaster of a life in which only three things can be relied on: fear, loneliness and the lack of money. . . .

The purity of Miss Rhys's style and her ability to be at once deadly serious and offhand make her books peculiarly timeless. Novels she wrote more than 40 years ago still seem contemporary, unlike those of many more popular authors. More important, her voice itself remains young. She was about 30 before she began to write—apparently having other things on her mind before that—yet the voice she created then, and still uses, is oddly youthful: light, clear, alert, casual and disabused, and uniquely concerned in simply telling the truth.

A. Alvarez. *The New York Times.*
March 17, 1974, pp. 6–7

Between 1927 and 1939 Jean Rhys published four novels and a collection of short stories. The novels all have in common a central figure who is an alienated woman and a modern setting, chiefly the years between the two world wars in Paris and London. Whether or not they are actually written in the first person, they adopt the point of view of their solitary heroines, of women who are more or less attractive and more or less mature, but who remain enigmatic and remote. Dependent on but invariably abandoned by men, they seem obscurely destined to drift from man to man and from one dingy hotel room to another. Although they come close to breakdown—this is most apparent in the fortyish Sasha Jansen of *Good Morning, Midnight*— the novels end characteristically with an abrupt gesture that stops the action short before breakdown can occur. Such, however, is not the case with Jean Rhys's latest heroine, the first wife of Charlotte Brontë's Rochester. In the remarkably new departure in her art that is *Wide Sargasso Sea,* which was first published in England in 1966, Jean Rhys follows her central character beyond the self-imposed limits of her earlier fiction and, as a result, gives fresh significance to her whole *oeuvre.* At the same time she subjects *Jane Eyre* itself to a provocatively new critical reading.

As Ford Madox Ford observed on the occasion of the publication of her earliest volume of short stories in 1927, Jean Rhys naturally assumes the point of view of the underdog. In her latest novel it is a point of view she consciously carries to an extreme. . . . The thematic continuity with Jean Rhys's preceding novels resides in the fact that she affirms in *Wide Sargasso Sea* that Bertha Rochester was not born mad but made so, and made so, both singly and collectively, by men.

Unlike her other novels with a contemporary setting, *Wide Sargasso Sea* derives its leading characters and their situation from another work of art. *Jane Eyre* provides the impulse for an imaginative *tour de force* and at the same time dictates a mode and a style that are new in Jean Rhys's fiction. This time she has written an historical novel with an exotic setting; in the words of a blurb on the paperback edition, it is "a novel of unforgettable romance and terror. A 'triumph' of Caribbean Gothic!" And the reasons for such a setting and such a mood are clear. In order to comment effectively on *Jane Eyre* and extend its meaning in previously unperceived ways, Jean

Rhys had to create a novel that would be largely continuous with Charlotte Brontë's work in terms of style and period and would stand comparison with the original. Thus although *Wide Sargasso Sea* is not a fully autonomous novel because an understanding of its meaning depends on our knowledge of *Jane Eyre,* it achieves its purpose because it is a remarkable work of art in its own right.

Dennis Porter. Massachusetts Review.
Autumn, 1976, pp. 540–41

Jean Rhys's early writing about the Caribbean has a wide range. Some of it is vivid recreation—mixing cocktails for her father in the holiday house, or portraying an illiterate Roseau newspaper editor. Other pieces are short stories, Chekhovian in their depth and economy. "The Day They Burnt the Books" encapsulates not only a conflict between mulatto and European, but between two ways of life. Mr. Sawyer, settled in Dominica with private means, tries to preserve his old way of life by filling his house full of books. He resents and insults his mulatto wife, and she, silently, resents and hates him. After his death, years of subdued anger explode. She builds a fire and has a ritual burning of his books, leaving for sale only those with fine bindings— and where the writer was a woman, even leather binding cannot save it. The scene is counterpointed against the attitude to the burning of their son— himself culturally divided—and the white girl who loves him. The relationships of white Creole and expatriate Dominicans with the black community are explored with even greater complexity in two more recent stories, "Oh Pioneers, Oh, Pioneers" and "Fishy Waters."

Imaginatively, perhaps the most remarkable achievement among her Caribbean stories is "Let Them Call It Jazz," which appeared in *The London Magazine* for 1962. In it, Jean Rhys writes—in dialect—from the point of view of a black girl from Martinique, living in Notting Hill, London. . . . In its evocation of black emotional warmth and essential awareness of musical rhythm, the story has an unassuming relationship to the insights of *negritude.*

The range of Jean Rhys's writing about the Caribbean has not been previously fully noticed, and when it has been taken into account at all, it has been seen as the primary material from which the masterpiece *Wide Sargasso Sea* was to be fashioned. Kenneth Ramchand's recent essay on the subject, for instance, while noting that Jean Rhys's *Voyage in the Dark* (1934) is "one of the most moving of the West Indian novels of exile," considers how the later work distances and develops the "too simple" divisions of *Voyage in the Dark.* While this is largely true, it can lead to a diminution of the importance of the earlier book. It was the first-written of all Jean Rhys's novels, and is still her favorite. It bears the same kind of relationship to *Wide Sargasso Sea* as Dickens's autobiographical *David Copperfield* bears to *Great Expectations.* Not only is one the mature reworking of the other, but what the earlier work lacks in symbolic objectivity, the first-written makes up in the freshness and poignancy of the personal element.

Louis James. *Ariel.* July, 1977, pp. 113–15

Although some articles on Rhys have appeared in popular magazines, she has received little critical attention, especially from women, despite her exceptional technical skill and the relevance of her subject matter to the women's environment. Is Rhys's relentless portrayal of passive, helpless heroines simply unpalatable to feminist critics? Or, perhaps more seriously, does Rhys's unremitting pessimism become an artistic failure that drives us to dismiss her vision despite her insight and control? Both questions, I believe, may be answered in the negative if we relinquish our expectation of a surface realism and adopt a psychological framework to explain the perversely self-destructive reactions of Rhys's heroines.

These reactions form the crux of Rhys's five novels, whose sparse and repetitive narratives are variations on the themes of failure and rejection. Although Rhys describes her heroines' progressive degeneration, often in excruciating detail, she fails to provide an adequate explanation for this process. A closer look at Rhys's recurrent heroine, however, reveals that in addition to her obvious passivity, she manifests several specific symptoms of schizophrenia: impoverished affect, apathy, obsessive thought and behavior coupled with the inability to take real initiative, a sense of the unreality of both the world and self, and a feeling of detachment from the body. Like schizophrenics, Rhys's heroines experience the world as a hostile environment and lead lives of isolation, detached from family and friends, unable to establish real contact with others. They all undergo periods in which they feel dissociated from bodies they experience as mechanical and alien, lose interest in a world they perceive as flat and gray, and succumb to obsessions that drive them in repetitive, unproductive patterns from which all pleasure has been drained. Rhys's heroines are not insane: they fall rather into the category sometimes referred to as ambulatory schizophrenia and sometimes as the schizoid (as opposed to the schizophrenic) state. They are disturbed in fairly distinctive ways, and seeing them within this specific context can illuminate aspects of their behavior which are otherwise obscure.

The particular approach to schizophrenia formulated by R. D. Laing is especially useful in analyzing the responses of Rhys's heroines. . . . Laing's insistence that schizophrenia is a legitimate and not uncommon response to certain interpersonal interactions provides a clue to understanding Rhys's heroines and thus the nucleus of Rhys's fiction. There is no question of influence here—Rhys wrote largely before Laing did—nor is the comparison directly demanded by the novels themselves, as it is by several of Doris Lessing's novels. Rather, Laing's account of the dynamics of schizophrenia provides a helpful framework for considering certain enigmatic features of Rhys's fiction.

Elizabeth Abel. *Contemporary Literature.*
Spring, 1979, pp. 155–57

Good Morning, Midnight represents a fulfillment of a loose but engaging dialectic between the self and the world that we can trace throughout Rhys's fiction. The earlier heroines fail to achieve an affirmation in their conflict with the world, but in *Good Morning, Midnight* Rhys finds in the deepest human resources a strength that confronts the terror—a strength at once fragile and human, but no longer merely defensive.

This synthesis is realized in *Good Morning, Midnight* through the character of Sasha. She is the most compelling and deeply sympathetic of Rhys's heroines. She is so, in the first place, because of her greater range of feeling and emotion. Her bitter humor and sardonic wisdom provide us with abundant clues to her deeper nature. Through Sasha we are able to see nowhere more clearly that conscious drive in Rhys's fiction to look past the awful bitterness of exclusion and defeat to a vision of sympathetic understanding and knowledge in a world of meager opportunities and easy despair. Hers is not a vision of fleeting and private harmony of the kind that holds Mrs. Ramsey together in *To the Lighthouse,* but rather one where the feminine psyche must find accommodation in the world itself. *Good Morning, Midnight* is similar to *To the Lighthouse* in that its themes and resonances reveal with clarity and force those fears which haunt the imagination, but its theme lies elsewhere, not in the passive, private world of the feminine but in an active life where human need triumphs over betrayal. There is no doubt that the women in Rhys's fiction have been crippled permanently by life, but what we also see—and nowhere more clearly than in *Good Morning, Midnight*— is that there is a new consciousness forming, one not formed only from anger and despair, but one imbued with an awareness that women must share equally in life's promises and defeats, and if they do not human life itself is lessened and even malformed. And this revelation is nowhere better expressed in Rhys's fiction than in *Good Morning, Midnight.*

Thomas F. Staley. *Jean Rhys: A Critical Study* (Austin: University of Texas Press, 1979), pp. 98–99

Finally, then, we arrive at an understanding of Rhys's increasingly focused and controlled mythopoesis. Having more or less consciously freed herself from the "utter misery" of her life in the writing of *Quartet* and the subsequent *After Leaving Mr. Mackenzie,* Rhys has become emotionally and psychologically strong enough to turn again to those writings of an earlier day, writings which generated at least as early as 1914 and possibly as early as 1910. Turning from the restricted male-centered vision of the first two novels, Rhys reconstructs the dim outlines of a female-centered reality which she had stumbled upon some twenty years earlier and which she had hinted at in the person of Julia's mother [in *After Leaving Mr. Mackenzie*], that dying old woman struggling for life. She takes her reader on a voyage, not chronologically but psychically, through her own maturing vision. Thus the male-dominated reality of a Marya Zelli *(Quartet)* yields to that of a Julia [*After*

Leaving Mr. Mackenzie], who survives in that same male structure almost on the verge of important self-discovery. Julia in turn apotheosizes into Anna, who having recognized herself (at least subconsciously) as her own "center" lies in bed following the abortion, thinking of "starting all over again."

Appropriately, all three women bear children—as does Zola's Nana—symbolic of their ancient natural, life-giving powers. But in the hands of Zola, the male writer, Nana the Golden Venus, in effect a sexually distorted creation of man's own needs, must be destroyed by her son for being what she is, just as the ancient goddess Anna—Grandmother of God—was destroyed by the engulfing patriarchal system. A Marya or a Julia, the product of that same male construct, must "lose" her child, a kind of symbolic sacrifice upon the altar of the male-universe which denigrates her life-giving powers and denies her economic and emotional survival. Anna, however, close to the reality of her own primal nature—a nature which is *not* a reflection of the masculine order—deliberately aborts her child; not for lack of money, not as a sacrifice to the conventions of the patriarchal, hypocritical white world. Anna aborts her child, without remorse, because, in the tradition of the Great Goddess, she is at once *creator* and *destroyer,* an independent force bearing the burden of no man! It is only when she has unconsciously but irrevocably acted in accordance with this duality of her own nature, aborting that which would destroy her, that the truth hidden in her unconscious can manifest itself and she can emerge whole.

And so we arrive at full awareness of Rhys's art and myth. Building on Zola's novel of a fallen woman, Nana, who was punished for her sins against man and his society, Rhys creates her own "story of a tart," Anna, a product of the sins committed against her nature by man and the society which he dominates. In moving from the perverted "Golden Venus" of Zola's male conception to the West-Indian-by-birth Anna Morgan, Rhys plucks—from the depths of her unconscious—sad melodies of mythic strain from the lyre of time, evoking memories of ancient sin against the life-giving female force. And in the siren song of different time and different way, she lulls us into hope that for the Annas of the world there might still be "mornings, and misty days, when anything might happen." But this hope, says Rhys, if it exists at all, lies in their awakening from the evil dream. Awakening from the illusory dream of safety which so long has held them captive, to take responsibility for their own lives, in whatever terms are right for them.

Helen Nebeker. *Jean Rhys: Woman in Passage* (Montreal: Eden Press Women's Publications, 1981), pp. 82–83

That Jean Rhys's personal life infused her fiction is obvious when her whole canon is placed against the background of her life. The exact nature of the interaction between her life and her writing is one of the more intriguing issues critics have addressed and will continue to address in the future. Because of the obvious fixation on her life that her fiction reveals, her memoirs were anticipated with great interest. Her unfinished autobiography [*Smile, Please*] issued after her death may be disappointing because of its incomplete state and because of its sketchiness. Even the first seventy-six pages, with which Rhys was reportedly content, presents a less detailed and less revealing rendering of her rich life than might be expected. This first section on her childhood contains some marvelous images, scenes and episodes, but many of the recollections are fairly pedestrian. The writing in this section is careful and meticulous, but it lacks the energy and integrity that marks her fiction. The unpolished draft covering another segment of her life and notes on later phases comprise the remainder of her book (to which an article originally printed in *Vogue* was appended by Diana Athill, although this was not the plan of Jean Rhys). On the whole, the book can only be said to be disappointing. Perhaps the greatest interest this book will hold is as a record of the last stage of a process, the final sifting of a life that had been sifted many times before when she wrote her fiction.

Mary Ann Klein. World Literature Today.
53 (1981), p. 324

Control is the key; there is no substitute for stylistic restraint in any art. Though Jean Rhys speaks for all those who pass through life without having a life, she does not shout. Her short, well-built declarative sentences glitter without blinding. Their spareness helps control our responses. Because of it, her rare figures of speech leap out; because of it, she commits us imaginatively to her characters and their problems. Nobody better understands the differences between art and propaganda than Jean Rhys. Very few practice a more severe economy of means. Her pared-down vocabulary and muted sentence rhythms have won Shirley Hazzard's highest praise—the comparing of her prose to great poetry: "For me her power lies in the very transformation of self-pity into literature—a feat of artistic strength seldom managed even by poets."

Poetic undertones in Jean Rhys stem from narrative strategy. Predicament all but replaces plot in her novels. Instead of telling a story, she places and then develops a situation. The basic one—that of the single city woman who has nothing and fits nowhere—had not been treated seriously before. . . .

The sealing-off of outlets for growth blocks character development in the usual sense. It promotes negation elsewhere, as well. The breakdown and withdrawal described in *Midnight* and *Sargasso* stem logically from what precedes. To exist sexually, as the Rhys heroine does, is to court ruin: hopelessness is a natural condition of sex, and deprival is a natural corollary of life in these curiously sex-free novels. "There is never an escape for the Rhys heroine," says Mellown; "happiness is always followed by sadness, and her last state is always worse than her first."

Peter Wolfe. Jean Rhys (Boston: Twayne,
1980), pp. 19–21

Even as a writer . . . Jean Rhys is only partly modern. Rather, she is timeless. For she explored her own age, its moods and changes, almost by accident. What she set out to explore were her own very personal feelings. We see the outside world through them, but only reflected and distorted by her concentration on what really concerned her: her own life, and her own suffering. She was entirely self-absorbed. She cut everything out of her writing but herself; and in order to write she did the same to her life. She became a near-recluse; though she suffered intensely from their separation, she never lived an ordinary family life with her daughter. As she grew older she pared more and more away in her writing—her present husbands, her present surroundings—so that all that was left were her deepest experience and her deepest feelings, and they were always the same. These experiences are what she wrote about over and over again, seeing herself and them more clearly each time: experiences of love and rejection, hate and revenge, fatality and fear.

Necessarily, therefore, Jean Rhys's novels are autobiographical: Not autobiographical in every detail, as readers sometimes suppose, but autobiographical they were. . . .

Following the heroines through the novels and stories, therefore, is following Jean's journey into self-knowledge—which is the point of all her life and work.

Carole Angier. *Jean Rhys* (New York: Viking Penguin, 1985), pp. 16–17

Rhys calculatingly works out a double perspective whereby two visions that should ostensibly be quite different turn out to be very much the same. We can assess society from the perspective of the author's alienated female protagonists, or we can assess those protagonists from the perspective of generally accepted social values. Presumably most of Rhys's readers and critics are more committed to social norms than to radical alienation and so are more likely to employ the second perspective than the first. Yet that second perspective readily brings in the first. . . .

We read Rhys, V. S. Naipaul has suggested, to see the whole world reflected in her "woman's half-world," the *"demi-monde"* that takes its "exact meaning" from "exile and dependence." As Naipaul concludes: "Out of her fidelity to her experience and her purity as a novelist, Jean Rhys thirty to forty years ago identified many of the themes that engage us today: isolation, an absence of society or community, the sense of things falling apart, dependence, loss. Her achievement is very grand." We read her, too, because what she writes she writes superlatively well, with a prose "reticent, unemphatic, precise, and yet supple, alive with feeling, as though the whole world she so coolly describes were shimmering with foreboding, with a lifetime's knowledge of unease and pain." We read her because of the personal triumph whereby that life of pain was transmuted and transcended. As much as any modern author, Rhys turned the transitory disasters of a disordered and mismanaged life into works of enduring art. And we read her, I would finally suggest, because of the paradoxical hope prompted by her hopeless fiction.

Arnold E. Davidson. *Jean Rhys* (New York: Frederick Ungar, 1985), pp. 137, 140

It is not only the thematic import of the novel [*Wide Sargasso Sea*] that carries the lesson but also the "aesthetic practice" demonstrated there that makes its most forceful assertion and furnishes the weight of its argument. The model of the woman's text, the dream-text, presents the strongest argument for the morality of the paradigm it offers, as well as providing evidence for our highest evaluation of the distinction of Rhys's literary achievement. . . .

We need feminine texts—that is to say, texts consciously founded in the mother-text: novels, fiction, narratives, essays—from both women and men. But the example offered in Rhys's presentation of the dream-text is not simply a "model." It is a paradigm. . . .

The moral of Rhys's story, and the morality of the text it displays, is what the woman's text—here, a woman's novel—can offer. Rhys offers new inflections on the "word of the father," the text that [Kenneth] Burke explicates at such length and upon which he rings so many changes without leaving its framework. Rhys offers a new grammar, the general principles on which new modes of verbal expression might rest: that of the woman's idiom. She is, however, using the form or genre called "the novel," which was given to us by the grammar of masculine preoccupation with the written word. She uses some of the customs of that convention, eschewing others, to offer the unconventional: a paradigm that gives us a set of new inflections to "express grammatical relationships," which is to say, the relationships that exist in our culture before we express them in the language we use with one another.

Nancy R. Harrison. *Jean Rhys and the Novel as Women's Text* (Chapel Hill: University of North Carolina Press, 1988), pp. 250–51

To view Jean Rhys as a woman writer only or to discuss her as a West Indian author or a European modernist exclusively limits our understanding of her work. For in each context, her writing remains outside the main current by virtue of its participation in the other two. I see her novels as textual sites both in between and intersecting these three important currents of twentieth-century cultural history and literature. . . .

The larger social context of these literary movements gives meaning to both the distorting mirror of the text and the truths we may see in it, and a sociocritical perspective can give us the wide focus we need to see the multiple contexts of Rhys's writing.

Mary Lou Emery. *Jean Rhys at "World's End": Novels of Colonial and Sexual Exile* (Austin: University of Texas, 1990), pp. 7–9

With *Wide Sargasso Sea*, Rhys produced not only a masterpiece of West Indian fiction, but most importantly a novel uniting the contradictory voices within the self, the voices controlling her writings. . . . The novel represents a dialogue between the two forces dividing Rhys's consciousness, closing with a vision of unity made possible by the final identification with one of the elements of this duality. Such interpretation requires close examination of the relationship between structure, characterization, images, and language in Rhys's last and major work of fiction.

This consideration makes possible the view of Rhys's entire *oeuvre* as a circular journey of self-discovery, beginning with *Voyage in the Dark,* the voyage within the darkness of the self. It marks Rhys's own departure from the island of her birth, the place where she identified with conflicting worlds and their values: that of the white Creole descendants of planters and that of the black islanders. The three novels usually referred to as Rhys's European works, because of their European setting, *Quartet, After Leaving Mr. Mackenzie,* and *Good Morning, Midnight,* correspond to the initiation phase during which the heroine experiences Europe, her father's land. Rhys's final novel, *Wide Sargasso Sea,* brings the heroine back home to Dominica, where she confronts for the last time the conflicting realities of her childhood world, Europe, and the West Indies, symbolized by Rochester and Antoinette. . . . But unlike the closure of the preceding novels, *Wide Sargasso Sea* ends with a solution to the identity crisis given symbolic representation in Rhys's fiction. The solution is implicit in the action prefigured by Antoinette's dream at the end of the novel. Through her plunge to death from Rochester's tower toward Tia, the West Indian black friend whose reflection she sees in the pool below, Antoinette achieves for Rhys the ultimate freedom, that of the self.

Pierrette Frickey. In Robert L. Ross, ed.
*International Literature in English: Essays
on the Major Writers* (New York: Garland,
1991), pp. 537–38

RIBEIRO TAVARES, ZULMIRA (BRAZIL) n.d.

O nome do bispo . . . tells of a hospital stay, a hemorrhoid operation, and the things that went through the mind of the patient, a man of fifty belonging to a "good" Paulist family. A title such as *The (B)Anal Operation of Heládio Marcondes Pompeu* would have hit the nail on the head by warning against the theme, most likely of small interest to those who have not undergone similar surgery and disagreeable to those who have.

Heládio is named after a bishop in the family; there is no other similarity between the two. The family history, told in the form of the ailing man's memories of it, seems typical enough, including as it does, some shady antecedents. The author uses the freedom freshly won by feminism to spice her story with the once-proscribed vocabulary designating sexual organs, the sexual act, and the climax, the details of the human anus. That must be the only (relative) novelty to her otherwise unremarkable work. It has its lively moments, especially when Oscar, an uncle, is involved, a man who dabbled in escapades, magic, and astronomy. His picturesque life, of which we glimpse several slices, would have made a better story.

G. M. Moser. *World Literature Today.*
60 (1986), p. 88

Although according to current Brazilian standards her literary output—four books in the last fifteen years—is relatively small, Zulmira Ribeiro Tavares has established herself, particularly since the publication of her award-winning novel *O Nome do Bispo* in 1985 . . . as one of the foremost contemporary writers from Brazil. *O Mandril* (The mandrill), a collection of forty-two pieces of short fiction and poetry, of which nine were originally published in newspapers and magazines, solidifies Tavares's well-deserved reputation.

Despite the diversity of the texts and the author's own claim in the final piece, "A casa desarrumada," that they are not parts of anything . . . the collection is unified by a distinctive world view and attitude toward literature. All the pieces reveal a humane concern for the precarious situation of the individual in the face of an ephemeral life, a silent God, burdensome restrictions imposed by family, culture, and gender roles on human freedom, and our own selfish disregard for one another. In reading the stories and verse of *O Mandril* we are asked to confront the basic paradox of our existence: that in spite of our existential loneliness, we are inexorably and inextricably connected. Magnificently depicted in the opening piece, from which the collection takes its title, this tension recurs in different forms throughout the volume, most particularly in the elegantly ironic "Coelho: Coelhos," in the frightfully powerful "Larvas e prodígios," in the delicately understated "Reserva," and in the moving "Humanidade(s)." Each of these pieces contains both an indictment of any attitude that results in turning the other into an object, from cruelty and contempt to pettiness and selfishness, and a plea for the recognition of the other as a subject conceived in our own likeness, one who mirrors our qualities and our foibles.

However, *O Mandril* is also a celebration of human resilience. Such pieces as "Crescendo (e dançando) para a carreira militar," "Circuitos latino-americanos," and "Mocinhamoringa" show that dreams, the imagination, and desire accomplish something invaluable by allowing us, at least temporarily, to go beyond the constraints of social conventions and the repetitiveness of the quotidian. "Uma quase pomba," "A perfeita coleção," and "Plácido, o abstêmio" bear witness to the redeeming power of love and generosity. Ultimately, literature matters because it partakes of the latter qualities. This is why in "A casa desarrumada" the author invites the reader to become involved as a collaborator in the project of bringing the texts to life: "arrumei a casa convidando calorosamente o leitor a desarrumá-la." As the poem "Torre de Pisa" suggests, Tavares conceives of literature not as a distant ivory tower but, like the famous leaning tower, as something created out of both human genius and human fallibility. Amid the skepticism and the often sterile self-referentiality of so much recent literature, Zulmira Ribeiro Tavares, although conscious of the limitations of the modern condition, stands out as a link with the best in the humanistic tradition.

Luiz Fernando Valente. World Literature
Today. 64, 1990, pp. 85–86

In *Jóias de família* (Family jewels) Zulmira Ribeiro Tavares continues the provocative but elegantly understated satire of the Brazilian family that she inaugurated in her first novel, *O nome do bispo.* Seen by the author as a microcosm of society, the family provides Tavares, who is uncomfortable with large panoramas and whose texts generally have an intimate quality, with a focal point for her social critique. The narrative centers on Maria Bráulia Munhoz, a dignified elderly widow who lives alone with her faithful black maid Maria Preta amid the trappings and rituals of more affluent days. As in her first novel, Tavares relies on an omniscient, completely reliable narrator, who, wielding language with the precision of a surgeon's scalpel, removes the protagonist's persona of propriety and formality layer by layer to expose a deeper, private self, ruled by repressed desire and engulfed in calculating lies.

As the title suggests, the novel is organized around variations on the motif of family jewels. From the very beginning a connection is established between family jewels and the antiquated values and empty traditions designed to preserve the social status quo. It is significant, therefore, that Maria Preta is ironically compared to a family jewel, for she has both passively accepted her role as a virtual slave of Maria Bráulia's family and unquestioningly adopted the values of her bosses. Like the financial situation of the family, though, the stability of these cherished values and traditions can no longer be taken for granted. . . . Above all, though, the motif of family jewels is symbolically liked to sexuality, particularly the two rubies of different shapes and sizes which Maria Bráulia has received as gifts from the two men around whom her life has revolved. The first ruby is a multifaceted gem, claimed to be from Ceylon, and given to Maria Bráulia as an engagement ring by her social-climbing fiancé, the staid and pompous Judge Munhoz, who turns out to be a closet homosexual. Only after marrying Munhoz does Maria Bráulia learn that, like her husband's feigned heterosexuality, this ruby is fake, a discovery that significantly takes place not long after she has surprised her husband and his male secretary in a compromising position. The social code by which Maria Bráulia lives requires, however, that she remain forever silent about the truth of both her husband's gift and his sexual preference.

Unlike the first ruby, the second one is authentic. Cut *en cabochon* and set into a pendant, it was a present to Maria Bráulia from Marcel de Souza Armand, a jeweler and friend of her husband's, who becomes her lover and finally fulfills her sexually. There is an obvious analogy between the pendant and Armand's genitals, an analogy made explicit by Armand himself during one of a series of private lessons on the secrets of gem-cutting with which he counterpoints Maria Bráulia's discovery of the mysteries of sex.

Although the omniscient point of view provides the distance necessary for satire to emerge, it also allows the reader to become intimately acquainted with Maria Bráulia. Despite the narrator's impassivity and irony, the reader does develop a certain degree of empathy for the protagonist, who, to a large extent, is a victim of a hypocritical society. Nevertheless, empathy is not allowed to become dominant. Indeed, the focus of the last chapter shifts from Maria Bráulia herself to the crystal swan on her dining table, which was first mentioned in the opening paragraph and which has reappeared as a leitmotiv throughout the narrative. A phallic symbol connected with Munhoz, the crystal swan, which, bathed in the faint light of the dawn, is said to resemble a dead chicken, stands for the artificiality and inauthenticity of society's rules, thereby serving as a constant reminder for the protagonist of her implacable guilt.

Even though Tavares does not consider herself a feminist, *Jóias de família* makes an eloquent statement about the situation of women in Brazilian society. Nevertheless, the novel also shows that the constraints society imposes on the individual victimize both women and men alike, by condemning them to a life of sham and self-deception. Tavares seems to be suggesting that there can be no liberation for women except in the context of a society that has been liberated of its dehumanizing prejudices and stale values, and that allows individuals of both genders the freedom to be true to their own selves.

Luiz Fernando Valente. *World Literature Today*. 65, 1991, pp. 684–85

RICH, ADRIENNE (UNITED STATES) 1929—

Miss Rich at twenty-one is a poet thoroughly trained by masters of verse whom she echoes at times but never slavishly. Thanks to her search for perfection, she has composed her poems with an almost flawless perception and sound ear. While one might say that she belongs to an age in which youth is skeptical of a world unmade by tottering elders, she is clearly aware of the artist's place in society, and this without special pleading or self-defenses. She is, in short, the kind of neo-classic poet who relies on true form. In this she resembles another young poet, somewhat older than herself, the perfectionist Richard Wilbur.

Alfred Kreymborg. *The New York Times.*
May 13, 1951, p. 27

Adrienne Cecile Rich is distinguished by her uncanny ability to write. Again and again her poetry communicates the peculiar excitement of exactness. Young poets of talent generally have one of two flaws; either they are afflicted with every kind of clumsiness, and must have their poems weeded clear of dead metaphors, extra feet, clichés, and dishonest rhetoric; either that, or they are gifted with easy competence and are plagued by not always sounding quite like themselves. Adrienne Cecile Rich falls into the second category, but she does not fall far. It is easy to greet several of her poems with familiarity: "How do you do, Mr. Frost? And you, Mr. Auden?" But even if one should decide to dismiss these poems (which would be foolish), there would be many left to which one could attach no name but the author's own.

The Diamond Cutters is Miss Rich's second volume, and it is superior to *A Change of World.* The earlier book was sometimes tame, and even a little smug about its ability to keep experience away from the door. In the second book, the wolf is inside and is busy writing poems about its successful campaign.

Donald Hall. *Poetry.* February, 1956, p. 301

Everybody thinks young things young, Sleeping Beauty beautiful—and the poet whom we see behind the clarity and gravity of Miss Rich's poems cannot help seeming to us a sort of princess in a fairy tale. Her scansion, even, is easy and limpid, close to water, close to air; she lives nearer to perfection (an all-too-easy, perfection, sometimes—there are a few of Schubert's pieces that are better the first time than they ever are again, and some of Miss Rich's poems are like this) than ordinary poets do, and her imperfections themselves are touching as the awkwardness of anything young and natural is touching. The reader feels that she has only begun to change; thinks, "This young thing, who knows what it may be, old?" Some of her poems are very different from the others, some of her nature is very far from the rest of it, so that one feels that she has room to live in and to grow out into; liking her for what she is is a way of liking her even better for what she may become.

Randall Jarrell. *Yale Review.* Autumn, 1956,
p. 100

Lynn Fontanne is said to speak our tongue without accent—neither British nor American, but "standard" English. Even so Adrienne Rich, and as in Miss Fontanne's case, there is nothing dull about decorum, nothing impersonal about propriety (indeed, the word means ownership), nothing weak about womanliness. The earlier work in *Snapshots of a Daughter-in-law,* fabricated on the careful loom responsible for the poems in Adrienne Rich's first two books, interest me most, though I can see that in the later pieces she is doing something new, generating a tenser tone, beyond cosiness, and the energy of this reaching style must stand surrogate for the knowingness of her past poems that seemed to be possessed of an effortless control. Naturally such ease is the triumph of hard work, a kind of verbal topiary, and its reward, as in the two most ambitious pieces of this collection, the title poem and "Readings of History," is a freedom, a sense of possibility apparently unhampered by even the strongest awareness of personal limitation.

Richard Howard. *Poetry.* July, 1963,
pp. 258–59

Adrienne Rich's *Snapshots of a Daughter-in-Law* . . . makes it evident that she is more than the able and delicate poetess some of her neat poems have implied. She has a hard vision and restlessness in the confines of her forms which save her from the monotony sometimes resulting from rather neutral language and standard versification. She hasn't the elegance of, say, Richard Wilbur in managing her stanzas and rhymes, nor the vitality and surprise of May Swenson. But she is more relentless than either in working at ragged human feelings, in catching the quality of our senseless isolation as we ride the random tide of history.

Judson Jerome. *Saturday Review of
Literature.* July 6, 1963, p. 31

Adrienne Rich has grown steadily more interesting from book to book and now in her fourth work, *Necessities of Life,* this advance, tortuous and sometimes tortured as it has been, is an arrival, a poised and intact completion. . . .

From the beginning, there was a yearning, a straining onward, a sense of disproportion between the life of looking and the life of living, tremors of discontent running through a style perhaps too beautiful and contented. After the perfection of *The Diamond Cutters* her work became in *Snapshots of a Daughter-in-law* more reckless. The opening poems are gnarled, sketchy and obscure. They read like jottings in a notebook, and looked like frayed threads in a spider web. Sometimes we seemed to be watching the terrible and only abstractly imaginable struggle of a beetle to get out of its beetle shell and yet remain a beetle.

Robert Lowell. *The New York Times.*
July 17, 1966, p. 5

The dominating quality of Adrienne Rich's work, the quality which knits all, sound, syntax, and sense, into a marvelous unitary structure, is what she herself calls "fierce attention." . . . Other words have been used for it—compression, concern, concentration—and none is exactly right; but the poetry shows what it is: a need not simply to confront experience—in this book [*Necessities of Life*] the experience, disconcerting enough, of a woman who is an artist—not simply to exclaim over it, to apostrophize it (one thinks of Sylvia Path), but to *solve* it; to make it come right. This is a small book, but compact. There is not a glib word in it, nor a wasted breath. The poems stand like the stones of Arizona, singly and distinct, some taller than others, all eroded; but with the natural resolution—balance, place, hardness—of stone.

Hayden Carruth. *Poetry.* January, 1967,
p. 267

Adrienne Rich, in her fifth book, *Leaflets,* comes to us so garlanded with honors that one tends to expect each poem to be a masterpiece. This is, of course, unfair. Yet she does manage, in the book as an entirety, to display complete mastery, absolute assurance of movement and tone. I did not find the book great, but I do find it faultless. One fashionable mode at the moment is poetry in free verse with surrealistic jumps between its lines and an ending of deliberate banality, a drop into flatness which constitutes the shock of the poem; another is free verse written with conscious flatness, whose last lines lift in sudden flight into sentimental lyricism, which the preceding lines pull back on like a kite string. Miss Rich avoids both of these over-used methods.

Mona Van Duyn. *Poetry.* March, 1970,
p. 433

Like other cultivated poets of her generation—like Merwin, Snodgrass and James Wright—Adrienne Rich is haunted into significance as much by what she has changed *from* as by changing at all or by what she is changing to. Recurrence, memory, any presentiment of the old order, of the poem as contraption, is what this poet obsessively, creatively combats. In her sixth book [*The Will to Change*], then, there will be a constant imagery of inconstancy, of breaking free, of fracturing, of shedding and molting. . . .

The governing (or anarchic) emblems in this taut, overturning book are more likely to be drawn from almost anywhere than from poetry, from anything but verse in its decorous accorded sense, the ritual of a departure and return, a refrain which is indeed a refraining as well, a reluctance to violate repetition. Rather the figures will be derived from dreams and dedications, letters, elegies, photographs, movies. . . . The movies . . . are the major representative form here, and the major piece in this book is an extended series of writings called, focally, "Shooting Script"—what Adrienne Rich herself calls a conversation of sounds melting constantly into rhythms, "a cycle whose rhythm begins to change the meanings of words."

Richard Howard. *Partisan Review.* Winter,
1971–72, pp. 484–85

The forcefulness of *Diving into the Wreck* comes from the wish not to huddle wounded, but to explore the caverns, the scars, the depths of the wreckage. At first these explorations must reactivate all the old wounds, inflame all the scar tissue, awaken all the suppressed anger, and inactivate the old language invented for dealing with the older self. But I find no betrayal of continuity in these later books, only courage in the refusal to write in forms felt to be outgrown. I hope that the curve into more complex expression visible in her earlier books will recur as Rich continues to publish, and that these dispatches from the battlefield will be assimilated into more complete poetry. Given Rich's precocious and sustained gifts, I see no reason to doubt her future. The title poem that closed *The Diamond Cutters* says that the poetic supply is endless: after one diamond has been cut, "Africa/ Will yield you more to do." When new books follow, these most recent poems will I think be seen as the transition to a new generosity and a new self-forgetfulness.

Helen Vendler. *Parnassus.* Fall–Winter,
1973, p. 33

It is rare that the poet-turned-activist survives as a poet. Adrienne Rich is an exception. In seven decisive steps from her first volume of poems to her most recent, she has increasingly closed the gap between her public and private selves, never criticizing what is outside herself without criticizing what is within. In so doing, she admits that oppression is as much the creation of the oppressed as the oppressor. To be "stern with herself" is thus the axis of her poetic and political commitment, and it is in this way that her poems are moral without being moralistic, sensitive without bleeding sap.

Language is the weapon of her revolution; the proper naming of her pain as woman, poet, activist, and human being in a decadent civilization is her strategy; the revolution of the human spirit is her goal.

Diving into the Wreck, her seventh volume of poems, is revolutionary in ways we ordinarily think revolutionary: it is feminist, anti-war, pro-ecology, anti-order; it rejects a whole tradition of formal poetry. But it is not a simple rendering of revolutionary themes.

Gale Flynn. *The Hollins Critic.* October,
1974, pp. 1–2

The poem "Diving into the Wreck" [presents] adventures behind the common definitions of sexuality and beyond the damages done by acculturation and conditioning. It is here also that Rich makes her strongest political identification with feminism, in her attempts to define experiences unique to women or to define the damages done by false definitions of sexual identity. Into her images she has been able to concentrate much of what has always been in her poetry: what it is like to feel oppressed, betrayed and unfulfilled. The explicit identification with feminism sometimes sets poems off balance. But this is a matter of presentation and not—as some critics have suggested— because Rich has radically changed the direction or interests of her writing. . . .

Twinned with the anger in [her] recent poems, there is also an enlarged awareness—a new voice, I think, in Rich's work—of the tragedy wrought into human relationships and into the attempts at dialogue and exchange.

There are two particularly important examples: on the level of social injustice, her "Meditations for a Savage Child" and, less general, a poem of blunted love, "Cartographies of Silence." "Meditations for a Savage Child" is a remarkable poem based on the documents Truffaut also used so movingly in his film *L'Enfant Sauvage,* the records of the French doctor, J. M. Itard (now published as *The Wild Boy of Aveyron*). Itard had observed and partly "civilized" a savage child in the late eighteenth century. Rich, perhaps following Truffaut, introduces excerpts from the doctor's accounts as points of departure for each of the five sections of her poem. Unlike Truffaut, who chose to play the part of Itard in his film, Rich often takes on the role of the child, or ponders what he has to teach her, as she engages in a series of meditative exchanges with the voice of Itard. The poem is partly a long historical register of Rich's own divided spirit. Itard is an adversary but not an enemy, as they gaze across the ambitious ruins of Enlightenment philosophy. In the solicitous elegance of his prose, she finds words which have been emptied of their meaning: humanity, administrators, protection of the government—the roots of much which would have once engaged her own ardor. But in the mysteries of childrearing, of miseducation, she locates everything which defeats that ardor. . . .

It is hard to know, now that some of Rich's force and passionate intelligence has been directed into prose, just what role poetry will come to play in her life and in her writing. Critics have in the past pointed out how much, in her commitment to the notation of present feelings, the pain of the moment, Rich has given up the traditional retrospective and shaping functions of verse. Poems like "Meditations for a Savage Child" and "Cartographies of Silence" show that whatever she has relinquished she has given up purposefully, that she understands the price of her ardor without giving up her rights to it.

David Kalstone. *Five Temperaments:
Elizabeth Bishop, Robert Lowell, James
Merrill, Adrienne Rich, John Ashbery* (New
York: Oxford University Press, 1977),
pp. 162, 165–66, 169

The interpenetration of psyche and history is . . . a major situation in Adrienne Rich's recent poems. She makes her analysis of individual consciousness and history by uniting the issues of sexuality and war. . . . The most intimate relations of love and marriage are traced out in her poems until they are revealed as a terrifying war, and war itself is seen as a fact originating in the patriarchal oppression of women. Domination, depersonalization, and dehumanization are the vectors of the patriarchal soul; multiplied and extended on a national scale, these male traits are, in Rich's view, an ur-political explanation for the Vietnam War and its atrocities. Social dislocation and war stem from an estrangement, at some original moment, between "male" and "female" components of the human psyche. Rich pursues this split, investigating its origins and its costs. In effect she is conducting a historical examination of the psychic life. . . .

The ultimate intention of *Diving into the Wreck* is to call this whole patriarchal myth into question. Rich does so by dramatizing the process of critique and self-exploration in a new myth that constructs her own version of the origin and history of consciousness. Nor is Rich's myth a simple reversal of [Erich] Neumann's model. For, unlike the fecund captive-treasure of the patriarchal myth, here the captive is dead, arrested in the strained posture of unfulfilled searching. Nothing can be won from this figure except the fact of death. The new "fruitful center" in Rich's myth has become the creative antagonism of the woman-hero to traditional consciousness and old patterns of myth—an antagonism motivated because that book of stories and explanations excludes her. So in the course of the journey an androgynous woman has been invented, one appropriating her own fruitfulness and power, and brought into being by her own creative momentum—that is, from the process of critique.

> Rachel Blau DuPlessis. In Sandra M.
> Gilbert and Susan Gubar, eds.
> *Shakespeare's Sisters: Feminist Essays on
> Women Poets* (Bloomington: Indiana
> University Press, 1979), pp. 291–92, 295

A Wild Patience Has Taken Me This Far assembles in chronological order the poems Adrienne Rich wrote between 1978 and 1981. These poems, given to rhetorical excesses and political simplifications, are far from her best work; but a fair portion of the collection is important. For some time, Rich has been moving towards the extreme of radical feminism; in this volume she arrives humorlessly at its pole. The irony that tempered her depiction of the conflict of the sexes in *The Dream of a Common Language,* her one great book, is gone now. What has survived is a poetry that will, and should, discomfit many readers; it will sometimes move them as well. . . .

Missing from . . . most . . . poems in the book, is a sense of balance. In Rich's worst poems, such as "Frame," she wilfully misrepresents men, committing the same act of distortion that she complains about elsewhere. "Frame" stoops to vicious clichés, portraying men as incurable rapists, invoking the stereotype of the Boston policeman who has nothing to do other than pursue and maim young women.

Fortunately, Rich can do better. The self-obsession that characterized much of her earlier work, which was largely concerned with an evolving autobiographical *mythos,* has widened into a concern with the "selves," past and present, around her. While her dream of a common language has never been realized in her own poems, Rich approaches it in pieces such as "Culture and Anarchy" and "The Spirit of Place," both of which call up for inspection the lives of earlier women.

> Jay Parini. *Times Literary Supplement.*
> November 12, 1982, p. 1251

In the 1970s, with the publication of *The Will to Change, Diving into the Wreck* and the essays "When We Dead Awaken: Writing as Re-Vision" (1971) and "The Anti-Feminist Woman" (1972), Adrienne Rich opened new areas of meaning for feminist discourse, a fact which engendered or provoked an important change in the state of affairs of the current criticism on her work. Indeed from that period there is a clearly distinguishable split among the critics of her work: those who accept her texts and her ways of approaching language, and those who reject this and who therefore do not attempt to read her following her own codes, and do not interpret the transformations as part of an on-going process, dismissing her for being too polemical, a feminist, or lesbian. . . . Both *The Dream of a Common Language* and *A Wild Patience Has Taken Me This Far* are further developments from her first irritations with the conventional world, which, although dispersed at the beginning, became inevitable. These two books contextualize woman-to-woman relations in North-American culture, another stage in Adrienne Rich's conscious act of creation and re-creation.

The Dream does not provide a "common language" but suggests its foundations. In this book Rich proposes the need to re-construct language by introducing new codes in order to build a new system of correlations for women in society.

Myriam Díaz-Diocaretz. *The Transforming Power of Language: The Poetry of Adrienne Rich* (Utrecht, Netherlands: H.E.S., 1984), pp. 17, 23

Rich's poems explore the possibilities of an authentic expression of what constitutes a woman's voice in a patriarchal world, and from this perspective her relationship to language and society emerges. The poet's changing world visions can be, for purposes of the present discussion, organized around four dominant *spectra:* the first one consists of the point of view of the woman growing up in a world that has been previously ordered and for which she must be equipped to exist as a subordinated being: that is, she has "to take the world as it was given." . . . The woman begins to perceive her individuality in a world in which her private experience is defined by pre-established conventions and previously assigned definitions about which there is little she can do. . . .

Second, the man–woman relationship set in context of a patriarchy-oriented society is first accepted, yet lived through with a certain distance, at times with restraint and suspicion, later confronted and critically rejected, and finally reexamined.

Third, the woman in the act of "re-vision" which brings her cognition of the need to establish her own true values in a man's world. As a consequence of this awareness, the image of the male figure becomes often the agent and instrument of social physical spiritual violence, or indifference, and also destruction (e.g., war) and self-destruction (e.g., suicide). A "visionary anger" arises and the poet explores the suffering and alienation felt as a woman, from the realization that man cannot stop being the perpetuator of patriarchal values and a potential enemy to himself.

Fourth, the woman-to-woman relationship becomes the answer to attain a meaningful existence, as a result of a gradual assertion of identity and identification with women in the past and the present as well. This development can be seen in the light of a movement from aesthetic detachment objectifying emotions and personal voice, to a direct lesbian-feminist vision. Man appears as an incidental presence, the occasional transgressor; this does not mean he has ceased to exist but that he is *deterritorialized* in the poet's presented vision. Woman is no longer living in a man's world; the critique of patriarchy and Rich's self assertion open a new territory for the bonding with other women through the "power of language, which is the ultimate relationship with everything in the universe."

Myriam Díaz-Diocaretz. *Translating Poetic Discourse* (Philadelphia: John Benjamins, 1985), p. 60–61

"Lesbian." For many, heterosexual or homosexual, the word still constricts the throat. Those "slimy" sibilants; those "nasty" nasalities. "Lesbian" makes even "feminist" sound lissome, decent, sane. In 1975, Adrienne Rich's reputation was secure. She might have eased up and toyed with honors. Yet, she was doing nothing less than seizing and caressing that word: "lesbian." She was working hard for "a whole new poetry" that was to begin in two women's "limitless desire". . . .

As Rich grounds women's thoughts and feelings in their bodies, she *naturalizes* them. Her poetry harvests the earth and the elements for its metaphors: the cave; trees; plants; flowers; fields; the volcano, at once peak to ascend and crater into which to descend, breast and genitals, cervix, womb. Rich, too, has absolute competence in composing a poem, in arranging implosive patterns of rhythm and sound. Because the quality of her verbal music and choreography is so assured, a reader learns to trust the palpability of a poem; its replication of the intellectual and emotional movements of experience.

Because of the pressure and magnetism of her metaphors; because of the surprising physicality of her lines; and because of her contempt for patriarchal culture, especially in its modern and urban forms, Rich may seem to be endorsing a feminized primitivism. However, she is far too intelligent a grammarian of reality to parse it into two opposing spheres of "nature" and "culture," and clamor only for the pristine ecological purities of the first. She constructs houses on her land. Rich's dream, her imaginative vision, is of an organic, but freeing, unity among body, nature, consciousness, vision, and community. Unequivocally, lyrically, she asks women to think through their maternal flesh and their own bodies, ". . . to connect what has been so cruelly disorganized—our great mental capacities, hardly used; our highly developed tactile sense; our genius for close observation; our complicated, pain-enduring, multi-pleasured physicality." In a leap of faith, she wants women to become the presiding geniuses of their bodies in order to create new life—biologically and culturally. Their thoughts and visions will transform politics, ". . . alter human existence," sustain a "new relationship to the universe."

Language lies. Language invents. Poetry lies. Poetry invents. Rich accepts that "truth." Writing tells stories that matter. Writing gives us images from the mind and of the body, for the relief of the body and the reconstruction of the mind. Rich accepts that "truth" as well. If some words ("lesbian") constrict the throat, say them. Open them up. Only then can we speak enough to wonder seriously if language lies, because it is language; if language invents, because it is language, or if language lies because people are liars who invent to control, rather than to dream, and justly please.

Catharine Stimpson. Parnassus. 12–13,
1985, pp. 249, 254–55, 265

Adrienne Rich has become an icon of American letters in her lifetime, a feat managed by few women writers of any time or place, by fewer poets than novelists, and probably by no other politically activist lesbian. Her poetry has inspired two generations of readers, and she has been far less ghettoized than most feminist writers. Not even the most hidebound of my traditionalist colleagues, male or female, dismiss Rich. They can't. The conceptual density and technical achievement of her poetry, together with the far-ranging knowledge of the Western intellectual tradition she demonstrates when she challenges that tradition in poetry or prose, are nearly impossible to patronize. Rich's poetry seems assured a secure place in the canon whose standards she rightly despises. With three new collections published by Norton since 1988 (*An Atlas of the Difficult World, Time's Power* and *Your Native Land, Your Life*), she has shown herself undiminished in creative power.

Like several of our best poets (I am thinking of, for instance, Maxine Kumin and Alicia Ostriker), Rich is building a parallel oeuvre of prose works, a body of culture criticism on American (and global) arts and politics. Beginning in some respects with *Of Woman Born*, these works now include essays collected under the titles *On Lies, Secrets, and Silence, Blood, Bread and Poetry* and this new volume, *What is Found There.* . . .

Rich sees "the life of North American poetry at the end of the century as a pulsing, racing convergence of tributaries . . . that, rising from lost or long-blocked springs, intersect and infuse each other." The river image is familiar, recurring in Rich's writing for years, rising here in her description of herself as poet: "I choose to sieve up old, sunken words, heave them, dripping with silt, turn them over, and bring them into the air of the present." If Rich's place in the life of the poetry she analyzes is certain, as I believe it is, does that mean it is "great?" The word itself betrays the anti-hierarchical imperatives she insists on in these essays; very well, then. Vital? Most needed? No, what I mean is great: I place a value judgment on the poems.

What about her poetics, delineated in these writings on poetry and politics? Are they in the same league as the poems? They explore much of the same subject-matter, but the poems almost always transcend their polemics as the prose sometimes does not. It's a matter of tone. In the essays she harangues. In the poems she sings; it's hard to sing in lists, even if we need them.

What I am saying flies in the face of Rich's most urgent thesis, here and elsewhere: that poetry not only *can* be political, but *is* by its very nature, as are all of our utterances; the American conviction that openly, explicitly political poetry cannot be good poetry is false, destructive, potentially lethal. "Arturo—would you agree?—we're unable to write love, as we so much wish to do, without writing politics." Yet she acknowledges sadly what love sometimes means: "Love might be put into action by firing a gun, yes—at whom? In what extremity?" Rich sets out to demonstrate—entirely successfully, for me—that a great deal of political poetry is also lyrically rich, linguistically sophisticated, imagistically successful by any measure.

Diana Hume George. *Women's Review of Books.* 11, December, 1993, pp. 1, 3

RICHARDSON, DOROTHY (GREAT BRITAIN) 1873–1957

By imposing very strict limitations on herself she has brought her art, her method, to a high pitch of perfection, so that her form seems to be newer than it perhaps is. She herself is unaware of the perfection of her method. She would probably deny that she had written with any deliberate method at all. . . . Obviously, she must not interfere; she must not analyze or comment or explain. Rather less obviously, she must not tell a story or handle a situation or set a scene; she must avoid drama as she avoids narration. And there are some things she must not be. She must not be the wise, all-knowing author. She must be Miriam Henderson. . . . She has taken Miriam's nature upon hers. . . . Of the persons who move through Miriam's world you know nothing but what Miriam knows. . . . Miriam is an acute observer, but she is very far from seeing the whole of these people. They are presented to us in the same vivid but fragmentary way in which they appeared to Miriam, the fragmentary way in which some people appear to most of us. Miss Richardson has only imposed on herself the conditions that life imposes on us all. . . .

To me these three novels show an art and method and form carried to punctilious perfection. [*Pointed Roofs, Backwater, Honeycomb*, Pts. I–III of *Pilgrimage*].

May Sinclair. *The Egoist.* April, 1918, p. 58

It seems to us that a comparison between M. Proust and Miss Richardson is not really very profitable—their work does not cover in the least the same ground. In certain ways their methods are alike. For instance, in the books of both authors it is often a little difficult to find out the outward circumstances of the person the working of whose mind we are shown. Both authors realize that it is not so much outward happenings that shape people's lives as the way in which these happenings are interpreted by the persons concerned. But while M. Proust's men and women are active, often restless in shaping their own destinies, altering, re-arranging, striving, Miss Richardson's derive a kind of ecstasy from passivity. It is, perhaps, this passivity that differentiates her work from that of Mr. James Joyce, which, however, it much more closely resembles than that of M. Proust. M. Proust has made what will probably remain for many generations of writers the ultimate analysis of one complete layer of life, not quite the intellectual layer, but what we might call the commonsense active layer. . . .

Mr. Joyce's ambitions take him down far below this daylight level to some strange, deep, passionate cave of consciousness. He storms into it, a revealing invader, flashing his lamp here and there on the beautiful and the grotesque and the obscene. But he is always the active explorer, finding things out, and is often in his own despite denunciatory. Miss Richardson, passive and still, sinks through events and states of mind quiet and dumb, and in this ecstasy of listening and waiting she reaches a layer of personality which is different to that either of Mr. James Joyce or M. Proust. . . .

Revolving Lights suffers more than do some of the other books from Miss Richardson's besetting sin—her tiresome twist towards feminism. It is the one blot upon her exquisite fairness and detachment. The reader cannot help constantly wishing that she would see how much any twist takes away from the value of her testimony on other points—Socialism, the territorial classes, Jews, Russians and what not.

The Spectator. June 30, 1923, pp. 1084–85

Miss Richardson's work is unique in fiction (none of her disciples has ever dared the full implications of her theory) and has a metaphysical value that is absent in Proust or Joyce. For neither of these writers is inspired by the mystical quality that is peculiar to Miss Richardson. . . . Dorothy Richardson has assumed the existence of a soul to which the consciousness has much the same relation that the intelligence has to the consciousness. . . . The great moments of Miriam's experience are not found in moving adventures nor in moments of physical stress, but at those times when she is most keenly aware of herself in relation to the spirit that moves beneath and animates every phenomenon of the great phantasmagoria we know as life and matter.

J. D. Beresford. *Tradition and Experiment in Present-Day Literature* (Oxford: Oxford University Press, 1929), p. 47

Dorothy Richardson is our first pioneer in a completely new direction. What she has done has never been done before. She has drawn her inspiration neither from man-imitating cleverness nor from narcissistic feminine charm but *from the abyss of the feminine subconscious*. . . . These quiet and penetrating books represent, in fact, the only attempt I am aware of to put into psychological fiction the real "philosophy," moral, aesthetic, spiritual, and that which underlies all these and escapes from all these and mocks at all these—of women where they differ most from men. . . . Miss Richardson is a far more original writer, a far greater writer, than the clever philistine-culture of our age has the sensitivity to understand. She is an authentic philosopher. . . . She has carried this philosophy of the "a-logical, innocent eye" into a new dimension, the dimension of women's secret, instinctive sensitiveness to the mystery of life.

J. C. Powys. *Dorothy Richardson* (n.p.:
Joiner and Steele, 1931), pp. 8, 17–18

She is perhaps the most perfect incarnation that has ever existed of one of the warring elements in the eternal sex war. Hers is—or perhaps I had better say appears to be—the authentic voice of essential woman using the distinctively feminine faculties to express the world. No doubt it was not by chance that she was first trying her hand at writing at the moment when the militant suffragette movement was at its height. Not that the suffragette way was her way. It was not by attempting to do what men do, or by "assimilating masculine culture" that women (according to Miriam) acted in their own true part. Miriam's part was to act, think, feel and experience life with the sentience that belongs to the feminine side of human nature and to do so in full consciousness of what she was doing. . . . Mrs. Virginia Woolf has immense power of presenting the feminine point of view, but she is not herself controlled by it, as Miss Richardson is. Miss Richardson not merely presents the feminine point of view; she is it. She is conscious of the fact, glories in it, and wages (through Miriam) relentless war on the amusing monstrosity of the male intelligence. . . . It is evident that the distinctive excellence for which Miss Richardson stands made it desirable for her to have just such a vehicle as she has chosen; her technique exactly serves her purpose. It lends itself—one might add—to artistic laziness—possibly a feminine defect?— to following the least line of resistance in recording the unordered flow of impressions as they pass through the mind.

R. A. Scott-James. *The London Mercury.*
December, 1935, pp. 202–3

The long trainload [*Pilgrimage*] draws by our platform, passes us with an inimical flash of female eyes, and proceeds on into how many more dry and gritty years. It set out in 1915 with some acclamation, carrying its embarrassing cargo—the stream of consciousness—saluted by many prominent bystanders—Miss West and Mrs. Woolf, Mr. Wells, Mr. Beresford, Mr. Swinnerton and Mr. Hugh Walpole.

Who could have foreseen in the first ordinary phrases this gigantic work which has now reached its two thousandth page, without any indication of a close? The Saratoga trunk becomes progressively more worn and labelled. There is no reason why the pilgrimage should ever end, except with the author's life, for she is attempting to represent the whole effect of every experience—friendship, politics, tea-parties, books, weather, what you will—on a woman's sensibility.

I am uncertain of my dates, but I should imagine Miss Richardson in her ponderous unwitty way has had an immense influence on such writers as Mrs. Woolf and Miss Stein, and through them on their disciples. Her novel, therefore, has something in common with Bowles's Sonnets. She herself became influenced about halfway through these four volumes (comprising twelve novels or installments) by the later novels of Henry James—the result, though it increased the obscurity of her sensibility, was to the good, for she began to shed the adjectives which in the first volume disguise any muscles her prose may possess. . . . Or was it simply that Miriam became a little older, unhappier, less lyrical? In the monstrous subjectivity of this novel the author is absorbed into her character. There is no longer a Miss Richardson: only Miriam. . . .

There are passages of admirable description, characters do sometimes emerge clearly from the stream of consciousness. . . . But the final effect, I fear, is one of weariness (that may be a tribute to Miss Richardson's integrity), the weariness of the best years of life shared with an earnest, rather sentimental and complacent woman. For one of the drawbacks of Miss Richardson's unironic and undetached method is that the compliments paid so frequently to the wit or intellect of Miriam seem addressed to the author herself. (We are reminded of those American women who remark to strangers, "They simply worshipped me.") And as for the method—it must have seemed in 1915 a revivifying change from the tyranny of the "plot." But time has taken its revenge: after twenty years of subjectivity, we are turning back with relief to the old dictatorship, to the detached and objective treatment. . . .

Graham Greene. *The Lost Childhood* (New York: Viking, 1951), pp. 84–85

The death of Dorothy Miller Richardson at eighty-four last June 17, in England, removed from our literary scene the last of the experimenters who in the century's opening years created the "inside-looking-out" novel—what we more commonly speak of as the "stream of consciousness" novel. The least read and the most unobtrusive of the experimenters, she had outlived them all, outlived, indeed, her own work and her own modest reputation. . . . Literary history bids fair to use *Pilgrimage* not so much for its exploration of the inner consciousness as for its vivid portraits of certain identifiable figures and its reflection of a certain era in English life and letters. For it is also, to a degree, a roman à clef and certain readers have already recognized the marked resemblance between Hypo Wilson and H. G. Wells. . . .

Certainly there can be no question of placing her now on an equality of footing with Proust and Joyce. Miss Richardson was a journeyman beside the nimble-minded Irishman, nor did she have the Frenchman's capacity for discovering a universe in a perfume. She must be written down rather as one of the hardy and plodding experimenters of literature, the axe-swingers and stump-pullers, those who have a single moment of vision which suffices for a lifetime. There was a kind of Zola in Miss Richardson, not in her work but in herself as the artist-type—the immense recording of data, the observation and note-taking, weight and solidity, the carrying out of a major project according to plan. . . . To re-read Miss Richardson now and to re-appraise her in her four thick volumes which embody her twelve novels or "chapters," is to marvel at her unflagging zeal: the book is a victory of resolution, patience, and sensibility over limited artistic means. *Pilgrimage* for all its sprawling minuteness, its endless internal monologue sensitively alert to sunlight and shadow, London streets and rooms, contains distinct qualities of strength, insight and feeling, and above all vitality—the vitality of a purposeful individual who cannot be swerved from a creative task, who indeed converts the task into a self-education.

In the novel we learn how Miss Richardson discovered *The Ambassadors* (Miriam reads it with intense excitement) and learned from Henry James the proper use of "point of view." The fascination of putting the reader into a given angle of vision and keeping him there: this was the lesson of the Master for Miss Richardson and she learned it well; it became the guiding light by which she worked. . . . Today we would call this the "camera eye," so accustomed are we to seeing it done in the cinema. Miss Richardson anticipated the moving picture camera; from the first she brought everything into the orbit of Miriam's eyes and her senses and sought to capture within a book the *ewige Weibliche*—not as men might express it, but as women experienced it. In undertaking to write "point of view" on so large a scale, Miss Richardson set herself a much more difficult task than Proust. . . .

Few men—few critics of their sex—have been willing to climb into Miss Richardson's boat; the journey is long, the "stream of consciousness" difficult—raw unabstracted data, the absence of the omniscient author to serve as guide, the consequent need to become the author so as to bring some order into the great grab-bag of feminine experience offered us; and then the need, Orlando-like, to become the girl or woman, to become Miriam if we are to be her consciousness. Few writers have placed so double-weighted a burden upon their readers. And yet if the challenge is met and the empathy achieved, Dorothy Richardson offers us, on certain pages, a remarkable emotional luminescence—as well as, historically speaking, a record of the trying out of a new technique, the opportunity to examine a turning point in the modern English novel. There is a distinct possibility that a new generation of readers—if there will continue to be readers at all—may truly discover Dorothy Richardson for the first time.

Leon Edel. Modern Fiction Studies.
Summer, 1958, pp. 165–68

Truly enough, Dorothy Richardson's propaganda reflects the period through which she wrote, and readers today are not likely to be stirred by *Pilgrimage* because they agree or disagree with her views on "the woman question." They will look for other values in her journey. One of these—and this has something to do with her subterranean influence on modern English writing— was her candid approach in dealing with the careers of women. *Pilgrimage*, then, was a long step toward Virginia Woolf's famous essay, "A Room of One's Own"—and that influence was even deeper than Mrs. Woolf's adaptations of the "stream of consciousness" technique to her own uses. Dorothy Richardson's example inspired self-confidence in other women writers and permitted them to assert their independence (in print) with far more ease than their predecessors had. *Pilgrimage* created an atmosphere in and from which other journeys could make their start. We must remember that its beginnings were actually gas-lit glimmerings out of Victorian darkness.

But the more enduring interest of *Pilgrimage* is very closely allied to the kind of journey taken by its heroine. We know at once that the journey has something to do with education, and from the predominant imagery of its first section, "Pointed Roofs," the journey moves from darkness toward light, toward hoped-for illuminations in the future. Miriam Henderson's journey, however realistic it may have been, had transcendental elements and associations. Her education included ardent readings in the essays of the American, Ralph Waldo Emerson, seemingly a strange choice for one so stoutly English in her likes and dislikes. But the choice is less strange if one assumes that she adopted him as a shining figure of Unitarianism—and of Protestant dissent.

Horace Gregory. Dorothy Richardson: An
Adventure in Self-Discovery (New York:
Holt, Rinehart and Winston, 1967),
pp. 108–9

The technique invented by Dorothy Richardson has become familiar to us through all those later writers who knowingly or not have derived something from her. It is hard for us today to grasp how difficult and strange her way of writing first appeared. Those early reactions of readers and critics, with their inevitable misunderstandings of her work, have dimmed her reputation to this day.

Some of her seeming limitations—occasional prosiness or blurred characterization, lack of compression or selection, or too much—these are part of her method, and therefore part of the cumulative effect of *Pilgrimage*.

The method was evolved to express her vision in the new world of the twentieth century with its changing ways and attitudes. A new kind of voice was needed: not specifically a woman's voice, but one expressing all the awareness and self-doubt of modern people in a world where traditional beliefs had been called into question.

She created, therefore, through her narrator Miriam just such a voice and viewpoint, taking nothing for granted, expressing nothing in the conventional or accepted way. It was a method belonging to the new age but stemming from the nineteenth-century analytical approach. It was closely equivalent to Impressionism in painting.

Pilgrimage might be called the first full-scale Impressionist novel. As never before in a novel, Dorothy Richardson attempted to show us what we really perceive, not what we accept as reality according to certain conventions. In her descriptions and also in depicting emotion and thought, her novel portrays reality as continual movement and fluctuation. To let this reality filter through as lucidly as possible, the novelist must keep his own voice from obtruding—from commenting, summarizing, drawing hard lines of demarcation of character or incident—just as the Impressionist painters had rejected the convention of firm outline. Similarly there could be no arbitrary "plot" imposed on the material, distorting the truth. If a novel were made alive enough by capturing the flow of reality, then its immediacy should be more exciting than any contrived plot. Dorothy Richardson's *Pilgrimage* bears marked resemblance to Proust's extended protagonist narration, for it too is an impressionistic portrayal of an evolving interpreting consciousness grappling simultaneously with external and internal realities. But Richardson's intensely intimate narrative . . . represents a third category, for it is cast in the form of third-person rather than first, a perspective that James calls "the indirect vision," and that I call third-person-subjective. Far from being omniscient or even multifarious, such a narrator as Richardson's anonymous and disembodied voice is myopic: "he" sees and feels with the eyes and senses of a single character, confining "himself" [with more or less consistency] to an individual perspective. . . .

The convention behind this narrative mode is that voice and order have been given not to the protagonist but to his thoughts and feelings, and that we can experience them directly and coherently, without such intermediary devices as participant narration employs. . . . Thus, despite the formal dissimilarity, Richardson's narrative voice is far closer to Proust's than to, say, Thackeray's arbitrarily shifting narrative perspective. For third-person-subjective has the force though not the form of protagonist narration, and both are equally congenial to impressionistic and stream-of-consciousness fictions.

Alan Warren Friedman. *Multivalence: The Moral Quality of Form in the Modern Novel* (Baton Rouge: Louisiana State University Press, 1978), pp. 21–22

Although Richardson lived and worked in comparative isolation and obscurity, she was very much attuned to the *Zeitgeist*. Indeed, her closest literary associates, H. G. Wells, J. D. Beresford, and John Cowper Powys, could hardly provide her with models or suggestions for the kind of novel which she began to write. But after the appearance of *Pointed Roofs* in 1915, she discovered that "the lonely track had turned out to be a populous highway," along which were traveling fellow pilgrims Proust, Woolf, and Joyce. . . .

As the title indicates, *Pilgrimage* is a spiritual journey, the object of which, in quite simple terms, is self-discovery. Richardson's persona, Miriam Henderson, is a young woman in whose consciousness both author and reader become immersed, whose impressions of experience and involuntary recollections associated with them are simply reported without intervening commentary or exposition. Miriam herself is conscious of her continual "registration of impressions" as "a thing that she must either do or lose hold of something essential." This is surely the most literal and extended representation in literature of the stream of consciousness of one character. Admittedly, over a fictional span of two decades and two thousand pages, it has its arid expanses. . . . The sense of identity as discovered through time, through the contemplation of the past as a living reality in the present, through the awareness of the future illuminating both present and past, through the experience of time not as discrete moments but an organic whole, these are the central themes of *Pilgrimage*. . . .

Miriam's pilgrimage, then, is not marked off by the conventional periods of minutes, hours, days, and years, nor is it concerned primarily with the outward events of her life—which are not extraordinary—she teaches in a girls' school in Germany, works as a dental assistant, rejects several proposals of marriage, visits friends, vacations in Switzerland and among Quakers in Sussex. But the true measure of time is contained in the recurrent moments, usually in solitude, on stairways, in halls and passages, deserted streets, empty rooms and railway carriages, when time seems to expand, bringing a flood of involuntary memories, along with a sense of illumination, a heightened awareness of the present moment accompanied by the feeling of *déjà vu*—described in *Clear Horizon* as "a loop in time, one of those occasions that bring with peculiar vividness the sense of identity, persistent, unchanging, personal identity, and return, in memory, inexhaustible."

This "feminine" treatment of time discards the traditional notion of time as continuous, linear, and quantitative. The discontinuous and impressionistic texture, the very style of *Pilgrimage* with its subtle, complex, Jamesian sentences, gives the sense of time experienced subjectively. The technical feat is the most striking quality of the work as well as the most commented upon.

Arline R. Thorn. *International Journal of Women's Studies*. March–April, 1978, pp. 214–15

Richardson's gradual formulation of her problem, the problem of being a woman, took two parallel lines of development. The first consists of how she lived her life, the second in how she wrote her fiction. Each may properly be called experimental. Her life was unusual for her repeated attempts variously to escape, overcome, modify or repudiate the traditional way of living she perceived to be expected of her by society—the way of love and marriage. Her writing is unusual in the intensity of its challenge to the structural devices in their traditional usages, and to the modes of apperception, of the novel as she knew it. What is especially remarkable and interesting is the way in which these two "experiments," in living and writing, clashed and coalesced, until the usually clear demarcation between them becomes, in her case, blurred and unhelpful. In one sense, that is, *Pilgrimage* is not fiction because the events recorded by its narrative and the characters it introduces, are direct replications of Richardson's own life experiences. On the other hand, it is not autobiography, since we are given no explicit chronology, no objective accounts of people and events and no assurance that the authorial voice and the persona's voice are always to be identified as synonymous. Richardson herself always insisted, perhaps ingenuously, that *Pilgrimage* was fiction and that she had chosen herself as its subject precisely because that was the subject about which she could be most authoritative. . . . In Richardson's case, too, her own statement is a good starting point; if her work is genuine fiction, however experimental, to what extent can we measure it according to traditional critical criteria? Is a woman's book different from a man's book just because Richardson says it is? *Pilgrimage* is clearly 'different' from the novels preceding it, but can its difference be adequately explained by reference to the fact that its author is a woman? . . .

What Richardson is doing in *Pilgrimage* is not a straightforward attempt to record the journey towards identity; it is an attempt to record the gestalt of her life. When she says, both explicitly and implicitly, that she wishes to show what a woman's consciousness is like, she means that though the events of her life occurred sequentially, they were not perceived sequentially. Richardson's inner life, like Miriam's, appears to have violated the chronology of events and to have consisted, also like Miriam's, in a collection of foreshadowings and portents, together with the juxtaposition of memories which bear a thematic relationship with one another, each of all these being as "real" as any point of experience in the outer world.

Gillian E. Hanscombe. *The Art of Life:*
Dorothy Richardson and the Development of
Feminist Consciousness (London:
Peter Owen, 1982), pp. 25–26, 33

If *Pilgrimage* is a meditation upon subjectivity, it is also an extended reflection upon language and writing, in which the subject-matter (sexuality/subjectivity) can be read as an 'alibi' in the formalist sense, for an exploration of signification and the signifying process. In Richardson's writing it is difficult to tell the story from the discourse, since, as the Foreword recounts, the writing of a story becomes the story of a writing. Writing here is many things:

an attempt to subordinate the past to language, an attempt to get beyond language to net or enmesh some pre-verbal state or being, and an investigation of the question of the subject in language. . . .

At narrative level, one can trace two different 'stories' about the subject and subjectivity in *Pilgrimage*. In the first, signified in Miriam's name (her myr-iad 'I-ams') the subject is presented as multiple, bisexual, contradictory. The constant disavowal of any fixed subject position constitutes a deconstruction of the 'sovereign' subject, master of all it surveys. Like Kristeva's *sujet-en-procès* (subject-in-process or subject-on-trial), Richardson's subject seems always in the process of 'becoming', always an effect of time, place and relationships.

> Jean Radford. *Dorothy Richardson*
> (Bloomington: Indiana University Press,
> 1992), pp. 116–19

RICHARDSON, HENRY HANDEL (pseud. ETHEL F. ROBERTSON) (AUSTRALIA) 1870–1946

There is a medical student in [*Maurice Guest*] who is delighted at the opportunity of watching the action of a rare poison on a frog. That is very much the position into which Mr. Richardson tries to put the reader. Maurice Guest is a thoroughly commonplace young man from an English provincial town who goes to Leipzig to study music. The book is the story of his infatuation for a girl student, the cast-off mistress of a young Polish musician. Guest catches her on the rebound, so to say; the friendship which with great difficulty he establishes develops into a stormy liaison, and we are spared no detail of his steady moral and physical degradation.

It is all very clever, and no doubt there are women who have the same effect on a lover as absinthe or morphia. But really this kind of thing has only a pathological interest. If the morals and manners of Leipzig musical students, girls as well as men, are faithfully represented by Mr. Richardson (who seems to know his theme), we imagine that a good many innocent parents in England will be greatly startled. Louise Dufrayer, the Circe of the story, remains a psychological puzzle—unspeakably vile.

> *Saturday Review* (London). September 26,
> 1908, pp. vii–viii

In the first volume of *The Fortunes of Richard Mahony* [*Australia Felix*], the hero, gazing on little Polly's oval face, vows to print only lines of happiness there. With somber patience, with relentless fidelity to character, the third [*Ultima Thule*] now achieves the melancholy irony of the author's purpose. From the first, the strain of diffidence, the haughtiness, the dreaminess, at once Richard's weakness and his apology, proves him no effective colonist. We find him back in Australia, for the third time, at the age of fifty, his fortune gone, partly by his own lack of foresight, partly by the rascality of others. . . .

Composed, deliberate, a little otiose as is the manner of this writer, a relentless sincerity harrows the record of life fairly begun, honorably continued, and lost in the everyday misery of false friends, the death of children, crushing debt, intimate altercation, and gradual insanity. Australia has been no friend to Richard, who never gave her his affection. Yet one feels the Spirit of the country behind the sorrowful story, choosing her own lovers, rejecting nostalgic hearts, flinging snares of her peculiar color, sound, and scent round the infants born on her soil, working out her destiny. It may need a patient reader to appreciate the patient method of Henry Handel Richardson—to realize the large scale of the picture, the come and go of minor characters, the minute psychology with its flashes of illumination. Whoever reads to the end must reflect how much is suffered, how much endured, how much resented, how much forgiven, in the history of an average pair of mortals seeking to feed and educate their children.

Rachel Annand Taylor. *The Spectator.*
January 12, 1929, p. 58

The full seizure of life which the nineteenth-century masters felt no scruples in attempting has largely disappeared. The Mahony trilogy restores to current fiction the full panoply of objective experience, grasped and mastered with an authority missing even in the fine chronicles with which it has won comparison—the Jacob Stahl novels of Beresford, Ford's Tietjens trilogy, and *The Forsyte Saga.* Those who demand in these ambitious histories more than a fortuitous calculation of the factors shaping an era or a lifetime are able to find Mahony a more significant index of the forces surrounding him in pioneer Australia than Beresford's hero or Soames Forsyte. Aided by a style both vivacious and compassionate, but always dominated by the sure detachment that creates the highest sympathy, Miss Richardson wrote a human story which must be designated, at whatever risk, a masterpiece. . . .

The profound sympathy in her novels overshadows such defects as have grown out of their massive themes and complex designs. *Maurice Guest* comes back in a new edition which should remind the reading public of the value of absolute aesthetic integrity. Such integrity has become so rare a commodity that Henry Handel Richardson's name may stand secure in any record of modern fiction. She has triumphantly survived the test of a revival within her own lifetime, and has restored to the English novel the quality of compassion which, though long surrendered to Continental writers, is really its own proper heritage.

Morton Dauwen Zabel. *The Nation.*
October 8, 1930, p. 380

[In 1908] nobody knew anything of Henry Handel Richardson, and *Maurice Guest,* being published, was praised in the newspapers, sold out its first edition, was reprinted seven months later, and thereafter seemed to be at the end of its active life. Never was such an assumption more false. The book remained out of print; but its life continued very extraordinarily, for writers of all kinds passed the word to each other that this was something of a masterpiece, and *Maurice Guest* was a legend in the professional world. The author published another novel, *The Getting of Wisdom,* in 1910, and this novel failed to repeat the mysterious success of *Maurice Guest,* so that just as the public ignored Henry Handel Richardson the writers knew him only as the unidentified author of a single book. . . .

Seven years passed before Henry Handel Richardson began to publish a three-volume history of the life of an Australian doctor named Richard Mahony; and at length a new edition of *Maurice Guest* made its appearance with what must have been one of the earliest prefaces written by Hugh Walpole. It was politely greeted (in 1922), and thereafter its admirers had less difficulty in obtaining copies for their friends; but even yet its great qualities have been insufficiently recognized. *Maurice Guest* is a very good novel indeed. It combines apparent literalness with subtlety, and passion with wisdom, in an altogether exceptional manner. For those interested in the technique of the novel, it shows as few other books do the possibility of combining narrative with Henry James's "blessed law of successive aspects," and the unromantic treatment of a romantic theme which yet leaves no tenderness and no conflict of mood and personality unrevealed. It is a book full of subtlety, as rich as living memory, as detached as a philosopher's mind. Although it moves slowly, it is never tedious; although, towards its end, the scenes turn upon a single note, it is never repetitive. Every scene takes us deeper and deeper into heart and nature. It might, we feel, be transcript; but no transcript could so surely keep to the essential.

Frank Swinnerton. *The Georgian Scene*
(New York: Farrar & Rinehart, 1934),
pp. 290–91

There are a good many angles from which one might approach this carefully grounded and delicately articulated historical romance [*The Young Cosima*]. It is a remarkable re-creation of the past, with its pictures of mid-nineteenth century Berlin, Zürich and Weimar and its evocation of the world of the romantic movement, as yet far from exhausted in its shaping of music and of life. Or viewed from another angle, it is a singularly informed and imaginative study of the processes of artistic creation, with its stresses and its ecstasies, its perennial absurdities and its spasmodic grandeurs. Indeed, one will go far to find a richer, more realistic, more understanding presentation of musical genius. There is nothing to be said against Wagner that is not here fully substantiated, and yet the spell of his tremendous energy, his wide-ranging humanity, his greatness and his charm is never broken. Indeed, the author has done nothing better than this portrait of the composer, which at once gives the excitement of genius and yet makes it seem possible and actual. . . .

But the age-old question will not down: are the rights of genius paramount in all regions? Hans [von Bülow] is a poor thing compared with either Richard or Cosima, but there is a realm in which even the second-rate have their rights. It would be unfair to say that the author is unaware of that, but her real strength lies in the brilliance with which she presents her two geniuses, pulled together by a magnetism which, one is sure, they will not ultimately resist.

Helen C. White. *Commonweal.*
May 19, 1939, pp. 108–9

This autobiography [*Myself When Young*] is not a work of art. The style in which it is written is bluff, pedestrian; it could be the style of some honest, natural person who had not written before. At a first glance, the object of the author might seem to be nothing more than to forge forward, at a steady pace, page by page, through time. Almost no passage directly illuminates the imagination of the reader; the selection of words would seem to have been, if not careless, utilitarian. The effect is domestic. And, in the matter of content, as to what has been set down, there could have been little discrimination other than memory's.

This was probably so. Henry Handel Richardson must have accepted that one remembers nothing that is not somehow, important; that memory is the editor of one's sense of life. In that case, she submitted herself, when writing *Myself When Young,* to an inner, arbitrary dictation. To do this was an abnegation on the part of the artist, for whom creativeness means, most of all, choice. . . . What she must have understood was, that in writing *Myself when Young* she was not creating, but, rather, contemplating what had created her. Her object, now, was not to set up illusion but to penetrate to its early source: she must, therefore, have fought shy of the magic that for any writer cannot but emanate from words. With the undiscriminating patience of a stenographer, she "took down." The result is, an objectivity rare in autobiography—rarest of all in the autobiography of a novelist, for whom it is exceedingly difficult not to select, place, evaluate, dramatize and, thereby, virtually, invent.

Elizabeth Bowen. (London) *Times Literary
Supplement.* July 17, 1948, p. 395

I'm not at all sure . . . that the theme of the trilogy [*The Fortunes of Richard Mahony*] is as representatively Australian as is often suggested. It is true that Richardson confessed her interest in "the misfits who were physically and mentally incapable of adapting themselves to this hard new world." And it's true that the novel itself seems often to posit a connection between the harshness of the Australian environment and the failure of the sensitive and civilized colonist to adjust to it. But we soon recognize that Richard Mahony is not a typical case of Colonial malaise at all. Mahony's malaise is deeper than, and in the last analysis independent of, his discontent as a colonist. And this, too, Richardson wanted to show. Mahony was created from memories of her father, "a well-meaning and upright man, but so morbidly thin-skinned that he could nowhere and at no time adapt himself to his surroundings." Within the trilogy these two rather different emphases seem to exist uneasily together, and they give rise to what is perhaps its most important preoccupation—the question of suffering and the very meaning of human life itself. Whether or not one finds the attempted exploration satisfactory, the book is unique among Australian novels in its serious and constant concern with the question. . . .

In the last analysis, *The Fortunes of Richard Mahony* seems to me to be a large and ambitious novel, but not a great one. Its earnest psychological study is deeply flawed by the kind of limitation the prose style indicates; its varying statements find no real synthesis; it fails, in fact, adequately to explore the fundamental problem of human existence with which it is most concerned. For all its scope and seriousness of intention, it is, I think, a minor achievement in our literary history.

Jennifer Dallimore. Quadrant. 4, 1960–61,
pp. 51, 59

Henry Handel Richardson's reading . . . makes clear the extent to which she was familiar with the realistic tradition before she began her writing career. And just as her intellectual life indicates a familiarity with the issues involved in realism, her detachment for objective observation, her interest in historical fact, her husband's knowledge as a scholar, and her knowledge of the religion, philosophy, and science of the age contributed significantly to her career in realism. Henry Handel's life, from the time of her settling in the house on Lyon Road, Harrow-on-the-Hill, until her husband's death in 1933, was the detached and solitary life of a writer. But her detachment had evolved from a lifelong habit of a realist's sense of objective approach to life. As a child in Australia, she first learned the value of detaching one's self from the group in order to observe people and events more objectively. The reasons for such a personality adjustment were clear; as the daughter of a doctor in an uneducated community, the opportunities were rare for group play with the miners' children. . . .

While she had learned detachment and objective observation, she had also learned the problems of existence; and it is the problems of existence in colonial Australia that H.H.R. portrays so vividly in *The Fortunes of Richard Mahony*. The confused memories of a year in Europe together with the practical annoyances of living in a two-room house in Koroit filled H.H.R.'s childhood. And because she experienced the last moves of [her father] Walter Richardson's life, she is able to describe them in such a strikingly objective manner in her trilogy.

William D. Elliott. Studies in the Novel.
Summer, 1972, pp. 144, 152

In England at the beginning of the century, Henry Handel Richardson's themes were both new and thought-provoking. Her work was a culmination of European thought and she stood in the vanguard of writers who were attempting to bridge the gap between English and European letters. True, she labored with an old-fashioned and outmoded technique. She had no desire to attempt the innovations in sentence structure and point of view which were so much a part of the works of Dostoyevsky, Joyce, and Faulkner. Thus, an approach to the relationship between theme [and] technique in Henry Handel Richardson's work must realize that while her themes are modern and highly sophisticated, her writing is not.

J. R. Nichols. *Art and Irony: The Tragic Voice of Henry Handel Richardson* (Lanham, Maryland: University Press of America, 1982), pp. 12–13

Her claims to classic status rest on *Maurice Guest, The Getting of Wisdom* and *The Fortunes of Richard Mahony.* The short stories in *The End of a Childhood* are not in this class, and *The Young Cosima* is a failure. Each of her three successes has been described on one occasion or another as her "best" book. Although the ironic stance of the narrator and the defiant heroine make *The Getting of Wisdom* an attractive novel, particularly to certain kinds of contemporary taste, I think it is perverse to suggest that is the best work of a writer who was most original and penetrating about characters of different moral and emotional outlooks bound together in intimate relationships. Between her other two novels it is harder to decide. The study of sexual obsession in *Maurice Guest* has extraordinary power, and the sheer exuberance of student life prevents the intensity of emotions from becoming stultifying. But one does not weep for Maurice as one does, I think, for Richard and Mary and Cuffy Mahony. The passions in *The Fortunes of Richard Mahony* are more humane, the circumstances that afflict Richard work with the grain of his character, so that the consequences are even more terrifying, and his relationship with his wife and son add immensely to the poignancy of the story. It is massive and, initially, discursive, but by the end it has acquired a tragic intensity. *Maurice Guest* has a colossal impact and a power to disturb by saying things which have rarely been said so directly, before or since. *The Fortunes of Richard Mahony* is a great tragic novel. Fortunately we do not have to cast one of them aside in order to save the other.

Henry Handel Richardson is a major novelist, a realist who explores the paradox at the core of human nature that people can never escape the hard facts of circumstance or their belief in their free-will to choose. She respects her characters too much to mock either their circumstances or their beliefs. Her range stretches from wry humor to obsessive passion, and from broad social observation to a tragic knowledge of the individual's inescapable need to be himself. Above all she is tough-minded and clear-sighted. She deserves to be read.

Karen McLeod. *Henry Handel Richardson:*
A Critical Study (New York: Cambridge
University Press, 1985, p. 243

Richardson's preoccupation with power relationships, particularly relationships concerning class and gender, is apparent throughout the trilogy. Her deprivileging of the European perspective and her identification of Richard with marginal characters is persistent. While critics have attacked her fiction over the years, claiming it was too shackled by realism or naturalism to be really convincing, I suspect she is manipulating genre rather than being manipulated by it, surprising the reader by upsetting expectations, subverting Victorian ideology as she seems to agree with it. Seen within the androcentric framework of genre the trilogy can, indeed, be said to fail, for Richard's death is foreordained and thus there is no room for character development. However, as I have suggested, Richardson's ironic point of view consistently unsettles the reader; the works, and particularly *Richard Mahony,* ask the reader to judge the nineteenth-century European world that perpetrated colonialism. After all, the anti-colonial motifs introduced in the Proem continue throughout the trilogy and are echoed at the novel's end, with Richard's burial. This is a novel about colonialism and the encoding of the values of imperialism. The trajectory of Richard's fortunes must be seen as ironic rather than tragic, for his death is only tragic if we see colonialism as positive and worthy of success.

The fact that Henry Handel Richardson began her writing at a time when modernism was emerging—and completed the bulk of *The Fortunes of Richard Mahony* when it already had been introduced and was carrying the day—has seemed to bias critics, many of whom explored the book as a nineteenth-century relic and missed the extraordinary challenge of her feminist and colonialist critique. Frequently ironic, her works present a skeptical view of the concepts of gender and class constructed by Victorian society. What I have tried to do is present some approaches to reading Richardson so that her radical vision, so long obscured, can emerge. Viewing Richardson's work through a feminist lens should allow us to appreciate her subversive qualities, especially apparent when seen alongside the current postcolonialist debate. Consistently in dialogue with social issues, the theory informing her approach to these issues is, consciously or unconsciously, activist.

Marian Arkin. In Robert L. Ross, ed.
International Literature in English: Essays
on the Major Writers. (New York: Garland,
1991), p. 325

The version of *The Getting of Wisdom* some readers might be familiar with is the 1981 Virago Modern Classic/Dial trade paperback, which features a brilliant introduction by Germaine Greer, who, like Richardson, was born in Melbourne. It is an edited version based upon a 1960 Heinemann reissue. A comparison of that text with the new unexpurgated Mercury House version exposes various deletions and "improvements," such as the substitution of "you" or "your" for "yer" in coach driver Patrick O'Donnell's dialogue; some politically correct rewording of dubious value (updating "Chinaman" to "Chinese," for example); and the truly incomprehensible omission of the Nietzsche quotations that originally appeared as chapter epigraphs. These brief excerpts from Nietzsche's writing cast a wry, frank light on the years between childhood and maturity, rescuing that period from the banal gloss with which so many adult chroniclers wish to coat and camouflage it. As Richardson herself wrote in a 1930 letter to Nettie Palmer, "Nietzsche was of such infinite value to German literature. His style . . . shows that German does not need to be ponderous and long-winded."

Although *The Getting of Wisdom* is her shortest and, seemingly, her breeziest fiction, Richardson packs a bigger emotional and intellectual wallop in this ironic novel than in her weightier tomes—which is not to say they are negligible. *The Getting of Wisdom,* a phrase from the Book of Proverbs that receives a rueful twist here, is actually a testament to the destruction of wisdom that occurs when the individual sacrifices originality to conformity. Sadly, it is the only Richardson title that appears in the current *Books in Print.* Let us hope that a farsighted, truly literary publisher wises up and fills this lamentable void before too long.

Patty O'Connell. *Women's Review of Books.*
10, July, 1993, p. 40

RIDING (JACKSON), LAURA (UNITED STATES) 1901–

Both these works [*Contemporaries and Snobs,* by Laura Riding and *A Survey of Modernist Poetry,* by Riding and Robert Graves] are based on a single thesis: poet, today and in the past, has nearly always forfeited his identity by yielding to the necessity imposed on him by criticism of expressing his own time. The term *Zeitgeist* represents the sum total of contemporary presence and criticism is its servant in an unholy alliance to prevent the poet from ever achieving a complete creative independence. The authors prefer to recognize the poet as an autonomous mind unaffected by the exigencies of time and space; as a hypothetical monster who works in a vacuum out of which all the elements but his own desire to write poetry have apparently been extracted.

It need scarcely be noted that such a view has much in common both with the vulgar conception of the poet as "eccentric" and with the credo of the "pure art" enthusiasts who would deposit him safely in a *tour d'ivoire*. Although neither is quite the role these critics reserve for the poet, they are never so explicit as to offer instances to illuminate their position. (Only Shakespeare and Blake manage to survive without damning qualifications.) They are thus embarrassed because actually no poet who ever wrote entirely escaped some mark of his own time. We have learned enough about the nature of the poetic mind to realize that its contents, structure, and mechanisms are determined by the age in a deeper sense than a mere contemporary coloration. The poetic vision cannot be interpreted otherwise than as a psychological phenomenon, and it becomes no less mysterious when described as the white hot crystallization of all the elements in the poet's consciousness, of which the contemporary elements form no small part. The esthetic idealism of Miss Riding and Mr. Graves unfortunately exceeds the actual limitations of the human mind. But their doctrinaire ardor, which expresses itself in a wholesale holocaust of contemporary reputations, does not prevent them from saying a number of fresh and pertinent things about poetry. Despite the arbitrary character of their diagnosis of the poetic corpus, their method has forced them to analyze with considerable minuteness the pretensions and technical aspects of such modern poets as T. S. Eliot, Marianne Moore, E. E. Cummings, Paul Valery, and the Sitwells. Not the least interesting chapter is the one devoted to a close textual interpretation of recent experiments in verse punctuation. For this and certain other incidental services, the two works merit the patience necessary to read them to the end.

Walter Troy. *The New Republic.* February 6, 1929, p. 328

The meat of this collection of essays [*Anarchism Is Not Enough*] is in a long article called "Jocasta," a criticism primarily of Wyndham Lewis and incidentally of most of the prominent writers of the day. Imperfectly translated from Miss Riding's jargon into something a little more like the King's English, her position seems to be this: both classicism and romanticism are wrong and, despite their quarrels, are wrong in the same way; what is right is pure individualism, standing completely outside the processes of nature and not to be judged with respect to any system of extrinsic values. Inasmuch as Miss Riding has some slight difficulty in making this position clear in a hundred-page essay, one can hardly hope to state it fairly in a two-hundred-word review. What is certain is that Miss Riding has found a point of view which, whatever else may be said about it, is, considered pragmatically, of some value, since it enables her to see authors in a new way and to say things about them that have not been said. It is this fact which encourages us to struggle with her obscurities and to pardon her eccentricities.

The Nation. March 13, 1929, p. 380

The labor of un-thinking and un-writing which Gertrude Stein and E. E. Cummings have done for poetry is by no means completely done. But even their energy flickers at times, and in their followers the purpose seems to have given way to the means. Miss Stein's counterpoint is constructed on less and less significant themes, and while Cumming's ideas have not weakened, he has of late called more and more attention to his typographical ingenuity, as was to be feared.

Laura Riding rests along a line of literary development. The development has always been too literary. Among Miss Riding's happiest works are those wherein she contrives to give the sensation which we get from reading Sapphic fragments, but this is an evasive technical device, like that of building ruins or sculpting shattered statues. She has contrived fresh word phrases; she has, as she says, a whole dictionary of un-words; but it is the syntax which she has not mastered. Most of her poems are too long, and while most of them are not clear enough, many, like *The Nightmare* with its unnecessary signposts, are too clear. It is conscious thought that she has not thought about.

Automatic writing is a therapeutic exercise for writers and readers because it uncovers otherwise unrecoverable layers of the mind. But the ultimate esthetic value of such discoveries depends entirely upon the intrinsic validity of the thought which is expressed. . . .

Not that Miss Riding's method is faulty so much as that she does not carry it far enough, and is content with sensorial effect. Nay more, she mistrusts intellectual effect. In *John and I* she sets out, much like Pirandello in his *Six Characters in Search of an Author,* to recount a story which has no inner consistency. At first it sounds quite interesting until she says, "Then strip the narrative of mystery." From then on the whole thing falls to pieces. At the close, we agree with her that "John and I are better off like this"— with the story left untold, as *Laura and Francisca* is untold. This is diverting, but interesting only to people who read too many detective stories.

Stream-of-consciousness writing ought to be at least as baffling as rational writing is to psycho-analysts. The trouble with these poems may be that anyone who might set out to psychoanalyze them would not make a fool of himself. If this is true of Miss Riding's work, it is because, like an inhibited patient, she cannot tell the truth:

> But we tell only half, fear to know all
> Lest all should be to tell.

How different this is from Disraeli's dying statement: "If I had been a Nihilist, I would have told all." When a literary movement, even in one of its minor representatives, has reached the impasse of fearing "lest all should be to tell," the time has come for a right-about-face. A literature lies before us in the rediscovery of clarity.

John Hall Wheelwright. *Poetry.* 40, August, 1932, pp. 288–90

Miss Riding prefaces her book of collected poems with an address to the reader which is remarkable for its pretentiousness. In it she answers the charge of obscurity by saying that those who find her work difficult are reading poetry for the wrong reasons. Her poems can only be read for the right reasons and are therefore written for the right reasons.

After the clarity and shrewdness of *A Pamphlet Against Anthologies,* this kind of mystic simplism is disturbing. After looking through the whole volume the total effect is also disturbing. Miss Riding's technical maturity is not to be questioned; there is felicity of phrase and originality in abundance, yet the bulk of the work seems to be a substitute for life rather than the product of integrated experience. There is such a barren rejection of all sensuality, (even word-color), such an imprisoning self-consciousness, such a dry dissection of the last cerebral quiver, that one is driven to psycho-analytical conjecture to find excuses for many of the poems.

It is true that the position of the woman artist in society is a difficult one. . . . Artists of real stature, like Miss Riding, are undoubtedly affected by this situation and react strongly in the opposite direction. In her poems she is apparently trying to capture certain enduring formal qualities. In so doing, however, she depends far too much on abstraction, she is too much afraid of letting direct experience creep in. She is indifferent to the salutary housecleanings of the imagists. Instead of honestly aiming at the target, she insists on looking into an arrangement of mirrors and firing over her shoulder.

In some ways her work is characteristic of the post-war era of expatriates, the era when most artists were completely dissociated from society, for there is no echo in her poems of anything that is going on in the world today, there is not even the general sense of revolt, which is present in surrealism, against an order of ideas. All her revolts take place internally. What is worse, only too many of them result in mere negation. . . .

It is to the poets of Miss Riding's generation that we must turn for maturity and technical finish, for elegant detail and firm use of language. But these qualities are not enough. . . .

How can Miss Riding with her magnificent sensitivity and her keenly analytical mind still feel that the dissection of her personal malaise, her expatriate consciousness, is an adequate and satisfying task for her fine poetic equipment?

H. R. Hays. Poetry. 54, May, 1939,
pp. 101–4

Laura Riding is not well known today because her career ran outside of the mainstream of American and English literature during the 1920s and 1930s. At a time when other poets were drifting from the aesthetics of modernism to the politics of commitment, Riding found a voice within herself that reached back to Shelley and forward to the epistemological poetry of our own time. She believed that the mind used language as a tool to reach self-consciousness and that poetry was the purest expression of this self-knowledge. Although she turned inward to find subjects and forms, she was confident that introspection would lead to the discovery of a universal human self. . . .

Although today Riding is only a minor literary figure, there is nothing minor about her poetry. Both her conception of poetry and her poems meet rigorous standards. She succeeded in making her reader aware of the thought process, particularly the relationship of language to consciousness. Many of Riding's poems are entirely about thought, but they seemed excessively abstract to her contemporaries. Other poems are more appealing because they describe the mind's response to emotional states like love, anger, fear, uncertainty. These poems seem more concrete, but in fact, Riding managed to make thought as vivid in her poems as sensory experience is in other poets' work.

Riding's concern with the relationship between sensory perception and intuitive knowledge eventually caused her to renounce poetry. Like a martyr, she denied herself what she loved most. Although she considered her own poems closer to truth than those of anyone else, she felt that poetry inevitably appealed to the senses and therefore could not express absolute truth.

Seeking an immutable setting for truth, she turned to linguistic study and lexicography to find a way to make the public more cognizant of the meanings of words than she was able to do in poetry. Because of her renunciation of poetry after the publication of her *Collected Poems* in 1938 and her subsequent reluctance to permit her poems to be reprinted, she is barely known today. . . .

Laura Riding is apparently unique among women writers up to the seventies in spelling out a systematic theory of literary criticism and a poetics, embodied in essays collected in four books published in 1927 and 1928. Though her poetry has long been held in high regard, Riding's theoretical books have been largely ignored despite her important and lasting contributions to poetry analysis. One of these books, *A Survey of Modernist Poetry* (1927), written in collaboration with Robert Graves, laid the technical groundwork for New Criticism. In *Seven Types of Ambiguity,* William Empson acknowledged this significant contribution to his "new" method of close reading as derived "from Miss Laura Riding's and Mr. Robert Graves' analysis of a Shakespeare sonnet, 'The Expense of Spirit in a Waste of Shame.'" Empson's book, in turn, received the lion's share of credit for "inventing" the New Critical method of close reading.

Riding's poetics is divided into three main parts: (1) the autonomy of the poem, (2) the method and aim of the poet, and (3) the obligation of the reader to the poem. Together, these parts form principles that support Riding's faith in the poem as the single absolute value, the only pure conception of self. The sum of Riding's poetics is that a poem *is* self:

When this self has been *isolated* from all that is impression and impurity of contact in an individual, then a "thing," a work, occurs, it is discharged from the individual, it is self; not *his* self, but Self. (*Anarchism,* 6) [Emphasis is Riding's]

Joyce Piehl Wexler. *Laura Riding's Pursuit of Truth* (Athens: Ohio University Press, 1979), pp. 5–6, 25–26

Driven out of idyllic Mallorca, where she and Robert Graves wrote poetry and published small volumes of esoteric writing at the Seizin Press, the poet Laura Riding wrote a manifesto. There is nothing odd about a poet writing a manifesto in the thirties. It would be an odd poet who didn't. This three-page document was recently on exhibit at the New York Public Library among a remarkable collection of manuscripts from the Berg Collection in "The Thirties in England," organized by curator Lola Szladits, famous for her acquisition of modern British writers' papers.

Across the room in another glass case were the drafts and typescript of Virginia Woolf's *Three Guineas* (1938). What's odd is how alike the two manifestoes are in theme and argument, though Woolf's pamphlet is written with a speed and grace of symbol and metaphor, sensuous appeals to the eye and ear and every literary trick in the bag—which Laura Riding, purest of pure poets, would have abhorred.

Woolf's anti-fascism was a tri-partite political stance of socialism, pacificism and feminism, her original contribution being the argument that the origin of fascism was not in nationalism but in the patriarchal family. Laura Riding also believed in women's superiority, but in her case it was linked to a belief that because of their domestic isolation, women are better at *thinking* than men. Because of female rationality, men, she suggests, ought to leave the running of the world to women so that war may be abolished and aggression stopped, locally and internationally.

Few feminist protests were heard in what Auden called that "low dishonest decade," especially when they were as high-minded and ferociously honest as Woolf's and Riding's. The last thing that men wanted to hear as they mounted the barricades in a fight for freedom was that war was related to irrational male sex drives. Riding did not get much response to her plea and she and Robert Graves left London for New Hope, Pennsylvania, where their last literary experiment in living broke up in a personal debacle, and Laura Riding married the poetry editor of *Time* magazine, Schuyler B. Jackson. She gave up poetry as too impure a medium for the pursuit of truth, and domestic *thinking* and linguistic study have been her occupation ever since. . . .

Riding ought to be restored to the ranks of writers like Hart Crane and Gertrude Stein, where she belongs as a shaper of our speech, a poet of powerful and original irony. In what Riding calls "the stuttering slow grammaring of self," it is language which makes us human. She is the least sentimental of love poets. For her, words are superior to acts. . . .

"Riding" is a name not only for a rhyme but also for districts or jurisdictions in a county. And since she named the press she ran with Robert Graves, Seizin Press, we could guess that another territorial imperative was being expressed, for "Seizin" means legal possession of freehold property. Both a "seizin" and a "riding" are far bigger chunks of territory for a woman writer to claim than the "room of one's own" Woolf modestly demanded. Is Riding's cult of domesticity feminist? Or does it simply lead to the inequalities of worship that cause poets like Robert Graves to make White Goddesses out of women?

"Analogy is always false," Riding argued, and tried to purge poetry of metaphor, symbol and myth. What else is left but pure language and thought? If, as she claims, things cannot be known by their resemblance to other things, then the poet is left with a purged language. The reader often finds the poems too abstract, but Riding would claim that thinking itself is not abstract. The title of her second volume of poems, *Love as Love, Death as Death,* conveys what she means. Riding published Gertrude Stein's poems at the Seizin Press in 1929, and her kinship with Stein is clear. In *Survey of Modernist Poetry,* a major influence on "the Auden generation," she praised repetition in Stein's work as having "the effect of breaking down the possible historical senses still inherent in the words." Since so much poetry alludes to past poetry, this is a revolutionary approach. Riding's abstract poetry reads like an extreme Modernist manifesto. It resembles nothing so much as the Russian revolutionary early Cubist/Constructivist paintings of Goncharova and Alexandra Exter. These lines from "In the Beginning," about a daughter's "unpentateuchal genesis," for example, might be painted by a surrealist: "She opens the heads of her brothers / And lets out the aeroplanes. / 'Now,' she says, 'you will be able to think better.'"

The life of the Riding/Graves circle in London in the late twenties consisted of couples, triangles, rectangles, and great bursts of creative activity. It included Robert Graves's wife, Nancy Nicholson, on a barge in the Thames with the children, the disruptions of the Irish poet Phibbs, the erring disciple, and Laura Riding's attempted suicide. She jumped out a window and broke her back but survived to pursue truth in words, an authoritative poet and critic, retreating from the limelight to the solitary pursuit of linguistic purity. Graves and her ex-disciples quarrel about her influence. In an early poem, "Forgotten Girlhood," Riding answers them:

> But don't call Mother Damnable names.
> The names will come back
> At the end of a nine-tailed Damnable Strap.
> Mother Damnable, Mother Damnable
> Good Mother Damnable.

Laura Riding's *Selected Poems* (Faber and Faber, 1970) or her *Collected Poems* (Random House, 1938) are good places for the reader to start. [B]oth

Lives of Wives (1939) and *A Trojan Ending* (1937) are fascinating. It was Virginia Woolf's Hogarth Press which published her first volume, *A Close Chaplet,* in 1926. Riding's integrity, her withdrawal from the world and her truth-telling suggest a modern Emily Dickinson. For her truth is "the muse that serves herself"; man's need to claim that his half truths are *the* truth leads to "Titanic dissipation." Let us read Laura Riding again, in an attempt to approach her abstract frontier of poetic truth. It is a world where there are no myths to deceive us.

Jane Marcus. *Iowa Review.* 12, 1981,
pp. 295, 298–99

RIDLER, ANNE (GREAT BRITAIN), 1912–

Mrs. Ridler's *Poems* are a far cry from the gracefully drawn, athletic line of Mr. MacNeice. She seems to work much too hard for her effects. The pressure of her hand makes a crabbed style of overloaded imagery and awkwardly inverted syntax, so that one feels a lack of elbow-room in the densely packed texture. But perhaps this is a characteristic of a first volume, which will pass with greater practice. . . .

Mrs. Ridler's intention is certainly uncommon and talented. Her language is underivative and fresh, and she used it with precision and the ability to fuse it with sharply articulated feelings. . . . One catches traces of Donne, and occasional lines have the air of early lyric . . . but Mrs. Ridler makes her own material and stamps it with the mark of a firmly independent, although still immature, poet.

Desmond Hawkins. *The Spectator.* June 30,
1939, p. 1140

Other poems in this volume [*The Golden Bird*]—as in all Anne Ridler's previous books—disarm the critic who is about to protest that she is a little too much under the influence of T. S. Eliot and George Herbert, too often apt to embark upon themes too large for her talent. But often she writes with exquisite delicacy of feeling, rich and true, though within the framework of a convention that includes occasional poems to her Head Mistress, and to her parents on their golden wedding. Amazing that domestic feelings and virtues still keep their flavor and ring true in such a world as this, as they do in Anne Ridler's best poems.

Kathleen Raine. *The New Republic.* June 23,
1952, p. 20

Mrs. Ridler's dignified and moving play [*The Trial of Thomas Cranmer*] has simplicity, exclusion and somewhat expensive tie-up with its modern corollary. The work is disarmingly modest in tone and she has stuck cleanly to her story. She has far too overtly commended her moral to our current woe. Her characters are believable, especially her hero . . . and we are all for the moment too vulnerable to the martyr-for-conscience theme to fail in our response to her spirit. The unwelcome fact remains that the total result is oddly thin, and that it falls between the loneliness of the majestic and the blood-knowledge of the common. . . .

One would guess Mrs. Ridler to be more dramatist than poet. There are indications that her sense of motion, of single purpose, of human values, might take her much further as a playwright. Poetry is another matter.

Josephine Jacobsen. Poetry. March, 1957,
pp. 380–82

Anne Ridler's best work arises from an almost antagonistic attitude towards her medium. She frequently refers to a fear that artistic form might allow us to "fool our minds." She is strongly aware of a need to struggle against making any false resolutions which distort the truth into a more acceptable shape. In "Exile," for instance, she is at her most pessimistic concerning poetry:

> Writing may gain on speech: worked with
> Wit and warmth, with scorn a sharp knife,
> Time and space as a frame, forgotten
> Like all good frames that point possession.
> So are set cliffs and seas on a stage:
> Over swamps, a road: on a flat canvas
> Three dimensions. O little comfort
> Comes to the maker, and when war ends
> Still *we are exiles from our fathers' land,*
> Exiles from heaven—pursue that no further.
> For still the raw material of pain
> Is changed into joy; for still a man
> Acts above reasonable expectation;
> Still the silence between men is broken;
> And these are glories.

Through her play on the various meanings of the word *still* here, she emphasises her doubt that writing can significantly assuage the pain of the human condition. . . .

Occasionally Anne Ridler's distrust of the form is a weakness in her work. After reading Ridler's poem "Geordie" Kathleen Raine told her, "you must trust your medium"—identifying her tendency to over-explicate and to weight the balance too much in favor of the skeptic. Her characteristic mode of protracted contemplation which embraces both doubt and belief within a poem and seeks a balance, is similar to the strategy in many of Yeats's late poems. In contrast with Yeats's tendency to leap into convinced affirmation through passionate rhetoric, Anne Ridler struggles to achieve even a tentative, qualified statement of belief. Her poetic statement is a quiet one, but nonetheless compelling.

Tracey Warr. *Poetry Review.* 73:1, 1983,
pp. 45–46

Anne Ridler's *New and Selected Poems* . . . begins with pale meditations on love and friendship. Gradually a note of religious despair takes over after personal encounters with tragedy. The imagery begins to echo seventeenth century religious mediations and combines with details drawn from incidents in her own life: a visit to a blood transfusion center, and the experience of a corneal graft. There is a further struggle with faith and with the concept of life after death which leads to a dismaying directness in recent poems, such as "A Taste for Truth," and a meditation on the ridiculous death of a French tailor who wanted to fly from the Eiffel Tower and whose plummet earthward was recorded on film.

English Studies. 71, 1990, p. 56

RILEY, JOAN (JAMAICA–GREAT BRITAIN) 1958–

Described as a "moving story of a woman's struggle for dignity," Joan Riley's second novel [*Waiting in the Twilight*] attempts to focus on the "forgotten and unglamorous" experience of the older generation of Afro-Caribbean women on coming to Britain, and the price that built my generation.

Adella, a talented seamstress, moves to Kingston, Jamaica. Her first experience with men has disastrous consequences; she is rescued by Stanton whom she follows to England. This too turns sour. Life is not easy, yet, through hard work, she buys her house and raises her children. At 32 she has a disabling stroke, loses her job and her husband. Reduced to a cleaner, she then loses her house and, eventually, has to give up work altogether to be looked after by one of her daughters. As a grandmother she reflects on her life.

With her second novel, Joan Riley again establishes herself as a writer who focuses on the negative. My attention having been grasped, I was propelled with a mixture of curiosity and disbelief: nothing good was ever going to happen to this Blackwoman. Adella becomes a combination of almost every depressing stereotype, a character defeated by circumstances, a passive victim to any discrimination around her. What makes her seem unreal is the almost total lack of any joy in her life. There is scanty evidence of any inner spark or humor that would keep her going: even her sustaining golden years with Stanton begin to seem like a dream. Men in Adella's life play a very limited role; she puts up with them in return for the "security" they offer. Joan Riley glosses over the physical and psychological abuse Adella meets at their hands.

There is a more positive aspect to the novel, in Adella's relationship to the women around her. In Jamaica she is surrounded by a community of spirited Blackwomen and we learn that the Blackwomen of Kingston's ghetto are equally supportive: "they shared together, helped each other out with a piece of saltfish here, rice there; or just by minding the children." In England her constant friendship with Lisa reflects this tradition. It is Lisa who looks after her children, offers her all kinds of priceless support and encouragement.

Unfortunately, Joan portrays a very one-sided relationship, the depths of which are never explored, only hinted at. The potential for intimacy is abruptly curbed: "What Lisa wanted her to know she told her, and everything else was not her business." Subsequently we are never shown those times when women speak as women to one another. I found myself wondering why, and how, they became and remained friends. Lisa's character remains undeveloped. We know no more about her by the end of the novel. She exists only to be there for Adella.

Joan leads us skillfully through the space and time of Adella's memories. As events in her life combine in a downward spiral, I found myself absorbed in their unfolding. She also uses language to good effect: the dialogue is in patois, while the rest of the narrative is in standard English, maintaining the strong sense of Adella's national identity. But in her desperate search for dignity and respect from others, Adella allows the idea of "shame" to rule her life. Viewing herself as a "cripple" only compounds her own lack of self-worth. It must be possible to examine the black woman, "too weak to stand and too strong to cry," without pathologizing our lives.

Dorothea Smartt. New Statesman.
March 13, 1987, pp. 27–28

Joan Riley's first two novels, *The Unbelonging* and *Waiting in the Twilight,* signaled the advent of one of the most original and uncompromising Caribbean writers to emerge in the 1980s. She has been praised for her insight into life in the Caribbean, her vivid, authentic evocation of its landscapes and her unflinching examination of the experiences of its people, most compellingly its women, both at home and as migrants in Britain. Her unglamorous portraits of poverty, dispossession and post-colonial disease are presented with lucid detachment, in a deft reworking of the conventions of realism; her resolute refusal of the exotic or the modish may account for the relative lack of attention to her work.

A Kindness to the Children, her fourth and most ambitious novel, displays, along with her familiar skills and preoccupations, her increasing command of technical intricacies, concealed by the deceptive clarity of her style. The shifts of third-person perspective in the fluid narrative strategy which

Riley employs allow the reader access to the thoughts and feelings of three women of contrasted sensibilities, who, as first-generation migrant, British-born, and deeply rooted Jamaican, embody conflicting aspects of Caribbean reality.

But realities are, as Riley's own shifting viewpoint illustrates, deceptive. *A Kindness to the Children* begins with the arrival of British-born Sylvia, recently widowed, well-to-do, educated and self-possessed in the Jamaica of her parents, and ends with her departure. But the novel soon subverts any expectations of a celebratory reclamation of lost roots and affinities. It is the turbulent Jean, Sylvia's cousin, who touches, from her first appearance, the novel's raw nerve-endings. It is for Jean—who has fled the deprivation of her rural Jamaican upbringing for an uneasily achieved measure of success in England—that Riley reserves her greatest sympathy. She is one of the unbelonging, scarred by a childhood of abuse, damaged by a collective heritage of oppression which, in spite of Jamaica's independence, persists in the prevalent attitudes of the culture at large. Jean shares her expatriate's life, with varying degrees of unhappiness, with the urbane Jimmy, an aspiring young black writer accorded token recognition by the white literary establishment; their children bear the marks of her struggle for survival. Her escape from the legacy of pain proves illusory, for in Riley's vision there is little redemption in self-exile, and none in turning back to abandoned concepts of home. Jean's return to the repressive surroundings of rural Jamaica unleashes her repressed traumas causing her to retreat into memory. Recollections of pain flash by in cinematic fragments in which she is at once performer and horrified observer: even the hallowed precincts of childhood faith are profaned by images of sexual violence, and the presiding icon of a male Christ—white or black—offers no salvation. The symbolic appearances of another manifestation of Caribbean life, the Ragged Woman—mocked as mad by the locals who use her as their whore-in-residence—mirror Jean's eventual fall.

Undone by a Jamaica that constantly reflects her own terminal despair, Jean loses herself in a wave of alcohol-abetted psychosis and desperate sexual adventure. Sylvia, in spite of her professional involvement with mental health, fails to see the social causes of the "madness" she diagnoses as an organic aberration. Her inept response to Jean's plight, like her inability to fathom or connect with Jamaica, is a symptom of her own alienation.

As always, Riley explores uncomfortable issues; but she is, as her many admirers will testify, primarily a novelist concerned with character, who uses language—particularly speech, with its many registers of status and difference—to examine its role in the shaping of identities. *A Kindness to the Children* is both a novel of characters and a novel of ideas: for character, in Riley's philosophy, is itself an idea, formed and determined by the environment in which it is created—a relentless and pessimistic philosophy, if one concurs with Riley's implied view of her protagonists as emblems of the contemporary Caribbean. An element of hope nevertheless resides in the salty, pragmatic minor characters she depicts with conviction and compassion. The novel's understated third perspective, which echoes their voice—that of the rooted Jamaican without thoughts of leaving—is provided by Pearl, Jean's apparently submissive sister-in-law. She is resigned to her place as wife, mother and undereducated, unpaid domestic worker, but a hidden desire for autonomy compels her to climb a daunting hill in search of fresh limes. The minor triumph of her ascent initiates a new process of liberation, revealing Riley's trust in the potential of neglected voices.

Aamer Hussein. (London) Times Literary Supplement. January 15, 1993, p. 22

[In *A Kindness to the Children*] Sylvia, a widow living in England, visits her late husband's family in Jamaica, because she feels a deep need to face up to his death and to ease her grieving as best she can. She imagines that by acquainting herself with his background history, including the people, places, and memories he was nurtured by before he emigrated from the island, she will be able to let go of her loss and lingering pain. Her first impressions of the new society are not without a certain ironic recall: "Sylvia thought of the years her parents had spent trying to convince her she was British. If only they had realized what it would mean: to be here where no English voice intruded and most every skin was black."

Sylvia's lofty idealism and her hasty visitor's wishful thinking are soon squashed by the unsettling realities of family discord and the island's social inequities she encounters. Indeed, she personifies the national airport as capable of producing "its usual mixture of petty irritations and endless discourtesies." She describes the transportation system as "ramshackle" and the black bourgeoisie and government leadership as concentrating their energies in "devising ways to rip the heart out of the country."

Her disheartening visit lasts only a week. Her traumatic disillusionment travels with her all the way back to England, where, as a child, she appreciated Jamaica, in an unreal sense, through "faded sepia prints, picture postcards . . . and posters on the curved walls of the London Underground." However, within the very brief duration of her stay, Sylvia manages to come to terms with the memory of her husband's death—but only in part. In the end, she says, "I suspect I was probably expecting too much." And much too soon, she may have added.

Joan Riley's novel reveals and highlights, in its riveting Dickensian details, a sustained metaphor of our impatience with loss: Sylvia's hurry in trying to lay to rest her own personal anguish and her reckless innocence in quickly relying on racial identification as a reliable source of social integration and lasting solace. Riley joins Caryl Phillips . . . in reversing the narrative order of the old Caribbean story. . . . George Lamming and Samuel Selvon gave us heroic views of ourselves, at the metropolitan center; these two recent novelists give us plain views of ourselves at home, and the new perspective is justly critical and brutally truthful.

Andrew Salkey. World Literature Today. 67, 1993, p. 658

RINSER, LUISE (GERMANY) 1911–

Luise Rinser has written in *Nina (Mitte des Lebens)* (1950; The middle of life; Nina) a love-story that has borrowed a little of the fire of D. H. Lawrence and something of the knock-about adventurousness of Hemingway. Her heroine is a woman who has taken part in the underground movement against the Nazi regime, has been imprisoned, has achieved some success as a writer after 1945 and, as we take leave of her, is on her way to take up work with an English family. But these events are only peripheral to a character whose main-spring of being lies in her passionate and unhappy sex life. This novel has an underlying tenderness and pity which are its most endearing qualities.

> H. M. Waidson. *German Life and Letters.*
> 1953–54, p. 246

Nina (Mitte des Lebens) . . . gives an interesting glimpse into postwar German writing. The novel is a study of the contradictions of the divided heart, unusual because it is a story of adult feeling and choice. . . .

Miss Rinser is admirable not only for the perception and originality of her theme, but for the way she has used conventions of the novel. She never descends to cheap effects. Yet it cannot be denied that nobility and high-mindedness are dangerous subjects for a woman. What is it that makes so many feel that long-suffering is attractive? Here Luise Rinser succumbs. Too many of the war incidents are of the stock variety, and in order to prove heroism at these junctures the book becomes an analysis of emotional states and of ideas rather than the presentation of people themselves.

> Mary Barrett. *Saturday Review of*
> *Literature.* December 1, 1956, p. 36

Die vollkommene Freude (The perfect joy). Luise Rinser is serious. She has no wish to provide the reader with distractions. Nor does she want to startle, stun, or provoke him. Rather, she endeavors gently to instruct us, to equip us with defenses against life's temptations and moral iniquities, and thus to contribute to our purification. This poet is concerned not with the reader's mind but with his heart and soul. Her goal is not art but edification.

> Marcel Reich-Ranicki. *Deutsche Literatur in*
> *West und Ost* (München: Piper, 1963), p. 298

Die vollkommene Freude . . . testifies once more to the author's instinct and talent for appealing to a feminine audience—for she addresses herself mostly to women—in those terms in which they can be reached most easily: the theme of woman's love and life.

There would be nothing new or noteworthy here if Luise Rinser's ambition did not in fact go further—so far, indeed, as to make the resources and possibilities of the novel subservient to her Christian "concern." In other words, the author consciously sets out to be placed in the category of edifying literature; but in contrast with her great contemporaries—men such as Bernanos, Mauriac, or Graham Greene—she includes in that category also the so-called stylish entertainment novel. Not only does she lack the naiveté required for that genre; she increases our discomfort by using the setting of high society, a practice that is current thanks to our pulp fiction yet tends to be self-defeating. Her cast of characters includes the best of everything, with the result that her unfortunate heroes act not like human begins but merely provide the cue words. The sole purpose is the explication, by means of one woman's life story, of what Luise Rinser calls "the perfect joy"; and that is nothing more and nothing less than the surrender to the will of God through a surrender in love to His creatures.

Ilse Leitenberger. *Welt und Wort.* 1965,
p. 634

Despite her voluminous and significant work as a writer and critic, Luise Rinser has so far attracted little attention among American experts, even though her novel *Nina (Mitte des Lebens),* for example, has been translated into twelve languages. . . . She is strongest and most effective in her positive attitude toward the fundamental questions of the present day, in her striving for truth, and in her portrayal of authentic human beings, working and suffering.

Albert Scholz. *German Quarterly.* 1967,
p. 392

Ich bin Tobias (I am Tobias). . . . Comparable stylistically to Uwe Johnson's shorter novella *Eine Reise wegwohin,* Tobias's quest for his real father leads him on a vertiginous journey through a series of "possibilities": the atheistic doctor, an old Jesuit, a store manager, etc., each of whom complicates the plot with his own philosophy of life, death, or the world in general.

Succeeding in containing form within a sporadic, unrestrained language, in too many cases the novel questions rather than answers, frustrates rather than reconciles. . . . And like so many contemporary works of its type, it redefines, indeed revitalizes, the problem without presenting a solution.

Thomas Hajewski. *Books Abroad.* 1967,
p. 317

In German-speaking countries, Luise Rinser is known as one of the most successful contemporary writers. She has made the bestseller list three times, in the 1950s and early 1960s with her novels *Mitte des Lebens* (Nina) and *Die vollkommene Freude* (Complete joy), and most recently, in 1981, with her autobiography *Den Wolf umarmen* (To embrace the wolf). *Nina* has been translated into twenty-two languages including Japanese and Hindu.

Despite this commercial success, literary critics have paid little attention to her works, a fate Rinser shares with most other German women writers even today. . . .

It was here that she wrote one of the most significant of her books, one of the earliest German works to be published immediately after the war and one of the few narrations of women's war experiences from a woman's perspective. *Gefangnistagebuch* (1946; Diary from prison) is a fascinating account of Rinser's prison experiences, but it focuses on the lives of other female inmates as well as on her own. In this diary the two recurring themes in Rinser's works are clearly discernible: her strong political *engagement,* which was unusual for a woman writer at that time, and her awareness of the plight of the oppressed, in this case women. . . .

Rinser's *Diary from Prison* is also significant because of its form. She wrote it in a fragmentary form as a diary, because that was the only possible means of expression for her, as she explained in a recent interview with me. She emphasized the documentary character of the book and also the fact that she had nothing but scraps of toilet paper to write notes on, which she hid in her straw. . . .

The diary form conveys immediacy, directness and truth, all undoubtedly reasons why Rinser developed it as an important structural element in her autobiographical and hitherto most successful novel *Mitte des Lebens* (Nina). Fictional diary entries and letters appear to interrupt and confuse the action of the novel, but at the same time they create, from various perspectives, a fascinating, intricate picture of Nina, the protagonist. The two themes . . . characteristic of Rinser's works [are] clearly visible in this novel, even though in different form. The problems of a woman emancipating herself in all areas of life and struggling against middle-class norms predominate over the discussion of purely political issues, although these are also part of the protagonist's emanicpatory process. . . .

Rinser's concern with Germany's political past has made her a conscientious and critical observer of today's political events. She has spoken out against violence, war, and oppression, and she has done so in a typical fashion, in four diaries: *Baustelle* (1970; Construction site), *Grenzubergange* (1972; Border crossing), *Kriegsspielzeug* (1978; Toy of war) and *Winterfrühling* (1982; Winter-spring). She has also done so in a more overtly political way on lecture tours, at political meetings, and in radio and television programs. As a consequence many political conservatives in The Federal Republic of Germany consider her a thorn in their side. In 1977 she was forbidden to lecture in the small Bavarian town Gerlingen because they believed a spurious article in the magazine *Quick* which had accused her of sympathizing with German terrorists. If one asks Rinser about her political beliefs, she answers that she declares herself in solidarity with all those "who want change for the sake of humanity, which seems to be of no importance in our capitalist world."

Finally, I would like to take a brief look at Rinser's latest work, her autobiography *To Embrace the Wolf* (1981). This book represents an effort to express her political, literary and religious ideas through personal experiences. It recreates her own life from 1911 to 1950 and focuses to a large extent on the years between 1933 and 1945. The difference from her other works is, however, that she describes and analyzes more directly her own problems and difficulties with the Hitler regime, even before she was imprisoned.

The wolf Rinser embraces is life in general, life which is beautiful and at the same time full of obstacles. She emphasizes her development as a woman and a writer towards independence, but as in so many autobiographies by women writers, she continuously asserts her self-worth.

Elke Frederiksen. In Alice Kessler-Harris
and William McBrien, eds. *Faith of a
(Woman) Writer* (1984; Westport,
Connecticut: Greenwood Press, 1988),
pp. 165–170

The association of "silver" with "guilt" in the title of Luise Rinser's latest narrative and her well-known chosen task as a writer of bearing witness to a "higher" reality from which we derive the sustenance of our lives may lead the reader to surmise that *Silberschuld* is a religious novel. However, the metaphorical richness inherent in the allusion to Judas's betrayal of Christ for thirty pieces of silver is here only incidental. The guilt alluded to in the title is that of a family actually occupied over centuries with the mining, owning, and trading of silver and whose wealth and status have derived from the exploitation of their fellow man. This collective guilt is now, in our day, thrust upon the principal figure in Rinser's novel, a young woman, youngest of the family, who must realize the guilt in order to propitiate it.

Propitiation is achieved not by traditional religious means—pilgrimage, meditation, ritual, good deeds, or the attainment of a "higher" reality—but rather by the conscious integration of the "lower" reality: of the dark or shadow side of the young woman's personality, which all of us reluctantly, if ever, confront and which breaks into our rational-rationalizing lives in such forms as dreams and psychoses. Evoking a journey to and through a surrealistic personal hell with the vividness of a sustained nightmare, Rinser, with language as distinct and precise as Kafka's, compels the reader, via the narrative "self" of the novel, to experience the examination of conscience, the coming-to-consciousness of personal responsibility for collective guilt.

The parallels between implications of *Silberschuld*—which incidentally extends a technique employed by Rinser in the last of her *Geschichten aus der Löwengrube* (1986). . . . and insights and conclusions of such studies on human consciousness as Erich Neumann's *Origins and History of Consciousness* and Jean Gebser's *Ever-Present Origin,* the deep draughts in the novel of certain mythological, symbolic-alchemic-hermetic traditions suggest that

Rinser has continued to extend her intuition and understanding of reality into the unknown and unmapped regions of experience far better than many so-called modernist and postmodernist writers. In this she has continued to fulfill the age-old responsibility of a poet to truth, to language, and to oneself best described in the words of another ostensibly conservative writer. In an argument germane to this review the poet-critic Allen Tate once asked: to whom is the poet responsible? And for what? "He is responsible," Tate concluded, "to his *conscience,* in the French sense of the word: the joint action of knowledge and judgment. . . [and] for the virtue proper to him as a poet, for his special *arête* for the mastery of disciplined language which will not shun the full report of the reality conveyed to him by his awareness: he must hold, in Yeats's great phrase, 'reality and justice in a single thought.'"

Noel Barstad. *World Literature Today.* 63,
1989, pp. 93–94

Though the title suggests poetry or fiction, the appended dates reveal that *Wachsender Mond, 1985–1988* is the continuation of *Im Dunkeln singen.* . . . and thus the sixth in the series of quasi-diaries begun in 1970 with *Baustelle.* Like the previous installments, the new book is not a true diary but rather an engaging collection of reflections, observations, and commentaries of varying length on the events and interests of Luise Rinser's life and work, which, as her readers know, encompass a very wide range. Remarkable in the present volume are the intensity and dedication of her concerns (and the extensive travels documented) at an age when others usually pursue more circumscribed tasks (she was born in 1911).

Wachsender Mond might indeed have been subtitled "A Philosopher's Travel Diary," for many of the finest reflections—whether on political, feminist, philosophical, theological, literary, or personal themes—ensue from encounters with new localities and situations: Albania, Finland, China, a women's prison, a Viennese congress on North Korea, Jean-Luc Godard's film about Mary and Joseph. Among other notable entries are reflections on her own work from the period documented *(Mirjam* and *Silberschuld)* . . . on East-West relations and prospects for peace with a letter to and answer from then East German premier Erich Honecker), on the Heinrich Mann and Elisabeth Langgässer prizes accorded her, on Ricarda Huch's heroic novel against the Nazification of the Prussian Academy in 1934, on the relation of religion and politics, on the nature of evil. Along with such serious and provocative themes there are also pieces no less vivid, cogent, and illuminating on private matters and the small joys of everyday life. . . .

It is to be hoped that Rinser . . . will also give us the second part of her autobiography (the first, *Den Wolf umarmen* [Embrace the wolf] covered only her first thirty-five years), which is not replaced by the six volumes of "almost a diary". . . .

Few writers' lives have been so inextricably interwoven with the questions and events of their time, in all their joys and terrors, promise and pain, as Luise Rinser's, and equally few writers have been able to "embrace the wolf" with equal conscience and intensity.

Noel Barstad. *World Literature Today.* 64,
1990, pp. 106–7

ROBERTS, MICHÈLE (GREAT BRITAIN) 1949–

Daughters of the House is an English novel about French Catholic provincial life; an overt but restrained feminism informs it and creates a sense of deep sadness. Cousins Thérèse and Léonie, born during the Occupation in a small Norman village, support each other through puberty and the death of Thérèse's mother, but are separated by Thérèse's vocation and by Léonie's marriage. Twenty years later, Thérèse returns, having decided to leave the convent, and finds their relationship has curdled.

Pervading both the extended picture of their adolescence in the 1950s, and the framing sections set twenty years later, is an awareness of what happened in the war. The question of their true parentage hangs over the two young women just as the memories of collaboration and doomed resistance hang over their community. Their journey into adulthood is a process of initiation into the language of their seniors, a language of angry reminiscence about what is past and unalterable. . . .

The strength of Michèle Roberts's writing has always grown out of ambivalence. . . .

The book is made up of short chapters, all but one of them having as its title the name of a domestic article, part of the house and the legacy which dominate the two women's lives. Where conventional Gothic novels portray houses which are haunted palaces of the mind, full of sliding panels and trapdoors for the unwary, this house is one where the trap of anguished memory is liable to be sprung by contemplation of a shard of a broken dish or a cellar key. The sense of rootedness is reinforced by these powerful everyday objects, but one problem it presents is that the vocabulary of hallucinatory intensity necessary to the presentation of Léonie's vision has already been exhausted in the kitchen.

Daughters of the House is an intense piece of writing, in which the transfigured mundane world of recipes, parental prohibitions and almost ritualized gossip is posed against official purity and religiosity, and shown to be superior. Both Thérèse and Léonie force the issue in order to get what they want, and both suffer as a result; there is no question which has chosen more wisely. This is a book in which choices have consequences, and stories morals, but Michèle Roberts has the wisdom not to make any of these overwhelming.

Roz Kaveney. (London) *Times Literary
Supplement.* September 18, 1992, p. 23

Daughters of the House begins with a full-blown nightmare, the image of a woman with dead, bleeding feet who clutches "a red handbag . . . full of shreds of dead flesh." Starting awake, Léonie runs to the bathroom gagging, feeling that it is her cousin Thérèse, expected home soon after many years in a convent, whom she is vomiting out. Threatened by real and symbolic manifestations of an unmother—a corpse, a nun—she feels compelled to discover the origin of her fear. What secrets in her family are hidden in her past?

In every way, the personalities and morality of "the daughters" are at odds. As a child, Léonie was granted a true vision of the Virgin, though her Lady of the Wood, in red and gold, may be an older divinity than the blue-and-white-robed Madonna worshiped in church, and claimed by Thérèse. And in Léonie's memories of her foster-mother, Rose, the girls' wet nurse (we're in rural France, pre-war), Michèle Roberts achieves a rhapsodic intensity, pushing the narrative towards poetry. "Sweetness was her and it, her two hands grasping, her mouth demanding and receiving the lively flow." There is no distinction between eroticism and religious ecstasy as described here. Thérèse, however, experiences neither. Like the village priest, who instigates the desecration of the shrine in the woods, she denies the possibilities of ecstasy in others and in herself. The antagonism between the cousins is carried forward in a satisfying plot involving the exposure of Nazi war crimes and family treachery. A mass grave hides the remains of a huddle of fugitive Jews and their protector.

In a lesser novel (such as those of Iris Murdoch in her middle period), Léonie and Thérèse might have become cyphers. This author allows her characters their full complexity. They are real children growing into adolescence, experimenting with sex, playing doctors—"the surgeon took her own clothes off as well as the patient's"—and coming to terms with the adult codes governing marriage and class. An unhappy, intelligent pair, their rivalry for maternal affection is to prove longer-lasting than any subsequent emotion. This is a fascinating story, full of psychological insight. Its necessary obscurities and slow unravelings are balanced by rich descriptive writing, "speckled beans . . . like tiny onyx eggs," celebrations of domesticity and femininity. Roberts has declared her admiration for Colette, whose influence is certainly evident in her own works. Short listed for the Booker Prize, this novel deserves to win.

Judy Cooke. *The New Statesman.* October
9, 1992, p. 21

These nine stories provide an excellent introduction to many of Michèle Roberts's preoccupations over the past five years: her compassion for weakness; her warm and witty nostalgia for a childhood spent between suburban England and rural France; her robustly unsentimental fascination for mystical experience and *la vie religieuse*; her unflinching exploration of the way in which taboos—cancer, childhood sexuality, incest—prey on consciousness.

They also show her considerable strengths, above all, her instinct for what makes the forbidden fruity.

Important influences—Toni Morrison's majestic *Beloved,* the sensual punning and mischief of Colette's Claudine stories—are near to the surface here. So is the autobiographical impulse: her struggle to come to terms with a complex, problematic Anglo-French heritage is harsher and more visible here than in the longer works. None the less, long-standing admirers of Roberts's fiction will see confirmed the ripening of confidence and power evident between *In The Red Kitchen* (1990) and the darkly seething *Daughters of the House* (1992).

Many of the ingredients brought so sumptuously to the boil in the latter novel are temptingly laid out. A reverence for everyday objects—a hand-glazed cup, a dark blue tin of Nivea, a pair of trainers—which provided the structure and the flavour of *Daughters of the House,* is sampled in *"Une Glossaire* (A glossary)," an autobiographical prose poem reminiscent of Gertrude Stein's *Tender Buttons.* And Roberts's great passions are to the fore: sin, sex and saturated fat.

For a generation terrorized and traumatized by food, Roberts is worth reading, if only for her promiscuous use of butter and cream. . . .

To say that the mother is the brooding presence linking these tales is to state the obvious. Rather, brooding itself, literally and metaphorically, is the keynote. . . .

This is not a collection praising or blaming mothers. That is not the point. The shrewish peasant woman Bertrande drops her baby in the fire in "Anger" with the same sureness of aim as the mother in "Fish" separates eggs for sauce ("let the white dangle down. Plop"). Instead, the mother-daughter bond—or lack of it—provides the starting-point for a series of meditations on love and power.

Trev Braughton. (London) Times Literary
Supplement. October 22, 1993, p. 21

ROBINSON, MARILYNNE (UNITED STATES) 1944–

In her first novel, *Housekeeping,* it is Marilynne Robinson's fate to tell a different story from most contemporary writers. Her very departure from the conventional demands our attention, in spite of the norms governing critical practice in the past. She presents a world almost exclusively populated by women, where experience filters through female consciousness and reflects the actions of women. This is not a world of Amazons or utopian androgynes—those presented by writers such as Ursula Le Guin, Joanna Russ, or Monique Wittig. It is not the milieu of Ernest Hemingway, Jack Kerouac, or Norman Mailer in reverse. If there are any resemblances, they are to the circumstances of women's lives as presented by writers such as [Mary Wilkins] Freeman and [Sarah Orne] Jewett, or to the motive that directs [Zora Neale] Hurston and [Alice] Walker to portray life within the black community. . . .

In *Housekeeping*, Robinson explodes the prevailing cultural mythos of motherhood and the nuclear family. Instead she offers a rare, momentary glimpse into the lives of women whose circumstances, both literal and metaphorical, seem strange despite their statistical frequency in our society. Without men and without mothers, the definitional status of women and family life changes radically. In her exploration of the question, the author is careful not to reduce women's diversity to a monolithic view. In other words, she resists the impulse to substitute a new model that merely replicates the reductive inadequacies of the old.

> Elizabeth A. Meese. *Crossing the Double-*
> *Cross: The Practice of Feminist Criticism*
> (Chapel Hill: University of North Carolina
> Press), 1986, pp. 57, 59

Marilynne Robinson's novel *Housekeeping* is an extraordinary work which explores the mythic significance of housekeeping both as primordial ritual and as a metaphor for art in the American literary tradition. It also challenges the nature-culture dichotomy characteristic of much American thought. In this it has profound implications both for the way we view ourselves and our work and the way we interpret the literary traditions of our past, in particular the so-called classic writers of the American canon. Not only is "the artistic acceptance of women's work a major step forward," as Kathryn Rabuzzi writes in *The Sacred and the Feminine: Toward a Theology of Housework,* but *Housekeeping* begins the re-examination of the very categories of nature and culture so necessary to our developing concepts of who we are and our relationship to the world.

In particular Robinson's novel addresses the preoccupation in American fiction with art—what Emerson called the mixture of man's will with nature—and its power to shape and order the apparent chaos and disorder of nature, a nature that was perceived as "thoroughly mediate" and "made to serve" man's will. . . .

Robinson's novel might be seen as a quest for what Hawthorne calls "our true parent." *Housekeeping* enacts and recommends, though not without ambivalence, a relinquishing of human arts, including housekeeping and society as we have known it, and a surrender to the forces of nature, which is conceived in the novel as very much a living entity. There is a rejection of the activities of *homo faber,* of man as artist ordering and subjecting the forces of nature to his power, and an evolution toward some unspecified union with the forces of nature. The gradual, graceful process of de-evolution, of de-civilizing, that the novel enacts is also a rejection of the patriarchal values that have dominated American culture and a return to values and modes of being that have been associated in myth and imagery with the province of the female.

Jane Kirkby. Tulsa Studies in Women's Literature. 5, 1986, p. 91–92

The challenge of *Housekeeping* lies in Robinson's refusal to "save" Ruth from herself, from Sylvie, and ultimately, from homelessness. Transients and runaways are not among society's favored or fortunate; and homelessness is a condition that evokes our pity or our tension—depending on how deeply it threatens our own rootedness—but never our assent. Like the townfolk of Fingerbone, we believe that people and things—like children, relationships, jobs, and houses—need to be made secure. We might permit, with tentative indulgence, a "stage" of rootlessness, a year or two of journeying. But ultimately, we will maintain, everyone and everything need a home. . . .

"My name is Ruth," the narrator quietly announces in the novel's opening sentence. And in such naming, Robinson suggests the presence of a significant predecessor for her character and a valuable precedent for her story of homelessness. The Book of Ruth provides an important touchstone for Robinson and her readers as we struggle to re-envision the terms and designs of dispossession. It ties the novel to a tradition of storytelling that speaks for fulfillment in the midst of wandering; and it links Ruth to a woman whose refusal to stay safely at home is a pledge of faith in the endurance of the human spirit and the human family. . . .

The Book of Ruth came out of a narrative tradition that sought to reveal the enactment of divine purpose in the reality of ordinary human history. Robinson's intentions seem equally substantial. Though her attention to theistic images and designs does not serve a primary theology, clearly she expects the resonance with sacred myth to deepen the vision of her own text. Essential to both is the belief that the order of the world is informed by mystery and should be received with awe. Central to *Housekeeping* is the solitary figure of a woman who moves easily in wind and water, and who invokes, with quiet power, the memory of revelation and the action of grace in human lives.

Anne-Marie Mallon. Critique. 30, 1988, pp. 95–96, 104

Robinson consciously sets her novel against the great texts of the American tradition. She opens *Housekeeping,* her first book, with a brief sentence that echoes the famous beginning of *Moby-Dick*—that prime American text about a castaway and survivor with a significant Biblical name: "My name is Ruth. I grew up with my younger sister, Lucille, under the care of my grandmother, Mrs. Sylvia Foster, and when she died, of her sisters-in-law, Misses Lily and Nona Foster, and when they fled, of her daughter, Mrs. Sylvia Fisher."

This genealogy of ordinary women, a revision of Biblical partrilinear genealogies, indicates at the outset how Robinson's language steeps her novel in textual traditions that recall the very foundations of our cultural inheritance while shifting the vantage point to a female perspective. Through style, theme, and symbolism that adapt American literary romanticism and nineteenth-century prototypes to twentieth-century womanhood, Robinson both resists and augments our native strain.

Martha Ravits. American Literature. 61,
1989, pp. 644–45

Robinson creates an alternative model for female relationships by first breaking the tie to the Law of the Father. She does this by disposing of the patriarch on whom the identities of literary heros and heroines supposedly depend and providing a different reason for creating stories. Housekeeping is narrated in a woman's voice that invokes the death of the Father and his Law. Her narrative counters Barthes's proclamation by "speak[ing] a conflict with the Law" as it falls on the shoulders of women; in so doing, it effaces the search for one's origins. She presents a legendary tale of a father who haunts the female characters and seems to determine their fates. But the novel also charts the efforts of its women to escape the memory and absence of the father. Using biblical motifs from the stories of Eve, Noah, and Ruth, Robinson has her women appropriate the father's myth. In so doing, they break free of its determining power.

Phyllis Lassner. In Mickey Pearlman, ed.
Mother Puzzles: Daughters and Mothers in
Contemporary American Literature
(Westport, Connecticut: Greenwood Press,
1989), p. 50

In at least three ways. . . . Housekeeping's subversion of symbolic structures opens up a new space for writing. The dissolution of the singular speaking subject in a merger with her loved ones dis-covers the other way of seeing, natural to mother-child relations but usually hidden beneath the symbolic order's insistence on the individual as a separate, closed entity. Objects and places seem to interpenetrate and time seems to circle when identity is in perpetual transition between self and other. Removing the wraps of the symbolic enables Robinson to articulate the language of facial reflection that always goes on, unacknowledged, beneath spoken conversations that pretend to tell the whole story. And threatening the linchpin of symbolic systems, the link between signifier and signified, by forcing language to articulate death—pure absence, "the signifier without a signified" . . . generates an impossible poetry whose metaphors make emptiness palpable, concrete.

Jean Wyatt. Reconstructing Desire: The
Role of the Unconscious in Women's
Reading and Writing (Chapel Hill:
University of North Carolina Press, 1990),
p. 100

In its meditations on the ambiguous nature of death, the deceptiveness of appearances, and the opposition between the values of a conventional and transient life, *Housekeeping* spills over convenient and culturally-conditioned critical enclosures to challenge both our perceptions and our conventional and taming critical terminology. . . . [T]he novel might be fruitfully understood as an unconventional primer on the mystical life, in which the basic accomplishment for both the protagonist, Ruth, and the reader is the expansion of consciousness through a process of border crossings—social, geographic, and perceptual. These crossings, in turn, are developed through the novel's central metaphor of transience. Transience implies pilgrimage, and the rigors and self-denials of the transient life are necessary spiritual conditioning for the valued crossing from the experience of a world of loss and fragmentation to the perception of a world that is whole and complete.

William M. Burke. *Modern Fiction Studies.*
37, 1991, p. 717

Marilynne Robinson's *Housekeeping* reacts against idols, notions of fixity, and narrative closure, i.e., "place" as keeper of the literary imagination, whether this takes the form of women who act as spokespeople, preservers of culture, or critics of the cultural imagination. Whereas the argument for androgynous vision is relevant to many contemporary feminist texts, the concept is not meaningful to Robinson: in *Housekeeping* (both the text and the institution) the male principle is expendable. . . . *Housekeeping* avoids the territory of marriage and male/female relationships because these are self-enclosed identities.

The tension between transience and fixity constantly negotiates positions and alliances among Sylvie, Ruth and Lucille. Transience in *Housekeeping* is that quality which is misunderstood and misrepresented by traditional social values, but is attained by those who have reconstructed (and so, recovered) their own history. Even before Ruth joins Sylvie in a life of transience, she feels comfortable with Sylvie's propensity for wandering:

> I was reassured by her [Sylvie's] sleeping on the lawn, and now and then in the car and by her interest in newspapers, irrespective of their dates, and by her pork-and-bean sandwiches. It seemed to me that if she could remain transient here, she would not have to leave.

This passage also illustrates the combining of traditionally opposing notions—although "keeping house" normally connotes "keeping order," in this passage and at the novel's end, housekeeping is inverted to privilege breaking fixed and closed ties to a house (and by implication, the standards that keep a woman enslaved within its confines) while preserving bonding between women.

Rosaria Champagne. *Women's Studies.* 20,
1992, p. 322

ROCHEFORT, CHRISTIANE (FRANCE) 1917–

The young French writers of today, especially the women, are reexcavating the oldest tradition of the French novel; its reputation for being scandalous. The latest *succès de scandale* to come to us from France is Christiane Rochefort's first novel, *Warrior's Rest* . . . which missed the Prix Femina by a vote, won another prize, [was a best-seller] . . . and greatly impressed the critics.

Warrior's Rest describes a journey to the end of the line—the line in this case being bed and the bottle. The two travelers are Genevieve . . . the narrator, a puritanical and priggish young *bourgeoise,* and Renaud . . . an idealist *manqué,* who has become an alcoholic and a nihilist with the searing contempt for normalcy of Colin Wilson's Outsider. Quite by accident, Genevieve saves Renaud's life after he has attempted suicide. She promptly falls in love with him and, since he is homeless and destitute, installs him in her Paris apartment. The candor, brutality, and demonic energy of his love-making bring about her sexual awakening, and she finds herself in bondage to a man who emerges from empty passivity only to lose himself in sex and drunkenness. A curious struggle ensues: Genevieve tries to coax Renaud toward a more human existence, and he, determined to destroy "the demons" of her puritanism, forces her into the lower depths of depravity and submits her to atrocious indignities. In the piercingly ironic conclusion, love conquers all—and defeats itself. For when Renaud, surrendering unconditionally, makes Genevieve marry him and begs her to help him enter "the Great Washing Machine" of ordinary life, Genevieve realizes that he has ceased to be the man she loved.

The robust vein of black comedy that runs through this nightmarish story makes it a singular fusion of the tragic, the erotic, and the comic. Slightly reminiscent of *Lolita,* it seems to me to move on two levels. On one, it is an audacious description of sexual obsession and of a season in hell. On the other, it parodies and punctures both the impulse of the amorous *bourgeoise* to tame her rogue male and the fashionable glorification of the Outsider. Christiane Rochefort, whom some readers will undoubtedly consider a moral monster, is unmistakably a writer of real talent.

Charles Rolo. *The Atlantic Monthly.*
October, 1959, p. 117

[In *Warrior's Rest,*] to make a long story short—it's too bad the author didn't—a good woman saves a bad man by the time-honored expedient of getting pregnant and persuading him to marry her. This conventional denouement is intended to be ironic, since the couple involved is trying very hard to be unconventional—they drink to excess, make love wildly, spend their capital, and tell each other, "We're all lost." In France, this novel won the Prix de la Nouvelle Vague and was considered shocking; in America its romantic concern with debauchery and the conquest of debauchery seems old-fashioned.

The New Yorker. November 28, 1959,
pp. 241–42

Beatnik heroine [in *Cats Don't Care for Money*] emerges from breakdown to marry a tall, blue-eyed bourgeois. Where popular fiction ends the quality novel begins, for marriage is more difficult than getting married. Céline gets off to a bad start at the wedding, drunk and funereally dressed, and spends the rest of the novel arguing with her husband. Originating as Style versus Confusion, the Philippe-Céline debate passes into Hypocrisy versus Truth. Philippe becomes a shadowy scapegoat for Céline's exuberance and by the end of the book she is looking for God, who is even less likely to answer back. Mlle. Rochefort's attacks on middle-class conformity are shrewd and she has managed to convey her heroine's splendors as well as her cuteness. The book amuses, gallops: sharp but not serious.

(London) *Times Literary Supplement*. May
5, 1966, p. 392

Closing the pages of *Children of Heaven,* it is possible, finally, to define the emotion it has engendered. It cannot be other than regret: regret for the society from which it evolved—which, sadly, may be all the world—and for something else, something far closer to the essence of this frequently compelling, always poignant account of a young girl—a child, really—growing up. I do not know whether Christiane Rochefort intended to write an indictment of either contemporary France or contemporary man. It is perhaps improbable that she would have attempted anything so sweeping in only 119 pages. Yet, here it is.

Through the eyes of Josyane, we look upon the rest of her family: her essentially indifferent parents; the eleven brothers and sisters who, highly individual though they are, are ultimately only chattels in their parents' never-ending drive toward the state's rewards for the bearing of children. For Josyane, forced to do the housework, to care for the younger children, it is a world without joy. Her premature—and altogether indiscriminate—sexual experiences become the one source of life in an otherwise drab, meaningless existence. For a time, they, at least, offer something to look forward to.

There is relatively little "plot" to *Children of Heaven*. It is giving away nothing to say that, in the end, Josyane does find a love to replace those fleeting moments of lust which had come to constitute her experience of being. It is the compassion of Christiane Rochefort's novel, not "what happens," that renders it vital and moving. And it is a compassion which appears in many forms, sometimes cloaked in bitterness, often deceptively, unwittingly, mirrored.

Throughout, there is a sense of what Graham Greene has called "the lost childhood"; one which, in this case at least, has been lost too soon (one wonders, of course, if it is not *always* too soon). Though her life, for several months, revolves around casual sexual encounters, Josyane, on another plane, has never really lost her innocence. In the sense that that "rebirth of wonder" for which poet Lawrence Ferlinghetti has cried out comes only to the *truly* innocent, Josyane has not forfeited it—and it is very close, really, to what she seeks. What she has done, perhaps, is to tinge it with that border of gray which should come only later.

The publishers couple Josyane with *Lolita*, which seems, on every level save that of sales, both unwise and inaccurate. Age is the only similarity; and it is not enough. The sardonic commentary of Nabokov is here replaced by a touching insight into childhood. There is a beautiful consistency in Josyane, in which the elements of youth and awakening experience come, at first dimly, then with startling clarity, into focus. If this is occasionally marred by the translator's excessive Anglicizing of dialog, that is a relatively small matter. Above all, Christiane Rochefort has known the world of childhood; known, remembered and imbued it with a flavor all its own, a flavor both nostalgic and frightening.

Catharine Hughes. *Commonweal.* 76,
July 27, 1962, p. 430

Future sociologists with an interest in the French society of the second half of the twentieth century will find a wealth of material in Christiane Rochefort's novels, especially in *Les Petits Enfants du siècle (Josyane and the Welfare), Printemps au parking* [Springtime in the parking lot] and *Les Stances à Sophie (Cats Don't Care for Money).*

It is not an entire society that forms the subject of Rochefort's rather satirical, yet humorous novels, but the lower bourgeois and the blue-collar working classes that live for the most part in the narrowly confined world of the *grands ensembles,* the French equivalent of public housing projects, big apartment blocks of steel and concrete, forming new cities all over France. Leftist intellectuals and anarchists also find a place in several of her novels. Historical events are absent, as are attempts to place the institutions that the author takes as the target of her implied social criticism into a political or economic context that would allow the apparent absurdities of the system to be viewed in a more subjective perspective.

In an interview the author once remarked: "I sadly realize the oppressive power of modern urbanism." Christiane Rochefort is one of the first French writers to have captured the atmosphere of the new cities that have sprung up on the periphery of Paris and all other big cities in France. The French housing authorities decided to build these huge structures to alleviate the critical housing shortage that had been plaguing France since World War II. Slum dwellers would finally be able to find the airy and spacious apartment, the modern conveniences in a green, park-like setting that they had so long been dreaming of. But their dreams most often turned into nightmares. The new cities that have emerged are inhabited by families uprooted from their homes in the old cities. Even though they may have been slums, they were nevertheless home to them, with neighbors and local traditions. . . .

The author proceeds by portraying salient features of contemporary French society through the experiences of adolescents and women. Her criticism bears mostly on the social institutions and technological inventions that rob modern people of dignity and soul. Gigantic steel and concrete housing projects of the new cities with their dehumanizing effect on the inhabitants arouse Rochefort's anger and often biting, yet humorous, and at times even lyrical satire. In *Les Petits Enfants du siècle* and *Printemps au parking* children and adolescents are the author's protagonists. They are also her favorite characters, not because they are model children, but because they are the exemplary victims of an oppressive society. They often suffer most in a world where human beings are reduced to the size of insects, overpowered by high-rise structures and where human qualities have been replaced by the efficiency of modern machines.

Through the experiences of her characters Christiane Rochefort shows that the inhabitants of the big housing projects, in addition to all their other problems, are faced with isolation, uniformity, boredom and an ensuing neurosis. At the heart of the matter lies the fact that their living quarters are anonymous, each building being exactly like the next one. The new structures are no longer built on a human scale. Rather the human being feels dwarfed by their dimensions.

In all her novels Rochefort underscores the dehumanizing aspect of our contemporary society. The large urban concentrations are shown to be a fitting frame and at the same time a reflection of our depersonalized society which has a stranglehold on its members. We have seen that it dictates man's outlook on all facets of life and affects human relationships: relationships between husband and wife, parents and children, and finally between the residents of the urban centers as members of a community. All of Rochefort's concerns are intimately linked to the questions of freedom and happiness.

> Anne D. Cordero. In Alice Kessler-Harris
> and William McBrien, eds. *Faith of a
> (Woman) Writer* (1984; Westport,
> Connecticut: Greenwood Press, 1988),
> pp. 83–85, 88

In *Ma vie revue et corrigée par l'auteur* (My life by the author) there lies the same moral conviction as can be found in Rochefort's journal/essay *C'est bizarre l'ecriture* (It's weird, writing): namely, that it is better to *éclairer* than it is to *endormir*. Both are works of demystification and de-toxification; in both there is a love of the facts ("Des faits on manque cruellement et ils ne font jamais de mal") and disgust—typically expressed with sardonic humor— with the various concoctions of lies and mistruths we tell ourselves about literature, life, the world. Rochefort uses the genre of autobiography—which means, happily, misuses it—in order to point up artifices and limits, and to suggest truths and possibilities. She gives us a process, not a conclusion; a context, not an abstraction; she refuses to make the whole greater than the sum of its parts; and her work ends, as she says, when the page remains white. If Rochefort's autobiography, like those of other women writers, undermines traditional autobiography as a genre belonging to the epic, masculine *moi*, it is above all intended to undermine our formal, "correct" (and therefore repressive) ways with words: "Nous n'avons pas à chercher les mots mais à les perdre; à construire les phrases qu'à les démanteler; car ce sont des forteresses qui nous enferment dans le mode de pensée régnante . . . Ecrire vraiment consiste à désécrire" [We don't have to seek words but lose them; put sentences together, but dismantle them; for they are fortresses that shut us up in the dominant way of thinking . . . writing really means unwriting].

Helen Bates McDermot. *Autobiography in French Literature,* French Literature Series (Columbia: University of South Carolina Press), 1985, p. 191

In *C'est bizarre l'ecriture* (1979; Writing is weird), the story of the creation of the novel *Printemps au parking* (1969; Springtime in the parking lot) as well as a commentary on *Une rose pour Morrison* (1966), Christiane Rochefort affirms the primacy of the unconscious in the process of literary creation. . . .

But Rochefort also says that writing most often consists in crossing out, in transforming the fine style that has been learned into a personal style. . . .

The desire to dismantle the language [is] expressed in *Une rose pour Morrison* (A rose for Morrison) by an abundant and highly original lexical creativity.

When this novel was published . . . DeGaulle's presidency was in full bloom, the Vietnam war was going full tilt. On the literary scene, linguistics was making itself felt, due notably to the translation of Roman Jakobson's *Essays in General Linguistics* (1963) and Roland Barthes's *Elements of Semiology.* In Paris, in Rochefort's own neighborhood, developers were razing entire blocks so as to build new ones. . . .

Une rose pour Morrison, a dystopian novel of the future whose daring humor underlines the author's anger and protest against society, is also a satire of precisely these political, literary, and social facts. . . .

In *Une rose pour Morrison,* lexical creation consists in various neologisms and is essentially and at one and the same creative burst, a breach with the polite and limited language of contemporary Western society and the dominant mode of thought that it expresses. . . .

Lexical creation makes possible a unified integration of form and content in a work that expresses "a certain state of frenzy" coming from its author and the rejection of the dominant order. . . .

Lexical creation in *Une rose pour Morrison* is one of the most interesting aspects of the novel. From a linguistic point of view, neologisms reveal . . . Rochefort's high degree of mastery, her erudition, her imagination, her sense of the comic, in a word, her talent as a writer.

For verbal creation, by its quality and its breadth, goes beyond linguistic interest to end up in a style of which that creation is a part. It is not simply ingenuity, acrobatics; it fills several stylistic functions. . . . Finally, lexical creation is essential to the demythification of the real and to the satire of the dominant way of thinking that Rochefort opposes. It is probably here that she achieves her deepest significance. For the dismantling of language, which is inseparable from all verbal invention, involves the taking of a political position.

In the Rabelaisian tradition, neologism in *Une rose pour Morrison,* is thus an organic part of the novel's fabric. By this lexical creation that simultaneously engenders and destroys, Rochefort has succeeded in integrating form and substance. "The process," she says, "when it is right is the visible face of the internal organism."

Monique Y. Crochet. Modern Philology. 83,
1986, pp. 379–80, 394

Christiane Rochefort's Medicis-crowned novel *La porte du fond* (The door beneath) is a chilling tale of incest, told, in conversational style and without self-pity, by the "survivor." It is the story of the person the narrator has become, because (or in spite?) of "the combat [which] lasted seven years. I lost every battle. But not the war," and of why, and how, she became a specialist in infamy. It is a tale too of broader implications about the frequent, if not general atrocities of family life in a patriarchal society, leading one to the conclusion that most, if not all of us would be better off could we but choose our relatives. It raises questions about psychology and psychologists, alluding to and agreeing or taking issue with Freud, Jeffrey Moussaïeff Masson, R. D. Laing, Françoise Dolto (who, as a woman, should most probably have known better), and others, and treats issues of psychic reality, the unreality of reality, and the possibility that disasters are only in the way one takes them.

No one—behind or in front of the door—is entirely innocent, but most particularly the narrator's parents, ill-matched in class, religion, character, and interests, are almost equally guilty. In explanation, self-defense, and self-disculpation her father uses all the shopworn arguments: it's common in families; everyone does it; you're better off learning from me; besides, I might not even be your father. Her mother neither knows nor wants to know, and nothing her daughter can do can please her. The daughter, who couldn't tell for fear it would kill her mother, for fear she herself would become an object of pity, has, during the seven-year struggle, "lost everything," including, not least of all, her illusions.

The sympathetic narrator understands childhood and (family) life without having lost all sympathy, not even for the only child of a loving family.

"One communicates," she says, "not by language, but by style." Fortunately she, like Rochefort, is ever a stylist.

Judith L. Greenberg. *World Literature Today.* 63, 1989, p. 451

RODOREDA, MERCÈ (SPAIN) 1909–83

One of the most important acts of rehabilitation that contemporary Catalan literature has benefited from, after its disintegration as a result of the latest civil war, is definitely that of Mercè Rodoreda, who, prior to her 1939 exile, published five novels and who, outside of Spain, in her Geneva retreat, maintained a silence . . . of approximately twenty years, at least as concerns the public appearance of her work.

I am writing these lines after reading the volume *Mi Cristina y otros cuentos* (1969; My Christina and other stories). . . . It goes almost without saying that the circumstances of the writer's long exile have influenced her work. On the one hand, there is the natural development and improvement of the style, the expressive elements—in general and in the strictly narrative sense. The years of exile correspond almost exactly with the second half of Merce Rodoreda's life to date, a period of maturity and, consequently, of improvement. But, on the other hand, it is obvious from the reading of each story and, even more clearly, from the reading of the entire volume, that there is one invariable idea in this book, one thread, by no means invisible, that gives a clear unity to all the stories. Loneliness is the central theme. Mercè Rodoreda's characters are alone. They often find themselves not within but rather at the margins of or confronting a society that excludes them or that challenges them in one way or another. And it is from here that the influence of the emotional situation shaped by exile is obvious. Although I do not wish to impose a strictly biographical reading, I do wish to indicate the author's experience as the logical source of an invariable thematic line. . . .

It does not seem that the sense of isolation created by exile has exacerbated the sadness in M. Rodoreda to the point of obscuring counterbalancing forces. It is just that the presence of sadness has remained within her, and that presence, translated into literary expression and creation, brings with it this negative vision of reality, this overwhelming "tragic sense of life.". . . .

It is in the very fact of her work as a writer that M. Rodoreda's fidelity to origins and her language are to be found. For there is no doubt that the greatest service that a writer, as such, can do for a country and an age is to confirm the linguistic mastery of her people. Anyone capable of such rich literary creation in a language is already providing an irrefutable argument against the abnormal situation imposed on that language by the fact that its natural evolution as a vehicle of life and culture has been suppressed.

F. Luis. *Cuadernos Hispanoamericanos.*
242, 1970, pp. 455, 467

In a sense, *The Time of the Doves (La Plaça del diamant)* is the story of most Spaniards during the 1930s and 1940s. But more profoundly, it explores what it feels like to be an ordinary woman in a Mediterranean country. Rodoreda uses a stream-of-consciousness technique to place us directly inside Natalia's sensibility, yet her technique is so subtle that we are aware only of the flow of Natalia's feelings. The author's literary skill never draws attention to itself. Instead, the heroine's mind plays obsessively over certain images, returning to them again and again until they become protagonists in her agony. Painfully sensitive but unable to objectify what she feels, Natalia is choked rather than educated by her experiences. A victim of history, she nonetheless lacks any historical sense. The book's densely-packed detail gives *The Time of the Doves* an almost hypnotic intensity and draws the reader into Natalia's private horrors.

David H. Rosenthal. Translor's introduction
to Mercè Rodoreda. *The Time of the Doves*
(Saint Paul, Minnesota: Graywolf, 1986),
pp. 8–9

Mercè Rodoreda . . . winner of the Premi d'Honor de les Lletres Catalanes 1980, the highest recognition an author can receive at home, is one of the very best Catalan storytellers. *The Time of the Doves* is a superb translation by David H. Rosenthal of the original *La plaça del Diamant,* a novel written by Rodoreda in 1960 and published by Club Editor in 1962. Beautifully composed in the so-called "spoken writing" technique, the work is a poignant account of a susceptible and naïve Barcelona shop girl, Natalia, who succeeds through tenacity and will in the face of the havoc produced by the Spanish Civil War (1936–39).

After a whirlwind courtship, the sensitive Natalia marries a man as dazzling as he is mercurial and whose obdurate ideas give her as much joy as sorrow. When her husband is killed, she experiences a virtual hell in her quest to ensure the well-being of her two small children. Amid the ravages of war and feminine, Natalia is a moving portrait of a simple heart struggling for survival in a complex and collapsing world while obsessed by her bittersweet memories of her short marriage—the time of the doves. The reader is awestruck at Natalia's private anguish and is relieved at her quiet redemption. The narrative is a powerful and strikingly original effort on the theme of a woman's capacity for love.

Rosenthal, as the poet he is, beautifully and accurately renders the most lyrical passages of Rodoreda's novel, and his "Translator's Note" situating the action historically and politically is most helpful for a better appreciation of the story.

Albert M. Forcadas. *World Literature Today.*
55, 1981, p. 458

The garden occupies a central place in the narrative vision of Mercè Rodoreda as it does in her own psychic life. The garden stands as a representation of the world of childhood with its promise of freedom, beauty and life, in opposition to the realities of isolation, enclosure and repression which characterize the adult world. . . .

The garden of Rodoreda's own childhood, the enticing but unreachable walled garden of a *torre* in the Barcelona barri de Sant Gervasi, comes to represent the lost world in which one's identity was secure, a safe refuge from the unknown dimensions of the city beyond its walls. It is this link between individual identity and nature which has given rise to the frequent characterization of Rodoreda's fiction as "lyrical" or "poetic," but the function of the garden, as the embodiment of the natural order, in the structuring of her fictional world lies much deeper than this description indicates.

The identity of both the male and female protagonists of Rodoreda's novels is intimately linked with the natural world. Whether the garden occupies the central space in the world of the novel, or a displaced, sacred space, it serves as the source of identity or self-renewal for the protagonist. The characters, who, being city dwellers, are not born into the edenic garden, turn to it to rediscover their identity; the characters who are expelled from the garden, or who escape into the larger world beyond its confines, long to return to the garden as to the irrecoverable innocent and secure self of youth.

Throughout Rodoreda's novels the garden functions as a place of escape from quotidian reality as well as of encounter with inner, psychic reality. The cyclical pattern of the natural order offers the characters the possibility of human renewal. For the female protagonists especially, the garden stands in contrast to enclosed space, to the room or house which forms her world. . . .

As women move in Rodoreda's novels from victims to survivors, the function of nature diminishes. The garden recedes into the background as the strong women emerge. . . .

The woman has emerged from the garden in Rodoreda's fiction to become solidly entrenched in the social and economic order, but she has lost herself in the process.

Mary Ellen Bieder. In Manuel Durán, et al.,
eds. *Actos del Segón Coloquio D'Estudis
Catalans a Nord-America* (Barcelona:
Publicaciones del'Abadia de Monserrat,
1982), pp. 253–54, 263

La Plaça del Diamant (1962) is considered the best Catalan novel of our century and has been translated into Castilian and eight other languages. The novel is written, or rather spoken, in the first person by Natàlia, a working-class woman in the Gràcia section of Barcelona. She tells about her life from shortly before the Second Republic to the years just after the Civil War; that span of Spanish history is the remote backdrop of her bare and restricted existence. The narrative is simple and linear; its language gives the impression of oral presentation.

The novel is about the pain of isolation and silence. It is a woman's story about a life turned in and imprisoned within itself. It looks out through doors, windows, cages and in at cracks in the woodwork where dust and the crumbs of wood borers accumulate and lie still and inert. The novel is not the story of a person who moves in a world with or against others, with or against forms of thought or feeling shared or disputed on the level of action. It is a reversed tapestry where the muted colors trace a pattern different from the outside design of historical events and acts. Its omissions shine and its silences are eloquent. Indeed, the narrator, the very person whose tale is a long lament, repeatedly protests her inability to speak, all the while telling us about an incommunicability imposed by herself in accord with a social world and a sexual role.

Natàlia speaks to us in Catalan, in the language which was, in the pre-war period, the language of the outside, of culture and politics, but which had become, through the Franco years and at the time the novel was written—in Geneva and at some temporal distance from the span of the narration—a language of the home, of the inside, a half-secret language of parents and children, and especially, because of woman's place in the home, of mothers and children. The Franco regime conscientiously suppressed Catalan; for many years publication in Catalan, schooling, and the public use of the language were forbidden. Castilian was, after all, the language of the Empire. Thus the history of the novel's language follows a process of interiorization that repeats the inward spiral of the plot. The contemporary history of Catalonia, the underground move of its language, the life of a woman in the grand and reified abstraction of "patriarchal society," run parallel and criss-crossing lines in the pages of the text. Language and sex, which are immanently and primarily social, are contained, circumscribed, suppressed, yet the reader hears the story of separation and silence in the language of a community. We have here an apparent contradiction, opposing narrative moves.

Toward the end of the novel Natàlia picks up a sea-shell, a decorative item in the house of her new husband, Antoni. She thinks to herself—she always thinks only to herself—that one would never know if within that seashell there were waves that could be heard when no ear was placed against its opening. . . .

Natàlia's Catalan is at once correct or literary and colloquial, popular. Without abandoning grammatical norms, Rodoreda creates the illusion of speech. . . . Rulfo's style creates the same illusion. Both writers take us into an oral culture, one that we know exists within or beneath a literate one. Nowhere in Natàlia's account do we find references to writing or to print;

there are no letters, books, newspapers, advertising, street signs. It is as if, amidst the timeless objectifications of the printed word, we stepped once again into the realm of verbal flux. Yet in the works of both Rodoreda and Rulfo, the narrator's spoken words are addressed to readers. This paradox has contrary effects: on the one hand, both narrator and *narrataire* are somewhat obscured and depersonalized; on the other, the sense of an audible delivery, a story-telling in *viva voce,* seems to give us an echo, faint enough, of a communal life prior to civilization and its discontents, prior to literature. In the same paradoxical way, literature comes to the rescue of characters who speak of passivity and impotence; the authors' writing is active and powerful. Natàlia's story of isolation and enclosure lives in the language of her city. The terrible experience of a woman's speechless imprisonment comes to us through the novel's implicit faith in the communal language. We put Natàlia's sea-shell up to our ear and hear the speech of a people.

Frances Wyers. Kentucky Romance
Quarterly. 30, 1983, pp. 301–2, 308

To begin, we must make a distinction between Rodoreda's novels and her short stories, and between the two exilic syntagms—expulsion and expatriation—that characterize them. For Rodoreda conceived of all adult life as a form of exile, whether lived within or without the borders of one's native country. Adulthood, particularly womanhood, is the stage that follows *expulsion* from the garden of childhood; the adolescent is banished, and may not return. It is around this universal experience of exile that all of Rodoreda's novels are structured. In many of her short stories, on the other hand, she deals with a particular or historic form of exile, that of the Catalan's *expatriation* after the fall of the Republic. The two formulations of the exile experience are complementary—indeed, she composed her stories interstitially with her novels—and both reflect her vision as a double outsider, female and Catalan.

Genesis provides the explicit paradigm for Rodoreda's novels of expulsion and stories of expatriation, but they deviate from this biblical model in two ways. First, they focus almost exclusively on Eve, and second, inverting the biblical scheme, they privilege Eve's postlapsarian sufferings over her Edenic misbehavior. This pattern is evident in all of Rodoreda's major novels, where it is usually a female adolescent who is beguiled away from her beloved childhood—or its objective correlative, the garden—to spend the rest of her fictional days, like Natàlia or Cecilia Ce or Teresa Goday de Valldaura, trying to reconstruct that magical green space.

In the stories, expatriation is also portrayed as a female, or, in several interesting cases, a feminizing experience of loss. The expatriates, male or female, live out Eve's curse, that is, the fall into gender and generation, with all of its corollaries: dependency, submission, and subjection to what we might call unwanted transformations. This conceptualization of exile as a gendered experience, or an experience of (the female) gender, appears to be unique in Rodoreda. . . .

Rodoreda's fictions about expatriation evolve over the twenty years that separate the writing of the first from the last. But just as the "real" face of the sexagenarian protagonist of "El mirall" could be found beneath the adventitious wrinkles, so too can the "real face" of these stories be discerned beneath their changes in subject matter, focus, style, and tone. In Rodoreda, the exile's face is that of Eve, or Everywoman: a creature "born," or suddenly become, inferior. Like women, Rodoreda's exiles are diminished beings, always less than the powers that be, from the "shadow" in the concentration camp, to the black servant stranded in France, to the literally shrinking diabetic and the sailor-turned-undocumented-alien. . . . Thus the exile, in Rodoreda's vision: a new-born creature whose destiny is gender, whose function is to be the Other, always the second sex.

Geraldine Cleary Nichols. *MLN.* 101, 1986, pp. 407, 414–15

Fantasy literature has been a neglected genre in Spanish literature of the last few decades. The so-called midcentury generation whose fundamental concern during the 1950s was social protest, had to make an effort in the sixties to go beyond this stage which, although it bore significant witness to Spanish life, impeded a narrative evolution in accord with universal developments. This was not the case with writers in exile, whose separation from their native soil allowed them to come to terms with the oppressive atmosphere of the peninsula, and, although this had importance resonances within their work, they nonetheless had to maintain the necessary balance between adapting and absorbing other contemporary influences and following more subjective directions.

Mercè Rodoreda . . . belongs to this latter group. Catalan by birth, she has spent a great part of her life outside of Spain, and this fact has been the most basic influence on her literary career. A recognized novelist, she also works in the short story form, publishing, in 1967, the original Catalan version of *Mi Cristina y otros cuentos.* Lyricism, realism, and fantasy are characteristics applicable to this entire collection. This study is a discussion of the fantasy elements, the exclusive nucleus of some of these stories. . . .

The goal of fantasy literature, like the aim of psychoanalysis, is the investigation of human reality from an unfamiliar angle. This affirmation could be the a posteriori conclusion obtained from reading Mercè Rodoreda's stories. If, in general terms, the assumption of a genre and a given form of expression are the unequivocal consequence of the content that the author desires to express, in the case of this writer they become simultaneous events. The perfect structure of the fantastic universe is the appropriate means of expression to project the reality of an overwhelming world that catches her protagonists. The exhibition of this ideology becomes dramatic if not more than that through the balancing action of the lyrical force, a characteristic present in all Rodoreda's prose. Imagination, reality, and poetry are three words inseparable from any valid judgment of the short story production of the Catalan writer.

Angeles Encinar. *Revista Canadiense de Estudios Hispanicos.* 11, 1986, pp. 1–2, 10

Rodoreda's first important narrative is *Aloma,* a poetic and symbolic novel set in prewar Barcelona, which was awarded the Crexells Prize of 1937 and published by the Institució de les Lletres Catalanes in 1938 (although *Women Writers of Spain* states that it remained unpublished until 1969, at which time it was substantially revised and rewritten). As is true of the remainder of Rodoreda's mature production, this novel focuses upon the character of a woman, almost an adolescent, emphasizing problems posed by the protagonist's gender and her sexual relationships. *Aloma* already contains the lyricism and many constant themes of the writer's definitive style. . . .

La plaça del Diamant (1962; *The Pigeon Girl,* 1967; *The Time of the Doves,* 1983; translation and introduction by David Rosenthal) has been rendered into at least seven languages, including two translations into English. This deceptively simple novel is an absolute masterpiece of European literature, a work of a level of significance and perfection that must have surprised even Rodoreda's most fervent admirers. Once again, she focuses upon daily life, choosing a lower-class woman as narrative point of view and protagonist. Natalia, the somewhat unlikely heroine, suffers in marriage almost as much as in the Civil War because of the blind egotism of men in the patriarchal society that has formed her and the men around her. . . .

Although *El carrer de les Camèlies* (1966; The street of camellias) has not been translated into English, there is a Spanish version, *La calle de las Camelias* (1970), which may be more accessible for those who do not read Catalan. The psychological study of solitude is continued via the personal narrative of Cecilia, abandoned as an infant on Camellia Street. Her psychosocial crisis begins as an identity problem, but is slowly compounded by a series of life experiences, inseparable from the history of the country and its frustrated attempt at autonomy (the defeat of the Republic). In the same way that the woman in a paternalistic and authoritarian society is merely an extension of the male, her functions defined by her relationship to him, the oppressed country's role has been defined by totalitarian forces.

Janet Pérez. *Contemporary Women Writers of Spain* (Boston: Twayne, 1988), pp. 77, 79, 81

In September 1964 *Serra d'Or,* an important Catholic journal of Barcelona that records and studies Catalonian culture, surveyed literary critics and novelists to determine the works that they perceived as the most important written during 1939–63. The runner–up was *Bearn,* a refined narration of a family's decadence by Lorenç Villalonga, a revered writer whose intelligent and rich prose can be compared to works by the Cuban Alejo Carpentier or the Spaniard master of style Juan Benet. The clear winner was *La Plaça del Diamant*, a Mercè Rodoreda novel published only two years before the survey was undertaken, when the author was over fifty years old. This novel, translated into English as *The Time of the Doves* in 1980, soon became a classic of peninsular literature and a popular film. . . .

The many translations of *La plaça del Diamant* and the favorable reception this novel continues to merit will surely establish Mercè Rodoreda's name among the best writers of Spain in this century. It should be clear how much suffering and difficulty she had to endure to attain this distinction, and her triple exile as a Republican, a Catalonian, and a woman should not be forgotten. "El meu exili ha estat dur" (My exile has been hard), she told an interviewer in 1966. Suffering deeply influenced her writing, which may in turn have saved her from the despair of some of her characters. Before Aloma closes down the ancestral house, lost by the folly of one of her brothers, she climbs to the attic where her other brother, a devoted reader, used to live, until he committed suicide. In homage to him Aloma leaves behind a daring book she has bought in a moment of freedom. Then she faces darkness, having decided to live and devote her life to the child who is growing within her. This was also Rodoreda's choice, to leave her work to us as a testimony of both the harshness of existence and the resilience of life.

> Randolph Pope. In Joan L. Brown, ed.
> *Women Writers of Contemporary Spain:*
> *Exiles in the Homeland* (Newark, Delaware:
> University of Delaware Press, 1991), pp. 116,
> 132–33

Mercè Rodoreda is known first and foremost as the author of *La plaça del Diamant,* a novel that won acclaim from the general public as well as from the critics. Joan Sales states in the preface to the fifth edition that it was the best novel to appear in Europe in many years—"de molts anys ençà." Not only did she give us this book, which the whole Catalan nation took to its heart, but she followed up this success with a series of other novels and four collections of short stories. . . . As the author of *La plaça del Diamant,* Rodoreda became known as the undisputed mistress of the narrative of everyday life. But this mistress of the quotidian also betrays an intense interest in the world of fantasy. The harsh reality of the everyday world is counterbalanced by the equally harsh vision of the world of the unseen. For one of the things that these two aspects of her writing have in common is an attitude of total pessimism. Neither the world of everyday fact nor the world of the imagination can offer any hope or comfort. It is almost impossible to find a single happy character in her writing. . . .

And we are left in no doubt that the [disenchanted] view [is] taken by all Rodoreda's principal characters—Aloma, joyless and oppressed even in her youth, Colometa penetrated by a nostalgia for a happiness she has never known, Cecília with her sad eyes and her fragmented life, Maria, the tragic child, both murderess and suicide, the bewildered hero of *Quanta, quanta guerra* . . . , materially and spiritually homeless—all these live in a world of disenchantment and futility. Some of them, like Aloma and Colometa, live entirely in the world of the quotidian; some, like La Salamandra, have moved wholly into the world of the fantastic. It is when, as in *Mirall Trencat,* her characters inhabit the dangerous territory between the two worlds, that Rodoreda's vision is at its most compelling, disturbing, and satisfying.

> Mercè Clarasó. In Catherine Davies, ed.
> *Women Writers in Spain and Spanish*
> *America* (Lewiston, New York: Edwin
> Mellen Press, 1993), pp. 43–44, 53–54

La plaça del Diamant (1962) by Mercè Rodoreda . . . is, as Arthur Terry points out, "perhaps the finest work of fiction to have appeared since the Civil War." Critics have variously praised its "human," "believable" and "epic" qualities. Like Laforet's *Nada,* Rodoreda's novel has a female protagonist and is set in Barcelona during the same time period (1930s–1940s). But here the similarity ends, for *Nada* concludes with the protagonist barely having left college, while the protagonist of Rodoreda's novel, Natàlia, gets married, has children, loses her husband as a result of the Civil War, remarries for the children's sake, and is middle-aged by the end of the novel. For this reason *La plaça del Diamant* is closer to the spirit of the *Bildungsroman* in that it plots the life of an individual from puberty to middle age and shows the protagonist as having achieved a deeper understanding of life's ironies by the end of the narrative. The knowledge that Natàlia has achieved, as we shall see, is quintessentially feminine in that it involves a knowledge of dispossession. Natàlia is shown to be twice removed from the corridors of power, first for being a woman, and second for being Catalan. . . .

In the main events of Natàlia's life, from courtship to the brink of suicide, she epitomizes the otherness of female identity in that she finds herself in a world she does not comprehend and in which she feels "lost." . . .

Natàlia's carving of her name on the door of her former apartment is . . . thus, not only to be seen as an (ambiguous) sexual metaphor but also as a political allegory of the *inscription* of a subaltern, Catalan culture which only exists in terms of repression. It is in this sense that Rodoreda's novel encapsulates the Otherness at once of the dispossessed female but also the repressed voice of Catalan culture which, like the Unconscious, sought to write its message publicly, in the civic arena of the Plaça del Diamant.

> Stephen M. Hart. *White Ink: Essays in*
> *Twentieth-Century Feminine Fiction in Spain*
> *and Latin America* (London: Tamesis, 1993),
> pp. 19–20, 25, 27–28

"They abandoned me on Camellia Street, in front of a garden gate, and the night watchman found me early the next morning."

So begins *Camellia Street,* a small masterpiece of fiction by Mercè Rodoreda, the Catalan novelist who died of cancer a decade ago. *Camellia Street* was first published in 1966 in the Catalan language. This new Graywolf edition, exquisitely translated by David H. Rosenthal, should introduce American readers to this important writer's work and, for that matter, to its meaning in the context of Catalan politics. . . .

Rodoreda's novel is written in the form of Cecilia's utterly unembellished, completely convincing stream of consciousness. The wall between the reader and what's read—between oneself and Cecilia—falls away, and it is only on reflection that the full achievement of this novel can be grasped. The work renders, first, the feeling of a woman abandoned by her parents, her lovers, and her miscarried children; second, it renders the plight of a people abandoned by the century; and third, most magnificently, it renders the basic experience of every human being—that we are all here on the earth as abandoned ones, that our lives are a long and futile search for "lost things."

In the face of the essential agony of the human condition, our books tell us, we can do only one of two things: offer the feeling up in prayer, or tell stories about it. Mercè Rodoreda, with *Camellia Street,* reminds us that even if prayer seems to have failed, stories have not.

James Carroll. *Ploughshares.* 19:4, 1993–94, pp. 221–23

ROMANO, LALLA (ITALY) 1909–

With some fifteen works to her credit, Lalla Romano continues to be one of Italy's most popular and prolific women writers. Indeed, with Natalia Ginzburg, Dacia Maraini, and Elsa Morante, Romano has given the most significant insights into the thinking and feeling of contemporary women. With *Nei mari estremi* (In the farthest seas) she has written another novel in which autobiographical facts, wishes, dreams, and fiction are expertly molded into an artistic whole. The image evoked by the volume's title, "In the Faraway Seas," taken from a short story by Hans Christian Andersen, has accompanied the author through the years as the embodiment of images of "extreme moments." Such moments of existence emerge and reemerge from the sea of memory as if they were out of time, bring visions where reality is fused to dream, and mysteriously convey images that are "openings" to wider horizons and a better understanding of life.

Nei mari estremi consists of a series of short chapters, none more than a page and a half long, flashes of love and death, "two universal and daily themes of life." These two themes appear and disappear like a musical composition: indeed, the text is like a series of musical variations on facts, feelings, thoughts, and dreams. The narration is both linear and cyclical; each life encounter reveals the importance of human relationships, while in the background there is the ever-present natural law of time that redimensions any lofty dream and levels all differences.

For Romano, however, it seems that the only valid time is that which is reflected in our consciousness. In memory, experiences overlap one another and are ordered not according to objective chronology but instead to subjective laws of association that require simultaneity of time and space. The sense of distance is not the result of the passage of time but rather is ontological. It is the distance between individual beings and, even more, the distance between our own beings and the reality surrounding us, existing but "unattainable," that makes the difference in life. *Nei mari estremi* is another significant and most interesting novel by a skillful writer who possesses humanitarian ideals and a love for life.

Mario B. Mignone. World Literature Today.
63, 1989, p. 82

Lalla Romano problematizes time extensively in her narrative fiction and exhibits a constant concern with the interplay between past and present, seeing both elements as equally important and necessary for the creation of the artistic object. A structural examination of two of Romano's main works, *La penombra che abbiamo attraversato* (The shade that we crossed) and *Le parole tra noi leggere* (Flighty words between us), illustrates the writer's sensitivity to recollection. An analysis of these novels not only reveals their inherent complexity but also highlights the rapport between what occurs at the actual moment of an individual's life and what has come before. . . .

La penombra che abbiamo attraversato and *Le parole tra noi leggere* both acquire their nonlinear structure from the narrators' recollections of the past. In the former, physical environment stimulates the narrator's memory and revives the past; in the latter, "documents" constitute the loose thread that leads the mind. The temporal scheme of the two novels projects a double movement from present to past and then back to present. Such a complex temporal itinerary, as well as opposition between past and present, serves a definite purpose. Romano has stated in various interviews that "we are the past"; she agrees with Poulet who writes: "The present is something that has not yet become past." According to Romano, earlier phases of human existence enlighten the present. Human experiences constitute a temporal process that transpires in time. The lessons of the past enable an understanding of the present and form a unified entity. In both novels, remembrances force the narrators' minds to confront their present selves with their former ones. In this sense, Romano's narratives are more than merely simple recollections of the past; they are enriching revisitations of it. Timelessness—a third temporal dimension—characterizes these novels. In the affective memory of the narrator, everything is; Ponte Stura remains as it appears in the present and as it used to be long ago. P. is unhappy both as a young man and as a child. By placing the past in direct contrast to the present and narrating the simple events of everyday life, Romano depicts the growth of a conscience and thereby represents the fascinating process of living that is always difficult and complex.

Flavia Brizio. In Santo L. Aricò, ed.
*Contemporary Women Writers in Italy: A
Modern Renaissance* (Amherst: University
of Massachusetts Press, 1990), pp. 63, 74

Einaudi, one of Italy's most prestigious publishing houses, has recently given birth to the latest work by one of its beloved children, Lalla Romano, a work whose title, "A Dream of the North," brings forth its strong evocative quality. Romano's association with Einaudi began in 1951, when she published her first work, *Le metamorfosi,* which she defined in 1984 as "a collection of dreams." It seems then that, in a way, at age eighty she felt the need to close a circle, within which one finds the whole of her narrative production, including such works as *Le parole tra noi leggere* (1969; Between us light words) and *Una gioventù inventata* (1979; An invented youth).

Romano (b. 1909) is one of Italy's most famous women writers, an author whose life and career span modern Italian history, with its tormented and painful events. Her life has obviously been eventful, for she met and became friends with some of Italy's and Europe's most gifted contemporary artists and intellectuals. She has often been described as a "writer of memory," a designation to which she once strongly reacted by saying that memory is in fact a means to make literature, that all writers are in a way "writers of memory," and that what is truly important is to question one's own life from a distance, almost drawing oneself out of it. This is in fact what she seems to be doing in *Un sogno del Nord:* it is not a novel, not a diary or a confession, but simply a collection of fragments grouped together in various sections with extremely evocative titles such as "Shadows," "Encounters," and "The Image and I." These fragments of memory follow one another by affinity rather than according to any chronological order: they are, we may say, attracted to one another by empathy and draw an expressionistic and pictorial ensemble. During her early years Romano became strongly interested in painting, and although after the war she decided to privilege writing, her narrative certainly shows clear signs of her passion for visual art, being as it is extremely vivid and imagistic.

Distant landscapes, places of the memory, stories of shadows, encounters with the friends of a lifetime, and personal reflections both literary and artistic intermingle here in a text whose confessional mode manages to assume the status of metaphor. Although Romano maintains that the various brief narratives are not intended to provide us with a depiction of History, her personal itinerary ends up coinciding with that of Italy in the aftermath of World War II and with that of contemporary European intellectual history.

Feelings, intimate images, remembrances of childhood, distant but never-lost gestures and events, fragments of a life written in a forty-year period are magnetically attracted to one another and highlight the "unsaid" as a bit of nostalgia or a mystery which gives the text a poetic flair and transcends the personal portrait to become that of an entire generation.

Manuela Gieri. World Literature Today. 65,
1991, p. 100

ROSE, WENDY (UNITED STATES) 1941–

Rose lives as a marginal woman on the lines between races, cultures, and languages. She is "foreign and familiar at once," the poet confesses, suffering and surviving on the limits of city and country. She stands her ground, however, in trenches of racial alienation, where mixed-bloods can exist neither Indian nor nonIndian, both and none. . . .

[Paula Gunn] Allen and Rose and other Indian women, born "breeds," decide to fight for their Indianness and to write about that choice. Like Indian meal leached from California buckeye on the Sierra slopes, acrid and poisonous until processed, Wendy Rose's art tempers the native sting in a daily staple. She nurtures herself on her own struggle. . . .

Wendy Rose writes with a contrary's come-and-go, the "backwards-forwards" clowning that steeled northern plains warriors, men and women, in a world of inversions. It is also Old Man Coyote's instinct for survival on the edges of village and wilderness. Rose dares reality with Trickster's nip-and-tuck, playing the serious game of life-and-death. She is a poet who barks and scudders for cover, who won't keep quiet or give in to oppression. She battles for native rights with a brave's honest sense of ambivalence toward the cost of life, without forsaking an artist's sensitivity. Hers is an old Lakota formula for a visionary leader, a sacred "word sender." She meets the world, too, with a skin "seven thumbs thick," as counseled among the eastern Iroquois when they spoke of leaders.

This poet-activist teeters in battle, rocklike, on the cliffs of vertical city walls: she opposes the violence of American city culture. She makes use of the energy of imbalance, a doubling self winding through the torque of Indian redefinition in contemporary society. The war, for her, is often fought in anthropological archives to defend Indian culture and still preserve, by way of her native and academic "twisted-twin birth," what otherwise would be lost. This woman's lineage traces to the mythic Hopi genatrix, "Hard Beings Woman" or *Huruing Wuhti.* . . .

Sensitivity blossoms among the rocks of her loss and anger, as Rose's imagination graces the politics of have-nots and the poetics of estrangement:

"touching ourselves / we touch everything," she claims in the poetry of *Academic Squaw.* . . .

This poet of a twisted throat knows her art to be by conventional white standards a language of mutation. She sings beyond semantics, out of the agony of being Indian/white. . . .

But in the irregularities of original voices, all poets stutter toward revelation, and no lines come easy. In the wake of stunned witness, a vision of things, some remain more open to their pain and awkward art than others (William Carlos Williams in contrast to Wallace Stevens, for example). Wendy Rose chisels her confusion powerfully, organically; her stone-sharpened poems run nicked on truth, never glazed simply in beauty. . . .

If the word "stone" were a stone, we could stand on it, and indeed imagine ourselves rooted in the earth. If "bone" *were* bone, we would flesh ourselves around it and remain firm. If "sage" were only sage, we could say it blessed and wise. If "copper" were copper, we would touch our hands and temper our voices to it. Wendy Rose, an alchemical Indian poet, has incarnated her words with native integrity. If "lost" were forever lost, then we would have no memory ringing in our language, no words to live by, no books of poetry like *Lost Copper,* which mine the losses and make alloys of native experience in American poetry.

Kenneth Lincoln. Parnassus. 10:1, 1982,
pp. 290–291, 293, 295–96

Rose is perhaps the most ritualistically oriented among American Indian poets. This is not always an advantage: fairly trite poems, put into ritualistic rhythms, at first seem more impressive than on second reading, while personal poems become weakened as emotion and experience gives way to an imposed ritual form. When ritual merges with contemporary American political consciousness, as in "Nuke Devils: the Indian women listen," Rose transforms anger into pride: "and nothing you can do / will stop us / as we re-make / your weapons into charms." The book's [*The Halfbreed Chronicles & Other Poems*] final section represents an interesting new direction for Rose's work, as she evokes personified voices—tortured social outcasts—whom she finds representative of her own state.

Rochelle Ratner. Library Journal. January,
1986, p. 89

The unique force of her poetry stems from the fact that she is also a professional anthropologist, at once "the subject and the object" of her own academic discipline. Faced with the need "to learn" her own native culture and to "look for its repaired form/in museums," she naturally feels repelled by a discourse which only knows her as "the other": "They give me, stretched across the desert, / their ethnography." "Us"—the community of white men describing Indians which was a continual reference point for [T. S.] Eliot and [William Carlos] Williams alike in their consistent use of the first person plural—has now become "them," but in the words of someone who also speaks "their" language. Anthropology's former plaything—the "other" as the classic object of ethnographic description—now talks back at the player, the white, male self that, in Rose's words, "paints" his face with words only. In the "other's" view of the anthropological self, poetic empathy turning ethnography into a "good read" is no better than an anthropology which hides its power to treat others as mere "ethno-data" behind a veil of scientific factuality. . . .

Whether or not we agree that "all discourse is colonial," Rose's poetry shows us how the hitherto oppressed other has learned to use—in Rose's own words—"the enemy's tool" so well that it can turn the language of colonialism (which for her seems to be epitomized by that of anthropology) against itself. "I test your speech like pottery," Rose warns the anthropologists, combining her "native" status of outsider with an academic insider's insight and treating the words of anthropologists as if *these* were the real collector's items and not the Indian artifacts. In spite of their own particular blind spots, however, Eliot and Williams already seem to share a dawning awareness that seeing with one's "own" eyes would entail the realization of what it means to see with ever so different eyes. What Eliot still cautiously *suppresses* is more emphatically *expressed* by Williams. My final point, however, is not simply that literature, by being more richly textured, can embody more truth than is to be found in scientific versions of human life. If poets have posed as anthropologists and anthropologists now sometimes like to present themselves as poets, Rose may serve as a reminder that, however flexible the stage opened up by the discovery of "writing" might be, different cultural assumptions do not interact there easily as long as human beings still seem unable to do so.

Christopher Irmscher. *Soundings.* 75, 1992,
pp. 599–600

The title of Rose's . . . new collection [*Going to War with All My Relations*] aptly points to the complexion of her poems. A descendant of the Hopi and Miwok tribes, the poet-as-shaman gives voice to her brothers and sisters: "I let my tongue lick / your bones back together . . . / I light the fire / to heat your lips. / I touch your spirit / that was never in danger," she intones in a poem about the Anishnabec Occupation. Meshing her own experience with revisionist history and newsworthy events, she carves a place for herself amid the cultures surrounding her, such as that of the Mormons, who "like to play / that I want to change, / that I don't mind ending myself / in their holy book." Culled from earlier books, and including a hefty selection of new work, this collection places 20 years of writing in perspective. Rose's concerns have remained consistent: ecological, archaeological and feminist. Assuming a sometimes ironic, sometimes angry cowboy-and-Indian stance, the speakers of many recent poems draw on the poet's experience as a university professor, dealing with interminable staff meetings and complacent students.

Throughout the volume, the writing is at times prosaic, rhetorical or gim-
micky, but the spirit rings true.

Penny Kaganoff. *Publishers Weekly.*
February 8, 1993, p. 81

ROTH, FRIEDERIKE (GERMANY) 1948–

Pfaff, a college professor [in *Ordnungstraume* (Dream of order)] shares his
life with a turtle that lives in his bathtub. He imagines living with a lover.
An immanent mystic, he fathoms the depths of his absurd, surrealistic and
Kafkaesque life by attempting to squeeze it into the framework of Hegel's
ideologies. This German metaphysician is widely quoted throughout the volume, with emphasis on his *Wissenschaft der Logik*. The book is a satire on
the Sense of Order that desires to arrange everyday events into a complete,
meaningful whole. The author convinces us that this is a sure way to chaos.
The poetic nature of this author's first prose volume is highly attractive.

H. Beerman. *World Literature Today.* 55,
1981, p. 101

January and February 1981 saw a great deal of Friederike Roth.

Her first play *Klavierspiele* (Piano playing) had its scandal-ridden premiere in Hamburg and was also performed on German television. Critics
called it a lyrical play by a lyrical poet and spoke of "feminist imagination
with the most trivial of all trivial plots." In discussing Roth's second volume
of poetry one is tempted to play a bit with this designation, perhaps, by
eliminating the word *lyrical* altogether and by adding another *trivial* or two.
I have no argument with the word *feminist*.

Most of the poems could be called trivial reflections on incidental observations of little consequence or depth, such as the following (my translation):
"Let's get / those grandpas who like to kiss / little girls; what / do they want,
go to the other side / of the lake when it is frozen, yeah?" True, behind these
observations there lurks a feeling of condensed social pessimism which, in
recent years, seems to take hold of every German writer at age thirty. Other
writers do not, however, show as much disenchantment with the traditions
of German poetry as does Roth. This disenchantment appears as a theme in
her poetry and also determines her poetic practice. At times the result seems
to be a dialectic between the critical writer's iconoclastic self and its double,
educated and steeped in tradition.

There is no denying that Roth is consistent in her effort to minimize the
importance of language as the creative force behind poetry. She prefers the
vernacular and tries hard to eliminate all "poetic" formality by using
the grammar of the carelessly spoken word and the casualness of chance

verbalizations. Many of her poems seem to be stream-of-consciousness effusions with a strong dose of inner monologue. The world of fairy tales and legends supplies her metaphors.

R. Terras. *World Literature Today.* 55, 1981,
p. 671

The first of [the negative] criticisms was that Friederike Roth's language is lyrical and that as a result the plays lack the dramatic element necessary to the theater. Her language certainly has lyrical and experimental qualities, but the plays also contain successful, swift moving dialogue alongside the associative passages and the direct monologues. It is also important to remember that a large part of the lyrical, associative language becomes much less obscure once we are aware of the various themes which preoccupy Friederike Roth. These themes . . . include originality and repetition, imagination and reality, and sexuality and morality. They are, for their own part, all to a greater or lesser extent interconnected. Their presence provides an underlying structure in the plays, a structure which may seem to be lacking at first glance. The separate scenes in *Klavierspiele,* for instance, appear to have little in common in terms of dramatic action, but the themes remain constant throughout. It cannot be denied that this pattern is complex and perhaps not quite what we expect when we speak of dramatic structure. The development in Friederike Roth's work tends to be circular rather than linear. In keeping with her awareness of the repetitiveness of life, the plays have a tendency to return to their starting points. We are given the impression that the whole thing, like the love affairs, the conversation, the attempts at self-discovery, could begin all over again. As is said in *Das Ganze ein Stück* (The whole of a part), "the old box in a box construction."

The second charge against her work, that it is of limited content, banal, and at best relevant only to a few, mostly women, can easily be refuted. Friederike Roth's plays are constructed on several levels, and critical observations of this type can stem only from a reading of the most obvious of these levels. The numerous themes in her work are relevant to a much wider audience. The mistaken view of Friederike Roth as not only a "woman playwright," but also a "woman's playwright," evolves from the preconceptions aroused by her at times lyrical and quiet language and by the continuing fallacy that female dramatic characters (as is all too often the case in traditional drama) are moved by less central and less comprehensive issues than those faced by men.

It can fairly be said that the plays of Friederike Roth are not easily accessible. Perhaps, to male actors and directors, they are not wholly acceptable either. The unprecedented aggression shown at the première of *Klavierspiele* in Hamburg would support this view. The writer herself provides only limited visual possibilities and a great deal of responsibility is put on the producer to draw out not only the dramatic qualities in the dialogue, but also

to convey to the audience sufficient of Friederike Roth's themes and concerns
to render the quieter episodes of the drama equally relevant and logical.

Lucinda Rennison. In W. G. Sebald, ed.
A Radical Stage: Theatre in Germany in the
1970s and 1980s (Oxford: Berg Publishers,
1988), pp. 62–63

ROY, GABRIELLE (CANADA) 1909–83

"Clear and sensible" is how the publishers, with a restraint almost unheard
of in dust-jacket prose, describe this chronicle [*The Tin Flute*] of poor French-
Canadians, and clear and sensible it is. Except that it has a tougher fiber and
an almost complete lack of humor, the book may remind you of *A Tree Grows
in Brooklyn* as it tells its story of an affectionate, not at all grim, family's life
in a Montreal slum. There are a ne'er-do-well father, a patient, loving mother,
a pretty older daughter who gets into what is known as trouble, and a number
of younger children. All these people long desperately for a life free from
poverty, but when the war brings government allowances and fat pay checks,
they find it too high a price for the comfort it provides. If the story isn't
quite as moving as it might be, this perhaps is because Miss Roy seems so
conscientiously determined not to overplay the pathos of her forlorn
characters.

The New Yorker. April 26, 1947, p. 93

If populism were not what it has been in France, an invention of aesthetes and
professors, I would say that [*Secondhand Happiness*] was the masterpiece of
populism. But through the fault of its creators, "populism" soon took on such
disagreeable connotations that I hesitate to use the term now. Gabrielle Roy
did not "live with" the common people, as they say, nor did she "study them"
with a curiosity tainted by condescension, admiring herself for being so good.
No, this authentic novelist, through the power of her sympathy (and perhaps,
who knows, through personal experience) lives the lives of the characters
she depicts. She suffers their sorrows, thrills to their joys, and experiences
all the sordid sense of destiny that a hopeless environment brings to weigh
on them. And because she knows what she is talking about, because
she knows the nature of these lives in all their mediocrity—and also because
she is a woman, in other words, better prepared than a man to penetrate the
details of the thousand and one trivial difficulties that constitute the necessity
of existence—she has succeeded in painting a picture of workers that is valid
for all the peoples of the world, not just those of Montreal.

Nevertheless, *Secondhand Happiness* is primarily a Canadian novel. For
the French public at least, it is a novel that shatters some clichés about

Canada and presents images of that country that are entirely new to us. The success of Jack London's works, some of which are admirable, and the astonishing popularity of [Louis Hémon's] *Maria Chapdelaine* have for some thirty years given France the idea of a nation of trappers and peasants, a land totally covered by snow, with vast plains and frozen rivers, a land in which the people struggle fiercely against a rebellious and awesome nature. Gabrielle Roy's novel suddenly makes us aware that Canada is also a country of great industrial cities.

> Francis Ambrière. *La revue de Paris.*
> December, 1947, pp. 137–38

Like Miss Roy's highly praised first novel, *The Tin Flute, Where Nests the Water Hen* is laid in the author's native Manitoba, in almost incredibly remote country ringed about by lakes connected with a network of unknown rivers. The place names are French, but the people who live in the few towns, the tiny hamlets and the isolated cabins come of stock from many other parts of the world as well—among them, the Ukraine, Hungary, Poland, Romania and, of course, the British Isles. Father Joseph-Marie, the Capuchin parish priest, had been born in Riga of a Belgian father and Russian mother and knew nearly a score of languages when he came to Toutes Aides, but he had to pick up at least a smattering of a half dozen more tongues, including even a few words of the Saultais Indians, to hear the confessions of his two or three hundred parishioners, scattered over about a hundred square miles. . . .

The largest part of this little book, which is not a novel strictly speaking, but three related long stories, is the tale of the school on Little Water Hen, which Mamma and Pap Tousignant created for their children with their hands and wits and love and some aid from their revered government. This and the other stories of Mamma Tousignant's annual journey and of Father Joseph-Marie's ministry, have appealing simplicity and modesty and compelling interest. The book captures the warmth and sincerity and charm of its chief characters. It is like Mamma Tousignant herself, who, whether at home or on one of her highly relished journeys, disposed the people about her to become aware that they had reasons for being happy.

> Mary Ross. *New York Herald Tribune.*
> October 21, 1951, p. 6

In the lake district of Northern Manitoba Gabrielle Roy is completely at home. True, she has the artist's faculty of making herself at home anywhere, and nobody would say that *Secondhand Happiness* fell short of perfection for any reason connected with the fact that its author was not a born Montrealer.

But a born Manitoban she actually is, and this lake area with its sparse and astoundingly mixed population is her home, and its ways are as familiar to her as they are strange and inexplicable to us. . . . The result of this familiarity combined with the author's technical skill is a clarity, a sharpness, a sunniness in the whole picture which has never been approached in any

Canadian writing about frontier life. *Maria Chapdelaine* is fuzzy and theoretical in comparison, making one feel that the idea came first and characters and situations were built to fit it. In *The Petite Poule d'Eau* (it is the name of a river) the characters are utterly self-sustaining; they are not the illustrations for something beyond themselves, they are the book. . . . Simple people doing simple things, but told with such loving care that they become universal, that the Little Water Hen River becomes a symbol of the world.

> B. K. Sandwell. *Saturday Night.* November
> 3, 1951, p. 23

Alexandre Chenevert, the cashier [in *Alexandre Chenevert, Cashier*], is a clerk in a city (Montreal, it happens to be), almost indistinguishable at first from the other coral creatures who make up the great barrier reefs of urban centers. He is a worrier and an insomniac, holder of a monotonous job, eater of cafeteria meals, taker of innumerable pills. As a groove in a victrola record reproduces sound, so his life reproduces one of the tracks civilization takes as it moves like a glacier across the rock of humanity.

The danger in writing a book like this is dullness. Doesn't the reader, after all, know all that? Doesn't he too hold a monotonous job, swear at the neighbor's radio, worry about the possibility of war, the necessity of doctor's bills, loose buttons on overcoats, lost umbrellas? Wouldn't he rather read about heroic adventures, as Alexandre himself once enjoyed doing? Quite frankly, this reader wondered for a while whether the minutiae of Alexandre's life were worth recording.

Then Alexandre began to transcend his type and Mlle. Roy's intention began to become clear. The minutiae add up to more than a chronicle. The cashier is more than a social statistic. Without knowing quite why the reader finds himself more and more deeply involved in the events of Alexandre's days—the jog-trot days of a man in his fifties, to whom nothing happens. Nothing happens to him, at any rate, that does not happen to everyone. . . . But—and here is Mlle. Roy's achievement—though Alexandre suffers what every man suffers, he is not Everyman. He is not a hollow symbol but a differentiated human being and thus the proper subject of fiction. He is individual, paradoxical, unpredictable. He is ridden by fear and also indomitable. People drive him to distraction and he is pathetic and noble, humble, cranky, irritating, original. . . .

He lives his outwardly dull life so intensely that the meaning of life shines through, just as it does through Joyce Cary's very different but equally intense characters. So we are reminded again that man is the measure of all things, and that no abstraction can be valued unless we reckon it by the value of such an individual as the cashier.

> Elizabeth Janeway. *The New York Times.*
> October 16, 1955, p. 5

[*Street of Riches*] is a pleasant book to read and a difficult one to criticize. As you turn the pages you are seldom excited or bored. The pace is even, the style is restrained, often lyrical but never passionate. But after you have finished, after you've gone about your business, you are likely to stop and think: "What was the name of that family, those French-Canadians in Manitoba?" You wonder about the family name because very quietly and with a subtle skill the author has impressed the character of the family upon your memory.

Street of Riches is the fourth of Miss Gabrielle Roy's books, and the first that I have read. The first thing that struck me was the apparent aimlessness of her method—it was as if she had merely reminisced. The next thing, far more accurate than the first, was the openness of her sensibility—her imagination and memory seem to meet and converse without inhibition. The third impression corrected the first, for at the end of the book one realizes that Miss Roy is an artist of clear purpose and of exact and delicate expression. . . .

No man could have written this book and yet its femininity is never cute or shrill. Miss Roy has fashioned a skillful subtlety of style without losing that "immediate dependence of language upon nature," which, as Emerson said, never loses its power to affect us.

Thomas F. Curley. *Commonweal.* October 25, 1957, pp. 107–8

In this century . . . we have met few novelists . . . who have looked with visionary clarity at the plight of wholly ordinary people in our modern cities.

Gabrielle Roy is one of these writers, and Theodore Dreiser (though he must bow to Zola as an influence in her work) is her chief American predecessor. But where Dreiser's typical hero is Clyde Griffiths, the sad dreamer of *An American Tragedy,* Gabrielle Roy's central figure is the frail banker Alexandre Chenevert, an experienced teller of our nation's true accounts. And though, like Dreiser, Gabrielle Roy recognizes that truth-telling is unwelcome to customers who hope for a large credit balance, she looks beyond mathematical calculations in a way that Dreiser does not. In the midst of this commercial Canadian time and place she is able to make a quiet affirmation. Her statement is more important than we have recognized. . . .

In Gabrielle Roy's imaginative landscape . . . big-city living, with its soot and noise, its mechanical routine and impersonality, suggests simultaneously both the pains of adulthood and the dislocations of this unhappy century. By contrast, the warm and simple life of the frontier and the provincial town is becoming a thing of the past—as dear, and as irrevocably lost as childhood innocence.

This perception of the controlling pattern in Gabrielle Roy's work is essential to an understanding of her statement. The values of the garden, childhood, innocence, and the past, array themselves against the forces of the city, adulthood, "experience," and the present. . . . It is true that, like

Willa Cather, Gabrielle Roy endorses the values of the past and the frontier. . . . Unlike Cather, however, Gabrielle Roy is unflinchingly aware that there is no real escape from the present. *Here* and *now* is where Everyman lives; and his greatest gifts in a world where both faith and justice have perished are his ability to endure and to love. The critics who have regarded *Rue Deschambault* (Deschambault street) and *The Petite Poule d'Eau* (The little water hen) as day-dreaming retreats from the present, then, are mistaken; these works are rediscoveries, deceptively gentle and subjective, of the meaning of valor, pain, aspiration and love.

Hugo McPherson. *Canadian Literature.*
Summer, 1959, pp. 46, 49

The Hidden Mountain can be appreciated as a novel only if the reader accepts or sympathizes with the conception of art which it expresses: a deeply religious conception that the artist serves a purpose similar to the priest's in leading man toward the fulfillment of his spirit. This conception is expressed when the master artist realizes near the end of Gabrielle Roy's story of Pierre that there are martyrs for art and that "there are more of them than we believe, perhaps even more than in religion—for the saints, for the martyrs for the cause, does hard-hearted creation keep any tally?" *The Hidden Mountain* is the record of a martyr for the cause. Pierre Cadorai's story is the story of the artist in any form of art, the story of Gabrielle herself. . . .

The Hidden Mountain has many faults as a work of fiction. It is not strong enough in narrative and has a tendency to lack strength and unity, although the author's reiteration of imagery among the three parts does contribute toward a unifying effect. The characters, aside from the main one, fail to be developed, and their comings and goings and their compassion for Pierre are a bit unbelievable at times. It is the subject matter, however, as much of Gabrielle Roy's vision of it as can be grasped (as in the case of Pierre's crude depictions of his mountain), which redeems whatever inadequacies are evident. Gabrielle Roy has attempted to capture the artistic process. The treatment of such a subject would seem inevitable in the career of every serious artist; like Pierre's compulsion to seek out his vision in the north, it is something that must be said. Gabrielle Roy, because she is a writer of fiction, depicts the artistic process in characters and events rather than defining it in expository prose. Such a depiction should always be valuable and interesting to the serious reader, who must bring his own creative powers to the image made by the artist.

John J. Murphy. *Renascence.* Fall, 1963,
pp. 53, 56

The frequent placing of the subject after the verb [in *The Secret Mountain*] gives the sentences a nobility and an individuality. The numerous inversions emphasize the unusualness and sublime strangeness of the setting. Except for a few moments of passion, the rhythm is slow. In this endlessly breathless era of ours, this novelist takes her time telling a story, stopping to muse about an idea she likes, lingering for a few lines to enjoy some little eccentricity.

The Hidden Mountain, which relates very simple things in a very simple style, has a certain biblical grandeur. . . .

Should the reader conclude that there has been an evolution in Gabrielle Roy's art from *Secondhand Happiness* to *The Hidden Mountain?* Although very few critics have studied her works, some of them did not like the style of *The Secret Mountain,* with its numerous inversions and overly refined constructions; they did not see that these techniques serve to contribute to the unity and grandeur of the narrative. *Secondhand Happiness* won a prize [the Prix Fémina]: therefore, its value is no longer debated; critics are satisfied with pointing out its merits. But they do not know what to think about her other novels, whose simplicity, spontaneity, and fidelity astonish them.

Since *Secondhand Happiness* Gabrielle Roy's art has indeed matured. I would even say that, compared to *The Hidden Mountain, Secondhand Happiness* is a novel of the senses. And it seems to me that to move from the psychological novel, the novel of manners, to the poetic novel is to progress, to move from the domain of the immediately visible into the domain of the invisible. The simpler plot, the more restrained style, and the slower rhythm all indicate that Gabrielle Roy is concentrating her effort so as to achieve greater intimacy. She has described her own life, she has brought fictional men and women to life, and she has depicted various ways of life; now she has touched the soul. If she continues to evolve in this direction, her work will gain more beauty and spirituality, but her novels will perhaps cease to be novels and become poetry.

Monique Genuist. *La Création romanesque chez Gabrielle Roy* (Ottawa: Cercle du Livre de France, 1966), pp. 129–30

[*The Road Past Altamont*] shows again [Roy's] strength in what most Canadian novelists lack: freshness of outlook, staying power, finesse. The book is quite outside the trend of modern fiction. There's little sex in it. Physical violence is scarcer than Zen's teeth—and no one froths at the mouth or moons about the Absurd. Yet, with a craft so adroit that it seems like instinct itself, it lights up many thoroughfares of the human heart.

At first glance, the book would seem to have two fatal strikes against it. Christine, the French-Canadian heroine, is a precocious, hypersensitive child of the type that usually cries out for euthanasia; and the simple people of her Manitoban family and acquaintance jar the ear with their dialogue. But soon the child becomes genuinely appealing, and the apparent incongruity of the dialogue takes on, in a curiously fabulistic way, a kind of supranaturalness. It is a mark of Miss Roy's talent that she can dare these hurdles and take them without a disastrous tumble into the spurious. . . .

This eternal tug-of-war between roots and change, between loyalty to kin and duty to desires, lies at the heart of the book; but it is only one of the emotional vectors in the complex physics of family life that Miss Roy captures so clearly. How she does it is hard to pin down. There is no real plot. Only incidents—and these, on the face of them, wispy rather than exclamatory. . . .

By drawing on the parables of lake, prairie ("this reminder of the total enigma") and hills, and with her gift for making an ounce of simple means carry a pound of implication, Miss Roy takes the very pulse of wonder. Incident and action become increasingly simple and luminous in her work, and the ineluctable flow of *time* and change becomes a leitmotif.

In her new novel, *Windflower*, these main themes come together with a gentle but piercing irony. The frontier "garden" of her earlier work has now become Canada's far north, perhaps the bleakest, purest landscape in the world; and the urban south is an unreal land of imagination in which the Eskimo heroine's half-caste son may find fulfillment perhaps in Vietnam, as far as she knows.

Miss Roy's original title, *La rivière sans repos,* is only partly echoed in *Windflower* (the short-lived, vivid red flower of the tundra), because her subject is indeed the inscrutable and unceasing river of time that has captured the imagination of artists throughout history. But it is not "sweet Thames," Niger, Amazon, Volga, or St. Lawrence. It is a cruel northern river.

Hugo McPherson. *The Tamarack Review.*
Spring, 1971, pp. 87–88

The qualities that entitle [Gabrielle Roy] to serious consideration as a distinguished novelist . . . are a talent for delicate, vibrant prose; a gentle understanding of the longing of the heart; and a warmly compassionate view of people. However, for a rounded estimate we must not blind ourselves to certain omissions. Her characters act intuitively; they do not engage in rational or irrational analysis; they are not torn by mental conflict; they are uninterested in ideas. . . .

Gabrielle Roy's world is not an easy one for her characters but it is one in which they never encounter the stalking figure of evil. Whether we view evil as a force possessing permanent reality, or as an inconvenience to be handled pragmatically as an unfortunate aspect of contingent circumstances, few adults would deny that its disordering presence forces itself upon our horrified attention from time to time. But it is not something that we tell children about; indeed, it is a terror from which we do all we can to shield them. It is in this sense that Mlle. Roy's characters are still treated as children not yet capable of venturing into the more somber areas of existence.

The characters never "surprise" us—an ability, E. M. Forster tells us, which is the ultimate test of a "round" character. I have emphasized that they are never faced with agonizing moral problems; like Faulkner's Dilsey, they "endure." Her characters are lovable, gentle creatures, but they are comparatively simple and childlike. Mlle. Roy totally ignores the darker specters that inhabit men's souls; nor does she ever allow her characters to experience those sudden revelations that unexpectedly open a precipice at our feet. Alexandre Chenevert frets about the death of Ghandi, and yet there is some justification for Eugénie's remonstrance, "After all, he was no relative of ours!"

Phyllis Grosskurth. Gabrielle Roy (Toronto:
Forum House, 1969), pp. 61–62

[<i>The Restless River</i>] . . . describes, in a restrained and profoundly moving manner, the destiny of Elsa, an Eskimo woman. Through her destiny the novel also describes the destiny of all the men and women of her race, who are led despite themselves—like the waters of the Koksoak River—toward a new life they did not desire. "Then who knows how we must live?" asks Elsa. An agonizing question, which she cannot succeed in answering.

Gabrielle Roy has the art to make her readers feel how much the Eskimo psychology is intimately linked to the harshness of the landscape of their rough homeland. Elsa is both simple and profound, dedicated to the impulses of love and the mirages of dreams. To succeed in expressing Elsa's evolution and inner contradictions, the novelist needed great sensitivity and a refined sense of nuance. . . .

Roy's fine novel makes us feel somewhat uneasy. Progress and happiness, as we already knew, are not synonymous.

The three stories [in the same volume] that serve as an introduction [to the novel] are excellent. . . . To tell these stories, Roy summons up a very individual kind of humor, which she seems to have borrowed from the Eskimos: she finds things funny and laughs at them, despite the old sadness that can never be permanently shaken off.

Constant Burniaux. Marginales. June–July,
1972, pp. 79–80

Cet été qui chantait [That summer that sang] is not a recollection of one particular summer. This summer is a symbolic season when all Nature is fulfilled, when the narrator leaves the city for a few months of peaceful contemplation in the country, much of it distinctly Wordsworthean. Nature has orchestrated a symphony surpassing any manmade composition. The wind conducts the pines and cherry trees, the ponds and river; finches, crows, and swallows sing their parts on high. The smallest insect is not forgotten in the theme of summer triumphant. And behind it all is the hand of God in a vision which is profoundly Christian. . . .

The beauty of <i>Cet été qui chantait</i> lies in the natural description recorded by a sensitive observer who participates in the processes she records. The weakness lies in the thinness of some of the parables. Mlle. Roy has to force much of the material to make it teach the lesson she wishes. She distrusts the reader's intelligence. Most of the tales are self-evident, but she feels compelled to point out explicitly, often more than once, the human implications of every situation. . . .

And so paradise is possible, but only if man does not destroy his environment. This book is Gabrielle Roy's contribution to the Ecology movement, dedicated to the children of the Earth. Unhappily the Whole Earth people have dwindled to smaller numbers recently precisely because they offer no viable answers for the 1970s.

                              Linda Shohet. *Journal of Canadian Fiction.*
                                            Spring, 1973, pp. 84–85

Early in her career, Gabrielle Roy expressed the belief that "in order to know people really well you have to be at their mercy." In her latest work, *Fragiles Lumières de la terre* (1978; *The Fragile Lights of Earth,* 1982) she repeated that belief which sums up her attitude towards life. Roy's faith in human nature, her excitement over life's possibilities, her sense of adventure, her strong awareness of human vulnerability, her balanced perception of man's tragic as well as comic potential, are all suggested by these words which stem from her contention that individuals must jump feet first into life to discover themselves and to achieve their full humanity. Roy, of course, is too subtle a person not to be fully aware of the risks involved in adopting such a stance. Human beings who take such risks are most vulnerable—indeed, at the mercy of all other men and women, of the social situations, and of the natural environments they encounter. Yet she shows that such individuals are most alive, most human. And so it happens, from first to last, that all of Roy's most touching characters are of this sort—from Rose-Anna (*Bonheur d'occasion,* 1945; *The Tin Flute,* 1947) and Luzina (*La Petite Poule d'eau,* 1950; *Where Nests the Water Hen,* 1951) to Elsa (*La Rivière sans repos,* 1970; *Windflower,* 1970), Martha (*Un Jardin au bout du monde,* 1975; *Garden in the Wind,* 1977), and the young teacher (*Ces Enfants de ma vie,* 1977; *Children of My Heart,* 1979). From their encounters, Roy has woven the rich and fragile fabric of their lives. . . .

Because of the widespread enthusiasm and recognition generated by Roy's Montreal masterpieces, *Bonheur d'occasion* and *Alexandre Chenevert* (1954; *The Cashier,* 1955), her numerous and moving books about the west have often been overlooked. . . .

Bonheur d'occasion and *Alexandre Chenevert* are Roy's only essentially urban novels, novels in which she polarizes city and country, and from which emerge one of the dominant motifs of her work—the cage. For it is the city, she posits, with its false promises of security, which traps the individual into relinquishing his liberty. The city itself remains the ultimate cage: the country—specifically the wilderness—the ultimate source of freedom. Although in *Bonheur d'occasion* the cage is an underlying image, it is in *Alexandre Chenevert* that it comes into greatest prominence as a symbol.

Bonheur d'occasion is undoubtedly a landmark in Canadian literature. Awarded the prestigious Prix Fémina in France, it helped Canadians in the forties—though particularly Francophones—to put aside their literary inferiority complexes, to take pride in the outstanding accomplishments of one of their own writers. No longer did Canadians feel compelled to continuously seek abroad for outstanding manifestations of aesthetic merit. Some critics in French Canada have even gone so far as to state that French-Canadian literature really came of age just after the Second World War—and specifically after the publication of *Bonheur d'occasion*.

> Allison Mitcham. *The Literary Achievement*
> *of Gabrielle Roy* (Fredericton, New
> Brunswick: York, 1983), pp. 7, 9, 24

The sociological and political awareness underlying the composition of *Bonheur d'occasion* and the author's avowed consciousness of her French-Canadian heritage as well as her deep sense of identity with Quebec have aroused some criticism because Roy has not taken part in the political debate dividing Canada. But in contrast to a Claude Jasmin or a Hugh MacLennan, for example—whose novels largely reflect Canada's contemporary political situation—Gabrielle Roy perceives her role as an artist somewhat differently.

Being an artist implies freedom for Roy—freedom that expresses itself on the most fundamental level to be oneself and extends on a more superficial level to the choice of subject and style.

The artist must always remain faithful to himself and cannot adopt a particular stance demanded by certain social or political happenings if he is to be true to himself. This is all the more important because only then can the artist be true to others. Thus if *Bonheur d'occasion* and her later works are seen not from a sociological or political point of view, but from the broader perspective of humanity, Roy's silence regarding Canada's current political dilemma is understandable.

> M. G. Hesse. *Gabrielle Roy* (Boston:
> Twayne, 1984), p. 86

Since the publication of *Bonheur d'occasion,* Gabrielle Roy has continued to dominate the literary scene in Quebec. She has written three additional novels, one of which, *La Rivière sans repos,* was published along with three short stories. Six collections of short stories have also appeared, as well as a recent compilation of some of her earlier journalistic writings and essays. She has, in addition, published two stories for children, the second one in honor of the International Year of the Child in 1979. Despite her determination to maintain a distance from the literary circles of Quebec and, in particular, despite her lack of an overt role in the contemporary political issues facing her province and country, Gabrielle Roy has remained one of the best known authors of francophone Canada. Her reputation both in French and English-speaking Canada, as well as her increasing international renown, have offered her a well-deserved, although still modest, place in the annals of world literature.

It was, perhaps, Roy's shying away from any direct involvement in the fervent literary activities of Quebec that caused the wide appeal of her fiction. . . .

Such an unusual attitude for a French-speaking Canadian author stems from the fact that Roy was born in Manitoba and not in Quebec. For this reason, plus her literary talent, her works have all been translated into English and have been highly regarded in English-speaking Canada. She has taken her place in Canadian literature, states Jones, because "the problems she explores, the way in which she resolves them and her over-all vision of life place her within the same imaginative world as that inhabited by the English-speaking writers. . . . She speaks for Canadians, both English and French." . . .

If each of Roy's texts remains open at its conclusion, inviting the next work to commence, her literary universe as a whole stands equally open, inviting its readers to hope and dream optimistically about the future of humanity and the world and beckoning them to work toward common, humanistic goals. It is a universe that has, in this sense, disengaged itself from an oppressive "garrison mentality." Like an increasing number of works of the current literature of Quebec, the fiction of Gabrielle Roy is universal.

Paula Gilbert Lewis. The Literary Vision of
Gabrielle Roy (Birmingham, Alabama:
Summa, 1984), pp. 7, 8, 20

Despite her compelling denunciation of the social and economic exploitation of French-Canadian, immigrant and native women, Gabrielle Roy has generally been considered a traditionalist on women's issues, or at best, a "feminist humanist." However unjust their fate, it would seem, her female characters nonetheless extol those virtues of traditional femininity, gentle resignation and tender altruism, exemplified by Roseanna Lacasse, the touching *mater dolorosa* of Roy's best-known novel, *Bonheur d'occasion*. Recently, however, scholars have begun to question the critical myths which underlie this conventional, albeit paradoxical, interpretation of Roy's portrayal of the female condition. . . .

As a woman writing in a male-dominated society, Roy has displayed the fundamental dilemma of the artist as a young woman in the shadows of her text, through a juxtaposition of dream and reality, private and public discourse. The implicit structures of the text expose the contradictions of the latter while at the same time validating the legitimacy of the former. Tracing the female process of self-realization initially *through* the other, Roy ultimately (dis)closes the possible reconciliation of artistic and personal identity *with,* or more precisely, *beside* the other, within a matriarchal social construct. Finally, then, it is this fundamentally anti-patriarchal re-vision of the portrait of the artist as young woman which renders *Children of My Heart* so "passionate and troubling."

Agnes Whitfield. In Janice Morgan and
Colette T. Hall, eds. Redefining
Autobiography in Twentieth-Century
Women's Fiction (New York: Garland, 1991),
pp. 209, 222

RUKEYSER, MURIEL (UNITED STATES) 1913–80

Theory of Flight is one of those rare first volumes which impress by their achievement more than by their promise. It is remarkable poetry to have been written by a girl of twenty-one, and would do credit to most of her elders. . . . Here is a well-stored, vigorous mind attempting to bring its world into some kind of imaginative and human order. . . . Miss Rukeyser's poems are among the few so far written in behalf of the revolutionary cause which combine craftsmanship, restraint, and intellectual honesty.

Philip Blair Rice. *The Nation.* January 29,
1936, p. 134

Miss Rukeyser's first book is remarkable for its self-confidence and lack of hesitation. At twenty-one, she has already covered much of the technical ground of modern American verse, and has learned how to pick up everything she feels capable of consolidating into a poem. . . . Miss Rukeyser's verse, however, unlike that of the immediately preceding generation of modernists, does not emanate from the decorative or phenomenalistic fascination alone; it contains a moral will, a will to make itself useful as statement, and a will to warm itself against the major human situations of our day. Thus the subjective, rarely quieted in her, is redirected towards recurrent themes of class-oppression, death, the historical background, revolution.

Harold Rosenberg. *Poetry.* May, 1936,
pp. 107–8

Though at first consideration she seems typical of our young class-conscious poets, she will be found to transcend them in nearly every respect. Her materials, like her contemporaries', is every-day life. . . . Her viewpoint, like theirs, has the clearness and objectivity of a photograph. But she is far more aware what an adaptable instrument the camera is, and achieves effects the poetic realist of the past never dreamed of. . . . Where her confreres tend to grasp only broad social phenomena, or only isolated examples, she captures both the general meaning and the specific detail, plays one against the other, thereby reaching a truer, more moving analysis.

Kerker Quinn. *New York Herald Tribune.*
February 20, 1938, p. 12

There are moments in *US 1* that are pretty dull, but that's bound to be the character of all good things if they are serious enough: when a devoted and determined person sets out to do a thing he isn't thinking first of being brilliant, he wants to get there even if he has to crawl on his face. When he is able to—whenever he is able to—he gets up and runs. . . . [But] I hope Miss Rukeyser does not lose herself in her injudicious haste for a "cause," accepting, uncritically, what she does as satisfactory, her intentions being of the best. I hope she will stick it out the hardest way, a tough road, and invent! make the form that will embody her rare gifts of intelligence and passion for a social rebirth the chief object of her labors.

William Carlos Williams. *The New Republic*.
March 9, 1938, pp. 141–42

What most distinguishes Muriel Rukeyser's third book, *A Turning Wind*, from her earlier work is an extension of method and point of view, which has greatly enriched her poetry and at the same time introduced a corresponding, though not, I believe, a necessary obscurity.

The extension of viewpoint may best be described in simplification as a shift of emphasis from the concrete to the abstract, from the immediate concern with evidence of social decay and its remedies to the more speculative concern with its causes, particularly psychological. . . . One reason, I believe, for the occasional failure to communicate is that Miss Rukeyser has not yet been wholly successful in extending her method to keep pace with the extension of viewpoint and subject matter.

Philip Horton. *The New Republic*. January
22, 1940, p. 123

What is exciting about Miss Rukeyser's work is the vitality and largeness of her ideas and feelings, and the amazing but controlled originality of her methods of expressing them. . . . Hers is an original and startling talent for the bright and expanding image, the concrete phantasy, the magical reality of a world of machines, cities, social forces, and nervous complexities. . . . Even when one cannot put his words on what all her "sources of power" are, one feels she has power. Beauty and thought are tremendously exciting even when we cannot measure their height, or compass their horizons.

Mildred Boie. *Atlantic Monthly*.
February, 1940, n.p.

If Muriel Rukeyser is—as I believe she is—the most inventive and challenging poet of the generation which has not yet reached thirty, it is because of her provocative language fully as much as because of her audacious ideas. . . . *Theory of Flight* announced a new symbolism as well as a new speech. The style was swift, abrupt, syncopated; it matched the speed of the strepitant post-war world, the crazy energy of murderous machines, the "intolerable contradiction" of flight. . . . For her the images of war and industry are all too natural. . . . It is the "agonies of decision" which Miss Rukeyser expresses for more than her own generation. . . . In the midst of desperate remedies and clamoring negatives, she affirms the life of people and the life of poetry—the life of the spirit giving all processes and inventions, the creative life which is the double answer to living slavery and to the wish for quick escapes, comforting death.

Louis Untermeyer. *Saturday Review of
Literature*. August 10, 1940, pp. 11–13

One of the most interesting phases of the transformation of the social poet in years of stress is the change in his use of language. In the case of Muriel Rukeyser, it moves from that of simple declarative exhortation, in the common phrases of the city man, to that of a gnarled, intellectual, almost private observation. In her earlier usage, images are apt to be simple and few; the whole approach is apt to be through the medium of urban speech. In the latter work, images become those of the psychologist, or of the surrealist, charged with increasing complication of symbols; the first are public, the last, even though they may represent universal issues, are privately conceived and privately endowed.

John Malcolm Brinnin. *Poetry*. January,
1943, p. 555

The dilemma of conflict rising from an unresolved dualism in viewpoint has characterized Muriel Rukeyser's recent work. . . . Hers is a poetry of confusion in a confused world—a poetry which submits to that confusion—falls back upon the non-rational; the myth, the dream, the supernatural; or selects as its mouth-pieces a "drunken girl," a "madboy," a "child." By so doing, the poet seemingly justifies lack of organization, disassociated images, abrupt shifts in person and tense, and enigmatical meaning. . . . It seems to me her poems are much more effective when she forgets myth, symbol and dream. . . . and turns to factual events or experiences common to the majority of men and women today.

Ruth Lechlitner. *New York Herald Tribune*.
December 31, 1944, p. 4

Muriel Rukeyser is a forcible writer with a considerable talent for emotional rhetoric, but she has a random melodramatic hand and rather unfortunate models and standards for her work—one feels about most of her poems pretty much as one feels about the girl on last year's calendar. . . . One feels, with dismay and delight, that one is listening to the Common Siren of our century, a siren photographed in a sequin bathing suit, on rocks like boiled potatoes, for the week-end edition of PM, in order to bring sex to the deserving poor. . . . Yet all the time the poem keeps repeating, keeps remembering to repeat, that it is a *good* girl—that it is, after all, dying for the people; the reader wanders, full of queasy delight, through the labyrinthine corridors of the strange, moral, sexual wishfantasy for which he is to be awarded, somehow, a gold star by the Perfect State.

Randall Jarrell. *The Nation*. May 8, 1948,
pp. 512–13

In a time of shrinking poets and shrinking critics here, at any rate, is one capable in both poetry and criticism, who expands and embraces. . . . Miss Rukeyser disowns little or nothing. With her poet's knack of seeing the symbolic meanings in events and the connections latent in them, and with various and deep reading she adduces and enriches from every quarter of contemporary life, from punctuation to the blues, from Fenellosa to Leadbelly. . . . Yet I have a disturbing sense that in these recent poems Miss Rukeyser's motile, ringing energies are becoming over-agitated. Frenetic is too harsh a word, but her images and rhythms, like Shelley's, seem humid and driven by a general passion behind and so external to all particular items of our experience.

James R. Caldwell. Saturday Review of
Literature. March 11, 1950, p. 26

Nonfiction? Fiction? A poem? Miss Rukeyser tells us in her foreword: "It is a book, a story, and a song." The bookmaking is beautiful, the story is Wendell Willkie's, and power (public and private) is the song.

One Life is episodic, dissonant, fragmented, and explosive—as Willkie's life was and as his country still is. Indeed, the temptation to condescend to Willkie's human failures, to faint-praise his history, is part of a reader's temptation to faint-praise Muriel Rukeyser's rhetoric, and to condescend to the faults of this book. Yet this is perhaps the most ambitious attempt since *Let Us Now Praise Famous Men* to define a segment of America, and for that it deserves any reader's praise. . . . The wonder, in all such history, is that Miss Rukeyser doesn't heroize Willkie; she sees, rather, heroic dimensions in his search for identity and in his capacity for growth. He becomes, somehow, a kind of political Sisyphus, in the act of failure succeeding most—all in the amorphous America for which Miss Rukeyser, too, risks so greatly.

Philip Booth. Saturday Review of Literature.
August 3, 1957, p. 12

Of her one does not use the world elegant; rather, primordial. She is long-swept Whitmanian without rhyme. She is not didactic. She has a love of life and sings of people and things. Her love and care for mankind are evident in every poem. The strength of her convictions coupled with her integrated conception of the world probably makes for the originality of her style, which is uncompromising in its difference from that of other poets and is always fresh, vibrant, profound.

Poetry is a personal thrusting and stance of being. It is thrown into the relations of mankind. It cannot exist without communication and is thus profoundly allied to society. Miss Rukeyser exemplifies these tenets. Hers is the great insolence of poetry and its great love. Never a cultist, never given to this fad or that, or labeled with the mark of only one decade, she submits her vision to art as a strong personal force and her delighting power to a lifetime of concentrated effort in a unitary plane. It is this striding vigor that I find most American. She is not a jewel-maker but a fire-thrower. It is the heavy brunt of meaning that we take on every page and in which many readers rejoice.

Richard Eberhart. The New York Times.
September 9, 1962, p. 4

Muriel Rukeyser has published a large body of work since her first collection, *Theory of Flight,* appeared when she was only twenty-one. It immediately marked her as an innovator, thoroughly American, Whitmanlike in method and scope. Characteristic of her poetry, of which we now have a survey in *Waterlily Fire (Poems 1935–1962),* is the big canvas, the broad stroke, love of primary color and primary emotion. Her method is the opposite of the designer's, her vision is never small, seldom introverted. Her consciousness of *others* around her, of being but one member of a great writhing body of humanity surging out of the past, filling the present, groping passionately toward the future, is a generating force in her work. She celebrates science as much as nature or the restless human heart. . . . Another main fulcrum of her work is psychological, even mystical (but it never departs from a physical, in fact a sexual base), and exploration of being and becoming and then of re-becoming, growing out of her interest in Eastern philosophy as well as Western primitivism.

May Swenson. *The Nation.* February 23,
1963, p. 164

In *The Orgy,* the poet and biographer Muriel Rukeyser has written a book that is less a conventional novel than a record of the experience of Puck Fair as felt through a thoroughly modern sensibility steeped in the literature of anthropology and psychology. It is hard, even, to guess to what extent this record is fiction; the otherwise unidentified narrator is addressed at one point as "Muriel," and there are a number of other references to well-known persons. Miss Rukeyser herself describes the book as a "free fantasy" on a real event, and the evidence at hand would appear to indicate that this is a precise and well-chosen term. . . . The narrator and her friends, responding to the dimly understood mysteries of the old, pagan religion, provide on one level a counterpoint of psychoanalysis and comparative anthropology, while on another level they are caught up in the orgiastic spirit of the fair, their partings and rejoinings seeming to have become powerfully infused with new and rather disturbing meanings.

This is a poet's book in a real sense—distilled, allusive, and more suggested than is in plain sight. I read it with great interest, with enthusiasm even, and still feel somewhat under the brooding influence of its dark and troubling beauty.

Kenneth Lamott. *New York Herald Tribune.*
February 28, 1965, p. 20

In a brief preface [to *The Orgy*] Miss Rukeyser's very knowledgeable book is stated to be a free fantasy on the event [Puck Fair in Ireland]. The goat, the fair and the orgy are real. Nevertheless there is so much dropping of actual names throughout her account that it is difficult to avoid regarding it as autobiographical. . . . The book itself is both exciting and intriguing. It is written in an unusual style that might, perhaps, be described as verse, under the disguise of free prose, rather than the more usual prose in the form of free verse. This method has many of the allusive qualities of poetry, together with its concomitant disregard for continuity, and some occasional doubts as to who or what the writer is referring. . . . Miss Rukeyser's technique also has a strong resemblance to that of the documentary cinema—a montage in which the writer piles up a catalogue of visual images, untrammeled on the whole by verbs, in the course of which, like the camera, she is able to focus the attention not on the scene as a whole but on some special element that impresses her. . . . One may perhaps wonder whether so subjective a method is suited to so extrovert an occasion—assuming, of course, that Puck Fair is the actual point of the book.

Denis Johnston. *The Nation.* March 15,
1965, pp. 202–3

Muriel Rukeyser is a poet of dark music, weighty and high-minded. *The Speed of Darkness,* the title of her new book, is indicative of the oracular soothsaying quality of much of her writing—for me, a defeating tendency of her style which often nullifies any attentiveness to detail. Her mystical vision is so dominant in the mentality of some poems, the writing becomes inscrutable, as she packs her lines with excessive symbolism or metaphorical density.

Her firmest art is the linear and straightforward delivery of her story-telling anecdotal poems, the longer biographical poems, and letter–poems to friends expressing an open declaration of personal faith. In all of these genres, her symbolism is balanced by clean, open statement. In "Endless" and "Poem" . . . personal lyrics irradiating pathos from the recollection of harrowing life-moments, Miss Rukeyser achieves a naïve forthrightness—an artlessness—which, as in the most lastingly valuable personal letters (those of Keats, for example), derives a universal moral faith from plainspoken events authentically observed and recorded. In these poems, Miss Rukeyser is most nearly able to make her experience—her recollected terror and madness—our own. Her absorptively sympathetic portrait of the German artist, Käthe Kollwitz, one portion of a continuing sequence of biographical works (*Lives*), is the most arresting long poem in the new collection. Miss Rukeyser displays wisdom as self-critic in choosing to adapt so many recent poems from biographical and historical studies, since the task of accurately restoring a human lifetime in verse compels a precision in the enumeration of items of dailiness that offsets her frequent tendency to drift into cloudy abstraction.

Laurence Lieberman. *Poetry.* April, 1969,
pp. 42–43

Rukeyser's first collection of poems, *Theory of Flight,* won the Yale Prize for Younger Poets in 1935. Since that year, new wars, changing attitudes toward minorities, women, the body and sex, and renewed interest in New England Transcendentalism, as well as the pursuit of a more profound understanding of complex and terrifying human relationships, cause us, in the seventies, to define Rukeyser as a poet far different from the one she has traditionally been assumed to be. The neglect her poetry has suffered has delayed recognition of her work as deeply rooted in the Whitman-Transcendental tradition.

Her belief in the unity of Being, her reliance on primary rather than on literary experience as the source of truth and the resultant emphasis on the self, the body and the senses, as well as the rhythmic forms and patterns that inevitably emerge from such beliefs, tie Rukeyser to her forebears in the nineteenth century. At the same time, through her highly personal contemporary voice, they project her into our era which, with its radical departures from traditional Transcendentalism, is yet a reaffirmation of it, with Rukeyser as one of its important figures.

Virginia R. Terris. *The American Poetry Review.* May–June, 1974, p. 10

Upon reading Muriel Rukeyser's latest volume of poems, upon going through *The Gates,* one feels silent, sad, instructed, grateful. No words of prose from a reviewer are needed to explain these poems; and to praise them is almost condescending. The woman who wrote them has been with us twentieth-century American readers almost a half a century: a gifted observer of this world; a person who can sing to us and make our duller, less responsive minds come more alive; and not least, someone who has proven it possible to be a sensible human being, a woman inclined to give, to extend herself toward others, and also a first-rate poet. We all struggle with the sin of pride; Muriel Rukeyser has been blessed with less narcissism than most of us— especially remarkable in such an introspective, sensitive, and self-aware person, who has for so long been committed to telling others what crosses her mind. She is saved from self-centeredness by a compassionate concern for others, all over the world, and by a wonderful capacity for self-mocking irony.

Robert Coles. *The American Poetry Review.* May–June, 1978, p. 15

The publication of Muriel Rukeyser's *Collected Poems* is an occasion for rejoicing. Not only is Miss Rukeyser one of those poets American literature would seem impoverished without, but, like William Carlos Williams, she has been an indestructible force for the good of poetry and poets for decades. For all that the poems have changed over the years, it is impossible to say that there has been a technical development. Miss Rukeyser seems to have been born poetically full-grown, and for this reason it is as rewarding to open the book at any point as to proceed systematically from beginning to end.

But wherever you begin, there is no sense in being niggling about Miss Rukeyser's rhapsodies in language. Yes, there are faults of construction. Yes, there are poems—such as "Tree of Rivers"—that begin, so to speak, in one key and end surprisingly in another. Never mind. However surprising, disturbing or rhetorically long-winded Miss Rukeyser's poems seem, they never bore you. It is always the same passionate and compassionate poet writing out of her extraordinary, iridescent imagination who confronts you, and although some of the earlier poems may seem dated (history itself is dated), what textbooks still pigeonhole as "social realism" makes for moving stories. Miss Rukeyser is fortunate in being among those poets who can tell stories in verse. . . .

Miss Rukeyser's collage method is effective, her indictment of war and American capitalism biting, and her feeling for the American wilderness and man's place in it is as fine as Faulkner's. . . .

Like Melville's, Miss Rukeyser's realism is really a bridge to an intensely visionary state of awareness. The line between world and world is indistinct. The threshold of the miraculous and mystical is never far away. It is as if life were always happening to her on two or three levels. Beneath her passion for social justice and her empathy with all sufferers lie deeper apprehensions of what existence and its paradoxes can lead to. . . .

It is inevitable that Miss Rukeyser will be compared with Whitman; indeed, *Leaves of Grass* must have shown her part of the way. Among modern poets she is the equal of Pablo Neruda, and like him, committed to a vision of humanity that acknowledges pain but leaves little room for despair. She is also patently a feminine poet—feminist but not bitchy. Love poems stud the volume. One of the most beautiful is "Song, the Brain Coral" (1939), which is more than a love poem. It condenses into one lyric a whole philosophy of linked humanity.

Anne Stevenson. *The New York Times.*
February 11, 1979, p. 12

Rukeyser is essentially a modern poet of possibility (a word which recurs in her writing and conversation) in the tradition of the transcendental writers of America's Golden Day: Emerson, Whitman, Thoreau. . . . Rukeyser's vision of possibility is . . . based in part on the marvels of technology, but her times—times of war, waiting for war, and living with the vast human devastation of the mid- and later twentieth century—and her personal exploration of the struggle of the individual in a corrupt society . . . caused her vision of possibility to rise from a more inclusive complexity than [Hart] Crane's. Yet the basic source of her vision is her self (in the Emersonian sense), which she sounds in poetic exploration and extends in human involvement thereby discovering the possibility to which all may aspire, despite repression, war, genocide, and the chorus of poets who sing . . . that "the humanistic way . . . has already been defeated." She believes that all her involvements, political, scholarly, artistic, are "ways of reaching the world and the Self," those two ever fertile sources of possibility. . . .

Words that come to mind after a reading of Rukeyser's lyrics are "strength" and "movement." Hers is not a tender but a strong lyricism that does not aim to distill or crystallize an emotion or an experience. Rukeyser's aim is to follow the powerful rhythms of experience in herself (and often in her imagining of another) in a world which in its fears about economics and war has conspired to be silent about the deepest human values and to repress impulses which interfere with "getting ahead." Rukeyser would not deny these rhythms, these impulses. She has said that talk about poetry which is "in terms of the start, the image, the crystallization" is inadequate. . . . In Rukeyser there is the no less rigorous, wide-ranging exploration of emotion and experience and the attempt to project them onto an imagined other, often a whole society; Rukeyser's world is always *there,* in her poetry. Dickinson is severely alone; there is little expression of an effort to reach another, through touch and speech, as in Rukeyser. Nor is there the expansive impulse (given form in Rukeyser's long lines) to reach the world, to include and transform an unfeeling other. There is no such impulse at exploration and inclusion in Rossetti and Brontë whose poetry is meditative—a distillation, again, a crystallization of very private emotions and experiences.

Louise Kertesz. The Poetic Vision of Muriel
Rukeyser (Baton Rouge: Louisiana State
University Press, 1980), pp. 46–47, 75–76

The early poems of Muriel Rukeyser are often flawed in ways which diminish their impact. In these poems, written from the 1930s to the mid-fifties, the poet tends to speak in a transcendental language which on analysis may seem merely vague. At the same time, Rukeyser's goals and values are stated or implied so incessantly that one's response to the poetry may depend greatly on how one reacts to the poet's relentless identification with causes and principles. Frequently in these poems, assuming the role of representative of humanity, Rukeyser orates and preaches. Randall Jarrell "with dismay and delight" sensed her to be "the Common Woman of our century," and William H. Pritchard has recently complained that "this Everywoman feels obliged to put her finger on Everything and render it significant." Pritchard does have a point, but the quality he identifies is mainly a problem in the early poetry, in which Rukeyser often appears to be trying to make whole the fragmented world of her experience by the force of her own will. It is a problem of tone and voice. The reader may feel that she overreaches herself, and reaction against her presumption may cancel out admiration for her goals and the successes among her early poems.

David S. Barber. Modern Poetry Studies.
11:1–2, 1982, p. 127

In an attempt to bridge [the] gap and embrace the positive aspects of both the male and female modes, Rukeyser has adapted the traditional forms to create a new myth—what might be called the woman's version of the odyssey. In her long poem "Searching/Not Searching," Rukeyser successfully releases woman from the passive cycle of private identity by sending her out instead on a poetic journey, epic in scope, which takes her imaginatively through her personal and cultural past and present—through history, politics, art, literature, memory, and technology, as well as through Asia, Europe, and modern urban America. Through this journey, Rukeyser reveals woman as both active seeker and receptor of experience—an explorer of both the inner and outer worlds of herself and society—as she searches for feminine role models, new identities, and re-vitalized relationships which will transform both men and women, as well as the political future of the world order.

Rukeyser clearly establishes in the opening line that this poem is a *woman's* quest. "What kind of woman goes searching and searching?" she asks. . . .

In this imaginative, global journey which also takes the poet into her personal and cultural past, Rukeyser suggests the epic scope a modern woman's odyssey can encompass by drawing upon the broad range of her own political interests which, among other things, sent her to war-torn Asia and involved her in other current events and world issues. The sense of political crisis in modern society, in fact, seems to be the original motive behind this poem which urges an active re-ordering of priorities to include the missing feminine relational values—the traditional values relegated by society to the private sphere of women's lives and for that reason missing in the destructively one-sided, public lives of technological nations following a patriarchal path toward possible annihilation.

The new era that Rukeyser hopes to set against this world of "murder" is a life-enhancing mode of existence that embraces both masculine and feminine values, that enables nations and individuals "to make" and "let [their] closeness be made." This political goal, prefigured by the personal relationship between the politically-conscious man and woman of the future, is celebrated in the triumphant image of sexual contact which concludes the poem: "In our bodies, we find each other. / On our mouths, inner greet." This shared "moment of revelation" completes the odyssey of this new kind of woman because it symbolically contains for Rukeyser the creative, revolutionary seeds of a new political world order.

Kathleen L. Nichols. Perspectives on
Contemporary Literature. 8, 1982, pp. 28, 32

The publication of *Out of Silence* is an event worthy of celebration. Finally, Muriel Rukeyser, one of this century's most distinguished, misunderstood and undervalued poets, is back in print. For a number of reasons, *Out of Silence* is a fitting title for Rukeyser's selected poems. Her reflection on her own death in "Then," from her 1973 collection *Breaking Open*, includes the lines: "I will still be making poems for you / out of silence." But after 1980 her own voice was "silenced" within the U.S. literary canon.

Author of eighteen books of poetry, five of prose—including two biographies, one play, a novel and an extended treatise on her poetic beliefs—and numerous poetry translations, Muriel Rukeyser was a major literary figure throughout her publishing years, from 1935 to 1980. She was a politically engaged poet whose aesthetic beliefs were at one with her lifelong anti-fascist and pacifist commitments. . . .

From a 1990s vantage point, Rukeyser's poetry does not overtly reflect a lesbian poetics, and yet careful reading reveals phrases and lines in which she clearly worked to break the silence dictated by homophobia. Many of her lines on taboos can be interpreted this way. . . .

She always wrote from an understanding that the personal is political, and vice versa. Her explicit writing about sex remains singular for her generation; in her work she refused to downplay her own body-consciousness. Testifying to her ardent pacifism and its connection to respect for the body, she wrote in "Waking this Morning":

> I want strong peace, and
> delight,
> the wild good.
> I want to make my touch poems:
> to find my morning, to find you entire
> alive moving among the anti-touch
> people.

[Kate] Daniels rightly points out that Rukeyser's work has always "been held in passionate regard by female readers." The titles of the two most important anthologies of women's poetry published in the 1970s, *No More Masks: An Anthology of Poetry by Women* (1973) and *The World Split Open: Four Centuries of Women Poets in England and America, 1552–1950* (1974) are taken directly from Rukeyser.

Anne Herzog. *Women's Review of Books.*
October 10, 1992, p. 15

From the publication of *Theory of Flight* in 1935 until her death in 1980, Muriel Rukeyser persistently broke the rules of the literary community, and because her poetry defied formal and aesthetic conventions, and was openly political as well, questions of poetic value have plagued her career. Rukeyser's work has been relegated until very recently to a kind of critical backwater reserved for women writers long dismissed by a Modernist male poetic sensibility.

The discomfort that critics felt at Rukeyser's overtly political poetry is clear from the earliest reviews of her work. . . .

What was so rare in the 1940s and 1950s is comparatively commonplace today—a woman speaking in a powerful, oracular voice, linking the self to the world, linking poetry explicitly to politics, and publicly confronting social injustice. In short, hers is a poetry of witness. . . .

Rukeyser's long forms explore the relation of the self to the world in a meditative and speculative manner (a characteristic she shares with Stevens and Auden, for example), but her speculation (unlike theirs) is distinctly non-rational, not necessarily logical, and always explicitly political. Rukeyser's meditative political sequence is a combination of public and private voices, emphasizing reflection, understanding, and self-knowledge within a particular historical/political milieu, and, most importantly, with the final aim of cultural and political transformation.

Michele S. Ware. *Women's Studies.* 22, 1993, pp. 297–99

EL-SAADAWI, NAWAL (EGYPT) 1930–

While few would dispute the fact that the interpretation of Islam is a factor in legislation concerning marriage, divorce and the legal status of women, it is not possible to consider the role of Islam outside the context of specific social and political conditions. The variability in interpretations of Islamic law and practice in itself suggests that factors other than religion are critical to an understanding of its impact on women and the family. It is the merit of *The Hidden Face of Eve* that it forces readers to confront this reality.

The stunning analysis of Arab women by the Egyptian feminist, novelist and doctor, Nawal el-Saadawi, addresses the full range of questions which the subject raises. El-Saadawi herself is no stranger to controversy. She lost her position as Director of Health Education in the Egyptian Ministry of Public Health as well as her post as editor in chief of the periodical *Health* as a result of her outspoken views. Writing about women in the Arab world, el-Saadawi claims, "is like picking your way through territory heavy with visible and hidden mines." Reading *The Hidden Face of Eve,* it is not difficult to see why the Egyptian Government—eager to show the West a liberal face—would find her work fundamentally subversive.

The critical point in el-Saadawi's interpretation is that the situation of women is not a women's problem alone. It is inseparable from the overall predicament of Arab society. She insists on the need for a historical and contemporary perspective to explain the perpetuation of patriarchal class society. This leads her to an investigation of the role of Islam and the uses to which it is and has been put by the state, and by Western governments that alternately denounce it as the source of fanatic intolerance and backwardness and simultaneously support its repressive power in the hands of reactionary regimes.

In response to Western feminists who have focused exclusively and too narrowly on the obvious limitations placed on women in the Arab world—and most recently on those in Iran—el-Saadawi insists on the need to see these limitations in their proper perspective. This in no sense means an apologetic stance. One has only to read her bitter denunciation of the practice of female circumcision, as well as her discussion of the need for radical change in legislation pertinent to marriage and the civil rights of women, and also of the circumstances they face in the labor force, to recognize the deep-seated roots of her own militancy. Hers is nothing if not an attempt at the total demystification of the Arab feminine mystique. But it is the special strength of her analysis that she is able to place the struggle for women's liberation in the broader context of the struggle taking place in Third World countries.

Hence, in the Iranian case, she pleads that solidarity on behalf of Iranian women be "exercised on the basis of a clear understanding of what is going on in the underdeveloped countries, lest it be used to serve other purposes diametrically opposed to the cause of equality and freedom for all peoples."

Irene Gendzier. *The Nation.* 231,
July 19–26, 1980, p. 91

Nawal el-Saadawi, the Egyptian physician, civil servant, feminist, political detainee (under Sadat) and novelist, writes in a tradition that ascribes to fiction the duty of social inquest and takes for granted the intersection of literature and politics. Born, like her characters in this book, in a village by the Nile, she bears down on social issues with directness and passion, transforming the systematic brutalization of peasants and of women into powerful allegory.

This directness may put off American readers. Ms. Saadawi is not a mediator. She doesn't try to make postcolonial Egypt's problems familiar to the West. She is impatient with psychology and motivation; her villagers are who they are because they have been betrayed by history and by religion.

She diagnoses: all religious, social and political authority in Egypt has become corrupt. And she prescribes: exterminate the tyrant.

The tyrant of *God Dies by the Nile* (the original Arabic edition appeared in Lebanon in 1974) is the unnamed Mayor of Kafr El Teen, an emblematic Nile village. The Mayor is half-English (a coded allusion, one presumes, to the colonial legacy as well as to the Sadats), privileged and manipulative. He runs his municipality the way crooked sheriffs and their deputies ran small Southern towns. He schemes and bribes, abducts, rapes and seduces. He falsely arrests and convicts. At least once he arranges to have a docile, Allah-fearing peasant murdered.

The avenger is Zakeya, an underfed, overworked, bitter, bewildered widow who lives in a hovel across the road from the Mayor's estate with her brother, two pretty nieces and a buffalo. The Mayor lusts after both nieces, seduces and abandons the older and tricks the younger into becoming his maid and mistress. In an act of final retribution, Zakeya rushes the Mayor with her hoe, a tool-turned-weapon of the peasant.

A favorite strategy of a politically aware author is the use of a politically naïve protagonist to press a message. Zakeya is not a rebel, but she does suffer crises in faith. The superstitious villagers equate doubt with devil-possession. One of the strongest scenes in the book (and its thematic center) occurs during her exorcism, when she reviews a litany of painful episodes embracing clitoridectomy, rape, abuse and every form of social and economic outrage in the feudal repertory.

In realistic fiction, these characters would seem flat, the action melodramatic. But historical reality encourages us to read this novel as a political allegory about Anwar el-Sadat's rule. The specific references to actual people and events are generally unfamiliar to American readers, but the allegorical intent here cannot be missed. The downtrodden *look* downtrodden. Zakeya breaks up stony fields all day; nights she comes home to a primitive shed and force-feeds herself pieces of dry bread, cheese and pickles. All the villagers lead mute, pointless lives. "They hated the policeman and his dogs, hated all policemen, all officers, all representatives of authority and the government. . . . They knew that in some way or another they had always been the victims, always been exploited, even if most of the time they could not understand how it was happening." Perversions are exaggerated. Freaks, victims, cheats and debauchers thrive in Kafr El Teen. Necrophilia, rape, bride-selling, bestiality seem little more than legal tender. In its handling of the perversions, *God Dies by the Nile* allegorizes the decaying of a society much as a Faulkner novel does. In Zakeya's final vision we learn that the enemy isn't just the Mayor. The true betrayer of Egyptian peasantry is Allah, symbol of all blind religious faith.

The translation by Sherif Hetata is vivid and simple. An alien world unfolds directly, even harshly, respecting the author's feel for the physical determination of peasant life—for sun, heat, wind and seasons.

While this novel may not feed our curiosity about "real life" behind the immediate headlines (one reason surely, that "exotic" novels are occasionally made available in English), *God Dies by the Nile* remains a moving political allegory.

Bharati Mukherjee. The New York Times.
July 27, 1986, p. 14

Nawal el-Saadawi wrote the original Arabic version of *The Circling Song* in 1973, published it two years later in Beirut (she was on the Egyptian government's blacklist at the time), and has now had it translated anonymously and published in the United Kingdom and the United States. From the dedication to the closing section, which is a two-page verbatim repetition of the opening, el-Saadawi's preoccupations reflect those of many contemporary Egyptian writers: children born out of wedlock and abandoned out of terror; children without childhoods; social obsessions with women's nubility and, above all, virginity. For readers familiar with the author's writings, there are many intertextual references: little girls raped by their fathers (cf. *The Fall of the Imam,* 1988); resourceless women pursued and persecuted by thugs in officials' clothing who finally use their bodies to survive (cf. *Woman at Point Zero,* 1983).

The title of the book renders more precisely its genre. *The Circling Song* is not so much a novel as it is a lyric meditation, a violent song about conflicting notions of self. El-Saadawi analyzes gender by hypothesizing gender ambiguity. Bodies undergo transformations at all levels: the male twin Hamido may find himself genitally deprived, as the female twin Hamida may find herself endowed; the twins become each other with a fluidity of identity boundaries that suggests the possible interchangeability of animal and human, dead and living, man (father/brother) and woman (mother/sister), master and servant. El-Saadawi subverts a static notion of socialization: gender and class identity are never fixed but are in constant flux; they are continually in the process of becoming.

The style of the whole is circular. Whenever the illusion of linearity is created, the line curls around to close the circle with, for example, a refrain from the beginning. This focus on circles and dots can also be seen in the writings of other Arab women, particularly the Beirut Decembrists. The language is imbued with sexuality and brutality. Particularly striking is the recurrent description of men as having a sharp/hard/rigid/erect implement/killing tool hanging down along their thighs. This phallic appendage is not biological but social. Again, gender identity is destabilized. *The Circling Song,* which el-Saadawi claims as her favorite novel, is a powerful example of the kind of anger and desperation to which Arab women writers are beginning to give vent.

Miriam Cooke. *World Literature Today.* 64,
1990, p. 187

[El-Saadawi] was the first feminist to publicly confront sexual issues such as prostitution, sexual diseases, clitoridectomy, incest, and various forms of sexual exploitation. For her daring writings on gender and sexuality, most notably *Al-Mara wa al-Jins* (1972; Woman and sex) she was dismissed from her job in the Ministry of Health. Her courage was applied equally to her private life; she left two oppressive husbands. In 1981, she was imprisoned for her writings and outspoken speech by Sadat. She has written about this experience in *Mudhakkirat fi Sijn al-Nisa* (Memoirs from the women's prison, Cairo, 1984 translated into French in 1984 as *Douze Femmes Dans Kanater,* and into English, 1987). Also inspired by this experience is her play, *Al-Insan* (1983; The human). Her books have been translated into English, French, German, Dutch, Danish, Swedish, Norwegian, Italian, Portuguese, and Persian.

Her twenty-four books include: *Mudhakkirat Tabiba* (1960; Memoirs of a woman doctor); *Al-Untha Hiya al-Asl* (1974; Female is the origin); *Al-Rajul wa-Jins* (1975; Man and sex); *Imraa Inda Nuqtat al-Sifr* (1975; Woman at point zero); *Al-Mara wa al-Sira al-Nafsi* (1976; Woman and psychological struggle); *Al-Wajh al-Ari Lil Mara al-Arabiya,* 1977 (translated into English as *The Hidden Face of Eve,* 1980); *Ughniyat al-Atfal al-Dairiyat* (1978; Children's songs).

[El-Saadawi's story] "Eyes" tells the story of an Egyptian man who is very strict with his daughter, only permitting her to work outside the home on the condition that she is completely isolated from men. The daughter finds that "ideal" job. Many months later, in the spring of 1988, this same man brings his veiled daughter to the office of Nawal el-Saadawi to see her in her capacity as a psychiatrist. "Eyes" is based on the young woman's story. Egyptian Television wanted to produce a film based on this story—on condition that the protagonist was not a veiled woman, as she had been in real life. Nawal el-Saadawi refused.

Margot Badran and Miriam Cooke. *Opening the Gates: A Century of Arab Feminist Writers* (London: Virago, 1990), pp. 201–2

It is perhaps no accident that the most vocal contemporary Arab feminist should also be a physician. The Egyptian Nawal el-Saadawi is without doubt the most articulate activist for woman's causes in the Arab world. Nowhere, also, is the importance of the literary body more evident than in Nawal el-Saadawi's corpus.

Virtually no form of modern prose is a stranger to Dr. el-Saadawi's pen: novels, plays, short stories, autobiography, prison memoirs, and travel literature. Her programmatic and theoretical works on sexuality threaten and vex readers just as much as does her literary corpus. Speaking of one of el-Saadawi's franker discussions, Hisham Sharabi notes that "it is difficult to explain to the non-Arab reader the effect [el-Saadawi's prose] can have on the Arab Muslim male." More than any other Arab woman writer, el-Saadawi has broken the barriers. . . .

A practicing physician and political activist, imprisoned under Sadat in 1981, Dr. el-Saadawi has deliberately chosen to break with the traditions of Arabic letters and adopt a simple yet powerful style, to make her work accessible to a wider Arabic readership. Many critics angrily deny literary importance to her considerable and varied literary corpus. Yet this is the sort of criticism that seems often like a tribute. One of Egypt's most distinguished academic critics (the name has been concealed to protect the guilty) privately said how much he admired her controversial latest novel, *Suqut al-Imam* (The fall of the imam). Unfortunately, he added, he felt that he could not say so in print. Had he done so, we might point out, his life might have been threatened, as was el-Saadawi's, and he might today be living with a twenty-four-hour guard on his building, as does el-Saadawi.

This, indeed, is the paradox of Nawal el-Saadawi's literary reputation. Though she is shunned by the official media, her books are published in Lebanese and Egyptian editions and eagerly sought by tens of thousands of readers across the Arab world. . . .

Nawal el-Saadawi develops the sexual politics of medicine in two ways: first, by using it as a vehicle for women to regain their lost power; and second, by making it the focus of her own call for the integration of traditionally male and female qualities.

This complex of elements is not, however, restricted to *Memoirs of a Woman Physician*. In *Two Women in One*, the author develops similar themes. . . .

Nawal el-Saadawi explores the relations of power, medicine, and the female condition in other ways than simply by centering on medicine as a career. This she does by focusing on the physician-patient relationship in a significant, and eminently characteristic, literary procedure.

In some highly innovative texts, Nawal el-Saadawi exploits a narrative technique that, though it brings her close to her medieval literary ancestor, Shahrazad, is most unusual in modern Arabic letters. This is a technique of embedding or enframing. A female physician, acting in her professional capacity, becomes the initial narrator who enframes a story told, eventually, by the patient. . . .

The universalization of social power is also its dissolution through the transcending of the oppositions dominating el-Saadawi's corpus and her heroines. It is not a coincidence that medicine escapes the dilemma of power (by becoming the point of fusion of science and art) in the context of a literary corpus—and a life—in which the role of medical practitioner has become fused with that of artist. Medicine becomes a space of purification, the locus where the raw social power of science is transmuted into the acceptable social power of art. As such, it is the ultimate woman's trick, but a modern one this time: linking individual with collective emancipation.

Fedwa Malti-Douglas. Woman's Body,
Woman's Word: Gender and Discourse in
Arabo-Islamic Writing (Princeton: Princeton
University Press, 1991), pp. 111, 113,
134–35, 143

Nawal el-Saadawi's latest novel, *Jannât wa-Iblîs,* differs from her previous works in that it emphasizes a subject matter that had thus far been circumvented in her novels. For the first time in her thirty-four years of literary production, the author of such relatively "secular" works as *Al-ghâ'ib* (1976; *Searching,* 1991) *Ugniyat al-atfâl al-dâ'irivyah* (1977; *The Circling Song,* 1989) and *Imra'ah 'nda nuqtat al-sifr* (1975; *Woman at point zero,* 1983) has written a novel in which religion is foregrounded and questioned in a way that may prove to be reminiscent of Rushdie's *Satanic Verses.* The title of the novel alone alerts the reader to its content. *Jannât* is the plural of *Jannah,* the Arabic word for *paradise,* and *Iblîs* is one of the names that is used to refer to the devil. In the novel, however, these are the names of two of the characters.

The narrative opens as Jannat is being escorted into a mental asylum where Nirjis, the matron in charge who has internalized the colonizer's ideology, and the male director, who sees himself literally as God, ensure that she is kept in a continuously drugged state. One of the patients, Iblis, who is described in terms that are later associated with the devil, observes the proceedings in silence. The novel is thus a series of recurring past and present events, as experienced by Jannat and other characters in the asylum. Jannat's recollections may remind the reader of certain characters in el-Saadawi's other novels, such as Firdaus in *Woman at Point Zero,* Bahiah in *Two Women in One,* and Fouada in *Searching.*

In reversing traditional roles, el-Saadawi purports to place the oppressor in the shoes of the oppressed and to question aspects not only of religion but also of language upon which those in power base their alleged superiority. For example, the word *sâqitah,* meaning "fallen woman," becomes *sâqet,* meaning "fallen man." People in the earlier lives of the characters also offer a powerful commentary on the role of religion in society. The Christian grandmother, who married a Muslim, "keeps her Bible hidden under her pillow." Misogynist fathers and grandfathers who view women as "the devil's allies," "the cause of sin, as is stated in the Bible," and "greatly cunning [*kaydihinna 'adhim*], as God said in his Holy Book," attempt to implant their views in the minds of their offspring. Such examples lead Jannat to understand that men use religion to oppress women by defining them as either virgins or whores, with nothing in between.

By the end of the novel, traditional and religious concepts of good and evil have been completely subverted. Iblis dies after jumping over the barbed wire in his attempt to follow Jannat, who is released after the director determines that she has lost her memory. Ironically, Iblis's innocence is then proclaimed by his killer (the director, known as God), who finds his dead body bathed in blood.

Ramzi M. Salti. *World Literature Today.* 67,
1993, pp. 437–38

SACHS, NELLY (GERMANY–SWEDEN) 1891–1970

Through the images of "Jagd" [Hunt] and "Flucht" [Flight], the author describes the fate of her people—a fate that has so darkened our era that it has become its symbol. The historical symbolic power of the sufferings of the Jews has restored their ancient meaning to the myths of Jewish Scripture. This author's work, then, also relates again and again to the Old Testament. The phenomena, events, and landscapes of the Old Testament provide the inexhaustible store of images and meanings that, like no other symbolism—neither that of classical antiquity nor that of the romantic-modern period—speaks to, and for, outcast and persecuted man. The fact that this hunted author wrote her poetic creation in the language of the very nation that handed her over to its "Schwarze Jäger" [Black hunters], the fact that the words of warning and of fear uttered by this Jewish woman stem from the intimately familiar German language of the Bible—these things touch upon an enigma of history that we may ponder but cannot solve.

Rainer Gruenter. *Neue Deutsche Hefte.*
November–December, 1960, pp. 829–30

Of late the name of Nelly Sachs is being mentioned with increasing frequency and great unanimity as that of the destined successor to Else Lasker-Schüler. And there actually is a good deal that links her with this great figure of a woman, who has dominated German lyric poetry for three decades. The question, who today really "is the greatest," seems idle trifling to me. There are a number of women who have written some very beautiful poems. The stature of a particular poem, of a particular work, can be determined—but of a human being? How is it to be weighed or measured? Nelly Sachs is a poet of great lines. Striking imagery and metaphors, harsh and beautiful, are juxtaposed in her poems. . . .

These poems speak over and over again of exodus, turmoil, and, softly and impossible to ignore, of a last refuge. . . .

Genuine profundity has been transmuted here into moving speech in a manner that should be marveled at, not discussed. We have reached a realm—"there, where tears signify eternity."

Wieland Schmied. *Wort und Wahrheit*. 1960,
p. 211

Flucht und Verwandlung (Flight and transformation). . . . The title of the present volume states its double theme; the fifty-four poems have no titles but vary this theme. They read like contourless improvisations—word-mobiles, if this is conceivable. Rarely is one phrase or line in focus out of context (which suggests a primacy of sensibility over intellect); and she avoids verbs—instead there are floating patterns of substantival and adjectival phrases, inlaid with genitive metaphors. . . . It is not clear what kind of rhythm is intended; the impression is even more attenuated by the decorative fluidity of meanings. One may be reminded of the gropings of Novalis, with whom Nelly Sachs has something in common. But it is an open question (piety apart) whether such gropings merit any title to truth, poetic or otherwise, or whether they are the intransitive extemporisings of an imagination whose exile from any given or non-fictive world deprives it of all nourishment.

J. C. Middleton. *German Life and Letters*.
1960–61, p. 315

Nelly Sachs is rooted in German-Jewish intellectual life before World War II. Relatively many authors of that period inclined toward mysticism, trying to force language into expressing the previously inexpressible. From German sources of mysticism she came to Jewish texts, Cabbala and Chassidic writings. When events heightened the emotional impact of her Jewishness, these views—interlocking life and death—became the themes she revealed and explored.

The first volumes of poems, all written after she emigrated, mirror the Nazi persecution of Jews: victims of brutality and concentration camps, wanderers seeking new places of physical and spiritual rest, are the main characters of her cast. In the later volumes historical events gradually recede; the mysteries of life and death remain, to be faced in loneliness. She never accuses; she etches experiences, always seeking, across desolation, a larger and unperturbed world.

Emma E. Kann. *Books Abroad.* 1962, p. 400

In her poems *Und neimand weiß weiter* (1957; And no one knows what next), a people's spirit achieves universal expression in plea and warning, lament and supplication—the formulary of an imageless faith for which the word signifies the vessel of all images. Her ecstasy resembles the transports of Jewish mysticism for which the word is the one way that man can come to wordless perfection. Thus a good deal of Nelly Sachs's metaphor may at first strike the reader as obscure, unfamiliar, and difficult to read. But that impression will disappear as soon as our ears, accustomed to the understatement of modern poetry, have learned the diction of this new and unspoiled language. . . .

What seemed impossible, considering that this poetry has sprung from suffering, did come to pass: out of a torment suffered to the full, the poetry of Nelly Sachs has gained a hitherto unfathomed degree of sublime lightness. The crushing subject matter did become so dematerialized that it began to sing.

Karl Schwedhelm. *Welt und Wort.* 1965,
p. 116

It was in exile—the Jewish form of life since the beginnings—that a decisive change began to find expression in her work. There came to be, in quick succession, those poetic cycles and scenic poems that established the fame of "Kafka's sister" as the "poetess of Jewish destiny." Through reading and meditation, Nelly Sachs gained access to the sources of Jewish religiosity and Christian mysticism; the prophets and psalmists of the Old Testament, the Book Sohar, works on Hassidism, and Jakob Böhme's tracts allowed her to escape the barbarous "hangman's era" and gave her the strength to overcome impulses clouded by emotion. Under the impact of her encounter with Jewish tradition her mastery of language and of form took on fresh vigor; in her new poems, modeled on the psalms, there flowered an original, concrete imagery that lets all that is within and behind things shine through.

Klaus Lazarowicz. In Hermann Kunisch,
ed. *Handbuch der deutschen
Gegenwartsliteratur* (Munich:
Nymphenburger, 1965), p. 501

She is that very rare exception, a poet who writes out of a life immersed in the horror of the actual nightmare, the deaths of those who were burned in ovens. Reading "O the Chimneys," one is there. One feels at once that here is a writer who does not make poetry out of material which she imagines from afar. Her poetry is the lived material itself.

Her poems have variety, but they might all be one poem, and each poem seems part of the suffering of her people in the camps, a death which in her imagination extraordinarily flows into the resurrection which is Israel. The idea of the Jewish people so prevails that the lives and the deaths seem aspects of the same consciousness. The history of destruction and rebuilding seems to happen at the same time, to be contained in a single moment of time, which is the concept of "my people."

Stephen Spender. *The New York Times.*
October 8, 1967, p. 5

Adorno maintains that after Auschwitz the writing of lyrical poetry had become impossible. But Nelly Sachs dared to record these colossal events which burst all the bounds of traditional forms and invested her language in her rhythmical-mellifluous structures with an intensity never heard before. She is a delicate human being, almost like a timid little bird, and it is a miracle that this fragile vehicle did not break when the fiery storm of these poetic inspirations erupted in her soul. The work of her early years disappears as irrelevant behind this new beginning and sinks below the horizon of her alert and conscious artistic existence. . . . I know most of the German poetry and prose grown out of the monstrous fate of the Jewish people: it is all left far behind by the genius of her achievement. . . .

The collection *In the Abodes of Death (In den Wohnungen des Todes)* starts off with a poem the last line of which runs, "And Israel's body in the smoke through the air" . . . Most of the other poems of this collection speak in the plural of children and old men, of the shoes of the dead and the hands of the hangmen and of the spectators. We recognize the Language of the Many at its most obvious in "Chorus after Midnight," in which all the things abandoned, the saved, the itinerant, the orphans, the dead, the shadows, the stones, the stars, the things invisible, the clouds, the trees, the comforters and the unborn come together. In these choruses the poetess joins the external universe and the universe of the soul in one lament for the dead. Some of the stanzas are headed by quotations from the Bible and from the mysticism of the Chassidim, and everywhere phrases charged with religious passion, representing death as the way into another life, penetrate the sombre song of the sufferings of Israel. And thus consolation and trust find their way into this opus of destruction. . . .

As with every author of rank, so with Nelly Sachs we encounter in each new work surprises both as to subject and language. In her sixties her excitable spirit was disturbed and agitated once again through the sensations pressing in on her from an environment difficult to bear and from which she retreated into the seclusion of a hospital where she felt protected by the care of the doctor and the nurses. There she began to write "Glühende Rätsel" (Glowing riddles). Compared with her previous poems these are distinguished by brevity and concentration. Many of them start from insignificant everyday happenings. . . . But they are only the starting points from which to advance

quickly into her inner life. . . . Sorrow and pain, wailing and weeping, departure and death, the way into eternity, nostalgia and mystery, resurrection and
reunion with the dead, all lived through and suffered through in the most
intensely personal manner, are her subjects, and any light that penetrates the
dark comes from the other side of the grave. The infinity of the world surrounding her merges with her dissolving self in innumerable phantastic
associations.

Walter A. Berendsohn. *Universitas.* 1968,
pp. 217–19, 224

The Zohar, a gigantic exegesis of the Pentateuch, was written in Spain in the
late thirteenth century. It became the central document of Kabbalah, a system of occult theosophy and mystical interpretation of the Scriptures in Jewish circles. . . .

The poems of Nelly Sachs's *Zohar* cycle [in *Und niemand weiß weiter*],
particularly appealing in their synoptical brevity, present an ideal subject for
a study of her concept of the word in the light of Jewish tradition. Both the
thought and the imagery of the cycle reveal the contribution of this heritage.
However, it also becomes apparent that the poetry of Nelly Sachs is universal
in its essence. From this Jewish background she develops a metaphysical *ars
poetica,* making of the word the instrument by which every creative act is
accomplished. Her esteem for the creative word makes it possible to discover
in her works a verbally oriented theosophy, the contemporary validity of
which is totally comprehensible on a nondogmatic plane.

W. V. Blomster. *Germanic Review.* 1969,
pp. 212–13

The link between critical recognition, artistic quality, and breadth of perspective is demonstrated in the case of Nelly Sachs, who received belated acclaim
for her work. In 1965 she was given the coveted Peace Prize of the German
book trade, and in 1966 she was awarded the Nobel Prize for literature. . . .

Being persecuted because of her "race" rather than her politics, Nelly
Sachs in adopting a representative stance and a historical perspective in
essence renounced the country of her birth. The loss of her homeland was a
deep emotional trauma, the more so since she remained dependent on the
German language as her artistic medium. Another exiled Jewish poet, Karl
Wolfskehl, reacted to this dilemma by postulating that his only true home,
from which he could not be expelled, was the word. Nelly Sachs in this
situation adopted neither a linguistic nor a political substitute for her lost
country of origin; instead she found compensation in the realm of mystical
contemplation.

Her outlook was expressed in the lines that she selected as the motto
for one of her major poetry collections: "In place of the homeland / I hold
the transmutations of the world" ("An Stelle von Heimat / halte ich die Ver-
wandlungen der Welt"). This formulation, cryptic though it may be, contains

the key to her thought. The word "transmutation" is a technical term from the Gnostic tradition and Nelly Sachs's use of it indicates that she had embraced this form of Jewish mysticism.

Egbert Krispyn. *Anti-Nazi Writers in Exile*
(Athens: University of Georgia Press, 1978),
pp. 169–70

Nelly Sachs left Germany for Stockholm in 1940, and lived there till her death in 1970. So unbearable did she find the memory of her German past that in a volume of essays and poems published to celebrate her 75th birthday in 1966 she requested that the bibliography should omit all reference to what she had written before she went to Sweden. 'Death was my master', she once said. 'What else could I have written about, since my images are my wounds? This is the only way to understand my work.' Titles such as *In den Wohnungen des Todes* (1947) and *Noch feiert Tod das Leben* (1965) tell their own story.

Ronald Taylor. *Literature and Society in
Germany, 1918–1945* (New York: Barnes &
Noble, 1980), p. 314

The *themes* of the Holocaust are explicit and not at all difficult to locate in Nelly Sachs's poetry, especially in the early volumes, which contain those many choruses of lamentation and beseeching—"Chorus of the Dead," "Chorus of the Rescued," "Chorus of the Orphans," etc. The language of these poems is typically direct (in many cases, perhaps too direct); their images—of burning chimneys, smoke-blackened stars, unsheathed knives, torn skin, etc.—are undisguised and equally direct; their tone, a mingling of elegiac sorrow and pained, ceaseless yearning. It is impossible, in other words, to read the early poetry of Nelly Sachs and not recognize the aptness of the poet's dedicatory inscription to her first book, *In den Wohnungen des Todes* (In the dwellings of death)—"for my dead brothers and sisters." Feeling her kinship to the dead as personal loss and national tragedy, she set out consciously and quite determinedly to commemorate them, and in poem after poem she intones her mournful, tender, always respectful dirge. Such poetry is, in her own words, a prolonged "music of agony"—grief-stricken, openly and effusively bereaved, the pained utterance of a wound that will not close until death itself arrives to heal it over.

While one can admire the nobility and tenacity of her undertaking in these early volumes, Nelly Sachs's most striking work is found elsewhere. For especially in her two final volumes—*Noch feiert Tod das Leben* (Death still celebrates life, 1965) and *Glühende Rätsel* (Glowing enigmas, 1963–1966)—the Holocaust shows its impact on her not only thematically but in poems whose language and forms begin to more closely approximate and reproduce her descent into night. . . .

"A sigh / is that the soul?" she queries. To find out—and to follow its fading music—she felt she had to stand in the very center of the world's wound. Only there might silence grant her its song, she believed. For in her day, after what she called "the sorrow-stone tragedy," language was to be retrieved, if at all, only by descending again into the darkness that precedes creation. That was her sphere as a poet and, in those late poems of all but total dispossession, Nelly Sachs returned to it time and again, with grace and a lingering beauty, carrying her quest to the very edge of articulation. There . . . just before the soul's sigh escaped into nothingness, she pursued and seemingly solved the most enigmatic of riddles: how language, expiring, can still find a voice: how "death still celebrates life." "Wait," she promises,

> Wait till the breath ends
> it will sing for you as well.

Alvin Rosenfeld. *American Poetry Review.*
7:6, November–December, 1978, pp. 41–42

Nelly Sachs has generally been recognized and acclaimed as a poet of the Holocaust. The *laudatio* at the award of the Nobel Prize in 1966 characterizes her work as such: "With moving intensity of feeling she has given voice to the world-wide tragedy of the Jewish people, which she has expressed in lyrical laments of painful beauty and in dramatic legends." In a similar vein, the citation reads: "For her outstanding lyrical and dramatic writings, which interpret Israel's destiny with touching strength." Calling her "the voice of . . . the suffering of Israel," Marie Syrkin says that "her work is measured by the magnitude of her theme," and the Swedish critic Olof Lagercrantz writes that "the name Nelly Sachs will always be connected with the great Jewish catastrophe."

But Nelly Sachs is also, and perhaps foremost, a poet of exile, not only because of the circumstances of her life, but also because exile is one of the central themes of her poetry. When she was awarded the Nobel Prize, she recited in lieu of an acceptance speech one of her poems on the theme of exile rather than on the Holocaust.

Her biography is not all that makes her a poet of exile. She wrote several volumes of poetry on the exile theme, grounded in Jewish tradition. It is Jewish literary tradition that provides the creative basis for her writings and supplies the images, the rhetoric, and the style of her work after 1940. The Bible and the literature of the Kabbalah and of Hasidism are the sources of her exile poetry. Judaism, in fact, is central to the understanding of Nelly Sachs's work, as has generally been recognized. Thus the exile theme in her work must be interpreted in this light as well.

Exile is one of the oldest concepts in Jewish theological, philosophical, and poetic thought. Beginning with the expulsion from Paradise, the exile theme continues through the Books of Moses, the Babylonian exile, and the return to Jerusalem, until the last exile after the second destruction of the Temple. Many of the Psalms are lamentations about exile, as for instance the 137th Psalm: "By the rivers of Babylon, there we sat down, yea, we wept, when we remembered Zion." Not only does the theme of exile appear in Kabbalism, Messianism, and Hasidism, but it also dominates Jewish prayer and worship, as well as modern Jewish political and social theory, including Zionism.

> Ehrhard Bahr. In John M. Spalek and
> Robert F. Bell, eds. *Exiles: The Writer's*
> *Experience* (Chapel Hill: University of
> North Carolina Press, 1982), pp. 267–68

SACKVILLE-WEST, VITA (GREAT BRITAIN) 1892–1962

Miss Sackville-West has already shown in her poetry and her first novel, *Heritage*, how deep and true is her passion for beauty, especially the beauty of the English countryside. She has interpreted the peculiar splendor of the Kentish weald admirably. In *The Dragon in Shallow Waters* she gave us terror, purgings through pity . . . but of all her work I think the most characteristic, the most memorable is her short story (not so very short, one hundred and twenty pages), *The Heir: A Love Story.* It is one of the world's perfect love stories . . . the growth of love in a man for a house. . . .

There is an amazing sense of quiet satisfaction to be got out of this story. We are made to feel that it really is one of the world's great love stories.

Miss Sackville-West's prose is a clarion call to slack Englishmen to look to the rock whence they were hewn and to make some effort to stem the foreign invasion. The old squirearchy are being displaced by commercial plutocrats who know nothing of, and care nothing for, the beauty of the English countryside. She strives to make us realize the heritage that is ours in such places as Knole before they are dismantled and changed.

> S. P. B. Mais. *Some Modern Authors*
> (London: Grant Richards, 1923),
> pp. 142, 144

She has done everything in her life, I imagine, simply because she thought it would be a delightful thing to do. The result of this is that she has made her own atmosphere, by collecting around her, quite unconsciously, a number of other atmospheres; first the atmosphere of Knole, English fields, houses, hills and rivers; the atmosphere of Persia and the East; the atmosphere of a certain kind of English society; the atmosphere of certain friends who seemed to her delightful people and therefore good friends to have. I would say that she has never definitely chosen anything or anybody all her life long, but that when a place or a person or a book has appeared close to her and has seemed the sort of place or person or book natural to her, she has attached it to herself without consciously thinking about it. This makes inevitably her position romantic, whether she wishes it or no, because the essence of romantic living is to find pleasure in the things around one, and she has found intense pleasure in them. This intensity of approach is at the basis of all her work.

I do not think that before *The Edwardians* she was a very good novelist. *The Dragon in Shallow Waters, Heritage* and *The Heir* are works of atmosphere, not of character creation, philosophical ideas or narrative force. Her cleverest book of this kind, *Seducers in Equador*, is a brilliant imitation rather than an original creation. Nevertheless I believe *The Heir* to be one of the best of modern long short-stories and I thought for some time that that was where her talent lay—in the creation of a beautiful place, its loveliness evoked by a poet, the figures in it like statues in a garden. . . .

Seducers in Equador was one of the earliest pupils in Mrs. Woolf's school for good writing. I do not know how highly Miss Sackville-West values this amusing little book. She may indignantly protest that it owes nothing at all to Mrs. Woolf. Authors are given to these indignations, but it is a further fact that Mrs. Woolf is Miss Sackville-West's closest friend among writers; they meet constantly and understand each other perfectly. All the more remarkable then that Miss Sackville-West has kept her independence, that most precious of her gifts, so resolutely, for *Seducers in Equador* is the only one of her books that shows any sign of Mrs. Woolf's influence. . . .

I do not think that I am claiming for Miss Sackville-West any of the extravagant things that personal friendship and interest sometimes blind one to claiming. I think that she is only in mid-career, but I must confess that I find among all the writers in England no one else who has achieved such distinction in so many different directions. The novelists who are also poets, the poets who are also novelists, are very rare always. Among the novelists now that Hardy is dead, Rudyard Kipling (who is not really a novelist), Ford Madox Ford and Rose Macaulay are almost the only examples of whom I can think as poets, and among the poets only Osbert Sitwell and Martin Armstrong as novelists.

Hugh Walpole. The Bookman. September,
1930, pp. 23, 26

Joan of Arc, as Miss Sackville-West truly says, "makes us think, makes us question; she uncovers the dark places into which we may fear to look." . . .

To settle the obstinate questionings of these invisible things, she determined [in *Saint Joan of Arc*] to go through the whole tragic history in all its tedious details, and to set it down as objectively as possible. Rightly, she has deliberately lowered the tone. Her style is as far removed from the rhapsody of De Quincey as from the ribaldry of Voltaire while it yet avoids the involuntary panegyrics of Anatole France and the curiously dubious admiration of Bernard Shaw. She shuns all poetry, and of set purpose keeps to the prose of the investigating historian. This is the correct attitude for one like her, who confesses that she is in "the position of anybody torn between an instinctive reliance on instinct and a reasonable reliance on reason."

E. E. Kellett. *The Spectator.* June 19, 1936,
p. 1141

Miss Sackville-West is traditional, even old-fashioned, both in matter and manner, and it may be said at once that this reluctance frequently fetters the spirit of her work, and encourages a personal timidity through which it is the duty of an artist to break. At its most repressive moments, it piles up poetic phrases in her work, conventionalizes emotions, and dodges behind literary echoes of form and diction. . . .

Indeed no lights are burning in the ivory tower. But that is not the only tower which this poet inhabits. I should say that it is a place where she retreats during certain moods of weariness of mind, of defeatism, when confidence falls low, and her sense of purpose wavers. She is not often to be found there. Her more natural place is in a tower not of ivory, but of brick, a richly colored house set in a richly colored land, and furnished with a collection of treasures gathered by her as she has ranged over time, scholarship, and life. This tower, not pallid and circular, but eight-sided, represents at each angle an idiosyncrasy of the persons within, whose vigor, sensuality, passion, practicalness, and common-sense are gathered thereby. . . .

Throughout her work . . . [the] quality of personal elegy, the celebration of emotions that at the time seemed inexhaustible and insurmountable, yet have been survived by her, persists as a sort of ground-bass, giving a deep tone to her verse, a Roman quality which has perhaps much to do with her attraction toward the work of Virgil, and the conscious modeling of *The Land* on the form and mood of *The Georgics.* . . .

Through that restriction of theme . . . she has mastered more than her subject. She has mastered also the waywardness and turbulence of her moods, bit down their vagueness to a precision that is hard and objective, given them a universal out of a personal value. She has put her hand to the plow in more senses than one. She says that "the country habit has me by the heart," and her heart, under that discipline, works the more harmoniously with her mind. This process, a hard one which cannot be mastered merely by willing, needs time, patience and experience before it can be acquired. Once acquired, however, it produces that essential poetry which is content with simple words, unliterary associations, and humble effects.

Richard Church. *Fortnightly Review.*
December, 1940, pp. 600–605

Ultimately what her work poses is a religious question: the validity of "order," determining or determined by qualities of the heart. Order has a repetitive motion in time; it keeps a social form in being; it is a vehicle for culture. Above and around the social order are those other orders of which she is acutely aware: the soil through the seasons, and the monastic, contemplative order, generating graces impalpable but potent. While the social order changes, is continually breaking down and reforming, the two other orders, those of the soil and the soul remain constant—the root of life and its ultimate flower. In *Pepita* Miss Sackville-West disclaims the title of novelist. "I hated writing novels," she tells her mother, "really only cared about writing poetry and other things." One need not take her too literally to see her as fulfilling her clearest intentions in her poetry and, of the "other things," in *The Eagle and the Dove,* also her *Saint Joan of Arc.* . . .

In her poetry Miss Sackville-West at times dreams of a hotter sun than ours. "But in this dear delusion of a South. . . . We northerners must turn towards our flowers." And so she turns to make bloom her Wealden clay of "yeavy spite." "The country habit has me by the heart." Emerging from the order of the great house in its heyday, she has based her poetry and her life latterly on the order of nature, with its wintry austerities, its flowery rewards; a type it may be of orders, but in an age of doubt at least a sure footing and foundation for a belief in life. Miss Sackville-West is fascinated by problems of the integral self and its sources. Like Keats she is "capable of being in uncertainties, mysteries, doubts, without any irritable reaching after fact and reason." Rather, in a mood of devout uncertainty she continues to develop and deepen.

(London) *Times Literary Supplement.*
February 6, 1953, p. 88

Miss Victoria Sackville-West prefaces her life of *La Grande Mademoiselle* with some sensible remarks about translation, and the difficulties of retaining the style of a past epoch even when the words themselves seem most easy to render into another language. . . . Miss Sackville-West has been right to approach her subject in an entirely unpretentious, easy-going manner. She never presents Mademoiselle as anything but a goose, and by the end one has a clear idea of just the sort of goose she was. . . .

Miss Sackville-West has produced a sympathetic and convincing picture—perhaps one should say tapestry.

Anthony Powell. *The Spectator.* April 10,
1959, p. 518

Vita Sackville-West's *All Passion Spent,* published in 1931, is as astonishingly feminist as Virginia Woolf's *A Room of One's Own* and Rebecca West's *Harriet Hume.* For what it eloquently demonstrates is that the life of a woman without a room of her own, without a work of her own, is the life of a somnambulist—is, in fact, no life at all. And in *All Passion Spent,* the woman's life as somnambulist is lived in the city—that social, political, and economic fortress erected by man to enable him to carry out his work while banishing all things natural, including human affection, and where he incarcerates the woman he has chosen to live his life with him, beside him, while he devotes himself to the task of building the British Empire.

Sackville-West had not always been the egalitarian pacifist feminist she seems to have become (at least for a time) in *All Passion Spent*. Nor had she always defined the city as the place from which men exerted their power; nor always manifested a contempt for the principles of patriarchy which lie at the root of the empire. . . .

Nigel Nicolson [her son] has stated that the roots of his mother's feminism can be traced, in part, to her resentment that she would not inherit Knole, gavelkind in Kent stipulating the entail of the house on male heirs only. Her life as a wife, coupled with her inability to inherit Knole, caused her to revise certain of her attitudes toward the aristocracy, toward patriarchal institutions, and, eventually, toward the city and the country as the places in which these institutions made their presences felt.

This change can be easily gauged by comparing *The Heir,* first privately printed in 1922, with *All Passion Spent,* published in 1931. *The Heir,* subtitled *A Love Story,* recounts how Mr. Peregrine Chase, manager of a small insurance office in Wolverhampton, a "sandy, weakly-looking little man, with thin reddish hair, freckles, and washy blue eyes," comes to love and refuse to part with Blackboys, an Elizabethan manor house with a Tudor moat, that has been left to him by an aunt that he has never met.

The Heir expresses that age-old romantically idealistic pastoral yearning that holds that everything evil exists in cities and everything wonderful occurs in the country where peacocks shriek and sheep graze. At the end of the novel, Chase looks forward to an idyllic life in the country, far away from the pressures and problems of his earlier life in the city.

In *The Land,* published in 1926, Sackville-West explores, as well, the nature of that country life which stands in such sharp contrast to life in the city. In one passage, events in the city are contrasted with the permanence of the land and the work of the yeoman who shapes the "fields, slow-paced, / Into their permanent design." On the one hand, there is the evanescence of the city and diplomacy, carried out by a male elite, the affairs of state changing and shifting with every change in age, point of view, and political philosophy; on the other hand, there is the permanence of the land and humble work, the work of the yeoman, the bee-keeper, the shepherd, the craftsman, in tune with the rhythms of the year which remain the same throughout the ages.

But in this hundred-odd-page celebration of country life, Sackville-West mentions the rightful work of women only a few times, as if women have no place in the country just as they have no place in the political and diplomatic affairs of the city, as if the idyll of life in the country does not extend to women. . . .

In *All Passion Spent,* Vita Sackville-West states that the city is the symbol of man's domination—not only of women, but also of the lower classes and of nature. In the city, diplomacy and politics prevail; they have been developed as the institutions through which men dominate women; through which the upper classes dominate the lower classes. In the city, materialism and acquisitiveness prevail; they are the outward manifestations of man's perversion of the nonstriving natural order of things; as material goods are the outward symbols of one person's wealth and ascendancy, of another's poverty and subservience. In the city, strife and conflict have become principles of existence—a Darwinian struggle in which the survival of the fittest through the domination or elimination of those defined as the weakest is the theoretical principle which both legitimates and masks the subjugation of one sex by another, one class by another. And the country is no better, except that in the country this struggle is more difficult to perceive because it is hidden beneath the myth of the goodness of the countryside. In the city or in the country, there is no hope for women, just as there is no hope for the poor or for the oppressed, unless the very structure of society is changed.

The conditions necessary to create art, or to create a life of one's own seem in *All Passions Spent* to be incompatible with the institution of marriage, the private ownership of property, and the striving ways of the city. Deborah must, in her youth, make of herself an island, either in a foreign city or in that border land between city and country, as her great-grandmother has done in the closing days of her life—an island unfettered by the ties of affection, ownership, or striving for material goods. Given the conditions imposed upon her by men, every woman, Vita Sackville-West insists, must, with the emotional strength and support of another woman, become an island unto herself if she is to live the life of a creator.

> Louise A. DeSalvo. In Susan Merrill Squier,
> ed. *Women Writers and the City* (Knoxville:
> University of Tennessee Press, 1984), pp. 97,
> 99–101, 111–112

SAGAN, FRANÇOISE (FRANCE) 1935–

What a conception of life! And, to start off with, what a conception of love! It is not that Françoise Sagan cultivates provocative obscenity. There is no cynicism in her books, regardless of what has been said. The symptoms revealed by her books are all the more alarming for this reason. Cynicism at least is combative: by flouting moral obligations, it recognizes their existence. Sagan does not defy anyone, and she does not seem to guess that she could possibly shock anyone at all. Do her heroines even know that their conduct is called profligacy? The truth is that they exceed certain limits without even perceiving them. The question is not one of modesty, but of a moral sense. Has a generation that has witnessed unheard-of and extreme changes linked propriety to those things revealed as no longer valid, and a moral sense to simple propriety? Quite determined not to be fooled by a society that, it feels, has proved itself dishonest and hypocritical, this generation has thrown everything overboard, indiscriminately, the eternal as well as the transitory. In anything that carries the stamp of tradition, it can only see conventions and arbitrary prohibitions. Therefore, each person can make his own experiment with life in total isolation. Clear-sightedness, a clear-sightedness that is corrosive and always on the alert, is the only virtue these moral orphans recognize. But the word "virtue" has grown rather old: they prefer to speak of honesty, of self-respect. . . .

Only clear-sightedness persists, a small pitiless light illuminating a life deprived of meaning and of orientation, stagnant, useless, and of an overwhelming boredom that can be fought off only with the help of fleeting and sharp pleasures, with the help of hard liquor.

André Blanchet. *Études*. May, 1956,
pp. 245–47

Hello, Sadness was a precocious book. It stamped a pattern of impossible, though amusing, events upon reality in a teen-age dream of wickedness, seduction, sophistication and power—for Cécile controlled and manipulated the adults about her at will. Her story was pure wishfulfillment, carried off by the intensity and immediacy with which it was told, but inclined, whenever the author's concentration faltered, to turn sheerly absurd. Cécile's fascination with, and rage against, the adult world—the world that is threatening to manipulate her—are very telling. But her revenge never gets out of the realm of day-dream or fairytale.

In *A Certain Smile* Mlle. Sagan has placed her young heroine, Dominique, in a situation which corresponds more closely with reality. Like Cécile, Dominique's central experience is of contact with the adult world; but it is a much more plausible contact. Indeed, Dominique's story is a retelling of one of the classic, one of the oldest, tales in the world: she falls in love with a man old enough to be her father.

Now the story of the young girl and the old magician who seduces her, initiates her and steals her from her young lover is positively legendary. Mlle. Sagan's version is valuable, however, on two counts. First, she manages to make the old legend moving in itself. And secondly, she tells it so honestly that the bare bones of her story indicate how the contemporary situation creates variations in the legend. . . .

To tell this story Mlle. Sagan employs a style which has been highly praised, but which seems to me to have serious drawbacks. Her technique is that of setting down a series of immediate perceptions, of particular sensations. Even Dominique's emotions—and she is narrator as well as central character—are given as separate events: "I was happy. I was sad." They seem merely things that happen to her. She is presented to us as a dotted outline, not as a defined character. The result is that Dominique, Luc and the rest seem to have little internal life of their own. They act without explaining themselves, and therefore they act abruptly and mysteriously. Mlle. Sagan may intend thus to convey the effect of ineluctable Fate moving among men; but the impression the reader actually receives is something different—that of a determined author manipulating her characters.

Elizabeth Janeway. *The New York Times*.
August 12, 1956, p. 1

The French language, by English standards, is inflexible—although the French don't think of it that way—and the more literate are constantly aware of separate, if overlapping sets of vocabulary. This makes for a somewhat different and more acute audience appreciation of not only the *mot*, but the style *juste,* than a writer in English could expect. Sagan's handling of literary French is classic and formal, and for a Frenchman, the conventions of tense and syntax used in a perfect academic fashion, have an expressiveness and charm quite apart from the ideas they help to convey. In the view of an academician like the respected critic of *Le Monde*, Emile Henriot (who has praised Sagan to the skies), such a demonstration of pure diction is doubtless, all by itself, a sign of major talent.

Robert Parris. *The New Republic*. August
20, 1956, p. 19

The novels written by Françoise Sagan have shown obviously and increasingly the sexual anarchy in which some adults and consequently many young people live. . . . Françoise Sagan has written about people she has met on the Côte d'Azur, at the University, and in the milieu of journalism, the theatre, and literature. Whatever may be the limits of her experience, it appears that she has put her finger on an illness of our period and the patient has flinched at her touch.

Georges Hourdin. *Le Cas Françoise Sagan*
(Editions du Cerf: Paris, 1958), pp. 73–74

What she has that is new is a rhythm. Whence her love of music and the musical allusions which appear so often. The common denominator of an air by Mozart and of a well-worn story is rhythm—more physical, more overpowering than melody. It pervades the very air we breathe, it changes systems of currents, and by almost physiological elements, it subjugates the reader. This is perhaps one of the factors of the prodigious success of [her] work.

Gérard Mourgue. *Françoise Sagan* (Paris:
Editions Universitaires, 1958), pp. 117–18

In order to write about people who do nothing, think nothing and bear no particular distinguishing mark, one has to be an observer—an angry one or a well-disposed one, but an observer. But one constantly has the feeling that Françoise Sagan is incapable of judging the people she talks about, for the reason that they are the very people she has lived among since the day she was born, whom she has seen every day of her life, and still does. Being unable to make her characters act in any significant way—to her everything they do is commonplace because their behavior is part and parcel of her own life—she determines to attempt to define them. . . . Her characters remain silhouettes; and what is worse, nothing ever happens to them.

Jean Bloch-Michel. *Partisan Review.* Winter,
1958, pp. 118–19

That *lucidité* which Sagan's characters never abandon for a second tells them that the absurdity of life and one's loneliness can only be escaped through love, but that theirs is no lasting flame (the leitmotiv of time's destruction, *dans un mois dans un an* occurs over and over again in these novels). . . . In Sagan's first two novels one could already suspect that, behind the rage to live that seemed to possess her characters, there lay a craving for an inaccessible ideal. The quest unremittingly goes on in *Aimez-vous Brahms?* . . . This . . . novel's poignant description of *la condition humaine* confirms, if it were necessary, Françoise Sagan's unusual literary gifts.

Michel Guggenheim. *Yale French Studies.*
Summer, 1959, p. 95

This deliberate limitation of her role to depicting the life of the bourgeois society she was born and brought up in is without doubt one of the keys to Sagan's popularity. She has described the vapid emptiness of this world without embellishment, and in doing so she has come to be recognized as one of the figures that best symbolize the bourgeois membership of France's first post-war generation. . . . In Sagan's hands the tortured philosophizings of Sartre have been turned into easily digestible clichés; the classic *roman d'amour* has been streamlined into the *roman démaquillé*—the novel without make-up. Its popularity goes hand in hand with the steadily expanding vogue for simplicity in everything: speech, gesture, dress.

Curtis Cate. *The Atlantic Monthly.* March,
1960, p. 94

Old critics and middle-aged women were responsible for Françoise Sagan's first success. What was there behind this stubborn little head? Through the heroine of *Hello, Sadness* these naïve readers sought to penetrate the secrets of youth. The author, not yet a legend, was troubling: nineteen years old, a high school graduate, consoling herself for failing an elementary college course by writing a novel at a lakeshore, the way vacation homework is rushed off, between swimming and tennis—where did her precocious experiment come from then? . . .

There is more sensuality in one page of a Mauriac novel than in the complete works of Sagan. But the public does not like genuine sensuality, which borders too closely on the death-wish; it only enjoys the shameless and trifling idea it has of sensuality. It does not displease the public that the characters make love the way one might steal a bar of chocolate. In the public's eye, *The Wonderful Clouds* serves more as a novelistic supplement to columns of advice to the lovelorn than as a *sexual digest*. How do rich kids fall in love? How do capricious young women choose their lovers? How does an American, a shy handsome boy, stand the ordeal of being cuckolded? People want to be informed, and promptly; therefore, the novels of Françoise Sagan are less reminiscent of studies of psychological crises . . . or of portraits of manners than of a parade of mannequins: high gallantry presents its latest fashions. Little flesh and no blood. But Françoise Sagan's private life prolongs that of her characters; the author's destiny overlaps theirs. The news items which are road-markers of Françoise's existence (car accident, marriage, friendships, divorce) and about which the mass-circulation press keeps us informed so obligingly, are like so many notes and commentaries on the margin of Sagan's work.

Willy de Spens. La table ronde. September,
1961, pp. 72, 75

I have no particular sympathy for Françoise Sagan—with whom I have never had the occasion to speak. Her political attitude is the kind that irritates me the most. Her novels merit attention and esteem because of their personal tone and voice, their very remarkable mastery in the art of handling a story full of intrigue, their subtle, valid touches in the creation of characters—in short, their gift of life. But these novels are of the category of high-quality merchandise for fancy stores rather than that of great art. Therefore, it is with a clear conscience that I say that *Violins Sometimes* deserves more than the reputation it has gotten and should be considered one of the interesting plays of the season.

The play is undoubtedly less agreeable, less finely poetic, than *Castle in Sweden*. There is something a little old-fashioned, a little like the plays of Henry Bernstein, in its central themes and its construction. The fact is that the audience is interested in the action and in the characters involved in it, and that in spite of some slowness in the first part, by the time the final curtain was lowered, I realized I had not been bored for a minute. . . .

The theme of the play is the destruction of purity in a rotten world. This theme is not extremely original. We find it in several of Anouilh's plays. But perhaps because Anouilh is a man, he likes to incarnate purity in the character of a girl; and perhaps because Sagan is a woman, she evokes purity through a young man. Another difference: Anouilh's pure characters are demanding, combative, impossible to deal with; Sagan's young man is unselfconscious and absentminded, whimsical and charming. Except for these details, the same purity is the subject of both playwrights, the purity which, through rebellion or disdain, opposes itself to the meanness of life and the power of money, the purity which we try to possess in love, in other words, which we try to attain and destroy at the same time.

Thierry Maulnier. La revue de Paris.
February, 1962, p. 150

The elements of Françoise Sagan's plays are in a way her own property—or at least are not instinctively used, or even borrowed, by other writers for the French theatre. For her, as a romantic, love is the fine flower of life—the most important gift you get or give—and it fades. As a modern intelligence, she perceives that between lovers the practice of ideas usually destroys emotions, that personal liberty is a dangerous necessity, that most human beings suffer from and give off ennui, and that fantasy is a final refuge from reality, especially for the French. This inventory she used in such perfect proportion in her *Chateau en Suède* that the play will likely be regarded for its delights as a personal period piece, and will be revived over time, like a minor theater classic.

Genêt. The New Yorker. January 26, 1963,
pp. 107–8

Poor old Françoise Sagan. Just one more old-fashioned old-timer, by-passed in the rush for the latest literary vogue and for youth. Superficially, her career in America resembles the life-span of those medieval beauties who flowered at fourteen, were deflowered at fifteen, were old at thirty and crones at forty. Miss Sagan is now only thirty-one, but the publication of her latest novel is almost like the return appearance of an elderly actress who was a sensation as an ingenue.

It was back there in 1954, when she was nineteen, that she published her first novel, *Hello, Sadness,* which was a literary sensation and a commercial success and which launched her well on the way to obscurity with serious critics. For, although her first book was astonishingly precocious, it dealt with relatively conventional materials of "French" sexual intrigue and it showed no slightest concern with new form. Her technique was close to that of the classic *nouvelle,* which Larousse defines as a short novel based on a recent incident. In an age of French literature where the philosophically rich fiction of Camus and Sartre and Mauriac was succeeded by the formal innovations of the New and the Anti Novel, there was not much left for Miss Sagan but popular success.

This is not an attempt to treat her as a neglected genius; still, after reading *The Drumroll,* I can agree with Brigid Brophy who, as usual, uses language precisely when she says: "Sagan is the most underestimated presence in post-war French writing." Underestimation is not to be replaced by overestimation. Miss Sagan is an accomplished entertainer of the particular reader. This is an ancient and honorable profession. . . . The traditional novel is dead and, according to the French, deader in France than elsewhere, until Miss Sagan writes another book and proves that Colette has a descendant. Not an equivalent but an active descendant.

Stanley Kauffmann. The New Republic.
October 29, 1966, pp. 21, 38

What label, exactly (or even approximately) is one to put on the books of Françoise Sagan? It is a question that has vexed more of us than would probably care to admit it, at least aloud. Is she, after all, nothing but an entertainer, a superficial romantic, or is she something disturbingly more subtle? True, her books have brought a suspicious amount of pleasure to a wide readership, mostly feminine; worse, they have proven easily transposable into a certain sort of motion picture. Why, then, does she trouble us?

Foremost is the problem of her subject matter—the frivolous people, the night clubs, the fast cars, the brittle affairs, the soft focus and the easy dooms, the hermetically sealed, bittersweet world of the love story. In terms of social consciousness, her books seem to have no more weight than their author's reflection in the mirror, no more relevance to the affairs of the real world than so much well-concocted marzipan.

And yet even among her most ardent (and, at the other end of the scale, studiously indifferent) detractors, there has dwelt a persistent, uneasy, and half-baffled sense that she is really up to more than she seems to be, that behind the mask there lurks a shrewd seriousness of intent that defies and perhaps even deliberately mocks analysis.

Scars on the Soul marks a radical and important departure from this sort of writing. It is not, I think, a significant work of literature, as such things are judged: its Ionesco-like effects are more than a trifle shopworn, and she cannot resist entertaining us even at the moments of greatest pain. But as a document of a writer's agonized self-appraisal, as a plea almost for help, and above all as a promissory note to be redeemed in the future, it deserves both our sympathy and close attention.

At the heart of the book is a typical Sagan novel. Surrounding it is a long personal meditation. The novel—brief, scattered, and fragmentary— brings back the van Milhems, an aristocratic brother and sister who were the protagonists of her early play, *Castle in Sweden*. . . . As the van Milhems become progressively disillusioned with their lot, so too does she, and she progressively abandons them to their fate, with pity and utter finality.

She bids them goodbye on the last page and, with them, all that she has written. It simply will not wash anymore; she has grown too old and life intrudes too much. If there are to be other books in her future, they will be of a very different sort. The time for drones and games is done, and the party is over at last.

L. J. Davis. *Book World*. April 28, 1974, p. 2

Both the autobiographical *Des bleus à l'âme* (Scars on the soul) and *Avec mon meilleur souvenir* (My best regards) are fundamentally celebrations of Sagan's rapport with writing. They appear disguised as something else, in the former case another novel of failed romance with authorial digressions, and in the latter a series of remembrances of artists Sagan has admired, as well as sketches of her great obsessions. However, each in its own way illustrates the basic but often overlooked fact that a writer, to paraphrase Barthes, writes. Or, to parody Descartes: "Sagan writes, therefore she is." She has said as much in an unusually earnest moment in 1977: "Writing is the only proof I have of my self, to my eyes it is the only tangible sign that I exist."

In *Des bleus à l'âme,* Sagan meanderingly portrays her writing as therapeutic for both herself and her readers. . . . Writing . . . protects [Sagan's writer character] F. S. and by extrapolation the author herself. In *Des bleus à l'âme,* Sagan directly transforms her emotional life into fiction.

While *Des bleus à l'âme* can be read as an attempt to resolve a personal crisis, *Avec mon meilleur souvenir,* beautifully orchestrated in ten movements of measured prose, reads like a meditation. The mood varies from essay to essay across a limited and tender spectrum. It ranges from nostalgia in the first piece on jazz singer Billie Holiday, to self-mocking dramatization in "Saint-Tropez," to charmed admiration in the much remarked upon "Lettre d'amour à Jean-Paul Sartre." Ironically inscribed within this controlled and sculpted form, the central concern emerges as a fascination with the outsized, the flamboyant, the totally absorbing. This preoccupation unites the diverse activities: gambling, speeding, rehearsing, relaxing, reading and the various personalities Sagan offers the readers—Holiday, Tennessee Williams, Orson Welles, Rudolf Nureyev, and Sartre. Whether the passion she exalts be the sea or sports cars, whether she recalls the anecdote of Billie Holiday's needle-marked arms or Orson Welles's monstrous genius, Sagan's subjects share the same emotional profile: unmediated, impassioned, unafraid. Each remembered risk, each memorialized artist merges in a fully engaged combat with the limits of the human condition. Speeding or Sartre both speak to living one's solitude aggressively. Gambling and Billie Holiday both evoke the intoxication of the fine line between absolute freedom and absolute collapse.

It is more than appropriate that Sagan chooses to cap all the essays in this volume by a reader's autobiography, a promenade through the texts that have formed her as a writer: Gide's *The Fruits of the Earth,* Camus's *The Rebel,* Rimbaud's *Illuminations,* and especially Proust's *Remembrance of Things Past.* No less meaningful is the thrill that literature has always provoked in her: "Since Rimbaud's *Illuminations,* literature has constantly made me feel there was a fire someplace—everywhere—and that it was up to me to put it out." All the earlier essays hint that her various enthusiasms are but permutations of this ultimate one. She thus equates the furor and necessity of gambling with the excitement of the opening of a new play, and indicates that passing behemoth trucks on the highway calls for the same psychological stamina as discovering the endless complexity of the writer's basic matter—humankind.

The penultimate essay, Sagan's radiant remembrance of Sartre, again serves to present her as the ever-grateful daughter of "the words": Sartre and Sagan, connected by the same birthday, by their fearlessness of big emotions, by their incapacity to live any other way than as though there were no tomorrow. The authors are connected, too, and this is Sagan's point in writing these memoirs, by the writer's passion, a passion that in Sagan's case both personalizes and intensifies her legendary heroes while setting her forth as one of their number.

Judith Graves Miller. *Françoise Sagan*
(Boston: Twayne, 1988), pp. 11, 13–14

In Sagan's works, the author usually creates a pair of women characters, the youthful protagonist and the older woman on whom she would like to pattern herself, but fears a loss of identity should she succeed in doing so. The dyad of Sagan's first three novels, *Bonjour Tristesse, A Certain Smile,* and *Those without Shadows,* disappears in *Aimez-vous Brahms* (1959; Do you like Brahms), leaving only the older woman. Paule is a successful thirty-nine-year-old interior designer who, like her predecessors Anne, Françoise, and Fanny, embodies a double image of female adulthood; while she is strong, independent, and clearly superior to her male counterpart, she is also fatally vulnerable to him for financial and/or emotional security. . . .

The title of the novel *La chamade* (1965; The drumroll), announces another failure, for the chamade is a roll on the drums to announce defeat. *La Chamade* is the story of a young woman whose sensitivity and love of life's pleasures are not enough to give her the courage needed to accept life's responsibilities. . . .

The female novel of development takes an interesting turn in *Des bleues à l'âme* (1972; Scars on the soul), with the brother–sister theme that is so important in Christiane Rochefort's utopian novel, *Archaos ou le jardin étincelant* (Archaos, or the sprakling garden), published in the same year. Instead of settling for being half a person, which is the same as being a self-destructive nonperson, the emerging woman often casts off her defined role and moves toward androgyny.

Lucille Frackman Becker. *Twentieth-Century*
French Women Novelists (Boston: Twayne,
1989), pp. 81–83

The leash referred to in the title of Françoise Sagan's most recent novel is the gilded leash attached to the charming gigolo Vincent; it is held by his beautiful wife Laurence. She treats him with the love and generosity that are the due of a faithful dog. Vincent's acceptance of his role stems from laziness, a flaw common to Sagan's privileged bourgeois characters. It was Vincent's lack of drive that led him to abandon what he alone believes might have been a promising career as a pianist.

Seven years of *dolce far niente* are interrupted one day when Vincent, in his usual desultory way, scribbles a dozen notes on a piece of paper. The twelve notes are more than are needed for the hit record that makes Vincent a millionaire. Scorned previously as a gigolo, he becomes respected and sought after, particularly by those who need capital for their various schemes. Laurence, however, feels the leash go slack and arranges to gain control of Vincent's money to keep him in check, but Vincent cannot give up his dreams of liberty—liberty in Sagan's universe is construed as not being responsible to anyone but oneself—and leaves Laurence. Only then does Sagan reveal that Laurence loves Vincent passionately. Unable to live without him, she kills herself.

Critics who have hailed *La laisse* (The leash) as a novel in which the man finally plays an admirable role have done so without understanding that it is a reprise of Sagan's first novel, *Bonjour tristesse*. Here the role of Cécile is played by Vincent. Like her, Vincent is lazy, self-indulgent, and self-centered; like her, he destroys the one person capable of sincere emotion in his superficial, uncaring milieu.

Lucille F. Becker. World Literature Today.
64, 1990, pp. 606–7